Warships of the Imperial Japanese Navy, 1869-1945

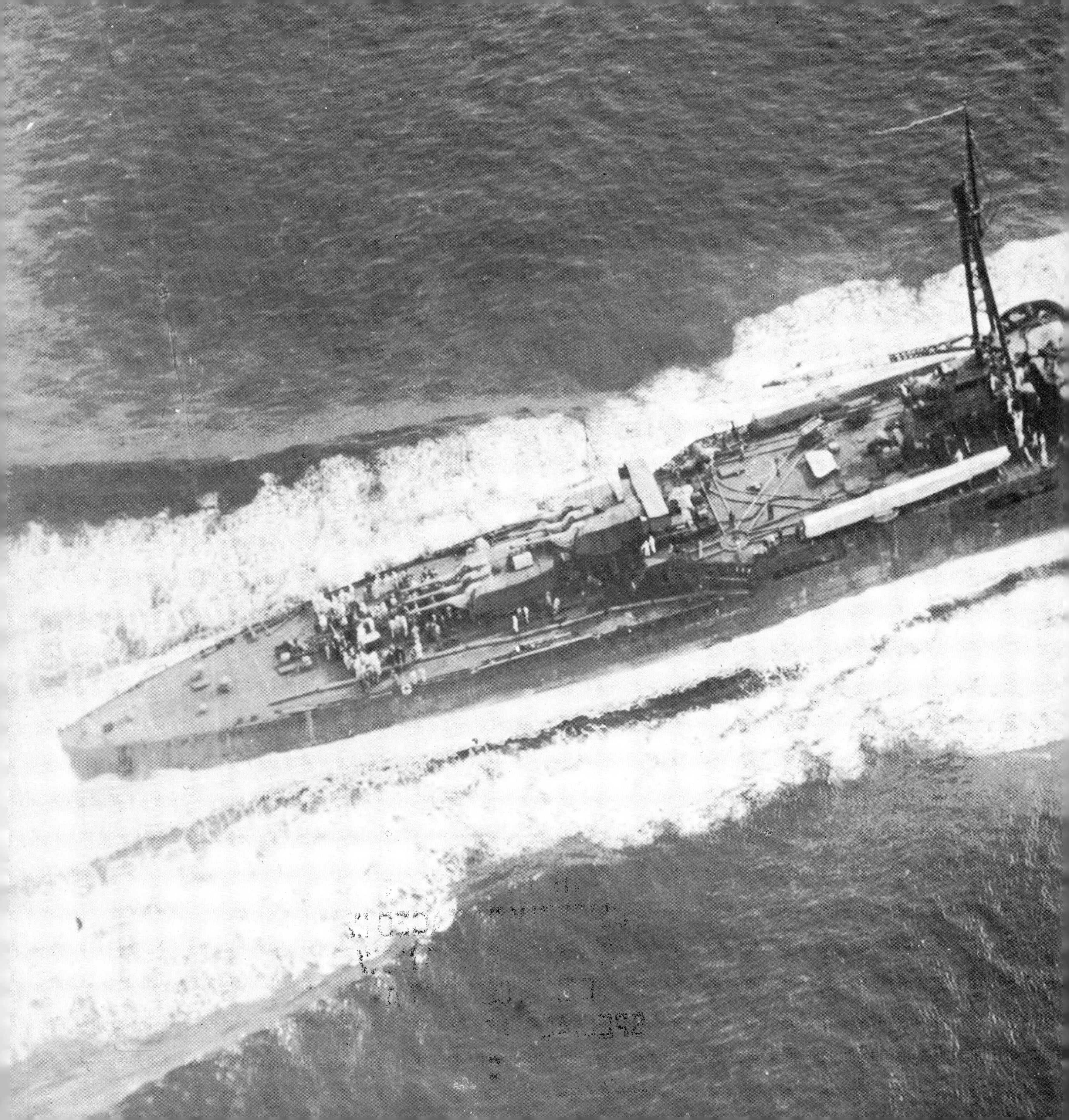

Warships of the Imperial Japanese Navy, 1869-1945

Hansgeorg Jentschura, Dieter Jung and Peter Mickel

Translated by Antony Preston and J. D. Brown

Arms and Armour

Preface

First published in 1977 by
Arms and Armour Press, Cassell plc
Wellington House
125 Strand
London WC2R 0BB

ISBN 0 85368 151 1

Publishing history:
First German-language edition, *Die Japanischen Kriegsschiffe 1869–1945*, published 1970 © J. F. Lehmanns Verlag, 1970
First English-language edition, revised with new material and photographs
© Lionel Leventhal Limited, 1977   Fourth impression 1986   Reprinted 1992
Reprinted 1996

All rights reserved. No part of this publication may be reproduced, stored in a retrieval system, or transmitted in any form by any means electrical, mechanical or otherwise, without first seeking the written permission of the copyright owner and of the publisher.

Title-spread illustration: the cruiser *Suzuya*, third unit of the *Mogami* class. While she was being built, major construction faults were discovered in her sister ships, as well as a lack of stability. Bulges were added, to cope with the latter problem, but at the time this photograph was taken — in 1935, on trials — the defective welding had not yet been made good. Note that only two of the four 5-inch DP mountings had then been installed. She was later re-armed as a heavy cruiser, and took part in the battle of Samar in October 1944, where she was badly damaged, and later scuttled. (Shizuo Fukui.)

Edited by Michael Boxall.
Printed in Great Britain at The Bath Press, Somerset

The origin of this book, and the gathering of material to be used for it, goes back over thirty years. The idea was that of Erich Gröner, historian of the German navy, and author of *Die Deutschen Kriegschiffe, 1815–1945*, (Lehmanns, Munich).

In October 1942, thanks to a special request by Hitler, the German Naval Attaché in Tokyo, Admiral Wenneker, was permitted to pay a short visit of inspection to a *Yamato* class "super-dreadnought" in a dockyard, and then to cable a very detailed description of the ship to Berlin. On 22nd August 1943, Gröner was shown this report at the Führer HQ for the purpose of interpretation and preparation of a design sketch drawing, under security supervision. Later, at the time of the collapse of the Third Reich, he rescued a copy of this sketch intending to use it as the frontispiece in a volume on Japanese warships. And after the war, hoping to put his plan into practice, Gröner embarked on an enthusiastic exchange of material with Shizuo Fukui, a Japanese naval constructor who planned similar publications in Japan.

Following Gröner's death, we decided to follow up the project. As Peter Mickel had already drawn a large number of plans of Japanese warships and discussed them with Gröner, continuity in this respect seemed assured. In the completion of this enormous task, he was later joined by F. Mrva, to whom special thanks are due for his utterly reliable assistance.

The task of preparing the text was undertaken by Hansgeorg Jentschura and Dieter Jung in the face of considerable difficulties. Original documents were not available for research, enquiries could not be made of individuals involved and no visits could be made to builders. Particular attention was paid to problems arising from varying transcriptions of Japanese characters — and which have led to the appearance in many publications of "phantom" ships. We give our heartfelt thanks to Dr. Wolfram Müller-Yokota of the University of Bochum for his help in clarifying these anomalies.

In the editing of material concerning units of the fleet, we were able to achieve complete coverage of all combat vessels down to submarines. In the listing of naval auxiliaries, military auxiliaries and "special" vessels, we had to forego encyclopaedic completeness: essentially, only ships and craft which were lost could be covered in detail.

The basis of this book therefore lies in the information forwarded to Gröner by Fukui in the 1950s, and for which we would again express our gratitude on Gröner's behalf; and the writings of Professor Dr. E. Lacroix of the University of Ghent in *The Belgian Shiplover* since 1959. To him we are grateful for the provision of special editions of his earlier writings.

As in previous publications, we were helped in our work by the selfless and loyal support of Messrs. N. Kelling, L.L. von Münching, Dr. J. Rohwer, P. Scarceriaux and W. Kähling. We are indebted to Mrs. H. Gröner for placing the material collected by her husband at our disposal, and we are eternally grateful to our original German publishers, Messrs. O. and B. Spatz, without whose helpful understanding of the difficulties of the task, its eventual completion would have been impossible.

For the current edition, now published in English, we have been able to take the opportunity to revise the text in the light of subsequent researches and to incorporate photographs and some extra drawings.

Hansgeorg Jentschura, Dr. Dieter Jung, Peter Mickel;
Berlin and Hamburg, 1977.

Introduction

This English version of *Die Japanischen Kriegsschiffe 1869–1945* is much more than a straight translation of the original German edition. The original authors have taken advantage of a complete re-presentation of the book to contribute a large amount of extra material which has come to light since the book first appeared. The translators have been able to take advantage of further information available in the United States and Great Britain, to amplify details and to make adjustments and amendments.

The most noticeable change from the original edition is in the illustrations. Drawings have been added and, in some cases, replaced, but—most important of all—photographs have now been included. Those students of the Japanese Navy who have tried without success to find sources of Japanese photographs will be delighted to see how many new views it has been possible to find. They come from many sources, in particular the collections of Shizuo Fukui and Hansgeorg Jentschura and the archives of the Netherlands Navy, the National Maritime Museum and the Bundesarchiv.

Despite the labours of the US Navy's technical mission after August 1945, and the work of historians in many countries during the past 30 years, there are still points of contention and doubt. One example is the Japanese predilection for rounded figures for gun-calibres. The 76mm (3inch)) gun, for example, started life as the British 12-pounder, but is referred to in Japanese records as an 80mm weapon. The translators have agreed to differ with the authors on such points, and the Japanese designation has been used for this edition. (A list of designations and calibres can be found on pages 10 and 11.)

The original combined index and 'abc' of ships has been simplified into a conventional index with a separate list of the requisitioned auxiliary gunboats, guardboats, transports, etc., which do not appear in the main text. A feature of the Imperial Japanese Navy's wartime policy was its prodigal attitude to mercantile shipping, and the reader will wonder at the enormous number of ships which the Japanese could apparently spare from normal mercantile service.

The one omission from this edition is of the Japanese/German translations of Japanese names, which were such an enjoyable feature of the German edition. These were the work of Dr. Wolfram Müller-Yokota of the University of the Ruhr, Bochum.

Grateful thanks are due to the following for their help in the translation, compilation and checking of material: D. H. Brown, R. Brown, David Lyon, George Osbon, Alan Raven, A. Stannett and Clive Taylor.

David Brown, Antony Preston, London, 1977.

Contents

Explanatory Notes	10
1. **Ironclads, Battleships and Battlecruisers**	12
2. **Aircraft Carriers and Aviation Transports**	40
Escort Carriers, 58 Seaplane Carriers, 62	
Army Aircraft Transports with Seaplane Tenders, 67	
Flight decks, 61 Aircraft Salvage Vessels, 69	
Merchant Aircraft Carriers, 62 Aircraft Transports, 71	
3. **Armoured Cruisers**	71
4. **Heavy Cruisers**	79
5. **Cruising Ships, 1857–1900**	88
6. **Protected Cruisers**	95
7. **Light Cruisers**	104
8. **Gunboats**	113
Merchant Ships used as Gunboats, 123	
9. **Torpedo Boats and Destroyers**	124
Torpedo Boats, 124 Destroyers, 130	
10. **Motor Torpedo Boats and Motor Gunboats**	154
Motor Torpedo Boats, 154 Motor Gunboats, 158	
11. **Submarines**	160
Midget Submarines, 183	
12. **Escort and Patrol Vessels**	186
13. **Minelayers**	197
Auxiliary Minelayers, 204	
Cable Ships, 205	
Netlayers, 206	
14. **Minesweepers**	207
Merchant Ships used as Minesweepers, 211	
15. **Submarine Chasers**	214
16. **Landing Ships and Landing Craft**	226
17. **Armed Merchant Cruisers**	234
18. **Submarine Depot Ships**	236
Auxiliary Submarine Depot Ships, 239	
Torpedo Recovery Vessels, 240	
19. **Repair Ships**	240
20. **Ammunition Ships**	243
21. **Transports**	244
22. **Supply Ships and Colliers**	247
23. **Oilers**	249
Merchant Ships used as Fleet Tankers, 252	
24. **Standard Merchant Ships**	255
25. **Hospital Ships**	262
26. **Survey Vessels**	263
27. **Research Ships and Icebreakers**	264
28. **Tugs**	266
29. **Utility Vessels**	269
30. **Training Ships**	270
31. **Target Ships**	271
32. **Miscellaneous Assault Craft**	272
33. **Royal Yacht**	273
34. **List of Miscellaneous Mercantile Auxiliary Vessels**	274
Index	281

Explanatory Notes

Beam
This is given in feet, and excludes folding structures, sponson extensions, bridge-wing extensions, etc.

Draught
This is given in feet at standard displacement.

Machinery
Propulsion machinery: the number and type of engines, the number and type of boilers, plus the number of shafts.

SHP
The heading SHP has been used throughout the tables, and is relevant in the vast majority of cases, which were turbine-driven warships. Where there are exceptions to this, the figure quoted has been qualified.
Turbine and diesel engines: the shaft horse-power (SHP), as measured by a torsion meter.
Reciprocating steam engines: indicated horse-power (ihp), as calculated from the available steam pressure and the swept volume of the cylinder(s); or nominal horse-power, a former mercantile measurement of the performance of reciprocating engines, without a fixed method of conversion to ihp. Used in *Lloyds Register of Shipping* until 1953.
bhp = brake horse-power; ehp = electrical horse-power.
Measured trials power output and speed are included in the notes, where information is available.
Astern power: in steam or diesel reciprocating engines, or engines working through reverse gear-boxes, the full output of the engine was available, whereas steam turbines, working through separate reverse turbines and gearing, yielded only 10 per cent to 30 per cent of the normal ahead power.

Speed
The maximum speed in knots (nautical miles per hour — 1 nm = 1.15 statute miles = 1.84 km) at normal displacement and full designed power. In the case of submarines, the figures are given for designed maximum speed on the surface and designed maximum speed submerged.

Fuel
The fuel stowage: coal, furnace fuel oil (for steam engines — FFO), and oil for diesel engines. Where two figures are given for the same type of fuel, these represent the stowage at normal and maximum displacements. FFO/oil stowage includes *all* liquid fuel, including aviation gasoline ("AvGas"), petrol for ships' boats, and domestic fuel.

Radius
The ship's endurance, shown as a range in nautical miles at a given speed, in knots, based on the maximum fuel capacity, irrespective of individual ships' limitations of stability, etc.
The conditions governing the range/speed data are not known, and these must therefore be regarded as theoretical design figures. To obtain an approximate radius of action by rule of thumb, the range should be halved, and the resulting figure reduced by 10-15 per cent, to allow for higher speeds and manoeuvring.

Armament
This column gives the number of guns, their calibre in millimetres (mm) and inches (generally when over 76.2mm/3in), the length of barrel in calibres, and the purpose of the guns (when less than 152 mm/6in). Gun calibres are expressed wherever possible in the original designations of manufacture. Some of the older heavy-calibre guns have been quoted in inches for consistency.

The number and position of torpedo tubes (TT) and diameter of torpedoes. Depth-charges and mines are also included.
AA Rocket-Launchers: 25mm AA triple mounting, adapted from 1944 to carry 28-barrelled rocket-launcher; the number of barrels later varied between as many as 30 in *Ise* and as few as 6 in *Shinano*. The 49lb projectile consisted of a 120mm/4.7in AA shell with a solid-fuel propellant, giving it a range of 1640 yds horizontally and 3300 ft vertically. Fired in a 12-second-long ripple from the 28-barrelled launcher, the rockets were intended to provide an AA barrage against dive- and torpedo-bombers.
Information concerning numbers of aircraft and types of special equipment (cranes on aircraft salvage vessels, for example), and the carrying-capacity of maintenance and landing craft is also included.
Flamethrowers, paravanes, explosive charges, minesweeping gear, etc., are not listed.

Comp
The personnel complement: a theoretical figure at the time of first commissioning, followed, where known, by subsequent increases in numbers.

Blanks, unknown data, etc.
In the tables, a blank space indicates identical information to the preceding entry ("ditto"); a dash ("—") indicates that there is no information in this column applicable to the entry; and a question mark ("?") indicates that the relevant information is not known.

General Notes, etc.
Below the data table for each ship, there is a concise summary of known information concerning the vessel, including General Notes (the construction, programme, purpose and quality of the ship), Armament (plus, where relevant, Re-armament and Reconstruction), Machinery notes and a brief resumé of the ship's Career. Service with the Imperial Navy begins with launching or purchase, and concludes with the date of loss, the date of surrender, or the place at which the ship was sold out of the service or broken up (BU). Before this final date, details are given of deletion from the Active List and reclassification as an auxiliary or special purpose vessel, hulk, target ship, etc. In cases of loss through destruction, information is included concerning the date (time, where given, is local time) and position of loss (given as a geographical location and, usually, as a latitude and longitude) as well as the cause and agency. The position given is that of actual sinking, not the subsequent surveyed position of the wreck.

Line Illustrations
A scale of 1:1,250 is used throughout for profile and plan drawings, as well as for detail drawings. Exceptionally, scales of 1:500 and 1:100 are used; these are clearly indicated as such.

Japanese Naval Guns (1920–45)

Type and date	Designation	Bore (in)		Projectile Weight (lb)	MV (fps)
94 1939	40cm 45-cal (46cm true)	18.11	BL	3220 AP 3000 HE	2556 2640
3rd Year 1918	40cm 45-cal (41cm true)	16.14	BL	2260 AP 2070 HE	2560 2640
41st Year c. 1905	36cm 45-cal (Vickers)	14	BL	1490 AP 1380 HE	2525 2640
3rd Year 1924	20cm 50-cal (20.32cm)	8	BL	278	2750

Type and date	Designation	Bore (in)		Projectile Weight (lb)	MV (fps)
3rd Year	15.5cm 60-cal	6.1	BL	123	3120
41st Year c. 1905	15cm 50-cal (15.24cm)	6	BL	100	2790
3rd Year 1915	14cm 50-cal	5.51	BL	84	2800
11th Year 1925	14cm 40-cal	5.51	QF LA	84	2300
3rd Year c. 1926	12.7cm 50-cal	5	BL	51	2960
88 and 89 1930/31	12.7cm 40-cal	5	QF DP	51	2400
3rd Year c. 1918	12cm 45-cal	4.72	QF LA	45	2560
11th Year c. 1927	12cm 45-cal	4.72	* LA	45	2750
10th Year 1927	12cm 45-cal	4.72	QF HA	45 HE 50 AA	2700
88 1930	10cm 50-cal	3.94	QF LA	28.7	2900
98 1940	10cm 65-cal	3.94	QF HA	28.7	3340
3rd Year c. 1915 and 88 1930	8cm** 40-cal	3	QF HA LA	13.2 13.2	2230 2230
11th Year c. 1926	8cm 40-cal	3	QF LA	12.5	2230
41st Year c. 1905	8cm 40-cal	3	QF LA	12.5	2230
41st Year "Short" c. 1905	8cm 25-cal (23-cal true)	3	QF HA	12.5	1475
5th Year c. 1914	8cm 23-cal (23-cal true)	3	QF LA	12.7	1475
98 1940	8cm 60-cal	3	QF LA	13.2	2950

* Types 'J' & 'K' were QF; Type 'L' was BL.
** All Japanese "8cm" guns were actually of 7.62cm calibre.

Lightweight Guns for defensively-armed merchant ships

Type and date	Designation	Bore (in)		Projectile Weight (lb)	MV (fps)
"Short Gun" 1941	12cm 12-cal	4.72	BL	28.7	1000
"Short Gun" 1943	20cm 12-cal (20.32cm)	8	BL	104	1000

QF = sliding breech; BL = screw breech; LA = low angle; HA = high angle; DP = dual purpose (LA/HA)

Japanese Automatic Anti-Aircraft Guns

Type and date		Maker/ designer	Calibre	Projectile weight	M/V (fps)	Ammunition supply	Rate of fire	Range (yds)	No. of guns
96	1935	Hotchkiss	25mm	0.55	2950	15 box	220	3300	1, 2, 3
92	1925	Vickers	40mm	2.00	1965	50 belt	200	3300	1, 2
93	1935	Hotchkiss	13.2mm	0.12	2600	30 box	450	1650	1, 2, 4
92F	1925	Vickers	7.7mm	0.03	2440	100 belt	900	1000	1
—	1925	Lewis	7.7mm	0.03	2500	47 drum	450	1000	1, 2

The date is that of adoption by the Imperial Japanese Navy.
The Rate of fire is the standard cyclic rate and not the actual rate of fire per minute; the magazine arrangement of the Hotchkiss guns resulted in such frequent changes of the magazine that the achievable rate of fire was barely half that of the cyclic.

List of Abbreviations

AA	anti-aircraft	HMS	His/Her Majesty's ship
A/S	anti-submarine	ihp	indicated horse-power
Avgas	aviation gasoline	IJN	Imperial Japanese Navy
AW	above water	LA	low-angle
bhp	brake horse-power	lwl	load waterline
BL	breech-loader (screw-breech)	m	mile(s)
BU	broken up, scrapped	ML	muzzle-loader
BW	below water	nhp	nominal horse-power
cal	calibre	nm	nautical mile(s), 1nm = 2000 yards
-cal	length of barrel in calibres, i.e. 45-cal	oa	overall
comp	complement	pdr	pounder
CSS	Confederate States' ship	pp	between perpendiculars
CT	conning-tower	QF	quick-firer (sliding-breech)
cwl	construction waterline	RML	rifled muzzle-loader
DC	depth-charge	SBML	smooth-bore muzzle-loader
DCT	depth-charge thrower	SC	submarine chaser
DE	destroyer escort	shp	shaft horse-power
DP	dual purpose	subm	submerged
DWT	deadweight tonnage	surf	surface
DY	dockyard	TF	task force
ehp	electrical horse-power	ts	tons
FFO	furnace fuel oil	TU	steam turbine
ft	foot, feet	TT	torpedo tubes
GRT	gross register tonnage	USS	United States' ship
GTU	geared turbine	VTE	vertical triple expansion
HA	high-angle	wl	waterline

The Starting Point

In April 1868, during the War of Restoration, six ships (including the *Moshun Maru*, *Hozui Maru* and *Yuhi Maru*) were placed at the disposal of the Imperial Fleet by the Aki, Chikuzen, Hizen, Kurume, Nagato, Satsuma and Tosa "clans", all of whom supported the young Emperor Meiji. These ships flew the Imperial ensign for the first time on the occasion of the Emperor's Review, off Osaka on 15th April 1968. After the surrender and abdication of the Shogun Yoshinobu (Keiki) in May 1868, the frigate *Kaiyo*, the corvette *Kaiten* and the gunboats *Banryu* and *Chiyoda-Gata* went over to the Imperial Fleet from the navy of the shogunate. They were followed by more ships from Daimyo, which had supported the last shogun.

Twenty-four clans in north-east Japan formed an alliance and continued to offer resistance to the Emperor even after the Shogun's surrender. On 4th October 1868, eight ex-shogunate vessels serving with the Imperial Fleet went over to the rebels, the deserters being led by Enomoto Takeaki (Buyo, known as Kamajiro), formerly Commander of the Shogunate Navy. After the loss of several vessels through shipwreck or re-capture by the Imperial Fleet, Enomoto was attacked by the latter off Hokkaido in June 1869. His last ship, the *Banryu*, was sunk on 20th June and, on 27th June, he was obliged to surrender at Goryokaku Castle. This brought to an end the opposition to the Emperor Meiji. Enomoto was imprisoned, but was later pardoned and finally became the Imperial ambassador to Russia, at St. Petersburg.

With the end of the rebellion, the less essential elements of the Imperial Navy were decommissioned, leaving only *Kotetsu*, *Fugi* and *Chiyoda-Gata*, as well as the transports *Kaifu*, *Hiryu*, *Osaka Maru* and *Hiyo* (probably *Hishun*) *Maru* to be retained as the nucleus of an eventual Imperial Fleet. Their modernisation was supervised by the Ministry of War (*Hyobu-sho*) from August 1869, and by the Admiralty (*Kaigun-sho*) from February 1872. This reorganisation must therefore be regarded as the true point of origin for the Imperial Japanese Navy.

EXPLANATORY NOTES 11

1. Ironclads, Battleships and Battlecruisers

Name	Builder	Date	Displ	Length ft in	Beam ft in	Draught ft in	Machinery	SHP	Speed	Fuel	Radius	Armament	Comp
AZUMA ex-*Kôtetsu* ex-*Staerkodder* ex-*Stonewall* ex-*Sphinx*	L'Arman Bros., Bordeaux	1863–1865	1560 F 1390 N	194 9 oa; 183 7 wl; 165 7 pp	31 6	15 8	2-screw horizontal direct-acting Mazeline engines 2 Mazeline rectangular boilers	1300 ihp	9	100 approx	?	1 × 9in BL in bow casemate; 2 × 6.3in BL (Armstrong)	135

Azuma (1866)

GENERAL NOTES
An ironclad ram designed by M. Arman, with a wooden hull and iron belt. The propellers were unusual, with twin coupled rudders and two keels. This unique arrangement was intended to give great manoeuvrability. Her sister ship *Cheops* became the Prussian *Prinz Adlbert*.

ARMOUR
Belt 4½in on waterline; 5½in on CT; 4in casemate. The upper deck was also enclosed by armoured bulwarks.

TRIALS
On 9 October 1864 she made 10.8 knots on full power and 5½ knots on one engine.

CAREER
Ordered for the Confederate States' Navy as the *Sphinx*; launched 21 June 1864, completed 25 October 1864; bought by Denmark and renamed *Staerkodder*, after being blockaded in Corunna by Federal warships *Sacramento* and *Niagara* the sale was not completed, and she was renamed CSS *Stonewall*; 1865 surrendered to Federal forces; bought for the Shogun's fleet in 1867 and arrived in Yokohama 24 April 1868 with an American crew. She was later taken back into American ownership and early in 1869 was handed over to the Emperor, with the new name *Kôtetsu* (the Armoured One); renamed *Azuma* in 1871 and rated as a coast-defence battleship; stricken 28 January 1888, and served for a further period as an accommodation ship.

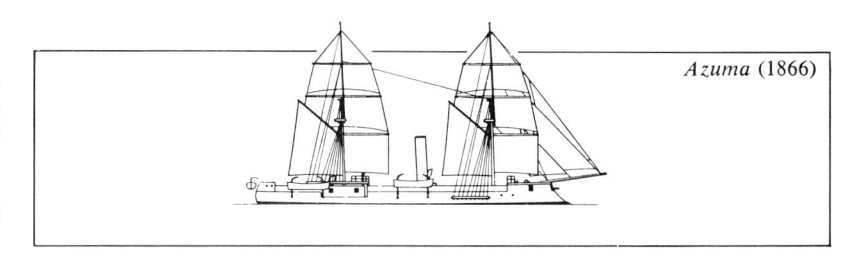

Name	Builder	Date	Displ	Length ft in	Beam ft in	Draught ft in	Machinery	SHP	Speed	Fuel	Radius	Armament	Comp
RYÛJÔ ex-*Ihosho Maru*	A. Hall, Aberdeen	1864–1869	1864 F 1429 N	210 9½ pp	38 10½	18 4 max; 17 4½ mean	Single-screw 2-cyl compound machinery	800 ihp	9	?	?	2 × 6.5in BL on central pivot mountings; 10 × 5.5in BL	275

GENERAL NOTES
An armoured corvette of composite (wood and iron) construction, with full rig.

ARMOUR
Waterline belt 4½in; casemates 4in.

RE-ARMAMENT NOTES
When rebuilt in 1894 as a gunnery training ship she was armed with 1 × 6.7in Krupp BL and 5 × 6.3in RML (64pdrs).

CAREER
Launched 1864 and completed 27 April 1869; Sold to Prince Kumamoto; arrived at Nagasaki in January 1870 and purchased the following May by Prince Higo as the *Ihosho Maru*; at the end of that year she was presented to the Emperor by the Kumamoto Princes as the *Ryûjô*; stricken in 1898 but was still in existence as a hulk in 1902; BU 1904.

The composite corvette *Ryujo* seen at Aberdeen in 1869, still under her original name of *Ihosho Maru*. (NMM.)

12 IRONCLADS, BATTLESHIPS AND BATTLECRUISERS

Name	Builder	Date	Displ	Length ft in	Beam ft in	Draught ft in	Machinery	SHP	Speed	Fuel	Radius	Armament	Comp
FUSO	Samuda Bros., Poplar	1876–1878	3718 inc to 3800 max after reconstruction	220 0 pp	48 0	18 0 inc to 20 max after reconstruction	2-screw horizontal Penn trunk engines 8 cyl boilers	3500 ihp 3932 ihp max	13 10½ by 1899	350 coal	4500 @ 10	4 × 9.4in Krupp BL 2 × 6.7in BL as built 6 small guns 5 MGs see re-armament notes for changes	250 later 386

General Notes
An armoured steel-hulled frigate or central battery ship with barque-rig, designed by Sir Edward Reed as a smaller edition of HMS *Iron Duke*. She was the first armoured ship to be built in England for Japan.

Armour
Waterline belt 9in; casemates 8in.

Re-armament and Reconstruction
In 1894 she was rebuilt and lost her barque rig and mainmast. The new armament was: 8 × 6in 50-cal QF; 7 MGs; 2 × 18in TT (AW). After her repair and refit in 1899–1900 she was again re-armed with 2 × 6in 50-cal; 4 × 4.7in 40-cal; 11 × 3pdrs QF; 3 × 18in TT (AW). From 1906 her complement was reduced to 377.

Career
Launched 14 April 1877, completed January 1878; lightly damaged 17 September 1894 in the battle of the Yalu River; sunk 29 October 1897 off Shikoku Island, following collision with the cruiser *Matsushima*; raised in September 1898 and repaired 1899/1900; served from 8 April 1900 as a coast-defence ship; stricken 1908 and BU 1910.

Fuso (1878)

Fuso (1898)

Name	Builder	Date	Displ	Length ft in	Beam ft in	Draught ft in	Machinery	SHP	Speed	Fuel	Radius	Armament	Comp
KONGÔ	Earle's SB & Eng. Co., Hull	1875–1878	3718 F	231 0 wl	41 0	18 0	Single-screw 2-cyl machinery cyl boilers	2450 ihp	13¾	280 coal	3100 @ 10	3 × 6.7in Krupp BL 6 × 5.9in Krupp BL 4 × 1pdr 7 MGs 2 × 14in TT (AW)	314
HIEI	Milford Haven SB & Eng. Co., Pembroke		2248 N	220 0 pp				2490 ihp	14				

General Notes
Built under the 1875 Programme, these armoured corvettes were designed by Sir Edward Reed. *Kongo* had a composite hull, *Hiei* had an all-iron hull.

Armour
Waterline belt 4½in.

Re-armament
In 1895 they were given a single 25mm QF. In 1903 they had 3 × 6.7in BL; 6 × 5.9in BL; 2 × 3in; 2 × 47mm; 6 MGs; 2 × 14in TT (AW).

Careers
Kongô
Launched April 1877 and completed in January 1878; on entering service she was rated as a coast-defence battleship; training ship in 1896; served until 1906 as a surveying vessel; stricken 1909, BU.

Hiei
Launched 12 June, 1877 and completed 23 March, 1878; damaged in the battle of the Yalu River, 17 September 1894; like *Kongo*, she served on surveying duties; stricken 1 April, 1911.

Hiei (1885)

Hiei, with yards crossed on her mainmast only. (Shizuo Fukui.)

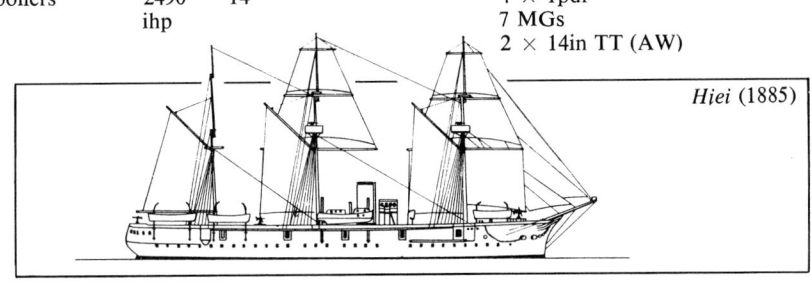

Hiei, seen after completion at Pembroke Dock in 1877 or 1878. Note that her telescopic funnel is half-lowered and that she has her original barque-rig. (Lawrence Phillips.)

Name	Builder	Date	Displ	Length ft in	Beam ft in	Draught ft in	Machinery	SHP	Speed	Fuel	Radius	Armament	Comp
HEIEN ex-*P'ing-yüan*	Foochow DY	1883–1890	2640 F 2150 N	230 0 wl 196 10¼ pp	40 0	13 9½	2-screw 3-cyl VTE cyl boilers	2400 ihp	10.2	350 coal	?	1 × 10.2in Krupp BL 2 × 6in 40-cal Krupp BL 8 × 3in 4 × 18in TT (AW)	201

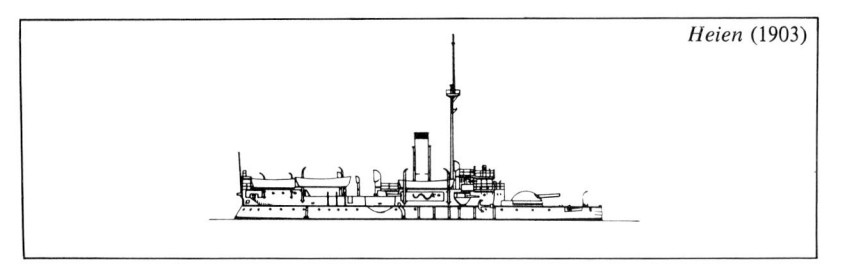

Heien (1903)

GENERAL NOTES
An armoured gunboat, built to German plans for the Chinese Navy; originally planned with similar dimensions to *Chen Yüan*.

ARMOUR
Belt 8in; turret 5in; deck 2in.

RE-ARMAMENT
About 1906 she was armed with Armstrong-pattern 6in in place of the Krupp guns.

CAREER
Launched 1890 and completed in that year for the Chinese Navy; captured 12 February, 1895 at Wei-hai-wei by the Japanese and incorporated into the Japanese Fleet as a 1st Class gunboat; sunk by a Russian mine West of Port Arthur 18 September 1904 (38°57′N, 120°56′E).

The former Chinese armoured gunboat *P'ing-Yüan* captured in 1895, but seen here in Japanese service prior to her loss in 1904. Her single Krupp 26cm gun can be seen on the forecastle, partly hidden under an awning. (Shizuo Fukui.)

Name	Builder	Date	Displ	Length ft in	Beam ft in	Draught ft in	Machinery	SHP	Speed	Fuel	Radius	Armament	Comp
CHIN'EN ex-*Chen Yüan*.	VulcanWorks, Stettin	1880–1885	7670 F 7220 N	308 0 oa 298 6½ wl	59 0	20 0	2-screw 3-cyl trunk engines, cyl boilers	6000 ihp	14½ normal 1000 max	650	4500 @ 10	4 × 12in 20-cal (Krupp) 2 × 5.9in 40-cal (Krupp) 8 × 1pdr 2 × 57mm 3 × 14in TT (AW)	250

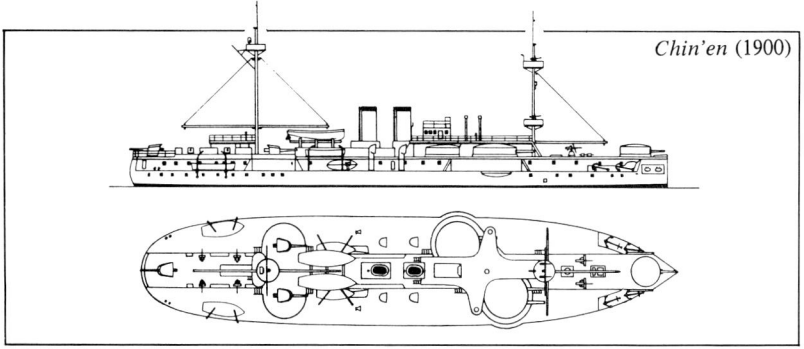

Chin'en (1900)

GENERAL NOTES
An armoured turret ship, sister ship of the Chinese *Ting-Yüan*.

ARMOUR
Belt 14in; turrets 12in; casemates 8in; deck 3in.

RE-ARMAMENT
In 1895/6 she was armed with 4 × 12in; 4 × 6in (Elswick); 2 × 57mm (Nordenfelt); 8 × 47mm.

CAREER
Launched 28 November 1882 and completed in 1885 for the Chinese Navy; damaged at battle of Yalu River 17 September 1894 and then surrendered at Wei-hai-wei 12 February, 1895; taken into the Japanese Fleet as a 2nd Class battleship; stricken 1911 and BU 1914.

The former Chinese battleship *Chen-Yüan* and her sister *Ting-Yüan* had their 12-inch guns mounted en echelon amidships, as in the British ship *Inflexible*. She surrendered after sustaining damage in the Battle of the Yalu River, and was renamed *Chin'En*. (Bundesarchiv.)

Name	Builder	Date	Displ	Length ft in	Beam ft in	Draught ft in	Machinery	SHP	Speed	Fuel	Radius	Armament	Comp
IKI ex-*Imperator Nikolai I*	New Admiralty Works, St. Petersburg	1886–1893	9960 F 8440 N	331 4 wl 327 11 pp	67 0	24 11	2-screw 3-cyl VTE 16 Belleville boilers	8000 ihp	16	850 normal 1000 max	4900 @ 10	2 × 12in 30-cal (1 × 2) 4 × 9in 35-cal 8 × 6in 35-cal 16 × 47mm 4 × 37mm 6 × 14in TT (AW)	611

Iki (1906)

GENERAL NOTES
Ex-Russian battleship, sister ship of *Imperator Alexander II*.

ARMOUR
Belt 14in; turrets 10in to 9in; casemates 6in; deck 2½in.

RECONSTRUCTION NOTES
Her machinery had been rebuilt between 1898 and 1900, and on trials on 30 October, 1900 she made 14.8 knots with 5000 ihp, as against the 8000 ihp anticipated. After being taken over in 1905 she was armed with 2 × 12in 30-cal; 6 × 6in 40-cal; 6 × 4.7in 40-cal; 6 × 3in. From 1910 she was armed with 2 × 12in 40-cal; 6 × 6in QF; 6 × 4.7in QF.

CAREER
Launched 27 October, 1889 and completed in 1893 for the Imperial Russian Navy; she surrendered near the Liancourt Reef after the battle of Tsushima, 28 May, 1905 having been part of Rear-Admiral Nebogatov's squadron; from 1905 to 1910 she was a gunnery training ship; from 1910 to 1915 she was a coast-defence ship and training ship for seamen and boys; stricken 1 May 1915 and sunk October 1915 as a target for the *Kongo* and *Hiei*.

Name	Builder	Date	Displ	Length ft in	Beam ft in	Draught ft in	Machinery	SHP	Speed	Fuel	Radius	Armament	Comp
MISHIMA ex-*Admiral Senyavin*	New Admiralty Works, St. Petersburg	1892–1895	4270 F 4165 N	277 6 wl	52 2	17 0¾	2-screw 3-cyl triple-expansion, Miyabara boilers	5250 ihp	16	260 normal 400 max coal	3000 @ 10	4 × 10in 45-cal 4 × 4.7in 45-cal 10 × 47mm 12 × 37mm 4 × 18in TT (AW)	406

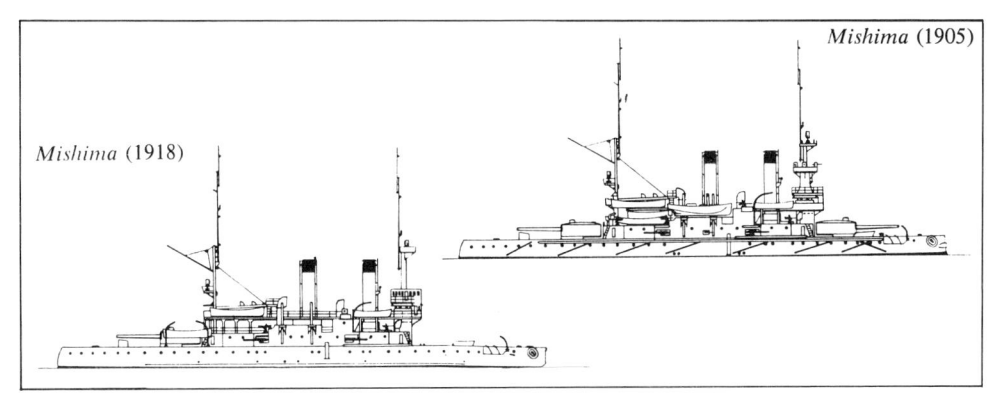

Mishima (1918)

Mishima (1905)

GENERAL NOTES
Ex-Russian coast-defence battleship, sister of *Admiral Ushakov*.

ARMOUR
Harvey compound steel. Belt on waterline 10in; turrets 8in; deck 3in.

MACHINERY
On her original trials she made 5327 ihp, = 16.1 knots.

RE-ARMAMENT
After repairs (March 1907) she carried 4 × 9.2in; 6 × 6in; from 1918 she carried only 2 × 9.2in and 6 × 6in.

CAREER
Launched 22 August 1894 and completed in 1895 for the Russian Navy; she surrendered 28 May, 1905 near the Liancourt Reef, having been slightly damaged at the battle of Tsushima; repaired at Mazuru; in the spring of 1907 she was badly damaged by an ammunition explosion, but was repaired; stricken in 1928 and became a submarine tender; hulked and renamed *Haikan No 7* 10 April 1936; sunk as a target in 1936.

The ex-Russian coast-defence battleship *Admiral Senyavin*, seen at Sasebo on 31st July 1905, just after recommissioning as the *Mishima*. She had been captured with only slight damage at Tsushima. (Shizuo Fukui.)

IRONCLADS, BATTLESHIPS AND BATTLECRUISERS

Name	Builder	Date	Displ	Length ft in	Beam ft in	Draught ft in	Machinery	SHP	Speed	Fuel	Radius	Armament	Comp
OKINOSHIMA ex-*General-Admiral Apraxin*	Baltic Works, St. Petersburg	1895–1898	5050 F 4126 N	227 6 wl	52 6	19 0	2-screw VTE 18 Belleville boilers	5250 ihp	16	260 normal 400 max coal	3000 @ 10	3 × 10in 45-cal 4 × 4.7in 45-cal QF 10 × 47mm 12 × 37mm 4 × 18in TT (AW)	404

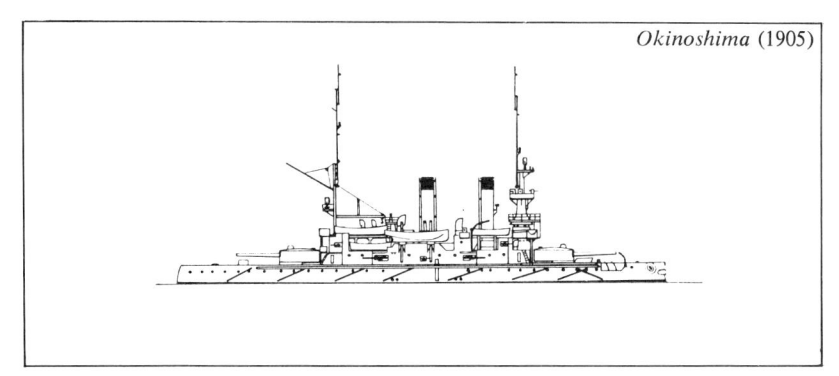

Okinoshima (1905)

GENERAL NOTES
Ex-Russian coast-defence ship, very similar to *Mishima*.

ARMOUR
Harvey compound steel. Belt 10in; turrets 8in; deck 3in.

MACHINERY NOTES
On original trials she reached 5757 ihp = 15.1 knots.

RE-ARMAMENT NOTES
From 1905 she had 3 × 10in; 6 × 6in, but later the 6in were replaced by 6 × 4.7in and finally she carried only 4 × 4.7in guns as a training hulk.

CAREER
Launched 12 May, 1896 and completed in 1898 for the Russian Navy; surrendered off Liancourt Reef 28 May, 1905; she was used as a training ship from 1905 to 1915; disarmed as an accommodation ship for cadets; stricken 1922 and hulked; BU 1939.

Okinoshima (ex-Russian *General-Admiral Apraxin*) was similar to the *Mishima*. She survived as a hulk until 1939. (Shizuo Fukui.)

Name	Builder	Date	Displ	Length ft in	Beam ft in	Draught ft in	Machinery	SHP	Speed	Fuel	Radius	Armament	Comp
FUJI	Thames Ironworks, Blackwall	1894–1897	12533 N *Fuji*	412 0 oa 400 0 wl	73 3	26 6	2-shaft 3-cyl VTE 14 cyl boilers	13500 ihp	18¼	700 normal 1200 max coal	4000 @ 10	4 × 12in 40-cal 10 × 6in 40-cal QF 24 × 47mm 5 × 18in TT (4 AW, 1 UW)	637
YASHIMA	Armstrong, Mitchell & Co., Elswick		12320 N *Yashima*	374 0 pp	73 9	26 3							

GENERAL NOTES
1894 Programme. *Fuji* was the first battleship built for the Japanese Navy. Unlike *Fuji*, *Yashima* had the keel cut away sharply towards the rudder.

ARMOUR
Harvey-nickel steel. Belt 18in over machinery spaces, thinning to 16in and 14in at the ends; bulkheads 14in forward, 12in aft; deck 2½in throughout; upper belt 4in carried to upper deck; barbettes 14in upper, 9in lower; casemates and turrets 6in; CT 14in.

MACHINERY NOTES
On trials, *Fuji* made 18½ knots with 14600 ihp and 16.8 knots with 10200 ihp. On a four-hour trial, *Yashima* made 19.227 knots with 14000 ihp. In both ships, the torpedoes could not be fired above 14 knots.

RE-ARMAMENT
Between 1900 and 1901, 16 of the 47mm (3pdr) guns were replaced by the same number of 3in (12pdrs) and complement was increased to 652 (later rose to 741). In 1910 *Fuji* was reboilered with ten Miyabara boilers, and her Armstrong-pattern guns were replaced by Japanese Model '41' 12in 40-cal guns. She was disarmed as a training hulk at Yokosuka (9179ts, 21.85ft draught); wooden deckhouses were fitted on the upper deck and the propellers were removed.

Fuji, the first Japanese battleship. (IWM.)

Fuji (1905)

Fuji (1912)

Fuji as a training hulk (1945)

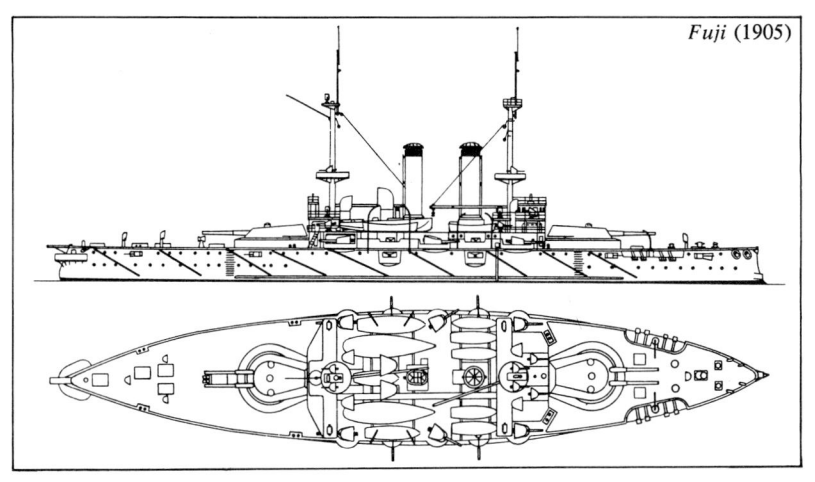

CAREERS

Fuji
Launched 31 March, 1896 and completed 17 August 1897; she and the other modern ships were the backbone of the fleet in the Russo-Japanese War; in 1910 she was rated as a 1st Class coast-defence ship and a training ship for gunners and seamen; disarmed 1922 and stricken 1 September 1922 and rated as a transport; training ship from 1 December 1922 (see Re-armament Notes above) but served until 1945 as a hulk in Yokosuka for training seamen and navigators; BU 1948 at Yokosuka.

Yashima
Launched 28 February 1896 and completed 9 September, 1897; on 15 May, 1904 she was badly damaged in a minefield laid by the Russian *Amur* 10 m SE of Port Arthur; while in tow she sank later the same day off Encounter Rock (38°34′ N, 121°40′ E).

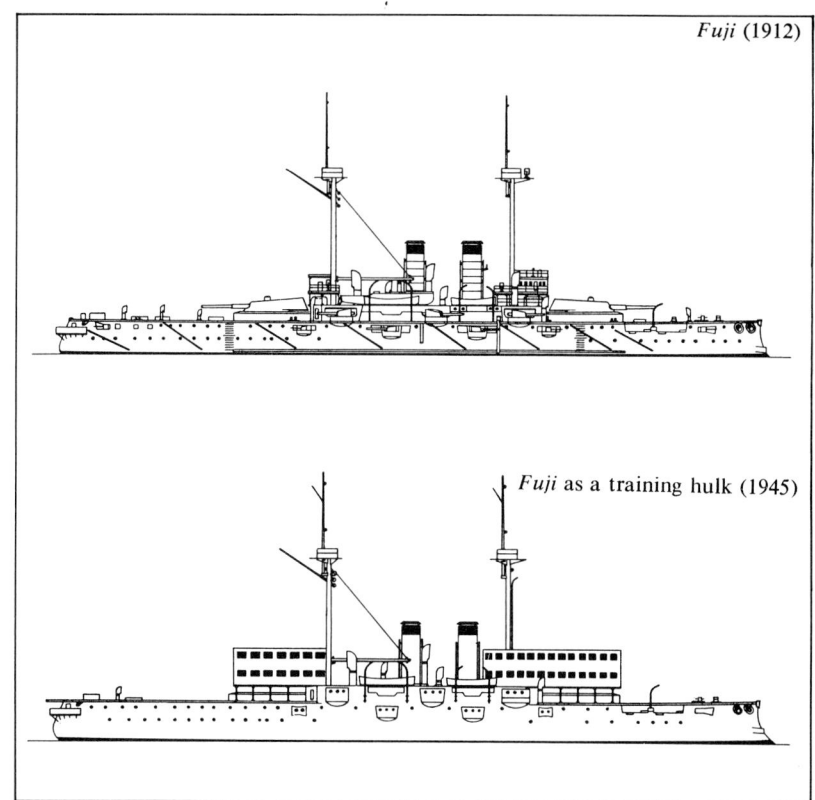

Name	Builder	Date	Displ	Length ft in	Beam ft in	Draught ft in	Machinery	SHP	Speed	Fuel	Radius	Armament	Comp
SHIKISHIMA **HATSUSE**	Thames Ironworks, Blackwall Armstrong Mitchell & Co., Elswick	1897– 1901	15453 F 14850 N *Shikishima* 15255 F 15000 N *Hatsuse*	438 0 oa (76 9 0 415 wl 400 0 pp	75 6 *Hatsuse*)	27 3 (27 0 *Hatsuse*)	2-shaft VTE 25 Belleville boilers	14500 ihp	18	700 1400 coal	5000 @ 10	4 × 12in 40-cal 14 × 6in 45-cal QF 20 × 3in QF 12 × 47mm 4 × 18in TT (UW) + 1 TT (AW) in *Shikishima*	741

Shikishima (1901)

Shikishima (1915)

Shikishima as a training hulk (1945)

GENERAL NOTES
Ordered after the Sino-Japanese War of 1894-5 as equivalents of the British *Formidable* class. *Shikishima* had a different hull-form from *Hatsuse* which resembled *Yashima*. *Hatsuse* had shorter topmasts.

ARMOUR
Harvey-nickel steel. Belt 9in (4in ends); deck 1.6in to 0.8in; barbettes 14in; casemates 6in.

RE-ARMAMENT
Shikishima was disarmed at Sasebo in 1922 (11275ts, 21.65ft draught).

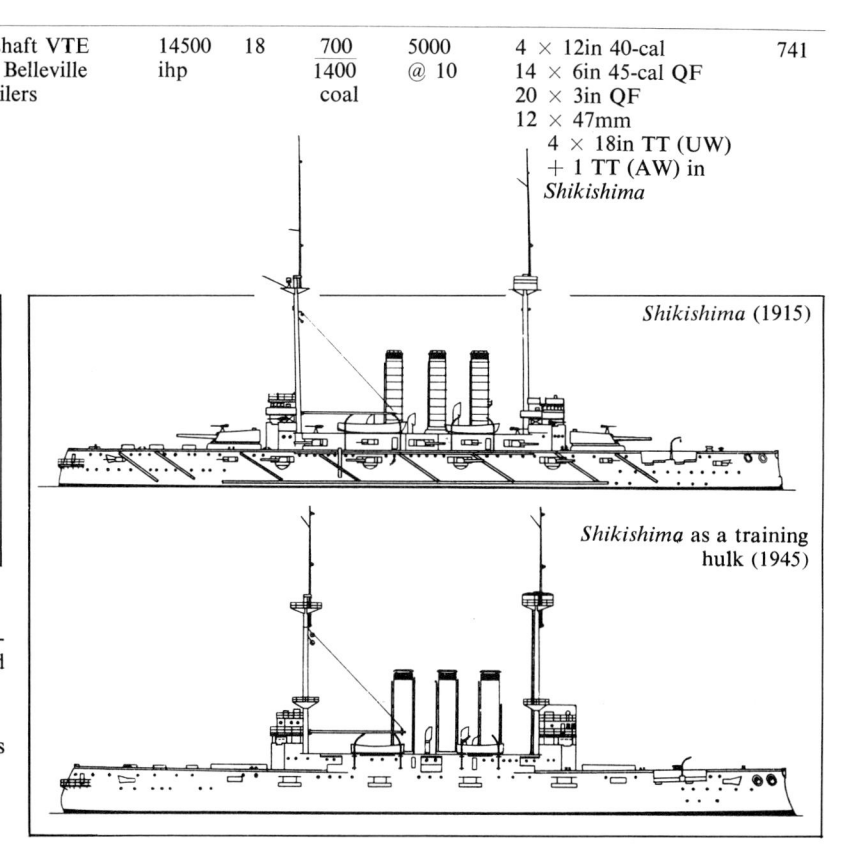

MACHINERY NOTES
On an eight-hour trial on 15 October 1899, *Shikishima* reached a maximum of 19.027 knots with 14667 ihp (averaging 18.78 knots).

CAREERS
Shikishima
Launched 1 November 1898 and completed 26 January 1900; she left Portsmouth on 27 January 1900 for Japan; served with main Fleet throughout the Russo-Japanese War; re-rated as a 1st Class coast defence ship on 1 September, 1921 and used as a training ship for submarine personnel; stricken 1923 and disarmed; rated as a transport from 1 April 1923; remained at Sasebo as a hulk until 1945; BU at Sasebo in 1948.

Hatsuse
Launched 27 June, 1899 and completed 18 January, 1901; on 15 May, 1904 she sank 10 m SE of Port Arthur (38°37′ N, 121°20′ E) after striking a mine laid by the Russian *Amur* the previous day.

Name	Builder	Date	Displ	Length ft in	Beam ft in	Draught ft in	Machinery	SHP	Speed	Fuel	Radius	Armament	Comp
ASAHI	John Brown & Co., Clydebank	1898–1900	15374 F 15200 N	425 3 oa 415 0 wl 400 3 pp	75 0	27 3	2-shaft 3-cyl VTE, 25 belleville boilers	15000 ihp	18	1000 / 2000 coal	9000 @ 10	4 × 12in 40-cal 14 × 6in 45-cal 20 × 3in QF 12 × 47mm (3- or 2½- pdrs) 4 × 18in-TT (UW)	773

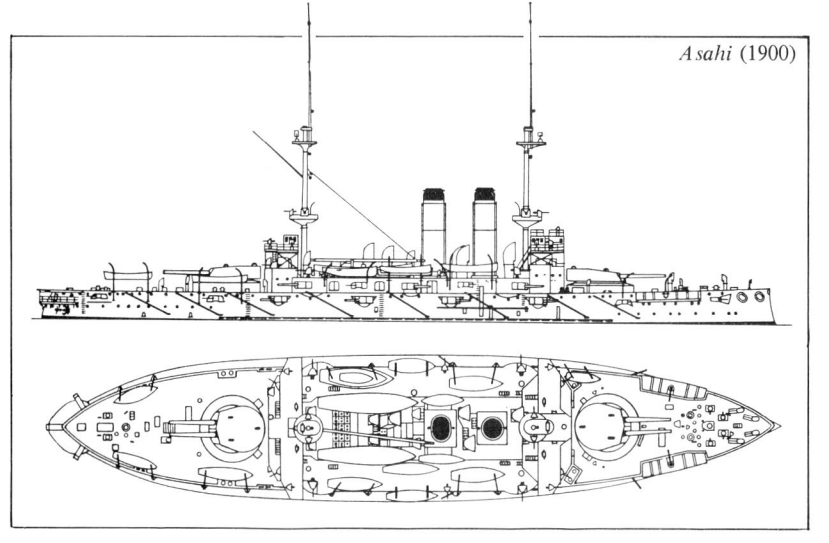

Asahi (1900)

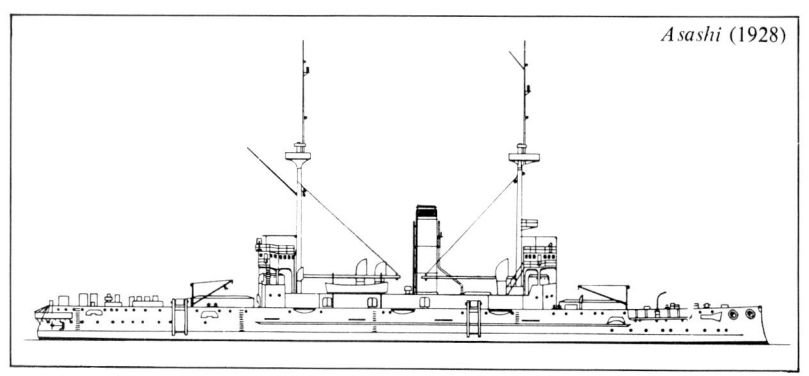

Asahi (1928)

GENERAL NOTES
Ordered under the post-war Programme of 1896–7. Apart from the number of funnels and the disposition of the 47mm guns, she was virtually a sister of the *Shikishima*.

ARMOUR
Harvey-nickel steel, and had a belt 250ft long, 8.2ft deep, extending 2.62ft below the waterline. Belt 9in maximum; barbettes 14in; turrets and casemates 6in; CT 14in to 3in.

RE-ARMAMENT AND RECONSTRUCTION
In 1917 the Armstrong-pattern 12in guns were replaced by Japanese Model '41' 12in 40-cal. Disarmed at Yokosuka in 1922, reducing displacement to 11441ts, speed to 12 knots. In 1927 she was reboilered with 4 Kampon Type RO boilers, and only one funnel.

CAREER
Launched 13 March, 1899 and completed 31 July, 1900; badly damaged by a Russian mine near Port Arthur 26 October, 1904; repaired at Sasebo by April 1905 and fought at Tsushima; in 1914 she became a gunnery training ship; re-rated as a 1st Class coast-defence ship in September 1921; on 1 April, 1923 she became a depot-, training- and repair-ship for submarines; disarmed in July 1923; on 25 May, 1942 she was torpedoed 100 m SW of Cape Paderan (10°00′ N, 110°00′ E) by the American submarine *Salmon*.

The battleship *Asahi* remained in service until 1923. Thereafter she was converted into a submarine depot- and repair-ship with one funnel removed and heavy lifting-frames on either side amidships. The port lifting frame can be seen just forward of the funnel. (NMM/Richard Perkins.)

Name	Builder	Date	Displ	Length ft in	Beam ft in	Draught ft in	Machinery	SHP	Speed	Fuel	Radius	Armament	Comp
MIKASA	Vickers, Sons & Co., Barrow	1899–1902	15179 F 15140 N	321 0 oa 414 8 wl 400 0 pp	76 0	27 2	2-shaft VTE 25 Belleville boilers	15000 ihp	18	1000 / 2000 coal	9000 @ 10	4 × 12in 40-cal 14 × 6in 45-cal QF 20 × 3in QF 12 × 47mm (3- or 2½- pdrs) 4 × 18in TT (UW)	756 / 935

IRONCLADS, BATTLESHIPS AND BATTLECRUISERS

GENERAL NOTES
Part of the post-war Programme of 1896–7, and the most modern unit in the battle fleet during the Russo-Japanese War.

ARMOUR
Harvey-nickel steel. Belt 9in to 4in; barbettes 14in to 6in; turrets 10in to 8in; casemates 6in; CT 14in to 4in.

MACHINERY
The machinery weighed 1355ts, and had a heating surface of 37458 sq ft and grate surface of 1270 sq ft. On trials in December 1901 she reached 16341 ihp = 18.45 knots (at 15140ts).

RE-ARMAMENT
After being salvaged at Sasebo in 1906–7, she was to have been rebuilt in similar fashion to the *Iwami* with 12in 45-cal and 14 × 6in 45-cal guns but was cancelled.

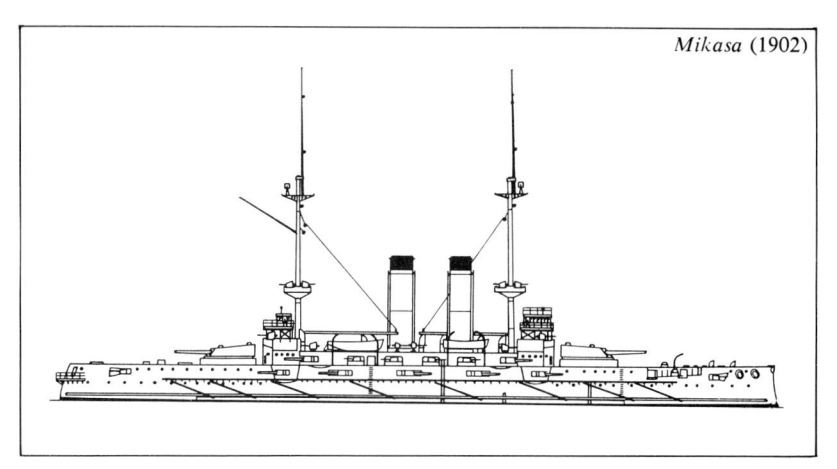

CAREER
Launched 8 November, 1900, and completed 1 March, 1902; she was Admiral Togo's flagship in the Russo-Japanese War; on the night of 11/12 September, 1905 she sank at her moorings in Sasebo after an ammunition and torpedo explosion; she was raised 7 August, 1906 and repaired at Sasebo; she re-entered service on 24 August, 1908; in September 1921 she was re-rated as a 1st Class coast-defence ship, but on 17 September in the same year she ran aground near Askold Island off Vladivostok; refloated and stricken 20 September, 1923; on 12 November, 1926 she was opened as a memorial by Prince Hirohito and Admiral Togo at Yokosuka, where she remained until 1945; she deteriorated between 1945 and 1959 but in 1960 she was restored.

Mikasa (1902)

Name	Builder	Date	Displ	Length ft in	Beam ft in	Draught ft in	Machinery	SHP	Speed	Fuel	Radius	Armament	Comp
TANGO ex-*Poltava*	New Admiralty Works, St. Petersburg	1892–1898	11400 F 10960 N	367 0 wl 340 1 pp	69 0	25 6	2-shaft 3-cyl VTE 14 cyl boilers	10600 ihp	17	700 / 1050 coal	1750 @ 16 4000 @ 10	4 × 12in 40-cal 12 × 6in 45-cal QF 16 × 47mm 12 × 37mm 6 × 15in TT (UW)	700

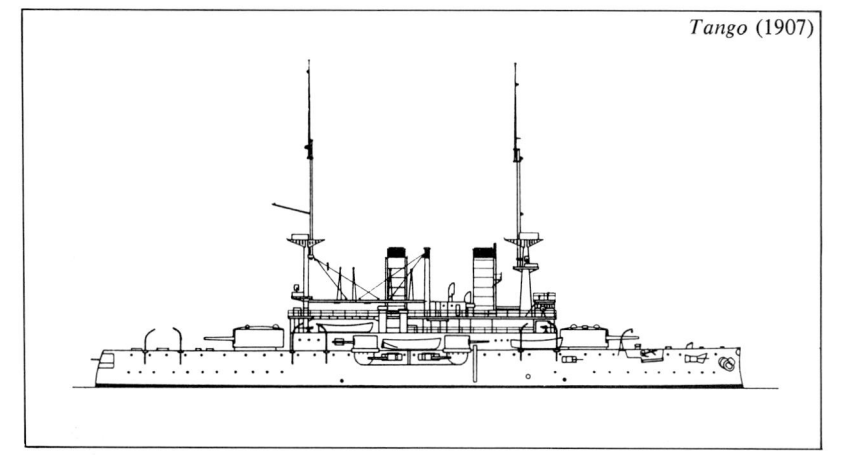

Tango (1907)

The ex-Russian *Tango* was rearmed after being raised at Port Arthur. She is seen here on her arrival at Maizuru, without guns or fittings, in 1907. (Marius Bar.)

GENERAL NOTES
An ex-Russian battleship, sister of the *Sevastopol* and *Petropavlovsk*.

ARMOUR
Harvey-nickel steel. Belt 15in to 3.9in; deck 2¾in; batteries and casemates 5in; turrets 10in to 6in; CT 9in.

RE-ARMAMENT
Refitted at Maizuru in 1908 with 16 Miyabara boilers and Armstrong-pattern weapons. The 47mm and 37mm positions at the bow, and the bow and stern TT were suppressed and replaced by 6 × 3.1in QF. The complement was increased to 750.

MACHINERY NOTES
On trials she reached 11255 ihp = 16.3 knots.

CAREER
Launched 6 November, 1894 and completed in 1898 for the Russian Navy; sunk at about 14.45 hrs 5 December, 1904 at Port Arthur by hits from Japanese 11in howitzer shells; fell into Japanese hands 2 January, 1905 and renamed *Tango* 21 July; in 1909 she was re-rated as a 1st Class coast-defence ship and served as a training ship for seamen and gunners; returned to Russia in March 1916 and renamed *Poltava* 5 April; renamed *Tchesma* in 1917; BU 1923.

Name	Builder	Date	Displ	Length ft in	Beam ft in	Draught ft in	Machinery	SHP	Speed	Fuel	Radius	Armament	Comp
SAGAMI ex-*Peresviet* **SUO** ex-*Pobieda*	Baltic Works, St. Petersburg	1895–1901 1898–1902	13500 F 12674 N	435 0 oa 424 0 wl 404 9½ pp	71 6	27 3	3-shaft VTE 30 Belleville boilers	14500 ihp	18	1060 / 2056 coal	6000 @ 10 10000 @ 10	4 × 10in 45-cal 11 × 6in 45-cal 20 × 75mm 60-cal 21 × 47mm 8 × 37mm 5 × 15in TT (3 AW, 2 UW)	732 / 775

IRONCLADS, BATTLESHIPS AND BATTLECRUISERS 19

Sagami (1908)

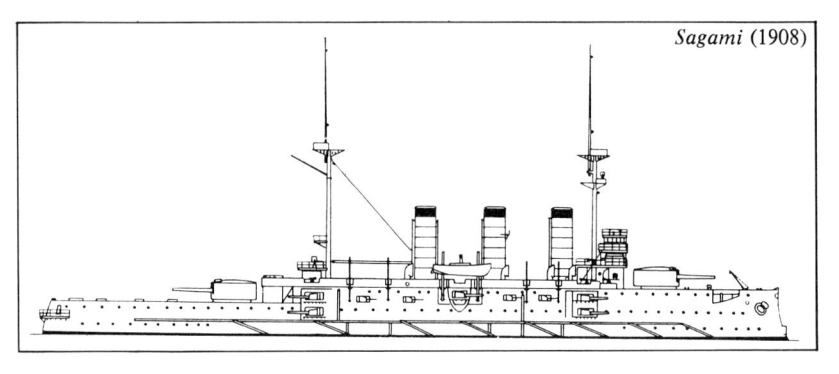

Suo (1908)

GENERAL NOTES
Ex-Russian battleships, sisters of the *Oslyabya*.

ARMOUR
Krupp steel. Belt 9in to 3.9in; deck 2.3in; batteries and casemates 5in; turrets 10in to 6in; CT 6in to 4in.

RE-ARMAMENT NOTES
Both repaired at Yokosuka in 1905–08 with Miyabara boilers and Armstrong-pattern guns: 4 × 12in 45-cal; 10 × 6in 45-cal; 16 × 3.1in; 26 small guns; 4 × 18in TT. The new hull dimensions were: displacement 12900ts; beam 71.76ft; draught 26.02ft. The fighting tops were removed from their masts.

MACHINERY NOTES
On trials, *Pobieda* reached 15442 ihp = 18½ knots.

CAREERS
Sagami
Launched 19 May, 1898 and completed in 1901 for Russian Navy; sunk in Port Arthur 6 December, 1904 by shellfire from Japanese 11in howitzers; fell into Japanese hands 2 January, 1905; salvaged 29 June, 1905: renamed *Sagami* and recommissioned in April 1908 at Yokosuka DY as a 1st Class coast-defence ship; returned to the Russians in March 1916 and renamed *Peresviet*; on 4 January, 1917 she struck a mine about 10 m from Port Said (laid by U.73) and sank with the loss of 116 lives.

Suo
Launched 24 May, 1900 and completed in 1902 for the Russian Navy; sunk at her moorings in Port Arthur by Japanese howitzer fire 7 December, 1904; fell into Japanese hands 2 January, 1905 and salvaged 17 October; renamed *Suo*: recommissioned in October 1908 as a 1st Class coast-defence ship and served as a training ship for engineers and cadets; disarmed at Kure in April 1922; stranded in Kure 13 July, 1922 and had her armour removed; hulked at Mitsugo Jima; BU after 1946 at Kure.

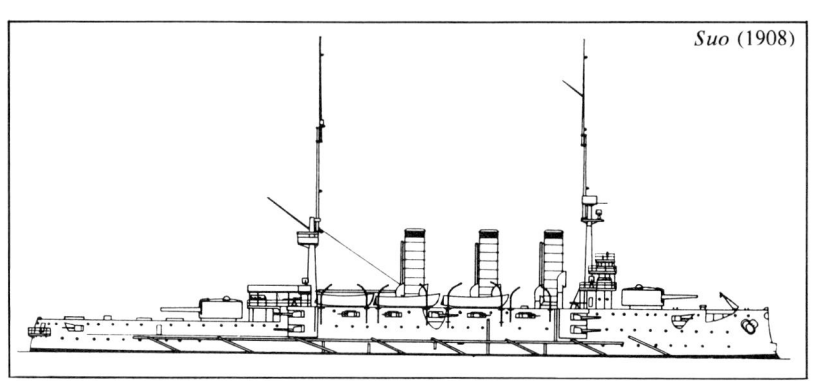

Suo, as the Russian battleship *Pobieda*, shortly after completion in 1902. (IWM.)

Name	Builder	Date	Displ	Length ft in	Beam ft in	Draught ft in	Machinery	SHP	Speed	Fuel	Radius	Armament	Comp
HIZEN ex-*Retvizan*	Wm Cramp & Sons, Philadelphia	1898–1902	12902 F 12700 N	383 10 oa 374 0 wl 372 0 pp	72 3	26 0	2-shaft 3-cyl VTE 24 Niclausse boilers	16000 ihp	18	1016 / 2000 coal	4000 @ 10 / 8800 @ 10	4 × 12in 40-cal 12 × 6in 45-cal QF 20 × 75mm QF 24 × 47mm 8 × 37mm 6 × 15in TT (4 AW, 2 UW)	778

GENERAL NOTES
American-built ex-Russian battleship.

ARMOUR
Krupp steel. Belt 9in to 3.9in; batteries and casemates 5in; deck 3in to 2in; turrets 10in to 9in; CT 10in.

RE-ARMAMENT
Repaired at Sasebo from January 1906 to November 1908, with Miyabara boilers and Armstrong-pattern guns: 4 × 12in 45-cal; 12 × 6in 45-cal QF; 20 × 3.1in QF; 20 × 47mm; 8 × 37mm; 4 × 18in TT (AW). Complement increased to 741.

MACHINERY NOTES
On trials she reached 16120 ihp = 18.8 knots.

CAREER
Launched 23 October, 1900 and completed in 1902 for Russian Navy; sunk at her moorings by Japanese 11in howitzer fire; fell into Japanese hands 2 January, 1905 and raised 22 September; renamed *Hizen* and entered service as a battleship in November 1908; re-rated as a 1st Class coast-defence ship in September 1921; disarmed at Sasebo in 1922; stricken 20 September, 1923 and sunk as a target in July 1924 in the Bungo Straits by the guns of the Combined Fleet.

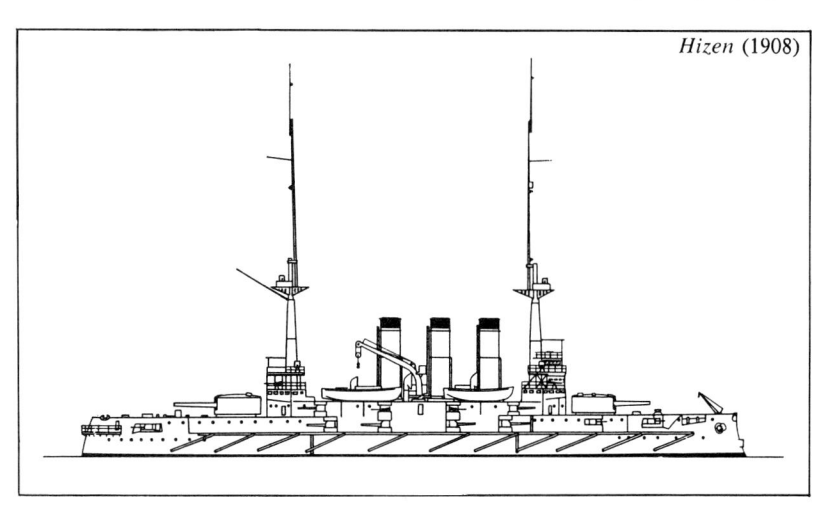

Hizen (1908)

The battleship *Hizen*. Formerly the Russian *Retvizan*, she was the only battleship built on American lines for a foreign navy at that time. She was sunk at her moorings at Port Arthur by gunfire and later salvaged. Note that the original prominent funnel-caps have been removed. (Shizuo Fukui.)

Name	Builder	Date	Displ	Length ft in	Beam ft in	Draught ft in	Machinery	SHP	Speed	Fuel	Radius	Armament	Comp
IWAMI ex-*Orel*	Franco-Russian Works, St. Petersburg	1900–1904	15300 F 13516 N	397 0 oa 376 5½ pp	76 0	26 0	2-shaft 4-cyl compound 20 Belleville boilers	15800 ihp	18	1250 / 2000 coal	5000 @ 10 8500 @ 10	4 × 12in 40-cal 12 × 6in 45-cal QF 20 × 75mm 60-cal QF 20 × 47mm 8 × 37mm 6 × 18in TT (4 AW, 2 UW)	740

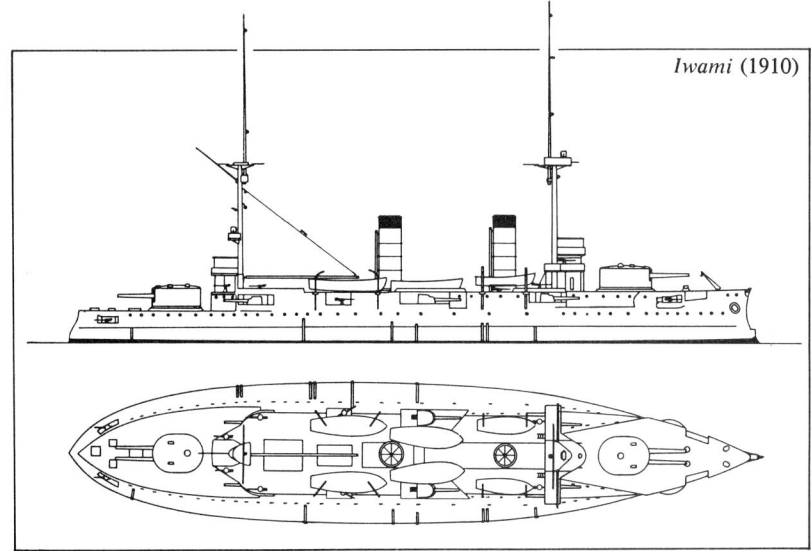

Iwami (1910)

MACHINERY NOTES
On trials she reached 16300 ihp = 17.6 knots.

CAREER
Launched 19 July, 1902 and completed in September 1904 for Russian Navy; heavily damaged by Japanese gunfire in battle of Tsushima 27 May, 1905; surrendered next day near the Liancourt Reef; renamed *Iwami* in 1907; re-rated as a 1st Class coast-defence ship in September 1921; disarmed in April 1922; stricken 1 September, 1922; sunk July 1924 off Miura as a target for aircraft.

GENERAL NOTES
Ex-Russian battleship, sole survivor of the *Borodino* Class (Sisters *Slava*, *Borodino*, *Imperator Alexander III*, *Kuiaz Suvorov*.

ARMOUR
Krupp steel. Belt 9in to 3.9in; deck 2¾in to 1½in; battery and casemates 5in; turrets 11in to 6in; CT 8in to 3in.

RE-ARMAMENT AND RECONSTRUCTION
Repairs completed at Kure DY by June 1907. The flying deck amidships was removed, the funnels were shortened, the main deck gun-positions were plated over, and the flying bridge and fighting tops were removed. The effect was to reduce the silhouette and improve stability. Other improvements were the substitution of Miyabara boilers and Armstrong-pattern guns: 4 × 12in 45-cal; 6 × 8in 45-cal; 16 × 3in 50-cal QF; 20 × 47mm; 8 × 37mm; 2 × 18in TT (UW). The complement was increased to 750.

Iwami off Tsingtao, in the early months of World War One. (IWM.)

IRONCLADS, BATTLESHIPS AND BATTLECRUISERS

Name	Builder	Date	Displ	Length		Beam		Draught		Machinery	SHP	Speed	Fuel	Radius	Armament	Comp
				ft	in	ft	in	ft	in							
KASHIMA	Vickers & Sons, Barrow	1904–1906	17200 F 16400 N	473 oa 455 wl 420 pp	7 0 0	78	2	26	4	2-shaft 4-cyl compound 20 Niclausse boilers	15800 ihp	18½	750 oil 2200 coal	3600 @ 18 12000 @ 11	4 × 12in 45-cal 4 × 10in 45-cal 12 × 6in 45-cal QF 16 × 3in QF 3 × 47mm 4 MGs 5 × 18in TT (UW) 2 × 56ft TBs 2nd Cl TBs	864/980
KATORI	Armstrong, Whitworth & Co., Elswick		16663 F 15950 N	456 oa 425 pp	3 0	78	0	27	0		16000 ihp		377 oil 2150 coal		4 × 12in 46.7-cal 4 × 10in 46.7-cal 12 × 6in 44-cal 12 × 3in QF 3 × 47mm 6 MGs 5 × 18in TT (UW) 2 × 56 ft 2nd Cl TBs	

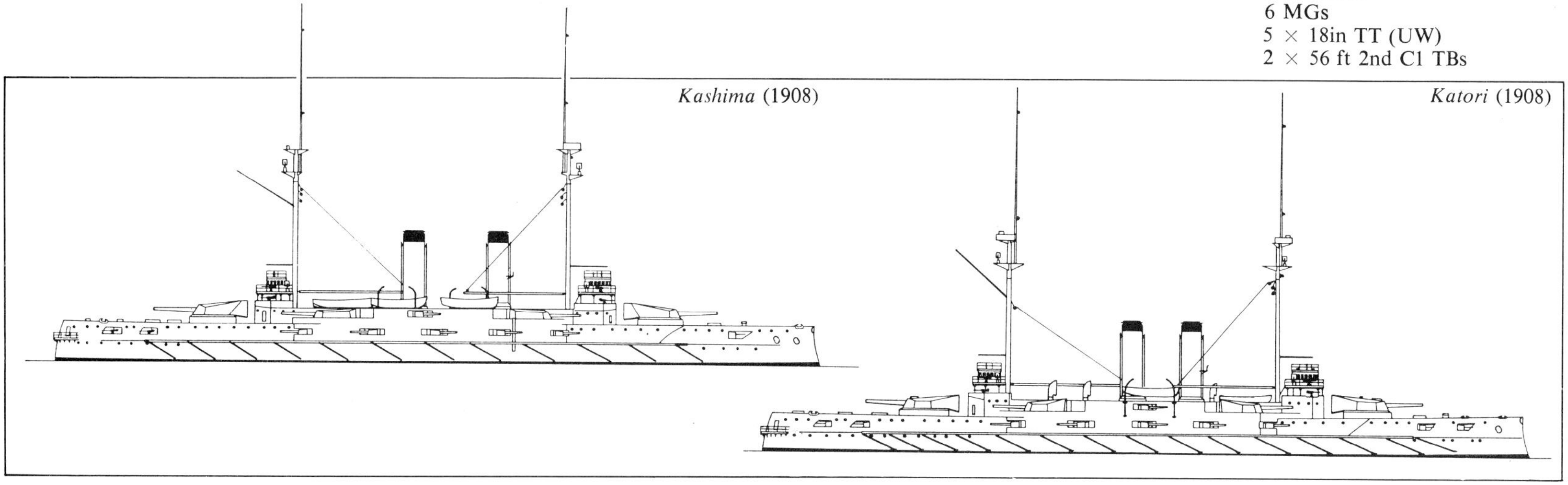

Kashima (1908)

Katori (1908)

General Notes
Built under the 1903 Programme, these were the last battleships to be built outside Japan. *Katori* was to have been launched at the same time as *Kashima* but the ceremony was delayed to coincide with the visit of Prince and Princess Arisugawa.

Armour
Krupp steel. Belt 9in to 3½in; deck 3in to 2in; casemates 10in to 6in.

Machinery Notes
Heating surface of boilers 44056 sq ft. Grate area 14359 sq ft. On trials on 4 April, 1906 *Kashima* made 19.24 knots with 17280 ihp; *Katori* made 19.5 knots on her trials, with 18500 ihp.

Careers
Kashima
Launched 22 March, 1905 and completed 23 May, 1906; disarmed at Maizuru in April 1922; stricken 1923 and BU by November 1924 by Mitsubishi at Nagasaki.
Katori
Launched 4 July, 1905 and completed 20 May, 1906; disarmed April 1922 at Maizuru; stricken 1923 and BU by January 1925 at Maizuru.

The *Kashima* was similar to the British *King Edward VII* class. (Shizuo Fukui.)

The sister ship of the *Kashima*, Vickers' Barrow yard in 1906. (Author's collection.)

Name	Builder	Date	Displ	Length ft in	Beam ft in	Draught ft in	Machinery	SHP	Speed	Fuel	Radius	Armament	Comp
— (1903/4 Design)	—	—	17000 N	450 0 wl 429 0 pp	80 0	27 10	?	?	18	?	?	8 × 12in 16 × 6in 4 × 4.7in 4 × 18in TT (UW)	?

GENERAL NOTES
Under the 1903 Programme a large but lightly armoured battleship was planned, but the design was totally recast and became the *Satsuma*.

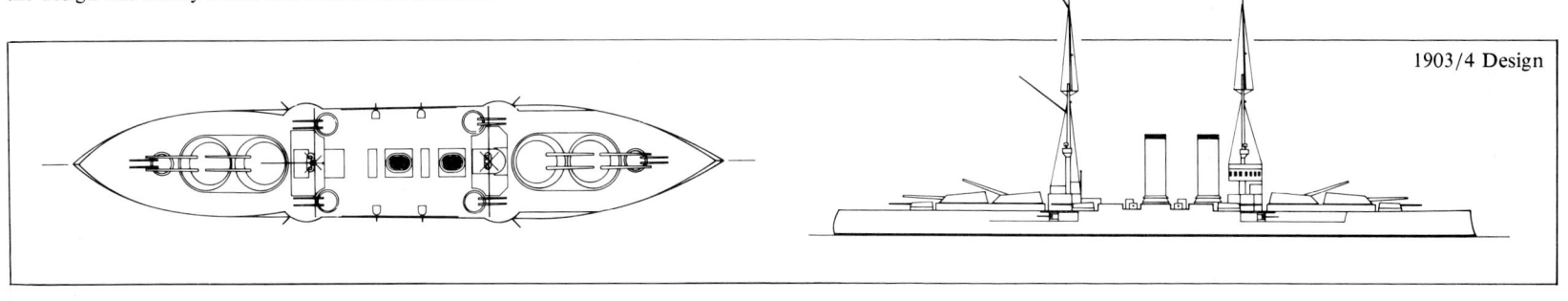

1903/4 Design

Name	Builder	Date	Displ	Length ft in	Beam ft in	Draught ft in	Machinery	SHP	Speed	Fuel	Radius	Armament	Comp
SATSUMA	Yokosuka DY	1905–1909	19700 F 19372 N	482 0 oa 479 0 wl 449 10 pp	83 6	27 6	2-shaft VTE 20 Miyabara boilers	17300 ihp	18¼	1000 2860 coal 377 oil	?	4 × 12in 45-cal 12 × 10in 45-cal 12 × 4.7in 50-cal QF 4 × 3.1in 40-cal QF 4 × 3.1in 28-cal QF 3 MGs 5 × 18in TT (UW)	800 940

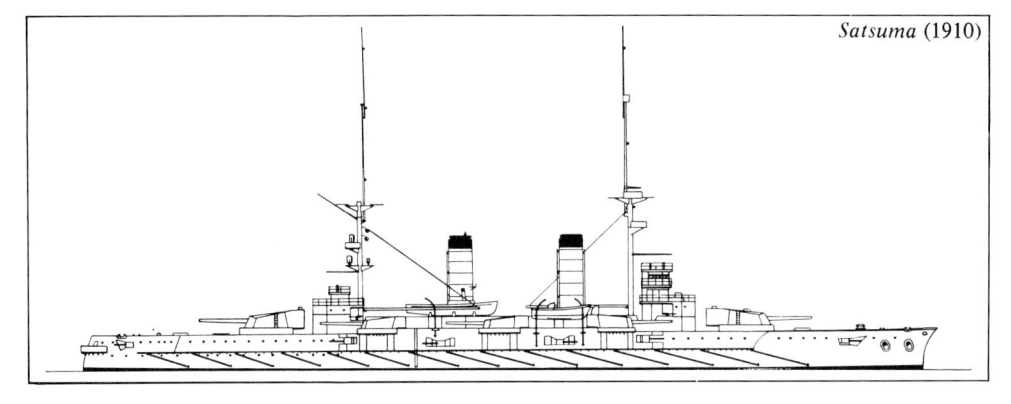

Satsuma (1910)

Satsuma seen here in 1924, stripped of armament, as a target ship. Note the ranging marks painted on her bow. (Shizuo Fukui.)

GENERAL NOTES
Built under the 1903 Programme, this was the first large warship built in Japan, and mainly from Japanese materials. She was a 'semi-dreadnought' or 'intermediate dreadnought' battleship, i.e. having a secondary battery of intermediate (8in to 10in) calibre.

ARMOUR
Krupp steel. Belt 9in to 4in; deck 3in to 2in; turrets 9½in to 7in; casemates 6in; CT 9.8in.

MACHINERY NOTES
On trials she reached 18.95 knots with 18507 ihp.

CAREER
Launched 15 November, 1906 and completed 25 March 1910; disarmed at Yokosuka in 1922 and then towed to Kure; stricken 20 September, 1923 and converted to a target-ship; sunk 7 September 1924 in Tokyo Bay as a target for the battleships *Mutsu* and *Nagato*.

Name	Builder	Date	Displ	Length ft in	Beam ft in	Draught ft in	Machinery	SHP	Speed	Fuel	Radius	Armament	Comp
AKI	Kure DY	1906–1911	21800 F 20100 N 19780 S	492 0 oa 483 0 wl 460 0 pp	83 7	27 6	2-shaft Curtis turbines, 15 Miyabara boilers	24000	20	1000 3000 coal 172 oil	?	4 × 12in 45-cal 12 × 10in 45-cal 8 × 6in 45-cal QF 8 × 3.1in 40-cal QF 4 × 3.1in 28-cal QF 3 MGs 5 × 18in TT (UW)	931

IRONCLADS, BATTLESHIPS AND BATTLECRUISERS

Aki (1911)

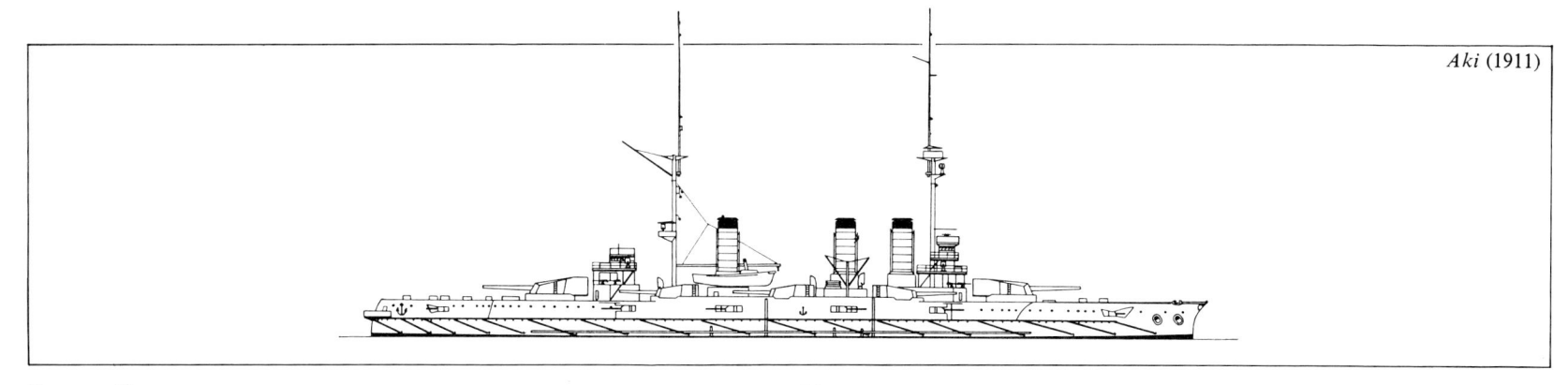

GENERAL NOTES
Semi-dreadnought battleship ordered under the 1903 Programme. Very similar to *Satsuma* in basic design.

ARMOUR
Krupp steel. Belt 9in to 4in; deck 3in to 2in; turrets 9½in to 7in; casemates 6in; CT 10in.

MACHINERY
On trials she reached 20¼ knots with 27740 shp.

CAREER
Launched 15 April 1907 and completed 11 March, 1911; disarmed at Yokosuka in 1922 and then towed to Kure; stricken in 1923 and used as target; Sunk 2 September, 1924 in Tokyo Bay as a target for the battlecruisers *Kongo* and *Hyuga*.

Name	Builder	Date	Displ	Length ft in	Beam ft in	Draught ft in	Machinery	SHP	Speed	Fuel	Radius	Armament	Comp
KAWACHI	Kure DY	1909–1912	21900 F 20823 N	526 0 oa	84 3 *Kawachi* 84 2 *Settsu*	27 0 *Kawachi* 27 10 *Settsu*	2-shaft Curtis turbines (Parsons in *Settsu*), 16 Miyabara boilers	25000	21	1000 / 2300 coal / 176 / 400 oil	2700 @ 18	4 × 12in 50-cal 8 × 12in 45-cal 10 × 6in 50-cal QF 8 × 4.7in 50-cal QF 12 × 3.1in 40-cal QF 4 × 3.1in 28-cal QF	999 1100
SETTSU	Yokosuka DY	1909–1912	21443 N										

Kawachi (1912)

Settsu (1912)

Settsu as target ship (1940)

GENERAL NOTES
These were the first Japanese dreadnought battleships, and were built under the 1907 Programme. They were also the first independent Japanese design, although Armstrong supplied the guns and mountings from England. The naming of these ships was performed at the keel-laying with great ceremony, and this procedure was adopted with all future warships.

ARMOUR
Krupp steel. Belt 12in to 4in; deck 12in; turrets 11in; casemates 6in; CT 10in to 6in.

APPEARANCE
Kawachi had a straight stem, but *Settsu* had a clipper bow.

RE-ARMAMENT AND RECONSTRUCTION
By 1918, twelve 3in were replaced by four 3.1in (80mm) AA guns; only three 18in TT were retained. In 1924, when *Settsu* became a target-ship all weapons and the side armour were removed. The centre funnel was removed and one boiler room suppressed, reducing speed to 16 knots and the tonnage to 16130. Between October 1935 and 1937 she was converted to a radio-controlled target at Kure DY; upperworks and funnels were remodelled, and she was modified to withstand shell-hits up to 8in and

24 IRONCLADS, BATTLESHIPS AND BATTLECRUISERS

10 kg bombs dropped from 4000 m. At this point she had 8 Myabara and 2 Kampon boilers, and displaced 16914ts. In 1940/41 she was again reboilered with 4 Miyabara and 4 Kampon boilers, giving 16000 shp = 18 knots. She was armed with 2 13mm MGs at this time, but in 1944 as 25mm mounting were added. The centre funnel was replaced, and the forefunnel was considerably shortened.

CAREERS

Kawachi
Launched 15 October, 1910 and completed 31 March, 1912; sunk by a magazine explosion in Tokuyama Bay on 12 July, 1918 (700 dead); stricken 2 September, 1918 and later BU.

Settsu
Launched 30 March 1911 and completed 1 July, 1912; disarmed at Kure in 1922; stricken 1 October, 1923; converted to a target-ship in 1924, and then to a wireless-controlled target in 1938, for training carrier pilots; sunk at Kure on 24 July, 1945 in shallow water by aircraft from Task Force 38; later salvaged and BU at Harima in 1947.

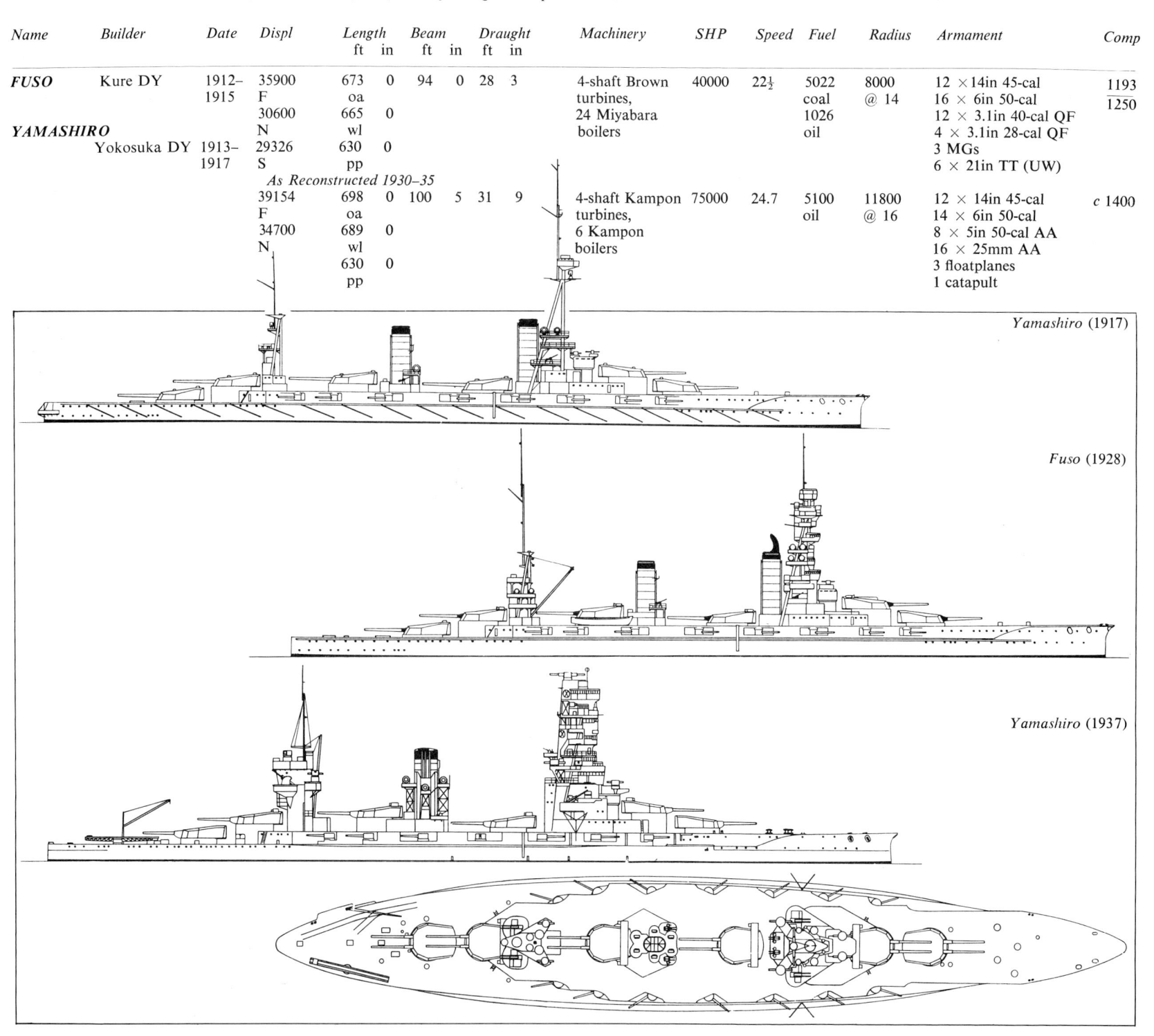

Name	Builder	Date	Displ	Length ft in	Beam ft in	Draught ft in	Machinery	SHP	Speed	Fuel	Radius	Armament	Comp
FUSO	Kure DY	1912–1915	35900 F 30600 N 29326 S	673 0 oa 665 0 wl 630 0 pp	94 0	28 3	4-shaft Brown turbines, 24 Miyabara boilers	40000	22½	5022 coal 1026 oil	8000 @ 14	12 ×14in 45-cal 16 × 6in 50-cal 12 × 3.1in 40-cal QF 4 × 3.1in 28-cal QF 3 MGs 6 × 21in TT (UW)	1193/1250
YAMASHIRO	Yokosuka DY	1913–1917											
As Reconstructed 1930–35			39154 F 34700 N	698 0 oa 689 0 wl 630 0 pp	100 5	31 9	4-shaft Kampon turbines, 6 Kampon boilers	75000	24.7	5100 oil	11800 @ 16	12 × 14in 45-cal 14 × 6in 50-cal 8 × 5in 50-cal AA 16 × 25mm AA 3 floatplanes 1 catapult	c 1400

Yamashiro (1917)

Fuso (1928)

Yamashiro (1937)

IRONCLADS, BATTLESHIPS AND BATTLECRUISERS 25

Fuso (1939)

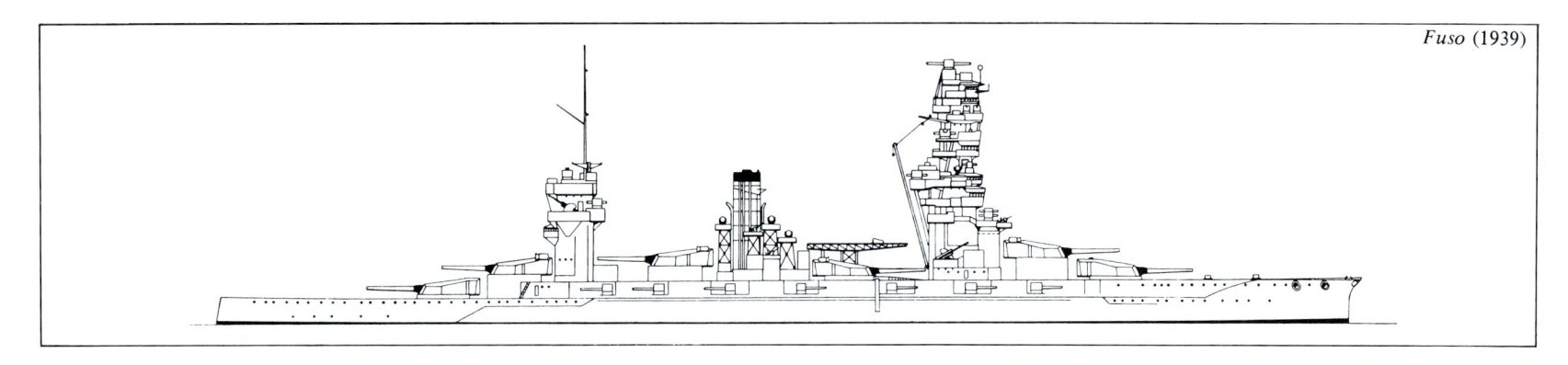

General Notes
These battleships, built under the 1911 and 1913 Programmes, respectively, were the first battleships built in Japan to use not only Japanese material but also Japanese-manufactured weapons.

Armour
Krupp steel. Belt 12in to 4in; bulkheads 12in to 4in; deck 2in to 1¼in; casemates 6in; barbettes 8in; turrets 12in to 4½in; CT 13¾in to 5.3in.

Machinery
On trials, *Fuso* reached 23 knots with 46500 shp, and *Yamashiro* reached 23.3 knots with 47730 shp. In 1930/35 both ships were given new machinery and boilers. On trials they averaged 76889 shp = 24¾ knots.

Reconstruction and Re-armament
In 1927/28, foremast in both ships was remodelled, with searchlights, fire-control platforms and 6 × 3.1in AA guns were added. In 1930–35 the armoured deck was increased to 3.8in to 2in and anti-torpedo bulges or 'blisters' were added. The elevation of main and secondary guns was increased, and the mast was rebuilt as a 'pagoda'. A planned conversion to carrier-battleships like *Hyuga* and *Ise* was cancelled. In December 1941 the AA armament was increased to twenty 25mm. In June 1944 it was increased to thirty-seven 25mm guns.

Careers
Fuso
Launched 28 March, 1914 and completed on 8 November, 1915; sunk in battle of Suriago Strait 25 October, 1944 (10° 25′ N, 125° 23′ E) by US battleships, cruisers and destroyers with gunfire and torpedoes

Yamashiro
Launched 3 November, 1915 and completed 31 March 1917; sunk in the battle of Suriago Strait 25 October, 1944 (10° 22′ N, 125° 21′ E) by US battleships and the destroyer *Killen* by gunfire and torpedoes.

The 'super-dreadnought' *Yamashiro* and her sister *Fuso* were the first battleships built entirely with Japanese materials and weapons. This photograph was taken at Yokosuka Dockyard on 20th April 1932, during her reconstruction. In the foreground can be seen the barbette with "Q" 14-inch gun turret removed; the original funnels are still in position. (Shizuo Fukui.)

Name	Builder	Date	Displ	Length ft in	Beam ft in	Draught ft in	Machinery	SHP	Speed	Fuel	Radius	Armament	Comp
ISE	Kawasaki, Kobe	1915–1917	36500 F	683 0 oa	94 0	29 1	4-shaft Curtis turbines (Parsons in *Hyuga*,) 24 Kampon boilers	45000	23½	4607 coal 1411 oil	9680 @ 14	12 × 14in 45-cal 20 × 5.5in 50-cal 12 × 3.1in 40-cal 4 × 3.1in 28-cal 3 MGs 6 × 21in TT (UW)	1360
HYÛGA	Mitsubishi, Nagasaki	1915–1918	31260 N 29980 S	675 0 wl 642 0 pp									
			As Reconstructed 1934–37										
	Ise		40169 F 35800 S 39657 36000 S	700 0 wl 642 0 pp	104 0	30 2	4-shaft Kampon turbines, 8 Kampon boilers	80825	25.3	5113 oil	7870 @ 16	12 × 14in 45-cal 16 × 5.5in 50-cal 8 × 5in AA 20 × 25mm AA 3 aircraft 1 catapult	1376
	Hyuga												
			As Reconstructed 1943–4										
			38676 F 35350 S				4-shaft Kampon turbines, 8 Kampon boilers	80825	25.3	4249 oil	9449 @ 16	8 × 14in 45-cal 16 × 5in AA 57 × 25mm AA 22 aircraft 2 catapults	1463

Ise (1918)

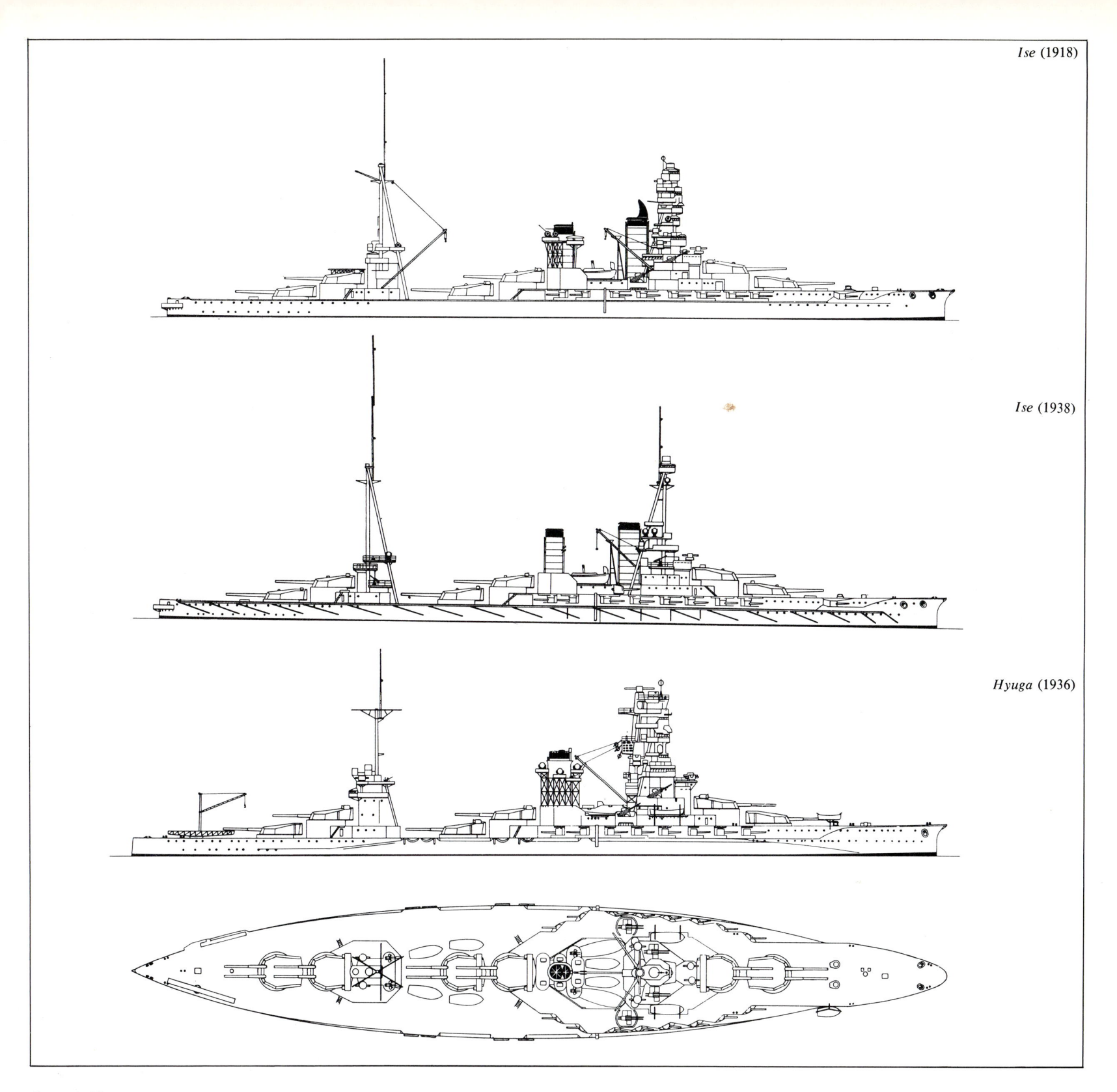

Ise (1938)

Hyuga (1936)

GENERAL NOTES
Ordered under the 1914 Programme as improved *Fuso* type, but armed with a new 5.5in secondary gun.

ARMOUR
Krupp steel. Belt 12in to 4in; deck 2¼in to 1¼in; casemates 6in; barbettes and turrets 12in; CT 12in to 6in.

IRONCLADS, BATTLESHIPS AND BATTLECRUISERS 27

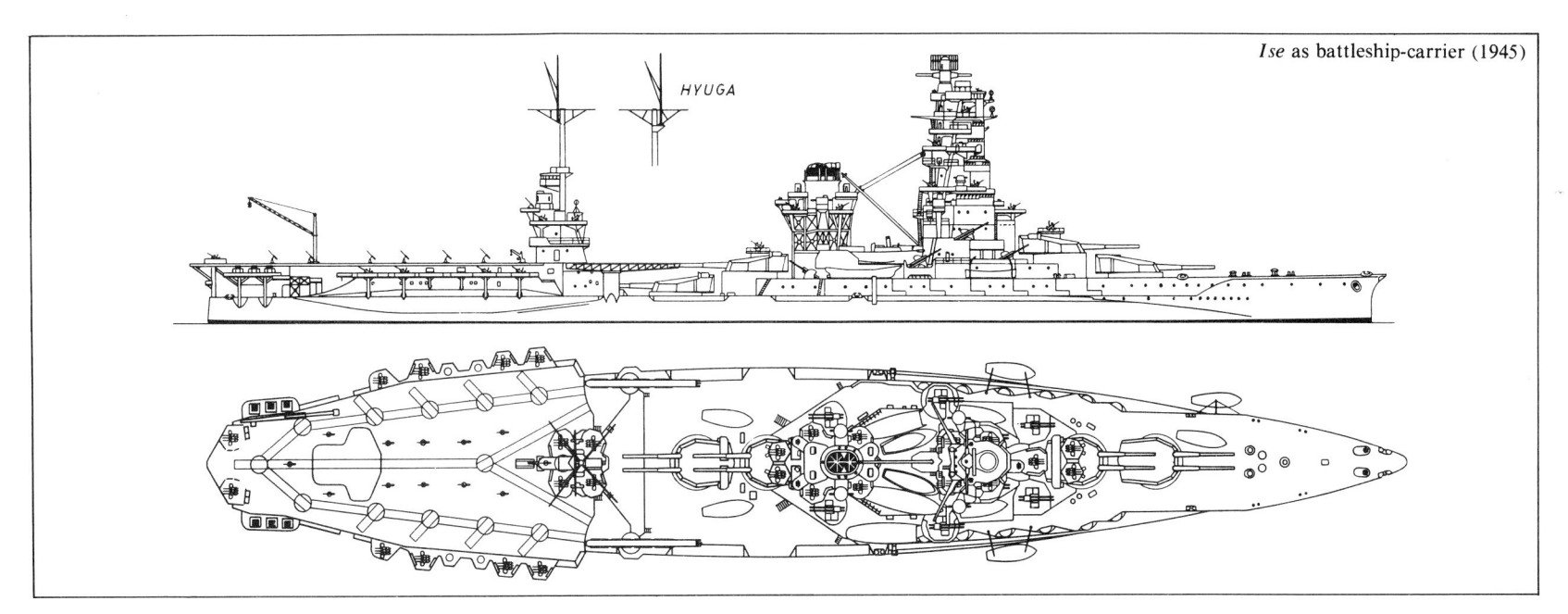

Ise as battleship-carrier (1945)

HYUGA

RECONSTRUCTION AND RE-ARMAMENT
From 1921, both carried 4 × 3.1in AA guns. Between 1926 and 1928 the foremast was rebuilt; both carried 1 or 2 floatplanes temporarily, but from 1933, 1 catapult and 3 floatplanes. In 1934–7 they were reconstructed (at Kure DY) with thicker deck armour, torpedo bulges, more elevation for main and secondary guns, removal of the forward funnel and a new 'pagoda' foremast. In 1943/44 to make good the losses of carriers at Midway, both ships were converted to battleship-carriers, with guns forward and a flight deck aft. In June 1944 104 25mm AA guns were carried, and by September, 180 5in rocket-launchers (6 × 30). In October 1944, the catapults were removed to improve the arcs of fire for 'P' & 'Q' turrets.

MACHINERY NOTES
On trials, *Ise* developed 56498 shp = 23.64 knots. In 1934/37, both ships were re-engined and re-boilered.

CAREERS
Ise
Launched 2 November, 1916 and completed on 15 December, 1917; sunk on 28 July, 1945 by aircraft of US Task Force 38, five m NW of Kure (34° 12′ N, 132° 31′ E); BU at Harima in 1946.

Hyuga
Launched 27 January, 1917 and completed on 30 April, 1918; sunk by US carrier aircraft of TF 38 at Kure on 24 July, 1945 (34° 10′ N, 132° 33′ E); raised in 1952 and BU.

Name	Builder	Date	Displ	Length ft in	Beam ft in	Draught ft in	Machinery	SHP	Speed	Fuel	Radius	Armament	Comp
NAGATO	Kure DY	1917–1920	38500 F	708 0 oa	95 0	30 0	4-shaft Gihon turbines 21 boilers	80000	26.7	1600 coal	5500 @ 16	8 × 16in 45-cal	1333
MUTSU	Yokosuka DY	1918–1921	33800 N 32720 S	699 9 wl 660 4 pp						3400 oil		20 × 5.5in 50-cal 4 × 3.1in AA 3 MGs 8 × 21in TT (4 AW, 4 UW)	
		After Reconstruction 1934–36	42850 F 39130 N	725 wl 660 pp	29 113 6 33	31 2	4-shaft Kampon turbines 10 Kampon boilers	82300	25	5650 oil	8650 @ 16	8 × 16in 45-cal 18 × 5.5in 50-cal 8 × 5in AA 20 × 25mm AA 3 aircraft 1 catapult	1368

GENERAL NOTES
Built under the 1916/17 Programme, and were the first battleships in the world to be armed with 16in guns. Designed by Admiral Hiraga.

ARMOUR
Belt 11.8in to 3.9in; deck 7in to 3in; barbettes 11.8in; casemates 1in to ¾in; turrets 14in; CT 14½in to 3.8in.

MACHINERY
On trials, *Nagato* reached 26.7 knots with 85500 shp, and *Mutsu* reached the same speed with 87500 shp.

RECONSTRUCTION AND RE-ARMAMENT
In 1921, the forward funnel had a clinker-screen added, but in 1924 the forward funnel was trunked aft. In 1930, *Mutsu* had a clipper-bow fitted, but this was not done to *Nagato* until 1936; from 1934 to 1936 both ships were reconstructed with torpedo-bulges, increased elevation for main armament, aircraft crane, etc. This involved various changes to the masts and bridgework. In June 1944, *Nagato* had radar aerials on both masts, but still had her 5.5in guns, with 68 25mm AA guns. In October 1944 she had 98 25mm AA guns (full load displacement 43581ts, speed 24.98 knots).

CAREERS
Nagato Launched 9 November, 1919 and completed 25 November 1920; damaged 18 July, 1945 in Yokosuka, by aircraft from US TF 38; surrendered in August 1945 and used as a target at Bikini Atoll in nuclear tests; lightly damaged 1 July 1946 (Test "Able") but totally destroyed in "Baker" test 24 July; wreck sunk 29 July, 1946.

Mutsu
Launched 31 May 1920 and completed 22 November 1921; sunk in Hiroshima Bay by magazine explosion 8 June 1943 (34° 05′ N, 132° 20′ E); raised on 7 June, 1970 and BU.

Nagato (1920)

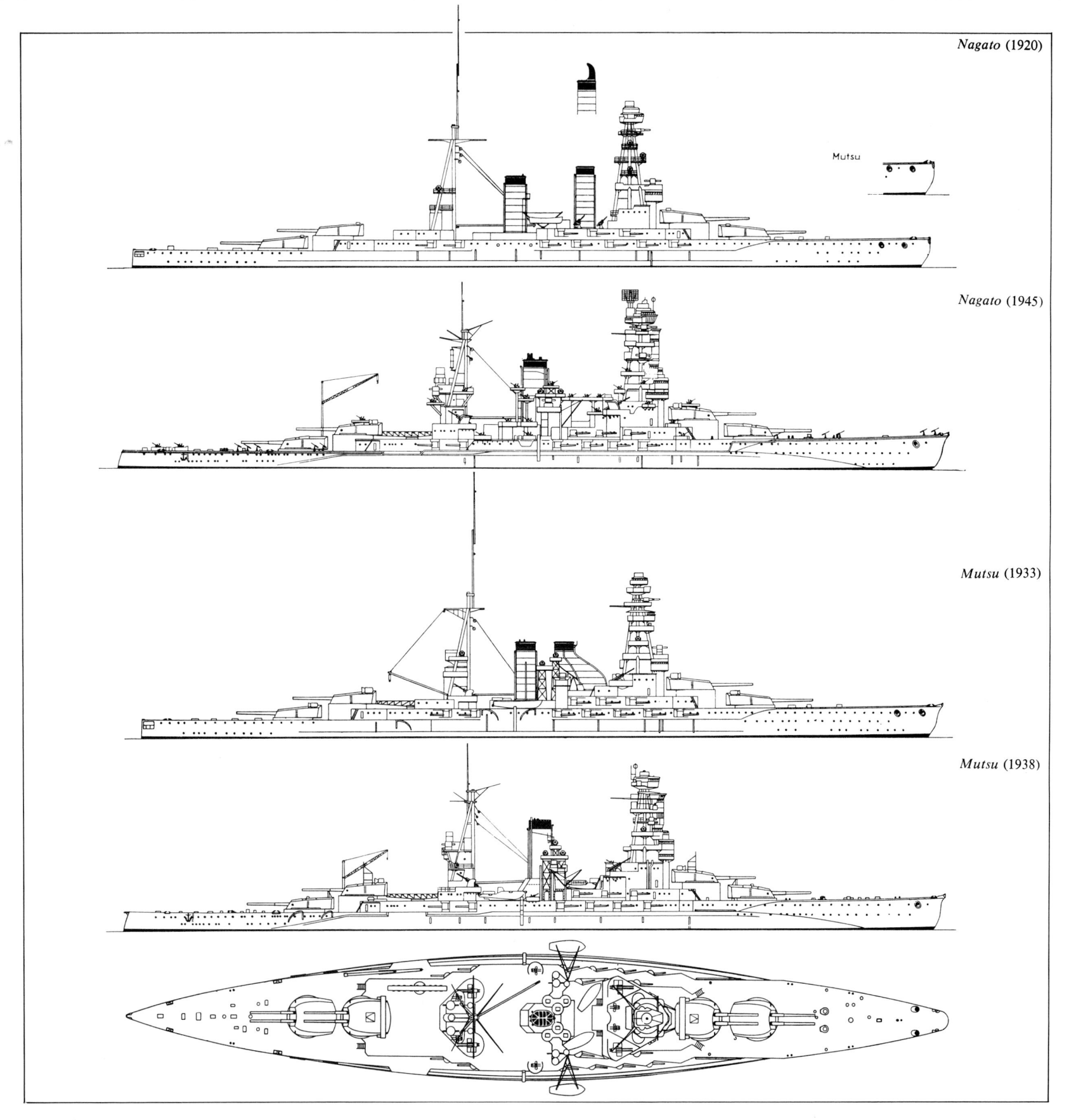

Mutsu

Nagato (1945)

Mutsu (1933)

Mutsu (1938)

IRONCLADS, BATTLESHIPS AND BATTLECRUISERS 29

Mutsu in dry dock, in 1921. (IWM.)

A photograph of *Mutsu* taken on 20th May 1936 at Yokosuka Dockyard, at the end of her reconstruction. The ship has been entirely rebuilt with a 'pagoda' foremast, a single funnel and a massive anti-torpedo 'bulge'. (Shizuo Fukui.)

Name	Builder	Date	Displ	Length ft in	Beam ft in	Draught ft in	Machinery	SHP	Speed	Fuel	Radius	Armament	Comp
TORGUD REIS ex-*Weissenburg*	AG Vulkan, Stettin	1890–1894	10670 F 10013 N	379 7 wl 373 8 pp	64 0	25 0	2-shaft 3-cyl VTE 12 cyl boilers	10242 ihp	16½	650 1050 coal 110 oil	4500 @ 10	4 × 11in 40-cal 2 × 11in 35-cal 2 × 4.1in 35-cal 8 × 3.4in 30-cal 2 × 18in TT (UW)	568

GENERAL NOTES
An 'armoured ship' or coast-defence battleship built for the German Navy to Marineamt plans. Steel-hulled. Reconstructed at Wilhelmshaven DY in 1902–04 and ceded to Japan as reparations after Armistice in 1918.

CAREER
Launched 14 December, 1891 and completed 5 June, 1894 for German Navy; 12 September, 1910 transferred to Turkey; allocated to Japan as war reparations by Allies, but not taken over; in 1924 she became a training hulk in the Bosphorus; BU 1938.

Name	Builder	Date	Displ	Length ft in	Beam ft in	Draught ft in	Machinery	SHP	Speed	Fuel	Radius	Armament	Comp
NASSAU	Wilhelmshaven DY	1907–1909	20535 F 18873 N	479 4 wl 477 8 pp	88 3	28 1	3-shaft 3-cyl VTE 12 Marine boilers	26244 ihp	20	950 3000 coal 160 oil	8100 @ 10	12 × 11in 45-cal 12 × 5.9in 45-cal 16 × 3.4in 45-cal 6 × 17.7in TT (UW)	1008

GENERAL NOTES
Ex-German battleship, built to Marineamt design of 1905/6.

CAREER
Launched 7 March, 1908 and completed 1 October, 1909; stricken 5 November, 1919 and ceded to Japan as 'B' on 7 April, 1920 as war-reparations; sold to a British firm in June 1920 and BU at Dordrecht.

Name	Builder	Date	Displ	Length ft in	Beam ft in	Draught ft in	Machinery	SHP	Speed	Fuel	Radius	Armament	Comp
OLDENBURG	F. Schichau, Danzig	1909–1912	24700 F 22808 N	548 6 wl 546 2½ pp	93 6	28 6	3-shaft 4-cyl compound, 15 Marine boilers	28000 ihp 34934 ihp max	21.3	900 3200 coal 197 oil	3600 @ 18	12 × 12in 50-cal 14 × 5.9in 45-cal 14 × 3.4in 45-cal 6 × 19.7in TT (UW)	1113

GENERAL NOTES
Ex-German battleship built to Marineamt design of 1907/8.

CAREER
Launched 30 June, 1910 and completed 1 May, 1912; stricken 5 November 1919 and transferred to Japan as 'M' 13 May, 1920 as war-reparations; sold to a British firm June 1920 and BU in 1921 at Dordrecht.

IRONCLADS, BATTLESHIPS AND BATTLECRUISERS

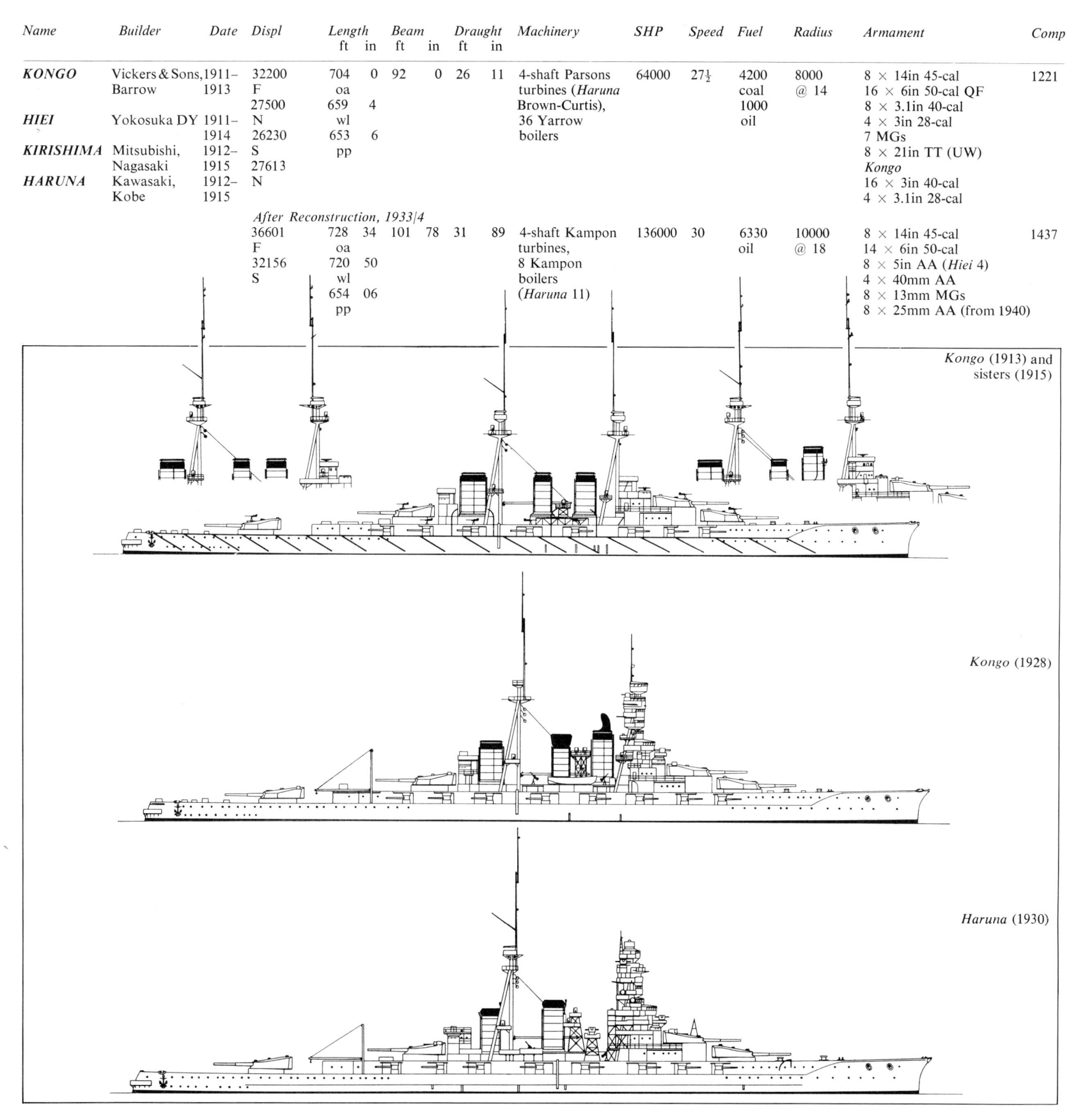

Name	Builder	Date	Displ	Length ft in	Beam ft in	Draught ft in	Machinery	SHP	Speed	Fuel	Radius	Armament	Comp
KONGO	Vickers & Sons, Barrow	1911–1913	32200 F 27500 N	704 0 oa 659 4 wl	92 0	26 11	4-shaft Parsons turbines (*Haruna* Brown-Curtis), 36 Yarrow boilers	64000	27½	4200 coal 1000 oil	8000 @ 14	8 × 14in 45-cal 16 × 6in 50-cal QF 8 × 3.1in 40-cal 4 × 3in 28-cal 7 MGs 8 × 21in TT (UW) *Kongo* 16 × 3in 40-cal 4 × 3.1in 28-cal	1221
HIEI	Yokosuka DY	1911–1914	26230	653 6									
KIRISHIMA	Mitsubishi, Nagasaki	1912–1915	S 27613 pp										
HARUNA	Kawasaki, Kobe	1912–1915	N										
			After Reconstruction, 1933/4										
			36601 F 32156 S	728 34 oa 720 50 wl 654 06 pp	101 78	31 89	4-shaft Kampon turbines, 8 Kampon boilers (*Haruna* 11)	136000	30	6330 oil	10000 @ 18	8 × 14in 45-cal 14 × 6in 50-cal 8 × 5in AA (*Hiei* 4) 4 × 40mm AA 8 × 13mm MGs 8 × 25mm AA (from 1940)	1437

Kongo (1913) and sisters (1915)

Kongo (1928)

Haruna (1930)

IRONCLADS, BATTLESHIPS AND BATTLECRUISERS

Haruna (1934)

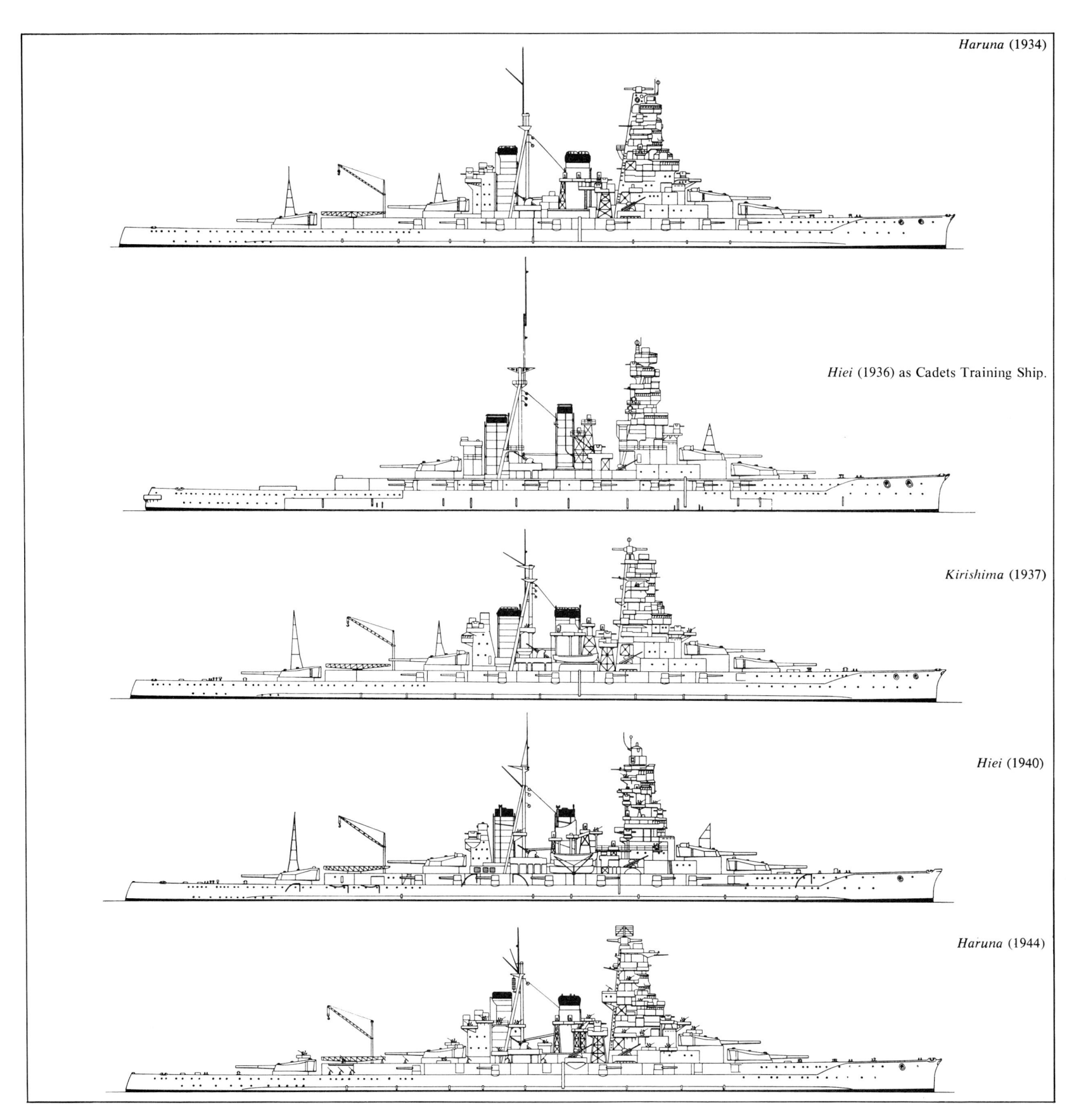

Hiei (1936) as Cadets Training Ship.

Kirishima (1937)

Hiei (1940)

Haruna (1944)

Hiei was built in Japan to the same plans as *Kongo*, and with gun-mountings imported from England. She is seen here running trials in 1914, before the forefunnel was raised. (IWM.)

After trials, the forefunnel of *Hiei* was raised to prevent the bridge from being smoked out. (IWM.)

This 1929 photograph shows the prominent funnel cap added to *Hiei*'s forefunnel in a further attempt to reduce the smoke nuisance. (IWM.)

IRONCLADS, BATTLESHIPS AND BATTLECRUISERS

In 1939, *Hiei* was taken in hand for "demilitarisation" to conform with the terms of the Washington Treaty. She lost one 14-inch gun turret, her side armour and the number of boilers was reduced. Despite this mutilation of her fighting power, she was brought back to the standard of her three sisters in time for World War Two. (IWM.)

Between 1927 and 1937, *Kirishima* and two of her sisters underwent a partial modernisation, which involved rebuilding the foremast and reducing the funnels from three to two. (Shizuo Fukui.)

This 1939 photograph of *Haruna* shows the final appearance of the class. Unlike *Kirishima* the forefunnel was lower than the after funnel. She was the only one of the class to survive the conflict at sea, but like so many other Japanese warships, she was sunk in harbour during the last weeks of the war. (Shizuo Fukui.)

GENERAL NOTES
These were the first true battlecruisers built for the Japanese Navy. They were designed by Sir George Thurston and were similar to HMS *Tiger*, but were slower and carried heavier armament. They were built under the 1910–11 Budget, and were later reclassified as battleships. *Kongo* was the last capital ship to be built outside Japan.

ARMOUR
Belt 8in to 3in; bulkheads 9in to 5.4in; barbettes 10in; turrets 9in; casemates 6in; CT 10in to 6in. The deck protection was greatly increased during reconstruction.

RE-ARMAMENT AND RECONSTRUCTION
In 1915 *Kongo* had her forward funnel raised 6½ft. In 1923–35, *Kongo* and *Hiei* were given caps to their forward funnels. In 1927–31, torpedo-bulges and thicker deck-armour were added, the 14in guns were given more elevation, and provision was made for 3 floatplanes. The number of funnels was reduced from 3 to 2, and after this reconstruction they were re-rated as battleships. From 1932 to 1936, *Hiei* had all her 6in guns removed.
From 1934 to 1940, all were lengthened by 26¼ft aft, and had new fire-control installed. *Hiei*'s foremast was a prototype for the *Yamato* Class, and she was the only unit of the class to have the forefunnel thinner than the after one. In 1943, *Kongo* and *Haruna* had 34 × 25mm AA guns, and in 1944 they received radar; their secondary armament was now 8 × 6in, 12 × 5in and 34 × 25mm AA. In October 1944 they had 100 × 25mm AA, and the final total was 118, and even depth-charges had been added.
The yards which carried out the various reconstructions were:
Kongo 1929–31, Yokosuka DY; 1936–7, Yokosuka DY
Hiei 1929–32, Kure DY; 1936–40, Kure DY
Kirishima 1927–30, Kure DY; 1935–6, Sasebo DY
Haruna 1927–8, Yokosuka DY; 1933–4, Kure DY

MACHINERY
To comply with the provisions of the Washington Treaty the ships were 'demilitarised' as follows:
Kongo & *Kirishima*: 16 Yarrow boilers, 13800 shp = 18 knots (armament 8 × 14in, 16 × 6in, 4 to 7 × 3.1in AA, 3 floatplanes and 1 catapult, 4 × 21in TT).
Haruna: Similarly armed but machinery as *Hiei*. Fuel increased to 2661ts coal and 3292ts oil = 9500 nm @ 14 knots.
Haruna & *Hiei*: 11 boilers, 13800 shp = 18 knots. *Hiei* had 6 × 14in, 16 × 6in, 4 × 3.1in AA.

Trials speeds:

	As Built	As Modernized
Kongo	27.54 knots (78275 shp)	30.27 knots
Kirishima	27.6 knots (82000 shp)	30.5 knots
Haruna	27.78 knots (80476 shp)	30.2 knots
Hiei	27.6 knots (shp not known)	29.7 knots

CAREERS
Kongo
Launched 18 May, 1912 and completed 16 August, 1913; torpedoed 21 November, 1944 by US submarine *Sealion* 65 nm NW of Keeling (26° 09′ N, 121° 23′ E).

Hiei
Launched 21 November, 1912 and completed 4 August, 1914; 1932 cadets' training ship; 1940 re-rated as a battleship; sunk 13 November, 1942 in battle of Savo Island by gunfire, torpedoes and air attacks from USS *Enterprise*, *Portland*, *San Francisco*, *Cushing*, *O'Bannon* and US Marine Corps aircraft (09° 00′ S, 159° 00′ E).

Kirishima
Launched 1 December, 1913 and completed 19 April, 1915; sunk 15 November, 1942 5 nm NW of Savo (09° 05′ S, 159° 42′ E) by US battleships *South Dakota* and *Washington*.

Haruna
Launched 14 December, 1913 and completed 19 April, 1915; damaged in South Pacific in 1917 by striking mine laid by German auxiliary cruiser *Wolf*; damaged at Kure 19 March, 1945; sunk in shallow water 8 nm NW of Kure 28 July 1945 by aircraft of US TF 38 (34° 15′ N, 132° 29′ E); BU 1946 at Harima.

Name	Builder	Date	Displ	Length ft in	Beam ft in	Draught ft in	Machinery	SHP	Speed	Fuel	Radius	Armament	Comp
KAGA	Kawasaki, Kobe	1920–	44200 F	768 1 oa	100 0	30 9	4-shaft Brown-Curtis turbines, 12 Kampon boilers	91000	26½	1700 oil 3600 oil	5500 @ 16	10 × 16in 45-cal 20 × 5.5in 50-cal 4 × 3.1in AA 8 × 24in TT (AW)	1333
TOSA	Mitsubishi, Nagasaki	1920–	39330 N 38500 S	760 2 wl 715 1 pp									

Kaga class (1918 design)

GENERAL NOTES
Laid down under the 1918 Programme as an improved *Nagato* type.

ARMOUR
Belt 11in (inclined at 15°); bulkheads 11in to 9in; barbettes 11.8in to 9in; CT 14in to 10in.

CAREERS
Kaga
Launched 17 November, 1921, but stricken in 1922 to comply with the Washington Treaty; building ceased 5 February, 1922 but the hull was later substituted for that of the damaged *Amagi* (scheduled for conversion to carrier) on 19 November, 1923 and she was completed as an aircraft carrier. (See under Aircraft Carriers)

Tosa
Launched 18 December, 1921 but cancelled under the terms of the Washington Treaty; building stopped on 5 February 1922; stricken 1 April, 1924 and the hull was sunk on 9 February, 1925 as a target in the Bungo Straits.

IRONCLADS, BATTLESHIPS AND BATTLECRUISERS 35

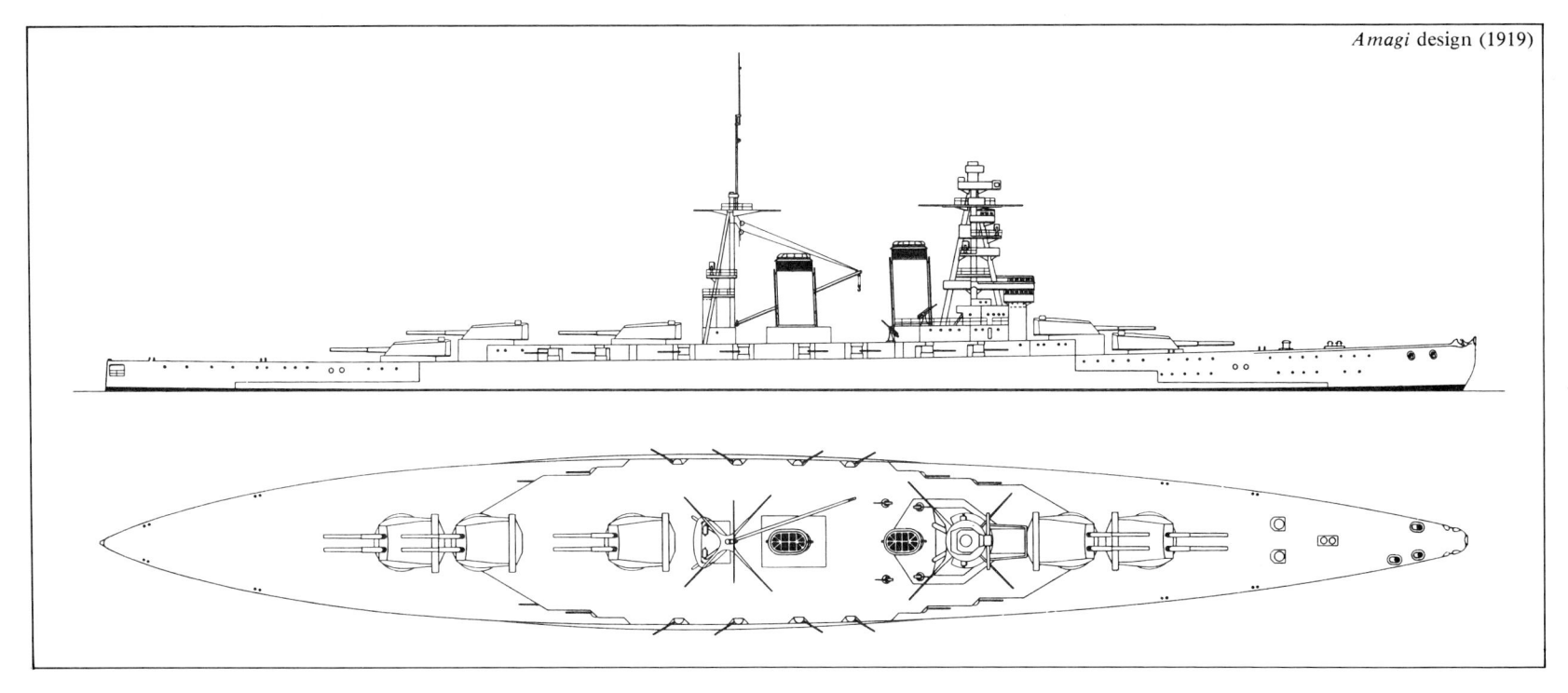

Name	Builder	Date	Displ	Length ft in	Beam ft in	Draught ft in	Machinery	SHP	Speed	Fuel	Radius	Armament	Comp
AMAGI	Yokosuka DY	1920–	47000 F	826 1 oa	101 0	31 0	4-shaft Gijutsu-Hombu geared turbines 19 Kampon boilers	131200	30	2500 coal 3900 oil	8000 @ 14	10 × 16in 45-cal 16 × 5.5in 50-cal 4 × 4.7in 45-cal AA 8 × 24in TT (UW)	?
AKAGI	Kure DY	1920	41217	820 3									
ATAGO	Kawasaki, Kobe	1921–	N 40000	wl 770 1									
TAKAO	Mitsubishi, Nagasaki	1921–	S	pp									

Amagi design (1919)

GENERAL NOTES
Ordered under the 1918–19 Budget, but cancelled in 1922.

ARMOUR
Belt 10in; bulkheads 11in to 9in; barbettes 11in to 9in; CT 14in to 3in.

CAREERS
Amagi
Laid down 6 December, 1920; stricken under the Washington Treaty and building stopped 5 February 1922 when 40% complete; she was meant to be finished as an aircraft carrier but her hull was badly damaged in an earthquake in 1923; stricken 31 July, 1922; BU begun 14 April, 1924.

Akagi
Keel laid 6 December, 1920 but stricken under Washington Treaty, and building stopped 5 February, 1922; from 19 November, 1923 work was resumed on conversion to an aircraft carrier (See under Aircraft Carriers).

Atago
Keel laid 22 November, 1921 but cancelled 31 July, 1922 to comply with the Washington Treaty; finally stricken 14 April, 1924 and BU on the slip.

Takao
Keel laid 19 December, 1921; building stopped 5 February, 1922; cancelled 31 July, 1922; finally stricken 14 April, 1924 and BU.

Name	Builder	Date	Displ	Length ft in	Beam ft in	Draught ft in	Machinery	SHP	Speed	Fuel	Radius	Armament	Comp
KII (No. 9)	Yokosuka DY	—	48500 F	826 9 oa	100 0	31 9	4-shaft Gijutsu-Hombu turbines, 19 Kampon boilers	131200	29¾	2500 coal 3900 oil	8000 @ 14	10 × 16in 45-cal 20 × 5.5in 50-cal 4 × 3.1in AA 8 × 24in TT (AW)	?
OWARI (No. 10)	Kure DY	—	42600	820 6									
No. 11	Kawasaki, Kobe	—	N 41400	wl 770 1									
No. 12	Mitsubishi, Nagasaki	—	S	pp									

GENERAL NOTES
Planned under the 1921 Programme as fast editions of the *Tosa* Class. *Owari* was planned to be laid down in 1922 for completion in 1925, and *Kii* was intended to follow in 1923, and to be completed in 1925.

ARMOUR
Belt 11½in; deck 4½in.

CAREERS
Kii
Cancelled 5 February, 1922, stricken 19 April, 1924.

Owari
Cancelled 5 February, 1922; stricken 19 November, 1923. *Nos. 11 & 12* cancelled at the same time, before contracts had been awarded; both stricken 19 November, 1923.

Name	Builder	Date	Displ	Length ft in	Beam ft in	Draught ft in	Machinery	SHP	Speed	Fuel	Radius	Armament	Comp
No. 13	Yokosuka DY	—	47500 N	915 4 oa	101 0	32 0	4-shaft Gijutsu-Hombu geared turbines, 22 Kampon boilers	150000	30	?	?	8 × 18in 45-cal	?
No. 14	Kure DY	—										16 × 5.5in 50-cal	
No. 15	Mitsubishi, Nagasaki	—		900 3 wl								4 × 5in AA	
No. 16	Kawasaki, Kobe	—		850 2 pp								8 × 24in TT (AW)	

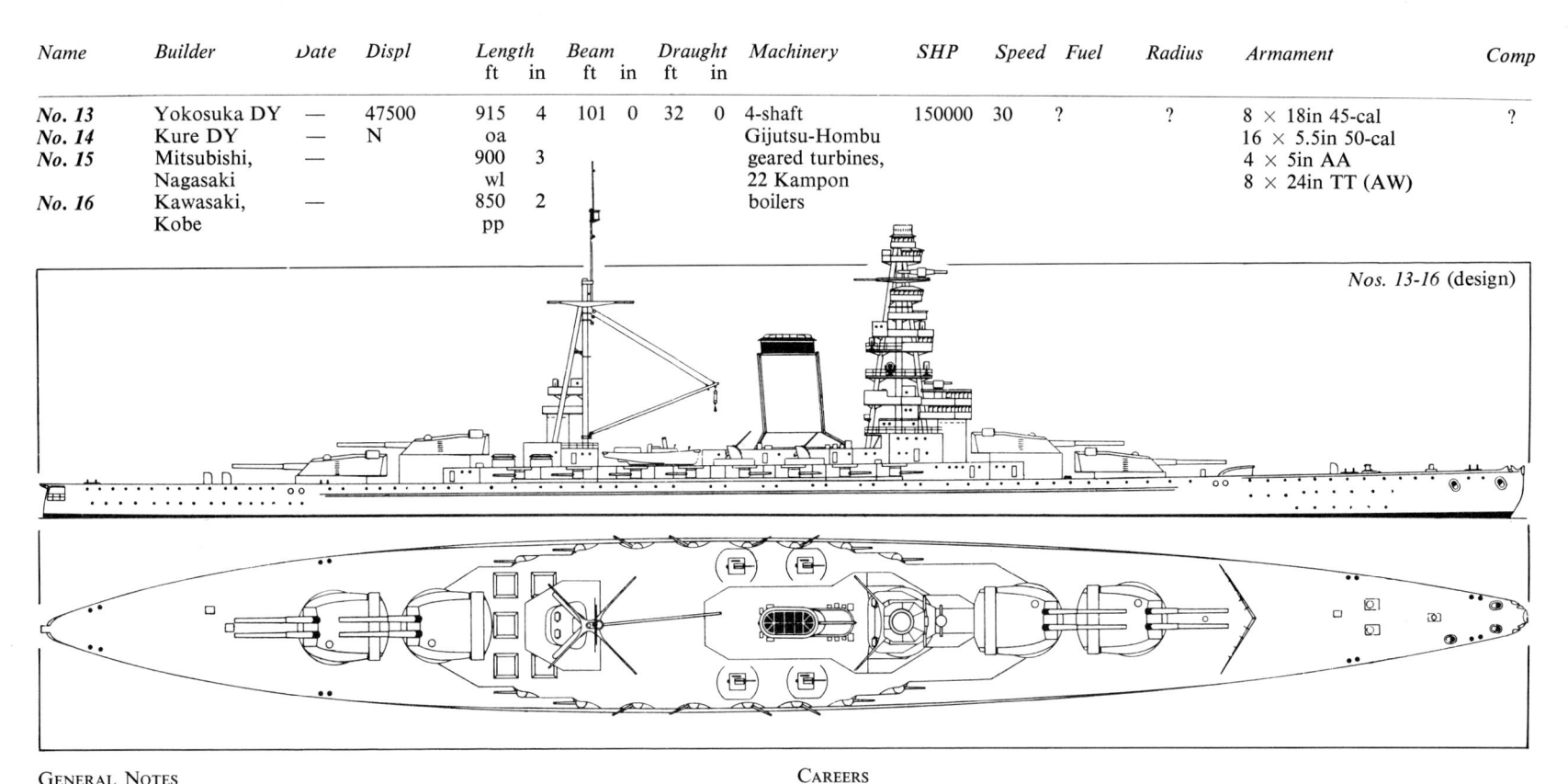

Nos. 13-16 (design)

GENERAL NOTES
Super-battleships with a similar armour-scheme to the *Tosa*, planned under the 1922 Programme.

ARMOUR
Belt 13in; deck 5in.

CAREERS
Keel-laying was planned for 1922–3 and completion for 1927. Stopped in 1922 under the Washington Treaty and contracts cancelled; stricken 19 November, 1923.

Name	Builder	Date	Displ	Length ft in	Beam ft in	Draught ft in	Machinery	SHP	Speed	Fuel	Radius	Armament	Comp
'**KONGO** Replacement'	—	—	39200 N 35000 S	761 1 wl	105 8	29 6	3 sets geared turbines	80000	26.3	?	?	10 × 16in 16 × 6in 8 × 5in AA 2 × 24in TT (UW) 2 floatplanes 1 catapult	?
'**FUSO** Replacement'	—	—	39250 N 35000 S	777 6 wl	105 0	28 6	4 sets geared turbines	73000	25.9	?	?	9 × 16in 12 × 6in 8 × 5in AA 2 floatplanes 1 catapult	?

GENERAL NOTES
Kongo replacement
A 1930 project designed by Admiral Hiraga.

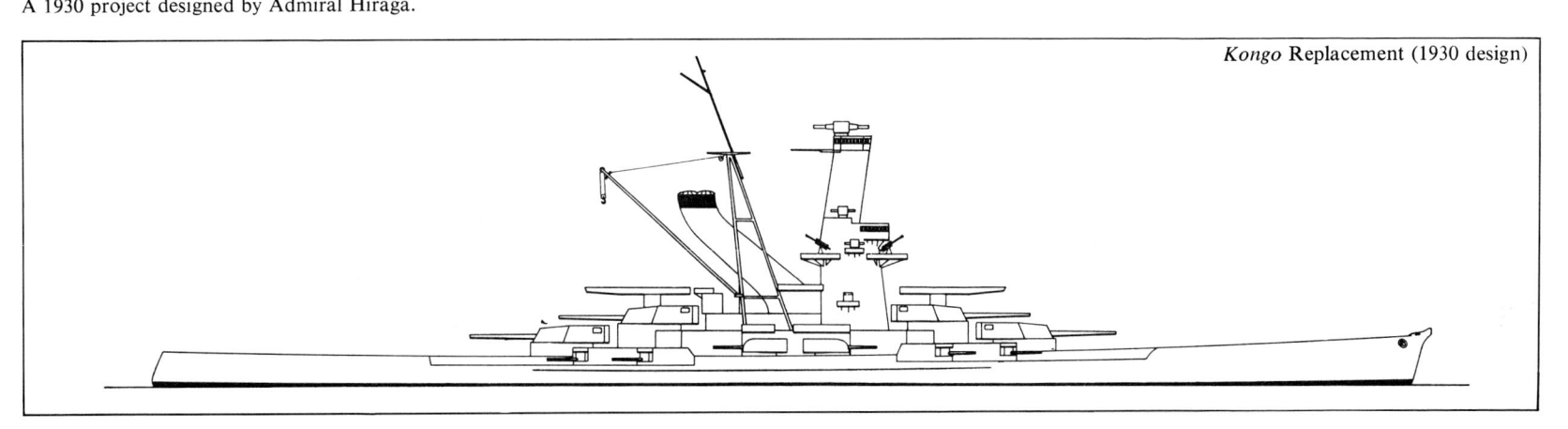

Kongo Replacement (1930 design)

IRONCLADS, BATTLESHIPS AND BATTLECRUISERS

Fuso Replacement (1930 design)

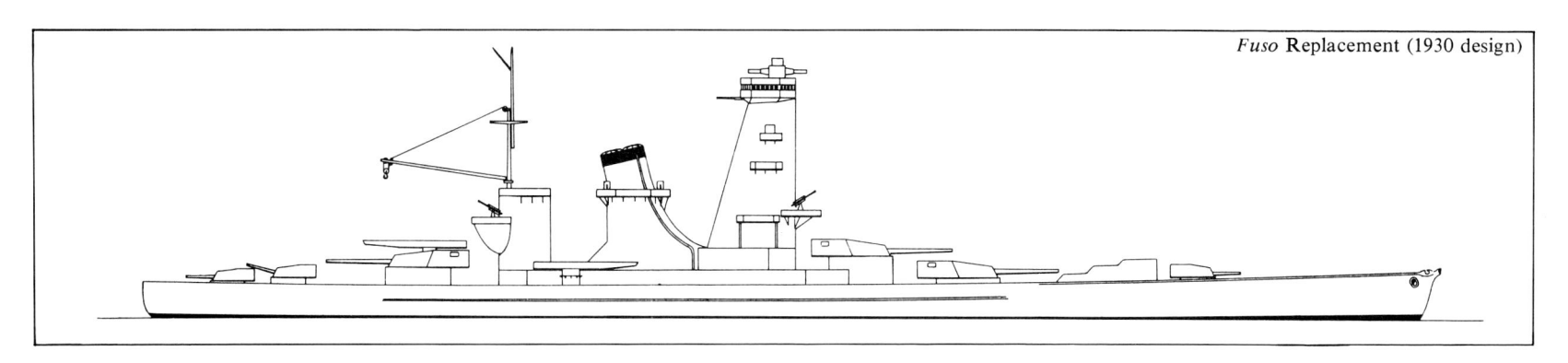

Fuso replacement
A 1930 projected design by Admiral Hiraga and Captain Fujimoto.

Name	Builder	Date	Displ	Length ft in	Beam ft in	Draught ft in	Machinery	SHP	Speed	Fuel	Radius	Armament	Comp
YAMATO	Kure DY	1937–1941	71659 F	862 10 oa	121 1	32 11	4-shaft Kampon geared turbines, 12 Kampon boilers	150000	27	6300 oil	7200 @ 16	9 × 18.1in 45-cal	2500
MUSASHI	Mitsubishi, Nagasaki	1938–1942	67123 N	839 10 wl								12 × 6.1in 55-cal	2800
SHINANO	Yokosuka DY	1940–	64000 S	800 6 pp								12 × 5in AA	
No. 111	Kure DY	1940–										24 × 25mm AA	
No. 797	—											4 × 13mm MGs	

7 floatplanes 2 catapults
Shinano, etc. were to have had: 9 × 18in 45-cal
6 × 6.1in 55-cal
16/20 3.9in 65-cal (probable)
numerous 25mm AA
7 aircraft, etc.

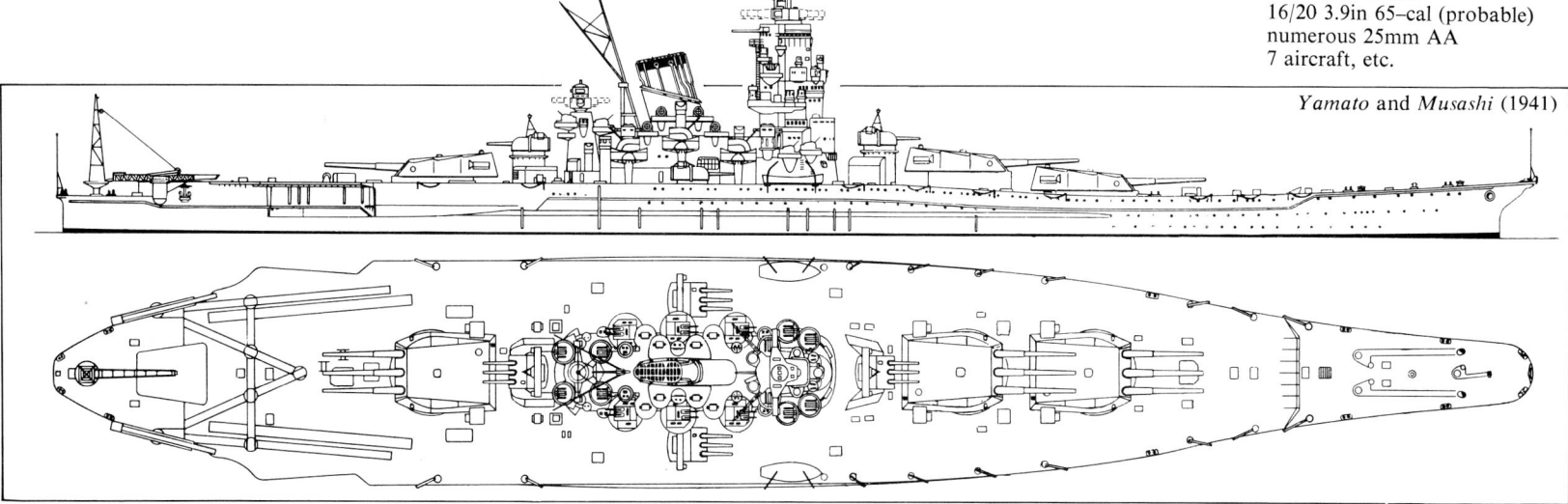

Yamato and *Musashi* (1941)

Yamato, running her trials on 30th October 1941. Note the long forecastle and the prominent ventilation-trunking below the upper-deck abreast of "Y" turret. The triple 6.1-inch guns on either side of the funnel amidships were later replaced by additional anti-aircraft guns. (Shizuo Fukui.)

IRONCLADS, BATTLESHIPS AND BATTLECRUISERS

Yamato (1945)

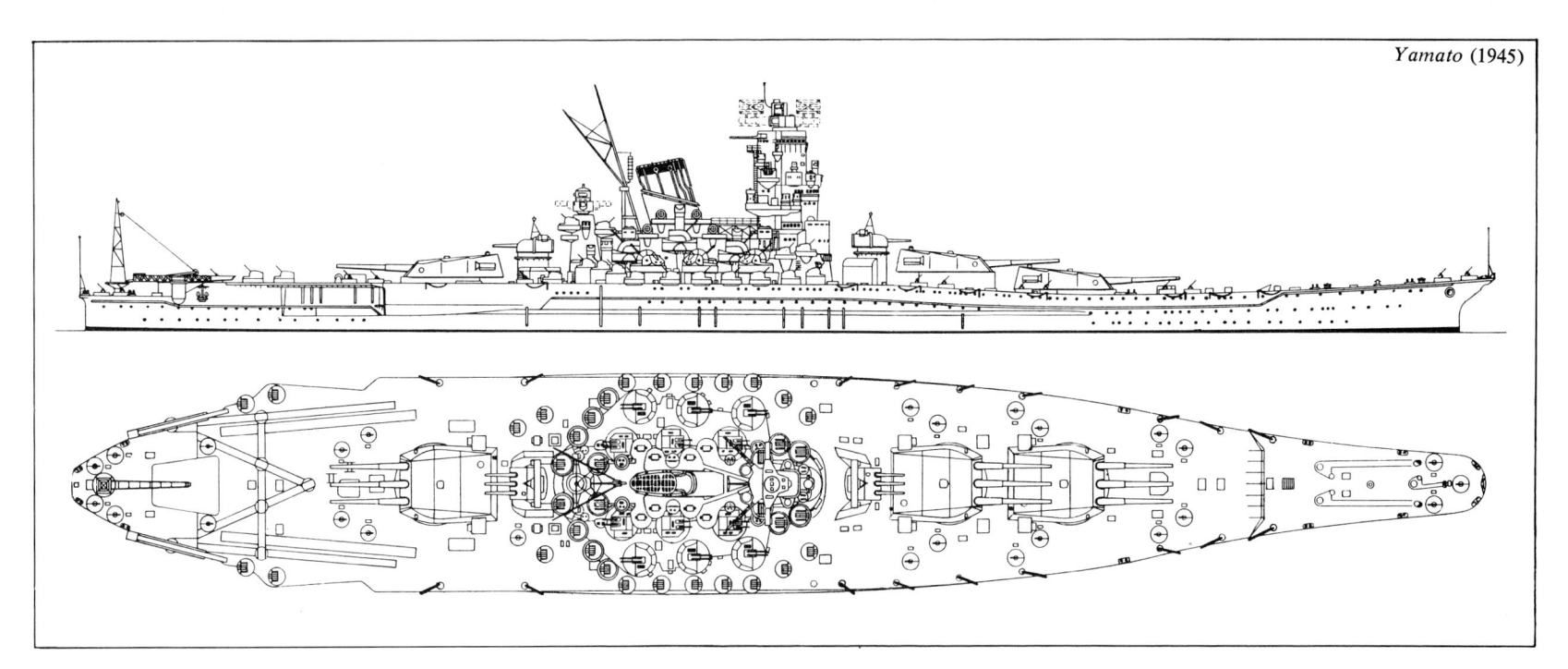

GENERAL NOTES
Ordered under the 1937–42 Programmes, these were the largest and most powerful battleships ever built.

ARMOUR
Belt 16.1in; bulkheads 11.8in; decks 9in to 7.8in; horizontal armour 2in to 1.1in; torpedo-bulkhead 11.8in to 3in; barbettes 22in to 2in; turrets 25.6in to 9.8in; CT 19.7in to 11.8in. *Shinano* and the later pair: belt 15.7in; deck 7.5in; barbettes 20.8in. The belt was 63ft deep.

SEARCHLIGHTS
8 fitted, 4.92ft in diameter.

MACHINERY
On trials *Yamato* reached 158000 shp = 27.7 knots, and 45000 shp astern. The boilers operated at 25 atmospheres/352°C.

FIRE-CONTROL
The main rangefinder was 50ft long, and the 18in turrets had a 50ft instrument apiece. There was a 32.8ft rangefinder on the after control, and 26.25ft instruments on the secondary turrets. A sonar set and 5 radar sets were fitted.

RE-ARMAMENT
In the autumn of 1943, both ships had their midships 6.1in triple turrets replaced by A.A: *Yamato*: from autumn 1943 36 × 25mm AA; from June 1944 24 × 5in AA; April 1944 98 × 25mm AA; July 1944 152 × 25mm AA; April 1945 150 × 25mm AA.
Musashi: Spring 1943 36 × 25mm AA; early 1944 54 × 25mm AA; April 1944 116 × 25mm AA; finally 130 × 25mm AA.

CAREERS
Yamato
Launched 8 August 1940 and completed 16 December, 1941; Fleet flagship in 1942; sunk 7 April, 1945 130 m WSW of Kagoshima (30° 22′ N, 128° 04′ E) by aircraft of US TF 38 (2498 dead).
Musashi
Launched 1 November, 1940 and completed 5 August, 1942; sunk 24 October, 1944 in the Visayan Sea, S of Luzon (12° 50′ N, 122° 35′ E) by aircraft of US TF 38.
Shinano
Laid down 4 May, 1940, but re-designed as a carrier and launched in 1944 (See under Aircraft Carriers).
No. 111
Laid down 7 November, 1940; construction stopped March 1942. Contract cancelled September 1942 and hull BU.
No. 797
Contract never awarded.

The giant battleship *Yamato* nears completion early in 1941. One of the 18-inch guns in "Y" turret can be seen at maximum elevation, and the 15-metre rangefinders on the forward and after control-towers. (Shizuo Fukui.)

IRONCLADS, BATTLESHIPS AND BATTLECRUISERS 39

Name	Builder	Date	Displ	Length ft in	Beam ft in	Draught ft in	Machinery	SHP	Speed	Fuel	Radius	Armament	Comp
No. 798	—	—	70000 N approx	?	?	?	?	?	27	?	?	6 × 20in	?
No. 799	—	—											

GENERAL NOTES
Two super *Yamato*-Class were planned under the 1942 Programme, but the contracts were never placed.

Name	Builder	Date	Displ	Length ft in	Beam ft in	Draught ft in	Machinery	SHP	Speed	Fuel	Radius	Armament	Comp
No. 795	—	—	34800 F	810 0 oa	89 3	28 10	4-shaft Kampon geared turbines 8 Kampon boilers	160000	33	4545 oil	8000 @ 18	9 × 12in 50-cal (Project 64) or 9 × 14in (Project 65) 16 × 3.9in 65-cal DP (probable) 12 × 25mm AA 8 × 13mm MGs 8 × 24in TT 3 floatplanes 1 catapult	?
No. 796	—	—	31495 S	787 4 wl									

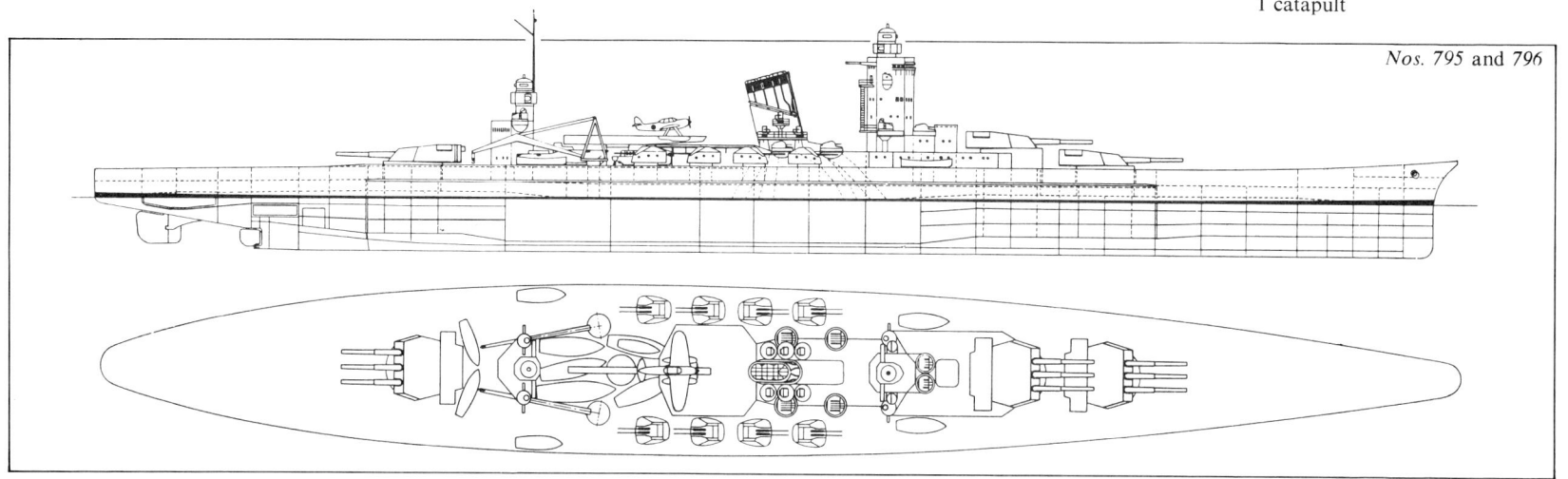

Nos. 795 and 796

GENERAL NOTES
Projected under the 1942 Programme. They were officially described as 'Super Type 'A' cruisers', not as battlecruiser editions of the *Yamato*.

ARMOUR
Belt 7½in to 0.8in; deck 4.7in. They were replanned as Project 65 in 1942, with 9 × 14in guns and no TT as a result of knowledge gained about the American *Alaska* Class.

CAREERS
They reached the planning stage only, and no contracts were placed.

2. Aircraft Carriers and Aviation Transports

Name	Builder	Date	Displ	Length ft in	Beam ft in	Draught ft in	Machinery	SHP	Speed	Fuel	Radius	Armament	Comp
HOSHO	Asano SB Co., Tsurumi	1919–1922	9630 N 7470 S	541 4 wl 510 0 pp	59 1	20 3	2 sets Parsons GT 8 Kampon boilers 2 shafts	30000	25	2695 oil 940 coal	8000 @ 15	4 × 140mm (5.5in) 40-cal LA	550
SHOKAKU Not built													

AIRCRAFT CARRIERS AND AVIATION TRANSPORTS

Hosho (1922)

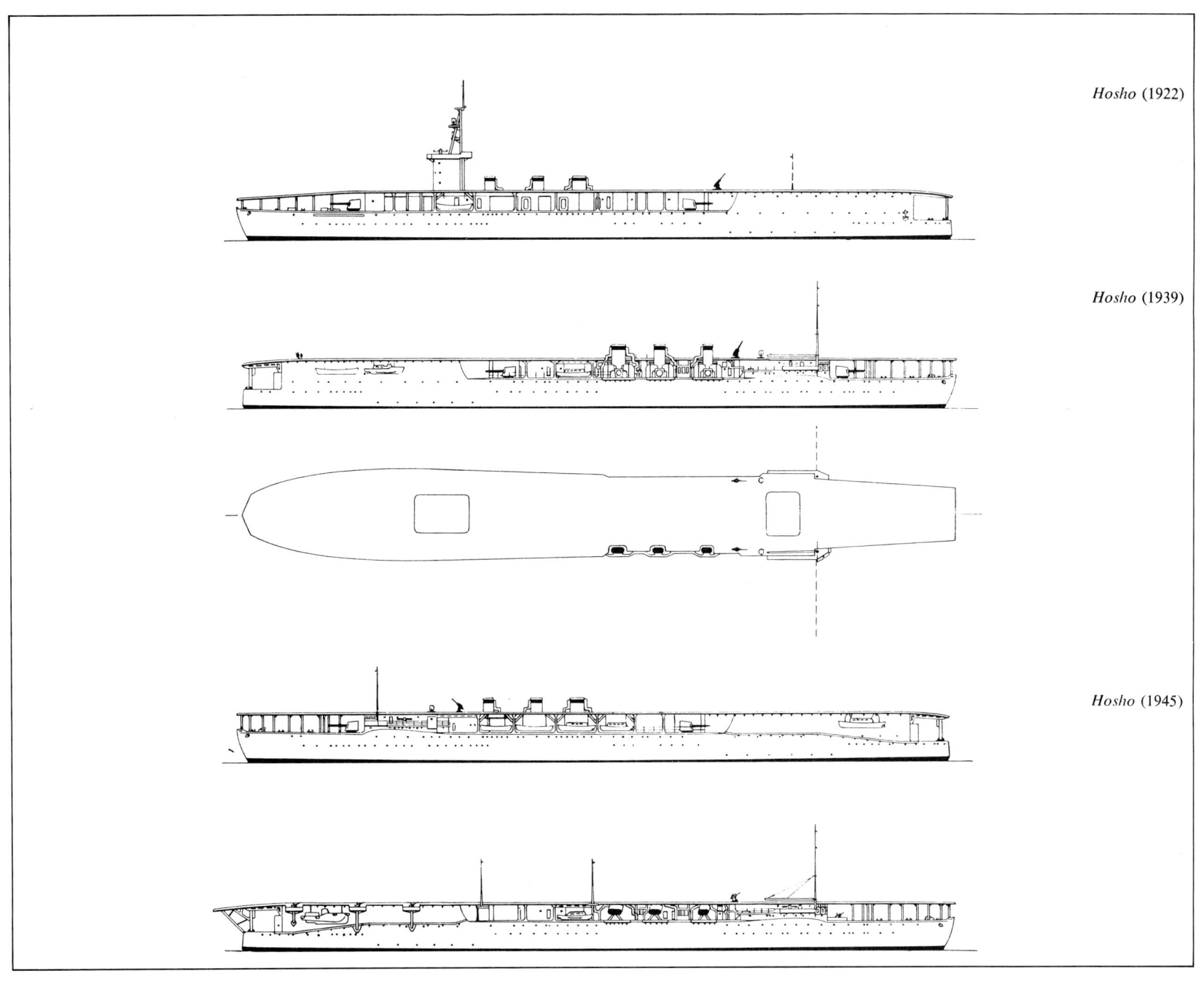

Hosho (1939)

Hosho (1945)

General Notes
Originally laid down 16 December, 1919 as an auxiliary, intended as a tanker, to be named *Hiryu*. Re-named *Hosho* in 1920, redesignated 13 October, 1921 as Aircraft Depot Ship (Kobubokan). A sister-ship, *Shokaku*, was planned, but construction never began, because of the limitations of the Washington Treaty.
'Through-deck' design; starboard-side island with tripod mast; downward-hinged deck-edge funnels; Sperry gyro-stabilization. Flight deck: 519ft × 74ft 6in.

Reconstruction and Re-armament
1923: island and tripod mast removed; 1934: funnels fixed in the upright position, aircraft stowage reduced to 21; 1936: 80mm AA guns replaced by 3 × 4 13.2mm AA (Hotchkiss) MGs; 1941: 4 × 2 25mm AA added; 1942: 140mm guns removed and replaced by another 4 × 2 25mm AA; 1944: flight deck extended to 593ft 2in; 1945: AA armament reduced to 6 × 25mm.

The first Japanese "flat-top": *Hosho*, as completed in 1922. The after lift is lowered, and the single W/T mast (on the starboard side) is raised, as is the quarter-deck ensign staff. (Jentschura.)

AIRCRAFT CARRIERS AND AVIATION TRANSPORTS 41

After the war, when being employed as a repatriation transport, the flight deck was partially dismantled in order to improve the field of view forward from the navigating bridge.

CAREERS

Hosho
Launched 13 November, 1921; completed 7 December, 1922; training carrier from 1941, but operationally deployed during the Midway campaign; superficially damaged 28 July, 1945 by US Task Force 38 air attack on Kure; handed over to the Allies at Kure in August 1945 and employed on Repatriation Service duties until 16 August, 1946; broken up at Hatachi Dockyard, Osaka, from 30 April, 1947.

Shokaku
Construction cancelled 19 November, 1923.

Name	Builder	Date	Displ	Length ft in	Beam ft in	Draught ft in	Machinery	SHP	Speed	Fuel	Radius	Armament	Comp
KAGA	Kawasaki DY Co., Kobe & Yokosuka DY	1920–1928	33693 N 26000 S	771 0 wl 715 1 pp	97 0	26 0	4 sets Brown-Curtiss GT 12 Kampon boilers 4 shafts	91000	28½	3600 oil 1700 coal	8000 @ 14	10 × 203mm (8in) 50-cal LA 12 × 120mm (4.7in) 45-cal HA 2 MGs 60 aircraft	1340
(modernisation)	Sasebo DY	1934–1935	42541 N 38200 S	812 6 wl 738 2 pp	106 8	31 1	4 sets Kampon GT 8 Kampon boilers	127400	28⅓	8208 oil	10000 @ 16	10 × 203mm (8in) 50-cal LA 16 × 127mm (5in) 40-cal DP (type '89') 22 × 25mm AA 90 aircraft	2016

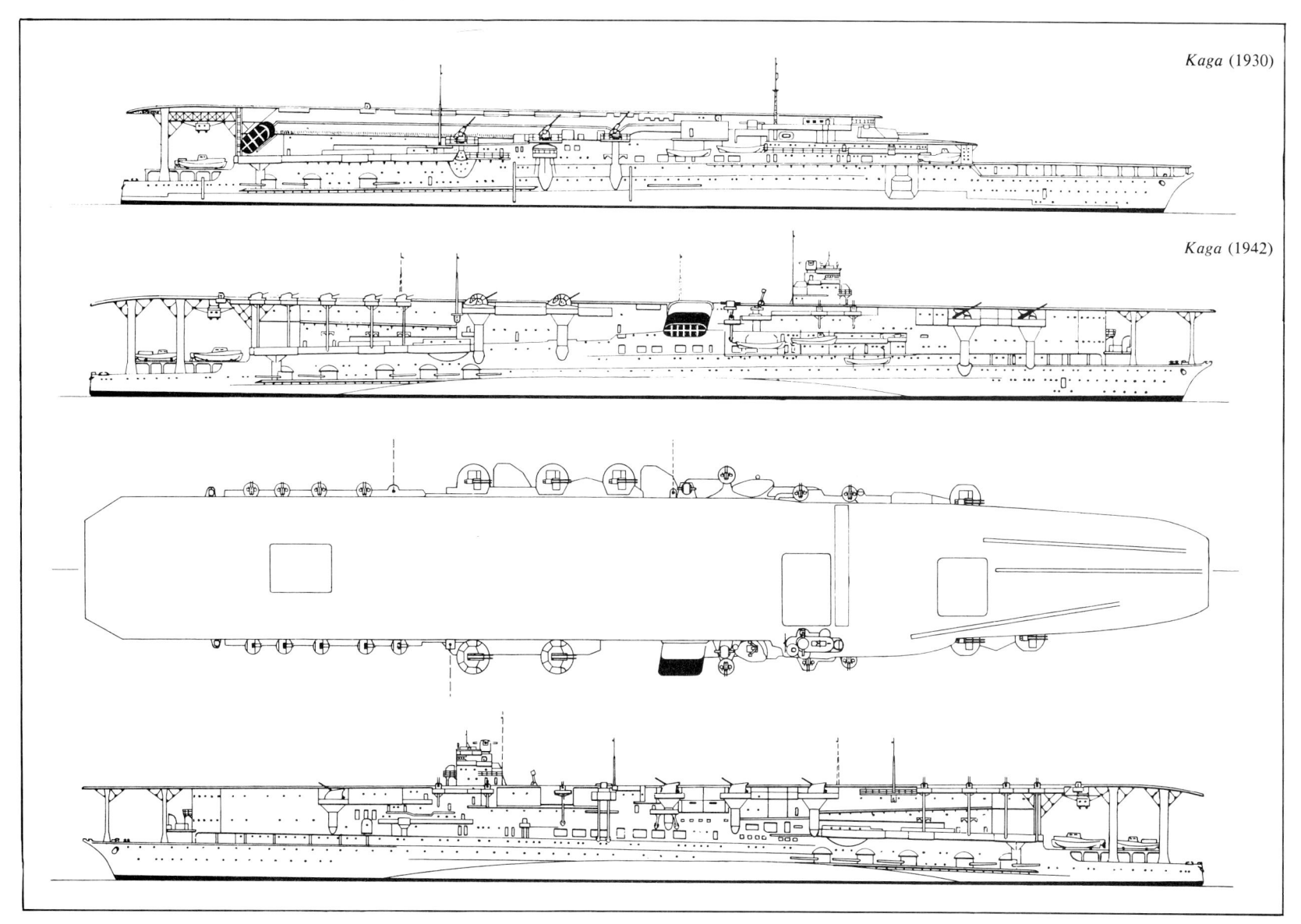

Kaga (1930)

Kaga (1942)

42 AIRCRAFT CARRIERS AND AVIATION TRANSPORTS

GENERAL NOTES
Launched as a battleship (see p. 35), completed as an aircraft carrier in place of *Amagi* (see p. 36) by the Yokosuka Naval Dockyard.
'Through-deck' design; armoured casemates and waterline belt. Flight deck 562ft × 100ft.

RECONSTRUCTION AND RE-ARMAMENT
25 June, 1934 to 25 June, 1935; reconstructed with full-length flight deck (815½ft × 100ft) and starboard-side island; 203mm all mounted in casemates; torpedo bulge protection.

CAREER
Launched 17 November, 1921; completed 31 March, 1926; sunk 4 June, 1942 NW of Midway (30° 20′ N, 179° 17′ W) after attack by aircraft from USS *Enterprise*. Campaigns and battles: China, Pearl Harbor, Rabaul, Darwin, Java, Midway.

Close-up detail of the midships section of *Kaga*, showing the open 4.7-inch AA mountings and their unusual supports, the horizontal smoke-ducts under the side of the flight-deck and the top "shelf" of the thick armoured belt. (IWM.)

Kaga was originally completed with two flying-off decks ahead of, and below, the 560-ft main flight deck. A twin 8-inch turret was located on either side of the upper flying-off deck, for use against surface targets only. (Jentschura.)

In 1935, *Kaga* emerged from Sasebo Navy Yard with a full-length (815-ft) flight deck, a starboard-side island and a large single, downward-facing funnel on the starboard side. (US Navy.)

AIRCRAFT CARRIERS AND AVIATION TRANSPORTS 43

Name	Builder	Date	Displ	Length ft in	Beam ft in	Draught ft in	Machinery	SHP	Speed	Fuel	Radius	Armament	Comp
AKAGI	Kure NY	1920–1927	34364 N 26900 S	816 7 wl 764 5 pp	95 0	26 6	4 sets Bihon GT 19 Kampon boilers 4 shafts	131200	31	3900 oil 2100 coal	8000 @ 14	10 × 203mm (8in) 50-cal LA 12 × 120mm (4.7in) 45-cal HA 22 MGs 60 aircraft	
(modernisation)	Sasebo NY	1936–1938	41300 N 36500 S	855 3 wl 770 0 pp	102 9	28 7		133000	31¼	5775 oil	8200 @ 16	6 × 203mm (8in) 50-cal LA 12 × 120mm (4.7in) 45-cal HA 28 × 25mm AA 91 aircraft	2000

General Notes
Laid down as a battlecruiser, completed as an aircraft carrier, work beginning on 17 November, 1923, following the Washington Treaty. The original ballast and trim arrangements had to be altered to preserve stability.
'Through-deck' design with armoured casemates and belt. Flight deck: 624ft × 100ft.

Reconstruction and Re-armament
24 October, 1935 to 31 August, 1938: reconstructed with full-length flight deck (817½ft × 100ft) and port-side island – the first of only two examples of this unusual arrangement; 203mm main armament reduced to 6 guns, all mounted in casemates.

Career
Launched 22 April, 1925; completed 25 March, 1927; severely damaged 4 June, 1942 NW of Midway by aircraft from USS *Enterprise*; 04.55 5 June: scuttled by destroyers *Nowake*, *Arashi*, *Hagikaze* 30° 30′ N, 179° 08′ W. Campaigns and battles: China, Pearl Harbor, Rabaul, Darwin, Java, Ceylon, Midway.

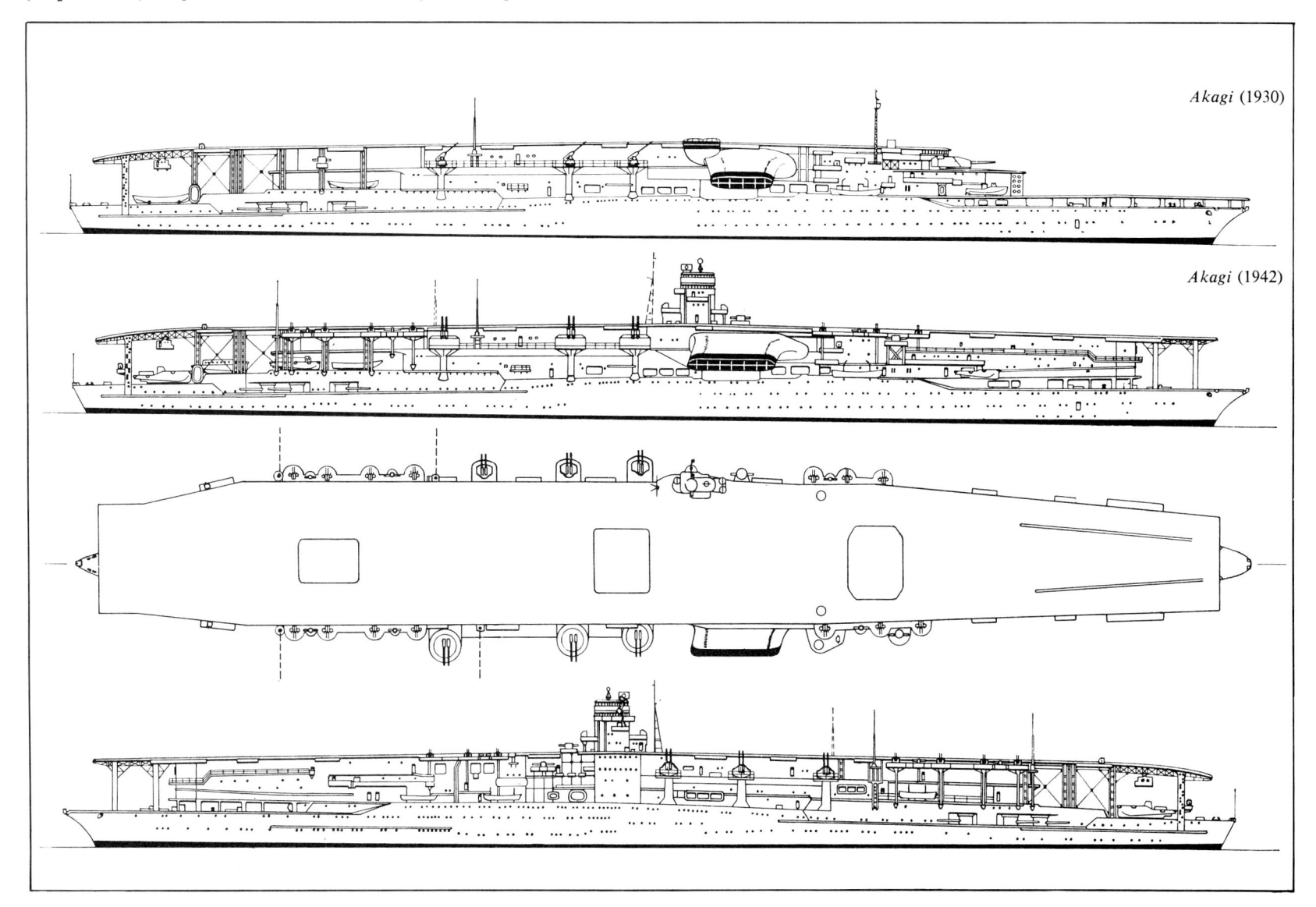

Akagi (1930)

Akagi (1942)

AIRCRAFT CARRIERS AND AVIATION TRANSPORTS

Akagi, seen in Sukumo Bay a year after she had commissioned, having been modernised with a port-side island and full-length flight deck. (US Navy.)

Name	Builder	Date	Displ	Length ft in	Beam ft in	Draught ft in	Machinery	SHP	Speed	Fuel	Radius	Armament	Comp
RYUJO	Yokohama DY Co.	1929–1931	10150 N 8000 S	575 5 wl 548 7 pp	66 8	18 3	2 sets GT 6 Kampon boilers 2 shafts	65000 (65270 on trials)	29 (29½)	2490 oil	10000 @ 14	12 × 127mm (5in) 40-cal DP 24 MGs 48 aircraft	600
(reconstruction)		1934–1936	12732 N 10600 S	590 7 oa 576 6 wl 550 4 pp	68 2	23 3		66269	29			8 × 127mm (5in) 40-cal DP 4 × 25mm AA 24 × 13.2mm AA 48 aircraft	924

Ryujo (1933)

Ryujo (1939)   *Ryujo* (1942)

Ryujo's forecastle remains dry, thanks to the considerable flare of the bows, despite the carrier's high speed in a short, steep swell. (US Navy.)

AIRCRAFT CARRIERS AND AVIATION TRANSPORTS   45

GENERAL NOTES
1927 Programme: fitted out at the Yokosuka Naval Dockyard. Designed as a flush-deck single-hangar ship, but a larger aircraft complement was demanded and she was completed with two hangar decks. Sperry gyro-stabilization; light side armour. Flight deck: 513½ft × 75½ft.

RECONSTRUCTION AND RE-ARMAMENT
1934–6: extensively modified to improve stability and sea-keeping qualities; 2 × 2 127mm AA removed and replaced by 2 × 2 25mm AA; ballast keel added, front-face of navigating bridge modified; 1940: forecastle raised.

CAREER
Launched 2 April, 1931; completed 9 May, 1933; sunk 24 August, 1942 near Bradley Reef (06° 20′ S, 160° 50′ E) by aircraft from USS *Saratoga*. Campaigns and battles: China, Philippines, East Indies, Indian Ocean, Aleutians, Eastern Solomons.

Right:
The hull of *Ryujo*, seen three weeks after launching, and before leaving the Yokohama Dockyard works for the Yokosuka Navy Yard, where the hangar and flight deck structure were added. The unconventional, but typical, Japanese sheer line, with the hull falling away from a flared bow to an almost level centre section and then dropping again to the stern, was employed to save structural weight, while giving the maximum freeboard where needed. (Jentschura.)

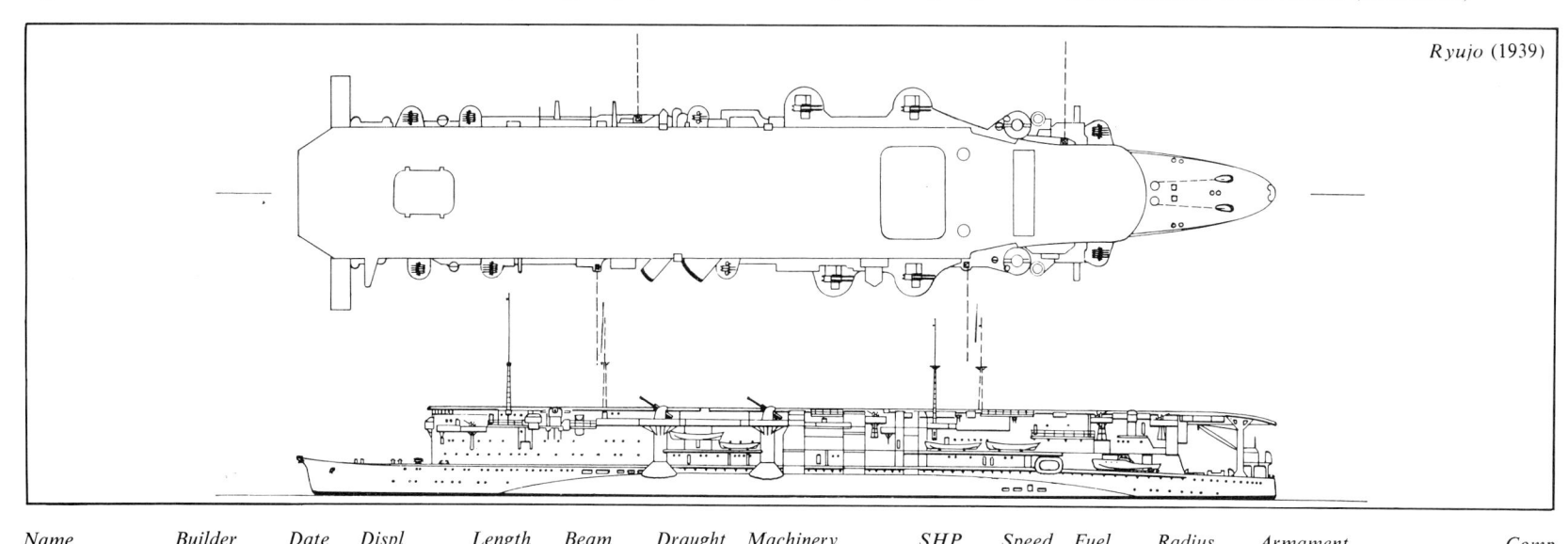

Ryujo (1939)

Name	Builder	Date	Displ	Length ft in	Beam ft in	Draught ft in	Machinery	SHP	Speed	Fuel	Radius	Armament	Comp
G.6 and G.8 Projects	—	—	17500 S	787 5 wl	—	—	GT	150000	—	—	—	6 × 203mm (8in) LA 5 × 155mm (6.1in) LA	

G6 design (1932)

G8 design (1933)

Sketch designs for *Soryu*-class.
G.6 Experimental design for 1932 'cruiser-carrier'.
G.8. Original 1933 design for *Soryu* class, replaced by the following design.

46 AIRCRAFT CARRIERS AND AVIATION TRANSPORTS

Name	Builder	Date	Displ	Length ft in	Beam ft in	Draught ft in	Machinery	SHP	Speed	Fuel	Radius	Armament	Comp
SORYU	Kure NY	1934–1937	18800 N 15900 S	746 5 oa 729 9 wl 677 7 pp	69 11	25 0	4 sets GT 8 Kampon boilers 4 shafts	152000	34½	3670	7750 @ 18	12 × 127mm (5in) 40-cal DP 28 × 25mm AA 71 aircraft	1100
HIRYU	Yokosuka NY	1936–1939	20250 N 17300 S	745 11 oa 721 9 wl 687 5 pp	73 3	25 9		153000	34⅓	4400 (approx)	10330 @ 18	12 × 127mm (5in) 40-cal DP 31 × 25mm AA 73 aircraft	1100

GENERAL NOTES
1931–2 Supplementary Programme: *Soryu*'s island on starboard side, *Hiryu*'s to port; 2 angled funnels starboard side amidships; light side armour. Flight deck: *Soryu* 711½ft × 85ft, *Hiryu* 711½ft × 88½ft.

CAREERS
Soryu
Launched 23 December, 1935; completed 29 December, 1937; sunk 4 June, 1942 NW of Midway (30° 38′ N, 179° 13′ W) by aircraft from USS *Yorktown*.

Hiryu
Launched 16 November, 1937; completed 5 July, 1939; severely damaged 4 June, 1942 NW of Midway by aircraft from *Yorktown* and *Enterprise*; 5 June: scuttled by destroyers *Kazegumo* and *Yugumo* 31° 38′ N, 178° 51′ W. Campaigns and battles: both ships, China, Pearl Harbor, Wake Island, Rabaul, Ambon Island, Timor, Darwin, Java, Ceylon, Midway.

Hiryu, running trials in June 1939. Nominally of the same class as *Soryu*, she was in fact of a revised design, with a greatly increased tonnage and slightly larger dimensions, quite apart from her port-side island layout. (Shizuo Fukui.)

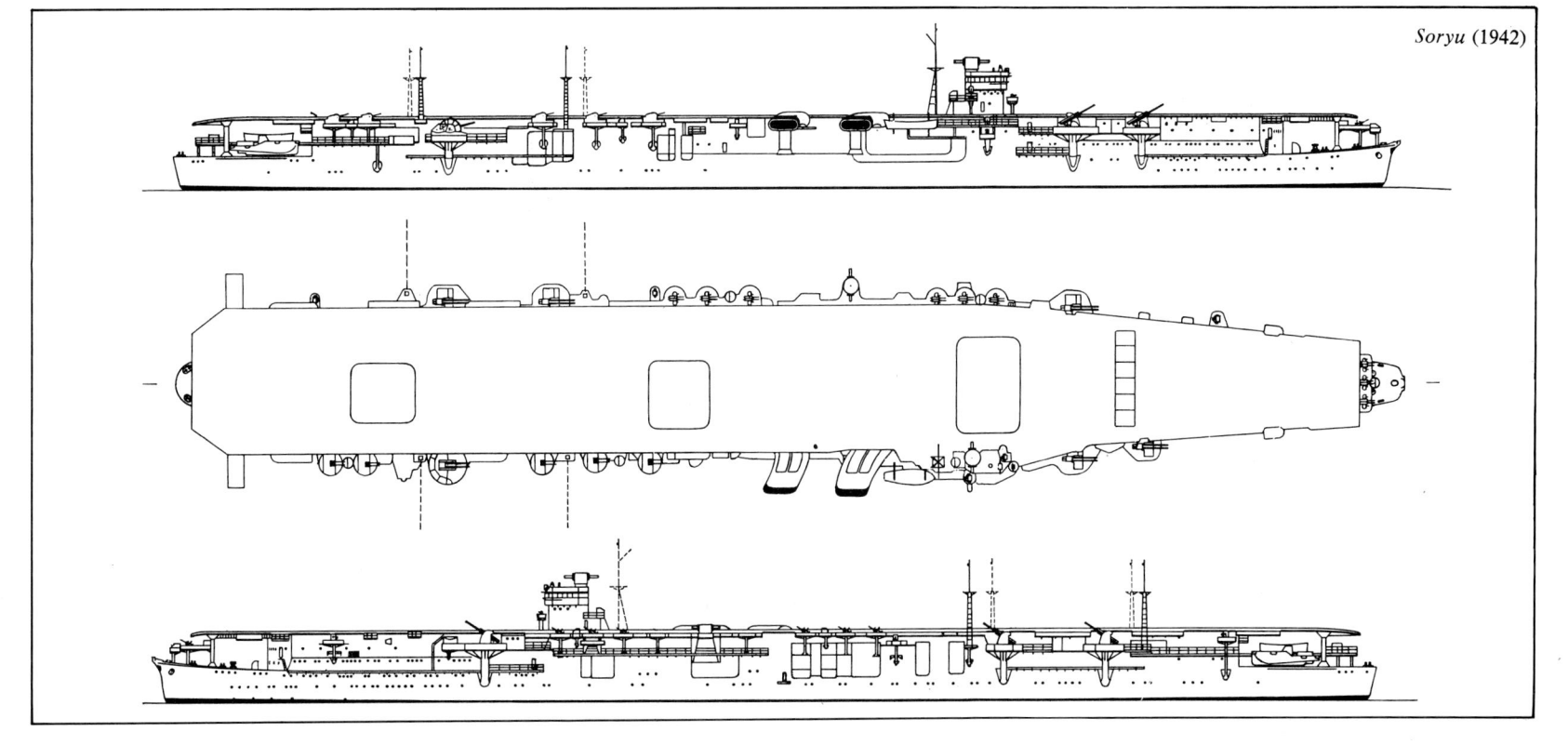

Soryu (1942)

AIRCRAFT CARRIERS AND AVIATION TRANSPORTS

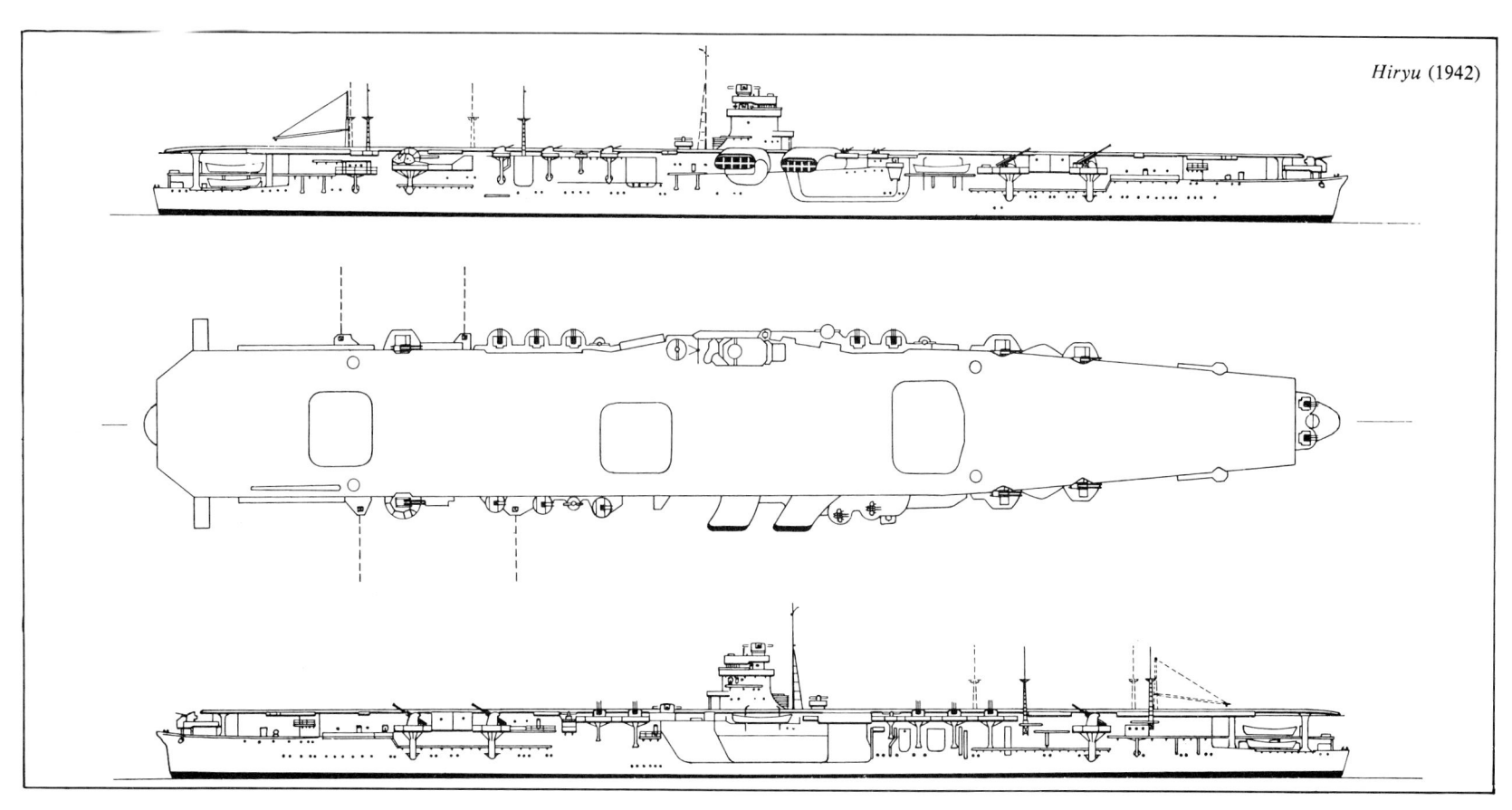

Hiryu (1942)

Zuiho (1941)

Name	Builder	Date	Displ	Length ft in	Beam ft in	Draught ft in	Machinery	SHP	Speed	Fuel	Radius	Armament	Comp
ZUIHO ex-*Takasaki*	Yokosuka NY	1935– 1940	13950 N	674 2 oa 660 11 wl 606 11 pp	59 8	21 7	2 sets GT 4 boilers 2 shafts	52000	28	2600 (approx)	7800 @ 18	8 × 127mm (5in)40-cal DP 8 × 25mm AA 30 aircraft	785
SHOHO ex-*Tsurugisaki*	Yokosuka NY	1941– 1942	11262 S										

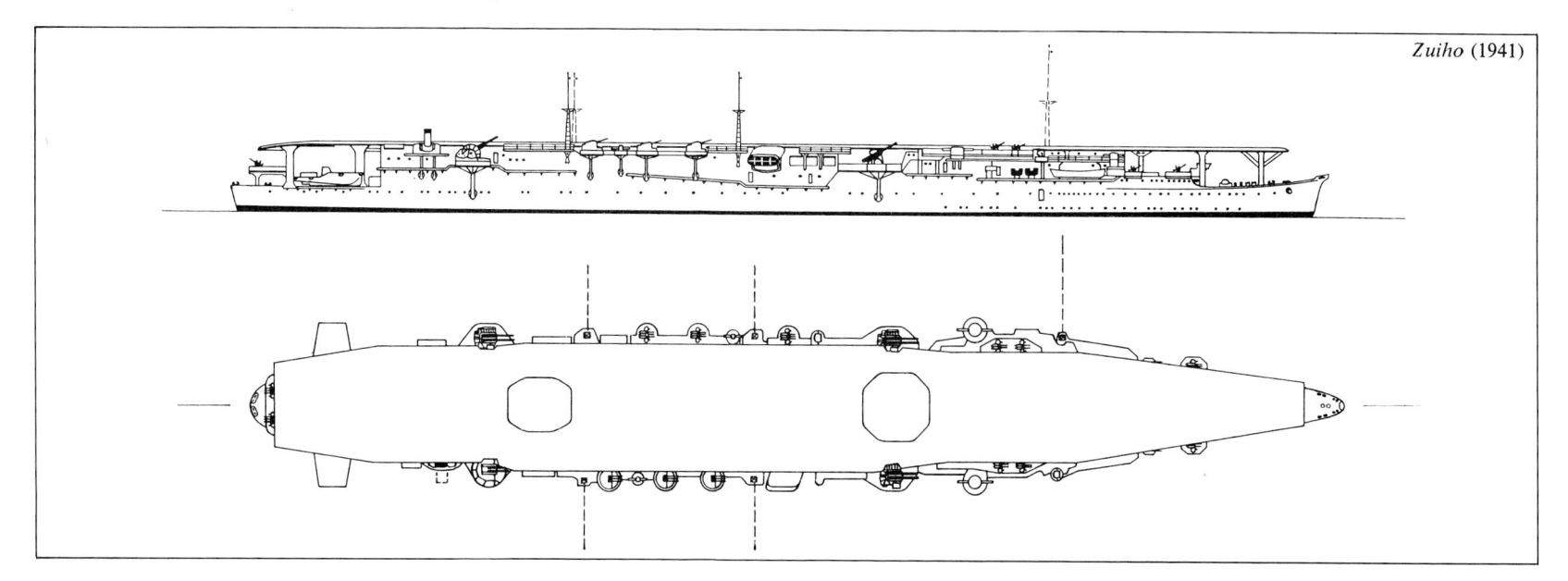

48 AIRCRAFT CARRIERS AND AVIATION TRANSPORTS

Shoho (1942)

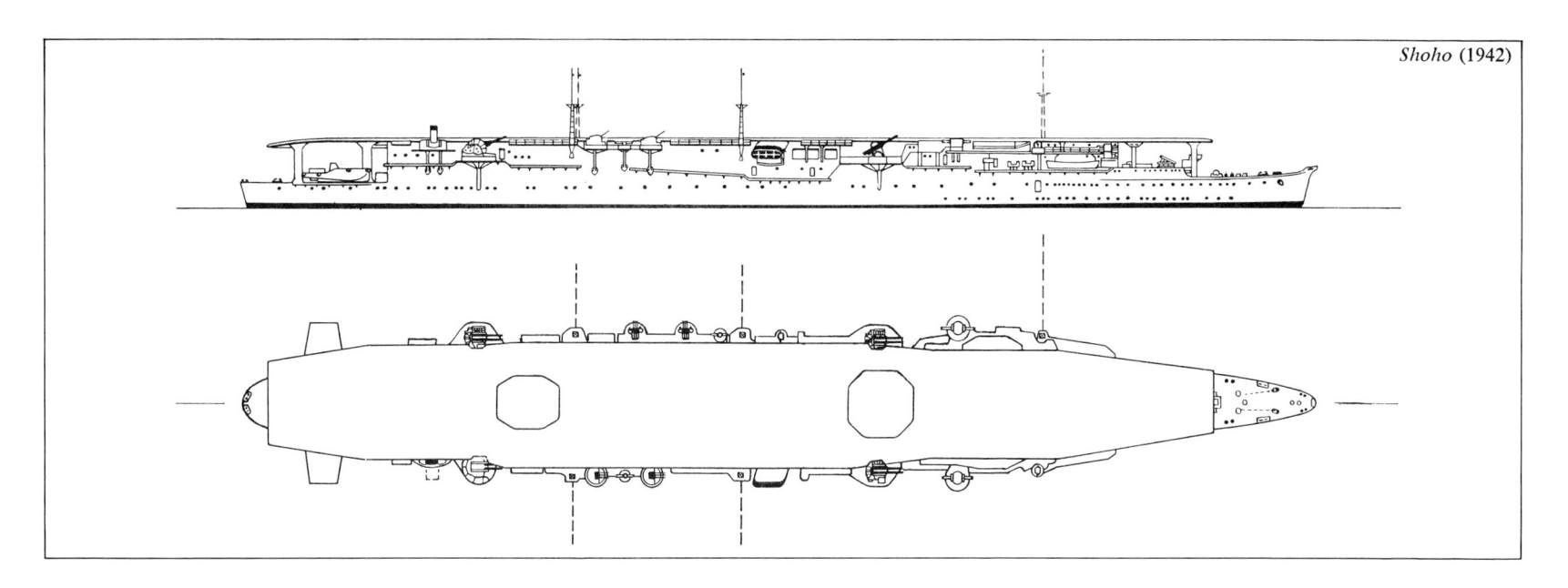

General Notes
Originally designed and launched as submarine support ships *Tsurugisaki* and *Takasaki* (see p. 238), the former being completed as such in 1939, four years after launching. *Takasaki* was taken in hand for reconstruction and renamed *Zuiho* while fitting out; *Tsurugisaki* was renamed *Shoho* in 1941, when she was rebuilt. The original Diesel engines were replaced by destroyer turbine machinery. Flight deck: 590½ft × 75½ft.

Re-armament
1943: (*Zuiho* only) AA armament increased to 48 × 25mm; 1944: armament further increased to 68 × 25mm, together with 6 × 28 AA rocket-launchers; flight deck extended to the bows.

Careers
Shoho
Launched 1 June, 1935 as *Tsurugisaki*; completed 15 January, 1939; renamed *Shoho* and reconstructed 1941, completed 26 January, 1942; sunk 7 May, 1942 18 nm S of Woodlark Island (10° 29′ S, 152° 55′ E) by aircraft from USS *Yorktown*.

Zuiho
Launched 19 June, 1936 as *Takasaki*; renamed and completed as *Zuiho* 27 December 1940; sunk 25 October, 1944 ENE of Cape Engano (19° 20′ N, 125° 15′ E) by aircraft from USS *Essex*, *Lexington*, *Franklin*, *Enterprise* and *San Jacinto*. Campaigns and battles: *Shoho* Coral Sea; *Zuiho* Philippines, Midway, Aleutians, Santa Cruz (damaged), Philippine Sea, Cape Engano.

Zuiho was commissioned four-and-a-half years after launching, the relatively simple conversion having taken an inordinately long period to complete. She is seen here running acceptance trials in Tokyo Bay, ten days before her official completion date. (Shizuo Fukui.)

Name	Builder	Date	Displ	Length ft in	Beam ft in	Draught ft in	Machinery	SHP	Speed	Fuel	Radius	Armament	Comp
RYUHO ex-*Taigei*	Yokosuka NY	1941–1942	15300 N 13360 S	707 6 oa / 689 0 wl / 647 4 pp	64 3	21 9	2 Sets GT 4 boilers 2 shafts	52000	26½	2900 (approx)	8000 @ 18	8 × 127mm (5in) 40-cal DP 38 × 25mm AA 31 aircraft	989

AIRCRAFT CARRIERS AND AVIATION TRANSPORTS

Ryuho (1944)

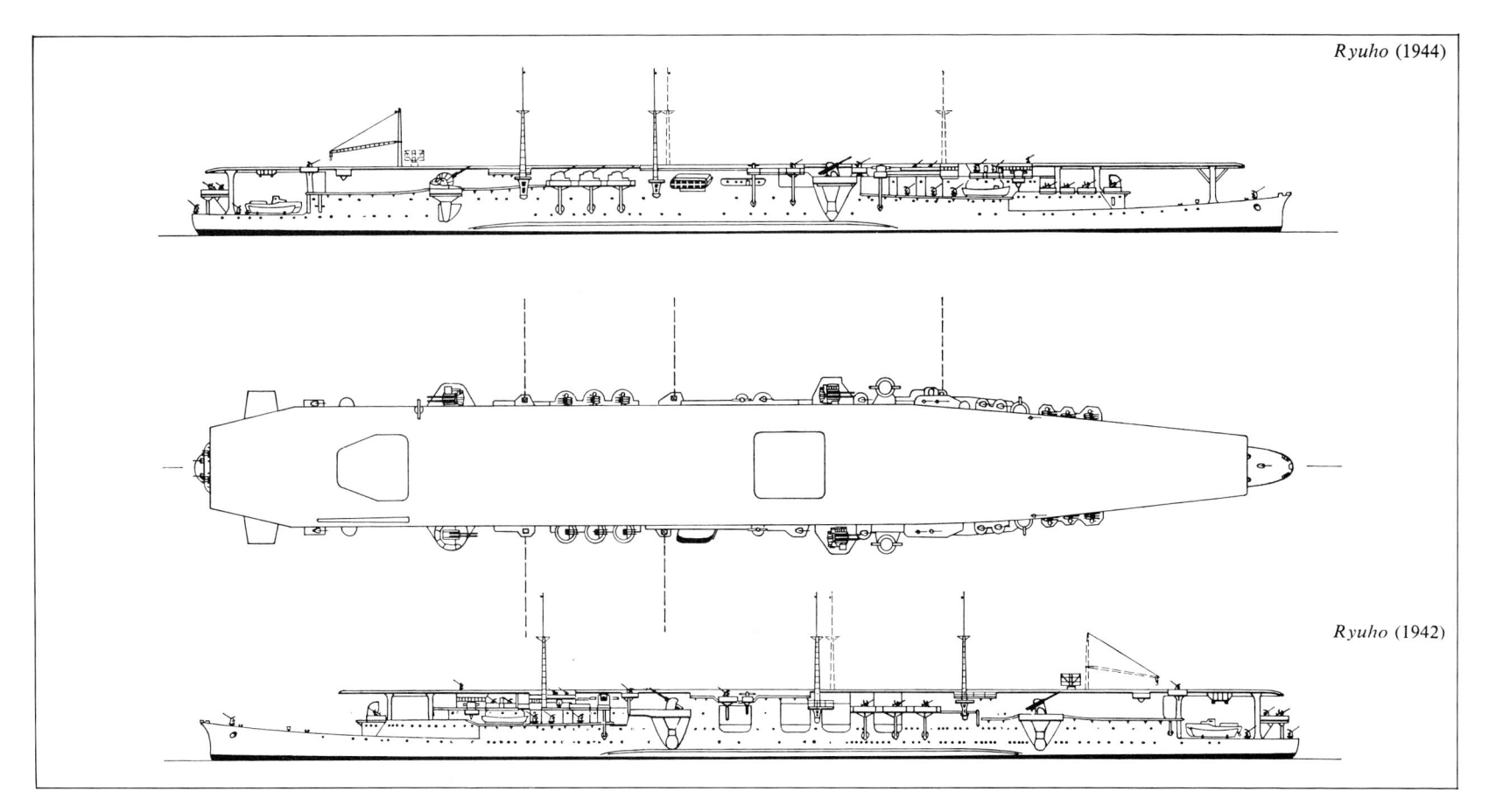

Ryuho (1942)

GENERAL NOTES
Submarine support ship *Taigei* (p. 238) rebuilt as a carrier as part of the 1941 secret mobilization plan. The Diesel engines were replaced by destroyer turbines to give a higher sea speed. This ship was an unsuccessful conversion of an unsuccessful original design. Poor internal sub-division and a weak hull structure limited her utility. Flight deck: 607ft × 75½ft.

RE-ARMAMENT
From 1943: 42 × 25mm AA, 6 × 13.2mm AA; June 1944: increased to 61 × 25mm, 28 × 13.2mm, together with 6 × 28 AA rocket-launchers; 6 depth-charges; flight deck extended to bows (650ft).

CAREER
Launched 16 November, 1933; completed as *Taigei* 31 March, 1935; renamed *Ryuho* 1941 when reconstruction commenced, completed 28 November, 1942; damaged in Kure harbour 19 March, 1945 by aircraft from US TF 58; not repaired, broken up at Kure 1946. Campaigns and battles; Philippine Sea (slightly damaged).

Zuikaku, seen on her commissioning day, 25th September 1941. (US Navy.)

Name	Builder	Date	Displ	Length ft in	Beam ft in	Draught ft in	Machinery	SHP	Speed	Fuel	Radius	Armament	Comp
SHOKAKU	Yokosuka NY	1937–1941	29800 N	844 oa 10	85 4	29 1	4 sets GT 8 Kampon boilers 4 shafts	160000	34¼	3500 oil	9700 @ 18	16 × 127mm (5in) 40-cal DP 42 × 25mm AA 84 aircraft	1660
ZUIKAKU	Kawasaki DY, Kobe	1938–1941	25675 S	820 wl 2 774 pp 6									

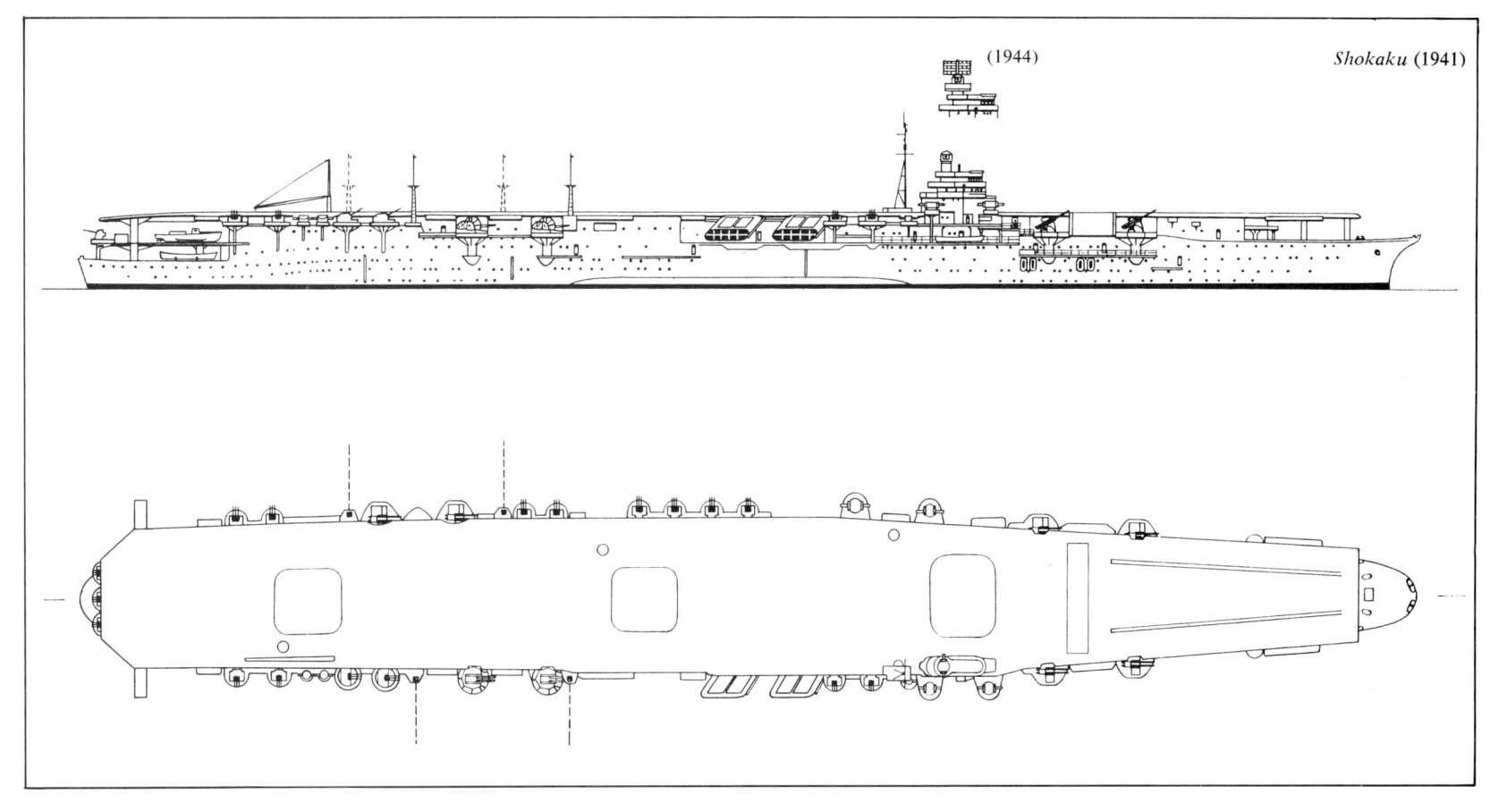

Shokaku (1941) (1944)

General Notes
1937 Supplementary Programme, modified *Hiryu* type with *Yamato*-design bow-form. Flight deck: 794ft × 95ft.

Armour
Belt 8.5in; deck 6.7in (total).

Armament
From 1943 both ships 70 × 25mm; July 1944 (*Zuikaku*) 96 × 25mm, 6 × 28 AA rocket-launchers.

Careers
Shokaku
Launched 1 June, 1939; completed 8 August, 1941; sunk 19 June, 1944 140 nm N of Yap Island (11° 40′ N, 137° 40′ E) by US submarine *Cavalla*.
Zuikaku
Launched 27 November, 1939; completed 25 September, 1941; sunk 25 October, 1944 220 nm ENE of Cape Engano (19° 20′ N, 125° 15′ E) by aircraft from USS *Essex* and *Lexington*. Campaigns and battles: both Pearl Harbor, Rabaul, Darwin, Java, Ceylon, Coral Sea (*Shokaku* damaged); *Zuikaku* Aleutians; both Eastern Solomons, Santa Cruz (*Shokaku* damaged), Philippine Sea (*Shokaku* sunk, *Zuikaku* damaged); Cape Engano (*Zuikaku* sunk).

The leading Aichi D3A "Val" dive-bomber takes off from *Shokaku*, to attack Pearl Harbor on 7th December 1941. (Koku Fan.)

AIRCRAFT CARRIERS AND AVIATION TRANSPORTS

Shokaku under attack during the Battle of the Coral Sea (5th May 1942), an aviation fire blazing forward and smoke rising from internal fires amidships. (US Navy.)

Name	Builder	Date	Displ	Length ft in	Beam ft in	Draught ft in	Machinery	SHP	Speed	Fuel	Radius	Armament	Comp
HIYO ex-*Izumo Maru*	Kawasaki DY, Kobe	1939– 1942	26949 N 24140 S	719 7 oa 706 4 wl 675 10 pp	87 7	26 9	2 sets GT 6 Kampon boilers 2 shafts	56250	25½	2800 oil approx	?	12 × 127mm (5in) 40-cal DP 24 × 25mm AA 53 aircraft	1187 to 1224
JUNYO ex-*Kashiwara Maru*	Mitsubishi SB, Nagasaki	1939– 1942					2 sets GT 4 Kampon and 2 Mitsubishi boilers 2 shafts						

GENERAL NOTES

Formerly *Kashiwara Maru* and *Izumo Maru*, laid down in 1939 as 27500 GRT, 24-knot liners for the NYK Line. Taken over by the Imperial Japanese Navy in August 1940 and completed as aircraft carriers. The fitting of new-pattern boilers was intended to raise the maximum speed by 1.5 knots, but in service, the ships seldom achieved more than 22–23 knots. The combined island and funnel was the first of its type in the Japanese Navy. Flight deck: 690ft × 89½ft.

Junyo (1945)

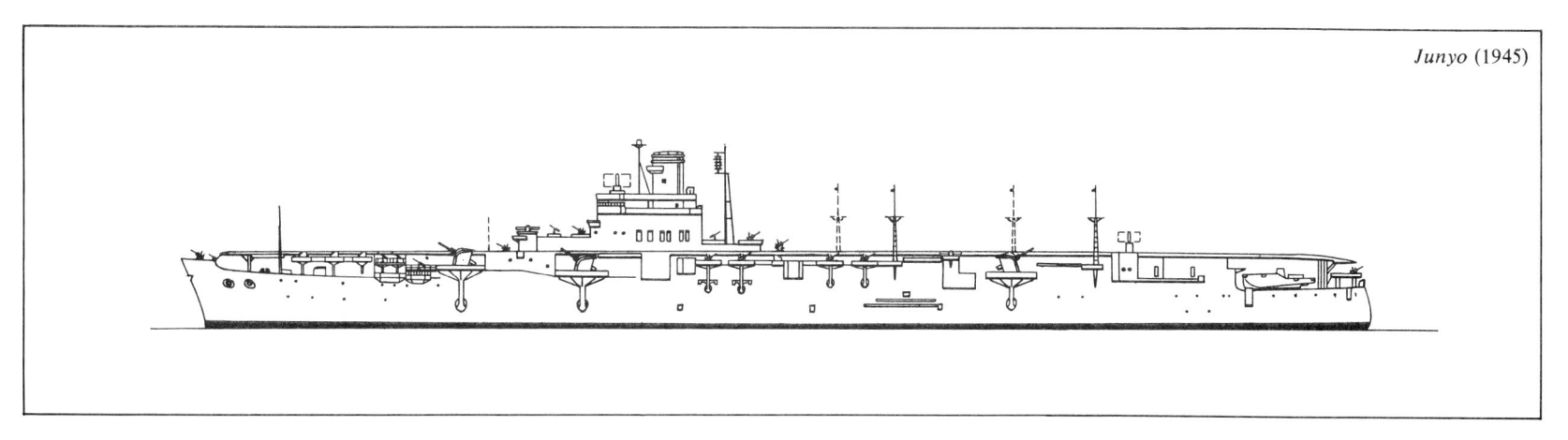

52 AIRCRAFT CARRIERS AND AVIATION TRANSPORTS

Junyo (1945)

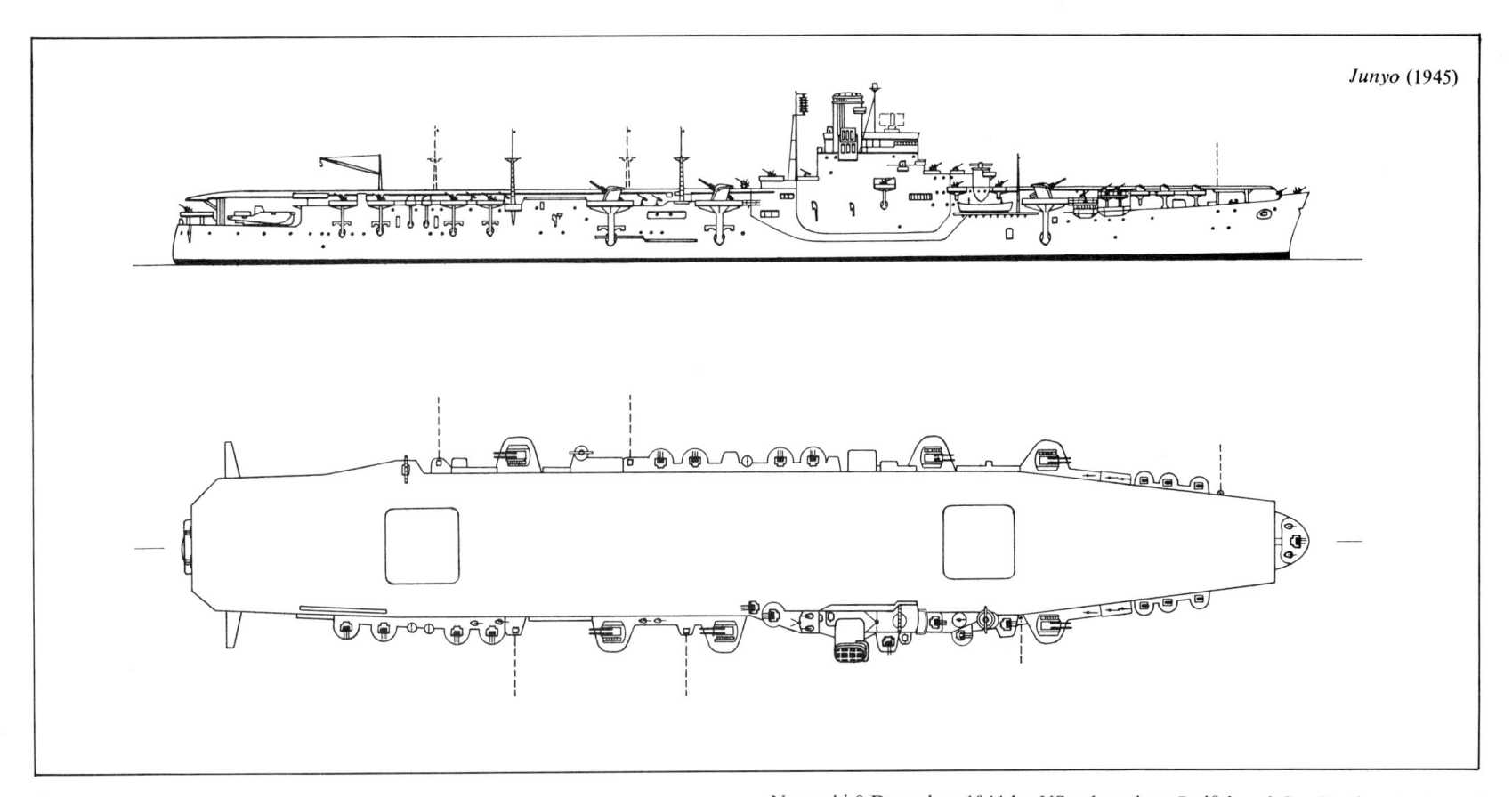

ARMAMENT
From 1943: 40 × 25mm AA; from July 1944 *Junyo*: 76 × 25mm, 6 × 28 AA rocket-launchers.

CAREERS
Junyo
Launched 26 June, 1941; completed 5 May, 1942; torpedoed and damaged off Nagasaki 9 December, 1944 by US submarines *Redfish* and *Sea Devil*; not returned to service, broken up at Sasebo, 1947.
Hiyo
Launched 24 June, 1941; completed 31 July, 1942; torpedoed and sunk 20 June, 1944 450 nm NW of Yap Island (15° 30′ N, 133° 50′ E) by aircraft from USS *Belleau Wood*. Campaigns and battles: *Junyo* Dutch Harbour, Aleutians, Santa Cruz; both Guadalcanal, Philippine Sea (*Hiyo* sunk).

Junyo, converted from an incomplete liner, was the first Japanese carrier to be built with the funnel in the island structure. She is seen here lying at Sasebo in September 1945. The radar antennae on the mainmast and forward of the funnel can be clearly made out. (US Navy.)

AIRCRAFT CARRIERS AND AVIATION TRANSPORTS 53

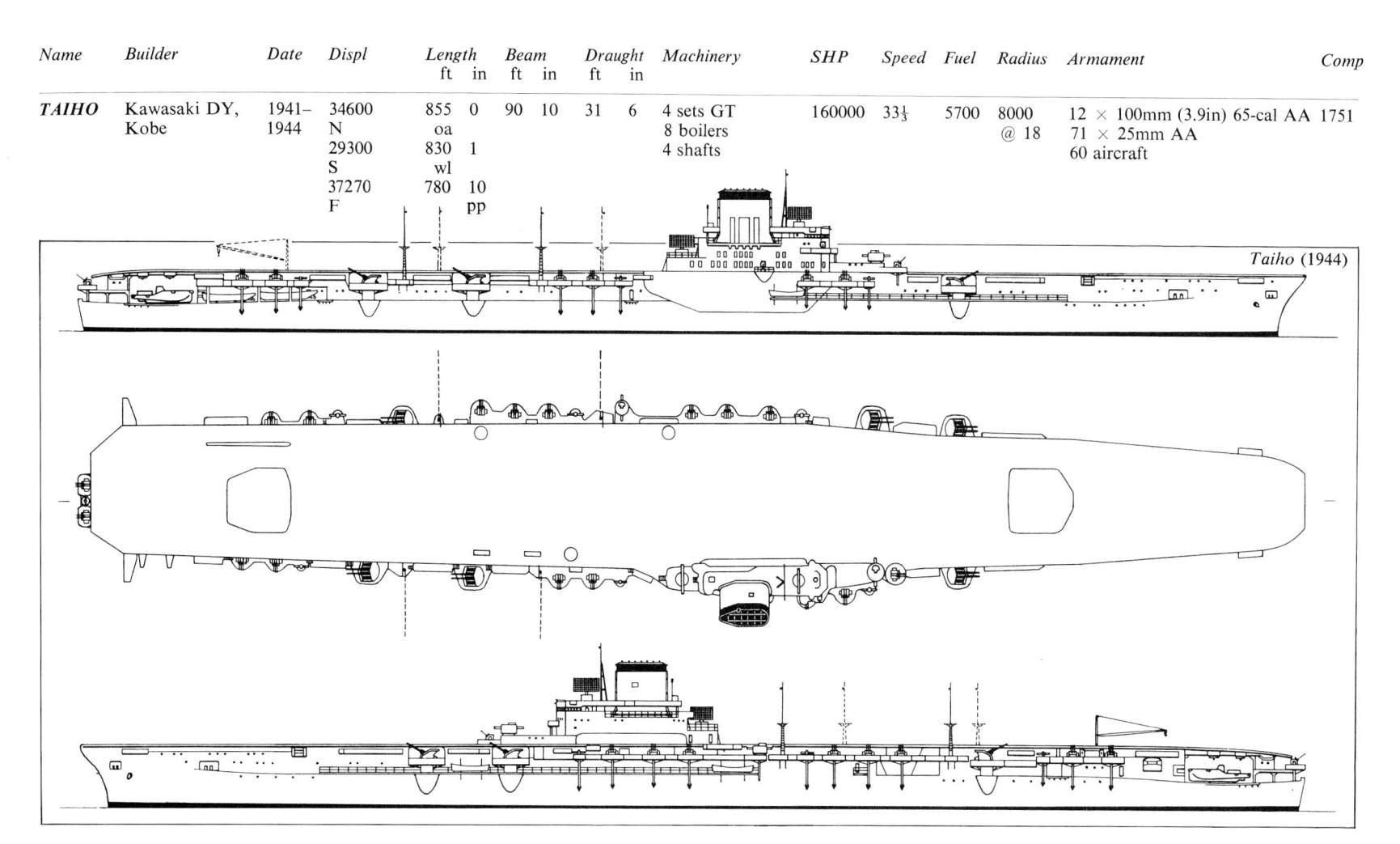

Name	Builder	Date	Displ	Length ft in	Beam ft in	Draught ft in	Machinery	SHP	Speed	Fuel	Radius	Armament	Comp
TAIHO	Kawasaki DY, Kobe	1941–1944	34600 N 29300 S 37270 F	855 0 oa / 830 1 wl / 780 10 pp	90 10	31 6	4 sets GT 8 boilers 4 shafts	160000	33⅓	5700	8000 @ 18	12 × 100mm (3.9in) 65-cal AA 71 × 25mm AA 60 aircraft	1751

Taiho (1944)

General Notes
4th Supplementary Programme, 1939: Japanese reply to the American *Essex*-class and British *Illustrious*-class carriers. First Japanese carrier with armoured flight deck. Five other units planned. Flight deck: 844ft × 98½ft.

Armour
Belt 5.9in; flight deck 3.9in; hangar deck 4.9in.

Career
Launched 7 April, 1943; completed 7 March, 1944; torpedoed 19 June, 1944 180 nm NNW of Yap Island (12° 05′ N, 138° 12′ E) by US submarine *Albacore*; sank seven hours later as the result of fuel explosions and fires.

Name	Builder	Date	Displ	Length ft in	Beam ft in	Draught ft in	Machinery	SHP	Speed	Fuel	Radius	Armament	Comp
Modified **TAIHO (G.15)** Job Nos. 801, 802 Job Nos. 5021–25	Naval Dockyards Kawasaki, Mitsubishi		30100 S 35300 N 30360 S	843 2 wl	91 10	31 8	8 boilers	160000	33	?	10000 @ 18	16 × 100mm (3.9in) 65-cal AA 66 × 25mm AA 53 aircraft	1800

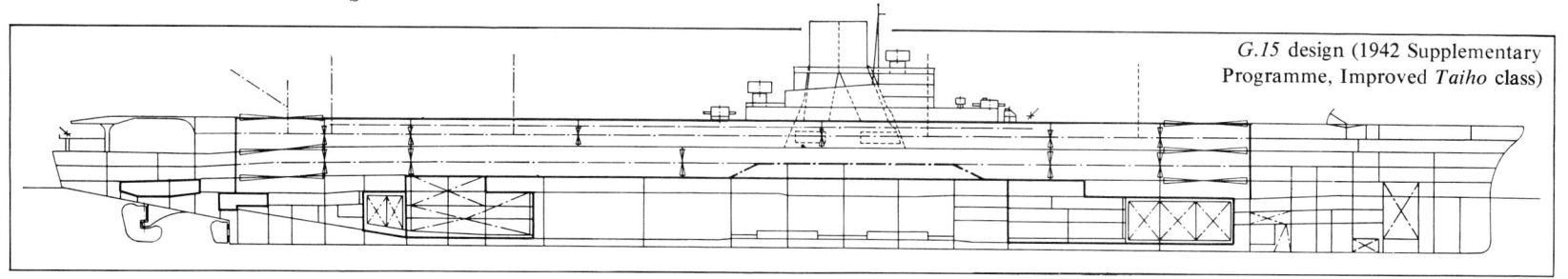

G.15 design (1942 Supplementary Programme, Improved Taiho class)

AIRCRAFT CARRIERS AND AVIATION TRANSPORTS

G.15 design (Improved Taiho class, plan)

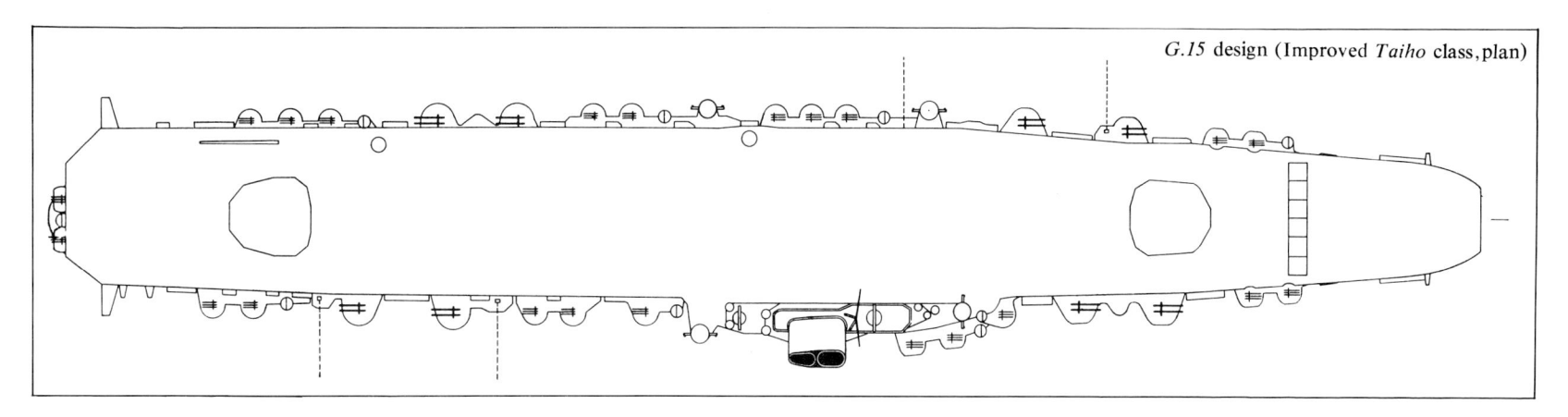

Modified Taiho class
Job Nos 801, 802: 1942 Programme, work never commenced.
Job Nos 5021–5: 1942 Supplementary Programme, considerably enlarged development of *Taiho* but with reduced aircraft complement. Flight deck: 858ft × 98½ft. Planned only.

Name	Builder	Date	Displ	Length ft in	Beam ft in	Draught ft in	Machinery	SHP	Speed	Fuel	Radius	Armament	Comp
SHINANO	Yokosuka NY	1940–1944	71890 F 68059 N 64800 S	872 2 oa 839 11 wl 800 6 pp	119 1	33 10	4 sets Kampon GT 12 Kampon boilers 4 shafts	150000	27	8904	10000 @ 18	16 × 127mm (5in) 40-cal DP 145 × 25mm AA 12 × 28 120mm (4.7in) AA rocket-launchers	2400

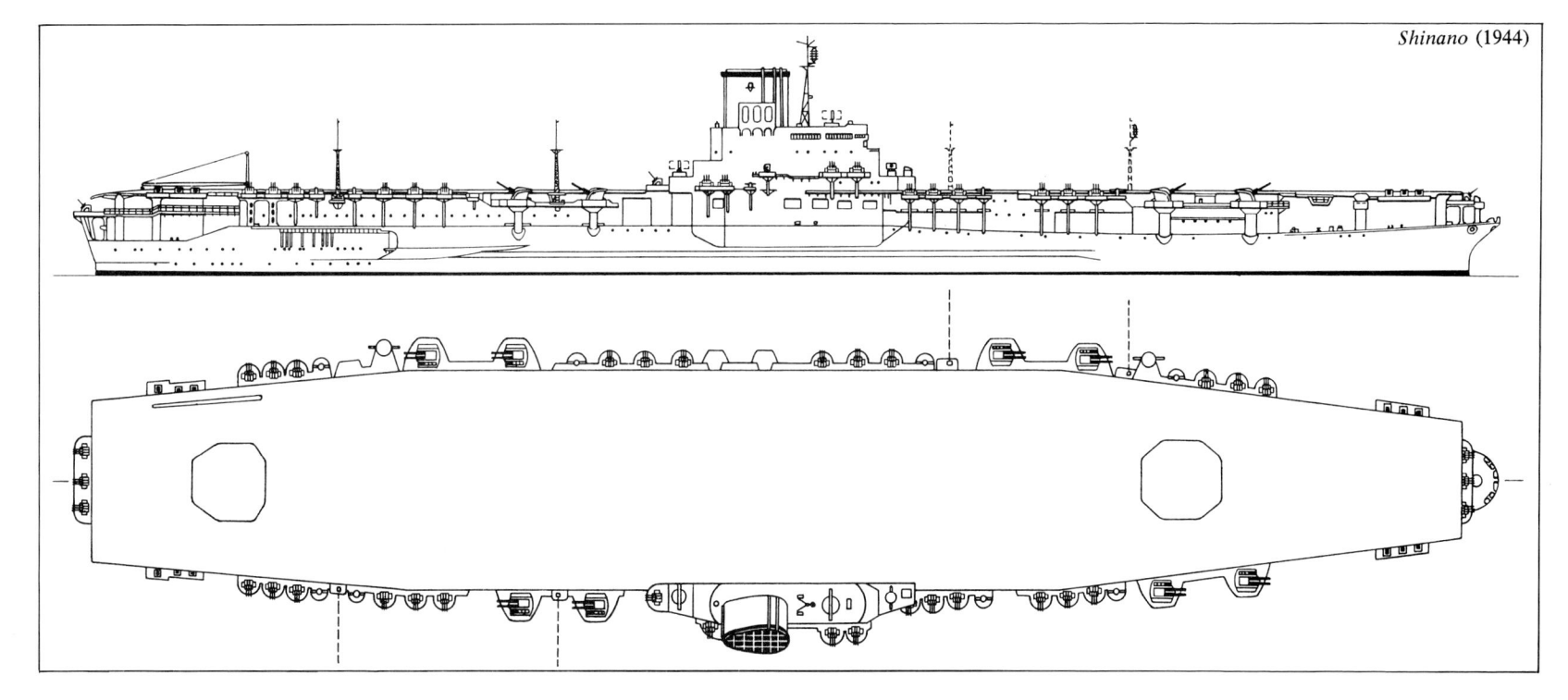

Shinano (1944)

General Notes
Laid down 4 May, 1940 as a *Yamato*-class battleship and converted while building to an aircraft carrier to make up for carrier losses at the battle of Midway. Compromise between battleship hull and carrier superstructure, with an armoured flight deck and 'open' hangar. As the result of her great fuel and ordnance stowage capacity, she was to have been fitted out as a replenishment and support ship for carrier task forces. The shell and charge hoists in the turret barbettes were converted for use as high-speed lifts for bombs and other air ordnance. Flight deck: 840ft × 131¾ft.

Armour
Belt 8.1in (magazines 13.8in); flight deck 3.15in; hangar deck 7.87in.

Career
Launched 8 October, 1944; completed for trials 19 November, 1944; torpedoed 29 November, 1944 by US submarine *Archerfish*, sank 160 nm SE of Cape Muroto (32° N, 137° E) as the result of uncontrolled flooding, the watertight doors for the extensive sub-division having not yet been fitted.

AIRCRAFT CARRIERS AND AVIATION TRANSPORTS

Name	Builder	Date	Displ	Length ft / in	Beam ft / in	Draught ft / in	Machinery	SHP	Speed	Fuel	Radius	Armament	Comp
UNRYU	Yokosuka NY	1942–1944	20100 N 17150 S	745 oa / 11, 731 wl / 8, 679 pp / 2	72 / 2	25 / 9	4 sets GT, 8 Kampon boilers, 4 shafts	152000	34	3670	8000 @ 18	12 × 127mm (5in) 40-cal DP (Type '89'), 51 × 25mm AA, 65 aircraft	1595
AMAGI	Mitsubishi, Nagasaki	1942–1944	20450 N 17460 S			28 / 8		152000	34			12 × 127mm DP, 89 × 25mm AA, 65 aircraft	1595
KATSURAGI	Kure NY	1942–1944	22534 F 20200 N 17260 S			25 / 6		104000	32 (32¾ on trials)			12 × 127mm DP, 89 × 25mm AA, 64 aircraft	1500
KASAGI not completed	Mitsubishi, Nagasaki	1943–	20400 N 17150 S			25 / 9		152000	34			12 × 127mm DP, 51 × 25mm AA, 64 aircraft	1595
ASO not completed	Kure NY	1943–	20100 N 17150 S			25 / 6		104000	32			12 × 127mm DP, 51 × 25mm AA, 64 aircraft	1500
IKOMA not completed	Kawasaki, Kobe	1943–	20450 N 17150 S			25 / 9		152000	34			12 × 127mm DP, 51 × 25mm AA, 53 aircraft	1595
Job Nos. 800, 5002, 5005, 5008–15 projected			20400 N 17150 S			25 / 9		152000	34			12 × 127mm (5in) 50-cal DP (Type '5'), 25mm AA, 64 aircraft	1595

Amagi (1945)

GENERAL NOTES
1941–2 War Construction Programme, modified *Hiryu* design. Cruiser-type geared turbines in all units except *Katsuragi* and *Aso*, which had destroyer-type turbines installed. *Kasagi* had hexagonal funnel uptakes. Flight deck: 712ft × 88½ft.

ARMOUR
Magazines 5.5in to 5.9in side, 2.17in deck; machinery 1.81in side, 1in deck.

ARMAMENT
1944–5: 6 × 28 120mm AA rocket-launchers added; *Unryu* 89 × 25mm AA.

CAREERS
Unryu
Launched 25 September, 1943; completed 6 August, 1944; torpedoed and sunk 19 December, 1944 by US submarine *Redfish* 200 nm SE of Shanghai (29° 59′ N, 124° 03′ E).

Amagi
Launched 15 October, 1943; completed 11 August, 1944; damaged at Kure 19 March, 1945 by TF 58 aircraft; sunk 24 July, 1945 in shallow water off Kurahashi Jima, Kure, by aircraft from TF 38; raised and broken up at Kure, 1947.

Katsuragi
Launched 19 January, 1944; completed 15 October, 1944; damaged by air attack at Kure 19 March, 1945; damaged at Kure 28 July, 1945 by TF 38 aircraft; taken over in August 1945 and used as repatriation transport until 11 November 1946; BU at Osaka, 1947.

Unryu (1944)

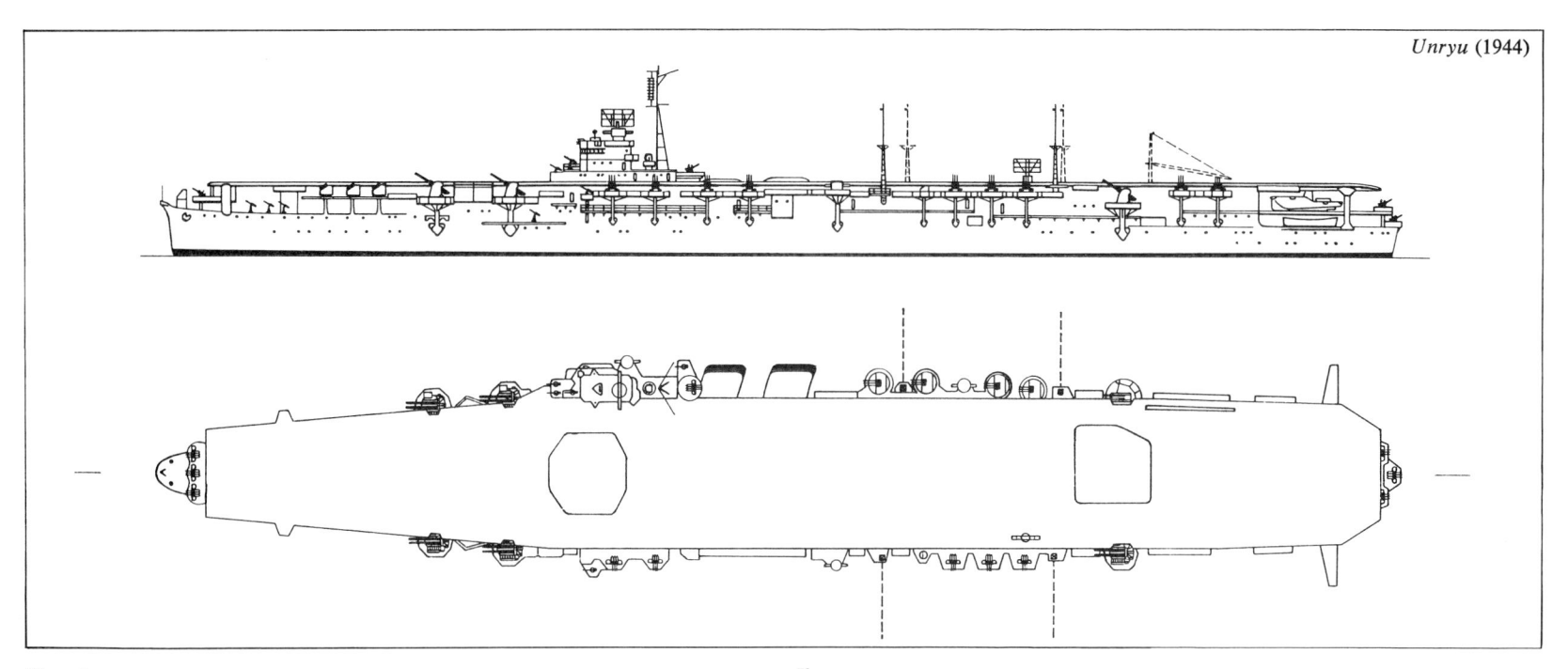

Kasagi
Launched 19 October, 1944; work suspended 1 April, 1945 when 85% complete; hull towed to Sasebo and BU in 1947.

Aso
Launched 1 November, 1944; work suspended January 1945 when 60% complete; hull heavily damaged at Kure 24 July, 1945 by TF 38 air attack; thereafter used as trials hulk for experiments with warheads for suicide weapons; BU at Sasebo, 1947.

Ikoma
Launched 17 November, 1944; work suspended January 1945, when 60% complete; hull heavily damaged in Ikei Bay 24 July, 1945 by TF 38 air attack; BU at Tamano, 1947.

Job Nos 800, 5002 (name *Kurama* considered), *5005, 5008–15*
1942 and 1942 Supplementary Programmes, building not commenced.

Name	Builder	Date	Displ	Length ft in	Beam ft in	Draught ft in	Machinery	SHP	Speed	Fuel	Radius	Armament	Comp
CHITOSE conversion	Sasebo NY	1943–1944	13647 N	631 7 oa	68 3	24 8	2 sets GT 4 Kampon boilers	44000	28.9	3600	11000 @ 18	8 × 127 mm (5in) 45-cal DP 30 × 25mm AA 30 aircraft	?
CHIYODA conversion see also p.64	Yokosuka NY	1942–1943	11190 S	605 10 wl 570 10 pp			2 Diesel engines 2 shafts	12800					

Chitose (1944)

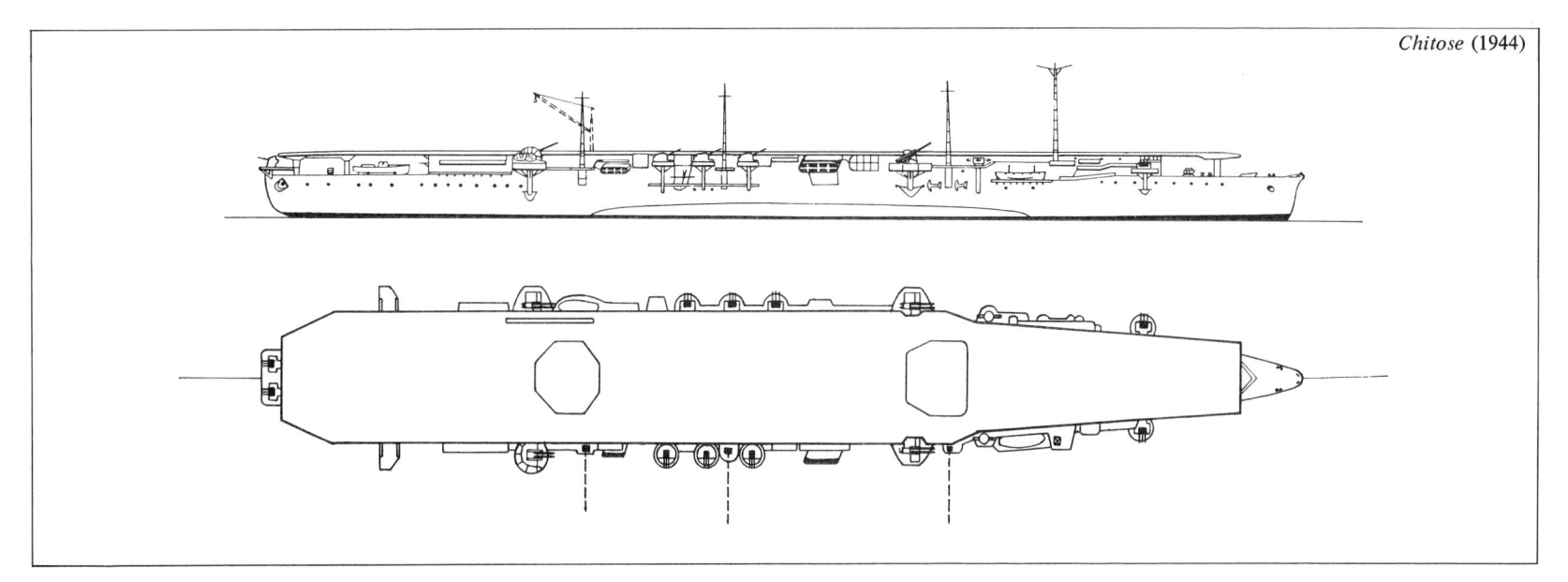

AIRCRAFT CARRIERS AND AVIATION TRANSPORTS

GENERAL NOTES
Seaplane Carriers (see p. 64) converted to aircraft carriers 1942–3. Flight deck: 590½ft × 75½ft.

ARMAMENT
From July 1943: 48 × 25mm AA.

CAREERS
Chitose
Launched 29 November, 1936; completed as seaplane carrier 25 July, 1938; conversion to light carrier completed 1 January, 1944; sunk 25 October, 1944 235 nm E of Cape Engano (19° 20′ N, 126° 20′ E) by aircraft from USS *Essex* and *Lexington*.

Chiyoda
Launched 19 November, 1937; completed as seaplane carrier 15 December, 1938; conversion to light carrier completed 31 October, 1943; damaged 25 October, 1944 by aircraft from USS *Lexington*, *Franklin* and *Langley*, and later sunk by US cruisers *Wichita*, *New Orleans*, *Santa Fe* and *Mobile*, 260 nm SE of Cape Engano (18° 37′ N, 126° 45′ E). Campaigns and battles (as carriers): Philippine Sea, Cape Engano.

Name	Builder	Date	Displ	Length ft in	Beam ft in	Draught ft in	Machinery	SHP	Speed	Fuel	Radius	Armament	Comp
IBUKI not completed	Kure NY and Sasebo NY	1942–	14800 N 12500 S	658 2 oa 650 9 wl 616 2 pp	69 7	20 8	2 sets GT 4 boilers 2 shafts	72000	29			4 × 80mm (actually 76.2mm–3in) 60-cal AA 48 × 25mm AA 120 mm AA rocket-launchers 27 aircraft 30 DCs	1015

Ibuki (1945)

GENERAL NOTES
Laid down as a heavy cruiser (see p. 87) at the Kure Naval Dockyard; work suspended summer 1943. Consideration given to conversion to a high-speed fleet oiler. In November 1943 towed to Sasebo and work commenced on conversion to a carrier.

Flight deck: 672½ft × 75½ft.

CAREER
Launched 21 May, 1943, work suspended March 1945 when 80% complete; BU at Sasebo, 1947.

Escort Carriers

Name	Builder	Date	Displ	Length ft in	Beam ft in	Draught ft in	Machinery	SHP	Speed	Fuel	Radius	Armament	Comp
TAIYO ex-*Kasuga Maru* conversion	Mitsubishi, Nagasaki and Sasebo NY	1940–1941 1941	20000 N 17830 S	591 4 oa 569 11 wl	73 10	26 3	2 sets GT 4 boilers 2 shafts	25200	21.1		6500 @ 18	6 × 120mm (4.7in) 45-cal HA 8 × 25mm AA 27 aircraft 8 × 127mm (5in) 40-cal DP	747 850
UNYO ex-*Yawata Maru* conversion	Mitsubishi and Kure NY	1938–1940 1942		551 2 pp		25 5			21.4			8 × 25mm AA 27 aircraft	
CHUYO ex-*Nitta Maru* conversion	Kure NY	1938–1940 1942				25 5			21.4				850

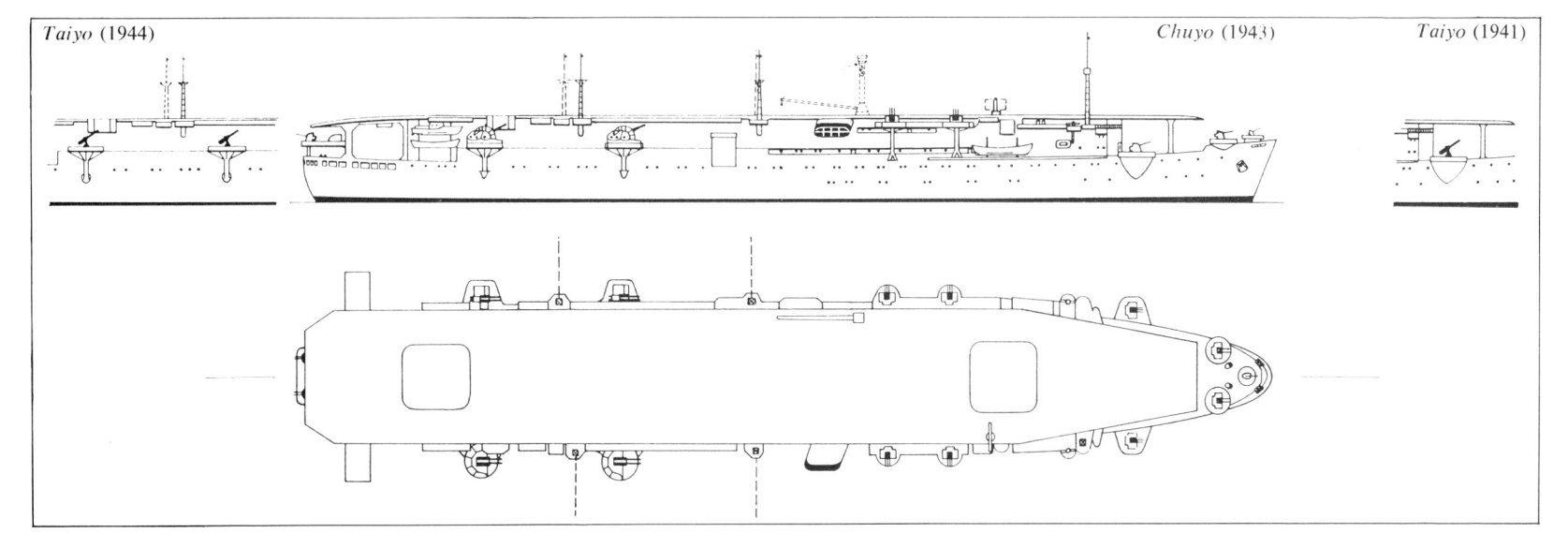

Taiyo (1944)   *Chuyo* (1943)   *Taiyo* (1941)

58 AIRCRAFT CARRIERS AND AVIATION TRANSPORTS

Chuyo (1943)

General Notes

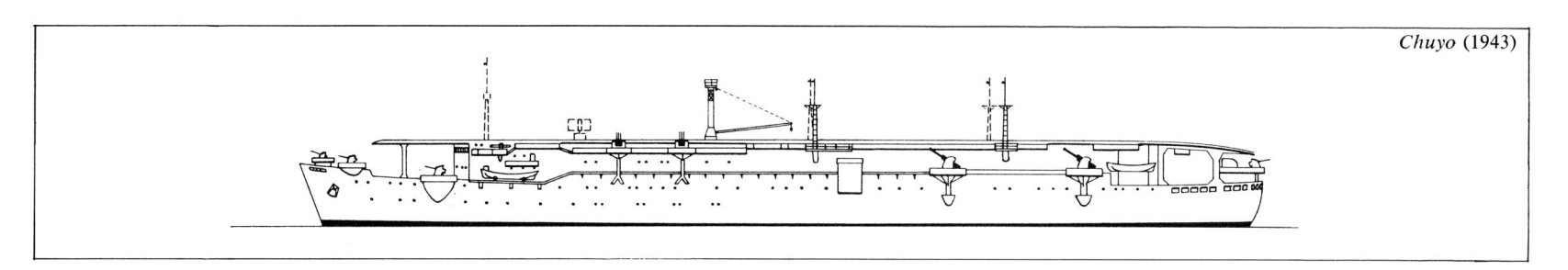

Kasuga Maru, launched as a 21-knot 17100 GRT liner for the NYK Line, Tokyo, was towed to Sasebo Naval Dockyard on 1 May, 1941 and completed as an auxiliary aircraft carrier. *Yawata Maru* and *Nitta Maru* were completed as 22.2-knot 17100 GRT ships for the NYK Line and were converted at Kure Naval Dockyard in 1942. These ships were the first such carrier conversions for the Imperial Japanese Navy, and elsewhere, only HMS *Audacity* (a much simpler conversion) preceded *Taiyo* into service. Employed exclusively as aircraft transports and as training carriers. Flight deck: 564¼ft × 77ft.

Armament

From 1943: *Chuyo* 22 × 25mm AA, 5 × 13.2mm AA, *Taiyo* and *Unyo* 24 × 25mm AA; from July 1944: 4 × 127mm 40-cal, 64 × 25mm, 10 × 13.2mm.

Careers

Taiyo
Launched 19 September, 1940 as *Kasuga Maru*, conversion commenced 1 May, 1941; commissioned 15 September, 1941; sunk 18 August, 1944 22 nm SW of Cape Bojeador, Luzon, Philippine Islands, (18° 16′ N, 120° 20′ E) by US submarine *Rasher*.

Unyo
Launched 31 October, 1939 as *Yawata Maru*, converted to escort carrier 1942, commissioned 31 May, 1942; sunk 16 September, 1944 220 nm SE of Hong Kong (19° 18′ N, 116° 26′ E) by US submarine *Barb*.

Chuyo
Launched 20 May, 1939 as *Nitta Maru*; converted to escort carrier 1942; commissioned 25 November, 1942; sunk 4 December, 1943 260 nm SE of Yokosuka (32° 37′ N, 143° 39′ E) by US submarine *Sailfish*.

Name	Builder	Date	Displ	Length ft in	Beam ft in	Draught ft in	Machinery	SHP	Speed	Fuel	Radius	Armament	Comp
KAIYO ex-*Argentina Maru*	Mitsubishi, Nagasaki	1938–1939 1942 1943	16748 N 13600 S	546 5 oa 523 7 wl 508 6 pp	71 10	27 1	2 sets Kampon GT 4 boilers 2 shafts	52100	23.8	?	?	8 × 127mm (5in) 45-cal DP 24 × 25mm AA 24 aircraft	829

Kaiyo (1944)

General Notes

Argentina Maru (12755 GRT, 21.5-knot) was a passenger liner built for the OSK Lines and served from the outbreak of war as a troop transport until she was taken in hand for conversion to an escort carrier in December 1942. The Diesel engines were replaced by destroyer-type turbines, raising the speed by 2 knots. Served as an escort carrier, aircraft transport and training carrier. Plans were drawn up for the conversion of her sister-ship, *Brazil Maru*, but she was sunk near Truk by USS *Greenling* on 5 August, 1942.

Armament

From July 1944: 44 × 25mm AA, 8 depth-charges, and a number of 120mm AA rocket-launchers.

Career

Launched 9 December, 1938 as *Argentina Maru*, requisitioned December 1941 as troop transport, taken in hand for conversion December 1942 and renamed; commissioned as escort carrier 23 November, 1943; severely damaged 24 July, 1945 10 nm NW of Oita, Beppu Bay (33° 21′ N, 131° 32′ E) by aircraft from HMS *Formidable*, *Indefatigable*, *Victorious*; BU at Beppu, 1948.

AIRCRAFT CARRIERS AND AVIATION TRANSPORTS

Name	Builder	Date	Displ	Length ft in	Beam ft in	Draught ft in	Machinery	SHP	Speed	Fuel	Radius	Armament	Comp
SHINYO ex-*Scharnhorst* conversion	Deschimag Werk AG, Bremen Kure DY	1934–1935 1942–1943	20916 N 17500 S	621 3 wl 606 11 pp	84 0	26 10	2 sets AEG turbines 4 water-tube boilers 2 shafts	26000	22	?	?	8 × 127mm (5in) 45-cal DP 30 × 25mm AA 33 aircraft	942

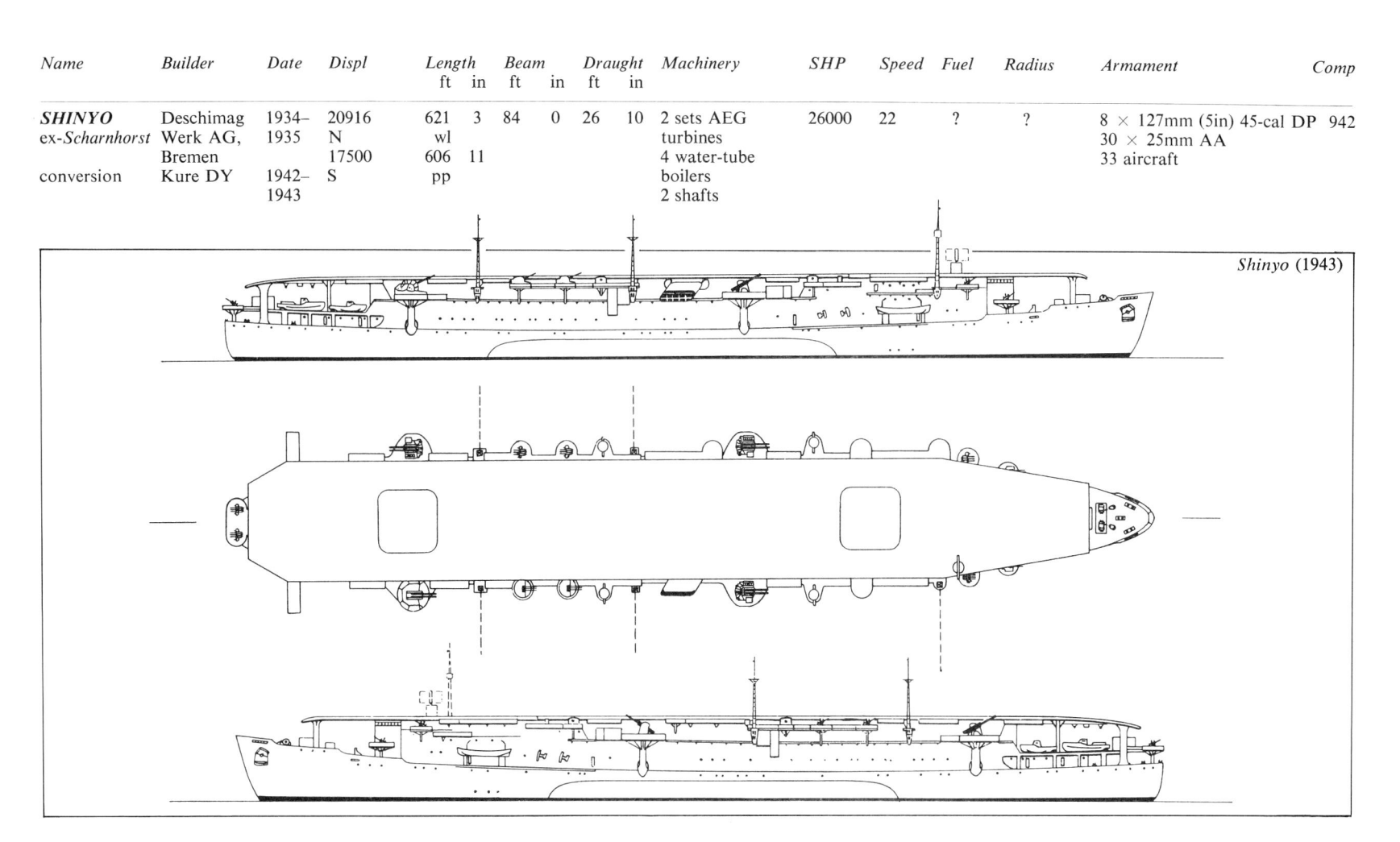

Shinyo (1943)

GENERAL NOTES
Scharnhorst (18184 GRT, 21-knot) was a passenger liner of the Nord-deutscher-Lloyd Line, Bremen, caught in the Far East by the outbreak of war in September 1939. Purchased and converted to an escort carrier, steel for the reconstruction coming from *Job No. 111*, the fourth unit of the *Yamato* class, cancelled while on the slip (see p. 38). Flight deck: 590½ft × 80½ft.

ARMAMENT
From early 1944: 42 × 25mm AA; July 1944: 50 × 25mm.

CAREER
Launched 14 December, 1934 as *Scharnhorst*, purchased by Imperial Japanese Navy 7 February, 1942; conversion commenced September 1942; commissioned as escort carrier 15 December, 1943; sunk 17 November, 1944 140 nm NE of Shanghai (33° 02′ N, 123° 33′ E) by US submarine *Spadefish*.
(*Gneisenau*: sister-ship, plans drawn up by Germans in 1942 for conversion to aircraft carrier).

Name	Builder	Date	Displ	Length ft in	Beam ft in	Draught ft in	Machinery	SHP	Speed	Fuel	Radius	Armament	Comp
KAMAKURA MARU (Project) ex-*Chichibu Maru*	Yokohama Dock Co.	1928–1930	16800 S	560 0 pp	73 10	27 7	2 8-cyl 4st Burmeister & Wain Diesels	16000	20	3190 oil	?	8 × 127mm (5in) DP 24 × 25mm AA 38 aircraft	

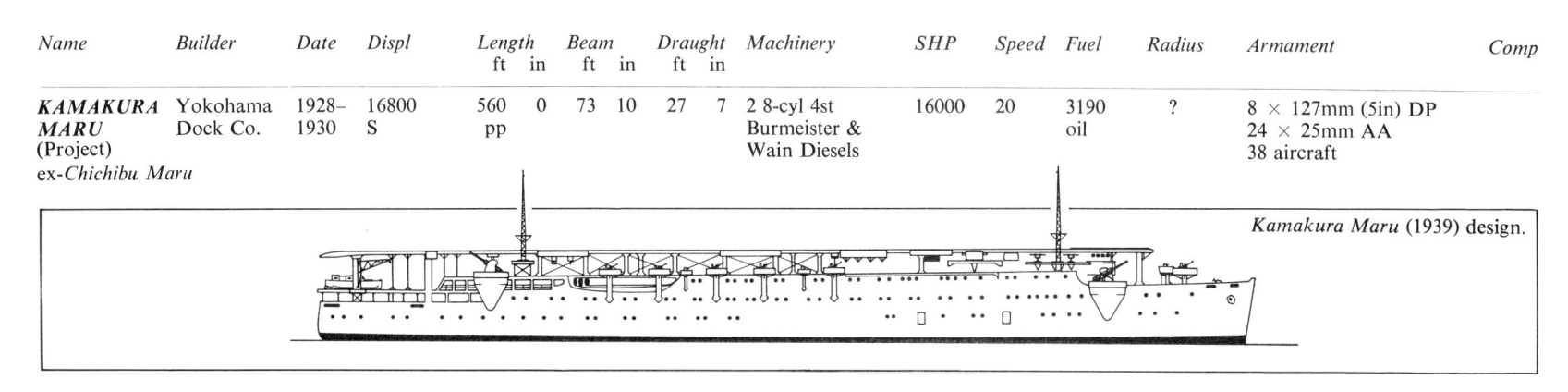

Kamakura Maru (1939) design.

GENERAL NOTES
Formerly *Chichibu Maru* (17526 GRT, 21-knot) NYK Lines passenger liner, renamed *Kamakura Maru* in 1939, and requisitioned in 1941 as a transport and hospital ship; was to have been taken in hand after the conversion of *Scharnhorst*/*Shinyo*, but was sunk by USS *Gudgeon* on 28 April, 1943.

60 AIRCRAFT CARRIERS AND AVIATION TRANSPORTS

Army Aircraft Transports with flight decks

Name	Builder	Date	Displ	Length ft in	Beam ft in	Draught ft in	Machinery	SHP	Speed	Fuel	Radius	Armament	Comp
AKITSU MARU	Harima SB,	1939–1942	11800 S	471 7 pp	64 0	25 9 / 37 9 max	2 sets GT 4 boilers 2 shafts	7500	20	?	?	2 × 75mm (2.9in) AA 10 × 75mm field guns 20 small aircraft 20 *Daihatsu* landing craft	?
NIGITSU MARU	Harima	1941–1943											

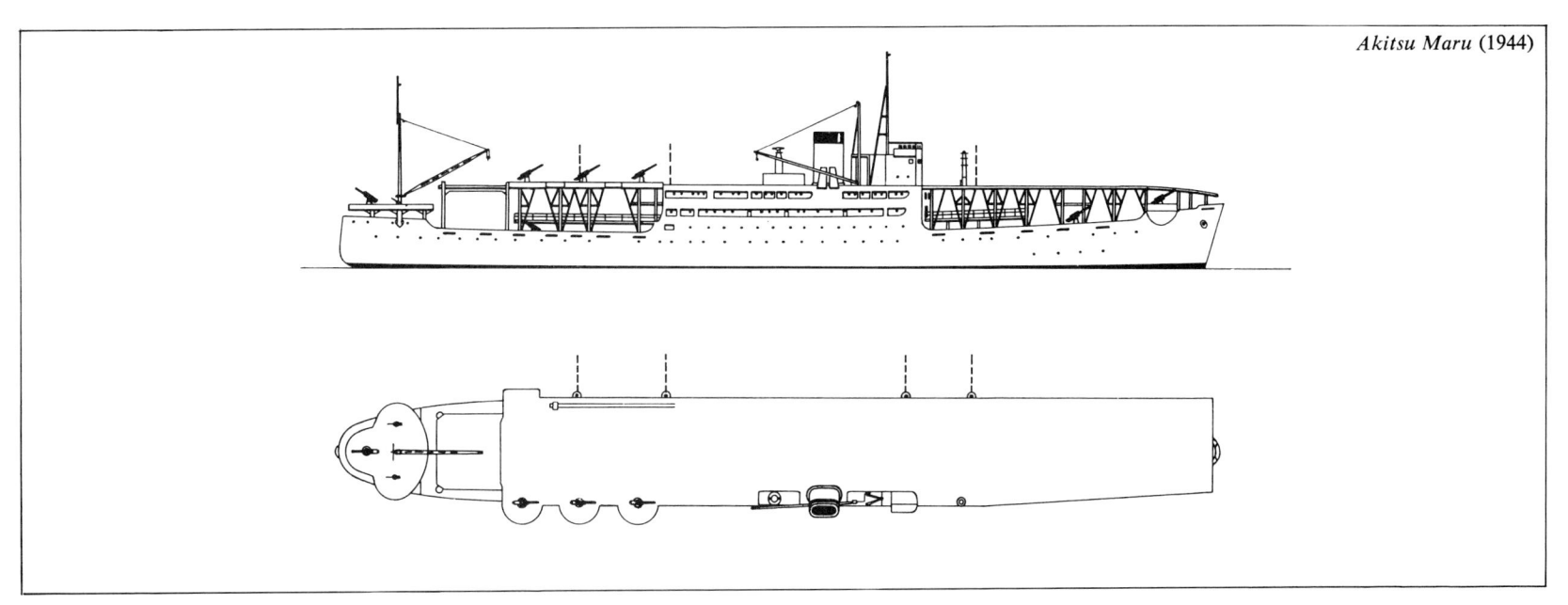

Akitsu Maru (1944)

GENERAL NOTES
Under construction from November 1939 until June 1941 as passenger liners for the Nippon Kaiun KK. Requisitioned by the Imperial Japanese Army for completion as Landing Ships fitted with flying-off decks, the installation of a large 'barracks' structure on the deck making landings impractical. In May 1944 plans were drawn up for the modification of *Akitsu Maru*'s flight deck in order to permit aircraft to land. Flight deck: 403½ft × 73¾ft.

CAREERS
Akitsu Maru
(9186 GRT) launched 1941, completed January 1942; sunk 15 November, 1944 in Korean Straits (33° 17′ N, 128° 11′ E) by US submarine *Queenfish*.
Nigitsu Maru
(9547 GRT) launched 1942, completed March 1943; sunk 12 January, 1944 near Rasa Island (23° 15′ N, 132° 51′ E) by US submarine *Hake*.

Name	Builder	Date	Displ	Length ft in	Beam ft in	Draught ft in	Machinery	SHP	Speed	Fuel	Radius	Armament	Comp
KUMANO MARU	Hitachi SB Co., Innoshima	1943–1945	10500 N / 8000 S	465 9 wl	64 3	23 0	2 sets GT 4 boilers 2 shafts	10000	19	?	6000 @ 17	8 × 75mm (2.9in) AA 6 × 25mm AA 37 small aircraft 13 *Daihatsu* craft 12 *Toku Daihatsu* craft	?

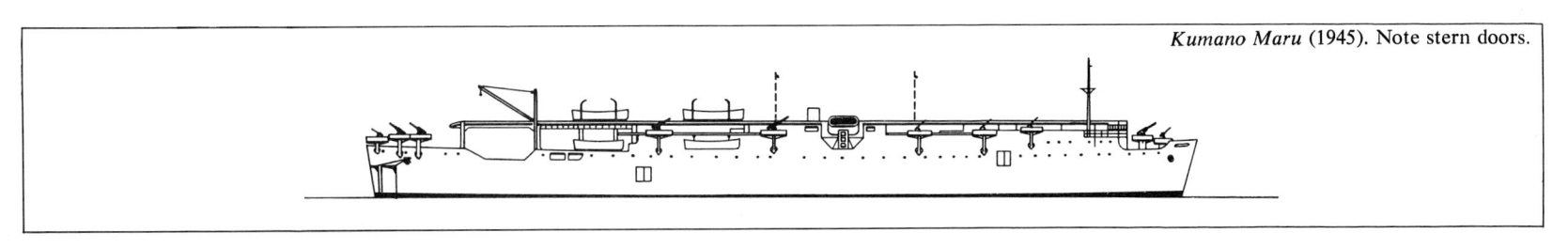

Kumano Maru (1945). Note stern doors.

GENERAL NOTES
1942 Plan: Type 'M' Military Special Service Vessel. Completed as Army Landing Ship with flying-off deck, to operate under naval administration. Flight deck: 361ft × 70½ft.

CAREER
(9502 GRT) launched 28 January, 1945; completed 31 March, 1945. Taken over at Kure in August 1945 and employed by Repatriation Service until 1947; disposed of to the Kawasaki Kisen KK shipping line; struck off list of warships in 1951.

AIRCRAFT CARRIERS AND AVIATION TRANSPORTS

Merchant Aircraft Carriers

Name	Builder	Date	Displ	Length ft in	Beam ft in	Draught ft in	Machinery	SHP	Speed	Fuel	Radius	Armament	Comp
SHIMANE MARU	Kawasaki, Kobe	1944–1945	14500 N	502 0 wl	65 7	29 10	1 set GT 2 boilers 1 shaft	8600	18.5	?	10000 @ 15	2 × 120mm (4.7in) HA 52 × 25mm AA 12 aircraft 16 DCs	?
OTAKISAN MARU		1944–1945	11800 S	491 1 pp									
Job Nos. 14 & 16 (projected)													

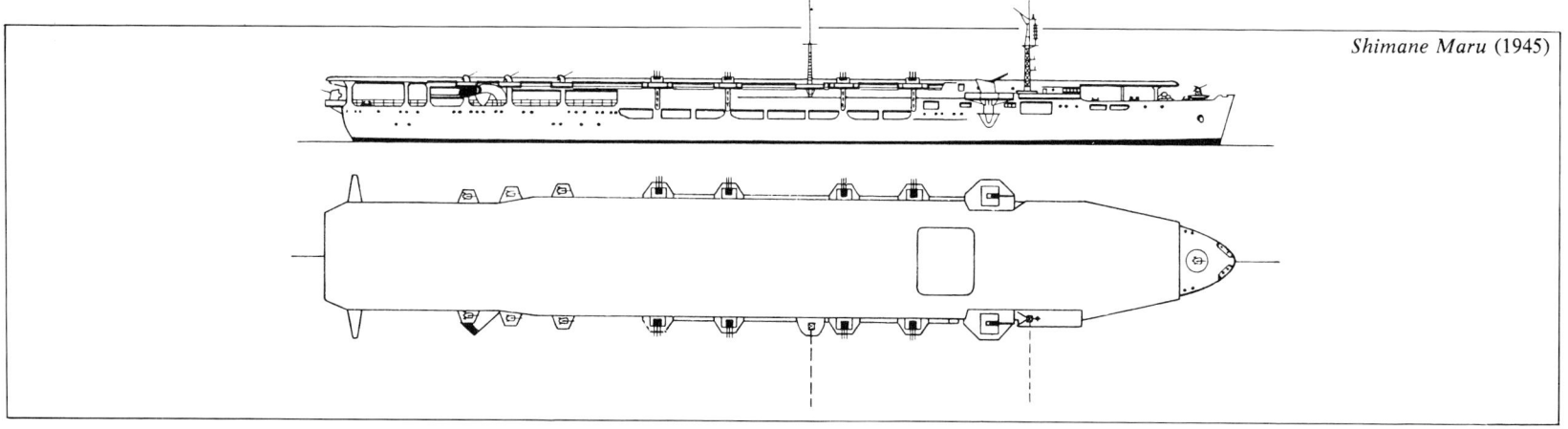

Shimane Maru (1945)

General Notes
Tanker-escort carriers based on Type 1TL War Standard hull (see p. 260). Built for the Mitsui Bussan Kaisha Line and entered service with the Ishiwara Steamship Co. on charter from the Navy. Official designation 'Special 1TL Type'. Plans to convert the ships to coal-burning freighters were not pursued. Flight deck: 508½ft × 75½ft.

Careers
Shimane Maru
(10002 GRT) launched 17 February, 1944; completed February 1945; sunk 24 July, 1945 in shallow water near Takamatsu (34° 20′ N, 134° 07′ E) by aircraft from US TF 38; BU at Naniwa, 1948.

Otakisan Maru
(10002 GRT) launched 14 January, 1945, construction halted when 70% complete; sunk 25 August, 1945 by mine in Kobe harbour; BU at Kobe, 1948.

Tanker Job Nos. *14* and *16* were to have been converted to tanker-carriers in the same manner, but the orders were cancelled in early 1945.

Name	Builder	Date	Displ	Length ft in	Beam ft in	Draught ft in	Machinery	SHP	Speed	Fuel	Radius	Armament	Comp
YAMASHIRO MARU	Mitsubishi, Yokohama	1944–1945	15864 N	485 7 pp	66 11	29 6	1 set GT 2 boilers 1 shaft	4500	15	?	9000 @ 13	16 × 25mm AA 8 aircraft 1 A/S projector 120 DCs	221
CHIGUSA MARU	Yokohama Dock Co.	1944–											

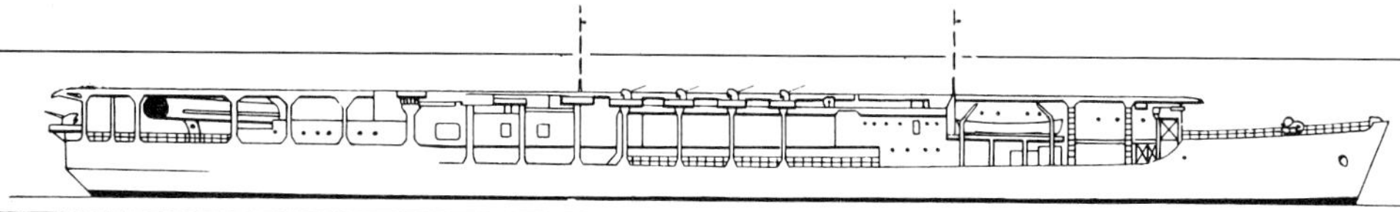

Yamashiro Maru (1945)

General Notes
Tanker-escort carriers based on Type 2TL War Standard hulls (see p. 260). Under construction for the Yamashita Line, to be operated by the NYK Line on charter from the Navy. Plans to convert the ships to coal-burning freighters were not pursued. Flight deck: 410ft × 75½ft.

Careers
Yamashiro Maru
(10100 GRT) launched 1944, completed 1945; sunk 17 February, 1945 in Yokohama harbour by aircraft from US TF 58; BU at Yokohama, 1947.

Chigusa Maru
(10100 GRT) launched 29 December, 1945 and work suspended; completed 1949 as 10325 GRT tanker for the Taiyo Gyogyo KK Line.

Seaplane Carriers

Name	Builder	Date	Displ	Length ft in	Beam ft in	Draught ft in	Machinery	SHP	Speed	Fuel	Radius	Armament	Comp
WAKAMIYA ex-*Lethington*	R. Duncan & Co. Ltd., Port Glasgow	1900–1901	7720 S	365 0 pp	48 2	19 0	1 set VTE 3 boilers 1 shaft	1600	9.5	851 coal	?	2 × 80mm (3in) LA 40-cal 2 × 47mm (1.82in) LA 4 floatplanes	

AIRCRAFT CARRIERS AND AVIATION TRANSPORTS

GENERAL NOTES
Former freighter *Lethington* (4421 GRT) of the WR Rea Shipping Co., Belfast, taken in prize W of Okinawa by *Torpedo Boat No. 72* on 12 January 1905; leased to the NYK Line from 1908; converted to seaplane carrier with canvas hangars and simple derricks in 1914. Flying-off deck erected over forecastle in 1920, first take-off made in June, by a British-built Sopwith Pup.

CAREER
Launched 21 September, 1901 and completed as British SS *Lethington*; 1 September, 1905: transport *Wakamiya Maru*; 17, August, 1914: seaplane carrier *Wakamiya*; 1 April, 1920: reclassified as an aircraft carrier; 1 April, 1931: removed from Active List.

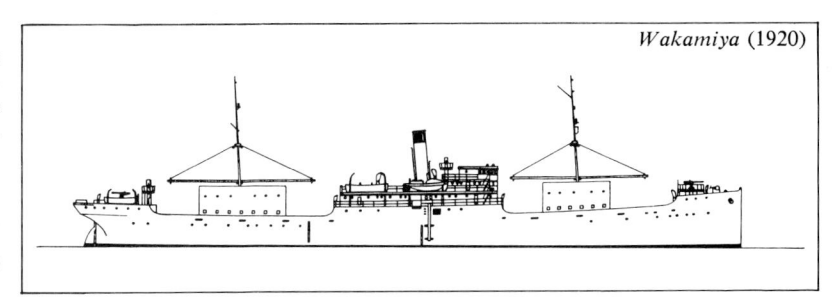

Wakamiya (1920)

Name	Builder	Date	Displ	Length ft in	Beam ft in	Draught ft in	Machinery	SHP	Speed	Fuel	Radius	Armament	Comp
NOTORO	Kawasaki, Kobe	1919–1920 1924	14050 S	455 8 pp	58 0	26 6	2 sets VTE 4 Miyabara boilers 2 shafts	5850	12	1000 oil		2 × 120mm (4.7in) 45-cal LA 2 × 80mm (3in) 40-cal HA 10 floatplanes	155
TSURUMI	Osaka Iron Works	1921–1922 1924											

Notoro (1933)

GENERAL NOTES
Fleet Oilers of *Shiretoko* class (p. 249). Modified in 1924 as Seaplane Carriers and Aircraft Transports.

CAREERS
Notoro
Launched 3 May, 1920; completed as oiler 10 August, 1920; converted to seaplane carrier 1924; re-converted to oiler at the end of 1942. (See p. 249).

Tsurumi
Launched 29 September, 1921; completed as oiler 14 March, 1922; converted to seaplane carrier 1924; re-converted to oiler 1931.

The tanker origins of the seaplane carriers *Kamoi* and *Notoro* are evident in these two views. Below, *Kamoi*'s covered forward seaplane stowage ("Alfs" and "Daves") makes her readily distinguishable from the earlier *Notoro* (right), seen in the Yangtse with one of her bomb-armed "Daves" on the water. (Author's Collection.)

AIRCRAFT CARRIERS AND AVIATION TRANSPORTS   63

Name	Builder	Date	Displ	Length ft in	Beam ft in	Draught ft in	Machinery	SHP	Speed	Fuel	Radius	Armament	Comp
KAMOI	New York SB Co., Camden and Uraga Dock Co., Tokyo	1921–1922 1932–1933	19550 N 17000 S	496 0 wl 488 6 pp	67 0	27 8	2 sets Curtiss turbo-electric 2 Yarrow boilers 2 shafts	9000	15	2500 coal	?	2 × 140mm (5.5in) 50-cal LA 2 × 80mm (3in) 40-cal HA 12 floatplanes	

Kamoi details: 1933. 1941. 1941. 1941.

Kamoi (1934)

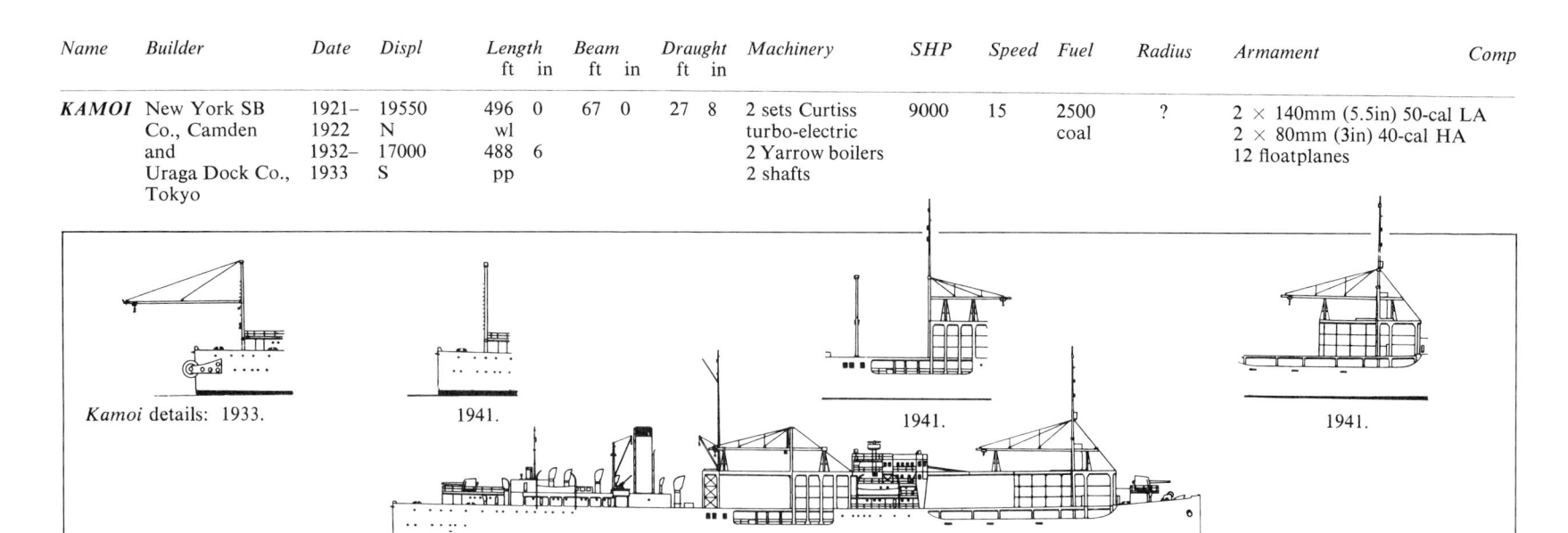

GENERAL NOTES
Former Fleet Oiler (10222 GRT) reconstructed in 1932–3 as a seaplane carrier for 10 to 14 floatplanes.

RECONSTRUCTION
1936–7: counter stern modified and fitted with German recovery gear and crane (Hein Mat Gear).

CAREER
Launched 8 June, 1922; completed as fleet oiler; seaplane carrier, June 1933; flying-boat tender, 1940; reclassified as fleet oiler, 1943.

Name	Builder	Date	Displ	Length ft in	Beam ft in	Draught ft in	Machinery	SHP	Speed	Fuel	Radius	Armament	Comp
CHITOSE	Kure DY	1934–1938	12550 N	631 7 oa 603 4 wl 570 10 pp	61 8	23 8	2 Sets GT 4 Kampon boilers	44000	29	3600 oil	8000 @ 18	4 × 127mm (5in) 40-cal DP 12 × 25mm AA 24 floatplanes 4 catapults	
CHIYODA		1936–1938	11023 S				2 Diesel engines 2 shafts	12800					

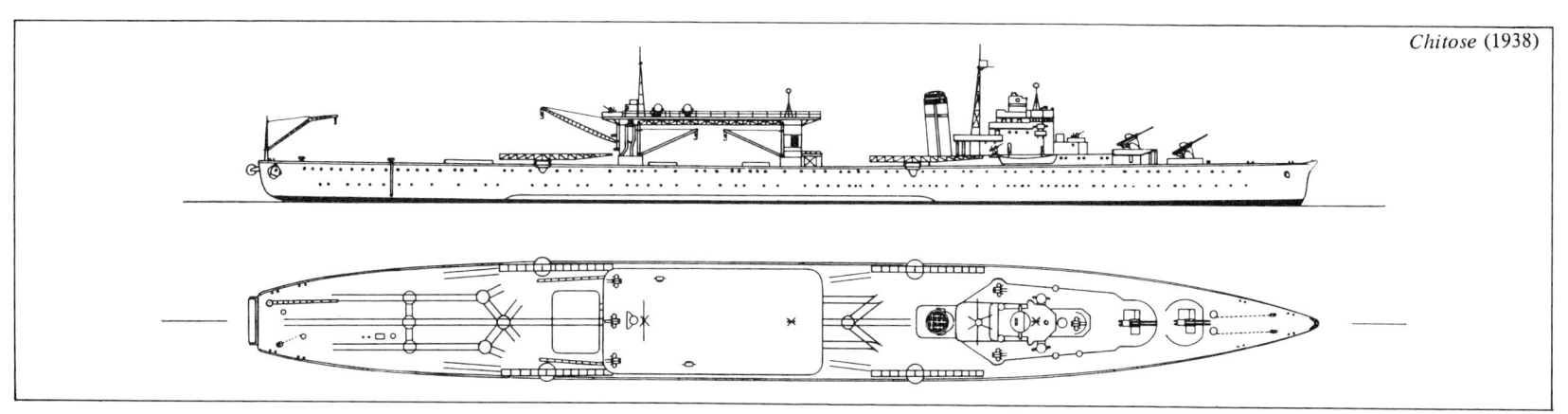

Chitose (1938)

GENERAL NOTES
Chitose and *Chiyoda* (see p. 57).
1931–2 Supplementary Programme: *Chitose* was the first seaplane carrier to be built as such, from the keel up, for the Imperial Japanese Navy. Officially classified as 'Seaplane Mother Ships'.

MODIFICATION
1941: modified as midget submarine transports, retaining stowage for 12 floatplanes. Twelve 46-ton Type 'A' midget submarines could be carried in the hangar and launched through two large steel doors in the stern.

CAREERS
Chitose
Launched 29 November, 1936; completed 25 July, 1938; converted to aircraft carrier 1943 (see p. 57).

Chiyoda
Launched 19 November, 1937; completed 15 December, 1938; converted to aircraft carrier 1942–3 (see p. 57).

Chiyoda in 1939, carrying Kawanishi "Alfs" and, in the covered central handling area, a Nakajima "Dave". The four pillars supporting the "roof" housed the machinery for six of the seven cranes. Note that *Chiyoda* does not have the Hein Mat Recovery Gear fittings on her stern. (Netherlands Navy.)

Name	Builder	Date	Displ	Length ft in	Beam ft in	Draught ft in	Machinery	SHP	Speed	Fuel	Radius	Armament	Comp
MIZUHO	Kawasaki, Kobe	1937–1939	12150 N 10929 S	602 4 wl 570 10 pp	61 8	23 3	2 4-cyl Diesels 2 shafts	15200	22	3600 oil	8000 @ 16	6 × 127mm (5in) 40-cal DP 12 × 25mm AA 24 floatplanes 4 catapults	

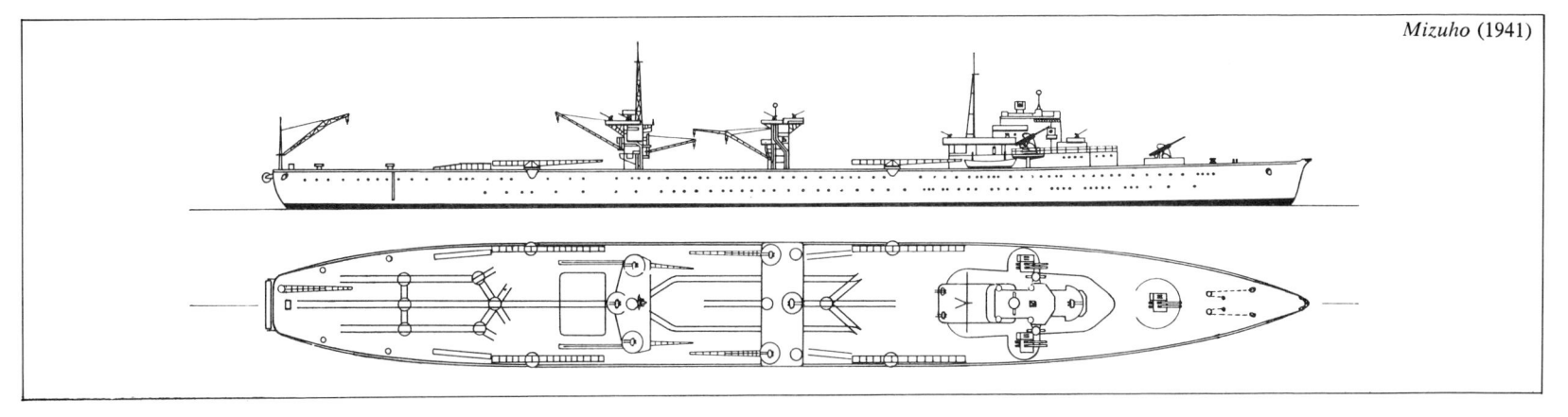

Mizuho (1941)

AIRCRAFT CARRIERS AND AVIATION TRANSPORTS

Mizuho was a diesel-engined follow-on to the *Chitose*-class seaplane carriers, intended for ocean operations with the Fleet. No roof is fitted over the centre hatch between the "goal-posts", and she does not have Hein Mat fittings on her stern. (Netherlands Navy.)

GENERAL NOTES
Diesel-engined improved *Chitose*-type. The engine exhausts were incorporated in the structure of the cranes. Modified to carry 12 Type 'A' midget submarines and 12 floatplanes.

ARMAMENT
From 1941: 18 × 25mm AA.

CAREER
Launched 16 May, 1938; completed 25 February, 1939; sunk 2 May, 1942 off Cape Omaisaki (34° 26′ N, 138° 14′ E) by US submarine *Drum*.

Name	Builder	Date	Displ	Length ft in	Beam ft in	Draught ft in	Machinery	SHP	Speed	Fuel	Radius	Armament	Comp
NISSHIN Job Nos. 863 and 864 (projected)	Kure DY	1938–1942	12500 N 11317 S 13500 S	616 10 pp	64 8	23 0	2 6-cyl Diesels 2 shafts	47000	28	?	11000 @ 18	6 × 127mm (5in) 40-cal DP 18 × 25mm AA 25 floatplanes 4 catapults	

Nisshin (1942)

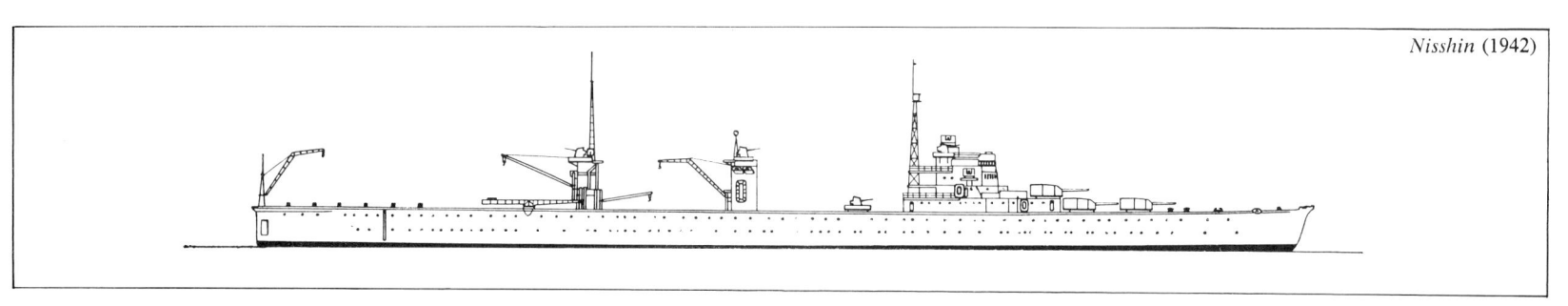

GENERAL NOTES
1937 Programme: Stowage for 20 floatplanes or 12 floatplanes and 700 mines; minelaying doors in stern.

MODIFICATION
1942: modified to carry Type 'A' midget submarines.

CAREERS
Nisshin
Launched 30 November, 1939; completed 27 February, 1942; sunk 22 July, 1943 17 nm W of Cape Alexander, Bougainville Island, (06° 35′ S, 156° 10′ E) by US aircraft.
Job Nos. 863 and 864
Modified *Nisshin* type, of 13500ts standard displacement; projected only.

See also:
Battleships *Ise* and *Hyuga* (p. 26).
Heavy Cruisers *Tone* and *Chikuma* (p. 87), *Mogami* (p. 85).
Merchant Conversions from 1941 (p. 67-68).
Fleet Oilers *Hayasui* and *Tamano* classes (p. 251).

Seaplane Tenders

Name	Builder	Date	Displ	Length ft in	Beam ft in	Draught ft in	Machinery	SHP	Speed	Fuel	Radius	Armament	Comp
AKITSUSHIMA	Kawasaki, Kobe	1940–1942	5000 N 4650 S	386 oa 11 / 370 wl 9 / 357 pp 7	51 10	17 9	4 Diesels 2 shafts	8000	19				

Akitsushima Class
1939 Programme (*Job No. 131*); 1941 War Programme (*Job No. 303*); 1942 War Programme 'M' (*Job Nos. 5031–33*). Flying Boat Support Ships – 'Hikotei-Bokan'.

CAREERS
Akitsushima
Launched 25 April, 1941; completed 29 April, 1942 (*Job No. 131*); sunk 24 September, 1944 in Coron Bay, Calamian Island (11° 59′ N, 120° 02′ E) by aircraft from US TF 38.
Chihaya
Cancelled (*Job No. 303*); *Job Nos. 5031–5033*: orders cancelled before keels laid.

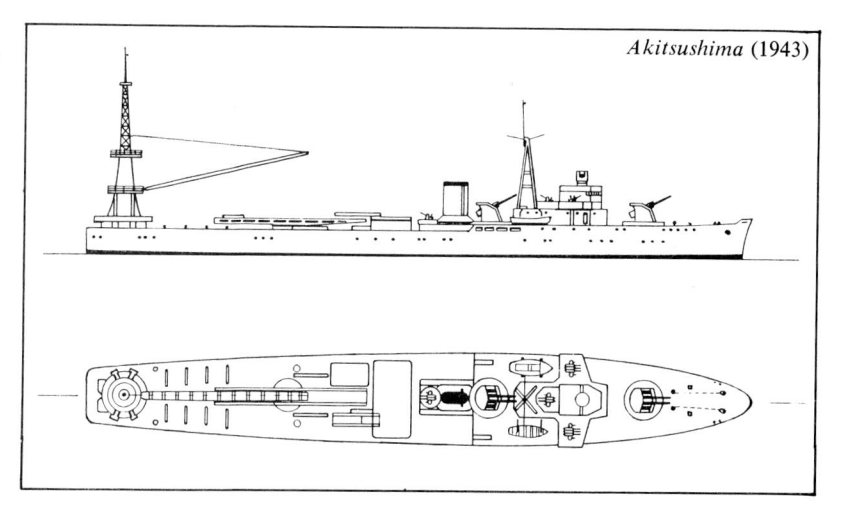

Akitsushima (1943)

Name	Builder	Date	Displ	Length ft in	Beam ft in	Draught ft in	Machinery	SHP	Speed	Fuel	Radius	Armament	Comp
Job No. 803–808			3300 S										
Job No. 809			11000 S										

Job Nos. 803 and 809 Types (projected)
1942 War Programme 'M' (*Job Nos. 803–808*), 'Sho-gata', 3300ts standard displacement small seaplane tender. 1942 Design Programme (*Job No. 809*), 'Chu-gata', 11000ts standard displacement medium-sized tender. Neither type proceeded beyond the design stage.

Name	Builder	Date	Displ GRT	Length ft in	Beam ft in	Draught ft in	Machinery	SHP approx	Speed	Fuel	Radius	Armament	Comp
KAGU MARU	Harima SB Co.	1936	6807	453 4 pp	61 0	31 0	1 7-cyl 2-stroke Kawasaki-M.A.N. Diesel engine 1 shaft	6000				All: 2×15mm & 140mm LA + light AA 2 catapults 12 aircraft (24 when ferrying)	
KAMIKAWA MARU	Kawasaki, Kobe	1937	6853	479 6 pp	62 4	30 4	1 7-cyl 2-stroke Kawasaki-M.A.N. Diesel engine 1 shaft	7600					
KUNIKAWA MARU			6863										
KIMIKAWA MARU			6863										
KIYOKAWA MARU			6863										
KINUGASA MARU	Kawasaki, Kobe	1936	8407	456 4 pp	61 0	30 4	1 7-cyl 2-stroke Kawasaki-M.A.N. Diesel engine	7600					
SAGARA MARU	Mitsubishi, Nagasaki	1940	7189	479 9 pp	62 4	32 3	2 8-cyl 2-stroke Mitsubishi-Sulzer Diesel engines 2 shafts	16000				2 catapults 8 aircraft	
SANUKI MARU		1939											
SAN'YO MARU	Mitsubishi, Nagoya	1930	8360	446 0 pp	60 6	40 0	unknown	unknown					

AIRCRAFT CARRIERS AND AVIATION TRANSPORTS

San'yo Maru (1942)

Kamikawa Maru (1943)

Sagara Maru (1942)

GENERAL NOTES

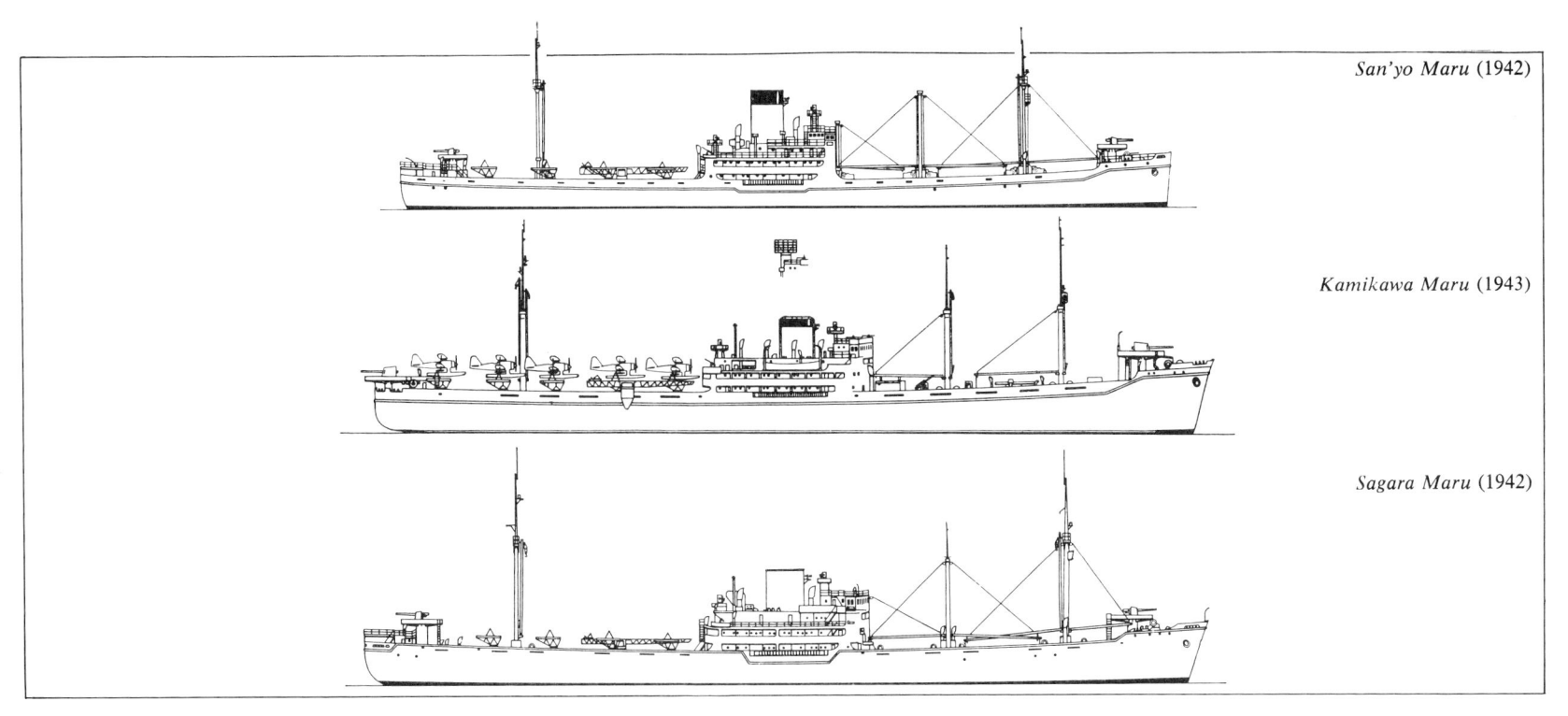

The following motor cargo vessels were requisitioned for use in support of flying-boats and subsequently converted as seaplane carriers with 1 or 2 17m (55¾ft) catapults and deck stowage for up to 8 to 12 floatplanes. Some units were converted as seaplane carriers immediately after requisition. The standard LA armament for these vessels consisted of 2 × 152mm (6in) 50-cal guns; AA armament was negligible: 2 × 13.2mm heavy AAMGs and, in *Kimikawa Maru* and *Kiyokawa Maru*, 2 × 80mm (3in) 40-cal guns.

CAREERS

Kagu Maru
Built 1936 for Kokusai Kisen KK; 1937: requisitioned for service as flying-boat tender; 1939: returned to owner; 1941: requisitioned as Transport; sunk 4 November, 1944 W of Luzon (15° 54′ N, 119° 45′ E) by US submarines *Bream* and *Ray*.

Kamikawa Maru
Built 1937 for (nominally) Kawasaki KKK; 1937: requisitioned as flying-boat tender; 1938: Aircraft Transport; 1939: Seaplane Carrier; sunk 28 April, 1943 N of New Ireland (01° 00′ S, 150° 18′ E) by US submarine *Scamp*.

Kimikawa Maru
Built 1937 as refrigerator ship for Kawasaki KKK; 1941: Seaplane Carrier; sunk 23 October, 1944 W of Luzon (18° 58′ N, 118° 46′ E) by US submarine *Sawfish*.

Kinugasa Maru
Built 1936 for Kokusai KKK; 1938: requisitioned as Seaplane Carrier; 1939: returned to owner; 1941: requisitioned as Transport; sunk 7 October, 1944 in South China Sea (14° 30′ N, 115° 48′ E) by US submarines *Baya* and *Hawkbill*.

Kiyokawa Maru
As *Kimikawa Maru* to 1942: Transport; beached 25 July, 1945 at Shida, Shimonoseki Straits, after US TF 38 air attack.

Kunikawa Maru
Built 1937 for Kawasaki KKK, 1942: requisitioned as Seaplane Carrier; 1943: Transport; sunk 30 April, 1945 in Makassar Straits (01° 15′ S, 116° 50′ E) by US aircraft.

Sagara Maru
Built 1940 for Nippon Yusen KK; 1941: requisitioned as Seaplane Carrier; 1942: Transport; beached 22 June, 1943 Omaezaki, Honshu (34° 52′ N, 138° 20′ E) after torpedo attack by US submarine *Harder*; deleted from Active List.

Sanuki Maru
Built 1939 for Nippon Yusen KK; 1941: requisitioned as Seaplane Carrier; 1942: Transport; sunk 28 January, 1945 NE of Shanghai (33° 55′ N, 122° 55′ E) by US submarine *Spadefish*.

San'yo Maru
Built 1930*; 1941: requisitioned as Seaplane Carrier; 1943: Transport; sunk 26 May, 1944 NNW of Menado, Celebes (02° 46′ N, 124° 22′ E) by US submarine *Cabrilla*.
(*This ship does not appear in *Lloyds Register of Shipping* under this name between 1930 and 1940, and the construction date may therefore be 1940; alternatively, the transcription from the Japanese ideogram may have been mistaken.)

Kamikawa Maru, off the Chinese coast in 1940, with "Alfs" aft and "Daves" forward. She is armed with 4.7-inch AA guns fore and aft, and twin 25mm AA guns in the bridge wings. She has no catapult. (Netherlands Navy.)

AIRCRAFT CARRIERS AND AVIATION TRANSPORTS

Aircraft Salvage Vessels

Name	Builder	Date	Displ	Length ft in	Beam ft in	Draught ft in	Machinery	SHP	Speed	Fuel	Radius	Armament	Comp
100-ton Type	Mitsubishi, Yokohama, etc.	1933	117.5 N 100 S	?	?	5 0	2 Diesels 2 shafts	520	13	?	?	1 3-tonne crane 1 floatplane	

GENERAL NOTES
100-Ton Type
Aircraft Salvage Craft (Hikoki-Kyunansen) originally projected as Tugs and Harbour Service Craft. Operated by the Naval Air Force for aircraft recovery, torpedo transport and similar tasks. First Japanese small craft with Diesel engines. About five units were built, details available only for:

CAREERS
No. 872
Launched 1933; served with Ominato Air Group; captured August 1945 at Ominato in derelict condition after damage sustained from air attack.
No. 873
Launched 1933; served with Sasebo Air Group from 31 March, 1934; captured August 1945 and used by Allies until 1948; 1949: MSDF *PS 61*, named *Iwashodori*; 1950: renumbered *PS 114*.

Name	Builder	Date	Displ	Length ft in	Beam ft in	Draught ft in	Machinery	SHP	Speed	Fuel	Radius	Armament	Comp
150-ton Type (1933)	Tsurumi, Yokohama	1933	145 N	131 4 wl 128 7 pp	18 4	4 3	2 Diesels 2 shafts	520	13			1 3-tonne crane 2 floatplanes	?
150-ton Type (1934)	various	1934–1935	141 N	124 0 wl 120 5 pp	17 1	5 7	2 Diesels 2 shafts	520	13			1 3-tonne crane 2 floatplanes	
150-ton Type (1936)	various	1936–1937	165 N	127 11 wl 125 4 pp	17 9	4 11	2 Diesels 2 shafts	520	13			1 3-tonne crane 2 floatplanes	

GENERAL NOTES
Improved 100-ton type. There were variations in appearance within the class (see line drawings) although dimensions, equipment and propulsive machinery were standardised. The design of the 3-tonne (2.95ts) crane also varied. Full details are not available of the number of craft built.

1933 Construction – several craft, including:
CAREERS
No. 870
Built 1933, Tsurumi, Yokohama; 1934: Yokosuka Air Group; captured August 1945 at Sanagawa, derelict; repaired and to MSDF in 1949 as *PS 50*; 1950: renumbered *PS 112*, named *Schimachidori*.

1934 Construction – approximately 5 craft, including:
CAREERS
No. 887
Built 1934–5, Harima, Aioi; 24 October, 1935: Saikai Air Group (also named *Saikai Maru No. 3*); 1945: ran aground at Matogahama.
No. 901
Built 1935, Mitsubishi, Yokohama, completed 30 June, 1935; sunk 28 July, 1945 alongside *Izumo* (see p. 74) at Takasu; raised 25 May, 1947 and scrapped.

No. 902
Built 1935, to Omura Air Group; captured August 1945 at Sasebo and used by Allies until 1948; 1949: MSDF *PS 43*; 1950: renumbered *PS 111*, named *Isochidori*.
No. 903
Career and fate unknown.

1936 Construction – approximately 5 units, including:
CAREERS
No. 929
Built 1936, Sakurajima, Osaka; 20 July, 1939: Kisarazu Air Group; captured August, 1945 at Tokyo and subsequently lost by accident off Shigaura.
No. 930
Built 1936, Harima, Aioi; 27 September, 1936: Chinkai Air Group; captured August, 1945 and employed by Minesweeping Service until laid up at Hakata in 1947; 1949: MSDF *MS 68*.
No. 931
Built 1936, Tsurumi, Yokohama, completed 2 November, 1936; sunk May 1945 (probably) in Sukumo Bay by TF 58 aircraft.
No. 932
Built 1936, Ujina SB Co., Hiroshima; 30 June, 1936: Kanoya Air Group; ran aground 1945 at Umigata.

Name	Builder	Date	Displ	Length ft in	Beam ft in	Draught ft in	Machinery	SHP	Speed	Fuel	Radius	Armament	Comp
200-ton Type	Tsurumi, Yokohama and Sakurajima, Osaka	1939 1940	189 N	126 4 wl 123 0 pp	19 4	6 4	2 Diesels 2 shafts	800	14			1 5-tonne crane 2 floatplanes	

GENERAL NOTES
Improved 150-ton type with superior sea-keeping qualities, higher maximum speed and 5-tonne (4.9t) crane. Between 5 and 8 units were built, including:

CAREERS
No. 1089
Completed 20 September, 1939; captured August 1945; 1949: MSDF *PS 49*; 1950: renumbered *PS 106*, named *Okichidori*.
No. 1090
Completed 15 August, 1939; captured August 1945 and used by Allies under name *Andorelia*; 1949: MSDF *MS 62*.

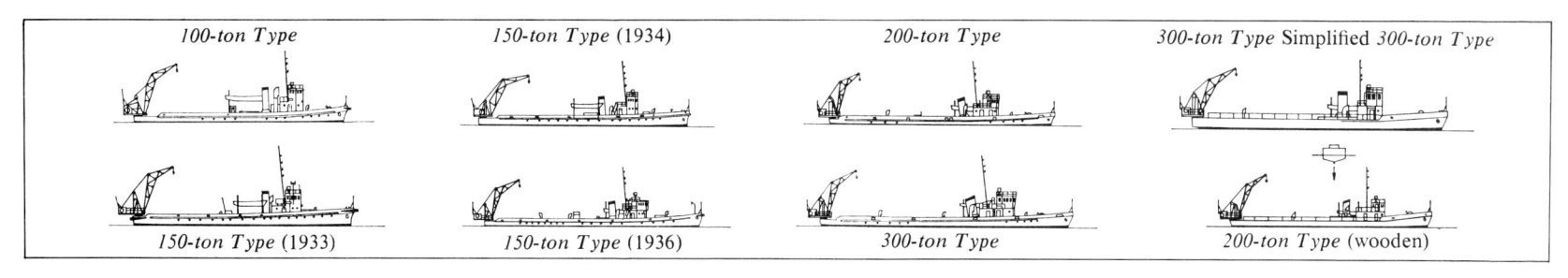

100-ton Type   *150-ton Type (1934)*   *200-ton Type*   *300-ton Type*   Simplified *300-ton Type*

150-ton Type (1933)   *150-ton Type (1936)*   *300-ton Type*   *200-ton Type (wooden)*

No. 1091
Completed 26 December, 1939; captured August, 1945 and used by Royal Navy under name *Lady Shirley*; 1949: MSDF *PS 57*; 1950: renumbered *PS 109*, named *Murachidori*.

No. 1264
Completed 4 December, 1940; captured August 1945; 1949: MSDF *PS 58*; 19 ? : renumbered *PS 105*, named *Tomochidori*.

No. 1 ?
Completed 20 January, 1941; Tateyama Air Group (also named *Tateyama Maru*); captured August 1945 derelict; January 1947: repaired and converted at Uraga.

Name	Builder	Date	Displ	Length ft in	Beam ft in	Draught ft in	Machinery	SHP	Speed	Fuel	Radius	Armament	Comp
300-ton Type	various	1940–1946	296 N	147 8 wl 141 1 pp	22 4	7 5	2 Diesels 2 shafts	800	14			1 × 13mm or 25 mm AA 1 5-tonne crane 2 floatplanes	

GENERAL NOTES
Improved 200-ton type, of standard construction and appearance. Later construction simplified: no sheer, solid bulwarks only around forecastle, vertical funnel and mast, transom stern. Built by Nakamura Sb Co., Horai Sb Co., Osaka Sb Co.
Builders: Ishikawajima Heavy Industry Co., Tokyo: 3 + 1 not completed
Horai Shipbuilding Co., Osaka: 1 not completed
Kawasaki Heavy Industry Co., Kobe: 4
Nakamura Shipbuilding Co., Matsue: 2 not completed
Osaka Shipbuilding Co., Osaka: 2 not completed
Ujina Shipbuilding Co., Hiroshima: 4
Approximately 30 units were built or ordered, including:

CAREERS
No. 1332
Built 1940, Ishikawajima; 12 December, 1940: Chitose Air Group, also known as *Akebono Maru*; captured August 1945 at Muroran; 1949: MSDF *PS 46*; 1950: renumbered *PS 103*, named *Asachidori*.
No. 1333
Built 1940, Ishikawajima; 12 December, 1940: Saikai Air Group, also known as *Saikai Maru No. 2*; captured August 1945 aground at Oita.
No. 1335
Built 1940, possibly by Kawasaki; Ibusuki Air Group; beached 1945 at Onejima.
No. 1336
Built 1940, possibly by Kawasaki; Usa Air Group, also known as *Usa Maru*; captured August 1945 when in service as Kyushu to Kochi ferry; employed by Royal Air Force at Sasebo; 1949: MSDF; 195?: Republic of Korea Navy as *Chung Mukong I*; deleted from Active List 1959.
No. 1337
Built 1940; captured August 1945; severely damaged 18 September 1945, removed from Active List and employed as a pontoon hulk.
No. 1338
Completed 7 February, 1941, Ishikawajima; captured August 1945 at Komatsujima in unserviceable condition; 1949: MSDF *PS 45*; 1950: *PS 102*, named *Hamachidori*.
No. 1339
Completed 17 March, 1941, Ishikawajima; to Chitose Air Group; captured August 1945 at Muroran and cannibalised to repair *No. 1332*.
No. 1341
Completed 1941; captured August 1945 at Yokosuka; 1949: MSDF *PS 48*; 195?: to Republic of Korea Navy as *Chung Mukong II*; deleted from Active List 1959.
No. 1440
Completed 1942, Ujina; subsequent fate unknown.
No. 1535
Completed 1942, to Kushimoto Air Group; captured August 1945 at Katsuura; 1946: *Kuroshio Maru*; 1950: Republic of Korea Navy *PC 22*, named *Hukchownan*; deleted from Active List 1959.

No. 1536
Completed 1942, Ujina; 31 March, 1943 to Saeki Air Group; ran aground 1945 at Oita, salvaged and (?) repaired as motor coaster *Narushio Maru* (228 GRT).
No. 1538
Completed 1942; captured August 1945 and employed as passenger vessel *Kyodo Maru* until 1946; 1949: MSDF *PS 56*, believed to be named *Yuchidori*.
No. 1539
Construction suspended 1944, Ishikawajima.
No. 1540
Launched 1943, completed 10 February, 1944; captured August 1945 and employed by Allies as *Sunning Hill*; 1949: MSDF *PS 44*; 1950: renumbered *PS 108*, named *Wakachidori*.
No. 1541
Completed 1943; to Oi Air Group, known in service as *Oi Maru*; captured August 1945 derelict; repaired; 1949: MSDF *PS 60*; 1950: *PS 105*, named *Haruchidori*.
No. 1579
Completed 1944, to Tarumi Air Group; lost September 1945 by stranding at Umigata; 1946: salvaged and repaired as motor coaster *Hatsushio Maru* (275 GRT).
No. 1???
Completion date unknown, Mitsubishi; to Otaka Air Group, known in service as *Otaka Maru*; captured August 1945 at Tadotsu; 1947–8: employed by Royal Air Force, Kochi; 1949: MSDF *Otaka Maru*; 195?: *PS 107*, believed to be named *Sawachidori*.
No. 1???
Completion date unknown; to Hakata Air Group, known in service as *Hakata Maru*; captured August 1945 at Shimonoseki; November 1946: Royal Air Force; 1949: MSDF *Hakata Maru* 195?: *PS 104*, named *Miochidori*.
No. 1???
Completion date unknown; to Saikai Air Group; captured August 1945; lost Autumn 1946 by stranding at Uppurui.
Nos. 1620 and 1644
Construction suspended September 1943, hulls still incomplete in 1948, Osaka SB Co.
No. 1???
Captured August 1945 incomplete, Ujina; commissioned for service by Royal Air Force 2 August, 1946; 1949 (possibly): MSDF *No. 16*; 195?: renumbered *PS 101*, named *Kawachidori*.
No. 1???
Order cancelled, Ujina.
No. 1???
Incomplete August 1945, Horai.
No. 1???
Incomplete August 1945, Nakamura; completed, possibly as *Shimane Maru No. 1*.
No. 1???
Incomplete August 1945, Nakamura; completed, possibly as *Shimane Maru No. 2*.

Name	Builder	Date	Displ	Length ft in	Beam ft in	Draught ft in	Machinery	SHP	Speed	Fuel	Radius	Armament	Comp
Wooden-hulled 200-ton Type	various	1944?	211 N	117 9 wl 116 6 pp	20 8	7 4	1 Diesel 1 shaft	400	12			1 5-tonne crane 1 floatplane	

GENERAL NOTES
Wood used for emergency construction because of shortage of steel in 1944; very simple design without sheer or flare, solid bulwarks only around forecastle, no bilge keel, concrete hull bottom. None completed or Numbers allocated before the end of the War.
Job No. 3127: Shikoku Dock Industrial Co., Takamatsu: keel laid 10 November, 1944.
Job No. 3128: as above – keel laid 16 December 1944.
Job No. 3129: Jin'en SB Ironworks, Moji: keel laid 12 December, 1944.
Job No. 3130: as above: keel laid 13 April, 1945.
Job No. 3131: Funaya SB Co., Hakodate: keel laid 10 January, 1945.
Job No. 3132: as above: keel laid 30 April, 1945.
Job No. 3133 and *3134*: Fukuoka SB Iron Works: work not commenced.
Job No. 3135: Yonago SB Co., work not commenced.
Job No. 3136: Shikoku Dock, Takamatsu: work not commenced.

Aircraft Transports

Name	Builder	Date	Displ	Length ft in	Beam ft in	Draught ft in	Machinery	SHP	Speed	Fuel	Radius	Armament	Comp
100-ton Type	various	1939–?	146 N 100 S	124 8 oa 118 1 pp	21 0	2 9	1 Diesel 1 shaft	80	7.5			2 aircraft and 5300lb (2400kg) bombs, etc.	

Aircraft Lighters (Hikoki-Umpansen): harbour service aircraft and bomb lighters with catamaran-type bow and 3 hatches. Number built and exact details not known.
No. 3780: built 1939, Sakurajima; 1945: at Yokosuka.
No. 3932: built 1941, Ujina; 1945: at Yokosuka.
No. 3933: built 1941, Ujina; 1945: at Sasebo.
No. 3934: built 1941, Ujina; fate unknown.

Name	Builder	Date	Displ	Length ft in	Beam ft in	Draught ft in	Machinery	SHP	Speed	Fuel	Radius	Armament	Comp
200-ton Type	various		200 S				2 Diesels 2 shafts	160				not known	

As 100-ton type, probably designed as such. Number built and exact details not known.
No. 4943: built 194?; 1945: at Sasebo.

3. Armoured Cruisers

Name	Builder	Date	Displ	Length ft in	Beam ft in	Draught ft in	Machinery	SHP	Speed	Fuel	Radius	Armament	Comp
CHIYODA	J. Brown, Clydebank	1888–1890	2400 N	310 0 wl 299 10 pp	42 0	14 0	2-shaft VTE 6 locomotive boilers	5600 ihp	18	330 / 420 coal	8000 @ 10	10 × 4.7in 40-cal QF 15 × 47mm 3 × 18in TT (AW)	350

Chiyoda shortly after completion. (Shizuo Fukui.)

Chiyoda (1891) (Insert 1902 modifications)

ARMOURED CRUISERS 71

GENERAL NOTES
A belted cruiser built as a replacement for the French-built *Unebi*. The planned armament of 12.6in Canet guns was not mounted because of the excessive topweight. The designation of armoured cruiser was not strictly appropriate because of her small displacement and light guns, but she was rated thus subsequently because of her relatively thick armour.

ARMOUR
Harvey chrome steel. Belt 4½in; deck 1½in to 1in.

RECONSTRUCTION NOTES
Reboilered in 1902 with 12 Belleville boilers, and given lighter masts.

CAREER
Launched 3 June, 1890, completed December 1890; severely damaged by mine near Port Arthur 26 July, 1904; re-rated as a 2nd Class coast-defence ship in 1912; submarine depot ship in 1920; stricken in April 1922 and disarmed at Kure; disposed of in 1927 and BU.

Name	Builder	Date	Displ	Length ft in	Beam ft in	Draught ft in	Machinery	SHP	Speed	Fuel	Radius	Armament	Comp
ASAMA	Armstrong, Whitworth	1896–1899	10519 F	442 oa	67 0	24 4	2-shaft 4-cyl compound boilers	18000 12 cyl ihp	21.3	600 / 1200 coal	10000 @ 10	4 × 8in 40-cal 14 × 6in 40-cal QF 12 × 3in QF 8 × 47mm 3 MGs 5 × 18in TT (1 AW, 4 UW)	676 / 726
TOKIWA	& Co., Elswick	1898–1899	*Asama* 10476 F *Tokiwa* 9700 N	408 0 pp									

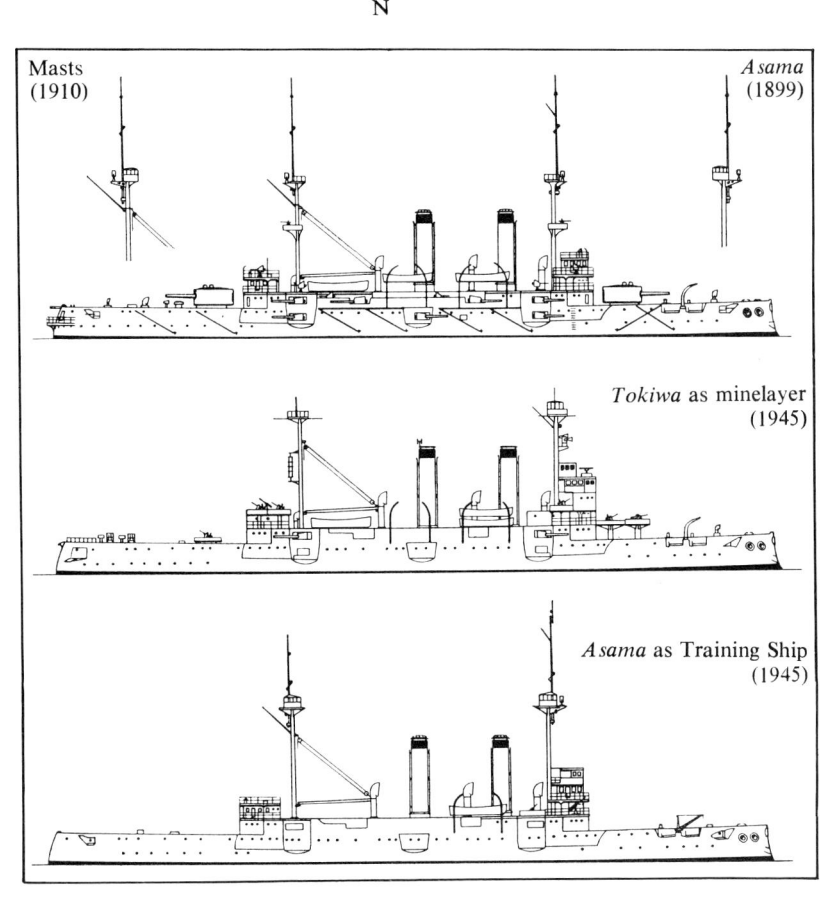

Masts (1910)

Asama (1899)

Tokiwa as minelayer (1945)

Asama as Training Ship (1945)

GENERAL NOTES
Ordered under the Post-war Programme of 1896–7. Both ships rendered sterling service in the Russo-Japanese War, when they formed part of the battle fleet.

ARMOUR
Harvey-nickel steel. Belt 7in to 3½in; deck 3in; turrets and casemates 6in; CT 14in.

MACHINERY NOTES
Both engined by Humphrys & Tennant, and averaged 18277 shp = 22.07 knots on trials (20556 shp = 23.09 knots max).

RE-ARMAMENT AND RECONSTRUCTIONS
Asama
Repaired between December 1915 and March 1917 with 16 Miyabara boilers; in 1922 she was armed with 8 × 3in 40-cal and 1 × 3.1in 40-cal AA guns; in 1937 she had 4 × 8in 40-cal, 8 × 6in 40-cal and some 3.1in.

Tokiwa
Was reboilered in 1910 with 16 Miyabara boilers, and partially re-armed with Japanese Model '41' 6in guns; in 1922 she was rebuilt as a minelayer, and had 2 × 8in 40-cal, 8 × 6in 40-cal, 2 × 3.1in 40-cal, 1 × 3.1in 40-cal AA, 3 MGs, 200 to 300 mines; her speed by this time was reduced to 16 knots; she was modernized between November 1937 and 1938 with 8 Kampon boilers (Type RO), = 18000 ihp = 16 knots, with 1383ts of coal; at this stage her armament was 3 × 6.5mm MGs, 2 × 13mm MGs, 500 Type 5 mines (TT removed).

Asama was one of the famous 'Elswick' armoured cruisers built on the Tyne. During the war against Russia, they were used virtually as 2nd Class battleships, and fought in the battle line at Tsushima. (Shizuo Fukui.)

Tokiwa was the sister of *Asama*, and is seen here late in her career, without torpedo-nets. Like her sister, she survived until 1945. (Shizuo Fukui.)

CAREERS
Asama
Launched 22 March, 1898, completed March 1899; on 3 December, 1914 she was badly damaged in Turtle Bay on the Pacific coast; wrecked on 31 January, 1915 in San Bartolomé Bay (27° 40′ N, 114° 50′ E): refloated on 8 May, 1915: under repair from 21 June, 1915 to March 1917; re-rated as a 1st class coast-defence ship in 1921; stricken 1937 and converted to a training ship for midshipmen at Kure; in 1944 she was towed to Osaka and then to Shimonoseki; surrendered in August 1945 and BU at Hatachi in 1947.

Tokiwa
Launched 6 July, 1898, completed April 1899; in 1921 re-rated at 1st Class coast-defence ship and used for training from 1920; recommissioned 1 April, 1922 as a minelayer; badly damaged in August 1927 by three mines (38 dead); repaired by April 1928; damaged by mine in May 1945 and repaired at Maizuru; sunk by aircraft bombs 8 August, 1945 near Ominato (41° 20′ N, 141° 60′ E); BU 1947 at Ominato.

Name	Builder	Date	Displ	Length ft in	Beam ft in	Draught ft in	Machinery	SHP	Speed	Fuel	Radius	Armament	Comp
AZUMA	Société des Chantiers de la Loire, St. Nazaire	1898–1900	9953 F 9278 N	452 5 oa 431 6 pp	59 3	23 6	2-shaft 4-cyl compound 24 Belleville boilers	18000 ihp	21	550 / 1200 coal	7000 @ 10	4 × 8in 40-cal 12 × 6in 40-cal QF 12 × 3in QF 12 × 47mm 5 × 18in TT (1 AW, 4 UW)	670 / 726

GENERAL NOTES
A French-designed armoured cruiser built under the Post-War Programme of 1896-7.

ARMOUR
Krupp steel. Belt 7in to 3½in; deck 2½in; casemates 6in; turrets 6.3in; CT 14in.

RE-ARMAMENT AND RECONSTRUCTION
In 1924 she had 12 × 6in 40-cal (Type '41') 8 × 3.1in 40-cal and 1 × 3.1in AA.
In 1930 she was armed with: 4 × 8in; 8 × 6in; 4 × 3.1in; 2 × 18in TT (UW). 9400 ihp = 16 knots, 650 men.

CAREER
Launched 24 June, 1899 and completed July 1900; formed part of the main battle fleet in the Russo-Japanese War; training ship in 1914; stricken in 1941 and hulked; badly damaged 18 July, 1945 by aircraft of TF 38 at Yokosuka (35° 18′ N, 139° 40′ E); BU 1946.

Azuma (1900)

Azuma (Jentschura.)

Name	Builder	Date	Displ	Length ft in	Beam ft in	Draught ft in	Machinery	SHP	Speed	Fuel	Radius	Armament	Comp
YAKUMO	AG Vulcan, Stettin	1898–1900	10288 F 9735 N	434 0 oa 408 11 pp	64 0	23 8	2-shaft 4-cyl compound 24 Belleville boilers	15500 ihp	20	500 / 1300 coal	7000 @ 10	4 × 8in 40-cal 12 × 6in 40-cal 12 × 3in 12 × 47mm 5 × 18in TT (UW)	670

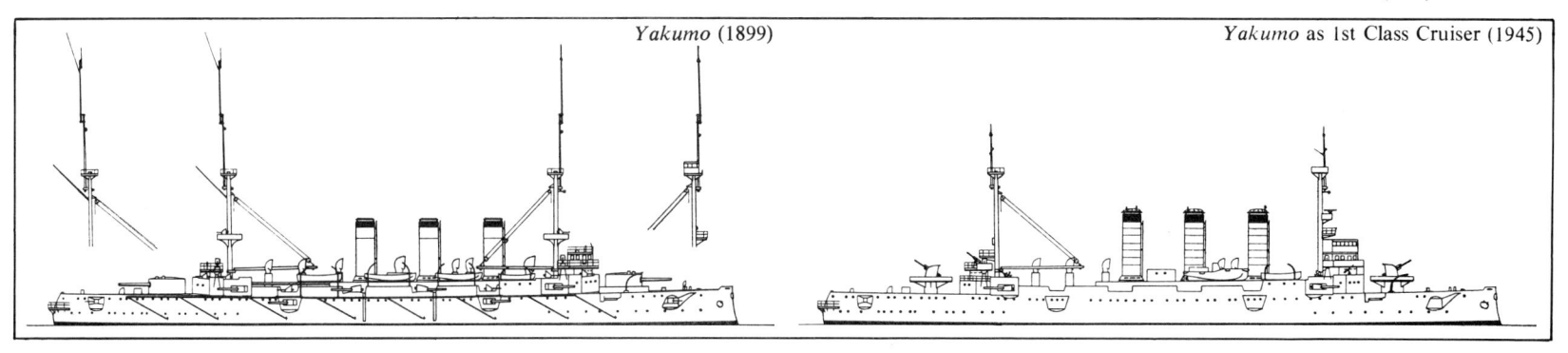

Yakumo (1899)

Yakumo as 1st Class Cruiser (1945)

ARMOURED CRUISERS 73

GENERAL NOTES
Ordered in Germany under the Post-war Programme of 1896–7.

ARMOUR
Krupp steel. Belt 7in to 3½in; deck 2½in; casemates 6in; turrets 6.3in; CT 14in.

RE-ARMAMENT AND RECONSTRUCTION
In 1924 she was armed with 12 × 6in 40-cal (Type '41'), 8 × 3.1in 40-cal, 1 × 3.1in AA; in 1927 reboilered with 6 Yarrow boilers from the *Haruna*, resulting in 7000 ihp = 16 knots; she then carried 1210ts coal and 306ts oil. In 1930–33 she was re-armed with 4 × 8in; 12 × 6in; 4 × 3.1in; 1 × 3.1in AA; 12 × 25mm AA.

MACHINERY
On trials she reached 16960 ihp = 21.005 knots on 9646ts. During the 1930–33 reconstruction (see above) the machinery was halved to 2 sets, and 6 boilers: 7000 ihp = 9 knots.

CAREER
Launched 8 July, 1899 and completed in June 1900; formed part of the main battle fleet in the Russo-Japanese War; reduced to a 1st Class coast-defence ship in 1921 and served as a training ship; in July 1942 she was re-rated as a 1st Class cruiser; surrendered in 1945 but served on repatriation duties until June 1946; BU at Maizuru.

The armoured cruiser *Yakumo* was built in Germany, and like the others, she had a long and distinguished career. She is seen here after 1912, when she was given masthead fire-control platforms. (P. A. Vicary.)

Name	Builder	Date	Displ	Length ft in	Beam ft in	Draught ft in	Machinery	SHP	Speed	Fuel	Radius	Armament	Comp
IZUMO	Armstrong, Whitworth, Elswick	1898–1901	10305 F 9750 N	435 8 oa 400 pp	68 6	24 3	2-shaft 4-cyl compound 24 Belleville boilers	14700 ihp	20¾	600 / 1550 coal	7000 @ 10	4 × 8in 40-cal 14 × 6in 40-cal QF 12 × 3in QF 8 × 47mm 5 × 18in TT (UW)	483 / 672
IWATE		1899–1901	10235 F 9750 N										

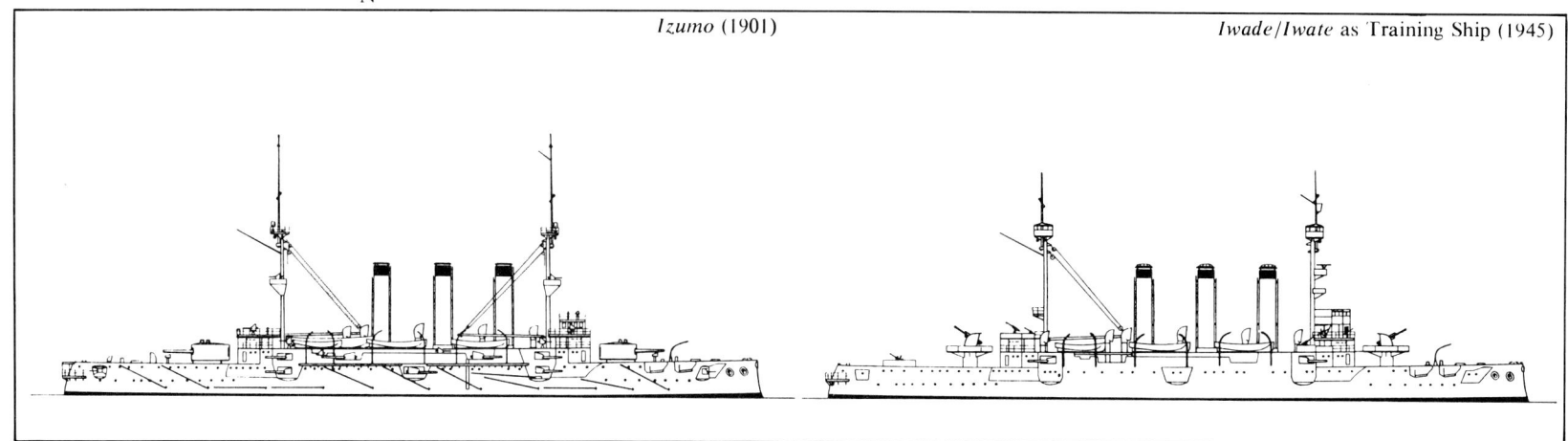

Izumo (1901)

Iwade/Iwate as Training Ship (1945)

GENERAL NOTES
Designed by Philip Watts and ordered under the Post-war Programme of 1896–7.

ARMOUR
Krupp steel. Belt 7in; deck 2½in; turrets 8in to 6in; casemates and barbettes 6in; CT 14in.

RE-ARMAMENT AND RECONSTRUCTION
In 1924, both ships were re-armed with 14 × 6in 40-cal (Type '41'); 8 × 3.1in 40-cal and 1 × 3.1in AA. In 1931 *Iwate* was reboilered with 6 Yarrow boilers, giving her 7000 ihp = 16 knots; she carried 1412ts coal and 324ts oil, and complement rose to 726; her TT were removed and the armament was 4 × 8in 40-cal; 8 × 6in 40-cal; 2 × 3.1in 40-cal; 3 × 3.1in AA, and 3 MGs. In 1936 the 8in guns were replaced by Japanese Type '41' model.
In 1935, *Izumo* was reboilered with 6 Kampon boilers, 7000 ihp = 16 knots; she carried 1405ts coal, and 324ts oil, and displaced 10692ts; her armament was 4 × 8in 40-cal; 8 × 6in 40-cal; returned to service in October 1935. In 1944–5 they were armed with 4 × 6in; 4 × 5in; 3 × 3.1in AA (*Izumo* only 1); 9 × 25mm AA (*Izumo* 14 × 25mm AA and 2 × 13mm), and speed reduced to 12 knots.

MACHINERY NOTES
On trials, *Izumo* reached 15739 ihp = 22.04 knots on 9733ts, and *Iwate* 16078 ihp = 21.74 knots on 9750ts. During the 1930–3 reconstruction, ihp was reduced to 7000 ihp = 16 knots, with 6 boilers (crew 726).

CAREERS
Izumo
Launched 19 September, 1899 and completed in September 1900; flagship of Admiral Kamimura at the battle of Tsushima; in 1921 re-rated as a 1st Class coast-defence ship; from 1932 to 1942 was flagship of the China Fleet; rated as a 1st Class cruiser in July 1942; training ship in 1943; sunk at Kure by aircraft 28 July, 1945 (34°14′N, 132° 30′ E); BU at Harima in 1947.

Iwate
Launched 29 March 1900 and completed 31 March, 1901; served in the main battle fleet during the Russo-Japanese War; re-rated as 1st Class coast-defence ship in 1921; training ship from 1923; rated in 1942 as a 1st Class Cruiser, and in 1943 as a training ship; sank 24 July, 1945, in shallow water at Kure 24 hours after a bombing raid by aircraft of US TF 38 (34° 14′ N, 132° 30′ E); BU at Harima in 1947.

74 ARMOURED CRUISERS

Izumo and her sister *Iwate* were the second pair of Elswick-built armoured cruisers. She is seen here some time after Tsushima, without torpedo-nets and her fighting tops replaced by fire-control platforms. (Jenschura.)

The armoured cruiser *Izumo* served as a flagship thoughout the "China Incident", and is here seen moored in the stream off Shanghai in 1938.

Name	Builder	Date	Displ	Length ft in	Beam ft in	Draught ft in	Machinery	SHP	Speed	Fuel	Radius	Armament	Comp
KASUGA ex-*Bernadino Rivadavia* ex-*Mitra*	Giovanni Ansaldo & Co., Sestri Ponente (Genoa)	1902– 1904	8591 F 7628 N	366 0 wl 344 0 pp	61 4	24 0 *Kasuga* 24 3 *Nisshin*	2-shaft 3-cyl VTE, 4 double-ended, 4 single-ended boilers	14800 ihp	20.6	500 / 1190 coal	5500 @ 10	*Kasuga* 1 × 10in 45-cal 2 × 8in 45-cal 14 × 6in 45-cal QF 10 × 3in 40-cal QF 6 × 47mm 2 MGs 4 × 18in TT (AW)	500 / 560
NISSHIN ex-*Mariano Moreno* ex-*Roca*		1902– 1904	8384 F 7698 N									*Nisshin* 4 × 8in 45-cal otherwise similar to *Kasuga*, except 4 × 47mm	

GENERAL NOTES

Armoured cruisers of the successful Italian *Garibaldi* type designed by Lieut-General Eduardo Masdea, they were launched as the Italian *Mitra* and *Roca*, and then bought by Argentina, who resold them to Japan in 1903-4.

ARMOUR

Krupp-Terni steel. Belt 5.9in to 3in; deck 1½in to 0.9in; turrets 5.9in; barbettes 5.9in to 4.7in; CT 5.9in.

RE-ARMAMENT AND RECONSTRUCTION

Kasuga's armament was altered in Japan after she had been taken over; both ships were modernized in 1914 with 12 Kampon boilers (Type 'I'); in 1924 they had 14 × 6in 40-cal Type '41'; 8 × 3.1in 40-cal; i × 3.1in AA. In August, 1933 *Kasuga* had 1 × 10in; 2 × 8in; 4 × 6in; 4 × 3.1in; 1 × 3.1in AA, 4 × 18in TT; her rated horse-power was 13500 shp and her complement was 600; she was hulked and totally disarmed in July 1942.

MACHINERY NOTES

On trials *Kasuga* reached 14944 ihp = 20.05 knots on 7283ts, and *Nisshin* reached 14896 ihp = 20.15 knots on 7296ts. By August 1933, *Kasuga* was reboilered with 12 Kampon boilers, and could achieve 13500 ihp.

CAREERS

Kasuga

Launched 22 October, 1902 and completed on 20 December 1903; formed part of the main battle fleet throughout the Russo-Japanese War; stranded 13 January, 1918 off Tandjon Delar in the Banka Straits; refloated by June 1918; in 1927 became a training ship for navigators and engineers; hulked in 1942 and sunk at Yokosuka by aircraft 18 July, 1945 (35° 18′ N, 139° 40′ E); BU at Uraga 1948.

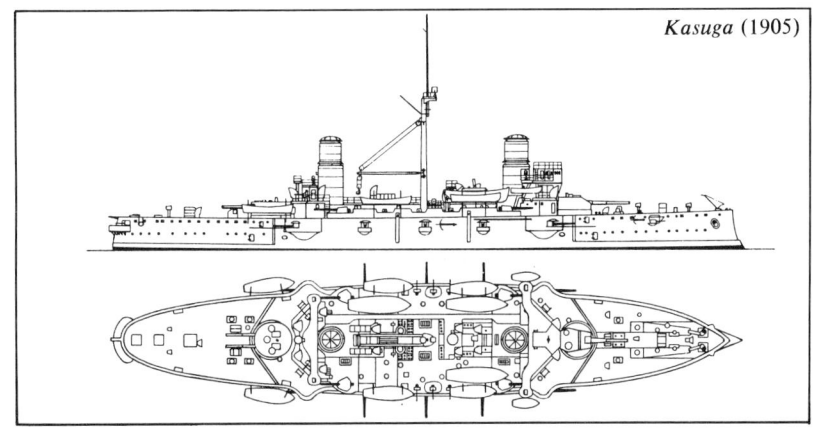

Kasuga (1905)

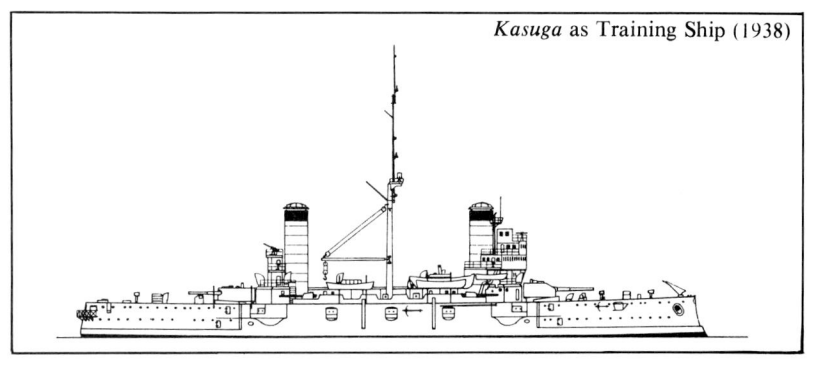

Kasuga as Training Ship (1938)

ARMOURED CRUISERS 75

Nisshin
Launched 9 February, 1903 and completed 17 January, 1904; formed part of the main battle fleet in the Russo-Japanese War; in 1927 she became a training ship and depot-ship at Yokosuka; stricken in 1935; and renamed *Hai Kan No 6*; she was sunk at Kamegakubi, near Kure in 1936, as a target for 18in shells, torpedoes and bombs. Raised in 1936 and BU.

Nisshin, at Port Said in October 1917. (IWM.)

The distinctive layout of *Kasuga*, with a single mast between two widely spaced funnels, betrays her Italian origin. Variants of the *Garibaldi* class were built for the Italian, Spanish and Argentine navies. This photograph shows her at about the time of the war against Russia. (Shizuo Fukui.)

Name	Builder	Date	Displ	Length ft in	Beam ft in	Draught ft in	Machinery	SHP	Speed	Fuel	Radius	Armament	Comp
ASO ex-*Bayan*	Forges et Chantiers de la Méditerranée, La Seyne, Toulon	1899–1903	7726 N	444 11 oa / 410 10 pp	57 0	22 0	2-shaft VTE 26 Belleville boilers	16500	21	750 / 1100 coal	7000 @ 10	2 × 8in 45-cal / 8 × 6in 45-cal QF / 20 × 75mm QF / 7 × 47mm / 5 × 15in TT (3 AW, 2 UW)	570

Aso as Minelayer (1923)

Aso (1908)

GENERAL NOTES
Ex-Russian armoured cruiser of French design.

ARMOUR
Krupp steel. Belt 8in to 4in; deck 2in to 1in; turrets 7in to 3½in; casemates 3.1in.

RE-ARMAMENT AND RECONSTRUCTION
Repaired at Maizuru in 1906–8 with Miyabara boilers and Armstrong-pattern guns: 2 × 8in; 8 × 6in; 16 × 3.1in. In 1913, the 8in guns were replaced by 2 × 6in 50-cal Armstrong-pattern guns. Rebuilt in 1920 as a minelayer, with 8in guns removed, and capacity for 420 mines.

MACHINERY NOTES
On trials in October 1902, she reached 17400 ihp = 22 knots.

CAREER
Launched 12 June, 1900 and completed in 1903 for the Russian Navy; sunk at Port Arthur 8 December, 1904 by Japanese howitzer-fire (heeled over in the eastern harbour); fell into Japanese hands 2 January, 1905 and raised later that year; joined the fleet in 1908, rated as an armoured cruiser; converted to a minelayer in 1920 (see above) and stricken 1 April, 1930 and renamed *Hai Kan No 4*; sunk as a target 8 August, 1932 by cruiser *Myoko*.

The armoured cruiser *Aso* was built as the Russian *Bayan*, and was sunk by gunfire at Port Arthur. This photograph shows her at Yokosuka around 1923, after conversion to a minelayer. (Shizuo Fukui.)

76 ARMOURED CRUISERS

Name	Builder	Date	Displ	Length ft in	Beam ft in	Draught ft in	Machinery	SHP	Speed	Fuel	Radius	Armament	Comp
TSUKUBA	Kure DY	1905–1907	15400 F	450 0 oa 445 0 wl 440 0 pp	75 0	26 0	2-shaft VTE 20 Miyabara boilers	20500 ihp	20½	600 / 1911 coal — 160 oil		4 × 12in 45-cal 12 × 6in 45-cal QF 12 × 4.7in 50-cal QF 4 × 3.1in 40-cal QF 2 × 3.1in 28-cal QF 3 MGs 3 × 18in TT (UW)	820
IKOMA		1905–1908	13750 N										

General Notes
These large armoured cruisers were first planned under the 3rd Fleet Law of 1903, and although orders were placed in June 1904 they were actually built under the Post-war Programme of 1907. *Tsukuba* was completed in two years, and the ship had many defects. They were later rated as battlecruisers, but *Ikoma* was re-rated as a 1st Class cruiser in 1921.

Machinery
On trials, *Tsukuba* reached 23260 ihp = 21.6 knots, and *Ikoma* reached 22670 ihp = 20.4 knots.

Armour
Krupp steel. Belt 7in to 4in; deck 2in; turrets 7in; casemates 5in; CT 8in to 6in. The depth of belt was 40.19ft.

Re-armament
In 1919, *Ikoma* was armed with 4 × 12in; 10 × 6in; 8 × 4.7in; 6 × 3.1in; 3 MGs; TT.

Careers
Tsukuba
Launched 26 December, 1905 and completed 14 January, 1907; sunk by magazine explosion 14 January, 1917 in Yokosuka Bay (305 dead); later raised and BU.
Ikoma
Launched 9 April, 1906 and completed 24 March, 1908; gunnery training ship in 1919; disarmed in 1922 at Sasebo under terms of the Washington Treaty; for disposal in 1923 and BU 13 November, 1924. by Mitsubishi at Nagasaki.

Ikoma, sistership of the *Tsukuba*, seen at a fleet review in Germany. After 1912 she was re-rated as a battlecruiser, when the term was introduced in the Royal Navy. (Bundesarchiv.)

Tsukuba (1907); details, *Ikoma* (1908)

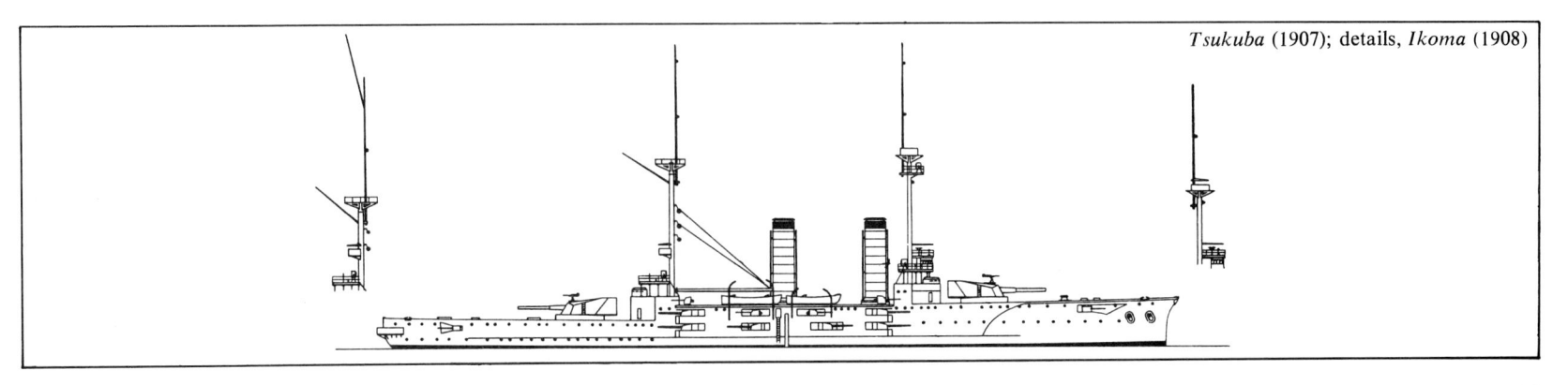

ARMOURED CRUISERS

Name	Builder	Date	Displ	Length ft in	Beam ft in	Draught ft in	Machinery	SHP	Speed	Fuel	Radius	Armament	Comp
KURAMA	Yokosuka DY	1905–1911	15595 F	485 0 oa	75 4	26 1	*Kurama* 2-shaft VTE 28 Miyabara boilers	22500 ihp	21¼	600 / 2000 coal	215	4 × 12in 45-cal	817
IBUKI	Kure DY		14636 N	451 0 wl								8 × 8in 45-cal	845
				449 0 pp			*Ibuki* 2-shaft Curtis turbines, 18 Miyabara boilers	24000	22½	oil		14 × 4.7in 50-cal QF 4 × 3.1in 40-cal QF 4 × 3.1in 28-cal QF 3 × 18in TT (UW)	

Ibuki (1909)

Kurama (1922)

GENERAL NOTES
Projected under the 3rd Fleet Law of 1903 but the cost was included under the 1907 Programme. They were improved versions of the *Tsukuba* and *Ikoma*, and were similarly re-rated as battlecruisers (from 1921, 1st Class cruisers).

ARMOUR
Krupp steel. Belt 7in to 6in; deck 2in; turrets 7in to 6in; casemates 5in; CT 8in to 6in.

MACHINERY
Ibuki was the first major Japanese warship with turbines. On trials, *Kurama* reached 23081 ihp = 21½ knots and *Ibuki* reached 27141 shp = 21 knots.

CAREERS
Kurama
Launched 21 October, 1907 and completed 28 February, 1911; disarmed in 1922 at Sasebo; for disposal in 1923; sold to Seiko Zosen for BU at Kobe.

Ibuki
Launched 21 November, 1907 and completed 1 November, 1909; disarmed at Kure in 1922; listed for disposal on 20 September, 1923; BU between 1923 and 9 December, 1924 by Kawasaki at Kobe.

Kurama was an improved version of the *Tsukuba* class, with the tripod masts associated with dreadnought battleships. (Shizuo Fukui.)

Ibuki was a sister of *Kurama*, but being completed earlier, she had the old-style pole masts. (Shizuo Fukui.)

4. Heavy Cruisers

Name	Builder	Date	Displ	Length ft in	Beam ft in	Draught ft in	Machinery	SHP	Speed	Fuel	Radius	Armament	Comp
FURUTAKA	Mitsubishi, Nagasaki	1922–1926	8586 N 7100 S	607 6 oa 602 2 wl 580 0 pp	51 9	18 3	2 sets Parsons GT 12 Kampon boilers 2 shafts (*Kako* Curtiss GT)	102000	34.5	1400 oil 450 coal	6000 @ 14	6 × 203mm (8in) (nominal 200mm) 50-cal LA 4 × 80mm (3in) 40-cal HA 10 MGs 12 × 610mm (24in) fixed TT 1 aircraft 1 take-off platform	625
KAKO	Kawasaki, Kobe	1922–1926											
Modernisation:													
FURUTAKA	Kure DY	1937–1939	10507 N	595 0 wl				103390	32.9	2000 oil	8000 @ 14	6 × 203mm 50-cal 4 × 120mm (4.7in) 45-cal HA 8 × 25mm AA 4 × 13.2mm AA 2 × 4 610mm rotating TT 2 aircraft 1 catapult	
KAKO	Sasebo DY	1936–1937	8700 S	580 0 pp									

Furutaka (1926)

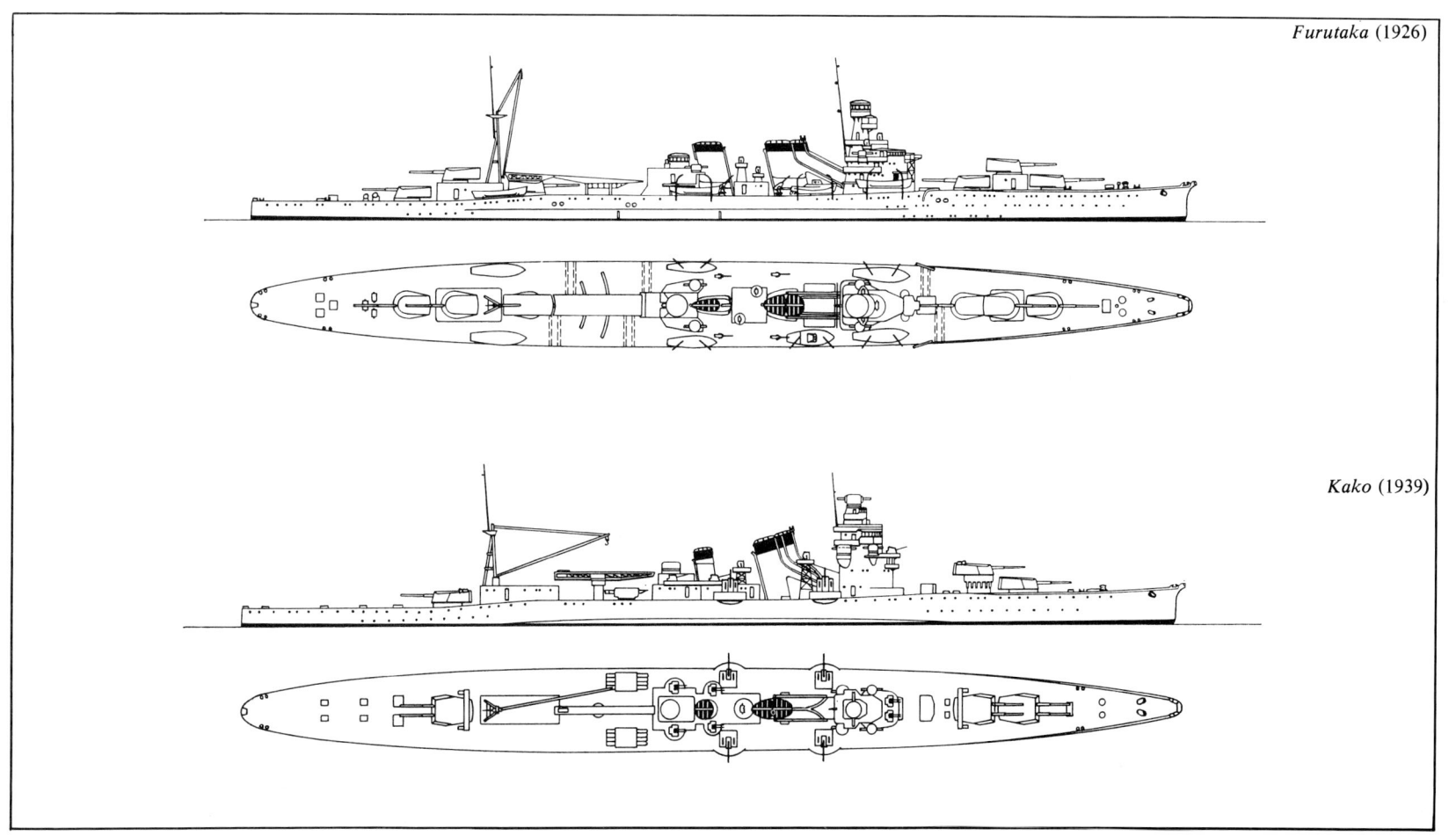

Kako (1939)

General Notes
First section of the first heavy cruiser division of the 1922–9 Programme which replaced the 1920–8 Programme, abandoned in compliance with the terms of the Washington Treaty. *Furutaka* was the first heavy cruiser designed and completed to conform to the Treaty limits. *Kako* attained 35.14 knots on 105845 shp on trials. 1934–5: 55¾ft catapult replaced by 62½ft catapult.

Armour
Belt 1in; main deck 2in.

Modernisation
1936–9: main armament redisposed in twin turrets (5in armour), fixed main deck TT removed and 2 quadruple rotating mounts installed on upper deck; anti-torpedo bulges added.

Careers
Furutaka
Launched 25 February, 1925; completed 31 March, 1926; modernized 1 April, 1937 to 30 April, 1939; sunk 11 October, 1942 by gunfire NE of Savo Island (09° 02′ S, 159° 34′ E) by US cruisers *Salt Lake City* and *Boise*.

Kako
Launched 10 April, 1925; completed 20 July, 1926; modernized 4 July, 1936 to 27 December 1937; sunk 10 August, 1942 off New Ireland (02° 15′ S, 152° 15′ E) by US submarine *S-44*.

Furutaka, in her original form, with first single 8-inch guns in lightly-protected gun-houses, installed as interim armament until the twin turret was available. The flying-off platform (not catapult) forward of the mainmast can just be seen. (Jentschura.)

Name	Builder	Date	Displ	Length ft in	Beam ft in	Draught ft in	Machinery	SHP	Fuel	Radius	Speed	Armament	Comp
AOBA	Mitsubishi, Nagasaki	1924–1926	8900 N	607 6 oa	51 10	18 9	4 sets Parsons GT (*Kinugasa* Curtiss GT) 12 Kampon boilers 4 shafts	102000	34.5 oil 450 coal	1800	6000 @ 14	6 × 203mm (8in) 50-cal 4 × 120mm (4.7in) 45-cal HA 10 MGs 12 × 610mm (24in) fixed TT 1 aircraft 1 catapult	625
KINUGASA	Kawasaki, Kobe	1924–1926	7100 S	602 4 wl 582 3 pp									
Modernisation: (both ships)	Sasebo NY	1938–1940	10822 N 9000 S	595 0 wl 582 3 pp	57 9	18 7		108456		2000	8000 @ 14	6 × 203mm 50-cal 4 × 120mm 45-cal 8 × 25mm AA 4 × 13,2mm AA 2 × 4 610mm rotating TT 2 aircraft 1 catapult	

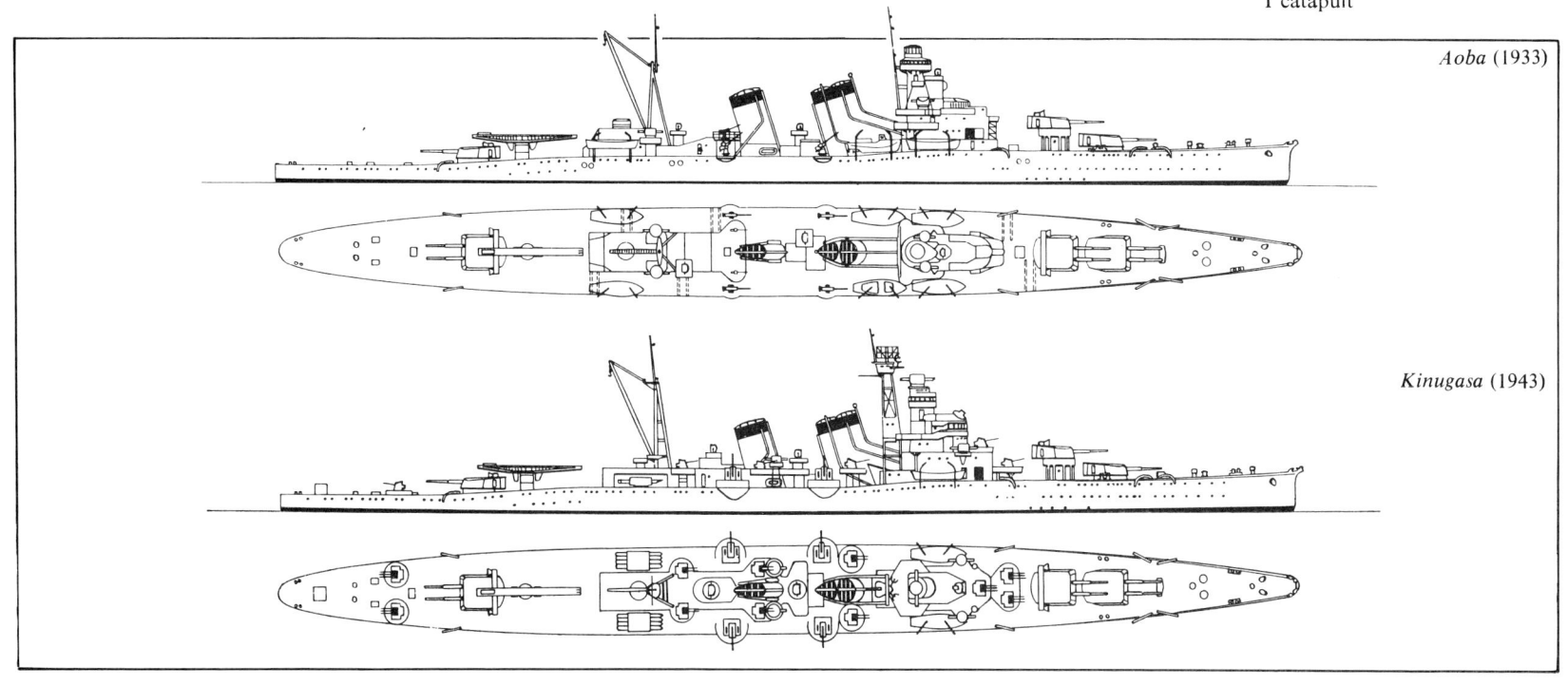

Aoba (1933)

Kinugasa (1943)

HEAVY CRUISERS

GENERAL NOTES
Improved *Furutaka* class, with main armament in twin turrets, and first catapult to be installed in Japanese cruiser.

ARMOUR
Belt 1in; deck 2in; turrets 5in.

ARMAMENT
1928: 62½ft catapult installed; 1934–5: 8 × 13.2mm AA added; 1938–40: TT moved from main deck to upper deck, anti-torpedo bulges added, AA armament 8 × 25mm, 4 × 13.2mm; May 1944: *Aoba* 15 × 25mm; July 1944: 42 × 25mm.

CAREERS
Aoba
Launched 25 September, 1926; completed 20 September, 1927; severely damaged 12 October, 1942 off Guadalcanal and the after 203mm turret was still inoperative when she was again damaged on 3 April, 1943 by US air attack at Kavieng. After repair, the maximum speed was reduced to 30 knots; severely damaged 24 October, 1944 in Manila Bay by US submarine *Bream*; attacked while under repair at Kure on 19 March and 25 July, 1945; aircraft from US TF 38 inflicting further heavy damage, finally settled on the bottom of Kure harbour on 28 July; BU 1948.
Kinugasa
Launched 24 October, 1926; completed 30 September, 1927; sunk 14 November, 1942 15 nm W of Rendova Island (08° 45′ S, 157° 00′ E) by aircraft from USS *Enterprise*.

Aoba, seen after installation of the 19m catapult abaft the mainmast, an immediately obvious difference between this ship and *Kinugasa*, and the modernised *Kako* and *Furutaka*, the only other Japanese heavy cruisers with three main armament turrets. (Jentschura.)

Name	Builder	Date	Displ	Length ft in	Beam ft in	Draught ft in	Machinery	SHP	Speed	Fuel	Radius	Armament	Comp
MYOKO	Yokosuka NY	1924–1929	12374 N	668 6 oa	56 11	19 4	4 sets GT 12 Kampon boilers 4 shafts	130000	35.5	2470 oil	8000 @ 14	10 × 203mm (8in) 50-cal 6 × 120mm (4.7in) 45-cal HA 10 MGs 12 × 610mm (24in) fixed TT 2 aircraft 1 catapult	773
NACHI	Kure NY	1924–1928	10000 S	661 1 wl									
HAGURO	Mitsubishi, Nagasaki	1925–1929		631 2 pp									
ASHIGARA	Kawasaki, Kobe	1925–1929											
Modernisation: (all ships)		1939–1941	14980 N 13000 S	661 9 wl 631 2 pp	68 0	20 9		130250	33.8		8500 @ 14	10 × 203mm 50-cal 8 × 127mm (5in) 40-cal DP 8 × 25mm AA 2 × 4 610mm rotating TT 3 aircraft 2 catapults	

HEAVY CRUISERS 81

Above: *Ashigara* in 1931. (Jentschura.)
Right and Below:
Ashigara was one of the most photographed Japanese ships of her generation, as a result of her visits to Britain and Germany in 1937. These views show most of the changes incorporated during refits between 1931 and 1936: twin 5-inch dual-purpose guns have replaced the single 4.7-inch AA guns; two catapults are installed, sponsored out to provide an open stowage, complete with "railway system", for the Nakajima "Dave" observation floatplanes. The top edge of the bulge, added in 1936 to compensate for increased topweight, is visible in the two views of the cruiser passing through the Kiel Canal. In the broadside view, the armoured tower bridge of *Admiral Graf Spee* can be seen under the jib of *Ashigara*'s seaplane derrick. (Bundesarchiv.)

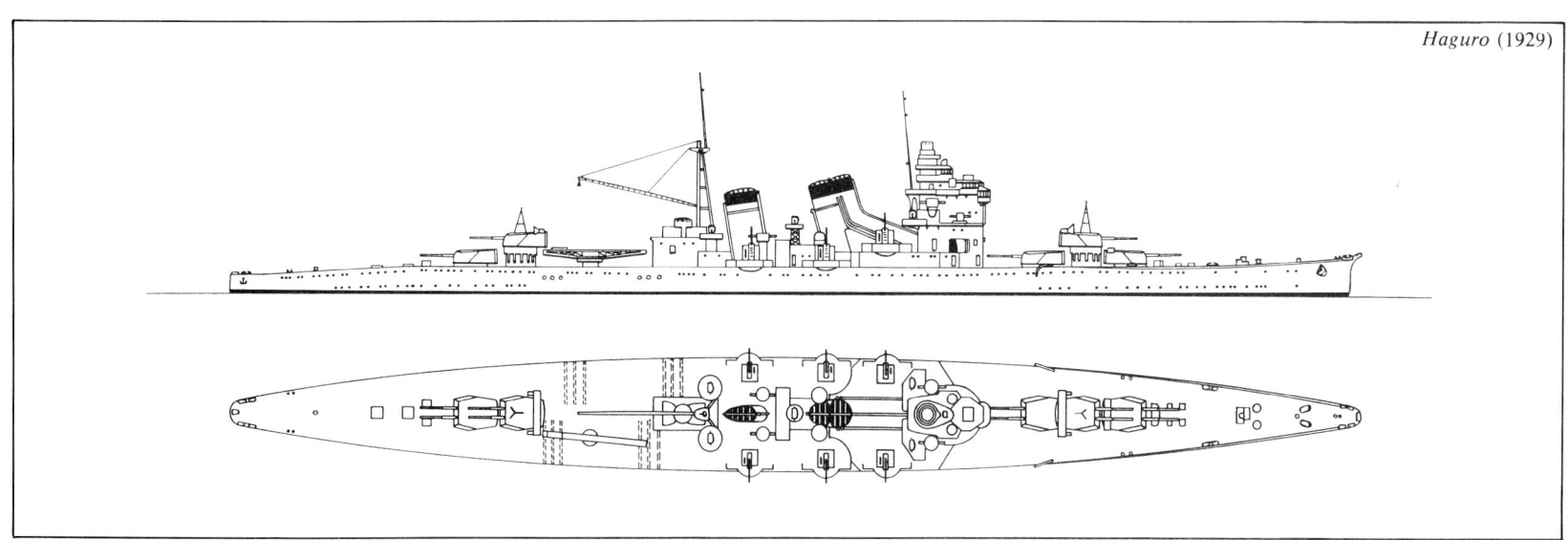

Haguro (1929)

82 HEAVY CRUISERS

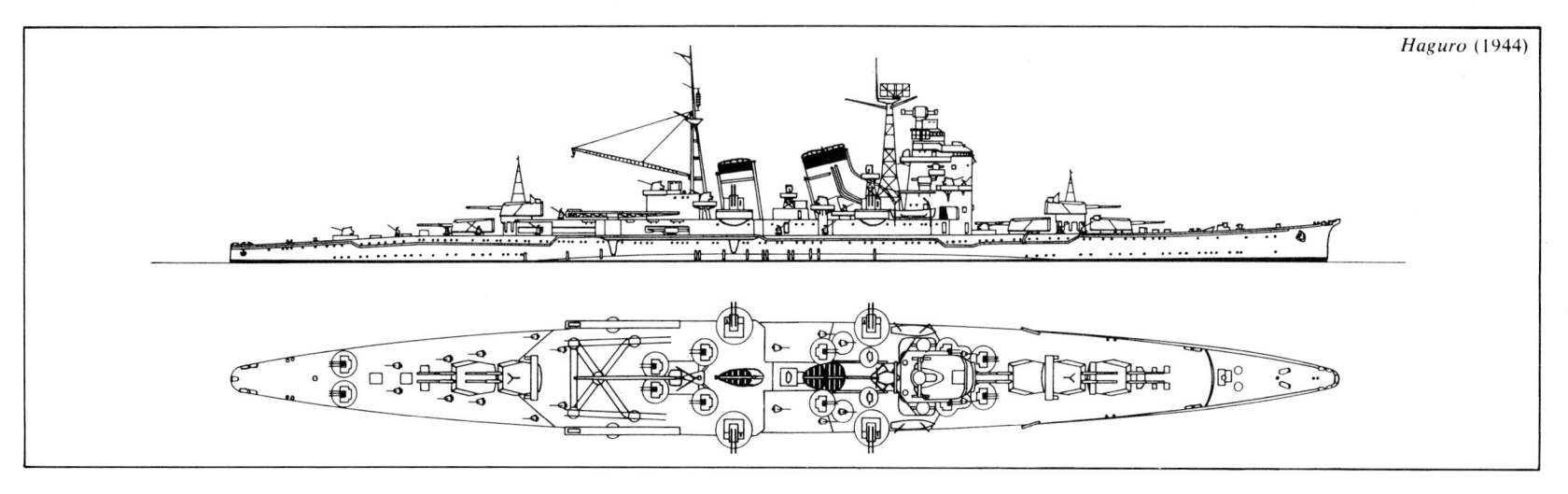

Haguro (1944)

General Notes
Second cruiser division of the 1922–9 Programme. Designed by Vice-Admiral Baron Y. Hiraga. Triple hull and extensive internal sub-division.

Armour
Belt 3in to 4in; deck 2in; turrets 6in, barbettes 3in.

Armament
1934–5: 4 × 13.2mm AA added; 1936: hull strengthened, fixed TT removed and replaced by by 2 quadruple rotating mounts on the upper deck; from May 1944: 24 × 25mm AA; July 1944: 52 × 25mm.

Careers
Myoko
Launched 16 April 1927, completed 31 July, 1929; severely damaged 13 December, 1944 off Royalist Bank, South China Sea, by US submarine *Bergall*; towed to Singapore but not repaired; scuttled by Royal Navy in the Malacca Straits on 8 July, 1946.
Nachi
Launched 15 June, 1927; completed 26 November, 1928; sunk 5 November, 1944 5 nm W of Corregidor by aircraft from USS *Lexington*.
Haguro
Launched 24 March, 1928; completed 25 April, 1929; torpedoed and sunk 16 May, 1945 55 nm WSW of Penang Island (05° 00′ N, 99° 30′ E) by British destroyers *Saumarez*, *Venus*, *Verulam*, *Vigilant* and *Virago*.
Ashigara
Launched 22 April, 1928; completed 20 August, 1929; sunk 8 June, 1945 14 nm WSW of Muntok, Banka Straits (01° 59′ S, 104° 57′ E) by British submarine *Trenchant*.

Name	Builder	Date	Displ	Length ft in	Beam ft in	Draught ft in	Machinery	SHP	Speed	Fuel	Radius	Armament	Comp
TAKAO	Yokosuka NY	1927–1932	12986 N	668 6 oa	59 2	20 0	4 sets GT 12 Kampon boilers 4 shafts	130000	35.5	2571 oil	8000 @ 14	10 × 203mm (8in) 50-cal 4 × 120mm (4.7in) 45-cal HA 2 × 40mm (2pdr) AA 4 × 2 610mm rotating TT 3 aircraft 2 catapults	773
ATAGO	Kure NY	1927–1932	9850 S	661 8 wl									
MAYA	Kawasaki, Kobe	1928–1932		631 8 pp									
CHOKAI	Mitsubishi, Nagasaki	1928–1932											
Modernisation:													
TAKAO & ATAGO		1938–1939	15781 F	661 9 wl	68 0	20 9		133100	34.2	2600 oil	8500 @ 14	10 × 203mm 50-cal 8 × 127mm (5in) 40-cal DP (*Takao* and *Atago*, 1941) 8 × 25mm AA 4 × 13.2mm AA 4 × 4 610mm rotating TT 3 aircraft 2 catapults	
MAYA & CHOKAI		1941	14838 N 13400 S	631 8 pp									

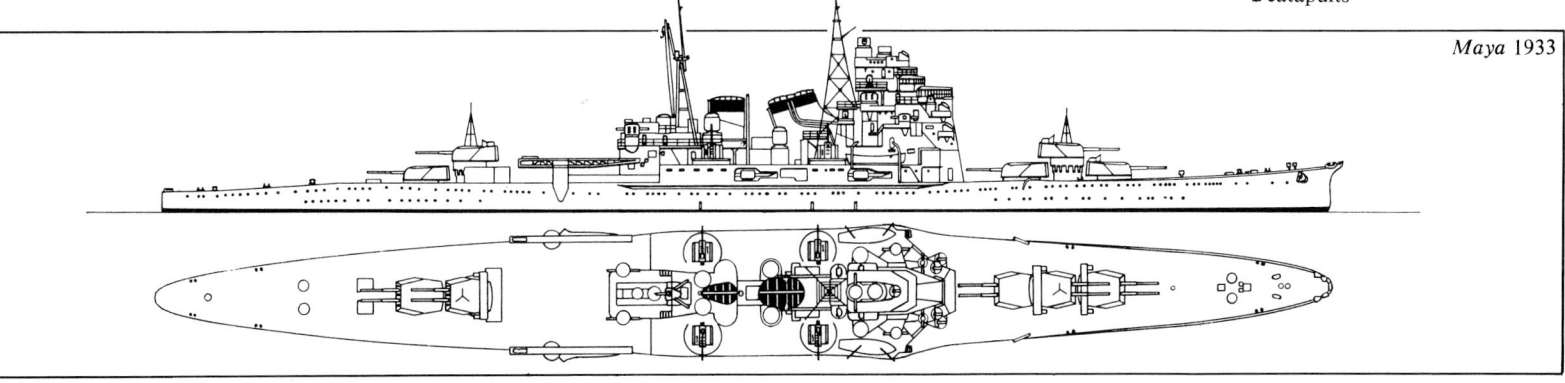

Maya 1933

HEAVY CRUISERS 83

Maya (1944)

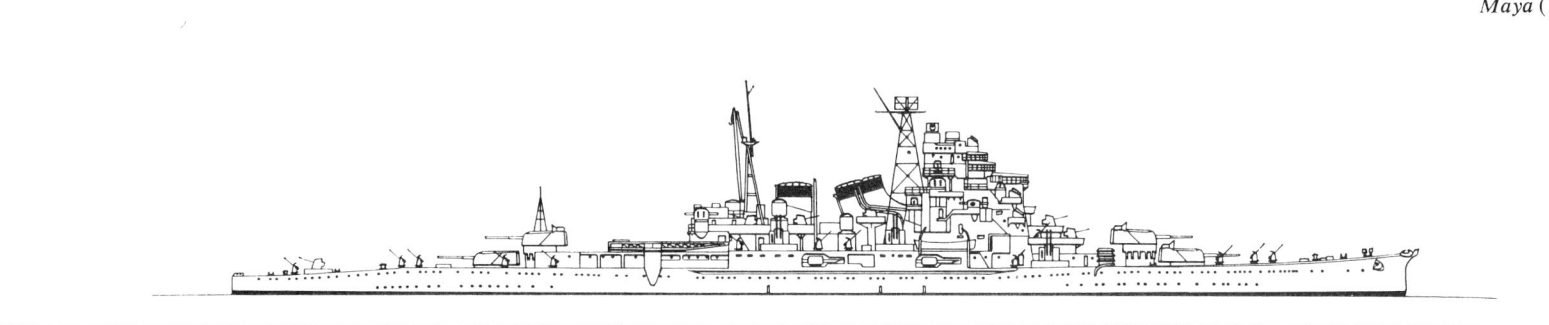

Atago class

GENERAL NOTES
1927–31 Supplementary Programme: modified *Myoko* design.

ARMOUR
Belt 4in to 5in; deck 2in; turrets 6in; barbettes 3in.

MODERNISATION AND ARMAMENT
1938–9: *Takao* and *Atago* modernised, torpedo armament doubled, mainmast stepped farther aft, abaft the catapults, forecastle deck extended aft to 'X' turret, aircraft stowage revised; *Maya* and *Chokai* 4 × 13.2mm AA added; 1941: *Maya* and *Chokai* modernised; summer 1942: 4 × 120mm HA replaced by 4 × 2 127mm DP; from March 1944: *Maya* 8 × 203mm, 12 × 127mm, 30 × 25mm AA; other ships 26 × 25mm AA; July 1944: 60 (*Maya* 66) × 25mm, depth-charges.

CAREERS
Takao
Launched 12 May, 1930; completed 31 May, 1932; severely damaged 23 October, 1944 in the Palawan Passage (09° 24′ N, 117° 11′ E) by US submarine *Darter*; again severely damaged 31 July, 1945 at Singapore by British midget submarine *XE-3* (towed to the Johore Straits by HM submarine *Stygian*); scuttled by Royal Navy 27 October, 1946 in Malacca Straits.
Atago
Launched 16 June, 1930; completed 30 March, 1932; sunk 23 October, 1944 in the Palawan Passage by *Darter*.
Maya
Launched 8 November, 1930; completed 30 June, 1932; sunk 23 October, 1944 in the Palawan Passage by US submarine *Dace*
Chokai
Launched 5 April, 1931; completed 30 June, 1932; damaged 25 October, 1944 by aircraft from US TU 77.4.3 during battle of Samar; scuttled 11° 26′ N, 126° 15′ E by destroyer *Fujinami*.

Left:
Maya, in 1933. The *Takao* class was immediately recognisable by the vertical second funnel, all other two-funnel heavy cruisers having appreciable rake on both funnels. (Jentschura.)

Above:
Chokai's massive bridge structure, complete with "greenhouses" at the three upper levels, would not have disgraced a battleship. Not surprisingly, this class proved to be somewhat top-heavy, and bulges were added some years after completion, to increase the hull beam amidships by nearly nine feet. (Netherlands Navy.)

Name	Builder	Date	Displ	Length ft in	Beam ft in	Draught ft in	Machinery	SHP	Speed	Fuel	Radius	Armament	Comp
MOGAMI	Kure DY	1931–1935	11169 N	646 4 wl	59 1	18 1	4 sets GT 10 Kampon boilers 4 shafts	152000	37	2163	8150 @ 14	15 × 155mm (6.1in) 60-cal 8 × 127mm (5in) 40-cal DP 4 × 40mm (2pdr) AA 4 × 3 610mm rotating TT 3 aircraft 2 catapults	850
MIKUMA	Mitsubishi, Nagasaki		8500 S	620 1 pp									

HEAVY CRUISERS

Name	Builder	Date	Displ	Length ft in	Beam ft in	Draught ft in	Machinery	SHP	Speed	Fuel	Radius	Armament	Comp
MOGAMI (rebuilt)	Kure NY	1936–1938	13440 N	649 10 wl	63 0	19 4			35			15 × 155mm 60-cal 8 × 127mm 40-cal DP 8 × 25mm AA 4 × 13.2mm AA	850
MIKUMA (rebuilt)	Kure NY		11200 S	661 2 pp									
SUZUYA	Yokosuka NY	1933–1937		656 0 oa	66 3	19 5	4 sets GT 8 Kampon boilers 4 shafts	15200	34.9	2163	8150 @ 14	4 × 3 610mm TT 3 aircraft 2 catapults	
KUMANO	Kawasaki, Kobe	1934–1937		649 7 wl									
Re-armament: (all ships)	Kure NY	1939–1940	13887 N									10 × 203mm (8in) 50-cal 8 × 127mm 40-cal DP, etc.	
MOGAMI (repairs)	Kure NY	1942–1943	12400 S 13890 N 12206 S	649 10 wl	66 3	19 4						6 × 203mm 50-cal 8 × 127mm 40-cal DP 30 × 25mm AA 4 × 3 610mm TT 11 aircraft 2 catapults	

Mikuma (1935)

Mogami (1943)

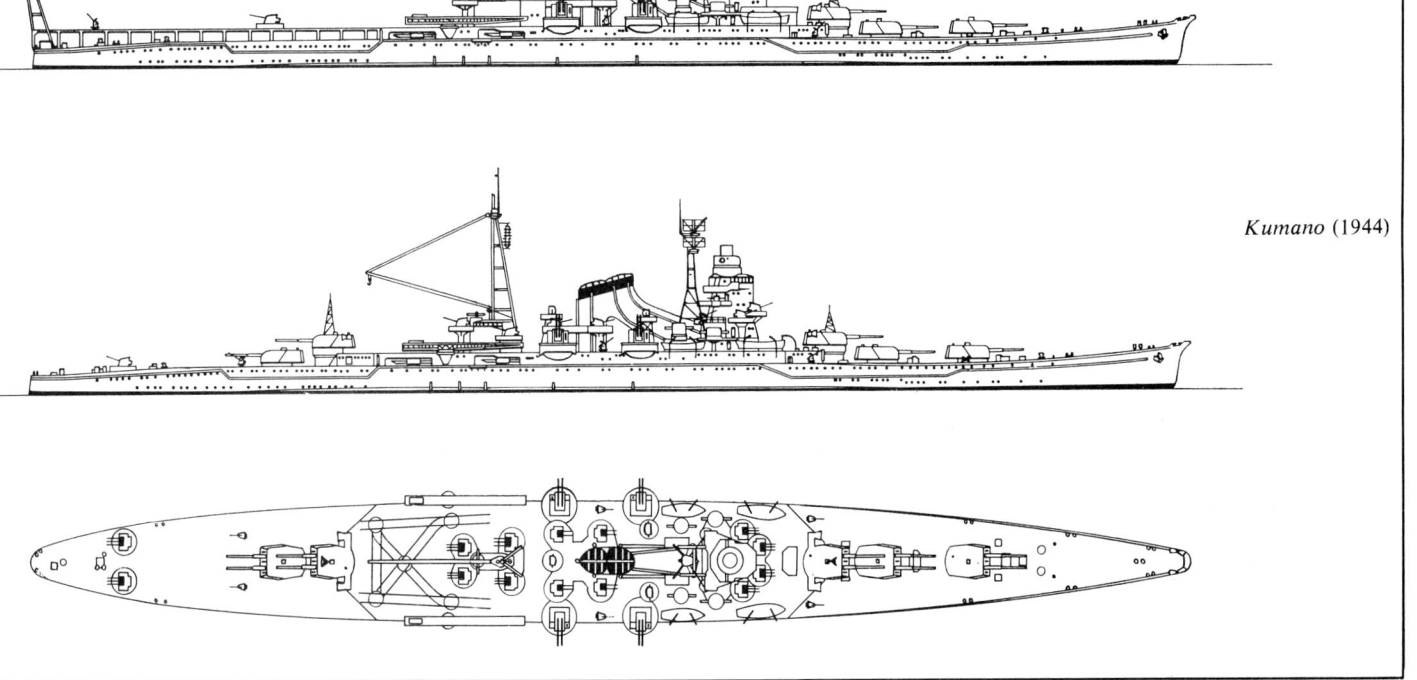

Kumano (1944)

HEAVY CRUISERS 85

Mogami class

GENERAL NOTES

1931 Supplementary Programme, drawn up following the 1930 London Naval Treaty. Built to within the Treaty's Light Cruiser limitations, *Mogami* and *Mikuma* had to be withdrawn from service less than a year after commissioning in order to rectify major faults in construction and also to improve stability. The welding defects were rectified and external bulges were added, the maximum speed being reduced to 35.9 knots in consequence. The lessons were immediately applied to *Suzuya* and *Kumano* both of which were still under construction.

ARMOUR

Belt 3.9in to 5.5in; deck 1.46in to 2in, all internal.

RE-ARMAMENT

1939–40: re-armed as heavy cruisers; from 1943: *Suzuya* and *Kumano* 20 × 25mm AA; January 1944: 30 × 25mm; July 1944: 50 × 25mm.

CAREERS

Mogami

Launched 14 March, 1934; completed 28 July, 1935; rebuilt April 1936 to February 1938; re-armed as heavy cruiser February 1939 to April 1940; severely damaged 5 June, 1942 by aircraft from USS *Enterprise* W of Midway Island; rebuilt as seaplane-carrier cruiser; severely damaged 5 November, 1943 at Rabaul by aircraft from USS *Saratoga* and *Princeton*; sunk 25 October, 1944 S of Bohol Island (09° 40′ N, 124° 50′ E) after night engagement with US light cruisers *Columbia*, *Denver*, and heavy cruisers *Minneapolis*, *Portland* and *Louisville* and collision with *Nachi*.

Mikuma

Launched 31 May, 1934; completed 29 August, 1935; rebuilt April 1936 to October 1937; re-armed as heavy cruiser May to October 1939; 5 June, 1942: in collision with *Mogami*; sunk 6 June W of Midway Island (29° 20′ N, 173° 30′ E) by aircraft from USS *Hornet* and *Enterprise*.

Suzuya

Launched 20 November, 1934; completed 31 October, 1937; re-armed as heavy cruiser February to December 1939; heavily damaged 25 October, 1944 by air attack during the battle of Samar, scuttled 11° 50′ N, 126° 25′ E by destroyer *Okinami*.

Kumano

Launched 15 October, 1936; completed 31 October, 1937; re-armed as heavy cruiser February to October 1939; torpedoed and damaged 25 October, 1944 during battle of Samar by US destroyer *Johnston*; damaged 26 October by air attack from TF 38; damaged 6 November off Cape Bolinao, Luzon, by US submarines *Guitarro*, *Bream* and *Raton*; towed to Dasol Bay, Luzon; sunk 25 November, 1944 by aircraft from USS *Ticonderoga*.

Above: *Mogami*, running trials in July 1935. These initial trials revealed a lack of stability, resulting from too much having been attempted on a small displacement. (Jentschura.)

Above: *Mikuma*, seen in service after interim modifications. (Jentschura.)

Below: *Suzuya* the third unit of the *Mogami* class.

Name	Builder	Date	Displ	Length ft in	Beam ft in	Draught ft in	Machinery	SHP	Speed	Fuel	Radius	Armament	Comp
TONE	Mitsubishi, Nagasaki	1934–1938	15200 F	649 7 wl	60 8	21 3	4 sets Kampon GT 8 Kampon boilers 4 shafts	152000	35.2	2950 Oil and AvGas	9000 @ 18	8 × 203mm (8in) 50-cal 8 × 127mm (5in) 40-cal DP 12 × 25mm AA 4 × 3 610mm (nominal rotating TT 5 aircraft 2 catapults	850
CHIKUMA		1935–1939	13320 N 11215 S	620 5 pp									

Tone class

GENERAL NOTES
2nd 1932 Supplementary Programme: originally designed as modified *Mogami*-class light cruisers within London Naval Treaty limitations of 8500ts and armed with 12 (4 × 3) 155mm guns. Floatplane-carrier cruisers, intended to operate with carrier task forces, providing long-range air scouting.

ARMOUR
Belt 3.9in to 5.7in; deck 2in to 2.2in.

RE-ARMAMENT
June 1944: 57 × 25mm AA.

CAREERS
Tone
Launched 21 November, 1937; completed 20 November, 1938; sunk 24 July, 1945 in shallow water near Kure (34° 14′ N, 132° 27′ E) by aircraft from US TF 38; salvaged and BU at Kure, 1948.
Chikuma
Launched 19 March, 1938; completed 20 May, 1939; severely damaged 25 October, 1944 by air torpedo attack from US TU 77.4.2 during battle of Samar and scuttled 11° 22′ N, 126° 16′ E by destroyer *Nowake*.

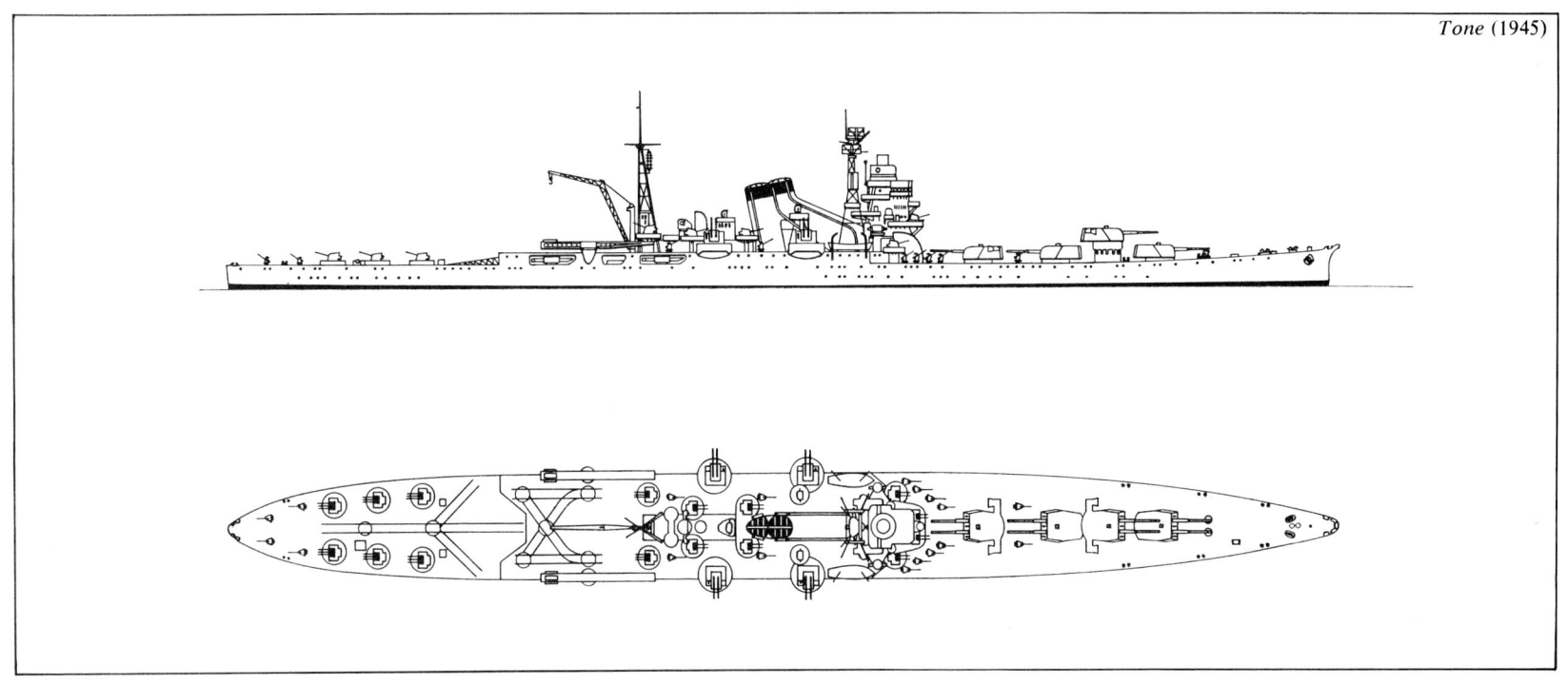

Tone (1945)

Name	Builder	Date	Displ	Length ft in	Beam ft in	Draught ft in	Machinery	SHP	Speed	Fuel	Radius	Armament	Comp
IBUKI Job No. 300)	Kure DY	1942–	14828 F	650 7 wl	63 0	19 10	4 sets GT 8 boilers 4 shafts	152000	33	2163	8150 @ 18	10 × 203mm (8in) 50-cal 8 × 127mm (5in) 40-cal DP 8 × 25mm AA 4 × 13.2mm 4 × 4 610mm (nominal rotating TT 3 aircraft 2 catapults	
Job No. 301 (neither completed – see p. 58)	Mitsubishi, Nagasaki	1942–	13890 N 12200 S	616 2 pp									

GENERAL NOTES
1941 Programme: intended as repeat *Tone*-class, but early war experience led to the rejection of the concept of concentration of armament forward; plans therefore altered to produce a repeat *Suzuya* design, incorporating all experience gained since her launch.

Ibuki (Job No. 300)
Launched 21 May, 1943; work suspended before decision to complete as an aircraft carrier (see p. 58).
Job No. 301
Laid down 1 June, 1942; work suspended July 1942 and material BU.

HEAVY CRUISERS

5. Cruising Ships 1857-1900

Name	Builder	Date	Displ	Length ft in	Beam ft in	Draught ft in	Machinery	SHP	Speed	Fuel	Radius	Armament	Comp
KANRIN ex-*Japan*	Fop Smit van Kinderdijk, Dordrecht	1857	700 F	163 0 wl	24 0	?	2-screw horizontal 1-cyl reciprocating machinery, rectangular boilers	100 nhp	6	?	?	12 guns	?
CHÔYÔ ex-*Yedo*	C. Gips & Sons, Dordrecht	1858	600 N	161 1 pp									

GENERAL NOTES
Screw despatch vessels with schooner-rig and wooden hull, ordered for the Shogun's fleet.

CAREERS
Kanrin
Launched 1856 and completed in 1857 as the *Japan*; delivered in Japan in August 1857 and renamed *Kanrin* (*Maru*?); in 1860 she made the first trans-Pacific crossing by a Japanese ship, when she visited San Francisco; in 1866 her machinery was replaced, and in 1868 she served under the rebel leader Enomoto; recaptured near Shimoda in April 1868 by the Government vessels *Fuji* (sometimes referred to in English sources as *Fujiyama*), *Musashi*, and *Hiryu*; taken over the same year by the Ministry of Finance; used as a transport by 1872, when she was wrecked near Hokkaido; later BU.
Choyo
Launched in 1856 and delivered in Japan as the *Yedo* in October 1858; renamed

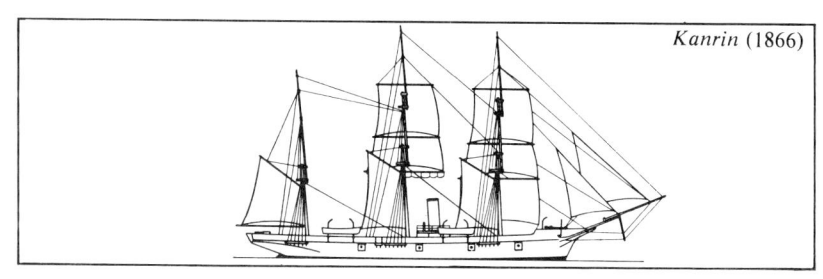

Kanrin (1866)

Choyo (*Maru*?) and rated as a corvette; in the Government fleet in 1868; training ship in 1869; sank 11 May, 1869 following a hit in the magazine during an action against the Enomoto rebels.

Name	Builder	Date	Displ	Length ft in	Beam ft in	Draught ft in	Machinery	SHP	Speed	Fuel	Radius	Armament	Comp
KANKO ex-*Soembing*	Amsterdam DY	1850–1852	781 N	172 10 oa / 170 0 wl	30 0	13 1	Paddle machinery, horizontal 1-cyl reciprocating, rectangular boilers	150 nhp	?	?	?	6 guns, including: 1 60pdr ML 2 long 30pdr ML 1 short 30pdr ML	?

GENERAL NOTES
A wooden despatch vessel with barque-rig, she was rated by the Dutch as a 3rd Class steamer (according to a model of this class in the Netherlands Historical Museum, Amsterdam).

CAREER
Launched 1852 and completed as the Dutch warship *Soembing*; given to the Shogun Iesada by the King of the Netherlands, and arrived in Japan in 1855; renamed *Kanko* and rated as a corvette; she became a training ship for the Shogunate fleet at Edo; joined the Government forces in 1868 and taken over by the Imperial Navy in 1869; BU in 1876.

Kanko (1870)

Name	Builder	Date	Displ	Length ft in	Beam ft in	Draught ft in	Machinery	SHP	Speed	Fuel	Radius	Armament	Comp
JINGEI	Yokosuka DY	1873–1881	1465	249 0 wl	31 2	14 5	Paddle, 1 diagonal 2-cyl reciprocating, 4 cyl boilers	1450 ihp	14	?	?	2 × 4.7in BL	170

GENERAL NOTES
A paddle despatch vessel, also rated as a corvette and as a royal yacht. She was the last wooden paddle vessel in the Japanese Navy, and took nine years to build, because of difficulties with her machinery.

CAREER
Launched in 1876 and completed in 1881 for service as a royal yacht and despatch vessel; stricken in 1894 and used as a training hull; BU subsequently.

Name	Builder	Date	Displ	Length ft in	Beam ft in	Draught ft in	Machinery	SHP	Speed	Fuel	Radius	Armament	Comp
FUJI	New York	1863–1865	1000 N	207 0 wl / 185 0 pp	33 9	10 9	Paddle, 1 horizontal direct-acting reciprocating engine; type of boilers unknown	350 nhp	13	?	?	1 × 6.3in MLR (?) / 2 × 5.9in (?) / 10 smaller guns	134

GENERAL NOTES
A fully-rigged paddle frigate, ordered for the Shogun's fleet.

RE-ARMAMENT AND RECONSTRUCTION NOTES
Later re-armed with 1 × 6.5in; 2 × 6in; new machinery in September 1868: 800 ihp = 9 knots. In 1876 the machinery was replaced.

CAREER
Launched in 1864 and completed in 1866; served in the Shogunate fleet, but in 1868 with the Government forces; in 1869 she was taken over by the Imperial Navy; training ship from January 1880; stricken May 1889 and hulked as a depot for torpedoes; sold August 1896.

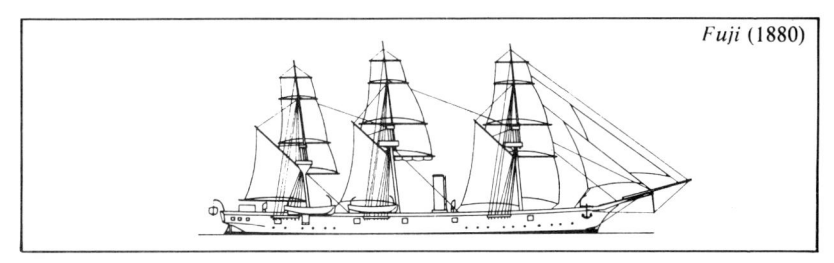

Fuji (1880)

Name	Builder	Date	Displ	Length ft in	Beam ft in	Draught ft in	Machinery	SHP	Speed	Fuel	Radius	Armament	Comp
KASUGA ex-*Kiangtse*	J. S. White, Cowes	1863	1289 N / 1015 BRT	248 6 wl / 212 0 pp	29 0	12 11	single horizontal reciprocating paddle machinery, type of boilers unknown	1217 ihp	9	?	?	1 × 7in ML (Forbes) / 4 × 4.5in BL / 2 × 30pdr ML	138 / 147

GENERAL NOTES
A fully-rigged wooden paddle frigate.

CAREER
Launched in 1863 and completed in 1863 (?) for China as the *Kiangtse* (properly spelled *Chiangtzu*); when the Imperial Chinese Government refused to ratify the purchase she was sold in 1867 to the Daimyo of Satsuma and renamed *Kasuga*; captured in 1868 at Hakodate by the Enomoto rebels; in 1869 she was taken over by the Imperial Navy; in 1894 she was a despatch vessel; stricken 1896 and BU.

Name	Builder	Date	Displ	Length ft in	Beam ft in	Draught ft in	Machinery	SHP	Speed	Fuel	Radius	Armament	Comp
YOSHUN ex-*Kaganokami* ex-*Sagamore*	unknown, Massachusetts	1861	530	178 9 wl / 167 3 pp	29 10	13 9	single (?)-shaft horizontal direct-acting reciprocating machinery, type of boilers unknown	280 ihp	12	?	?	6 guns	?

GENERAL NOTES
A fully-rigged wooden screw corvette
Launched in 1861 and completed the same year as the USS *Sagamore*; transferred in 1865 but sold to the Akita Clan in 1867 and renamed *Kaganokami*; in 1868 she joined the Shogun's fleet as the *Yoshun*; at the end of 1868 she was taken over by the Government forces, and in October 1870 taken over by the Ministry of Defence; sold in 1871 and BU.

Name	Builder	Date	Displ	Length ft in	Beam ft in	Draught ft in	Machinery	SHP	Speed	Fuel	Radius	Armament	Comp
TSUKUBA ex-*Malacca*	Mould, Moulmein (Burma)	1851–1855	1978 BOM	197 11 wl / 190 10 pp	35 1	17 10	single-screw horizontal direct-acting reciprocating, type of boilers unknown	526 ihp	10	?	?	6 × 4.5in BLR / 2 × 30pdr / 2 × 24pdr	275 / 301

Tsukuba (1880)

The old British sloop *Malacca* in Australia in April 1880, as the *Tsukuba*. (NMM.)

CRUISING SHIPS 1857–1900　89

GENERAL NOTES
An ex-Royal Navy wooden screw corvette with full ship-rig.

RE-ARMAMENT NOTES
From 1892 she was armed with 4 × 6in QF.

CAREER
Launched 9 April, 1853 and completed in 1854 as HMS *Malacca*; sold June 1869; re-sold to Japan in 1870 and renamed *Tsukuba*; in about 1900 she became a stationary training ship; stricken 1906 and BU.

Name	Builder	Date	Displ	Length ft in	Beam ft in	Draught ft in	Machinery	SHP	Speed	Fuel	Radius	Armament	Comp
NISSHIN	C. Gips & Sons, Dordrecht	1869	1490 N 780 BRT	203 1 pp	28 10	13 11	reciprocating machinery, number of shafts and boilers unknown	710 ihp	11	?	?	1 × 7in BLR (Armstrong) 6 × 30pdr	145

GENERAL NOTES
A wooden screw barque-rigged corvette, ordered for the Shogunate fleet.

RE-ARMAMENT NOTES
After 1888 she had 6 × 4.7in BL (Krupp).

CAREER
Launched 1869 and completed 1870 for the Hizen Clan; transferred to Imperial Navy in May 1870; re-rated as cruiser 1883; stricken 30 May 1892; BU 1893.

Nisshin (1880)

Name	Builder	Date	Displ	Length ft in	Beam ft in	Draught ft in	Machinery	SHP	Speed	Fuel	Radius	Armament	Comp
ASAMA ex-*Hokkai Maru*	unknown, France	1868	1422	228 8 pp	28 10	14 1	single-shaft horizontal compound reciprocating, boilers unknown	300 ihp	10	?	?	8 × 6.7in BL (Krupp) 4 × 4.5in BL	?

GENERAL NOTES
A screw composite-built corvette, built for the Hokkaido Transport Dept.

CAREER
Launched 1869 and completed July 1874 as the *Hokkai Maru*; taken over by Imperial Navy in 1874; gunnery training ship in 1887; stricken 3 March 1891 and hulked as a torpedo school at Yokosuka sold; 3 December 1896.

Name	Builder	Date	Displ	Length ft in	Beam ft in	Draught ft in	Machinery	SHP	Speed	Fuel	Radius	Armament	Comp
SEIKI	Yokosuka DY	1873–1876	897	203 9 wl 192 3 pp	30 6	13 1	single-shaft 3-cyl compound reciprocating machinery, 2 cyl boilers	443 ihp	9½	?	?	1 × 5.9in 22-cal BL (Krupp) 1 × 4.7in 25-cal BL (Krupp) 1 × 3in BL 1 × 47mm 3 × 1in Nordenfelt MGs	167

Seiki (1876)

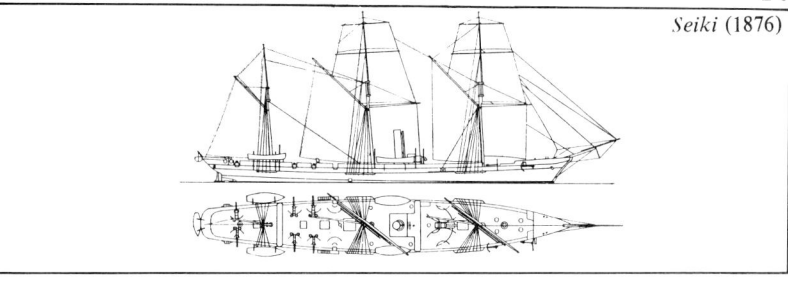

GENERAL NOTES
A despatch vessel or sloop-of-war with barque-rig, she was the first warship built at Yokosuka and the first wooden warship built in Japan. Designed by the French Verny shipyard.

CAREER
Launched 5 May, 1875 and completed June 1876; lost by stranding 7 December 1888 in the Fuji Estuary, off Suruga-wan (35° 07′ N, 138° 40′ E).

Name	Builder	Date	Displ	Length ft in	Beam ft in	Draught ft in	Machinery	SHP	Speed	Fuel	Radius	Armament	Comp
AMAGI	Yokosuka DY	1875–1878	1030 F 911 N	214 3 wl 204 0 pp	35 9	14 4	single-shaft 3-cyl compound reciprocating machinery, 2 cyl boilers	720 ihp	11	150 coal		1 × 6.7in BL (Krupp) 4 × 4.7in BL 3 × 3.1in BL 3 MGs	159

GENERAL NOTES
A wooden despatch vessel with barque-rig, built to the design of the French Verny shipyard.

RE-ARMAMENT NOTES
From 1898 she had 6 × 4.7in QF; 2 × 47mm.

CAREER
Launched March 1877 and completed April 1878; in 1898 she was re-rated as a gunboat; sold 1903 and BU.

Amagi

A French-designed wooden sloop built in 1875–8, *Amagi* was sold just before the war against Russia. (Shizuo Fukui.)

Name	Builder	Date	Displ	Length ft in	Beam ft in	Draught ft in	Machinery	SHP	Speed	Fuel	Radius	Armament	Comp
KAIMON	Yokosuka DY	1877–1884	1429 F 1350 N	210 10 pp	32 6	16 4	single-shaft 2-cyl compound reciprocating machinery, 4 cyl boilers	1267 ihp	12	197 coal	?	1 × 6.7in BL (Krupp) 6 × 4.5in BL (Krupp) 1 × 3in BL 4 MGs	210

GENERAL NOTES
A wooden despatch vessel built to a Japanese design.

CAREER
Launched September 1882 and completed 13 August, 1884; in 1894 she was employed as a transport; sunk by mine 5 July, 1904 off Nan!Nan-San-Shan Tao Island in Talien-Wan Bay (38° 50′ N, 121° 50′ E), with 16 dead.

Name	Builder	Date	Displ	Length ft in	Beam ft in	Draught ft in	Machinery	SHP	Speed	Fuel	Radius	Armament	Comp
TENRYÛ	Yokosuka DY	1878–1885	1525 N	210 3 pp	35 6	17 0	single-shaft horizontal compound machinery, 4 cyl boilers	1267 ihp	12	204	?	1 × 6.7in BL (Krupp) 6 × 4.7in BL (Krupp) 4 MGs 1 3in BL (Krupp)	214

GENERAL NOTES
A Japanese-designed wooden despatch vessel.

CAREER
Launched September 1883 and completed March 1885; served in 1894 as a transport; possibly sunk during the Russo-Japanese War; stricken 1906 and BU.

Name	Builder	Date	Displ	Length ft in	Beam ft in	Draught ft in	Machinery	SHP	Speed	Fuel	Radius	Armament	Comp
KATSURAGI	Yokosuka DY	1882–1887	1478 N	206 9 wl	35 0	15 3	single-shaft horizontal 2-cyl compound reciprocating machinery, 6 cyl boilers	1622 ihp	13	100 151 coal	?	2 × 6.7in BL (Krupp) 5 × 4.7in BL (Krupp) 1 × 3in QF (Krupp) 4 MGs 2 × 15in TT (AW?)	231
YAMATO	Onohama, Kobe	1883–1887		201 0 pp									
MUSASHI	Yokosuka DY	1884–1888											

Three composite sloops, or unprotected cruisers, were built in Japan during the years 1882–8. *Musashi* is seen here after her 1900 modernisation, which involved rearmament and the removal of her barque-rig. (Jentschura.)

A clearer view of *Yamato* after reconstruction, showing the forward gun embrasures (Shizuo Fukui.)

CRUISING SHIPS 1857–1900   91

GENERAL NOTES
Despatch vessels or unprotected cruisers of composite construction.

RE-ARMAMENT NOTES
After reconstruction they were armed with 8 × 47mm QF; 6 MGs and 2 × 18in TT.
After 1907 they were armed with 4 × 3in QF.

CAREERS
Katsuragi
Launched 31 March, 1885 and completed in October 1887; rated as a coast-defence ship in 1898; sank 13 October, 1900; raised in 1901 and repaired; in 1907 she became a survey ship; stricken 1912; sold 1913 and BU.
Yamato
Launched April 1885 and completed October 1887; rated as a coast-defence ship in 1898; stricken 1907 and became a survey ship; stricken 1935 and became a drillship in Uraga Harbour; she sank in a storm 18 September, 1945; BU in 1950.
Musashi
Launched 30 March, 1886 and completed February 1888; coast-defence ship in 1898; wrecked 30 April, 1902 near Nemoro but re-floated June 21; and repaired; converted 1922 to a survey ship; hulked as *Hai Kan No 5*, 6 July, 1928; BU 1931.

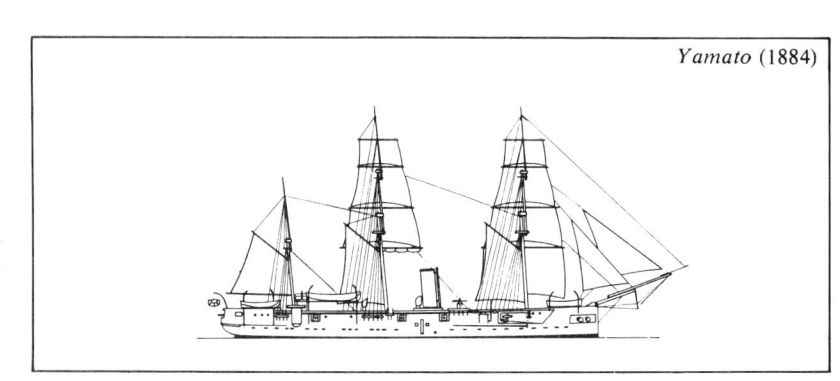

Yamato (1884)

Name	Builder	Date	Displ	Length ft in	Beam ft in	Draught ft in	Machinery	SHP	Speed	Fuel	Radius	Armament	Comp
TSUKUSHI ex-*Arturo Prat*	Armstrong, Mitchell & Co., Elswick	1879–1883	1542 F 1350 N	210 0 pp	32 0	17 6	2-shaft horizontal 2-cyl compound reciprocating machinery, 4 boilers	2600 ihp	16	250 / 300 coal	2887 @ 16½ 5000 @ 8	2 × 10in BL 4 × 4.7in BL 2 × 3in 4 × MGs 2 × 15in TT (AW?)	177 / 186

GENERAL NOTES
A Gunboat or partially protected cruiser of steel construction. She was designed by Sir Edward Reed for Chile, and had a ram-bow. Bought by Japan after completion.

RE-ARMAMENT NOTES
From 1898 she had 1 × 3in QF; 2 × 47mm QF; 2 MGs and 2 × 18in TT.

CAREER
Launched 11 August, 1880 and completed June 1883 for the Chilean Navy; in 1885 she was bought by the Japanese naval mission under Admiral Ito; in 1898 she was re-rated as a gunboat; stricken 1906 and re-rated as a training ship; BU about 1910.

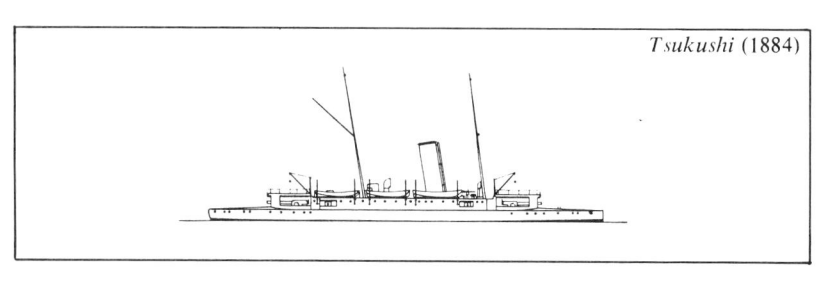

Tsukushi (1884)

Name	Builder	Date	Displ	Length ft in	Beam ft in	Draught ft in	Machinery	SHP	Speed	Fuel	Radius	Armament	Comp
TAKAO	Yokosuka DY	1886–1889	1927 F 1750 N	232 11 wl 231 0 pp	34 6	13 2	2-shaft horizontal 2-cyl compound reciprocating machinery, 5 cyl boilers	2332 ihp	15	300 coal	3000 @ 10	4 × 6in QF 1 × 4.7in QF 1 × 57mm 2 MGs 2 × 15in TT (AW?)	222 / 250

GENERAL NOTES
Despatch vessel or unprotected cruiser of steel and iron construction. She was designed by Emile Bertin and had a double-bottom.

RE-ARMAMENT NOTES
About 1900 she was armed with 4 × 6in QF; 2 × 47mm; 6 MGs; 2 × 18in TT.

CAREER
Launched 15 October 1888, completed 16 November 1889; March 1898 re-rated as a 3rd Class coast-defence ship; stricken 1 April 1911 but served as a survey ship until 1918, and then BU.

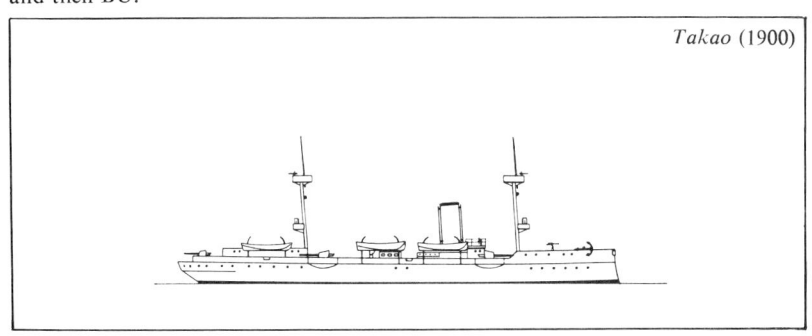

Takao (1900)

Seen here at Sasebo on 23rd July 1905, *Takao* was an unprotected sloop designed by the great Frenchman Emile Bertin in 1885. In 1900 her rig was cut down and her armament modernised (Shizuo Fukui.)

CRUISING SHIPS 1857–1900

Name	Builder	Date	Displ	Length ft in	Beam ft in	Draught ft in	Machinery,	SHP	Speed	Fuel	Radius	Armament	Comp
YAEYAMA	Yokosuka DY	1887–1892	1584 N	317 11 pp	34 6	13 4	2-shaft horizontal 3-cyl triple-expansion machinery, 6 cyl boilers	5400 ihp	21	350 coal	5000 @ 10	3 × 4.7in QF (Krupp) 8 × 47mm 2 × 15in TT (AW)	217

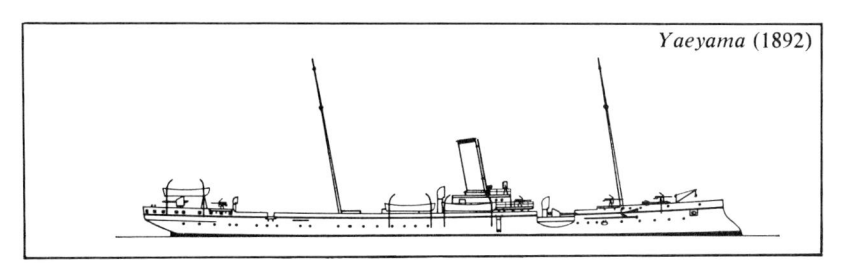

Yaeyama (1892)

GENERAL NOTES
A steel unprotected cruiser designed by Emile Bertin.

RECONSTRUCTION NOTES
Reboilered in 1902, with 8 Niclausse boilers. In 1906–8 she was the trials ship for the introduction of oil-firing.

CAREER
Launched March 1889, completed March 1892; stranded 11 May, 1902 near Nemoro, and towed off 1 September; repaired and reboilered; stricken 1906 but used for trials with oil-fired boilers; stricken 1911 and BU.

Name	Builder	Date	Displ	Length ft in	Beam ft in	Draught ft in	Machinery	SHP	Speed	Fuel	Radius	Armament	Comp
CHISHIMA	Société des Chantiers de la Loire, St. Nazaire	1890–1892	741 N	232 11 pp	25 3	16 1	2-shaft VTE 4 boilers	3500 ihp	22	?	?	2 × 4.7in QF 4 × 47mm 4 × 18in TT (AW)	?

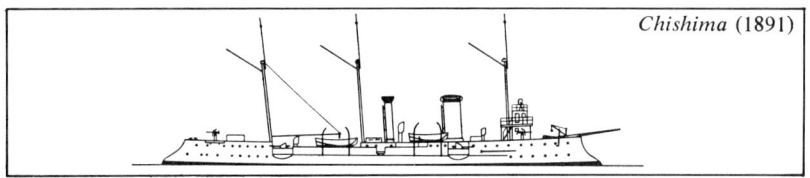

Chishima (1891)

GENERAL NOTES
An unprotected cruiser, designed by Emile Bertin.

CAREER
Launched November 1890, completed April 1892; sunk 30 November, 1892 in collision with the British steamer *Ravenna* while on a voyage from Nagasaki to Kobe in the Inland Sea.

Name	Builder	Date	Displ	Length ft in	Beam ft in	Draught ft in	Machinery	SHP	Speed	Fuel	Radius	Armament	Comp
TATSUTA	Armstrong, Mitchell & Co., Elswick	1893–1894	830 N	240 0 pp	27 6	9 6	2-shaft 3-cyl VTE 4 cyl boilers	5000 ihp	21	200 coal	?	2 × 4.7in QF 4 × 47mm 5 × 37mm 5 × 15in TT (AW)	107

The torpedo gunboat *Tatsuta* was completed in England in 1894. (NMM.)

CRUISING SHIPS 1857–1900

GENERAL NOTES
An unprotected cruiser, ordered as a replacement for the *Chishima*.

RE-ARMAMENT AND RECONSTRUCTION NOTES
Reboiled in 1903 with 4 Kampon boilers (3 funnels), and re-armed in 1905 with 2 × 4.7in QF; 4 × 3in QF; 5 × 18in TT.

CAREER
Launched 6 April, 1894, completed August 1894; wrecked 15 May, 1904 on Kuan Lun Tao in the Elliot Islands (39° 08′ N, 122° 22′ E); salvaged and completed repairs at Yokosuka by 30 August, 1904; in 1918 she was a submarine depot- and repair-ship, and renamed *Nagaura* (*Maru*); stricken 1925 and BU.

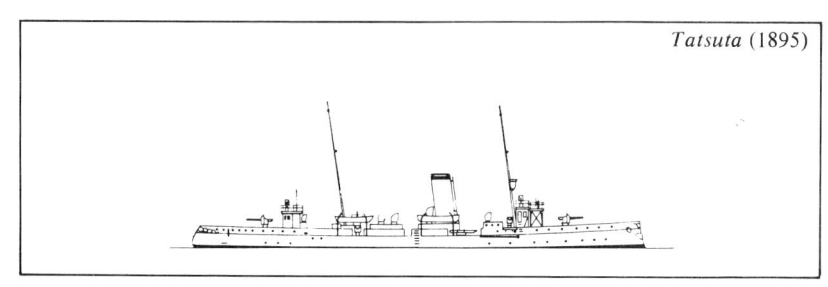

Tatsuta (1895)

Name	Builder	Date	Displ	Length ft in	Beam ft in	Draught ft in	Machinery	SHP	Speed	Fuel	Radius	Armament	Comp
KOHEI-GO ex-*Kuang-P'ing*	Foochow DY, China	? – 1892	1335 N	262 6 pp	30 6	13 5	details unknown	2400 ihp	17	?	?	3 × 4.7in 40-cal QF 4 × 47mm 4 MGs 4 × 15in TT (AW?)	?

Kohei-go, a little torpedo gunboat captured from the Chinese as the *Kuang P'ing* in 1895. This photograph was taken shortly before her loss in a storm off the Pescadores Islands. (Shizuo Fukui.)

GENERAL NOTES
Steel-built despatch vessel or torpedo-gunboat built for China.

CAREER
Launched in 1891 and completed 1892 for the Imperial Chinese Navy; captured at Wei-hai-wei 12 February, 1895 and renamed 17 February; foundered 21 December, 1895 in a storm near the Pescadores Islands

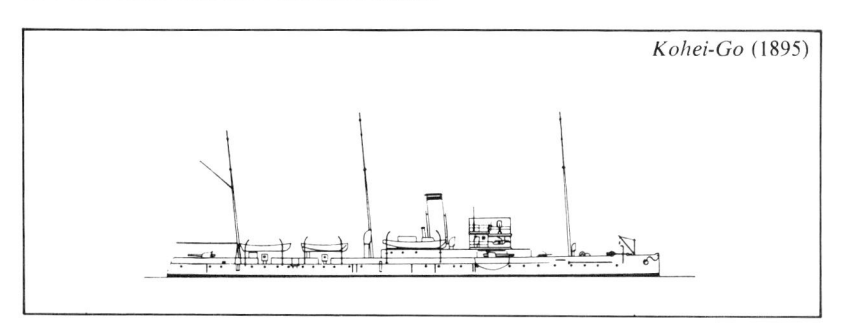

Kohei-Go (1895)

Name	Builder	Date	Displ	Length ft in	Beam ft in	Draught ft in	Machinery	SHP	Speed	Fuel	Radius	Armament	Comp
MIYAKO	Kure DY	1894–1890	1772 N	315 0 pp	34 5	14 0	2-shaft 3-cyl VTE 8 cyl boilers	6130 ihp	20	400 coal	5000 @ 10	2 × 4.7in 40-cal QF 10 × 47mm 2 × 15in TT (AW?)	217

A small sloop or unprotected cruiser, *Miyako* resembled contemporary British types. (Shizuo Fukui.)

94 CRUISING SHIPS 1857–1900

Miyako (1903)

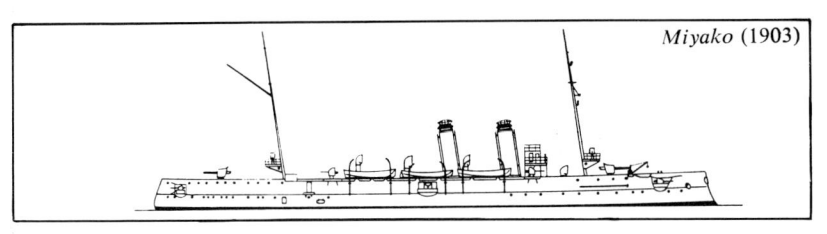

GENERAL NOTES
Built under the 1894 Programme as 'cruiser-type despatch vessels.

CAREER
Launched October 1898 and completed March 1899; mined and sunk 14 May, 1904 off Cape Robinson, NE of Port Arthur (39° 02′ N, 121° 22½′ E) with only 8 survivors; hull later salvaged and BU.

Name	Builder	Date	Displ	Length ft in	Beam ft in	Draught ft in	Machinery	SHP	Speed	Fuel	Radius	Armament	Comp
CHIHAYA	Yokosuka DY	1898–1901	1464 F 1243 N	287 8 oa 272 11 pp	31 7	9 10	2-shaft 3-cyl VTE 4 Normand boilers	6100 ihp	21	250 / 344 coal	?	2 × 4.7in 40-cal QF 4 × 3in (12pdr) QF 5 × 18in TT (AW?)	125 / 163

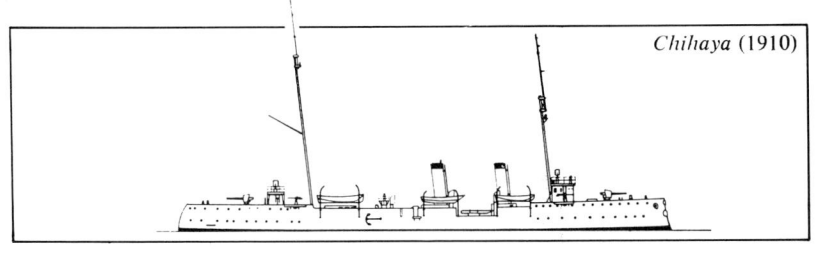

Chihaya (1910)

GENERAL NOTES
An unprotected cruiser built under the Post-war Programme of 1896–7.

MACHINERY NOTES
On trials she reached 5700 ihp = 21.43 knots, @ 1268ts.

CAREER
Launched 26 May, 1900 and completed September 1901; stricken 1927 and served as a cadets' training ship at Etajima Naval Academy until 1939; she was still in existence as a hulk at the Urazaki Depot in Kure in August 1945.

Chihaya was similar to *Miyako*, but had smaller funnels. (Shizuo Fukui.)

6. Protected Cruisers

Name	Builder	Date	Displ	Length ft in	Beam ft in	Draught ft in	Machinery	SHP	Speed	Fuel	Radius	Armament	Comp
NANIWA TAKACHIHO	Armstrong, Mitchell & Co., Low Walker	1884–1886	4150 F 3650 N	299 0 pp	46 0	18 6	3-shaft horizontal 2-cyl compound reciprocating machinery, 6 cyl boilers	7500 ihp	18	350 / 800 coal	8880 @ 10 3480 @ 14½	2 × 10.2in 35-cal (Krupp) 6 × 5.9in 35-cal (Krupp) 6 × 47mm 14 MGs 4 × 15in TT (AW)	338 / 365

GENERAL NOTES
These 2nd Class cruisers were ordered in England by Admiral Ito's Naval Mission, and were the first steel cruisers in the Japanese Navy. Their ram-bows were made of mild steel. They were designed by W. H. White, and achieved 18.7 knots with 7604 ihp. When built, they were the most powerful cruisers in the world.

ARMOUR
Decks 3in to 2in; barbettes 10in to 1½in; CT 2in.

RE-ARMAMENT NOTES
In 1900–1 they were re-armed with 8 × 6in 40-cal QF; 2 × 57mm; 2 MGs; 4 × 18in TT (AW). *Takachiho* converted to a minelayer in 1907.

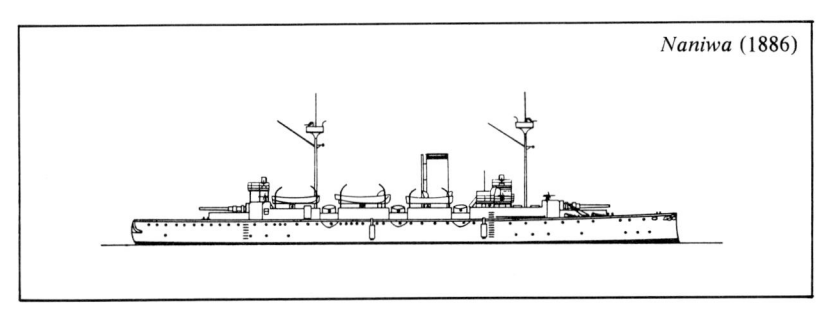

Naniwa (1886)

PROTECTED CRUISERS 95

CAREERS
Naniwa
Launched 18 March 1885 and completed 1 December 1885; from 14 December, 1891 to February 1895 she was commanded by the future Admiral Togo, and fired the opening shot of the Sino-Japanese War 25 July 1894 against the Chinese cruiser *Ch'i Yuan*; on 26 June, 1912 she was wrecked on Uruppu Island in the Kuriles (46° 30′ N, 15° 10′ E) and became a total loss on 18 July, wreck abandoned 5 August.
Takachiho
Launched 16 May, 1885 and completed 26 March, 1886; converted to a minelayer in 1907; on 18 October, 1914 she was torpedoed by the German TB *S. 90* 60 m off Tsingtau (264 dead).

Naniwa, one of the famous 'Elswick' protected cruisers, seen coaling at Malta on her way out to Japan, towards the end of 1885. (Shizuo Fukui.)

Name	Builder	Date	Displ	Length ft in	Beam ft in	Draught ft in	Machinery	SHP	Speed	Fuel	Radius	Armament	Comp
UNEBI	Société des Forges et Chantiers, Le Havre	1884–1886	3615 N	321 6 pp	42 8	18 9	2-shaft horizontal 3-cyl VTE 6 cyl boilers	6000 ihp	17½	?	5600 @ 10	4 × 9.4in 35-cal BL (Krupp) 7 × 5.9in 35-cal BL 2 × 47mm 14 MGs 4 × 15in TT (AW)	280

GENERAL NOTES
A 2nd Class cruiser designed by Ing. Marmièsse. Her elongated ram-bow was made of steel. To reduce topweight the hull was given exaggerated 'tumblehome', and so the 9.4in guns had to be sponsoned out. The weight of guns was 400ts = 11% of the total displacement. She had a three-masted barque-rig, with a sail area of more than 12000 sq ft, and this probably contributed to her loss.

ARMOUR
Deck 2.3in; CT ¾in. Depth of belt 27.9ft.

CAREER
Launched 6 April, 1886, completed October 1886; taken over 3 December, 1886; lost by foundering in October 1887 while *en route* from Singapore to Japan.

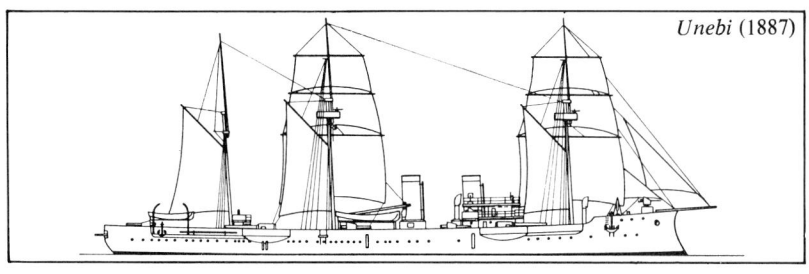

Unebi (1887)

A protected cruiser, *Unebi* was designed by M. Marmièsse and built in France; she is seen here at Le Havre. (Shizuo Fukui.)

Name	Builder	Date	Displ	Length ft in	Beam ft in	Draught ft in	Machinery	SHP	Speed	Fuel	Radius	Armament	Comp
ITSUKUSHIMA MATSUSHIMA	Société des Forges et Chantiers, La Seyne	1888–1891	4217 N	301 2 wl 294 11 pp	51 1	19 10	2-shaft horizontal 3-cyl triple-expansion machinery, 6 cyl boilers	5400 ihp	16½	400 / 680 coal	6000 @ 10	1 × 12.6in 38-cal (Canet) 11 × 4.7in 40-cal QF 5 × 57mm 11 × 47mm 4 × 5in TT	360 / 430
HASHIDATE	Yokosuka DY	1888–1894											

GENERAL NOTES
These 2nd Class cruisers were designed by Emile Bertin, who also reorganised the Japanese dockyards. *Hashidate* was built to the same plans, and was the first armoured ship to be built in Japan. She took almost 6½ years to build.

ARMOUR
Harvey steel. Deck 1½in; turret 12in; barbette 3.9in.

RE-ARMAMENT AND RECONSTRUCTION NOTES
In 1901 *Itsukushima* and *Matsushima* were reboilered with 8 Belleville boilers; *Hashidate* was given 8 Miyabara boilers in 1902.

CAREERS
Itsukushima
Launched 11 July, 1889, completed August 1891; damaged 2 September, 1894 by 8 hits (8 dead); repaired and became a training ship from 1906 to 1918; stricken 1919 and used as a submarine tender until 1922; BU.
Matsushima
Launched 22 January, 1890, completed March 1891; badly damaged by gunfire from Chinese battleships in the battle of the Yalu River 17 September, 1894, but repaired subsequently; training ship in 1906; lost 30 April, 1908 by a magazine explosion in Makung Harbour in the Pescadores Islands (141 dead).

Hashidate
Launched 24 March, 1891, completed June 1894; rated as a coast-defence ship; training ship from 1906 to 1918; from 1918 to 1923 she was a training ship for conscripts, but stricken in 1923 and used as a training hulk for seamen and boys until 1927; BU.

Itsukushima (1889)

French influence over Japanese shipbuilding lasted until the end of the 1880s. Among the last French ships built for Japan were three 2nd Class cruisers, armed with one 12.6-inch Canet gun. *Itsukushima* is seen here at Toulon in 1891. (Marius Bar/Havet Collection.)

Matsushima (1890)

In 1901, *Itsukushima* was modernised and lost the trailing struts to her mast. She is seen here at Sasebo on 30th June, 1905. (Shizuo Fukui.)

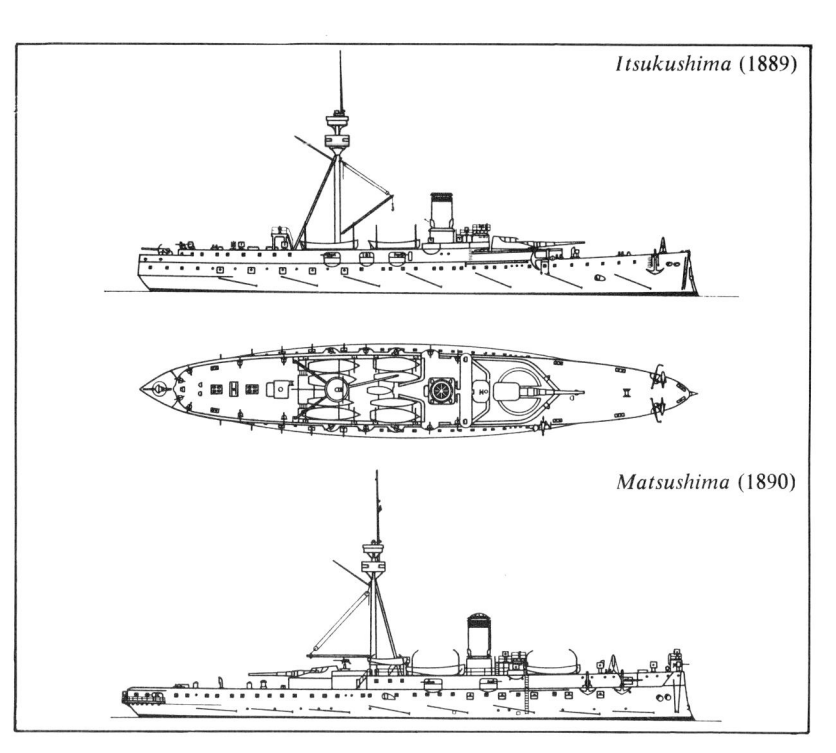

Matsushima differed from her two sisters in having the 12.6-inch Canet gun aft, theoretically giving her better seakeeping. She was sunk by a magazine explosion in 1908. (Marius Bar.)

Name	Builder	Date	Displ	Length ft in	Beam ft in	Draught ft in	Machinery	SHP	Speed	Fuel	Radius	Armament	Comp
AKITSUSHIMA	Yokosuka DY	1890–1894	3100 N	301 11 wl 300 10 pp	33 1	17 5	2-shaft horizontal 3-cyl triple-expansion machinery, 6 cyl boilers	8516 ihp	19	550 coal	?	1 × 12.6in 38-cal (Canet) 12 × 4.7in 42-cal QF 8 × 47mm 4 × 15in TT	330

Akitsushima originally mounted a Canet gun, like the *Itsukushima* class, but in 1894–5 she was reconstructed and given a more conventional armament of 6-inch and 4.7-inch guns. (Shizuo Fukui.)

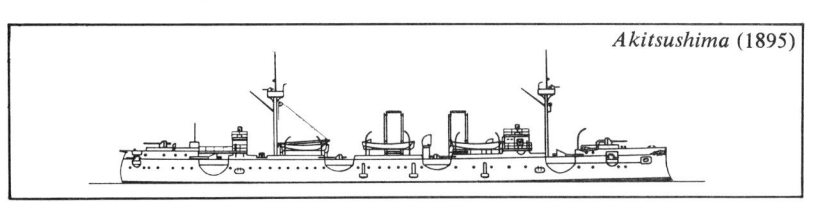

Akitsushima (1895)

PROTECTED CRUISERS 97

GENERAL NOTES
This 3rd Class cruiser was the last warship to be built of imported steel.

ARMOUR
Deck 3in to 1½in.

RE-ARMAMENT AND RECONSTRUCTION NOTES
About 1894–5 she was re-armed with 4 × 6in 40-cal QF; 6 × 4.7in 40-cal QF; 18 × 47mm; 4 × 18in TT (AW). In 1908 her cylindrical boilers were replaced by Miyabara type.

CAREER
Launched 6 July, 1892, completed February 1894; stricken in 1921 and converted to a submarine depot-ship; BU in 1927.

Name	Builder	Date	Displ	Length ft in	Beam ft in	Draught ft in	Machinery	SHP	Speed	Fuel	Radius	Armament	Comp
YOSHINO	Armstrong, Mitchell & Co., Elswick	1892–1893	4150 N	360 pp 0	46 6	17 0	2-shaft 4-cyl compound 12 boilers	15750 ihp	23	350 / 1000 coal	9000 @ 10	4 × 6in 40-cal QF 8 × 4.7in 40-cal QF 22 × 47mm 5 × 14in TT (AW)	360

GENERAL NOTES
A 2nd Class cruiser designed by Philip Watts. The machinery was built by Humphrys & Tennant, and in her day she was the fastest cruiser in the world.

ARMOUR
Harvey steel. Deck 4½in to 1½in guns 4in; CT 4in.

RE-ARMAMENT NOTES
About 1900 re-armed with 5 × 18in TT (AW).

CAREER
Launched 20 December, 1892, completed September 1893; sunk in collision with the armoured cruiser *Kasuga* 15 May, 1904 N of the Chang Tuan promontory (about 03.30 hrs 38° 07′ N, 122° 33′ E); the cruiser's ram hit *Yoshino* on the port side, high up in the engine room, and she sank with only 19 survivors.

Yoshino (1892)

Another of the long series of Elswick cruisers, *Yoshino* was designed by Sir Philip Watts, and enjoyed a high reputation after her performance in the war against China. (Bundesarchiv.)

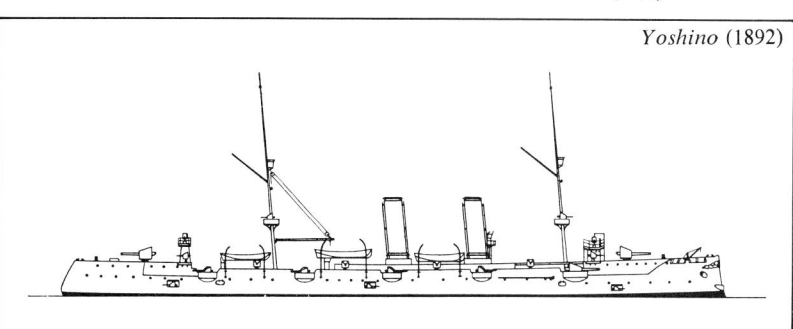

Another view of *Yoshino*, at Yokosuka in 1894. (Shizuo Fukui.)

Name	Builder	Date	Displ	Length ft in	Beam ft in	Draught ft in	Machinery	SHP	Speed	Fuel	Radius	Armament	Comp
IZUMI ex-*Esmeralda*	Armstrong, Mitchell & Co., Elswick	1881–1884	2920 N	270 pp 0	42 0	18 3	2-shaft horizontal 2-cyl compound reciprocating machinery, double-ended boilers	5500 ihp	18	400 / 600 coal	2200 @ 10	2 × 10in 30-cal 6 × 6in 26-cal BL 2 × 57mm 7 MGs 3 × 15in TT (AW)	300

Izumi seen here at Kure in 1905. (Shizuo Fukui.)

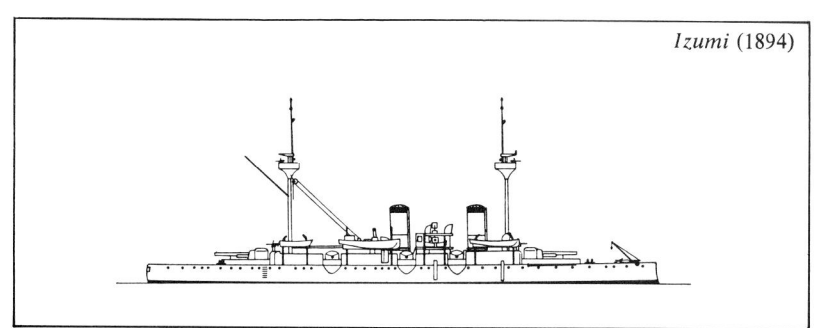

Izumi (1894)

98   PROTECTED CRUISERS

GENERAL NOTES
A 3rd Class cruiser originally designed by George Rendel for Chile.

ARMOUR
Deck 3in to 1in; guns 2¼in; CT 2in.

RE-ARMAMENT NOTES
(1) about 1899 she was armed with 2 × 10in; 6 × 4.7in 40-cal; 2 × 57mm; 6 × 47mm; 3 × 15in TT.

(2) In 1901/2 she was armed with 2 × 6in 40-cal QF; 6 × 4.7in 40-cal QF; 2 × 57mm; 6 × 47mm; 3 × 18in TT. After this refit she displaced 2800ts and developed 6500 ihp.

CAREER
Launched 6 June, 1883 and completed 15 July, 1884 as the Chilean *Esmeralda*; transferred 15, November 1894 via Ecuador as a 'cargo vessel'; served in various subsidiary roles until stricken 1 April 1912; BU.

Name	Builder	Date	Displ	Length ft in	Beam ft in	Draught ft in	Machinery	SHP	Speed	Fuel	Radius	Armament	Comp
SAI-EN ex-*Ch'i-Yüan*	AG Vulcan, Stettin	1880–1885	2440 N	246 0 wl 236 3 pp	35 0	15 4	2-shaft compound reciprocating machinery, 2 cyl boilers	2800 ihp	15	230 coal	?	2 × 8.3in 35-cal 1 × 5.9in 35-cal 4 × 57mm 9 MGs 4 × 15in TT (AW?)	200/254

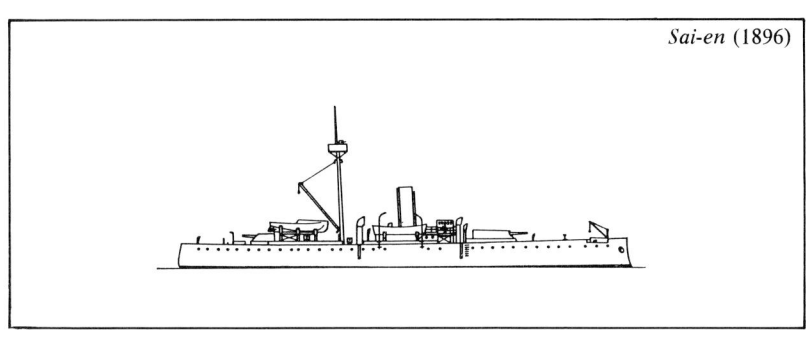

Sai-en (1896)

Left: *Sai-en*. (Bundesarchiv.)

GENERAL NOTES
A 3rd Class cruiser built for China.

ARMOUR
Compound (iron faced with steel). Deck 3in; guns 9.8in to 2in.

RE-ARMAMENT NOTES
About 1898 she was re-armed with 2 × 8.3in; 1 × 5.9in; 8 × 47mm; 4 × 18in TT.

CAREER
Launched in 1883 and completed in 1885 for the Chinese Navy as the *Ch'i-Yüan*; damaged 25 July and again on 17 September, 1894 by Japanese units; fell into Japanese hands 12 February 1895 at Wei Hai Wei and renamed *Sai-en*; sank 30 November, 1904 after striking a mine W of Port Arthur (38° 51′ N, 121° 05′ E).

Name	Builder	Date	Displ	Length ft in	Beam ft in	Draught ft in	Machinery	SHP	Speed	Fuel	Radius	Armament	Comp
SUMA AKASHI	Yokosuka DY	1892–1896 1894–1899	2657 N 2756 N	306 8 wl *Suma* 295 3 pp *Akashi*	40 1 *Suma* 41 8 *Akashi*	15 1 *Suma* 15 9 *Akashi*	2-shaft 3-cyl VTE 8 cyl boilers *Akashi* 9 single-ended boilers	*Suma* 8384 ihp *Akashi* 7890 ihp	20 19½	200/600 coal	12000 @ 10	2 × 6in 40-cal QF 6 × 4.7in 40-cal QF 10 × 47mm 4 × 42mm 4 MGs 2 × 15in TT	275

GENERAL NOTES
These 3rd Class cruisers were the first armoured warships built with Japanese material, in a Japanese yard, to Japanese plans. They had fighting tops, and *Akashi* could be distinguished by her higher foremast with a W/T aerial. *Suma* proved a bad seaboat because she lacked stability, and so *Akashi* was modified during construction.

ARMOUR
Harvey steel. Deck 2in to 1in

MACHINERY
Suma's cylindrical boilers were replaced by Miyabara type in 1908; *Akashi* had her boilers replaced by 9 Niclausse type in 1912.

CAREERS
Suma
Launched March 1895, completed December 1896; disarmed in 1922 under Washington Treaty; stricken 1923; hulked and BU in 1928.

Left: *Akashi* is seen here as completed, and before she was fitted with a topmast carrying radio aerials. (Shizuo Fukui.)

PROTECTED CRUISERS 99

Akashi
Launched 18 December, 1897, completed March 1899; damaged by mine 11 m S of Port Arthur, 10 December, 1904; repaired by April 1905, and later became a training ship; in 1922 she was disarmed under the terms of the Washington Treaty; stricken 1923; hulked and renamed *Hai Kan No 2* on 6 July, 1928; sunk in August 1930 in Tokyo Bay as a target for aerial torpedoes.

Name	Builder	Date	Displ	Length ft in	Beam ft in	Draught ft in	Machinery	SHP	Speed	Fuel	Radius	Armament	Comp
TAKASAGO	Armstrong, Mitchell & Co., Elswick	1896–1898	5260 F 4160 N	387 8 oa 360 0 pp	47 6	17 0	2-shaft 4-cyl compound 4 single-ended and 4 double-ended boilers	15500 ihp	23½	800 / 1000 coal	5500 @ 10	2 × 8in 40-cal QF 10 × 4.7in 40-cal QF 12 × 3in 40-cal QF 6 × 47mm 5 × 18in TT (AW)	425

GENERAL NOTES
A 2nd Class cruiser built under the Post-war Programmes of 1896–7, she was designed by Philip Watts.

ARMOUR
Harvey steel. Deck 4½in; guns 4½in to 2in; CT 4½in.

MACHINERY NOTES
On trials she reached 22.9 knots with 12990 ihp on 4463ts.

CAREER
Launched 18 May, 1897, completed 6 April, 1898; mined and sunk on night of 12/13 December 1904 37 m S of Port Arthur (38° 10′ N, 121° 15′ E).

Takasago was completed in 1898, as a 2nd Class cruiser armed with 8-inch guns — a heavy armament for a vessel displacing only 5,000 tons. (Shizuo Fukui.)

Name	Builder	Date	Displ	Length ft in	Beam ft in	Draught ft in	Machinery	SHP	Speed	Fuel	Radius	Armament	Comp
KASAGI	Wm Cramp & Sons, Philadelphia	1896–1898	6066 (K) F 4900 N	401 9 oa 374 6 pp	48 10	20 9	2-shaft 4-cyl compound 12 single-ended boilers	12500 ihp	22.7	350 / 1000 coal	4200 @ 11½	2 × 8in 45-cal QF 10 × 4.7in 40-cal QF 12 × 3in 40-cal QF 6 × 42mm 5 × 18in TT (AW)	440
CHITOSE	Union Iron-works, San Francisco		5598 (C) F 4760 N	395 0 oa 377 0 pp	49 2	19 9			22.9		4500 @ 11		

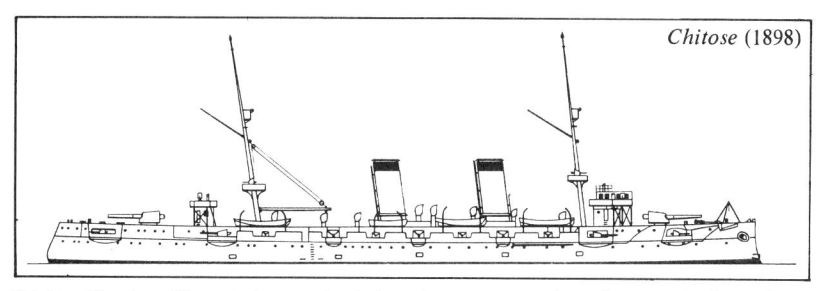

Chitose (1898)

Right: The two *Kasagi* class protected cruisers were an American equivalent of *Takasago*, but they displaced about 1,000 tons more. *Kasagi* is seen here at Toulon in 1898. (Marius Bar.)

GENERAL NOTES
Ordered under the Post-war Programme of 1896–7, these 2nd Class cruisers were an improved *Yoshino* design. They were the first warships purchased from the USA since 1865, a gesture to show Japan's gratitude for American neutrality in the Sino-Japanese War.

Chitose, in Japanese waters at about the time of the war against Russia. (Shizuo Fukui.)

RE-ARMAMENT AND RECONSTRUCTION
In 1912 *Chitose* was reboilered with Miyabara boilers; *Kasagi* similarly reboilered in 1910. In 1924 *Chitose* was armed with 10 × 3.1in 40-cal and 1 × 3.1in AA guns.

ARMOUR
Harvey steel. Deck 4½in to 1¾in; guns 4½in.

MACHINERY
On trials *Kasagi* reached 22¾ knots with 13492 ihp on 5416ts.

CAREERS
Kasagi
Launched 20 January, 1898, completed December 1898; badly damaged 27 May, 1905 at battle of Tsushima by gunfire from Russian cruiser *Svjetlana*; repaired subsequently; training ship from 1910 to 1916; wrecked 20 July, 1916 in Tsugaru Straits during an attempt to assist a merchant ship in distress; the wreck was abandoned as a total loss 13 August, 1916.

Chitose
Launched 23 January, 1898 and completed in March 1899; disarmed in 1922 to comply with the Washington Treaty and re-rated as a 2nd Class coast-defence ship; stricken and renamed *Hai Kan No 1* 6 July, 1928; sunk 19 July, 1931 as an aircraft and gunnery target in Saeki Bay, Bungo Straits.

Name	Builder	Date	Displ	Length ft in	Beam ft in	Draught ft in	Machinery	SHP	Speed	Fuel	Radius	Armament	Comp
NIITAKA	Yokosuka DY	1902–1904	3716 F	339 3 wl	44 1	16 1	2-shaft 4-cyl compound 16 Niclausse boilers	9400 ihp	20	280 / 600 coal	4000 @ 10	6 × 6in 40-cal QF 10 × 3in 40-cal QF 4 × 42mm	320
TSUSHIMA	Kure DY	1901–1904	3366 N 3120 S	334 8 pp									

GENERAL NOTES
3rd Class cruisers built under the Post-war Programme of 1896–7.

ARMOUR
Krupp steel. Deck 2½in to 1½in; CT 4in.

RE-ARMAMENT
In 1924 *Tsushima* had 8 × 3.1in 40-cal and 1 × 3.1in AA.

CAREERS
Niitaka
Launched 15 November, 1902 and completed 27 January, 1904; on 1 September, 1921 she was re-rated as a 2nd Class coast-defence ship; foundered in a typhoon off the coast of Kamchatka 26 August, 1922 (284 dead); the wreck was abandoned.

Tsushima
Launched 15 December, 1902, completed 14 February, 1904; re-rated as a 2nd Class coast-defence ship; disarmed 1930 and stricken 1936; served as *Hai Kan No. 10* at Yokosuka until 1939; a hulk by 1944, when she was sunk, probably by US aircraft.

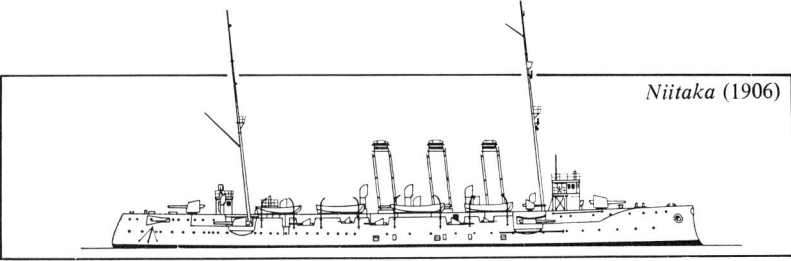

Niitaka (1906)

Tsushima resembled the small cruisers built for the Royal Navy, both in appearance and disposition of guns. (Shizuo Fukui.)

PROTECTED CRUISERS 101

Name	Builder	Date	Displ	Length ft in	Beam ft in	Draught ft in	Machinery	SHP	Speed	Fuel	Radius	Armament	Comp
OTOWA	Yokosuka DY	1903–1904	3388 3000 N 2800 S	340 9 oa 321 6 pp	41 5	15 11	2-shaft 4-cyl compound 10 Kampon boilers	10000 ihp	21	600 $\overline{875}$ coal	7000 @ 10	2 × 6in 50-cal QF 6 × 4.7in 40-cal QF 4 × 3in 40-cal QF 2 MGs 2 × 18in TT (AW)	320

GENERAL NOTES
A 3rd Class cruiser built under the Post-war Programme of 1896–7.

ARMOUR
Harvey-nickel steel. Deck 3in to 2in; guns 1½in; CT 4in.

CAREERS
Launched 2 November, 1903 and completed 6 September, 1904; wrecked 25 July, 1917 near Daio Saki, Mieken, Shima Hanto (approx 34° 14′ N, 136° 53′ E); the hull broke in two and the wreck was later abandoned; stricken in 1917.

Otowa was slightly smaller than *Niitaka* and *Tsushima*, but otherwise similar. She is seen here at Kobe on 3rd September 1906. (Shizuo Fukui.)

Name	Builder	Date	Displ	Length ft in	Beam ft in	Draught ft in	Machinery	SHP	Speed	Fuel	Radius	Armament	Comp
TSUGARU ex-*Pallada*	Franco-Russian Yard, St. Petersburg	1896–1902	6932 F 6731 N	413 3 wl 399 11 pp	55 9	21	2-shaft VTE 24 Belleville boilers	11600 ihp	20	910 $\overline{1430}$ coal	3700 @ 10	8 × 6in 45-cal QF 22 × 3in 60-cal QF 8 × 37mm 4 × 18in TT	422 $\overline{570}$

GENERAL NOTES
An ex-Russian protected cruiser, built under the 1895–6 Programme. Her sisters were the *Diana* and *Aurora*.

ARMOUR
Harvey-nickel steel. Deck 2½in to 2in; CT 6in.

RE-ARMAMENT AND RECONSTRUCTION NOTES
Rebuilt at Sasebo and recommissioned in 1910, with Miyabara boilers and 8 × 6in; 22 × 3in guns. After 1920 she had only 7 × 6in and carried 300 mines.

MACHINERY NOTES
On her original trials she reached 19.3 knots with 13100 ihp, but after reboilering she reached 22¾ knots.

CAREER
Launched 26 August, 1899 and completed in 1902 for the Russian Navy as the *Pallada*; sank in shallow water (upper deck awash) at Port Arthur 7 December, 1904 following damage sustained on previous days from Japanese 11in howitzer shells; fell into Japanese hands 2 January, 1905; raised and recommissioned for service as a training ship in May 1910; in 1920 she became a minelayer; stricken 1922 and sunk 27 May, 1924 as a target for bombs.

Name	Builder	Date	Displ	Length ft in	Beam ft in	Draught ft in	Machinery	SHP	Speed	Fuel	Radius	Armament	Comp
SOYA ex-*Varyag*	Wm Cramp & Sons, Philadelphia	1898–1900	6500 N	416 0 wl 399 11 pp	51 11	19 6	2-shaft 4-cyl compound 30 Niclausse boilers	20000 ihp	23	770 $\overline{1250}$ coal	4500 @ 10	12 × 6in 45-cal QF 12 × 3in 60-cal QF 8 × 47mm 6 × 18in TT	571

GENERAL NOTES
An ex-Russian protected cruiser.

ARMOUR
Krupp steel. Deck 3in to 1½in; CT 6in.

RE-ARMAMENT AND RECONSTRUCTION NOTES
Repaired and rebuilt at Yokosuka DY in 1906–7, with Miyabara boilers and Armstrong-pattern guns; 12 × 6in 45-cal; 10 × 3in; 2 × 42mm; 2 × 18in TT.

MACHINERY NOTES
On trials in July 1900 she reached 24.6 knots with 20000 ihp.

CAREER
Launched 31 October, 1899, completed July 1900 for Russian Navy as the *Varyag*; sank in shallow water at about 18.00 hrs 9 February, 1905 after hits from Japanese cruisers, off Inchon, Korea (37° N, 126° 34′ E); raised -8 August 1905 and all movable material including funnels and guns were removed by the salvage vessels *Santo Maru* and *Kyoto Maru*; she was repaired at Yokosuka and became a training ship; in March 1916 she was returned to Russia, and was handed over and renamed *Varjag* 5 April, 1916; by orders of the British Government she was disarmed at Liverpool in June 1917; stranded 15 February, 1918 while in tow off the Irish coast; raised and used by RN until 1919 as a depot-ship; in 1920 she was for disposal and sold for BU, but later that year she was wrecked on the coast of Scotland while in tow; BU in 1922.

Name	Builder	Date	Displ	Length ft in	Beam ft in	Draught ft in	Machinery	SHP	Speed	Fuel	Radius	Armament	Comp
SUZUYA ex-*Novik*	F. Schichau, Danzig	1899–1901	3080 N	360 10 oa 347 1 pp	40 0	16 5	2-shaft 4-cyl compound 12 Thornycroft boilers	18000 ihp	25	500 coal	5000 @ 10 $\overline{500}$ @ 20	6 × 4.7in 45-cal QF 8 × 47mm QF 2 × 37mm 5 × 18in TT	340

GENERAL NOTES
An ex-Russian protected cruiser of German design.

ARMOUR
Krupp nickel steel. Deck 2in; CT 1.1in.

RE-ARMAMENT AND RECONSTRUCTION NOTES
Repaired and rebuilt at Yokosuka in 1906 with Miyabara boilers and Armstrong-pattern guns: 2 × 6in 50-cal QF; 4 × 4.7in QF. In 1908 the armament was changed to 2 × 4.7in; 4 × 3.1in 40-cal QF; 6 × 47mm; 2 × 37mm.

MACHINERY NOTES
On her original trials she reached 25.6 knots with 19000 ihp, but by 1908 her speed had dropped to 20 knots.

CAREER
Launched 15 August, 1900, completed 1901 as the Russian *Novik*; damaged 20 August, 1904 by gunfire of Japanese cruiser *Tsushima* off Sakhalien; on 21 August, sank in Korsakow anchorage after damage from the cruiser *Chitose*; she fell into Japanese hands on 5 July, 1905 and was salvaged 16 July, 1906; repaired at Yokosuka; renamed *Suzuya* 11 July, 1908 and repairs completed in December 1908; stricken 1 April, 1913 and BU.

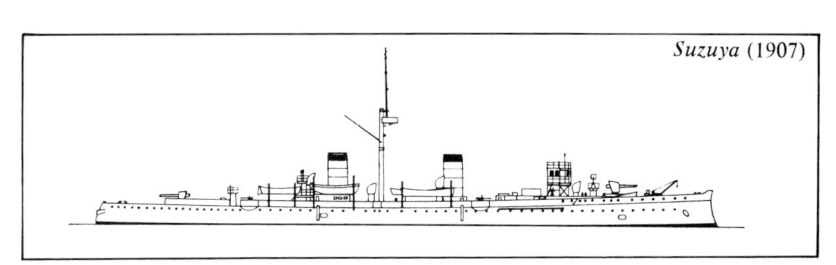

Suzuya (1907)

The Russian cruiser *Novik* became *Suzuya* after she fell into Japanese hands in 1904. She is seen here at Kure on 1st July 1908. (Shizuo Fukui.)

Name	Builder	Date	Displ	Length ft in	Beam ft in	Draught ft in	Machinery	SHP	Speed	Fuel	Radius	Armament	Comp
TONE	Sasebo DY	1905–1910	4900 F 4100 N 3760 S	373 4 wl 359 10 pp	46 11	16 9	2-shaft 4-cyl compound 16 Miyabara boilers	15000 ihp	23	903 coal 124 oil	7340 @ 10	2 × 6in 50-cal QF 10 × 4.7in 50-cal QF 2 × 3.1in 48-cal QF 1 MG 3 × 18in TT (AW)	392

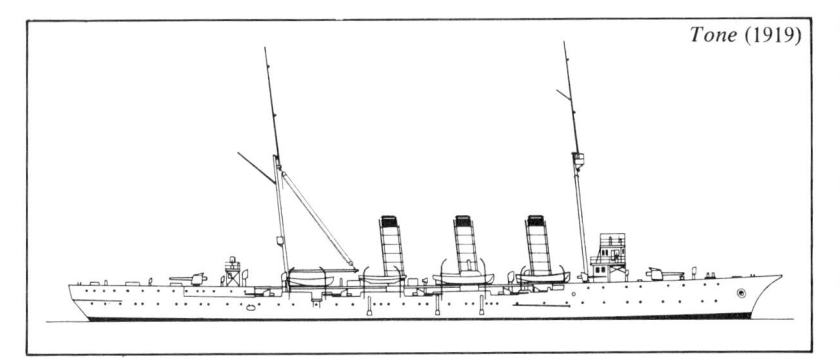

Tone (1919)

GENERAL NOTES
A 2nd Class cruiser laid down under the Third Fleet Law of 1903.

ARMOUR
Krupp steel. Deck 3in to 1½in; CT 4in.

MACHINERY
On trials she reached 23.37 knots with 15215 ihp.

CAREER
Launched 24 October, 1904 and completed 15 May, 1910; stricken 1 April, 1931; renamed *Hai Kan No 2* and used for trials; sunk in April 1933 by aircraft off Amami-O-Shima.

Tone, a graceful cruiser, built under the 3rd Fleet Law of 1903. She could be distinguished by her pronounced clipper bow, which was to become a feature of Japanese ships thereafter. (Shizuo Fukui.)

Name	Builder	Date	Displ	Length ft in	Beam ft in	Draught ft in	Machinery	SHP	Speed	Fuel	Radius	Armament	Comp
YODO	Kawasaki, Kobe	1908	1250 N	305 5 oa 280 pp	32 1	9 9	2-shaft 4 cyl compound 4 Miyabara boilers	6500 ihp	22	125 340 coal 76 oil	3600 @ 10	2 × 4.7in 50-cal QF 4 × 3.1in 40-cal QF 2 × 18in TT (AW) 1 MG	180

PROTECTED CRUISERS 103

Name	Builder	Date	Displ	Length ft in	Beam ft in	Draught ft in	Machinery	SHP	Speed	Fuel	Radius	Armament	Comp
MOGAMI	Mitsubishi, Nagasaki	1907–1908	1350 N	315 11 oa / 300 pp	31 8	9 9	2-shaft Parsons TU, 6 Miyabara boilers	8000 ihp	23	352 coal / 68 oil	3300 @ 10	2 × 4.7in 50-cal QF / 4 × 3.1in 40-cal QF / 2 × 18in TT (AW) / 1 MG	180

GENERAL NOTES
Protected cruisers or despatch vessels, but also rated as gunboats.

ARMOUR
Krupp steel. Deck 2½in; CT 2in.

RE-ARMAMENT NOTES
As a survey ship *Yodo* had only 2 × 3in.
Mainmast fitted 1931, tripod derrick between funnels, deckhouse on poop. She was re-armed with two 3.1in QF, one 6.5mm MG.

CAREERS
Yodo
Launched 18 November, 1907, completed 8 April 1908; in 1927–8 she became a survey ship; stricken 1 April, 1940; hulked and renamed *Hai Kan No. 13* at Hikari, Tokuyama; surrendered in August 1945 and BU.
Mogami
Launched 25 March, 1908, completed 16 September, 1908; stricken 1928 and renamed *Hai Kan No. 3*; BU in 1931.

The gunboat *Yodo* differed from her sister *Mogami*, in having only two funnels and a clipper bow. The cruiser *Izumi* appears behind her, dating the photograph at between 1908 and 1911. (NMM.)

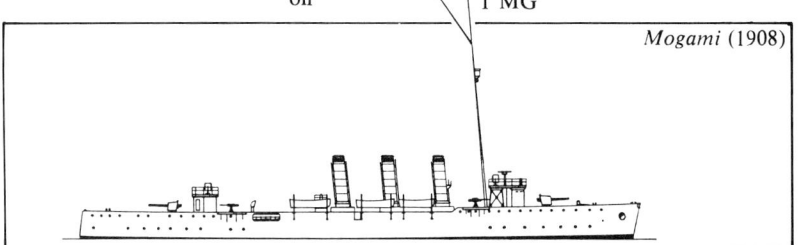

Mogami (1908)

7. Light Cruisers

Name	Builder	Date	Displ	Length ft in	Beam ft in	Draught ft in	Machinery	SHP	Speed	Fuel	Radius	Armament	Comp
CHIKUMA	Sasebo DY	1910–1912	5040 F / 5000 N	475 0 oa / 460 11 wl	46 7	16 9	2-shaft Curtis geared turbines 16 Kampon boilers	22500 ihp	26	1128 coal / 300 oil	10000 @ 10	8 × 6in 50-cal QF / 4 × 3.1in 40-cal QF / 2 MGs / 3 × 18in TT (AW)	390 / 450
HIRADO	Kawasaki, Kobe		4400 S	440 0 pp						1098 coal / 312 oil			
YAHAGI	Mitsubishi, Nagasaki						4-shaft Parsons geared turbines etc			1122 coal / 378 oil			

GENERAL NOTES
Light cruisers built under the Third Fleet Law of 1903.

ARMOUR
Krupp steel. Waterline belt 3in to 2in; deck 2in to 1½in; CT 4in.

MACHINERY
On trials *Chikuma* reached 26.8 knots with 24794 shp; *Yahagi* reached the same speed with 27408 shp. Reboilered in 1924 with 6 Kampon boilers.

Three 6-inch gunned cruisers, modelled on the British 'Town' class, were built in 1910–12. *Hirado* is seen here as built. (Shizuo Fukui.)

Hirado (1912)

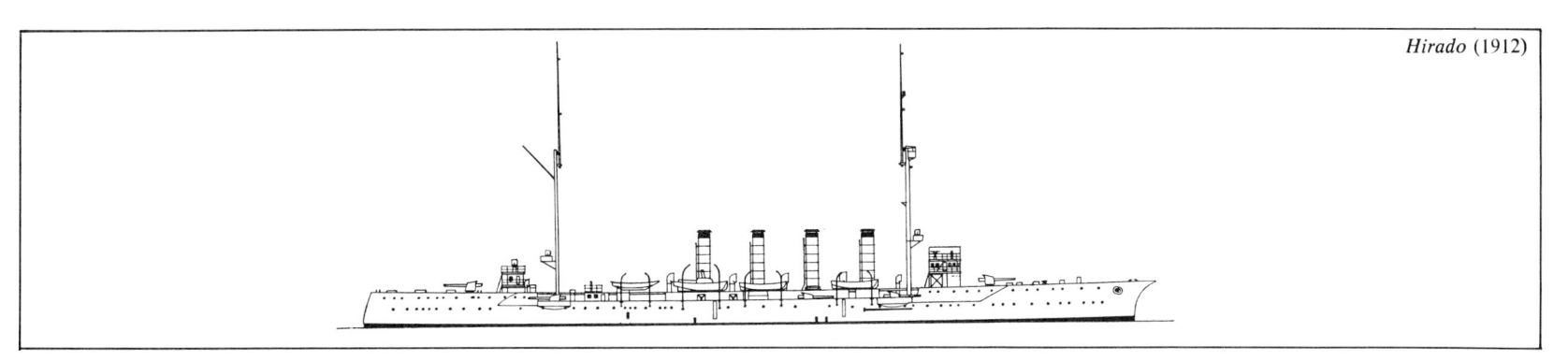

RE-ARMAMENT
In 1924 they were re-armed, with 2 × 3.1in AA guns replacing 2 of the 4 × 3.1in QF, and 4 × 21in TT replacing the 3 × 18in.

CAREERS
Chikuma
Launched 1 April, 1911, completed 17 May, 1912; stricken 1 April, 1931 and became *Hai Kan No. 3*; subsequent fate unknown.

Hirado
Launched 29 June, 1911, completed 17 June, 1912; stricken 1939 and became *Hai Kan No. 11* at Kure; hull BU in July 1947.

Yahagi
Launched 3 October, 1911, completed 27 July, 1912; stricken in 1940 and became *Hai Kan No. 12* at Etajima; in 1944 she was a training ship for submarine crew at Otake; BU by 8 July, 1947 at Kasado.

Name	Builder	Date	Displ	Length ft in	Beam ft in	Draught ft in	Machinery	SHP	Speed	Fuel	Radius	Armament	Comp
TENRYŪ	Yokosuka DY	1917–1919	4350 F	468 11 oa	40 6	13 0	3-shaft Brown-Curtis GTU	51000	33	150 coal	6000 @ 10	4 × 5.5in 50-cal	332
TATSUTA	Sasebo DY		3948 N	457 10 wl			10 Kampon boilers			920 oil	1250 @ 31	1 × 3.1in 40-cal AA 2 MGs 6 × 21in TT (AW) provision for mines	
			3230 S	440 pp									

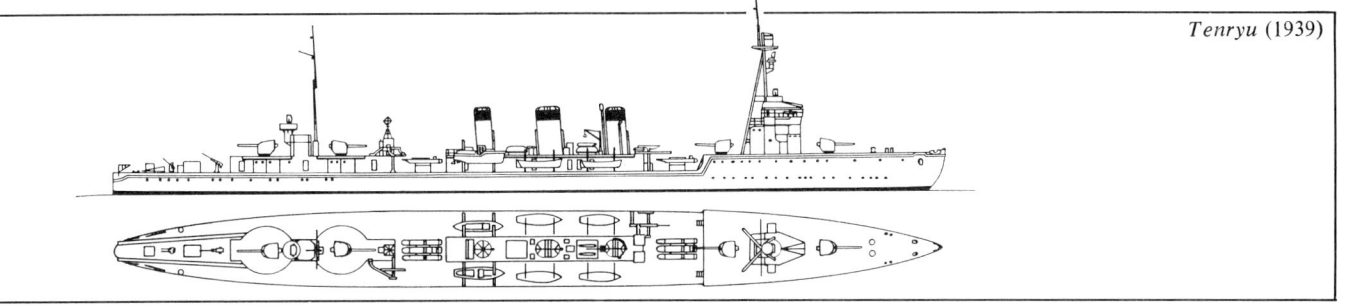

Tenryu (1939)

GENERAL NOTES
Built under the 1916 Programme, these were the first modern light cruisers in the Japanese Navy and were inspired by the British *Arethusa* and 'C' Classes. They were designed to act as flagships for the destroyer flotillas, and were the first units armed with triple TT.

ARMOUR
Waterline belt 2in; deck 1½in.

RE-ARMAMENT NOTES
During her March 1927–March 1930 refit, *Tenryu* was given a tripod foremast, and *Tatsuta* was similarly altered in 1931. In 1939 both ships were given 2 × 13mm AA guns.

CAREERS
Tenryu
Launched 11 March, 1918, completed 20 November, 1919; torpedoed 18 December, 1942 by US submarine *Albacore* 10 m E of Madang (05° 11′ S, 145° 57′ E).

Tatsuta
Launched 29 May, 1918, completed 13 March, 1919; torpedoed by US submarine *Sandlance* 13 March, 1944 145 m SSW of Yokosuka (32° 58′ N, 138° 52′ E).

Name	Builder	Date	Displ	Length ft in	Beam ft in	Draught ft in	Machinery	SHP	Speed	Fuel	Radius	Armament	Comp
ex-AUGSBURG	Kiel DY	1908–1910	4915 F	428 0 wl	42 8	18 3 max	4-shaft Parsons GTU	19000	25½	400 1010 coal	3630 @ 14	6 × 5.9in 50-cal	367
			4362 N metric	426 6 pp		17 8 mean	15 Marine boilers			115 oil		2 × 88mm 45-cal AA 2 × 17.7in TT (UW) 2 × 19.7in TT (AW) 100 mines	

GENERAL NOTES
She was built for the Imperial German Navy and was built to a Marineamt design of 1906–7 for a 'small' cruiser. She was steel-built, with longitudinal and transverse framing.

CAREER
Launched 10 July, 1909, completed 1 November, 1910; served as a gunnery training ship from 1912, but from 1914 she served on coast-defence, and with the fleet handed over to Allies on 3 September, 1920 as Ship *Y*, being part of Japan's share of German tonnage; BU 1922 at Dordrecht.

LIGHT CRUISERS 105

Name	Builder	Date	Displ	Length ft in	Beam ft in	Draught ft in	Machinery	SHP	Speed	Fuel	Radius	Armament	Comp
KUMA	Sasebo DY	1918–1920	5832 F	532 0 oa	46 6	15 9	4-shaft Gihon GTU	90000	36	350 coal	9000 @ 10	7 × 5.5in 50-cal	439
TAMA	Mitsubishi, Nagasaki	1918–1921	5500 N	520 1 wl			12 Kampon boilers			700	5000 @ 17	2 × 3.1in 40-cal AA 2 MGs	
KITAKAMI	Sasebo DY		metric	500 0 pp						1260 oil		8 × 21in TT (AW)	
OI	Kawasaki, Kobe	1919–1921	5100 S										
KISO	Mitsubishi, Nagasaki												

Oi (1922)

Kuma (1935)

Kiso (1943)

General Notes
These ships were built under the 1917–18 Budget and were the first of the so-called 5500-ton series. They were a development of the *Tenryu* Class.

Armour
Waterline belt 2½in; deck 1¼in.

Re-armament and Reconstruction
In 1927 all were given a floatplane and catapult. In 1929–30 *Kuma* was given funnel-caps. *Kuma* and *Tama* were given catapults and tripod mainmasts in 1934–35. In 1940, they were re-armed with 24in TT in place of the 21in, but in 1941 *Oi* and *Kitakami* were rebuilt as torpedo-cruisers. Their armament was: 4 × 5.5in, 8 × 25mm AA, 40 × 24in (in 10 quadruple mountings). By 1943, *Oi* had 4 × 5in 50-cal DP guns, 36 × 25mm AA, and 40 24in TT. In 1942–3 *Kitakami* had only 32 × 24in TT (8 mountings) and carried 14m Daihatsu landing craft. In January 1944, she carried 4 × 5in DP, 10 × 25mm AA, 4 × 13mm MGs and only 24 × 24in. TT. Her boilers had been reduced, giving her 78000 shp = 31.7 knots and 4000 m endurance @ 14 knots. In January 1945 she had 4 × 5in DP, 67 × 25mm AA, 18 DCs, 8 Kaiten midget submarines, and a 20t crane. By this time she had only 2 turbines, developing 35110 shp = 23 knots.
Tama and *Kiso* in July 1944 were armed with 5 × 5.5in 50-cal, 2 × 5in AA, 44 × 45-mm AA, 6 × 13mm MGs.

The light cruiser *Kitakami* before reconstruction. (Author's Collection.)

CAREERS

Kuma
Launched 14 July, 1919, completed 31 August, 1920; torpedoed 11 January, 1944 by British submarine *Tally Ho* 10 m NW of Penang (6° N, 39° E).

Tama
Launched 10 February, 1920, completed 29 January, 1921; damaged 25 October 1944 by aircraft of US carriers *Essex* and *Lexington*; torpedoed the same day by submarine *Jallao* 320 miles NE of Cape Engano (21° 32′ N, 129° 17′E).

Kitakami
Launched 3 July, 1920, completed 15 April, 1921; surrendered August 1945; in September 1945 she was stationed at Kagoshima as a repair ship for units of the Repatriation Service; stricken 10 August, 1946 and BU at Nanao by 31 March 1947.

Oi
Launched 15 July, 1920, completed 4 May, 1921; torpedoed 19 July, 1944 by submarine USS *Flasher* 570 m S of Hong Kong (12° 45′ N, 114° 20′ E).

Kiso
Launched 14 December, 1920, completed 3 October, 1921; sunk 13 November, 1944 by aircraft of US TF 38, 8 m W of Manila (14° 35′ N, 120° 50′ E).

The light cruiser *Kitakami*, seen shortly before reconstruction as a "Torpedo Cruiser". No catapult pedestal is visible between the guns ahead of the mainmast. (Author's Collection.)

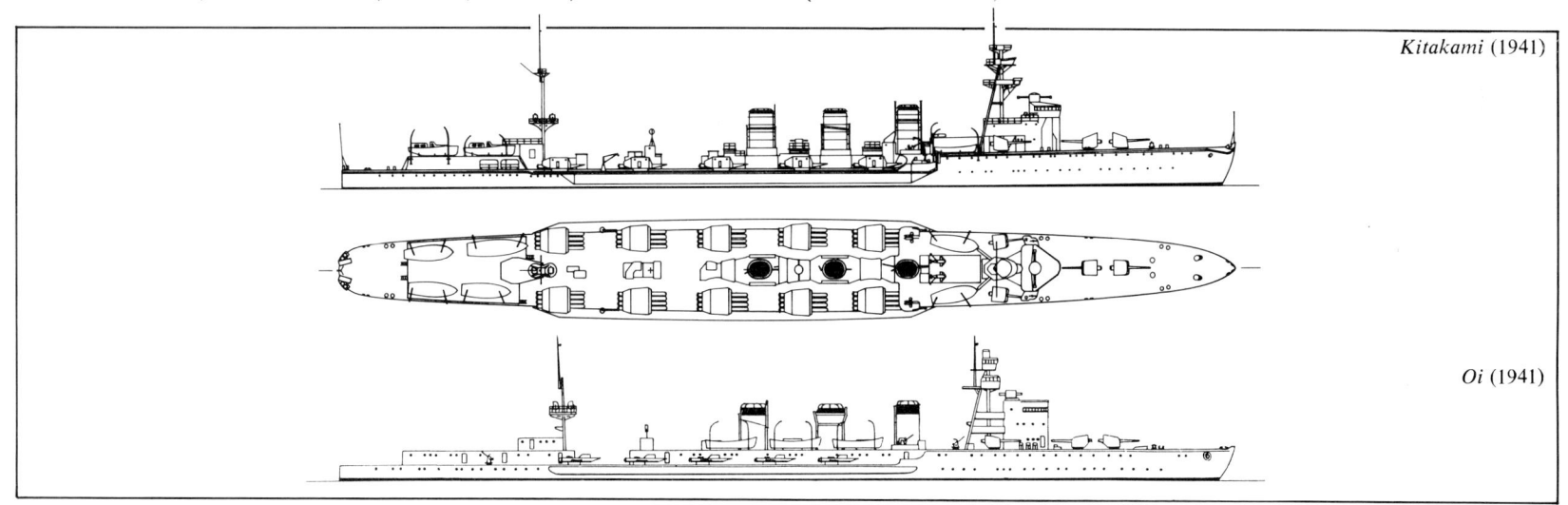

Kitakami (1941)

Oi (1941)

Name	Builder	Date	Displ	Length ft in	Beam ft in	Draught ft in	Machinery	SHP	Speed	Fuel	Radius	Armament	Comp
NAGARA	Sasebo DY	1920–1922	5570 N metric	534 9 oa	48 5	16 0	4-shaft Gihon GTU	90000	36	350 coal	9000 @ 10	7 × 5.5in 50-cal	438
ISUZU	Uraga Dock, Tokyo	1920–1923	5170 S	520 0 wl			12 Kampon boilers (8 oil-fired, 4 coal-fired):			700 —— 1260 oil	1500 @ 33	2 × 3.1in 40-cal AA 6 MGs 8 × 24in TT (AW) provision for mines	
YURA ex-*Suzuka*	Sasebo DY	1921–1923		500 0 pp			*Kinu* had Curtis turbines and boilers						
NATORI	Mitsubishi, Nagasaki	1920–1922											
KINU ex-*Otonase*	Kawasaki, Kobe	1921–1922											
ABUKUMA ex-*Minase*	Uraga Dock, Tokyo	1921–1925											

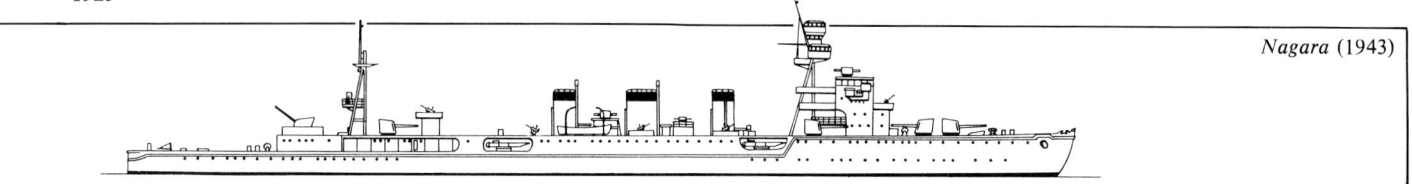

Nagara (1943)

GENERAL NOTES
These ships were similar to the *Kuma* Class, and were designed in 1916 for the 1920 Programme. They were designed as flagships for cruiser-, destroyer- and submarine-squadrons.

ARMOUR
Waterline belt 2½in; deck 1¼in;

NOMENCLATURE
Suzuka, *Otonase* and *Minase* were renamed in November 1921.

RECONSTRUCTION AND RE-ARMAMENT
In 1927 they were given a catapult and 1 floatplane. The ships were altered with tripod mainmast and the catapult moved aft as follows: *Natori* from July 1931 to September 1932, *Isuzu* May 1932 to 1933, *Nagara* October 1932 to September 1933, *Kinu* Nov-

ember 1933 to August 1934, *Yura* January 1936 to December 1936. After her collision in 1930, *Abukuma* was given a bow similar to *Naka* and *Jintsu*. In 1943 the armament was altered to: 5 × 5.5in 50-cal; 2 × 5in 50-cal DP; 22 × 25mm AA; 2 × 13mm AA; 24 × 24in TT. In June 1944, the survivors had 36 × 25mm AA; their displacement was listed as 6050ts and speed at 33.4 knots. In 1944, *Isuzu* was re-armed as an AA cruiser and flagship for anti-submarine groups (CH17, 18, 23, 37 & 38).

The *Kuma* class light cruisers, built between 1918 and 1921, were followed by the similar *Nagara* class, which were built between 1920 and 1925. *Yura* is seen here as altered in 1927, with a flying-off platform for aircraft over the forward guns. (This was later replaced by a catapult.) Note also that the funnels are unmodified. (Shizuo Fukui.)

CAREERS

Nagara
Launched 25 April, 1921, completed 21 April, 1922; torpedoed 7 August, 1944 by US submarine *Croaker* 35 m S of Nagasaki (32° 09′ N, 129° 53′ E).

Isuzu
Launched 29 October, 1921, completed 15 August, 1923; torpedoed 7 April, 1945 30 m N of Soembawa Island, Java Sea (07° 38′ S, 118° 09′ E) by US submarines *Charr* and *Gabilan*.

Yura
Launched 15 February, 1922, completed 20 March, 1923; badly damaged 25 October, 1942 by US naval aircraft at Guadalcanal; she was sunk the same day by the Japanese destroyers *Harusame* and *Yudachi* 30 m NNE of Savo (08° 40′ S, 160° E).

Natori
Launched 16 February, 1922, completed 15 September, 1922; torpedoed 18 August, 1944 by US submarine *Hardhead* 250 m NE of Surigao (12° 29′ N, 128° 49′ E).

Kinu
Launched 29 May, 1922, completed 10 November, 1922; sunk 26 October, 1944 by aircraft of Task Group 77/44 SW of Masbate (11° 46′ N, 123° 11′ E).

Abukuma
Launched 16 March, 1923, completed 26 May, 1925; on 20 October, 1930 she was damaged in collision with the *Kitakami* during manoeuvres in Tokyo Bay; she lost her bow as far as 'A' gun and was repaired at Kure DY; badly damaged 24/25 October, 1944 by US MTB *PT.137*; sunk next day (26 October) by USAF aircraft 10 m SE of Negros Coast (09° 20′ N, 122° 30′ E).

Above: *Nagara* leaves Kure during 1938. (Authors' Collection.)

Above: *Kinu*. (Shizuo Fukui.)

Below: *Abukuma*. (Shizuo Fukui.)

Name	Builder	Date	Displ	Length ft in	Beam ft in	Draught ft in	Machinery	SHP	Speed	Fuel	Radius	Armament	Comp
NAKA	Mitsubishi, Yokohama	1922–1925	7100 F	534 9 oa	48 5	16 1	4-shaft Gihon GTU (*Jintsu* Curtis GTU) 12 Kampon boilers	90000	35¼	300 570 coal 1010 oil	7800 @ 10 1300 @ 33	7 × 5.5in 50-cal 2 × 3.1in 40-cal AA 2 MGs 8 × 24in TT (AW) 80 mines	450
SENDAI	Mitsubishi, Nagasaki	1922–1924	5595 metric	520 0 wl									
JINTSU	Kawasaki, Kobe	1922–1925	5195 N	500 0 pp									

108 LIGHT CRUISERS

Sendai (1926)

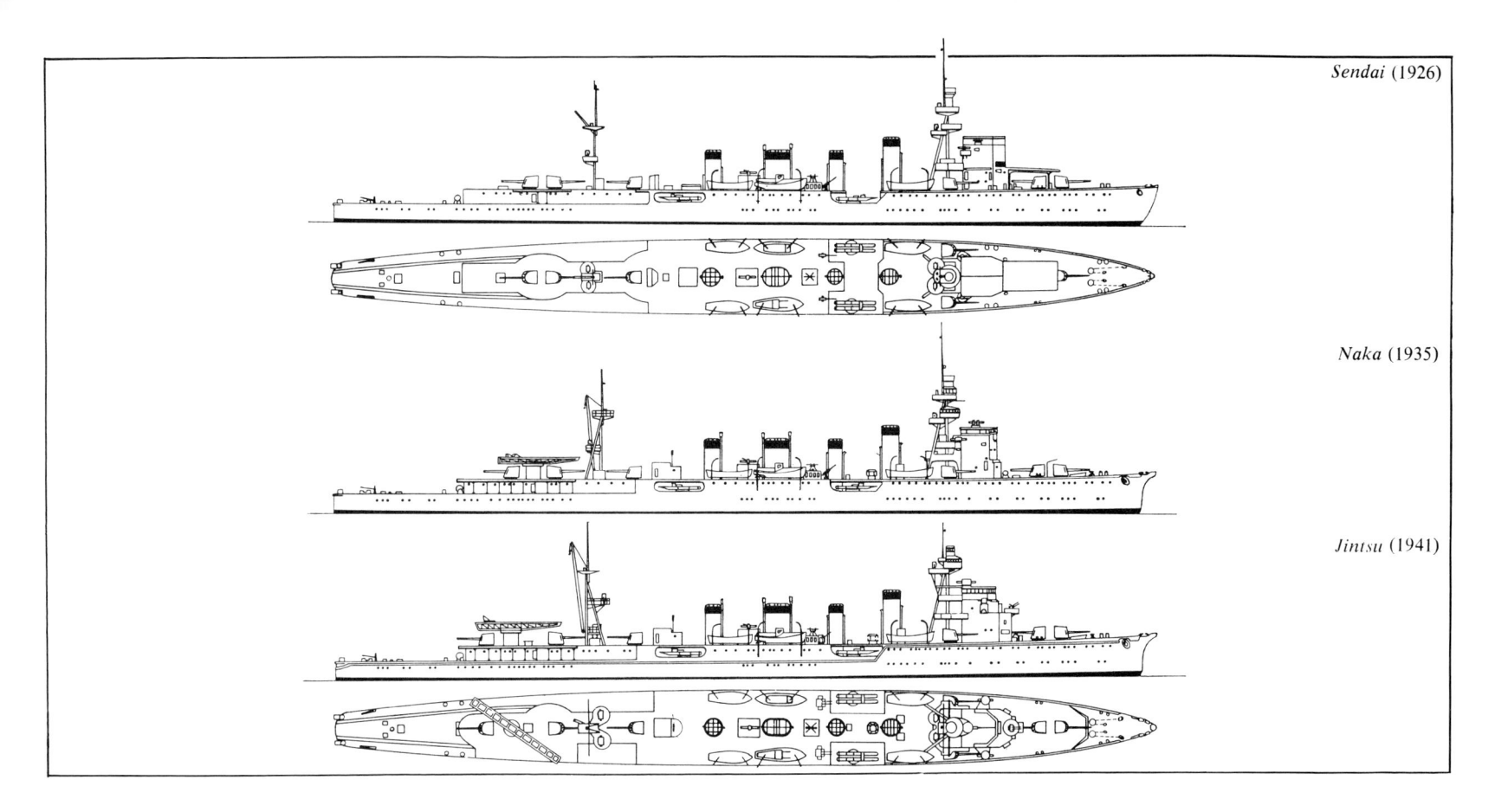

Naka (1935)

Jintsu (1941)

GENERAL NOTES
Built under the 1922 Budget, this was the last of the 5500t series. The last three units of the programme were cancelled under the Washington Treaty.

ARMOUR
Waterline belt 2½in to 2in; deck 2in; CT 2in.

RE-ARMAMENT AND RECONSTRUCTION
After her collision *Jintsu* was refitted in 1927-8 with a bow like *Naka*. In 1934, all three received a catapult and aircraft, and the bridge was rebuilt. In 1943 the armament was 7 × 5.5in 50-cal; 2 × 5in 50-cal DP; 44 × 25mm AA; 6 × 13mm AA.

Naka in September 1931, before modernisation. (Shizuo Fukui.)

CAREERS
Naka
Launched 24 March, 1925, completed 30 November, 1925; sunk 17 February, 1944 by aircraft from US carriers *Bunker Hill* and *Cowpens* 35 m W of Truk (07° 15′ N, 151° 15′ E).
Sendai
Launched 30 October, 1923, completed 29 April, 1924; sunk 2 November, 1943 by aircraft of TF 39 in Empress Augusta Bay (06° 10′ S, 154° 19′ E).
Jintsu
Launched 8 December, 1923, completed 31 July, 1925; damaged 24 August, 1927 in collision with the destroyer *Warabi*; repaired at Maizuru DY; sunk 13 July, 1943 by gunfire and torpedoes from three light cruisers and ten destroyers of TF 18, 14 m N of Kolombangara (07° 41′ S, 157° 15′ E).

LIGHT CRUISERS 109

Sendai, and her sisters of the *Naka* class, resembled the *Nagara* class, but had an extra funnel. As completed, *Sendai* an aircraft platform forward, which was later replaced by a catapult abaft the mainmast. (Shizuo Fukui.)

Name	Builder	Date	Displ	Length ft in	Beam ft in	Draught ft in	Machinery	SHP	Speed	Fuel	Radius	Armament	Comp
YUBARI	Sasebo DY	1922–1923	3587 F 3141 *metric* 2890 N	450 0 wl 436 0 pp	39 6	11 9	3-shaft Gihon GTU 8 Kampon boilers	57900	35½	100 coal 210 640 oil	5500 @ 10 1400 @ 33	6 × 5.5in 50-cal 1 × 3.1in 40-cal AA 2 MGs 4 × 24in TT (AW) 34 mines	328

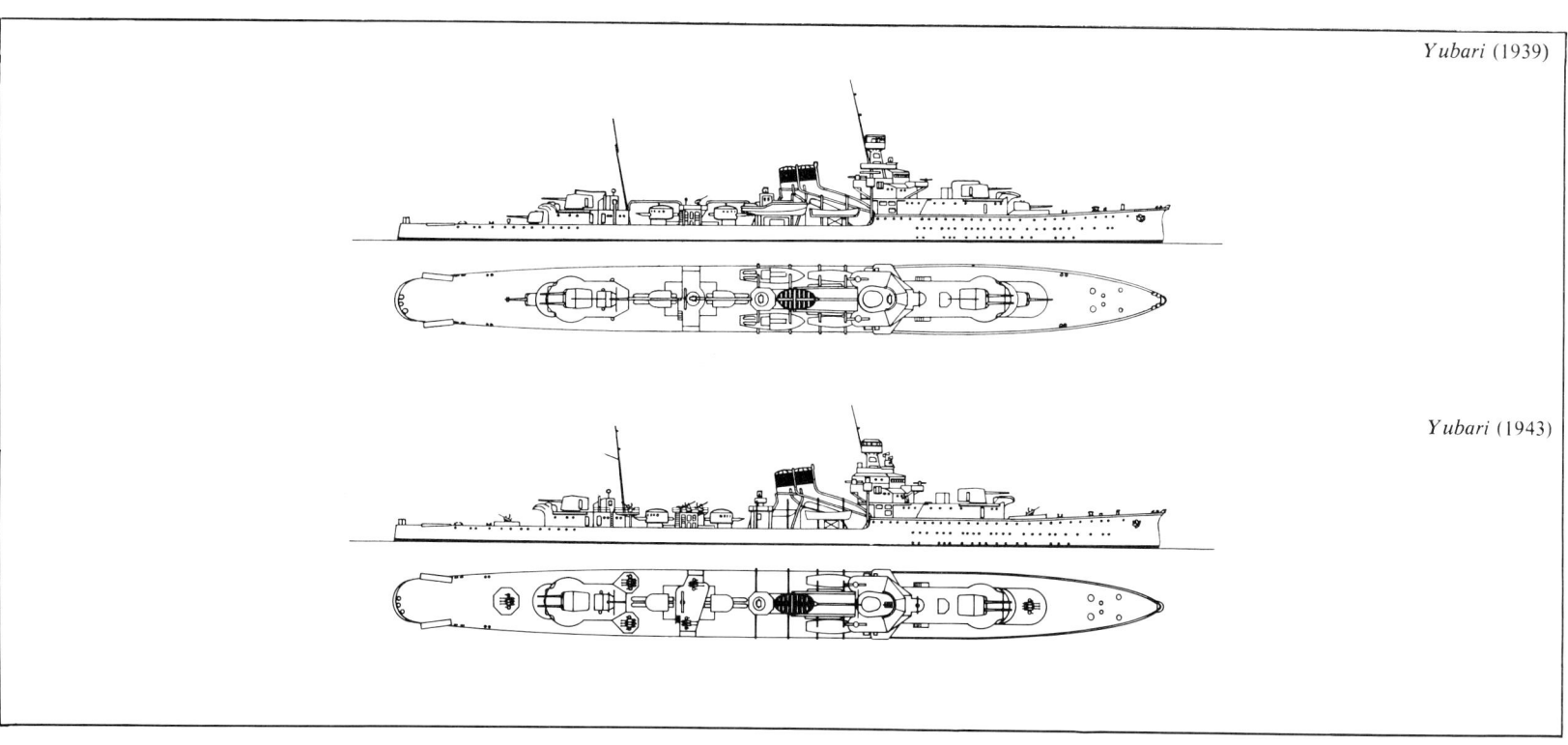

Yubari (1939)

Yubari (1943)

GENERAL NOTES
This cruiser was designed by Admiral Hiraga, and was built under the 1922 Budget as the twenty-fifth cruiser projected for the period 1922–7. She had originally been planned under the 1917 Programme as a small cruiser with experimental machinery to be named *Ayase*.

ARMOUR
Waterline belt 2in; deck 1in.

RE-ARMAMENT
In 1927 the shields to the TT were enlarged and the funnel raised. In 1943 she had four 5.5in 50-cal; 12 × 25mm AA; 8 × 13mm AA, 4 × 24in TT. Her displacement rose to 4448/3780/3510ts and her speed dropped to 32 knots with 58943 shp.

CAREER
Launched 5 March, 1923, completed 31 July, 1923; torpedoed 27 April, 1944 by US submarine *Bluegill* near Palau (05° 20′ N, 132° 16′ E).

The light cruiser *Yubari*, on completion in 1923, with her original short funnel and mine-rails on the quarter-deck. (Shizuo Fukui.)

A view of *Yubari* taken after her 1927 modifications, which included raising the funnel and fitting larger shields to the torpedo-tubes. (Shizuo Fukui.)

Name	Builder	Date	Displ	Length ft in	Beam ft in	Draught ft in	Machinery	SHP	Speed	Fuel	Radius	Armament	Comp
KATORI	Mitsubishi, Yokohama	1938– 1940	6280 N	425 9 wl	52 4	18 10	2-shaft GTU and 2 Diesels 3 Kampon boilers	8000	18			4 × 5.5in 50-cal 2 × 5in 40-cal DP 4 × 25mm AA 4 × 21in TT (AW) 1 catapult and floatplane	
KASHIMA		1938– 1940	5890 S	405 2 pp									
KASHII		1940– 1941	5800 S										
KASHIWARA		1941–											
Nos. 815–818													

GENERAL NOTES
Ordered under the 1937–9 Programmes as training cruisers.

ARMOUR
Deck 2in.

RE-ARMAMENT
In 1943 they were armed with 4 × 5.5in 50-cal, 6 × 5in 40-cal DP, 20 × 25mm AA. By July 1944 the catapult was replaced by 30 × 25mm AA, 8 × 13mm AA and 100 DCs.

CAREERS
Kashima
Launched 25 September 1939, completed 31 May, 1940; in 1945 she was the flagship of the China Coast Escort Squadron; damaged on 30 July, 1945 at Maizuru by aircraft of the TF 38; surrendered in August 1945 and used on repatriation duty until 15 November, 1946; BU at Nagasaki by 15 June, 1947.

Katori
Launched 17 June, 1939 and completed 20 April, 1940; flagship of 6th Submarine Fleet; damaged 17 February, 1944 at Truk by aircraft of TF 58 and sunk the same day by US cruisers *Minneapolis* and *New Orleans* and destroyers *Radford* and *Burns* 40 m NW of Truk (07° 45′ N, 151° 20′ E).

Kashii
Launched 15 October, 1940 and completed 15 July, 1941; flagship of 1st South Seas Flotilla at Seletar until 1944; sunk 12 January, 1945 by aircraft of TF 38 55 m N of Cape Varela (13° 50′, 109° 20′ E).

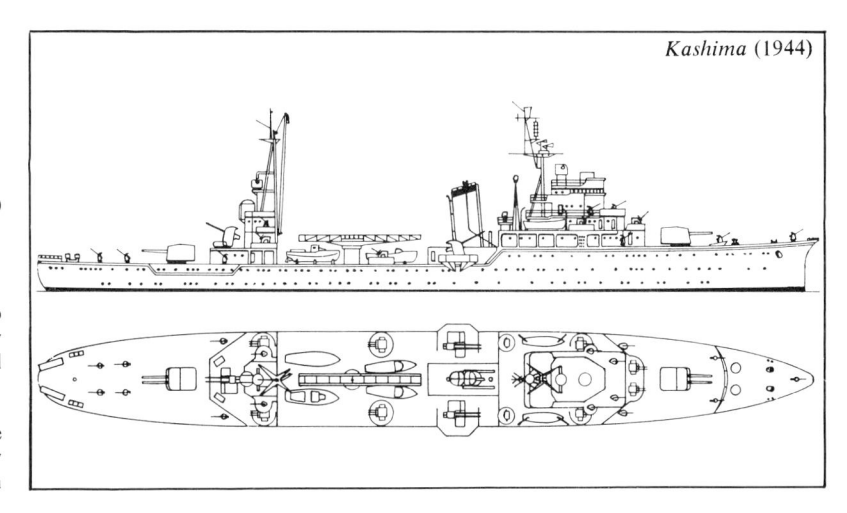

Kashima (1944)

Kashiwara
Building No. 237; laid down 23 June, 1941 but work stopped on 6 November 1941 and material BU.

Nos. 815–818 Projected under the 1942 Programme, but never begun.

Name	Builder	Date	Displ	Length ft in	Beam ft in	Draught ft in	Machinery	SHP	Speed	Fuel	Radius	Armament	Comp
AGANO	Sasebo DY	1940– 1942	8534 F	571 0 oa	49 10	18 5	4-shaft GTU 6 Kampon boilers	100000	35	1405 oil	6300 @ 18	6 × 6in 50-cal 4 × 3.1in 65-cal AA 32 × 25mm 65-cal AA 8 × 24in TT (AW) 16 DCs 1 catapult 2 floatplanes	
NOSHIRO	Yokosuka DY	1941– 1943	7895 F	563 0 wl									
YAHAGI	Sasebo DY	1941– 1943	7710 F	531 6 pp									
SAKAWA	Sasebo DY	1942– 1944	6652 F										

GENERAL NOTES
Built under the 1939 Programme, and were unusual in having a flush deck, with marked sheet to the forecastle. A bulbous bow was fitted for the first time. They were intended to act as flagships for destroyer flotillas.

RE-ARMAMENT
In 1944 they were armed with 46 × 25mm AA, but by March of that year an additional 6 × 25mm AA guns had been added; by July 1944, 61 × 25mm AA were mounted.

LIGHT CRUISERS 111

CAREERS

Agano
Launched 22 October, 1941, completed 31 October, 1942; torpedoed 17 February, 1944 at about 13.50 hrs, by US submarine *Skate* 160 m N of Truk (10° 11′ N, 151° 42′ E).

Noshiro
Launched 19 July, 1942, completed 30 June, 1943; sunk 26 October 1944 by aircraft of US carriers *Hornet* and *Wasp*.

Yahagi
Launched 25 October, 1942, completed 29 December, 1943; sunk 7 April, 1945 at about 14.05 hrs, in company with the *Yamato* by aircraft of TF 58 130 m WSW of Kagoshima (30° 47′ N, 128° 80′ E).

Sakawa
Launched 9 April, 1944, completed 30 November, 1944; surrendered in August 1945 at Maizuru; repatriation duties; badly damaged 1 July, 1946 as a target in the atom bomb tests at Bikini Atoll; the wreck sank the next day.

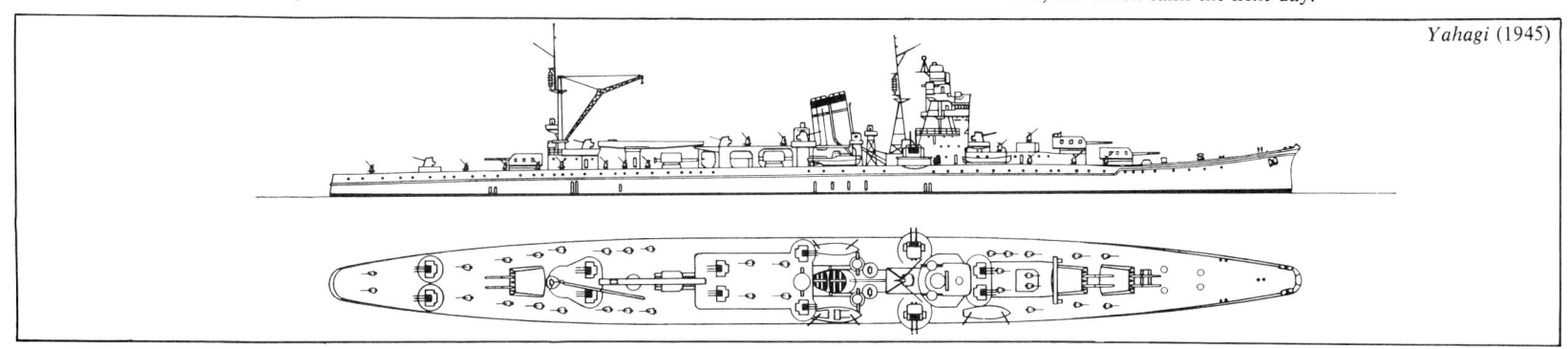

Yahagi (1945)

The new light cruiser *Yahagi*, seen on 19th December 1943, just before she entered service. (Shizuo Fukui.)

Name	Builder	Date	Displ	Length ft in	Beam ft in	Draught ft in	Machinery	SHP	Speed	Fuel	Radius	Armament	Comp
OYODO	Kure DY	1941–1943	11433 F	630 0 oa	51 5	19 6	4-shaft GTU 6 Kampon boilers	110430	36	2360 oil	10600 @ 18	6 × 6.1in 60-cal 8 × 3.9in 65-cal AA 12 × 25mm AA 1 catapult 2 floatplanes	?
NIYODO	—		10417 N 8164 S	618 0 wl 590 6 pp									
Nos. 810–814	—		8500 S						37½				
Nos. 5037–5038	—		8520 S										

Oyodo (1945)

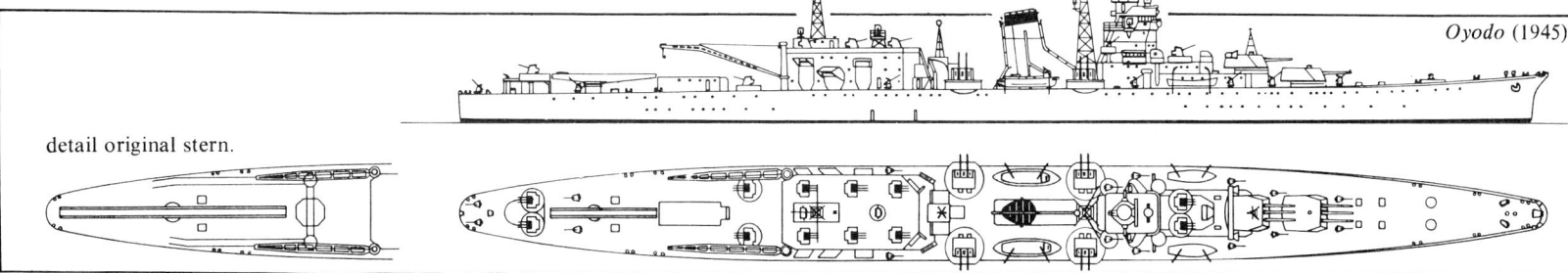

detail original stern.

GENERAL NOTES
Built under the 1939 Programme. They were an improved *Agano* type, and retained the flush deck and bulbous bow of that class. They were planned as flagships for the submarine flotillas, and would have carried 6 floatplanes.

RE-ARMAMENT
In 1944 *Oyodo* was rebuilt at Yokosuka; the large catapult was replaced by one of normal length, and the hangar was rebuilt as staff accommodation. In 1945 she was armed with 52 × 25mm AA.

CAREERS

Oyodo
Launched 2 April, 1942, completed 28 April, 1943; badly damaged on 19 March, 1945 by aircraft of TF 58 at Kure; after temporary repairs she was sent to Edachi; sunk 28 July, 1945 after attack by aircraft of TF 38, moored in shallow water at Edachi (34° 13′ N, 132° 25′ E); BU by 30 June, 1948 at Harima, Kure.

Niyodo
Not laid down because the contract was cancelled. Nos. 810–814 and 5037–5038 were projected under the 1942 Programme but never ordered.

Name	Builder	Date	Displ	Length ft in	Beam ft in	Draught ft in	Machinery	SHP	Speed	Fuel	Radius	Armament	Comp
IOSHIMA ex-*Ning Hai*	Harima Zosensho KK, Harima	1930– 1932	2500 N	360 0 oa 350 0 pp	39 0	13 0	2-shaft GTU	9500	22			6 × 5.5in 50-cal 6 × 3in AA 8 MGs 4 × 21in TT (AW)	340
YASOSHIMA ex-*P'ing Hai*	Chiang Nan Dock Co., Shanghai	1931– 1936											

GENERAL NOTES
Built as small cruisers for the Chinese Navy and designed for 2 aircraft.

ARMOUR
Deck 1in; turrets 1in.

MACHINERY
On trials they averaged 10500 shp = 24 knots.

CAREERS
Ioshima
Launched 1 October, 1931, completed in 1932 for the Chinese Navy; captured 13 December, 1937 in the Yangtse River; served from 1939 to 1942 in the Nanking Government Fleet; taken over by Japan in 1943 and renamed *Ioshima* 28 June, 1944; rated as a coast-defence ship; torpedoed 19 September, 1944 by US submarine *Shad* S of Honshu (33° 40′ N, 138° 18′ E).

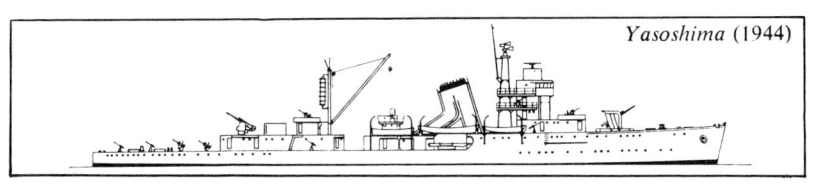

Yasoshima (1944)

Yasoshima
Launched 29 September, 1935, completed 18 June, 1936 for the Chinese Navy; sunk 23 September, 1937 in shallow water in the Yangtse by Japanese warships; raised and repaired and served in the Nanking Government Fleet from 1938 to 1943; taken over by Japan in 1943 and renamed *Yasoshima* 10 June, 1944; sunk 25 November, 1944 by aircraft of TF 38/3 in Santa Cruz Bay, Luzon (15° 40′ N, 119° 45′ E); wreck raised and returned to China for BU.

8. Gunboats

Name	Builder	Date	Displ	Length ft in	Beam ft in	Draught ft in	Machinery	SHP	Speed	Fuel	Radius	Armament	Comp
CHIYODA	Ishikawajima Z., Tokyo	1862– 1866	138 N	103 4 wl 97 5 pp	16 0	6 9	single-shaft horizontal 2-cyl trunk engine 2 locomotive boilers	60.84 (nom.)	5			1 × 5.5in (?ML) 2 smaller guns	35

GENERAL NOTES
3rd Class wooden gunboat with brig rig, she was the first warship built in Japan.

CAREER
Launched 2 July, 1863, completed May 1866 for the fleet of the Shogun; in May 1868 she was taken over by the Government, and was captured by rebels 4 October, 1868; recaptured by Imperial Navy forces at Hakodate; stricken June 1869; 28 January, 1888 and sold to a whaling company; served until 1911 before being BU.

Chiyoda (1861)

Name	Builder	Date	Displ	Length ft in	Beam ft in	Draught ft in	Machinery	SHP	Speed	Fuel	Radius	Armament	Comp
TEIBO No. 1 ex-*Teibo Maru No. 1* ex-*Hinda*	Unknown, London	1867	236 N	125 2 wl 120 0 pp	20 10	7 11 max 7 6 mean	single-shaft single cyl direct-acting engine, rectangular boiler	60 (nom.)	10			No. 1 1 × 5.9in ML 1 × 5.5in Krupp BL No. 2 2 × 6.5in Krupp BL 2 smaller guns	65 87
TEIBO No. 2 ex-*Teibo Maru No. 2* ex-*Assunta*		1866											

GENERAL NOTES
3rd Class wooden gunboats, barque-rigged.

CAREERS
Teibo No 1
Launched 1867, completed the same year as the British steamer *Hinda*; bought by the Choshu Clan as *Teibo Maru No. 1*; transferred in 1868 to the Government fleet and armed in March 1869; in July that year she was returned to the Choshu Clan; transferred to the Emperor as a gift in 1870; she became a survey ship in 1873; wrecked in 1875 in the Kuriles.

Teibo No 2
Launched in 1866 and completed 1867 as the British *Assunta*; in 1868 acquired by the Choshu Clan as *Teibo Maru No. 2* and given by the Clan to the Emperor in 1870; stricken 1885 and wrecked 2 April, 1885 near Aomori, Shima.

Name	Builder	Date	Displ	Length ft in	Beam ft in	Draught ft in	Machinery	SHP	Speed	Fuel	Radius	Armament	Comp
MOSHUN ex-*Moshun Maru* ex-*Eugenie*	Unknown, London	1865–1867	357 F 305 N	149 11 oa 143 1 wl 131 pp	22 0	7 11 max 7 7 mean	single-screw horizontal direct-acting engine rectangular boilers	120 nhp	10			1 × 7in Forbes ML 1 × 5.5in Krupp BL 2 smaller guns	65 / 88

GENERAL NOTES
A 3rd Class composite gunboat with schooner rig.

CAREER
Launched 1865 and completed 1867 as the British steamer *Eugenie*; sold in February 1868 to the Hizen Clan as *Moshun Maru*; taken over in March 1868 by the Government but returned in July 1869; given to the Emperor by the Clan in 1870 and renamed *Moshun*; she was a hulk by 1887 and was subsequently BU.

Left:
The composite gunboat *Moshun* was built in England before the end of the Shogunate, but survived until 1887 or later. (Shizuo Fukui.)

Name	Builder	Date	Displ	Length ft in	Beam ft in	Draught ft in	Machinery	SHP	Speed	Fuel	Radius	Armament	Comp
UN'YO ex-*Wunya Maru* (see note below)	? A. Hall & Co., Aberdeen	1868–1870	270 N	126 0 wl 119 9 pp	24 0	10 10	single-screw horizontal single-cyl direct-acting engine ?rectangular boilers	60 nhp	10			1 × 6.3in RML 1 × 5.5in 2 smaller guns	65

GENERAL NOTES
A 3rd Class brig-rigged gunboat, she was composite-built and had a ram bow.

CAREER
Launched in 1868 and completed 1870 as the steamer *Wunya Maru* (this must be simply a bad transliteration of *Un'yo Maru* as the sound 'wu' does not exist in the Japanese language); in July 1870 she was taken over by the Nagato Clan but in the same year she was given to the Emperor and renamed *Un'yo*; wrecked 31 October, 1876 near Oshima Kishu Bay of Atawa; later BU.

Name	Builder	Date	Displ	Length ft in	Beam ft in	Draught ft in	Machinery	SHP	Speed	Fuel	Radius	Armament	Comp
HOSHO ex-*Ho Sho*	A. Hall & Co., Aberdeen	1868–1869	316 N	144 0 pp	22 0	6 9	single-screw horizontal direct-acting engine, ?rectangular boilers	217 ihp	10	810 coal		1 × 7in BL (Armstrong) 1 × 5.5in BL (Armstrong) 2 smaller guns	65

GENERAL NOTES
A 3rd Class gunboat, composite-built and barque-rigged.

CAREER
Launched in 1868 and completed 1869 as the British steamer *Ho Sho*; sold in June 1870 to Japan and renamed *Hosho*; rated as a tender; re-rated 2nd Class gunboat March 1898; stricken 13 March, 1899 and BU.

Hosho (1880)

Name	Builder	Date	Displ	Length ft in	Beam ft in	Draught ft in	Machinery	SHP	Speed	Fuel	Radius	Armament	Comp
RAIDEN ex-*Raiden Maru* ex-*Emperor* ex-*Banryu* ex-HMS *Emperor*	Unknown, Blackwall	1856– 1857	400 N 370 gross	135 0 wl	22 0	8 6	single-shaft horizontal single-cyl direct-acting engine rectangular boilers	60 nhp	9			4 ML guns	

GENERAL NOTES
This vessel was an armed yacht or 3rd Class gunboat, and had an iron hull and brigantine rig. She was built to the order of the British Government for presentation to the Japanese Emperor, which accounts for the fact that she was originally known as HMS *Emperor*.

RE-ARMAMENT
In 1877 she was re-armed with 2 × 4.7in (40pdr) Armstrong BL guns.

CAREER
Launched in 1856 and completed in 1857 as HMS *Emperor*; transferred in July 1858 at Shinagawa and renamed *Banryu*; joined the Government fleet in March 1868 but in October of that year she went over to the rebels; in the May of 1869 she was sunk by units of the Imperial Navy; the wreck was repaired by an American firm which renamed her SS *Emperor*; in 1873 she was returned to the Imperial Government as *Raiden Maru* and in 1877 she was transferred to the Navy as the gunboat *Raiden*; afterwards she served as a transport; stricken in 1888 and sold to a Japanese shipping firm; rebuilt as a whaler and renamed *Raiden Maru*; BU about 1899 at Osaka.

Raiden (1880)

Name	Builder	Date	Displ	Length ft in	Beam ft in	Draught ft in	Machinery	SHP	Speed	Fuel	Radius	Armament	Comp
BANJO	Yokosuka DY	1877– 1880	708 F 656 N	153 10 pp	25 10	12 9	single-shaft horizontal 2-cyl compound machinery 4 rectangular boilers	659 ihp	10	60/120 coal	?	1 × 5.9in 22-cal BL (Krupp) 1 × 4.7in 25-cal BL (Krupp) 2 × 3.1in BL (Krupp) 3 MGs	112

GENERAL NOTES
A wooden-hulled gunboat.

CAREER
Launched July 1878 and completed August 1880; stricken in 1907 and served as a fishery protection vessel until 1913; BU.

Name	Builder	Date	Displ	Length ft in	Beam ft in	Draught ft in	Machinery	SHP	Speed	Fuel	Radius	Armament	Comp
MAYA	Onohama, Kobe	1885– 1887	612 N	154 2 pp	26 10	9 8	2-shaft 2-cyl horizontal compound machinery 2 cyl boilers	963 ihp	12	60 coal	?	1 × 8.3in 22-cal BL (Krupp) 1 × 4.7in 25-cal BL (Krupp) 2 MGs (see Armament Notes)	104
CHOKAI	Ishikawajima, Tokyo	1885– 1888											
ATAGO	Yokosuka DY	1886– 1889											
AKAGI	Onohama, Kobe	1886– 1890											

GENERAL NOTES
These were the first Japanese gunboats to use iron in their construction, but only *Maya* and *Chokai* had iron hulls; *Atago* was composite wood-and-iron and *Agaki* was built of steel. They were schooner-rigged and had ram bows.

ARMAMENT
Probably only *Chokai* and *Atago* were fitted with 8.3in and 4.7in guns. In about 1887, *Maya* had 2 × 5.9in 25-cal (Krupp); 2 × 57mm (Nordenfelt); 2 MGs. In 1906 she had 4 × 4.7in 40-cal QF; 2 × 47mm (Hotchkiss). In 1894 *Akagi* had 4 × 4.7in 40-cal QF; 6 × 47mm (Hotchkiss).

CAREERS
Maya
Launched 18 August, 1886, completed December 1887; stricken 1908 but served as a fishery protection vessel until 1913; BU.
Chokai
Launched August 1887 and completed in October 1888; stricken 1908; served as a fishery protection vessel until 1914; BU.
Atago
Launched June 1887, completed March 1889; sank 6 November, 1904 SW of Port Arthur (38° 24′ N, 120° 55′ E) after running into a cliff in fog.

The composite gunboat *Atago* was completed in 1889. Two of her sisters were steel-hulled, and a third was built of 'compound' iron and steel (Shizuo Fukui.)

GUNBOATS 115

Name	Builder	Date	Displ	Length ft in	Beam ft in	Draught ft in	Machinery	SHP	Speed	Fuel	Radius	Armament	Comp
OSHIMA	Onohama, Kobe	1889–1892	630 N	175 6 pp	26 3	9 0	2-shaft VTE 2 cyl boilers	1216 ihp	16	140 coal	?	4 × 4.7in 40-cal 5 × 47mm (Hotchkiss)	130

GENERAL NOTES
This steel gunboat was the first Japanese warship with triple expansion machinery. The machinery was built by Yokosuka DY.

ARMAMENT
At some stage in her career she was re-armed with 4 × 4.7in 40-cal; 7 × 40mm and 1 MG.

CAREER
Launched September 1891, completed February 1892; heavily damaged 16 May, 1904 in collision with the *Akagi* in fog NE of Port Arthur (39° 01′ N, 121° 08′ E); she sank the next day at about 3.38 hrs.

Ohshima was a steel gunboat, completed in 1892. She was the first Japanese ship fitted with triple-expansion steam machinery (Shizui Fukui.)

Name	Builder	Date	Displ	Length ft in	Beam ft in	Draught ft in	Machinery	SHP	Speed	Fuel	Radius	Armament	Comp
SOKO ex-*Ts'aochiang*	Unknown, Shanghai	1869–1879	600 N	156 8 pp	28 3	10 4	Horizontal reciprocating machinery cyl boilers	400 ihp	9	?	?	2 × 6in on Vavasseur mountings 2 MGs	79

GENERAL NOTES
A gunboat built for the Chinese Navy.

ARMAMENT
About 1898 she was armed with 2 × 3in 40-cal QF (Armstrong pattern).

CAREER
Launched *c* 1876 and completed *c* 1879 for the Chinese Navy; captured 25 July, 1894 by cruiser *Akitsushima* off the W Coast of Korea (she surrendered without a fight); renamed *Soko*; stricken 1902 and on the disposal list in 1904; BU.

Soko (1897)

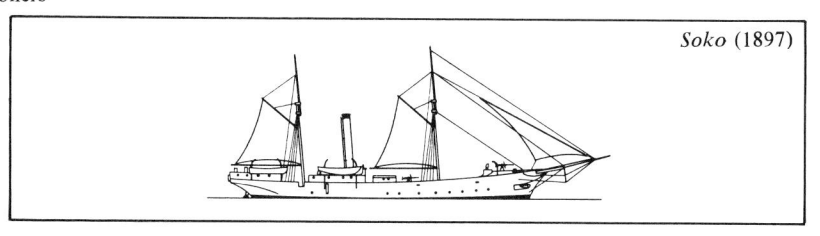

Name	Builder	Date	Displ	Length ft in	Beam ft in	Draught ft in	Machinery	SHP	Speed	Fuel	Radius	Armament	Comp
CHINCHU ex-*Chen Chung* ex-*Iota*	Armstrong, Mitchell & Co., Elswick	1881	500	125 0 pp	29 0	9 10	2-shaft horizontal machinery, cyl boiler	455 ihp	10.4	50 coal	?	1 × 11in 23-cal MLR 2 × 3in 4 MGs	28
CHINTO ex-*Chen Tung* ex-*Epsilon*		1879	490	125 0 pp	29 0	9 6		472 ihp	10.2	50 coal			
CHIMPEN ex-*Chen Pien* ex-*Kappa*		1878–1880	440	125 7 pp	29 0	9 3		455 ihp	10.4	50 coal			
CHINHOKU ex-*Chen Pei* ex-*Theta*								472 ihp	10.2	50 coal			
CHINNAN ex-*Chen Nan* ex-*Eta*													
CHINSEI ex-*Chen Hsi* ex-*Zeta*													

Chinto (1895)   *Chinchu* (1895)

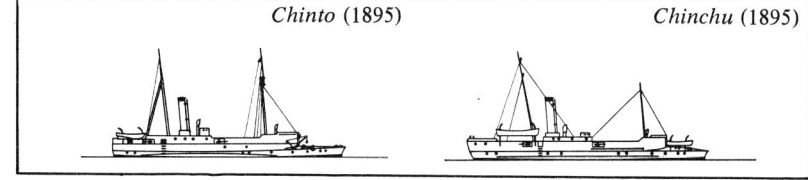

GENERAL NOTES
These steel gunboats were designed by Sir George Rendel as improved *Staunch* type. They had a simple fore-and-aft rig with two tripod masts, and the gun was in an embrasure in the bow. To aid manoeuvrability a bow rudder was fitted. The class were originally named after letters of the Greek alphabet.

ARMAMENT
About 1898 they were re-armed with: 1 × 11in (35t RML); 2 × 3in 40-cal QF and 4 MGs.

CAREERS
Chimpen
Launched 1880, completed 1881 as Chinese *Chen Pien*; captured 12 February, 1895 at Wei Hai Wei; taken over 17 February; for disposal in 1906 and BU 1906–7.
Chinchu
Launched 1880 and completed 1881 as Chinese *Chen Chung*; captured and taken over as *Chinpen* above; disposal as *Chinpen*.
Chinhoku
Launched 1879, completed 1880 as Chinese *Chen Pei*; capture and disposal as *Chinpen* above.
Chinto
Launched 1879, completed 1880 as Chinese *Chen Tung*; capture and disposal as *Chinpen* above.
Chinnan
Launched 1879, completed 1880 as Chinese *Chen Nan*; capture and disposal as *Chimpen* above.
Chinsei
Launched 1879, completed 1880 as Chinese *Chen Hsi*; capture and disposal as *Chinpen* above.

Chimpen was a former Chinese gunboat of the British Rendel or 'flat iron' type, surrendered at Weihaiwei in 1895. Eleven were built for China between 1878 and 1881, originally with Greek alphabetical names. (Shizuo Fukui.)

Name	Builder	Date	Displ	Length ft in	Beam ft in	Draught ft in	Machinery	SHP	Speed	Fuel	Radius	Armament	Comp
UJI	Kure DY	1902–1903	620 N 540 light	189 6 oa 180 5 pp	27 7	7 0	2-shaft 3 cyl VTE 2 Kampon boilers	1000 ihp	13	100/180 coal	?	4 × 3in 40-cal QF 6 MGs	86

GENERAL NOTES
A 1st Class steel-hulled gunboat built under the 1896–7 War Programme.

CAREER
Launched 14 March, 1903 and completed in August 1903; stricken 1932 and BU.

Uji (1903)

Name	Builder	Date	Displ	Length ft in	Beam ft in	Draught ft in	Machinery	SHP	Speed	Fuel	Radius	Armament	Comp
MAKIKUMO ex-*Vsadnik*	Crichton, Abo	1893	400 light	190 3 pp	23 11	11 2	2-shaft VTE machinery 2 locomotive boilers	3000 ihp	22	90 coal	4000 @ 10	6 × 47mm QF 3 × 37mm 2 × 15in TT (AW)	64
SHIKINAMI ex-*Gaidamak*	Crichton, Abo												

GENERAL NOTES
Steel torpedo gunboats built for the Russian Navy.

ARMAMENT
During their repairs in 1906 they were reboilered with Miyabara boilers and the Russian guns were replaced by Armstrong-pattern guns.

MACHINERY
On original trials they averaged 21 knots with 3350 ihp; after reboilering they were good for 22 knots with 3600 ihp.

CAREERS
Makikumo
Launched 1893 and completed that year as the Russian *Vsadnik*; sunk 15 December, 1904 in Port Arthur by Japanese artillery; fell into Japanese hands on 2 January, 1905; salvaged 23–30 October, 1905; repaired and renamed *Makikumo*; stricken 1913 and BU 1914.
Shikinami
Launched 1893 and completed the same year as the Russian *Gaidamak*; scuttled 1 January, 1905 in Port Arthur and fell into Japanese hands next day; raised 7 October, 1905 and renamed *Shikinami* during repairs; stricken 1913 and BU 1914.

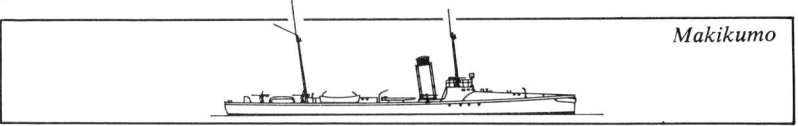

Makikumo

Name	Builder	Date	Displ	Length ft in	Beam ft in	Draught ft in	Machinery	SHP	Speed	Fuel	Radius	Armament	Comp
SAGA	Sasebo DY	1912–1913	785 F 685 N	208 8 pp	29 6	7 3	2-shaft VTE 2 Kampon boilers	1600 ihp	15	90/190 coal	?	1 × 4.7in 45-cal QF 3 × 3.1in 40-cal 3 MGs	98
BIUN ex-*Mei Yün*													

GUNBOATS 117

GENERAL NOTES
1st Class steel gunboat.

ARMAMENT
By 1941 the 3.1in guns were replaced by AA guns of the same calibre, and 3 MGs were added.

CAREER
Launched 27 September, 1912, completed 16 November, 1912; sunk 22 January, 1945 in Hong Kong by USAF aircraft; officially stricken 10 March, 1945.

Saga (1937)

Name	Builder	Date	Displ	Length ft in	Beam ft in	Draught ft in	Machinery	SHP	Speed	Fuel	Radius	Armament	Comp
ATAKA ex-*Nakoso*	Yokohama Dock Co.	1920–1922	880 N 725 *light*	222 0 pp	29 6	7 5	2-shaft VTE 2 Kampon boilers	1700 ihp	16	235 coal	?	2 × 4.7in 45-cal 2 × 3.1in 40-cal 6 MGs	118

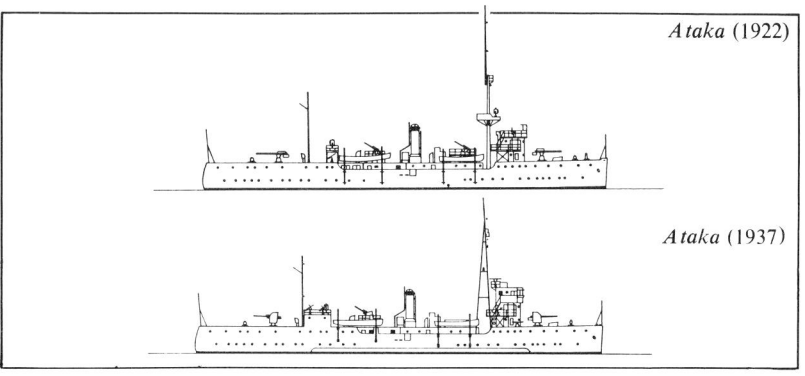

Ataka (1922)

Ataka (1937)

GENERAL NOTES
Built under the 1920–8 Fleet Construction Programme as a gunboat and submarine tender. She had a vertical stem and higher freeboard than had been usual in Japanese warships.

RE-ARMAMENT AND RECONSTRUCTION
In 1937 she was re-armed at Kure and given a tripod mast. Her armament was now 1 × 4.7in 45-cal; 2 × 3.1in AA; 4 × 13mm AA; 4 MGs, DCs, Bulges were added to increase stability. Her particulars were now: displacement 1094ts; beam 32.09ft. From 1939 she had 8 × 13mm AA.

CAREER
Launched 11 April, 1922 and completed 12 August, 1923 (renamed *Ataka* in November 1921); served as the permanent flagship of the Yangtze Flotilla; surrendered in August 1945 at Singapore and transferred to China as *An Tung*; captured in 1949 by Communists.

Two views of the gunboat *Ataka*. Left, on completion in 1922; right, after her 1936–37 refit at Kure, with a tripod mast and larger bridge. (Shizuo Fukui.)

Name	Builder	Date	Displ	Length ft in	Beam ft in	Draught ft in	Machinery	SHP	Speed	Fuel	Radius	Armament	Comp
HASHIDATE UJI No. 867	Sakurajima, Osaka	1939–1941	1204 F 1100 N 999 *light* 1860 S	257 6 wl 249 4 pp	31 9	8 0	2-shaft GTU 2 Kampon boilers	4600	19½	?	3460 @ 14	3 × 4.7in 45-cal 4 × 25mm AA	170

GENERAL NOTES
Gunboats fitted to act as flagships, built under the 1937 Programme.

MACHINERY
On trials they averaged 20.15 knots on 1205ts.

118 GUNBOATS

RE-ARMAMENT
Their wartime AA was 9 × 25mm, and DCs were carried.

CAREERS
Hashidate
Launched 23 December, 1939, completed 30 June, 1940; torpedoed 22 May, 1944 by US submarine *Picuda* off Pratas Island (21° 08′ N, 117° 20′ E); officially stricken 10 July, 1944.

Uji
Launched 29 September 1940, completed 30 April 1941; surrendered August 1945 and transferred to China as *Chang Chi*; taken over by Communists in 1949 and re-armed by 1955.

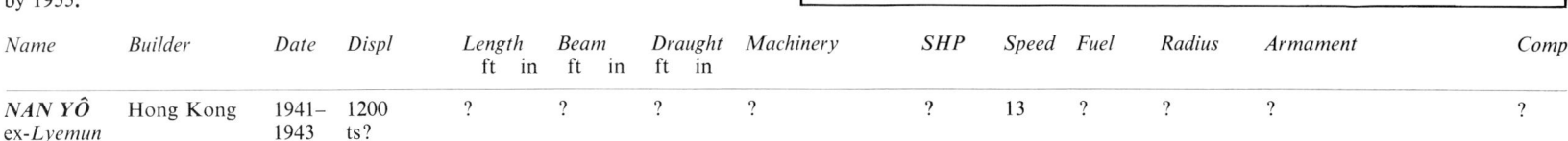

Hashidate (1940)

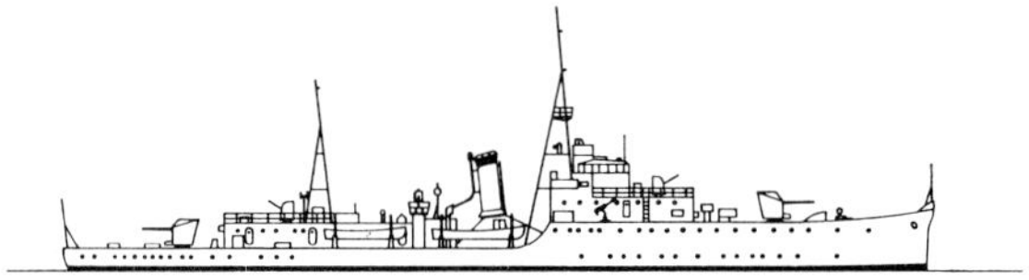

Name	Builder	Date	Displ	Length ft in	Beam ft in	Draught ft in	Machinery	SHP	Speed	Fuel	Radius	Armament	Comp
NAN YÔ ex-*Lyemun* ex-*Looe*	Hong Kong	1941–1943	1200 ts? N	?	?	?	?	?	13	?	?	?	?

She was completed as a gunboat, but details of a sister-ship completed as a sweeper will be found on page 210.

GENERAL NOTES
A former British minesweeper of the *Bangor* Class taken over on the slips. As the original displacement was 672ts, the tonnage given in Japanese records is either wrong or the dimensions were enlarged. The planned measurements were 171.5ft × 28.5ft × 8.23ft.

CAREER
Begun as HMS *Looe* but renamed *Lyemun*; demolished at Hong Kong while half-complete in December 1941; launched by the Japanese in 1942 and completed 2 March, 1943; sunk 23 December, 1943 by US carrier aircraft 35 m S of Formosa Straits (25° 30′ N, 119° 30′ E).

Name	Builder	Date	Displ	Length ft in	Beam ft in	Draught ft in	Machinery	SHP	Speed	Fuel	Radius	Armament	Comp
NANSHIN ex-*Ram*	Droogdok Mij., Tandjong Priok	1941–	2400 N	281 6 wl 253 3	36 1	12 6	2-shaft Diesels	4800 bhp	18	?	?	3 × 3.1in 4 × 25mm AA DCs, mines	120
NANKAI ex-*Regulus*	Droogdok Mij., Soerabaja	1942–1944		pp								4 × 4.7in 45-cal 4 × 25mm AA DCs, mines	

GENERAL NOTES
Dutch minelayers rebuilt by the Japanese as gunboats.

CAREERS
Nanshin
Launched 10 December, 1941 as *Ram*; hull towed to Tjilatjap in January 1942, but scuttled 2 March, 1942; raised by Japanese but cannibalised and never completed; surrendered 1945 and BU.

Nankai
Begun as *Regulus* but scuttled half-completed on 2 March, 1942 at Soerabaja;

Nanshin as projected; *Nankai* similar

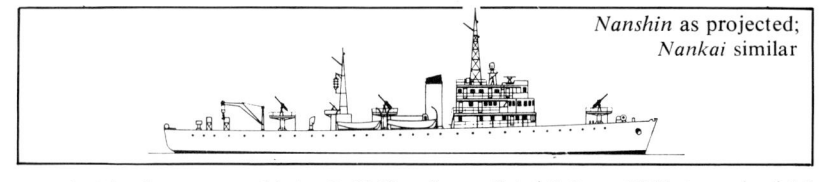

launched by Japanese on 21 April, 1943 and completed 7 June, 1944; torpedoed 16 July, 1945 by submarine 150 m W of Soerabaja; officially stricken 30 July, 1945.

Name	Builder	Date	Displ	Length ft in	Beam ft in	Draught ft in	Machinery	SHP	Speed	Fuel	Radius	Armament	Comp
OKITSU ex-*Lepanto*	Cantieri Navale Riuniti, Ancona	1925–1927	615	216 6 oa 204 0 pp	28 6	8 6	2-shaft VTE 2 water-tube boilers	1500 ihp	14	75 oil	3500 @ 10	2 × 4in 47-cal 1 × 3in 40-cal AA 4 MGs 80 mines	66

GENERAL NOTES
An ex-Italian minelayer of the *Ostia* type, designed to serve as a minesweeper as well.

RE-ARMAMENT
In 1944 she was armed with 1 × 3.1in 40-cal; 8 × 25mm AA; 36 DCs.

CAREER
Launched 22 May, 1927, completed 1927 as the Italian *Lepanto*; scuttled 9 September, 1943 at Shanghai; raised in February 1944 and repaired; re-rated as a gunboat on 1 March, 1944 and renamed *Okitsu*; damaged 21 March, 1945 near Cape Hung Hua by US aircraft; surrendered August 1945 in the Chusan Archipelago; transferred to China as the *Chienning*; stricken 1956 and BU.

Okitsu (1944)

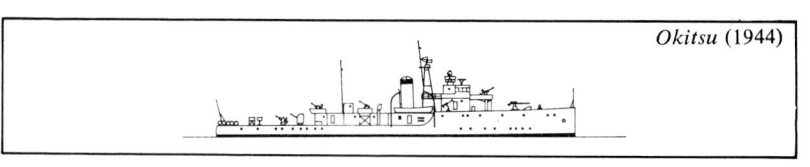

Name	Builder	Date	Displ	Length ft in	Beam ft in	Draught ft in	Machinery	SHP	Speed	Fuel	Radius	Armament	Comp
SUMIDA	John I. Thornycroft & Sons, Woolston	1903–1906	126 N 105 light	145 0 pp	23 7	1 11	3-shaft VTE Thornycroft boilers	550 ihp	13	40 coal	?	2 × 47mm 40-cal 4 MGs	40

GUNBOATS 119

GENERAL NOTES
Built under the Post-War Programme of 1896–7, this river gunboat was built in England, sent to Japan in sections and re-assembled between October 1903 and April 1906.

CAREER
Launched 26 June, 1903 and completed August 1903 by builders; stricken 1935 and BU.

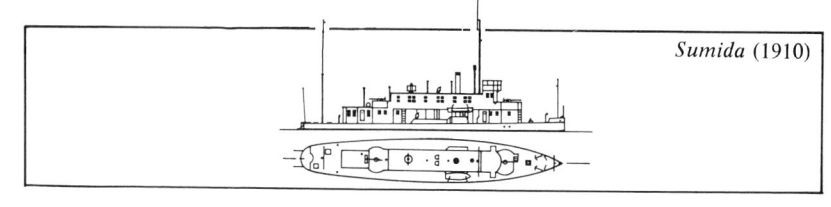

Sumida (1910)

Name	Builder	Date	Displ	Length ft in	Beam ft in	Draught ft in	Machinery	SHP	Speed	Fuel	Radius	Armament	Comp
FUSHIMI	Yarrow & Co., Scotstoun	1903–1906	180 N 150 light	159 9 pp	24 3	2 3	VTE Yarrow boilers	900 ihp	14	25 coal	?	2 × 57mm 40-cal 3 MGs	45

GENERAL NOTES
River gunboat built under the Post-War Programme of 1896–7. She was the last gunboat built outside Japan, and was sent out to Japan in sections in October 1906. At the end of 1906 she was stripped by Kawasaki for re-assembly for the second time at Shanghai.

CAREER
Launched 5 August, 1906, completed October 1906 by builders; stricken 1935 and BU.

Name	Builder	Date	Displ	Length ft in	Beam ft in	Draught ft in	Machinery	SHP	Speed	Fuel	Radius	Armament	Comp
TOBA	Sasebo DY	–1911	291 F 250 N 215 light	180 0 pp	27 0	2 7	3-shaft 3-cyl VTE 2 cyl boilers	1400 ihp	15	81 coal	?	2 × 3.1in 28-cal 6 MGs	59

GENERAL NOTES
This river gunboat was built under the 1910 Budget. She had extra cabins added aft.

RE-ARMAMENT
She later had 2 × 3.1in 40-cal; 6 MGs, but from 1940 she had 2 × 3.1in 40-cal; 3 × 25mm AA; 1 × 13mm AA. In 1945 her guns were removed for use on land.

CAREER
Launched 7 November, 1911, completed 17 November, 1911; surrendered August 1945 at Shanghai and handed over to China as *Yang Ch'i*; she fell into Communist hands in 1949 and became *Ho Hsüeh* (?).

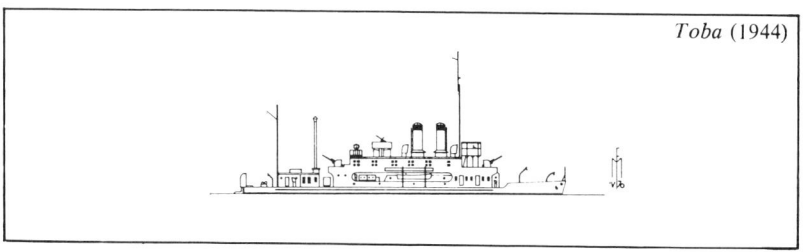

Toba (1944)

Name	Builder	Date	Displ	Length ft in	Beam ft in	Draught ft in	Machinery	SHP	Speed	Fuel	Radius	Armament	Comp
SETA KATATA HIRA HOZU	Harima Z. KK, Harima Mitsubishi, Kobe	1920–1923	340 N 305 light	184 0 oa 180 0 pp	27 0	3 4	2-shaft 2-cyl compound 2 Kampon boilers	2100 ihp	16	74 coal 25 oil	1750 @ 10	2 × 3.1in 40-cal 3/6 13mm MGs	62

GENERAL NOTES
River gunboats built under the Fleet Building Programme of 1920–8, on the same dimensions as the *Toba*. They were built in sections; *Seta* and *Katata* were re-assembled by Tunghwa Shipbuilding Co., Shanghai, and the other pair by Yangtze Engineering Co., Hankow.

RE-ARMAMENT AND RECONSTRUCTION
About 1940 they were armed with 2 × 3.1in 40-cal AA; 6 × 25mm AA. *Seta* and *Katata* later had 5 × 13mm AA in place of the 25mm. In 1945 their guns were removed for use on land. In some the funnels were shortened, and given mushroom-topped ventilators.

Hozu (1943)

CAREERS
Seta
Launched 30 June, 1922, completed 6 October, 1923; damaged 6 June, 1943 in Yangtze by Chinese aircraft; surrendered August 1945 at Shanghai and transferred to China as *Chang Teh*; fell into Communist hands in 1949.
Katata
Launched 16 July, 1922, completed 20 October, 1923; badly damaged 12 December, 1944 at Kiukiang on the Yangtze by USAF aircraft (29° 35′ N, 116° 10′ E) and grounded; salvaged and towed to Shanghai; damaged 2 April, 1945 at Shanghai by USAF aircraft; surrendered August 1945 and BU.
Hira
Launched 14 March, 1923, completed 24 August, 1923; badly damaged 26 November, 1944 by Chinese aircraft near Anking on Yangtze; BU in Spring 1945 but officially stricken 10 May, 1945.
Hozu
Launched 19 April, 1923, completed 7 November, 1923; sunk 26 November, 1944 in shallow water near Anking by Chinese aircraft (30° 30′ N, 117° E); BU in Spring 1945 but officially stricken 10 May, 1945.

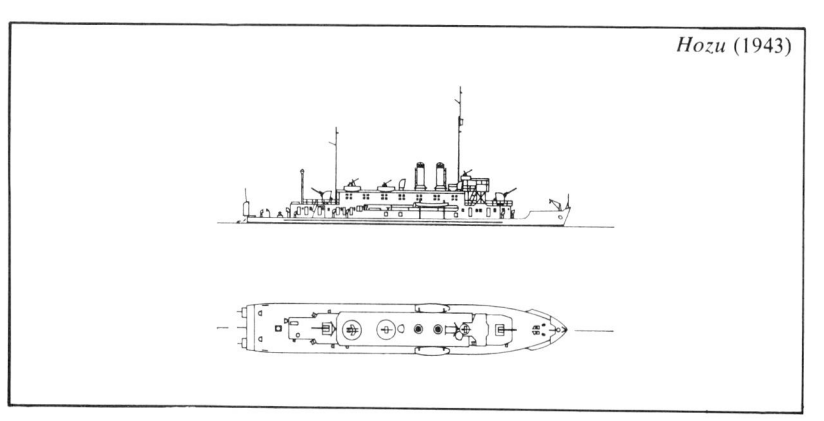

The river gunboat *Fushimi* was built on the Clyde, and then re-assembled at Kobe in 1906. (IWM.)

The river gunboat *Toba* was similar to the British-built *Sumida* and *Fushimi*, but was built at Sasebo Dockyard. (Shizuo Fukui.)

Atami was completed in 1929 for service in China, and survived World War Two. (Shizuo Fukui.)

Name	Builder	Date	Displ	Length ft in	Beam ft in	Draught ft in	Machinery	SHP	Speed	Fuel	Radius	Armament	Comp
ATAMI	Tama Fujinagata,	1928–1929	225 N	151 11 oa	22 3	3 8	2-shaft 2-cyl compound	1300 ihp	16¾	28 coal	?	1 × 3.1in 28-cal AA 1 × 13mm	54/77
FUTAMI	Osaka	1928–1930	206 light	148 7 wl 148 7 pp			2 Kampon boilers			34 oil		5 × 7.7mm MGs	

GENERAL NOTES
Improved *Sata* type built under the 1927 Programme.

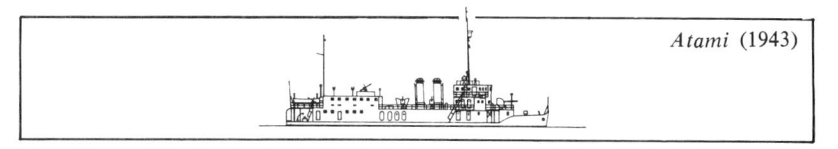

RE-ARMAMENT
About 1940 they were armed with 1 × 3.1in 40-cal AA, 5 × 25mm AA; In 1945 they were disarmed and the guns were sent ashore for land service.

CAREERS
Atami
Launched 30 March, 1929, completed 30 June, 1929; damaged 10 June, 1943 near Tung Ting Lake on the Yangtze by Chinese aircraft; surrendered in August 1945 at Shanghai and transferred to China as *Yung Ping*; taken over by Communists in 1949.

Futami
Launched 20 November, 1929, completed 28 February, 1930; surrendered August 1945 at Shanghai and given to China as *Yung An*; taken over by Communists in 1949.

Atami (1943)

Name	Builder	Date	Displ	Length ft in	Beam ft in	Draught ft in	Machinery	SHP	Speed	Fuel	Radius	Armament	Comp
KOTAKA	Mitsui, Tamano	1929–1930	62.7 N 50 light	100 0 oa 98 5 pp	16 10	2 1	2-shaft 2-cyl Diesels	540 bhp	15½	? oil	?	5 MGs	?

GENERAL NOTES
Built under the 1927 Programme for service on the Upper Yangtze. She had a depth of hold of only 4.59ft, and was carried to the Yangtze on board the transport *Seito*.

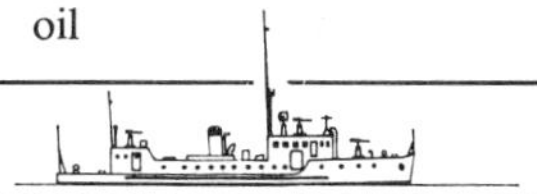

ARMAMENT
Her final armament was 3 × .303in Lewis MGs.

Kotaka (1944)

CAREER
Launched 18 January, 1930, completed 11 January 1930; about 1942 she was serving as a passenger vessel on the Yangtze; sunk 31 May, 1944 on Yangtze by Chinese aircraft.

GUNBOATS 121

Name	Builder	Date	Displ	Length ft in	Beam ft in	Draught ft in	Machinery	SHP	Speed	Fuel	Radius	Armament	Comp
FUSHIMI	Fujinagata, Z., Osaka	1938–1939	374 F	164 0 wl	32 1	4 1	2-shaft GTU 2 Kampon boilers	2200	17	oil	1500 @ 14	1 × 3.1in 28-cal 2 × 25mm AA	64
SUMIDA		1939–1940	350 N 304 light	159 1 pp									
Nos. 868–869			360 N 310 light										

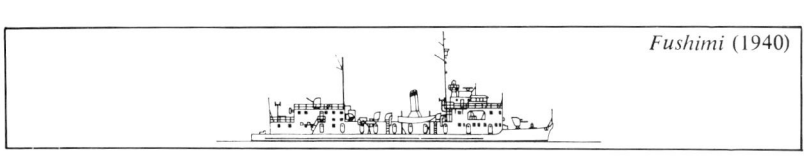

GENERAL NOTES
These river gunboats of the 1937 Programme were the last ordered for the Japanese Navy. The depth of hold was 7.38ft. Nos. 868–9 were projected under the 1942 Programme but not ordered.

ARMAMENT
In 1942/3 the AA armament was increased to 8 × 25mm, but in 1945 both were disarmed.

CAREERS
Launched 26 March, 1939, completed 15 July, 1939; sunk 25 November, 1944 by Chinese aircraft in shallow water near Anking on the Yangtze (30° 30′ N, 117° E); salvaged and towed to Shanghai; surrendered at Shanghai in August 1945 and transferred to China as *Kiang Hsi*; became the Communist *Chiang Feng* in 1949.
Sumida
Launched 30 October, 1939, completed 31 May, 1940; damaged 25 November, 1944 by Chinese aircraft near Anking; surrendered August 1945 Shanghai and transferred to China as *Nan Chang*, but renamed *Chiang Hsi* when she fell into Communist hands in 1949.

Fushimi (1940)

Name	Builder	Date	Displ	Length ft in	Beam ft in	Draught ft in	Machinery	SHP	Speed	Fuel	Radius	Armament	Comp
TATARA ex-*Wake* (PR.3) ex-*Guam* (PG. 43)	Kiangnan, Shanghai	1926–1927	370 S	159 9 oa 149 11 pp	26 11	5 3	2-shaft 3-cyl VTE 2 Thornycroft boilers	1950 ihp	12½	75 oil	?	2 × 3in 13 × 25mm AA	70
SUMA ex-*Moth*	Sunderland SB Co., Sunderland	1914–1916	650 N 625 light	237 6 oa 230 0 pp	36 0	4 0	2-shaft VTE 2 Yarrow boilers	2000 ihp	14	76 oil	?	2 × 6in 1 × 3in AA	65
KARATSU ex-*Luzon* (PR.7)	Kiangnan, Shanghai	1926–1928	560 S	214 7 wl 196 10 pp	31 3	5 9	2-shaft 3-cyl VTE 2 Thornycroft boilers	3150 ihp	16	? oil	173	2 × 3in 10 MGs	82
MAIKO ex-*Macau*	Yarrow, Scotstoun	1909–1910	133 N 95 light	119 9 pp	19 9	2 2	2-shaft 3-cyl VTE 1 Yarrow boiler	250 ihp	11.8	? coal	?	2 × 57mm 3 MGs	24
NARUMI ex-*Ermanno Carlotto*	Shanghai Dock & Eng. Co.	1919–1921	180 S	160 1 pp	24 6	2 9	2-shaft 3-cyl VTE 2 Yarrow boilers	1100 ihp	14	56 oil	?	2 × 3in 6 MGs	60

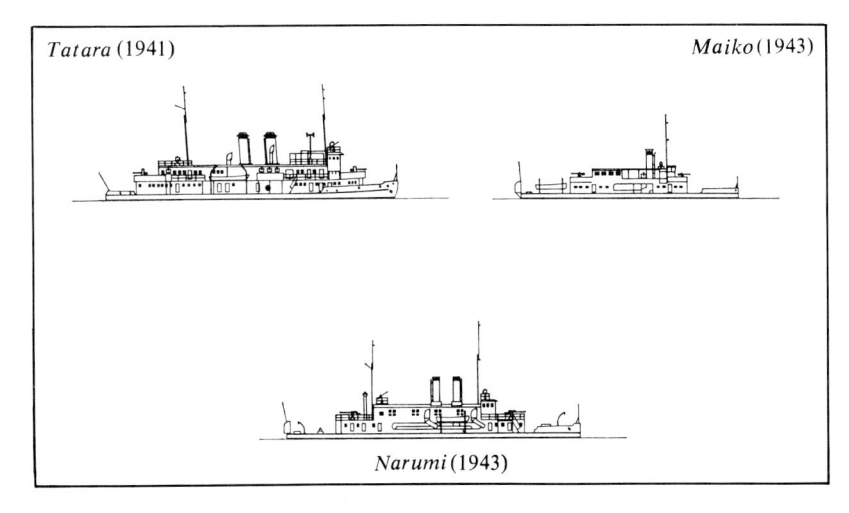

Tatara (1941) *Maiko* (1943)

Narumi (1943)

GENERAL NOTES
River gunboats captured from the British, American, Portuguese and Italian Navies.

RE-ARMAMENT
All units were re-armed but details are unknown.

CAREERS
Tatara
Launched 28 May, 1927, completed 1927 as USS *Guam*; renamed *Wake* 194?; fell into Japanese hands 8 December, 1941 at Shanghai; renamed *Tatara* 15 December; disarmed in 1945 and surrendered at Shanghai; became Chinese *Tai Yüan* in 1946, but taken over by Communists in 1949.
Suma
Launched 9 October, 1915, completed early 1916 as HMS *Moth*; scuttled 12 December, 1941 at Hong Kong; salvaged 1 July, 1942 and renamed *Suma*; sunk by mine 19 March, 1945 near Kiangying on the Yangtze (32° N, 120° E); officially stricken 10 May, 1945.
Karatsu
Launched 12 September, 1927 and completed 1928 as USS *Luzon*; sunk 5 May, 1942

Suma (1942)

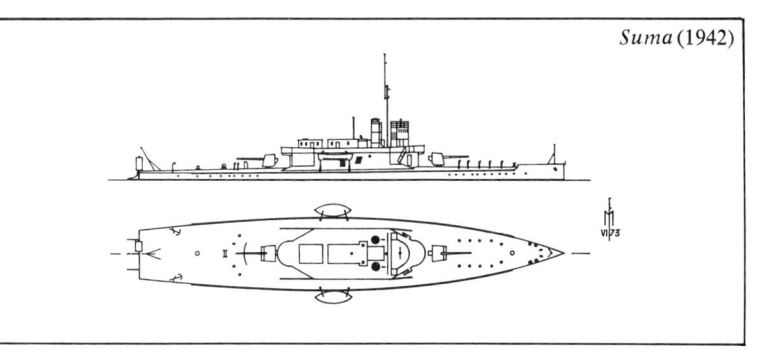

by Japanese artillery at Corregidor, Manila Bay; salvaged 1 August, 1942 and renamed *Karatsu*; 3 March, 1944 badly damaged 20 m NE of Dapitan, Mindanao (08° 25′ N, 123° 23′ E) by US submarine *Narwhal*; towed to Manila and sunk there 3 February, 1945; BU 10 May, 1945.

Maiko
Launched 1909 and completed 1910 as the Portuguese *Macau*; acquired by Japan in 1943 and renamed *Maiko* 15 August, 1943; surrendered at Canton in August 1945 and transferred to China in 1946 as *Wu Feng*; taken over by Communists 1949.

Narumi
Launched 28 February, 1921, completed 1921 as *Ermanno Carlotto*; sunk 9 September, 1943 at Shanghai; salvaged and taken over 15 October, 1943; renamed *Narumi*; damaged 15 January, 1945 by USAF aircraft near Hankow; disarmed 1945 and guns used ashore; surrendered August 1945 and handed over to China in 1946 as *Kiang Kun*; taken over by Communists in 1949.

Merchant Ships used as Gunboats

The following merchant ships were armed and used as gunboats:

Name	Tonnage	Date	Type
Anshu Maru	2601	1937	steamer
Aso Maru	703	1932	motor ship
Busho Maru	2569	1921	passenger steamer
Choan Maru No. 2	2632	1927	motor passenger ship
Chohakusan Maru	2120	1928	passenger steamer
Chojusan Maru	2131	1928	passenger steamer
Choko Maru No. 2	2629	1927	steamer
Chosa Maru	2538	1921	passenger steamer
Choun Maru	1914	1940	motor ship
Chowa Maru	2719	1940	?
Chuwa Maru	2719	1940	?
Daido Maru	2962	1935	passenger steamer
Daigen Maru No. 7	1289	1937	steamer
Delhi Maru	2205	1922	passenger steamer
Edo Maru	1299	1937	steamer
Ehimo Maru	623	1903	steamer
Eifuku Maru	3520	1939	?
Eiko Maru	3011	1937	turbine passenger steamer
Fukuei Maru No. 10	847	1936	motor ship
Fukuyama Maru	3581	1936	steamer
Fuso Maru	319	1895	steamer
Hakkai Maru	2921	1939	steamer
Hakkaisan Maru	3311	1937	steamer
Heijo Maru	1201	1903	steamer
Heijo Maru	2627	1941	?
Hijikawa Maru No. 5	564	1897	steamer
Hino Maru No. 2	998	1935	motor ship
Hino Maru No. 5	2935	1940	?
Hirota Maru	2922	1940	?
Hirotama Maru	1911	1933	?
Hiyoshi Maru No. 2	1287	1936	steamer
Hokoku Maru	1274	1936	steamer
Hongkong Maru	2797	1935	turbine passenger ship
Hyakufuku Maru	986	1928	passenger steamer
Ikushima Maru	3943	1936	turbine steamer
Ikuta Maru	2968	1936	steamer
Imizu Maru	2924	1940	?
Kagawa Maru	613	1903	steamer
Kahoku Maru	3311	1931	motor passenger ship
Kaiho Maru	1093	1941	?
Kaijo Maru	284	1902	steamer
Kamitsu Maru	2721	1937	turbine steamer
Kanko Maru	2929	1938	steamer
Kasagi Maru	3140	1928	passenger steamer
Katori Maru	1920	1938	steamer
Katsura Maru No. 2	1368	1937	steamer
Kazan Maru	2103	1936	steamer
Keijo Maru	2626	1940	steamer
Keiko Maru	2929	1938	steamer
Keishin Maru	1434	1940	steamer
Kenzan Maru	951	1938	steamer
Kiikawa Maru	209	1892	steamer
Kinjosan Maru	3262	1936	steamer
Kiso Maru	703	1932	motor ship
Kongosan Maru	2119	1927	passenger steamer
Kosho Maru	564	1883	steamer
Kosho Maru	1365	1940	?
Kowa Maru	1106	1940	?
Kugogawa Maru	417	1893	steamer
Magane Maru	3120	1940	?
Manda Maru	248	1900	steamer
Manyo Maru	2904	1937	?
Meiji Maru No. 1	1934	1937	steamer
Miyoshima Maru	273	1902	steamer
Mukogawa Maru	418	1893	steamer
Myoken Maru	4124	1938	turbine steamer
Nachi Maru	1605	1926	motor ship
Nagata Maru	2969	1936	steamer
Nampo Maru	1206	1940	?
Nikkai Maru	2562	1938	steamer
Nissho Maru No. 2	1386	1941	?
Nissho Maru No. 12	1199	1936	steamer
Okuyo Maru	2904	1938	steamer
Otagawa Maru	408	1893	steamer
Peking Maru	2288	1937	steamer
Sabagawa Maru	313	1890	steamer
Saikyo Maru	1296	1936	steamer
Santo Maru	3266	1931	motor passenger ship
Seian Maru	3712	1938	motor passenger ship
Seikai Maru	2693	1940	?
Seikyo Maru	2608	1934	steamer
Sen-yo Maru	2904	1937	steamer
Shinko Maru No. 1	935	1938	motor ship
Shinko Maru No. 2	2577	1939	?
Shinkyo Maru	2672	1932	passenger steamer
Shinyo Maru	414	1903	steamer
Shoei Maru	1986	1936	steamer
Shoei Maru	3580	1936	steamer
Shoko Maru	1933	1939	?
Shosei Maru	998	1929	passenger steamer
Shotoku Maru	1964	1938	steamer
Sumanoura Maru	3519	1940	?
Taiko Maru	498	1891	steamer
Taiko Maru	2984	1937	steamer
Terushima Maru	3110	1937	turbine steamer
Tomitsu Maru	2933	1937	turbine steamer
Tosho Maru	1289	1937	steamer
Toyotsu Maru	2930	1937	turbine steamer
Tozan Maru	2103	1926	passenger steamer
Unkai Maru No. 10	851	1939	?
Un-yo Maru No. 1	2039	1936	steamer
Yoshida Maru	2920	1941	?
Yoshidagawa Maru	310	1890	steamer
Zuiko Maru	2577	1939	steamer

9. Torpedo Boats and Destroyers

Torpedo Boats

Name	Builder	Date	Displ	Length ft in	Beam ft in	Draught ft in	Machinery	SHP	Speed	Fuel	Radius	Armament	Comp
TBs. 1 to 4	Yarrow & Co., Poplar	1878–1880	40 N	96 6 pp	12 1	3 3	single-shaft horizontal compound, 1 locomotive boiler	430 ihp	22	coal	?	2 × 37mm, 3 × 14in TT (AW)	?
TBs. 5 to 14, 16 to 19	Ch. de Chalons-sur-Saone	1890–1894	54	114 10	11 0	2 11	single-shaft 2-cyl horizontal, 1 locomotive boiler	525 ihp	19	3/8 coal	200 @ 20, 500 @ 20	2 × 37mm, 2 × 15in TT (AW)	16
TBs. 15 to 20	Normand, Le Havre	1891–1893	53	111 6	11 6	3 3	single-shaft 2-cyl horizontal compound, 1 Normand boiler	657 ihp	20	5 coal	?	2 × 37mm, 2 × 15in TT (AW)	20
TBs. 21 to 24	Normand, Le Havre; Kure DY	1891–1892, 1895	80	118 1	13 1	5 3	single-shaft, 3-cyl horizontal compound, 1 Normand boiler	1121 ihp	20.7	10 coal	1800 @ 10	2 × 37mm, 3 × 15in TT (AW)	21

GENERAL NOTES
TBs. *1* to *4* were modelled by Sir Edward Reed on the RN 100ft type. They were re-assembled in Japan, and were rated as 3rd Class boats. *Nos. 5 to 14*, etc., were built under the 1882 Programme, and were modified versions of the French 35m type. *Nos. 15 to 20* were similarly based on the French 34m type, and *21* and *24* were similar to the French *No. 126*. Material for *No. 24* had to be imported from France (depth of hull 8.69ft).

CAREERS
Nos. 1 to 4
Launched 1879, completed 1880; harbour service until 1904, and then BU.
Nos. 5 to 7
Launched 1890, completed 1892; stricken 1907 and BU.
No. 8
Launched 1891, completed 1892; wrecked 4 February, 1895 at Wei Hai Wei; raised and repaired; stricken 1908, BU.
No. 9
Launched 1891, completed 1892; badly damaged 4 February, 1895 at Wei Hai Wei by Chinese warships and shore batteries (6 dead); later repaired; stricken 1908 and BU.
No. 10
Launched September 1891, completed 1892; stricken 1910 and BU.
Nos. 11 to 13
Launched 1891, completed 1893–4; stricken 1908–10 and BU.
No. 14
Launched 1892, completed 1893; wrecked 4 February, 1895 at Wei Hai Wei but repaired; stricken 1908 and BU.
No. 15
Launched 1892, completed 1893; stricken 1900 and BU.
No. 16
Launched 1892, completed 1893; capsized 11 May, 1895 off the Pescadores Islands (23° 30′ N, 119° 30′ E).
Nos. 17 to 20
Launched 1892, completed 1893–4; stricken 1910 and BU.
No. 21
Launched 1892, completed 1894; stricken 1911 and BU.
No. 24
Launched 1895, completed 1894–5; stricken 1911 and BU.

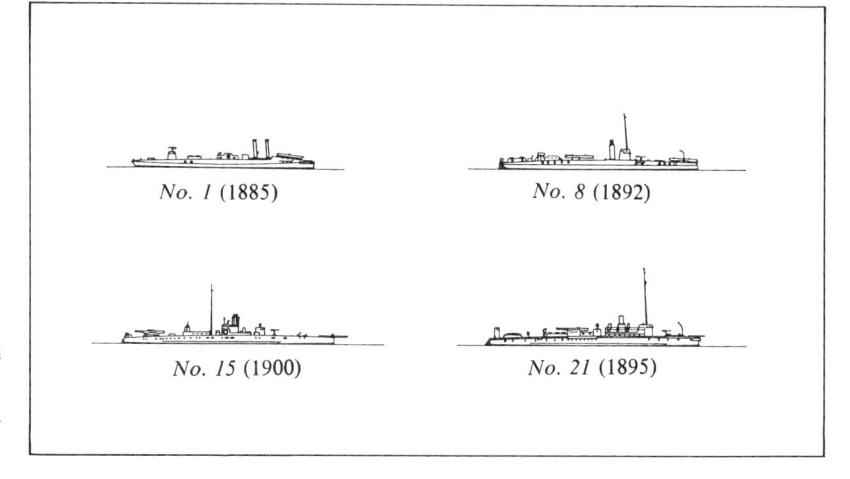

No. 1 (1885)   *No. 8* (1892)

No. 15 (1900)   *No. 21* (1895)

The French-built torpedo-boat *No. 12* was typical of the contemporary 35-metre Type, built by Normand for the French Navy in the late 1880s. (Shizuo Fukui.)

124 TORPEDO BOATS AND DESTROYERS

Name	Builder	Date	Displ	Length ft in	Beam ft in	Draught ft in	Machinery	SHP	Speed	Fuel	Radius	Armament	Comp
TBs. 22 to 23,	Schichau, Elbing (Nos. 444–5)	1891–1892	85 N	127 11	15 9	3 6	single-shaft 3-cyl VTE 1 locomotive boiler	990 ihp / 904 ihp	19	24 coal	300 @ 15	2 × 37mm 3 × 14in TT (AW)	20
TB. 25	Onohama, Nagasaki	1895											
TBs. 26 27	AG Vulcan, Stettin	1894 1894	66 74	110 7 110 4	11 6 14 0	3 6 3 7	single-shaft compound, 1 locomotive boiler	338 ihp 442 ihp	13.8 15.5	coal	? ?	2 × 37mm 2 × 14in TT (AW)	? ?
TB. 28		1885	16	62 1	8 10	?		91 ihp	10.6		?	1 × 37mm 1 × 14in TT (AW)	?

GENERAL NOTES

Nos. 22, 23 and 25 were 2nd Class torpedo-boats built under the 1882 Programme, and corresponded to the German 39m type, or S.7. Nos. 22 and 24 were re-assembled in, Japan in 1893 but No. 25 was built with material imported from Germany. Depth of hold 6.56ft.

Nos. 26 to 28 were 3rd Class torpedo-boats captured from the Chinese in 1895.

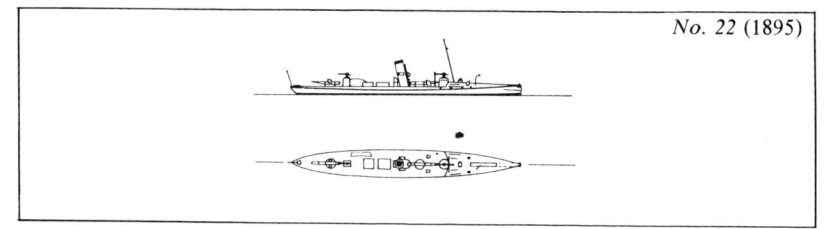

No. 22 (1895)

CAREERS

No. 22
Launched 1892, completed 1893; wrecked 4 February, 1894, but raised; stricken 1897 and BU.
No. 23
Launched 1892, completed 1893; wrecked 20 July, 1898; stricken 13 August, 1899
No. 25
Launched 1894, completed 1895; stricken 1913 and BU

No. 26 and 27
Launched 1894, completed ?...; captured from Chinese near Wei Hai Wei; 7 February, 1895; renamed TB No. 26; stricken 1908 and BU.
No. 28
Launched 1885, completed ?...; captured near Wei Hai Wei 7 February, 1895; stricken 1902 and BU.

Name	Builder	Date	Displ	Length ft in	Beam ft in	Draught ft in	Machinery	SHP	Speed	Fuel	Radius	Armament	Comp
TBs. 29, 30	Normand, Le Havre	1898	88 N	121 4 pp	13 6	4 ?	single-shaft 3-cyl VTE, 2 Normand water-tube boilers	2000 ihp	22.5	15 coal	?	1 × 47mm 3 × 14in TT	20
TBs. 31 to 38, 44 to 49, 60, 61	Schichau, Elbing (Nos. 621–8) Kawasaki, Kobe (Nos. 622–7, 677–8)	1898–1900 1899–1901	89 N 83 light	127 11 pp	15 9	3 6	single-shaft 3-cyl VTE, 2 Schichau water-tube boilers	1200 ihp	24	15 coal	2100 @ 10	2 × 42mm 3 × 14in TT (AW)	20
TBs. 39 to 43, 62 to 66	Yarrow, Poplar	1899–1901	102 N	152 6	15 3	5 2	single-shaft 3-cyl VTE, 2 Yarrow boilers	1920 ihp	26	25 coal	1600 @ 8	2 × 47mm 3 × 14in TT (AW)	20
TBs. 50 to 55, 56 to 58	Yokosuka DY Kure DY	1899–1902	54 N	111 6	11 6	3 3	single-shaft 3-cyl VTE, 1 Normand water-tube boiler	660 ihp	20	14 coal	?	1 × 47mm 2 × 14in TT	16
TBs. 67, 68 TBs. 69 to 75	Yokosuka DY various (see notes)	1902–1903	87 N	131 6 pp	16 4	3 6	single-shaft 3-cyl VTE, 2 Yarrow water-tube boilers	1200 ihp	23½	26½ coal	?	2 × 47mm 3 × 14in TT	24

GENERAL NOTES

All these 2nd Class torpedo-boats were built under the Post-War Programme of 1896–7. Nos. 29 and 30 were similar to the French No. 212 of the 39m type; Nos. 31 to 36 were assembled by Kawasaki, 37 and 38 by Mitsubishi; 39 to 43 were similar to the Austrian *Viper*; 44 to 49 and 60 to 61 were built from imported material; Nos. 50 to 59 were built in Japan to Normand plans and were similar to the French No. 130. Nos. 67 to 75 were built to Yarrow's plans and were similar to the British No. 82. The builders of 69 to 75 are not known individually but they include Sasebo DY, and Kawasaki as well as Yokosuka DY.

No. 37 (1910)   *No. 39 (1910)*

No. 57 (1902)   *No. 72 (1910)*

CAREERS

No. 29
Launched 1899, completed 1900; stricken 1916 and BU.
No. 30
Launched 1899, completed 1900; stricken 1913 and BU.

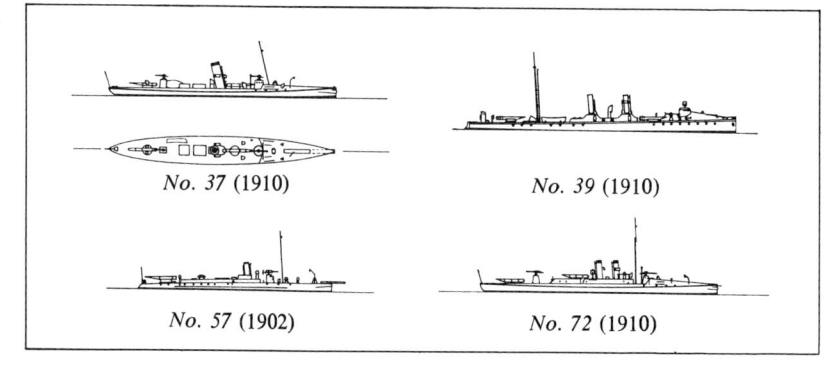

TORPEDO BOATS AND DESTROYERS

Nos. 31 and 32
Launched 1899, completed 1900; stricken 1913 but used on auxiliary duties before being BU.
No. 33
Launched 1899, completed 1900; sunk 11 November, 1914 by German mine in Kiaiachow Bay (10 dead).
Nos. 34 and 35
Launched 1899, completed 1900; both sunk 27 May, 1905 by Russian gunfire at battle of Tsushima.
No. 36
Launched 1899, completed 1900; stricken 1913 but used on auxiliary service before being BU.
No. 37
Launched 10 May, 1899, completed 23 March 1900; stricken 1913 but used on auxiliary duties before being BU.
No. 38
Launched 22 May, 1899, completed 23 March 1900; damaged 11 August, 1904 off Port Arthur but repaired; stricken 1914–15, BU.
Nos. 39 to 41
Launched 1900, completed 1901; stricken 1913 but served on auxiliary duties until BU.
No. 42
Launched 1900, completed 1901; sunk 15 December, 1904 by Russian destroyer *Serdity* E of Cape Liao Ti Chan (38° 45′ N, 121° 14′ E) following damage from Russian ships sustained during night attack on the battleship *Sevastopol*.
Nos. 43 to 46
Launched 1900, completed 190?; stricken 1913, but served on auxiliary duties before being BU.
No. 47
Launched 10 June, 1900, completed 1 October, 1900; Foundered in typhoon 22–23 September, 1912 (34° 33′ N, 136° 32′ E).
No. 48
Launched 1900, completed 1900; mined 12 May, 1904 (7 dead) NE of Dalny Bay (39° 01′ N, 121° 55′ E).
No. 49
Launched 1900, completed 1900; stricken 1915 and BU.
No. 50
Launched 1900, completed 1900; stricken 1912 and BU.
No. 51
Launched 1900, completed 1900; wrecked 28 June, 1904 at about 04.00 hrs 9 m NW of San-Shantao Island (30° 58′ N, 121° 59′ E).
No. 52
Launched 1900, completed 1901; stricken 1912 and BU.

Torpedo Boat *No. 58* was one of the first group to be built in Japan. The plans were supplied by Normand, and resembled the French *No. 130*. (Shizuo Fukui.)

No. 53
Launched 1900, completed 1901; mined 14 December, 1904 off Cape Liao Ti Chan, Port Arthur (38° 44′ N,121′ E) during night attack on Russian ships.
Nos. 54 to 58
Launched 1900, completed 1901/02; stricken 1913–15 and BU.
No. 59
Launched December 1901, completed 1902; stricken 1915 and BU.
Nos. 60 and 61
Launched 1901, completed 1901; stricken 1915 and BU.
Nos. 62 to 65
Launched 1901, completed 1902; stricken 1913 but subsequently used for auxiliary duties before BU.
No. 66
Launched 1901, completed 1902; badly damaged 23 November, 1904 SE of Cape Liao Ti Chan; stricken 1916 and BU.
No. 67
Launched 1902, completed 1903; badly damaged 3 May, 1904 SE of Cape Liao Ti Chan; stricken 1922 and BU.
No. 68
Launched 1902, completed 190?; stricken 1922 and BU.
No. 69
Launched 30 March, 1903; completed 26 September, 1903; badly damaged 27 May, 1905 by Russian gunfire at Tsushima and sank next day in collision with destroyer *Akatsuki*; stricken 14 June 1905.
Nos. 70 to 74
Launched 1903, completed 190?; stricken 1922–3 and BU.
No. 75
Launched 10 November, 1903, completed 190?; stricken 1923 and BU.

Name	Builder	Date	Displ	Length ft in	Beam ft in	Draught ft in	Machinery	SHP	Speed	Fuel	Radius	Armament	Comp
KAWASEMI ex-*Fungo*, No. 8	Kawasaki, Kobe	1906	96 N	134 10 pp	15 9	7 2	single-shaft, 3-cyl VTE, 1 Normand water-tube boiler	1200 ihp	23	18 coal	?	2 × 47mm 3 × 14in TT (AW)	40

GENERAL NOTES
An old Chinese 2nd Class torpedo-boat, engined by Normand.

RE-ARMAMENT
In 1937 she had 1 × 65mm and 1 MG and her speed was 13 knots.

CAREER
Launched 1906, completed 190? for China; sunk 8 October, 1937 in Yangtze by Japanese aircraft; salvaged and renamed *Kawasemi* in 1939–40; later stricken and BU.

Name	Builder	Date	Displ	Length ft in	Beam ft in	Draught ft in	Machinery	SHP	Speed	Fuel	Radius	Armament	Comp
KOTAKA	Yarrow & Co., Poplar	1885–1886	203 N	165 0 pp	19 0	5 7	2-shaft, 2-cyl compound, 2 locomotive boilers	1217 ihp	19	30 coal	?	4 × 37mm 6 × 15in TT (AW)	?

GENERAL NOTES
A 1st Class torpedo-boat built under the 1882 Programme. She was re-assembled in Japan. Her machinery was re-built by 28 April, 1916 and she was re-classified as *Hai Sen* (discarded ship); from February 1917 to October 1926 renamed *Kotaka Maru* as 'Zatsueki Sen'(miscellaneous vessel); BU 27 January, 1927.

ARMOUR
She was protected with 1in plating over her machinery.

Kotaka (1900)

CAREER
Launched 1887, completed October, 1888; stricken 1908 but subsequently used as a target; BU.

The 1st Class torpedo-boat *Kotaka* was built on the Clyde, and reassembled at Yokosuka in 1888. (Authors' Collection.)

Name	Builder	Date	Displ	Length ft in	Beam ft in	Draught ft in	Machinery	SHP	Speed	Fuel	Radius	Armament	Comp
FUKURYU ex-*Fulung*	Germania, Kiel	1886	115	140 3 pp	16 5	5 1	single-shaft 2-cyl compound, 1 locomotive boiler	1015 ihp	20	18 coal	?	2 × 37mm 4 × 14in TT (AW)	?

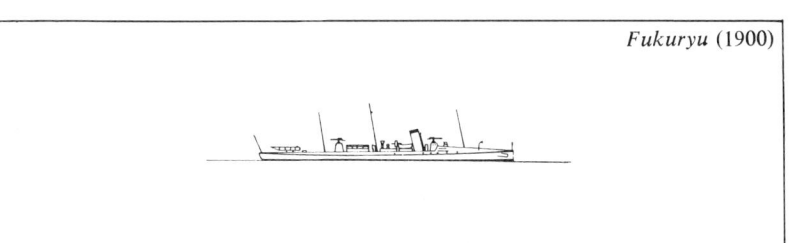

Fukuryu (1900)

GENERAL NOTES
A 1st Class torpedo-boat built originally for China.

CAREER
Launched 1885, completed 1886 as *Fulung*; captured 8 February, 1895 at Wei Hai Wei, and renamed *Fukuryu*; stricken 1908 and BU.

Right: *Fukuryu* was built by the German firm of Schichau, for China as the *Fulung*, but fell into Japanese hands in 1895. (Authors' Collection.)

Name	Builder	Date	Displ	Length ft in	Beam ft in	Draught ft in	Machinery	SHP	Speed	Fuel	Radius	Armament	Comp
SHIRATAKA	Schichau, Elbing (No. 629)	1897– 1898	127 N	152 6 pp	16 9	41 8	2-shaft 3-cyl VTE 2 Schichau water-tube boilers	2600 ihp	28	30 coal	?	3 × 42mm 3 × 15in TT (AW)	26

GENERAL NOTES
Built under the Post-War Programme of 1896–7 as a 1st Class torpedo-boat, and re-assembled by Mitsubishi between January 1899 and April 1900.

RE-ARMAMENT
Later she had 1 × 3in 40-cal and 2 × 57mm guns.

CAREER
Launched 10 June, 1899, completed 22 June, 1900; stricken 1923 and BU.

Shirataka (1900)

Name	Builder	Date	Displ	Length ft in	Beam ft in	Draught ft in	Machinery	SHP	Speed	Fuel	Radius	Armament	Comp
HAYABUSA Class (4 units)	Normand, Le Havre	1899– 1901	152	147 8 pp	16 1	4 9	2-shaft 3-cyl VTE 2 Normand water-tube boilers	3500 ihp	28½	26 coal	c 2000 @ 10	1 × 57mm 2 × 42mm 3 × 18in TT	26

TORPEDO BOATS AND DESTROYERS

Chidori (1900)

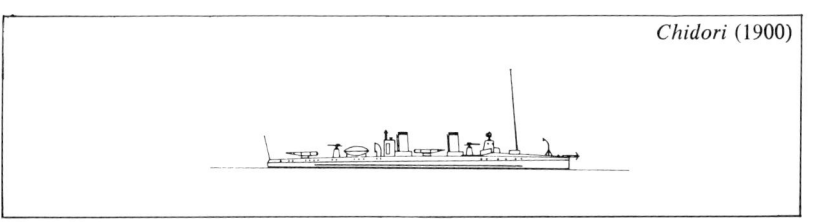

GENERAL NOTES
Ordered under the 1897–8 Programme, these 1st Class torpedo-boats were based on the French *Cyclone* type. They were re-assembled in Japan in 1900–1.

CAREERS
Hayabusa
Launched 1899, completed 1899; harbour service 1910; stricken 1919 and BU.
Kasasagi
Launched 1900 and completed 1900; harbour service 1910; stricken 1919 and BU.
Manazuru
Launched 1900, completed 1900; harbour service 1910; for disposal in 1921 and BU.
Chidori
Launched 1901, completed the same year; harbour service 1910; stricken 1919 and BU.

Chidori was a French-built torpedo-boat of the *Hayabusa* class, reassembled in Japan in 1900. (Shizuo Fukui.)

Name	Builder	Date	Displ	Length ft in	Beam ft in	Draught ft in	Machinery	SHP	Speed	Fuel	Radius	Armament	Comp
AOTAKA Class (11 units)	various	1902–1904	152 N	147 8 pp	16 1	4 9	2-shaft 3-cyl VTE 2 Normand water-tube boilers	3500 ihp	28	26 coal	2000 @ 10	1 × 57mm 2 × 42mm 3 × 18in TT (AW)	30

GENERAL NOTES
These 1st Class torpedo-boats were built under the 1896–7 Post-War Programme as Japanese copies of the *Hayabusa* Class.

CAREERS
Aotaka
Launched February 1903 by Kure DY; completed 1903; stricken 1922 and BU.
Kari
Launched 14 March 1903 by Kure DY; completed 1903; stricken 1922 and BU.
Hato
Launched July 1903 by Kure DY; completed 1903; stricken 1923 and BU.
Hibari
Launched October 1903 by Kure DY; completed 1904; stricken 1923 and BU.
Kiji
Launched November 1903 by Kure DY; completed 1904; stricken 1923 and BU.

Tsubame
Launched August 1903 by Kure DY; completed 1904; stricken 1922 and BU.
Hashitaka
Launched December 1903 by Kawasaki, Kobe; completed 1904; stricken 1923 and BU.
Sagi
Launched December 1903 by Kawasaki, Kobe; completed 1904; stricken 1923 and BU.
Kamome
Launched April 1904 by Kawasaki, Kobe; completed 1904; stricken 1923 and BU.
Otori
Launched April 1904 by Kawasaki, Kobe; completed 1904; stricken 1923 and BU.
Uzura
Launched February 1904 by Kawasaki, Kobe; completed 1904; stricken 1923 and BU.

Name	Builder	Date	Displ	Length ft in	Beam ft in	Draught ft in	Machinery	SHP	Speed	Fuel	Radius	Armament	Comp
TOMOZURU Class (4 units)	various	1931–1934	737 F 651 N 535 light	269 0 oa 259 2 wl 254 3 pp	24 3	8 2	2-shaft GTU 2 Kampon boilers	11000	30	150 oil	9000 @ 10	3 × 5in 50-cal DP 1 × 40mm 4 × 21in TT (AW)	113

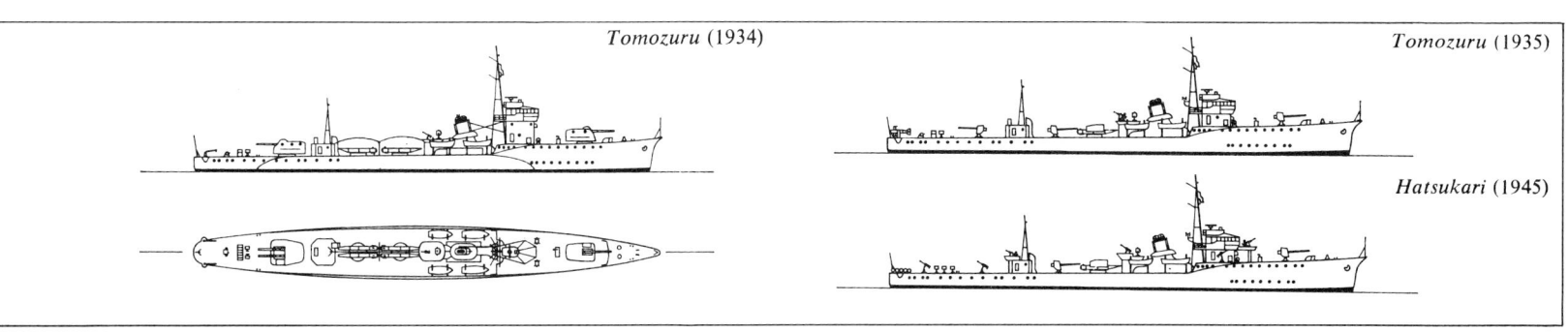

Tomozuru (1934)

Tomozuru (1935)

Hatsukari (1945)

128   TORPEDO BOATS AND DESTROYERS

GENERAL NOTES
These were fleet torpedo-boats, virtually small destroyers, and were built under the 1931 Programme. They suffered from excessive topweight as a result of trying to keep within the tonnage limit imposed by the London Treaty.

RE-ARMAMENT AND RECONSTRUCTION
Between August and December, 1936, Maizuru DY carried out various alterations. Bridges, masts and funnels were reduced in height, the armament was reduced, and permanent ballast and a 23.6ft keel were added. The new tonnages were 600ts (S), 770ts (N) and 815ts (F).
After reconstruction, the armament was: 3 × 4.7in 50-cal DP; 1 × 7.7mm MG; 2 × 21in TT. In 1942 they had 2 × 4.7in 50-cal; 10 × 25mm AA; 2 × TT; 48 DCs.

CAREERS
Tomozuru
Launched 1 October, 1933, completed 24 February, 1934; capsized in a storm 12 March, 1934 7 m S of Dai Tatsu Shima, SW of Sasebo (32° 55′ N, 129° 30′ E) (90 dead); raised keel uppermost and rebuilt; sunk 24 March, 1945 by US aircraft of TF 58 230 m SE of Shanghai (28° 25′ N, 124° 32′ E).
Chidori
Launched 1 April, 1933, completed 20 November, 1933; torpedoed 24 December, 1944 by USS *Tilefish* 90 m WSW of Yokosuka (34° 30′ N, 138° 02′ E).
Manazuru
Launched 11 July, 1933, completed 31 November, 1934; sunk 1 March, 1945 by aircraft of TF 58 off Okinawa (26° 17′ N, 127° 35′ E).
Hatsukari
Launched 19 December, 1933, completed 15 July, 1934; surrendered August 1945 at Hong Kong and BU.

Below: When torpedo-boats were started again in 1931, traditional names were chosen. *Chidori* is seen here on trials, following drastic reconstruction in 1934, to improve her stability. (Shizuo Fukui.)

Name	Builder	Date	Displ	Length ft in	Beam ft in	Draught ft in	Machinery	SHP	Speed	Fuel	Radius	Armament	Comp
OTORI Class (8 units + 8)	various	1934–1937	1040 F 960 N 840 light	290 4 oa 284 9 wl 278 10 pp	26 10	9 1	2-shaft GTU 2 Kampon boilers	19000	30½	150 oil	4000 @ 14	3 × 4.7in 45-cal 1 × 40mm 3 × 21in TT (AW)	113

GENERAL NOTES
Ordered under the 1934 Programme as Torpedo-boats 5 to 20, these were improved *Tomozuru* Class fleet TBs/small destroyers/fast escorts. From September 1935 their hulls were strengthened to incorporate the lessons learned from the *Tomozuru* débâcle.

RE-ARMAMENT
In 1944 the survivors had 2 × 4.7in DP (55° elevation); 11 × 25mm AA; 48 DCs, and their displacement was 1043ts.

CAREERS
Otori
Launched 25 April, 1935 by Maizuru DY; completed 10 October, 1936; sunk 12 June, 1944 by aircraft of TF 58 180 m NW of Saipan (17° 32′ N, 144° E).
Kasasagi
Launched 28 October, 1935 by Osaka Tekkosho; completed 15 January, 1937; torpedoed 26 September, 1943 by US submarine *Bluefin* 25 m S of Flores Sea (05° 0′ S, 121° 57′ E).
Hiyodori
Launched 25 October, 1935 at Ishikawajima Zosensho, Tokyo; completed 20 December, 1936; torpedoed 17 November, 1944 by US submarine *Gunnel* 140 m ENE of Cape Tourane (16° 56′ N, 110° 30′ E).
Hayabusa
Launched 28 October, 1935 by Yokohama Docks; completed 7 December, 1936; sunk 24 September, 1944 by aircraft of TF 38 110 m SSE of Manila (13° N, 122° E).
Hato
Launched 25 January, 1937 by Ishikawajima Zosensho, Tokyo; completed 7 August, 1937; sunk 16 October, 1944 by aircraft of TF 38 130 m ESE of Hong Kong (21° 54′ N, 116° 30′ E).
Sagi
Launched 30 January, 1937 by Harima Zosensho KK; completed 31 July, 1937; torpedoed 8 November, 1944 by US submarine *Gunnel* 60 m WSW of Cape Bolinao (16° 09′ N, 118° 56′ E).

TORPEDO BOATS AND DESTROYERS

Kari
Launched 20 January, 1937 by Mitsubishi, Yokohama; completed 20 September, 1937; torpedoed 16 July, 1945 by US submarine *Baya* 220 m WSW of Makassar (05° 48′ S, 115° 53′ E).
Kiji
Launched 26 January, 1937 by Tama Zosensho KK, Okayama; surrendered at Soerabaja in August 1945; after repatriation duties she was handed over to the USSR and was subsequently renamed and re-armed.
Nos. 13 to 20
No contracts were placed for these units as the order was changed in favour of subchasers *4* to *11* (q.v.). The names projected were: *Hatsutaka, Aotaka, Wakataka, Kumataka, Yamadori, Mizudori, Umidori,* and *Komadori*.

The torpedo-boat *Hayabusa*, off Woosung in 1938, with additional AA machine-guns mounted on the forecastle. The numeral on her bow is not an individual pendant number, but denotes that she is in the 1st Torpedo-Boat Flotilla. (Tappman Collection.)

Kiji belonged to the *Otori* class torpedo-boats or coastal destroyers, which were improved versions of the *Tomozuru* type. She is seen here with a sister, at Shanghai in 1936. (Shizuo Fukui.)

Destroyers

Name	Builder	Date	Displ	Length ft in	Beam ft in	Draught ft in	Machinery	SHP	Speed	Fuel	Radius	Armament	Comp
IKAZUCHI Class (6 units)	Yarrow & Co., Poplar	1897–1900	410 F 305 N	224 6 oa 220 8 pp	20 6	5 2	2-shaft 4-cyl VTE 4 Yarrow boilers	6000 ihp 7000 max	31	40 110 coal	?	2 × 3in 40–cal 4 × 57mm 2 × 18in TT (AW)	55

GENERAL NOTES
These 3rd Class destroyers were built under the 1897 Programme, and were similar to the British '30-knotter' types.

MACHINERY
Niji ran trials to Admiralty specifications and on 12 December, 1899 reached 31.15 knots. The contract specified 31 knots for three hours.

CAREERS
Ikazuchi
Launched 15 November, 1898; completed 1899; badly damaged 27 May, 1905 at Tsushima by Russian gunfire, but repaired; sunk 10 October, 1913 by boiler explosion; the wreck was subsequently BU.
Inazuma
Launched 28 January, 1899; completed 1899; sunk December 1909 in collision with a schooner 30 m S of Hakodate; the wreck broke in two and was salvaged in the summer of 1910 but not repaired; stricken 1910 and BU.

Akebono (1899)

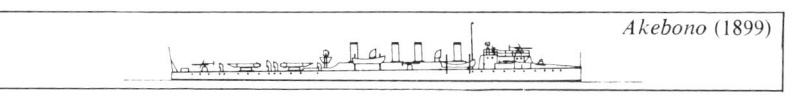

Niji
Launched 17 December, 1899; completed 1900; wrecked 29 July, 1900 in Japanese Waters.
Akebono
Launched 25 April, 1899, completed 1899; badly damaged 10 March, 1904 by Russian gunfire at Port Arthur, but repaired; reclassified as a tender in 1918; BU July 1921.
Oboro
Launched 5 October, 1899, completed 1900; badly damaged 2 November, 1904 by mine (?) SSW of Port Arthur, but repaired; reclassified as a tender in 1918; stricken 1921 and BU.
Sazanami
Launched 8 August, 1899, completed 1900; stricken 1921.

Sazanami was one of the *Ikazuchi* class, the first Japanese destroyers. They were very similar to the Yarrow-built '30-knotter' destroyers, built for the Royal Navy. (Bundesarchiv.)

Akebono was another destroyer of the *Ikazuchi* class. (Marius Bar.)

130 TORPEDO BOATS AND DESTROYERS

Name	Builder	Date	Displ	Length ft in	Beam ft in	Draught ft in	Machinery	SHP	Speed	Fuel	Radius	Armament	Comp
MURAKUMO Class (6 units)	J. Thornycroft & Co., Chiswick	1897–1900	361 F 275 light	215 oa 207 pp 5 4	19 6	5 8	2-shaft 4-cyl compound 3 Thornycroft water-tube boilers	5470 ihp	30	40/80 coal	?	2 × 3in 40-cal QF 4 × 57mm QF 2 × 18in TT (AW)	60

GENERAL NOTES
These 3rd Class destroyers were built under the 1898 Programme, and were similar to the '30-knotters' building for the Royal Navy.

MACHINERY
Usugumo made 30.602 knots on her trials on 23 January, 1900 although 35ts overweight, and averaged 30.37 knots for three hours. *Kagero* made 30.45 knots in a three-hour trial, and *Shiranui* 30.517 knots.

CAREERS
Murakumo
Launched November 1898, completed 1899; 10 May, 1909 wrecked in typhoon, but salvaged and repaired at Toba DY; stricken 1921 and then served as a depot-ship for minesweepers and torpedo-boats before being BU.
Shinonome
Launched 15 December, 1898, completed 1899; wrecked 10 May, 1909 during a typhoon; raised and repaired at Yokosuka in August 1910; sank 20 July, 1913 in typhoon off Formosa.
Yugure
Launched 26 January, 1899, completed 1899; badly damaged 27 May, 1905 by Russian gunfire at Tsushima; but repaired; stricken 1921 and served as depot-ship for sweepers and TBs; BU.
Shiranui
Launched 14 March, 1899, completed 1899; stricken 1918 and served as a tender; for disposal April 1922 at Kure, and BU 1923.
Kagero
Launched 22 August, 1899, completed 1900; stricken 1918 but served as a tender; for disposal at Kure in April 1922, and BU 1923.
Usugumo
Launched 26 January, 1900, completed 1900; wrecked July 1913 in a typhoon but repaired; stricken 1922 and BU 1927.

Right: *Usugumo*, shortly after completion in 1900. (IWM.)

Shiranui (1900)

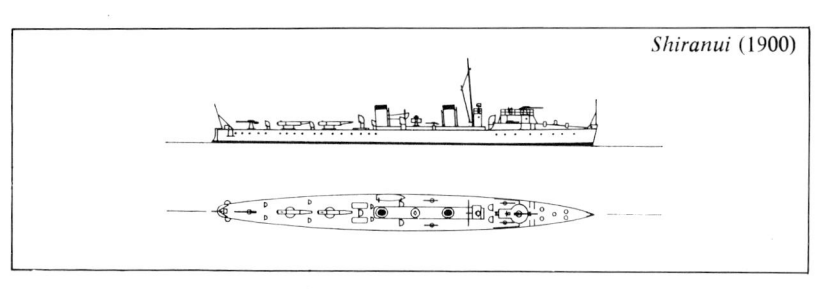

Shiranui, and her sisters of the *Murakumo* class, were similar to the Thornycroft-built '30-knotters'. (Marius Bar.)

Name	Builder	Date	Displ	Length ft in	Beam ft in	Draught ft in	Machinery	SHP	Speed	Fuel	Radius	Armament	Comp
SHIRAKUMO ASASHIO	J. Thornycroft & Co., Chiswick	1901–1902	428 F 342 N	221 6 oa 216 2 pp	20 9	6 0	2-shaft 4-cyl compound 4 Thornycroft water-tube boilers	7000 ihp	31	40/95 coal	?	2 × 3in 40-cal QF 4 × 57mm QF 2 × 18in TT	60

Shirakumo in 1902. (IWM.)

Asashio. (IWM.)

TORPEDO BOATS AND DESTROYERS

GENERAL NOTES
Ordered under the 1898 Programme.

MACHINERY
Shirakumo ran a six-mile trial in January 1902 and reached 31.819 knots. In a three-hour trial *Asashio* reached 31.058 knots with 7224 ihp.

CAREERS
Shirakumo
Launched 1 October, 1901, completed 1902; stricken April 1922; disarmed at Kure in 1923 and BU.

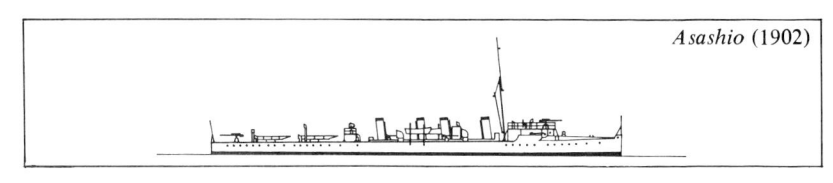

Asashio (1902)

Asashio
Launched 10 January, 1902, completed 1902; stricken April 1922; disarmed at Kure in 1923 and BU.

Name	Builder	Date	Displ	Length ft in	Beam ft in	Draught ft in	Machinery	SHP	Speed	Fuel	Radius	Armament	Comp
AKATSUKI	Yarrow & Co.,	1901–1902	415 F	224 7 oa	20 6	5 8	2-shaft 4-cyl compound	6000 ihp	31	40/89 coal	?	2 × 3in 40-cal QF	60
KASUMI	Poplar		363 N	220 8 pp			4 Yarrow water-tube boilers					4 × 57mm QF 2 × 18in TT	

GENERAL NOTES
Built under the 1898 Programme and rated as 3rd Class destroyers.

MACHINERY
On trials on 20 November, 1901, *Akatsuki* made 31.121 knots for three hours; on a six-mile trial she reached 31.3 knots with 6450 ihp. On 29 January, 1902, *Kasumi* reached 31.075 knots over the measured mile and averaged 31.295 knots on a three-hour trial.

CAREERS
Akatsuki
Launched 13 November, 1901, completed 1902; mined 17 May, 1904 8 m SSW of Cape Liao Ti Chan, Port Arthur (38° 38′ N, 121° 05′ E).

Kasumi
Launched 23 January, 1902, completed 1902; stricken 1913 and served as a target until 1920 or later before being BU.

Right: *Kasumi* in 1903. (IWM.)

Name	Builder	Date	Displ	Length ft in	Beam ft in	Draught ft in	Machinery	SHP	Speed	Fuel	Radius	Armament	Comp
HARUSAME Class (7 units)	various	1902–1905	435 F 375 N	234 3 oa 227 0 pp	21 7	6 0	2-shaft 4-cyl compound 4 Kampon boilers	6000 ihp	29	40/100 coal	1200 @ 10	2 × 3in 40-cal QF 4 × 57mm QF 2 × 18in TT (AW)	55/60

GENERAL NOTES
Third Class destroyers, built under the 1896–7 Post-War Programme to Thornycroft plans. On trials they averaged 28.952 knots with 5250 ihp, on a tonnage of 378.5.

CAREERS
Harusame
Launched 31 October, 1902 at Yokosuka DY; completed 1903; badly damaged 27 May, 1905 by Russian gunfire at Tsushima, but repaired; stranded 24 November 1911 in storm in Sea of Japan (34° 25′ N, 137° E) with 45 dead, wreck abandoned December 1911; stricken 1 April, 1912.

Murasame, and the rest of the *Harusame* class, were built to Thornycroft plans in Japanese yards in 1902–5. (Shizuo Fukui.)

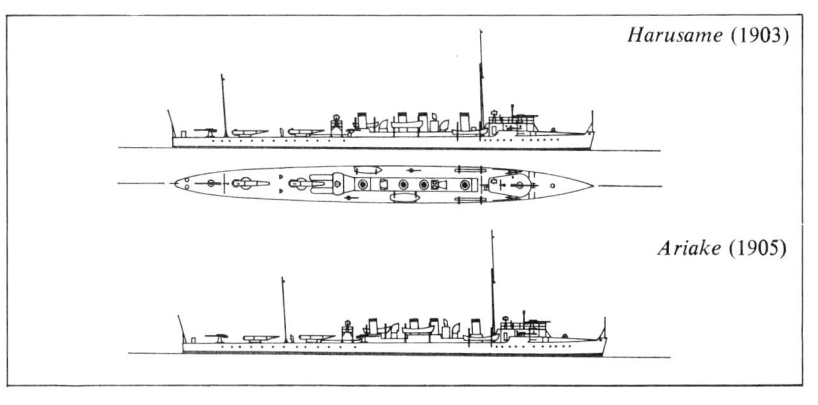

Harusame (1903)

Ariake (1905)

132   TORPEDO BOATS AND DESTROYERS

Hayatori
Launched March 1903 at Yokosuka DY; completed 1903; mined 3 September, 1904 2 m S of Lun Wan Tan, Port Arthur (38° 47′ N, 121° 30′ E) while on blockade duty.
Murasame
Launched November 1902, Yokosuka DY; completed 1903; stricken 1922, then target service and BU 1923.
Asagiri
Launched April 1903 at Yokosuka DY; completed 1903; stricken 1922, then target service and BU.

Ariake
Launched 7 December, 1904, Kure DY; completed 24 March, 1905; stricken 1925 and BU 1926.
Arare
Launched 5 April, 1905, Kure DY; completed 10 May, 1905; stricken 1924 and BU 1926.
Fubuki
Launched 21 January, 1905 at Kure DY; completed 28 February 1905; stricken 1925 and BU 1926.

Name	Builder	Date	Displ	Length ft in	Beam ft in	Draught ft in	Machinery	SHP	Speed	Fuel	Radius	Armament	Comp
ASAKAZE Class (32 units)	various	1905–1909	450 F 381 N	234 0 oa / 227 0 pp	21 7	6 0	2-shaft 4-cyl compound 4 Kampon boilers	6000 ihp	29	40 / 150 coal 15 / 20 oil	1200 @ 15	4 × 3.1in 28-cal 2 × 3.1in 40-cal 2 × 18in TT (AW)	70

General Notes
These were almost exact copies of the *Harusame* Class, and were built under the 1904 War Programme.

Re-armament
In 1922–6 they were given 2 × 4.7in 45-cal; 2 × 3.1in 40-cal when converted for minesweeping.

Careers
Asakaze
Launched 28 October, 1905 by Kawasaki, Kobe; completed 1 April, 1906; converted to minesweeper 1923; stricken 1928 and BU.
Wakaba
Launched 25 November, 1905 at Yokosuka DY; completed 28 February, 1906; converted to minesweeper 1923; stricken 1928 and BU.
Ushio
Launched 18 July, 1905 at Kure DY; completed 15 July, 1905; re-rated as a minesweeper in 1923; stricken 1928 and BU.
Ne-no-hi
Launched 30 August, 1905 at Kure DY; completed 1 October, 1905; reclassed as a minesweeper 1923; stricken 1928 and BU.
Kisaragi
Launched 6 September, 1905 at Yokosuka DY; completed 19 October, 1905; reclassified as a minesweeper 1923; stricken 1928 and BU.
Kamikaze
Launched 15 July, 1905 at Yokosuka DY; completed 16 August, 1905; reclassified as a minesweeper 1923; stricken 1928 and BU.
Hatsushimo
Launched 13 May, 1905 at Yokosuka DY; completed 18 August, 1905; reclassified as a minesweeper 1923; stricken 1928 and BU.
Yugure
Launched 17 November, 1905 at Sasebo DY; completed 26 May, 1906; reclassified as a minesweeper 1923; stricken 1928 and BU.
Harukaze
Launched 25 December 1905 by Kawasaki, Kobe; completed 14 May, 1906; reclassified as a minesweeper 1923; stricken 1928 and BU.
Yayoi
Launched 7 August, 1905 at Yokosuka DY; completed 23 September, 1905; stricken 1925; served as target and BU August 1926.
Oite
Launched 10 January 1906 at Maizuru DY; completed 21 August, 1906; stricken 1925 and hulked 1926.
Hibiki
Launched 31 March, 1906 at Yokosuka DY; completed 6 September, 1906; reclassified as a minesweeper 1923; stricken 1928 and BU.
Hatsuyuki
Launched 8 March, 1906 at Yokosuka DY; completed 17 May, 1906; reclassified as a minesweeper 1923; stricken 1928 and BU.
Yudachi
Launched 26 March, 1906 at Sasebo DY; completed 16 July, 1906; reclassified as a minesweeper 1923; stricken 1923 and BU.
Nowaki
Launched 25 July, 1906 at Sasebo DY; completed 1 November, 1906; stricken 1924 and BU.
Mikazuki
Launched 26 May, 1906 at Sasebo DY; completed 12 September, 1906; stricken 1928 and BU.
Shigure
Launched March 1906 by Kawasaki, Kobe; stricken 1925 and BU.
Hatsuharu
Launched 12 May, 1906 by Kawasaki, Kobe; completed 1 March, 1907; stricken 1925 and BU.
Asatsuyu
Launched 2 April, 1906 by Osaka Tekkosho, Osaka; completed 16 November, 1906, wrecked 10 November, 1913 off Shichi-Towan, Noto Hanto; wreck abandoned.
Shirotae
Launched 30 July, 1906 by Mitsubishi, Nagasaki and completed 21 January, 1907; wrecked 3 September, 1914 in fog in Kiao Chao Bay; she was destroyed the same day by German shore batteries and by the gunboat *Jaguar*; wreck BU 1915.
Shiratsuyu
Launched 12 February, 1906 by Mitsubishi, Nagasaki and completed 23 August, 1906; stricken 1928 and BU.
Shirayuki
Launched 19 May, 1906 by Mitsubishi, Nagasaki and completed 6 August, 1906; stricken 1928 and BU.
Matsukaze
Launched 23 December, 1906 by Mitsubishi, Nagasaki and completed 15 March, 1907; stricken 1925 and BU 1926 (?) after use as target.
Nagatsuki
Launched 15 December, 1906 by Uraga Dock, Tokyo; completed 31 July, 1907; reclassified as *Minesweeper No. 11* in 1926; BU February 1930.
Yunagi
Launched 22 August, 1906 at Maizuru DY; completed 25 December, 1906; stricken 1925 and BU.
Uzuki
Launched 20 September, 1906 by Kawasaki, Kobe; completed 6 March, 1907; stricken 1925 and BU.
Minazuki
Launched 5 November, 1906 by Mitsubishi, Nagasaki and completed 14 February, 1907; reclassified as *Minesweeper No. 10* in 1926; BU in February 1930.
Hayate
Launched 22 May, 1906 by Osaka Tekkosho, Osaka; completed 13 June, 1907; stricken 1925 and BU.
Kikuzuki
Launched 18 April, 1907 by Uraga Dock, Tokyo; completed 20 September, 1907; reclassified as *Minesweeper No. 12* in 1926; BU in February 1920.
Uranami
Launched 8 December, 1907 at Maizuru DY; completed 2 October, 1908; reclassified as *Minesweeper No. 8* in 1926; BU February 1930.
Isonami
Launched 21 November, 1908 at Maizuru DY; completed 2 April, 1909; reclassified as *Minesweeper No. 7* in 1926; BU February 1930.
Ayanami
Launched 20 March, 1909 at Maizuru DY; completed 26 June, 1909; reclassified as *Minesweeper No. 9* 1926; BU February 1930.

Name	Builder	Date	Displ	Length ft in	Beam ft in	Draught ft in	Machinery	SHP	Speed	Fuel	Radius	Armament	Comp
FUMIZUKI ex-*Silny* ex-*Baklan*	Nevskii Yard, St. Petersburg	1901–1902	240 N	197 0 pp	18 8	7 6	2-shaft 3-cyl VTE 4 Yarrow boilers	3800 ihp	27½	60 coal	?	1 × 3in 50-cal QF 3 × 47mm QF 2 × 18in TT (AW)	51
YAMABIKO ex-*Akatsuki* ex-*Riechitelny* ex-*Kondor*													
SATSUKI ex-*Biedovy* ex-*Keta*	Nevskii Yard, St. Petersburg	1902	356 N	209 11 pp	21 0	5 11	2-shaft 3-cyl VTE 4 Yarrow boilers	5700 ihp	26½	80 coal	1200 @ 10	1 × 3in 50-cal QF 5 × 47mm QF 2 × 18in TT (AW)	62

GENERAL NOTES
Ex-Russian destroyers which had been re-erected at Port Arthur in 1901–4. The *Satsuki* was a Laird design.

RE-ARMAMENT AND RECONSTRUCTION
In 1905–6 they were refitted with Miyabara boilers and British-pattern guns. *Fumizuki* and *Yamabiko* were armed with 3 × 47mm guns and 2 × 18in TT; *Satsuki* had 5 × 47mm and 3 × 18in TT.

MACHINERY
After reboilering, *Fumizuki* and *Yamabiko* made 27 knots with 3800 ihp, and *Satsuki* made 26 knots with 5700 ihp.

CAREERS
Fumizuki
Launched 1901, completed 1902 as *Baklan* for Russian Navy; renamed *Silny* 22 March, 1902; badly damaged 11 November, 1904 by a mine off Port Arthur; scuttled at Port Arthur 1 January, 1905 and fell into Japanese hands the next day; raised 22 August, 1905 and repaired at Takeshiki; renamed *Fumizuki*; stricken 1913 and BU.
Yamabiko
Launched 1901, completed 1902 as the Russian *Kondor*; renamed *Riechitelny* 22 March, 1902; interned 11 August, 1904 by China at Chifu, but fell into Japanese hands the next day; renamed *Akatsuki*; badly damaged 27 May, 1905 by Russian gunfire at Tsushima; repaired and renamed *Yamabiko*; stricken 1917 and BU.
Satsuki
Launched 1902 and completed the same year as the Russian *Keta*; renamed *Biedovy* 22 March, 1902; captured 28 May, 1905 by Japanese destroyers *Sazanami* and *Kagero* S of Uldshin (with the badly wounded Admiral Rozhestvenski on board); later renamed *Satsuki*; stricken 1913 but served as a target until BU in 1922.

Right: *Fumitsuki* was built to the British plans, as the Russian *Silny* in 1902. She fell into Japanese hands at Port Arthur in 1905. (Shizuo Fukui.)

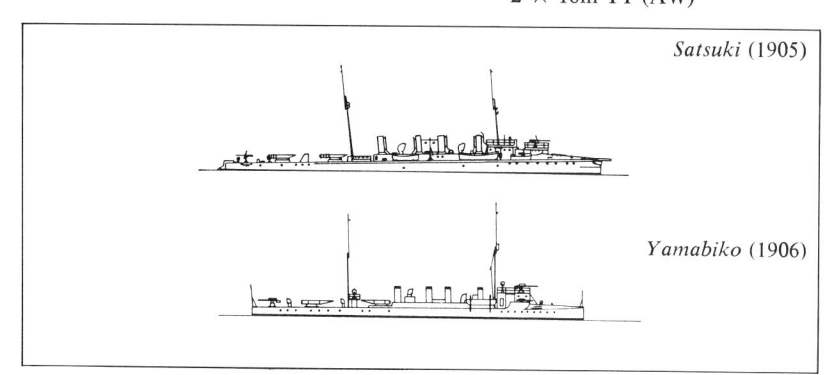

Satsuki (1905)

Yamabiko (1906)

Name	Builder	Date	Displ	Length ft in	Beam ft in	Draught ft in	Machinery	SHP	Speed	Fuel	Radius	Armament	Comp
YAMASEMI ex-*Chien Kang* ex-*Fu Po*	Schichau, Elbing (No. 876)	1911–1912	390 N	196 10 pp	21 4	5 11	2-shaft 3-cyl VTE 3 Schichau water-tube boilers	6000 ihp	32	80 coal	?	2 × 3in QF 2 × 47mm QF 2 × 18in TT	85

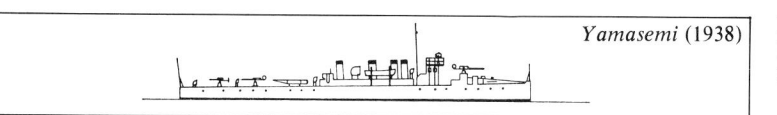

Yamasemi (1938)

RE-ARMAMENT
In 1937 she had 2 × 3in, 4 × 47mm and 2 × 18in TT, and her speed had fallen to 20 knots.

GENERAL NOTES
An ex-Chinese 3rd Class destroyer. She was unusual in that she was equipped for mixed firing.

CAREER
Launched 1912 and completed the same year as the Chinese *Fu Po*; later renamed *Chien Kang*; sunk by Japanese aircraft at Shanghai on 27 September, 1937; raised and renamed *Yamasemi*; stricken 1939 and BU.

Name	Builder	Date	Displ	Length ft in	Beam ft in	Draught ft in	Machinery	SHP	Speed	Fuel	Radius	Armament	Comp
SAKURA *TACHIBANA*	Maizuru DY	1911–1912	830 F 605 N 530 light	274 0 oa 270 0 wl 260 0 pp	24 0	7 3	3-shaft 4-cyl compound 5 Kampon boilers	9500 ihp	30	228 coal 30 oil	2400 @ 15	1 × 4.7in 40-cal QF 4 × 3.1in 40-cal QF 4 × 18in TT (AW)	92

134   TORPEDO BOATS AND DESTROYERS

GENERAL NOTES
Built under the 1910 Programme as 2nd Class destroyers. They had mixed firing and were the first Japanese-designed destroyers.

CAREERS
Sakura
Launched 20 December, 1911, completed 21 May, 1912; stricken 1931; for disposal 1933 and BU.
Tachibana
Launched 27 January, 1912, completed 25 June, 1912; stricken 1931; for disposal 1933 and BU.

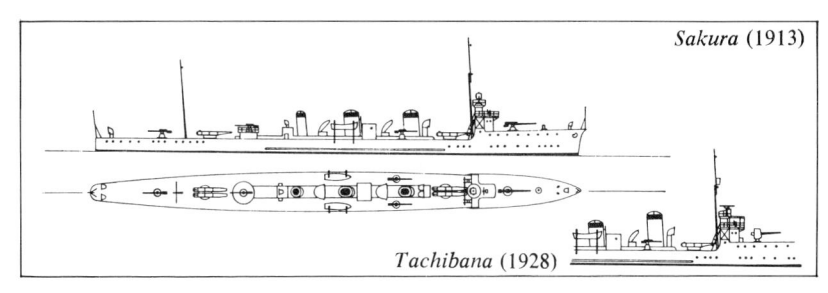

Sakura (1913)

Tachibana (1928)

Name	Builder	Date	Displ	Length ft in	Beam ft in	Draught ft in	Machinery	SHP	Speed	Fuel	Radius	Armament	Comp
KABA Class (10 units)	various	1914–1915	850 F 665 N 595 light	274 0 oa 270 0 wl 260 0 pp	24 0	7 9	3-shaft 4-cyl compound 4 Kampon boilers	9500 ihp	30	100 coal 137 oil	1600 @ 15	1 × 4.7in 40-cal QF 4 × 3.2in 40-cal QF 4 × 18in TT (AW)	92

GENERAL NOTES
These 2nd Class destroyers were built under the War Budget of September 1914. A further twelve were built for France as the *Algérien* Class, the first warships built for a European navy in Japan. Like the previous class they had mixed firing. The after TT could only fire less than 55° astern.

CAREERS
Kaba
Launched 6 February 1915 at Yokosuka DY; completed 5 March, 1915; stricken November 1931 and BU.
Matsu
Launched 5 March, 1915 by Mitsubishi, Nagasaki; completed 6 April, 1915; damaged 1 September, 1923 in earthquake but repaired; stricken November 1931 and BU.
Kashiwa
Launched 14 February, 1915 by Mitsubishi, Nagasaki; completed 4 April, 1915; damaged 1 September, 1923 in earthquake but repaired; stricken November 1931 and BU.
Katsura
Launched 4 March, 1915 at Kure DY; completed 31 March, 1915; stricken November 1931 and BU.
Kaede
Launched 20 February, 1915 at Maizuru DY; completed 25 March, 1915; stricken November 1931 and BU.
Kiri
Launched 28 February, 1915 by Uraga Dock, Tokyo; completed 22 March, 1915; stricken November 1931 and BU.
Kusunoki
Launched 5 March, 1915 by Kawasaki, Kobe; completed 31 March, 1915; stricken November 1931 and BU.
Ume
Launched 27 February, 1915 at Sasebo DY; completed 31 March, 1915; stricken November 1931 and BU.

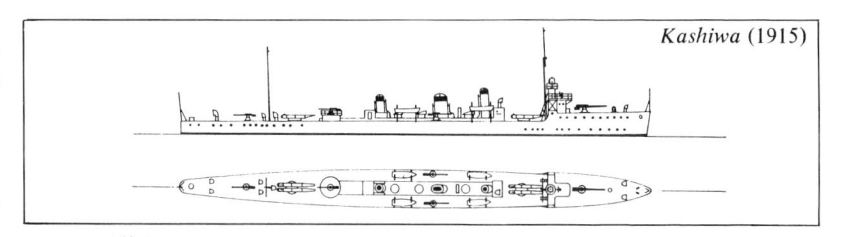

Kashiwa (1915)

Three destroyers of the *Kaba* class at Corfu on 28th April 1917. Several of this class served in the Mediterranean in 1917–18, and twelve were built for the French Navy as the *Algérien* class in 1917. (IWM.)

Sakaki
Launched 15 February, 1915 at Sasebo DY; completed 26 March, 1915; badly damaged 11 June, 1917 by Austrian *U.27*'s torpedo in the Mediterranean, NE of Cengotto (36° 10′ N, 23° 30′ E) but repaired; stricken November 1931 and BU.
Sugi
Launched 16 February, 1915 by Mitsubishi, Yokohama; completed 7 April, 1915; stricken November 1931 and BU.

Name	Builder	Date	Displ	Length ft in	Beam ft in	Draught ft in	Machinery	SHP	Speed	Fuel	Radius	Armament	Comp
MOMO Class (4 units)	various	1916–1917	1080 F 835 N 755 light	281 8 wl 275 0 pp	25 4	7 9	2-shaft Curtis TU 4 Kampon boilers	16000	31½	92 coal 212 oil	2400 @ 15	3 × 4.7in 40-cal 2 × 7.7mm MGs 6 × 18in TT (AW)	110

Momo (1917)

TORPEDO BOATS AND DESTROYERS

GENERAL NOTES
Built under the 1915 Programme as 2nd Class destroyers, they were the first Japanese ships with triple TT.

RE-ARMAMENT
Yanagi was hulked as a training ship in 1940 without armament.

MACHINERY
The first Japanese destroyers with turbines. Mixed firing retained, but oil fuel increased

CAREERS
Momo
Launched 12 October, 1916 at Sasebo DY; completed 23 December, 1916; stricken 1940 and BU.
Kashi
Launched 1 December, 1916 at Maizuru DY; completed 31 March, 1917; transferred 1937 to Manchukuo Navy and renamed *Hai Wei*; in 1943–4 she returned to Japanese control for service as an auxiliary escort and was renamed *Kali*; sunk 10 October, 1944 off Okinawa by aircraft of TF 38.
Hinoki
Launched 25 December, 1916 at Sasebo DY; completed 31 March, 1917; stricken 1940 and BU.

Yanagi
Launched 24 February, 1917 at Maizuru DY; completed 5 May, 1917; stricken 1 April, 1940 as a training hulk; BU 1 April, 1947 at Ominato.

Momo and her three sisters were built in 1916–17, and were the first Japanese destroyers with triple torpedo-tubes. Note also the novel bow-form, which was peculiar to this class and several successors. (Marius Bar.)

Name	Builder	Date	Displ	Length ft in	Beam ft in	Draught ft in	Machinery	SHP	Speed	Fuel	Radius	Armament	Comp
ENOKI Class (6 units)	various	1917–1918	1100 F 850 N 770 light	281 8 wl 275 pp	25 4	7 9	2-shaft Curtis TU 4 Kampon boilers	17500	31½	98 coal 212 oil	2400 @ 15	3 × 4.7in 40-cal 2 × 7.7mm MGs 6 × 18in TT (AW)	110

GENERAL NOTES
These were very similar to the *Momo* Class in nearly all respects.

RE-ARMAMENT
Enoki and *Nara* were converted to minesweepers in 1930; their armament was reduced to 2 × 4.7in 45-cal and 2 MGs.

CAREERS
Enoki
Launched 5 March, 1918 at Maizuru DY; completed 30 April, 1918; reclassified as *Minesweeper No. 10* 1 June, 1930; stricken 1938 and BU.
Nara
Launched 28 March, 1918 at Yokosuka DY; completed 30 April, 1918; reclassified as *Minesweeper No. 9* 1 June, 1930; stricken 1938 and BU.

Tsubaki
Launched 23 February, 1918 at Kure DY; completed 30 April, 1918; stricken 1 April, 1932 and BU.
Kuwa
Launched 23 February, 1918 at Kure DY; completed 31 March, 1918; stricken 1 April, 1932 and BU.
Keyaki
Launched 15 January, 1918 at Sasebo DY; completed 20 April, 1918; stricken 1 April, 1932 and BU.
Maki
Launched 28 December, 1917 at Sasebo DY; completed 7 April, 1918; stricken 1 April, 1932 and BU.

Name	Builder	Date	Displ	Length ft in	Beam ft in	Draught ft in	Machinery	SHP	Speed	Fuel	Radius	Armament	Comp
T. 181 ex-*V. 181*	AG Vulcan, Stettin	1909–1910	783 F 650 light	242 5 wl 241 5 pp	25 9	10 6 / 10 3	2-shaft AEG-Vulcan TU 4 Marine boilers	18000 / 17640	33.3 / 32	121 coal 76 oil	1250 @ 17	2 × 88mm 45-cal QF 4 × 19.7in TT (AW)	84
S. 51	Schichau, Elbing	1914–1915	1074 F 802 N	261 2 wl 259 2 pp	27 5	11 11 / 9 2	2-shaft Schichau TU, 3 Marine boilers	25015 / 24000	36.6 / 34	252 oil	1605 @ 17	3 × 88mm 45-cal QF 6 × 19.7in TT (AW) 24 mines	85
S. 60	Schichau, Elbing	1914–1916	1170 F 919 N	272 7 wl 270 8 pp	25 9	12 9 / 11 9	2-shaft Schichau TU, 1 cruising TU, 3 Marine boilers	25900 / 24000	35.1 / 34	305 oil	1960 @ 17	3 × 4.1in 45-cal QF 6 × 19.7in TT (AW) 24 mines	85
V. 80	AG Vulcan, Stettin	1914–1916	1188 F 924 N	269 0 wl 265 9 pp	27 3	12 9 / 11 2	2-shaft AEG TU 3 Marine boilers	24400 / 23500	36.6 / 34	306 oil	2050 @ 17	3 × 4.1in 45-cal QF 6 × 19.7in TT (AW) 24 mines	85
V. 127	AG Vulcan, Stettin	1916–1917	1188 F 924 N	269 0 wl 267 0 pp	27 3	13 6 / 11 5	2-shaft AEG TU 3 Marine boilers	25150 / 23500	34.6 / 34	298 oil	2050 @ 17	3 × 4.1in 45-cal QF 6 × 19.7in TT (AW) 24 mines	105

General Notes
Ex-German destroyers, built under the 1909 Programme (*T. 181*), 1914 War Programme (*S. 51*, *S. 60*, *V. 80*) and 1916 War Programme (*V. 127*).

Machinery
S.60 was unusual in having a cruising turbine coupled to the starboard shaft.

Careers
T. 181
Launched 6 November, 1909, completed 11 March, 1910 as German *V. 181*; renamed *T. 181* on 22 February, 1918; handed over to Japan 20 August, 1920 as war reparations; not taken over but BU at Dordrecht 1922.

S. 51
Launched 29 April, 1915, completed 7 September, 1915 as German *S.51*; interned 22 November, 1918 at Scapa Flow; beached after scuttling 21 June, 1919; raised July 1919 and transferred to Japan as war reparations; not taken over but sold; BU at Rosyth 1922.

S. 60
Launched 3 April, 1916, completed 15 August, 1916 as German *S. 60*; interned 22 November, 1918 at Scapa Flow; allocated to Japan as war reparations but not taken over; sold June 1920 and BU in England.

V. 80
Launched 28 April, 1916, completed 6 July, 1916 as German *V. 80*; interned 22 November, 1918 at Scapa Flow; allocated to Japan as war reparations but not taken over; sold June 1920 and BU in England.

V. 127
Launched 28 July, 1917, completed 23 October, 1917 as *V. 127*; interned 22 November 1918 at Scapa Flow; allocated to Japan as war reparations but not taken over; sold June 1920 and BU in 1922 at Dordrecht.

Name	Builder	Date	Displ	Length ft in	Beam ft in	Draught ft in	Machinery	SHP	Speed	Fuel	Radius	Armament	Comp
SENDAN ex-*Minstrel*	Thornycroft, Woolston	1911	740 N	246 6 oa	25 6	7 10	3-shaft Parsons TU 4 Yarrow boilers	13500	27	90 / 170 oil	2250 @ 13	2 × 4in QF 2 × 3in 40-cal QF 2 × 21in TT (AW)	72 / 76
KANRAN ex-*Nemesis*	Hawthorn, Leslie, Tyne	1910–1911	730 light	240 0 pp									

General Notes
Royal Navy 'H' or *Acorn*-Class destroyers of Admiralty design, lent to Japan for escort work in 1917.

Machinery
On an 8-hour trial *Nemesis* reached 27.05 knots with 14351 shp and *Minstrel* reached 28.938 knots with 15976 shp.

Careers
Sendan
Launched 2 February, 1911, completed 1911 as HMS *Minstrel*; lent June 1917 to Japan; returned 1919; sold 1 December, 1921 and BU.

Kanran
Launched 9 August, 1910, completed 7 March, 1911 as HMS *Nemesis*; lent June 1917 to Japan as *Kanran*; returned 1919; sold 26 November, 1921 and BU.

Kanran, Sendan (1917)

Name	Builder	Date	Displ	Length ft in	Beam ft in	Draught ft in	Machinery	SHP	Speed	Fuel	Radius	Armament	Comp
MOMI Class (21 units)	various	1919–1923	1020 F 850 N 770 light	280 0 wl 275 0 pp	26 0	8 0	2-shaft TU 3 Kampon boilers	21500	36	240 / 275 oil	3000 @ 15	3 × 4.7in 45-cal 2 × 7.7mm MGs 4 × 21in TT (AW)	110

General Notes
Built under the 1918 Programme (8 *Momi* group), 1919 Programme (5 *Fuji* group) and 1920 Programme (8 *Ashi* group) respectively. They were the first Japanese destroyers armed with 21in TT.

Machinery
Kaki, Tsuga, Nire, Hagi, Susuki, Hishi and *Hasu* fitted with Parsons turbines; *Sumire* and *Yomogi* had Zoelly turbines.

Re-armament and Reconstruction
In 1939, *Fuji, Kiku, Aoi, Susuki, Tsuta, Hishi, Yomogi* and *Tade* had 2 × 4.7in; 6 × 25mm AA; 60 DCs. Their displacement was 935/1162ts, with 12000 shp = 18 knots.
In 1940, *Nire, Take, Kaki, Ashi* and *Sumire*, had 1 × or 2 × 4.7in 2 × 21in TT; their displacement was 755ts, with 9000 shp = 14 knots.
In 1941, *Nos. 32* to *39* had the stern rebuilt for launching a Daihatsu landing craft.
In 1942–3, *No. 31* had 2 × 4.7in 8 × 25mm AA; 60 DCs: *Nos. 34* to *36, 38* and *39* had 2 × 4.7in; 6 × 25mm AA; one Daihatsu landing craft.
In 1937, *Fuji, Susuki, Hishi, Hasu, Tsuka, Yanogi* and *Tade* had their funnels raised and capped. In 1944, *Osu* and *Mitaka* were disarmed and fitted with wooden deckhouses for accommodation and training.

Careers
Momi
Launched 10 June, 1919 at Yokosuka DY; completed 27 December, 1919; stricken 1 April, 1932 but retained as a hulk in Yokosuka; BU later.

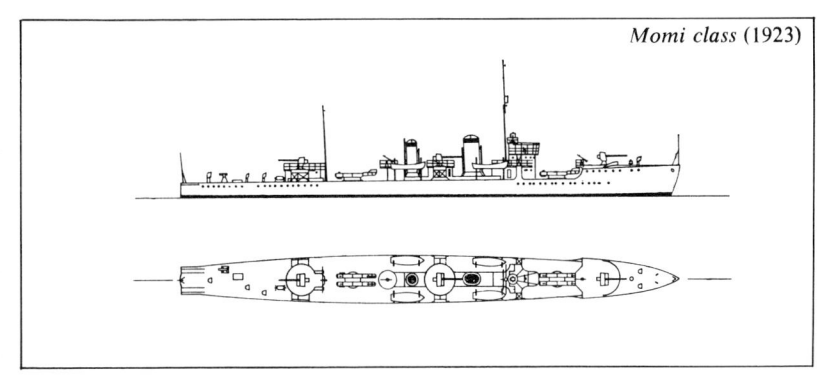

Momi class (1923)

Kaya
Launched 10 June, 1919 at Yokosuka DY; completed 28 March, 1920; stricken 1939 and BU.

Nire
Launched 22 December, 1919 at Kure DY; completed 31 March, 1920; disarmed 1939; tender 1940; on 15 December, 1944 she became training ship *Tomariura No. 1*; surrendered August 1945; BU by 15 August, 1948 at Uraga.

TORPEDO BOATS AND DESTROYERS

Nashi
Launched 26 August, 1919 by Kawasaki, Kobe; completed 10 December, 1919; stricken 1939 and BU.

Take
Launched 26 August, 1919 by Kawasaki, Kobe; completed 25 December, 1919; disarmed 1939; tender 1940; surrendered August 1945; BU 1947 at Maizuru.

Kaki
Launched 20 October, 1919 by Uraga Dock, Tokyo; completed 8 August, 1920; disarmed 1939; tender 1940; became training ship *Osu* 23 February, 1945; surrendered August 1945; BU at Kure 1947.

Kuri
Launched 19 March, 1920 at Kure DY; completed 30 April, 1920; surrendered at Tsingtao September 1945; mined 8 October, 1945 off Pusan, Korea.

Tsuga
Launched 17 April, 1920 at Ishikawajima Zosensho, Tokyo; completed 20 July, 1920; sunk 15 January, 1945 Makung Harbour, Pescadores Islands (23° 33′ N, 119° 33′ E) by aircraft of TF 38.

Fuji
Launched 27 November, 1920 by Fujinagata Zosensho, Osaka; completed 31 May, 1921; renamed *Patrol Boat No. 36* in 1939; 17 May, 1945 damaged at Soerabaja by aircraft from carriers HMS *Illustrious* and USS *Saratoga*; surrendered August 1945 while still under repair at Soerabaya; in July 1946 ceded to Netherlands and BU 1947.

Kiku
Launched 13 October, 1920 by Kawasaki, Kobe; completed 10 December, 1920; renamed *Patrol Boat No. 31* in 1939; sunk 30 March, 1944 by US aircraft of TF 58 off Palau (07° 30′ N, 134° 30′ E).

Aoi
Launched 9 November, 1920 by Kawasaki, Kobe; completed 20 December, 1920; renamed *Patrol Boat No. 32* in 1939; beached and sunk 23 December, 1941 after damage by US coastal batteries on Wake Island (19° 17′ N, 166° 37′ E).

Hagi
Launched 29 October, 1920 by Uraga Dock, Tokyo; completed 20 April, 1921; renamed *Patrol Boat No. 33* in 1939; beached and sunk 23 December, 1941 after damage by US coastal batteries on Wake Island (with *No. 32*, ex-*Aoi*).

Susuki
Launched 21 February, 1921 by Ishikawajima Z., Tokyo; completed 25 May, 1921; renamed *Patrol Boat No. 34* in 1939; badly damaged 6 March, 1943 S of Kavieng after collision with target ship *Yakaze*; returned to Truk for repairs but sunk there by air attack 3 July, 1944; stricken officially 30 November, 1945.

Ashi
Launched 3 September, 1921 by Kawasaki, Kobe; completed 29 October, 1921; disarmed 1939; tender 1940; became training ship *Tomariura No. 2* 15 December, 1944; surrendered August 1945 at Yokohama and BU 1947.

Tsuta
Launched 9 May, 1921 by Kawasaki, Kobe; originally be have been named *Tsuru*; completed 30 June, 1921; became *Patrol Boat No. 35* in 1939; sunk 2 September, 1943 by USAF aircraft in Lae Harbour, New Guinea (06° 45′ S, 147° E).

Warabi
Launched 28 September, 1921 by Fujinagata Z., Osaka (originally to have been named *Toko*) completed 19 December, 1921; sunk 24 August, 1927 in collision with cruiser *Jintsu* at Maizuru (106 dead).

Hasu
Launched 8 December, 1921 by Uraga Dock, Tokyo; completed 31 July, 1922; badly damaged 16 January, 1945 at Hong Kong by aircraft of TF 38; surrendered September 1945 at Tsingtao and BU 1946 at Sasebo.

Hishi
Launched 19 May, 1921 by Uraga Dock, Tokyo; completed 23 March, 1922; became *Patrol Boat No. 37* in 1939; badly damaged 24 January, 1942 by gunfire and torpedoes of US destroyers *Pope* and *Parrott* near Balikpapan (01° 24′ S, 117° 02′ E); raised and BU.

Sumire
Launched 14 December, 1921 by Ishikawajima Z., Tokyo; completed 31 March, 1923; disarmed 1939; tender 1940; became training ship *Mitaka*; surrendered August 1945 at Etajima, Kure; BU March 1948 at Harima.

Yomogi
Launched 14 March, 1922 by Ishikawajima Z., Tokyo; completed 19 August, 1922; became *Patrol Boat No. 38* in 1939; torpedoed 25 November, 1944 by US submarine *Atule* 100 m N of Cape Engano (20° 12′ N, 121° 51′ E); officially stricken 10 March, 1945.

Tade
Launched 15 March, 1922 by Fujinagata Z., Osaka (originally to have been named *Fuyo*); completed 31 July, 1922; became *Patrol Boat No. 39* in 1939; torpedoed 23 April, 1943 by US submarine *Seawolf* 150 m NE of Formosa (23° 45′ N, 122° 45′ E); officially stricken 1 July, 1943.

The destroyer *Kuri*, seen making 35.2 knots on trials in April 1920. The numerous *Momi* class were built between 1919 and 1923, and were converted to escorts for service in World War Two. (Shizuo Fukui.)

Sumire, of the *Momi* class, in 1927. The siting of the torpedo-tubes, in the break of the forecastle forward of the bridge, was copied from pre-1914 German practice. (Shizuo Fukui.)

Name	Builder	Date	Displ	Length ft in	Beam ft in	Draught ft in	Machinery	SHP	Speed	Fuel	Radius	Armament	Comp
WAKATAKE Class (formerly YURI Class) (8 units + 4)	various	1922–1924	1100 F 900 N 820 light	280 0 wl 275 0 pp	26 6	8 3	2-shaft Parsons TU 3 Kampon boilers	21500	35½	244 / 275 oil	3000 @ 15	3 × 4.7in 45-cal 2 × 7.7mm MGs 4 × 21in TT (AW)	110

GENERAL NOTES
Built under the 1921 Programme, these were improved *Momi*s and were the last 2nd Class destroyers built. They were also rated as minelayers and minesweepers. Originally 13 units were planned but the class was reduced to 9 units, and then *No. 14* was cancelled in 1922. From 1 August, 1928 the remaining units were given names once more.

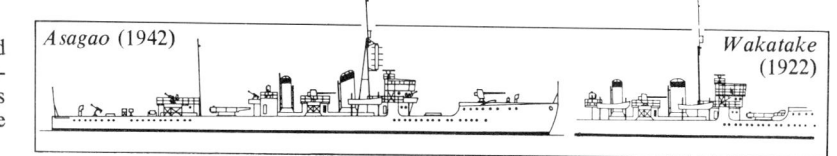

Re-armament and Reconstruction
In 1939–40, *Yugao* had 2 × 4.7in 45-cal; 8 × 25mm AA; 60 DCs. The horsepower was reduced to 10000 shp and speed to 18 knots, and the displacement was 910/1130ts. In 1941–2 they had 2 × 4.7in QF; 6 × 25mm AA; some 13mm AA; 36/48 DCs (*Asagao* had 2 × 21in TT).

In 1938 *Wakatake* and *Sanae* had the forefunnel capped and additional ballast; displacement rose to 1113ts and speed was 31 knots.

Machinery
Most units had Parsons turbines but *Wakatake*, *Kuretake*, *Fuyo* and *Karukaya* had Brown-Curtis.

Careers
Wakatake
Launched 24 July, 1922 by Kawasaki, Kobe; completed 30 September, 1922 as *No. 2* (ex-*Kikyo*); sunk 30 March, 1944 by aircraft of TF 58 60 m N of Palau (07° 50′ N, 134° 20′ E).

Kuretake
Launched 21 October, 1922 by Kawasaki, Kobe; completed 21 December, 1922 as *No. 4* (ex-*Yuri*); torpedoed 30 December, 1944 by US submarine *Razorback* 65 m SE of Formosa (21° N, 121° 24′ E).

Sanae
Launched 15 February, 1923 by Uraga Dock, Tokyo; completed 5 November, 1923 as *No. 5* (ex-*Ayame*); torpedoed 18 November, 1943 by US submarine *Bluefish* 90 m S of Basilan Island (04° 52′ N, 122° 07′ E).

Sawarabi
Launched 1 September, 1923 by Uraga Dock, Tokyo; completed 24 July, 1924 as *No. 8* (ex-*Kaido*); foundered at 14.00 hrs 5 December, 1932 in storm 100 m NE of Keelung Formosa Straits (27° 17′ N, 122° 12′ E).

Asagao
Launched 4 November, 1922 by Ishikawajima Z., Tokyo; completed 10 May, 1923 as *No. 10* (ex-*Kakitsubata*); badly damaged by mine at about 16.35 hrs on 22 August, 1945 at the western exit of the Straits of Shimonoseki; surrendered in same condition at Shimonoseki and BU at Yoshimi 10 June, 1948.

Yugao
Launched 14 April, 1923 by Ishikawajima Z., Tokyo; completed 31 May, 1924 as *No. 12* (ex-*Tsutsuji*); re-rated as *Patrol Boat No. 46* in 1942; torpedoed 10 November, 1944 by US submarine *Greenling* 75 m SW of Yokosuka (34° 30′ N, 138° 34′ E).

No. 14
Originally to have been called *Shian*; contract cancelled in 1922 (Kawasaki, Kobe).

Fuyo
Launched 23 September 1922 by Fujinagata Z., Osaka; completed 16 March, 1923 as *No. 16* (ex-*Ajisai*), torpedoed 20 December, 1943 by US submarine *Puffer* 60 m W of Manila (14° 44′ N, 119° 55′ E).

Karukaya
Launched 19 March, 1923 by Fujinagata Z., Osaka; completed 20 August, 1923 as *No. 18*; torpedoed 10 May, 1944 by US submarine *Cod* 35 m WNW of Iba, Luzon (15° 38′ N, 119° 25′ E).

No. 20
Ordered as *Omodoka* from Kawasaki, Kobe; laid down 1922; cotnract cancelled and material BU.

No. 22
To have been ordered as *Nadeshiko* from Fujinagata Z., Osaka; contract cancelled.

No. 24
To have been ordered as *Botan* from Uraga Dock, Tokyo; contract cancelled.

No. 26
To have been ordered as *Basho* from Ishikawajima Z., Tokyo; contract cancelled.

A *Wakatake* class "2nd-class" destroyer, at Shanghai in 1938. Tied up alongside is one of a number of requisitioned craft, used for river patrols. (Tappman Collection.)

The *Wakatake* class were a development of the *Momi* class, and also served as escorts in World War Two. *Sanae* is seen here in August 1930. (Shizuo Fukui.)

Name	Builder	Date	Displ	Length ft in	Beam ft in	Draught ft in	Machinery	SHP	Speed	Fuel	Radius	Armament	Comp
UMIKAZE	Maizuru DY	1909–1911	1500 F	323 3 oa	28 1	9 0	3-shaft Parsons TU 8 Kampon boilers	20500	33	250 coal 180 oil	2700 @ 15	2 × 4.7in 40-cal QF 5 × 3.1in 40-cal QF 4 × 18in TT (AW) (*Yamakaze* 3 TT)	140
YAMAKAZE	Mitsubishi, Nagasaki		1150 N 1030 light	321 1 wl 310 1 pp									

General Notes
1st Class destroyers built under the 1907 Programme. They had mixed-firing boilers.

Re-armament and Reconstruction
They were converted to minesweepers in 1929, and were re-armed with 1 × 4.7in 40-cal, 4 × 3.1in 40-cal; displacement was 1030ts and speed reduced to 24 knots.

Careers
Umikaze
Launched 10 October, 1910; completed 28 September, 1911; reclassified as *Minesweeper No. 7* in 1930; stricken 1936 and BU.

Yamakaze
Launched 21 January, 1911, completed 21 October, 1911; reclassified as *Minesweeper No. 8* in 1930; stricken 1936 and BU.

Yamakaze (1911)

Yamakaze as Minesweeper No. 8

TORPEDO BOATS AND DESTROYERS

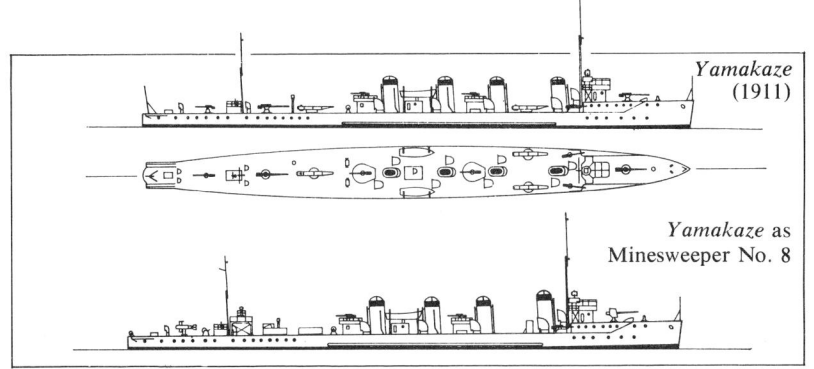

Name	Builder	Date	Displ	Length ft in	Beam ft in	Draught ft in	Machinery	SHP	Speed	Fuel	Radius	Armament	Comp
URAKAZE	Yarrow & Co.,	1913–	1085	286 3	27 7	8 0	2-shaft	22000	28	248	1800	1 × 4.7in 45-cal QF	120
KAWAKAZE	Scotstoun	1916	F	oa			Brown-Curtis			oil	@ 15	4 × 3.1in 40-cal QF	
			907	284 4			GTU					4 × 21in TT (AW)	
			N	wl			3 Yarrow boilers						
			810	275 3									
			light	pp									

GENERAL NOTES
Ordered under the 1912 Programme as 1st Class destroyers. They were built to a Yarrow design as the first oil-fired Japanese destroyers.

RE-ARMAMENT
In 1936 *Urakaze* was disarmed and hulked.

MACHINERY
They were originally planned to have Diesel machinery. *Urakaze* made 30.26 knots on trials.

CAREERS
Urakaze
Launched 16 February, 1915, completed 14 October, 1915 but not delivered to Japan until 1919; stricken 1936; hulked at Yokosuka and renamed *Haikan No. 18*; sunk 18 July, 1945 by aircraft of TF 38 at Yokosuka; BU there 9 September, 1948.

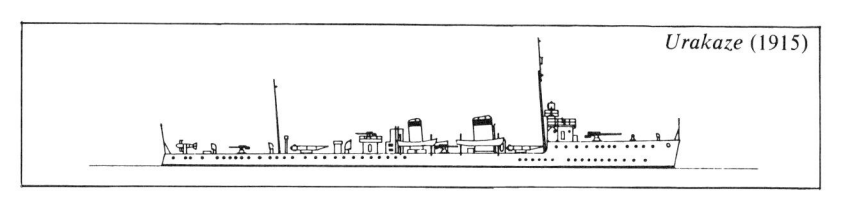

Urakaze (1915)

Kawakaze
Launched 27 September, 1916, completed 23 December, 1916; sold to Italy 1916 and renamed *Audace* (re-armed); re-rated as torpedo-boat 1935; converted to W/T control ship for target vessel *San Marco* 1938; 12 September, 1943 captured by Germans; became *TA. 20* in October 1943; sunk at 22.30 hrs on 1 November, 1944 N of Zara, off Pago Island (44° 24′ N, 15° 02′ E) by British destroyers *Avon Vale* and *Wheatland*.

Name	Builder	Date	Displ	Length ft in	Beam ft in	Draught ft in	Machinery	SHP	Speed	Fuel	Radius	Armament	Comp
AMATSUKAZE	various	1916–	1570	326 6	27 11	9 3	3-shaft Parsons	27000	34	147	4000	4 × 4.7in 40-cal	128
Class		1917	F	oa			TU (*Amatsukaze*			coal	@ 15	2 × 7.7mm MGs	
(4 units)			1227	317 2			Curtis TU)			297		6 × 18in TT	
			N	wl			5 Kampon boilers			oil			
			1105	310 0									
			light	pp									

GENERAL NOTES
These 1st Class destroyers were built under the 1915 Programme, and reverted to mixed firing.

RECONSTRUCTION
In 1935, *Tokitsukaze* was converted to a training hulk without armament.

CAREERS
Amatsukaze
Launched 5 October 1916 at Kure DY; completed 14 April, 1917; stricken 1 April, 1935 and BU the same year.
Isokaze
Launched 5 October, 1916 at Kure DY; completed 28 February, 1917; stricken 1 April, 1935 and BU the same year.
Tokitsukaze
Launched 27 December, 1916 by Kawasaki, Kobe; completed 31 May, 1917; broke in two on 25 March, 1918 off the coast of Kyushu; raised July 1918 and repaired at Maizuru by February 1920; stricken 1 April, 1935; hulked at Etajima as *Haikan No. 20*; BU 1 March, 1948 at Kure.

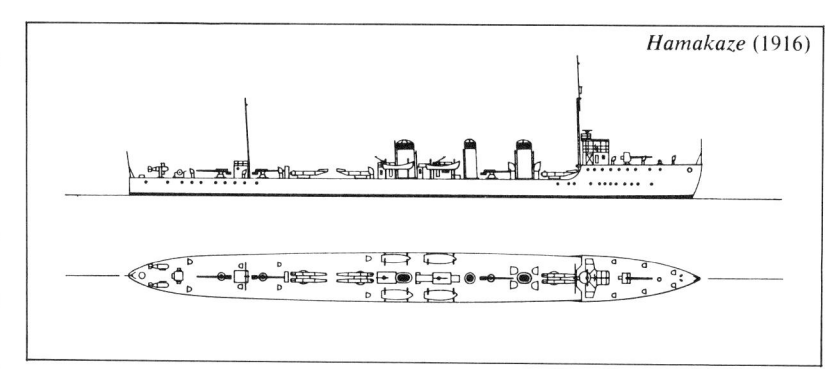

Hamakaze (1916)

Hamakaze
Launched 30 October, 1916 by Mitsubishi, Nagasaki; completed 28 March, 1917; stricken 1 April, 1935 and BU the same year.

Name	Builder	Date	Displ	Length ft in	Beam ft in	Draught ft in	Machinery	SHP	Speed	Fuel	Radius	Armament	Comp
TANIKAZE	Maizuru DY	1916–	1580	336 6	29 0	9 3	2-shaft (*Tanikaze*	34000	37½	380	4000	3 × 4.7in 45-cal	128
		1919	F	oa			Curtis TU)			oil	@ 15	2 × 7.7mm MGs	
KAWAKAZE	Yokosuka DY		1300	326 9			Parsons GTU					6 × 21in TT	
			N	wl			4 Kampon boilers						
			1180	320 0									
			light	pp									

GENERAL NOTES
Built under the 1916 Programme and rated as 1st Class destroyers, they were improved *Amatsukaze*s.

RE-ARMAMENT AND RECONSTRUCTION
Later re-armed with 2 triple TT in place of 3 twin mounts.

Tanikaze (1919)

140 TORPEDO BOATS AND DESTROYERS

CAREERS
Kawakaze
Launched 10 October 1917, completed November 1918; stricken 1 April, 1934 and BU.

Tanikaze
Launched 20 July, 1918, completed 30 January, 1919; stricken 1 April, 1935 and hulked as *Haikan No. 19*; became a training ship for Kaitens in 1944; later scuttled as a breakwater at Kure and subsequently BU.

Name	Builder	Date	Displ	Length ft in	Beam ft in	Draught ft in	Machinery	SHP	Speed	Fuel	Radius	Armament	Comp
MINEKAZE Class (15 units)	various	1918– 1922	1650 F 1345 N 1215 light	336 6 oa 326 6 wl 320 0 pp	29 8	9 6	2-shaft Parsons GTU, 4 Kampon boilers	38500	39	395 oil	3600 @ 14 900 @ 34	4 × 4.7in 45-cal 2 × 7.7mm MGs 6 × 21in TT (AW) 20 mines	148

GENERAL NOTES
The first 2 units were built under the 1917 Programme, then 5 each under the 1918 and 1919 Programmes, and 3 under the 1920 Programme. They were also classed as minesweepers.

MACHINERY
On trials *Shimakaze* reached over 40 knots. The 4 units rebuilt as patrol vessels in 1939–40 had 2 boilers removed, 19250 shp = 20 knots.

RECONSTRUCTION AND RE-ARMAMENT
In 1937, *Yakaze* was refitted at Kure as a control ship for the wireless target *Settsu*; her TT were removed and her armament was reduced by 1 or 2 × 4.7in 45-cal. In 1937–8 the rest of the class had their hulls strengthened, funnel caps fitted and their fuel capacity reduced as follows: *Minekaze*, *Okikaze* 275ts, *Shimakaze*, *Akikaze*, *Shiokaze*, *Yukaze*, *Nadakaze* 230ts, *Hakaze*, *Hokaze*, *Tachikaze* 295ts; displacement 1552ts, speed 36 knots maximum.
In 1939, *Nokaze*, *Numakaze* and *Namikaze* had their hulls strengthened, additional ballast, raked funnel caps. Their displacement was increased to 1692ts, and speed reduced to 34½ knots maximum.
In 1939/40, *Nadakaze* and *Shimakaze* were rebuilt as patrol vessels displacing 1390/1700ts. They had 2 × 4.7in DP; 10 × 25mm AA; 2 × 21in TT and 16 DCs. By the end of 1941 this was altered to 1 × 4.7in 50-cal DP; two Daihatsu landing craft, 250 troops, 18 DCs.
In 1944, *Nadakaze* had 16 × 25mm AA, and the remaining ships had 13 × to 20 × 25mm AA, 5 × 13mm MGs; displacement was 1350ts.
Namikaze was rebuilt as a Kaiten-carrier with three boilers, 22000 shp = 28 knots. Her armament was: 1 × 4.7in 50-cal DP; 20 × 25mm AA; 8 × 13mm MGs; 2 Kaiten. Similarly, from February 1945 *Shiokaze* had 1 × 4.7in 50-cal DP; 11 × 25mm AA and 4 Kaitens, with an additional 50ts of oil in 7 Kaiten hulls stowed in No. 1 boiler room.
In 1945, *Yukaze* had 2 × 4.7in 50-cal DP; 12 × 25mm AA; 2 × 21in TT; 36 DC.1
In August 1945, *Sawakaze* had 1 × 4.7in 50-cal DP; 10 × 25mm AA; 1 × 5.9in A/S rocket-launcher (wire barrage); speed was 16 knots.

CAREERS
Minekaze
Launched 8 February, 1919 at Maizuru DY; completed 29 May, 1920; torpedoed 10 February, 1944 by US submarine *Pogy* 85 m NNE of Formosa (23° 12′ N, 121° 30′ E).

Sawakaze
Launched 7 January, 1919 by Mitsubishi, Nagasaki; completed 16 March, 1920; became an aircraft rescue ship 1939; patrol vessel 1941; surrendered August 1945 at Yokosuka; BU 1948.

Okikaze
Launched 3 October, 1919 at Maizuru DY; completed 17 August, 1920; stricken 1938 but reinstated as a destroyer in 1941; torpedoed 10 January, 1943 by US submarine *Trigger* 35 m SE of Yokosuka (35° 02′ N, 140° 12′ E).

Hakaze
Launched 21 June, 1920 by Mitsubishi Nagasaki; completed 16 September, 1920; torpedoed 23 January, 1943 by US submarine *Guardfish* 15 m SW of Kavieng (02° 47′ S, 150° 38′ E).

Yakaze
Launched 10 April, 1920 by Mitsubishi, Nagasaki; completed 19 July, 1920; in September 1942 she became an aircraft target (1531ts, 11260 shp = 24 knots, 1 × 50mm gun); badly damaged 18 July, 1945 by aircraft of TF 38 at Yokosuka; surrendered August 1945 and BU.

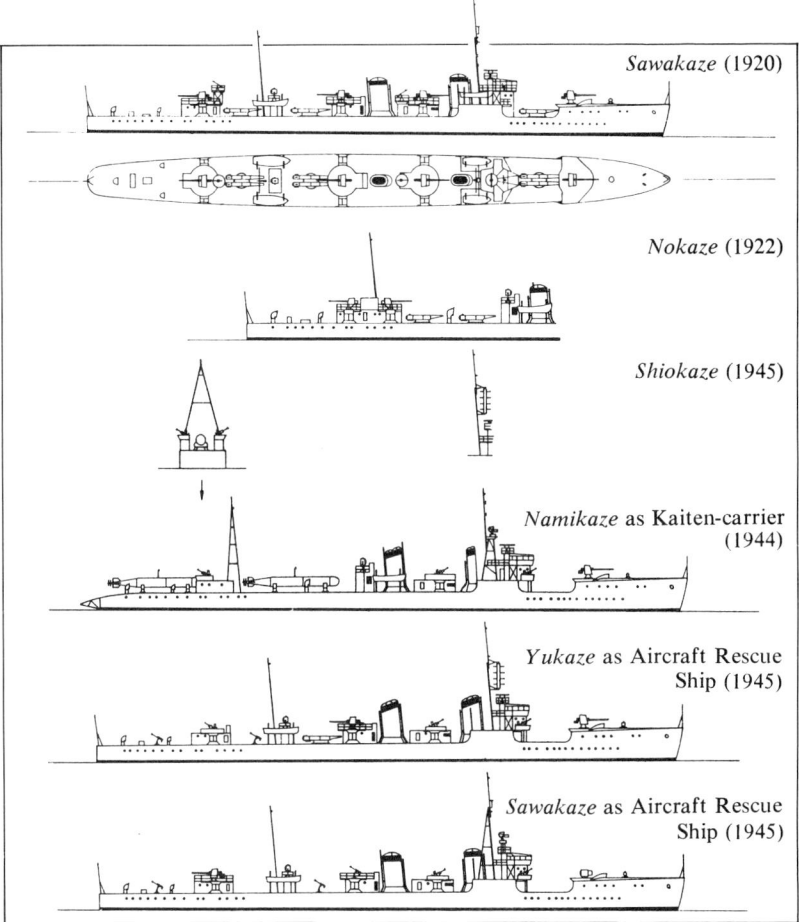

Sawakaze (1920)

Nokaze (1922)

Shiokaze (1945)

Namikaze as Kaiten-carrier (1944)

Yukaze as Aircraft Rescue Ship (1945)

Sawakaze as Aircraft Rescue Ship (1945)

Shimakaze was a unit of the *Minekaze* class, another development of the *Momi* design. She was lost in 1943, as an escort. (Y. Bertrand.)

TORPEDO BOATS AND DESTROYERS

Nadakaze
Launched 26 June, 1920 at Maizuru DY; completed 30 September, 1921; became *Patrol Boat No. 2* in 1939; torpedoed 25 July, 1945 by British submarine 175 m E of Soerabaja (07° 06′ S, 115° 42′ E); officially stricken 15 September, 1945.

Shimakaze
Launched 31 March, 1920 at Maizuru DY; completed 15 November, 1920; became *Patrol Boat No. 1* in 1939; torpedoed 13 January, 1943 by US submarine *Guardfish* 65 m WSW of Kavieng (02° 51′ S, 149° 43′ E).

Akikaze
Launched 14 December, 1920 by Mitsubishi, Nagasaki; completed 1 April, 1921; torpedoed 3 November, 1944 by US submarine *Pintado* 160 m W of Cape Bolinao (16° 48′ N, 117° 17′ E).

Shiokaze
Launched 22 October, 1920 at Maizuru DY; completed 29 July, 1921; badly damaged 31 January, 1945 by US aircraft off Formosa; towed to Japan and converted to a Kaiten-carrier; surrendered in an unseaworthy condition in August 1945 but later used on repatriation service; BU 1948.

Yukaze
Launched 28 May, 1921 by Mitsubishi, Nagasaki; completed 24 August, 1921; surrendered in August 1945 and used on repatriation duties; handed over to Great Britain in 1947 and towed to Singapore for BU.

Hokaze
Launched 12 July, 1921 at Maizuru DY; completed 22 December, 1921; torpedoed 6 July, 1944 by US submarine *Paddle* 105 m NNE of Men do in the Celebes Sea (03° 24′ N, 125° 28′ E).

Tachikaze
Launched 31 March, 1921 at Maizuru DY; completed 5 December, 1921; sunk 17 February, 1944 by aircraft of TF 38 at Truk Atoll (07° 04′ N, 151° 55′ E).

Nokaze
Launched 1 October, 1921 at Maizuru DY; completed 31 March, 1922; torpedoed 20 February, 1945 by US submarine *Pargo* near Cape Varella (12° 48′ N, 109° 38′ E).

Namikaze
Launched 24 June, 1922 at Maizuru DY; completed 11 November, 1922; badly damaged 8 September, 1944 by US submarine in Sea of Okhotsk; repaired and converted to a Kaiten-carrier; surrendered at Kure in August 1945 and used on repatriation duties; transferred to China on 3 October, 1947 and renamed *Shen Yang*; disarmed and BU.

Numakaze
Launched 25 February, 1922 at Maizuru DY; completed 24 July, 1922; torpedoed 19 December, 1943 by US submarine *Grayback* 50 m ENE of Naha, Okinawa (26° 29′ N, 128° 26′ E).

Name	Builder	Date	Displ	Length ft in	Beam ft in	Draught ft in	Machinery	SHP	Speed	Fuel	Radius	Armament	Comp
KAMIKAZE Class (9 units)	various	1921–1925	1720 F 1400 N 1270 light	336 6 oa 327 0 wl 320 0 pp	30 0	9 7	2-shaft Parsons GTU 4 Kampon boilers	38500 ihp	37.3	420 oil	3600 @ 14	As completed 4 × 4.7in 50-cal DP 2 × 7.7in MGs 6 × 21in TT (AW) 1941–2: 3 × 4.7in 50-cal DP 10 × 25mm AA 4 × 21in TT 18 DCs	148

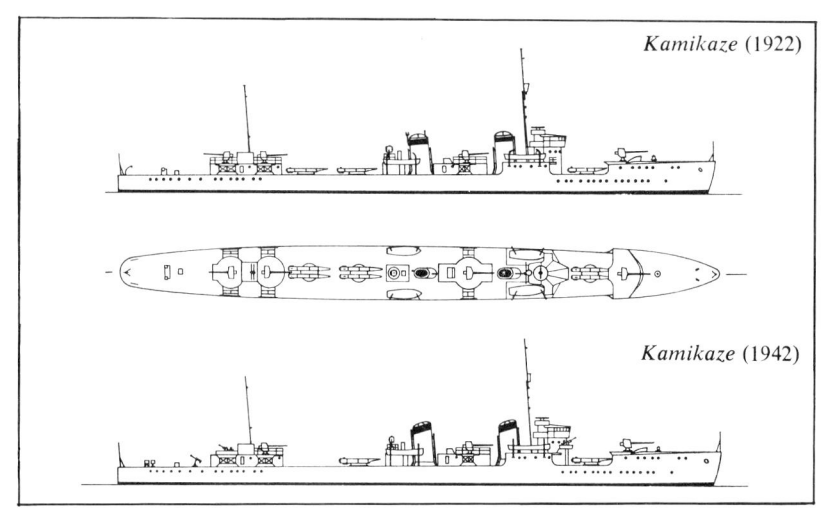

Kamikaze (1922)

Kamikaze (1942)

Oite, of the *Kamikaze* class, seen on completion in 1925. (Shizuo Fukui.)

GENERAL NOTES
Built under the 1921–2 Programmes as improved *Minekaze* type. Although first commissioned with numbers instead of names, they were renamed in 1928.

RECONSTRUCTION AND RE-ARMAMENT
After reconstruction in 1941/2 the normal displacement was increased to 1523ts and the light displacement to 1300ts. By June 1944 the survivors had 13 × to 20 × 25mm AA and 4 × 13mm. Speed was reduced to 35 knots.

CAREERS
Kamikaze
Launched 25 September, 1922 by Mitsubishi, Nagasaki; completed 28 December, 1922 as *Destroyer No. 1* (originally to have been named *Kiyokaze* or *Shirushikaze*); surrendered at Singapore in August 1945 and served on repatriation duties; wrecked 7 June, 1946 near Omaezaki; BU by 31 October, 1947 at Suruga-Wan.

Asakaze
Launched 8 December, 1922 by Mitsubishi, Nagasaki; completed 16 June, 1923 as *Destroyer No. 3* (originally to have been named *Karuikaze* or *Suzukaze*); torpedoed 23 August, 1944 by US submarine *Haddo* 20 m SW of Cape Bolinao (16° 06′ N, 119° 44′ E).

Harukaze
Launched 18 December, 1922 at Maizuru DY; completed 31 May, 1923 as *No. 5* (ex-*Makaze*); badly damaged by mine 4 November, 1944; badly damaged 21 January, 1945 by aircraft of TF 38 near Makung, Formosa; towed to Japan but was surrendered unrepaired at Sasebo in August 1945; BU 1947.

Matsukaze
Launched 30 October, 1923 at Maizuru DY; completed 5 April, 1924 as *No. 7*; torpedoed 9 June, 1944 by submarine *Swordfish* 70 m SE of Chichijima, Bonin (26° 59′ N, 143° 13′ E).

Hatakaze
Launched 15 March, 1924 at Maizuru DY; completed 30 August, 1924 as *No. 9*; sunk 15 January, 1945 by US aircraft of TF 38 at Takao Harbour, Formosa (22° 37′ N, 120° 15′ E).

Oite
Launched 27 November, 1924, by Uraga Dock, Tokyo; completed 30 October, 1925 as *No. 11*; sunk 17 February, 1944 by aircraft of TF 38 while carrying survivors of the cruiser *Agano*, at Truk (07° 40′ N, 151° 45′ E).

Hayate
Launched 23 March, 1925 by Ishikawajima Z., Tokyo; completed 21 December, 1925 as *No. 13*; sunk 11 December, 1941 by US coastal batteries, 2 m SW of Wake Island (19° 16′ N, 166° 37′ E); she was the first Japanese warship to be sunk during the Second World War.

Asanagi
Launched 21 April, 1924 by Fujinagata Z., Osaka; completed 29 December, 1925 as *No. 15*; torpedoed 22 May, 1944 by submarine *Pollack* 200 m WNW of Chichijima, Bonin (28° 20′ N, 138° 57′ E).

Yunagi
Launched 23 April, 1924 at Sasebo DY; completed 24 April, 1925 as *No. 17*; torpedoed 25 August, 1944 by submarine *Picuda* 20 m NNE of Cape Bojeador (18° 46′ N, 20° 46′ E).

Two more units, *Okaze* and *Tsumikaze* were stricken in 1922 under the Washington Treaty and the contracts were cancelled.

Name	Builder	Date	Displ	Length ft in	Beam ft in	Draught ft in	Machinery	SHP	Speed	Fuel	Radius	Armament	Comp
MUTSUKI Class (12 units)	various	1924–1927	1772 N 1315 light	338 9 wl 320 0 pp	30 0	9 8	2-shaft Parsons GTU 4 Kampon boilers	38500	37¼	420 oil	4000 @ 15	As built 4 × 4.7in 45-cal DP 2 × 7.7mm MGs 6 × 24in TT (AW) (10 torpedoes) 16 mines 18 DCs 1941–2: 2 × 4.7in 50-cal DP 10 × 25mm AA 6 × 24in TT 36 DCs	150

GENERAL NOTES
Built under the 1923 Programme as an improved *Kamikaze* type, and also rated as minesweepers and minelayers. They were the first destroyers with 24in torpedoes. Although numbered at first, they were given names in 1928.

MACHINERY
The highest speed reached in full load condition was only 33½ knots. Two of the class were engined with foreign turbines for comparison; *Yayoi* with Rateau turbines, and *Nagatsuki* with Zoelly. *Nagatsuki* ran trials in April 1927 and reached 36.3 knots with 40787 shp.

RECONSTRUCTION AND RE-ARMAMENT
In 1935–6 *Satsuki*, *Minazuki*, *Fumizuki*, *Nagatsuki*, *Kikuzuki* and *Mikazuki* had their hulls strengthened, raked funnel caps fitted and shields to the TT. They were rebuilt in 1941–2 as fast transports (normal displacement 1913ts, light 1590ts, 20 × 25mm AA and 5 × 13mm).

CAREERS
Mutsuki
Launched 23 July, 1925 at Sasebo DY; completed 25 March, 1926 as *No. 19*; sunk 2 August, 1942 by US B17 bombers 40 m NE of San Isabel (07° 47′ S 160° 13′ E).

Kisaragi
Launched 5 June, 1925 at Maizuru DY; completed 21 December, 1925 as *No. 21*; sunk 11 December, 1941 by US bombers 30 m SW of Wake Island (18° 55′ N, 166° 17′ E).

Yayoi
Launched 11 July, 1925 by Uraga Dock, Tokyo; completed 28 August, 1926 as *No. 23*; sunk 11 September, 1942 by British and US aircraft 8 m NW of Vakuta (08° 45′ S, 151° 25′ E).

Uzuki
Launched 15 October, 1925 by Ishikawajima Z., Tokyo; completed 14 September, 1926 as *No. 25*; torpedoed 12 December, 1944 by US *PT. 490* and *PT. 492* 50 m NE of Cebu (11° 03′ N, 124° 23′ E).

Satsuki
Launched 25 March, 1925 by Fujinagata Z., Osaka; completed 15 November, 1925 as *No. 27*; sunk 21 September, 1944 by aircraft of TF 38 in Manila Bay (15° 35′ N, 120° 55′ E).

Minazuki
Launched 25 May, 1926 by Uraga Dock, Tokyo; completed 22 March, 1927 as *No. 28*; torpedoed 6 June, 1944 by US submarine *Harder* 150 m ENE of Tarakan, Celebes Sea (04° 05′ N, 119° 30′ E).

Fumizuki
Launched 16 February, 1926 by Fujinagata Z., Osaka; completed 3 July, 1926 as *No. 29*; sunk 18 February, 1944 by aircraft of USS *Enterprise* at Truk (07° 24′ N, 151° 44′ E).

Nagatsuki
Launched 6 October, 1926 by Ishikawajima Z., Tokyo; completed 30 April, 1927 as *No. 30*; wrecked 6 July, 1943 near Bambari Harbour, 5 m N of Vila (08° 02′ S, 157° 12′ E) and sunk the same day by US aircraft.

Kikuzuki
Launched 15 May, 1926 at Maizuru DY; completed 20 November, 1926 as *No. 31*; sunk 4 May, 1942 by aircraft from USS *Yorktown* at Tulagi Harbour (09° 07′ S, 160° 12′ E).

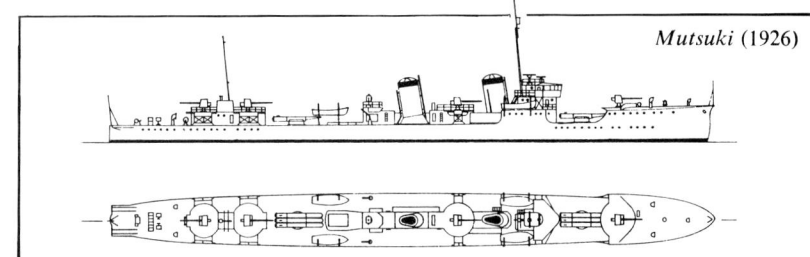

Mutsuki (1926)

Mikazuki, seen at Sasebo in 1938. (Tappman Collection.)

The *Mutsuki* class were the last variants of the *Momi* class to be built, but they differed in having a clipper bow, and introduced the 24-inch torpedo. The photograph shows *Mutsuki* herself. (Shizuo Fukui.)

TORPEDO BOATS AND DESTROYERS 143

Mikazuki
Launched 12 July, 1926 at Sasebo DY; completed 7 May, 1927 as *No. 32*; wrecked 27 July, 1943 off Cape Gloucester (05° 27′ S, 148° 25′ E), and sunk the next day by B-25 bombers.

Mochizuki
Launched 28 April, 1927 by Uraga Dock, Tokyo; completed 31 October, 1927 as *No. 33*; sunk 24 October, 1943 by US Marine Corps aircraft 90 m SSW of Rabaul (05° 42′ S, 151° 40′ E).

Yuzuki
Launched 4 March, 1927 by Fujinagata Z., Osaka; completed 25 July, 1927 as *No. 34*; sunk 12 December, 1944 by US Marine Corps aircraft 65 m NNE of Cebu (11° 20′ N, 124° 10′ E).

Name	Builder	Date	Displ	Length ft in	Beam ft in	Draught ft in	Machinery	SHP	Speed	Fuel	Radius	Armament	Comp
FUBUKI Class (20 units)	various	1926–1928	2090 N 1750 light	378 3 wl / 367 0 pp	34 0	10 6	2-shaft Parsons GTU 4 Kampon boilers	50000	38	500 oil	4700 @ 15 / 1100 @ 34	6 × 5in 50-cal DP 2 × 13mm AA 9 × 24in TT (AW) 18 torpedoes 18 mines 18 DCs	197

GENERAL NOTES
Built under the 1923 Programme (*Nos. 35 to 39*), 1926 Programme (*Nos. 40 to 43*), and 1927 Programme (*Nos. 44 to 54*). They were referred to as the 'special type' and were the world's first destroyers with guns in enclosed mountings. *Nos. 35 to 44* had the Model 'A' 5in gun with 40° elevation, but *Nos. 45 to 54* had the Model 'B' with 75° elevation. Normally 150 rounds per gun, but 180 max. When mines were not carried, 36 DCs were carried.

RE-ARMAMENT AND RECONSTRUCTION
In *Nos. 35–44*, 2 × 7.7mm MGs were substituted for the 13mm AA on completion. In *Nos. 35–44*, shields to the TT were added. Rebuilt in 1935 to improve stability, and had bridges and funnels reduced in height. Ballast was added, bringing the tonnage up to 2090(S) 2427 (F), and reducing speed to 34 knots: oil fuel 490-500ts, complement 215–221, and only 12 torpedoes (new type) carried.
In 1943–4 they were rearmed with 4 × 5in 50-cal DP (75° elevation), 14 × 25mm AA, 4 × 13mm, 36 DCs; complement 238/250.
By June 1944 the survivors had 22 × 25mm AA and 10 × 13mm (draught 12ft).

CAREERS
Fubuki
Launched 15 November, 1927 at Maizuru DY; completed 10 August, 1928 (ex-*No. 35*); sunk 11 October, 1942 by US Task Group 64.2 (4 cruisers and 5 destroyers) off Cape Esperance (09° 06′ S, 159° 38′ E).

Shinonome
Launched 26 November, 1927 at Sasebo DY; completed 25 July, 1928 (ex- *No. 40*); sank after striking a Dutch mine 18 December, 1941 near Miri, Borneo (04° 24′ N, 114° E).

Usugumo
Launched 26 December, 1927 by Ishikawajima Z., Tokyo; completed 26 July, 1928 (ex-*No. 41*); torpedoed 7 July, 1944 by US submarine *Skate* near Atsukeshi in the Sea of Okhotsk, 330 m WSW of Paramushir (47° 43′ N, 147° 55′ E).

Shirakumo
Launched 27 December, 1927 by Fujinagata Z., Osaka; completed 28 July, 1928 (ex-*No. 42*); torpedoed 16 March, 1944 by US submarine *Tautog* 170 m E of Muroran, Hokkaido (42° 25′ N, 144° 55′ E).

Isonami
Launched 24 November, 1927 by Uraga Dock, Tokyo; completed 30 June, 1928 (ex-*No. 43*); torpedoed 9 April, 1943 by US submarine *Tautog* 35 m SE of Wangiwangi Island (05° 26′ S, 123° 04′ E).

Shirayuki
Launched 20 March, 1928 by Yokohama Docks; completed 18 December, 1928 (ex-*No. 36*); sunk 3 March, 1943 by US aircraft 55 m SE of Finchhafen (07° 15′ S, 148° 30′ E).

Hatsuyuki
Launched 29 September, 1927 by Maizuru DY; completed 30 March, 1929 (ex-*No. 37*); badly damaged in a storm on 27 September 1935 but repaired; sunk 17 July, 1943 by US aircraft at Kahili, Bougainville (06° 50′ S, 155° 47′ E).

Miyuki
Launched 26 June, 1928 by Uraga Dock, Tokyo; completed 29 June, 1929 (ex-*No. 38*); sank 29 June, 1934 on manoeuvres off Cheju Do (33° N, 125° 30′ E) after collision with destroyer *Inazuma*; stricken 15 August, 1934.

Murakumo
Launched 27 September, 1927 by Fujinagata Z., Osaka; completed 10 May, 1929 (ex-*No. 39*); sank 12 October, 1942 after damage by US aircraft 90 m WNW of Savo Island (08° 40′ S, 159° 20′ E).

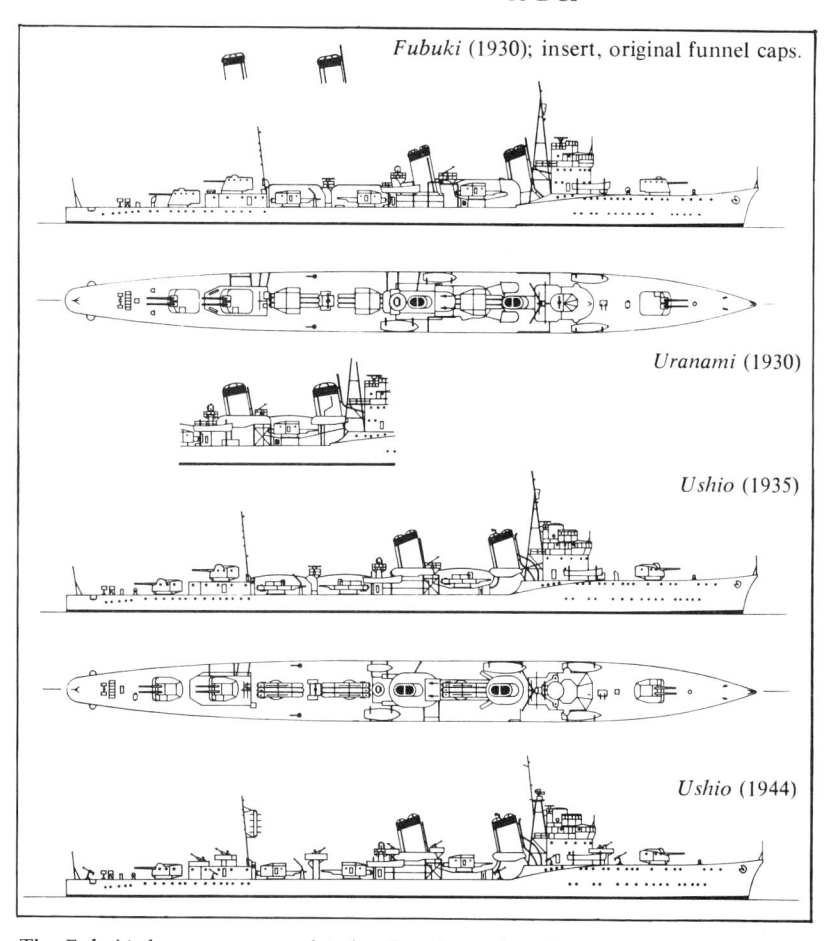

Fubuki (1930); insert, original funnel caps.

Uranami (1930)

Ushio (1935)

Ushio (1944)

The *Fubuki* class were a complete break with previous Japanese destroyers — in size, fighting power and appearance. *Shirayuki* in seen here in 1931, showing the distinctive profile of the class. (Shizuo Fukui.)

Uranami
Launched 29 November, 1928 by Sasebo DY; completed 30 June, 1929 (ex-*No. 44*); sunk 26 October, 1944 by US Task Group 77.4.2 70 m NNE of Iloilo, Panay (11° 50′ N, 123° E).
Shikinami
Launched 22 June, 1929 at Maizuru DY; completed 24 December, 1929 (ex-*No. 46*); torpedoed 12 September 1944 by US submarine *Growler* 240 m S of Hong Kong (18° 16′ N, 114° 40′ E).
Ayanami
Launched 5 October, 1929 by Fujinagata Z., Osaka; completed 30 April, 1930 (ex-*No. 45*); sunk 15 November, 1942 by gunfire of battleship USS *Washington* SE of Savo (09° 10′ S, 159° 52′ E).
Asagiri
Launched 18 November, 1929 at Sasebo DY; completed 30 June, 1930 (ex-*No. 47*); sunk 28 August, 1942 by US Marine Corps aircraft near Santa Isabel 60 m NNE of Savo (08° S, 160° 10′ E).
Sagiri
Launched 23 December, 1929 by Uraga Dock, Tokyo; completed 31 January, 1931 (ex-*No. 50*); torpedoed 24 December, 1941 by Dutch submarine *K.16* near Kuching, Sarawak (01° 34′ N, 110° 21′ E).
Yugiri
Launched 12 May, 1930 at Maizuru DY; completed 3 December, 1930 (ex-*No. 48*); sunk 25 November, 1943 by gunfire of US destroyers *Ausburne*, *Claxton* and *Dyson* 50 m E of Cape St George (04° 44′ S, 154° E).
Amagiri
Launched 27 February, 1930 by Ishikawajima Z., Tokyo; completed 10 November, 1930 (ex-*No. 49*); mined 23 April, 1944 55 m S of Balikpapan, Borneo (02° 10′ S, 116° 45′ E).
Oboro
Launched 8 November, 1930 at Sasebo DY; completed 31 October, 1931 (ex-*No. 51*); sunk 16 October, 1942 by B-24 bombers 30 m NE of Kiska (52° 17′ N, 178° 08′ E).

Ayanami, of the *Fubuki* class, seen at Yokohama on 5th September 1930. (Jentschura.)

Akebono
Launched 7 November, 1930 by Fujinagata Z., Osaka; completed 31 July, 1931 (ex-*No. 52*); sunk 13 November, 1944 by US aircraft of TF 38 in Manila Bay (14° 35′ N, 120° 50′ E).
Sazanami
Launched 6 June, 1931 at Maizuru DY; completed 19 May, 1932 (ex-*No. 53*); torpedoed 14 January, 1944 by US submarine *Albacore* 300 m SE of Yap (05° 15′ N, 141° 15′ E).
Ushio
Launched 17 November, 1930 by Uraga Dock, Tokyo; completed 14 November, 1931 (ex-*No. 54*); badly damaged 14 November, 1944 by aircraft of TF 38 in Manila Bay; later towed to Yokosuka and surrendered there in August 1945; BU 4 August, 1948 Shimasaki Dokku.

Name	Builder	Date	Displ	Length ft in	Beam ft in	Draught ft in	Machinery	SHP	Speed	Fuel	Radius	Armament	Comp
AKATSUKI Class (4 units)	various	1931–1933	1980 N 1680 light	371 8 wl 350 0 pp	34 0	10 9	2-shaft Parsons GTU 3 Kampon boilers	50000	38	475 oil	4700 @ 15 1100 @ 34	6 × 5in 50-cal DP 2 × 13mm AA 14 DCs 9 × 24in TT (AW)	197 (by 1941/2 238–250

GENERAL NOTES
Built under the 1927 Programme as 1st Class destroyers, very similar to the *Fubuki* Class. The *Hibiki* was the first welded ship in the Japanese Navy.

RE-ARMAMENT AND RECONSTRUCTION
In 1935/7 they were rebuilt like the *Fubuki* Class, with tonnage increased to 1980 (S) 2300 (F), oil fuel 490–500ts and speed cut to 34 knots (221 men). In 1941/2 they were re-armed with 4 × 5in 50-cal DP; 14 × 25mm AA; 4 × 13mm; 36 DCs.
   In June 1944 the survivors had 22 × 25mm AA and 10 × 13 mm. In 1945 *Hibiki* had 28 × 25mm AA.

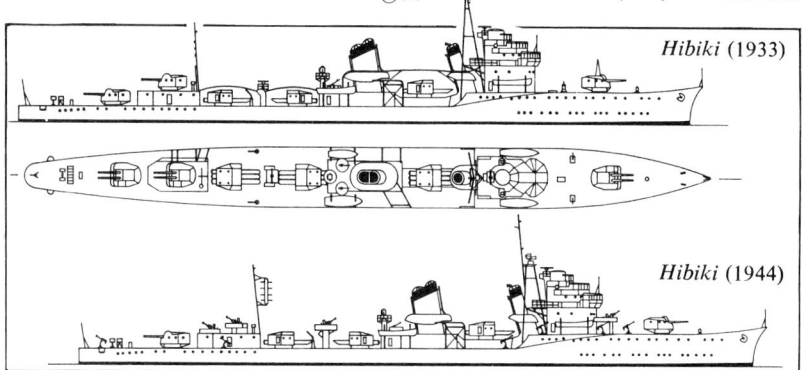

CAREERS
Akatsuki
Launched 7 May, 1932 at Sasebo DY; completed 30 November, 1932 (ex-*No. 55*); sunk 13 November, 1942 by gunfire of US warships near Savo (09° 17′ S, 159° 56′ E).
Hibiki
Launched 16 June, 1932 at Maizuru DY; completed 31 March, 1933 (ex-*No. 56*); damaged 29 April, 1945 by mine near Himejima; surrendered at Maizuru and served on repatriation duties; handed over to Soviet Union 5 April, 1947 and renamed *Pritky* (?); subsequently re-armed.
Ikazuchi
Launched 22 October, 1931 by Uraga Dock, Tokyo; completed 15 August, 1932 (ex-*No. 57*); torpedoed 14 April, 1944 by US submarine *Harder* 200 m SSE of Guam (10° 13′ N, 143° 51′ E).
Inazuma
Launched 25 February, 1932 by Fujinagata Z., Osaka; completed 15 November, 1932 (ex-*No. 58*); badly damaged 29 June, 1934 in collision with destroyer *Miyuki*; repaired from 20 October 1934 at Kure DY; torpedoed 14 May, 1944 by US submarine *Bonefish* near Tawi Tawi E of Borneo (05° 08′ N, 119° 38′ E).

Hibiki (1933)

Hibiki (1944)

Hibiki was the first all-welded destroyer in the Japanese Navy. Note the increased elevation possible with the 5-inch guns, and the small funnel uptake from the single forward boiler. (Tappman Collection.)

TORPEDO BOATS AND DESTROYERS 145

Name	Builder	Date	Displ	Length ft in	Beam ft in	Draught ft in	Machinery	SHP	Speed	Fuel	Radius	Armament	Comp
HATSUHARU Class (6 units)	various	1931–1935	1802 F 1680 N 1490 light	359 3 oa 346 1 wl 339 7 pp	32 9	9 11	2-shaft GTU 3 Kampon boilers	42000	36½	500 oil	6000 @ 15 / 1020 @ 34	5 × 5in 50-cal DP 2 × 13mm AA 14 DCs 9 × 24in TT (AW)	200

GENERAL NOTES
Built under the 1931 Programme as improved editions of the *Fubuki* Class, with lighter armament.

RE-ARMAMENT AND RECONSTRUCTION
In 1935/7 *Hatsuharu*, *Wakaba*, *Hatsushimo* and *Nenohi* were altered like the *Fubuki*s to improve stability. These modifications were incorporated during construction of the remaining units, and delayed their completion. Tonnage was increased to 1715 (S) 2099 (F) and speed was reduced to 33.3 knots. One set of TT was removed. In 1942/3 the armament was reduced to 4 × 5in 50-cal; 13 × to 21 × 25mm AA; 4 × 13mm; 36 DCs.

CAREERS
Hatsuharu
Launched 27 February, 1933 at Sasebo DY; completed 30 September, 1933; sunk 13 November, 1944 by aircraft of TF 38 in Manila Bay (14° 35′ N, 120° 50′ E).
Nenohi
Launched 22 December, 1932 by Uraga Dock, Tokyo; completed 30 September, 1933; torpedoed 4 July, 1942 by US submarine *Triton* at Agattu (52° 15′ N, 173° 51′ E).
Hatsushimo
Her intended launching on 31 October, 1933 failed, and she did not take the water until 4 November, 1933 at Uraga Dock, Tokyo; completed 27 September, 1934; mined 30 July, 1945 in Miyatsu Bay 12 m WNW of Maizuru (35° 33′ N, 135° 12′ E).
Wakaba
Launched 18 March, 1934 at Sasebo DY; completed 31 October, 1934; sunk 24 October, 1944 by aircraft of USS *Franklin* off W coast of Panay (11° 50′ N, 121° 25′ E).
Yugure
Launched 6 May, 1934 at Maizuru DY; completed 13 April, 1935; sunk 20/21 July, 1943 by US Marine Corps aircraft in Vella Lavella Gulf (07° 25′ S, 156° 45′ E).
Ariake
Launched 23 September, 1934 by Kawasaki, Kobe; completed 25 March, 1935; wrecked 27 July, 1943 on a reef near Cape Gloucester (05° 27′ S, 148° 25′ E); the wreck was destroyed on 28 July, 1943 by B–25 bombers.

Hatsuharu (1935)

Hatsuharu (1937)
Nenohi similar before rebuilding

Hatsushimo (1943)

Nenohi, after the super-firing gun forward had been removed to the quarter-deck. The enclosed gun-house was extremely narrow, and conditions inside must have been cramped. (Tappman Collection.)

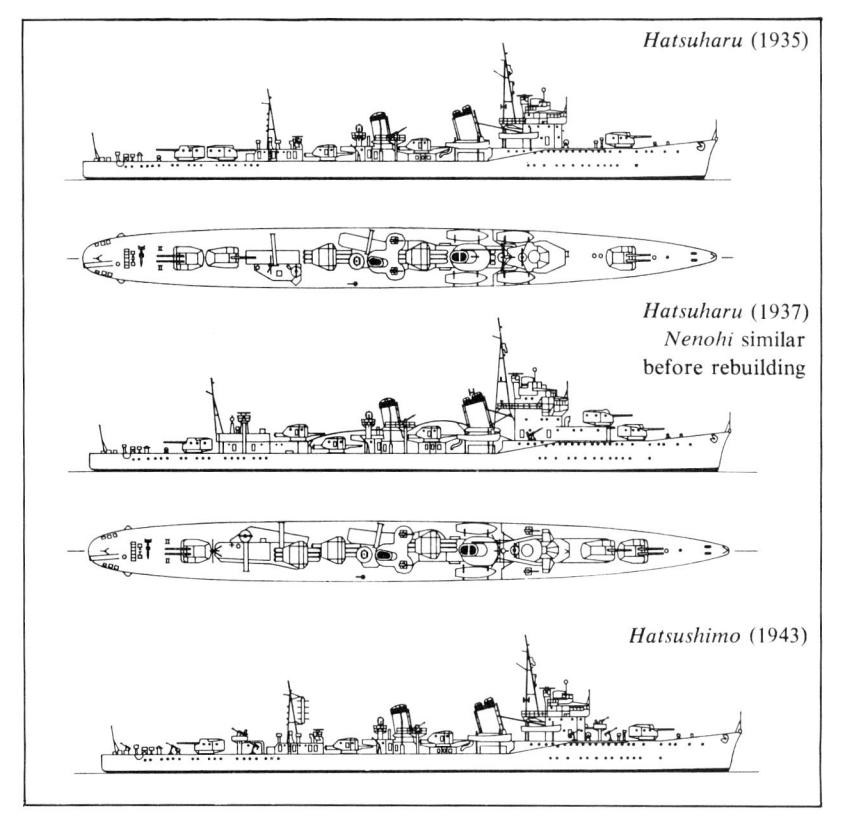

Ariake was to have been a sister-ship of *Nenohi*, but she was still under construction when the lack of stability and strength of the design became apparent. She was therefore completed with the single gun aft, and an enlarged bridge structure. (Tappman Collection.)

Name	Builder	Date	Displ	Length ft in	Beam ft in	Draught ft in	Machinery	SHP	Speed	Fuel	Radius	Armament	Comp
SHIRATSUYU Class (10 units)	various	1933–1937	1980 N 1685 light	352 8 wl 339 7 pp	32 6	11 6	2-shaft GTU 3 Kampon boilers	42000	34	500 oil	6000 @ 15 / 1020 @ 34	5 × 5in 50-cal DP 2 × 13mm AA 16 DCs 8 × 24in TT (AW)	180

TORPEDO BOATS AND DESTROYERS

GENERAL NOTES

Built under the 1931 Programme (first 6 units) and the 1934 Programme as an improved *Hatsuharu* type. They were the first Japanese destroyers armed with quadruple TT.

RE-ARMAMENT

In 1942/3 they were armed with 4 × 5in 50-cal DP; 13 × to 21 × 25mm AA; 4 × 13mm and 36 DCs, and the displacement had risen to 2075ts (F).

CAREERS

Shiratsuyu
Launched 5 April, 1935 at Sasebo DY; completed 20 August, 1936; sunk 15 June, 1944 in collision with tanker *Seiyo Maru* 90 m SE of Surigao Strait (09° 09′ N, 126° 51′ E).

Shigure
Launched 18 May, 1935 by Uraga Dock, Tokyo; completed 7 September, 1936; torpedoed 24 January, 1945 by US submarine *Blackfin* 160 m E of Khota Bharu, Malaya (06° N, 103° 48′ E).

Murasame
Launched 20 June, 1935 by Fujinagata Z., Osaka; completed 7 January, 1937 badly damaged 6 March, 1943 by gunfire of US cruisers *Cleveland*, *Denver* and destroyers *Conway*, and *Cony* near Bambari Harbour, Kolombangara; later torpedoed by the destroyer *Waller* (08° 03′ S, 157° 13′ E).

Yudachi
Launched 21 June, 1936 at Sasebo DY; completed 7 January, 1937; damaged 12/13 November, 1942 by US destroyers near Savo; on 13 November she was sunk by gunfire of US cruiser *Portland* SE of Savo (09° 14′ S, 159° 52′ E).

Samidare
Launched 6 July, 1935 by Uraga Dock, Tokyo; completed 29 January, 1937; wrecked 18 August, 1944 off Palau Island and torpedoed 25 August by US submarine *Batfish*.

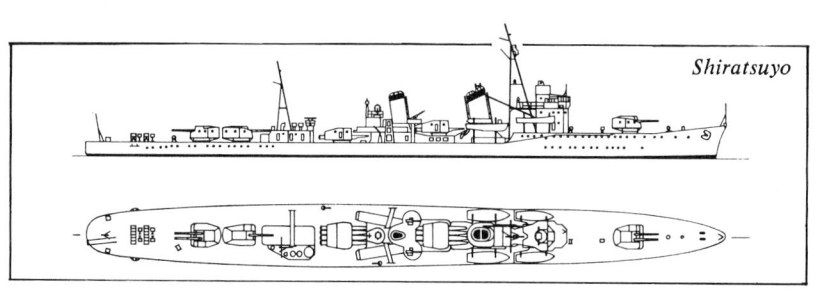

Harusame
Launched 21 September, 1935 by Uraga Dock, Tokyo; completed 26 August, 1937; sunke 8 June, 1944 by B-24 bombers and P-38 fighters 30 m NW of Cape of Good Hope near Manokawari (00° 05′ S, 132° 45′ E).

Yamakaze
Launched 21 February, 1936 by Uraga Dock, Tokyo; completed 30 June, 1937; torpedoed 25 June, 1942 by US submarine *Nautilus* 60 m SE of Yokosuka (34° 34′ N, 14° 26′ E).

Kawakaze
Launched 1 November, 1936 by Fujinagata Z., Osaka; completed 30 April, 1937; torpedoed 6 August, 1943 by US destroyers *Dunlap*, *Craven* and *Maury* near Kolombangara (07° 50′ S, 156° 54′ E).

Umikaze
Launched 27 November, 1936 at Maizuru DY; completed 31 May, 1937; torpedoed 1 February, 1944 by US submarine *Guardfish* S of Truk Atoll (07° 10′ N, 151° 43′ E).

Suzukaze
Launched 11 March, 1937 by Uraga Dock, Tokyo; completed 31 August, 1937; torpedoed 26 January, 1944 by US submarine *Skipjack* 140 m NNW of Ponape Island (08° 51′ N, 157° 10′ E).

Shiratsuyo

The 'improved *Hatsuharu*' class were developments of the original *Fubuki* design, and introduced quadruple 24-inch torpedo-tubes. *Kawakaze*, seen here, carries her after 5-inch guns back-to-back to reduce topweight. (Tappman Collection.)

Name	Builder	Date	Displ	Length ft in	Beam ft in	Draught ft in	Machinery	SHP	Speed	Fuel	Radius	Armament	Comp
ASASHIO Class (10 units)	various	1935–1939	2370 N 1961 light	388 0 oa 377 3 wl 364 2 pp	33 11	12 1	2-shaft GTU 3 Kampon boilers	50000	35	500 oil	5700 @ 10 960 @34	6 × 5in 50-cal DP 4 × 25mm AA 16 DCs 8 × 24 in TT (AW)	200

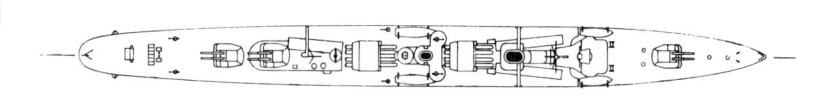

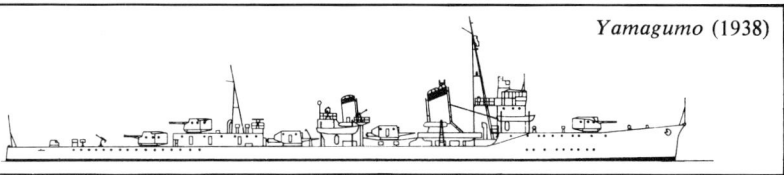

Yamagumo (1938)

TORPEDO BOATS AND DESTROYERS 147

GENERAL NOTES
Built under the 1934 Programme as a so-called 'cruiser' type, although they were only improved *Shiratsuyu*s. On her trials, *Asashio* showed very bad manoeuvrability.

RE-ARMAMENT AND RECONSTRUCTION
About 1941 the stern and rudder arrangements were altered in all units. In 1943/4 the survivors had 4 × 5in 50-cal DP, 15 × 25mm AA. By June 1944 the armament had been increased to 28 × 25mm AA; 4 × 13mm; 36 Dcs and displacement had risen to 2000/2400/2635ts; 50280 shp = 35·29 knots.

MACHINERY
This class was fitted with new, advanced steam turbines.

CAREERS
Asashio
Launched 16 December, 1936 at Sasebo DY; completed 31 August, 1937; sunk 4 March, 1943 by B-25 bombers 45 m SE of Finschhafen (07° 15′ S, 148° 15′ E).

Oshio
Launched 19 April, 1937 at Mazuru DY; completed 31 October, 1937; torpedoed 20 February, 1943 by US submarine *Albacore* 70 m NW of Manus Island (00° 50′ S, 146° 06′ E).

Michishio
Launched 15 March, 1937 by Fujinagata Z., Osaka; completed 31 October, 1937; damaged 25 October, 1944 by US destroyer *McDermut* in Surigao Straits, and sunk the same day by the destroyer *Hutchins* (10° 25′ N, 125° 23′ E).

Arashio
Launched 26 May, 1937 by Kawasaki, Kobe; completed 20 December, 1937; sunk 4 March, 1943 by B-17 bombers 55 m SE of Finschhafen (07° 15′ S, 148° 30′ E).

Natsugumo
Launched 26 May, 1937 at Sasebo DY; completed 10 February, 1938; sunk 12 October, 1942 by US Marine Corps SBD aircraft while rescuing the survivors of the heavy cruiser *Furutaka* and the destroyer *Fubuki*, 8 m WSW of Savo (09° 10′ S, 159° 40′ E).

Yamagumo
Launched 24 July, 1937 by Fujinagata Z., Osaka; completed 15 January, 1938; sunk 25 October, 1944 by US destroyer *McDermut* in Suriago Strait (10° 16′ N, 125° 23′ E).

Minegumo
Launched 4 November, 1937 by Fujinagata Z., Osaka; completed 30 April, 1938; sunk 5/6 March, 1943 by gunfire of US light cruisers *Montpelier* and *Cleveland* and destroyers *Cony*, *Waller* and *Conway* in Kula Gulf (08° 01′ S, 157° 14′ E).

Asagumo
Launched 5 November, 1937 by Kawasaki, Kobe; completed 31 March, 1938; badly damaged 25 October, 1944 by US destroyer *McDermutt* in Surigao Strait, and sunk the same day by gunfire from the light cruiser *Denver* at the entrance to the strait (10° 04′ N, 125° 21′ E).

Arare
Launched 16 November, 1937 by Maizuru DY; completed 15 April, 1939; torpedoed 5 July, 1942 by US submarine *Growler* 7 m E of Kiska Harbour (52° N, 177° 40′ E).

Asashio, name-ship of her class, re-introduced the six-gun main armament and superimposed turret aft. She was also the first destroyer to be armed with the Type 96 25mm (Hotchkiss) AA gun. The port-side twin 25mm gun can be seen abreast the after funnel, and the AA director is immediately abaft the funnel. The bridge structure is uncluttered, and reflects the Japanese efforts to reduce topweight after experience with earlier destroyer designs. (Tappman Collection.)

Kasumi
Launched 18 November, 1937 by Uraga Dock, Tokyo; completed 28 June, 1939; badly damaged 7 April, 1945 by aircraft of TF 58 and sank at 16.57 hrs 150 m SW of Nagasaki (31° N, 128° E).

Name	Builder	Date	Displ	Length ft in	Beam ft in	Draught ft in	Machinery	SHP	Speed	Fuel	Radius	Armament	Comp
KAGERO Class (18 units)	various	1937–1941	2490 N 2033 F	388 oa 9 381 wl 3 364 pp 2	35 5	12 4	2-shaft GTU 3 Kampon boilers	52000	35	?	5000 @ 18	6 × 5in 50-cal DP 4 × 25mm AA 16 DCs 8 × 24in TT (AW)	240

GENERAL NOTES
Built under the 1937·Programme (first 15 units) and the 1939 Programme (*Arashi*, *Hagikaze* and *Tanikaze*). They were improved *Arashio*s, known as Type 'A' or 'Cruiser' type.

RE-ARMAMENT
In 1943–4 they had 4 × 5in 50-cal DP; 14 × 25mm AA; 36 DCs. By June 1944 the survivors had 18 × to 24 × 35mm AA and 4 × 13mm. *Hamakaze* was the first Japanese destroyer fitted with radar.

CAREERS
Kagero
Launched 27 September, 1938 at Maizuru DY; completed 6 November, 1939; badly damaged 7/8 May, 1943 by mine off Rendova, and sunk 8 May by US Marine Corps aircraft SW of Rendova (08° 08′ S, 156° 55′ E).

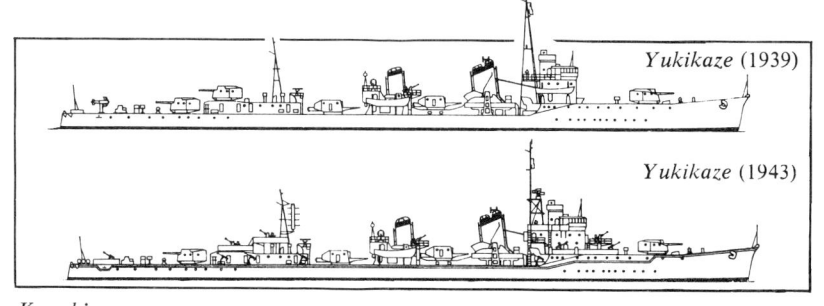

Yukikaze (1939)

Yukikaze (1943)

Kuroshio
Launched 25 October, 1938 by Fujinagata Z., Osaka; completed 27 January, 1940; sunk 7/8 May, 1943 by mine SW of Rendova.

Oyashio
Launched 29 November, 1938 at Maizuru DY; completed 20 August, 1940; badly damaged 7/8 May, 1943 by mine SW of Rendova; sunk 8 May by naval aircraft 5 m SW of Rendova (08° 08′ S, 156° 55′ E).
Hatsukaze
Launched 24 January, 1939 by Kawasaki, Kobe; completed 15 February, 1940; badly damaged 2 November, 1943 in collision with heavy cruiser *Myoko* in Augusta Bay; sunk later the same day by gunfire from the destroyers *Spence*, *Ausburne*, *Dyson*, *Claxton* and *Stanley* (06° 01′ S, 153° 58′ E).
Natsushio
Launched 23 February, 1939 by Fujinagata Z., Osaka; completed 31 August, 1940; torpedoed 8 February, 1942 by US submarine *S.37* 22 m S of Makassar, Celebes (05° 10′ S, 119° 24′ E).
Yukikaze
Launched 24 March, 1939 at Sasebo DY; completed 20 January, 1940; damaged 30 July, 1945 by mine near Miyatsu; surrendered August 1945 at Maizuru and used on repatriation service; transferred to China 6 July, 1947 as the *Tan Yang*; BU in 1971 at Kaohsiung, Taiwan.
Hayashio
Launched 19 April, 1939 by Uraga Dock, Tokyo; completed 31 August, 1940; sunk 24 November, 1942 by B-17 bombers in Guna Bay, Huon Gulf (07° S, 147° 30′ E).
Maikaze
Launched 15 March, 1941 by Fujinagata Z., Osaka; completed 15 July, 1941; sunk 17 February, 1944 by gunfire of Task Group 50.3 (2 battleships, 2 heavy cruisers and 4 destroyers) 40 m NW of Truk (07° 45′ N, 151° 20′ E).
Isokaze
Launched 19 June, 1939 at Sasebo DY; completed 30 November, 1940; badly damaged 7 April, 1945 by aircraft of TF 58 and sank at about 22.40 hrs on the same day, 150 m SW of Nagasaki (30° 46′ N, 128° 92′ E).
Shiranui
Launched 28 June, 1938 by Uraga Dock, Tokyo; completed 20 December, 1939; sunk by TF 77 80 m N of Iloilo, Panay (12° N, 122° 30′ E); 27 October 1944.
Amatsukaze
Launched 19 October 1939 at Maizuru DY; completed 26 October, 1940; sunk 6 April, 1945 by B-25 bombers 6 m E of Amoy (24° 30′ N, 118° 10′ E).
Tokitsukaze
Launched 10 November, 1939 by Uraga Dock, Tokyo; completed 15 February, 1940; sunk 3 March, 1943 by aircraft 55 m SE of Finchhafen (07° 15′ S, 148° 30′ E).
Urakaze
Launched 10 April, 1940 by Fujinagata Z., Osaka; completed 15 December, 1940; torpedoed 21 November, 1944 by US submarine *Sealion* 65 m NNW of Keelung, Formosa (26° 09′ N, 121° 23′ E).
Hamakaze
Launched 25 November, 1940 by Uraga Dock, Tokyo; completed 30 June, 1941; sunk 7 April, 1945 by aircraft from carriers *Hornet* and *Cabot* 150 m SW of Nagasaki (30° 47′ N, 128° 08′ E).
Nowaki
Launched 17 September, 1940 at Maizuru DY; completed 28 April, 1941; sunk 26 November, 1944 by gunfire of cruisers and destroyers 65 m SSE of Legazpi, Luzon (13° N, 124° 54′ E).
Arashi
Launched 22 April 1940 at Maizuru DY; completed 27 January, 1941; sunk 6/7 August, 1943 by gunfire and torpedoes of US destroyers *Dunlap*, *Craven*, and *Maury* between Kolombangara and Vella Lavella (07° 50′ S, 156° 55′ E).
Hagikaze
Launched 18 June, 1940 by Uraga Dock, Tokyo; completed 31 March, 1941; sunk 6/7 August, 1943 by torpedoes of US destroyers *Dunlap*, *Craven* and *Maury* between Kolombangara and Vella Lavella (07° 49′ S, 156° 55′ E).
Tanikaze
Launched 1 November, 1940 by Fujinagata Z., Osaka; completed 25 April, 1941; torpedoed 9 June, 1944 by US submarine *Harder* in Sibutu Passage 90 m SW of Basilan (05° 42′ N, 120° 41′ E).

Name	Builder	Date	Displ	Length ft in	Beam ft in	Draught ft in	Machinery	SHP	Speed	Fuel	Radius	Armament	Comp
SHIMAKAZE Nos. 733–748	Maizuru DY	1941–1943	3048 N 2567 light	413 4 wl 395 4 pp	36 9	13 7	2-shaft GTU 3 Kampon boilers	75000	39	?	1400 @ 30	6 × 5in 50-cal DP 6 × 25mm AA 18 DCs 15 × 24in TT	?

GENERAL NOTES
Built under the 1939 Programme as the prototype for a new 'cruiser' type with advanced machinery.

RE-ARMAMENT
In 1944 she had 4 × 5in 50-cal DP, 14 × 25mm AA, and by June 1944 her light armament had been increased to 28 × 25mm AA and 4 × 13mm.

MACHINERY
The turbines were of a new type, designed to produce nearly 50% more power than previous installations. On trials she reached 40.9 knots with 79240 shp.

CAREER
Laid down 8 August, 1941, completed 10 May, 1943; sunk 11 November, 1944 by aircraft of TF 38 55 m NE of Cebu (10° 50′ N, 124° 35′ E).

Nos. 733–748
A further 16 units were planned under the 1942 Programme (2750ts S) but contracts were not placed.

Shimakaze (1943)

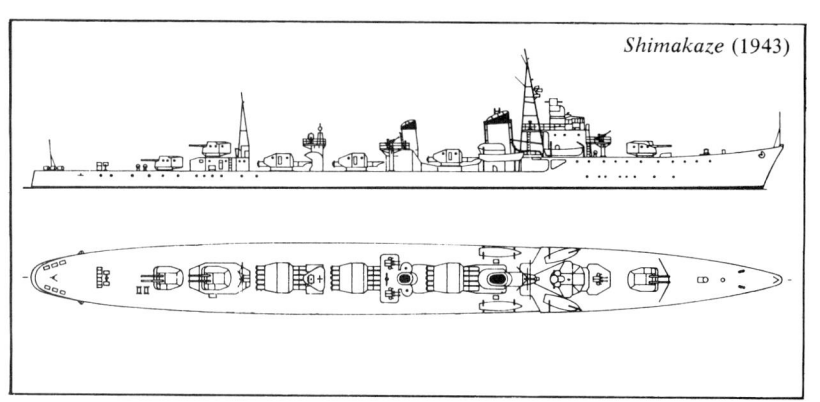

The only known photograph of the experimental destroyer *Shimakaze*, running at 40 knots, late in 1944. The sixteen sister ships were never laid down. (Shizuo Fukui.)

Name	Builder	Date	Displ	Length ft in	Beam ft in	Draught ft in	Machinery	SHP	Speed	Fuel	Radius	Armament	Comp
YUGUMO Class (20 units)	various	1940–1944	2520 N 2077 light	390 oa 11 383 wl 10 365 pp 11	35 5	12 4	2-shaft GTU 3 Kampon boilers	52000	35	oil		6 × 5in 50-cal DP 4 × 25mm AA 36 DCs 8 × 24in TT (AW)	228

Kiyoshimo (1944)

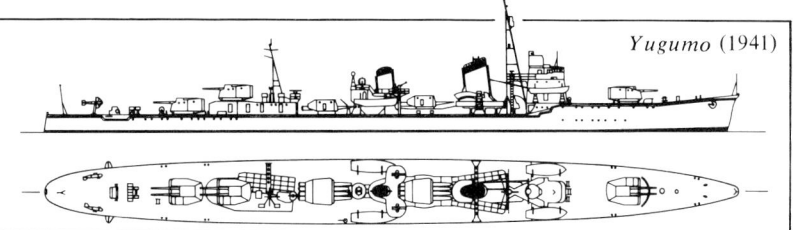

Yugumo (1941)

GENERAL NOTES
Built under the 1939 Programme (first 12 units) and 1941 Programme as an improved *Kagero* 'cruiser' type.

RE-ARMAMENT
In 1943 they had modifications to their radar and received 2 extra 25mm AA. During 1943–4 the armament was changed to 4 × 5in 50-cal DP; 15 × 25mm AA. By June 1944 the survivors had 15 × to 28 × 25mm AA and 4 × 13mm, but some units had 2 × 5in 50-cal DP; 2 × 5in 40-cal AA and 12 × 25mm AA.

CAREERS
Yugumo
Launched 16 March, 1941 at Maizuru DY; completed 5 December, 1941; sunk 6/7 November, 1943 by torpedoes and gunfire of US destroyers *Chevalier* and *Selfridge* 15 m NW of Vella Lavella (07° 33′ S, 156° 14′ E).
Akigumo
Launched 11 April, 1941 by Uraga Dock, Tokyo; completed 27 September, 1941; torpedoed 11 April, 1944 by US submarine *Redfin* 30 m SE of Zamboanga (06° 43′ N, 122° 23′ E).
Kazekumo
Launched 26 September, 1941 by Uraga Dock, Tokyo; completed 18 March, 1942; torpedoed 8 June, 1944 by US submarine *Rake* near Davao Gulf, Mindonoro (06° 03′ N, 124° 57′ E).
Makikumo
Launched 5 November, 1941 by Fujinagata Z., Osaka, completed 14 March, 1942; sunk 1 February, 1943 by mine 3 m SSW of Savo (09° 15′ S, 159° 47′ E).
Makinami
Launched 27 December, 1941 at Maizuru DY; completed 18 August, 1942; sunk 25 November, 1943 by torpedoes and gunfire of US destroyers *Ausburne*, *Claxton*, *Dyson*, *Spence* and *Converse* 55 m ESE of Cape St George (05° 14′ S, 153° 50′ E).
Takanami
Launched 16 March, 1942 by Uraga Dock, Tokyo; completed 31 August, 1942; badly damaged 30 November to 1 December, 1942 by TF 67 (5 light cruisers and 6 destroyers) 10 m SSW of Savo; she sank at about 01.37 hrs on 1 December (09° 18′ S, 159° 56′ E).
Naganami
Launched 5 March, 1942 by Fujinagata Z., Osaka; completed 30 June, 1942; sunk 11 November, 1944 by aircraft of TF 38 55 m NE of Cebu (10° 50′ N, 124° 35′ E).
Tamanami
Launched 26 December, 1942 by Fujinagata Z., Osaka; completed 30 April, 1943; torpedoed 7 July, 1944 by US submarine *Mingo* 150 m WSW of Manila (13° 55′ N, 118° 30′ E).
Suzunami
Launched 12 March, 1943 by Uraga Dock, Tokyo; completed 27 July, 1943; sunk 11 November, 1943 by aircraft of Task Group 50.3 in Rabaul Harbour (04° 13′ S, 152° 11′ E).
Onami
Launched 13 August, 1942 by Fujinagata Z., Osaka; completed 29 December, 1942; torpedoed 25 November, 1943 by US destroyers *Ausburne*, *Claxton* and *Dyson* 55 m ESE of Cape St George (05° 15′ S, 153° 49′ E).
Fujinami
Launched 20 April, 1943 by Fujinagata Z., Osaka; completed 31 July, 1943; sunk 27 October, 1944 by aircraft of TF 38 80 m N of Iloilo (12° N, 122° 30′ E).
Kishinami
Launched 19 August, 1943 by Uraga Dock, Tokyo; completed 3 December, 1943; torpedoed 4 December, 1944 by US submarine *Flasher* 270 m WSW of Luzon Straits (13° 12′ N, 116° 37′ E).
Hayanami
Launched 19 December, 1942 at Maizuru DY; completed 31 July, 1943; torpedoed 7 June, 1944 by US submarine *Harder* 35 m E of Borneo (04° 43′ N, 120° 03′ E).
Kiyonami
Launched 17 August, 1942 by Uraga Dock, Tokyo; completed 25 January, 1943; sunk 20 July, 1943 by aircraft 42 m NNW of Kolombangara (07° 13′ S, 156° 45′ E).
Okinami
Launched 18 July, 1943 at Maizuru DY; completed 10 December, 1943; sunk 13 November, 1944 by aircraft of TF 38 8 m W of Manila (14° 35′ N, 120° 50′ E).
Hamanami
Launched 18 April, 1943 at Maizuru DY; completed 15 October, 1943; sunk 11 November, 1944 by aircraft of TF 38 55 m NE of Debu (10° 50′ N, 124° 35′ E).
Asashimo
Launched 18 July, 1943 by Fujinagata Z., Osaka; completed 27 November, 1943; sunk 7 April, 1945 by aircraft of TF 58 150 m SW of Nagasaki (31° N, 128° E).
Kiyoshimo
Launched 29 February, 1944 by Uraga Dock, Tokyo; completed 15 May, 1944; sunk 26 December, 1944 by aircraft and PT-boats 145 m S of Manila (12° 20′ N, 121° E).
Hayashimo
Launched November, 1943 at Maizuru DY; completed 20 February, 1944; sunk 26 October, 1944 by aircraft of TF 38 40 m SE of Mindoro after she had been wrecked (12° 50′ N, 121° 21′ E).
Akishimo
Launched 5 December, 1943 by Fujinagata Z., Osaka; completed 11 March, 1944; sunk 13 November, 1944 by aircraft of TF 38 8 m W of Manila (14° 35′ N, 120° 55′ E).
Nos 5041–5048
These units of the 1941 Programme were never ordered. They were an improved design (2077ts) and would have been named: *Umigiri, Yamagiri, Tanigiri, Kawagiri, Taekaze, Kiyokaze, Satokaze* and *Murakaze*.

Name	Builder	Date	Displ	Length ft in	Beam ft in	Draught ft in	Machinery	SHP	Speed	Fuel	Radius	Armament	Comp
AKIZUKI Class (13 units + 3)	various	1940–1945	3700 F 3485 N 2701 light	440 oa 3 433 wl 1 413 pp 4	38 1	13 7	2-shaft Kampon GTU 3 Kampon boilers	52000	33	1097 oil	8300 @ 18	8 × 3.9in 65-cal DP 4 × 25mm AA 72 DCs (*Suzutsuki* 34) 4 × 24in TT (AW) 8 torpedoes	300

150 TORPEDO BOATS AND DESTROYERS

GENERAL NOTES

These unique vessels were originally planned as AA cruisers but were completed as destroyers, with torpedo-armament. The *Akizuki* group were built under the 1939 Programme, and the *Shimotsuki* group under the 1941 Programme. *Nos. 777–785* were projected under the 1942 Programme, and *Nos. 5061–5083* under the 1942 'M' Programme.

RE-ARMAMENT

On completion in 1943 the armament was increased to 15 × 25mm AA. In June 1944 they had 29 × 25mm AA and 4 × 13mm. In 1945 the survivors carried 40 × to 51 × 25mm AA.

CAREERS

Akizuki
Launched 2 July, 1941 at Maizuru DY; completed 11 June 1942; sunk 25 October, 1944 by aircraft of TF 38 ENE of Cape Engano (20° 29′ N, 126° 30′ E).

Teruzuki
Launched 21 November, 1941 by Mitsubishi, Nagasaki; completed 31 August, 1942; torpedoed 12 December, 1942 by US PT-Boats 20 m NE of Kolombangara (07° 50′ S, 157° 30′ E).

Suzutsuki
Launched 4 March, 1942 by Mitsubishi, Nagasaki; completed 29 December, 1942; badly damaged on 16 January, 1944 when she lost her bow and stern; repaired in three months, but was badly damaged once more on 7 April, 1945 by aircraft of TF 58 S of Kyushu; she was surrendered unrepaired at Sasebo in August 1945; used as a breakwater in the harbour at Takamatsu and later BU.

Hatsutsuki
Launched 3 April, 1942 at Maizuru DY; completed 29 December, 1942; sunk 25 October, 1944 by gunfire of 4 heavy cruisers, 12 destroyers at about 20.57 hrs ENE of Cape Engano (20° 24′ N, 126° 20′ E).

Niizuki
Launched 29 June, 1942 by Mitsubishi, Nagasaki; completed 31 March, 1943; sunk 6 July, 1943 by gunfire of US cruisers and destroyers 5 m E of Kolombangara (07° 57′ S, 157° 12′ E).

Wakatsuki
Launched 24 November, 1942 by Mitsubishi, Nagasaki; completed 31 May, 1943; sunk 11 November, 1944 by aircraft of TF 38 at 11.30 hrs 55 m N of Cebu (10° 50′ N, 124° 35′ E).

Shimotsuki
Launched 7 April, 1943 by Mitsubishi, Nagasaki; completed 31 March, 1944; torpedoed 25 November, 1944 by US submarine *Cavalla* at 04.40 hrs 220 m ENE of Singapore (02° 21′ N, 107° 20′ E).

Fuyutsuki
Launched 20 January, 1944 at Maizuru DY; completed 25 May, 1944; mined in the Inland Sea 24 August, 1945 and lost her stern; surrendered at Moji without armament and used later as a breakwater at Takamatsu; subsequently BU.

Hanatsuki
Launched 10 October, 1944 at Maizuru DY; completed 26 December, 1944; damaged at Kure 24 July, 1945 and was surrendered there a month later; after repatriation duties she was transferred to the USN 28 August, 1947 without armament and renamed *DD-934*; BU following various trials in 1948.

Yoizuki
Launched 25 September, 1944 by Uraga Dock, Tokyo; completed 31 January, 1945; damaged by mine near Himejima 5 June, 1945 and surrendered at Kure in August; after serving on repatriation duties she was transferred to China 29 August, 1947 in disarmed condition and renamed *Fen Yang*; BU 1963.

Harutsuki
Launched 3 August, 1944 at Sasebo DY; completed 28 December, 1944; surrendered at Kure August 1945, and transferred 28 August, 1947 to Soviet Union without armament; renamed *Pospeshny*.

Natsuzuki
Launched 2 December, 1944 at Sasebo DY; completed 8 August, 1945; badly

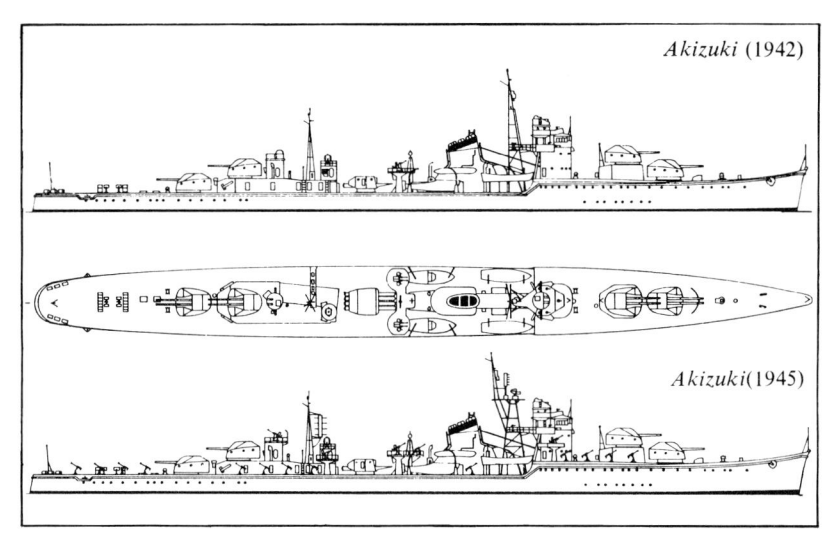

Akizuki (1942)

Akizuki (1945)

Akizuki class destroyer *Fuyutsuki*, shortly after completion in May 1944. (Shizuo Fukui.)

damaged by mine 16 June and surrendered at Kure in August; served on repatriation duties and transferred 3 September, 1947 to Great Britain without armament; BU 1 March, 1948 by Uraga Dock.

Mochizuki
Laid down 3 January, 1945 but building stopped March and BU on the stocks.

Kiyotsuki
Ordered from Maizuru DY but the contract was cancelled.

Ozuki
Ordered from Mitsubishi, Nagasaki but the contract was cancelled.

Hazuki
Ordered from Maizuru DY but the contract was cancelled.

Nos. 770–785
These improved units would have displaced 2980ts (light) but the contracts were cancelled. Their names were to have been: *Arashikaru, Asahikari, Chugao, Hikugumo, Hikushio, Hitonozi, Kaosame, Karuiyuki, Kitakaze, Natsukaze, Nishikaze, Nobikaze, Shimushio, Soragumo, Yugachio* and *Yugao*.

Nos 5061–5083
Were to have displaced 2701ts but their contracts were also cancelled. The names would have been: *Yamatsuki, Amagumo, Aogumo, Asagochi, Fuyukaze, Fuyugumo, Hae, Harugumo, Hatsunatsu, Hatsuaki, Hayaharu, Hayakaze, Kitakaze, Kochi, Natsukaze, Nishikaze, Okitsugumo, Okaze, Shimokaze, Uruzuki, Yaegumo* and *Yukigumo*.

Name	Builder	Date	Displ	Length ft in	Beam ft in	Draught ft in	Machinery	SHP	Speed	Fuel	Radius	Armament	Comp
MATSU Class	various	1943–1945	1530 N 1262 light	328 1 oa 321 6 wl 302 3 pp	30 8	10 10	2-shaft GTU 2 Kampon boilers	19000	27.8	oil	4680 @ 16	3 × 5in 40-cal AA 24 × 25mm AA 36 DCs 4 × 24in TT (AW)	?

TORPEDO BOATS AND DESTROYERS

GENERAL NOTES
Built under the 1942 'M' Programme as escort destroyers (*Nos.* 5481 to 5509). They were equipped with Type '31' radar and originally were to have had 6 × 21in TT in a sextuple mounting. They took from 5 to 9 months to build.

RE-ARMAMENT AND RECONSTRUCTION
By 1945 they each carried up to 29 × 25mm AA. *Take* and others were modified to carry Kaitens.

MACHINERY
For the first time, each boiler and each turbine was in its own compartment to localize damage.

CAREERS
Matsu
Launched 3 February, 1944 at Maizuru DY; completed 29 April, 1944; sunk 4 August, 1944 by gunfire of US destroyers *Ingersoll*, *Knapp* and *Cogswell* 50 m NW of Chichi-jima Retto (27° 40′ N, 141° 48′ E); officially stricken 10 August, 1944.

Momo
Launched 25 March, 1944 at Maizuru DY; completed 10 June, 1944; torpedoed 15 December, 1944 by US submarine *Hawkbill* 140 m WSW of Cape Bolinao, Luzon (16° N, 117° 39′ E).

Take
Launched 28 March, 1944 at Yokosuka DY; completed 16 June, 1944; damaged 25 November, 1944 near Luzon by aircraft of TF 38 (13° 32′ N, 121° 52′ E); surrendered August 1945 and served on repatriation duties until 1947; transferred 16 July, 1947 to Great Britain and BU.

Ume
Launched 24 April, 1944 by Fujinagata Z., Osaka; completed 28 June, 1944; sunk 31 January, 1945 by B-25 and P-38 aircraft 20 m S of Formosa (22° 30′ N, 120° E).

Kuwa
Launched 25 May, 1944 by Fujinagata Z., Osaka; completed 25 July, 1944; sunk 3 December, 1944 by gunfire of US destroyers *Cooper*, *Allen M. Sumner* and *Moale* in Ormoc Bay, Leyte (10° 50′ N, 124° 35′ E).

Maki
Launched 10 June, 1944 by Maizuru DY; completed 10 August, 1944; badly damaged 9 December, 1944 by US submarine *Plaice* 30 m off Meshima (32° 15′ N, 129° E'); repaired and surrendered August 1945; used on repatriation service and then transferred 14 August, 1947 to Great Britain and BU.

Kiri
Launched 27 May, 1944 at Yokosuka DY; completed 14 August, 1944; badly damaged 12 December, 1944 by US aircraft in Ormuc Bay, Leyte; repaired and surrendered August 1945; on repatriation service 1945–47; transferred to Soviet Union 29 July, 1947.

Sugi
Launched 3 July, 1944 by Fujinagata Z., Osaka; completed 25 August, 1944; damaged 21 January, 1945 by US aircraft at Takao, Formosa; surrendered August 1945 and then served on repatriation duties; transferred to China 31 July, 1947 and renamed *Hui Yang*.

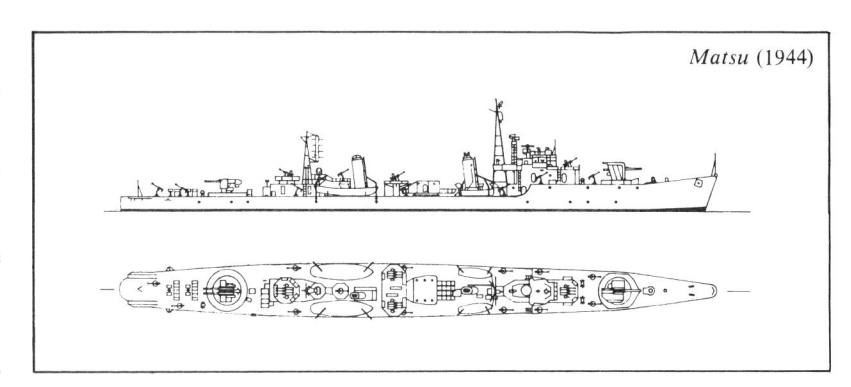

Momi
Launched 16 June, 1944 by Yokosuka DY; completed 3 September, 1944; sunk 5 January, 1945 by aircraft of TF 38, 28 m WSW of Manila (14° N, 120° 20′ E); officially stricken 10 March, 1945.

Hinoki
Launched 4 July, 1944 at Yokosuka DY; completed 3 September 1944; sunk 7 January, 1945 by gunfire of US destroyers *Ausburne*, *Shaw*, *Braine* and *Russell* in the western part of Manila Bay (14° 30′ N, 119° 30′ E).

Kashi
Launched 13 August, 1944 by Fujinagata Z., Osaka; completed 30 September, 1944; damaged 21 January, 1945 by aircraft of TF 38 at Takao, Formosa; surrendered at Kure August 1945 and served on repatriation duties; transferred to USA 7 August, 1947 and BU 20 March, 1948 by Kasado KB, Kobe.

Kaya
Launched 30 July, 1944 at Maizuru DY; completed 30 September, 1944; surrendered at Kure August 1945 and then served on repatriation duties; transferred to Soviet Union 5 July, 1947.

Kaede
Launched 25 July, 1944 at Yokosuka DY; completed 30 October, 1944; badly damaged 31 January, 1945 by B-25 and P-38 aircraft 20 m S of Formosa (22° 30′ N, 12° E); repaired and surrendered in August 1945; served on repatriation duties; transferred to China 6 July, 1947 and renamed *Heng Yang*; later hulked.

Sakura
Launched 6 September, 1944 at Yokosuka DY; completed 25 November, 1944; mined 11 July, 1945 in Osaka Harbour (34° 36′ N, 135° 28′ E); officially stricken 10 August, 1945.

The *Matsu* class escort destroyers adopted the unit system of staggered boilers and machinery, and so had widely-spaced funnels. *Momi* is seen here on 4th September 1944, during trials. (Shizuo Fukui.)

Nara
Launched 12 October, 1944 by Fujinagata Z., Osaka; completed 26 November, 1944; badly damaged by mine 30 June, 1945, 6 m WSW of Shimonoseki (33° 54′ N, 130° 49′ E) and unable to steam; disarmed 15 July, 1945 and towed to Moji; BU 1 July, 1948 at Shimonoseki.

Tsubaki
Launched 30 September, 1944 at Maizuru DY; completed 30 November, 1944; damaged 24 July, 1945 near Okayama by aircraft of TF 38 (34° 38′ N, 133° 50′ E); towed to Kure and surrendered there in August; BU 28 July, 1948 at Kure.

Keyaki
Launched 30 September, 1944 at Yokosuka DY; completed 15 December, 1944; disarmed at Maizuru 15 July, 1945 and surrendered August; repatriation duties 1945–7; transferred to USA 5 July, 1947 and sunk as a target.

Yanagi
Launched 25 November, 1944 by Fujinagata Z., Osaka; completed 8 January, 1945; wrecked 14 July, 1945 near Ashizaki, Tsugaru Straits; raised and towed to Ominato; damaged there 9 August by aircraft of TF 38; BU 1 April, 1947 at Ominato.

11 Units (their numbers are included in the series 5481–5509) had their contracts cancelled in the summer of 1944, but no keels had been laid.

Name	Builder	Date	Displ	Length ft in	Beam ft in	Draught ft in	Machinery	SHP	Speed	Fuel	Radius	Armament	Comp
TACHIBANA Class (23 units)	various	1944–1945	580 N 1289 light	328 1 oa / 322 6 wl / 302 3 pp	30 8	11 1	2-shaft GTU 2 Kampon boilers	19000	27.8	oil	4680 @ 16	3 × 5in 40-cal AA / 24 × 25mm AA / 60 DCs / 4 × 24in TT (UW)	?

GENERAL NOTES
Built under the 1942 'M' Programme (*Nos. 5510 to 5522*) and the 1943–4 Programme (*Nos. 4801 to 4820*) as escort destroyers. They were *Matsu*s simplified without curves or tumblehome. Like the previous class they were intended to have sextuple 21in TT, and were completed with Type '13' radar.

Tachibana class: as *Matsu* except

CAREERS

Tachibana
Launched 14 October, 1944 at Yokosuka DY; completed 20 January, 1945; sunk 14 July, 1945 by TF 38 in Hakodate Harbour, Hokkaido (41° 48′ N, 141° 41′ E) officially stricken 15 September, 1945.

Nire
Launched 25 November, 1944 at Maizuru DY; completed 31 January, 1945; damaged 22 June, 1945 at Kure by B-29 bombers; placed in reserve 15 July, 1945 and surrendered August; BU at Kure 20 April, 1948.

Tsuta
Launched 2 November, 1944 at Yokosuka DY; completed 8 January, 1945; surrendered August 1945 and served on repatriation duties; transferred to China 31 July, 1947 as *Hua Yang*; later hulked.

Hagi
Launched 27 November, 1944 at Yokosuka DY; completed 1 March, 1945; damaged 24 July, 1945 at Kure by aircraft of TF 38; surrendered August and served on repatriation duties 1945–7; transferred to Great Britain 16 July, 1947 and BU.

Kaki
Launched 11 December, 1944 at Yokosuka DY; completed 5 March, 1945; damaged at Osuka 19 March by aircraft of TF 38; placed in reserve at Maizuru 15 July, and surrendered August; repatriation service 1945–7; transferred to USA 4 July, 1947 and BU.

Shii
Launched 13 January, 1945 at Maizuru DY; completed 13 March, 1945; damaged by mine 5 June, 1945 in Bungo Straits; surrendered August; repatriation service 1945–7; transferred to Soviet Union 5 July, 1947.

Nashi
Launched 17 January, 1945 by Kawasaki, Kobe; completed 15 March, 1945; sunk 28 July, 1945 by aircraft of TF 38 at Mitajirizaki, Kure (34° 14′ N, 132° 30′ E); officially stricken 15 September, 1945; raised 1955 and repaired at Kure DY; purchased by Japanese Maritime Self-Defence Force and renamed *Wakaba* 31 May, 1956; used as a radar trials ship and BU 1972–3.

Sumire
Launched 27 December, 1944 at Yokosuka DY; completed 26 March, 1945; disarmed at Maizuru 15 July and surrendered August; repatriation service 1945–7; transferred to Great Britain 20 August, 1947 and sunk as a target.

Enoki
Launched 27 January, 1945 at Maizuru DY; completed 31 March, 1945; sunk by mine 26 June, 1945 in shallow water at Obama Wan, Fukui (35° 28′ N, 135° 44′ E); wreck raised and BU 1 July, 1948 by Mitsubishi, Nanao.

Kusunoki
Launched 18 January, 1945 at Yokosuka DY; completed 28 April, 1945; disarmed 15 July at Maizuru and surrendered August; repatriation service 1945–7; transferred to Great Britain 16 July, 1947 and BU.

Odake
Launched 10 March, 1945 at Maizuru DY; completed 15 May, 1945; disarmed at Maizuru 15 July and surrendered August; repatriation service 1945–7; transferred 4 July, 1947 to USA and BU.

Hatsuzakura
Launched 10 February, 1945 as the *Susuki* at Yokosuka DY; completed 28 May, 1945; disarmed 15 July at Yokosuka and surrendered August; repatriation service 1945–7; transferred 29 July, 1947 to Soviet Union; later became trials ship *TSL.24*.

Kaba
Launched 27 February, 1945 by Fujinagata Z., Osaka; completed 29 May, 1945; damaged 24 July and 11 August by aircraft of TF 38; surrendered August and used on repatriation duties 1945–7; transferred 4 August, 1947 to USA; BU by Mitsui, Tamano.

Hatsuume
Launched 25 May, 1945 at Maizuru DY; completed 18 June, 1945; damaged 26 June by mine at Maizuru; disarmed 15 July and surrendered August; repatriation service 1945–7 and transferred to China 6 July, 1947 as *Hsin Yang*; later renamed *No. 82*.

Yaezakura
Launched 17 March, 1945 at Yokosuka DY; building stopped June 1945 when 60% complete; hull destroyed by aircraft of TF 38 18 July, 1945.

Tochi
Launched 28 May, 1945 at ——————? building stopped June 1945 when 60% complete; hull surrendered August and BU 1946–8.

Yadake
Launched 1 May, 1945 at Yokosuka DY; building stopped June 1945 when 60% complete; hull surrendered August and BU 1946–8.

Katsura
Launched 23 June, 1945 by Fujinagata Z., Osaka; building stopped June 1945 when 60% complete; hull surrendered August and BU 1946–8.

Wakazakura
Laid down 15 January, 1945 by Fujinagata Z., Osaka; stopped March 1945 and material diverted to midget submarines.

Azura
Laid down 29 December, 1944 at Yokosuka DY; building stopped March 1945 and material diverted to midget submarines.

Sakaki
Laid down 29 December, 1944 at Yokosuka DY; building stopped March 1945 and material diverted to midget submarines.

Kuzu
Laid down 2 March, 1945 at Yokosuka DY; building stopped March 1945 and material diverted to midget submarines.

Hishi
Laid down 10 February, 1945 at Maizuru DY; building stopped March 1945 and material diverted to midget submarines.

10 Units (among *Nos. 4801 to 4820*) had their contracts cancelled in March 1945. A further 80 'Improved *Tachibana*' Class were projected for 1944–5 but contracts were never placed.

TORPEDO BOATS AND DESTROYERS

10. Motor Torpedo Boats and Motor Gunboats

Motor Torpedo Boats

Name	Builder	Date	Displ	Length ft in	Beam ft in	Draught ft in	Machinery	SHP	Speed	Fuel	Radius	Armament	Comp
55-ft CMB Type	Thornycroft, Southampton	1920	14 N	55 0 oa	11 1	3 3	2-shaft petrol engines	1000	40	? petrol	200 @ 40	2 × .303in MGs 2 × 18in TT 2 DCs	5

GENERAL NOTES
Experimental boats copied from the British coastal motor boats, they were rated as Naikatei or motor boats. They were wooden-hulled with a stepped keel, and reached 43 knots on trials.

CAREERS
Naikatei No. 615
Launched 1920 and purchased 1920–2 and named 'Experimental Motor Boat 615'; later attached to the engineering school at Yokosuka; stricken by 1938.
2nd Boat (number unknown)
Launched 1920 and purchased 1920–2 as *No. 615*; attached to the engineering school at Yokosuka and stricken by 1938.
3rd Boat (number unknown)
Launched 1920 and purchased 1920–2 but nothing further known.
Naikatei No. 1149
Launched 1920 and purchased 1920–2 as *No. 1149*; later a torpedo-recovery vessel and despatch boat at Kure DY; still in existence in 1945.
5th Boat
Launched 1934 and completed 1935 for China as *Motor Boat No. 1* or *No. 2*; fell into Japanese hands at Canton in 1938; in 1939 she became an experimental motor boat (number unknown); attached to torpedo school at Yokosuka in 1940; possibly stricken 1944.

A captured Chinese Coastal Motor Boat (Thornycroft 55-foot type), seen making over 30 knots in the Whangpoa River. (Tappman Collection.)

Name	Builder	Date	Displ	Length ft in	Beam ft in	Draught ft in	Machinery	SHP	Speed	Fuel	Radius	Armament	Comp
19-METRE Experimental Type	Yokohama Yacht Co., Tsurumi	1940	18.7 N	62 4 oa	14 2	3 11	2-shaft Type '94' petrol engines 1 M cruising engine	1800 / 60 hp	35 8	?	270 @ 30 / 830 @ 8	1 × .303in MG 2 × 18in TT	7

GENERAL NOTES
This craft was the first Japanese MTB, known as the Type 'B' Otsu-gata. She was classified as a Gyoraitei or motor torpedo boat, and had a wooden V-section hull 6.89ft deep.

CAREER
She appears to have had neither name nor number, but was launched in 1940 and completed the same year. She ran trials against the former Chinese CMB and the purchased Italian MAS (see under *Hayabusa No.1*, p. 158); from 1943 she was at Kisarazu.

Name	Builder	Date	Displ	Length ft in	Beam ft in	Draught ft in	Machinery	SHP	Speed	Fuel	Radius	Armament	Comp
T 1 Type Nos. 1 to 6	Yokohama Yacht Co., Tsurumi	1941	20.5 F 17 N	60 ? oa	14 1	2 1	2-shaft Type '94' petrol engines 1 M cruising engine	1800 / 60 hp	38½	?	210 @ 30	2 × .303in MGs 2 × 18in torpedo-launchers or 6 DCs	7

GENERAL NOTES
These were a modified version of the 19m experimental design, with a similar V-section wooden hull.

MACHINERY
It is believed that the trials were run with propellers of different types.

CAREERS
Gyoraitei No. 1
Launched 21 August, 1941 and completed 25 October, 1941; badly damaged in a storm in the Marshall Islands, 14 December, 1942; repaired and used for training at the Yokosuka torpedo school.
Gyoraitei No. 2
Launched 28 August, 1941 and completed 25 October, 1941; sunk 19 September, 1943 by aircraft from carriers *Lexington*, *Princeton* and *Belleau Wood* off Tarawa, Marshall Islands.
Gyoraitei No. 3
Launched 6 October, 1941 and completed 1 November, 1941; sunk with *Gyoraitei No. 2*.
Gyoraitei No. 4
Launched 18 October, 1941 and completed 15 November, 1941; sunk by aircraft at Wake Island 24 March, 1944 (19° N, 167° E).

Gyoraitei No. 5
Launched 30 October, 1941 and completed 30 November, 1941; sunk January, 1944 at Wake Island by aircraft attack.

Gyoraitei No. 6
Launched 11 November, 1941 and completed 6 December, 1941; sunk January, 1944 by aircraft at Wake Island.

Name	Builder	Date	Displ	Length ft in	Beam ft in	Draught ft in	Machinery	SHP	Speed	Fuel	Radius	Armament	Comp
T51 Type Nos. 10, 13–16	Yokohama Yacht Co., Tsurumi	1942–1945	90 F 80 S	106 3 oa	16 5	3 8	4-shaft Type '71' petrol engines (*No. 10* had 2 shafts, with Vulcan gearing)	3600	29	?	1000 @ 16 340 @ 28	*No. 10* 2 × 25mm 2 × 18in torpedo-launchers *Others* 3 × 25mm 2 × 18in torpedo-launchers or 4/8 DCs	18
Nos. 11–12, 14–15, 17–27, 5441–5458	Choshi	1943–1945	84.2 F 75 S										

GENERAL NOTES
This type, known as 'Type A Ro-gata' was based on German schnellboot plans, and were intended to act as division boats. Not a success as they suffered from structural weakness and were the wrong length for the Pacific waves.

CONVERSION
Alterations were incorporated in later craft following experience with *No. 10*. but without success. After building ceased, the boats in hand were altered to guard-boats and sub-chasers. In these vessels two petrol engines were removed.

Gyoraitei No. 10
Launched 1943 and completed 20 November, 1943; sunk 17 February, 1944 by aircraft at Truk (07° 31′ N, 151° 59′ E).

Gyoraitei No. 11
Launched 1943 and completed 1944; found in wrecked condition at Uraga in 1945; BU.

Gyoraitei No. 12
Launched 1943 and completed 1944; sunk 20 August, 1944 by petrol explosion at Nagaura Pier, Yokosuka (35° 15′ N, 139° 40′ E).

Gyoraitei No. 13
Launched 1943 and completed 1944; destroyed by fire at Uraga in February 1946.

Gyoraitei No. 14
Launched and completed 1944; in wrecked condition at Uraga 1945; BU.

Gyoraitei No. 15
Launched and completed 1944; at Uraga in 1945; sunk subsequently in collision at Uraga (35° 15′ N, 139° 43′ E).

Gyoraitei No. 16
Launched 1944 and completed 194?; at Sasebo in wrecked condition 1945; later sunk, but raised and BU.

Gyoraitei No. 17
Launched 1944 and completed 194?; in wrecked condition at Uraga in July 1946; BU.

Gyoraitei No. 18
Not launched, but on 5 March, 1945 she was renamed *Raitei No. 111* and used as a torpedo-launcher for the submarine base at Yokosuka.

Gyoraitei No. 19
Incomplete by August 1945.

Gyoraitei Nos. 20–27, 5441–5458
Contracts cancelled.

Name	Builder	Date	Displ	Length ft in	Beam ft in	Draught ft in	Machinery	SHP	Speed	Fuel	Radius	Armament	Comp
T23 Type Nos. 201–207	Yokosuka DY Mitsubishi, Yokohama	1943–1945	25.4 F 20 S	59 1 oa	14 1	2 1	1-shaft Type '91' hp petrol engine 1 cruising engine	450 80	17	?	310 @ 14	1 × 13mm or 25mm 2 × 18in torpedo-launchers	7
Nos. 401–410 Nos. 451–456	Sasebo DY												
T25 Type No. 468 Nos. 484–488	Sasebo DY	1943–1945	25.4 F 20 S	59 1 oa	14 1	2 1	1-shaft Type '71' petrol engine 1 cruising engine	920 80	21½	?	?	1 × 13mm or 25mm 2 × 18in torpedo-launchers	7
T31 Type Nos. 208–240	Yokosuka DY, Mitsubishi, Yokohama	1943–1945	24 F 20 S	59 1 oa	14 1	2 5	2-shaft Hispano-Suiza petrol engines	800	20		340 @ 18½	1 × 13mm or 25mm 2 × 18in torpedo-launchers	7
T32 Type Nos. 301–308	Kure DY	1943–194?	24.2 F 20 S	59 1 oa	14 1	2 5	2-shaft Hispano-Suiza petrol engines	1000	21½	?	300 @ 19½	1 × 13mm or 25mm 2 × 18in torpedo-launchers	7
T33 Type Nos. 500–505	Maizuru DY	1943–1948	24½ F 20 S	59 1 oa	14 1	2 5	2-shaft Type '91' petrol engines	900	21	?	300 @ 19½	1 × 13mm or 25mm 2 × 18in torpedo-launchers	7
T34 Type Nos. 151–165	various	1943–194?	24 F 20 S	59 1 oa	14 1	2 5	2-shaft Lorraine petrol engines	1400	27½	?	250 @ 26	1 × 13mm or 25mm 2 × 18in torpedo-launchers	7
T35 Type Nos. 469 482–483 494–499 801–837	Sasebo DY	1943–194?	24½ F 20 S	59 1 oa	14 1	2 5	2-shaft Type '91' petrol engines	1840	35	?	290 @ 33	1 × 25mm 2 × 18in torpedo-launchers	7
529–537	Maizuru DY												
T36 Type	Sasebo DY	1943–	24	59 1	14 1	2 5	2-shaft air-cooled	800	21½	?	300	1 × 25mm	7

Name	Builder	Date	Displ	Length ft in	Beam ft in	Draught ft in	Machinery	SHP	Speed	Fuel	Radius	Armament	Comp
Nos. 411–450 Nos. 470–473		1948	F 20 S	oa			Kotobuki Type '3' petrol engine	hp			@ 21	2 × 18in torpedo-launchers	
T37 Type Nos. 327–	Kure DY	1943–194?	24.7 F 20 S	59 1 oa	14 1	2 5	2-shaft air-cooled Myojo Type '2' petrol engine	1200 hp	25	?	250 @ 24	1 × 25mm 2 × 18in torpedo-launchers	7
T38 Type Nos. 241–286 Nos. 457–467 Nos. 506–528	Yokosuka DY Sasebo DY Maizuru DY	1943–194?	24.3 F 20 S	59 1 oa	14 1	2 5	2-shaft air-cooled Kinsei Type '41' petrol engine	1400 hp	27½	?	220 @ 26	1 × 25mm 2 × 18in torpedo-launchers	7
T39 Type Nos. 474–	Sasebo DY	1943–194?	24½ F 20 S	59 1 oa	14 1	2 5	2-shaft air-cooled Shinten Type '21' petrol engine	1440 hp	27	?	220 @ 25½	1 × 25mm 2 × 18in torpedo-launchers	7

GENERAL NOTES
These were modified versions of the *T1* Type, using aircraft engines to make up for the shortage of petrol engines. The *T23*, *T31–33* and *T37* types had steel hulls. The *T36–39* types had air-intakes amidships. The hull was 6.56ft deep. Assembly of hulls etc., was done by Okamoto Shipbuilding Co., Kysei Gumi Co., and Hasegawa Shipbuilding Co.

CONVERSION
For lack of fast motors, 238 boats were completed as Raitei (torpedo-launches).

CAREERS
It has proved very difficult to obtain full details of the careers and fates of the vessels.
T23 Type
Gyoraitei No. 402
Sunk 18 March, 1944 off Boronga, Burma by British aircraft.
Gyoraitei No. 453
Sunk 18 March, 1944 off Boronga, Burma by British aircraft.
T31 Type
Gyoraitei No. 219
Damaged at Toba 1945.
Gyoraitei No. 220
Damaged at Toba 1945.
Gyoraitei No. 222
Damaged at Toba 1945.
Gyoraitei No. 223
Damaged at Toba 1945; sunk 2 November, 1946 in a tidal wave.
Gyoraitei No. 225
Taken over by USA at Yokosuka in 1945 and BU.
Gyoraitei No. 228
Was a hulk at Uraga in July 1946.
Gyoraitei No. 232
Damaged at Komatsujima in 1945.
Gyoraitei No. 233
Sunk at Naruto (date unknown); wreck still in existence in 1945.
Gyoraitei No. 235
Undamaged at Nraga in 1945.

Gyoraitei No. 239
Taken over by US at Yokosuka in 1945 and BU.
T33 Type
Gyoraitei No. 500
Sunk 10 October, 1944 by aircraft of TF 38 at Okinawa (26° 30′ N, 128° E).
T35 Type
Gyoraitei No. 482
Sunk 14 September, 1944 by aircraft of TF 38 N off Cebu (11° N, 124° E).
Gyoraitei No. 483
Sunk 12 September, 1944 by aircraft of TF 38 off Cebu (10° 17′ N, 123° 54′ E).
Gyoraitei No. 493
Sunk 10 October, 1944 by aircraft of TF 38 off Okinawa (26° 30′ N, 128° E).
Gyoraitei No. 496, 498, 805, 806, 810, 812, 813, 814, 820 and *823*.
Sunk as *No. 493*.
T36 Type
Gyoraitei No. 416
Sunk July/September 1944 off Palau (07° 25′ N, 134° 30′ E).
Gyoraitei No. 245
Sunk at Uraga (date unknown) but hulk still in existence in 1945.
Gyoraitei No. 246
Damaged at Ominato 1945.
Gyoraitei No. 247
Damaged at Ominato 1945 but reparable.
Gyoraitei No. 249
Damaged at Ominato 1945.
Gyoraitei No. 250
As *No. 249*.
Gyoraitei No. 251
Stricken 11 July, 1944 at Kushiro after irreparable machinery damage.
Gyoraitei No. 254
Damaged at Uraga in 1945, and beached.
Gyoraitei No. 256
Badly damaged at Yokosuka, 18 July, 1945 by aircraft of TF 38; taken over by USA and later sunk.
Gyoraitei No. 258
Damaged at Uraga 1945, and beached.

Name	Builder	Date	Displ	Length ft in	Beam ft in	Draught ft in	Machinery	SHP	Speed	Fuel	Radius	Armament	Comp
No. 114 ex-*Q.III*	Thornycroft, Southampton	1939	40 N	65 0 oa	13 3	3 7	3-shaft Thornycroft RY.12 12-cyl petrol engines	1800 bhp	39	?	?	2 × 13mm 2 × 18in torpedo-launchers DCs	?

GENERAL NOTES
This craft was an enlarged edition of the 55ft Thornycroft CMB, built for the Philippines Navy. She was built of wood and had a depth of hold of 8.20ft. On trials she reached 41 knots.

CAREER
Launched 1939 and completed 1940 for the Philippines Navy as *Q.3*; sunk at Cavite in May 1942 but raised; recommissioned 12 April, 1943 as *Gyoraitei No. 114*; sunk in 1944 or 1945 in the Philippines.

Name	Builder	Date	Displ	Length ft in	Beam ft in	Draught ft in	Machinery	SHP	Speed	Fuel	Radius	Armament	Comp
T14 Type Nos. 538–555 Nos. 871–900 Nos. 838–850	Maizuru DY Mitsubishi, Nagasaki	1944–1945	14½ F	49 2 oa	12 0	2 0	1-shaft Type '71' petrol engine	920	33	?	?	1 × 13mm or 25mm 2 × 18in torpedo-launchers	7
T15 Type Nos. 1001–1008 Nos. 1101–1131	Sasebo DY various, including Mitsubishi, Nagasaki	1944–1945	15 F	49 10 oa	12 5	2 1	1-shaft Type '71' petrol engine	920 hp	35	?	?	1 × 13mm or 25mm 2 × 18in torpedo-launchers	7

GENERAL NOTES
These were improved Type 23, but the *T14* type had the V-form hull, whereas the *T15* had a single-stepped hull. Both types were wooden, with a depth of 5.91ft.

CAREERS
Details of the vessels and their fates are obscure.
Type *T14*
Gyoraitei No. 549
Sunk at Nagoya (date unknown), but wreck still in existence in 1945.
Gyoraitei No. 869
As *No. 549.*
Gyoraitei No. 870
As *No. 549.*
Gyoraitei No. 871
As *No. 549.*
Gyoraitei No. 872.
As *No. 549.*
Gyoraitei No. 873
As *No. 549.*
Gyoraitei No. 874
As *No. 549.*
Gyoraitei No. 875
As *No. 549.*
Gyoraitei No. 876
As *No. 549.*
Gyoraitei No. 877
As *No. 549.*
Gyoraitei No. 879
As *No. 549.*
Gyoraitei No. 882
Damaged at Kadokawa in 1945.
Gyoraitei No. 883
Sunk at Saeki (date unknown); wreck still in existence in 1945.
Type *T15*
Gyoraitei No. 1113
Sunk at Sasebo (date unknown); wreck still in existence in 1945.

Name	Builder	Date	Displ	Length ft in	Beam ft in	Draught ft in	Machinery	SHP	Speed	Fuel	Radius	Armament	Comp
No. 101 ex *TM.3*	Soerabaja DY	1938	15 N approx	59 1 oa approx	12 5 approx	3 3 approx	2-shaft Otto aero-engines	1260 hp	38	?	?	unarmed	6
Nos. 102–113 Nos. 115–120 ex-*TM.4-21*	Soerabaja DY	1940–1944	19.2 F 13.1 N	59 1 oa	12 5	2 3	3-shaft Lorraine petrol engines	1350 bhp	33.3	?	310 @ 30 370 @ 18	1 × .303in MG 2 × 18in torpedo-launchers 4DCs	7

GENERAL NOTES
These vessels were all built for the Dutch Navy in the East Indies. They had steel hulls. *TM.3* had permanent engine trouble and was not seaworthy.

CONVERSION
From 1944 the recommissioned boats had 1 × 13mm or 25mm gun and a speed of 20 knots.

CAREERS
Note that there is some doubt about many of the former Dutch numbers of these craft.
Gyoraitei No. 101
Launched and completed 1938 as Dutch *TM.3*; scuttled 2 March, 1942 at Soerabaja; raised 1942 and renamed *Gyoraitei No. 101*; she probably never put to sea because of the problems with her machinery.
Gyoraitei No. 102
Launched 1940 and completed as *TM.4*; scuttled at Soerabaja 2 March, 1942 but raised and became *Gyoraitei No. 102*; badly damaged 1 August, 1945 at Nagasaki by US aircraft; later BU?.
Gyoraitei No. 103
Launched 1940 and completed as *TM.6*; scuttled at Soerabaja 2 March, 1942 but raised and became *Gyoraitei No. 103*; in 1942 became a training boat at Yokosuka Torpedo School; taken over by USA in 1945.
Gyoraitei No. 104
Launched 1940 and completed as *TM.8*; scuttled at Soerabaja 2 March, 1942 but raised and became *Gyoraitei No. 104*; training duties at Yokosuka Torpedo School; taken over by USA in 1945.
Gyoraitei No. 105
Launched 1941 and completed as *TM.9*; scuttled at Soerabaja 2 March, 1942 but raised and became *Gyoraitei No. 105*; training duties at Yokosuka Torpedo School; taken over by USA in 1945.
Gyoraitei No. 106
Launched and completed 1941 as *TM.10*; scuttled at Soerabaja 2 March, 1942 but repaired as *Gyoraitei No. 106*; fate as *No. 105.*
Gyoraitei No. 107
Launched and completed 1941 as *TM.11*; scuttled at Soerabaja 2 March, 1942 but repaired as *Gyoraitei No. 107*; fate as *No. 105.*
Gyoraitei No. 108
Launched 1941 and completed as *TM.12*; scuttled at Soerabaja 2 March, 1942; repaired as *Gyoraitei No. 108*; fate as *No. 105.*
Gyoraitei No. 109
Launched 1941 and completed as *TM.13*; scuttled at Soerabaja 2 March, 1942; repaired as *Gyoraitei No. 109* (completed 9 October, 1943); later sunk.
Gyoraitei No. 110
Launched 1941 and completed January, 1942 as *TM.14*; scuttled 2 March, 1942 at Soerabaja but repaired as *Gyoraitei No. 110* (completed 9 October, 1943); accidentally lost.
Gyoraitei No. 111
Launched 1942 and completed 17 February, 1942 as *TM.15*; scuttled 2 March, 1942 at Soerabaja; repaired as *Gyoraitei No. 111*, completed 6 May, 1943; accidentally lost.
Gyoraitei No. 112
Launched and completed 1940 as *TM.5*; scuttled 2 March, 1942 at Soerabaja; completed repairs as *Gyoraitei No. 112* on 6 May, 1943; sunk 2 August, 1943 by aircraft at Lae, New Guinea (07° N, 147° E).
Gyoraitei No. 113

Launched and completed 1940 as *TM.7*; scuttled 2 March, 1942 at Soerabaja; completed repairs as *Gyoraitei No. 113* on 6 May, 1943; badly damaged by air attack 2 August, 1943 at Lae, New Guinea.

Gyoraitei No. 115
Launched as *TM.16* but scuttled incomplete at Soerabaja 2 March, 1942; completed repairs as *Gyoraitei No. 115* on 6 May, 1943; sunk 26 July, 1943 by petrol explosion at Rabaul (04° 12′ S, 152° 12′ E).

Gyoraitei No. 116
Launched as *TM.17* but scuttled incomplete at Soerabaja 2 March, 1942; completed repairs as *Gyoraitei No. 116* on 6 May, 1943; sunk at Rabaul in 1944.

Gyoraitei No. 117
Launched as *TM.18* but scuttled incomplete at Soerabaja 2 March, 1942; completed 6 May, 1943 as *Gyoraitei No. 117*; sunk 1944 off Rabaul.

Gyoraitei No. 118
Material assembled for building *TM.19* was demolished at Soerabaja in March 1942, but building recommenced and she was finished as *Gyoraitei No. 118* 13 October, 1943.

Gyoraitei No. 119
Material assembled for *TM.20* was demolished at Soerabaja in March 1942, but building recommenced and she was finished as *Gyoraitei No. 119* on 15 November, 1944.

Gyoraitei No. 120
Material assembled for *TM.21* was demolished at Soerabaja in March 1942, but building recommenced and finished on 15 November, 1944 as *Gyoraitei No. 120*.

Motor Gunboats

Name	Builder	Date	Displ	Length ft in	Beam ft in	Draught ft in	Machinery	SHP	Speed	Fuel	Radius	Armament	Comp
H1 Type No. 1	Baglietto, Varazze	1940	26 N	59 1 oa	14 9	2 8	2-shaft Isotta-Fraschini petrol engines	1840 bhp	33	?	?	2 × 20mm 2 DCs	?

GENERAL NOTES
An experimental vessel of the Italian *MAS*-type, similar to the Bagliettio-built *MAS. 451–2*. Wooden-hulled with two steps.

MACHINERY
She was delivered with 2 sets of Alfa-Romeo cruising engines of 100 bhp, giving 8 knots and an endurance of 800 nm. She reached 50 knots on trials with a total of 2300 bhp but in 1941 after lengthy trials, the cruising engines were removed and the main engines were de-rated to 1840 bhp.

CONVERSION
The original armament was 1 × 13mm gun and 2 × 17.7in TT but she entered service as a motor gunboat with new armament.

CAREER
Launched and completed 1940 for trials; entered service 1941 as *Hayabusa-Tei No. 1*; sunk 1944 off Rabaul.

Name	Builder	Date	Displ	Length ft in	Beam ft in	Draught ft in	Machinery	SHP	Speed	Fuel	Radius	Armament	Comp
H2 Type Nos. 2–9	Yokosuka DY	1943– 194?	24.7 N	59 1 oa	14 9	3 0	2-shaft Kasei petrol engines	2100 bhp	33½	?	140 @ 30	2 × 20mm 2 × .303in MGs DCs	8
H35 Type Nos. 27–32 Nos. 201, 217	Yokosuka DY Kure DY	1943– 194?	25 N	59 1 oa	14 1	2 5	2-shaft Type '71' Model 6 petrol engines	1840 bhp	34	?	290 @ 33	3 × 25mm 4 DCs	7
H38 Type Nos. 10–26 Nos. 51–100	Yokosuka DY Kure DY	1943– 194?	24.8 N	59 1 oa	14 1	2 5	2-shaft Kinsei air-cooled petrol engines	1400 bhp	27	?	220 @ 26	3 × 25mm 4 DCs	7

GENERAL NOTES
These were motor gunboats developed from the Gyoraitei or MTBs (*H35* and *H38* were ex-*T35* and *T38* hulls), with hulls of V-section). The *H35* group were built of wood, but the others were of steel. The *H38* group had a distinctive air-intake amidships. The depth of hull varied from 6.56ft (*H35* and *H38*) to 7.19ft (*H2*). Hull-assembly etc, was done by Matsuo Heavy Industry Co., Osaka. A total of 105 was completed, including Type 61.

CONVERSION
In 1945, torpedo-launchers were installed and boats were re-rated as *Gyoraitei*. Vessels with weaker motors were completed as *Raitei*.

CAREERS
Details of the fates are obscure.
H2 Type
Hayabusa-Tei No. 3
Sunk 1944/5 off Rabaul.
Hayabusa-Tei No. 4
While being transferred from Truk to Rabaul in tow of *Choko Maru No. 2* she was badly damaged 12 January, 1944 by US submarine *Albacore* and had to be sunk by gunfire of a Japanese escort (03° 37′ N, 147° 27′ E).
Hayabusa-Tei No. 5
Sunk 1944/5 off Rabaul.
Hayabusa-Tei No. 7
Sunk 1944/5 off Rabaul.
Hayabusa-Tei No. 8
Sunk 1944/5 off Rabaul.
H35 Type
No. 28
Sunk 18 May, 1945 by aircraft of TF 38 at Yokosuka (35° 19′ N, 139° 40′ E).
H38 Type
No. 10
Damaged at Ominato 1945
No. 11, 19 and 20.
As No. 10.
No. 25
Badly damaged 25 September, 1944 in storm off Bonin Island (27° N, 142° E); later sank.
No. 52
Sunk 12 September, 1944 by aircraft of TF 38 at Cebu (10° 17′ N, 123° 54′ E).
No. 55, 61, 62 and 67.
As No. 52.

Name	Builder	Date	Displ	Length ft in	Beam ft in	Draught ft in	Machinery	SHP	Speed	Fuel	Radius	Armament	Comp
H 61 Type Nos. 101–124 Nos. 33–46 Nos. 218–245	Sasebo DY Kure DY	1944– 1945	25.6 N	62 4 oa	14 4	2 5	2-shaft Type '51' Diesels	600 bhp	17½	?	?	3 × 25mm 4 DCs	7

GENERAL NOTES
This was the first Diesel-engined MGBs, and the V-section steel hull was retained. The depth of hull was 6.27ft.

CONVERSION
Two 18in torpedo-launchers were added in 1945 to convert them to *Gyoraitei*.

CAREERS
As with the others, fates are obscure.
Hayabusa-Tei No. 33
At Ito in 1945.
Hayabusa-Tei No. 34
At Uraga in 1945.
Hayabusa-Tei No. 35
At Yokosuka in 1945 and taken over by USA.
Hayabusa-Tei No. 36
At Uraga in 1945.
Hayabusa-Tei No. 41
Damaged at Kure in 1945.
Hayabusa-Tei No. 46
Sunk at Saeki (date unknown) but her hull was in existence in 1945.
Hayabusa-Tei No. 102
Badly damaged 1 August, 1945 by US aircraft at Nagasaki (this may be confused with *Gyoraitei No. 102*).
Hayabusa-Tei No. 106
At Furue in 1945, and taken over by USA.
Hayabusa-Tei No. 113
Sunk in Omura Bay (date unknown); hull in existence in 1945.
Hayabusa-Tei No. 222
At Fukae in 1945.
Hayabusa-Tei No. 223
At Hirao in 1945.

Name	Builder	Date	Displ	Length ft in	Beam ft in	Draught ft in	Machinery	SHP	Speed	Fuel	Radius	Armament	Comp
19-METRE Type (river gunboat) *Nos. 3537* etc	Yokosuka DY, etc.	193?– 1938	10 N approx	62 4 oa	13 1	1 0	1 aero-engine, driving airscrews	500 bhp approx	19	?	?	1 × .303in MG	?

GENERAL NOTES
These MGBs were designed for use in inland waters in China, and were developed from excursion craft. They had wooden hulls and were classed as *Naikatei No. 3*, etc. As transports they could carry 100 men.

CAREERS
Although 48 boats were completed, no individual information is available.

Name	Builder	Date	Displ	Length ft in	Beam ft in	Draught ft in	Machinery	SHP	Speed	Fuel	Radius	Armament	Comp
15-METRE Type (river gunboat) *Nos.1035* etc	Yokohama Yacht Co. Sumidagawa Co., Tokyo	1938– 1939	10 N approx	62 4 oa	10 10	1 11	2 Buda, or single Hispano-Suiza, or single Lorraine petrol engines	120 bhp	11 approx	?	?	1 × 12mm or .303in MG	?

GENERAL NOTES
Like the 19m type these were designed for service on Chinese rivers and had wooden hulls. They were numbered *Naikatei No. 1*.

MACHINERY AND ARMAMENT
17 boats had 2 Buda petrol engines, and 3 boats had a 12mm gun aft.

CAREERS
Although 40 boats were completed, no details of service are available.

25-ton River Gunboats

Name	Builder	Date	Displ	Length ft in	Beam ft in	Draught ft in	Machinery	SHP	Speed	Fuel	Radius	Armament	Comp
25-TON Type (river gunboat) *Nos.1164–1173, 1179–1180,* etc. *Nos. 1357–1366* approx 20 boats 7 boats	Yokosuka DY Nagasaki DY Ujina DY Sasebo DY	1940– 1944	26 N	59 1 oa	11 6	2 3	2-shaft Diesels	300 bhp	11	?	400 @ 12	2 × 13mm	?

GENERAL NOTES
These MGBs had an all-welded hull, with 5mm decks and 4mm sides of Ducol steel. The depth of hold was 4.92ft and a speed of 12½ knots was reached on trials. They were classified as *Naikatei No. 1*.

CONVERSION
Because of the time taken to build them, many were completed for different functions, e.g. guardboats, sub-chasers and commercial craft.

CAREERS
Although 80 boats were completed, no individual details are available.

T 51 Type (1944)

19-metre Experimental Type (1940) *H1 Type* (1940) *T.1. Type* (1941) *H.35 Type* (1943) *H.38 Type* (1943) *H.61 Type* (1944)

T.25 Type (1943) *T.38 Type* (1943) *T 31 Type* (1943) *25-ton Type* Gunboat *T.14 Type* (1944) *T 15 Type* (1942)

MOTOR TORPEDO BOATS AND MOTOR GUNBOATS

11. Submarines

Name	Builder	Date	Displ	Length ft in	Beam ft in	Draught ft in	Machinery	SHP	Speed	Fuel	Radius	Armament	Comp
HOLLAND Type Nos. 1–5	Fore River Yard, Quincy, Mass.	1904–1905	103 surf 124 subm	67 0 oa / 60 0 pp	11 11	10 3	1-shaft 4-cyl petrol engine / 1 electric motor	180 bhp / 70 ehp	8 / 7	2 oil	184 @ 8 / 21 @ 7	1 × 18in TT 2 torpedoes	13

GENERAL NOTES
These coastal submersibles were built to the design of John P. Holland and were similar to the US 'A' Class. They were single-hulled boats.
Originally planned to be operational during the Russo-Japanese War but delayed. The order was placed 14 June, 1904, work finished on 5 October and all 5 were delivered in sections at Yokohama on 12 December, 1904. After reassembly the first was ready in August 1905.

CAREERS
No. 1
Launched 30 March, 1905 and completed 1 August, 1905; stricken 1921 and BU.
No. 2
Launched 2 May, 1905 and completed 5 September, 1905; stricken 1921 and BU.
No. 3
Launched 16 May, 1905 and completed 5 September, 1905; stricken 1921 and BU.
No. 4
Launched 27 May, 1905 and completed 1 October, 1905; sunk 14 November, 1916 at Kure by petrol explosion; raised and repaired; stricken 1921 and BU.
No. 5
Launched 13 May, 1905 and completed 1 October, 1905; stricken 1921 and BU.

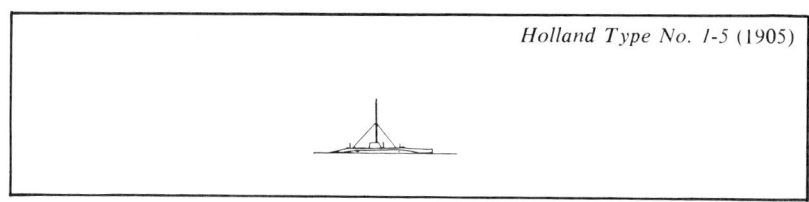

Holland Type No. 1-5 (1905)

Name	Builder	Date	Displ	Length ft in	Beam ft in	Draught ft in	Machinery	SHP	Speed	Fuel	Radius	Armament	Comp
KAIGUN HOLLAND Type No. 6	Kawasaki, Kobe	1904–1906	57 surf 63 subm	73 10 oa / 69 4 pp	7 0	6 8	1-shaft petrol engine / 1 electric motor	300 bhp / 22 ehp	8½ / 4	1.4 oil / –	184 @ 8 / 12 @ 4	1 × 18in TT 1 torpedo	14
KAIGUN HOLLAND Type No. 7	Kawasaki, Kobe	1904–1906	78 surf 95 subm	84 4 oa / 80 1 pp	7 11	7 8	1-shaft petrol engine / 1 electric motor	300 bhp / 22 ehp	8½ / 4	1.7 oil / –	184 @ 8 / 12 @ 4	1 × 18in TT 1 torpedo	14

GENERAL NOTES
These were modified versions of the Holland design, and were the first submarines built in Japan.

CAREERS
No. 6
Launched 28 September, 1905 and completed 30 March, 1906; sank 15 April, 1910 after a petrol explosion at Kure; (16 dead) raised 16 April, 1910 and repaired by August 1910; stricken 1920 and preserved as a memorial at Kure.
No. 7
Launched 28 September, 1906 and completed 30 March, 1906; stricken 1920 and BU.

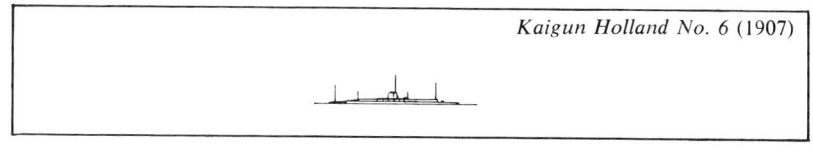

Kaigun Holland No. 6 (1907)

Name	Builder	Date	Displ	Length ft in	Beam ft in	Draught ft in	Machinery	SHP	Speed	Fuel	Radius	Armament	Comp
VICKERS C(1) Type Nos. 8–9	Vickers, Sons & Maxim, Barrow	1907–1909	286 surf 321 subm	142 3 oa / 131 6 pp	13 7	11 3	1-shaft Vickers Diesel engine / 1 electric motor	600 bhp / 300 ehp	12 / 8½	15 oil	660 @ 12 / 60 @ 4	2 × 18in TT 2 torpedoes 1 MG	26

GENERAL NOTES
These single-hulled coastal submarines were ordered from England under the 1907 Programme, and were similar to the RN's 'C' Class.

CAREERS
No. 8
Launched 19 May, 1908 and completed 26 February, 1909; renumbered *Ha.1* 1924; stricken 1 December, 1928 and BU.
No. 9
Launched 19 May, 1908 and completed 9 March, 1909; renumbered *Ha.2* in 1924; stricken 1 December, 1928 and BU.

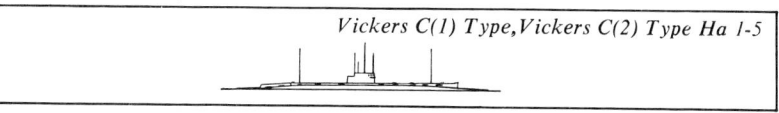

Vickers C(1) Type, Vickers C(2) Type Ha 1-5

Name	Builder	Date	Displ	Length ft in	Beam ft in	Draught ft in	Machinery	SHP	Speed	Fuel	Radius	Armament	Comp
VICKERS C(2) Type *Nos. 10–12*	Vickers, Barrow	1910–1911	291 surf 326 subm	142 3 oa 131 6 pp	13 7	11 3	1-shaft Vickers Diesel engine 1 electric motor	600 bhp 300 ehp	12 8½	15½ oil —	660 @ 12 60 @ 4	2 × 18in TT 2 torpedoes 1 MG	25

GENERAL NOTES
Single-hulled coastal submarines ordered under the 1910 Programme, they were similar to the previous class. They were shipped in sections to Kure and then re-assembled.

CAREERS
No. 10
Launched 4 March, 1911 and completed 12 August, 1911; renumbered *Ha.3* in 1923; stricken 1 December, 1928 and BU.

No. 11
Launched 18 March, 1911 and completed 26 August, 1911; renumbered *Ha.4* in 1923; stricken 1 December, 1928 and BU.

No. 12
Launched 27 March, 1911 and completed 3 August, 1911; renumbered *Ha.5* in 1923; stricken 1 December, 1928 and BU.

Name	Builder	Date	Displ	Length ft in	Beam ft in	Draught ft in	Machinery	SHP	Speed	Fuel	Radius	Armament	Comp
VICKERS C(3) Type *Ha. 7, Ha. 8* ex–*Nos. 16, 17*	Kure DY	1916	290 surf 326 subm	143 8 oa 134 10 pp	13 7	11 3	1-shaft Vickers Diesel engine 1 electric motor	600 bhp 300 ehp	12 8½	18.2 oil —	660 @ 12 60 @ 4	2 × 18in TT 4 torpedoes	26

GENERAL NOTES
These were virtually repeat editions of the previous two classes, ordered under the 1915 Programme, and were similar to the British 'C' Class. Ordered as *Nos. 16* and *17* but renumbered in 1914.

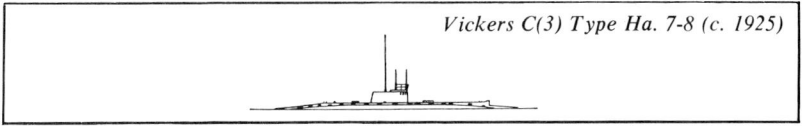

CAREERS
No. 16
Launched 15 March, 1916 and completed 1 November, 1916; renumbered *Ha.7* in 1923; stricken 1 December, 1928 and BU.

No. 17
Launched 15 March, 1916 and completed 2 February, 1917; renumbered *Ha.8* in 1923; stricken 1 December, 1928 and BU.

Vickers C(3) Type Ha. 7-8 (c. 1925)

Name	Builder	Date	Displ	Length ft in	Beam ft in	Draught ft in	Machinery	SHP	Speed	Fuel	Radius	Armament	Comp
VICKERS/ KAWASAKI Type *No. 13*	Kawasaki, Kobe	1910–1912	304 surf 340 subm	126 9 oa 125 pp	12 7	10 0	1-shaft petrol engine 1 electric motor	1000 bhp 300 ehp	10.8 8	17.8 oil —	? ?	2 × 18in TT 2 torpedoes	26

GENERAL NOTES
Ordered under the 1910 Programme as a Japanese revision of the original Vickers design. She was a single-hulled boat similar to the 'C' Class.

CAREER
Launched 18 July, 1912 and completed 30 September, 1912; renumbered *Ha.6* in 1923; stricken 1 December, 1928 and BU.

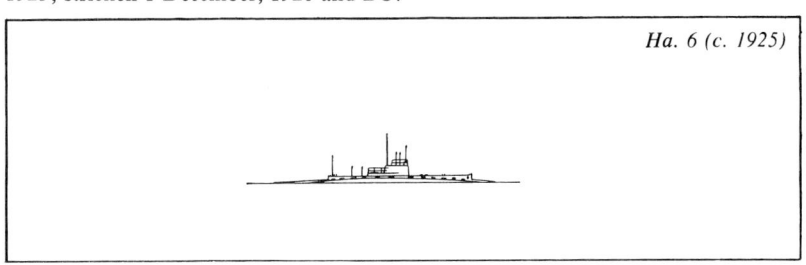

Ha. 6 (c. 1925)

The Kaigun Holland submarine *No. 6*, the first submarine to be built in Japan. She is seen here at Yokosuka in 1907, shortly after completion. (Shizuo Fukui.)

Name	Builder	Date	Displ	Length ft in	Beam ft in	Draught ft in	Machinery	SHP	Speed	Fuel	Radius	Armament	Comp
SCHNEIDER-LAUBEUF Type *No. 14 (i) No. 15*	Schneider, Chalons-sur-Saone	1913–1917	457 F 418 surf 665 subm	186 1 oa 184 4 pp	17 1	10 2	2-shaft Schneider Diesel engine 2 electric motors	2000 bhp 850 ehp	17 10	32 oil —	2050 @ 10 60 @ 4	4 × 18in TT 8 torpedoes 1 × 2pdr AA	30 approx

SUBMARINES 161

Name	Builder	Date	Displ	Length ft in	Beam ft in	Draught ft in	Machinery	SHP	Speed	Fuel	Radius	Armament	Comp
No. 14 (ii)	Kure DY	1918–1920	529 F 480 surf 737 subm	192 3 oa	17 0	10 8	2-shaft Schneider Diesel engine 2 electric motors	1800 bhp 850 ehp	16½ 9½	35 oil	2050 @ 10 60 @ 4	6 × 18in TT 8 torpedoes 1 MG	30 approx

GENERAL NOTES
Two boats were ordered from France, under the 1912 Programme, of which one was taken over by the French Navy, and one was a replacement ordered in 1916. They were the first sea-going submarines built for the Japanese Navy. The replacement for *No. 14* was built under licence in Japan, but some improvements were incorporated, making her somewhat larger than her sisters.

ARMAMENT
In 1919 *No. 14 (i)* and *No. 15* were armed with 1 × 3in 40-cal deck gun.

CAREERS
No. 14 (i)
Laid down in November 1913 but taken over for French Navy in June 1915; launched July 1915 as *Armide* and commissioned June 1916; stricken July 1932.

No. 15
Launched 7 April, 1914 and completed 20 July, 1917; renumbered *Ha.10* in 1923; stricken 1 December, 1928 and BU.

No. 14 (ii)
Ordered as a replacement for the previous *No. 14*; launched 8 July, 1918 and completed 30 April, 1920; renumbered *Ha.9* in 1923; stricken 1 December, 1928 and BU.

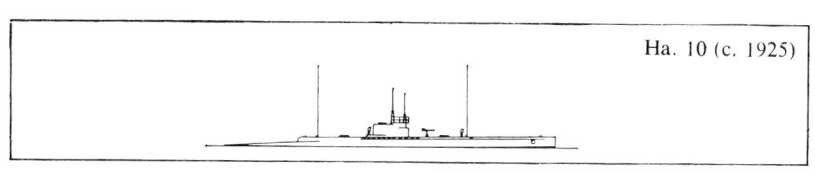

Ha. 10 (c. 1925)

Name	Builder	Date	Displ	Length ft in	Beam ft in	Draught ft in	Machinery	SHP	Speed	Fuel	Radius	Armament	Comp
FIAT-LAURENTI Type Nos. 18, 21	Kawasaki, Kobe	1917–1920	717 F 689 surf 1047 subm	215 1 oa 198 7 pp	19 11	13 9	2-shaft Fiat Diesels 2 Savigliano electric motors	2800 bhp 1200 ehp	13 8	58.4 oil	3500 @ 10 75 @ 4	5 × 18in TT 8 torpedoes 1 MG	43
FIAT-LAURENTI Type Nos. 31–33	Kawasaki, Kobe	1919–1922	74 F 689 surf 1047 subm	215 1 oa 198 7 pp	19 11	13 3	2-shaft Fiat Diesels 2 Savigliano electric motors	2600 ehp 1200 ehp	18 8	58.4 oil	3500 @ 10 75 @ 4	5 × 18in TT 8 torpedoes	43

GENERAL NOTES
Two classes were built under licence from the Italian Fiat-Laurenti firm, 2 boats under the 1915–16 Programme and 3 under the 1918 Programme. They had a diving depth of 130ft, and they mark the beginning of Japan's interest in ocean-going submarines. They were of single-hull design.

ARMAMENT
Shortly after completion they were armed with 1 × 3in 40-cal deck gun.

CAREERS
No. 18
Launched 28 July, 1919 and completed 31 March, 1920; renumbered *RO.1* in 1924; stricken 1930.

No. 21
Launched 22 November, 1919 and completed 20 April, 1920; renumbered *RO.2* in 1924; stricken 1930.

No. 31
Launched 10 March, 1921; completed 17 July, 1922; renumbered *RO.3* 1 November, 1924; stricken 1930.

No. 32
Launched 22 June, 1921; completed 5 May, 1922; renumbered *RO.4* 1 November, 1924; stricken 1930.

No. 33
Launched 17 September, 1921; completed 9 March, 1922; renumbered *RO.5* 1 November, 1924; stricken 1930.

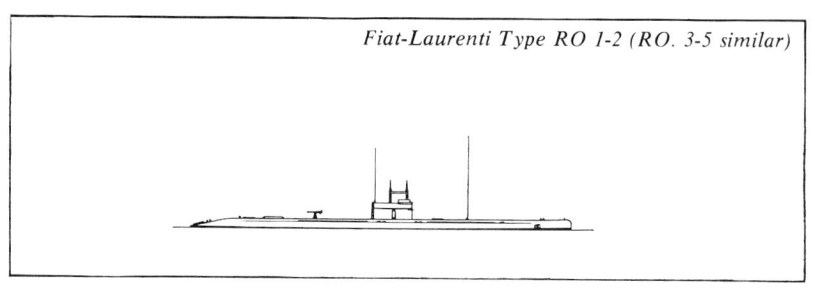

Fiat-Laurenti Type RO 1-2 (RO. 3-5 similar)

Name	Builder	Date	Displ	Length ft in	Beam ft in	Draught ft in	Machinery	SHP	Speed	Fuel	Radius	Armament	Comp
VICKERS L (1) Type Nos. 25, 26	Mitsubishi, Kobe	1918–1920	902 max 893 surf 1195 subm	231 7 oa 220 3 pp	23 6	12 9	2-shaft Vickers Diesels 2 electric motors	2400 bhp 1600 ehp	17 8	75 oil	5500 @ 10 80 @ 4	6 × 18in TT 10 torpedoes 1 × 3.1in 28-cal AA 1 MG	48

GENERAL NOTES
These boats were built under the 1917 Programmes to the same design as the British 'L' Class. They were double-hulled and could dive to 200ft. They were later rated as 2nd Class submarines. *Ro.51* refitted 1928.

CAREERS
No. 25
Launched 25 October, 1919 and completed 30 June, 1920; renumbered *RO.51* 1 November, 1924 and stricken 1940.

162 SUBMARINES

No. 26
Launched 9 March, 1920 and completed 30 November, 1920; sank 29 October, 1923 in Kure as a result of an error in flooding; raised 17 November the same year and used for trials; renumbered *RO.52* 1 November, 1924; stricken 1 April, 1932.

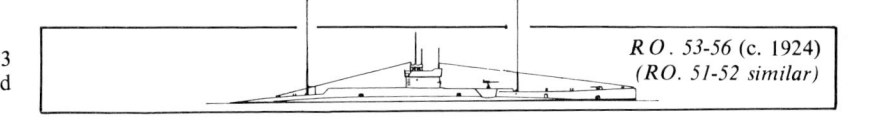

RO. 53-56 (c. 1924)
(RO. 51-52 similar)

Name	Builder	Date	Displ	Length ft in	Beam ft in	Draught ft in	Machinery	SHP	Speed	Fuel	Radius	Armament	Comp
VICKERS L (2) Type Nos. 27–30	Mitsubishi, Kobe	1919–1921	902 max 893 surf 1195 subm	231 7 oa 220 3 pp	23 6	12 11	2-shaft Vickers Diesels 2 electric motors	2400 bhp 1600 ehp	17 8	80 oil –	5500 @ 10 80 @ 4	4 × 18in TT 10 torpedoes 1 × 3.1in 40-cal 1 MG	48

GENERAL NOTES
Built under the 1918 programme to Vickers plans based on the British 'L' Class, they were slightly improved versions of the previous group. *RO.54–56* were refitted in 1927 and *RO.53* in 1928.

CAREERS
No. 27
Launched 6 July, 1920 and completed 10 March, 1921; renumbered *RO.53* 1 November, 1924 and stricken 1938.

No. 28
Launched 13 October, 1920 and completed 10 September, 1921; renumbered *RO.54* 1 November, 1924 and stricken 1939.

No. 29
Launched 10 February, 1921 and completed 15 November, 1921; lost by accident 29 October, 1923 off Kobe, but raised and renumbered *RO.55* 1 November, 1924; stricken 1939.

No. 30
Launched 11 May, 1921 and completed 16 January, 1922; renumbered *RO.56* 1 November, 1924 and stricken 1940.

Name	Builder	Date	Displ	Length ft in	Beam ft in	Draught ft in	Machinery	SHP	Speed	Fuel	Radius	Armament	Comp
VICKERS L (3) Type Nos. 46, 47, 57	Mitsubishi, Kobe	1920–1922	897 max 889 surf 1195 subm	250 0 oa 242 9 wl	23 6	13 0	2-shaft Vickers Diesels 2 electric motors	2400 bhp 1600 ehp	17 8	98 oil –	7000 @ 10 85 @ 4	4 × 21in TT 10 torpedoes 1 × 3.1in 40-cal 1 MG	48

GENERAL NOTES
Built under the 1919–20 Programme as slightly improved editions of the previous groups. In 1933 the fuel was increased to 117ts. *RO.57–59* were refitted in 1934.

CAREERS
No. 46
Launched 3 December, 1921 and completed 30 July, 1922; renumbered *RO.57* 1 November 1924; training boat in 1941; stricken 1 May 1945 and used for training midget submarine crews at Shodojima; BU in 1946.

No. 47
Launched 2 March, 1922 and completed 25 November, 1922; renumbered *RO.58* 1 November 1924; training boat in 1941; stricken 1 May, 1945; at Yokosuka August 1945; BU in 1946.

Nos. 48–50
Contracts cancelled 1920 and replaced by minelayers.

No. 57
Launched 28 June, 1922 and completed 20 March, 1923; renumbered *RO.59* 1 November, 1924; training boat in 1924; stricken 1 May, 1945 and used as a training hulk at the Submarine School, Otake; BU.

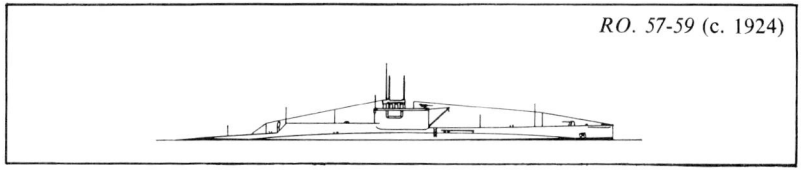

RO. 57-59 (c. 1924)

Name	Builder	Date	Displ GRT	Length ft in	Beam ft in	Draught ft in	Machinery	SHP approx	Speed	Fuel	Radius	Armament	Comp
VICKERS L (4) Type Nos. 59, 72, 73 No. 84 RO. 64–68	Mitsubishi, Kobe	1921–1927	996 max 988 surf 1322 subm	250 0 oa 243 0 wl	24 2	12 4	2-shaft Vickers Diesels 2 electric motors	2400 bhp 1600 ehp	16 8	101 oil –	7000 @ 10 85 @ 4	6 × 21in TT 10 torpedoes 1 × 3.1in 28-cal AA 1 MG	47–60

GENERAL NOTES
This class was the last to be built under licence from British plans. They were a modification of the Vickers design and were built under the 1921-8 Programme. Later rated as 2nd Class submarines. *RO.60–62* were rebuilt in 1928 and *Ro. 63–68* were re-fitted in 1934.

CAREERS
No. 59
Launched 22 December, 1922 and completed 17 September 1923; renumbered *RO.60* 1 November, 1924; wrecked 29 December, 1941 at about 02.00 hrs on the northern point of Kwajalein Atoll (09° N, 167° 30′ E).

Nos. 60–61
Contracts cancelled in 1921.

No. 72
Launched 19 May, 1923 and completed February 1924; renumbered *RO.61* shortly afterwards; sunk 31 August, 1942 by US destroyer *Reid* and aircraft off Atka (52° 36′ N, 173° 57′ W).

No. 73
Launched 19 September, 1923 and completed 23 July, 1924; renumbered *RO.62* shortly afterwards; training boat 15 November, 1942; surrendered at Kure in August 1945 and BU.

No. 84
Launched 24 January, 1924 and completed 20 December, 1924 as *RO.63*; training boat 25 September, 1942; surrendered at Hure August 1945 and BU.

RO.64
Launched 19 August, 1924 and completed 30 April, 1925; training boat 25 September,

SUBMARINES 163

1942; sunk by mine 12 April, 1945 at 14.28 hrs off Kobe (34° 14′ N, 132° 16′ E).
RO.65
Launched 25 September, 1925 and completed 30 June, 1926; sank 4 November, 1942 after diving onto a reef while avoiding aircraft attack in Kiska Harbour (51° 58′ N, 177° 33′ E).
RO.66
Launched 25 October, 1926 and completed 28 July, 1927; sunk 17 December, 1941 at 20.30 hrs after collision with *RO.62* off Wake (19° 10′ N, 166° 28′ E).
RO.67
Launched 18 March, 1926 and completed 15 December, 1926; training boat 15

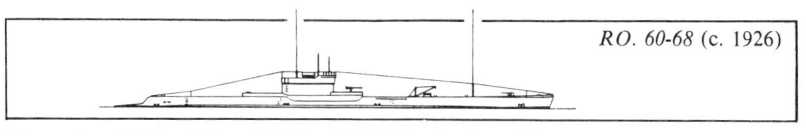

RO. 60-68 (c. 1926)

November, 1942; stricken 20 July, 1945 following bomb damage; at Sasebo in August 1945 and later BU.
RO.68
Launched 23 February, 1925 and completed 27 October, 1926; training boat 25 September, 1942; surrendered at Maizuru in August 1945; BU.

Name	Builder	Date	Displ	Length ft in	Beam ft in	Draught ft in	Machinery	SHP	Speed	Fuel	Radius	Armament	Comp
KAICHU (1) Type *Nos. 19; 20*	Kure DY	1917–1919	735 F 720 surf 1030 subm	227 0 oa	20 10	11 3	2-shaft Diesels	2600 bhp	18	60 oil	4000 @ 10	6 × 18in TT 10 torpedoes 1 × 3.1in 28-cal AA	44
							2 electric motors	1200 ehp	9	–	85 @ 4		

GENERAL NOTES
Built under the 1916 Programme and later rated as 2nd Class boats. The name is derived from Kai (gun)-chu = medium Navy design, but they were based on the Schneider-Laubeuf double-hulled designs with stronger pressure hull.

No. 20
Launched 1 December, 1917 and completed 18 September, 1919; renumbered *RO.12* in 1924; stricken 1931.

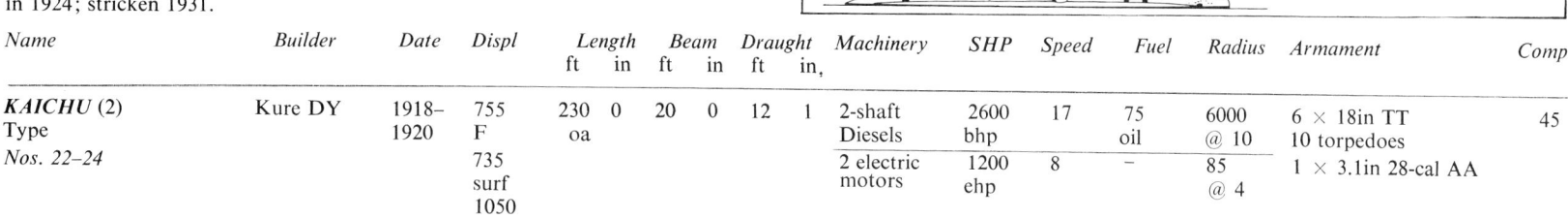

CAREERS
No. 19
Launched 15 October, 1917 and completed 31 July, 1919; renumbered *RO.11* in 1924; stricken 1931.

Kaichu (1) Type. RO. 11-12

Name	Builder	Date	Displ	Length ft in	Beam ft in	Draught ft in	Machinery	SHP	Speed	Fuel	Radius	Armament	Comp
KAICHU (2) Type *Nos. 22–24*	Kure DY	1918–1920	755 F 735 surf 1050 subm	230 0 oa	20 0	12 1	2-shaft Diesels	2600 bhp	17	75 oil	6000 @ 10	6 × 18in TT 10 torpedoes 1 × 3.1in 28-cal AA	45
							2 electric motors	1200 ehp	8	–	85 @ 4		

GENERAL NOTES
Slightly improved versions of the previous class.

CAREERS
No. 22
Launched 31 March, 1919 and completed 17 February, 1921; renumbered *RO.14* 1 November, 1924; stricken 1931 but was still in existence in 1940 as a training hulk; BU at Harima in September 1948.
No. 23
Launched 26 August, 1919 and completed 30 September, 1920; renumbered *RO.13* 1 November, 1924; stricken 1 April, 1932.

No. 24
Launched 14 October, 1920 and completed 30 June, 1921; renumbered *RO.15* 1, November, 1924; stricken 1931.

Kaichu (2) Type. RO. 13-15

Name	Builder	Date	Displ	Length ft in	Beam ft in	Draught ft in	Machinery	SHP	Speed	Fuel	Radius	Armament	Comp
KAICHU (3) Type *Nos. 34–37* *Nos. 38–41* *Nos. 42–43*	Kure DY Yokosuka DY Sasebo DY	1920–1922	755 F 736 surf 1050 subm	230 0 oa 220 0 pp	20 1	12 1	2-shaft Diesels	2600 bhp	17	75 oil	6000 @ 10	6 × 18in TT 10 torpedoes 1 × 3.1in 28-cal AA	45
							2 electric motors	1200 ehp	8	–	85 @ 4		

GENERAL NOTES
Built under the 1918 Programme as slightly improved versions of the previous class.

CAREERS
No. 34
Launched 24 February, 1921 and completed 20 October, 1921; renumbered *RO.17* 7 November, 1924; stricken 1 April, 1932.
No. 35
Launched 25 March, 1921 and completed 15 December, 1921; renumbered *RO.18* 1 November, 1924; stricken 1 April, 1936.
No. 36
Launched 28 December, 1920 and completed 15 March, 1922; renumbered *RO.19* 1 November, 1924; stricken 1 April, 1936 and became training hulk *Haikan No. 4* at

Tokuyama; BU at Naniwa in 1948.
No. 37
Launched 22 April, 1921 and completed 29 April, 1922; renumbered *RO.16* 1 November, 1924; stricken 1 April, 1936.
No. 38
Launched 26 October, 1920 and completed 1 February, 1922; renumbered *RO.20* 1 November, 1924; stricken 1 April, 1932 and sold to Kanagawa Prefecture for 5000 Yen and used for fishery conservation (scuttled to provide a breeding-place).
No. 39
Launched 26 October, 1920 and completed 1 February, 1922; renumbered *RO.21* 1 November, 1924; stricken 1 April, 1932 and sold with *RO.20* to Kanagawa Prefecture for use in fishery conservation as *RO.20*.

No. 40
Launched 15 October, 1921; completed 10 October, 1922; renumbered *RO.22* 1 November, 1924; stricken 1 April, 1932.
No. 41
Launched 25 October, 1921; completed 28 April, 1923; renumbered *RO.23* 1 November, 1924; stricken 1 April, 1932.
No. 42
Launched 8 December, 1919 and completed 30 November, 1920; renumbered *RO.24* 1 November, 1924; stricken 1 April, 1932.
No. 43
Launched 17 July, 1920 and completed 25 October, 1921; renumbered *RO.25* 1 November, 1924; sunk 19 March, 1924 in collision with light cruiser *Tatsuta* off Sasebo; raised 25 April, 1924 and used for trials at Sasebo; stricken 1 April, 1936 and BU.

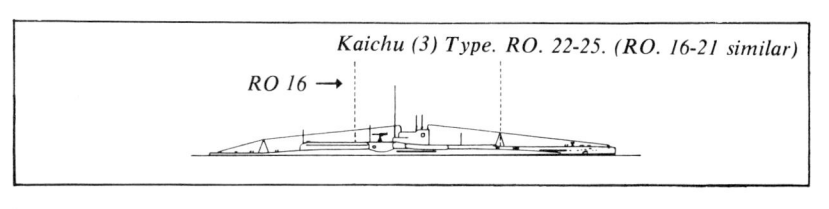

Kaichu (3) Type. RO. 22-25. (RO. 16-21 similar)

Name	Builder	Date	Displ	Length ft in	Beam ft in	Draught ft in	Machinery	SHP	Speed	Fuel	Radius	Armament	Comp
KAICHU (4) Type Nos. 45, 62 No. 58	Sasebo DY Yokosuka DY	1921–1923	770 F 746 surf 1080 subm	243 6 oa 230 0 pp	20 1	12 3	2-shaft Sulzer Diesels 2 electric motors	2600 bhp 1200 ehp	16 8	75 oil –	6000 @ 10 85 @ 4	4 × 21in TT 8 torpedoes 1 MG 1 × 3.1in 28-cal AA	45

GENERAL NOTES
These were slightly improved editions of the previous class, *RO.26* refitted 1932, *RO.27* and *RO.28* in 1934.

CAREERS
No. 45
Launched 18 October, 1921 and completed 25 January, 1923; renumbered *RO.26* 1 November, 1924; stricken 1 April, 1940 and BU at Kanagawa in April 1948.
No. 58
Launched 22 July, 1922 and completed 13 July, 1924; renumbered *RO.27* 1 November, 1924; stricken 1 April, 1940 and BU at Iwakuni in October 1947.

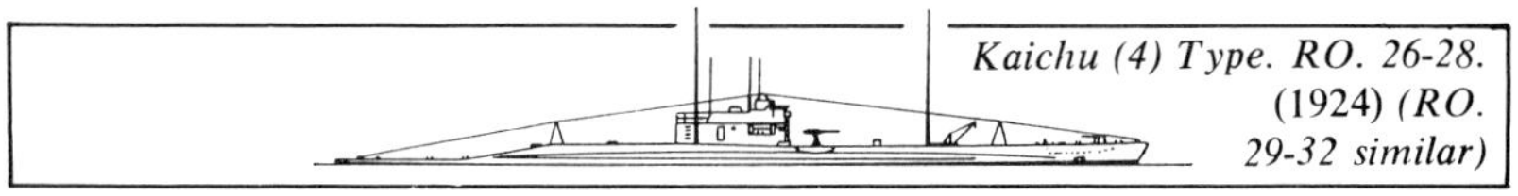

Kaichu (4) Type. RO. 26-28. (1924) (RO. 29-32 similar)

No. 62
Launched 13 April, 1922 and completed 30 November, 1923; renumbered *RO.28* 1 November, 1924; stricken 1 April, 1940 and BU at Kumagaya Gumi in May 1948.
Nos. 63–67
Contracts cancelled 1922 to comply with the Washington Treaty (*No. 64* probably never ordered).

Name	Builder	Date	Displ	Length ft in	Beam ft in	Draught ft in	Machinery	SHP	Speed	Fuel	Radius	Armament	Comp
KAITOKU CHU Type Nos. 68–71	Kawasaki, Kobe	1921–1923	665 surf 1030 subm	243 6 oa 230 0 pp	20 1	12 3	2-shaft Fiat Diesels 2 electric motors	1200 bhp 1200 ehp	13 8	113 oil	8000 @ 10 85 @ 4	4 × 21in TT 8 torpedoes 1 × 4.7in 45-cal 1 MG	43

GENERAL NOTES
These boats were built under the 1918 Programme and were later rated as 2nd Class. Kai-toku-chu = medium special Navy type, and the design was based on French Schneider-Laubeuf plans, with a double hull. They had heavier armament than the Kaichu Types 1–5, but at the expense of reduced surface speed.

CAREERS
No. 68
Launched 5 December, 1922 and completed 15 September, 1923; renumbered *RO.29* 1 November, 1924; stricken 1 April, 1936.
No. 69
Launched 18 January, 1923 and completed 29 April, 1924; renumbered *RO.30* on 1 November in the same year; training duties 1940; stricken 1 April, 1942 and used as a stationary training hulk at the Submarine School, Otake; BU after August 1945.
No. 70
Launched February 1923; on 21 August, 1923 while running trials she was accidentally lost off Kobe; she was salvaged in November 1924 and returned to service 25 September, 1926; renumbered *RO.31* on 10 May, 1927; used for training, and stricken 25 May, 1945; surrendered at Sasebo September 1945 and scuttled there on 5 April, 1946 by US Navy.
No. 71
Launched 19 March, 1923 and completed 31 May, 1924; renumbered *RO.32* 1 November, 1924; training boat in 1940; stricken 1 April, 1942 and became a stationary hulk at the Submarine School, Otake; BU after August 1945.
Nos. 72–87
Cancelled 1922 to comply with the Washington Treaty: no contracts had been placed.

Name	Builder	Date	Displ	Length ft in	Beam ft in	Draught ft in	Machinery	SHP	Speed	Fuel	Radius	Armament	Comp
KAICHU (5) Type RO. 33 RO. 34	Kure DY Mitsubishi, Kobe	1933–1937	940 F 700 surf	248 4 oa 234 7 wl	21 11	12 11	2-shaft Diesels 2 electric motors	2900 bhp 1200 ehp	19 8.2	?	8000 @ 12 90 @ 3½	4 × 21in TT 10 torpedoes 1 × 3.1in 40-cal AA 1 × 13mm AA	42

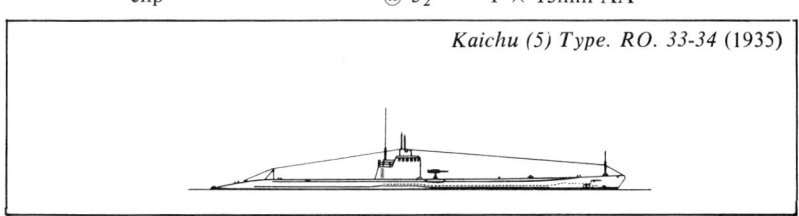

Kaichu (5) Type. RO. 33-34 (1935)

The 2nd Class submarine *RO.33* is seen here on completion in 1935. (Shizuo Fukui.)

SUBMARINES 165

General Notes
This class was built under the Fleet Replenishment Law of 1931, and were a purely Japanese design. They were experimental prototypes for an emergency wartime type. They were most successful, with good sea-keeping, and had a diving depth of 250ft.

Careers
RO.33
Launched 10 October, 1934 and completed 7 October, 1935; sunk 29 August, 1942 by Australian destroyer *Arunta* 10 m SE of Port Moresby (09° 36′ S, 147° 06′ E).
RO.34
Launched 12 December, 1935 and completed 31 May, 1937; sunk 5 April, 1943 near Russell Island, Solomons (08° 15′ S, 158° 55′ E) by US destroyer *O'Bannon*.

Name	Builder	Date	Displ	Length ft in	Beam ft in	Draught ft in	Machinery	SHP	Speed	Fuel	Radius	Armament	Comp
KAICHU (6) Type RO. 35–38 RO. 40, 41, 43 RO. 45–46, 48 RO. 39, 42 RO. 44, 47, 49 RO. 50, 55	Mitsubishi, Kobe Sasebo DY Tamano Z., Tamano	1941– 0000	1115 F 960 surf 1447 subm	259 2 oa 251 0 wl	23 1	13 2	2 shaft Diesels 2 electric motors	4200 bhp 1200 ehp	19.7 8	? –	5000 @ 16 45 @ 5	4 × 21in TT 10 torpedoes 1 × 3in AA 2 × 25mm AA	54

RO. 56 (ex- RO. 75) RO. 51–54 RO. 70–74 RO. 76–99 RO. 200–227 Nos. 715–723

General Notes
These 2nd Class submarines were built under the 1940–42 Programmes of the 4th and 5th Fleet Replenishment Laws and the wartime programmes. They were designed by K. Nakamura as an improved *Kaichu* (5) type, and introduced the Type '95' torpedo. They were the best Japanese design with good sea-keeping and manoeuvrability. Their diving depth was 260ft. At the end of 1943 the remainder of the class was cancelled.

Re-armament and Reconstruction
The 3in gun was not included in the original planned armament. In 1942–3 the conning-tower was rebuilt in *RO.41*, and *46–9*, etc. In these boats, the sides of the conning-tower were sloped to deflect enemy radar, but as this measure had little effect it was not extended to the rest of the class.

Careers
RO. 35
Launched 4 June, 1942 and completed 31 March, 1943; missing from 25 August, 1943 and probably sunk on that date by US destroyer *Patterson* 170 m SE of San Cristobal (12° 57′ S, 164° 23′ E).
RO. 36
Launched 14 October, 1942 and completed 31 May, 1943; sunk 13 June, 1944 by US destroyer *Melvin* at 23.30 hrs, 75 m E of Saipan (15° 21′ N, 147° E).
RO.37
Launched 30 June, 1942 and completed 30 June, 1943; sunk 22 January, 1944 by US destroyer *Buchanan* at 22.41 hrs 130 m ESE of San Cristobal (11° 47′ S, 164° 17′ E).
RO.38
Launched 24 December, 1942 and completed 31 July, 1943; went missing *en route* from Truk to Gilbert Island, after 19 November, 1943.
RO.39
Launched 6 March, 1943 and completed 12 September, 1943; sunk 2 February, 1944 by US destroyer *Walker* at 05.00 hrs, 10 m E of Wotje (09° 24′ N, 170° 32′ E).
RO.40
Launched 6 March, 1943 and completed 28 September, 1943; sunk 16 February, 1944 by US destroyer *Phelps* and minesweeper *Sage* at 17.50 hrs, 45 m NW of Kwajalein Atoll (09° 50′ N, 166° 35′ E).
RO.41
Launched 5 May, 1943 and completed 26 November, 1943; missing in Okinawa area from 22 March, 1945 and possibly sunk 23 March by US destroyer *Haggard* at 01.00 hrs, 320 m SE of Okinawa (22° 57′ N, 132° 19′ E).
RO.42
Launched 25 October, 1942 and completed 27 August, 1943; sunk 10/11 June, 1943 by US destroyer escort *Bangust* 90 m ENE of Roi, Kwajalein Atoll (10° 05′ N, 168° 22′ E).
RO.43
Launched 5 June, 1943 and completed 16 December, 1943; sunk 26 February, 1945 by aircraft of US escort carrier *Anzio* 50 m WNW of Iwo Jima (25° 07′ N, 140° 19′ E).
RO.44
Launched 1943 and completed 12 September, 1943; sunk 16 June, 1944 by US destroyer escort *Burden R. Hastings* 110 m E of Eniwetok (11° 13′ N, 164° 15′ E).
RO.45
Launched 1943 and completed 11 January, 1944; missing from 30 April, 1944 and possibly sunk that day at 07.00 hrs, 65 m SSW of Truk (06° 13′ N, 151° 19′ E) by US destroyers *McDonough* and *Stephen Potter* and aircraft from carrier *Monterey*.
RO.46
Launched 1943 and completed 11 February, 1944; missing from 17 April, 1945 and possibly sunk 25 April off Okinawa by US destroyer escort *Horace H. Bass*.
RO.47
Launched 1943 and completed 31 January, 1944; missing from 24 September, 1944 and possibly sunk 26 September by US destroyer escort *McCoy Reynolds* 80 m W of Yap (09° 19′ N, 136° 44′ E).
RO.48
Launched 1943 and completed 31 March, 1944; missing from 14 July, 1944 and possibly sunk at 08.75 hrs the same day by US destroyer escort *William C. Miller* 75 m W of Saipan (15° 18′ N, 144° 26′ E).
RO.49
Launched 1943 and completed 19 May, 1944; missing from 25 March, 1945 but possibly sunk 5 April at 08.00 hrs by US destroyer *Hudson* 60 m W of Okinawa (26° 22′ N, 126° 30′ E).
RO.50
Launched 1943 and completed 31 July, 1944; surrendered at Sasebo in September 1945; scuttled 1 April, 1946 near Goto by US Navy.
RO.51–54
Contracts cancelled 1943 and not laid down.
RO.55
Launched 1944 and completed 30 September, 1944; sunk 7 February, 1945 at 23.30 hrs by US destroyer escort *Thomason* off Iba, Luzon (15° 27′ N, 119° 25′ E).
RO.56
Launched 1944 and completed 15 November, 1944; missing from 18 March, 1945, and possibly sunk 9 April, at 07.00 hrs by US destroyers *Mertz* and *Monssen* 45 m E of Okinawa (26° 09′ N, 130° 21′ E).
RO.70–74
Contracts cancelled 1943, and none laid down.
RO.75
Renumbered *RO.56* in 1943 (see above).
RO.76–99
RO.200–227
Contracts cancelled 1943 before any had been laid down.
Hull Nos. 715–723 were projected in 1942 but contracts were not allocated.

Kaichu (6) Type. RO. 35–47 (1942-43)

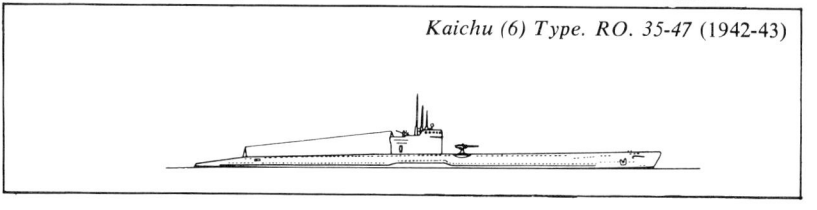

Name	Builder	Date	Displ	Length ft in	Beam ft in	Draught ft in	Machinery	SHP	Speed	Fuel	Radius	Armament	Comp
KAISHO Type RO. 100, 103 RO. 106, 107 RO. 101, 102 RO. 104, 105 RO. 108–117 I–IX	Kure DY Kawasaki, Kobe	1941– 1944	601 max 525 surf 782 subm	194 4 wl 188 4 pp	19 8	11 6	2-shaft Diesels 2 electric motors	1100 bhp 760 ehp	14.2 8	? –	3500 @ 12 60 @ 3	4 × 21in TT 8 torpedoes 2 × 25mm AA	38

GENERAL NOTES
These 2nd Class submarines were built under the 1940–41 Programme (4th Fleet Replenishment Law, War Programme). The name derives from Kai(gun)-sho = small Admiralty type, and they were designed to defend the small island air-bases to be established in the Pacific. They took 12 months to build, and their diving depth was 250ft.

CAREERS
RO.100
Launched 6 December, 1941 and completed 23 September, 1942; sunk by aircraft or mine 25 November, 1943 2 m W of Omai (06° 50′ S, 155° 58′ E).
RO.101
Launched 17 April, 1942 and completed 31 October, 1942; missing from 15 September, 1943, but probably sunk that day by US destroyer *Saufley* and aircraft 100 m E of San Cristobal (10° 57′ S, 163° 56′ E).
RO.102
Launched 17 April, 1942 and completed 17 November, 1942; missing from 9 May, 1943 but probably sunk 14 May by US *PT-150* and *PT-152* in Vitiaz Strait (06° 55′ S, 147° 34′ E).
RO.103
Launched 6 December, 1941 and completed 21 October, 1942; missing from 28 July, 1943 in Vanganu area.
RO.104
Launched 11 July, 1942; completed 25 February, 1943; sunk 23 May, 1944 by US DE *England* 250 m NNW of Kavieng (01° 26′ N, 149° 20′ E).
RO.105
Launched 11 July, 1942; completed 5 March, 1943; sunk 31 May, 1944 by US DE *England* 200 m NNW of Kavieng (08° 47′ N, 149° 56′ E).
RO.106
Launched 30 May, 1942; completed 26 December, 1942 sunk 22 May, 1944 by US DE *England* 250 m N of Kavienga (01° 40′ N, 150° 31′ E).
RO.107
Launched 30 May, 1942; completed 26 December, 1942; missing from 6 July, 1943 and probably sunk 12 July by US destroyer *Taylor* at 05.10 hrs 15 m E of Kolombangara (08° S, 157° 19′ E).
RO.108
Launched 26 October, 1942; completed 20 April, 1943; sunk 26 May, 1944 at 23.23 hrs 110 m NE of Manus Island by US DE *England* (00° 32′ S, 148° 35′ E).
RO.109
Launched 1942; completed 30 April, 1943; missing from 12 April, 1945 and probably sunk 29 April, 1945 by aircraft from US carrier *Tulagi* 220 m SE of Okinawa (24° 15′ N, 131° 16′ E).
RO.110
Launched 1943; completed 10 July, 1943; sunk 11 February, 1944 by Indian sloop *Jumna* and Australian sweepers *Ipswich* and *Launceston* 17 m S of Vizagapatam (17° 25′ N, 83° 21′ E).
RO.111
Launched 1943; completed 20 July, 1943; missing from 4 June, 1944 but probably sunk 10 June by US destroyer *Taylor* at 15.58 hrs 210 m NNW of Kavieng (00° 26′ N, 149° 16′ E).
RO.112
Launched 1943; completed 12 September, 1943; torpedoed 11 February, 1945 by US submarine *Batfish* at 22.02 hrs off Camiguin (18° 53′ N, 121° 50′ E).
RO.113
Launched 1943; completed 15 October, 1943; torpedoed by US submarine *Batfish* at 04.50 hrs 12 February, 1945 off Babuyah (19° 10′ N, 121° 23′ E).
RO.114
Launched 1943; completed 25 November, 1943; sunk 17 June, 1944 by US destroyers *Melvin* and *Wadleigh* at 01.45 hrs 80 m W of Tinian (15° 02′ N, 144° 10′ E).
RO.115
Launched 1943; completed 25 November, 1943; missing from 22 January, 1945 but probably sunk 31 January at 24.00 hrs by US destroyers *Jenkins*, *O'Bannon* and *Bell* and DE *Ulvert M. Moore* 125 m SW of Manila (13° 20′ N, 119° 20′ E).
RO.116
Launched 1943; completed 31 January, 1944; sunk 24 May, 1944 by US DE *England* at 02.00 hrs 225 m NNW of Kavieng (00° 53′ N, 149° 14′ E).
RO.117
Launched 1943; completed 31 January, 1944; sunk 17 June, 1944 by US Marine Corps aircraft 350 m SE of Saipan (11° 05′ N, 150° 31′ E).
Nos. I to IX were projected in 1942 but not begun.

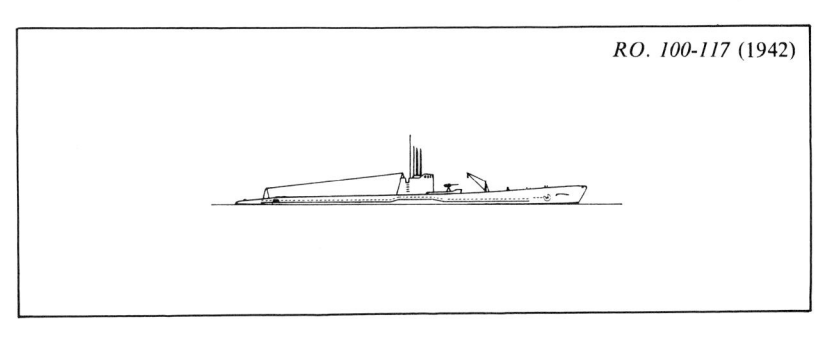

RO. 100-117 (1942)

Name	Builder	Date	Displ	Length ft in	Beam ft in	Draught ft in	Machinery	SHP	Speed	Fuel	Radius	Armament	Comp
SEN-YU-SHO Type Ha.101, 104 Ha. 106–108, Ha. 110 Ha. 102, 103, Ha. 105, 109 Ha.110–112, Ha. 113–200	Kawasaki, Tanagawa Mitsubishi, Kobe	1944– 1945	429 max 370 surf 493 subm	144 4 wl 138 5 pp	20 0	13 3	single-shaft Diesel 1 electric motor	400 bhp 150 ehp	10 5	? –	3000 @ 10 46 @ 2.3	60ts of cargo or 3630 cu ft 1 × 25mm AA	21

Ha. 101-200 (1944)

GENERAL NOTES
These 2nd Class submarines were built under the 1943–4 War Programme. The name is short for Sensuikan Yuso Sho = small supply submarines. They were intended as replacements for the large supply submarines which were planned in 1943. The construction was simple, and building time was only 5 months. They had 15 days' en-

durance and could dive to about 350ft. The programme was cut back at the end of 1944.

CAREERS

Ha.101
Launched 1944 and completed 22 November, 1944; surrendered August 1945 and at Uraga and BU.

Ha.102
Launched 1944 and completed 6 December, 1944; surrendered at Uraga August 1945 and BU.

Ha.103
Launched 1944 and completed 3 February, 1945; surrendered at Kure in August 1945; sunk 1 April, 1946 off Goto by US Navy (32° 30′ N, 128° 40′ E).

Ha.104
Launched 1944 and completed 1 December, 1944; surrendered at Uraga in August 1945 and BU.

Ha.105
Launched 1945 and completed 19 February, 1945; surrendered at Kure in August 1945; scuttled 1 April, 1946 off Goto by USN (32° 30′ N, 128° 40′ E).

Ha.106
Launched 1944 and completed 15 December, 1944 surrendered at Kure in August 1945; scuttled 1 April, 1946 by USN off Goto.

Ha.107
Launched 1945 and completed 7 February, 1945; surrendered August 1945 at Maizuru; scuttled 1 April, 1946 by USN off Goto.

Ha.108
Launched 1945 and completed 6 May, 1945; surrendered August 1945 at Maizuru; scuttled 1 April, 1946 by USN off Goto.

Ha.109
Launched 1945; completed 10 March; surrendered at Saeki in August 1945; scuttled off Goto 1 April, 1946 by USN.

Ha.110
Launched 1945 but still fitting out in August 1945; sprang a leak and sank at Kawasaki 16 April, 1946.

Ha.111
Launched 1945; completed 13 July; surrendered August at Saeki; scuttled off Goto by USN 1 April, 1946.

Ha.112
Launched 1945 and still fitting out in August; later BU.

Ha.113–200
Projected in 1944–5 but no contracts were placed.

Name	Builder	Date	Displ	Length ft in	Beam ft in	Draught ft in	Machinery	SHP	Speed	Fuel	Radius	Armament	Comp
Experimental Boat *No. 71*	Kure DY	1937–1938	213 max 195 surf 240 subm	140 5 oa	10 10	10 2	single-shaft Daimler-Benz Diesel	1200 bhp	18	16 oil	3830 @ 12½	3 × 18in TT 3 torpedoes	11
							1 electric motor	1800 ehp	25	—	33 @ 7		

GENERAL NOTES

This experimental boat was given the camouflage designation of *Vessel No. 71*. She was the first Japanese submarine built for maximum submerged speed, but she had no influence on designs outside Japan. She was a single-hulled boat with a diving depth of 280ft.

MACHINERY

She was originally meant to have Daimler-Benz Diesels but when these were not delivered she was engined with Japanese Diesels. Her speed was then 13.2/21.3 knots with 300/1200 bhp; endurance was 2200 nm at 12 knots (surf) and 38 nm at 7 knots (subm).

CAREER

Began December 1937; launched (lowered into water by crane) complete in August 1938; scrapped after completion of trials in 1940.

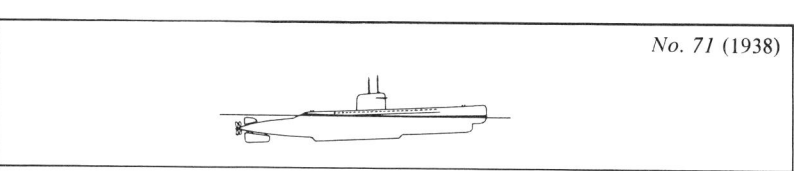

No. 71 (1938)

Name	Builder	Date	Displ	Length ft in	Beam ft in	Draught ft in	Machinery	SHP	Speed	Fuel	Radius	Armament	Comp
SEN-TAKA-SHÔ Type Ha.201–205 Ha.207–210 Ha.215–219 Ha.228–232 Ha.241–245 Ha.254–258 Ha.267–271 Ha.206, Ha.211 Ha.220, Ha.222 Ha.233, Ha.235 Ha.246 Ha.212, Ha.221 Ha.223, Ha.234 Ha.236 Ha.247–249 Ha.259–262 Ha.272–275 Ha.213, Ha.214 Ha.224–227 Ha.237–240 Ha.250–253 Ha.263–266 Ha.276–279	Sasebo DY Kawasaki, Tanagawa Kawasaki, Kobe Mitsubishi, Kobe	1945	377 max 320 surf 440 subm	146 8 wl 164 0 pp	13 1	11 3	single-shaft Diesel	400 bhp	10½	?	3000 @ 10	2 × 21in TT 4 torpedoes 1 × .303in MG	22
							1 electric motor	1250 ehp	13	—	100 @ 2		

GENERAL NOTES

These small 2nd Class submarines were meant for coastal operations and were built under the 1943–4 Programme. The designation is short for Sensui Taka Sho = small fast submarines. They were 'true' submarines designed for 15 days submerged endurance. The diving depth was 330ft. The hull was welded and built in sections at various yards, and the time taken was as follows: Sasebo 5 months, Mitsubishi 4 and Kawasaki 4, making a total of 13 months.

MACHINERY

On trials they made 13½ knots and had an endurance of 5500 nm, considerably in excess of the designed figures.

CAREERS

Ha.201
Launched 1945, completed 31 May; surrendered August 1945 at Sasebo and scuttled 1 April, 1946 by US Navy off Goto.

Ha.202
Launched 1945, completed 31 May; scuttled as *Ha.201*.

Ha.203
Launched 1945, completed 26 June; surrendered August 1945; BU by Nishimura Zosen in 1948.

Ha.204
Launched 1945, completed 25 June; surrendered August 1945; wrecked 29 October, 1945 in Aburatsu Bay.
Ha.205
Launched 1945, completed 3 July, 1945; surrendered August 1945 at Sasebo and later BU.
Ha.206
Launched 10 July, 1945; surrendered incomplete August 1945 and lost in a storm at Kobe, 25 August.
Ha.207
Launched 1945 and surrendered incomplete at Sasebo; scuttled 5 April, 1946 by USN off Sasebo (33° 10′ N, 129° 43′ E).
Ha.208
Launched 1945 and surrendered incomplete at Sasebo; scuttled 1 April, 1946 by USN off Goto.
Ha.209
Launched 1945; completed 4 August, and surrendered at Shimonoseki; used as target by USN and BU in 1946 at Shimoneseki.
Ha.210
Launched 1945; completed 11 August, and scuttled 5 April, 1946 off Sasebo.
Ha.211
Launched 24 April, 1946 to clear slip, and hull BU.
Ha.212
Launched 25 June, 1945 and surrendered incomplete; BU.
Ha.213
Launched 29 July, 1945 and surrendered incomplete; BU.
Ha.214
Launched 15 August, 1935 and surrendered incomplete; BU.
Ha.215
Launched 15 June, 1945 but not completed; scuttled with *Ha.207*, etc.
Ha.216
Launched 1945 but not completed; scuttled with *Ha.207*, etc.
Ha.217
Launched 26 June, 1945 but not completed; scuttled with *Ha.207*, etc.
Ha.218
Launched 2 July, 1945 but not completed; hull wrecked in Sasebo harbour; BU December 1946.
Ha.219
Launched 12 July, 1945 but not completed; scuttled with *Ha.207*, etc.
Ha.220
BU on slip by Kawasaki in June 1946.
Ha.221
Launched 4 August, 1945 but not completed; BU.
Ha.222
BU on slip by Kawasaki in June 1946.
Ha.223–227
BU on slip by Kawasaki in June 1946.
Ha.228
Launched 18 July, 1945 but not completed; scuttled with *Ha.207*, etc.
Ha.229
Launched 27 July, 1945 but not completed; hull wrecked in Sasebo harbour, and BU December 1946.
Ha.230
Launched 1946 but not completed; hull wrecked as *Ha.229*.
Ha.231–233
BU on slip at Sasebo.
Ha.234
BU on slip by Kawasaki in June 1946.
Ha.235–236
BU on slip by Kawasaki.
Ha.237–240
BU on slip by Mitsubishi, Kobe in June 1946.
Ha.241–245
Ordered from Sasebo but not begun.
Ha.246
BU on slip by Kawasaki.
Ha.247–249, *Ha.259–262*, *Ha.272–275*
Ordered from Kawasaki but not begun.
Ha.250–253, *Ha.263–266*, *Ha.276–279*
Ordered from Mitsubishi but not begun.
Ha.254–258, *Ha.267–271*
Ordered from Sasebo DY but not begun.
Nos. I–X
Projected in 1945 but contracts not placed.

Ha. 201-271 (1945)

Name	Builder	Date	Displ	Length ft in	Beam ft in	Draught ft in	Machinery	SHP	Speed	Fuel	Radius	Armament	Comp
KAIDAI Type 1 *No. 44*	Kure DY	1921–1924	1500 max 1390 surf 2430 subm	300 0 oa 285 5 wl	28 11	15 1	4-shaft Sulzer Diesels 4 electric motors	5200 bhp 2000 ehp	20 10	338 oil —	20000 @ 10 100 @ 4	1 × 4.7in 40-cal 1 × 3.1in 40-cal AA 8 × 21in TT 24 torpedoes	60

GENERAL NOTES
1st Class or cruiser-type submarines laid down under the 1919 Programme. Kai(gun) Dai = large Admiralty type. She was an experimental boat based on the large British submarines, and could dive to about 200ft.

RECONSTRUCTION
In 1932 she had 2 Diesels and 2 propeller-shafts removed, and had the 3.1in gun removed.

CAREER
Launched 29 November, 1921; completed 20 June, 1924 as *No. 44*; renumbered *I.51* 1 November, 1924; relegated to training between 1930 and 1939 at Kure; stricken 1941.

I. 51 (1924)

Name	Builder	Date	Displ	Length ft in	Beam ft in	Draught ft in	Machinery	SHP	Speed	Fuel	Radius	Armament	Comp
KAIDAI Type 2 *Nos. 52–56*	Kure DY	1922–1925	1500 max 1390 surf 2500 subm	330 10 oa 310 4 wl	25 1	16 10	2-shaft Sulzer Diesels 2 electric motors	6800 bhp 2000 ehp	22 10	230 oil —	10000 @ 10 100 @ 4	1 × 4.7in 40-cal 1 × 3.1in 40-cal 8 × 21in TT 16 torpedoes	60

GENERAL NOTES
A 1st class cruiser-submarine built under the 1920 Programme, she was an experimental boat based on the German *U.139*. She was a double-hulled type with a diving depth of nearly 200ft.

CAREER
Launched 12 June, 1922 and completed 20 May, 1925 as *I.52*; refitted 1932; renumbered *I.152* on 20 May, 1942; put into reserve on 14 July the same year and then cannibalized; stricken and BU at Harima by September 1948.
Nos. 52–56 were stricken in 1922 under the Washington Treaty (the contract for *No. 52* had not been placed).

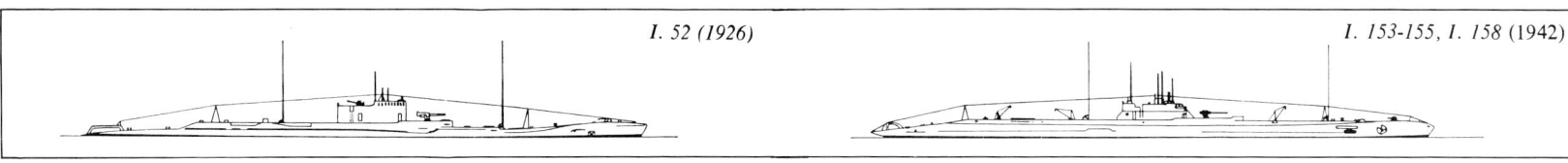

I. 52 (1926)   *I. 153-155, I. 158 (1942)*

Name	Builder	Date	Displ	Length ft in	Beam ft in	Draught ft in	Machinery	SHP	Speed	Fuel	Radius	Armament	Comp
KAIDAI Type 3A		1924– 1928	1800 max 1635 surf 2300 subm	330 10 oa 309 0 wl	26 2	15 10	2-shaft Kampon 8-cyl 2-stroke Diesels 2 electric motors	6800 bhp 1800 ehp	20 8	233 oil —	10000 @ 10 90 @ 3	1 × 4.7in 45-cal 8 × 21in TT 16 torpedoes	64
I.53 ex-*No. 64*	Kure DY												
I.55 ex-*No. 78*	Sasebo DY												
I.54 ex-*No. 77*	Yokosuka DY												
I.58													

GENERAL NOTES
1st Class submarines built under the 1923–8 Fleet Law. They were the first purely Japanese-designed cruiser-submarines, with higher surface speed to enable them to work with the Fleet.

APPEARANCE
There were minor differences between all four, in conning-tower and bow-shape.

RECONSTRUCTION
All refitted 1934–5.

CAREERS
I.53
Ordered as *No. 64* but launched as *I.53* on 5 August, 1925; completed 30 March, 1927; reduced to training 10 March, 1942 and renumbered *I.153* 20 May; laid up in reserve 31 January, 1944; damaged at Maizuru 30 July, 1945 by aircraft of US TF 38; BU in 1948.
I.54
Ordered as *No. 77* but launched 15 March, 1926 as *I.54*; completed 15 December, 1927; reduced to training 10 March, 1942 and renumbered *I.154* 20 May; laid up in Reserve 31 January, 1944; surrendered at Otake in August 1945; BU.
I.55
Ordered as *No. 78* but launched 21 September, 1925 as *I.555*; completed 5 September, 1927; training duties 10 March, 1942 and renumbered *I.155* 20 May; laid up in Reserve 20 July, 1945 and surrendered at Kure in August; BU.
I.58
Launched 3 October, 1925 and completed 15 May, 1928; renumbered *I.158* 20 May, 1942 and reduced to training 10 July; damaged 17 March, 1945 while at Mitsubishi's yard, Kobe and repaired as a 'Kaiten' carrier; back in service 20 April, and surrendered at Sasebo in September; scuttled 1 April, 1946 off Goto by USN.

Name	Builder	Date	Displ	Length ft in	Beam ft in	Draught ft in	Machinery	SHP	Speed	Fuel	Radius	Armament	Comp
KAIDAI Type 3B		1926– 1930	1800 max 1635 surf 2300 subm	331 4 oa 308 5 pp	25 11	15 11	2-shaft Kampon 8-cyl 2-stroke Diesels 2 electric motors	6800 bhp 1800 ehp	20 8	230 oil —	10000 @ 10 90 @ 3	1 × 4.7in 45-cal 1 × .303in MG 8 × 21in TT 16 torpedoes	63
I.56, I.57	Kure DY												
I.60, I.63	Sasebo DY												
I.59	Yokosuka DY												

GENERAL NOTES
1st Class Fleet submarines built under the 1923–8 Fleet Law, and very similar to the Type 3A apart from a different bow-form. The depth of hull was 22ft and they could dive to 200ft.

RECONSTRUCTION
I.59, I.63 refitted 1934, *I.56–57* in 1935 and *I.60* in 1937.
From mid-1944 schnorkels were fitted to the survivors and in 1945 they became 'Kaiten' carriers.

CAREERS
I.56
Launched 23 March, 1928 and completed 31 March, 1929; renumbered *I.156* on 20 May, 1942; reduced to training 10 July; became a 'Kaiten' carrier 1 April, 1945 and surrendered at Sasebo in September; scuttled off Goto 1 April, 1946 by USN.
I.57
Launched 1 October, 1928 and completed 24 December, 1929; renumbered *I.157* 20 May, 1942 and reduced to training 10 July; became a 'Kaiten' carrier 20 April, 1945 and surrendered at Sasebo in September; scuttled off Goto 1 April, 1946.
I.59
Launched 25 March, 1929 and completed 31 March, 1930; renumbered *I.159* on 20 May, 1942 and reduced to training 10 July; became a 'Kaiten' carrier 20 April, 1945 and surrendered at Sasebo in September; scuttled off Goto 1 April, 1946.
I.60
Launched 24 April, 1929 and completed December 1929; sunk 17 January, 1942 by British destroyer *Jupiter* at about 16.00 hrs 25 m WNW of Krakatoa (06° S, 105° E).
I.63
Launched 28 September, 1927 and completed 20 December, 1928; sunk 2 February, 1939 in collision with *I.60* off Kyushu in the Bungo Straits (81 dead); raised by repair ship *Asapi* 22 January, 1940 and BU at Kure.

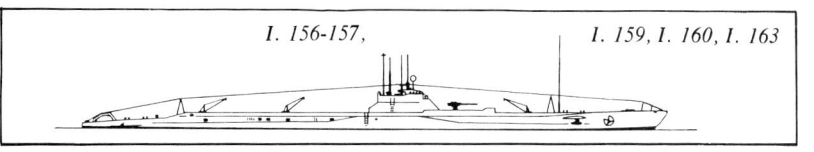

I. 156-157,   *I. 159, I. 160, I. 163*

I.59 was similarly renamed *I.159* in May 1942, shortly before being relegated to training. She is seen here on 14th July 1930 at Yokosuka. (Shizuo Fukui.)

The big submarine-cruiser *I.57* was completed in 1929, but was renumbered *I.157* in May 1942. (Shizuo Fukui.)

The Kaidai Type 4 boats of the *I.61* class were similar to the *I.57* class, and were renumbered in May 1942. The exception was *I.61*, seen here before the war, as she was lost accidentally shortly before the outbreak of war in 1941. (Shizuo Fukui.)

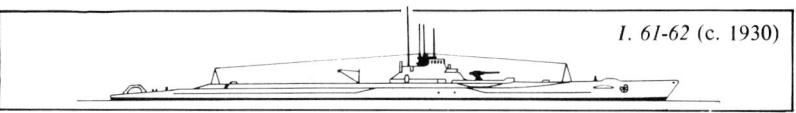

I. 61-62 (c. 1930)

Name	Builder	Date	Displ	Length ft in	Beam ft in	Draught ft in	Machinery	SHP	Speed	Fuel	Radius	Armament	Comp
KAIDAI Type 4 *I.61, I.62* *I.64*	Mitsubishi, Kobe Kure DY	1926–1930	1720 max 1635 surf 2300 subm	310 6 oa 298 6 pp	25 7	15 10	2-shaft Kampon 10-cyl 4-stroke Diesels 2 electric motors	6000 bhp 1800 ehp	20 8½	230 oil	10800 @ 10 60 @ 3	1 × 4.7-in 45-cal 1 × .303in MG 6 × 21in TT 14 torpedoes	58

GENERAL NOTES
Improved Type 3A and B built under the same Fleet Law. Their diving depth was about 200ft.

RECONSTRUCTION
All refitted 1936.

CAREERS
I.61
Launched 12 November, 1927 and completed 6 April, 1929; sunk 2 October, 1941 in collision with a gunboat off Iki (approx 33° 40′ N, 129° 40′ E); raised February 1942 and BU at Sasebo.
I.62
Launched 29 November, 1928 and completed 24 April, 1930; renumbered *I.162* 20 May, 1942; reduced to training 1 July, 1944; became a 'Kaiten' carrier 1 April, 1945 and surrendered at Sasebo in September; scuttled off Goto 1 April, 1946.
I.64
Launched 5 October, 1929 and completed 30 August, 1930; torpedoed 17 May, 1942 by US submarine *Triton* 230 m SE of Kagoshima (29° 25′ N, 134° 09′ E); on 20 May she was renumbered *I.164* before her loss became known.

Name	Builder	Date	Displ	Length ft in	Beam ft in	Draught ft in	Machinery	SHP	Speed	Fuel	Radius	Armament	Comp
KAIDAI Type 5 *I.65* *I.66* *I.67*	Kure DY Sasebo DY Mitsubishi, Kobe	1929–1932	1705 max 1575 surf 2330 subm	310 6 oa 296 11 pp	26 11	15 5	2-shaft Kampon 8-cyl 2-stroke Diesels 2 electric motors	6800 bhp 1800 ehp	20½ 8.2	230 oil	10800 @ 10 60 3 @	1 × 3.9in 50-cal AA 1 × 12mm AA 1 × .303in MG 6 × 21in TT 14 torpedoes	62–82

GENERAL NOTES
These were improved versions of the Type 4 boats built under the 1927–31 Fleet Law, with a depth of hull of 23·13ft and a diving depth of 230ft.

RECONSTRUCTION
All refitted 1935. In 1945, *I.165* became a 'Kaiten' carrier.

CAREERS
I.65
Launched 2 June, 1931 and completed 1 December, 1932; renumbered *I.165* 20 May, 1942; reduced to training 15 December, 1944 but became a 'Kaiten' carrier on 1 April, 1945; lost at the end of June, probably sunk 27 June by US Marine Corps aircraft 450 m E of Saipan (15° 28′ N, 153° 39′ E).

I.66
Launched 2 June, 1931 and completed November 1932; renumbered *I.166* 20 May, 1942; torpedoed 17 July, 1944 at about 10.00 hrs by British submarine *Telemachus* off Singapore (01° 10′ N, 103° 45′ E).
I.67
Launched 7 April, 1931 and completed 8 August, 1932; lost accidentally 29 August, 1940 during fleet manoeuvres off Bonin Island (87 missing).

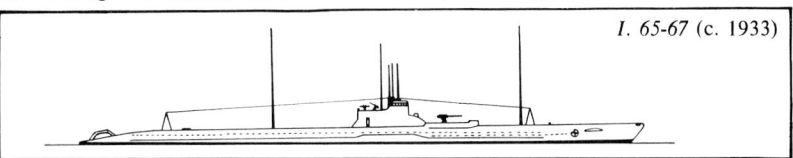

I. 65-67 (c. 1933)

Name	Builder	Date	Displ	Length ft in	Beam ft in	Draught ft in	Machinery	SHP	Speed	Fuel	Radius	Armament	Comp
KAIDAI Type 6A *I.68* *I.69, I.72* *I.70* *I.71, I.73*	Kure DY Mitsubishi, Kobe Sasebo DY Kawasaki, Kobe	1934–1938	1785 max 1400 surf 2440 subm	336 7 wl 322 10 pp	26 11	15 0	2-shaft Kampon 2-stroke Diesels 2 electric motors	9000 bhp 1800 ehp	23 8.2	341 —	14000 @ 10 65 @ 3	1 × 4in AA 1 × 13mm AA 6 × 21in TT 14 torpedoes	60–84

SUBMARINES 171

GENERAL NOTES
These improved Type 5 boats were built under the 1931 Fleet Law. Their pressure hulls were stronger and they introduced a new double-acting 2-stroke Diesel motor. The depth of hull was 23ft and the diving depth was nearly 250ft (*I.68* and *I.69* only 230ft). *I. 68–70* refitted 1938 and improvements made to machinery.

RECONSTRUCTION
I.171–173 were re-armed with 1 × 5in gun in place of the 4in AA weapon.

CAREERS
I.68
Launched 26 June, 1933, completed 31 July, 1934; renumbered *I.168* 20 May, 1942; missing from 27 July, 1943 and probably torpedoed at 18.09 hrs on that day by US submarine *Scamp* 60 m off New Hanover (2° 50′ S, 149° 01′ E).
I.69
Launched 15 February, 1934 and completed 28 September, 1935; renumbered *I.165* 20 May, 1942; sank 09.50 hrs 4 April 1944 at Truk after flooding during US air attacks and salvage proved impossible.
I.70
Launched 14 June, 1934 and completed 9 November, 1935; sunk 10 December, 1941 by aircraft from carrier *Enterprise* NE of Pearl Harbor (23° 45′ N, 155° 35′ W).
I.71
Launched 25 August, 1934 and completed 24 December, 1935; renumbered *I.171* 20 May, 1942; sunk 1 February, 1944 by US destroyers *Guest* and *Hudson* 15 m W of Buka Island (5° 37′ S, 154° 14′ E).
I.72
Launched 20 June, 1935, completed 7 January, 1937; renumbered *I.172* 20 May, 1942; missing from 28 October, 1942 but probably sunk 10 November by US destroyer *Southard* at 10.00 hrs off Cape Recherché (10° 13′ S, 161° 09′ E).
I.73
Launched 20 June, 1935, completed 7 January, 1937; torpedoed 27 January, 1942 by US submarine *Gudgeon* at 09.10 hrs 240 m W of Midway (28° 24′ N, 178° 35′ E).

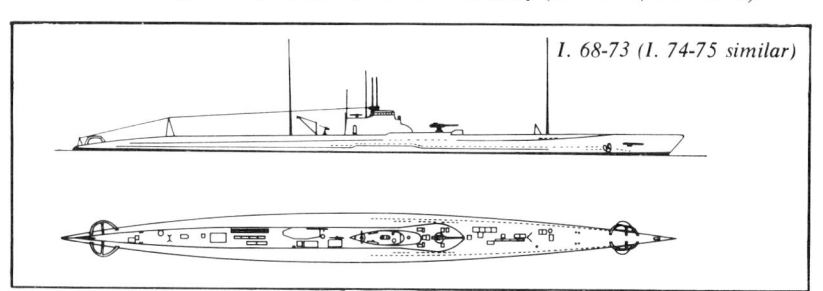

I. 68-73 (I. 74-75 similar)

The Kaidai series of submarine-cruisers was in production from 1921 to 1943. *I.73*, seen here on 24th April 1939 in Ariake Bay, was a 1,785-ton Kaidai Type 6A boat. (Shizuo Fukui.)

Name	Builder	Date	Displ	Length ft in	Beam ft in	Draught ft in	Machinery	SHP	Speed	Fuel	Radius	Armament	Comp
KAIDAI Type 6B		1934–1938	1810 max	336 7 wl	26 11	15 2	2-shaft Kampon 2-stroke Diesels	9000 bhp	23	350	10000 @ 16	1 × 5in 59-cal 2 × 13mm AA	60–84
I.74	Sasebo DY		1420 surf	322 10 pp			2 electric motors	1800 ehp	8		65 @ 3	6 × 21in TT 14 torpedoes	
I.75	Mitsubishi, Kobe		2564 subm										

CAREERS
I.74
Launched 28 March, 1937, completed 15 August, 1938; renumbered *I.174* 20 May, 1942; missing from 11 April, 1944, probably sunk 12 April by US Marine Corps aircraft N of Truk.

GENERAL NOTES
These were slightly improved Type 6A boats with stronger armament, built under the 1934 Fleet Law.

I.75
Launched 16 September, 1936, completed 18 December, 1938; renumbered *I.175* 20 November, 1942; missing from 30 January, 1944, probably sunk 4 February at 00.50 hrs by US destroyer *Charrette* and DE *Fair* 100 m NW of Jaluit (06° 48′ N, 168° 08′ E).

Name	Builder	Date	Displ	Length ft in	Beam ft in	Draught ft in	Machinery	SHP	Speed	Fuel	Radius	Armament	Comp
KAIDAI Type 7		1940–1943	1833 max	336 7 wl	27 1	15 1	2-shaft Kampon 2-stroke Diesels	8000 bhp	23.1	?	8000 @ 16	1 × 5in 50-cal 2 × 25mm AA	88
I.76–85 I–X	Various		1630 surf 2602 subm	323 6 pp			2 electric motors	1800 ehp	8		50 @ 5	6 × 21in TT 12 torpedoes	

GENERAL NOTES
These improved Type 6A boats were built under the 4th 1939 Fleet Law. They could dive to 260ft.

RE-ARMAMENT
Originally planned to have 4 × 25mm AA guns but because of production difficulties 2 were replaced by a 5in. The conning-tower was altered accordingly.

CAREERS
I.176
Launched 7 June, 1941 as *I.76* and completed 4 August, 1942 as *I.176*; sunk 16/17 May, 1944 by US destroyers *Franks*, *Haggard* and *Johnston* 150 m N of Cape Alexander (4° 01′ S, 156° 29′ E).

I.177
Launched 20 December, 1941 as *I.77* and completed 28 December, 1942 as *I.177*; missing from 24 September, 1944 off Palau, probably sunk 3 October by US DE *Samuel B. Miles* at 04.40 hrs 60 m NNE of Angaur (7° 48′ N, 133° 28′ E).
I.178
Launched 24 February, 1942 as *I.78*, and completed 26 December, 1942 as *I.178*; missing from end of May 1943, probably sunk 28 May by US SC.669 30 m W of Espiritu Santu (15° 35′ S, 166° 17′ E).
I.179
Launched 16 July, 1942 as *I.79* and completed 18 June, 1943 as *I.179*; sunk accidentally 14 July, 1943 off Akizaki (33° 40′ N, 132° 40′ N); raised 23 February, 1957 and used for trials by Maritime Self-Defence Force.

I.180
Launched 7 February, 1942 as *I.80* and completed 15 January, 1943 as *I.180*; sunk 26 April, 1944 at 01.07 hrs by US DE *Gilmore* 120 m SW of Kodiak (55° 10′ N, 155° 40′ W).

I.181
Launched 2 May, 1942 as *I.81* and completed 24 May, 1943 as *I.181*; missing from 13 January, 1944, probably sunk 16 January by US forces off Gali, New Guinea.

I.182
Launched 30 May, 1942 as *I.82* and completed 10 May, 1943 as *I.182*; missing from 22 August, 1943, probably sunk 1 September by US destroyer *Wadsworth* off Espiritu Santo (approx 15° 38′ S, 166° 57′ E).

I.183
Launched 21 January, 1943 as *I.83* and completed 31 October, 1943 as *I.183*; torpedoed 28/29 April, 1944 by US submarine *Pogy* 30 m S of Cape Ashizuri (32° 07′ N, 133° 03′ E).

I.184
Launched 12 December, 1942 as *I.84* and completed 15 October, 1943 as *I.184*; missing from 15 June, 1944, probably sunk 19 June by aircraft of US escort carrier *Suwannee* 20 m S of Guam (13° 01′ N, 144° 53′ E).

I.185
Launched 16 September, 1943 as *I.85* and completed 23 September, 1943 as *I.185*; missing from 15 June, 1944, probably sunk 22 June at 11.44 hrs by US destroyer *Newcomb* and sweeper *Chandler* 90 m ENE of Saipan (15° 50′ N, 147° 08′ E).

Nos. I–X
Projected in 1942 but not ordered.

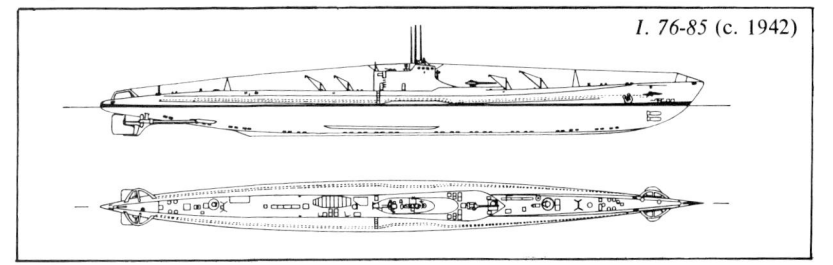

I. 76-85 (c. 1942)

Name	Builder	Date	Displ	Length ft in	Beam ft in	Draught ft in	Machinery	SHP	Speed	Fuel	Radius	Armament	Comp
JUNSEN Type 1 I.1–3 (ex-Nos. 74–76) I.4 (ex-*No. 61*)	Kawasaki, Kobe	1923–1929	2135 max 1970 surf 2791 subm	319 10 oa 308 5 wl	30 3	17 6	2-shaft M.A.N. 10-cyl 4-stroke Diesels 2 electric motors	6000 bhp 2600 ehp	18 8	545 oil 60	24400 @ 10 @ 3	2 × 5.5in 40-cal 1 × .303in MG 6 × 21in TT 20 torpedoes	62–92

GENERAL NOTES
These 1st Class cruiser-submarines were built under the 1922–8 Fleet Law and the 1923–8 Law. Jun (yo) Sen (suikan) = cruiser submarine. The hull and conning-tower were lightly armoured. They were double-hulled and were based on Krupp's plans for *U.142* type, with M.A.N. Diesels bought in Germany. From December 1924 to April 1925 construction was under the supervision of Dr. Ing. H. Techel, formerly of Krupp's Germania Yard. They could dive to 260ft.

MACHINERY
On trials, *I.1* made 18.8 knots and *I.2* and *I.3* made 19.1 knots.

RE-ARMAMENT
In 1939–41 they were re-armed with the Type '95' oxygen-driven torpedo.

CAREERS
I.1
Launched 15 October, 1924 as *No. 74* but completed 10 March, 1926 as *I.1*; wrecked 29 January, 1943 at 21.05 hrs in Kamimbo Bay (09° 13′ S, 159° 40′ E); she blew up after being heavily damaged by the New Zealand corvettes *Kiwi* and *Moa* (gunfire and ramming).

I.2
Launched 23 February, 1925 as *No.75* but completed 24 July, 1926 as *I.2*; sunk 7 April, 1944 by US destroyer *Saufley* at 07.23 hrs, 50 m WNW of New Hanover (2° 17′ S, 149° 14′ E).

I.3
Launched 8 June, 1925 as *No. 76* but completed 30 November, 1936 as *I.3*; torpedoed 9/10 December, 1942 by US PT-59, 3 m NE of Kamimbo Bay (09° 12′ S, 159° 42′ E).

I.4
Launched 22 May, 1928 as *No. 61* and completed 4 December, 1929; missing from 21 December, 1942, probably torpedoed 25 December by PT-122 off the mouth of the Kumusu River (8° 32′ S, 148° 17′ E).

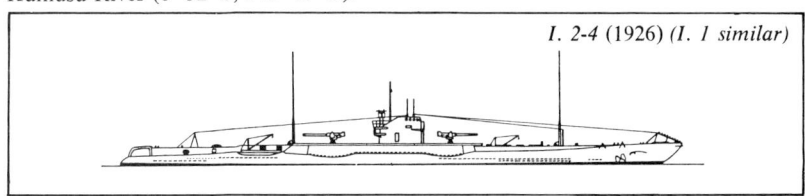

I. 2-4 (1926) (I. 1 similar)

Name	Builder	Date	Displ	Length ft in	Beam ft in	Draught ft in	Machinery	SHP	Speed	Fuel	Radius	Armament	Comp
JUNSEN Type 1M I.5	Kawasaki, Kobe	1930–1932	2243 max 2080 surf 2921 subm	308 7 wl 308 8 pp	29 8	17 8	2-shaft M.A.N. 10-cyl 4-stroke Diesels 2 electric motors	6000 bhp 2600 ehp	18 8	548 oil 60	24000 @ 10 @ 3	2 × 5.5in 40-cal 1 × 12mm AA 1 × .303in MG 6 × 21in TT 20 torpedoes, 1 seaplane	68–93

GENERAL NOTES
A 1st Class cruiser-submarine, developed from the *Junsen* Type 1, but with a hangar and crane for handling a seaplane. She was built under the 1927 Fleet Law. Like the Type 1 *Junsen* she had a hull-depth of 24.87ft.

RE-ARMAMENT AND RECONSTRUCTION
From February to July 1936, 1 × 5.5in gun was replaced by a 5in 40-cal AA gun. In 1940 the hangar and crane were removed, and she was armed with Type '95' torpedoes.

CAREER
Launched 19 June, 1931 and completed 31 July, 1932; missing from 19 July, 1944, probably sunk at 01.30 hrs that day by US DE *Wyman* 360 m of E Guam (13° 01′ N, 151° 58′ E).

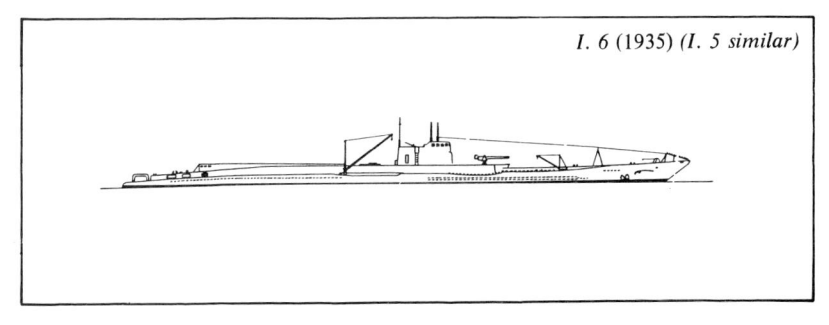

I. 6 (1935) (I. 5 similar)

SUBMARINES 173

Name	Builder	Date	Displ	Length ft in	Beam ft in	Draught ft in	Machinery	SHP	Speed	Fuel	Radius	Armament	Comp
JUNSEN Type 2 *I.6*	Kawasaki, Kobe	1932–1935	2243 max 1900 surf 3061 subm	323 2 oa 302 2 pp	29 9	17 5	2-shaft Kampon Diesels 2 electric motors	8000 bhp 2600 ehp	20 7½	580	20000 @ 10 60 @ 3	1 × 5in 40-cal AA 1 × 13mm MG AA 1 aircraft 6 × 21in TT 17 torpedoes	97

GENERAL NOTES

1st Class cruiser-submarine built under the 1st Fleet Replenishment Law of 1931. She was a double-hulled boat based on the German *U.139*, but incorporated a floatplane and catapult, the first Japanese submarine so equipped. The hull and conning-tower were lightly armoured. She was designed with 2 × 5in guns but was completed with only one, positioned forward of the conning-tower.

CAREER

Launched 31 March, 1934 and completed 15 May, 1935; missing from 30 June, 1944 in the Saipan area, and stricken 10 September.

Name	Builder	Date	Displ	Length ft in	Beam ft in	Draught ft in	Machinery	SHP	Speed	Fuel	Radius	Armament	Comp
JUNSEN Type 3 *I.7* *I.8*	Kure DY Kawasaki, Kobe	1934–1938	2525 max 2231 surf 3538 subm	355 4 oa 340 6 pp	29 10	17 3	2-shaft Kampon Diesels 2 electric motors	11200 bhp 2800 ehp	23 8	800	14000 @ 16 60 @ 3	2 × 5.5in 40-cal 2 × 13mm MG AA 6 × 21in TT 20 torpedoes 1 aircraft	100

GENERAL NOTES

1st Class cruiser-submarines built under the 2nd Fleet Replenishment Law of 1934. They were an enlarged and modified Kaidai type of purely Japanese design, with double hulls. The design included 2 hangars sunk in the deck casing, and the diving depth was 330ft. Both boats were fitted as flagships.

RE-ARMAMENT AND RECONSTRUCTION

In 1943 they had 2 × 25mm AA guns and 1 × 13mm. In 1945 *I.8* had the floatplane and catapult removed on conversion to a 'Kaiten' carrier; four 'Kaiten' were carried on the after casing.

CAREERS

I.7

Launched 3 July, 1935 and completed 31 March, 1937; badly damaged 22 June, 1943 by gunfire of US destroyer *Monaghan*, 10 m S of Cape Hita; at 23.00 hrs she ran aground 12 m SSW of Kiska (51° 49′ N, 177° 20′ E); the wreck was destroyed by US bombers on 5 July.

I.8

Launched 20 July, 1935 and completed 5 December, 1938; sunk 31 March, 1945 at 04.12 hrs 65 m SE of Okinawa (25° 29′ N, 128° 35′ E) by US destroyers *Morrison* and *Stockton*.

I. 7-8 (1939)

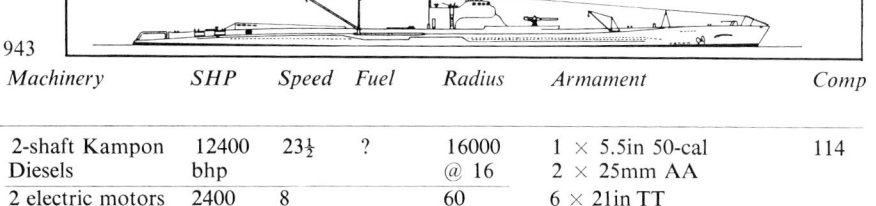

Name	Builder	Date	Displ	Length ft in	Beam ft in	Draught ft in	Machinery	SHP	Speed	Fuel	Radius	Armament	Comp
A(1) Type *I.9* *I.10*, *I.11* Nos. 700, 701	Kure DY Kawasaki, Kobe	1938–1942	2919 max 2434 surf 4149 subm	367 5 wl 356 8 pp	31 4	17 7	2-shaft Kampon Diesels 2 electric motors	12400 bhp 2400 ehp	23½ 8	?	16000 @ 16 60 @ 3	1 × 5.5in 50-cal 2 × 25mm AA 6 × 21in TT 18 torpedoes 1 aircraft	114

GENERAL NOTES

These 1st class cruiser-submarines were built under the 3rd and 4th Fleet Laws of 1937 and 1939. The double-hulled design was by Kogata and was based on the *Junsen* Type 3. They were fitted as flagships for submarine flotillas, and could dive to 330ft.

CAREERS

I.9

Launched 20 May, 1940 and completed 13 February, 1941; missing from 15 June, 1944, probably sunk 13 June, at 18.30 hrs by US destroyer *Frazier* 10 m NNE of Kiska (52° 08′ N, 177° 38′ E).

I.10

Launched 20 September, 1939 and completed 31 October, 1941; missing from 28 June, 1944, probably sunk 4 July at 18.30 hrs by US DE *Riddle* and destroyer *David W. Taylor* 65 m ENE of Saipan (15° 26′ N, 147° 48′ E).

I.11

Launched 28 February, 1941 and completed 16 May, 1942; missing from 11 January, 1944 off Samoa.

Nos. 700–701

Projected in 1942 but not begun.

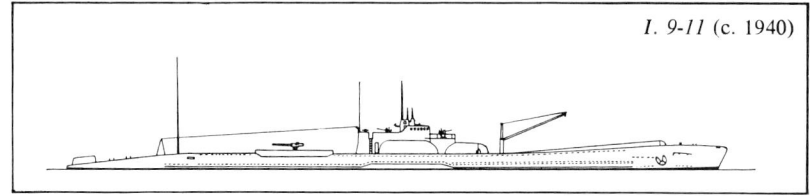

I. 9-11 (c. 1940)

Name	Builder	Date	Displ	Length ft in	Beam ft in	Draught ft in	Machinery	SHP	Speed	Fuel	Radius	Armament	Comp
A(2) Type *I.12*	Kawasaki, Kobe	1942–1944	2934 max 2390 surf 4172 subm	367 5 wl 355 8 pp	31 4	17 8	2-shaft Diesel motors 2 electric motors	4700 bhp 1200 ehp	17.7 6.2	?	22000 @ 16 75 @ 3	1 × 5.5in 50-cal 2 × 25mm AA 6 × 21in TT 18 torpedoes 1 floatplane	114

GENERAL NOTES

1st Class cruiser-submarine built under the 1941 War Programme. Similar to the *A(1)* Type but had lower power in order to increase her radius.

CAREER

Launched 1943 and completed 25 April, 1944; missing from 5 January, 1945 in the Central Pacific.

Name	Builder	Date	Displ	Length ft in	Beam ft in	Draught ft in	Machinery	SHP	Speed	Fuel	Radius	Armament	Comp
Modified *A* Type *I.1, I.13–15* Nos. 5094–5096	Kawasaki, Kobe	1943	3603 max 2620 surf 4762 subm	340 3 oa 355 8 wl	38 5	19 4	2-shaft Kampon Diesels	4400 bhp	16.7	?	21000 @ 16	1 × 5.5in 50-cal 7 × 25mm AA	?
							2 electric motors	600 ehp	5.5		60 @ 3	6 × 21in TT 12 torpedoes 1 floatplane	

GENERAL NOTES
These 1st Class cruiser-submarines were built under the 1941 War Programme. The design was known as the Kai-ko-taka and was based on the *A(2)* Type, but was originally intended to be a repeat of the *I.9* group. Diving depth 330ft.

MODIFICATIONS
The class was altered to carry 2 floatplane bombers like the *Sen-Toku* Type. Bulges were fitted to increase freeboard and reserve buoyancy. The hangar was on the centreline, and so the conning-tower was offset to port. The class was fitted with a Schnorkel.

CAREERS
I.13
Launched 1944 and completed 16 December, 1944; sunk 16 July, 1945 at 11.40 hrs by US DE *Lawrence C. Taylor* and escort carrier *Anzio* 550 m E of Yokosuka (34° 28′ N, 150° 55′ E).
I.14
Launched 1944 and completed 14 March, 1945; surrendered at sea 27 August, 1945, 200 m SE of Yokosuka; later BU.

I.15
Launched 12 April, 1944; construction stopped March 1945, and BU.
I.1
Launched 10 June, 1944; construction stopped March 1945; the hull sank in a storm at Kobe on 18 September, and was finally BU in July 1947 by Kawasaki.
Nos. 5094–5096
Never begun, and contracts cancelled in 1943.

I. 13-14 (1945) carrying two aircraft.

Name	Builder	Date	Displ	Length ft in	Beam ft in	Draught ft in	Machinery	SHP	Speed	Fuel	Radius	Armament	Comp
B(1) Type *I.15, I.26* *I.30, I.37* } Kure DY *I.17, I.23* *I.29, I.31* } Yokosuka DY *I.36* *I.21* Kawasaki, Kobe *I.19, I.25* *I.28, I.33* } Mitsubishi, Kobe *I.35* *I.27, I.32* *I.34* } Sasebo DY *I.38, I.39*		1938– 1943	2589 max 2198 surf 3654 subm	350 8 wl 335 10 pp	30 6	16 10	2-shaft Diesels	12400 bhp	23.6	?	14000 @ 16	1 × 5.5in 50-cal 2 × 25mm AA	101
							2 electric motors	2000 ehp	8		96 @ 3	6 × 21in TT 17 torpedoes 1 floatplane	

GENERAL NOTES
1st Class cruiser-submarines, built under the 4th Fleet Replenishment Law of 1939. The design was known as the Otsu-gata and was based on the *Kaidai (6A)* type. Very similar to the *A(1)* type with some improvements. The diving depth was about 330ft.

RE-ARMAMENT
From 1941, some boats had the aircraft and catapult replaced by an extra 5.5in gun. In 1944 *I.36* and *I.37* were rebuilt as 'Kaiten'-carriers, with *I.36* carrying 6 Kaiten and *I.37*, 4.

CAREERS
I.15
Launched 7 March, 1939 and completed 30 September, 1940; missing from 3 November, 1942, probably sunk 2 November by US destroyer *McCalla* N of San Cristobal (10° 53′ S, 161° 50′ E).
I.17
Launched 19 July, 1939 and completed 24 January, 1941; sunk at 10.00 hrs 19 August, 1943, by New Zealand corvette *Tui* and US naval aircraft 40 m SE of Noumea (23° 26′ S, 166° 50′ E).
I.19
Launched 16 September, 1939 and completed 28 April, 1941; sunk 25 November, 1943 by US destroyer *Radford* at 23.44 hrs 50 m W of Makin (03° 10′ N, 171° 55′ E).
I.21
Launched 24 February, 1940 and completed 15 July, 1941; missing from 27 November, 1943 off Tarawa.
I.23
Launched 24 November, 1939 and completed 27 September, 1941; missing from 15 February, 1942 S of Oahu.

I.25
Launched 8 June, 1940 and completed 15 October, 1941; missing from 20 September, 1943.
I.26
Launched 10 April, 1940 and completed 6 November, 1941; missing from 25 October 1944, probably sunk at 15.00 hrs 28 October by US destroyers *Gridley* and *Helm* 125 m NE of Surigao (10° 56′ N, 127° 13′ E).
I.27
Launched 6 June, 1940 and completed 24 February, 1942; sunk 12 February, 1944 by British destroyers *Paladin* and *Petard*.
I.28
Launched 17 December, 1940 and completed 6 February, 1942; torpedoed 17 May the same year by US submarine *Tautog* 45 m SSE of Truk (06° 30′ N, 152° E).
I.29
Launched 29 September, 1940 and completed 27 February, 1942; torpedoed 26 July, 1944 by US Submarine *Sawfish* ay 16.45 hrs in Balintang Channel (20° 10′ N, 121° 55′ E).
I.30
Launched 17 September, 1940 and completed 28 February, 1942; mined 13 October, 1942 at 16.30 hrs 3 m E of Singapore; she had been running the blockade from Brest, and part of her cargo was recovered; later salvaged and surrendered.
I.31
Launched 13 March, 1941 and completed 30 May, 1942; missing from 13 May, 1943 off Attu.
I.32
Launched 17 December, 1940 and completed 26 April, 1942; sunk at 04.30 hrs by DE *Manlove* and aircraft, 50 m S of Wotje (08° 30′ N, 170° 10′ E).
I.33
Launched 1 May, 1941 and completed 10 June, 1942; sunk 26 September, 1942 by aircraft bomb while under repair in Truk; raised and refitted at Kure, and returned to service 1 June, 1944; sunk 13 June, 1944 by accident on her trials 20 m SW of Matsuyama (33° 40′ N, 132° 30′ E); raised July 1953 and BU.
I.34
Launched 24 September 1941 and completed 31 August, 1942; torpedoed 13 November, 1943 at 07.30 hrs by British submarine *Taurus* off Muka Lighthouse, Penang (05° 26′ N, 100° 06′ E).

SUBMARINES 175

I.35
Launched 24 September, 1941 and completed 31 August, 1942; sunk by ramming and gunfire from DE *Frazier* at 17.27 hrs 22 November, 1943 off Tarawa (01° 22′ N, 172° 47′ E).
I.36
Launched 1 November, 1941 and completed 30 September, 1942; surrendered August 1945 at Sasebo; scuttled by USN off Goto 1 April, 1946.
I.37
Launched 22 October, 1941 and completed 10 March, 1943; missing from 20 November, 1944 while on Kaiten mission against Palau, probably sunk at 17.00 hrs 19 November by US DE *Conklin* and *McCoy Reynolds* in NW Kossol Passage (08° 07′ N, 134° 16′ E).

I.38
Launched 15 April, 1942 and completed 31 January, 1943; missing from 5 November, 1944, probably sunk 12 November by US destroyer *Nicholas* 85 m S of Yap (08° 04′ N, 138° 92′ E).
I.39
Launched 15 April, 1942 and completed 22 April, 1943; missing from 3 December, 1943.

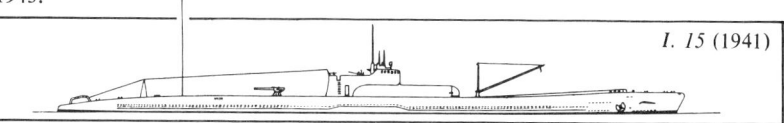

I. 15 (1941)

A development of the cruiser-submarine was the Junsen series of aircraft-carrying boats. *I.29*, seen here on completion in February 1942, was a unit of the *I.15* or Otsu-Gata Type. (Shizuo Fukui.)

Right: Many of the aircraft-carrying submarines had their floatplane and catapult removed, to allow conversion to supply-carriers. *I.30* is seen here on 5th August 1942 at Lorient in France, bringing precious rubber, and other scarce raw materials, from the Far East. She was sunk on her homeward voyage. (Authors' Collection.)

Name	Builder	Date	Displ	Length ft in wl / pp	Beam ft in	Draught ft in	Machinery	SHP	Speed	Fuel	Radius	Armament	Comp
B(2) Type *I.40–42* *I.43, I.45* *I.44* Nos. 702–709	Kure DY Sasebo DY Yokosuka DY	1942– 1944	2624 max 2230 surf 3700 subm	350 8 wl 335 10 pp	30 6	17 0	2-shaft Diesels 2 electric motors	11000 bhp 2000 ehp	23½ 8	?	14000 @ 16 96 @ 3	1 × 5.5in 50-cal 2 × 25mm AA 6 × 21in TT 17 torpedoes 1 floatplane	101

GENERAL NOTES
1st Class cruiser-submarines built under the 1941 War Programme. Virtually identical with the *B(1)* Type but with less powerful machinery and minor differences in displacement and draught.

CAREERS
I.40
Launched 1942 and completed 31 July, 1943; missing from December 1943 off Gilbert Islands.
I.41
Launched 1943 and completed 18 September, 1943; sunk 18 November, 1944 at 06.30 hrs by US DE *Lawrence C. Taylor* and escort carrier *Anzio* E of Samar (12° 44′ N, 130° 42′ E).
I.42
Launched 1943 and completed 3 November, 1943; torpedoed 23 March, 1944 by US submarine *Tunny* 6 m SW of Angaur (06° 40′ N, 130° 42′ E).
I.43
Launched 1943 and completed 5 November, 1943; torpedoed 15 February, 1944 by US submarine *Aspro* 280 m ESE of Guam (12° 42′ N, 149°′10′ E).
I.44
Launched 1943 and completed 31 January, 1944; missing from 4 April, 1945 on a Kaiten mission to Okinawa, probably sunk 10 April by US DE *Fieberling* 300 m SE of Okinawa (23° 12′ N, 132° 23′ E).
I.45
Launched 1943 and completed 28 December, 1943; missing from 27 October, 1944 in Leyte area, probably sunk 28 October by US DE *Whitehurst* 120 m ENE of Surigao (10° 10′ N, 127° 28′ E).
Nos. 702–709
Projected in 1942 but not authorised.

Name	Builder	Date	Displ	Length ft in wl / pp	Beam ft in	Draught ft in	Machinery	SHP	Speed	Fuel	Radius	Armament	Comp
B(3) Type *I.54, I.56, I.58* *I.62, I.64–66* Nos. 5101–5114	Yokosuka DY	1942– 1944	2607 max 2140 surf 3688 subm	350 9 wl 335 11 pp	30 6	17 0	2-shaft Diesels 2 electric motors	4700 bhp 1200 ehp	17.7 6.5	?	21000 @ 16 105 @ 3	1 × 5.5in 40–cal 2 × 25mm AA 6 × 21in TT 19 torpedoes 1 floatplane	101

GENERAL NOTES
1st Class cruiser-submarines built under the 1941–2 War Programme. Similar to the *B(1)* type but with less powerful machinery to allow greater endurance.

RECONSTRUCTION
In 1945, *I.56* and *I.58* had the aircraft and catapult removed to allow them to carry 6 Kaiten.

CAREERS
I.54
Launched 1943 and completed 31 March, 1944; missing from 23 October, 1944 off Leyte, probably sunk 24 October at 09.15 hrs by US DE *Richard M. Rowell* 7o m E of Surigao (09° 45′ N, 126° 45′ E).
I.56
Launched 1943 and completed 8 June, 1944; missing from 31 March, 1945 on Kaiten mission to Okinawa, probably sunk 18 April at 14.00 hrs by US carrier *Bataan* and destroyers *Collett, Heermann, McCord, Mertz* and *Uhlmann* 160 m E of Okinawa (26° 42′ N, 130° 38′ E).
I.58
Launched 1944 and completed 7 September, 1944; surrendered at Sasebo August 1945; scuttled by US Navy off Goto on 1 April, 1946.
I.62, I.64–66
Not laid down; cancelled 1943.
Nos. 5101–5114
Not laid down; cancelled 1943.

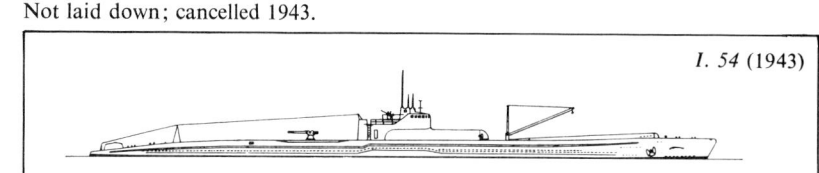

I. 54 (1943)

I. 58 carrying Amphibious Tanks Type 4.(see p. 272).

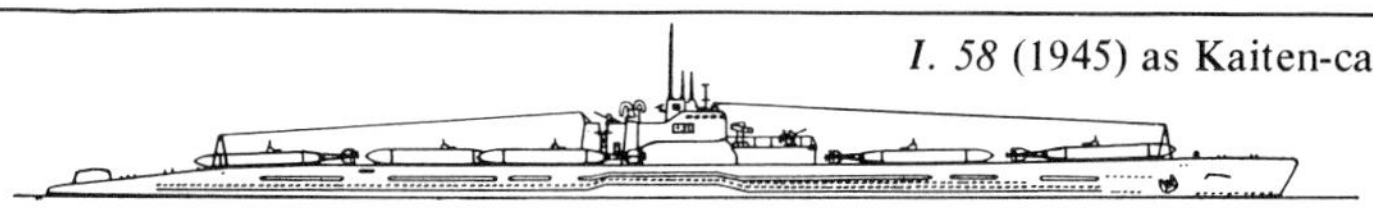

I. 58 (1945) as Kaiten-carrier.

Name	Builder	Date	Displ	Length ft in	Beam ft in	Draught ft in	Machinery	SHP	Speed	Fuel	Radius	Armament	Comp
B(4) Type	—	—	2800 surf	?	?	?	2-shaft Diesels	?	22.4	?	?	1 × 5.5in	
Nos. 5115–5132							2 electric motors	?	?		?	2 × 25mm AA 8 × 21in TT 16 torpedoes 8 mines 1 floatplane	?

GENERAL NOTES
This class of modified *B(3)* type was to have been ordered under a modification to the 5th Fleet Replenishment Law.
CAREERS
Nos. 5115–5132 were never begun and the contracts were cancelled in 1943.

Name	Builder	Date	Displ	Length ft in	Beam ft in	Draught ft in	Machinery	SHP	Speed	Fuel	Radius	Armament	Comp
C(1) Type		1937–	2554 max	350 10 wl	29 10	17 6	2-shaft Diesels	12400 bhp	23.6	?	14000 @ 16	1 × 5.5in 40-cal	101
I.16, I.20	Mitsubishi, Kobe	1941										2 × 25mm AA	
I.18, I.24	Sasebo DY		2184 surf	340 6 pp			2 electric motors	2000 hp	8		60 @ 3	8 × 21in TT	
I.22	Kawasaki, Kobe		3561 subm									20 torpedoes	

GENERAL NOTES
1st Class cruiser-submarines built under the 3rd Fleet Replenishment Law of 1937. The design was known as the Hei-gata and was based on the *Kaidai 6A* type. They were very similar to the *A(1)* and *B(1)* types, but as they were designated attack submarines they dispensed with the floatplane and catapult. They were of double-hull design, with a hull depth of 25.6ft and a diving depth of 330ft.

RE-ARMAMENT
For the Pearl Harbor attack they were fitted to carry a midget submarine on deck.

CAREERS
I.16
Launched 28 July, 1938 and completed 30 March, 1940; sunk 19 May, 1944 by US DE *England* at 13.40 hrs, 140 m NE of Cape Alexander (05° 10′ S, 158° 17′ E).
I.18
Launched 12 November, 1938 and completed 31 January, 1941; sunk 11 February, 1943 at 12.38 hrs by US destroyer *Fletcher* 200 m S of San Cristobal (14° 15′ S, 161° 59′ E).
I.20
Launched 25 January, 1939 and completed 26 September, 1940; missing from 30 August, 1943, probably sunk 3 September at 21.00 hrs by US destroyer *Ellett* 150 m NE of Espiritu Santo (13° 10′ S, 165° 28′ E).
I.22
Launched 23 December, 1938 and completed 10 March, 1941; missing from 5 October, 1942 W of Malaita.
I.24
Launched 12 November, 1939 and completed 31 October, 1941; missing from 7 June, 1943, probably rammed by US *PC.487* 10 June, 50 m NE of Attu (53° 16′ N, 174° 24′ E).

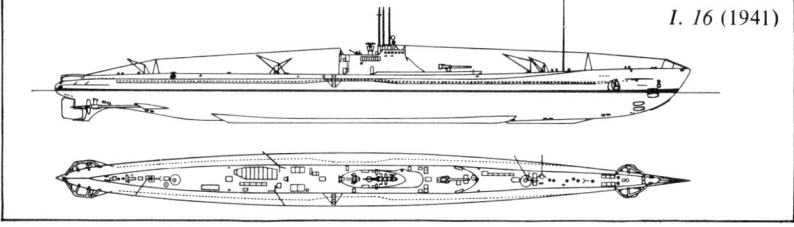

I. 16 (1941)

Name	Builder	Date	Displ	Length ft in	Beam ft in	Draught ft in	Machinery	SHP	Speed	Fuel	Radius	Armament	Comp
C(2) Type		1942–	2557 max	350 10 wl	29 10	17 6	2-shaft Diesel motors	11000 bhp	23½	?	14000 @ 16	1 × 5.5in 40-cal	101
I.46–48	Sasebo DY	1944										2 × 25mm AA	
I.49–51	—		2184 surf	340 6 pp			2 electric motors	2000 hp	8		60 @ 3	8 × 21in TT	
Nos. 710–713	—		3564 subm									20 torpedoes	

GENERAL NOTES
1st Class cruiser-submarines built under the 1941 War Programme, and very similar to the *C(1)* type apart from minor differences in displacement. Also similar to the *Junsen (3)* and *B(1)* types.

CAREERS
I.46
Launched 1943 and completed 29 February, 1944; missing from 27 October, 1944 E of Leyte.
I.47
Launched 1943 and completed 10 July, 1944; surrendered at Kure August 1945 and scuttled off Goto on 1 April, 1946 by USN.
I.48
Launched 1944 and completed, 5 September, 1944; missing from 20 January, 1945 on a Kaiten mission to Ulithi, probably sunk 23 January by US DE *Conklin, Corbesier* and *Raby* 25 m NE of Yap (09° 45′ N, 138° 20′ E).

SUBMARINES 177

I.49–51
Not begun and cancelled in 1943.

Nos. 710–713
Projected in 1942 but not started.

Name	Builder	Date	Displ	Length ft in	Beam ft in	Draught ft in	Machinery	SHP	Speed	Fuel	Radius	Armament	Comp
C(3) Type I.52, I.53 I.55 I.57, I.59 Nos. 5141–5155	Kure DY	1942–1944	2564 max 2095 surf 3644 subm	350 9 wl 335 11 pp	30 6	16 10	2-shaft Diesel motors 2 electric motors	4700 bhp 1200 hp	17.7 6½	?	21000 @ 16 105 @ 3	2 × 5.5in 40-cal 2 × 25mm AA 6 × 21in TT 19 torpedoes	101

GENERAL NOTES
1st Class cruiser-submarines built under the 1941–2 War Programme, and very similar to the *C(1)* type apart from less powerful machinery to give greater range.

RE-ARMAMENT
In 1944–5, *I.53* was altered to carry 6 Kaiten.

CAREERS
I.52
Launched 1943 and completed 18 December, 1943; sunk 24 June, 1944 by US escort carrier *Bogue* 800 m SW of Fayal, in the Azores (15° 16′ N, 39° 55′ W).
I.53
Launched 1943 and completed 20 February, 1944; surrendered at Kure August 1945 and scuttled off Goto by USN 1 April, 1946.
I.55
Launched 1943 and completed 20 April, 1944; missing from 14 July, 1944 off Tinian, probably sunk 28 July at 18.15 hrs by US DEs *Reynolds* and *Wyman* 400 m E of Tinian (14° 26′ N, 152° 16′ E).
I.57, I.59
Not begun and cancelled 1943.

Name	Builder	Date	Displ	Length ft in	Beam ft in	Draught ft in	Machinery	SHP	Speed	Fuel	Radius	Armament	Comp
C(4) Type Nos. 5156–5180	—	—	2756 surf	?	?	?	2-shaft Diesel motors 2 electric motors	? ?	20.4 ?	? ?	? ?	1 × 5.5in 40-cal 2 × 25mm AA, 8 × 21in TT	?

GENERAL NOTES
These modified *C(3)* type were projected under the modified 5th Fleet Replenishment Law.

CAREERS
Nos. 5156–5180 were never started and were cancelled in 1943.

Name	Builder	Date	Displ	Length ft in	Beam ft in	Draught ft in	Machinery	SHP	Speed	Fuel	Radius	Armament	Comp
SEN-TAKA Type I.201–223 I-LXXVI	Kure DY	1944	1291 max 1070 surf 1450 subm	257 6 wl 249 4 pp	19 0	17 11	2-shaft M.A.N. Diesel motors 2 electric motors	2750 bhp 5000 hp	15.8 19	?	5800 @ 14 135 @ 3 or 17 @ 19 and 36 @ 3	2 × 25mm AA 4 × 21in TT 10 torpedoes	31

GENERAL NOTES
These 1st Class submarines were designed primarily for high underwater speed and resembled the German Type XXI. Sen (suikan) Taka = fast submarine. The double-hull principle was retained, but the welded outer hull was streamlined. The hull was built in sections. Depth of hull was 22ft and the boats could dive to 360ft.

MACHINERY
Lightweight M.A.N. Diesels were used, and the battery capacity was greatly enlarged.

RECONSTRUCTION
The hulls of the later boats were altered to allow greater battery capacity.

CAREERS
I.201
Launched 1944 and completed 2 February, 1945; surrendered at Maizuru August 1945 and taken back to USA for trials.
I.202
Launched 1944 and completed 12 February, 1945; handed over damaged at Maizuru in August 1945; scuttled 5 April, 1946 off Sasebo by USN.
I.203
Launched 1944 and completed 29 May, 1945; surrendered August 1945 at Maizuru and taken over by USN.
I.204
Launched 16 December, 1944 and sunk incomplete at Kure on 22 June, 1945 by US aircraft bombs; BU at Harima in April 1948.
I.205
Launched 15 February, 1945 but sunk incomplete in a dry dock at Kure 19 March, 1945, by bombs from US TF 58; repaired but badly damaged 28 July by aircraft fo TF 38; BU at Harima in July 1948.
I.206
Launched 26 March, 1945 but not completed; BU at Harima in November 1946.
I.207–208
Building stopped April 1945 and BU at Harima in April 1946.
I.209–223
Not begun and cancelled 1945.
I–LXXVI
Projected 1944–5 but contracts not awarded.

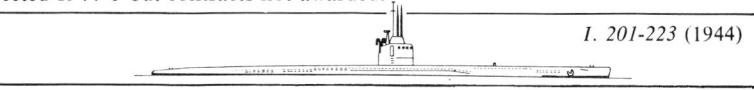

I. 201-223 (1944)

After surrendering in 1945, *I.203* lies moored alongside (from left to right) *Ha.203*, *Ha.204* and *Ha.106*. (US Navy.)

Name	Builder	Date	Displ	Length ft in	Beam ft in	Draught ft in	Machinery	SHP	Speed	Fuel	Radius	Armament	Comp
KIRAI-SEN Type *I.21–23* *I.*(ex-*Nos. 48–50*) *I.24* (ex-*No. 60*) *I.25*, *I.26* (ex-*Nos. 52, 63*)	Kawasaki, Kobe	1924– 1928	1383 max 1142 surf 1768 subm	279 7 oa 269 wl	24 8 5	14 6 max 14 1	2-shaft M.A.N. 6-cyl 4-stroke Diesel motors 2 electric motors	2400 bhp 1100 hp	14½ 7	225 oil	10500 @ 8 40 @ 4½	1 × 5.5in 40-cal 1 × 7.7mm MG 4 × 21in TT 42 torpedoes 42 mines	51–70

GENERAL NOTES
Large submarine-minelayers, rated as 1st Class submarines and built under the 1919 Programme. They were based on the ex-German *U.125* (see *O.6*) taken over as war booty, and were the only minelaying submarines built by the Japanese. They could dive to about 250ft.

CAREERS
I.21
Ordered as *No. 48* but launched 30 March, 1926 as *I.21*; completed 31 March, 1927; renumbered *I.121* 1 June, 1938; relegated to training 15 August, 1942: surrendered at Maizuru in August 1945 and BU.
I.22
Ordered as *No. 49* but launched 8 November, 1926 as *I.22*; completed 28 October, 1927; renumbered *I.122* 1 June, 1938; torpedoed 10 June, 1945 by US submarine *Skate* 6 m off Cape Rokugo Lighthouse (37° 29′ N, 137° 25′ E).
I.23
Ordered as *No. 50* but launched 19 March, 1927 as *I.23*; completed 28, April, 1928; renumbered *I.123* 1 June, 1938; sunk 29 August, 1942 at 11.47 hrs by US minelayer *Gamble* 60 m ESE of Savo (09° 21′ S, 160° 43′ E).
I.24
Ordered as *No. 60* Launched 12 December, 1927 and completed 10 December, 1928; renumbered *I.124* 1 June, 1938; sunk 20 January, 1942 at 19.45 hrs by US destroyer *Edsall* and Australian minesweeper *Deloraine* in western entrance to Clarence Strait (12° 05′ S, 130° 06′ E).
I.25–26
Projected as *No. 52* and *No. 63* but cancelled 1924.

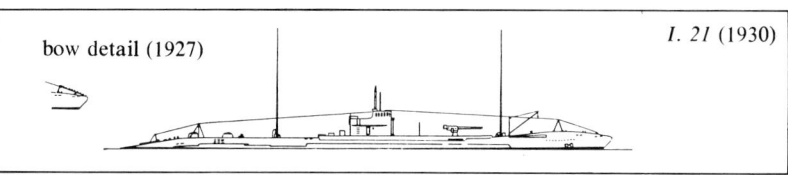

bow detail (1927)

I. 21 (1930)

Name	Builder	Date	Displ	Length ft in	Beam ft in	Draught ft in	Machinery	SHP	Speed	Fuel	Radius	Armament	Comp
SEN-TOKU Type *I.400, I.404* *I.401, I.402* *I.405* *I.403, I.406–17*	Kure DY Sasebo DY Kawasaki, Kobe —	1943	5223 max 3530 surf 6560 subm	394 0 wl 380 6 pp	39 4	23 0	2-shaft M.A.N. Diesels (4 bhp motors) 2 electric motors	7700 2400	18.7 6½	?	37500 @ 14 60 @ 3	1 × 5.5in 40-cal 10 × 25mm AA 8 × 21in TT 20 torpedoes 3 floatplanes	144

GENERAL NOTES
Aircraft-carrying 1st Class submarines, built under the 5th Fleet Replenishment Programme of 1942. Sen (suikan) Toku = Special Submarine, designed in response to a project of Admiral Yamamoto to bomb the Panama Canal. The twin hull was designed in the form of a horizontal 00 to aid stability, and had 2 Diesel engines in each half-cylinder coupled to a shaft. The conning-tower was offset to port, to allow space for a 110ft horizontal cylindrical hangar for 3 floatplane bombers offset to starboard. The 115ft catapult was offset to starboard on the forward casing, with a folding crane to port.

ALTERATIONS
Originally planned to have only 2 floatplanes, on a maximum tonnage of 4550. They were temporarily fitted with dummy funnels to conceal them in Home waters.

CAREERS
I.400
Launched 1944 and completed 30 December that year; surrendered at sea 200 m SE of Yokosuka 27 August, 1945; taken to USA in 1946 and scuttled in US Waters.
I.401
Launched 1944 and completed 8 January, 1945; surrendered at sea 25 August, 1945; taken to USA in 1946 and scuttled there.
I.402
Launched 1944 and converted to a tanker; in service 24 July, 1945; surrendered at Kure August; scuttled off Goto by USN 1 April, 1946.
I.403
Not begun; contract cancelled March 1945.
I.404
Launched 7 July, 1944; building stopped March 1945 when 90% complete; hull sunk at Kure 28 July by US aircraft of TF 38; raised and BU at Harima July 1946.
I.405
Building stopped March 1945 and BU.
I.406–417
Not begun, and contracts cancelled in 1945.

A deck-view of the 5,000-ton *I.400*, alongside the US depot-ship *Fulton* after the surrender. Apart from giving an impression of her size, the photo also shows clearly the hangar door, the offset conning-tower and the schnorchel mast lying stowed on deck. (US Navy.)

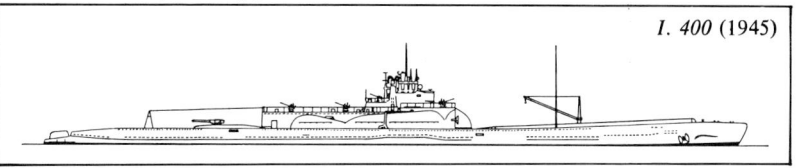

I. 400 (1945)

SUBMARINES 179

Name	Builder	Date	Displ	Length ft in	Beam ft in	Draught ft in	Machinery	SHP	Speed	Fuel	Radius	Armament	Comp
SEN-HO Type *I.351–353* I–III	Kure DY	1943	3512 max 2650 surf 4290 subm	360 10 wl 351 0 pp	33 3	20 1	2-shaft Diesels 2 electric motors	3700 bhp 1200	15.8 6.3	?	13000 @ 14 100 @ 3	2 × 80mm mortars 7 × 25mm AA 4 × 21in TT 4 torpedoes 390ts cargo	77+13

GENERAL NOTES
Designed as submarine oil-tankers under the 5th Fleet Replenishment Programme of 1942. Sen (suikan) Ho = Support Submarine. They were to act as seaplane tenders, with sufficient fuel to refuel 3 flying boats, 365ts of gasoline in the ballast tanks, 11ts of fresh water, 1½ts of supplies, and 15ts of aircraft bombs and torpedoes. They could remain at sea for 60 days and could dive to 300 ft.

RE-ARMAMENT
Originally intended to have 1 × 5·5in and 4 × 25mm AA.

CAREERS
I.351
Launched 1944 and completed 28 January, 1945; torpedoed 14 July by US submarine *Bluefish* 100 m ENE of Natuna Besar (04° 30′ N, 110° E).
I.352
Launched 23 April, 1944 and sunk incomplete by US air attack at Kure 22 June, 1945.
I.353, I–III
Projected 1941 but not begun; cancelled 1943.

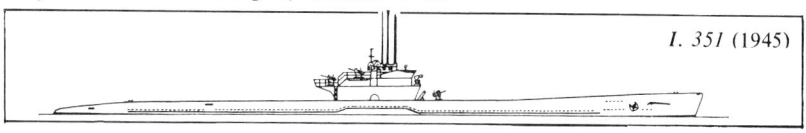

I. 351 (1945)

Name	Builder	Date	Displ	Length ft in	Beam ft in	Draught ft in	Machinery	SHP	Speed	Fuel	Radius	Armament	Comp
D(1) Type *I.361, I.363* *I.362, I.364* *I.366, I.367* *I.370 I·371* *I.365 I.368* *I.369, I.372* I–XCII	Kure DY Mitsubishi, Kobe Yokosuka DY	1943	1779 max 1440 surf 2215 subm —	239 6 wl 231 5 pp	29 2	15 7	2-shaft Diesel motors 2 electric motors	1850 bhp 1200	13 6½	?	15000 @ 10 120 @ 3	1 × 5.5in 40-cal 2 × 25mm AA 2 landing craft 82ts cargo 110 men	60

GENERAL NOTES
Built under the 5th Modified Fleet Replenishment Programme of 1942 as transport submarines, known as the Tei-gata design, two 13m landing craft were carried in wells on the after casing, outside the pressure-hull. Cargo capacity was 62½ts internally and 20ts externally, handled with electric winches as in the 1st Class transports. Diving depth was 250ft.

RECONSTRUCTION
Originally fitted with two 21in bow TT, but trials with *I.361* showed that the full lines and stowage space on deck produced a conspicuous bow-wave. The tubes were removed from all subsequent boats and the original conning-tower was modified to an 'anti-radar' type similar to the *Kaichu* (6) type boats. In 1944–5, *I.361, I.363* and *I.366–370* were converted to Kaiten-carriers with reduced armament.

CAREERS
I.361
Launched 1943 and completed 25 May, 1944; missing from 24 May, 1945 on a Kaiten mission, probably sunk 30 May by US escort carrier *Anzio* 400 m SE of Okinawa (22° 22′ N, 134° 09′ E).
I.362
Launched 1943 and completed 23 May, 1944; missing from 1 January, 1945, probably sunk 13 January by US DE *Fleming* 320 m NNE of Truk (12° 08′ N, 154° 27′ E).
I.363
Launched 1943 and completed 8 July, 1944; surrendered August 1945 but mined at 12.45 hrs 29 October off Kyushu while on passage to Sasebo (approx 32° N, 131° 40′ E).
I.354
Launched 1943 and completed 14 June, 1944; missing from 14 September, probably torpedoed next day by US submarine *Sea Devil* 300 m ESE of Yokosuka (34° 30′ N, 145° 23′ E).

I. 367 (1944)
I. 361 (1944)
I. 363 (1945) as Kaiten-carrier

I.365
Launched 1944 and completed 1 August, 1944 torpedoed 28 November by US submarine *Scabbardfish* 75 m SE of Yokosuka (34° 44′ N, 141° 01′ E).
I.366
Launched 1944 and completed 3 August the same year; surrendered August 1945 and scuttled off Goto 1 April, 1946 by USN.
I.367
Launched 1944 and completed 15 August the same year; surrendered and scuttled as *I.366*.
I.368
Launched 1944 and completed 25 August, 1944; sunk 27 February, 1945 by US escort carrier Anzio 35 m W of Iwo Jima (24° 43′ N, 140° 37′ E).
I.369
Launched 1944 and completed 9 October, 1944; surrendered at Yokosuka August 1945 and BU.
I.370
Launched 1944 and completed 4 September, 1944; sunk at 10.10 hrs on 26 February, 1945 by US DE *Finnegan* 120 m S of Iwo Jima (22° 45′ N, 141° 27′ E).
I.371
Launched 1944 and completed 2 October, 1944; missing from 31 January, 1945, probably torpedoed 24 February by US submarine *Lagarto* off Bungo Suido (32° 40′ N, 132° 33′ E).

Name	Builder	Date	Displ	Length ft in	Beam ft in	Draught ft in	Machinery	SHP	Speed	Fuel	Radius	Armament	Comp
D(2) Type *I.373–378* I–CLX	Yokosuka DY	1944	1926 max 1660 surf 2240 subm	241 3 wl 230 0 pp	29 2	16 7	2-shaft Diesel motors 2 electric motors	1750 bhp 1200	13 6½	?	15000 @ 10 100 @ 3	1 × 5.5in 40-cal 2 × 25mm AA 1 landing craft 110ts cargo, 150ts gasoline	60

GENERAL NOTES
1st Class transport submarines built under the 1943–4 War Programme, and similar to the *D(1)* type but with stronger hulls. A landing craft was carried in a watertight well on the after casing and the cargo included 100ts internally, 10ts externally and 150ts of gasoline. The diving depth was about 330ft.

RE-ARMAMENT
Originally designed without armament. In 1945, *I.372* became a Kaiten-carrier.

CAREERS
I.372
Launched 1944 and completed 8 November, 1944; sunk 18 July, 1945 by aircraft of TF 38 in Yokosuka harbour; raised and scuttled in deep water in August 1946.

I.373
Launched 1944 and completed 14 April, 1945; torpedoed 14 August at 05.00 hrs by US submarine *Spikefish* 190 m SE of Shanghai (29° 02′ N, 123° 53′ E).

I.374
Building stopped April 1945 and BU on slip.

I.375–378
Not begun, and cancelled 1945.

I–CLX
Projected 1943–4 but no contracts awarded.

Name	Builder	Date	Displ	Length ft in	Beam ft in	Draught ft in	Machinery	SHP	Speed	Fuel	Radius	Armament	Comp
YU.1–12	Hitachi SB Co., Kasado	1943–1944	273 surf 370 subm	134 oa 2 129 wl 7	12 9	9 8	2-single-shaft Diesels	400 bhp	10	?	1500 @ 8	1 × 37mm AA 40ts cargo	13
							1 electric motor	75	5		32 @ 4		
YU.1001–1014	Chosen Machine Co., Wonsan (Jinsen)	1944–1945	392 surf	160 9 oa	16 3	8 9	2 single-shaft Diesels	700 bhp	12	?	1500 @ 8	40ts cargo	?
							1 electric motor	?	?		32 @ 4		
YU.2001–	Ando Ironworks, Tokyo	1945	?	?	?	?	2 single-shaft Diesels	?	?	?	?	?	?
							1 electric motor	?	?	?	?	?	?

GENERAL NOTES
These transport submarines were designed by Army officers as the 'Maru-Yu' series. They were based on the *Sen-yu-sho* type but were smaller and simpler in construction. The *YU-1001* series was slightly larger.

CAREERS
Very little information about these boats has survived.

YU.1
Launched 16 October, 1943 and completed the same year; sunk.

YU.10
Launched 194? and completed 194?; sank in a storm off Kuchinotsu in 1946; raised and BU in January 1947 by Kawanami, Nagasaki.

YU.12
As *YU.10* but BU February 1947.

YU.25
Launched 194? and completed 194?; BU at Naniwa in December 1947.

YU.1007
Launched 1944 and completed 194?; sank in a storm off Mikuriya in 1946; raised and BU in January 1948 by Kawanami, Nagasaki.

YU.1011, YU.1013
Fate as *YU.1007*

YU.1014
Launched 194? and completed 194?; lost in storm as *YU.1011* and *YU.1013* but BU December 1947 at Uranosaki.

YU.1 (1944)

YU.1013 (1945)

Name	Builder	Date	Displ	Length ft in	Beam ft in	Draught ft in	Machinery	SHP	Speed	Fuel	Radius	Armament	Comp
O.1 ex-U.125	Blohm & Voss, Hamburg	1917–1918	1163 surf 1468 subm	269 0 oa	24 4	13 10	2-shaft M.A.N. 6-cyl 4-stroke Diesels	2400 bhp	14.7	220 oil	11470 @ 8	1 × 5.9in 45-cal 4 × 19.7in TT 14 torpedoes	40
							2 SSW electric motors	1235	7.2		35 @ 4½	2 mine-tubes 42 mines	

GENERAL NOTES
A large minelaying submarine built under the German War Programme 'L' to official designs. She was fitted with 2 stern mine-tubes for laying mines but could also be fitted with 2 stern torpedo-tubes and carry only 30 mines instead. She was of double-hull design and could dive to 250ft.

CAREER
Launched 26 May, 1918; completed 4 September as the German *U.125*; handed over to Japan 26 November 1918 as war booty; BU at Kure in 1922, but the remains of the hull became a berthing pontoon for submarines at Kure after March 1928.

Name	Builder	Date	Displ	Length ft in	Beam ft in	Draught ft in	Machinery	SHP	Speed	Fuel	Radius	Armament	Comp
O.2 ex-U.46 U.43	Danzig DY	1913–1916	725 surf 940 subm	213 3 oa	20 4	12 3	2-shaft M.A.N. 6-cyl 4-stroke Diesels	2000 bhp	15.2	110 oil	8100 @ 8	2 × 3.4in 30-cal 4 × 19.7in TT 6 torpedoes	36
							2 SSW electric motors	1200	9.7		51 @ 5		
O.3 ex-U.55	Krupp, Germania (Kiel)	1915–1916	786 surf 954 subm	213 11 oa	20 9	12 5	2-shaft M.A.N. 6-cyl 4-stroke Diesels	2400 bhp	17.1	115 oil	9000 @ 8	1 × 4.1in 45-cal 1 × 3.4in 30-cal 4 × 19.7in TT 7 torpedoes	36
							2 SSW electric motors	1200	9.1		55 @ 5		

GENERAL NOTES
Built under the German War Programme 'A', to standard official double-hulled design. Diving depth 160ft.

CAREERS
O.2
Launched 18 May, 1915 and completed 17 December, 1915 as German *U.46*; handed over to Japan on 26 November, 1918 as war booty; BU at Kure 1922.

U.43
Launched 26 September, 1914 and completed 30 April 1915 as *U.43* for German Navy; handed over to Japan as war booty on 20 January, 1919 but not renamed or taken over; BU at Swansea 1922.

Name	Builder	Date	Displ	Length ft in	Beam ft in	Draught ft in	Machinery	SHP	Speed	Fuel	Radius	Armament	Comp
O.4 ex-*UC.90*	Blohm & Voss, Hamburg	1917–1918	491 surf 571 subm	185 5 oa	18 2	12 4	2-shaft M.A.N. 6-cyl 4-stroke Diesels	600 bhp	11½	77 oil	9850 @ 7	1 × 4.1in 45-cal 3 × 19.7in TT 7 torpedoes 6 mine chutes 14 mines	32
O.5 ex-*UC.99*							2 SSW electric motors	770	6.6		40 @ 4½		

GENERAL NOTES
Built for German Navy under War Programme 'S' as *UC.III* type twin-hulled minelayers.

CAREERS
O.4
Launched 19 January, 1918 and completed 15 July as German *UC.90*; interned 13 November at Karlskrona and delivered to Japan as war booty 1 December, 1918; BU at Kure in 1921.

O.5
Launched 17 March, 1918 and completed 20 September as German *UC.99*; handed over to Japan as war booty 22 November, 1918; BU in 1921 at Sasebo.

O.3
Launched 18 March, 1916 and completed 8 June, 1916 as German *U.55*; handed over to Japan as war booty 26 November, 1918; BU 1922 at Sasebo.

Name	Builder	Date	Displ	Length ft in	Beam ft in	Draught ft in	Machinery	SHP	Speed	Fuel	Radius	Armament	Comp
O.6 ex-*UB.125*	AG Weser, Bremen	1917–1918	512 surf 643 subm	183 4 oa	19	12 2	2-shaft Körting 6-cyl 4-stroke Diesels	1060 bhp	13.9	78 oil	7280 @ 6	1 × 4.1in 45-cal 5 × 19.7in TT 10 torpedoes	34
							2 SSW electric motors	788	7.6		55 @ 4		
O.7 ex-*UB.143*	AG Weser, Bremen	1918	523 surf 653 subm	183 3 oa	19 0	12 3	2-shaft Benz 6-cyl 4-stroke Diesels	1060 bhp	13½	78 oil	7280 @ 6	1 × 4.1in 45-cal 5 × 19.7in TT 10 torpedoes	34
							2 Schiffsunion electric motors	788	7½		50 @ 4		

GENERAL NOTES
UB.III double-hulled U-Boats built under the War Programmes 'Q' and 'T' for the German Navy. Diving depth 160ft.

CAREERS
O.6
Launched 16 April, 1918 and completed 18 May as German *UB.125*; handed over to Japan 20 November, 1918 as war booty; BU in 1921 at Kure.

O.7
Launched 21 August, 1918 and completed 3 October as German *UB.143*; interned at Karlskrona 13 November and handed over to Japan 26 November, 1918; BU at Yokosuka in 1921.

Name	Builder	Date	Displ	Length ft in	Beam ft in	Draught ft in	Machinery	SHP	Speed	Fuel	Radius	Armament	Comp
RO.500 ex-*U.511*	Deutsche Werft, Hamburg	1941	1137 surf 1232 subm	251 10 oa	22 2	15 5	2-shaft M.A.N. 9-cyl 4-stroke Diesel motors	4400 bhp	18.3	208 oil	13450 @ 10	1 × 4.1in 45-cal 2 × 20mm AA 6 × 21in TT 22 torpedoes	48
							2 SSW electric motors	1000	7.3		59 @ 4		
RO.501 ex-*U.1224*	Deutsche Werft, Hamburg	1943	1144 surf 1257 subm	251 10 oa	22 6	15 4	2-shaft M.A.N. 9-cyl 4-stroke Diesel motors	4400 bhp	18.3	214 oil	13850 @ 10	1 × 4.1in 45-cal 4 × 20mm AA 6 × 21in TT 22 torpedoes	48
							2 SSW electric motors	1000	7.3		63 @ 4		
I.501 ex-*U.181* *I.502* ex-*U.862*	Deschimag, Bremen	1941–1943	1616 surf 1804 subm	287 4 oa	24 7	17 6	2-shaft M.A.N. 9-cyl 4-stroke Diesel motors + 2MWM 6-cyl 4-stroke Cruising Diesel motors	4400 bhp +1000 bhp	19.2	441 oil	31500 @ 10	1 × 4.1in 45-cal 1 × 37mm AA 4 × 20mm AA 6 × 21in TT 24 torpedoes	60
							2 SSW electric motors	1000	6.9		57 @ 4		
I.506 ex-*U.195*			1610 surf 1799 subm				2 Germania 6-cyl 4-stroke Diesel motors	3000 bhp		203 oil	12750 @ 10	1 × 37mm AA 4 × 20mm AA + cargo	60
							2 SSW electric motors	1000	6.9		115 @ 4		

GENERAL NOTES
U.511 was a Type *IXC* ocean-going submarine developed from the Type *IX*. She was double-hulled and could dive to 200m. *U.1224* was of the Type *IXC/40*, another development of the Type *IX*, while *U.181* and *U.862* were of the 1939–40 Type *IXD$_2$* group. *I.506* was a Type *IXD$_1$* boat with the forward casing reduced in width to decrease her diving time.

CAREERS
RO.500
Launched 22 September, 1941; completed 8 December, 1941 as German *U.511*; transferred to Japan in July 1943 and temporarily renamed *Satsuki No. 1*; handed over at Kure August, and commissioned 16 September, 1943 as *RO.500* for experimental purposes; surrendered August 1945 at Maizuru; scuttled 30 April, 1946 by USN in Gulf of Maizuru.

RO.501
Launched 7 July, 1943; completed 20 October, 1943 as German *U.1224*; transferred to Japan in 1943 under the temporary name of *Satsuki No. 2*; commissioned as *RO.501* at Kiel, but sunk 31 May, 1944 by US DE *Francis M. Robinson* while on passage 400 m SSW of Azores (18° 08′ N, 33° 13′ W).

I.501
Launched 30 December, 1941; completed 9 May, 1942 as German *U.181*; taken over by Japan in May 1945 and renumbered *I.501* 15 July; surrendered at Singapore 16 August and scuttled 12 February, 1946.

I.502
Launched 5 June, 1943; completed 7 October, 1943 as German *U.862*; taken over with *U.181* and renumbered *I.502* 15 July, 1945; surrendered at Singapore 16 August; scuttled off Singapore 12 February, 1946.

I.506
Launched 1942; completed 5 September, 1942 as German *U.195*; taken over by Japan May 1945 and renumbered 15 July; surrendered at Soerabaya August 1945; BU in 1947.

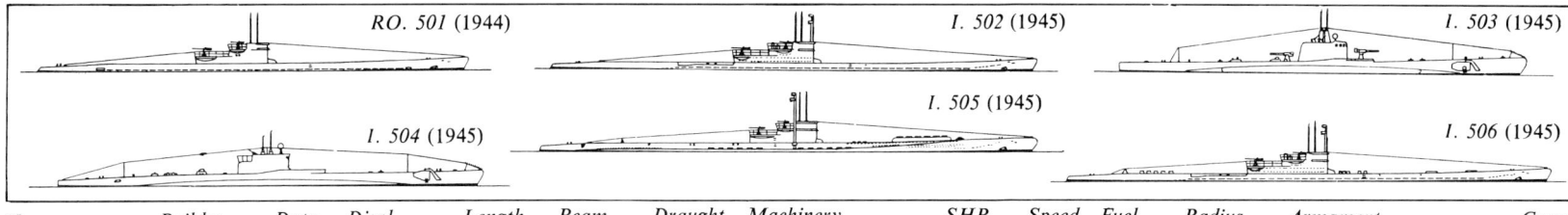

Name	Builder	Date	Displ	Length ft in	Beam ft in	Draught ft in	Machinery	SHP	Speed	Fuel	Radius	Armament	Comp
I.503 ex-*UIT.24* ex-*Comandante Cappellini*	Odero-Terni-Orlando, La Spezia	1938–1939	1060 surf 1313 subm	239 10 oa	26 9	16 9	2 Fiat 6-cyl 4-stroke Diesel motors	3000 bhp	17.4	108 oil approx	7500 @ 9.4	2 × 3.9in 45-cal 8 × 21in TT 12 torpedoes	60
							2 CRDA-Modyn	1300	8		80 @ 4		
I.504 ex-*UIT.25* ex-*Luigi Torelli*	Odero-Terni-Orlando, La Spezia	1939–1940	1191 surf 1489 subm	249 6 oa	25 11	15 6	2 CRDA 6-cyl 4-stroke Diesel motors	3600 bhp	18	?	10500 @ 8	1 × 3.9in 45-cal 8 × 21in TT 12 torpedoes	60
							2 C-Marelli-Modyn electric motors	1240	8		110 @ 3		
I.505 ex-*U.219*	Germania-werft, Kiel	1941–1942	1763 surf 2177 subm	294 7 oa	30 2	15 5	2 Germania 9-cyl 4-stroke Diesel motors	4500 bhp	17	368 oil	18450 @ 10	1 × 37mm AA 4 × 20mm AA 2 × 21in TT	52
							2 AEG electric motors	1100	7		93 @ 4	15 torpedoes 30 mine-tubes 66 mines	

GENERAL NOTES
The ex-Italian submarine *UIT.24* was one of the *Marcello* Class designed by Bernardis, and was a partially double-hulled boat capable of diving to 100m. The ex-*UIT.25* was one of the *Marconi* Class designed by Bernardis, of the same basic type as the *Marcello* Class.
U.219 was a former minelayer or Type *XB* U-Boat designed in 1938. She was converted to a transport with storage spaces in her pressure hull.

CAREERS
I.503
Launched 14 May, 1939; completed 23 September, 1939 as Italian *Commandante Cappellini*; taken over 10 September, 1943 as German *UIT.24*; taken over in May 1945 by Japan and renumbered *I.503* 15 July; surrendered at Kobe in August; scuttled off Kobe 15 April, 1946 by USN.

I.504
Launched 6 January, 1940; completed 15 May, 1940 as Italian *Luigi Torelli*; taken over 10 September, 1943 as German *UIT.25*; taken over in May 1945 by Japan and renumbered *I.504* 15 July; surrendered at Kobe in August; scuttled off Kobe 16 April, 1946 by USN.

I.505
Launched 6 October, 1942; completed 12 December, 1942 as German *U.219*; used as a transport from 1943; taken over by Japan in May 1945 and renumbered *I.505* 15 July; surrendered at Djakarta in August and BU 1947.

Midget Submarines

Name	Builder	Date	Displ	Length ft in	Beam ft in	Draught ft in	Machinery	SHP	Speed	Fuel	Radius	Armament	Comp
Type A No. 1, No. 2	Kure DY	1934	46 N	78 5 oa	6 1	6 1	Single-shaft electric motor	600	24		80 @ 6	2 × 18in TT	2
Ha. 1, Ha 2 Ha. 3–52 Ha. 54–61(?)	Ourazaki, Kure	1936 1938–1942						600 600	23 19				
Type B Ha. 53	Ourazaki, Kure	1943	49 N	81 oa	8 6 2	6 2	1 Diesel generator	40 bhp	6.5		350 @ 6.5	2 × 18in TT	3
Type C Ha. 62–76		1944					1 electric motor	600	18.5		120 @ 4		

GENERAL NOTES
Types 'A–C'
The first large series of midget submarines, these boats were first designed in 1933 to support the battle fleet; their depot ships were the *Chiyoda* and *Chitose* (see p. 64). The code-name was A-Hyoteki, or 'A-Target' for *Nos. 1–2*, and Ko-Hyotelei for *Ha 1–2*, and production was begun by Kure DY and Ourizaki under total secrecy. From the outbreak of war the Type 'A' midgets were used in operations against Pearl Harbor, Sydney and Diego Suarez, but later they were relegated to local defence of

SUBMARINES 183

island bases. Endurance of the Type 'A' was limited, and so the experimental Type 'B' *Ha 53* was designed with greater radius. It had a generator to allow the re-charging of batteries. The production series Type 'C' (*Ha 62–76*) were identical.

MODIFICATIONS
Speed was reduced by the various alterations. Propeller-guards and caps for the TT were added to later boats (the TT were originally free-flooding). Some Type 'C' boats were fitted with an enlarged conning-tower and 2 periscopes for training.

FATES
Type 'A'
4 boats sunk at Pearl Harbor 7 December, 1941; 3 at Diego Suarez 30 May, 1942; 4 in Sydney Harbour 31 May, 1942; *Ha 8*, *Ha 22*, *Ha 38* and 5 other boats lost off Guadalcanal in 1942; 3 boats lost in the Aleutians in 1942–3.
Type 'C'
4 boats sunk off Cebu in 1944–5; 2 at Zamboanga in 1944–5; 2 off Dava in 1944–5.

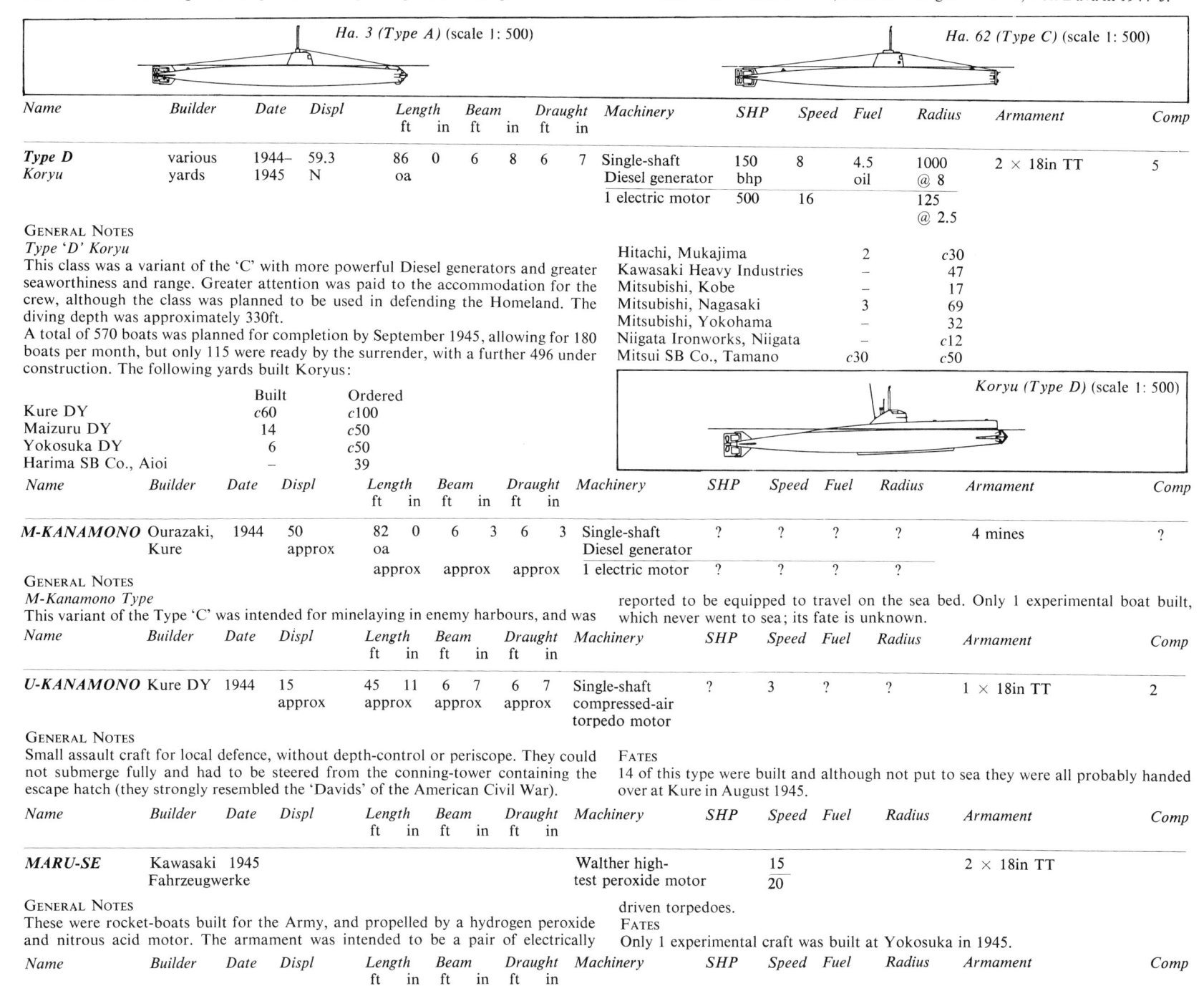

Ha. 3 (Type A) (scale 1: 500)

Ha. 62 (Type C) (scale 1: 500)

Name	Builder	Date	Displ	Length ft in	Beam ft in	Draught ft in	Machinery	SHP	Speed	Fuel	Radius	Armament	Comp
Type D *Koryu*	various yards	1944–1945	59.3 N	86 0 oa	6 8	6 7	Single-shaft Diesel generator	150 bhp	8	4.5 oil	1000 @ 8	2 × 18in TT	5
							1 electric motor	500	16		125 @ 2.5		

GENERAL NOTES
Type 'D' Koryu
This class was a variant of the 'C' with more powerful Diesel generators and greater seaworthiness and range. Greater attention was paid to the accommodation for the crew, although the class was planned to be used in defending the Homeland. The diving depth was approximately 330ft.

A total of 570 boats was planned for completion by September 1945, allowing for 180 boats per month, but only 115 were ready by the surrender, with a further 496 under construction. The following yards built Koryus:

	Built	Ordered
Kure DY	c60	c100
Maizuru DY	14	c50
Yokosuka DY	6	c50
Harima SB Co., Aioi	–	39

Hitachi, Mukajima	2	c30
Kawasaki Heavy Industries	–	47
Mitsubishi, Kobe	–	17
Mitsubishi, Nagasaki	3	69
Mitsubishi, Yokohama	–	32
Niigata Ironworks, Niigata	–	c12
Mitsui SB Co., Tamano	c30	c50

Koryu (Type D) (scale 1: 500)

Name	Builder	Date	Displ	Length ft in	Beam ft in	Draught ft in	Machinery	SHP	Speed	Fuel	Radius	Armament	Comp
M-KANAMONO	Ourazaki, Kure	1944	50 approx	82 0 oa approx	6 3 approx	6 3 approx	Single-shaft Diesel generator	?	?	?	?	4 mines	?
							1 electric motor	?	?	?	?		

GENERAL NOTES
M-Kanamono Type
This variant of the Type 'C' was intended for minelaying in enemy harbours, and was reported to be equipped to travel on the sea bed. Only 1 experimental boat built, which never went to sea; its fate is unknown.

Name	Builder	Date	Displ	Length ft in	Beam ft in	Draught ft in	Machinery	SHP	Speed	Fuel	Radius	Armament	Comp
U-KANAMONO	Kure DY	1944	15 approx	45 11 approx	6 7 approx	6 7 approx	Single-shaft compressed-air torpedo motor	?	3	?	?	1 × 18in TT	2

GENERAL NOTES
Small assault craft for local defence, without depth-control or periscope. They could not submerge fully and had to be steered from the conning-tower containing the escape hatch (they strongly resembled the 'Davids' of the American Civil War).

FATES
14 of this type were built and although not put to sea they were all probably handed over at Kure in August 1945.

Name	Builder	Date	Displ	Length ft in	Beam ft in	Draught ft in	Machinery	SHP	Speed	Fuel	Radius	Armament	Comp
MARU-SE	Kawasaki Fahrzeugwerke	1945					Walther high-test peroxide motor		15/20			2 × 18in TT	

GENERAL NOTES
These were rocket-boats built for the Army, and propelled by a hydrogen peroxide and nitrous acid motor. The armament was intended to be a pair of electrically driven torpedoes.

FATES
Only 1 experimental craft was built at Yokosuka in 1945.

Name	Builder	Date	Displ	Length ft in	Beam ft in	Draught ft in	Machinery	SHP	Speed	Fuel	Radius	Armament	Comp
SHINKAI	Ourazaki, Kure	1944	11.5	41 0 wl	5 5	3 11	Single-shaft electric motor	20	9	?	?	1 × 1-ton explosive charge	2

GENERAL NOTES
The smallest type of midget submarine, intended to attack ships anchored in Pacific atolls. More advanced mechanical and magnetic guidance was under development.

FATES
The design was known as '9-Kanamono'. It incorporated an oval hull-form with side ballast tanks. Only 1 boat was built for trials, and did not get to sea. Its career is unknown

Shinkai (scale 1: 200)   *U. Kanumono* (scale unspecified)

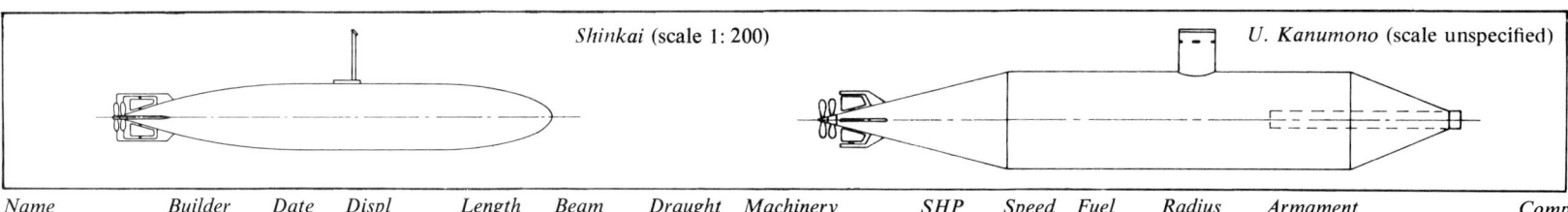

Name	Builder	Date	Displ	Length ft in	Beam ft in	Draught ft in	Machinery	SHP	Speed	Fuel	Radius	Armament	Comp
S-KANAMONO	Ourazaki, Kure	1943–1944	45	?	?	?	?	?	?	?	?	?	?

GENERAL NOTES
A very small midget with fixed side-fins, it was an experimental prototype for the *Kairyiu* Type.

FATE
Only 1 built, and fate unknown.

Name	Builder	Date	Displ	Length ft in	Beam ft in	Draught ft in	Machinery	SHP	Speed	Fuel	Radius	Armament	Comp
KAIRYU	Various yards	1945	19.24 surf 19.27 subm	56 11 wl	4 3 aft	4 3	1 single-shaft Isuzu gasoline engine	85 bhp	7.5	?	450 @ 5	2 × 18in TT or 1 600kg charge	2
							1 electric motor	80	10		36 @ 3		

GENERAL NOTES
Fitted with fixed side-fins, and diving rudders on the conning-tower and aft. The design was developed by modifying a Type 'A' midget with fins, and preliminary trials were carried out at the training base at Yokosuka in 1944. They were originally designed for local defence, to serve with the *Koryu* Type, but lack of torpedoes meant that they had to be used as suicide craft with a simple explosive charge in the nose.

MODIFICATIONS
An enlarged 40t version was planned in 1945.

FATES
It was intended to have 760 *Kairyu* ready by September 1945, but by the surrender in August, only 213 had been delivered, with a further 207 still under construction. The yards' production is shown below:

Yard	Completed	Building
Yokosuka DY	207	c30
Hakodate Dock Co., Hakodate	–	41
Hayashikane Heavy Industry, Shimonoseki	–	c10
Hitachi/Innoshima SY, Habu	–	5
Hitachi/Kasado	6	2
Fujinagata SB Co., Osaka	–	10
Mitsubishi, Yokohama	–	35
Osaka SB Co., Osaka	–	10
Hitachi/Sakurajima, Osaka	–	4
Uraga Dock Co., Uraga	–	c50
Kawaminami Industry, Uranosaki	–	c10

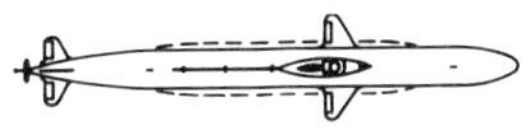

Kairyu (scale 1: 500)

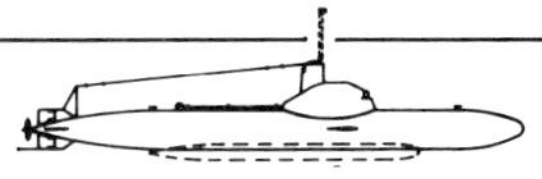

Name	Builder	Date	Displ	Length ft in	Beam ft in	Draught ft in	Machinery	SHP	Speed	Fuel	Radius	Armament	Comp
KAITEN Type 1	Naval yards	1944–1945	8.3	48 4 wl	3 3	3 3	2 Type '93' torpedo motors	550 bhp	30	?	78 @ 12	1 × 1.55t charge	1
KAITEN Type 2	Naval yards	1945	18.4	55 2 wl	4 5	4 5	1 Type '6' torpedo motor	1500 bhp	40	?	83 @ 20	1 × 1.55t charge	2
KAITEN Type 4	Naval yards	1945	18.2	55 2 wl	4 4	4 5	1 Type '6' torpedo motor	1800 bhp	40	?	62 @ 20	1 × 1.55t charge	2

A captured Kaiten Type 2 midget submarine, which can be seen today at Washington Navy Yard. Note the Japanese 18-inch gun in the background. (John Batchelor.)

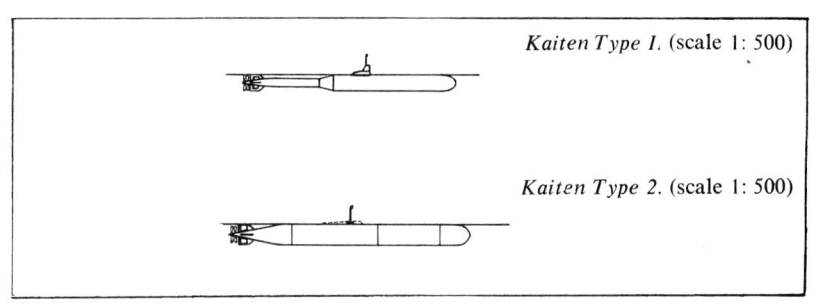

Kaiten Type 1. (scale 1: 500)

Kaiten Type 2. (scale 1: 500)

Name	Builder	Date	Displ	Length ft in	Beam ft in	Draught ft in	Machinery	SHP	Speed	Fuel	Radius	Armament	Comp
SENSUI SAGYO-SEN	Kure DY	1939–1940	20	42 0 oa	6 1	5 11	1 electric motor 1 reserve motor	16	4.4	?	?	None	?

SUBMARINES 185

GENERAL NOTES

Originally designed by Mitsubishi, Yokohama in 1935 to collect coral, but when the submarine *I.63* was lost accidentally on 2 February, 1939 the submersible was bought by the Navy. She was adapted as a rescue vessel on the lines of the German *Grundhai*, with mechanical 'arms' fitted with suction cups and capable of diving to a depth of 650ft. A similar submersible numbered *001* was built in 1970 by the Gabler Maschinenbau GmbH, Lübeck for the Kuo Feng Ocean Development Co., Taipeh, and proved capable of diving to a depth of nearly 1000ft.

FATES

The total number of submersibles built cannot be established, but at least 1 and possibly 2 were surrendered at Kure in August 1945.

Sensui Sagyo-sen (scale 1: 100)

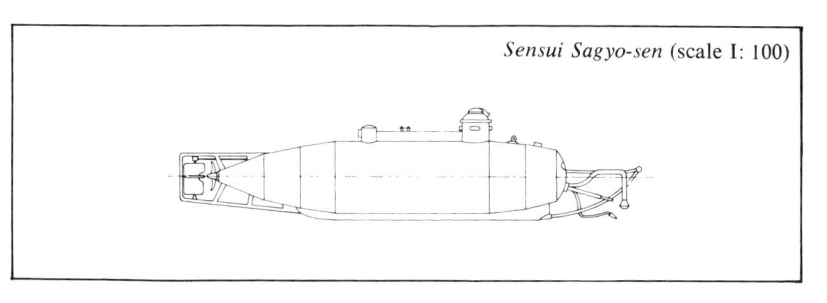

Name	Builder	Date	Displ	Length ft in	Beam ft in	Draught ft in	Machinery	SHP	Speed	Fuel	Radius	Armament	Comp
TOKUGATA UNKATO	Kure DY	1942–1943	43.9	77 1 oa	5 11	5 11	Compressed air engine	?	?	—	?	8–10ts of stores	1–2
UNKATO, L	Kure DY	1943	544	135 6 oa	16 1	16 1	None	—	?	—	—	9200 cu ft of stores	?
UNKATO, M	Kure DY	1943–1944	280	108 7 oa	12 10	12 10	None	—	?	—	—	6500 cu ft of stores	?
UNKATO, S	Kure DY	1943–1944	88.5	80 4 oa	8 0	8 0	None	—	?	—	—	2000 cu ft of stores	?

GENERAL NOTES
Tokugata Unkato

Small submarine-like stores vessels designed for one-way replenishment of the Solomon Islands garrisons. They had no ballast tanks and could only submerge when fully loaded. The bow portion was attached with bolts, to allow it to be left on shore after the craft had beached. The boats normally made a one-way passage and were then allowed to sink after reaching their destination.

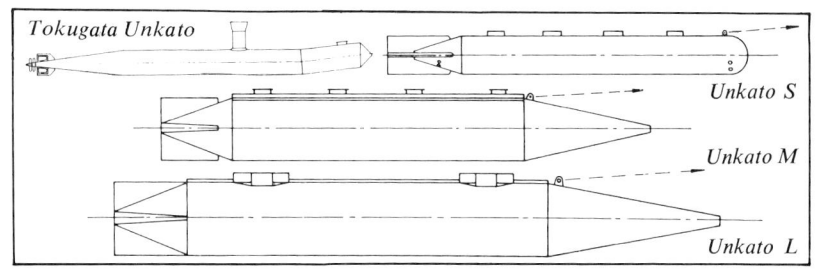

Tokugata Unkato

Unkato S

Unkato M

Unkato L

FATES
The total built is unknown, but 1 example survived at Ourazaki in 1945.

Unkato, Types L, M and S

GENERAL NOTES
An underwater towed container for revictualling island garrisons that had been cut off. The hull was designed to submerge when the towed speed reached 4–5 knots. The reserve of buoyancy was: *Type L* 1.5ts, *Type M* 1.2ts, *Type S* 1.2ts. The maximum depth when loaded was: *Type L* 400ft, *Type M* 450ft, *Type S* 180ft. Maintaining trim was extremely difficult, and few reached their destination.

CONSTRUCTION
The hulls were made in sections, either 2 (*Type L*) or 4 (*Types M* and *S*).

FATES
2 units of *Type L* were built in May 1943, and were tried with the submarine *I.37*. No. 1 was taken to Rabaul in the autumn of 1943. 10 to 20 of the *M* and *S* types were built, and some were surrendered at Kure in August 1945. 2 were used post-war by the Shell Co. for carrying supplies to the CRA copper mines in Bougainville.

12. Escort and Patrol Vessels

Name	Builder	Date	Displ	Length ft in	Beam ft in	Draught ft in	Machinery	SHP	Speed	Fuel	Radius	Armament	Comp
SHIMUSHU Type (4 units)	various yards	1938–1941	1020 F 860 S	255 0 oa 250 0 wl 237 10 pp	29 10	10 0	2-shaft Diesel motors	4200 bhp	19.7	?	8000 @ 16	3 × 4.7in 45-cal 4 × 25mm AA 12 DGs	150

GENERAL NOTES
Built under the 1937 Programme as *Nos. 9–12*; a repeat group was ordered under the 1942 Programme as *Nos. 790–792*. They were known as Type 'A' and also rated as minesweepers. The top 5 feet of the funnel was bulbous in shape.

RE-ARMAMENT
In May 1942 they were rebuilt and the minesweeping gear was replaced by 24 DCs. By August 1943 the armament was 15 × 25mm AA, 60 DCs, one 3in A/S mortar.

CAREERS
Shimushu
Launched 13 December, 1939; completed 30 June, 1940 by Mitsui, Tamano; damaged 25 November, 1944 by US submarine in western part of Manila Bay (14° N, 119° 25′ E); repaired at Maizuru with new bow; surrendered August 1945 and used on repatriation until 1947; handed over to Soviet Union 5 July, 1947.

Hachijo
Launched 10 April, 1940; completed 31 March, 1941 by Sasebo DY; badly damaged

11 May, 1945 in Kataoka Bay (50° 55′ N, 156° 25′ E); taken to Maizuru; BU 5 April, 1948 by Ino, Maizuru.

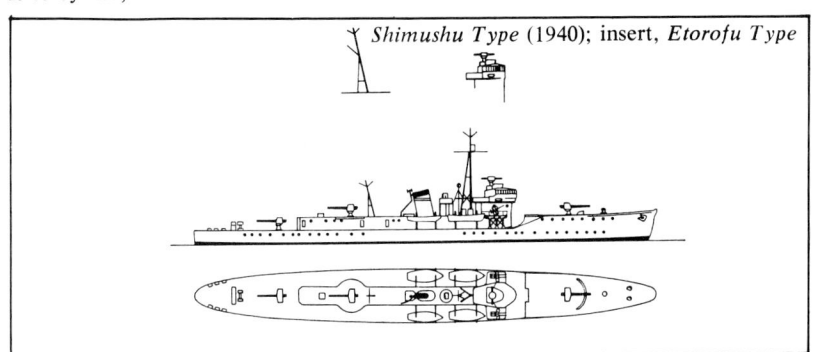

Shimushu Type (1940); insert, *Etorofu Type*

Kunashiri
Launched 6 May, 1940; completed 3 October, 1940 by Tsurumi; surrendered August 1945; repatriation service 1945–6; wrecked off Omaezaki, Suruga Wan (34° 35′ N, 138° 15′ E) 4 June, 1946; abandoned 25 June and stricken.
Ishigaki
Launched 14 September, 1940 and completed 15 February, 1941 by Mitsui, Tamano; torpedoed 31 May, 1944 by US submarine *Herring* 70 m W of Matsuwa, in the Kuriles (48° 30′ N, 151° 30′ E); stricken 10 July, 1944.
Nos. 790–793
Projected but contracts never placed.

Shimushu Type (1944)

Name	Builder	Date	Displ	Length ft in	Beam ft in	Draught ft in	Machinery	SHP	Speed	Fuel	Radius	Armament	Comp
ETOROFU Type (14 units)	various yards	1942–1944	1020 F 870 S	255 0 oa 250 0 wl 237 10 pp	29 10	10 0	2-shaft Diesel motors	4200 bhp	19.7	?	8000 @ 16	3 × 4.7in 45-cal 4 × 25mm AA (*Kanju* only 2) 36 DCs	147

GENERAL NOTES
Built under the War Programme of 1941 as *Nos. 310–339*, an improved *Shimushu* type without the bulbous funnel and with a more conventional bow form.

RE-ARMAMENT
By August 1943 they were armed with 15 × 25mm AA (*Kanju* had 21), 60 DCs and a 3in A/S mortar.

CAREERS
Etorofu
Launched 29 January, 1943; completed 25 March, 1943 by Hitachi, Sakurajima; surrendered August 1945; repatriation service until 1947; handed over to USA 5 August, 1947 and BU at Kure 13 October.
Oki
Launched 20 December, 1942; completed 31 March, 1943 by Uraga, Tokyo; surrendered August 1945 and used on repatriation duties until 1947; handed over to China 29 August, 1947 as *Ch'ang Pai* but fell into Communist hands 1949; re-armed 1955.
Sado
Launched 28 November, 1942; completed 1 April, 1943 by Tsurumi; torpedoed 22, August, 1944 by US submarine *Haddo* 35 m W of Manila (14° 15′ N, 120° 25′ E).
Matsuwa
Launched 19 April, 1942; completed 1 April, 1943 by Mitsui, Tamano; torpedoed 22 August, 1944 by US submarine *Harder* 55 m WSW of Manila (14° 15′ N, 120° 05′ E).
Fukue
Launched 2 April, 1943; completed 15 July, 1943 by Uraga Dock, Tokyo; surrendered August 1945 and used on repatriation until 1947; handed over to Great Britain and BU.
Tsushima
Launched 20 March, 1943; completed 15 August, 1943 by Tsurumi; surrendered August 1945 and used on repatriation service until 1947; handed over to China 31 July, 1947 and renamed *Lin An*.

Mutsure
Launched 10 April, 1943; completed 15 August, 1943 by Hitachi, Sakurajima; torpedoed 2 September, 1943 by US submarine *Snapper* 85 m NNW of Truk (08° 40′ N, 151° 31′ E); stricken 1 November, 1943.
Wakamiya
Launched 19 April, 1943; completed 25 August, 1943 by Mitsui, Tamano; torpedoed 23 November, 1943 by US submarine *Gudgeon* 70 m S of Shushan Island, China (28° 49′ N, 122° 11′ E); stricken 5 January, 1944.
Kanju
Launched 7 August, 1943; completed 30 October, 1943 by Uraga Dock, Tokyo; sunk 15 August, 1945 by Russian aircraft near Wansan, Korea (39° 10′ N, 127° 27′ E).
Hirado
Launched 30 June, 1943; completed 1 November, 1943 by Hitachi, Sakurajima; torpedoed 12 September, 1944 by US submarine *Growler* 250 m E of Hainan Island (17° 54′ N, 114° 49′ E); stricken 10 November.
Amakusa
Launched 31 September, 1943; completed 20 November, 1943 by Hitachi, Sakurajima; sunk 9 August, 1945 by aircraft of TF 38 in Onagawa harbour (38° 26′ N, 141° 30′ E).
Manju
Launched 31 July, 1943; completed 30 November, 1943 by Mitsui, Tamano; badly damaged 3 April, 1945 by air attack in Hong Kong but probably repaired; surrendered in August and BU in 1946.
Kasado
Launched 9 December, 1943; completed 30 March, 1944 by Uraga Dock, Tokyo; damaged 15 July, 1945 by aircraft of TF 38 but probably repaired; towed to Ominato and temporarily repaired; moved to Sasebo under her own power 20 August, 1945; BU 31 May, 1948 by Amakusa Kaiji.
Iki
Launched 5 February, 1943; completed 10 April, 1944 by Mitsui, Tamano; torpedoed 24 May, 1944 by US submarine *Raton* 240 m W of Singapore (01° 17′ N, 107° 53′ E).

Name	Builder	Date	Displ	Length ft in	Beam ft in	Draught ft in	Machinery	SHP	Speed	Fuel	Radius	Armament	Comp
MIKURA Type (8 units)	various yards	1942–1944	1020 F 940 S	258 6 oa 254 3 wl 237 10 pp	29 7	10	2-shaft Diesel motors	4200 bhp	19.5	?	5000 @ 16	3 × 4.7in AA 4 × 25mm AA 1 × 3in A/S mortar 120 DCs	150

GENERAL NOTES
Built under the 1941 War Programme (*Nos. 310–339*) as 'B' Type, or an improved *Etorofu*; also rated as minesweepers. In March 1944 *Chiburi* was the first ship to have Type '3' underwater detection gear. Building time was 6 to 12 months.

RE-ARMAMENT
In 1944–5 they had 14 × to 18 × 25mm AA; in 1945 the minesweeping gear was replaced by greater DC stowage. *Miyake* was armed with 16 × 25mm AA.

CAREERS
Mikura
Launched 16 July, 1943; completed 30 October, 1943 by Tsurumi; damaged in Formosa Straits 10 February, 1945 (23° 51′ N, 117° 25′ E) in collision with Japanese escort *No. 33*; missing 2 May and stricken 25 May.
Miyake
Launched 30 August, 1943; completed 30 November, 1943 by Tsurumi; badly damaged 21 August, 1945 by ground mine near Moji (33° 58′ N, 131° E); towed to Kure and repaired, then earmarked for repatriation but did not carry out any work; BU at Sasebo 1 July, 1948.
Awaji
Launched 30 October, 1943; completed 15 February, 1944 by Hitachi, Sakurajima; torpedoed 2 June, 1944 by US submarine *Guitarro* near Yasho Island, Formosa (22° 34′ N, 121° 51′ E), stricken 10 July.
Kurahashi
Launched 15 October, 1943; completed 10 March, 1944 by Tsurumi; surrendered August 1945 and used as minesweeper 1945–7; handed over to Great Britain 14 September, 1947 and BU.

Awaji was an improved *Etorofu* class anti-submarine escort, launched in October 1943. She is seen here in Osaka harbour just after completion. (Shizuo Fukui.)

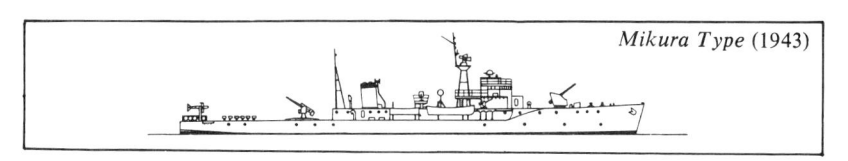

Mikura Type (1943)

Nomi
Launched 3 December, 1943; completed 15 March, 1944 by Tsurumi; torpedoed 14 April, 1945 by US submarine *Tirante* NW of Chezhudo (23° 25′ N, 126° 15′ E); stricken 25 May.
Chiburi
Launched 30 November, 1943; completed 13 May, 1944 by Tsurumi; sunk 12 January, 1945 by US TF 38 45 m E of Cape San Jacques (10° 20′ N, 107° 50′ E).
Yashiro
Launched 16 February, 1944; completed 3 June, 1944 by Hitachi, Sakurajima; surrendered August 1945; minesweeping duties 1945–7; handed over to China 29 August, 1947 and renamed *Cheng An*.
Kusagaki
Launched 22 January, 1944; completed 1 July, 1944 by Tsurumi; torpedoed 7 August, 1944 by US submarine *Guitarro* 60 m W of Manila (14° 51′ N, 119° 59′ E); stricken 10 October.

Nomi in 1944. (Jentschura.)

Name	Builder	Date	Displ	Length ft in	Beam ft in	Draught ft in	Machinery	SHP	Speed	Fuel	Radius	Armament	Comp
UKURU Type (33 units)	various yards	1944–1945	1020 F 940 S	258 5 oa 251 0 wl 237 10 pp	29 10	10 0	2-shaft Diesel motors	4200 bhp	19.5	?	5000 @ 16	3 × 4.7in AA 6 × 25mm AA 1 × 3in A/S mortar 120 DCs	150

GENERAL NOTES
Built under 1941 Programme (*Nos. 310–39* – *Ukuru* Group), 1942 Programme (*Nos. 5251–5284* – *Yaku* Class) and 1943–4 Programme (*Nos. 4701–4721* – *Inagi* Class) as improved *Mikuras*. They were probably completed with more depth-charge throwers in place of racks. To assist prefabrication, curved plating was eliminated, and the funnel was made six-sided, and building time was reduced to 4–5 months per unit.

ARMAMENT
In 1944–5 the AA armament was altered during completion to allow 16 × to 20 × 25mm to be carried.

CAREERS
Ukuru
Launched 15 May, 1944; completed 16 October, 1944 by Tsurumi; surrendered August 1945 and used from 1945 to 1947 on minesweeping service as a tender for other sweepers; transferred to Maritime Self-Defence Force in 1948 and renamed *Satsuma* (*PL.104*) in 1955.
Hiburi
Launched 10 April, 1944; completed 4 August, 1944 by Hitachi, Sakurajima; torpedoed 22 August, 1944 by US submarine *Harder* 35 m WSW of Manila (14° 15′ N, 120° 25′ E); stricken 10 October.

Shonan
Launched 19 May, 1944; completed 7 August, 1944 by Hitachi; torpedoed 25 February, 1945 by US submarine *Hoe* S of Hainan Island (17° 52′ N, 110° 05′ E); stricken 10 April.
Daito
Launched 24 June, 1944; completed 11 September, 1944 by Hitachi; surrendered August 1945 and used on minesweeping duties; sunk by floating mine 16 November, 1945 at about 11.00 hrs in the Eastern Sound of the Tsushima Straits.
Okinawa
Launched 19 June, 1944; completed 3 October, 1944 by Tsurumi; sunk 30 July, 1945 by US TF 38 in shallow water 6 m NNW of Maizuru (35° 30′ N, 135° 21′ E).
Kume
Launched 15 August, 1944; completed 3 November, 1944 by Hitachi; torpedoed

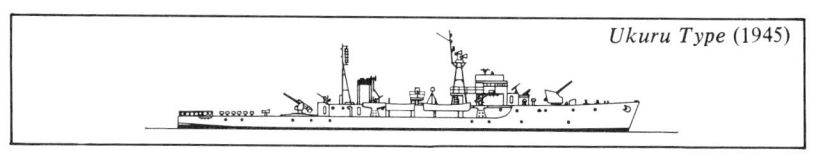

Ukuru Type (1945)

ESCORT AND PATROL VESSELS

28 January, 1945 by US submarine *Spadefish* SE of Tsingtau (33° 54′ N, 122° 55′ E); stricken 10 March.

Ikuna
Launched 4 September, 1944; completed 15 November, 1944 by Hitachi; surrendered August 1945 and attached to minesweeping force 1945–7 as a tender for sweepers at Kobe; to Maritime Self-Defence Force in 1948 and renamed *Okija (PL.102)* in 1945.

Shinnan
Launched 5 September, 1944; completed 26 November, 1944 by Uraga Dock, Tokyo; surrendered August 1945 and attached to minesweeping forces as a tender for sweepers at Sasebo; to Maritime Self-Defence Force 1948 and renamed *Tsugaru* in 1955.

Yaku
Launched 5 September, 1944; completed 5 December, 1944 by Uraga Dock, Tokyo; torpedoed 23 February, 1945 by US submarine *Hammerhead* 15 m S of Cape Varella (12° 44′ N, 109° 29′ E); stricken 10 April.

Aguni
Launched 21 September, 1944; completed 17 January, 1945 by Tsurumi; badly damaged 27 May, 1945 by mine off Maizuru; not repaired when surrendered August 1945; BU 20 May, 1948 by Iino, Maizuru.

Mokuto
Launched 7 January, 1945; completed in the spring by Hitachi; sunk by mine 4 April, 1945 at 09.05 hrs in the Shimonoseki Straits (33° 53′ N, 131° 03′ E).

Inagi
Launched 25 September, 1944; completed 26 January, 1945; by Mitsui, Tamano; sunk 9 August, 1945 by US TF 38 in Hachinohe harbour (40° 32′ N, 141° 30′ E)

Uku
Launched 12 November, 1944; completed 8 February, 1945 by Sasebo DY; damaged by mine 9 May 4 m SE of Shimonoseki, but repaired; surrendered August 1945 and served on repatriation service until 1947; handed over to US 4 July, 1947 and BU.

Chikubu
Launched 24 November, 1944; completed 26 February, 1945 by Uraga Dock; surrendered August 1945 and used on minesweeping duties until 1947 and as a tender for sweepers; to Maritime Self-Defence Force 1948 and renamed *Atsumi (PL.103)* in 1955.

Habushi
Launched 20 November, 1944; completed 20 February, 1945 by Mitsui, Tamano; surrendered August 1945 and used on repatriation service until 1946; handed over to US 6 September, 1947 and BU.

Sakito
Launched 29 November, 1944; completed 28 February, 1945 by Hitachi; damaged by mine 27 June in Changgu Sound, Korea (34° 13′ N, 126° 36′ E); temporarily repaired at Pusan and ended war at Sasebo; BU 30 November, 1947 at Sasebo.

Kuga
Launched 19 November, 1944; completed 5 March, 1945 at Sasebo DY; badly damaged by mine 25 June off Maizuru; surrendered unrepaired in August and BU 30 May, 1948 by Iino at Maizuru.

Oga
Launched 30 December, 1944; completed 5 April, 1945 by Mitsui, Tamano; torpedoed 2 May, by US submarine *Springer* in Yellow Sea (33° 56′ N, 122° 49′ E); stricken 25 May.

Kozu
Launched 31 December, 1944; completed 3 May, 1945 by Uraga Dock; surrendered August 1945 and used on minesweeping service until 1947; handed over to Soviet Union 28 August, 1947.

Kanawa
Launched 15 November, 1944; completed 5 May, 1945 by Mitsui; surrendered August 1945 and used on repatriation service until 1947; handed over to Great Britain 14 August, 1947 and BU.

Shiga
Launched 9 February, 1945; completed 13 May, 1945 at Sasebo DY; surrendered August 1945 and used on minesweeping service until 1947 as a ferry between Pusan and Hakata; to Maritime Self-Defence Force 1948 and renamed *Kojima (PL.106)* in 1955.

Amami
Launched 30 November, 1944; completed 27 May, 1945 by Tsurumi; surrendered August 1945 and used on repatriation service until 1947; handed over to Great Britain 20 December, 1947 and BU at Hiroshima.

Hodaka
Launched 28 January, 1945; completed 3 June, 1945 by Uraga Dock; surrendered August 1945 and used on repatriation service until 1947; handed over to US 19 July, 1947 and BU 1 March, 1948 at Uraga.

Habuto
Launched 28 February, 1945; completed 10 June, 1945 by Hitachi; surrendered August 1945 and used on repatriation service until 1947; in January 1947 she became an accommodation ship in Otake; handed over to Great Britain 16 July, 1947 and BU.

Io
Launched 12 February, 1945; completed June 1945 at Maizuru DY; surrendered August 1945 and served on repatriation service until 1946; in April 1946 she became an accommodation ship at Senzaki; BU at Sasebo 1 July, 1946.

Takane
Launched 13 February, 1945; completed 3 July, 1945 by Mitsui; damaged near Maizuru 30 July by US TF 38 and surrendered August; BU at Kure 27 November, 1947.

Ikara
Launched 22 February, 1945; completed 23 July, 1945 by Uraga; damaged 1 August in Koguch Channel, Nanao Wan (37° 05′ N, 137° E); subsequently sunk by sudden flooding; hull raised and BU.

Shisaka
Launched 31 October, 1944; completed July 1945 by Hitachi; surrendered August and served until 1947 on repatriation service; handed over to China 6 July, 1947 as *Hui An*; Communist China 1949 and disarmed in 1955.

Ikino
Launched 11 March, 1945; completed July 1945 by Uraga Dock; surrendered August and served on repatriation duties until 1947; handed over to Soviet Union 29 July, 1947.

Otsu
Launched 10 May, 1945 by Hitachi; probably sunk during fitting-out between 24 July and August by TF 38(?); BU 25 March, 1948 by Hitachi.

Urumi
Launched 1945; completed August 1945 by Uraga Dock; BU.

Murotsu
Launched 15 June, 1945; completed August 1945 by Uraga Dock; BU.

Tomishiri
Laid down 5 March, 1945 by Sakurajima, Osaka; 20% complete at war's end; material BU at Osaka 23 October, 1947.

Nos. 5251–5284
18 units of the *Yaku* Class, contracts cancelled August 1944.

Nos. 4701–4721
12 units of the *Inagi* Class, contracts cancelled August 1944. 79 units planned 1944–5 but contracts not placed.

Name	Builder	Date	Displ	Length ft in	Beam ft in	Draught ft in	Machinery	SHP	Speed	Fuel	Radius	Armament	Comp
TYPE C (Odd numbers) (118 units)	various yards	1943– 1945	810 F 745 S	221 5 oa 216 6 wl 206 8 pp	27 7	9 6	2-shaft Diesel motors	1900 bhp	16.5	?	6500 @ 14	2 × 4.7in AA 4 × to 6 × 25mm AA 1 × 3in A/S mortar 120 DCs	136

GENERAL NOTES
Ordered under the 1943–4 Programme (*Nos. 2401–2532*) and 1944–5 Programme (168 units) as reduced editions of the *Ukuru* type. Prefabrication was used and the design avoided the use of scarce materials as far as possible. Welding was used and building time averaged 3–8 months. The anti-submarine armament was 1 depth-charge rack and 12 throwers. Builders were: Mitsubishi; Kobe; Tsurumi; Nihonkai Dock; Tayama; Maizuru DY; Naniwa, Osaka; Kyowa, Osaka.

MODIFICATIONS
As they trimmed by the bow, stern ballast had to be added. In 1944–5 the AA armament was increased to 12 to 16 × 25mm.

CAREERS
No. 1
Launched 1944; completed 2 April, 1944; sunk by B-24 aircraft 6 April, 1945, 40 m SSW of Amoy (23° 55′ N, 117° 40′ E); stricken 25 May.

No. 3
Launched 1944; completed 30 March, 1944; sunk by TF 38 9 January, 1945 off Keelung, Formosa (25° 10′ N, 121° 45′ E); stricken 10 March.

No. 5
Launched 1944; completed 11 April, 1944; sunk by TF 38 21 September, 1944 near Masinloc, Luzan (150° 30′ N, 119° 50′ E); stricken 25 May, 1945.

No. 7
Launched 1944; completed 18 April, 1944; torpedoed 14 November, 1944 by US submarine *Ray* 165 m NW of Cape Bolinao (17° 46′ N, 117° 57′ E); stricken 10 January, 1945.

No. 9
Launched 1944; completed 28 March, 1944: torpedoed 14 February, 1945 by US submarine *Gato* SW of Chezhudo (32° 43′ N, 125° 37′ E); stricken 10 April, 1945.

No. 11
Launched 1944; completed 5 April, 1944; sunk 10 November, 1944 by US aircraft off Ormuc, Leyte (10° 51′ N, 124° 32′ E); stricken 10 January, 1945.

No. 13
Launched 1944; completed 26 April, 1944; torpedoed 14 August, 1945 by US submarine *Torsk* WNW of Maizuru (35° 41′ N, 134° 38′ E); stricken 15 September, 1945.

No. 15
Launched 1944; completed 1 May, 1944; torpedoed 6 June, 1944 by US submarine *Raton* SE of Cape San Jacques (8° 58′ N, 109° 30′ E); stricken 10 May, 1945.

No. 17
Launched 1944; completed 7 May, 1944; sunk 12 January, 1945 by US TF 38, 45 m E of Cape San Jacques (10° 20′ N, 107° 50′ E); stricken 10 March, 1945.

No. 19
Launched 1944; completed 20 May, 1944; sunk 12 January, 1945 as *No. 17* above.

No. 21
Launched 1944; completed 18 August, 1944; torpedoed 6 October, 1944 by US submarine *Seahorse* 140 m NW of Cape Bojeador, Luzon (19° 45′ N, 118° 22′ E); stricken 10 January, 1945.

No. 23
Launched 1944; completed 29 October, 1944; sunk 3 May, 1945 by US TF 38 N of Bay of Quinhon (14° 15′ N, 109° 10′ E); stricken 10 March, 1945.

No. 25
Launched 1944; completed 30 July, 1944; torpedoed 3 May, 1945 by US submarine *Springer* 180 m WSW of Mokpo, Korea (33° 56′ N, 122° 49′ E); stricken 25 May, 1945.

No. 27
Launched 1944; completed 16 August, 1944; surrendered August 1945, and served on repatriation duties until 1947; handed over to Great Britain 1947 and BU.

No. 29
Launched 1944; completed 13 October, 1944; badly damaged 28 May, 1945 by mine near Sasebo (33° 07′ N, 129° 44′ E); probably repaired by August, and surrendered; BU at Sasebo by 1 February, 1948.

No. 31
Launched 1944; completed 13 October, 1944; torpedoed 14 April, 1945 by US submarine *Tirante* near Chezhudo (33° 25′ N, 126° 15′ E); stricken 25 May, 1945.

No. 33
Launched 1944; completed 13 October, 1944; sunk 28 March, 1945 by aircraft of US TF 58 SSE of Miyazaki (31° 45′ N, 131° 45′ E); stricken 25 May, 1945.

No. 35
Launched 1944; completed 21 November, 1944; sunk 12 January, 1945 by aircraft of US TF 38 7 m SW of Cape Padaran (11° 10′ N, 108° 55′ E); stricken 10 March, 1945.

No. 37
Launched 1944; completed 1944; surrendered August 1945 and used on repatriation duties; 4 September, 1947 handed over to US Navy; BU by Kawasaki 30 November, 1947.

No. 39
Launched 1944; completed 9 November, 1944; sunk 7 August, 1945 by US aircraft off Kuche Island, Korea (35° 06′ N, 129° 03′ E); stricken 10 September, 1945.

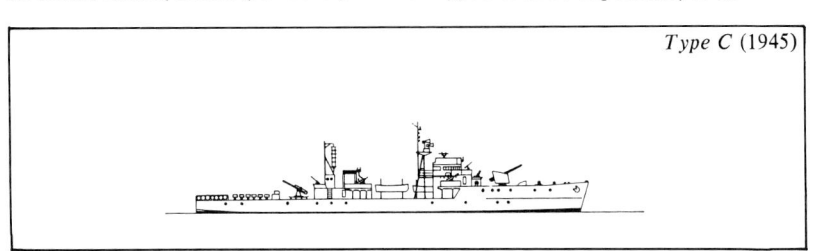

Type C (1945)

No. 41
Launched 1944; completed 26 November, 1944; torpedoed 9 June, 1945 by US submarine *Sea Owl* 50 m SE of Mokpo, Korea (34° 18′ N, 127° 18′ E); stricken 10 August, 1945.

No. 43
Launched 1944; completed 10 September, 1944; sunk 12 January, 1945 by US aircraft of TF 38 7 m SW of Cape Padaran (11° 10′ N, 108° 55′ E); stricken 10 March, 1945.

No. 45
Launched 1944; completed 1944; badly damaged 28 July, 1945 by aircraft of US TF 38 off Owase (34° 05′ N, 136° 15′ E); BU at Owase 30 April, 1948.

No. 47
Launched 1944; completed 1944; torpedoed 14 August, 1945 by US submarine *Torsk* 14 m WNW of Maizuru (35° 41′ N, 134° 38′ E).

No. 49
Launched 1944; completed 1944; surrendered August 1945 and used on minesweeping until 1947; handed over to USA 1 September, 1947 and BU at Shimizu 2 January, 1948.

No. 51
Launched 1944; completed 29 October 1944; sunk by her own depth-charges 12 January, 1945 after attack from aircraft of US TF 38 N of Quinhon Bay (14° 15′ N, 109° 10′ E); stricken 10 March 1945.

No. 53
Launched 1944; completed 18 January, 1945; torpedoed 7 February, 1945 by US submarine *Besugo* near Cainranh Bay (11° 55′ N, 109° 20′ E); stricken 10 April, 1945.

No. 55
Launched 1944; completed 1 February, 1945; surrendered August 1945 and used on repatriation duties until 1947; handed over to Great Britain and BU.

No. 57
Launched 1944; completed 28 February, 1945; surrendered August 1945 and used on repatriation duties until 1947; BU 1947.

No. 59
Launched 1945; completed 5 April, 1945; surrendered August 1945 and used on repatriation duties until 1946; hulked at Kure in May 1946 but on 30 July sank after colliding with the wreck of the battleship *Hyuga*; repaired at Kure and stricken 7 September, 1946; BU at Kure 1 February, 1947.

No. 61
Launched 1944; completed 20 November, 1944; badly damaged by mine 9 February, 1945 10 m off Cape San Jacques (10° 10′ N, 106° 55′ E); towed to Saigon but not repaired; disarmed 15 August and put into Reserve; BU at Saigon.

No. 63
Launched 1944; completed 1944; mined 10 August, 1945 at 18.30 hrs at Ogudii Seto in Nanao Bay (37° 08′ N, 136° 50′ E) and sank with her bow out of the water; BU at Nanao 25 June, 1948.

No. 65
Launched 1944; completed 1 April, 1945; sunk 14 July, 1945 by aircraft of US TF 38, 15 m S of Muroran, Hokkaido (42° 21′ N, 140° 59′ E).

No. 67
Launched 1944; completed 28 December, 1944; surrendered August 1945 and served on repatriation duties until 1947; transferred to China 6 July, 1947 a *Ying K'ou*; later renamed *Swe An*, and in 1955 *Jui An*.

No. 69
Launched 1944; completed 1 February, 1945; badly damaged by US aircraft 8 March, 1945 E of Hainan Island (19° 02′ N, 111° 50′ E); sank in tow 16 March 8 m off Cape Hong Kong (22° N, 113° 40′ E); stricken 10 May.

No. 71
Launched 1945; completed 20 May, 1945; surrendered August 1945 and used on repatriation duties until 1947; handed over to Soviet Union 28 August, 1947.

No. 73
Launched 1945; completed 1945; torpedoed 16 April, 1945 by US submarine *Sunfish* 2 m off Todosaki (39° 36′ N, 142° 05′ E).

No. 75
Launched 1945; completed 1945; lost 23 August, 1945 while on passage from Wakhanai to Hokkaido, probably mined.

No. 77
Launched 1945; completed 1945; surrendered August 1945 and used on mine clearance until 1946; handed over to Soviet Union 28 August, 1947.

No. 79
Launched 1945; completed 16 July, 1945; surrendered August 1945 and used on repatriation duties until 1947; handed over to Soviet Union 29 July, 1947.

No. 81
Launched 1944; completed 25 January, 1945; surrendered August 1945 and used on repatriation duties until 1947; handed over to China as *Mukden* 29 August, 1947 and later became *Huang An*; 1949 became Communist *Sheng Yang*; believed sunk by air attack 16 March, 1949 100 m off Takao (Hsuchow).

No. 83
Launched 16 January, 1945; by Kiyawa, Osaka but completed by Naniwa Yard; while still incomplete towed to Osaka and surrendered there in August; BU at Naniwa 17 March, 1948.

No. 85
Launched 1945; completed 31 May, 1945; surrendered August 1945 and used on repatriation duties until 1947; handed over to China as *Shin An*; 1949 taken over by Communists and later hulked.

No. 87
Launched 1945; completed June 1945; surrendered August 1945; served on repatriation duties until 1947; handed over to USA 29 July, 1947 and BU at Kawanami 15 May, 1948.

No. 89
Launched 3 May, 1945; moored incomplete, without machinery at Nihonkai, Toyama; surrendered August 1945; BU at Toyana 30 November, 1947.

No. 91
Contract No. 2246 cancelled August 1944.

No. 93
Contract No. 2247: keel laid by Kyowa, Osaka, but work stopped early in 1945 and the material was BU.

No. 95
Launched 1945; completed July 1945; badly damaged in collision 5 July, 1945 in Tsurumi Harbour, Tokyo Bay; damaged again by mine in Yokosuka, 8 July; BU 20 July, 1948 at Tsurumi.

No. 97
Launched 25 May, 1945; surrendered incomplete at Tsurumi August 1945; completion continued post-war for service on repatriation duties, but because of the shortage of spares she never made a single voyage; she was moored at Kure until 1947 and was BU at Kure by 27 November, 1947.

No. 99
Contract No. 2250 cancelled August 1944.

No. 101
Contract No. 2251 begun by Kyawa, Osaka, but work stopped early in 1945 and the material was BU.

No. 103
Contract No. 2252 cancelled August 1944.

No. 105
Contract No. 2253 ready for launching at surrender in August 1945; launched January 1946 at Tsurumi and completed April; repatriation duties 1946–7; handed over to Soviet Union 5 July, 1947.

No. 107
Contract No. 2254 as *No. 105* but launched 16 March, 1946 and completed May; handed over to China 29 August, 1947 as *Ch'ao An*.

No. 109
Contract No. 2255 begun at Nichankai, Toyama but contract cancelled early in 1945.

No. 111, *No. 113* and *No. 115*
Contracts 2256–2258 cancelled August 1944.

No. 117
Contract No. 2459 laid down at Tsurumi, Yokohama but cancelled March 1945.

No. 119–No. 203
Contract Nos. 2460–2502 (43 units) cancelled August 1944.

No. 205
Launched 1944; completed 16 December, 1944; surrendered August 1945 and used for repatriation until 1947; handed over to China 31 July, 1947 as *Hsin An*; wrecked 26 September, 1954 in Pescadores Islands; hulked and renamed *Ch'ang An*.

No. 207
Launched 1944; completed 21 November, 1944; surrendered August 1945 and used for repatriation until 1947; handed over to USA 4 July, 1947 and BU.

No. 209 and *No. 211*
Contract Nos. 2505 and 2506 cancelled August 1944.

No. 213
Launched 1944; completed 23 March, 1945; sunk 18 August, 1945 by Soviet aircraft off Pusan, Korea (35° 10′ N, 129° E).

No. 215
Launched 1945; completed 1945 and surrendered August; used for repatriation until 1947; handed over to China 6 June, 1947 as *Liao Hai*; later hulked and renamed *Tsing Pai*.

No. 217
Launched 1945; completed 1945 and surrendered August; used for minesweeping until 1947; handed over to Great Britain 5 September, 1947 and BU 10 February, 1948 by Kawanami.

No. 219
Launched 1945; completed 1945; sunk by aircraft of US TF 38 15 July, 1945 2 m SW of Hakodate (41° 48′ N, 140° 41′ E).

No. 221
Launched 1945; completed 1945; surrendered August 1945; used for repatriation until 1947; handed over to Soviet Union 29 July, 1947.

No. 223
Launched 4 July, 1945; surrendered incomplete at Mitsubishi, Kobe; no more work was done on her and she was BU at Kobe by 23 October, 1947.

No. 225
Launched 1945; in August 1945 she lay at Kure disabled for lack of spares; BU 30 April, 1948 by Amakisa Kaiji.

No. 227
Launched 1945; completed 1945 and surrendered August; repatriation service until 1946; handed over to Soviet Union 5 July, 1947.

No. 229
Contract No. 2515 for Mitsubishi, Kobe suspended March 1945.

No. 231 and *No. 233*
Contract Nos. 2516 nd 2517 cancelled 1944–5.

No. 235
Contract No. 2518 for Niigata yard suspended March 1945.

No. 237–No. 263
Contract Nos. 2519–2532 (14 units) cancelled between August 1944 and March 1945.

No. 265 onwards
Unnumbered contracts for a further 168 units were not placed.

Name	Builder	Date	Displ	Length ft in	Beam ft in	Draught ft in	Machinery	SHP	Speed	Fuel	Radius	Armament	Comp
TYPE D (Even numbers) (102 units)	various yards	1943–1945	940 F 740 S	228 0 oa 223 1 wl 213 3 pp	28 3	10 0	Single-shaft Turbine, 2 Kampon boilers	2500	17.5	?	4500 @ 14	2 × 4.7in AA 6 × 25mm 1 × 3in A/S mortar 120 DCs	160

GENERAL NOTES
Ordered under the 1943–4 Programme (*Nos. 2701–2843*, and a further 60 units), and very similar to the Type 'C'. They adopted the same turbines as the standard Type 2A freighters, and some units were completed in less than 75 days. A full-size *wooden* prototype was built on land at Mukaijima to test the concept. One depth-charge rack and 12 throwers were carried.

MODIFICATIONS
In 1944–5 AA armament was increased to 12 × to 16 × 25mm guns. In January 1945, shortage of oil caused a conversion to coal-firing boilers.

CAREERS
No. 2
Launched 1944; completed 30 March, 1944; sunk 30 July, 1945 in shallow water in Maizuru by aircraft of US TF 38; BU 20 July, 1948 by Iino, Maizuru.

No. 4
Launched 1944; completed 5 April, 1944; torpedoed 13 August, 1945 by US submarine *Atule*, 50 m off Cerino Saki, Hokkaido (42° 16′ N, 142° 12′ E); stricken 15 September, 1945.

No. 6
Launched 1944; completed 2 April, 1944; badly damaged on 24, 25 and 28 July, 1945

by US aircraft off Toba in Mie Prefecture (34° 28′ N, 136° 42′ E); BU at Tokai 30 June, 1948.

No. 8
Launched 11 January, 1944; completed 29 February, 1944; surrendered August 1945 and used on repatriation duties until 1947; handed over to Great Britain 16 July, 1947 and BU.

No. 10
Launched 11 January, 1944; completed 29 February, 1944; torpedoed 27 September, 1944 by US submarine *Plaice* 100 m NNW of Amami-Oshima (29° 26′ N, 128° 50′ E); stricken 10 November, 1944.

No. 12
Launched 1944; completed 14 April, 1944; surrendered August 1945 and used for mine clearance until 1946; handed over to USA 5 September, 1947 and BU at Sasebo.

No. 14
Launched 1944; completed 5 May, 1944; surrendered August 1945 and used for repatriation until 1947; handed over to China 6 July, 1947 as *Chieh 5*; became Communist *Wu Chang* in 1949.

No. 16
Launched 1944; completed 25 April, 1944; surrendered August 1945 and used for repatriation until 1947; handed over to Great Britain 14 August, 1947 and BU.

No. 18
Launched 11 January, 1944; completed 8 March, 1944; sunk 29 March, 1945 by US aircraft 110 m N of Cape Varella (14° 44′ N, 109° 16′ E'; stricken 25 May, 1945.

No. 20
Launched 11 January, 1944; completed 11 April, 1944; sunk December 1944 by US aircraft NW of San Fernando Harbour, Luzon (16° 43′ N, 120° 18′ E); stricken 25 May, 1945.

No. 22
Launched 27 January, 1944; completed 24 April, 1944; surrendered August 1945 and used for mine clearance until 1946; handed over to USA 5 September, 1947 and BU at Sasebo

No. 24
Launched 27 January, 1944; completed 28 March, 1944; torpedoed 28 June, 1944 by US submarine *Archerfish* 30 m W of Iwo Jima (24° 44′ N, 140° 20′ E); stricken 20 August, 1944.

No. 26
Launched 11 April, 1944; completed 31 May, 1944; surrendered August 1945 and used for mine clearance until 1946; handed over to USA 6 September, 1947 and BU 13 October, 1947 at Kure.

No. 28
Launched 11 April, 1944; completed 31 May, 1944; torpedoed 14 December, 1944 by US submarine *Blenny*, 3 m W of Hermana Island, Luzon (15° 46′ N, 119° 45′ E); stricken 10 February, 1945.

No. 30
Launched 10 May, 1944; completed 26 July, 1944; sunk 28 July, 1945 by aircraft of US TF 38 in Yura Straits (34° 20′ N, 135° E); stricken 15 September, 1945.

No. 32
Launched 10 May, 1944; completed 30 June, 1944; surrendered August 1945 and used for repatriation until 1947; handed over to Great Britain 16 July, 1947 and BU.

No. 34
Launched 1944; completed 4 November, 1944; surrendered August 1945 and used for repatriation until 1947; handed over to Soviet Union 5 July, 1947.

No. 36
Launched 1944; completed 28 December, 1944; surrendered August 1945 and used on repatriation duties until 1947; handed over to USA 19 July, 1947 and BU by Tsurumi.

No. 38
Launched 1944; completed 6 November, 1944; torpedoed 25 November, 1944 by US submarine *Hardhead* 60 m W of Manila (14° 22′ N, 119° 57′ E); stricken 10 January, 1945.

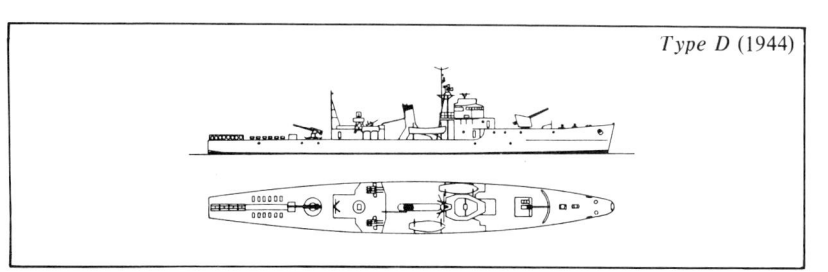

No. 40
Launched 1944; completed 1 February, 1945; surrendered August 1945 and used on mine clearance until 1946; handed over to China 29 August, 1947 as *Ch'eng An*.

No. 42
Launched 7 July, 1944; completed 25 August, 1944; torpedoed 10 January, 1945 by US submarine *Puffer*, 100 m W of Okinawa (270° 01′ N, 126° 34′ E).

No. 44
Launched 7 July, 1944; completed 21 August, 1944; surrendered August 1945 and used for repatriation until 1947; handed over to USA 5 July, 1947 and BU.

No. 46
Launched 1944; completed 8 October, 1944; mined and sank 17 August, 1945 off Mokpo, Korea (34° 51′ N, 126° 02′ E); stricken 15 September.

No. 48
Launched 1944; completed 1945 and surrendered August; used for mine clearance until 1946; handed over to Soviet Union 28 August, 1947.

No. 50
Launched 1944; completed 5 December, 1944; badly damaged by US submarine torpedo 1 May, 1945 off Wakayama, Kii Suido (34° 15′ N, 135° 05′ E); probably repaired before being surrendered in August at Osaka; BU at Osaka by 30 April, 1948.

No. 52
Launched 7 August, 1944; completed 25 September, 1944; surrendered August 1945 and used for repatriation; handed over to Soviet Union 29 July, 1947.

No. 54
Launched 7 August, 1944; completed 30 September, 1944; sunk 15 December, 1944 by aircraft of US TF 38 in Luzon Straits (19° 25′ N, 121° 25′ E); stricken 10 February, 1945.

No. 56
Launched 1944; completed 1944; torpedoed 17 February, 1945 by US submarine *Bowfin*, 5 m E of Mikurajina (33° 54′ N, 139° 43′ E).

No. 58
Launched 1945; surrendered incomplete in August 1945 but completed post-war for repatriation duties 1946–7; handed over to USA 31 July, 1947 and BU at Sasebo.

No. 60
Launched 1944; completed 16 December, 1944; surrendered August 1945 and used for repatriation until 1947; handed over to Great Britain 14 August, 1947 and BU.

No. 62
Launched 1945 but surrendered incomplete at Mukaijima, Ohanichi in August 1945; towed to Kure 18 December, 1945 and completed for repatriation service; sprang a leak in Kure 14 January, 1946 but raised 27 March; BU 31 May, 1948 by Amakusa Kaiji.

No. 64
Launched 5 September, 1944; completed 19 October, 1944; torpedoed 3 December, 1944 by US submarine *Pipefish* SE of Hainan Island (18° 36′ N, 111° 54′ E); stricken 10 February, 1945.

No. 66
Launched 5 September, 1944; completed 21 October, 1944; sunk 13 March, 1945 by US aircraft off South China (23° 30′ N, 117° 10′ E); stricken 25 April.

No. 68
Launched 1944; completed 1945; sunk 24 March by aircraft of US TF 58 170 m off Amami-Oshima (30° N, 126° 36′ E); stricken 10 May, 1945.

No. 70
Contract No. 2735 laid down 1945 at Hitachi, Onamichi but work stopped in March.

No. 72
Launched 1944; completed 31 January, 1945; torpedoed 1 July, 1945 by US submarine *Haddo* off Changsan, W. Korea (38° 08′ N, 124° 38′ E); stricken 10 August.

No. 74
Launched 1944; completed 10 December, 1944; sunk 14 July, 1945 by aircraft of US TF 38, 15 m S of Muroran, Hokkaido (42° 21′ N, 140° 59′ E).

No. 76
Launched 1944; completed 20 February, 1945; surrendered August 1945 and used on mine clearance until 1946; handed over to Soviet Union 28 August, 1947.

No. 78
Launched 1945 but surrendered incomplete in August; completed 4 April, 1946 for repatriation duties until 1947; handed over to Soviet Union 29 July, 1947.

No. 80
Contract No. 2740 laid down 1945 by Mukaijima, but work stopped in March.

No. 82
Launched 18 November, 1944; completed 3 December, 1945; sunk 10 August by Russian aircraft 7 m SSW of Kumsudan, Korea (41° 21′ N, 130° E); stricken 15 September.

Type D (1944)

No. 84
Launched, 18 November, 1944; completed 31 December, 1945; torpedoed 29 March by US submarine *Hammerhead* 115 m N of Cape Varella (14° 44′ N, 109° 16′ E); stricken 10 May.
No. 86–No. 100
Contract Nos. 2743–2750 (8 units) cancelled August 1944.
No. 102
Launched 4 December, 1944; completed 20 January, 1945; surrendered August 1945 and used for mine clearance until 1947; handed over to Soviet Union 28 August, 1947.
No. 104
Launched 16 December, 1944; completed 31 January, 1945; surrendered August 1945 and used for mine clearance until 1947; handed over to China 29 August, 1947 as *T'ai An.*
No. 106
Launched 1944; completed 5 March, 1945; surrendered August and used for repatriation until 1947; handed over to USA 5 July, 1947 and BU.
No.108 and *No.110*
Contract Nos. 2754–2755 cancelled Spring 1944.
No. 112
Launched 1944, completed 8 December, 1944; torpedoed 18 July, 1945 by US submarine *Barb* in Bay of Aniwa (46° 06′ N, 142° 16′ E); stricken 15 September.
No. 114
Contract No. 2757 cancelled Spring 1944.
No. 116
Launched 1945 but surrendered incomplete in August; completed post-war for repatriation service; ran aground 25 March, 1946 off Makurazaki, Kyushu (31° 16′ N, 130° 18′ E); BU.
No. 118
Launched 1944; completed 27 December, 1944; surrendered August 1945 and used for repatriation until 1947; handed over to China 31 July, 1947 as *Chieh 12;* became Communist *Ch'ang Sha* 1949.
No. 120
Contract No. 2760 cancelled Spring 1944.
No. 122
Contract No. 2761 laid down at Ishikawajima, Tokyo but suspended March 1945.
No. 124
Launched 1944; completed 1945; badly damaged 10 April at 15.47 hrs by mine off Futaojima, Shimonoseki; probably repaired before surrender in August; BU at Kawanami by 10 February, 1948.
No. 126
Launched 1944; completed 1945 and used for repatriation until 1947; handed over to Great Britain 14 August, 1947 and BU.
Nr.128
Contract No. 2764 cancelled Spring 1944.
No. 130
Launched 1944; completed 20 November, 1944; sunk 29 March, 1945 by US aircraft 105 m N of Cape Varella (14° 39′ N, 109° 16′ E); stricken 10 May.
No. 132
Launched 1944; completed 18 October, 1944; surrendered August 1945 and used for repatriation until 1946; BU 1 July, 1948 at Sasebo.
No. 134
Launched 1944; completed 11 November, 1944; sunk 6 April, 1945 by US B-24 aircraft 50 m SSW of Amoy (23° 55′ N, 117° 40′ E); stricken 10 May, 1945.
No. 136
Contract No. 2768 cancelled Autumn 1944.
No. 138
Launched 1944; completed 5 December, 1944; sunk 2 January, 1945 by aircraft off San Fernando, Luzon (16° 37′ N, 120° 19′ E); stricken 10 March, 1945.
No. 140
Contract No. 2770 cancelled Autumn 1944.
No. 142
Launched 1945 but surrendered incomplete in August; completed post-war for repatriation service 1946–7; handed over to Soviet Union 29 July, 1947.
No. 144
Launched 1944; completed 1944; torpedoed 2 February, 1945 by US submarine *Besugo* E of Cape Laguan (04° 11′ N, 104° 35′ E); stricken 10 April.
No. 146 and *No. 148*
Contract Nos. 2773 and 2774 cancelled Autumn 1944.
No. 150
Launched 1944; completed 8 February, 1945; surrendered August 1945 and used for repatriation until 1947; handed over to USA 5 July, 1947 and BU.

No. 152
Contract No. 2776 cancelled Autumn, 1947.
No. 154
Launched 1945; completed 23 March, 1945; surrendered August 1945 and used for mine clearance until 1946; handed over to Great Britain 10 September, 1947 and BU 1 March, 1948 by Urabe, Takuma.
No. 156
Launched and completed 1945; surrendered August 1945 and used for mine clearance until 1946; handed over to Great Britain 4 September, 1947 and BU 11 December, 1947 by Iino, Maizuru.
No. 158
Launched and completed 1945; surrendered August 1945 and used for repatriation until 1947; handed over to USA 25 July, 1947; BU 31 December, 1947 by Iino, Maizuru.
No. 160
Launched and completed 1945; surrendered August 1945 and used for repatriation until 1947; handed over to Great Britain 8 September, 1947 and BU 10 February, 1948 by Nanao.
No. 162–No. 184
Contracts Nos. 2781–2792 (12 units) cancelled Autumn 1944.
No. 186
Launched 30 December, 1944; completed 15 February, 1945; sunk 2 April, 1945 by US TF 58 in Bay of Seai, Amami-Oshima (28° 07′ N, 129° 09′ E).
No. 188
Contract No. 2794 cancelled Autumn 1944.
No. 190
Launched 16 January, 1945; completed 21 February, 1945; damaged 28 July by US TF 38 in Straits of Yura; surrendered at Shimonoseki in August and BU 1 April, 1948 by Moji.
No. 192
Launched 30 January, 1945; completed 28 February, 1945; surrendered August and used for repatriation until 1947; handed over to China 31 July, 1947 as *T'ung An.*
No. 194
Launched 15 February, 1945; completed 15 March, 1945; surrendered August and used for repatriation until 1947; handed over to China 6 July, 1947 as *Chieh 6;* later became *Wei Hai* and in 1949 became Communist *Chi An.*
No. 196
Launched 26 February, 1945 and completed 31 March, 1945; surrendered August and used for repatriation to 1947; handed over to Soviet Union 5 July, 1947.
No. 198
Launched 26 February, 1945 and completed 31 March; surrendered August and used for repatriation until 1947; handed over to China 31 July, 1947 as *Chieh 14;* fell into Communist hands in 1949 and became *Si Nam.*
No. 200
Launched 19 March, 1945; completed 20 April, 1945; badly damaged 17 May by mine in Bay of Miyazu, W of Maizuru; surrendered August and BU 1 July, 1948 by Iino, Maizuru.
No. 202
Launched 2 April, 1945 and completed 7 July; surrendered August with mine damage; BU 31 December, 1947 at Sasebo.
No. 204
Launched 14 April, 1945; completed 11 July, 1945; damaged 17 July, 1945 in Bay of Senzaki, Honshu; surrendered in August and BU 31 January, 1948 at Nagasaki.

The Type 'D' escorts were distinguished from the Type 'C' by a thinner funnel. *No. 22*, seen here, was completed in April 1944 and survived the war. (Shizuo Fukui.)

No. 206–No. 286
Contract Nos. 2803–2843 (41 units) cancelled autumn 1944.

No. 288 et seq.
60 units planned for 1944–5 but not ordered.

Name	Builder	Date	Displ	Length ft in	Beam ft in	Draught ft in	Machinery	SHP	Speed	Fuel	Radius	Armament	Comp
TYPE A CDa Nos. 1–2	various yards	1945	282 N 278 designed	159 1 wl 150 11 pp	17 9	7 9	2-shaft Diesel motors	800 bhp	15.0	?	?	1 × 40mm AA 6 × 25mm AA 2 Kaiten 4 DCs	?
TYPE B CDa Nos. 101–157	various yards	1945	290 N 280 designed	123 0 wl 114 10 pp	19 11	8 0	2-shaft Diesel motors	800 bhp	12.5	?	?	1 × 40mm AA 6 × 25mm AA 1 Kaiten 8 DCs	?

GENERAL NOTES
Light escorts, completed as Kaiten-carriers as part of the anti-invasion planning. Type 'A' built under the 1943–4 Programme (*Nos. 1851–1870*), with steel hulls. Type 'B' built under the same programme (*Nos. 1701–1760*) but had wooden hulls. A further 40 unnumbered units of Type 'B' were ordered under the 1944–5 Programme.

Type A CDa Nos. 1-2 (1945)   *Type B CDa Nos. 101-157 (1945)*

RE-ARMAMENT NOTES
They were partially modified for service as coastal escorts. The new displacement was 270ts (Type 'A') to 285ts (Type 'B'), with 60 DCs in place of the Kaiten midget submarine.

CAREERS
CDa No. 1
Launched June 1945 by Kawanami, Uranosaki; 50% complete when surrendered in August; sunk 19 September, 1945 after she sprang a leak.
CDa No. 2
Launched June 1945 as *No. 1*; lost 19 September, 1945 after she sprang a leak.
18 units
Contract Nos. 1853–1870 not laid down, and cancelled.
CDa No. 101
Contract No. 1701 laid down at Funaya, Hakodate; not launched by August 1945; material utilized for civil shipping built post-war.
CDa No. 103
Contract No. 1703 laid down at Yamanishi, Ishinomaki; fate as *No. 101*.
CDa No. 104
Contract No. 1704 laid down at Yamanishi, Ishinomaki; fate as *No. 101*.
CDa No. 109
Contract No. 1709 laid down at Murakami, Ishinomaki; fate as *No. 101*.
CDa No. 113
Contract No. 1713 laid down at Miho, Shimizu; fate as *No. 101*.
CDa No. 118
Contract No. 1718 laid down at Koyanagi, Shizuoka; fate as *No. 101*.
CDa No. 119
Contract No. 1719 laid down at Kayanagi, Shizuoka; fate as *No. 101*.
CDa No. 122
Contract No. 1722 laid down at Ishikawa, Ujiyamada; fate as *No. 101*.
CDa No. 125
Contract No. 1725 laid down at Goriki, Ujiyamada; fate as *No. 101*.
CDa No. 126
Contract No. 1726 laid down at Goriki, Ujiyamada; fate as *No. 101*.
CDa No. 128
Contract No. 1728 laid down at Nishii, Ujiyamada; fate as *No. 101*.
CDa No. 131
Contract No. 1731 laid down at Takamatsu, Shikoku; fate as *No. 101*.
CDa No. 132
Contract No. 1732 laid down at Takamatsu, Shikoku; fate as *No. 101*.
CDa No. 133
Contract No. 1733 laid down at Takamatsu, Shikoku; fate as *No. 101*.
CDa No. 137
Contract No. 1737 laid down at Tokushima; fate as *No. 101*.
CDa No. 138
Contract No. 1738 laid down at Tokushima; fate as *No. 101*.
CDa No. 139
Contract No. 1739 laid down at Tokushima; fate as *No. 101*.
CDa No. 141
Contract No. 1741 laid down at Fukushima, Matsue; fate as *No. 101*.
CDa No. 144
Contract No. 1744 laid down at Hayashikane, Shimonoseki; fate as *No. 101*.
CDa No. 148
Contract No. 1748 laid down at Jin'en, Moji; fate as *No. 101*.
CDa No. 151
Contract No. 1751 laid down at Fukuoka; fate as *No. 101*.
CDa No. 157
Contract No. 1757 laid down at Takaoka, Saga; fate as *No. 101*.
38 units
Contract Nos. 1702–1760 cancelled before laying down.
40 units
Projected in 1944–5 but not ordered.

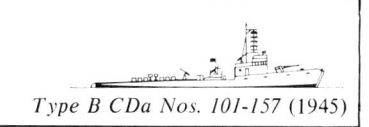

Name	Builder	Date	Displ	Length ft in	Beam ft in	Draught ft in	Machinery	SHP	Speed	Fuel	Radius	Armament	Comp
P No. 101 ex-*Thracian* (HMS)	Hawthorn, Leslie & Co., Hebburn-on-Tyne	1920– 1923	1233 F 2090 N 905 S	276 0 oa 265 0 pp	26 10	9 10	2 × 2-shaft Brown-Curtis turbines 3 Yarrow water-tube boilers	10000	25	300 oil	?	3 × 3.9in 1 × .303in MG 4 × 24in TT DCs	90 approx
P No. 102 ex-*Stewart* (USS)	Cramp & Sons, Philadelphia	1919– 1920	1539 N	311 4 wl 303 1 pp	30 10	10 10	2-shaft Turbines 4 boilers	28500	26	375 oil	2500 @ 12	2 × 3in AA 2 × 13mm AA	120 approx
P No. 103 ex-*Finch* (USS)	Standard SB Co., New York	1918	1100 N 980 S	173 10 wl	35 5	8 10	Single-shaft triple-expansion 2 Babcock boilers	1400 ihp	13	275 oil	1400 @ 10	2 × 3in AA 48 DCs	70 approx
P No. 104 ex-*Valk* (Dutch)	Mij., Fijenoood, Rotterdam	1929– 1930	775 S	230 0 oa 218 1 pp	29 6	9 2	2-shaft VTE 2 cyl boilers	3350 ihp	15	? oil	?	1 × 3in AA 2 × 13mm AA 8 × 25mm AA 48 DCs	265

194 ESCORT AND PATROL VESSELS

Name	Builder	Date	Displ	Length ft in	Beam ft in	Draught ft in	Machinery	SHP	Speed	Fuel	Radius	Armament	Comp
P No. 105 ex-*Arayat* (USS)	?	?	1200 N	?	?	?	?	?	?	?	?	?	?
P No. 106 ex-*Banckert* (Dutch)	Burgerhouts Masch, Rotterdam	1928–1930	1316 S	322 0 oa 307 0 pp	31 2	9 10	2-shaft Parsons turbines 4 Yarrow boilers	31000	36	330 oil	?	2 AA 12 AA 24 DCs 2 14m Daiharsu	140 approx
P No. 107 ex-*Genessee* ex-*Monocacy*	Maryland Steel Co., Sparrows Pt.	1905	1180 N 1000 official	180 5 wl 174 5 pp	29 1	11 1	Single-shaft 3-cyl VTE	1000 ihp	15	286 coal	?	2 × 3in AA 48 DCs	?
P No. 108 ex-*Arend*	Mij. Fijenoord, Rotterdam	1929–1930	775 S	230 oa 218 2 pp	29 7	9 2	2-shaft VTE, 2 cyl boilers	3350 ihp	15	?	?	1 × 3in AA 8 × 25mm AA 2 × 13mm AA 48 DCs	65 approx
P No. 109 ex-*Fazant*	Marinewerft, Soerabaja	1930–1931	623 S	156 9 wl 153 3 pp	27 6	8 10	Single-shaft 3-cyl VTE, 2-cyl boilers	525 ihp	12	?	?	1 × 3in AA 48 DCs	40 approx

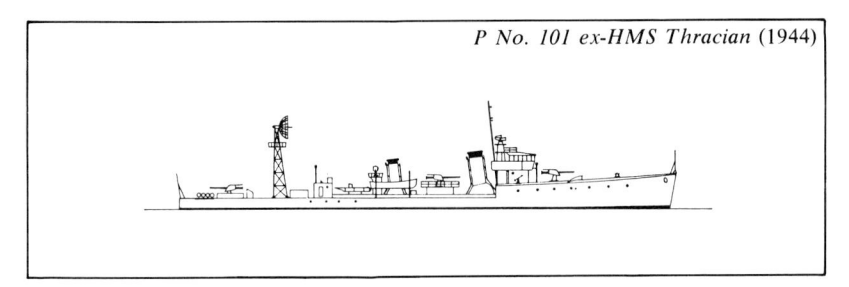

P No. 101 ex-HMS Thracian (1944)

GENERAL NOTES

No. 101 was an ex-British destroyer of the Admiralty 'S' Class (905ts, 2 × 4in and 1 × 3in gun, mines).

No. 102 was an ex-US destroyer of the *Semmes* Class (1215ts, 4 × 4in and 5 × 20mm AA guns, 6 × 21in TT).

No. 103 was an ex-US minesweeper of the *Bittern* type (840ts, 2 × 3in AA).

Nos. 104 and *108* were ex-Dutch customs and fishery protection patrol craft (1011ts, 2 × 75mm and 2 MGs).

No. 105 has an obscure origin, but could have been an ex-US gunboat captured from Spain in 1898 and sold for commercial use in 1910.

No. 106 was an ex-Dutch destroyer of the *Van Galen* Class (1316ts, 4 × 4in 50-cal, 1 × 75mm AA and 4 × 40mm AA guns, 6 × 21in TT, 1 aircraft).

No. 107 was a former US tug (745ts, 2 × 3in AA).

No. 109 was an ex-Dutch customs patrol craft (623ts, 1 × 75mm and 1 MG).

RECONSTRUCTION

No. 101 was reboilered with only 2 boilers, and re-armed with 25mm AA guns and possibly 13mm. In 1944 she was completely rebuilt as a radar trials ship. *No. 102* was rebuilt with 3 boilers, and had the 2 foremost funnels trunked together to change her silhouette entirely from the original 'flush-decker' profile. In November 1944 she was armed with 2 × 80mm and 16 × 25mm AA guns, and 72 DCs. She then had a tripod mast, shortened funnels and enlarged bilge keels.

CAREERS

P No. 101

Launched 5 March, 1920 and completed 1 April, 1922 as HMS *Thracian*; beached at Hong Kong on 25 December, 1941; fell into Japanese hands and renamed *Patrol Vessel No. 101* on 10 July, 1942; repairs completed at Hong Kong by 25 November, 1942; reclassified as a training ship on 15 March, 1944 and renamed *Toku 1 Go Renshu-Tei* (special training ship No. 1) at Yokosuka; returned to the British in Hong Kong in October 1945 and BU there in February 1946.

P No. 102

Launched 4 March, 1920 and completed 15 September, 1920 as USS *Stewart*; capsized in dry dock at Soerabaya on 20 February, 1942 while under repair, following attack by Japanese aircraft; scuttled 2 March but raised by Japanese in February 1943; rebuilt and on 15 June, 1943 she was reclassified as *Patrol Vessel No. 102*; repairs completed 20 September, 1943; surrendered at Kure 15 October, 1945 and returned to USA on 3 November; sunk off San Francisco 24 May, 1946 as a target for US warships.

P No. 103

Launched 30 March, 1918 and completed 10 September, 1918 as USS *Finch*; sunk 11 April, 1942 by Japanese gunfire at Manila; raised by the Japanese and reclassified 1 April, 1943 as *Patrol Vessel No. 103*; sunk 12 January, 1945 by US aircraft of TF 38 7 m SW of Cape Padaran (11° 10′ N, 108° 55′ E); stricken 10 March.

P No. 104

Launched 19 October, 1929 and completed 1930 as Dutch *Valk*; scuttled 8 March, 1942 as a blockship in Tjilatjap Harbour after being damaged by air attack; raised by the Japanese in April 1943 and reclassified as *Patrol Vessel No. 104* 1 September, 1943; completed repairs 31 January, 1944; badly damaged 25 May, 1945 3 m off the Kammon Straits; laid up disarmed in Maizuru; surrendered in August 1945 but mined off Nishiyama 24 August, 1945.

P No. 105

Possibly an ex-Spanish gunboat, and if so she was launched at Cavite in 1888, sunk in the Pasig River in 1898 and taken into the USN after salvage; sold 1910 for commercial use and taken over by the Japanese in 1942 (the origin of this vessel is obscure); reclassified as *Patrol Vessel No. 105* 1 September, 1943; torpedoed 29 November, 1944 by US MTB *PT.127* in Ormuc Bay (10° 59′ N, 124° 33′ E); stricken 10 January, 1945.

P No. 106

Launched 14 November, 1929 and completed 4 November, 1930 as HNethMS *Banckert*; damaged by Japanese air attack off Soerabaya on 24 and 28 February sunk, 2 March, at Soerabaya but salvaged by Japanese; reclassified 20 April, 1944 as *Patrol Vessel No. 106* but not completed, although her machinery was reported to be capable of 26 knots; surrendered at Soerabaya in August 1945 and sunk as a target by Netherlands Navy September 1949 in Madura Straits.

P No. 107

Launched and completed 1905 as commercial tug *Monocacy* (617 GRT); taken over by USN 1917 as USS *Genessee* (AT.55); sunk 5 May, 1942 off Corregidor but later raised by Japanese; reclassified 20 April, 1944 as *Patrol Vessel No. 107*; sunk 5 November, 1944 by aircraft of US TF 38 off Corregidor (13° 50′ N, 120° 20′ E); stricken 10 January, 1945.

P No. 108

Launched 21 May, 1929 and completed 16 January, 1930 as Dutch *Arend*; sunk off Tandjong Priok 1 March, 1942 but salvaged by Japanese 29 February, 1944; reclassified 31 July, 1944 as *Patrol Vessel No. 108*; sunk 28 March, 1945 by US aircraft of TF 38 60 m NNW of Macassar (04° 15′ S, 119° 05′ E); stricken 10 May, 1945.

P No. 109

Launched 1930 and completed 1931 as the Dutch *Fazant*; sunk 1 March, 1942 at Tandjong Priok but raised by Japanese; reclassified 15 October, 1944 as *Patrol Vessel No. 109*; surrendered at Batavia in August 1945 and handed over to Netherlands Navy 21 April, 1946; transferred to Indonesia in 1951 as the *Kartika*; stricken 1954 and BU.

Name	Builder	Date	Displ	Length ft in	Beam ft in	Draught ft in	Machinery	SHP	Speed	Fuel	Radius	Armament	Comp
Type *Pa No. 1*	various yards	1944–1945	250 N 238 S	97 9 wl 93 6 pp	20 1	7 8	Single-shaft Diesel motor	400 bhp	9	?	3500 @ 9	2 × 25mm AA 3 × 13mm AA 8 DCs	?

A typical small trawler, used for various combatant and auxiliary duties.

GENERAL NOTES
Built under the 1943–4 Programme (*Nos. 2121–2400*) as auxiliary patrol vessels, they were also intended for post-war conversion to fishing craft. They had wooden hulls and were intended to have auxiliary sailpower. 16 private yards specializing in fishing craft built the hulls, but machinery was installed in naval yards.

ARMAMENT
2 torpedo-launchers were originally planned. In January 1945 they had 4 × 25mm AA, 2 × 4.7m rocket-launchers and 12 DCs.

APPEARANCE
Some units had thinner funnels and a foremast abaft the bridge.

CAREERS
Pa No. 1
Launched 1945 at Yamanishi (*No. 2121*); probably surrendered at Yokosuka in August 1945.
Pa No. 2
Launched 1945; at Yamanishi (*No. 2122*); surrendered at Yokohama in August 1945, and lay at Kawasaki, Kobe until 1947.
Pa No. 3
Launched 1945 at Yamanishi (*No. 2123*); surrendered at Yokosuka in August 1945; transferred to Japanese mercantile marine 1947.
Pa No. 4
Launched 1945 at Yamanishi (*No. 2124*); still fitting out in August 1945 but completed post-war for mercantile use.
Pa No. 25
Launched 1945 at Marakami (*No. 2125*); damaged 22 May, 1945 by US aircraft off Southern Honshu; surrendered at Shimanoseki in August but lost in a storm 19 September, 1945.
Pa No. 26
Launched 1945 at Murakami (*No. 2146*); fate as *No. 3*.
Pa No. 27
Launched 1945 at Murakami (*No. 2147*); incomplete in August 1945 and BU subsequently.
Pa No. 31
Launched 1945 at Funaya (*No. 2151*); surrendered August 1945 and used for mine clearance until 1947; transferred to MSDF in 1948 as *MS.18* and renamed *Ukishima* in 1956.
Pa No. 32
Launched 1945 at Funaya (*No. 2152*); still fitting out in August 1945; lay at Ominato in December 1946; probably became merchant ship in 1947.
Pa No. 33 and *Pa No. 34*
Built at Funaya (*Nos. 2153–2154*) but BU on stocks after August 1945.
Pa No. 37
Launched 1945 at Mino (*No. 2157*); sunk 18 July, 1945 by US aircraft of TF 38 in Yokosuka Harbour.
Pa No. 38
Built at Mino as *No. 2158* but still under construction in August 1945, and later BU.
Pa No. 54
Launched 1945 at Kayanagi (*No. 2174*); surrendered August 1945 but lost subsequently as a result of a leak.
Pa No. 55
Built at Kayanagi (*No. 2175*) but still under construction in August 1945; fate as *No. 4*.
Pa No. 64
Launched 1945 at Saga (*No. 2184*); surrendered August 1945 and used for repatriation until 1947; fate as *No. 3*.
Pa No. 65
Launched 1945 at Saga (*No. 2185*) but still building at surrender; fate unknown.
Pa No. 66
Built at Saga (*No. 2186*) but not completed, and BU after surrender.
Pa No. 84
Launched 1945 at Yanago (*No. 2204*); surrendered August 1945 and used for mine clearance until 1947; handed over to MSDF as *MS.19* and renamed *Tsurushima* in 1965.
Pa No. 85
Built at Yanago (*No. 2205*) but still under construction in August 1945; fate as *No. 4*.
Pa No. 86
Built at Yanago (*No. 2206*) but scrapped incomplete after August 1945.
Pa No. 90
Launched 1945 at Ishikawa (*No. 2210*); lost by unknown cause off Sakata in August or September 1945.
Pa No. 91
Launched 1945 at Ishikawa (*No. 2211*) but still completing in August 1945; fate unknown.
Pa No. 92
Launched 1945 at Ishikawa (*No. 2212*) but still completing in August 1945; fate unknown.
Pa No. 93
Launched 1945 at Ishikawa (*No. 2213*) but still completing in August 1945; fate unknown.
Pa No. 110
Launched 1945 at Nishii (*No. 2230*); sunk 18 July, 1945 by aircraft of US TF 38 in Yokosuka Harbour.
Pa No. 111
Launched 1945 at Nishii (*No. 2231*); almost complete in August 1945; probably sunk post-war.
Pa No. 122
Launched 1945 at Goriki (*No. 2242*); badly damaged 18 July, 1945 by aircraft of TF 38 in Yokosuka Harbour and later sank.
Pa No. 123
Launched 1945 at Goriki (*No. 2243*); almost complete in August 1945 but fate unknown.
Pa No. 134
Launched 1945 at Shikoku (*No. 2254*) and completed 20 January; surrendered August 1945 and used for mine clearance; transferred 1948 to MSDF as *MS.20* but renamed *Otoshima* in 1956.
Pa No. 135
Launched 1945 at Shikoku (*No. 2255*); surrendered August 1945 and used for mine clearance until 1947; transferred to MSDF in 1948 as *MS.21* and renamed *Matsushima* in 1956.
Pa No. 136
Launched 1945 at Shikoku (*No. 2256*); surrendered August 1945 and used for mine clearance until 1947; transferred to MSDF in 1948 as *MS.22* and renamed *Himeshima* in 1956.
Pa No. 137
Launched 1945 at Shikoku (*No. 2257*); surrendered August 1945 and used for mine clearance until 1947; ran aground and sank 18 April, 1946 near Yoshimi/Shimonoseki.
Pa No. 138
Launched 1945 at Shikoku (*No. 2258*); surrendered August 1945 and used on mine clearance until 1947; transferred to MSDF in 1948 as *MS.23* and renamed *Awashima* in 1956.
Pa No. 139
Launched at Shikoku (*No. 2259*); surrendered at Kure in August 1945 and completed post-war for mine clearance until 1947; transferred to MSDF in 1948 as *MS.24*; renamed *Kurushima* in 1956.

Pa No. 140
Launched 1945 at Shikoku (*No. 2260*).
Pa No. 152
Launched 1945 at Fukushima (*No. 2272*); surrendered August 1945 and used for mine clearance until 1947; transferred to MSDF as *MS.26* in 1948; renamed *Kamoshima*.
Pa No. 153
Launched 1945 at Fukushima (*No. 2273*); surrendered August 1945 and was completed for mine clearance service lasting until 1947; handed over to MSDF in 1948 as *MS.26*; renamed *Takashima* in 1956.
Pa No. 154
Launched 1945 at Fukushima (*No. 2274*); surrendered August, 1945 and completed for mine clearance, 1945–7; transferred to MSDF in 1948 as *MS.27*; mined 23 May, 1949 at 13.47 hrs (4 dead) near Manju Island, at the eastern exit of the Straits of Shimonoseki.
Pa No. 155
Launched 1945 at Fukushima (*No. 2275*); almost complete by August 1945 but fate unknown.
Pa No. 156
Built at Fukushima (*No. 2276*); construction stopped April 1945 and later BU.
Pa No. 163
Launched 1945 at Hayashikane (*No. 2283*); mined 22 August, 1945 in Bay of Nano.
Pa No. 164
Launched 1945 at Hayashikane (*No. 2284*); wrecked 30 May, 1945 S of Kyushu; BU.
Pa No. 165
Launched 1945 at Hayashikane (*No. 2285*); surrendered at Yokosuka in August 1945 but later sank after springing a leak.
Pa No. 166
Launched 1945 at Hayashikane (*No. 2286*); sunk 12 August, 1945 by air attack 5 m SE of Urasaki.
Pa No. 173
Launched 1945 at Tokushima (*No. 2293*); mined and sunk 29 March, 1945 in Wakamatsu Harbour; raised 18 May but not repaired; surrendered at Hikoshima in August 1945 and later BU.

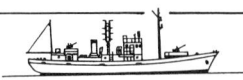

Pa No. 174
Launched 1945 at Tokushima (*No. 2294*); surrendered August 1945 but fate unknown.
Pa No. 175
Launched 1945 at Tokushima (*No. 2295*); surrendered August 1945 and used for mine clearance until 1947; transferred to MSDF in 1948 as *MS.28*; wrecked on reef off Suzaki in Shizuoka Prefecture 30 October, 1950.
Pa No. 176
Launched 1945 at Tokushima (*No. 2296*); surrendered August 1945 and used for mine clearance until 1946; ran aground 18 April, 1946 in rough weather near Yoshimi, Shimonoseki.
Pa No. 177
Launched 1945 at Tokushima (*No. 2297*) probably destroyed by fire on 4 July, 1945 following attack by US B-29 bombers during completion.
Pa No. 178
Built at Tokushima (*No. 2298*); fate as *No. 177*.
Pa No. 179
Launched 1945 at Jin'en (*No. 2299*); surrendered August 1945 and used for mine clearance until 1947; transferred to MSDF in 1948 as *MS.29*; renamed *Oshima* in 1956.
Pa No. 180
Launched 1945 at Jin'en (*No. 2300*); nearly complete by August 1945; lost post-war after springing a leak.
Pa No. 181
Built at Jin'en (*No. 2301*); still building in August 1945 but fate unknown.
Pa No. 191
Launched 1945 at Fukuoka (*No. 2311*); surrendered August 1945 and used for mine clearance until 1947; transferred to MSDF as *MS.30* in 1948; wrecked 27 October, 1950 on a reef near Koriyama.
Pa No. 192
Launched 1945 at Fukuoka (*No. 2312*); surrendered August 1945 at Wansan, Korea; fate unknown.
Pa No. 193
Built at Fukuoka (*No. 2313*); still building in August 1945 but the hull was destroyed in a storm on 18 September, 1945, and the material was later BU.
23 units numbered between 2121 and 2320 were building in sections. On 2 July, 1945 the assembly was stopped and the contracts cancelled. A further 120 units in the same series were cancelled early in 1945. 80 units numbered 2321–2400 were not ordered.

Par No. 1 (1945)

13. Minelayers

Name	Builder	Date	Displ	Length ft in	Beam ft in	Draught ft in	Machinery	SHP	Spd	Fuel	Radius	Armament	Comp
KATSURIKI	Kure DY	1916–1917	2000 N 1540 S	240 0 wl	39 0	14 0	2 sets VTE 2 Kampon boilers 2 shafts	1800 ihp	13	449 coal	1800 @ 10	3 × 80mm 40-cal LA 150 mines	?

Katsurika (1918)

GENERAL NOTES
1915/16 Programme. Fitted out with 4 wooden minelaying and minesweeping gallows.

CAREER
Launched 5 October, 1916, completed January 1917; employed as survey vessel from 1936 – officially classified as such in July 1942; torpedoed 21 September, 1944, by US submarine *Haddo* 80 nm SW of Manila (13° 35′ N, 119° 06′ E).

Name	Builder	Date	Displ	Length ft in	Beam ft in	Draught ft in	Machinery	SHP	Speed	Fuel	Radius	Armament	Comp
SHIRATAKA	Ishikawa-jima, Tokyo	1927–1929	1692 F 1540 N	1345 S	275 7 wl 259 10 pp	37 11	9 2	2 sets VTE 2 Kampon boilers 2 Shafts	2000 ihp	16	300 coal	2200 @ 10	3 × 4.7in 50-cal AA 1 MG 100 mines 6 A/S nets	175

MINELAYERS 197

GENERAL NOTES
1923 Programme. Fitted out as dual-purpose minelayer/netlayer.

RECONSTRUCTION AND RE-ARMAMENT
In 1935 she had 250ts of permanent ballast added, increasing draught to 10ft 2in. The bridge was lowered and the armament altered to 2 × 4.7in 40-cal AA Model 3.
1940: reconstructed as escort vessel – 36 DCs added in vicinity of the after 4·7in guns; bridge lowered by one deck and funnel size reduced to compensate added topweight.

CAREER
Launched 25 January, 1929, completed 9 April, 1929; sunk 31 August, 1944, by US submarine *Sealion* W of Itbayat (Batan Islands) in Luzon Straits (20° 55′ N, 121° 07 E); stricken 10 October, 1944.

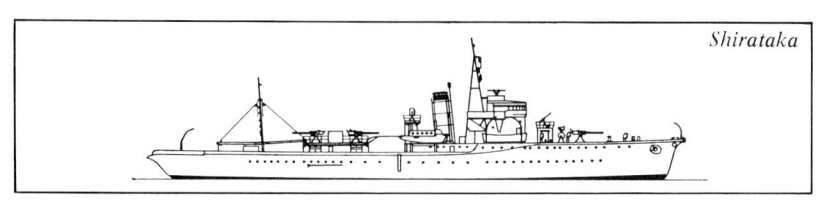

Shirataka

The minelayer (ex-netlayer) *Shirataka*, seen at Shanghai during the war against China. In 1940 she was rebuilt as an escort vessel, with a smaller funnel. (Bundesarchiv.)

Name	Builder	Date	Displ	Length ft in	Beam ft in	Draught ft in	Machinery	SHP	Speed	Fuel	Radius	Armament	Comp
ITSUKU-SHIMA	Uraga Dock, Tokyo	1928–1929	2408 F 2080 N 1970 S	341 wl 328 pp	38 10	10 7	3 M.A.N. 4-cyl Diesels 3 shafts	3000	17	295 oil	5000 @ 10	3 × 140mm(5.5in)50-cal LA 2 × 80mm 40-cal HA 300 mines 2 DC throwers	235
	refit	1944	2330 S									3 × 5.5in 3 × 25mm AA 6 × 13.2mm AA 400 mines	

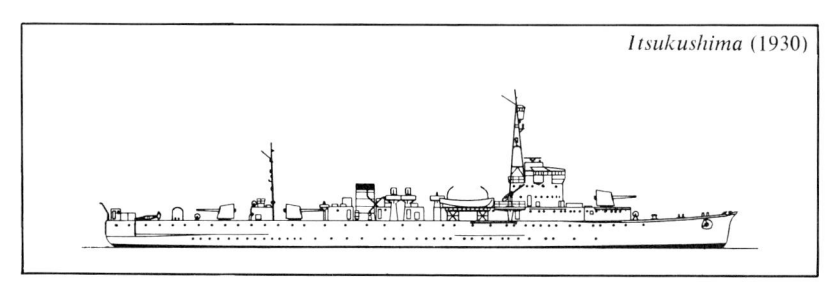

Itsukushima (1930)

GENERAL NOTES
1923 Programme. First large Diesel-powered Japanese ship, fitted out as dual-purpose minelayer/netlayer; followed the example of the larger, British *Adventure*.

RE-ARMAMENT
In 1938 the 80mm guns were replaced by 4 × 13mm AA and 2 × 47 mm Yamaguchi 'short' guns.

CAREER
Launched 22 May, 1929, completed December 1929; sunk 7 October, 1944, by Netherlands submarine *Zwaardvisch* SE of Bawaen Island, Java Sea (05° 26′ S, 113° 48′ E); stricken 10 January, 1945.

The minelayer *Itsukushima* was the first large Japanese warship to be driven by diesels, and her design was based on the British *Adventure*. She is seen here at Shanghai on 13 December 1938 (Bundesarchiv.)

The minelayer *Itsukushima* (Tappman Collection.)

198   MINELAYERS

Name	Builder	Date	Displ	Length ft in	Beam ft in	Draught ft in	Machinery	SHP	Speed	Fuel	Radius	Armament	Comp
YAEYAMA	Kure NY	1930–1932	1384 F 1380 N 1135 S	292 0 wl 280 6 pp	34 11	9 2	2 sets VTE 2 Kampon boilers 2 shafts	4800 ihp	20	278 coal 164 oil	4800 @ 10	2 × 120mm (4.7in) 45-cal HA 2 × 12mm MGs 185 mines	150

GENERAL NOTES

1927 Programme. Fitted out as dual-purpose minelayer/netlayer, alternative coal/oil burning; 1943/4: refitted as escort vessel, 36 DCs installed over the mine-tracks.

CAREER

Launched 15 October, 1931, completed 31 August, 1932; sunk 24 September, 1944, by TF 58 aircraft S of Mindoro (12° 15′ N, 121° 00′ E); stricken 3 October, 1944.

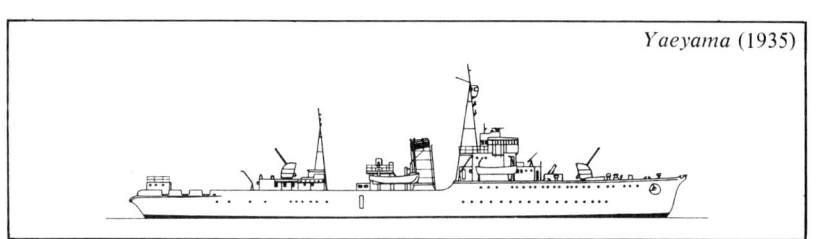

The small dual-purpose minelayer/netlayer *Yaeyama* was armed with two 4.7-inch AA guns, the forward one of which was enclosed in a shield of the type first seen aboard the heavy cruiser *Nachi*. (Tappman Collection.)

Yaeyama (1935)

Yaeyama was smaller than *Itsukushima*. (Tappman Collection.)

Name	Builder	Date	Displ	Length ft in	Beam ft in	Draught ft in	Machinery	SHP	Speed	Fuel	Radius	Armament	Comp
KAMOME	Osaka IW	1928–1929	557 F	214 11 wl	23 7	6 11	2 sets VTE 2 Kampon boilers 2 shafts	2500 ihp	19	45 coal 35 oil	2500 @ 10	1 × 80mm (3in) 40-cal HA 1 × 12mm AAMG 120 mines (or 3 A/S nets + 80 mines)	56–80
TSUBAME	Mistubishi, Yokohama		510 N	206 8 pp									
NATSU-SHIMA	Ishikawa-jima, Tokyo	1931–1933	450 S	229 8 wl	24 7	6 3	2 Diesels 2 shafts	2300	19	?	2100 @ 10	2 × 80mm (3in) 40-cal HA 1 × 13.2mm AAMG 120 mines	?
NASAMI	Harima, Aioi			219 10 pp									
SARUSHIMA	Mitsubishi, Yokohama	1933–1934	583 N 566 S			6 1		2100	18	?	2100 @ 10		?

GENERAL NOTES

1923 and 1931 Programmes. Fitted out as minelayers/netlayers, but also intended as coastal A/S escorts. 1943/4: *Kamome, Tsubame, Sarushima* refitted as escort vessels, 36 DCs installed over mine-tracks.

CAREERS

Kamome
Launched 27 April, 1929, completed 30 August, 1929; sunk 27 April, 1944, by US submarine *Halibut* W of Tokunoshima, Nansei Shoto (27° 37′ N, 128° 11′ E).

Tsubame
Launched 24 April, 1929, completed 15 July, 1929; sunk 1 March, 1945, at Ishigaki-shima (Yaeyama Retto) by TF 58 aircraft.

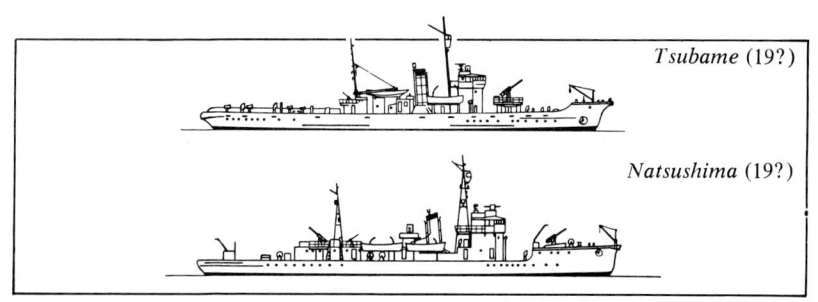

Tsubame (19?)

Natsushima (19?)

MINELAYERS 199

Natsushima
Launched 24 March, 1933, completed 31 July, 1933; sunk 22 February, 1944, by gunfire of US destroyers *Ausburne, Dyson* and *Stanley*, near Tingwon Island, New Ireland (02° 40′ S, 149° 40′ E).

Nasami
Launched 26 March, 1934, completed 20 September, 1934; severely damaged by air attack in Rabaul Harbour 30 March, 1944, and sank on 1 April.

Sarushima
Launched 16 December, 1933, completed 20 July, 1934; sunk 4 July, 1944, by aircraft from TF 58 off W coast of Anijima (Ogasawara Gunto) (27° 06′ N, 142° 10′ E).

Name	Builder	Date	Displ	Length ft in	Beam ft in	Draught ft in	Machinery	SHP	Speed	Fuel	Radius	Armament	Comp
OKINO-SHIMA	Harima, Harima	1934–1936	5000 N 4400 S	391 4 wl 370 9 pp	51 8	18 0	2 sets GT 4 Kampon boilers 2 shafts	9000	20	? oil	9000 @ 10	4 × 140mm(5.5in) 50-cal LA 2 × 80mm(3in) 40-cal HA 500 mines 1 catapult 1 floatplane	?

GENERAL NOTES
1931 Programme. Minelaying cruiser and escort vessel.

CAREER
Launched 15 November, 1935, completed 30 September, 1936; sunk 11 May, 1942, by US submarine *S.42* in St George's Channel, Bismarck Sea (05° 06′ S, 153° 48′ E).

The large minelayer *Okinoshima* could also be employed as an escort, and was well-armed with two twin 5.5-inch guns in open shields and a Kawanishi E7K "Alf" long-range reconnaissance floatplane on her catapult. (Tappman Collection.)

Name	Builder	Date	Displ	Length ft in	Beam ft in	Draught ft in	Machinery	SHP	Speed	Fuel	Radius	Armament	Comp
TSUGARU	Yokosuka DY	1939–1941	4400 N 4000 S	408 6 oa 397 0 wl 372 8 pp	51 3	16 2	2 sets GT 4 Kampon boilers 2 shafts	9000	20	? oil	?	4 × 5in 40-cal DP 4 × 25mm AA 600 mines 1 catapult 1 floatplane	?

GENERAL NOTES
1937 Programme, improved *Okinoshima* design, Type 'B'.

CAREER
Launched 5 June, 1940, completed 22 October, 1941; in March 1942, during the struggle for Lae and Salamaua, she was damaged by aircraft from the US carriers *Lexington* and *Yorktown*; sunk 29 June, 1944, by US submarine *Darter* W of Morotai Island (02° 19′ N, 127° 57′ E).
2 further units of the *Tsugaru* type (Job Nos. 898, 899) were projected in 1942 but were never ordered. They were to have displaced 4100ts standard and 4500ts full load.
Note: see also Type 'A' minelayer *Nisshin*, page 66.

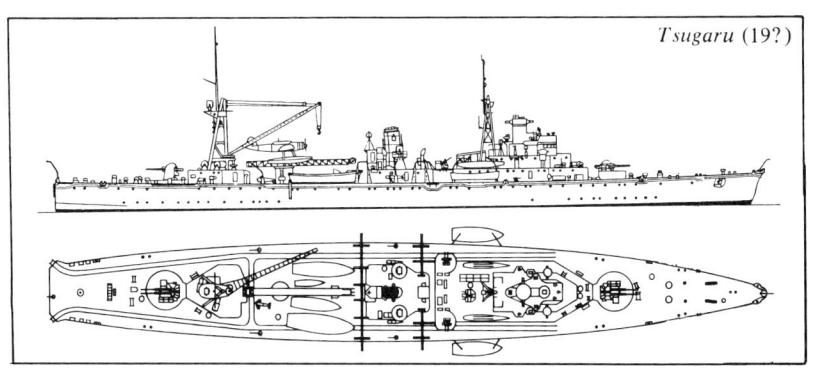

Tsugaru (19?)

Name	Builder	Date	Displ	Length ft in	Beam ft in	Draught ft in	Machinery	SHP	Speed	Fuel	Radius	Armament	Comp
SOKUTEN Class	various	1937–1940	750 N 720 S	247 8 oa 241 2 wl 228 0 pp	25 9	8 6	2 Diesels 2 shafts	3600	20	35 tonnes oil	2550 @ 14	2 × 2pdr AA (Vickers) 2 × 13.2mm AAMG 120 mines	100
HIRASHIMA Class	various	1939–1942						3500				1 × 80mm (3in) HA 2 × 13.2mm AAMG 120 mines 36 DCs	

GENERAL NOTES
1937 Programme: *Sokuten* class (Job Nos. 57–61).
1939 Programme: *Hirashima* class (Job Nos. 170–179).
1941 Programme: *Ajiro* class (improved *Hirashima* class, Job Nos. 460–473).

1942 Programme: *Ajiro* class (Job Nos. 850–857) and improved *Ajiro* class (Job Nos. 5421–5432). Small dual-purpose minelayers/netlayers; 1943: water ballast tanks modified to carry 53ts of oil fuel (radius of action 5000 nm at 10 knots) 36 DCs added; 1944: *Sokuten* and *Hirashima* classes had 13.2mm AAMGs replaced by 6 × 25mm AA (*Saishu* 15 × 25mm).

CAREERS

Sokuten
Launched 27 April, 1938, completed 28 December 1938, by Mitsubishi, Yokohama; sunk 25 July, 1944, by TF 58 aircraft in Malakal Harbour, Palau (07° 20′ N, 134° 27′ E).

Shirakami
Launched 25 June, 1938, completed 25 April, 1939, by Ishikawajima, Tokyo; collided with Army Transport *Nichiran Maru* (6503 GRT) 3 March, 1944, in a storm S of Urup Island, Kuriles (approx 45° 30′ N, 150° E), and sank

Naryu
Launched 28 August, 1939, completed 20 June, 1940, by Mitsubishi, Yokohama; sunk 16 February, 1945, by US submarine *Sennet* S of Honshu (32° 10′ N, 139° 58′ E).

Kyosai
Launched 29 June, 1939, completed 27 December, 1939, by Ishikawajima, Tokyo; damaged 6 August, 1945, by TF 58 aircraft E of Nojimazaki; captured and used by Repatriation Service 1945-7; 20 November, 1947: to Britain as reparation; BU in Japan 1948.

Ukishima
Launched 9 December, 1939, completed 31 October, 1940, by Ishikawajima, Tokyo; lost 16 November, 1943, 11 nm SE of Hatsushima, Sagami Nada (34° 55′ N, 139° 22′ E) cause unknown.

Hirashima
Launched 6 June, 1940, completed 24 December, 1940; sunk 27 July, 1943, by US submarine *Sawfish* near Osezaki, Fukueshima (Goto Retto) (32° 32′ N, 127° 41′ E).

Hoko
Launched 8 September, 1941, completed December 1941; sunk 28 September, 1943, by US aircraft 20 nm E of Buka Island, Solomons (05° 00′ S, 154° 30′ E).

Ishizaki
Launched 13 August, 1941, completed 28 February, 1942; captured August 1945 and employed by Allied Minesweeping Service until 1947; 1 October, 1947: to USA and believed to have been BU.

Takashima
Launched 18 October, 1941, completed 28 March, 1942; sunk 10 October, 1944, by TF 38 aircraft near Okinawa (26° 39′ N, 127° 52′ E).

Saishu
Launched 15 November, 1941, completed 25 April, 1942; captured August 1945 and used by Repatriation Service until 1947; 3 October, 1947: to China, renamed *Yung Ching*.

Niizaki
Launched 2 March, 1942, completed 31 August, 1942; captured August 1945 and employed by Allied Minesweeping Service; severely damaged off Muroran 4 October, 1945, and laid up at Muroran until scrapped in 1947.

Yurijima
Launched 4 July, 1942, completed 25 November, 1942; sunk 14 January, 1945, by US submarine *Cobia* 70 nm SE of Kota Bharu, Malaysia (05° 51′ N, 103° 16′ E).

Nuwashima
Launched 31 July, 1942, completed 15 November, 1942; September 1943: Trials ship for direction-finding gear; damaged 7 May, 1945, and beached in Saeki Bay (32° 56′ N, 131° 05′ E) – attacked by US naval aircraft; later BU.

Maeshima
Launched 18 April, 1943, completed 31 July, 1943; beached 18 October, 1944, near Salomague, Luzon (17° 46′ N, 120° 25′ E) after attack by TF 38 aircraft.

Moroshima
Order cancelled in 1942 before keel laid.

Name	Builder	Date	Displ	Length ft in	Beam ft in	Draught ft in	Machinery	SHP	Speed	Fuel	Radius	Armament	Comp
AJIRO Class	various	1943–										1 × 80mm (3in) HA 6 × 25mm AA 120 mines 36 DCs	

CAREERS

Ajiro
Launched 1943, completed July 1943 at Innoshima; sunk 1 October, 1944, by US submarine *Snapper* WNW of Ogasawara Gunto (28° 20′ N, 139° 25′ E).
13 further units of this class were cancelled in 1943 before any had been laid down. The proposed names were: *Kamishima, Shinoshima, Muso, Namizaki, Terajima, Kyobun, Kosei, Futsutsu* (?), *Sugashima, Niijima, Hikoshima, Himeshima,* and *Tateshima* (Job Nos. 461–473).
The 8 *Ajiro* class units proposed in the 1942 Programme were never ordered, and the 12 Improved *Ajiro* class units of the same Programme were cancelled in 1943, before any had been laid down.

Name	Builder	Date	Displ	Length ft in	Beam ft in	Draught ft in	Machinery	SHP	Speed	Fuel	Radius	Armament	Comp
HATSUTAKA Class	Harima, Aioi	1938–1941	1890 N 1608 S	298 3 oa 283 10 wl 270 8 pp	37 1	13 1½	2 sets GT 3 boilers 2 shafts	6000	20	? coal /oil	3000 @ 14	4 × 2pdr AA *Wakatake* 2 × 80mm (3in) HA 4 × 25mm AA 360 mines	?

GENERAL NOTES
1937–42 Programmes (see below). Dual-purpose minelayers/netlayers carrying 24 A/S nets and 110 mines as alternative to full mine load; alternative coal/oil fuel. 1943/4: mine rails removed and replaced by 36 DCs; 1945: *Wakatake* overall length reduced by 17-20ft after repair to bows; 4 × 13.2mm AAMG added.

CAREERS

Hatsutaka
1937 Programme: launched 28 April, 1939, completed 31 October, 1939; sunk 16 May, 1945, by US submarine *Hawkbill* near Cape Labuan (04° 49′ N, 103° 31′ E).

Aotaka
1937 Programme: launched 5 February, 1940, completed 30 June, 1940; sunk 26 September, 1944, by US submarine *Pargo* 120 nm NNE of Labuan (07° 00′ N, 116° 00′ E).

Wakatake
1939 Programme: launched 12 July, 1941, completed 30 November, 1941; 27 March, 1945: bow blown off by mine 5 nm S of Kapulauan Kangean, Sumbawa Islands; repaired at Soerabaya, where captured in September 1945; used by Repatriation Service 1946-7; 17 October, 1947: to Britain, renamed *Laburnum* and served with Malayan Navy until stricken in 1956; BU.

Asadori
1942M Programme: (Job No. 5039) cancelled in 1943 before keel laid.
1 1942 Programme unit of an improved *Wakatake* class (Job No. 819, 1650ts standard) planned but not ordered.

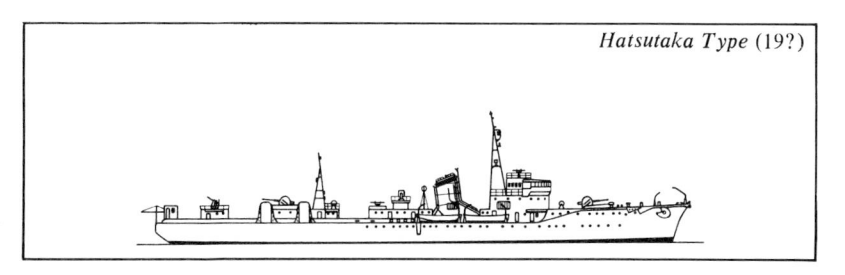

Hatsutaka Type (19?)

Name	Builder	Date	Displ	Length ft in	Beam ft in	Draught ft in	Machinery	SHP	Speed	Fuel	Radius	Armament	Comp
KAMI-SHIMA Class	Sasebo NY	1945–	800 N 766 S	244 5 oa 240 6 wl 228 0 pp	25 9	8 6	2 Diesels 2 shafts	1900	16.5	? oil	?	4 × 2pdr AA 13 × 25mm AA 120 mines 36 DCs	?

GENERAL NOTES
1944 Programme. Simplified construction without sheer or cambered plates: hexagonal funnel, hence a short building time: originally intended to carry 9 × 25mm AA.

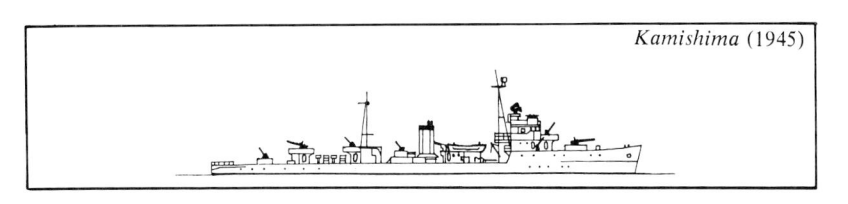

CAREERS
Kamishima
Launched 12 June, 1945, completed 30 July, 1945; captured August, 1945 and used by Repatriation Service until 1947; 1 October, 1947: to USSR.
Awashima
Launched 1945, not completed until 18 April, 1946; used by Repatriation Service until 1947; 1 October, 1947: to USA and probably scrapped.
7 more units of this class (Job Nos. 1803–9) were to have been built by Sasebo Navy Yard and Mitsubishi, Kobe, but the order was cancelled in 1945 before the ships were laid down
11 units projected in the 1944/5 Planning Programme were not ordered.

Kamishima (1945)

Name	Builder	Date	Displ	Length ft in	Beam ft in	Draught ft in	Machinery	SHP	Speed	Fuel	Radius	Armament	Comp
EIJO	Kiangnan, Shanghai	1944–1945	5200 N 3224 S	300 9 oa 283 0 wl 278 10 pp	44 1	19 2	*Eijo* 1 set VTE 1 boiler 1 shaft	1200 ihp	11	? coal	?	1 × 120mm (4.7in) HA 14 × 25mm AA 380 mines 24 DCs	?
MINO	Naniwa, Osaka						*Mino* 1 set GT 1-cyl boiler 1 shaft	1200	11				

GENERAL NOTES
Minelaying conversion of Type 2D Standard Merchant Vessel (2,274 GRT/3850 dwt). Additional transverse bulkheads installed between the boiler room and engine room and also in the hold, the latter being fitted out as the mine stowage. Intended for use as transports, the cargo derricks being retained.

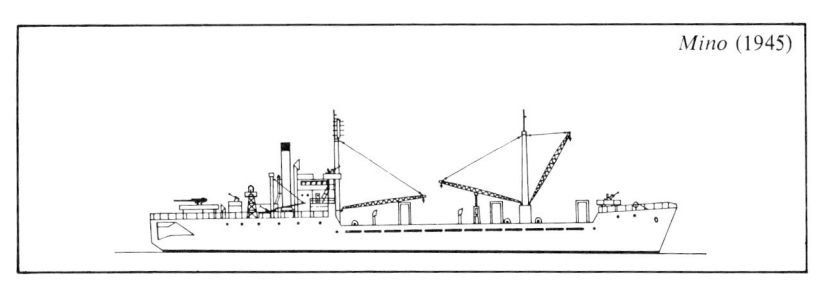

CAREERS
Eijo (also known as *Eijo Maru*)
Launched 1944 as a Type 2DRS Standard Freighter, requisitioned at the beginning of 1945 and completed 10 March, 1945 at Kure NY as a minelayer; sunk 17 June, 1945, by US submarine *Spadefish* near Motsutanozaki, W of Hokkaido (42° 43′ N, 139° 57′ E).
Mino
Laid down November 1944 as Type 2D Standard Freighter (Job No. 1821), requisitioned by the Navy in December 1944 and completed 5 August, 1945, as a minelayer at Kure NY; August, 1945: captured and used by Repatriation Service until 1947; BU 1947 at Urabe, Innoshima.

Mino (1945)

1 unit laid down 1 February, 1945 (Job No. 1822) at Naniwa, Osaka; work suspended New Year 1945, planned for completion as *Mino* class minelayer; June 1948: completed as mercantile *Kenshin Maru*.
8 Improved Type 2DT Standard Freighters were included in the 1944/5 Planning for completion as *Mino* class but were not ordered.

Name	Builder	Date	Displ	Length ft in	Beam ft in	Draught ft in	Machinery	SHP	Speed	Fuel	Radius	Armament	Comp
NATSU-SHIMA Class	various Navy Yards	1911–1920	420 N 405 S	149 11	24 11	7 7	1 set VTE 1 boiler 1 shaft (2 propellers)	600 ihp	12.8	? coal	600 @ 10	2 × 80mm (3in) 40-cal HA 2 MGs 45 mines	?
	refit	1941–1942										1 × 80mm (3in) 40-cal HA 120 Type 4 mines 1 or 2 13.2mm AAMG added later	

GENERAL NOTES
Coastal and harbour minelayers, also fitted for minesweeping; in some units the mainmast was offset to starboard or stepped above the engine room.

CAREERS
Natsushima
Launched March 1911, completed 1911 at Yokosuka; BU 1932.
Sokuten
Launched March 1913, completed 1913 at Maizuru; BU 1937.
Toshima
Launched October, 1914, completed 1914 at Maizuru; sunk 30 July, 1945 at Maizuru by Allied carrier aircraft.
Kuroshima
Launched October 1914, completed 1914 at Maizuru; August 1945: captured and used by Repatriation Service until 1947; 14 November, 1947: to China, renamed *Chieh 29*.
Ashizaki
Launched October 1915, completed 1915 at Maizuru; August, 1945: captured;

Kurosaki (1945)

17 November, 1945: ran aground at Hayakawa during a storm, abandoned.
Katoku
Launched October 1915, completed 1915 at Maizuru; August 1945: captured and used by Repatriation Service until 1947; to USA but handed back to Japan in 1948: MSDF Patrol Boat *PS 29* (also used as a Buoy Tender at Hiroshima); stricken 1953/4 and scrapped.
Kurokami
Launched February 1917, completed 1917 at Kure; August 1945: captured and employed by Allied Minesweeping Service until 1947; 14 November, 1947: to Britain, scrapped in Japan
Katashima
Launched February 1917, completed 1917 at Maizuru; August 1945: captured and employed by the Allied Minesweeping Service until 1947; 3 October, 1947: to USSR.
Ento (shown in several Fleet Lists as *Maroshimo*)
Launched March 1917, completed 1917 at Maizuru; severely damaged 15 January, 1945, by TF 38 aircraft at Fangliao, Taiwan; August, 1945: captured at Takao and scrapped
Enoshima
Launched and completed in 1917 at Maizuru; severely damaged 14 October, 1944, by TF 38 aircraft in Takao Harbour, Taiwan; August 1945: captured in Taiwan and scrapped.
Kurosaki
Launched and completed in 1918 at Yokosuka; August 1945: captured; 18 November, 1945: ran aground in rough seas and broke up off Hachinohe.
Ninoshima
Launched and completed in 1918 at Kure; August 1945: captured in Taiwan and BU.
Washizaki
Launched and completed in 1920 at Yokosuka; August 1945: captured and used by Repatriation Service until 1947; 24 November, 1947: to Britain; scrapped at Sasebo in 1948.

Name	Builder	Date	Displ	Length ft in	Beam ft in	Draught ft in	Machinery	SHP	Speed	Fuel	Radius	Armament	Comp
MA 1–4	Uraga Dock, Tokyo	1941–1942	288 N 215 S	115 2 oa 103 4 wl 99 7 pp	20 3	7 10	1 Diesel 1 shaft	400	9.5	?	?	1 × 80mm (3in) 40-cal HA 2 × 13.2mm AAMG 40 mines 16 DCs	?

GENERAL NOTES
1940 Programme. Coastal and harbour minelayers, similar to *Wa 1* Class minesweepers (see below), designed for post-war use as fishing craft. AA armament later increased by addition of extra 13.2mm and 25mm guns.

CAREERS
Ma 1 (Job No. 257)
Launched 20 August, 1941, completed 28 February, 1942; sunk 27 March, 1945, 5 nm NE of Belawan Deli, Sumatra, by mine laid by British minelayer *Porpoise*.
Ma 2 (Job No. 258)
Launched 30 August, 1941, completed 10 April, 1942; mined and sunk 31 December, 1942, in entrance to Soerabaya Harbour.
Ma 3 (Job No. 259)
Launched 14 January, 1942, completed 30 June, 1942; damaged by aircraft 18 September, 1944, at Enderby Island, Caroline Islands; August, 1945: captured at Truk and scrapped.
Ma 4 (Job No. 260)
Launched 24 January, 1942, completed 20 August, 1942; sunk 20 November, 1944, by British submarine *Tally-Ho* S of Great Nicobar Island.

Name	Builder	Date	Displ	Length ft in	Beam ft in	Draught ft in	Machinery	SHP	Speed	Fuel	Radius	Armament	Comp
Ma 101 (ex-HMS Barlight)	Lobnitz, Renfrew	1938	900 N 730 S	173 9 oa 150 pp	32 3	9 6	1 set VTE 2 coupled boilers 1 shaft	850 ihp	10	coal	?	1 × 80mm (3in) 40-cal HA 6 × 25mm AA ? mines	30

GENERAL NOTES
Captured Royal Navy Boom Defence Vessel HMS *Barlight* (730ts standard, 1 × 3in AA gun).

CAREER
Ma 101
Launched 9 September, 1938, completed 12 December, 1938; 19 December, 1941: scuttled at Hong Kong; raised and repaired, commissioned by Japanese as minelayer *Ma 101* on 20 September, 1942; August 1945: recaptured; sold to China in 1947 and taken by Chinese Communist forces 1949.

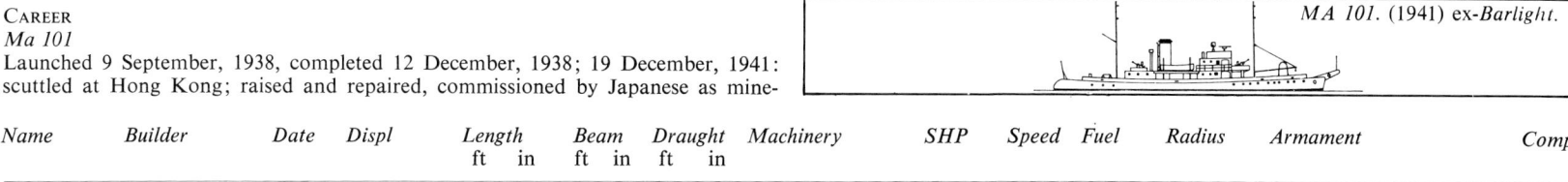

MA 101. (1941) ex-*Barlight*.

Name	Builder	Date	Displ	Length ft in	Beam ft in	Draught ft in	Machinery	SHP	Speed	Fuel	Radius	Armament	Comp
Harbour Minelayers (*Tuhs*) 100-tonne Type (*Eisen No. 690*, etc.)	various	?	100 S	91 10 pp	17 9	5 5	1 set VTE 1 boiler 1 shaft	300 ihp	12	coal	?	15–20 mines	?
150-tonne Type (*No. 709*, etc.)		?	150 S	118 1	19 8	5 1		450 ihp	12			20–30 mines	?
No. 879		1934	155 N 150 S	137 2 oa	18 4	5 2	2 Diesels 2 shafts	520	13	?	?	1 × 25mm AA 12 mines 2 DC throwers	?
150-tonne Diesel Type (*No. 1008*, etc.)	various	1938–1945	180 N 175 S	120 9 wl 118 1 pp	18 4	6 0	2 Diesels 2 shafts	800	14	?	1,180 @ 14	1 × 25mm or 13.2mm AA 20 mines or 14 DCs	?

MINELAYERS 203

GENERAL NOTES
Harbour minelayers built and numbered as tugs, although not fitted with towing gear; also ordered for the use of the Navy Yards as general-purpose trials craft. Approximately 30 100-tonne and 150-tonne craft built.

CAREERS
100-tonne type: a few built with clipper bow (e.g. *No 690*).
Eisen No. 690
Captured 1945 and employed by Minesweeping Service until 1947, thereafter harbour craft at Uraga.
Eisen No. 691
Captured 1945 and employed by Minesweeping Service.
Eisen No. 777
Captured 1945 and employed by Minesweeping Service in Sasebo area until 1947.
Eisen No. 778
Captured 1945 and employed by Minesweeping Service in Ominato area until 1947.
Eisen No. 800
Captured at Sasebo in 1945.
Eisen No. 904
Captured at Kure in 1945.

150-tonne type: Appearance differed depending upon the builders. Some fitted with clipper bow.
Eisen No. 709
Captured 1945 and employed by Minesweeping Service; lost (date unknown) by stranding near Mera, Chiba Prefecture.
Eisen No. 710
Lost by stranding near Yoshima after the War.
Eisen No. 740
Captured 1945 and used by Repatriation Service.
Eisen No. 827
Captured 1945 and employed by Minesweeping Service in Kobe area until 1947.
2 craft of this type were completed as minelayers at Ujina in 1938 but further details and ultimate fates are not known.

Experimental type:
Eisen No. 879 launched 1934, completed August 1934; captured 1945 and

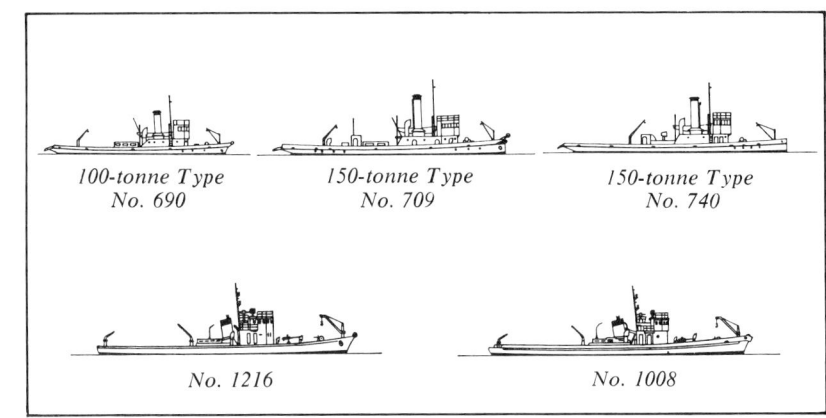

100-tonne Type No. 690
150-tonne Type No. 709
150-tonne Type No. 740
No. 1216
No. 1008

employed by Minesweeping Service until 1947; thereafter employed by Japanese merchant marine at Otake, Hiroshima Prefecture.

150-tonne Diesel type: Diesel-powered version of 150-tonne type; first units (Nos. *1008, 1009, 1120, 1121*) fitted with protective plating which was dispensed with in later craft. Approximately 20 craft of this type were built by Mitsubishi Yokohama (2), Mitsubishi, Kobe (4), Ujina, Hiroshima (7–8), Fujinagata, Osaka (2), Kyushu Hyuga Yard, Kadokawa (3).
Eisen Nos. 1008, 1009, 1120, 1121, 1216, 1217, 1268, 1269, 1313, 1314, 1372, 1373 were built between 1938 and 1945 by various yards. These craft were employed by the Allied naval forces occupying Korea, from 16 November, 1946, until 15 May 1947. *No. 1268* was then scrapped, but the others were handed over to the Republic of Korea Navy and re-designated *JML* (later *AMC*) *301–304, 306* (sunk by mine off Chinnampo 5 May, 1951), *307–310, 313, 315*.
3 more craft of this type were lying incomplete at Kadokawa at the end of the War and of these, one was completed in 1947 for the MSDF as *PS 1007*, later named *Kabashima*.

Auxiliary Minelayers

Various warships were employed as minelayers during both World Wars (see armoured cruisers, destroyers and torpedo-boats).
During the First World War a great number of steam trawlers were placed in service as auxiliary minelayers. 33 continued to appear in the Fleet List between 1920 and 1944, under the numbers *1–44*, omitting *10, 12, 16–20, 34* and *38–40*; no ultimate fates are known, and original identities can be established only for the following:
No. 1: ex-*Shinten Maru No. 7* (1901, 320 GRT).
No. 5: ex-*Ominato Maru No. 2* (1900, 302 GRT).
No. 11: ex-*Takeshiki Maru* (1899, 366 GRT).
No. 12: ex-*Nasami Maru* (1899, 287 GRT).
No. 21: ex-*Shinten Maru No. 3* (1888, completed 15 October 1888 by Mitsubishi, 295 GRT).
No. 24: ex-*Keikan Maru* (135 GRT).
No. 26: ex-*Kaiten Maru No. 2* (1900, 284 GRT).
No. 29: ex-*Shinten Maru No. 5* (1898, 315 GRT).
No. 41: ex-*Tenkyo Maru No. 1* (1899, 304 GRT).
The following merchant ships were requisitioned as minelayers:
Kahoku Maru
Built 1931 as 3311 GRT motor vessel; requisitioned as gunboat 1941; minelayer 1941; sunk 8 June, 1943, by US submarine *Finback* N of Palau (08° 58′ N, 134° 14′ E).
Kinjo Maru
Built 1935 as 330 GRT motor vessel; requisitioned as minelayer 1941, subsequently returned to civilian owner.
Koei Maru
Built 1934 as 6774 GRT motor refrigerator ship; requisitioned as minelayer 1941; August 1945: captured and used by Repatriation Service; returned to civilian owner 1947.
Koryo Maru
Built 1903, 745 GRT; requisitioned as minelayer 1904; returned to owners 1905; scrapped c.1948.
Mogamigawa Maru
Built 1934 as 7469 GRT motor vessel *Getsuyo Maru*; requisitioned as minelayer 1941;

aircraft transport 1942; sunk 31 July, 1943, by US submarine *Pogy* NW of Truk (11° 08′ N, 153° 18′ E).
Nagato Maru
Built 1912 as 211 GRT *Nagato Maru No. 6*; requisitioned as minelayer 1914; sunk 2 October, 1914, off Tsingtao by mine laid by SMS *Lauting*.
Nichiyu Maru
Built 1938 as 6871 GRT steamer; requisitioned as minelayer 1940; sunk 16 June, 1944 by surface ship bombardment in Apra Harbour, Guam.
Shinko Maru
Built 1935 as 6480 GRT motor passenger liner; requisitioned as minelayer 1940; sunk 18 October, 1944, by TF 38 aircraft off Aparri, Luzon.
Shonan Maru No. 2 & No. 3
Steam trawlers requisitioned as minelayers in 1914; no further details known.
Taihoku Maru
Built 1891 as 2796 GRT SS *Priok*, renamed *Guinee*, renamed *London City*; purchased 1904 as minelayer, sold 1905; scrapped 1933.
Takachiho Maru
Built probably 1937 as 343 GRT motor vessel; requisitioned as minelayer 1941; August 1945: captured and returned to civilian owners.

Kahoku Maru (1941)

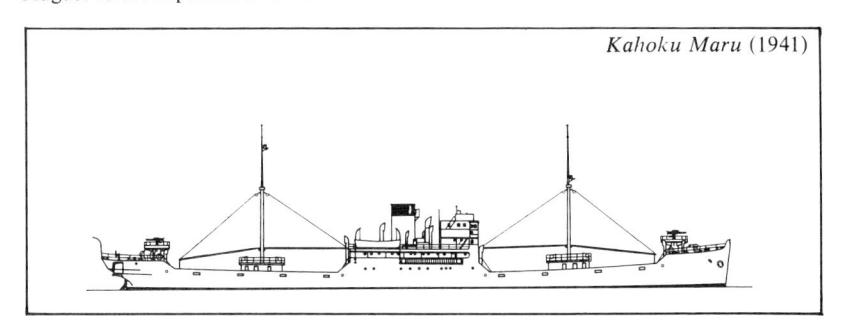

Shinko Maru (1942)

Tatsuharu Maru
Built 1939, 6345 GRT; requisitioned as minelayer 1941; sunk 19 March, 1945, by US submarine *Balao* N of Shanghai.

Tatsumiya Maru
Built 1938 as 6343 GRT steamer (turbine); requisitioned as minelayer 1941; subsequently returned to civilian owners.

Ten-yo Maru
Built 1935 as 6843 GRT motor passenger liner; requisitioned as minelayer 1941; sunk 10 March, 1942, off Lae, New Guinea by aircraft from USS *Lexington*.

Uwajima Maru No. 6
Built 1901 as 444 GRT steamer; purchased 1904 as minelayer, sold 1905; lost 12 May, 1925, by stranding off Nagasaki.

Cable Ships

Name	Builder	Date	Displ	Length ft in	Beam ft in	Draught ft in	Machinery	SHP	Speed	Fuel	Radius	Armament	Comp
HATSU-SHIMA Class	various	1939–1941	1700 N 1564 S	262 3 oa 225 5 pp	35 5	11 7	2 sets VTE 2 Kampon boilers 2 shafts	2300 ihp	14	coal	?	1 × 80mm (3in) 40-cal HA 2 × 13.2mm AAMG 12 mines	?
	refit	1943 1944										1 × 80mm 6 × 25mm AA 12 mines DCs	

GENERAL NOTES
1939 Programme. Cable-ships with minelaying capability (21870yds of cable in cable-room amidships, abaft the bridge).

CAREERS
Hatsushima (also known as *Hashima*)
Launched and completed 1940 by Kawasaki, Kobe; sunk 28 April, 1945, by US submarine *Sennet* 24 nm off Mikizaki (33° 58′ N, 136° 17′ E).

Tsurushima
Launched 24 May, 1940, completed 28 March, 1941, by Kawasaki, Kobe; August 1945: captured and employed in service of the Transport Administration of the Allied Occupation Forces as *Tsurushima Maru*; 1948–56: JMSDF; 1956: to the Nippon Public Telegraph and Telephone Company.

Odate
Launched 11 December, 1940, completed 31 July, 1941, by Harima SB Co.; sunk 27 March, 1945, by US submarine *Trigger* 142 nm off Ibusuki, Kyushu (30° 40′ N, 127′ 50′ E).

Tateishi
Launched 1 March, 1941, completed 31 August, 1941, by Harima; sunk 21 March, 1945, by aircraft 6 nm N of Cam Ranh Bay (11° 50′ N, 109° 18′ E).

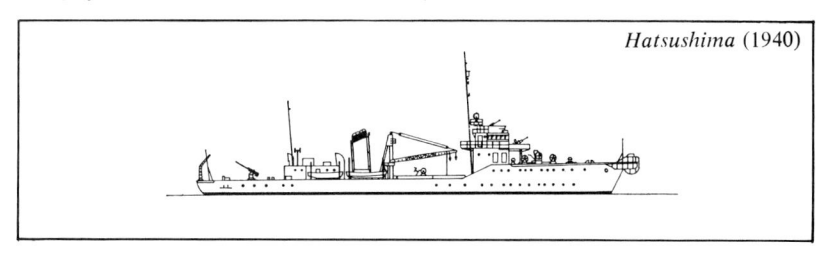

Hatsushima (1940)

Name	Builder	Date	Displ	Length ft in	Beam ft in	Draught ft in	Machinery	SHP	Speed	Fuel	Radius	Armament	Comp
HARUSHIMA (ex-*Harushima Maru*, ex-*Colonel GFE Harrison*)	not known		700 grt	?	?	?	2 sets VTE 2 boilers 2 shafts	?	11	?	?	1 × 80mm (3in) HA ? × 25mm AA ? mines	?

Harushima
Formerly the US Army Cable-Ship *Colonel GFE Harrison*, captured in Mariveles Bay, Luzon, at the beginning of 1942 and repaired; 19 October, 1942: classified as an auxiliary cable-ship – *Harushima Maru*; 15 July, 1943: re-classified as cable-ship *Harushima*; 15 February, 1944: transferred to Yokosuka and re-classified as submarine-chaser; 18 July, 1945: sunk by TF 38 aircraft in Yokosuka Harbour.

The following merchant cable-ships were requisitioned:

Ogasawara Maru
Built 1906 as 1456 GRT Government Cable Vessel; requisitioned 1941; sunk 22 August, 1945, by mine in Inland Sea.

Okinawa Maru
Built 1896, 2221 GRT; requisitioned 1904 and returned 1905; again requisitioned 1941; sunk 10 May, 1944, by US submarine *Silversides* SE of Guam (11° 31′ N, 143° 41′ E).

Yamabato Maru
Built 1937, 2256 GRT; requisitioned 1941; sunk 29 March, 1943, by US submarine *Wahoo* W of Yakushima (30° 26′ N, 129° 41′ E).

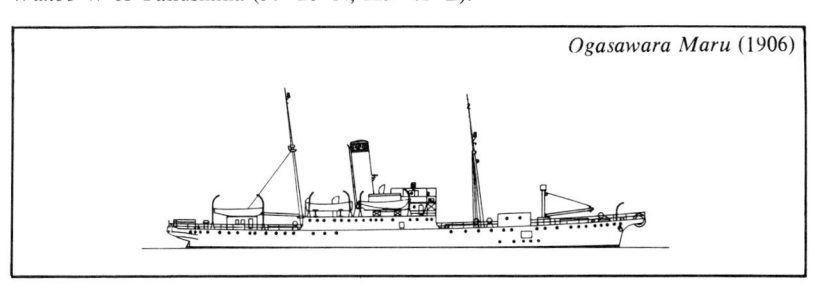

Ogasawara Maru (1906)

MINELAYERS

Netlayers

The following merchant vessels were employed as auxiliary netlayers.

Agata Maru
Built 1931 as 302 GRT motor passenger vessel; requisitioned as netlayer 194?; sunk 11 April, 1945, by British aircraft NE of Nicobar Islands.

Choko Maru
Built 1940 as 889 GRT merchant vessel; requisitioned 1941; August 1945: captured and employed on Repatriation Service until 1947.

Eiryu Maru
Built 1928 as 758 GRT passenger vessel; requisitioned as netlayer 194?; sunk 4 May, 1944, by US submarine *Pargo* E of Mindanao.

Fuji Maru
Built 1932 as 703 GRT motor vessel; requisitioned as netlayer 1941; sunk 25 March, 1945, by US submarine *Tirante* off Torishima.

Fukuei Maru No. 15
Built 1939 as 867 GRT motor vessel; requisitioned as netlayer 1941; 1945: at Ominato.

Himetaka Maru
Built 1940 as 554 GRT ?; requisitioned as netlayer 194?; sunk 2 July, 1945, by USAAF aircraft at Kure.

Hinoki Maru
Built 1939 as 599 GRT ?; requisitioned as netlayer 1942; sunk 11 September, 1944, by US submarine *Pargo* in Java Sea.

Hiro Maru
Built 1927 as 549 GRT passenger vessel; requisitioned as netlayer 194?; sunk 31 January, 1944, by US submarine *Tullibee* NNW of Saipan.

Iwato Maru
Built 1939 as 526 GRT ?; requisitioned as netlayer 194?; sunk 4 January, 1945, by TF 38 aircraft NE of Taiwan.

Kainan Maru
Built 1940 as 525 GRT ?; requisitioned as netlayer 1941; sunk 21 March, 1945, by US submarine *Baya* in Cam Ranh Bay.

Kanko Maru
Built 1941 as 909 GRT ?; requisitioned as netlayer 194?; sunk (with *Shunsen Maru*) 5 January, 1945, by US submarine *Cavalla* in Java Sea.

Kashi Maru
Built 1940, 654 GRT; requisitioned as netlayer 194?; sunk 2 July, 1943, by US aircraft off New Georgia.

Kashima Maru
Built 1938 as 879 GRT motor vessel; requisitioned as netlayer 1941; 1 February, 1942: damaged by aircraft from USS *Enterprise* at Kwajalein and later stricken.

Kashiwa Maru
Built 1918 as 976 GRT steamer *Mitsu Maru No. 1*; requisitioned as netlayer 194?; Army Transport 1943; sunk 25 April, 1944, by US submarine *Crevalle* N of Borneo.

Kashiwa Maru
Built 1938 as. 515 GRT motor vessel; requisitioned 194?; sunk 21 December, 1943, by US submarine *Grayback* SSW of Kagoshima.

Katsura Maru
Built 1938 as 541 GRT motor vessel; requisitioned as netlayer 1941; sunk 31 January, 1944, off Eniwetok by aircraft of TG 58.3 and gunfire of US destroyer *Harrison*.

Kiku Maru
Built 1929 as 760 GRT motor passenger vessel; requisitioned as netlayer 1941; hospital ship 1945; 1945: captured and used by Repatriation Service, 1947: returned to original owners.

Kishin Maru
Built 1941, 869 GRT; requisitioned as netlayer 194?; August 1945: captured and used by Repatriation Service; 1950: returned to original owners.

Koa Maru
Built 1939, 623 GRT; requisitioned as netlayer 194?; sunk 24 December, 1943, by aircraft in Marcus Bay, New Britain.

Koei Maru
Built 1941, 863 GRT; requisitioned as netlayer 1941; sunk 21 September, 1942, by US submarine *Trout* S of Truk.

Kogi Maru
Built 1940, 857 GRT; requisitioned as netlayer 1941; sunk 5 July, 1944, by US submarine *Plaice* off Ototojima.

Kokko Maru
Built 1938 as 717 GRT motor vessel; requisitioned as netlayer 1941; sunk 12 June, 1944, by TG 58.4 aircraft 180 nm NW of Saipan.

Korei Maru
Built 1939, 540 GRT; requisitioned as netlayer 1941; sunk 12 September, 1944, by TF 38 aircraft off Cebu.

Kosei Maru
Built 1915, 1026 GRT; requisitioned as netlayer 1941; subsequently returned to original owners.

Kotobuki Maru No. 3
Built 1936 as 723 GRT steamer; requisitioned as netlayer 1941; August 1945: captured and subsequently returned to original owners.

Kotobuki Maru No. 5
Built 1939, 720 GRT; requisitioned as netlayer 1941; sunk 25 October, 1942, by aircraft at Rabaul.

Kumano Maru
Built 1941, 872 GRT; requisitioned as netlayer 194?; sunk 30 November, 1944, by British submarine in Malacca Straits.

Kyosei Maru
Built 1938 as 556 GRT motor vessel; requisitioned as netlayer 194?; sunk 22 February, 1944, in Isabel Channel, New Hanover by gunfire of US Destroyer Division 45.

Kyushu Maru
Built 1936 as 632 GRT steamer; requisitioned as netlayer 194?; sunk 27 June, 1945, by US aircraft E of Otsu.

Matsu Maru
Built 1938, 509 GRT; requisitioned as netlayer 194?; sunk 15 February, 1944, by aircraft at Rabaul.

Nagara Maru
Built 1940, 855 GRT; requisitioned as netlayer 194?; sunk 5 March, 1945, by US submarine *Sea Robin* off Bawean.

Nissho Maru No. 3
Built 1928 as 676 GRT SS *Tsunekiko Maru*; requisitioned as netlayer 194?; August 1945: captured and used by Repatriation Service; 1947: returned to previous owners.

Nissho Maru No. 5
Built 1935 as 782 GRT motor vessel; requisitioned as netlayer 194?; sunk 30 March, 1944, by TF 58 aircraft at Palau.

Nissho Maru No. 16
Built 1939, 1173 GRT; requisitioned as gunboat 1941; netlayer 1943; sunk 1 February, 1945, by mine, off Mokpo, Korea.

Sakae Maru
Built 1938 as 540 GRT motor vessel; requisitioned as netlayer 194?; August 1945: captured; 1948: returned to civilian ownership as *Shinto Maru No. 3*.

Seiko Maru
Built 1938 as 708 GRT motor vessel; requisitioned as netlayer 194?; sunk 3 August, 1944, by US submarine off Mangole, Molucca Sea.

Shinto Maru No. 2
Built 1938 as 540 GRT motor vessel; requisitioned as netlayer 194?; sunk 5 April, 1945, by shore artillery in Naha Harbour, Okinawa.

Shirataka Maru
Built 1929, 1327 GRT; requisitioned as netlayer 1941; sunk 20 March, 1944, by US submarine *Pollack* SW of Torishima.

Shofuku Maru
Built 1941, 891 GRT; requisitioned as netlayer 1941; sunk 7 August, 1942, by US submarine *Tambor* off Wotje, Marshall Islands.

Shosei Maru
Built 1928 as 773 GRT passenger steamer; requisitioned as netlayer 194?; beached 30 March, 1944, after air attack on Palau by TF 58.

Shuko Maru
Built 1939, 889 GRT; requisitioned as netlayer 194? sunk 29 January, 1944 by US submarine *Angler* SSE of Iwo Jima.

Shunsen Maru
Built 1920, 971 GRT; requisitioned as netlayer 1941; sunk 5 January 1945

Taiko Maru
Built 1941, 897 GRT; requisitioned 194?; sunk 4 July, 1944, by TF 58 aircraft off Onagawa Retto.

Tatsu Maru
Built 1939 as 501 GRT motor vessel; requisitioned as netlayer 194?; sunk 24 January, 1944, by US aircraft, off Manus.

Tokachi Maru
500 GRT; requisitioned as netlayer 194?; sunk by aircraft (date unknown) off Cape Cambodia.

Toko Maru No. 1
Built 1938 as motor vessel *Toko Maru*, 721 GRT; requisitioned as netlayer 1941; sunk 19 September, 1944, by aircraft in Manila Harbour.

Uji Maru
Built 1940, 872 GRT; requisitioned as netlayer 1941; sunk 29 January, 1944 by TG 58.1 aircraft in Marshall Islands.

Wakamiya Maru
Built 1937 as 547 GRT motor vessel; requisitioned as netlayer 194?; August 1945: captured and returned to civilian owners.

14. Minesweepers

Name	Builder	Date	Displ	Length ft in	Beam ft in	Draught ft in	Machinery	SHP	Speed	Fuel	Radius	Armament	Comp
W.1–4	various	1922–1925	702 N 615 S	250 oa 243 wl 235 pp / 2 9 0	26 4	7 6	2 sets VTE 3 Kampon boilers 2 shafts	4000 ihp	20	186 coal	3000 @ 10	2 × 120mm (4.7in) 45-cal HA 1 × 80mm (3in) 40-cal AA 2 DC throwers	91
W.5 & 6	various	1927–1929	717 N 620 S	252 oa 246 wl 236 pp / 8 1 3	27 1	7 5			21	176 coal	2000 @ 14	as W1, plus 1 × 12mm MG	91

GENERAL NOTES
1922 Programme (*W 1–4*) and 1927 Programme (*W.5* and *W.6*). Armed with DCs and throwers to enable ships to be used as escorts. *W.5* and *W.6* were slightly larger and had minor differences in appearance as well as stepping a tripod mast. Alternative coal/oil fuel.

RECONSTRUCTION AND RE-ARMAMENT
In 1927 *W 1–4* had their funnels raised and in 1934–5 *W 5–6* had their hulls strengthened, with permanent ballast added. 1 × 80mm AA gun was removed to reduce topweight; the tonnage was now 826(F). In 1938 *W 1–4* were similarly refitted and their tonnage was 807(F). 1944: minesweeping gear removed; 1 × 4.7in, 5 × 25mm, 36 DCs.

CAREERS
W.1
Launched 6 March, 1923, completed 30 June, 1923, at Harima; sunk 10 August, 1945, by TF 38 aircraft in Yamada Bay.
W.2
Launched 17 March, 1923, completed 30 June, 1923, at Tama; sunk 1 March, 1942, by mine in Bantam Bay, Java.
W.3
Launched 29 March, 1923, completed 30 June, 1923, at Osaka; sunk 9 April, 1945, by US submarine *Parche* 65 nm NE of Sendai (39° 07′ N, 141° 57′ E).
W.4
Launched 24 April, 1924, completed 29 April, 1925, at Sasebo; August 1945: captured at Singapore; scuttled 13 July, 1946, by British in Malacca Straits.
W.5
Launched 30 October, 1928, completed 25 February, 1929, by Mitsui; sunk 4 November, 1944, by British minesweeper *Terrapin* E of Sumatra (03° 44′ N, 99° 50′ E).
W.6
Launched 29 October 1928, completed 25 February, 1929, by Hitachi; sunk 26 December, 1941, by Dutch Army aircraft off Sarawak (01° 34′ N, 110° 21′ E).

W1. Type (1944) Insert W5-6.

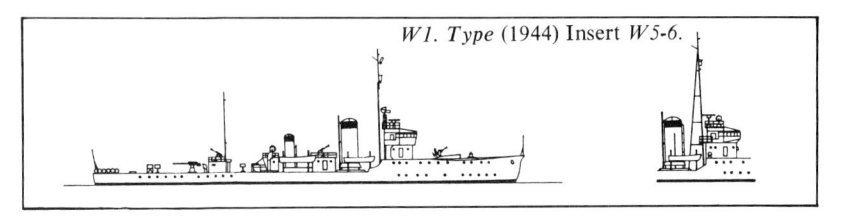

Close-ups of the minesweepers *W.2* (Left) and *W.6*. (Tappman Collection.)

ex-ASAKAZE Class
Six 3rd Class destroyers of the 1904 *Asakaze*-class were fitted out as Fleet minesweepers in 1926, armament being reduced to 2 × 3in LA. The following conversions served until 1930, when they were scrapped:
Sokaitei No. 7, ex-*Isonami*.
Sokaitei No. 8, ex-*Uranami*.
Sokaitei No. 9, ex-*Ayanami*.
Sokaitei No. 10, ex-*Minazuki*.
Sokaitei No. 11, ex-*Nagatsuki*.
Sokaitei No. 12, ex-*Kikuzuki*.

ex-ENOKI Class
In 1930, *Sokaitei Nos. 9* and *10* were replaced by the 1917-Programme 2nd class destroyers *Nara* and *Enoki*, whose armament had been reduced to 2 × 4.7in LA guns. These two ships served until 1938.

ex-UMIKAZE Class
In 1930, *Sokaitei Nos. 7* and *8* were replaced by the 1907-Programme 1st Class destroyers *Umizake* and *Yamazake*, armament reduced to 1 × 4.7in LA and 4 × 3in LA. These ships served until scrapped in 1936. No further conversions were made to replace *Nos. 11* and *12*.

Name	Builder	Date	Displ	Length ft in	Beam ft in	Draught ft in	Machinery	SHP	Speed	Fuel	Radius	Armament	Comp
W.13 Class	various	1931–1934	560 N 500 S	242 9 oa / 236 3 wl / 226 4 pp	26 11	6 9	2 sets VTE 2 Kampon boilers 2 shafts	3200 ihp	20	?	2600 @ 12	2 × 120mm (4.7in) 45-cal LA 2 AAMG DCs	?
	refit	1935	800 N 691 S						18				

GENERAL NOTES
1931 Programme; alternative coal/oil fuel; 1935: bridge and funnel reduced in size and ballast keel added to improve stability, tonnage increased as in table. 1944: minesweeping gear removed from *W 15*: 2 × 4.7 in 45-cal., 5 × 25mm, 36 DCs.

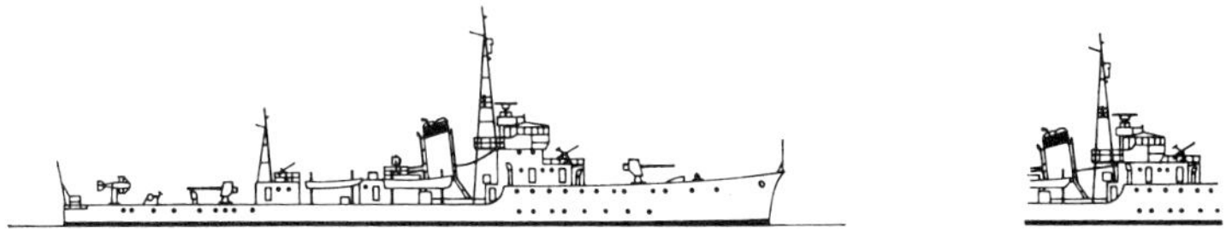

CAREERS
W.13
Launched 30 March, 1933, completed 31 August, 1933, by Fujinagata; sunk 12 January, 1942, by Dutch Army coastal battery off Tarakan, Borneo.
W.14
Launched 20 May, 1933, completed 30 September, 1943, by Hitachi; 12 January, 1942; sunk with *W 13*.
W.15
Launched 14 February, 1934, completed 21 August, 1934, by Fujinagata; severely damaged 5 March, 1945, by US submarine *Tilefish* – beached on Akuseshima (29° 30′ N, 129° 33′ E) and abandoned.
W.16
Launched 30 March, 1934, completed 29 September, 1934, by Mitsui; sunk 11 September, 1943 by mine 60 nm S of Makassar, Celebes (06° 08′ S, 119° 20′ E).

Right:
The *W.13* Type minesweepers were completed in 1933–4. *W.13* is seen here on completion (Shizuo Fukui.)

W 14 on completion. (Shizuo Fukui.)

W13. Type (1933)

The minesweeper *W.14*, seen here at Kure after completion in 1933. (Shizuo Fukui.)

Name	Builder	Date	Displ	Length ft in	Beam ft in	Draught ft in	Machinery	SHP	Speed	Fuel	Radius	Armament	Comp
W.17 W.18	Hitachi, Sakurajima Mitsui, Tama	1935–1936	707 N 578 S	237 10 oa 229 8 wl 220 10 pp	25 9	8 3	2 sets GT 2 boilers 2 shafts	3200	19	?	2600 @ 12	2 × 120mm (4.7in) 45-cal LA 2 × 13.2mm AAMG DCs	?

GENERAL NOTES
1931 Programme; improved *W 13* type with alternative coal/oil fuel; 1943/4: magnetic mine sweeping gear installed; 2 × 4.7in 45-cal. 5 × 25mm, 36 DCs.

CAREERS
W.17
Launched 3 August, 1935, completed 15 January, 1936; damaged 2 August, 1945, by mine S of Korea (36° 06′ N, 128° 40′ E); August 1945: captured at Sasebo and scrapped in 1947.

W.18
Launched 19 September, 1935, completed 30 April, 1936; sunk 26 November, 1944, by aircraft SW of Hainan Island (16° 52′ N, 108° 38′ E).

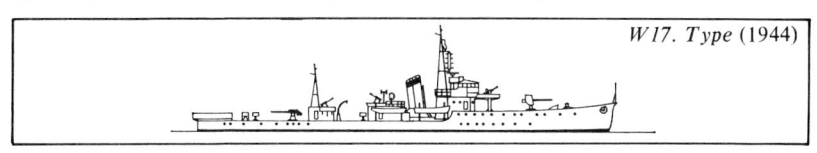

W17. Type (1944)

Name	Builder	Date	Displ	Length ft in	Beam ft in	Draught ft in	Machinery	SHP	Speed	Fuel	Radius	Armament	Comp
W.7 Class	various	1937–1939	750 N 630 S	237 10 oa 233 11 wl 220 10 pp	25 9	6 7	2 sets GTU 2 Kampon boilers 2 shafts	3850	20	?	2000 @ 14	2 × 120mm (4.7in) 45-cal LA 2 × 25mm AA DCs	88

GENERAL NOTES
1937 Programme; similar to *W 13* with alternative coal/oil fuel. Numbered out of sequence to fill gap left by withdrawal of the converted destroyers (see above) 1944: minesweeping gear removed; 2 × 4.7in 45-cal, 9 × 25mm, 36 DCs.

CAREERS
W.7
Launched 16 June, 1938, completed 15 December, 1938, by Mitsui; sunk 15 April, 1944 by British submarine *Storm* SE of Port Blair, Andaman Islands (11° 34′ N, 93° 08′ E).

W.8
Launched 28 May, 1938, completed 15 February, 1939, at Uraga; August 1945: captured at Soerabaya; scuttled 13 July, 1946, by British in Malacca Straits.

W.9
Launched 10 September, 1938, completed 15 February, 1939 at Maizuru; sunk 2 February, 1942, by mine off Ambon (03° 42′ S, 128° 10′ E).

W.10
Launched 22 September, 1938, completed 15 February, 1939, by Ishikawajima; sunk 10 December, 1941, by USAAF aircraft off Vigan, Luzon (17° 32′ N, 120° 22′ E).

W.11
Launched 28 December, 1937, completed 15 July, 1939, by Uraga; sunk 28 March, 1945, by US aircraft off Makassar (05° 06′ S, 119° 14′ E).

W.12
Launched 18 February, 1939, completed 15 August, 1939 by Ishikawajima; sunk 6 April, 1945 by US submarine *Besugo* off Sumbawa Island (08° 13′ S, 119° 14′ E).

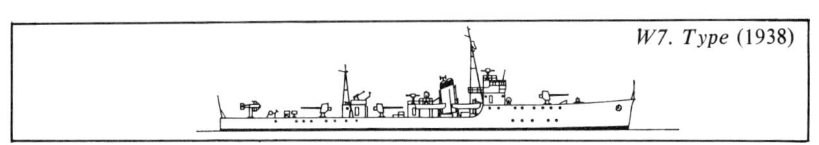

W7. Type (1938)

Name	Builder	Date	Displ	Length ft in	Beam ft in	Draught ft in	Machinery	SHP	Speed	Fuel	Radius	Armament	Comp
W.19 Class	various	1940–1944	755 N 648 S	237 10 oa 233 11 wl 220 10 pp	25 9	8 7	2 sets GT 2 boilers 2 shafts	3850	20	?	2000 @ 14	3 × 120mm (4.7in) 45-cal HA 2 × 25mm AA DCs	?

GENERAL NOTES
1939 Programme (Job Nos. 164–169); 1941 Programme (Job Nos. 410–437); 1942M Programme (Job Nos. 5301–5336); 1942 Planning Programme (Job Nos. 820–829); slightly simplified *W 7* type, retaining alternative fuel; 1944: minesweeping gear removed; 2 × 4.7in HA, 9 × 25mm, 36 DCs (except *W 19* and *W 26*).

CAREERS
W.19
Launched 18 February, 1941, completed 31 May, 1941; severely damaged 10 December, 1941 by air attack and beached on North Luzon (18° 22′ N, 121° 38′ E); abandoned but classified as 'Reserve Unit' 15 January, 1942; stricken 30 November, 1945.

W.20
Launched 17 September, 1941, completed 15 December, 1941; sunk 4 May, 1945, by US submarine *Trepang* 140 nm SE of Mokpo, Korea (34° 16′ N, 123° 37′ E).

W.21
Launched 28 February, 1941, completed 30 June, 1942; August 1945: captured at Tsingtao and used by Repatriation Service until 1947; 1 October, 1947: to USA, scrapped.

W.22
Launched 28 April, 1942, completed 31 July, 1942; sunk 11 November, 1944, by mine near Babelthuap, Palau.

W.23
Launched 13 January, 1943, completed 31 March, 1943; August 1945: captured and employed by Allied Minesweeping Service until 1947; 3 October, 1947: to USSR.

W.24
Launched 26 September, 1942, completed 25 January, 1943; sunk 15 July, 1945, by TF 38 aircraft near Omasaki (41° 38′ N, 141° 00′ E).

W.25
Launched 1942, completed 30 April, 1943; sunk 4 July, 1944 by TF 58 aircraft in Ogasawara Gunto area (28° 35′ N, 141° 04′ E).

W.26
Launched 1942, completed 31 March, 1943; severely damaged 2 November, 1943, by aircraft from USS *Saratoga* at Rabaul; sunk unrepaired 17 February, 1944, by aircraft at Rabaul.

W.27
Launched 1942, completed 31 July, 1943; sunk 10 July, 1945, by US submarine

MINESWEEPERS 209

Runner off Tadosaki (39° 20′ N, 142° 07′ E).
W 28
Launched 1943, completed 28 June, 1943; sunk 29 August, 1944 by US submarine *Jack* 70 nm NW of Manado, Celebes (02° 15′ N, 123° 29′ E).
W 29
Launched 1943, completed 22 October, 1943; sunk 7 May, 1945, by mine off Kinzurusaki (34° 02′ N, 130° 54′ E).
W 30
Launched 1943, completed 5 February, 1944; sunk 11 November, 1944, by TF 38 aircraft in Ormoc Bay, Leyte (10° 50′ N, 124° 31′ E).
W 33
Launched 1943, completed 31 July, 1943; sunk 9 August, 1945 by Allied carrier aircraft in Onagawa Bay.
W 34
Launched 1943, completed 29 May, 1944; sunk 21 May, 1945 by US submarine *Chub* NNE of Kepulauan (06° 18′ S, 116° 14′ E).
W 38
Launched 1944, completed 10 June, 1944; sunk 20 November, 1944, by US submarine *Atule* 75 nm SW of Taiwan (21° 21′ N, 119° 45′ E).
W 39
Launched 1944, completed 31 May, 1944; sunk 20 July, 1945, by US submarine *Threadfin* NW of Mokpo, Korea (35° 01′ N, 125° 42′ E).
W 41
Launched 1944, completed 17 July, 1944; beached 4 January, 1945, near Takao, Taiwan, after attack by TF 38 aircraft; abandoned.

Units cancelled before commencement of construction (1942–3): *W 31* (Job No. 416), *W 32* (Job No. 417), *W 35–37* (Job Nos. 420–422), *W 40* (Job No. 425), *W 42–52* (Job Nos. 427–437). (1944) *W 53–88* (Job Nos. 5301–5336 – to have been built by Harima and Ishikawajima).
Units planned but not ordered: Job Nos. 820–829.

W19. Type (1944)

Name	Builder	Date	Displ	Length ft in	Beam ft in	Draught ft in	Machinery	SHP	Speed	Fuel	Radius	Armament	Comp
W 101 (ex-HMS *Taitam*) *W 102* (ex-HMS *Waglan*)	Taikoo, Hong Kong	1941–1944	678 N 580 S	180 0 oa 177 6 wl 171 6 pp	28 6	8 4	2 sets VTE 2 boilers 2 shafts	2200 ihp	15.8	? oil	1900 @ 15.7	1 × 120mm (4.7in) 45-cal LA 8 × 25mm AA 36 DCs	60 approx

GENERAL NOTES
British *Bangor* class (Reciprocating) Fleet minesweepers captured on the slipway at Hong Kong in 1941; originally 550ts standard, 1 × 3in, 1 2pdr AA.

CAREERS
W 101
Laid down 12 July, 1941, as HMS *Taitam* (originally *Portland*); captured on the stocks December 1941; launched February 1943 and commissioned 10 April, 1944 as *W 101*; sunk 12 January, 1945 by TF 38 aircraft 7 nm SW of Cape Padaran (11° 10′ N, 108° 55′ E).
W 102
Laid down 12 July, 1941, as HMS *Waglan* (originally *Seaford*); captured on the stocks December 1941; launched March 1943 and commissioned 28 September, 1944 as *W 102*; severely damaged 3 February, 1945 (cause unknown) N of Haitan Island (25° 40′ N, 119° 50′ E); repaired; August 1945: recaptured and employed by Allied Minesweeping Service until 1947; 20 November, 1947: returned to Britain and scrapped at Uraga in 1948.

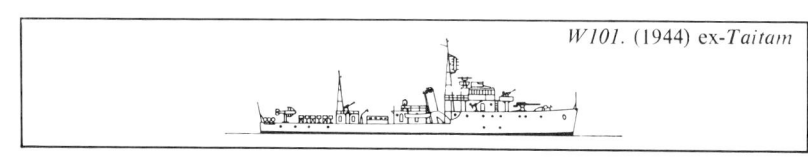

W101. (1944) ex-*Taitam*

Name	Builder	Date	Displ	Length ft in	Beam ft in	Draught ft in	Machinery	SHP	Speed	Fuel	Radius	Armament	Comp
Wa 1 Class	various	1941–1943	222 N 215 S	97 0 wl 95 0 pp	19 5	7 10	1 Diesel 1 shaft	300	9.5	?	1700 @ 9.5	1 × 80mm (3in) 23-cal AA ? 1 × 7.7mm MG 6 DCs	

GENERAL NOTES
These auxiliary minesweepers were built under the 1940 Programme (hull Nos. 251–256), and the 1941 Programme (Nos. 480–495). They were wooden-hulled trawler-type craft with a freeboard of 9ft 8in. The builders were Hitachi, Sakurajima; Naniwa, Osaka; Mitsubishi, Shimonoseki; Sanoyago, Osaka; Namura, Osaka.

RE-ARMAMENT
In 1943–4 they received 2–4 × 25mm AA guns and the DCs were increased to 15.

CAREERS
Wa 1
Launched 9 November, 1941, completed 31 January, 1942; sunk 4 May, 1942, by aircraft from USS *Yorktown* in Gavutu harbour, Florida Island, Solomons (09° 07′ S, 160° 12′ E).
Wa 2
Launched 9 November, 1941, completed 28 February, 1942; sunk with *Wa 1*.
Wa 3
Launched 31 March, 1942, completed 30 May, 1942; sunk 24 July, 1945, by US aircraft in Soerabaya harbour.
Wa 4
Launched 10 March, 1942, completed 29 June, 1942; sunk 19 July, 1944, by British aircraft in Dili harbour, Timor (08° 38′ S, 125° 26′ E).
Wa 5
Launched 31 March, 1942, completed 30 June, 1942; damaged 18 September, 1944, by US aircraft at Enderby Island, in the Carolines; surrendered unrepaired at Truk in August 1945; BU.
Wa 6
Launched 18 July, 1942, completed 30 October, 1942; badly damaged and run aground 10 August, 1945, after attack by US TF 38 in Yamada Bay (39° 29′ N, 141° 58′ E); raised and repaired for transfer to Mercantile Marine in 1946.
Wa 7
Launched 16 July, 1942, completed 28 December, 1942; surrendered at Singapore August 1945 and operated as a passenger ferry under British control until July 1946; believed to have been sold subsequently.
Wa 8
Launched 16 July, 1942, completed 31 January, 1943; sunk 21 October, 1944, by US TF 38 NE of Panay Island (11° 30′ N, 123° 20′ E).

Wa 1. Type (1941)

Wa 9
Launched 25 January, 1943, completed 14 April, 1943; surrendered at Singapore in August 1945; fate as *Wa 7*.
Wa 10
Launched 25 January, 1943, completed 14 May, 1943; sunk 11 January, 1945, by gunfire from US destroyers S of Vigan, Luzon (17° 20′ N, 120° E).
Wa 11
Launched 1942; surrendered August 1945 and used for mine clearance until 1947; handed over to Great Britain 14 November, 1947, and BU at Kure in 1948.
Wa 12
Launched 1942; surrendered August 1945 and used for mine clearance until 1947; handed over to USSR 3 October, 1947.
Wa 13
Launched 25 January, 1943, completed 14 April, 1943; surrendered August 1945; used for mine clearance until 1947; handed over to USA 1 October, 1947 and BU.
Wa 14
Launched 25 January, 1943, completed 14 May, 1943; surrendered August 1945 and used for mine clearance until 1947; handed over to China 3 October, 1947, and renumbered *No. 201*; captured 1949 by Communist Chinese forces.
Wa 15
Launched 1943; surrendered in Korea August 1945, but not taken over; BU.
Wa 16
Launched 1943; surrendered in Korea August 1945 and served on mine clearance until 1947; handed over to Great Britain 14 November, 1947, and BU at Kure in 1948.
W 17
Launched 1943; surrendered August 1945 and used for mine clearance until 1947; handed over to USSR 3 October, 1947.
W 18
Launched 1943; surrendered August 1945 and used for mine clearance until 1947; handed over to USA 1 October, 1947, and BU.
W 19
Launched 1943; surrendered August 1945 and used on Repatriation Service until 1946; handed over to China 3 October, 1947, and renumbered *No. 202*; later renamed *Chiang Yung*.
Wa 20
Launched 1943; surrendered August 1945 and used on Repatriation Service until 1946; handed over to USSR 3 October, 1947.
Wa 21
Launched 11 March, 1943, completed 15 June, 1943; surrendered August 1945 and used for mine clearance until 1947; handed over to USA 1 October, 1947, and BU.
Wa 22
Launched 1943 and completed 20 October, 1943; surrendered August 1945 and used for mine clearance until 1947; handed over to China 3 October, 1947, and renumbered *No. 203*; later renamed *Chiang*.

Name	Builder	Date	Displ	Length ft in	Beam ft in	Draught ft in	Machinery	SHP	Speed	Fuel	Radius	Armament	Comp
Wa 101 (ex-*Flores*)	Droogdok Mij. Tandjong Priok	1941– 1943	175 N 170 S	114 2 wl 106 8 pp	18 8	6 3	1 'Enterprise' Diesel 1 shaft	360	12.5	?	?	3 × 25mm AA 1 × 13.2mm AAMG 6 DCs	14
Wa 102 (ex-*Fakfak*)													
Wa 103 (ex-*Garoet*)													
Wa 105 (ex-*Grissee*)													
Wa 104 (ex-*Djember*)	Droogdok Mij. Tandjong Priok	1940– 1942	175 N 170 S	113 7 wl 106 8 pp	18 8	6 3	1 Benz Diesel 1 'Enterprise' Diesel 1 shaft	350	10.5	?	?	as *Wa 101*, etc.	12
Wa 106 (ex-*Djombang*)													
Wa 107 (ex-*Enggano*)													

GENERAL NOTES
Flores, Fakfak, Garoet and *Grissee* were Dutch *Gouvernementsmarine* patrol craft of the 'FG' Type, or improved 'DE' Type, designed for wartime use as minesweepers. *Djember, Djombang* and *Enggano* belonged to the 'DE' Type, which were derived from the 'ABC' Type.

CAREERS
Wa 101
Launched 1942; scuttled while incomplete 2 March, 1942; repaired by the Japanese and launched 17 October 1942 as *Wa 101*; completed 25 June, 1943; sunk 13 October, 1943 by mine near Madura Island (07° 11′ S,112° 45′ E); raised: destroyed in dock 17 May, 1945 by aircraft from USS *Saratoga* and HMS *Illustrious* at Soerabaya; surrendered unrepaired August 1945 and returned to Netherlands Navy; repaired and transferred to Indonesia in 1950.
Wa 102
Launched 1942; scuttled 2 March, 1942 while still completing; repaired by the Japanese and launched 17 October, 1942 as *Wa 102*; completed 30 June, 1943; surrendered at Soerabaya in August 1945; subsequent fate unknown.
Wa 103
Launched 1942; scuttled 2 March, 1942 by Dutch naval personnel in the building yard; repaired by the Japanese and re-launched 20 November, 1942 as *Wa 103*; completed 7 May 1943; surrendered at Djakarta in August 1945; subsequent fate unknown.
Wa 104
Launched 1940 as *Djember*; renumbered Auxiliary Minesweeper *No. 19* in 1942; sunk 2 March, 1942 at Tandjong Priok; repaired by the Japanese and put into service 20 February, 1943 as *Wa 104*; torpedoed 12 April, 1945 by British submarine *Stygian* SW of Bali (08° 55′ S, 115° 15′ E).
Wa 105
Launched 1943; scuttled 2 March, 1942 by Dutch naval personnel in the building yard; repaired by the Japanese and re-launched 15 February, 1943; completed 31 August, 1943; torpedoed 25 May, 1945 by British submarine *Trenchant* near Tandjong Bugel, Java (06° 21′ S, 110° 57′ E); stricken 10 July, 1945.
Wa 106
Launched 1942 as Dutch *Djombang* but renumbered Auxiliary Minesweeper *No. 20*; scuttled 2 March, 1942, at Tandjong Priok; repaired by the Japanese and commissioned 31 August, 1943, as *Wa 106*; surrendered at Djakarta August 1945 and returned to Netherlands Navy; transferred to Indonesia in 1950.
Wa 107
Launched 1941 as Dutch *Enggano* but renumbered Auxiliary Minesweeper *No. 21* in 1942; scuttled 2 March, 1942 at Tandjong Priok; repaired by the Japanese and commissioned 31 August, 1944, as *Wa 107* (she also bore the interim name *Hino Maru*); surrendered at Djakarta August 1945 and returned to Netherlands Navy; transferred to Indonesia in 1950.

Wa 101. (1944)   *Wa 104.* (1944)

Merchant Ships converted to Minesweepers

CAREERS
Aioi Maru
Built 1935 as 358 GRT motor passenger vessel; converted August 1941; returned to Nippon Kaisen KK, Kobe, after August 1945.
Asahi Maru No. 2 ex-*Fukuei Maru No. 3*
Converted August 1941; returned to mercantile service as a vehicle ferry 1 June, 1945.

MINESWEEPERS 211

Ataka Maru
Built 1921 as 275 GRT steam trawler; converted 1941; taken over by USA in August 1945 and BU.

Atsu Maru
Built 1934 as 160 GRT motor cargo vessel; converted 1942; returned to mercantile service in 1945 as a vehicle ferry; renamed *Showa Maru* 1961; lost 6 December, 1962.

Banshu Maru No. 18
Built 1922 as 264 GRT steam trawler; converted 1941; sunk 28 July, 1945, by US TF 38 off Owase (34° 04′ N, 136° 15′ E); later raised and returned to mercantile service.

Banshu Maru No. 51 ex-*Banshu Maru*
Built 1921 as 234 GRT steam trawler; conversion date unknown; returned to mercantile service 1945 as *Taiyo Maru No. 8*.

Banshu Maru No. 52 ex-*Banshu Maru No. 2*
Built 1921 as 234 GRT steam trawler; converted 1941; mined 20 January, 1942, in Subic Bay, Luzon (14° 45′ N, 120° 17′ E).

Banshu Maru No. 56 ex-*Meiji Maru*
Built 1920 as 267 GRT steam trawler; converted 1941; sunk 11 January, 1945, as a blockship in the S entrance to Manila Bay, Luzon.

Bisan Maru
Built 1922 as 344 GRT steam passenger vessel; converted 1941; surrendered August 1945; returned to mercantile service.

Chitose Maru
Built 1937 as 246 GRT motor cargo vessel; converted 1941; sunk 24 March, 1945, by US TF 38 off Amami-Oshima (29° 12′ N, 126° 13′ E).

Choun Maru
Built 1935 as 330 GRT passenger vessel; converted 1941.

Choun Maru No. 6
Built 1932 as 167 GRT motor cargo vessel; converted 1941; returned to mercantile service 1945.

Choun Maru No. 7
Built 1934 as 163 GRT motor cargo vessel; converted 1941; sunk (torpedoed?) 14 December, 1944, off Balawan (approx. 03° 55′ N, 98° 50′ E).

Choun Maru No. 8
Built 1933 as 168 GRT motor cargo vessel; converted 1941; returned to mercantile service 1945; later renamed *Miyatsu Maru*.

Choun Maru No. 18
Built 1935 as 195 GRT motor cargo vessel; converted 1941; sunk 12 September, 1944, by US TF 38 off Cebu (10° 20′ N, 124° E).

Choun Maru No. 21
Built 1935 as 195 GRT motor cargo vessel; converted 1941; sunk 25 November, 1944, as blockship in Manila Harbour, Luzon.

Choyo Maru No. 2
80 GRT; conversion date unknown; sunk 14 July, 1945, by US TF 38 5 m off Kikonai (Tsugaru-Kaikyo) (41° 38′ N, 140° 35′ E).

Eguchi Maru No. 3
Built 1935 as 198 GRT motor cargo vessel; converted 1941; torpedoed 6 September, 1944, by US submarine *Shad* in entrance to Kii Suido (33° 27′ N, 135° 33′ E).

Fuji Maru
Built 1929 as 231 GRT motor passenger vessel; converted 1941; stranded 15 July, 1945, off Hakodate, Hokkaido following bomb damage; subsequently salvaged and returned to mercantile service.

Fukuei Maru No. 7
Built 1934 as 285 GRT motor cargo vessel; converted 1941; returned to mercantile service 1948.

Fumi Maru No. 2
Built 1939 as 304 GRT whalecatcher; converted 1941; used as minelayer from 1942; torpedoed 21 September, 1944, by US submarine *Shad* 18 m E of Nii-jima, Izuschhito (34° 45′ N, 139° 40′ E).

Genchi Maru
525 GRT; conversion date unknown; sunk 26 November, 1943, by US aircraft in Chianghai Bay, Canton (approx 21° 33′ N, 112° E).

Hagoromo Maru
Built 1920 as 234 GRT steam trawler; converted 1941; surrendered August 1945 and returned to mercantile service.

Hakata Maru No. 6
Built 1922 as 262 GRT steam trawler; converted 1941; sunk 16 October, 1944, by US aircraft off Minami, Daito Island (approx 25° 30′ N, 131° E).

Hakata Maru No. 7
Built 1923 as 257 GRT steam trawler; converted 1941; later returned to mercantile service.

Himeshima Maru
Built 1927 as 274 GRT steam trawler; converted 1941; surrendered in August 1945.

Hinode Maru No. 17 ex-*Inaba Maru,* ex-*Kakuwa Maru No. 17*
Built 1919 as 235 GRT steam trawler; converted 1941; torpedoed 11 April, 1945, by US submarine *Spadefish* off Tokchok-Kundo (37° 13′ N, 125° 11′ E).

Hinode Maru No. 18 ex-*Izumo Maru,* ex-*Kakuwa Maru No. 18*
Built 1919 as 235 GRT steam trawler; converted 1941; sunk 26 July, 1945, by US aircraft W of Häzhyu-man, Korea (37° 58′ N, 126° 40′ E).

Hinode Maru No. 20 ex-*Kokusai Maru No. 100*
Built 1930 as 281 GRT steam trawler; converted 1941; torpedoed 21 August, 1944, by US submarine *Barb* S of Formosa (21° 21′ N, 121° 11′ E).

Hoei Maru
Built 1919 as 219 GRT steam trawler; conversion date unknown; torpedoed 29 September, 1944, by US submarine *Skate* off Yoronjima (27° 14′ N, 128° 29′ E).

Kaiyo Maru
Built 1911, 212 GRT; conversion date unknown; sunk 1 October, 1944, by mine off Kiachou (Tsingtao).

Kaiyo Maru No. 1
Built 1939 as 150 GRT Government motor vessel; conversion date unknown; mine clearance 1945–7.

Kaiyo Maru No. 3
Built 1938, 150 GRT; conversion date unknown; mine clearance 1945–7.

Keijin Maru No. 1
Built 1937 as 425 GRT motor cargo vessel; converted 1941; ran aground 28 July, 1945, off Owase (34° 05′ N, 136° 14′ E); raised 1946? and returned to mercantile service.

Keijin Maru No. 2
Built 1937 as 433 GRT motor cargo vessel; converted 1941; subsequently returned to mercantile service.

Keijin Maru No. 3
Built 1937 as 433 GRT motor cargo vessel; converted 1942; sunk 14 July, 1945, by US TF 38 NE of Shiriya-saki (41° 30′ N, 141° 30′ E).

Keijin Maru No. 5
Built 1937 as 433 GRT motor cargo vessel; converted 1941; mine clearance 1945–7 and then returned to mercantile service 1948.

Keinan Maru
Built 1938 as 316 GRT steam trawler; converted 1941; subsequently returned to mercantile service.

Kiri Maru No. 5
Built 1937 as 335 GRT motor cargo vessel; converted 1941; later returned to mercantile service.

Kongo Maru No. 2
Built 1941 as 216 GRT steam trawler; converted 1941; sunk 10 August, 1945, by US TF 38 off Onagawa (38° 30′ N, 141° 29′ E).

Kosan Maru
Built 1934, 278 GRT; converted 1941; later returned to mercantile service.

Kyo Maru No. 1
Built 1937 as 340 GRT steam whalecatcher; converted 1941; sunk 15 January, 1945, by mine S of Penang (05° 18′ N, 100° 20′ E).

Kyo Maru No. 3
Built 1938 as 341 GRT steam whaler; converted 1941; sunk 26 February, 1943, by mine off Rangoon (approx 15° 36′ N, 96° 15′ E).

Mejima Maru
Built 1928 as 336 GRT steam cargo vessel; converted 1941; sunk 26 April, 1945, by mine in Shimonoseki Straits.

Misago No. 1
Built 1920 as 265 GRT steam trawler; converted 1941; torpedoed 15 April, 1945, by US submarine *Cero* off Todo-saki (39° 35′ N, 142° 06′ E).

Misago No. 3
Built 1921 as 267 GRT steam trawler; converted 1941; sunk 27 May, 1945, by US aircraft in entrance to Ise Wan (34° 37′ N, 137° 19′ E).

Misago Maru No. 8
Built 1922 as 281 GRT steam trawler; converted 1941; surrendered August 1945 and BU.

Misago Maru No. 11
Built 1928 as 318 GRT steam trawler; converted 1941; lost (cause unknown) December 1943 in Ogasawara-gunto area.

Miyo Maru ex-*Miwa Maru*
Built 1937 as 355 GRT motor cargo vessel; converted 1941; later returned to mercantile service.

Musashi Maru
Built 1920 as 227 GRT steam trawler; converted 1941; torpedoed 16 July, 1942, by US submarine *Narwhal* or *Cachalot* 100 m E of Nojimasaki (approx. 34° 50′ N, 142′ E).

Nagato Maru No. 3
Built 1911 as 213 GRT steam trawler; auxiliary minesweeper August 1914; sunk 1 October, 1914, near Tsingtao by mine laid by SMS *Lauting*.

Nagato Maru ex-*Nagato Maru No. 6*
Built 1912 as 211 GRT steam trawler; auxiliary minesweeper August 1914; mined 1 October, 1914, as *Nagato Maru No. 3*.

Naruo Maru
Built 1922 as 215 GRT steam trawler; converted 1941; torpedoed 25 December, 1943, by US submarine *Gurnard* NE of Daiozaki.

Noshiro Maru No. 2
Built 1923 as 216 GRT steam trawler; converted 1941; torpedoed 1 April, 1944, by US submarine Haddock 120 m E of Haha-jima (26° N, 142° E).

Oi Maru
Built 1939 as 396 GRT motor cargo vessel; converted 1941; stricken 10 May, 1944.

Otowa Maru
Built 1920 as 220 GRT steam trawler; converted 1941; sunk 12 January, 1945, by US TF 38 in Cam Ranh Bay (11° 50′ N, 109° E).

Ranzan Maru
Built 1920 as 219 GRT steam trawler; conversion date unknown; lost in Chinese Waters.

Reisui Maru
Built 1920 as 219 GRT steam trawler; converted 1941; torpedoed 25 December, 1944, by British submarine off Labuan Roekoe lighthouse in Malacca Straits (03° 19′ N, 99° 45′ E).

Rikuzen Maru
Built 1920 as 221 GRT steam trawler; converted 1941; sunk 26 July, 1945, in Häzhuman delta, Korea (37° 58′ N, 125° 40′ E).

Rokko Maru
Built 1919, 225 GRT; converted 1941; lost.

Saishu Maru Nos. 1, 2, 6, 7
Conversion dates and fates unknown.

Sakaki Maru
Built 1934 as 275 GRT motor cargo vessel; converted 1942; mine clearance 1945–7 and then returned to mercantile service.

Seki Maru
Built 1937 as 297 GRT motor cargo vessel; converted 1942; sunk 24 March, 1945, by US TG 58/1 W of Tokara-gunto (30° N, 126° 30′ E).

Seki Maru No. 3
Built 1939 as 304 GRT whalecatcher (?); converted 1941; minelayer 1942; later returned to mercantile service.

Sen'yu Maru No. 2
Built 1934 as 281 GRT motor cargo vessel; converted 1941; surrendered August 1945; mine clearance until 1947 and then returned to mercantile service.

Sen'yu Maru No. 3
Built 1936 as 327 GRT motor cargo vessel; career as *Sen'yu Maru No. 2*.

Shimpo Maru
Built 1936 as 294 GRT motor cargo vessel; converted 1941; sunk 10 October, 1944, by US TF 38 off Naha, Okinawa (26° 13′ N, 127° 40′ E).

Shintohoku Maru
Built 1925 as 305 GRT steam passenger vessel; converted 1941; returned to mercantile service in 1945.

Shonan Maru No. 16
Built 1940 as 354 GRT steam whalecatcher; converted 1941; sunk 24 March, 1945, by US TG 58/1 W of Amami-Oshima (29° 12′ N, 126° 13′ E).

Showa Maru Nos. 7–8, 10
Built 1936 as 264 GRT steam whalecatchers; converted 1941; all later returned to mercantile service.

Sonobe Maru
Built 1920 as 220 GRT steam trawler; converted 1941; sunk 14 July, 1945, by US TF 38 12 m off Hiroo, Hokkaido (42° 11′ N, 143° 36′ E).

Taian Maru
Built 1930 as 193 GRT motor cargo vessel; date of conversion unknown; returned to mercantile service in 1945.

Taihei Maru No. 3
Built 1930 as 197 GRT motor cargo vessel; date of conversion unknown; returned to mercantile service.

Taisei Maru
Built 1932 as 228 GRT motor cargo vessel; converted 1941; Repatriation Service 1945; returned to mercantile service in 1947.

Taito Maru
Built 1932 as 267 GRT motor cargo vessel; converted 1941; torpedoed 16 August, 1944, by US submarine *Croaker* W of Korea (36° 15′ N, 125° 52′ E).

Takao Maru
Built 1920 as 220 GRT steam trawler; converted 1941; used as submarine-chaser 1943; sunk 12 September, 1944, by US TF 38 between Cebu and Biliran.

Takasago Maru
Built 1921 as 275 GRT steam trawler; converted 1941; later returned to mercantile service.

Takashima Maru No. 2
162 GRT motor passenger vessel: converted 1941; later returned to mercantile service.

Takashima Maru No. 3
162 GRT motor passenger vessel; converted 1941; mine clearance 1945; returned to mercantile service 1947.

Takunan Maru No. 1
343 GRT steam whalecatcher; converted 1941; sunk 10 October, 1944, by US TF 38 off Okinodaitoshima (25° 30′ N, 131° E).

Takunan Maru No. 3
Built 1937 as 343 GRT steam whalecatcher; converted 1941; submarine-chaser 1944; returned to mercantile service 1945.

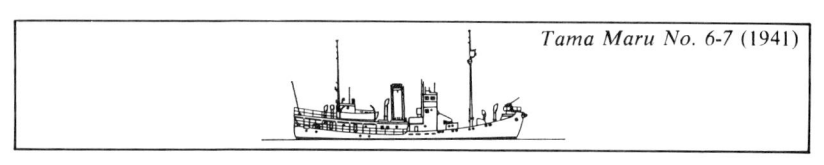

Tama Maru No. 6-7 (1941)

Tama Maru
Built 1936 as 264 GRT steam whalecatcher; converted 1941; sunk 4 May, 1945, by aircraft of US carrier *Yorktown* off Gavutu, Tulagi (09° 07′ S, 160° 12′ E).

Tama Maru
Built 1939 as 396 GRT motor vessel; converted 1941; submarine-chaser 1944; torpedoed 8 April, 1945, by US submarine *Seadevil* 10 m E of Sohuksando, Korea (34° 05′ N, 125° 25′ E).

Tama Maru No. 2
Built 1936 as 264 GRT steam whalecatcher; converted 1941; no further details.

Tama Maru No. 3
Built 1936 as 258 GRT steam whalecatcher; converted 1941; submarine-chaser 1944; later returned to mercantile service.

Tama Maru No. 5
Built 1936 as 258 GRT steam whalecatcher; converted 1941; submarine-chaser 1944.

Tama Maru No. 6
275 GRT steam whalecatcher; converted 1941; submarine-chaser 1944 (q.v.).

Tama Maru No. 7
275 GRT steam whalecatcher; converted 1941; submarine-chaser 1944 (q.v.).

Tamazono Maru No. 1
Built 1920 as 313 GRT steam trawler; converted 1941; returned to mercantile service 1945; later renamed *Awaji Maru*.

Tamazono Maru No. 2
Built 1920 as 316 GRT steam trawler; converted 1941; sunk 14 July, 1945, by US TF 38 at Kushiro Pier, Hokkaido (42° 58′ N, 144° 25′ E); raised and returned to mercantile service; renamed *Naruto Maru* and in 1956 became *Kiku Maru*.

Tamazono Maru No. 3
Built 1920 as 316 GRT steam trawler; converted 1941; later returned to mercantile service.

Tamura Maru
Built 1920 as 255 GRT steam trawler; converted 1941; later returned to mercantile service.

Togo Maru
Built 1923 as 302 GRT steam passenger vessel; converted 1941; torpedoed 15 April, 1945, by US submarine *Cero* off Todosaki (39° 30′ N, 142° 10′ E).

Tokuho Maru No. 5
Built 1934 as 238 GRT motor cargo vessel; converted 1941; returned to mercantile service 1945.

Tokuho Maru No. 10
353 GRT motor cargo vessel; converted 1941; returned to mercantile service 1945.

Torishima Maru
Built 1922 as 256 GRT steam trawler; converted 1941; surrendered April 1945; returned to mercantile service.
Toshi Maru Nos. 1–2
Built 1937 as 294 GRT steam whalecatcher; converted 1941; no further details.
Toshi Maru No. 5
Built 1937 as 298 GRT steam whalecatcher; converted 1941; sunk 4 July, 1944, off Hahajima (26° 20′ N, 141° 50′ E).
Toshi Maru No. 7
Built 1937 as 297 GRT steam whalecatcher; converted 1941; wrecked 22 July, 1945, off Sata-Misaki (31° N, 130° 40′ E).
Toshi Maru No. 8
Built 1937 as 298 GRT steam whalecatcher; converted 1941; sunk 31 August, 1944, by US TF 38 off Iojima (250° N, 141° 50′ E).
Tsukushi Maru
Built 1920 as 220 GRT steam trawler; converted 1940; sunk 30 September, 1943, by US aircraft in Kuangchou Bay (21° 12′ N, 110° 24′ E).
Yachiyo Maru
Built 1937 as 271 GRT motor passenger vessel; converted 1941; returned to mercantile service in 1945.
Yoshino Maru
Built 1920 as 220 GRT steam trawler; converted 1941; torpedoed 14 May, 1945, by US submarine *Sandlance* 18 m off Erimosaki, Hokkaido (32° N, 143° 36′ E).
Yoshitomo Maru
Built 1934 as 209 GRT motor passenger vessel; converted 1941; returned to mercantile service 1945.
Yuki Maru
Built 1929 as 389 GRT motor trawler; conversion date unknown; surrendered August 1945 and used for mine clearance until 1947.

15. Submarine Chasers

Name	Builder	Date	Displ	Length ft in	Beam ft in	Draught ft in	Machinery	SHP	Speed	Fuel	Radius	Armament	Comp
Ch 1	Uraga Dock Co., Tokyo	1933–1934	280 N	210 0 wl	19 5	4 8	2 Diesel engines 2 shafts	3400	24	–	1500 @ 14	2 × 40mm (2pdr) AA 2 × 7.7mm AA 36 DCs	45
Ch 2	Ishikawajima, Tokyo		266 S	203 5 pp									
Reconstruction:		1935	400 F 376 S						21.1				

GENERAL NOTES
First 1931 Fleet Supplementary Programme. First Japanese-built submarine chasers and smallest units in the fleet. Fitted with 2 rudders and two depth-charge throwers (DCT). These craft suffered from excessive topweight and after the *Tomodzuru* disaster (p. 128) they were rebuilt with a ballast keel and additional permanent ballast.

RE-ARMAMENT
1944: 3 × 25mm AA replaced 2 × 7.7mm MGs.

CAREERS
Ch 1
Launched 23 December, 1933; completed 24 March, 1934; beached 14 November, 1944 at Sablayan, Mindoro, after air attack by TF 38; salvaged and repaired; captured August 1945 and scuttled 11 July, 1946 by US Navy off Singapore.
Ch 2
Launched 20 December, 1933; completed 25 March, 1934; sunk 27 June, 1945 N of Lombok (07° 30′ S, 116° 15′ E) by US submarine *Blueback*.

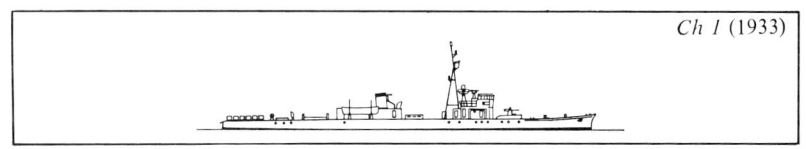

Ch 1 (1933)

Name	Builder	Date	Displ	Length ft in	Beam ft in	Draught ft in	Machinery	SHP	Speed	Fuel	Radius	Armament	Comp
Ch 3	Tsurumi, Yokohama	1935–1936	285 N 270 S	180 4 wl 173 11 pp	18 4	6 11	2 Diesel engines 2 shafts	2500	20	–	1500 @ 14	2 × 40mm (2pdr) AA 36 DCs	45

Submarine chaser *No. 3* seen on trials in 1936. The 2-pounder pom-pom is mounted behind a "Zareba" and the sea-boat davits are on the port side, unlike *Ch.1* and *2* in which they were to starboard. (Authors' Collection.)

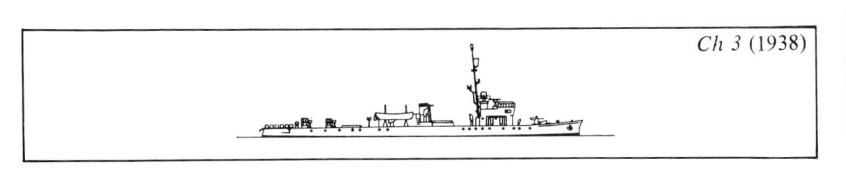

Ch 3 (1938)

214 SUBMARINE CHASERS

GENERAL NOTES
2nd 1934 Fleet Supplementary Programme. Modified *Ch 1* design with less topweight and 1 rudder. 2 DCTs.

RE-ARMAMENT
1944: 3 × 25mm added.

CAREER
Launched 6 June, 1936; completed 5 October, 1936; captured at Soerabaya August 1945; scuttled off Singapore 11 July, 1946.

Name	Builder	Date	Displ	Length ft in	Beam ft in	Draught ft in	Machinery	SHP	Speed	Fuel	Radius	Armament	Comp
Ch 51	Tsurumi,	1936–	175 N	146 0 wl	15 9	5 7	2 Diesel engines	3000	23	–	–	1 × 40mm (2pdr) AA	–
Ch 52	Yokohama	1937	170 S	141 9 pp			2 shafts					18 DCs	
Ch 53	Sakurajima, Osaka	1937	180 N 170 S	146 0 wl 141 9 pp	15 9	5 8	2 sets GT 2 sets Kampon boilers 2 shafts	3000	23			1 × 40mm (2pdr) AA 18 DCs	

GENERAL NOTES
2nd 1934 Fleet Supplementary Programme. Experimental craft of a smaller design, with turbines and Diesel engines fitted in hulls of the same basic layout, featuring negative sheer aft. The manoeuvrability of *Ch 51* and *Ch 53* was poor and they were modified by lengthening the hull aft by 3.3ft and the fitting of new rudders. *Ch 52* was modified while building, to incorporate the modified stern which had proved successful in trials. *Ch 53*'s funnel was offset to starboard. 1 rudder, 2 DCTs.

RE-ARMAMENT
1944: 20 to 30 DCs.

CAREERS
Ch 51
Launched 9 June, 1937; completed 30 September, 1937; 20 May, 1943 re-designated Auxiliary Submarine Chaser (SC) *Cha 251*; 28 August, 1944 redesignated Tug *Eisen No. 1658*, attached to the Yokosuka Anti-Submarine School; captured at Uraga August 1945.

Ch 52
Launched 25 August, 1937; completed 25 July, 1939; 20 May, 1943 redesignated as Auxiliary SC *Cha 252*; 15 February, 1944 redesignated Tug *Eisen No. 1650*, attached to the Yokosuka A/S School; captured at Uraga August 1945.

Ch 53
Launched 15 July, 1937; completed 31 October, 1937; 20 May 1943 redesignated Auxiliary SC *Cha 253*; 15 February 1944, redesignated Tug *Eisen No. 1651*, attached to the Yokosuka A/S School; captured at Uraga August 1945; sank August 1946 through flooding caused by leaks.

Ch 53, as *Eisen No. 1651* (1944)   *Ch 52*, as *Eisen No. 1650* (1944)
(1937)

Name	Builder	Date	Displ	Length ft in	Beam ft in	Draught ft in	Machinery	SHP	Speed	Fuel	Radius	Armament	Comp
Ch 4, 10	Sakurajima, Osaka	1937– 1939	309 N	184 5 wl	18 4	7 4	2 Diesel engines 2 shafts	2600	20			2 × 40mm (2pdr) AA 36 DCs	
Ch 5, 9	Mitsubishi, Yokohama		291 S	173 11 pp									
Ch 6, 7, 11	Tsurumi, Yokohama												
Ch 8, 12	Tama Slipway, Tamano												

GENERAL NOTES
3rd 1937 Fleet Supplementary Programme. Officially designated '*Ch 1*-type' but significant differences included a long, low bridge structure and negative sheer to the hull aft. The class was also known as the '*Ch-7*-class', *Ch 7* being the first unit completed. *Ch 9–12* featured an inclined front face to the bridge. 1 Rudder, 2 DCTs.

RE-ARMAMENT
1944–5: 3 × 25mm and Type '13' radar added.

CAREERS
Ch 4
Launched 13 September, 1938; completed 28 December, 1938; captured August 1945 at Bandjermasin, Borneo, and sold; ultimate fate unknown.

Ch 5
Launched 28 July, 1938; completed 8 December, 1938; captured August 1945 in seriously damaged condition at Djakarta; scuttled 11 July, 1946 off Singapore.

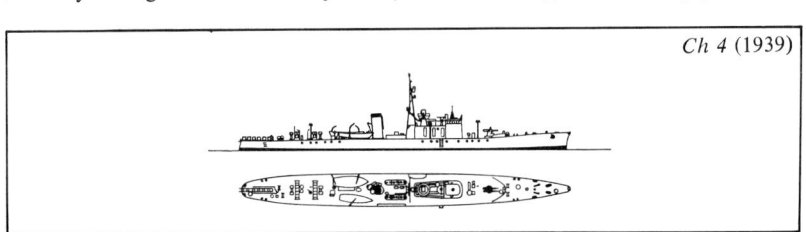

Ch 6
Launched 6 February, 1939; completed 20 May, 1939; beached at Babelthuap, Palau 30 March, 1944 after TF 58 air attack; deleted from Active List 10 October, 1944.

Ch 7
Launched 10 June, 1938; completed 20 November, 1938; sunk 11 April, 1945 E of Car Nicobar (08° 57′ N, 93° 38′ E) by Royal Air Force aircraft.

Ch 8
Launched 9 August, 1938; completed 30 November, 1938; sunk 4 March, 1945 85 nm Sof Penang (04° 04′ N, 100° 35′ E) by gunfire of HM Submarines *Trenchant* and *Terrapin*.

Ch 9
Launched 15 October, 1938; completed 9 May, 1939; captured August 1945 at Penang; employed on Repatriation Service until laid up in early 1946; handed over to China 3 October, 1947; renamed *Fu Ling*, then *Hai Ta*; post-1949 *Min Chiang*.

Ch 10
Launched 31 January, 1939; completed 15 June, 1939; lost 2 May, 1944 through stranding in the Palaus (approx. 07° 20′ N, 134° 30′ E); deleted from Active List 30 September, 1945.

Ch 11
Launched 28 June, 1938; completed 2 February, 1939; sunk 6 November, 1943 W of Buka (05° 26′ S, 154° 35′ E) by US aircraft.

Ch 12
Launched 8 February, 1939; completed 30 April, 1939; lost off the Palaus August 1944, cause unknown; deleted from Active List 30 September, 1945.

Ch 4 (1939)

Name	Builder	Date	Displ	Length ft in	Beam ft in	Draught ft in	Machinery	SHP	Speed	Fuel	Radius	Armament	Comp
Ch 13–27	various yards	1939–1942	460 N 438 S	167 4 wl 152 7 pp	22 0	9 0	2 Diesel engines 2 shafts	1700	16			1 × 80mm (3in) HA 40-cal 2 × 13.2mm AA (*Ch 23*: 26 × 25mm AA) 136 DCs	

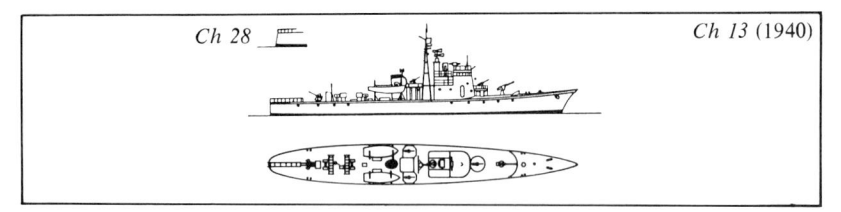

Ch 28   *Ch 13* (1940)

GENERAL NOTES
4th 1939 Fleet Supplementary Programme, 1940 Additional Programme. Standard type based on *Ch 1* and *Ch 4* classes but with much more compact appearance and distinctive clipper bow. Very seaworthy. Small tripod mast. 1 rudder, 2 DCTs.

RECONSTRUCTION AND RE-ARMAMENT
Funnel heightened by 3.3ft in some units; from 15 September, 1944: 36 × 25mm AA (in *Ch 17*, *18*, *23* and *56* – 56 × 25mm); DC release trap, 2 Type '94' DCTs, Type '93' A/S hydrophone. Type '22' Radar, Radar intercept receiver.

CAREERS
Ch 13
Launched 30 March, 1940; completed 15 July, 1940; sunk 3 April, 1943 SE of Shiriyasaki (41° 03′ N, 141° 58′ E) by US submarine *Pickerel*.
Ch 14
Launched 29 November, 1940; completed 31 March, 1941; sunk 28 July, 1945 at Owase (34° 05′ E, 136° 15′ E) by aircraft from TF 38; deleted from Active List 30 November, 1945 and BU.
Ch 15
Launched 23 December, 1940; completed 31 March, 1941; captured August 1945 at Uraga; BU 1948.
Ch 16
Launched 19 November, 1940; completed 5 April, 1941; sunk 4 July, 1944 at Chichi Jima, Bonin Islands, by aircraft from US TF 38.

Ch 17
Launched 3 May, 1941; completed 31 July, 1941; sunk 28 April, 1945 S of Fukueshima (32° 25′ N, 128° 46′ E) by US submarine *Springer*.
Ch 18
Launched 23 April, 1941; completed 31 July, 1941; sunk 30 December, 1944 off Santiago, Luzon, (17° 00′ N, 123° 00′ E) by US aircraft.
Ch 19
Launched 3 June 1941; completed 20 September, 1941; captured August 1945 in severely damaged condition at Kure; laid up at Sasebo and BU in 1948.
Ch 20
Launched 29 May, 1941; completed 20 August, 1941; captured August 1945 in damaged condition at Kure; laid up at Sasebo in 1947; BU 1948.
Ch 21
Launched 21 May, 1941; completed 20 August, 1941; captured August 1945 and employed on Repatriation Service; laid up at Sasebo in early 1946; taken over by Great Britain 17 October, 1947 and BU at Singapore.
Ch 22
Launched 29 May, 1941; completed 12 October, 1941; sunk 19 February, 1944 in the exit from Stephen Strait, New Ireland (03° 04′ S, 150° 42′ E) by US aircraft.
Ch 23
Launched 13 August, 1941; completed 15 November, 1941; captured August 1945 while laid up unserviceable at Tsingtao; BU in 1948.
Ch 24
Launched 10 October, 1941; completed 20 December, 1941; sunk 17 February, 1944 W of Truk (07° 10′ N, 150° 35′ E) by gunfire of USS *Burns*.
Ch 25
Launched 7 October, 1941; completed 29 December, 1941; sunk 15 July, 1942 off Kiska (52° 02′ N, 177° 42′ E) by US submarine *Grunion*.
Ch 26
Launched 28 August, 1941; completed 20 December, 1941; sunk 30 July, 1945 in Korea Strait (34° 47′ N, 128° 27′ E) by aircraft from US TF 38.
Ch 27
Launched 5 November, 1941; completed 28 January, 1942; sunk 15 July, 1942 off Kiska by US submarine *Grunion*.

Name	Builder	Date	Displ	Length ft in	Beam ft in	Draught ft in	Machinery	SHP	Speed	Fuel	Radius	Armament	Comp
Ch 28–58, 60, 61, 63 Ch 59, 62, Ch 64–89	various yards	1941–1944	442 N 420 S	160 9 wl 152 7 pp	22 0	8 8	2 Diesel engines 2 shafts	1700	16			1 × 80mm (3in) HA 40-cal 2 × 13.2mm AA (*Ch 38*: 26 × 25mm AA) 36 DCs	

GENERAL NOTES
1941–2 Fleet Programme. Standard type, scarcely changed from *Ch 13* design. Counter modified (see drawing). 1 rudder, 2 DCTs.

RE-ARMAMENT
From 1944: 3 × 25mm AA added; from 15 September 1944: (*Ch 37*, *38*) 56 × 25mm; Type '22' Radar in all surviving units.

CAREERS
Ch 28
Launched 30 January, 1942; completed 15 May, 1942; sunk 2 February, 1945 off Camiguin, Mindanao, (09° 05′ N, 124° 40′ E) by US aircraft.
Ch 29
Launched 10 December, 1941; completed 30 April, 1942; sunk 18 February, 1944 off Truk (07° 25′ N, 151° 45′ E) by aircraft from US TF 58.
Ch 30
Launched 30 January, 1942; completed 13 May, 1942; sunk 24 December, 1944 NE of Kuching, Sarawak (02° 42′ N, 111° 05′ E) possibly by US submarine *Barbero*.
Ch 31
Launched 7 March, 1942; completed 15 June, 1942; sunk 12 January, 1945 7 nm W of Cape Padaran, Indo-China (11° 10′ N, 108° 55′ E) by aircraft from US TF 38.

Ch 32
Launched 22 May, 1942; completed 19 August, 1942; sunk 24 December, 1944 S of Mindoro (12° 15′ N, 121° 50′ E) by aircraft from US TF 38.
Ch 33
Launched 16 May, 1942; completed 15 August, 1942; sunk 21 March, 1945 S of Cape Varella, Indo-China (12° 30′ N, 109° 00′ E) by aircraft from TF 38.
Ch 34
Launched 20 December, 1941; completed 31 August, 1942; sunk 26 March, 1945 E of Khota Andaman (10° 38′ N, 94° 42′ E) by gunfire of HMS *Saumarez*, *Volage*, *Vigilant* and *Virago*.
Ch 35
Launched 31 December, 1942; completed 28 February, 1943; sunk 23 February, 1945 off Cape Padaran (11° 30′ N, 109° 00′ E) by US aircraft.
Ch 36
Launched 28 July, 1942; completed 15 October, 1942; sunk 19 November, 1944 off Subic Bay (14° 43′ N, 120° 10′ E) by aircraft from US TF 38.
Ch 37
Launched 10 August, 1942; completed 31 October, 1942; sunk 22 May, 1945 W of Taira Shima (29° 45′ N, 129° 10′ E) by aircraft from US TF 58.

Ch 38
Launched 31 August, 1942; completed 10 December, 1942; captured August 1945 at Tsingtsao and employed by the Minesweeping Service. Handed over to the USSR 3 October, 1947.

Ch 39
Launched 26 May, 1942; completed 31 October, 1942; sunk 16 February, 1944 off Kavieng, New Ireland, by US aircraft.

Ch 40
Launched 1942; completed 31 March, 1943; sunk 19 February, 1944 (with *Ch 22*) in Stephen Strait, New Ireland, by US aircraft.

Ch 41
Launched 1942; completed 31 January, 1943; captured August 1945 at Singapore; scuttled off Singapore 11 July, 1946.

Ch 42
Launched 1942; completed 1 May, 1943; damaged 3 August, 1945 off Ozaki (38° 24′ N, 141° 15′ E) by US submarine; sunk 10 August, 1945 in Onagawa Wan by aircraft from Allied TFs 38 and 37.

Ch 43
Launched 1942; completed 7 April, 1943; sunk 12 January, 1945 in the Camranh Bay area, Indo-china by aircraft from US TF 38.

Ch 44
Launched 1942; completed 15 May, 1943; captured August 1945 and laid up at Uraga; BU 1948.

Ch 45
Launched 1943; completed 15 October, 1943; sunk 29 November, 1944 W of Leyte Island (10° 45′ N, 124° 00′ E). by US aircraft.

Ch 46
Launched 1943; completed 30 September, 1943; sunk 25 November, 1944 off Masbate Island (12° 00′ N, 123° 58′ E) by US aircraft.

Ch 47
Launched 1943; completed 21 August, 1943; captured August 1945 and employed on Repatriation Service until laid up at Yokosuka in early 1946; handed over to USA 1 October, 1947.

Ch 48
Launched 1943; completed 31 July, 1943; sunk 14 July 1945 off Kamaishi (30° 20′ N, 141° 58′ E) by aircraft from US TF 38.

Ch 49
Launched 1943; completed 31 January, 1944; captured August 1945 and employed on Repatriation Service until laid up at Yokosuka in early 1946; handed over to China 3 October, 1947; renamed *Yai Lung*, post-1949 *Hai Hung*; 1955 *Chu Chiang*.

Ch 50
Launched 1943; completed 30 November, 1943; sunk 18 July, 1944 200 nm NW of Chichi Jima (29° 22′ N, 139° 14′ E) by US submarine *Plaice*.

Ch 51
Launched 1943; completed 8 November, 1943; captured August 1945 in severely damaged condition (sustained in air attack 7 March, 1945) at Sasebo; sank 10 December, 1945 at Sasebo and BU.

Ch 52
Launched 1943; completed 30 November, 1943; captured August 1945 in unserviceable condition at Sasebo; BU 1948.

Ch 53
Launched 1943; completed 20 March, 1944; sunk 28 November, 1944 off Ormoc Bay, Leyte (10° 48′ N, 124° 35′ E) by gunfire of USS *Waller*, *Saufley*, *Renshaw*, *Pringle*.

Ch 54
Launched 1943; completed 12 November, 1943; sunk 25 March, 1944 75 nm N of Chichi Jima (28° 34′ N, 142° 14′ E) by US submarine *Pollack*.

Ch 55
Launched 1943; completed 31 May, 1944; sunk 12 September, 1944 3 nm NE of Cebu (10° 20′ N, 124° 00′ E) by aircraft from US TF 38.

Ch 56
Launched 1944; completed 26 July, 1944; captured August 1945 at Soerabaya and BU.

Ch 57
Launched 1944; completed 28 October, 1944; sunk 12 June, 1945 45 nm NW of Sabang (06° 20′ N, 94° 45′ E) by gunfire of HMS *Tartar*, *Eskimo* and *Nubian*.

Ch 58
Launched 1943; completed 26 January, 1944; sunk 22 May, 1945 W of Taira Shima (with *Ch 37*) by aircraft from US TF 58.

Ch 59
Contract cancelled in 1943.

Ch 60
Launched 1943; completed 28 March, 1944; captured August 1945 and employed on Repatriation Service until laid up at Sasebo in early 1946; BU 1948.

Ch 61
Launched 1944; completed 8 May, 1944; sunk 9 January 1945 NW of Takao (22° 40′ N, 121° 04′ E) by aircraft from US TF 38.

Ch 62
Contract cancelled in 1943.

Ch 63
Launched 1944; completed 30 June, 1944; sunk 26 March, 1945 E of Khota Andaman (with *Ch 34*) by torpedoes from HMS *Volage*, *Vigilant* and *Virago*.

Ch 64 to Ch 89
Contracts cancelled in 1943.

Name	Builder	Date	Displ	Length ft in	Beam ft in	Draught ft in	Machinery	SHP	Speed	Fuel	Radius	Armament	Comp
Cha 1 Class	various (see text)	1939–1944	135 N 130 S	85 4 wl 84 8 pp	18 4	6 6	1 Diesel engine 1 shaft	400	11		1000 @ 10	1 × 7.7mm MG 22 DCs	23

GENERAL NOTES
1941–3 Programmes. Auxiliary Submarine Chasers, design based on that of the experimental 'tugs' *Eisen No. 1182* and *No. 1183* (see p. 267), the intention being to employ them after the War as fishing vessels. Built by 16 commercial shipyards specialising in the construction of fishing craft, armed and equipped by the Naval Dockyards at Yokosuka, Kure, Maizuru and Sasebo. (From 1944, the similar *Pa 1*-class harbour defence craft were built by the same firms, see p. 198.) Wooden construction. 4mm armour on bridge and engine rooms.

Builders:
Fukuoka Shipbuilding Ironworks, Fukuoka: 10
Fukushima Shipbuilding Co., Matsue: 13
Funaya Shipbuilding Co., Hakodate: 7
Goriki Shipbuilding Co., Ujiyamada: 12
Hayashikawa Heavy Industrial Co., Shimonoseki: 20
Ichikawa Shipbuilding Co., Ujiyamada: 16
Jin'en Shipbuilding Iron Works, Moji: 12
Koyanagi Shipbuilding Co., Shizuoka: 12
Miho Shipbuilding Co., Shimizu: 13
Murakami Shipbuilding Co., Ishinomaki: 8
Nishii Shipbuilding Co., Ujiyamada: 13
Saga Shipbuilding Co., Takaoka: 18
Shikoku Dock Industrial Co., Takamatsu: 20
Tokushima Shipbuilding Co., Tokushima: 3
Yamanishi Shipbuilding Ironworks, Ishinomaki: 17
Yokosuka Naval Dockyard: 1
Yonago Shipbuilding Co., Yonago: 6

RE-ARMAMENT
1943: 1 × 13.2mm AA added except in units in overseas areas – 2 × 13.2mm, 10 DCs; 1944–5: 13.2mm replaced by 25mm AA; from March 1945: craft in Home Waters converted as minesweepers.

Cha 1
Captured August 1945 and employed by Minesweeping Service until 1947; 1948: MSDF *PS 18*; 1952: renamed *Chidori*; 1955: renumbered *PS 134*; deleted from Active List in October 1960.

Cha 2
Sunk 6 October, 1944 110 nm W of Penang (04° 20′ N, 98° 24′ E) by HM submarine *Tally-ho*.

Cha 3
Remained in the Rabaul area, fate unknown.

Cha 1 class (1941)

Cha 4
Captured August 1945 and employed by Minesweeping Service until 1947; 1948: MSDF *PS 20*; 1952: named *Kiji*; deleted from Active List 1959.

Cha 5
Sunk 18 August, 1943 N of Vella Lavella (07° 26′ S, 156° 45′ E) by gunfire of USS *Nicholas*, *Chevalier*, *O'Bannon*, *Taylor*.

Cha 6
Sunk 7 July, 1944 off Rabaul by US submarine.

Cha 7
Heavily damaged 14 October, 1944 at Takao by aircraft from US TF 38; decommissioned.

Cha 8
Sunk 9 September, 1944 by mine 7 nm NE of Belawan Deli, Sumatra (03° 54′ N, 98° 44′ E).

Cha 9
Mined off Sumatra 9 September, 1944.

Cha 10
Sunk 18 March, 1944 off Mushu, Wewak (03° 30′ S, 144° 00′ E) by gunfire of US warships.

Cha 11
Captured August 1939 at Hong Kong, intended for the Minesweeping Service, but no record of activity; ultimate fate unknown.

Cha 12
Sunk 18 August, 1943 N of Vella Lavella with *Cha 5*.

Cha 13
Sunk 1 November, 1943 W of Shortland Island (07° 00′ S, 155° 30′ E) by US aircraft.

Cha 14
Sunk 30 January, 1944 at Mili Atoll, Marshal Islands by US aircraft.

Cha 15
Sunk 22 October, 1944 W of Tabals, Philippines (12° 55′ N, 122° 35′ E) by aircraft from US TF 38.

Cha 16
Sunk 16 February, 1944 off Kavieng, New Ireland (02° 24′ S, 150° 06′ E) by US aircraft.

Cha 17
Sunk 18 February, 1944 off Kavieng (02° 30′ S, 150° 30′ E) by US aircraft.

Cha 18
Sunk 30 January, 1944 at Kwajalein, Marshall Islands, by aircraft from US TF 58.

Cha 19
Sunk 30 January, 1944 at Mili, Marshall Islands, by aircraft from US TF 58.

Cha 20
Moderately damaged 22 July, 1945 by mine in Kure harbour; captured August 1945 while under repair; BU 1948.

Cha 21
Sunk 30 January, 1944 at Kwajalein, Marshall Islands, by aircraft from US TF 58.

Cha 22
Sunk 30 March, 1944 at Palau (07° 30′ N, 134° 30′ E) by aircraft from US TF 58.

Cha 23
Sunk 9 July, 1944 at Rabaul by Royal New Zealand Air Force aircraft.

Cha 24
Captured August 1944 at Hong Kong; subsequent fate unknown.

Cha 25
Sunk 31 January, 1944 at Nauru Island (00° 30′ S, 167° 00′ E) by US aircraft; salvaged and BU at Kure in 1946.

Cha 26
Sunk 30 March, 1944 at Palau by aircraft from US TF 58.

Cha 27
Captured August 1945 and employed by Minesweeping Service until laid up at Yokosuka in 1947; 1948: MSDF *PS 23*; deleted from Active List 1952.

Cha 28
Sunk 30 January, 1944 at Mili by aircraft from US TF 58.

Cha 29
Sunk 22 February, 1944 near Kavieng by US aircraft.

Cha 30
Sunk 4 November, 1943 near Kieta, Bougainville Island (06° 10′ S, 155° 35′ E) by US aircraft.

Cha 31
Sunk 16 October, 1943 off Cape Lambert, New Britain (04° 10′ S, 151° 30′ E) by US aircraft.

Cha 32
Sunk 24 September 1944 S of Mindoro (12° 15′ N, 121° 00′ E) by aircraft from US TF 38.

Cha 33
Sunk 31 January, 1944 at Nauru Island by US aircraft.

Cha 34
Sunk 19 February, 1944 10 nm S of Kavieng (02° 45′ S, 150° 47′ E) by US aircraft.

Cha 35
Possibly captured at Truk in August 1945.

Cha 36
Captured August 1945 at Soerabaya; handed over to Great Britain at Singapore 3 August, 1946; ultimate fate unknown.

Cha 37
Sunk 5 July, 1945 22 nm SW of Bali (08° 10′ S, 114° 50′ E) by US submarine *Lizardfish*.

Cha 38
Sunk 30 April, 1944 at Truk by aircraft from US TF 58.

Cha 39
Sunk 21 September, 1944 in the Sibuyan Sea (12° 18′ N, 122° 46′ E) by aircraft from US TF 38.

Cha 40
Sunk 22 January, 1944 8 nm N of Lorengau, Admiralty Island (01° 50′ S, 147° 20′ E) by US aircraft.

Cha 41
Captured August 1945 at Soerabaya; handed over to Great Britain at Singapore 3 August, 1946; ultimate fate unknown.

Cha 42
Sunk 23 June, 1945 80 nm E of Bawean Island, Java Sea (05° 50′ S, 114° 18′ E) by US submarine *Hardhead*.

Cha 43
Reclassified 15 February, 1944 as a tug, *Eisen No. 1648*; captured August 1945 at Uraga and employed as a harbour craft until laid up in 1947.

Cha 44
Reclassified 15 February, 1944 as a tug, *Eisen No. 1649*; captured August 1945 at Uraga; burned out April 1946 and sank at Uraga.

Cha 45
Captured August 1945 at Singapore and employed as a transport; handed over to Great Britain July 1946.

Cha 46
Sunk 5 April, 1944 at Wake Island by US aircraft.

Cha 47
Sunk 20 March, 1944 130 nm E of Hollandia (02° 55′ S, 143° 40′ E) by US aircraft.

Cha 48
Sunk 21 February, 1944 off New Hannover, Admiralty Island (02° 30′ S, 149° 55′ E) by US aircraft.

Cha 49
Sunk 20 March, 1944 130 nm E of Hollandia with *Cha 47*.

Cha 50
Sunk 9 July, 1945 NE of Singapore (02° 20′ N, 105° 05′ E) by US submarine *Bluefish*.

Cha 51
Lost in the Rabaul area.

Cha 52
Lost 25 October, 1944 at Palau (07° 30′ N, 134° 30′ E).

Cha 53
Sunk 30 March, 1944 at Palau by aircraft from US TF 58.

Cha 54
Sunk 15 June, 1944 at Rota, Mariana Island, by aircraft from US TF 58.

Cha 55
Captured August 1945 at Singapore and employed as a transport; handed over to Great Britain July 1946.

Cha 56
Sunk 17 June, 1944 at Rota, Mariana Island, by aircraft from US TF 58.

Cha 57
Captured August 1945 and employed by Minesweeping Service until laid up at Maizuru in 1947; 1948: MSDF *PS 21*, named *Kawasemi*; 1955 renumbered *PS 136*; deleted from Active List in 1957.

Cha 58
Captured August 1945 and employed by Minesweeping Service until laid up at

Yokosuka in 1947; 1948: MSDF *PS 32*, named *Uzura*; 1955: renumbered *PS 140*; deleted from Active List in October 1960.

Cha 59
Sunk July 1945 by US submarine off Singapore.

Cha 60
Captured August 1945 at Shimonoseki in an unserviceable condition; BU in 1946.

Cha 61
Captured August 1945 at Singapore and employed as a transport; handed over to Great Britain July 1946.

Cha 62
Sunk 20 March, 1944 130 nm E of Hollandia with *Cha 47* and *Cha 49*.

Cha 63
Sunk 10 June, 1945 by collision W of Mokpo, Korea (34° 50′ N, 126° 10′ E).

Cha 64
Sunk 6 January, 1945 off Pulau Condore, (08° 55′ N, 106° 30′ E) by US aircraft.

Cha 65
Captured August 1945 and employed by Minesweeping Service; Sunk 14 December, 1945 20 nm S of Hachinoe (41° 00′ N, 141° 30′ E), ran aground and subsequently BU.

Cha 66
Sunk 7 August, 1945 at Truk by US aircraft.

Cha 67
Captured August 1945 in unseaworthy condition at Yulin, Hainan.

Cha 68
Captured August 1945 and employed by Minesweeping Service until laid up at Yokosuka in 1947; 1948: MSDF *PS 27* named *Kamome*; 1955: renumbered *PS 139*.

Cha 69
Captured August 1945 in unserviceable condition at Kure.

Cha 70
Captured August 1945 at Penang.

Cha 71
Captured August 1945 and employed by Minesweeping Service until laid up at Sasebo in 1947; 1948: MSDF *PS 39*, named *Ho'ojiro*; 1955: renumbered *PS 143*.

Cha 72
Captured August 1945 and employed by Minesweeping Service until laid up at Yokosuka in 1947; 1948: MSDF *MS 07*, named *Umitsubame*; 1957: redesignated *MSI 697*; 1961: redesignated *YAM 23*.

Cha 73
Sunk 26 June, 1945 S of Onnekotan Island, Kurile Island (49° 40′ N, 155° 30′ E) by gunfire of USS *Bearss*, *John Hood*, *Jarvis* and *Porter*.

Cha 74
Captured August 1945 Keelung, Formosa.

Cha 75
Captured August 1945 at Keelung, Formosa.

Cha 76
Sunk 11 December, 1944 between Goto and Tsushima by US submarine.

Cha 77
Sunk 28 August, 1944 off Paramushiro, Kurile Island, (50° 30′ N, 156° 20′ E) by US aircraft.

Cha 78
Captured August 1945 and employed by Minesweeping Service until laid up at Yokosuka in 1947; 1948: MSDF *PS 28*, named *Otori*; 1953: redesignated *MS 82*; deleted from Active List in 1959.

Cha 79
Captured August 1945 at Chinhae, Korea, and employed by Minesweeping Service until laid up at Maizuru in 1947; 1948: MSDF *MS 08*, named *Yuhibari*; deleted from Active List 1959.

Cha 80
Captured August 1945 at Chinhae and employed by Minesweeping Service until laid up at Sasebo in 1947; 1948: MSDF *PS 08*, named *Sekirei*; 1955: renumbered *PS 128*.

Cha 81
Captured August 1945 and employed by Minesweeping Service; lost 18 April, 1946 off Matsushima – ran aground on a reef; caught fire 21 February, 1947 – fore end of ship destroyed.

Cha 82
Sunk 22 November, 1944 off Balabac Island, Philippines (08° 00′ N 117° 00′ E) by US aircraft.

Cha 83
Captured August 1945 at Makung, Pescadores Islands; subsequent fate not known.

Cha 84
Sunk 12 November, 1944 N of Banggi Island, Sabah (07° 40′ N, 117° 10′ E) by US aircraft.

Cha 85
Sunk 8 July, 1945 in Shaisu Straits, South Korea, by US submarine.

Cha 86
Captured August 1945 at Chinhae and employed by Minesweeping Service until laid up at Maizuru in 1947; 1948: MSDF *MS 09*, named *Hayataka*; deleted from Active List in 1959.

Cha 87
Sunk 12 October, 1944 in Ryukyu Islands by aircraft from US TF 38.

Cha 88
Captured August 1945 and employed by Minesweeping Service until laid up at Yokosuka in 1947; 1948: MSDF *MS 10*, named *Yukari*; 1957: redesignated *MSI 692*; 1961: redesignated *YAM 30*.

Cha 89
Captured August 1945 and employed by Minesweeping Service until laid up at Sasebo in 1947; subsequent fate unknown.

Cha 90
Captured August 1945 and employed by Minesweeping Service until laid up at Sasebo in 1947; 1948: MSDF *MS 11*, named *Hakuo*; deleted from the Active List 1959.

Cha 91
Sunk 25 January 1945 NW of Kyushu by US submarine.

Cha 92
Abandoned 4 October, 1944 after running aground in the entrance to the Sabtang Channel, N of Luzon (20° 20′ N, 122° 00′ E).

Cha 93
Captured August 1945 at Chinhae and employed by Minesweeping Service until laid up at Sasebo in 1947; 1948: MSDF *MS 12*, named *Miyakodori*; deleted from Active List 1959.

Cha 94
Sank 23 September, 1944 in typhoon off Sabtang, Luzon (20° 00′ N, 122° 00′ E).

Cha 95
Sunk 18 October, 1944 at Takao, Formosa, by aircraft from US TF 38.

Cha 96
Captured August 1945 at Makung, Pescadores Islands; subsequent fate unknown.

Cha 97
Sunk 19 April, 1945 in the Kii Channel (33° 35′ N, 135° 23′ E) by US submarine *Sennet*.

Cha 98
Sunk 24 July, 1945 at Moji (33° 58′ N, 130° 58′ E) by aircraft from US TF 38.

Cha 99
Captured August 1945 and employed by Minesweeping Service until laid up at Sasebo in 1947; 1948: MSDF *MS 13*, named *Iwatsubame*; 1957: redesignated *MSI 698*; 1961: redesignated *YAM 31*.

Cha 100
Captured August 1945 at Chinhae; subsequent fate unknown.

Cha 101 to 118
Ex-Dutch (see pp 222–223).

Cha 151
Lost 15 April, 1945 by grounding SE of the Pescadores Islands (23° 30′ N, 119° 40′ E).

Cha 152
Lost off Formosa late 1944.

Cha 153
Mined 6 July 1945 in Niigata harbour.

Cha 154
Captured August 1945 and employed by Minesweeping Service until laid up at Sasebo in 1947; 1948: MSDF *PS 06*, named *Ugusui*; 1955: renumbered *PS 126*; deleted from Active List in October 1960.

Cha 155
Captured August 1945 and employed by Minesweeping Service until laid up at Yokosuka in 1947; 1948: MSDF *PS 26*, named *Shigi*; 1955: renumbered *PS 155*; deleted from the Active List in 1957.

Cha 156
Sunk 29 March, 1945 4 nm N of Takao (22° 40′ N, 120° 15′ E) by US aircraft.

Cha 157
Captured August 1945 and employed by Minesweeping Service until laid up at Maizuru in 1947; 1948: MSDF *PS 37*, named *Aosagi*; 1955: renumbered *PS 141*.

Cha 158
Captured August 1945 and employed by Minesweeping Service until 1947; deleted from Active List in 1948.

Cha 159
Captured August 1945 and employed by Minesweeping Service until laid up at Yokosuka in 1947; 1948: MSDF *PS 38*, named *Hinazuru*; 1955: renumbered *PS 142*.

Cha 160
Ran aground 18 September, 1944 S of Yoshimi during typhoon; deleted from Active List 30 November 1945.

Cha 161
Captured August 1945 and employed by Minesweeping Service until laid up at Yokosuka in 1947; 1948: MSDF *PS 24*, named *Kotaka*; 1955: renumbered *PS 137*; deleted from Active List 1956.

Cha 162
Captured August 1945 and employed by Minesweeping Service until laid up at Maizuru in 1947; subsequent fate unknown.

Cha 163
Abandoned 4 January, 1945 after suffering damage in the Formosa Straits from aircraft of US TF 38.

Cha 164
Captured August 1945 at Shimonoseki; employed by the Minesweeping Service from 1946 until laid up at Maizuru in 1947; subsequent fate unknown.

Cha 165
Sunk 11 September, 1944 S of Kagoshima (32° 20′ N, 131° 50′ E) by US submarine *Albacore*.

Cha 166
Captured August 1945 and employed by Minesweeping Service until laid up at Maizuru in 1947; 1948: MSDF *PS 17*, named *Hato*; 1955: renumbered *PS 133*.

Cha 167
Sunk by accident 15 August 1945 at Kure.

Cha 168
Captured August 1945 and employed by Minesweeping Service until laid up at Sasebo; 1948: MSDF *MS 57*, named *Nishikidori*; deleted from Active List in 1959.

Cha 169
Captured August 1945 and employed by Minesweeping Service until laid up at Sasebo in 1947; 1948: MSDF *PS 11*, named *Yamasemi*; 1955: renumbered *PS 130*; deleted from Active List in 1956.

Cha 170
Captured August 1945 in unserviceable condition at Tadotsu; BU.

Cha 171
Captured August 1945 and employed by Minesweeping Service until laid up at Yokosuka in 1947; 1948: MSDF *MS 01*, named *Chiyozuru*; 1957: redesignated *MSI 695*; 1961: redesignated *YAM 22*.

Cha 172
Sunk 26 May, 1945 by mine off Fushiki (36° 48′ N, 137° 05′ E).

Cha 173
Captured August 1945 and employed by Minesweeping Service until laid up at Sasebo in 1947: 1948 MSDF *PS 40*, named *Shirataka*; 1955: renumbered *PS 144*; deleted from Active List in 1959.

Cha 174
Captured August 1945 and employed by Minesweeping Service; lost 1 September, 1946 through fire at Otake.

Cha 175
Captured August 1945 and employed by Minesweeping Service until laid up at Maizuru in 1947; 1948: MSDF *PS 01*, named *Kasasagi*; 1955: renumbered *PS 121*; deleted from Active List in 1959.

Cha 176
Lost 4 January, 1945 in Formosa Straits after attack by aircraft from US TF 38.

Cha 177
Captured August 1945 at Takao; fate unknown.

Cha 178
Mined 11 August, 1945 and ran aground in the Shimonoseki Straits.

Cha 179
Captured August 1945 and employed by Minesweeping Service until laid up at Maizuru in 1947; 1948 MSDF *PS 41*, named *Yamagara*; 1955: renumbered *PS 145*; deleted from Active List in October 1960.

Cha 180
Captured August 1945 and employed by Minesweeping Service; towed out to sea 25/26 March 1946 and sunk, after fire in Osaka Harbour.

Cha 181
Captured August 1945 and employed by Minesweeping Service until laid up at Yokosuka in 1947; 1948: MSDF *PS 16*, named *Hibari*; 1955: renumbered *PS 132*.

Cha 182
Heavily damaged at Ito 30 July, 1945 by aircraft from US TF 38; broken up at Yokosuka in 1946.

Cha 183
Captured August 1945 and employed by Minesweeping Service until laid up at Yokosuka in 1947; 1948: MSDF *PS 12*, named *Benizuru*; deleted from Active List 1955.

Cha 184
Captured August 1945 and employed by Minesweeping Service; deleted from Active List 25 December, 1946; BU in 1947.

Cha 185
Captured August 1945 and employed by Minesweeping Service until laid up at Yokosuka in 1947; 1948: MSDF *PS 19*, named *Hayabusa*; 1955: renumbered *PS 135*; deleted from Active List 1958.

Cha 186
Captured August 1945 and employed by Minesweeping Service until laid up at Maizuru in 1947; 1948: MSDF *PS 13*, named *Hatsukari*; 1955: renumbered *PS 131*.

Cha 187
Captured August 1945 and employed by Minesweeping Service until laid up at Maizuru in 1947; 1948: MSDF *PS 04*, named *Yamadori*; 1955: renumbered *PS 124*; deleted from Active List 1958.

Cha 188
Mined 2 July, 1945 off Mutsure Light (33° 59′ N, 130° 52′ E).

Cha 189
Sunk 29 March, 1945 at Takao by US aircraft.

Cha 190
Captured August 1945 at Takao; fate unknown.

Cha 191
Captured August 1945 at Hong Kong; fate unknown.

Cha 192
Sunk 29 March, 1945 4 nm off Takao (22° 40′ N, 120° 15′ E) by US aircraft.

Cha 193
Captured August 1945 and employed by Minesweeping Service until deleted from Active List in May 1946.

Cha 194
Captured August 1945 and employed by Allied Minesweeping Service until laid up at Yokosuka in 1947; 1948: MSDF *PS 42*, named *Mizutori*; 1955: renumbered *PS 146*.

Cha 195
Mined 6 June, 1945 and sunk in Nanao Bay, Honshu (37° 10′ N, 137° 05′ E); salvaged and under repair in August 1945; deleted from Active List 30 November, 1945; BU 1947.

Cha 196
Captured August 1945 and employed by Minesweeping Service until laid up at Yokosuka in 1947; 1948: MSDF *PS 25*, named *Wakataka*; 1953: redesignated *MS 58*; deleted from Active List 1959.

Cha 197
Sunk 18 June, 1945 by mine off Mojisaki Light (33° 58′ N, 130° 56′ E).

Cha 198
Captured August 1945 aground in Saeki Bay; salvaged 1946 and employed by Minesweeping Service until laid up at Maizuru in 1947; 1948: MSDF *PS 02*, named *Wakasagi*; 1955; renumbered *PS 122*.

Cha 199
Mined April 1945 off Mutsure Light.

Cha 200
Sunk 29 March, 1945 W of Sata Misaki, Kyushu (31° 05′ N, 130° 39′ E) by aircraft from US TF 58.

Cha 201
Captured August 1945; lost 24 February, 1946 after running aground on the southern point of Chezhu do.

Cha 202
Captured August 1945 and employed by Minesweeping Service until laid up at Yokosuka in 1947; 1948: MSDF *MS 14*; sunk 17 October, 1950 by mine in Yong Hung Bay (39° 20′ N, 127° 30′ E).

Cha 203
Captured August 1945 and employed by Minesweeping Service until laid up at Yokosuka in 1947; 1948: MSDF *PS 22*, named *Hiyodori*; 1953: redesignated *MS 84*; 1957: redesignated *MSI 700*.

Cha 204
Found wrecked at Amoy August 1945; fate unknown.

Cha 205
Sunk 29 March, 1945 at Kuchinoerabujima, Kyushu (30° 30′ N, 130° 10′ E) by aircraft from US TF 58.

Cha 206
Sunk 26 June, 1945 off Onnekotan, Kurile Island (49° 40′ N, 155° 30′ E) by gunfire of US destroyers.

Cha 207
Captured August 1945 in unserviceable condition at Sasebo; deleted from Active List 30 November 1945; BU 1946.
Cha 208
Captured August 1945 in unserviceable condition at Shimonoseki; BU 1946.
Cha 209
Sunk 26 June, 1945 with *Cha 73* and *Cha 206* off Onnekotan, Kurile Island, by gunfire of US destroyers.
Cha 210
Sunk 4 January, 1945 in Formosa Straits by aircraft from US TF 38.
Cha 211
Damaged 18 July, 1945 and beached in Mujina Bay, Yokosuka, after attack by aircraft from US TF 38.
Cha 212
Captured August 1945 and employed by Minesweeping Service until laid up at Yokosuka in 1947; deleted from Active List 1948.
Cha 213
Captured August 1945 in unserviceable condition at Yokosuka; ultimate fate unknown.
Cha 214
Allocated to the Karafuto Naval District (Sakhalin) as a Fishery Protection gunboat July 1944.
Replacement Cha 214
Captured August 1945 and employed by Minesweeping Service until laid up at Maizuru in 1947; 1948: MSDF *MS 15*, named *Hayatori*; 1955: redesignated *MSI 699*.
Cha 215
Captured August 1945 and employed by Minesweeping Service until laid up at Maizuru in 1948: MSDF *MS 16*, named *Tomozoru*; 1957: redesignated *MSI 693*.
Cha 216
Captured August 1945 in sinking condition at Hsinchu, Formosa; fate unknown.
Cha 217
Captured August 1945 and employed by Minesweeping Service until laid up at Maizuru in 1947; 1948 MSDF *PS 07*, named *Tsugumi*; 1955: renumbered *PS 127*; deleted from Active List October 1960.
Cha 218
Captured August 1945 and employed by Minesweeping Service until deleted from Active List in 1946.
Cha 219
Captured August 1945 and employed by Minesweeping Service until laid up at Maizuru in 1947; 1948: MSDF *PS 14*, named *Shirasagi*; 1953: redesignated *MS 85*; deleted from Active List 1959.
Cha 220
Captured August 1945 by Chinese at Shanghai, named *Kao Ming*, later renamed *Hsien Feng*; 1949: to People's Republic of China.
Cha 221
Captured August 1945 and employed by Minesweeping Service until laid up at Yokosuka in 1947; 1948: MSDF *MS 02*, named *Yoshikiri*; 1957: redesignated *MSI 690*; 1961: redesignated *YAS 29*.
Cha 222
Captured August 1945 and employed by Minesweeping Service until laid up at Maizuru in 1947; 1948: MSDF *MS 03*, named *Hatsutaka*; 1957: redesignated *MSI 696*.
Cha 223
Captured August 1945 at Keelung, Formosa; 1947: to China, named *Kuang Kuo*; 1949: to People's Republic of China.
Cha 224
Sunk 5 March, 1945 at Makung, Pescadores (23° 32′ N, 119° 40′ E) by aircraft from US TF 58.
Cha 225
Sunk 18 July, 1945 in Nagaura Bay, Yokosuka, by aircraft from US TF 38.
Cha 226
Mined 1 April, 1945 in the Kii Channel; captured August 1945 in damaged condition at Moji; scrapped at Kure in 1947.
Cha 227
Captured August 1945 and employed by Minesweeping Service until laid up at Maizuru in 1947; 1948: MSDF *PS 05*, named *Oshidori*; 1955: renumbered *PS 125*; deleted from Active List 1956.
Cha 228
Captured August 1945 at Sasebo; lost 18 September, 1945 at Sasebo after springing a leak in a storm.

Cha 229
Captured August 1945 while under repair at Kure; fate unknown.
Cha 230
Sunk 5 June, 1945 in collision with Army Transport *Azusa Maru* off S coast of Korea (34° 00′ N, 127° 18′ E).
Cha 231
Captured August 1945 and employed by Minesweeping Service until laid up at Sasebo in 1947; 1948: MSDF *MS 17*, named *Shiratori*; 1957: redesignated *MSI 694*.
Cha 232
Captured August 1945 and employed by Minesweeping Service until laid up at Maizuru in 1947; 1948: MSDF *PS 09*, named *Otaka*; 1953; redesignated *MS 86*; deleted from Active List 1959.
Cha 233
Sunk 31 March, 1945 W of Amakusa Shimojima (32° 19′ N, 129° 50′ E) by aircraft from US TF 58.
Cha 234
Captured August 1945 and employed by Minesweeping Service until laid up at Sasebo in 1947; deleted from Active List 1948.
Cha 235
Captured August 1945 at Hong Kong in damaged condition (damaged 14 March, 1945 by aircraft off Mako, Formosa), subsequent fate unknown.
Cha 236
Captured August 1945 and employed by Minesweeping Service until laid up at Maizuru in 1947; 1948: MSDF *PS 15*, named *Komadori*; deleted from Active List 1954.
Cha 237
Sunk 11 June, 1945 E of Irakosaki (34° 30′ N, 137° 06′ E) by US aircraft.
Cha 238
Captured August 1945 at Keelung in damaged condition; subsequent fate unknown.
Cha 239
Captured August 1945 and employed by Minesweeping Service until laid up at Maizuru in 1947; 1948: MSDF *PS 10*, named *Kari*; 1955: renumbered *PS 129*; deleted from Active List 1955.
Cha 240
Captured August 1945 at Shanghai; possibly handed over to China.
Cha 241
Captured August 1945 and employed by Minesweeping Service until laid up at Yokosuka in 1947; 1948: MSDF *MS 04*, named *Furutaka*; deleted from Active List 1959.
Cha 242
Captured August 1945 at Wonsan and employed by Minesweeping Service until deleted from Active List in 1946.
Cha 243
Captured August 1945 at Keelung, Formosa; fate unknown.
Cha 244
Sunk 20 May, 1945 225 nm S of Okinawa (22° 35′ N, 128° 51′ E) by aircraft from US TF 58.
Cha 245
Captured August 1945 and employed by Minesweeping Service until laid up at Maizuru in 1947; 1948: MSDF *PS 03*, named *Manazuru*; 1955: renumbered *PS 123*.
Cha 246
Captured August 1945 and employed by Minesweeping Service until laid up at Maizuru in 1947; 1948: MSDF *MS 05*, named *Yamabato*; deleted from Active List 1959.
Cha 247
Captured August 1945 at Chinhae and employed by Minesweeping Service until laid up at Sasebo in 1947; deleted from Active List 1948.
Cha 248
Captured August 1945 and employed by Minesweeping Service; sunk 25 January, 1946 by mine in Iki Sound (33° 40′ N, 129° 40′ E).
Cha 249
Captured August 1945 and employed by Minesweeping Service until laid up at Sasebo in 1947; 1948: MSDF *MS 06*, named *Kamozuru*; 1957: redesignated *MSI 691*.
Cha 250
Captured August 1945 and employed by Minesweeping Service until laid up at Sasebo in 1947; deleted from Active List 1948.
Cha 251, ex-*Ch 51*: see p. 217.
Cha 252, ex-*Ch 52*: see p. 217.
Cha 253, ex-*Ch 53*: see p. 217.
Kaii, ex-*Hai Wei*, ex-*Kashi*: see p. 135.

SUBMARINE CHASERS 221

Name	Builder	Date	Displ	Length ft in	Beam ft in	Draught ft in	Machinery	SHP	Speed	Fuel	Radius	Armament	Comp
Cha 101 ex-*Tjerimei*	Batavia SB Co.	1942	80 N 67 S	74 6 wl 68 11 pp	14 3	4 11	1 Diesel motor 1 shaft	135	10			2 × 13.2mm AA 5 DCs	c 15

GENERAL NOTES
Netherlands East Indies Government patrol vessel of the *Merapi* class.

CAREER
Completed at Batavia in 1942; sunk 2 March, 1942 at Tanjong Priok; raised and repaired by Japanese, commissioned as *Cha 101* 4 August, 1942; sunk 8 April, 1945 SE of Celebes (04° 43′ S, 122° 17′ E) by US aircraft.

Name	Builder	Date	Displ	Length ft in	Beam ft in	Draught ft in	Machinery	SHP	Speed	Fuel	Radius	Armament	Comp
Cha 102 ex-*Ardjoeno* class (5 units)	Soerabaya Dry Dock Co.	1937	75 N 51 S	86 11 wl	14 7	3 3	2 Carmouth petrol engines 2 shafts	1000	15			2 × 13.2mm AA 4 DCs	

GENERAL NOTES
Netherlands East Indies Government patrol vessels and auxiliary minesweepers of *Ardjoeno* class.

CAREERS
Cha 102
Launched 1937 as Dutch *Ardjoeno*; 1942: *Hulpmijnenveger No. 000* (Auxiliary Minesweeper); sunk 3 March, 1942 at Soerabaya; raised by Japanese and commissioned as *Cha 102* 6 August, 1942; captured August 1945 at Soerabaya.
Cha 104
Launched 1937 as Dutch *Gedeh*; 1942: *Hulpmijnenveger No. 14*, fitted also as danlayer; sunk 2 March, 1942 at Soerabaya; raised by Japanese and commissioned as *Cha 104* 15 October 1942; captured August 1945 at Djakarta.
Cha 109
Launched 1937 as Dutch *Kawi*; 1939: *Hulpmijnenveger No. 7*; sunk 2 March, 1942 at Soerabaya; raised by Japanese and commissioned as *Cha 109* 15 March, 1943; sunk 14 August, 943 at Balikpapan, Borneo, by US aircraft.
Cha 110
Launched 1937 as Dutch *Lawoe*; 1939: *Hulpmijnenveger No. 15*, employed as danlayer; sunk 2 March, 1942 at Soerabaya; raised by Japanese and commissioned as *Cha 110* 27 September, 1943; captured August 1945 at Soerabaya.
Cha 118
Launched 1937 as Dutch *Salak*; 1939: *Hulpmijnenveger No. 8*; sunk 2 March, 1942 at Soerabaya; raised by Japanese and commissioned as *Cha 118* 31 July 1944; damaged 6 November, 1944 off Sumba Island by air attack; captured August 1945 in unserviceable condition at Soerabaya.

Note:
The details given for the *Ardjoeno* class agree essentially with the most frequently quoted Japanese sources, rather than with the Dutch specification. The former completely contradicts the specification for the machinery installation (a single engine with an output of only 135 hp). In spite of the fact that three craft were recovered in a serviceable condition after the War, none of them appears in post-1945 lists of Royal Netherlands Navy units.
Four patrol craft of the *P 9* class (*P 11, 12, 15* and *16*) were recovered and given their original numbers after the War, but the use to which they were put by the Japanese is still not clear. Japanese information indicates that *Cha 102* and her sister-ships were identical in appearance with *Cha 111*; the *P 9s'* engine installation was identical with that of *Cha 111* (and different from that in the *Ardjoeno* class), establishing them as being of the same type. This contradicts the official Dutch specification, which could not until now be corrected.

Name	Builder	Date	Displ	Length ft in	Beam ft in	Draught ft in	Machinery	SHP	Speed	Fuel	Radius	Armament	Comp
Cha 111 ex-*P 13* or *14*	Tandjong Priok Dry Dock Co.	1941	26 S	62 0 oa	12 10	3 9	2 Buda-Lanova Diesel motors 2 shafts	300	14.5			2 × 13.2mm AA 4 DCs	c 10

General appearance of *Cha 102, 104, 109, 110, 118.*

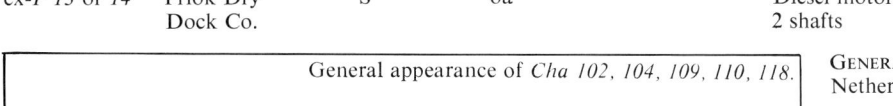

GENERAL NOTES
Netherlands East Indies patrol craft of the *P 9* class.

CAREER
Launched 1941 as patrol craft *P 13* or *P 14*; sunk March 1942; raised by Japanese and planned to be commissioned as *Cha 111* on 21 October, 1943; sunk 22 July, 1943 at Soerabaya by aircraft.

Name	Builder	Date	Displ	Length ft in	Beam ft in	Draught ft in	Machinery	SHP	Speed	Fuel	Radius	Armament	Comp
Cha 103 type ex-*B 1* class (7 units)	RNethN DY and Soerabaya Dry Dock Co.	1942– 1943	130 S	149 9 oa 139 1 pp	16 5	4 7	*Cha 103, 114, 115*: 2 petrol engines *Cha 105*: 4 Carmouth petrol engines *Cha 106*: 3 Lorraine petrol engines *Cha 107, 108*: 4 Lorraine petrol engines	1500 1800 1200 1800	19 19 16.5 19			1 × 47mm (3pdr) 1 × 13.2mm AA 1 × 7.7mm MG 32 DCs	c 18

GENERAL NOTES
Netherlands East Indies patrol craft of *B 1* class, under construction at Soerabaya at the time of the Japanese capture of Java.

CAREERS
Cha 103
Launched 1942 as *B 1*; completed and commissioned as *Cha 103* 31 August, 1942;

captured August 1945 at Amboina; handed over to Australia 22 September, 1945; subsequent fate unknown.

Cha 105
Captured before launch; launched 11 January, 1943 and commissioned as *Cha 195* 25 January, 1944; sunk 16 June, 1945 N of Soerabaya (06° 52′ S, 111° 45′ E) by US submarine *Hardhead*.

Cha 106
Launched 24 March, 1943 by Japanese and commissioned as *Cha 106* 2 September, 1944; captured August 1945 at Djakarta.

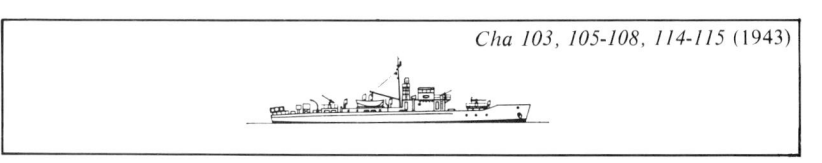

Cha 103, 105-108, 114-115 (1943)

Cha 107
Launched 27 February, 1943 by Japanese and commissioned as *Cha 107* 30 January, 1945; captured August 1945 at Djakarta; returned to Dutch and laid up until 1947, when used as an accommodation vessel.

Cha 108
Launched 22 April, 1943 by Japanese and not yet commissioned as *Cha 108* when sunk 17 May, 1944 at Soerabaya by aircraft from USS *Saratoga* and HMS *Illustrious*; raised and under repair in August 1945.

Cha 114
Launched 30 November, 1943 by Japanese and commissioned as *Cha 114* 23 June, 1944; torpedoed and heavily damaged 15 April, 1945 by USS *Hawkbill*; captured August 1945 at Soerabaya still in damaged condition.

Cha 115
Launched 30 November, 1943 by Japanese and commissioned as *Cha 115* 2 September, 1944; captured August 1945 at Soerabaya, restored to Dutch and employed as a ferry between Soerabaya and Madura.

Name	Builder	Date	Displ	Length ft in	Beam ft in	Draught ft in	Machinery	SHP	Speed	Fuel	Radius	Armament	Comp
Cha 177 ex-*Bantam*	Tandjong Priok Dry Dock Co.	1938	145 N 131 S	103 8 wl 96 2 pp	17 11	6 0	1 Stork Diesel motor 1 shaft	300	12			1 × 47mm (3pdr) 1 × 13.2mm AA 1 × 7.7mm MG 32 DCs	c 17

GENERAL NOTES
Netherlands East Indies Government Service vessel of the *ABC* class. Guardboat and patrol craft with accommodation for 12 passengers.

CAREER
Cha 117
Launched 1938 as *Bantam*; 1939: *Hulpmijnenveger No. 3*; sunk 3 March, 1942 at Tandjong Priok; raised by Japanese and commissioned as *Cha 117* 10 August, 1943; sunk 23 July, 1945 23 nm SSE of Bali (08° 10′ S, 115° 29′ E) by US submarine *Hardhead*.

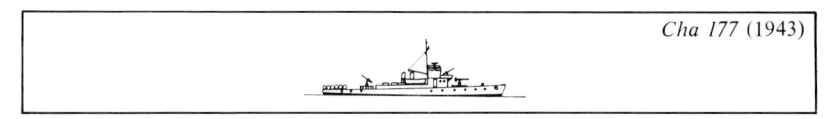

Cha 177 (1943)

Name	Builder	Date	Displ	Length ft in	Beam ft in	Draught ft in	Machinery	SHP	Speed	Fuel	Radius	Armament	Comp
Cha 112 type ex-*ABC* class (3 units)	Willemsoord Royal DY	1928	179 S	147 8 oa 140 5 pp	19 8	4 11	2 VTE engines 1 water-tube boiler ihp 2 shafts	700	14.5	40 oil		1 × 47mm (3pdr) 3 × 25mm AA 1 × 13.2mm AA 8 DCs	c 30

GENERAL NOTES
Shallow-draught minesweepers for service in the East Indies, design based on that of the German *FM* class.

CAREERS
Cha 112
Launched 24 September, 1929; completed 4 August, 1930 as Dutch *Minesweeper B*; sunk 2 March, 1942 at Tandjong Priok; raised by Japanese and commissioned as *Cha 112* 20 December 1942; sunk 4 June, 1945 off Laut Ketjil, Java Sea (05° 00′ S, 116° 04′ E) by US aircraft.

Cha 113
Launched 19 April, 1929; completed 4 August, 1930 as Dutch *Minesweeper A*; sunk 1 March, 1942 at Soerabaya; raised by Japanese and commissioned as *Cha 113* 17 January, 1943; sunk 23 June, 1945 off Talembau, Java (05° 44′ S, 114° 16′ E) by US submarine *Hardhead*.

Cha 116
Launched 1929; completed 4 August, 1930 as Dutch *Minesweeper C*; sunk 6 March, 1942 at Soerabaya; raised by Japanese and commissioned as *Cha 116* 8 April, 1943; sunk 13 November, 1944 20 nm W of Cavite, Luzon (14° 30′ N, 120° 45′ E) by aircraft from US TF 38.

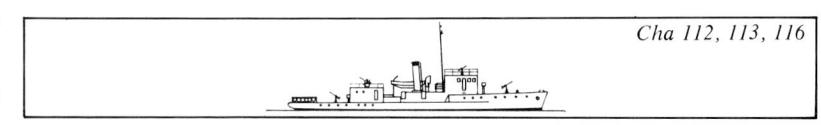

Cha 112, 113, 116

Name	Builder	Date	Displ	Length ft in	Beam ft in	Draught ft in	Machinery	SHP	Speed	Fuel	Radius	Armament	Comp
SUIKEI No. 11 ex-*HDML 1062*	Walker, Son, & Co., Singapore	1941	54 N 46 S	72 0 oa 70 0 pp	15 10	5 6	2 Gleniffer petrol engines 2 shafts	320	12½	7 oil		1 × 47mm (3pdr) 1 × 7.7mm MG 4 DCs	c 10

GENERAL NOTES
Thornycroft-type Harbour Defence Motor Launch; plywood hull.

CAREER
Suikei No. 11
Built 1941 as Royal Navy HM/*HMDL 1062*; sunk 16 February, 1942 in Banka Straits by gunfire of Japanese ships; raised and commissioned as *Suikei No. 11*, serving as a harbour gunboat; March 1943; redesignated *Kusentai No. 101* as a pilot boat and patrol craft; ultimate fate unknown.

Three other craft of the same type were captured at the Royal Naval Dockyard, Singapore, but these were not completed, being scrapped in 1942.

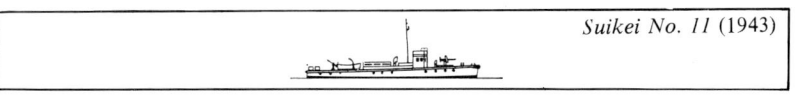

Suikei No. 11 (1943)

SUBMARINE CHASERS 223

Name	Builder	Date	Displ	Length ft in	Beam ft in	Draught ft in	Machinery	SHP	Speed	Fuel	Radius	Armament	Comp
SUIKEI No. 12 ex-*ML 310* and **KUSENTAI No. 111** ex-*ML 3???*	Singapore Harbour Board Voss Ltd., Singapore	1940–1943	130 N 80 S approx	112 0 oa	17 10	5 0	2 Hall-Scott petrol engines 2 shafts	1200	20	12 oil	1500 @ 12	1 × 47mm (3pdr) 2 × 7.7mm MGs 8 DCs 1 × 13.2mm AA 8 DCs	c 15

GENERAL NOTES
Fairmile type 'B' Motor Launches; plywood hull.
Suikei No. 12
Built 1941 as Royal Navy HM/*ML 310*; sunk 14 February, 1942 by Japanese Army Artillery fire off Singapore Island; raised and commissioned as harbour gunboat *Suikei No. 12*; March 1943: redesignated *Kusentai No. 102*, pilot boat and patrol craft; ultimate fate unknown.
Kusentai No. 111
Under construction as Royal Navy *ML 3??* when captured 50% complete in March 1942; launched 5 May, 1943 by Japanese, as pilot boat and patrol craft *Kusentai No. 111*; fate unknown.
These two craft were completed with only two engines, instead of the three installed in the standard British Fairmile 'B', with a consequent reduction in maximum speed to 18 knots from 20 knots. A third ML captured at Singapore was intended for completion by the Japanese but obviously this was not achieved.

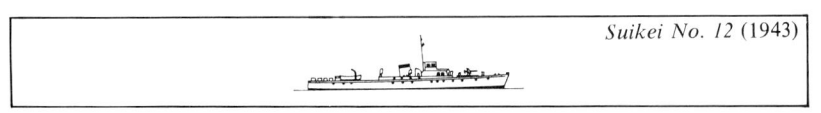

Suikei No. 12 (1943)

Name	Builder	Date	Displ	Length ft in	Beam ft in	Draught ft in	Machinery	SHP	Speed	Fuel	Radius	Armament	Comp
SUIKEI No. 21 ex-*Jeram*	Taikoo Dock, Hong Kong	1940	approx 393 S 210 GRT	137 10 oa 126 4 pp	21 4	8 0	1 compound engine 2 boilers 1 shaft	approx 400 ihp	9			1 × 80mm (3in) 40-cal HA 2 × 7.7mm MGs 6 DCs	

GENERAL NOTES
Merchant construction, requisitioned by Royal Navy as an Auxiliary Minesweeper.
CAREER
Suikei No. 21
Launched 1927 as merchant ship *Jeram*; requisitioned October 1939 for service as Auxiliary Minesweeper HMS *Jeram*; captured 15 February, 1942 at Singapore and commissioned as *Suikei No. 21*; fate unknown.

Suikei No. 21 (1943)

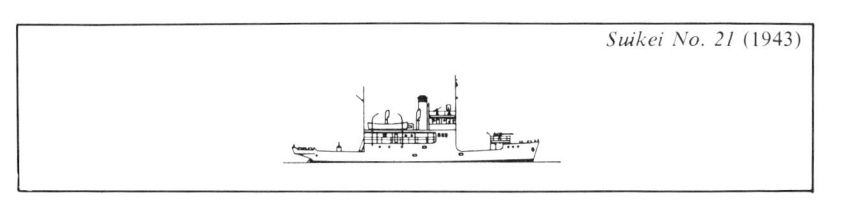

Name	Builder	Date	Displ	Length ft in	Beam ft in	Draught ft in	Machinery	SHP	Speed	Fuel	Radius	Armament	Comp
SUIKEI No. 2? ex-*Rhu*	Straits SS Co., Penang		254 GRT	126 0 wl	27 0	6 9	1 5-cyl, 4 stroke KHD Diesel		9			No details known (Other details from *Lloyds Register* 1941–1942)	

CAREER
Launched 1940 as merchant ship *Rhu*; requisitioned 22 October, 1941 for service as Auxiliary Minelayer; captured 15 February, 1942 off Singapore and commissioned as *Sukei No. 2?*; 1 September, 1943 redesignated *Kusentai No. 105*; torpedoed 29 November, 1944 and sunk in Ormoc Bay, Leyte, by USS *PT 128* and *PT 191*.

Name	Builder	Date	Displ	Length ft in	Beam ft in	Draught ft in	Machinery	SHP	Speed	Fuel	Radius	Armament	Comp
SUIKEI No. 22 ex-*Kelena*			295 S	108 0 oa approx	– –	– –	1 VTE engine 2 boilers 1 shaft		8			1 × 80mm (3in) 40-cal HA 2 × 7.7mm MG 6 DCs	

GENERAL NOTES
Coastal passenger craft.
CAREER
Built 1941 as coastal ferry *Kelena*; requisitioned by Royal Navy 1941; under conversion as patrol craft when scuttled in Keppel Harbour, Singapore, 15 February, 1942; raised and repaired by Japanese, commissioned as harbour defence gunboat *Suikei No. 22*, named *Kiri Maru*; despatched to Penang March 1943; fate thereafter not known.

The following merchant vessels (trawlers, whalers, etc.) were commissioned as Auxiliary Submarine Chasers:
Akitsu Maru
97ts; sunk 12 October, 1944 off Formosa by TF 38 aircraft.
Asahi Maru No. 9
277ts; 1939; steam vessel; sunk 6 November, 1943 W of Buka, Solomon Islands by aircraft.
Ayukawa Maru
189ts; 1925; steam freighter; sunk 18 February, 1945 NW of Iowa Jima by USS *Dortch*.
Banshu Maru No. 53
267ts; 1920; steam trawler; sunk 30 July, 1945 at Obama, Honshu, by TF 38 aircraft.
Bunzan Maru
97ts; sunk 15 July, 1945 at Hachinohe, Honshu, by TF 38 aircraft.
Byoritsu Maru
99ts; sunk 16 July, 1945 in Chongjin Bay, Korea, by mine.
Chikuto Maru
89ts; sunk 29 March, 1945 in Kagoshima Bay, Kyushu, by TF 58 aircraft.
Chikuzen Maru
52ts; sunk 30 July, 1945 at Imaura by TF 38 aircraft.
Chikuyu Maru
89ts; 1934; motor trawler; sunk 22 April, 1945 S of Toshijima by aircraft.

Fuji Maru No. 11
135ts; sunk 6 February, 1944 at Kwajalein by TF 58 aircraft.
Fumi Maru
360ts; 1938; motor whaler; captured August 1945 but returned and reconverted as whaler.
Fumi Maru No. 3
370ts; 1940; whaler; captured August 1945; returned to service as whaler.
Fumi Maru No. 5
384ts; 1942; whaler; captured August 1945; returned to service 1951 as whaler.
Ganjitsu Maru No. 1
216ts; 1926; sunk 14 January, 1943 E of Mindanao by USS *Searaven*.
Hakko Maru
76ts; sunk 26 January, 1945 off Corregidor Island by aircraft.
Hakusan Maru No. 2
43ts; sunk 17 May, 1945 at Ishigaki, Sakishima, by British aircraft.
Hakusan Maru No. 2, ex-*Hakusan Maru*
89ts; 1928; motor trawler; sunk 5 June, 1944 at Menokwari, N Guinea, by aircraft.
Hakuyo Maru
219ts; 1920; sunk 15 January, 1945 as blockship at southern entrance to Manila Bay.
Hino Maru No. 25
247ts; 1945; ran aground 5 August, 1945 in Bungo Suido.
Hino Maru No. 43
258ts; 1945; sunk 7 June 1945 at Miyanoura, Goto Island, by aircraft.
Hino Maru No. 63
240ts; 1945; sunk 8 August, 1945 W of Koje do, Korea, by aircraft.
Hinode Maru No. 15, ex-*Daifuku Maru*
220ts; 1920; steam trawler; sunk 14 September, 1944 in Manila Harbour, cause unknown.
Kaiko Maru
233ts; 1921; steam trawler; sunk 13 April, 1945 SE of Haiphong by US aircraft.
Kaio Maru No. 2
62ts; sunk 21 July 1944 30 nm N of Iwo Jima by USS *Cobia*.
Kaiyo Maru No. 2
143ts; sunk 15 October, 1944 off north coast of Java by USS *Dace*.
Kamoi Maru No. 9
260ts; 1945; War Standard trawler; ran aground 31 July, 1945 at Ukushima.
Kamo Maru
234ts; 1920; steam trawler; sunk 18 July, 1944 off Balabac Straits, Sabah, by USS *Lapon*.
Keihin Maru
76ts; sunk 14 March, 1945 W of Salembu Island, Java Sea, by USS *Sea Robin*.
Keisho Maru
75ts; 1929; motor trawler; sunk 18 December, 1944 at Nagoya; raised and repaired; sunk 30 July, 1945 at Imaura by TF 38 aircraft.
Kenkai Maru
89ts; sunk 20 November, 1944 in SW Pacific area.
Kiku Maru
233ts; 1920; steam trawler; sunk 4 March, 1945 off NW Sumatra by HMS/M *Selene*.
Kinsui Maru
89ts; beached 9 January, 1945 after air attack by TF 38 off Formosa.
Kongo Maru
270ts; 1934; motor coaster; sunk 14 October, 1944 at Amoy by aircraft.
Koshun Maru
88ts; 1928; motor trawler; ran aground 22 May, 1945 off Yurasaki, Kyushu.
Kumi Maru
75ts; 1929; motor trawler; damaged 6 May, 1945 off Koji do, Korea, by aircraft.
Kurama Maru
233ts; 1921; steam trawler; sunk 18 July, 1944 150 nm NW of Jesselton, Sabah, by USS *Lapon*.
Kyo Maru No. 2
340ts; 1938; steam whaler; sunk 7 August, 1944 W of Mindanao by USS *Puffer*.
Kyo Maru No. 6
341ts; 1938; steam whaler; ran aground 27 November, 1943 on Namu Island, Marshall Islands.
Kyo Maru No. 7
341ts; 1938; steam whaler; sunk 26 December, 1944 off Okinomisaki, Bonin Island, by gunfire of USS *Fanning*.
Kyo Maru No. 8 and *No. 10*
341ts; 1938; steam whalers; both deleted from Active List 31 March, 1944; possibly sunk by aircraft at Saipan 23 February, 1944.

Kyo Maru No. 11
385ts; 1938; steam turbine whaler; sunk 2 March, 1942 in Subic Bay, Luzon, by aircraft.
Kyo Maru No. 12
344ts; 1941; whaler; sunk 12 September, 1944 off Cebu, Philippine Islands, by aircraft.
Kyo Maru No. 13
340ts; 1941; whaler; sunk 26 January, 1945 by mine off Singapore.
Minakami Maru
97ts; slightly damaged 14 July, 1945 by TF 38 aircraft off Usujiri; captured August 1945; fate not known.
Misago Maru
154ts; sunk 13 August, 1944 N of Cape San Augustin, Mindanao, by USS *Bluegill*.
Misago Maru No. 2
265ts; 1920; steam trawler; sunk 2 September, 1944 N of Mindanao by aircraft.
Mogami Maru
498ts; 1938; motor trawler; sunk 12 September 1944, off Cebu Island by aircraft.
Myoken Maru
185ts; sunk 12 June, 1945 at Atsuta, Honshu, by aircraft.
Nan-Ho Maru
122ts; sunk 12 September, 1944 off Cebu by TF 38 aircraft, or sunk 31 March, 1945 at Macassar by aircraft.
Nanshin Maru
52ts; sunk 27 August, 1944 W of Mindoro Island by USS *Guitarro*.
Nippon Maru No. 2, ex-*Nippon Maru*
88ts; 1933; motor trawler; sunk 30 July, 1945 in Usami Bay by TF 38 aircraft.
Nisui Maru
89ts; sunk 26 March, 1945 E of Fukushima by TF 58 aircraft.
Nitto Maru No. 19 and *No. 20*
96ts; both sunk 8 July, 1944 at Rabaul by aircraft.
Nitto Maru No. 22
95ts; sunk 9 January, 1945 at Keelung, Formosa, by TF 38 aircraft.
Oshima Maru
184ts; sunk 31 March, 1945 off Makassar by aircraft.
Rumoe Maru
220ts; 1920; steam trawler; sunk 7 August, 1945 at My Tho, near Saigon, by aircraft.
Ryusei Maru
99ts; sunk 8 November, 1944 off Uji Gunto, south of Kyushu, by USS *Queenfish*.
Sankyo Maru
89ts; suffered slight damage from air attack 9 October, 1944 off Okinawa; subsequent fate unknown.
Sapporo Maru
400ts; 1930; motor trawler; sunk 4 May, 1944 at Truk by aircraft.
Seki Maru No. 2
359ts; 1938; motor whaler; captured August 1945 and subsequently returned to owner.
Shinan Maru
111ts; sunk 30 March, 1945 off Yulin, Hainan Island, by aircraft.
Shiratori Maru
269ts; 1936; motor trawler; sunk 12 April, 1945 E of Tanega Shima by submarine.
Shonan Maru No. 2
350ts; 1938; steam whaler; captured August 1945 and returned to original owner; 1948: Dutch *AM 12*; 1949: *Egbert Vinke*.
Shonan Maru No. 1 and *3*
350ts; 1938; steam whalers; captured August 1945 and returned to original owner.
Shonan Maru No. 5
350ts; 1938; steam whaler; sunk 23 August, 1944 NW of Chichi Jima by TF 58 aircraft.
Shonan Maru No. 6
356ts; 1938; steam whaler; captured August 1945 and returned to original owner.
Shonan Maru No. 7
356ts; 1938; steam whaler; sunk 22 September, 1944 W of Luzon by TF 38 aircraft.
Shonan Maru No. 8
355ts; 1938; steam whaler; captured August 1945 and returned to original owner.
Shonan Maru No. 10
350ts; 1938; steam whaler; sunk 1 February 1942 at Kwajalein by aircraft from USS *Enterprise*.
Shonan Maru No. 11
350ts; 1938; steam whaler; captured August 1945 and returned to original owner.
Shonan Maru No. 12
355ts; 1939; steam whaler; sunk 30 April, 1943 at Rangoon by British aircraft.

Shonan Maru No. 15
355ts; 1939; steam whaler; possibly sunk 17 February, 1944 at Truk by TF 58 aircraft.
Shonan Maru No. 17
356ts; 1940; steam whaler; captured August 1945 and returned to original owner; 1948: Dutch *AM 11*; 1949: *Trudy Vinke*.
Showa Maru
187ts; 1928; steam coaster; captured August 1945.
Showa Maru No. 2
195ts; 1930; steam whaler; captured August 1945.
Showa Maru No. 3, ex-*Leslie*
222ts; 1926; steam whaler; sunk 30 May, 1944 by mine E of the Kurile Islands.
Showa Maru No. 5
217ts; 1924; steam whaler; sunk 30 March, 1944 at Palau by TF 58 aircraft.
Showa Maru No. 6, ex-*William Wilson*
217ts; 1925; whaler; ran aground 6 August, 1943 in Naha Harbour, Okinawa.
Shunsei Maru No. 5
92ts; sunk 31 May, 1942 190 nm S of the Kii Channel, possibly by USS *Silversides*.
Shun'yo Maru
76ts; sunk 26 January, 1945 off Corregidor Island by aircraft.
Sobun Maru
99ts; severely damaged 25 March, 1945 by air attack between Yakujima and Amami-O-shima; fate unknown.
Suzuya Maru No. 1
88ts; 1934; fishery protection gunboat; sunk 22 September, 1944 off San Fernando, Luzon, by TF 38 aircraft.
Suzuya Maru No. 2
68ts; damaged 22 September, 1944 off San Fernando by TF 38 aircraft; fate unknown.
Takunan Maru No. 2
343ts; 1937; steam whaler; removed from Active List 10 August 1943; returned to owner 1945.
Takunan Maru No. 3
343ts; 1937; steam whaler; 1941–4: auxiliary minesweeper; 1944–5: auxiliary SC; returned to original owner.
Takunan Maru No. 5
340ts; 1937; steam whaler; August 1945: captured and returned to original owner; 1948: Dutch *AM 10*; 1949: *Nellie Vinke*.
Takunan Maru No. 6
343ts; 1937; steam whaler; sunk 10 August, 1945 at Onagawa Wan by TF 38 or TF 37 aircraft; raised and returned to original owner.
Takunan Maru No. 7
343ts; 1937; steam whaler; sunk 4 December, 1944 at Kwajalein by aircraft from TF 50.
Takunan Maru No. 8
343ts; 1937; steam whaler; 1941–4: auxiliary minesweeper; 1944: auxiliary SC; sunk 29 January, 1945 NW of Chichi Jima by aircraft.
Takunan Maru No. 10
343ts; 1937; steam whaler; captured August 1945 and returned to original owner.
Tama Maru No. 3, No. 5, No. 7
260–275ts; 1936; steam whalers; 1941–4: auxiliary minesweepers; 1944–5: auxiliary SCs; 1945: returned to original owner.

Suikei No. 22   Kyo Maru No. 11   Shonan Maru No 7

Tama Maru No. 6
275ts; 1936; steam whaler; 1941–4: auxiliary minesweeper; 1944: auxiliary SC; sunk 9 August, 1944 W of Chichi Jima by submarine.
Tama Maru No. 8
279ts; 1936; steam whaler; sunk 23 February, 1944 at Kavieng, New Ireland, by aircraft.
Tatsui Maru
99ts; burned out 14 February, 1945 after air attack off Formosa.
Toseki Maru
89ts; sunk 10 August, 1944 E of Celebes by submarine.
Toshi Maru No. 3
298ts; 1937; steam whaler; captured August 1945 and returned to original owner; 1957: *Katsu Maru No. 2*.
Ujina Maru
227ts; 1920; steam trawler; sunk 5 March, 1945 off Tourane (Da Nang), by aircraft.
Uruppu Maru
224ts; 1926; sunk 31 October, 1944 off Mindoro Island, by aircraft.
Wafu Maru
88ts; 1934; motor trawler; sunk 17 February, 1945 off Omaesaki Light, by USS *Haynsworth*.
Wakatake Maru
45ts; sunk 16 June, 1945 at Keelung, Formosa, by aircraft.
Yaryu Maru
97ts; severely damaged 15 July, 1945 at Hachinoe by TF 38 aircraft.
Yatsushiro Maru
398ts; 1930; motor trawler; sunk 14 March, 1945 S of Wenchow by aircraft.
Yobai Maru
99ts; damaged 17 May, 1945 at Ishigaki, Sakishima, by TF 57 aircraft.
Yusen Maru No. 1
194ts; sunk 21 July, 1944 with *Kaio Maru No. 2* by US submarine *Cobia*.
Yusen Maru No. 9 and *No. 10*
196ts; sunk September 1944 in Leyte area.
Yusen Maru No. 11
245ts; 1944: standard war programme trawler; sunk 5 March, 1945 off Okinawa, possibly by USS *Balao*.
Yusen Maru No. 16
245ts; standard trawler; sunk 22 September, 1944 off Cebu by TF 38 aircraft.
Yusen Maru No. 27
245ts; 1944; standard trawler; sunk 27 March, 1945 in Kuchinoerabu Bay, Kyushu, by TF 58 aircraft.
Yusen Maru No. 31
245ts; 1944; standard trawler; sunk 27 April, 1945 off Amami-O-shima by TF 58 aircraft.
Yusen Maru No. 43
257ts; sunk 18 March, 1945 45 nm SW of Satamisaki Light by TF 58 aircraft.

16. Landing Ships and Landing Craft

Name	Builder	Date	Displ	Length ft in	Beam ft in	Draught ft in	Machinery	SHP	Speed	Fuel	Radius	Armament	Comp
T.I Type	various	1943–1945	1800 (tonnes) N 1500 (ts) S	315 0 oa 308 4 wl 292 0 pp	33 6	11 9½	Single-screw geared turbine, 2 boilers	9500	22	?	3700 @ 18 4700 @ 18	2 × 5in 40-cal AA 15 × 25mm AA	?

GENERAL NOTES

Built under the 1943 Programme (Hull Nos. 2901–2946) by Kure DY and Mitsubishi, Yokohama. They were fast and powerfully armed transports designed to carry landing craft and amphibious tanks. The construction was simplified, with a welded flush-decked hull without sheer or tumble home. The sections were assembled at Kure, and construction took 3–6 months. Four 'Daihatsu' landing craft or 260ts of cargo could be carried, and the landing craft were launched over the stern, using rollers. Alternative loads were 7 Type 2 amphibious tanks and 220ts of cargo, 2 Koryu midget submarines and 184ts of cargo, 6 Kaiten human torpedoes and 243ts of cargo, 450–500ts of cargo, or 480 marines.

T.9 (1944)

RE-ARMAMENT AND MODIFICATIONS

By May 1944 they were armed with 42 DCs, and by September 1944 the armament included 26 × 25mm AA guns and 5 × 13mm MGs. In 1945, Type '22' Radar was added. A breakwater was added aft to prevent water from washing over the after deck.

CAREERS

T.1
Launched 1944, completed 10 May, 1944; sunk 27 July, 1944 by aircraft of US TF 58 off Palau (07° 30′ N, 134° 30′ E).

T.2
Launched 1944, completed 25 June, 1944; sunk 5 August, 1944, by aircraft of US TF 58 off Chichijima Retto (27° 05′ N, 142° 09′ E).

T.3
Launched 1944, completed 29 June, 1944; ran aground 14 September, 1944, on reef S of Mindanao (05° 35′ N, 125° 20′ E).

T.4
Launched 1944, completed 15 June, 1944; sunk 4 August, 1944, by aircraft of US TF 58 off Chichijima Retto (27° 07′ N, 142° 12′ E).

T.5
Launched 1944, completed 14 September, 1944; sunk 14 September, 1944 by aircraft of US TF 38 in Gulf of Davao, Mindanao (06° 10′ N, 126° E).

T.6
Launched 1944, completed 19 August, 1944; sunk 25 November, 1944, by aircraft of US TF 38 in Balanacan Harbour (13° 32′ N, 121° 52′ E).

T.7
Launched 1944, completed 15 August, 1944; sunk 27 December, 1944, by gunfire of US destroyers E of Kazan Retto (24° 47′ N, 141° 20′ E).

T.8
Launched 1944, completed 13 August, 1944; sunk 24 December, 1944, by gunfire of US destroyer *Case* 72 m off Chichijima Retto (25° 10′ N, 141° E).

T.9
Launched 1944, completed 28 August, 1944; surrendered August 1945 and used on Repatriation Service until 1946; used subsequently as a depot-ship for whalecatchers and then handed over to USA; BU by Ishikawajima 26 June, 1948.

T.10
Launched 1944, completed September, 1944; sunk 25 November, 1944 by aircraft of US TF 38 in Balanacan Harbour.

T.11
Launched 1944, completed 5 November, 1944; sunk 7 December, 1944 by US aircraft 5 m N of Leyte (11° 23′ N, 124° 18′ E).

T.12
Launched 1944, completed 11 November, 1944; torpedoed 13 December, 1944, by US submarine *Pintado* 200 m SE of Takao, Formosa (20° 34′ N, 118° 45′ E).

T.13
Launched 1944, completed 1 November, 1944; surrendered in August 1945 and used on Repatriation Service until 1947; handed over to USSR 8 August, 1947.

T.14
Launched 1944, completed 18 December, 1944; sunk 15 January, 1945, by US TF 38 off Takao, Formosa (22° 37′ N, 120° 15′ E).

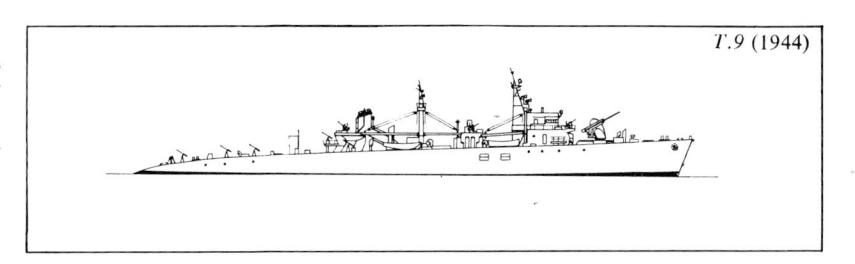

T.15
Launched 1944, completed 20 December, 1941; torpedoed 17 January, 1945, by US submarine *Tautog* off Kagoshima, Kyushu (31° 06′ N, 130° 34′ E).

T.16
Launched 1944, completed 31 December, 1944; surrendered August 1945 and used on Repatriation Service until 1947; handed over to China on 29 August, 1947, and renamed *Wu I*.

T.17
Launched 1944, completed 8 February, 1945; sunk 2 April, 1945, by US TF 38 off Amami-Oshima (28° 07′ N, 129° 09′ E).

T.18
Launched 1944, completed 12 February, 1945; missing from 18 March, 1945, near Mutsurejima, NW of Kyushu.

T.19
Launched 1945, completed 16 March, 1945; surrendered August 1945 and used on Repatriation Service until 1947; handed over to Great Britain 20 November, 1947, but retroceded and BU at Uraga in 1948.

T.20
Launched 1945, completed 23 April, 1945; surrendered August 1945 and used on Repatriation Service; ran aground 25 September, 1946, off Chipei-hsiaotao Island, in the Pescadores; stricken 1 November, 1946.

T.21
Launched 1945, completed 15 July, 1945; damaged 9 August, 1945, by US aircraft and sank the next day off Tsuwajima Island, in Ehime Prefecture (33° 59′ N, 132° 31′ E).

T.22
Launched 25 April, 1945, at Kure; work stopped 23 June when 90 per cent complete- BU post-war.

T.23–46
A further 24 units numbered 2923–2946 were not laid down; the contracts were cancelled in May 1945 and the material was dispersed.

The Type *T.1* fast transports were designed to carry landing craft and amphibious tanks. *T.5* is seen here in 1944, with two Koryu midget submarines aft. (Shizuo Fukui.)

Name	Builder	Date	Displ	Length ft in	Beam ft in	Draught ft in	Machinery	SHP	Speed	Fuel	Radius	Armament	Comp
T.101 Type	various	1943–1944	1010 (tonnes) N 950 (ts) S	264 0 oa 246 1 wl 236 3 pp	29 10	9 6	3-shaft Diesels	1200 bhp	13½	?	3000 @ 13½	1 × 80mm 40-cal AA 6 × 25mm AA	90

LANDING SHIPS AND LANDING CRAFT

Name	Builder	Date	Displ	Length ft in	Beam ft in	Draught ft in	Machinery	SHP	Speed	Fuel	Radius	Armament	Comp
T.103 Type	various	1944–1945	1020 (tonnes) N 950 (ts) S	264 0 oa 246 1 wl 236 3 pp	29 10	9 8	single-shaft geared turbine 2 Kampon boilers	2500	16	?	2500 @ 14	1 × 80mm 40-cal AA 6 × 25mm AA	90

GENERAL NOTES
Built under the 1943 Programme (Nos. 1501–1603) by Osaka, Uranosaki and Hitachi, Mukaijima. They were officially known as Type SB, the Type *101* being the SBD group (Diesel-engined) and the Type *103* the SBT group (turbine-driven). The design included a bow door and the bow was fitted with a double skeg. Only 6 of the SBD group were completed (*T.101–102, 127–8, 149–150*). The SBT group had their hulls strengthened during construction, increasing tonnage to 887 (S), 1129 (N) and draught to 10ft 3in. The cargo that could be carried included: 14 Type 95 7-ton tanks, 9 Type 97 15-ton tanks, 7 Type 2 amphibious tanks, 5 Type 3 amphibious tanks, 4–5 Type 4 amphibious tanks, 218ts of cargo, or 120 marines and 67.4ts of cargo.

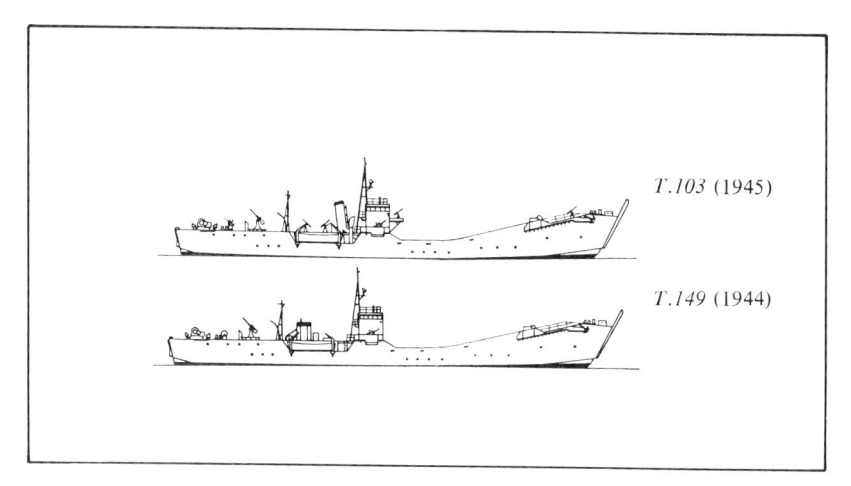

RE-ARMAMENT AND RECONSTRUCTION
In May 1944 they were armed with 8 × 25mm AA and 12 DCs, but by September 1944 they carried 21 × 25mm guns. In 1945 the Radar was improved. *T.147* was converted to coal-firing and given a raised funnel, and all vessels built after January 1945 were similarly treated.

T.103 (1945)

T.149 (1944)

CAREERS
T.101
Launched 1944 (Hull No. 1501); sunk 28 October, 1944, by US aircraft off Ormuc, Lyete (11° N, 123° E).
T.102
Launched 1944, completed ?; sunk 26 October, 1944, by aircraft of US carrier *Hancock* while passing through the Guimaras Straits (11° N, 123° E).
T.103
Launched 1944, completed ?; sunk 4 July, 1944, by US TF 58 108 m off Chichijima Retto (27° 05′ N, 142° 09′ E).
T.104
Launched 1944, completed ?; torpedoed 13 December, 1944, by US submarine *Pintado* 200 m SE of Takao (20° 34′ N, 118° 45′ E).
T.105
Launched 1944, completed ?; torpedoed 11 October, 1944, by US submarine *Trepang* 150 m SSW of Yokosuka (33° 07′ N, 137° 38′ E).
Nos. 1506–1509 Contracts for the Army.
T.106
Launched 1944 as *SB.120* (Army) but transferred October 1955 to Navy as *T.106*; sunk 15 December, 1944, by US TF 39 near Dasol Bay, Luzon (15° 54′ N, 119° 50′ E).
T.107
Launched 1944 as *SB.123* (Army) but transferred October 1944 to Navy as *T.107*; sunk 5 January, 1945, by gunfire of US destroyers off Hahajima Retto (26° 27′ N, 141° 11′ E).
T.108
Launched 1945 as *SB.125* (Army) but transferred ? October 1944 to Navy, as *T.108*; badly damaged 16 January, 1945, by US TF 38 at Hong Kong; surrendered in damaged condition August 1945 and not allocated; BU.
T.109
This number was not allocated.
T.110
Launched 1944; surrendered August 1945 and used on Repatriation Service until 1947; handed over to Great Britain 17 October, 1947, and BU.
T.111
Launched 1944, abandoned and sunk 24 November, 1944, after heavy damage from US air attack in Cataingan Bay, Masbate Island (11° 58′ N, 123° 59′ E).
T.112
Launched 1944; run aground and abandoned 5 November, 1944, on N coast of Luzon (18° 35′ N, 120° 45′ E).
T.113
Launched 1944; sunk 25 November, 1944, by US TF 38 S of Santa Cruz, Luzon (15° 40′ N, 119° 45′ E).

T.114
Launched 1944; sunk 17 February, 1945, by US aircraft off Shanghai (31° 20′ N, 122° E); stricken 10 April, 1945.
T.115
Launched 1944; badly damaged 1 February, 1945, in Luzon Straits (approx 20° N, 121° E); beyond repair and stricken 15 September, 1945; BU.
Nos. 1516–1526. Contracts for the Army. (*T.116–126* did not appear on the Navy List.)
T.127
Launched 1944; sunk 24 September, 1944, by US TF 38 near Manila (14° 35′ N, 120° 59′ E).
T.128
Launched 1944; sunk 4 June, 1944, by US aircraft 120 m NE of Morotai (04° N, 129° 55′ E).
T.129
Launched 1944; torpedoed 14 August, 1944, by US destroyer *Cole* S of Boeroe Island, Banda Sea (04° 04′ S, 126° 59′ E).
T.130
Launched 1944; sunk 4 July, 1944, off E coast of Iojima, Kazan Retto (24° 47′ N, 141° 20′ E).
T.131
Launched 1944, completed 24 June, 1944; badly damaged 12 January, 1945, by US aircraft near Saigon Harbour; following repairs on 10 February, 1945, she was re-classified as a passenger ferry, *Kuroshio No. 1* (armed with 1 × 76mm AA gun, 6 × 25mm AA and 12 DCs); surrendered August 1945 at Saigon and later BU.
T.132
Launched 1944, completed ?; sunk 27 December, 1944, by gunfire of US destroyers off E coast of Iojima, Kazan Retto (24° 47′ N, 141° 20′ E).
T.133
Launched 1944; abandoned 4 August, 1944, following heavy damage from US TF 58 near Iojima, Kazan Retto (24° 47′ N, 141° 20′ E).
T.134
Launched 1944; run aground and abandoned off E coast of Iojima, Kazan Retto.
T.135
Launched 1944; sunk 18 October, 1944, by US TF 38 near Salamague, Luzon (17° 46′ N, 141° 20′ E).
T.136
Launched 1945; lost with *T.135* 18 October, 1944.
T.137
Launched 1945; surrendered August 1945 and used on Repatriation Service until 1947; handed over to USSR 3 October, 1947.

228 LANDING SHIPS AND LANDING CRAFT

T.138
Launched 1944; torpedoed 26 October, 1944, by US submarine *Kingfish* 30 m NNE of Iojima (25° 22′ N, 141° 31′ E).
T.139
Launched 1944; sunk 6 November, 1944, by US TF 38 in Silanguin Bay, Luzon.
T.140
Launched 1944; sunk 12 January, 1945, by US TF 38 in Saigon Harbour.
T.141
Launched 1944; sunk 25 November, 1944, by US aircraft in Cataingan Bay, Masbate Island (11° 58′ N, 123° 59′ E).
T.142
Launched 1944; sunk 25 November, 1944, by US TF 38 in S part of Santa Cruz Harbour, Luzon (15° 40′ N, 119° 45′ E).
T.143
Launched 1944; run aground and abandoned 8 February, 1945, SE of Pescadores (approx 23° 30′ N, 119° 40′ E).
T.144
Launched 1944; surrendered August 1945, but not taken over; BU.
Nos. 1544–1548. Contracts for the Army.
T.145
Launched 1944 as *SB.115*; transferred to Navy 25 January, 1945, as *T.145*; badly damaged 2 April, 1945, by US TF 58 near Amami-Oshima; ran aground 4 April (28° 07′ N, 129° 09′ E); salvaged 3 September, 1945, but sank once more off Oshima Seto, Amami-Oshima; stricken 15 September, 1945.
T.146
Launched 1944 as *SB.118*; transferred to Navy as *T.146* 25 January, 1945; torpedoed 28 April, 1945, by US submarine *Trepang* off Osezaki (32° 24′ N, 128° 40′ E); stricken 25 May, 1945.
T.147
Launched 1944 as *SB.112*; transferred to Navy as *T.147* 15 January 1945; surrendered August 1945 and used by Repatriation Service until 1947; handed over to Great Britain 13 November, 1947, and BU in 1948 at Innoshima.
T.148
Number not allocated.
T.149
Launched 1944 and completed 20 February, 1944, by Mukajima; badly damaged 12 January, 1945, by US TF 38 near Cape St Jacques (10° 20′ N, 107° 50′ E); after repairs, reclassified as a passenger ferry, *Kuroshio No. 2* (armament 1 × 76mm AA, 6 × 25mm AA, 12 DCs); surrendered at Saigon in August 1945; BU.
T.150
Launched 1944 and completed by Mukajima; sunk 27 July, 1944, by US TF 58 near Palau (07° 30′ N, 134° 30′ E).
T.151
Launched 1944; torpedoed 23 November, 1944, by US submarine *Besugo* 20 m W of Palawan Island (11° 22′ N, 119° 07′ E).
T.152
Launched 1944; foundered in storm 2 August, 1945 between Chichijima Retto and Iojima, Kazan Retto.

T.153
Launched 1944; surrendered August 1945 in damaged condition at Kure; stricken 30 November, 1945, and BU 1947/48.
T.154
Launched 1944; sunk 5 January, 1945, by US destroyers near Iojima, Kazan Retto (24° 47′ N, 141° 20′ E).
Nos. 1555–1556. Army contracts.
T.157
Launched 1944; sunk 24 December, 1944, by US destroyers *Case* and *Roe* off Iojima, Kazan Retto (25° N, 141° E).
T.158
Launched 1944; sunk 10 October, 1944, by US TF 38 30 m NNW of Okinawa (26° 38′ N, 127° 52′ E).
T.159
Launched 1944; attacked 12 December, 1944, by US aircraft and abandoned, N of Camotes Island (11° 20′ N, 124° 10′ E).
T.160
Launched 1944; abandoned and sunk 24 November, 1944, following heavy damage by US aircraft in Cataingan Bay, Masbate Island; stricken 10 May, 1945.
T.161
Launched 1944; sunk 25 November, 1944, in S part of Santa Cruz Harbour, Luzon.
Nos. 1562–1563. Army contracts.
T.164–165
Keels laid April 1945 by Osaka SB Co., Osaka; work stopped in May and material BU.
Nos. 1566–1571. Army contracts.
T.172
Launched 1945; surrendered August 1945 and used by Repatriation Service until 1947; handed over to China 3 October, 1947, and renamed *Lu Shan*.
T.173
Launched 1945; sunk 22 May, 1945, by US TF 58 150 m SSW of Kagoshima (29° 45′ N, 129° 10′ E).
T.174
Launched 1945; surrendered in damaged condition in August 1945; stationed at Hakataka, Kyushu until 1947 as a repair ship for the vessels engaged on Repatriation Service; BU 1948.
T.175
Launched 11 April, 1945, by Uranosaki, Kawaminami (Hull No. 1575); work stopped 17 August, 1945; the hull sank in a storm off Imari, in Saga Prefecture, 18 September, 1945.
T.176
Launched 25 June, 1945, by Uranosaki (Hull No. 1576) and suffered the same fate as *T.175*.
Nos. 1577–1603
Contracts for 27 units of the *T.101* type placed at the end of 1944 were cancelled in March 1945.

Name	Builder	Date	Displ	Length ft in	Beam ft in	Draught ft in	Machinery	SHP	Speed	Fuel	Radius	Armament	Comp
SB. 101 Type	various	1944–1945	1020 (tonnes) N 870 (ts) S	264 0 oa 246 1 wl 263 3 pp	29 10	9 8	single-shaft geared turbines 2 Kampon water-tube boilers	2500	16	?	2500 @ 14	1 × 76mm AA 6 × 25mm AA	90 approx

GENERAL NOTES
These were naval-type *T.103* landing craft built for the Army. Several of this group were fitted to burn coal and therefore had taller funnels: *SB.101–102, 105, 108, 113, 126*. During building the hull was strengthened, increasing tonnage to 887 (S)/1129 (N) and draught to 10ft 3in. The cargo capacity was the same as the *T.103* type.

RE-ARMAMENT
In 1945 the armament was increased to 16 × 25mm AA guns.

CAREERS
SB.101
Launched 1944; surrendered August 1945; although earmarked on Repatriation Service duty she did not make any voyages; BU 1947.

SB.102
Launched 1944; surrendered August 1945; stranded near Moji; BU.
SB.103
Launched 1944; surrendered August 1945; BU 1947.
SB.104
Launched 1944; fate as *SB.103*.
SB.105
Launched 1944; fate as *SB.103*.
SB.106
Launched 1944; fate as *SB.103*.
SB.107
Launched 1944; lost March 1945 near Tsushima, cause unknown.

SB.108
Launched 1944; fate as *SB.103*.
SB.109
Launched 1944; surrendered August 1945 and used on Repatriation Service until 1946 and then BU.
SB.110
Launched 1944; surrendered August 1945; damaged October 1945 by boiler-explosion; lay at Hataka until BU in 1948.
SB.111
Launched 1944; fate as *SB.103*.
SB.112
Launched 1944; transferred to Navy as *T.147* (see above) 21 January, 1945.
SB.113
Launched 1944; sunk 28 July, 1945, by US TF 38 near Innoshima, Habu Island (33° 25′ N, 133° 15′ E).
SB.114
Launched 1944; fate as *SB.109*.
SB.115
Launched 1944; transferred to Navy 25 January, 1945 as *T.145*.
SB.116–117
Launched 1944; fate as *SB.103*.
SB.118
Launched 1944; transferred to Navy 25 January, 1945, as *T.146*.

SB.119
Launched 1944; fate as *SB.103*.
SB.120
Launched 1944; transferred to Navy October 1944 as *T.106*.
SB.121
Launched 1944; fate as *SB.103*.
SB.122
Launched 1944; fate as *SB.103*.
SB.123
Launched 1944; transferred to Navy October 1944 as *T.107*.
SB.124
Launched 1944; fate as *SB.103*.
SB.125
Launched 1945; transferred to Navy October 1944 as *T.108*.
SB.126
Launched 1944; fate as *SB.103*.
SB.127
Launched 10 April, 1945, by Osaka SB Co., Osaka; 80 per cent complete at time of surrender in August 1945; BU 1947–8.
SB.128
Launched 11 August, 1945, by Osaka SB Co.; work stopped 17 August, 1945, when 60 per cent complete; BU 1947–8.

Name	Builder	Date	Displ	Length ft in	Beam ft in	Draught ft in	Machinery	SHP	Speed	Fuel	Radius	Armament	Comp
SS.1 Type	various	1941–1945	948 (tonnes) N	206 9 oa 193 7 pp	31 6	9 2	2-shaft 6-cyl 4-stroke Diesels	1100 bhp	13½	?	2000 @ 12	1 × 75mm AA 4 × 20mm AA 4 × 7.7mm MGs 1 mortar DCs	?

GENERAL NOTES

Known as the Navy ES Type, these landing craft were also built under naval supervision for the Army. They had bow doors 16½ft × 10ft and a freeboard of 15ft. The hull was based on an icebreaker and could lift 4 Type 97 tanks (15-ton), 1 truck and 170 marines. The first ship of the class, the *Koryu Maru* (623 GRT, 14½ knots) was used as a trials ship in 1942–4.

RE-ARMAMENT

In 1944–5 the 20mm guns were replaced by 25mm.

CAREERS

SS.1
Launched 1942, completed 10 April, 1942, by Harima as *Koryu Maru* (see above); renumbered *SS.1* in 1944; sunk 13 January, 1945, by US aircraft at Lingayen, Luzon (16° 02′ N, 120° 22′ E).
SS.2
Launched 1943, completed 31 July, 1943, by Harima as *Banryu Maru* (780 GRT); renumbered *SS.2* in 1944; sunk 13 September, 1944, by US aircraft near Cebu Island (10° 20′ N, 124°).
SS.3
Launched 1943 as *Kairyu Maru*; renumbered *SS.3* in 1944; sunk (torpedoed?) 27 March, 1944 by submarine (Allied?) near Manokwari, New Guinea (01° S, 134° 10′ E).
SS.4
Launched 1943; lost (cause unknown) in autumn of 1944 in Philippines.
SS.5
Launched 1943; sunk 30 November, 1944, by US aircraft near Masbate Island 12° N, 123° 30′ E).
SS.6
Launched 1943; sunk 4 December, 1944 by US aircraft near Mindoro Island.
SS.7
Launched 1943; surrendered August 1945 and used on Repatriation Service until 1946; converted to mercantile use and renamed *Kiku Mary No. 7*; later became *Kiku Maru No. 10*.
SS.8
Launched 1943; believed lost, date and cause unknown.
SS.9
Launched 1943; sunk 4 December, 1944, by US aircraft near Mindoro Island.
SS.10
Launched 1943; believed lost, date and cause unknown.

SS.11
Launched 1943; believed sunk in the Spring of 1945 near Shiranoe or near Moji.
SS.12
Launched 1942; surrendered August 1945 and used on Repatriation Service until 1946; converted for mercantile use as *Taishu Maru* (830 GRT), belonging to Kyushin YKK, Fukuoka.
SS.13
Launched 1943; ran aground August 1945 near Moji; repaired post-war and converted to a merchant ship, *Nagasaki Maru*, owned by Kaburaki Kisen KK, Tokyo; about 1960 renamed *Mishima Maru*.
SS.14
Launched 1944; lost during the War, date and cause unknown.
SS.15
Launched 1944; fate as *SS.14*.
SS.16
Launched 1944; lost April 1946 (?) at Yohimi; raised and remained at Moji until 1947; BU.
SS.17
Launched 1944; sunk 5 June, 1945, by US aircraft near Talien (38° 45′ N, 121° 20′ E).
SS.18
Launched 1944; surrendered August 1945 and served on Repatriation Service until 1946; converted to merchant ship *Tenkei Maru*, owned by Hakuyo Kisen KK, Osaka; in 1963 renamed *Hokko Maru No. 21*.
SS.19
Launched 1944; surrendered August 1945 and served on Repatriation Service from December 1945 to December 1946; converted to merchant ship *Yokohama Maru*, owned by Nippon Sempaku KK, Osaka.
SS.20
Launched 1944; ran aground 20 May, 1945, near Shodoshima; raised 17 September, 1945 but lost during a storm, while under repair; raised again and completed conversion at Harima in July 1946; renamed *Kimishima Maru* (701 GRT)
SS.21
Launched 1944; sunk 1 June, 1945, by US aircraft near Osaka; raised and completed as the merchant ship *Tomi Maru*, owned by Sanko SS Co.
SS.22
Launched 1944; sunk 8 August, 1945, by US TF 38 off coast of Asamushi, near Aomori.

1 unit laid down 10 March, 1944, by Ohara, Osaka; incomplete hull, sunk by US aircraft in 1945.

3 units laid down at Kowloon, Hong Kong in 1944; not completed and material BU.

1 unit launched 1944 (with SS number) by Sanko, Osaka; badly damaged by air attack while fitting out; surrendered in unrepaired condition August 1945 and believed to have been converted to the merchantman *Otowa Maru* (Kansai Kisen KK, Osaka – 909 GRT).

Name	Builder	Date	Displ	Length ft in	Beam ft in	Draught ft in	Machinery	SHP	Speed	Fuel	Radius	Armament	Comp
SHIUSHU MARU	Harima SB Co., Harima	1934–1935	12000 (tonnes) N 9000 (ts) S 8160 GRT	492 1 pp	72 2	26 9	2-shaft geared turbines	8000	19	?	?	5 × 75mm AA (later 8) 26 small floatplanes 20 Diahatsu landing craft	?

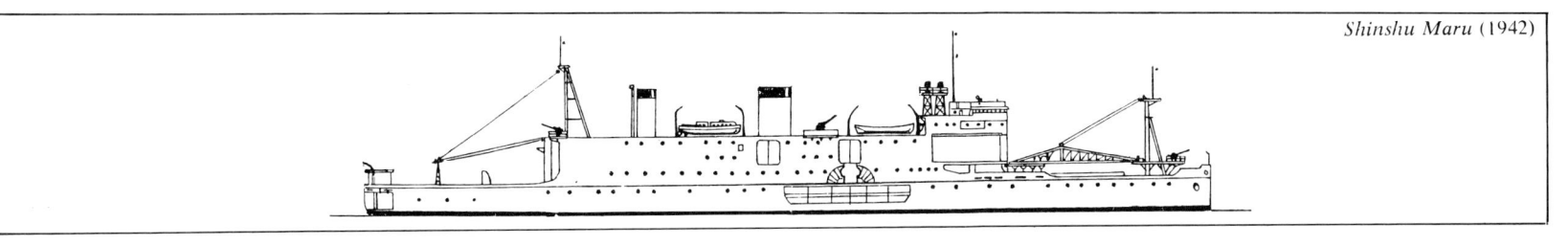

Shinshu Maru (1942)

The purpose-built landing craft carrier *Shinshu Maru*. Procured by the Japanese Army, she was the first ship of her type in the world. She is seen here during operations off Woosung, in November 1937. Note the "Daihatsu" being loaded fore and aft and through the upward hinging cargo doors amidships; powerful searchlights are mounted on lattice masts on either bridge-wing, to permit night operations. (Tappman Collection.)

Shinshu Maru

GENERAL NOTES

Known as the MT Type, this was the world's first specially designed landing ship. She was built in great secrecy. There was an aircraft hangar in the superstructure, but catapults on either side of the bridge were not installed. Internally, there was a through-deck for carrying 20 fully laden landing craft, which could be discharged two at a time through stern doors, or lifted out through the forward hatch by crane. Tanks and heavy cargo could be taken on board through two loading ports amidships. The ship was taken over from the Army during construction, and completed as a landing craft depot ship. The freeboard was 39ft.

RECONSTRUCTION

To remedy poor stability, extra ballast was added, and a torpedo-bulkhead was built internally.

CAREER

Launched 1935; completed 1935; during the War she carried a false name, either *Ryujo Maru* or *Fuso Maru*, for security reasons; torpedoed 1 March, 1942, in shallow water in Banten Bay, Java (06° 56′ S, 106° 07′ E), probably by the destroyer *Fubuki*; raised and repaired in 1943; badly damaged by submarine torpedo 3 January, 1945, between Manila and Takao; sunk 5 January by TF 38 40 m SW of Takao (21° 57′ N 119° 44′ E).

Name	Builder	Date	Displ	Length ft in	Beam ft in	Draught ft in	Machinery	SHP	Speed	Fuel	Radius	Armament	Comp
MAYASAN MARU TAMATSU MARU	Mitsui, Tamano	1941–1944	11910 (tonnes) N 7000 (ts) S 9433 GRT (MM) 9589 GRT (TM) 4617 DW	459 1	62 4	23 1	2-shaft Diesels	10800 bhp	208	?	?	6 × 75mm AA 20 MGs 20 Diahatsu landing craft	?

GENERAL NOTES

These two ships were originally motor-ships laid down in 1941–2 for the Mitsui Line and Osaka Shosen KK respectively. They were taken over from the Army and completed as landing craft depot ships, with stern doors. The freeboard was 38ft 9in.

CAREERS

Mayasan Maru

Launched 1942, completed December 1942; torpedoed 17 November, 1944, by US submarine *Picuda* in E China Sea (33° 17′ N, 124° 41′ E).

Tamatsu Maru

Launched 1943, completed January 1944; torpedoed 19 August, 1944, by US submarine *Spadefish* near Cape Bojeador, Luzon (18° 12′ N, 120° 20′ E).

LANDING SHIPS AND LANDING CRAFT 231

Name	Builder	Date	Displ	Length ft in	Beam ft in	Draught ft in	Machinery	SHP	Speed	Fuel	Radius	Armament	Comp
TAKATSU MARU	Uraga Dock Co., Tokyo	1942–1944	9500 (tonnes) N 5000 (ts) S 5350 GRT	?	?	?	2-shaft geared turbines	5000	17½	?	?	6 × 75mm AA 20 Daihatsu landing craft	?

Takatsu Maru

GENERAL NOTES
Laid down in 1942 for the Yamashita Line, and taken over from the Army for completion as a landing craft depot ship.

CAREER
Launched 1943 and completed January 1944; sunk 10 November, 1944, by US aircraft in Ormuc Bay (10° 50′ N, 124° 35′ E).

Name	Builder	Date	Displ	Length ft in	Beam ft in	Draught ft in	Machinery	SHP	Speed	Fuel	Radius	Armament	Comp
KIBITSU MARU HYUGA MARU SETTSU MARU TOKITSU MARU	Hitachi SB Co., Inoshima	1942–1945	12000 (tonnes) F 10500 (tonnes) N 8000 (ts) S	500 3 oa 465 10 pp	64 3	23 0	2-shaft geared turbines 3-cyl water-tube boilers	10000	19	?	?	8 × 75mm AA (later) up to 60 × 25 mm AA 2 mortars 13 Daihatsu landing craft 12 Toku landing boats	

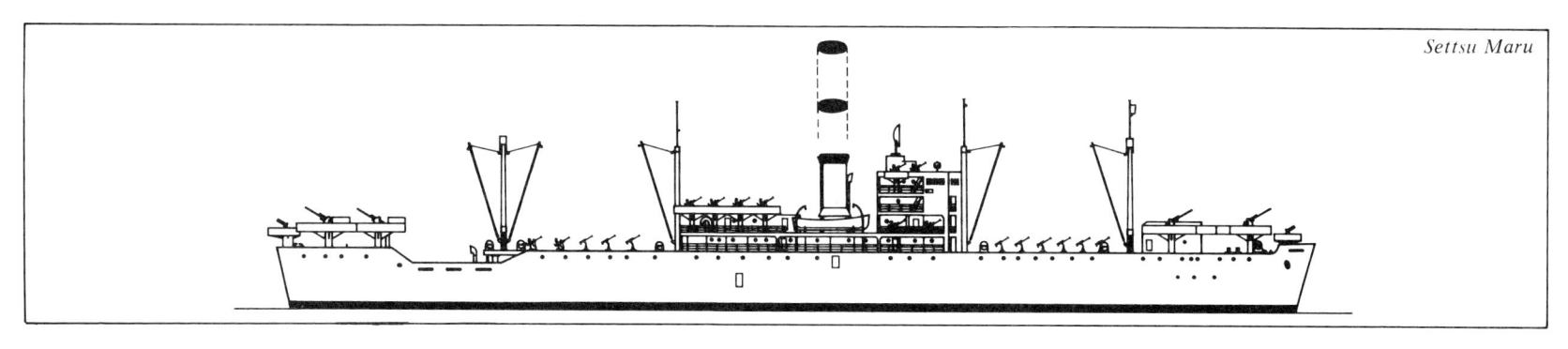

Settsu Maru

GENERAL NOTES
Projected in 1942 as Standard Type 1 MA. Taken over from the Army and converted to dock landing ships with stern doors. They had two funnels side-by-side, and the freeboard was 39ft 3in.

The tonnage varied between the four ships:
Kibitsu Maru   9574 GRT
Hyuga Maru   9687 GRT
Settsu Maru   9725 GRT
Tokitsu Maru   9554 GRT

RECONSTRUCTION
Shortly after completion, the *Settsu Maru* was converted to a merchant ship with coal-fired boilers. She displaced 11360ts and her machinery developed 2700 SHP = 12 knots.

CAREERS
Kibitsu Maru
Launched 1943, completed 29 December, 1943; damaged by mine 7 August, 1945, and ran aground 250 m E of Hiraiso, near Kobe (34° 37′ N, 135° 04′ E); BU.

Hyuga Maru
Launched 1944, completed 15 January, 1945; mined 30 May, 1945, and ran aground 2 m SSE of Genkajima, in the outer harbour of Hakata (33° 45′ N, 130° E).

Settsu Maru
Launched 1944, completed 15 January, 1945; surrendered August 1945 and used on Repatriation Service until 1947; transferred to Japanese mercantile marine (Nippon Suisan KK, Osaka – 9329 GRT) in 1948.

Tokitsu Maru
Laid down 14 October, 1944; work stopped in March 1945; completed as a merchant ship for Nippon Kaiun KK, Tokyo, and launched 2 May, 1946 (9554 GRT).

The following landing craft depot ships with flight decks were reclassified as aircraft transports, and are fully described on p. 61.
  Akitsu Maru Launched 1941
  Nigitsu Maru Launched 1942
  Kumano Maru Launched 1945

Name	Builder	Date	Displ	Length ft in	Beam ft in	Draught ft in	Machinery	SHP	Speed	Fuel	Radius	Armament	Comd
10-METRE 'Shohatsu' Type (Army SB-C Type)	various	–1945	605 (tonnes) N	34 9 oa	8 0	1 11	single-shaft oil engine	60 bhp	7½	?	60 @ 7½	1 × 7.7mm MG 35 men or 3.3 ts of cargo	5

232   LANDING SHIPS AND LANDING CRAFT

Name	Builder	Date	Displ	Length ft in	Beam ft in	Draught ft in	Machinery	SHP	Speed	Fuel	Radius	Armament	Comp
13-METRE 'Chuhatsu' Type	various	–1945	15.5 (tonnes) N	42 8 oa	9 6	2 7	single-shaft oil engine	60 bhp	8	?	70 @ 8	1 × 7.7mm MG or 1 × 13mm MG 60 men or 10 ts of cargo	6
15-METRE 'Moku Daihatsu' Type	various	1944–1945	17 (tonnes) N	49 2 oa	11 10	1 9	2 oil engines	80 bhp	8	?	70 @ 8	2 × 7.7mm MGs 80 men or 8ts of cargo	6
14-METRE 'Daihatsu' Type (Army LB-D Type)	various	1935–1945	20–21.4 (tonnes) N	47 10 oa	11 0	2 6	various types	60–150 hp	7½ –8½	?	100 @ 7½ 50 @ 8½	2 × 7.7mm MGs or 2/3 × 25mm AA 1 Type 95 7.4t tank or 70 men or 10ts of cargo	12
17-METRE 'Toku Daihatsu' Type (Army N-L-BD Type)	various	–1945	32.6–37.2 (tonnes) N	57 9 oa	12 2	3 3	various types	120–150 hp	8 10	?	100 @ 8 300 @ 10	1 × 13mm AA or 3 × 25mm AA or 2 × 7.7 MGs 1 Type 97 15.6t tank or 100 men or 16ts of cargo	15

GENERAL NOTES
These landing craft were all steel-built, except the wooden 15-metre type. Most were fitted with bow ramps, apart from the 10-metre type, which had a motorboat-type hull. The freeboard of the 10-metre type was 3ft 11in and that of the 15-metre type, 4ft 11in.

MACHINERY
The following engines were fitted:
14-metre Type A1: 1 60 hp Army Diesel, 7½ knots.
14-metre Type AB1: 1 60 hp HS Diesel, 7½ knots.
14-metre Type B1: 1 80 hp Navy petrol engine, 8 knots.
14-metre Type C2: 2 40 hp automobile engines, 8 knots.
14-metre Type D: 1 60 hp Diesel, 8 knots.
14-metre Type E1: 1 150 hp Diesel, 8½ knots.
17-metre Type A2: 2 60 hp Army Diesels, 8 knots.
17-metre Type AB2: 2 60 hp HS Diesels, 8 knots.
17-metre Type B1: 1 150 hp Diesel, 8 knots.
17-metre Type B2: 2 150 hp Diesels, 10 knots.

CONSTRUCTION AND FATES
The Navy ordered 20 10-metre type, probably 3 13-metre type, 1140 15-metre type, 3229 14-metre type, and 163 17-metre type. The only exact information to survive is about the following boats built by Mitsubishi:
14-metre Daihatsu Type
Nos. 5029–5033, 5048–5052, 5067–5071, 5087–5091, 5112–5117, 5138–5143, 5160–5165, 5188–5189 (all 1942).
17-metre Toku Daihatsu Type
Nos. 2049–2068, 2081–2099, 2526–2531 (1943-4).
Note: See also p.159 for 19-metre river gunboats, which were used to carry about 100 men.

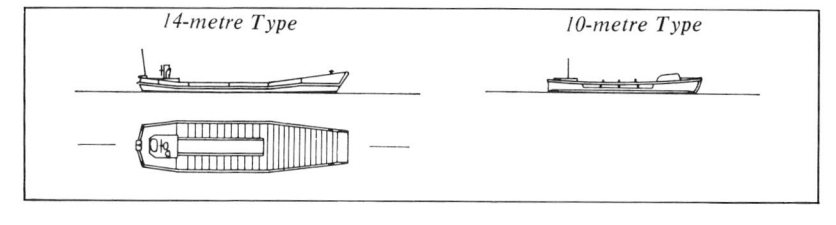

14-metre Type   *10-metre Type*

Typical early 14-metre "Daihatsu" in laden condition. (Tappman Collection.)

Name	Builder	Date	Displ	Length ft in	Beam ft in	Draught ft in	Machinery	SHP	Speed	Fuel	Radius	Armament	Comp
'UMPOTO' Type	Kure DY	1941–1942	36.7 (tonnes) N	70 4 oa	14 3	4 4	2 compressed-air motors	?	?	?	?	15ts deadweight of cargo 4 field-guns or 2 × 20mm	

Umpoto Type (scale 1: 500)

GENERAL NOTES
The 'Umpoto' Type landing craft was designed to be carried in three sections as a deck-cargo aboard submarines, for transport in the Solomon Islands. They were driven by two compressed air motors designed for torpedoes.
The total built is not known, but many survived at the end of the War in Kure, Yokosuka and other yards.

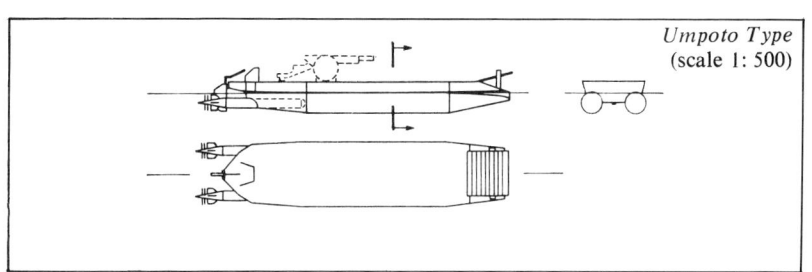

Name	Builder	Date	Displ	Length ft in	Beam ft in	Draught ft in	Machinery	SHP	Speed	Fuel	Radius	Armament	Comp
Type 2	Mitsubishi	–1945	12.5 (tonnes) N	24 oa 7	9 2	5 10	1 Diesel tank engine	70–120 bhp	5–6	?	?	1 × 37mm 3 × 7.7mm MGs	3
Type 3	Mitsubishi	1943–1945	28.3 (tonnes) N	32 oa 9	9 10	8 2	1 Mitsubishi 12-cyl Diesel	240 bhp	6	?	?	1 × 46mm 4 × 7.7mm MGs	7
Type 4	?	1944–1945	19.2 (tonnes) N	36 oa 1	10 10	7 6*	1 Mitsubishi 12-cyl Diesel	240 bhp	5	?	?	2 × 13mm AA 10 tons of cargo	3

GENERAL NOTES

The Type 2 was known as *Toku 2-shiki Naikatei*, the others as *Toku-3*, etc., and *Toku-4*, etc. The draughts quoted in the tables above* refer to the depth between the lower caterpillar-track and the 'deck' of the hull. Type 2 had two fixed propellers, two hoisting rudders and two detachable floatation tanks. There were five variants: the first series was driven by an 8-cyl 90 hp Diesel, and the remainder by a 6-cyl 120 hp Diesel, or a 4-cyl Mitsubishi 70 hp Diesel, or an air-cooled OHV Diesel. Type 3 had twin hoisting propellers as well as rudders, and two flotation tanks. They were a considerable improvement over the Type 2, with a pressure-tight hull to allow them to be carried as deck-cargo in submarines. The first trials vehicles were completed in 1943. Production problems resulted in only a few being built, and none was used operationally. Type 4 had two hoisting propellers and rudders. They were built to carry 10ts of cargo, as replacements for the highly dangerous Daihatsu landing craft. Because of material shortages only 18 units were built, and these were converted to small assault units armed with torpedoes (see p. 272).

CAREERS

No individual fates are known. Between 200 and 300 Type 2 were built, about 10 Type 3 and 18 Type 4.

17. Armed Merchant Cruisers

Name	Builder	Date	Displ	Length ft in	Beam ft in	Draught ft in	Machinery	SHP	Speed	Fuel	Radius	Armament	Comp
NOSHIRO MARU	Mitsubishi, Nagasaki	1933–1934	7184 GRT	448 pp 6	62 4	27 8	1 7-cyl 2-stroke Mitsubishi Diesel engine 1 shaft	6700	18.5	1500	?	4 × 140mm (5.51in) 50-cal LA + light automatic AA	
AKAGI MARU	Mitsubishi	1935–1936	7387 GRT	462 pp 8	62 3	27 7	1 8-cyl 2-stroke Mitsubishi-Sulzer Diesel engine 1 shaft	8000	19	?	?	4 × 152mm (6in) 50-cal LA + light AA	
ASAKA MARU **AWATA MARU**	Mitsubishi	1937 1937	7399 GRT 7398	478 oa 0	61 0	26 11	1 7-cyl 2-stroke Mitsubishi-Sulzer Diesel engine 1 shaft	7600	18	1430	?	4 × 140mm (5.51in) 50-cal LA + light AA	
KIYOZUMI MARU	Kawasaki, Kobe	1934	GRT 8613 GRT	453 pp 9									

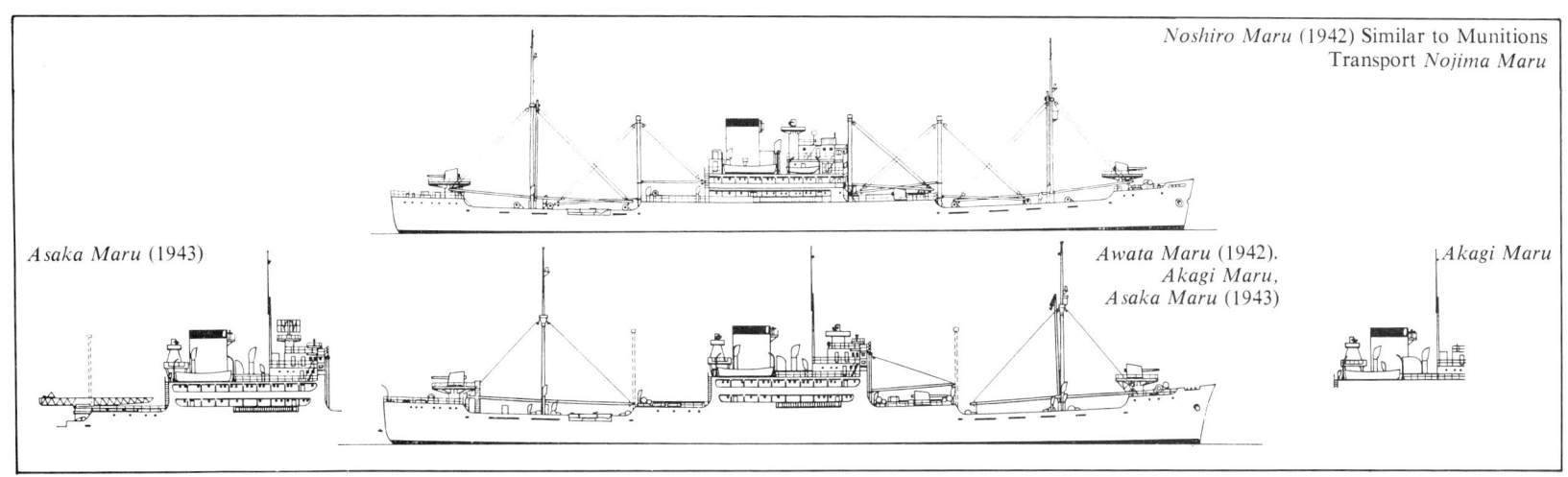

Noshiro Maru (1942) Similar to Munitions Transport *Nojima Maru*

Asaka Maru (1943)

Awata Maru (1942). *Akagi Maru*, *Asaka Maru* (1943)

Akagi Maru

Name	Builder	Date	Displ	Length ft in	Beam ft in	Draught ft in	Machinery	SHP	Speed	Fuel	Radius	Armament	Comp
KONGO MARU	Harima SB Co.	1935	8624	450 0 pp	61 0	27 11	1 8-cyl 2-stroke Kawasaki-M.A.N. Diesel engine 1 shaft	7600	18	1430		4 × 140mm (5.51in) + light AA	
UKISHIMA MARU	Mitsui, Tama	1936	4730	355 7 pp	51 6	23 0	1 8-cyl 2-stroke Mitsui-B & W Diesel engine 1 shaft	748 (Lloyds registered hp)	16.5	219		6 × 120mm (4.7in) 45-cal LA 1 × 7.7mm MG	
BANGKOK MARU	Mitsubishi, Kobe	1937	5451	376 4 pp	55 9	23 0	2 8-cyl 2-stroke Mitsubishi-Sulzer Diesel engines 1 shaft (hydraulic gearbox)		18			4 × 120mm (4.7in) 45-cal LA 1 × 7.7mm MG 500 mines	
SAIGON MARU			5350										
KINRYU MARU	Kawasaki, Kobe	1938	9309	475 7 pp	62 9	26 0	1 8-cyl 2-stroke Kawasaki-M.A.N. Diesel engine 1 shaft	9200	18			4 × 152mm (6in) 50-cal LA + light AA	
AIKOKU MARU	Tama SB, Tama	1940	10437	490 10 pp	66 5	26 0	2 Mitsui-B & W Diesel engines 2 shafts	13000	21			8 × 140mm (5.51in) 4 × 533mm (20.6in) TTs 2 aircraft	
HOKOKU MARU		1940	10438										
GOKOKU MARU		1941	10438										

General Notes
During the 1894–5 Sino-Japanese War and the 1904–5 Russo-Japanese War, a very large number of cargo ships and passenger ships were commissioned into the Imperial Japanese Navy as auxiliary cruisers. The names of all that could be traced are listed in the Index.

Careers
Noshiro Maru
Launched 28 June, 1934; completed 30 November, 1934 for Nippon Yusen KK, Tokyo; April: 1942: AMC; 1942–3: Transport; damaged 19 August, 1944 NW of Luzon by US submarine *Rasher*; sunk 24 September, 1944 in Manila Harbour by aircraft from US TF 38.

Akagi Maru
Launched 6 June, 1936; completed 10 September, 1936 for Nippon Yusen KK, Tokyo; 1 January, 1942: AMC; sunk 17 February, 1944 NW of Truk (07° 54′ N, 151° 25′ E) by TF 58 aircraft.

Asaka Maru
Launched 7 July, 1937; completed 30 November, 1937; for Nippon Yusen KK, Tokyo; August 1941: AMC; 1943: Transport; sunk 12 October, 1944 off Pescadores (23° 33′ N, 119° 34′ E) by TF 38 aircraft.

Awata Maru
Launched 5 August, 1937; completed 23 December, 1937 for Nippon Yusen KK, Tokyo; August 1941: AMC; 1943: Transport; sunk 22 October, 1943 in China Sea (26° 30′ N, 125° 05′ E) by US submarine *Grayback*.

Kiyozumi Maru
Launched 1934; completed October 1934, for Kokusai KKK, Tokyo; August 1941: AMC; 1943: Transport; heavily damaged 1 January, 1944 S of Truk by US submarine *Balao*; sunk 17 February, 1944 at Truk by TF 58 aircraft.

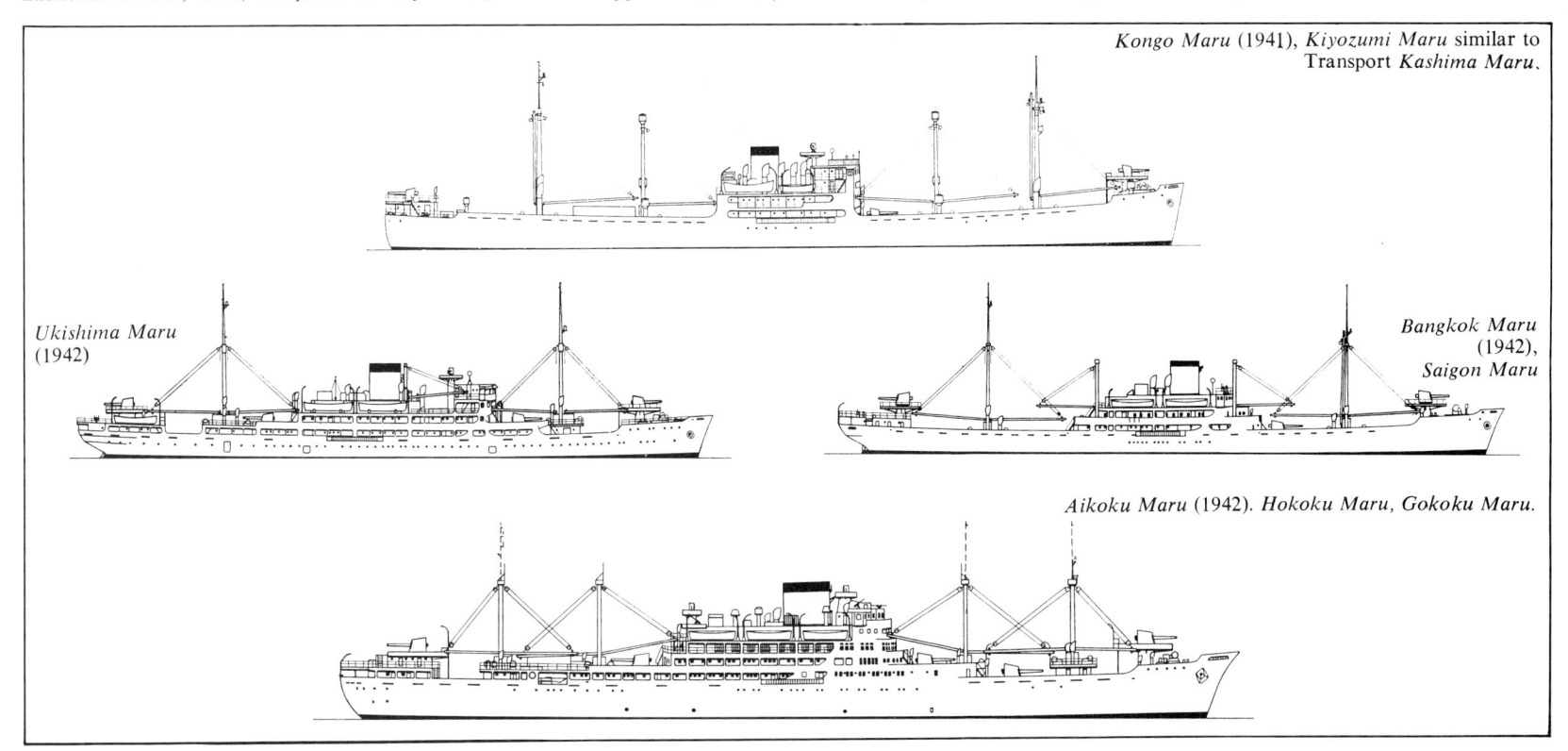

Kongo Maru (1941), *Kiyozumi Maru* similar to Transport *Kashima Maru*.

Ukishima Maru (1942)

Bangkok Maru (1942), *Saigon Maru*

Aikoku Maru (1942). *Hokoku Maru*, *Gokoku Maru*.

ARMED MERCHANT CRUISERS

Kongo Maru
Launched 1934; completed February 1935 for Kokusai KKK, Tokyo; August 1941: AMC; sunk 10 March, 1942 at Salamaua, New Guinea, by aircraft from USS *Lexington* and *Yorktown*.

Ukishima Maru
Launched and completed 1936 for Osaka Shosen KK, Osaka; April 1942: AMC; severely damaged 26 January, 1943 SE of Palau by three torpedo hits, probably fired by US submarine *Wahoo*; repaired and employed as a gunboat; 1945: Transport; ultimate fate unknown.

Bangkok Maru
Launched and completed 1937 for Osaka Shosen KK, Osaka; August 1941: AMC; sunk 20 March, 1943 E of Jaluit Atoll, Marshall Islands (05° 47′ N, 169° 42′ E) by US submarine *Pollack*.

Saigon Maru
Launched and completed 1937 for Osaka Shosen KK, Osaka; August 1941: AMC; 20 January, 1944: redesignated Auxiliary Gunboat; sunk 18 September, 1944 off Manila Bay (14° 20′ N, 120° 05′ E) by US submarine *Flasher*.

Kinryu Maru
Launched and completed 1937 for Kokusai KKK, Tokyo; August 1941: AMC; 14 July, 1942: Transport; sunk 25 August, 1942 N of Guadalcanal Island (07° 47′ S, 160° 13′ E) by US Marine Corps aircraft.

Aikoku Maru
Launched 1939 and completed 1940 for Osaka Shosen KK, Osaka; August 1941: AMC; 1943: Transport; sunk 17 February, 1944 at Truk by TF 58 aircraft.

Hokoku Maru
Launched August 1939 and completed 1940 for Osaka Shosen KK, Osaka; August 1941: AMC; sunk 11 November, 1942 550 nm SSW of the Cocos Islands (20° 00′ S, 93° 00′ E) by RIN minesweeper *Bengal* and Dutch tanker *Ondina* (6341 GRT, 1 × 4in LA).

Gokoku Maru
Launched and completed 1941 for Osaka Shosen KK, Osaka; August 1941: AMC; 1 October, 1943: Transport; sunk 10 October, 1944 NW of Hiradoshima, Kyushu (33° 31′ N, 129° 10′ E) by US submarine *Barb*.

18. Submarine Depot Ships

Name	Builder	Date	Displ	Length ft in	Beam ft in	Draught ft in	Machinery	SHP	Speed	Fuel	Radius	Armament	Comp
TOYOHASHI ex-*Flintshire*	London & Glasgow SB Co., Ltd.	1888	4055 S	344 0 pp	40 2	16 7	1 set VTE 1 shaft	400 nominal	12			2 × 120mm (4.7in) LA 6 × 47mm (3pdr) LA	

Toyohashi (1905)

GENERAL NOTES
Purchased merchant freighter.

CAREER
Launched 1888, completed 1889 as British SS *Flintshire* (Jenkins & Co., London); August 1894: purchased by IJN from Nippon Yusen Kaisha and commissioned as Torpedo Depot Ship *Toyohashi*; 1911: Submarine Depot Ship; 1922: deleted from Active List.

Name	Builder	Date	Displ	Length ft in	Beam ft in	Draught ft in	Machinery	SHP	Speed	Fuel	Radius	Armament	Comp
KARASAKI ex-*Ekaterinoslav*	Hawthorn Leslie & Co., Newcastle-on-Tyne	1896	9570 S	449 10 oa 419 0 pp	49 6	17 3	2 sets VTE 4 Hiyabara boilers 2 shafts	3200 ihp	12.6			2 × 80mm (3in) 40-cal LA 4 × 47mm (3pdr) LA 1 MG	

GENERAL NOTES
Captured passenger liner; clipper bow; 5267 GRT.

CAREER
Launched 1896 as SS *Ekaterinoslav*; to Russian Volunteer Fleet; captured 6 February 1904 off Pusan; December 1904: auxiliary vessel *Karasaki Maru*; 4 July 1905: commissioned as Torpedo Depot Ship *Karasaki*; August 1906: Submarine Repair Ship; 28 August, 1912: Coast Guard vessel; 1 April, 1920: Torpedo Depot Ship; 1 December, 1924: Submarine Depot Ship; 1939: hulked at Kure; 1940: *Haikau No. 9* scrapped 1946.

The submarine depot ship *Karasaki* was an English-built merchant ship of the Russian Volunteer Fleet, captured in 1904. She was stricken in 1939. (Shizuo Fukui.)

Name	Builder	Date	Displ	Length ft in	Beam ft in	Draught ft in	Machinery	SHP	Speed	Fuel	Radius	Armament	Comp
KOMAHASHI	Kure DY	1913–1924	1250 N 1125 S	210 0 pp	35 0	12 8	1 set VTE 2 Hiyabara boilers 1 shaft	1825 ihp	14	230 coal		2 × 80mm (3in) 40-cal LA 1 × 80mm etc. 40-cal HA	

General Notes
Three-island merchant freighter design, 1911 Programme. Rebuilt 1914–15 as Depot Ship, with after well-deck filled in; 1932: re-engined with two Ikegai Diesel engines; unknown date: 2 × 80mm HA guns replaced AA MG, DCs added.

Career
Launched 21 May, 1913; completed 20 January, 1914 as *Komashashi Maru*; 16 August 1914: Submarine Tender *Komahashi*; 1920: Torpedo Depot Ship; December 1924: Submarine Depot Ship; 1933: Survey Vessel; 20 July, 1942: Submarine Depot Ship (?); sunk 28 July 1945 in shallow water at Owase by aircraft of US TF 38; salvaged and scrapped 1947.

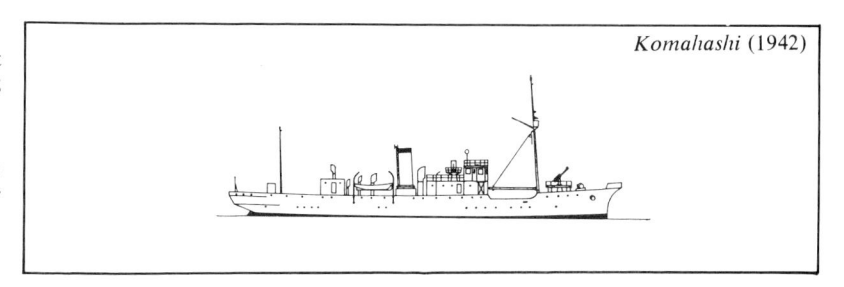

Komahashi (1942)

Name	Builder	Date	Displ	Length ft in	Beam ft in	Draught ft in	Machinery	SHP	Speed	Fuel	Radius	Armament	Comp
JINGEI CHOGEI (modified)	Mitsubishi, Nagasaki	1922–1923 1922–1924 1935–1936	8500 N 5160 S 8600 N 6600 S	405 2 wl 380 0 pp 405 2 wl 380 0 pp	53 0 56 6	22 8 21 6	2 sets Parsons GT 6 (*Chogei*) Kampon boilers 2 shafts	7500	18	2300		4 × 140mm (5.51in) 50-cal LA 2 × 80mm (3in) 40-cal HA 2 MGs 1 floatplane	399

General Notes
1920–28 Fleet Programme: first submarine depot ships to be designed and built for IJN, fitted out as submarine flotilla flagships.

Reconstruction and Re-armament
1935: bulges added to improve stability; 1941: 2 × 80mm HA guns replaced by 4 × 25mm AA, 26 × 7.7mm MGs and 2 × 47mm Yamaguchi 'short guns' (A/S howitzers); 1944: 25mm AA increased to 18 (6 × 3), DCs.

Careers
Jingei
Launched 4 May, 1923; completed 20 August, 1923; sunk 10 October, 1944 NNE of Okinawa (26° 39′ N, 127° 52′ E) by aircraft from US TF 38.

Chogei
Launched 24 March, 1924; completed 2 August, 1924; damaged 30 July, 1945 by direct hit on bridge in US TF 38 air attack on Ine, near Maizuru; repaired with new bridge (as in drawing) and employed by Repatriation Service from August 1945 until deleted from Active List 15 August, 1946; broken up by Hitachi SB Co., Mukajima 1946–7.

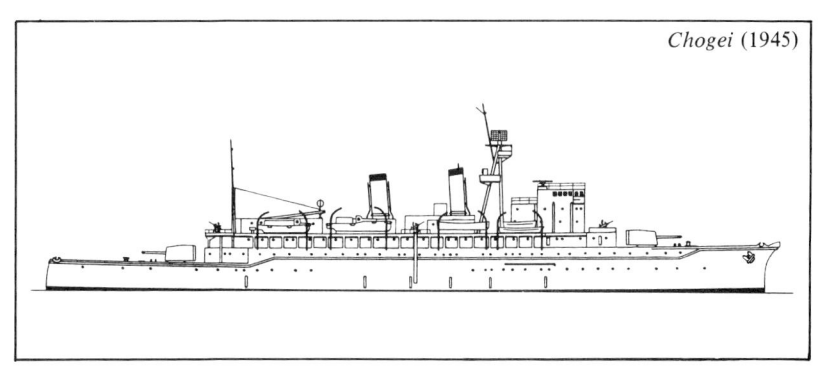

Chogei (1945)

Chogei was designed to operate with the fleet, controlling her submarine flotilla on operations, as well as maintaining the boats in harbour. No catapult was provided for the Kawanishi "Alf" floatplane. (Tappman Collection.)

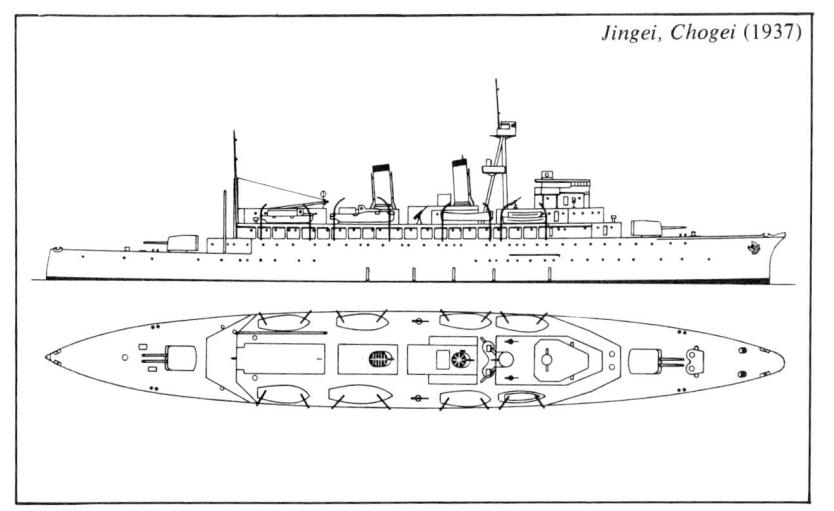

Jingei, Chogei (1937)

SUBMARINE DEPOT SHIPS 237

Name	Builder	Date	Displ	Length ft in	Beam ft in	Draught ft in	Machinery	SHP	Speed	Fuel	Radius	Armament	Comp
TAIGEI (modified)	Yokosuka DY	1933–1934 S 1936–1937 S	10000 10500	692 8 wl 647 4 pp	59 3	17 6	4 Diesel engines 2 shafts	14000	20	3570	8000 @ 14	4 × 127mm (5in) 40-cal DP 12 × 13.2mm AA 2 catapults 3 floatplanes	413+ 414

GENERAL NOTES
1933 Supplementary Estimates: designed as a sea-going submarine flotilla flagship, carrying aircraft for scouting purposes. Built with very high freeboard and shallow draught, resulting in poor sea-keeping; extensively welded construction which proved to be defective.

RECONSTRUCTION
1936–7: modified to strengthen hull and bulges added to improve stability.

CAREER
Launched 16 November, 1933, completed 31 March, 1934; saw only limited service from 1941; 1942: converted as aircraft carrier *Ryuho* (see p. 50).

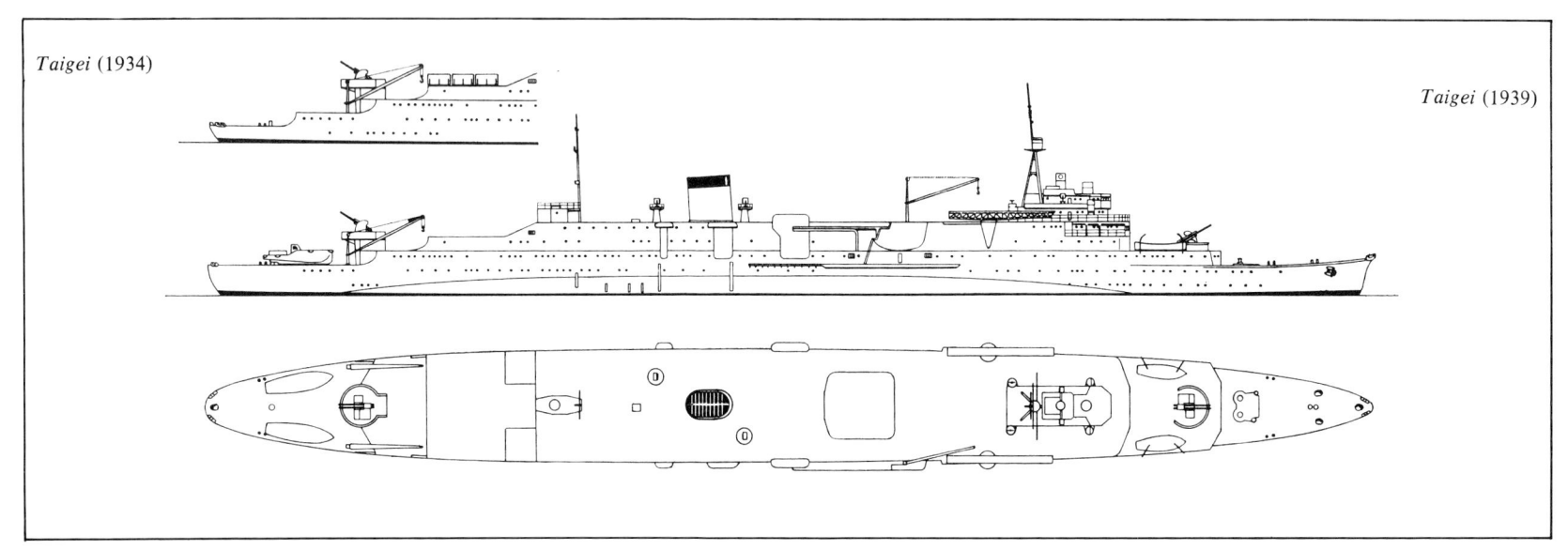

Taigei (1934)

Taigei (1939)

Name	Builder	Date	Displ	Length ft in	Beam ft in	Draught ft in	Machinery	SHP	Speed	Fuel	Radius	Armament	Comp
TSURIGISAKI **TAKASAKI**	Yokosuka DY	1935–1939 1935–?	13000 N 9500 S	661 5 wl 606 11 pp	59 8	22 1	8 Diesel engines 2 shafts	56000	29			4 × 127mm (5in) 40-cal DP 12 × 13.2mm AA 2 catapults 3 floatplanes	

GENERAL NOTES
Tsurugisaki Class
2nd 1934 Supplementary Programme: new design, incorporating the experience gained with the unsuccessful *Taigei* and capable of conversion to light carriers, in accordance with the mobilisation plan.

CAREERS
Tsurugisaki
Launched 20 July, 1935; completed 15 January, 1939; 1941: converted as aircraft carrier *Shoho* (see p. 49).

Takasaki
Launched 19 June, 1936; conversion to aircraft carrier *Zuiho* commenced before completion as depot ship (see p. 49).

'*Sensui-Bokan Nos. 865 & 866*'
5th 1942 Supplementary Programme: improved *Tsurigisaki*-Class design; not proceeded with and no further details known.

'*Sensui-Bokan Nos. 5034–36*'
Amended 5th 1942 Supplementary Programme: new design, cancelled 1943. No further details known.

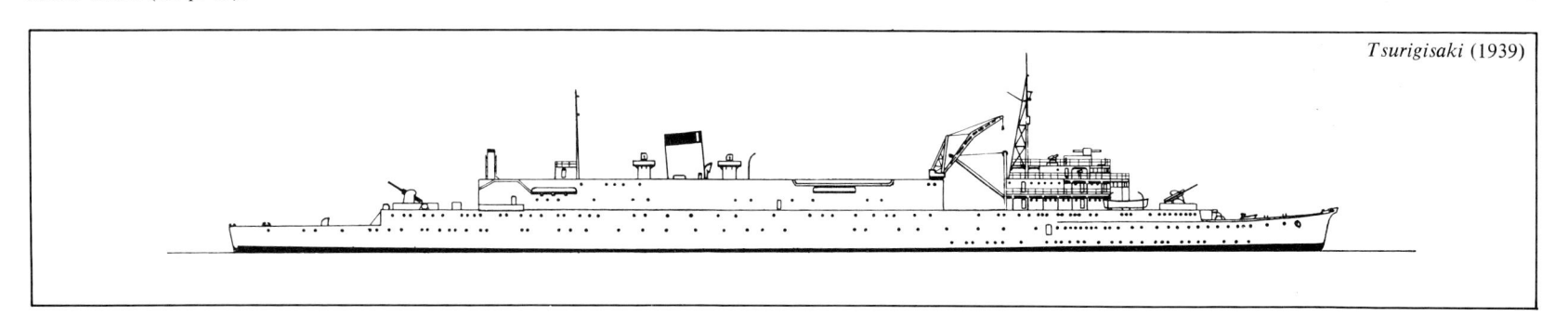

Tsurigisaki (1939)

238 SUBMARINE DEPOT SHIPS

Auxiliary Submarine Depot Ships

Name	Builder	Date	Displ GRT	Length ft in	Beam ft in	Draught ft in	Machinery	SHP	Speed	Fuel	Radius	Armament	Comp
HEIAN MARU	Osaka Iron Works Ltd.	1930	11616	511 pp 8	66 0	30 0	2 8-cyl 4-stroke Burmeister & Wain Diesel engines 2 shafts	7600 approx				2 × 120mm (4.7in) LA MGs	
MANJU MARU ex-Santos Maru	unknown	1925	7266	unknown			Diesel engines	unknown				unknown	
NAGOYA MARU	Mitsubishi, Nagoya	1932	6072	406 pp 9	55 6		1 set GT hydraulically coupled to 1 shaft	unknown				unknown	
RIO DE JANEIRO MARU	Mitsubishi, Nagoya	1930	9627	461 pp 3	62 0	26 0	2 6-cyl 2-stroke Diesel engines	6500 approx					
TSUKUSHI MARU	Mitsubishi, Nagoya	1941	8135	unknown			Diesel engines						
YASUKUNI MARU	Mitsubishi, Nagoya	1930	11933	507 pp 6	64 0		2 8-cyl 4-stroke Krupp Germania Diesel engines with reduction gearing 2 shafts					2 × 80mm 40-cal HA MGs	

GENERAL NOTES
The following merchant ships were requisitioned as Submarine Depot Ships.

CAREERS

Heian Maru
Built 1930 as passenger liner for Nippon Yusen KK; 1941: requisitioned as Submarine Depot Ship, 1st Submarine Squadron; sunk 17 February, 1944 at Truk by aircraft from US TF 58.

Manju Maru
Built 1925 as passenger liner *Santos Maru* (7266 GRT); 1941: requisitioned as Submarine Depot Ship, 2nd Submarine Squadron to 20 August, 1942: Kure Submarine Squadron to 25 March 1943; renamed *Manju Maru*, miscellaneous Auxiliary; sunk 29 November, 1943 in the Luzon Strait (20° 14′ N, 121° 40′ E) by US submarine *Atule*.

Hie Maru
Built 1930 as passenger liner for Nippon Yusen KK (11621 GRT); 1942: requisitioned as Submarine Depot Ship, 8th Submarine Squadron from 10 March, 1942 until sunk 17 November, 1943 300 nm NNW of New Ireland (01° 45′ N, 148° 35′ E) by US submarine *Drum*.

Nagoya Maru
Built 1932 as passenger liner for Nanyo Kaiun KK (6072 GRT); 1941: requisitioned as Submarine Depot Ship, 4th Submarine Squadron to 10 March, 1942: converted to Aircraft Transport; sunk 1 January, 1944 100 nm SW of Hachijojima (32° 15′ N, 138° 02′ E) by US submarine *Herring*.

Rio de Janeiro Maru
Built 1930 as passenger liner for Osaka Shosen KK (9627 GRT); 1940: requisitioned as Submarine Depot Ship, 5th Submarine Squadron to 10 July 1942; Attached Force, South-West Area Fleet to 15 September, 1943: employed as Transport; sunk 17 February, 1944 at Truk by aircraft from US TF 58.

Tsukushi Maru
Built 1941 (8135 GRT); 1943: requisitioned as Submarine Depot Ship; 1 April, 1943: to 11th Submarine Squadron until 20 July 1944: to 6th Fleet Base Force until 20 January, 1945: Transport, damaged 4 July, 1945 by mine SE of Shimonoseki (33° 50′ N, 131° 19′ E); captured August 1945, repaired and employed by Repatriation Service until 1947, returned to original owner; 1952: sold to Pan-Islamic Steam Ship Co.

Yasukuni Maru
Built 1930 as passenger liner for Nippon Yusen KK (11933 GRT); requisitioned 1940 as Submarine Depot Ship, 1st Submarine Squadron to 15 December 1941: 3rd Submarine Squadron to 15 September 1943: Attached Force, Sixth Fleet; sunk 31 January 1944 NW of Truk (09° 12′ N, 147° 13′ E) by US submarine *Trigger*.

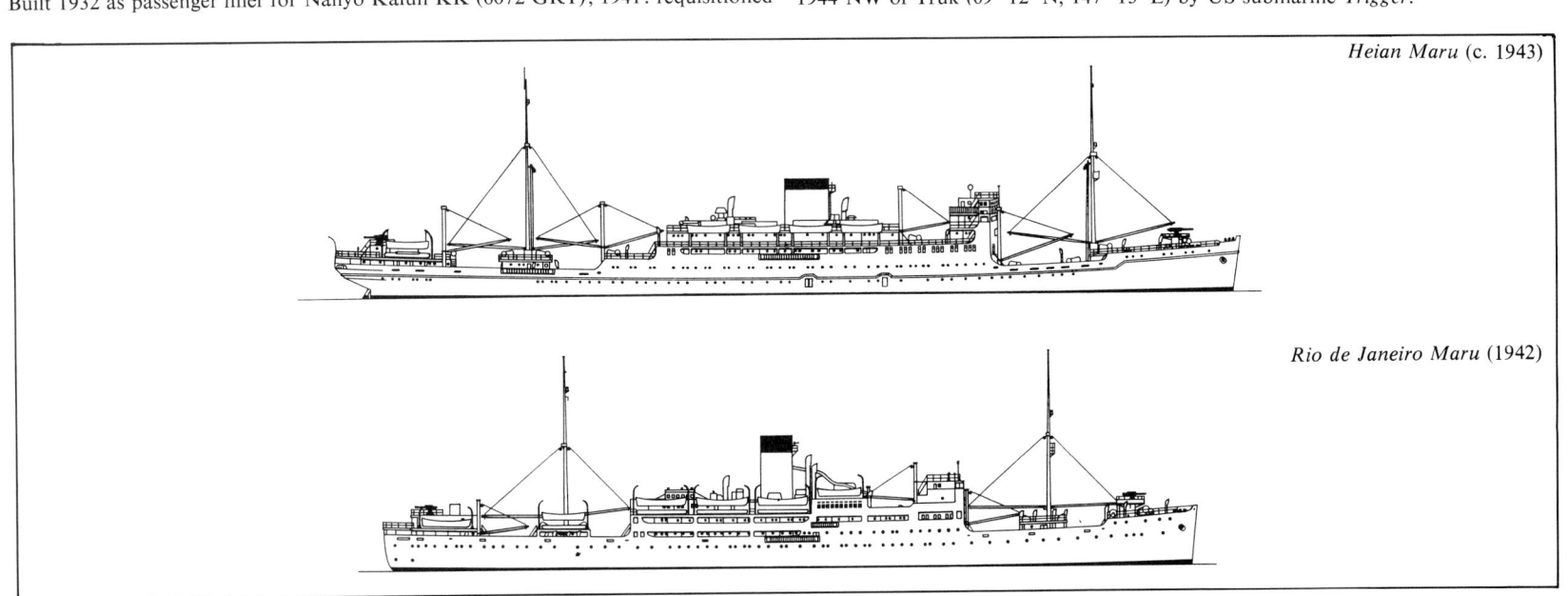

Heian Maru (c. 1943)

Rio de Janeiro Maru (1942)

SUBMARINE DEPOT SHIPS

Yasukuni Maru (1942)

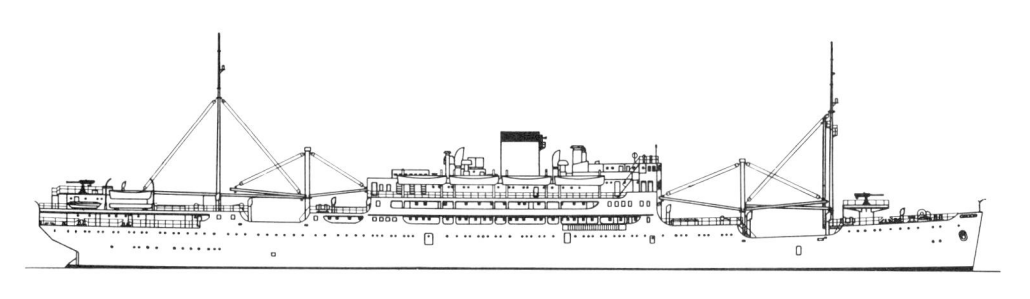

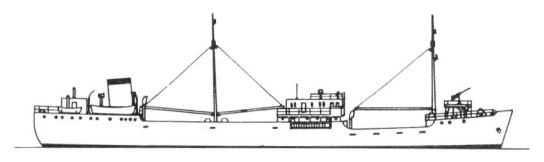

Teishu Maru (1942)

Torpedo Recovery Vessels

Name	Builder	Date	Displ	Length ft in	Beam ft in	Draught ft in	Machinery	SHP	Speed	Fuel	Radius	Armament	Comp
18-metre Torpedo Recovery Vessels	Yokohama Yacht Co., Chosi	1944	20 S	59 oa 1	14 6	2 7	2 Petrol engines 2 shafts	1840	44	?	170 @ 42	nil	6
SAGYOTEI Type	Kure DY and others	1945	9.7 S	49 oa 3	10 10	1 9	1 Petrol engine 1 shaft	80	9 approx	?	50 @ 9	nil	

GENERAL NOTES

59-foot Torpedo Recovery Vessels
Designed as torpedo recovery and *Kaiten* training craft; based on Italian *MAS* trials craft (Type *H1* – see p. 158). Wooden construction, two-step hull. Three completed, fates unknown.

'Sagyotei' Type
Training, torpedo recovery and tugs for *Kaiten*. Work boats designed without sheer or camber but of very robust construction. Equipped to tow 2 *Kaiten* alongside. 20 'Sagyotei' were built at Kure and between 50 and 80 others were on order, under construction and, possibly, completed by August 1945, in various naval and private yards: No details of fates known.

19. Repair Ships

Name	Builder	Date	Displ	Length ft in	Beam ft in	Draught ft in	Machinery	SHP	Speed	Fuel	Radius	Armament	Comp
KANTO ex-*Manchuria*	Burmeister & Wain, Copenhagen	1897–1900	10000 S	410 0 wl	49 4		1 set VTE 4 boilers 1 shaft	2500 ihp	10			2 × 120mm (4.7in) LA	
AKASHI	Sasebo DY	1937–1939	10500 N 9000 S 10630 N 9600 S	507 5 wl 479 0 pp	67 3	18 4	2 Diesel engines 2 shafts	10000	19.2			2 × 127mm (5in) 40-cal DP and smaller 3 heavy cranes	650
Job Nos. 840, 841, 5416, and 5417	Not built			Otherwise as *Akashi*									

Akashi (1940)

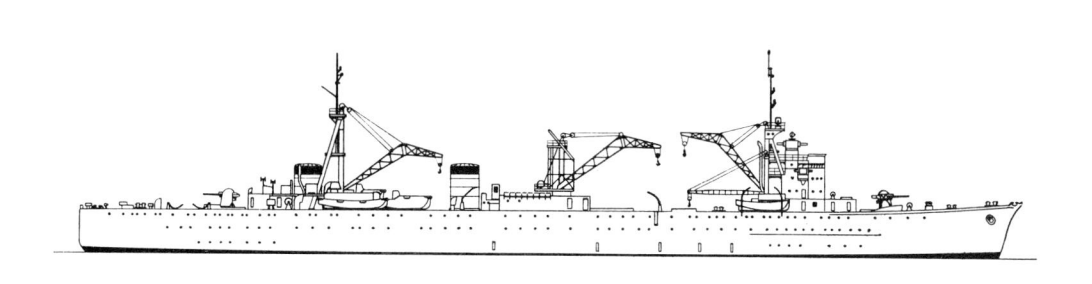

Kanto

GENERAL NOTES

ex-Russian SS *Manchuria* (6193 GRT) of the Russia-East Asia Steam Shipping Company.

CAREER

Launched 1900, completed 1903 as *Manchuria*; captured 9 February, 1904 SE of Port Arthur by cruiser *Takasago*; 14 February 1904: entered service as auxiliary cruiser repair ship *Kanto Maru*; 1906: Repair Ship *Kanto*; ran aground 12 December, 1924 and abandoned in storm off Odawara (30 nm SW of Yokosuka), subsequently broke up.
1937 Programme: Repair Ship, official designation 'Kosakukan'.

Akashi

CAREER

Launched 29 June, 1938; completed July 1939; sunk 30 March 1944 at Palau (07° 30′ N, 134° 30′ E) by aircraft from US TF 38

Akashi-type

Job Nos. 840 & 841: 1942 War Programme, not ordered.

Job Nos. 5416 & 5417: 1942M War Programme, order cancelled 1943.
Ex-Chinese river gunboat: 600t, 1 × 120mm (4.7in) LA, 1 × 100mm (3.9in) LA, 1 × 76.2mm (3in) HA, 2 × 20mm AA.

Below:
The Repair Ship *Akashi* resembled contemporary British submarine depot ships, but was diesel-engined, with two low exhaust stacks, and was flush-decked, with a much lower profile. (Shizuo Fukui.)

REPAIR SHIPS 241

Name	Builder	Date	Displ	Length ft in	Beam ft in	Draught ft in	Machinery	SHP	Speed	Fuel	Radius	Armament	Comp
HITONOSE ex-*Ming Sen*	Kiangnan Dock Co., Shanghai	1930–1932	600 N 460 S	210 0 pp	27 0	6 6	2 sets VTE 2 shafts	3600 ihp	18	?	?	several MGs	115 approx
HAYASE ex-*Chin Chiang*	unknown	unknown	800 S	unknown			unknown	unknown	12	?	?	several MGs	

Hitonose
CAREER
Launched 1931, completed 1932 as Chinese *Ming Sen*; sunk 3 September, 1937 in shallow water at Hankow by Japanese aircraft; captured 16 November, 1938 by Japanese, salvaged between May and June 1939; 27 December, 1939: Repair Ship *Hitonose*; sunk 21 December, 1944 in Shih harbour on Yangtse River through collision with freighter *Kosho* (3378 GRT); raised but later mined.

Hayase
Ex-Chinese tug.

CAREER
Built as Chinese *Chin Chiang*; 1937: captured by Japanese; 25 October, 1938: Repair Ship *Hayase*; damaged 20 September, 1943 at Ch'iu-chiang, Yangtse River, by Chinese aircraft; subsequent fate unknown.

Name	Builder	Date	Displ	Length ft in	Beam ft in	Draught ft in	Machinery	SHP	Speed	Fuel	Radius	Armament	Comp
SEISHU	Ishikawajima, Tokyo	1927	2035 S (1300 GRT)	200 2 pp	50 0	9 2	1 set VTE 2 boilers 1 shaft	1400 ihp	9–10.2		1500 @ 7	1 × 80mm (3in) 40-cal LA 1 150-tonne (147t) crane 1 20-tonne (19.7t) crane	

GENERAL NOTES
Specialised Crane Ship and transport vessel for handling the 305mm (12in) turrets of old battleships disarmed in accordance with the 1922 Washington Treaty. After removal and overhaul, the turrets were transported to various localities for use in a coast-defence role. Official designation of the crane ship was 'Kijukisen'.

CAREER
Launched 1926; completed 1927; captured August 1945 at Singapore; July 1946: sank in typhoon in Hong Kong area.

Seishu (1939)

The 150-tonne crane, which was the main *raison d'être* of *Seishu*, seen in the stowed position, as the "Craneship and Special Transport" lies at anchor at Shanghai in late 1937. By this time, *Seishu* was being employed as a salvage vessel. (Tappman Collection.)

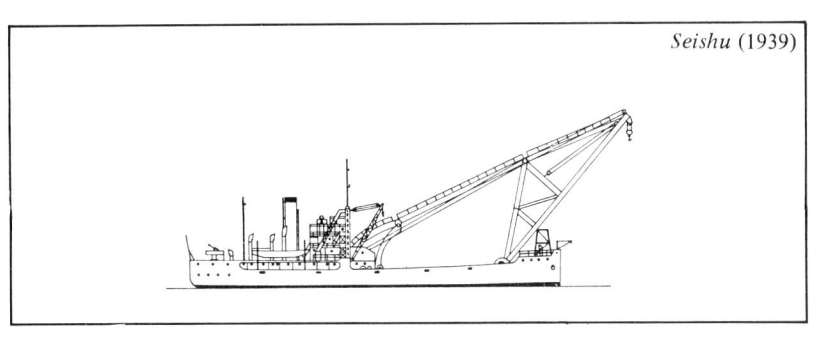

20. Ammunition Ships

Name	Builder	Date	Displ	Length ft in	Beam ft in	Draught ft in	Machinery	SHP	Speed	Fuel	Radius	Armament	Comp
KASHINO	Mitsubishi, Nagasaki	1939–1940	10360 S	451 1 oa / 442 11 wl / 426 6 pp	61 8	21 11	2 sets GT / 2 Lamont boilers and / 2 Kampon boilers (see text) / 2 shafts	4500	14	?	?	2 × 120mm (4.7in)45-cal HA / 4 × 13.2mm AA / 5800 (5700t) tonnes cargo	

GENERAL NOTES
1937 Programme. Special Service Transport and Ammunition Ship designed to support the construction of the *Yamato*-class battleships, carrying the Type '94' 457mm (18.1in) guns, turrets and ordnance material to the yards where the ships were being built from the Naval Ordnance Factory, Kure. The main propulsion machinery was an experimental installation of BBC reaction turbines and Lamont High-Pressure superheated steam boilers. The deep double bottoms and the sides of the ship were distorted by a grounding accident which, with other accidents, delayed her entry into service, thus inconveniencing the battleship building programme.

CAREER
Launched 26 January, 1940; completed 10 July, 1940; torpedoed 4 September, 1942 and sunk in the Formosa Straits (25° 45' N, 121° 41' E) by US submarine *Growler*.

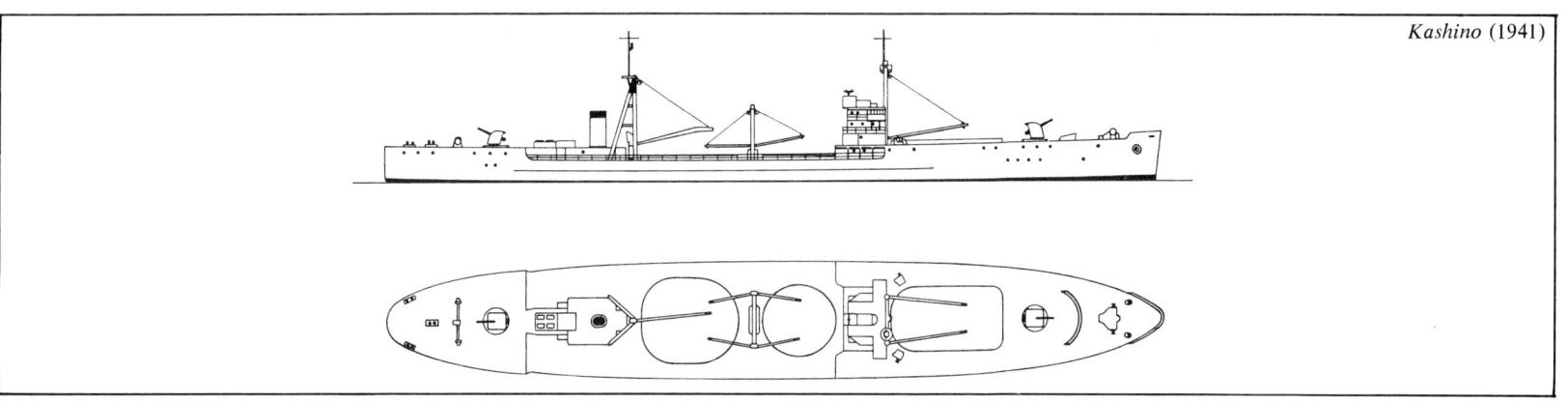

Kashino (1941)

Name	Builder	Date	Displ	Length ft in	Beam ft in	Draught ft in	Machinery	SHP	Speed	Fuel	Radius	Armament	Comp
150-ton Torpedo Transports	Ujina, Hiroshima / Sakurajima, Osaka	1936–	156 S	80 5 pp	– –	5 3	1 Diesel engine / 1 shaft	200	10	?		nil	

GENERAL NOTES
150-ton Torpedo Transports
Designed to mercantile standards with engine aft and one cargo hatch; early units built by Ujina had 145 hp engines. Full details of class not known.

No. 3161: built 1937, Ujina; at Kure 1947.
No. 3162: built 1937, Ujina; nothing further known.
No. 3243: built 1938, Sakurajima; nothing further known.
No. 4980: possibly completed 1947; at Kure 1947.

Name	Builder	Date	Displ	Length ft in	Beam ft in	Draught ft in	Machinery	SHP	Speed	Fuel	Radius	Armament	Comp
SOYA ex-*ChiryoMaru*	Kawaminami, Koyakijima	1936–1938	3800 S (2224 GRT)	257 2 pp	42 0	20 3	1 set VTE / 2 boilers / 1 shaft	1597 ihp	12.4	?	?	1 × 80mm (3in) 40-cal HA / 2 × 25mm AA / 10 DCs	

GENERAL NOTES
Freighter (2224 GRT) ordered by the Soviet Union; bought while on the stocks and requisitioned by the IJN in 1939. Rebuilt at Yokosuka Navy Dockyard as an ammunition ship with an ice-breaking bow, for service in northern waters; also equipped as a survey vessel. Official designation 'Kyuheikan'. Sister ships: *Tenryo Maru*, *Minryo Maru*.

Soya (1945)

AMMUNITION SHIPS   243

CAREER
Launched 16 February, 1938; completed 10 July, 1938 as *Chiryo Maru*; November 1939: requisitioned for service as Ammunition Transport – conversion completed 10 June, 1940; captured August 1945 and employed by Repatriation Service; 1949: MSDF as lighthouse tender; 1956–8: rebuilt as trials ship – 4365t, 4800 SHP Diesel engines, 4 helicopters.

21. Transports

Name	Builder	Date	Displ	Length ft in	Beam ft in	Draught ft in	Machinery	SHP	Speed	Fuel	Radius	Armament	Comp
ANEGAWA ex-*Angara*	Clydebank, Glasgow	1898	11700 GRT	487 0 pp	58 2	– –	2 sets VTE 30 Belleville water-tube boilers 2 shafts	16500 ihp	20			4 × 120mm (4.7in) LA	
MATSUE ex-*Sungari* ex-*May*	J. Scott, Kinghorn	1898	2550 S	237 5 pp	34 1	– –	1 set VTE 2 boilers 1 shaft	1500 ihp	13			2 × 80mm (3in) 40-cal LA	
MANSHU ex-*Manchuria*	Stabilimento Tecnico, Trieste	1901	3916 GRT	349 5 oa 337 7 pp	43 0	– –	2 sets VTE 5 boilers 2 shafts	5000 ihp	17.6			2 × 80mm etc. LA 2 × 47mm (3pdr) LA	
TAKASAKI ex-*Roseley*	Duncan, Port Glasgow	1902	5181 S	375 0 pp	47 11	15 9	1 set VTE 2 boilers 1 shaft	1850 ihp	10			2 × 80mm etc. LA	
KOSHU ex-*Michael Jebsen*	Howaldswerke, Kiel	1905	2080 S	252 6 pp	36 0	12 2	1 set VTE 1 shaft	800 ihp	10.3			2 × 80mm etc. LA	

GENERAL NOTES
From 31 March 1920, all naval Transports had the suffix 'Maru' added to their names.

CAREERS

Anegawa
Built as a three-funnelled, clipper-bow passenger liner.
Launched August 1898 as Russian *Angara* (Russian Volunteer Fleet); March 1904: in service at Port Arthur as Hospital Ship; sunk 19 October, 1904 in the west harbour of Port Arthur by Japanese Army howitzer fire; 12 May 1905: raised after capture, repaired and commissioned as Transport and Torpedo Depot Ship *Anegawa*; 1911: returned to Russia and renamed *Moskva*; November 1916: Torpedo Boat Depot Ship *Pechenga*; October 1923: at Vladivostock with unserviceable engines and boilers – subsequent fate unknown.

Matsue
Launched June 1898 as British SS *May* (2981 GRT); 1898: Russian *Sungari* (Chinese Eastern Railway Company, Vladivostock); sunk 9 February, 1904 off Inchon, Korea; raised 6 August, 1905 by Japanese, repaired and commissioned as Gunboat *Matsue*; 1918: Transport and Survey Vessel; Deleted from Active List 1929.

Manshu
Launched April 1901 as Russian SS *Manchuria* (Chinese Eastern Railway Company, Vladivostock); seized 10 February, 1904 at Nagasaki; 17 February 1905: commissioned as Armed Merchant Cruiser *Manshu*; March 1906: Transport, Despatch Vessel and Survey Vessel; 28 August, 1912: 2nd Class Coastal-Defence Vessel; deleted from Active List 1 April, 1932: target hulk *Haikau No. 5*; scrapped 1933.

Takasaki
Launched April 1902 as British SS *Roseley* (WR Rea, Belfast – 4370 GRT); 11 January 1905: taken as prize off Okinoshima; January 1905: commissioned as Armed Merchant Cruiser *Takasaki*; 1 September, 1905: Transport; 1928: laid up at Kure; deleted from Active List 1 April 1932; 27 February, 1933: to Army as hulk, at Ujina; 1944: target ship for suicide motor boat training; December 1944: sank at Ujina following suicide boat explosion.

Koshu
Built 1904 as German SS *Michael Jebsen* (Michael Jebsen, Apenrade – 1521 GRT); scuttled 28 October, 1914 as blockship at Tsingtao with *Ellen Rickmers* and *Dorendart*; 1915: raised by Japanese, repaired and commissioned as Transport *Koshu*; April 1922: Ice-breaker and Survey Vessel; deleted from Active List 1939.

Name	Builder	Date	Displ	Length ft in	Beam ft in	Draught ft in	Machinery	SHP	Speed	Fuel	Radius	Armament	Comp
ROZAN ex-*Ellen Rickmers*	RC Rickmers, Geestemünde	1906	unknown	367 0 pp	47 7	– –	1 set VTE 1 shaft	1600 ihp	11			2 × 80mm etc. LA	
SEITO ex-*Durendart*	Flensburger Schiffsbau, Flensburg	1906	7542 S	341 2 pp	49 2	– –	1 set VTE 1 shaft	1525 ihp	10			2 × 80mm etc. LA	
TAKECHI Nos. 1–6	Mitsui, Sone	1944– 1945	1200 S	196 10 pp	40 0	16 5	1 Diesel engine 1 shaft	800	8.5			nil	

Rozan
Built 1906 as German *Ellen Rickmers* (Rickmers Reederei, Bremerhaven – 4117 GRT); scuttled 14 October, 1914 as blockship at Tsingtao; 1915: raised by Japanese, repaired and commissioned as Transport *Rozan*; wrecked 15 June, 1922 off Shiriya-saki (Hokkaido).

Seito
Built 1906 as German SS *Durendart* (Roland Lines Ltd., Bremen – 3844 GRT); scuttled 14 October, 1914 as blockship at Tsingtao; 1915: raised by Japanese, repaired and to Merchant Marine as SS *Tsingtao Maru*; 1917: requisitioned and commissioned as Transport *Seito*; 1 April 1939: Target hulk *Hakau No. 8*; destroyed 30 April 1936 in target practice.

Takechi Nos. 1–6
GENERAL NOTES
Coaster-type Transports, concrete construction: 840 GRT, 110 dwt; designed jointly by Kure Navy Dockyard and the Naval Transport Division, Osaka.

CAREERS
Takechi No. 1.
Built 1944; 1945: at Kure, unserviceable.
Takechi No. 2.
Built 1944; 1945: at Osaka
Takechi No. 3.
Built 1945, fate unknown.
Takechi No. 4.
Launched 1945; August 1945: incomplete, hull aground at Sanko SB Co., Kobe.
Takechi No. 5.
Uncompleted due to lack of material.

Many other vessels were requisitioned for use as Transports, during both World Wars. Losses were heavy, due initially to the depredations of US submarines and the inability of the Imperial Japanese Navy to provide efficient A/S escorts, and latterly to the wide-ranging US carrier aircraft. As the Second World War progressed, many large fast ships had to be taken from other auxiliary duties and re-categorised as Transports: in the attack on Truk in mid-February 1944, aircraft from Task Force 58 destroyed six such re-categorised vessels, totalling 54600t. No fewer than 92 out of 142 ships commissioned as Transports between 1941 and 1945 were sunk while serving as such.

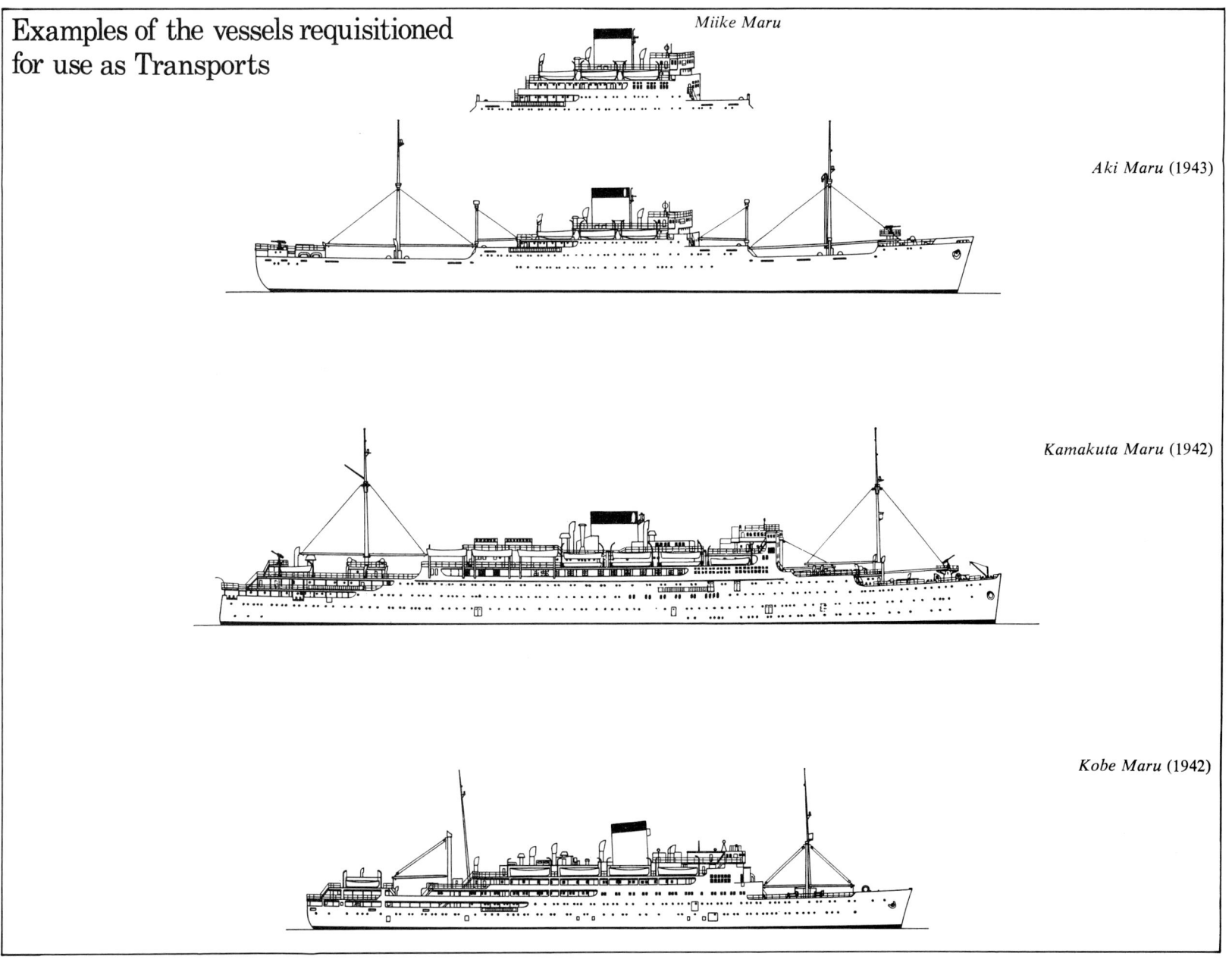

Examples of the vessels requisitioned for use as Transports

Miike Maru

Aki Maru (1943)

Kamakuta Maru (1942)

Kobe Maru (1942)

TRANSPORTS 245

Canberra Maru (1942)

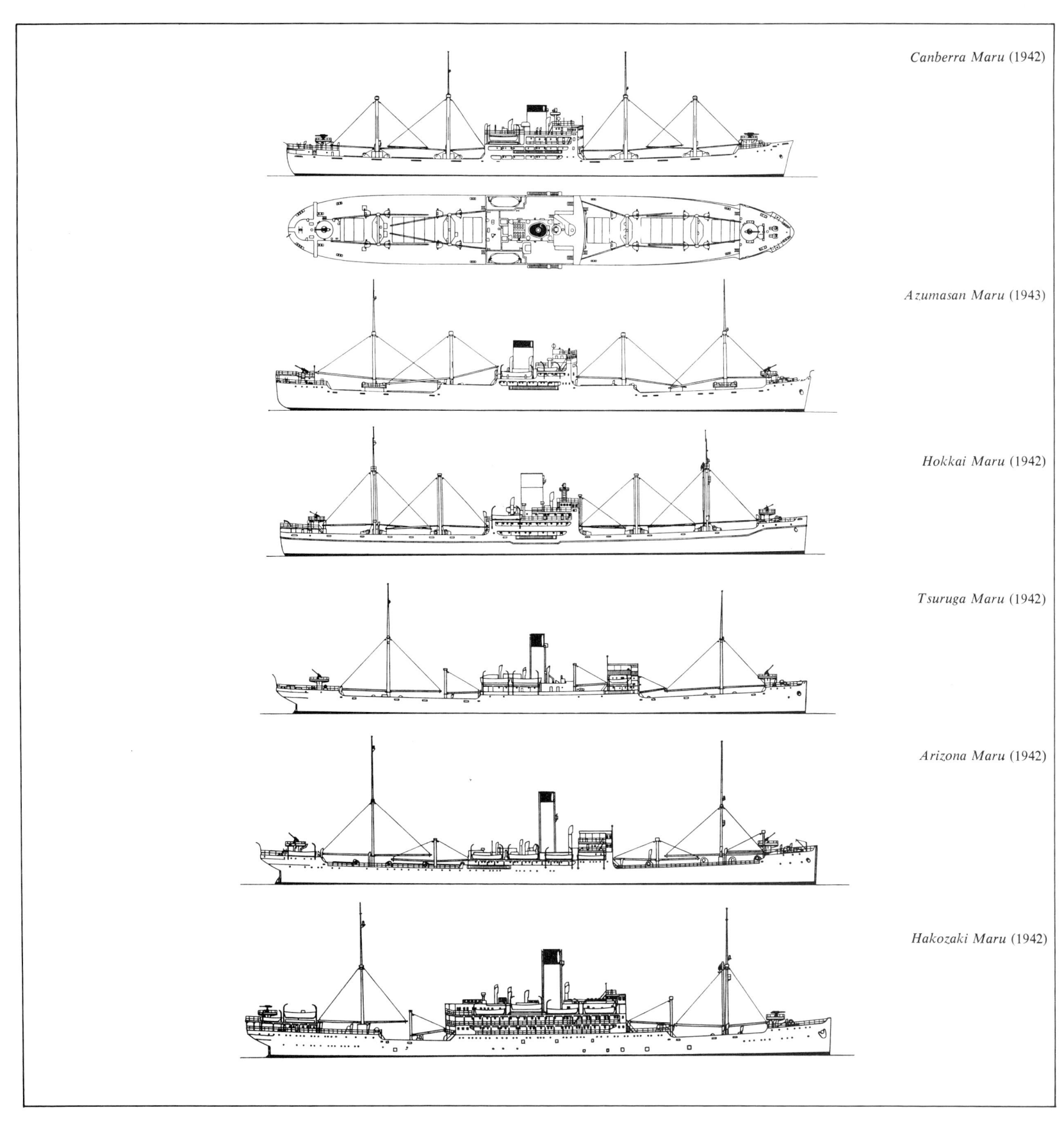

Azumasan Maru (1943)

Hokkai Maru (1942)

Tsuruga Maru (1942)

Arizona Maru (1942)

Hakozaki Maru (1942)

246 TRANSPORTS

22. Supply Ships and Colliers

Name	Builder	Date	Displ	Length ft in	Beam ft in	Draught ft in	Machinery	SHP	Speed	Fuel	Radius	Armament	Comp
MAMIYA	Kawasaki, Kobe	1920–1923	17500 N 15820 S	475 0 pp	61 0	27 8	2 sets VTE 8 Kampon boilers 2 shafts	10000 ihp	14	3414 coal 2134 oil	?	2 × 140mm (5.51in) 50-cal LA 2 × 80mm (actual 3in) 40-cal HA	284
KURASAKI ex-*Oha Maru*	Harima SB, Aioi	1927–1928	2371 N	220 2 pp	34 0	14 3	1 set VTE 1 shaft	1000 ihp	9	?	?	1 × 80mm etc. 40-cal HA	
NOZAKI ex-*Nankai*	Mitsubishi, Shimonoseki	1939–1941	660 N 640 S	160 10 wl 158 8 pp	26 11	9 5	2 Diesel engines 2 shafts	1200	13	?	?	1 × 80mm etc. 40-cal HA	
KINEZAKI Class and *Job Nos. 5401–7*	Sakurajima, Osaka	1940–1942	950 N 920 S	194 9 wl 190 3 pp	30 10	10 2	2 Diesel engines 2 shafts	1600	15	?	?	1 × 80mm etc. 40-cal HA 3 × 13.2mm AA 84.5 tonnes coal 58 tonnes water	
IRAKO Class	Kawasaki, Kobe	1940–1941	11100 N 9570 S	476 0 wl 467 6 pp	62 4	19 10	2 sets GT 6 Kampon boilers 2 shafts	8300	17.5	?	?	4 × 127mm (5in) 40-cal DP 13 × 25mm AA DCs	
KUSUMI			9719 S										

GENERAL NOTES
Mamiya
1920–8 Programme: Supply Ship with refrigerated store-rooms. Provisions carried for 16000 men for 3 weeks and stalls for 50 head of cattle. Pole mainmast replaced by tripod after completion.

CAREER
Launched 26 October, 1923; completed 15 July, 1924; sunk 20 December, 1944 250 nm E of Hainan (17° 48′ N, 114° 09′ E) by US submarine *Sealion*.

GENERAL NOTES
Kurasaki
Requisitioned merchant refrigerator ship.

CAREER
Launched 1927, completed March 1928 as *Oha Maru* (989 GRT) for Kita Kabofuto SKK; May 1944: requisitioned as Naval Supply Ship *Kurasaki*; sunk 14 November, 1944 NNW of Cape Bolinao, Luzon (17° 40′ N, 118° 00′ E) by US submarine *Raton*.

GENERAL NOTES
Nozaki
4th 1939 Supplementary Programme: Refrigerated Supply Ship.

CAREER
Launched 22 July, 1940; completed 18 March, 1941; as *Nankai*; 1 April 1942: renamed *Nozaki*; sunk 28 December, 1944 off Cape Varella (12° 39′ N, 109° 30′ E) by US submarine *Dace*

GENERAL NOTES
Kinezaki class
4th 1939 Supplementary Programme and 1940 Supplementary Programme: Medium-size Refrigerated Supply Ships.

CAREERS
Kinezaki
Launched 27 June 1940, completed 30 September 1940 as *Nanshin*; April 1942: renamed *Kinezaki*; sunk 1 March, 1945 in Kiji Bay, Amami O (28° 10′ N, 129° 05′ E) by aircraft from US TF 58.
Hayasaki
Launched 12 May 1942, completed 31 August, 1942; August 1945: captured at Singapore and employed by Repatriation Service until laid up at Sasebo in 1947; 3 October 1947: delivered to USSR at Nakhodka.
Shirasaki
Launched 5 November, 1942, completed 31 December, 1942; captured August 1945 and employed by Repatriation Service until laid up at Sasebo in 1947; 3 October 1947: delivered to China at Tsingtao – renamed *Wu Ling*.
Arasaki
Launched 27 February 1943, completed 29 May, 1943; captured August 1945 and employed by Repatriation Service until laid up at Sasebo in 1947; 1949: MDSF as training ship *Kaiyo Maru*.
Nos. 5401–5407 ordered under 5th 1942 Supplementary Programme but not commenced.

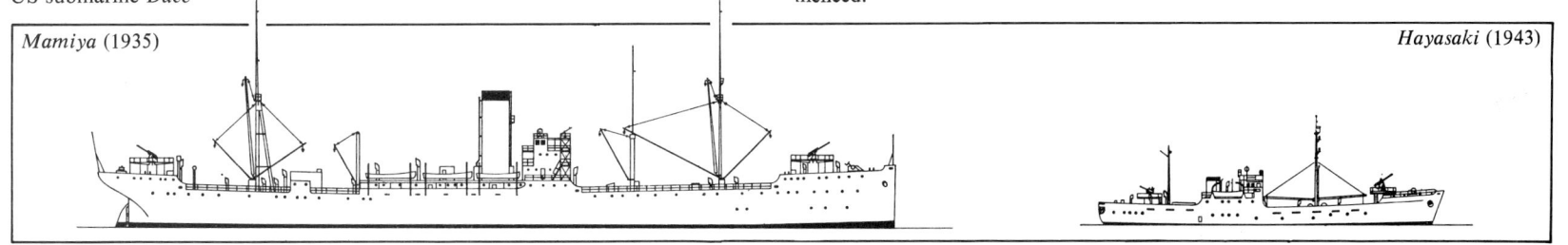

Mamiya (1935)

Hayasaki (1943)

SUPPLY SHIPS AND COLLIERS 247

GENERAL NOTES
Irako class
3rd 1937 Supplementary Programme: Large Fleet Refrigerated Supply Ship.

CAREERS
Launched 14 February, 1941, completed 5 December, 1941; beached 24 September, 1944 in Coron Bay, Calamian Island (11° 59′ N, 120° 02′ E) after suffering severe damage in air attack by aircraft from US TF 38; total loss.

Job No. 8450
Provided for in the 5th 1942 Supplementary Programme but not commenced.
Kusumi
Provided for in the Modified 5th 1942 Supplementary Programme but not commenced.
Nos. 5409 & 5410
Modified 5th 1942 Supplementary Programme: fast Refrigerator Ships, 5300ts standard displacement. No further details known, not commenced.

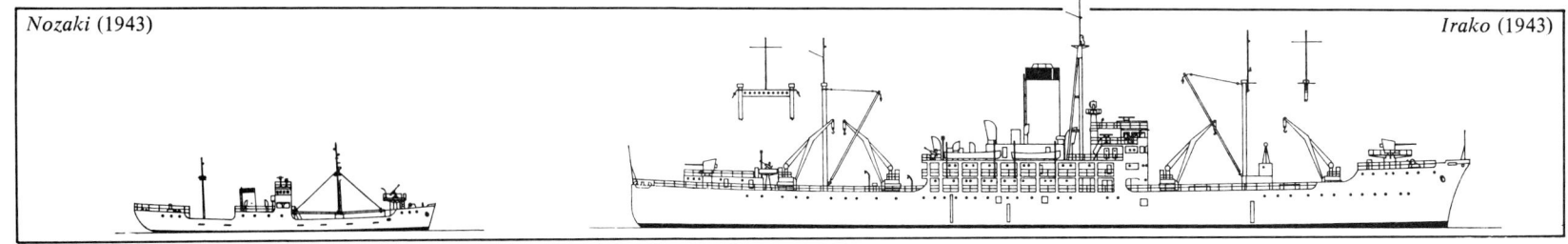

Nozaki (1943)

Irako (1943)

Name	Builder	Date	Displ	Length ft in	Beam ft in	Draught ft in	Machinery	SHP	Speed	Fuel	Radius	Armament	Comp
MUROTO Class	Mitsubishi, Kobe	1918–1919	8750 N 8215 S	345 0 wl	50 0	23 11	2 sets VTE 2 shafts	2600 ihp	12.5			2 × 120mm (4.7in) 50-cal LA 2 × 80mm etc. 40-cal LA 877 tonnes coal	

GENERAL NOTES
1918–19 Special Estimates: Large Fleet Colliers and Supply Ships. 1928–32: *Muroto* fitted with 2 Kampon boilers, *Noshima*, with 3 Hiyabara boilers.

CAREERS
Muroto
Launched 23 October, 1918; completed 7 December, 1918; 1941: refitted as Supply Ship; sunk 22 October, 1944 SSW of Kagoshima (29° 19′ N, 129° 44′ E) by US submarine *Seadog*.
Noshima
Launched 3 February, 1919; completed 31 March, 1919; 1941: refitted as Supply Ship; sunk 3 March, 1943 50 nm SE of Finschafen, New Guinea (07° 15′ S, 148° 30′ E) by US aircraft.

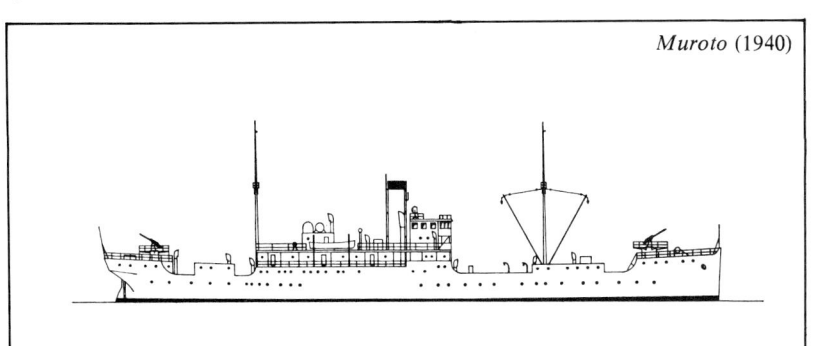

Muroto (1940)

The following merchant ships were employed as Colliers:
Asakaze Maru
(6517 GRT) built 138; sunk 5 December, 1943 by aircraft at Roi, Kwajalein.
Hikosan Maru
(3712 GRT) built 1892; taken prize 1904 – ex-British *Carradale*; returned 1905.
Iwashiro Maru
(3559 GRT) built 1939; sunk 15 January, 1943 off Kwajalein by US submarine *Whale*.
Kamoi Maru
(5355 GRT) built 1937; sunk 10 October, 1942 off Bougainville Island by US submarine *Wahoo*.
Kosei Maru +
(6667 GRT) built 1933; sunk 10 March, 1942 in Cam Ranh Bay by mine.
Nittei Maru
(2728 GRT) built 194?; ran aground 6 January, 1945 in Owari Bay area.
Ryuko Maru
(5636 GRT) built 1936; sunk 4 August, 1944 NW of Osagawara Gunto by aircraft.
Sansei Maru (i)
(2386 GRT) built 1936; sunk 28 June, 1944 off Tsushima by US submarine *Sealion* (ii).
Sansei Maru (ii)
(641 GRT) built 1942; damaged 15 September, 1943 N of Truk by US submarine *Haddock*.
Shinsei Maru No. 6
(4298 GRT) built 1938; sunk 21 August, 1942 off Ponape Island by US submarine *Tambor*.
Shinyubari Maru
(5354 GRT) built 1936; sunk 23 February, 1944 W of Saipan by US submarine *Sunfish*.
Soyo Maru +
(6081 GRT) built 1931; sunk 7 December, 1943 N of Truk by US submarine *Pogy*.
Unyo Maru No. 2
(2827 GRT) built 1937; sunk 26 December, 1941 off Kuching, Sarawak by Dutch aircraft.
Yodogawa Maru +
(6441 GRT) built 1939; sunk 11 May, 1943 NW of Kavieng by US submarine.
Yubari Maru
(4109 GRT) built 1930; sunk 27 March 1942 off Kupang, Timor by Dutch aircraft.
(All ships were steamers (turbine or triple expansion) with the exception of those marked '+', which were Diesel-driven.)

The collier *Noshima*, seen operating as a stores ship off Shanghai late in 1937. (Netherlands Navy).

SUPPLY SHIPS AND COLLIERS

23. Oilers

Name	Builder	Date	Displ	Length ft in	Beam ft in	Draught ft in	Machinery	SHP	Speed	Fuel	Radius	Armament	Comp
SHIJIKI	Kure DY	1916	5300 S	300 0 pp	42 0	20 0	1 set VTE 6 Kampon boilers 1 shaft	2500 ihp	12	345 coal 3000 tonnes oil		2 × 80mm (3in)40-cal LA	
TSURUGISAKI	Kure DY	1917	1970 S	210 0 pp	31 0	14 0	1 4-stroke Diesel engine 1 shaft	1000	11	135 oil 1100 tonnes oil		2 × 80mm etc. LA	
SUNOSAKI	Yokosuka NDY	1917–1918	9800 N 8800 S	400 0 pp	50 0	23 0	2 sets VTE 6 Kampon boilers 2 shafts	6000 ihp	14	800 coal 2000 oil		2 × 120mm (4.7in) 45-cal LA 2 × 80mm etc. HA 5000 tonnes oil	
NOMA ex-*War Wazir*	R. Duncan & Co., Port Glasgow	1919	11400 N 10605 S	412 0 oa 400 0 pp	52 0	25 1	1 set VTE 3 boilers 1 shaft	3000 ihp	10	900 coal 7290 tonnes oil		2 × 140mm (5.51in) 50-cal LA 2 × 80mm etc. HA	

GENERAL NOTES
1915–16 Naval Estimates: first Large Fleet Tanker.
CAREER
Launched 15 March, 1916; completed 15 May, 1916 as *Shijiki Maru*; August 1919: renamed *Shijiki*; lost 15 August, 1919 off Tanegashima in Typhoon.
GENERAL NOTES
1916 Naval Estimates.
CAREER
Launched 21 June, 1917; removed from Active List and re-employed as Fishery Protection vessel *Kaiho Maru* from 1933; 1941: commissioned as Gunboat; sunk 19 April, 1945 off Shizunai, Hokkaido, by US submarine *Sunfish*.
GENERAL NOTES
1916 Naval Estimates.
CAREER
Launched 22 June, 1918; completed 28 September, 1918; deleted from Active List 1939; 1 April, 1940: employed as target hulk *Haikau No. 14*.
GENERAL NOTES
British Standard Tanker Type 'Z' – designed by Swan Hunter and Wigham Richardson Ltd., Hebburn-on-Tyne, Newcastle: 5800 GRT.
CAREER
Launched 29 January, 1919; completed 28 May, 1919 as British tanker *War Wazir* (D Rowan); 6 August. 1919: sold to Japan, renamed *Noma*; 6 July 1928: deleted from Active List and employed as target hulk *Haikau No. 7* March or October 1929: to Department of the Interior as an Exhibition Ship; 1931: sold as merchant *Nippon Maru* (Jiho Shoji KK, Tokyo); lost 28 May, 1933 off Point Arguello, California.

Name	Builder	Date	Displ	Length ft in	Beam ft in	Draught ft in	Machinery	SHP	Speed	Fuel	Radius	Armament	Comp
SHIRETOKO ERIMO NOTORO ONDO	Kawasaki, Kobe	1920–1923	15450 N 14050 S	470 8 wl 455 0 pp	58 0	26 6	1 set VTE 4 boilers 2 shafts	5500 ihp	14	1350 coal 1000 oil		2 × 140mm (5.51in) 50-cal LA 2 × 80mm etc. HA 8000 tonnes oil	160
SHIRIYA SATA	Yokohama Dock Co.	1920–1922											
TSURUMI IRO	Osaka Iron Works	1921–1922											
HAYAMOTO	Kure DY	1922–1924											
NARUTO	Yokosuka DY	1922–1924											

Ondo (1926); Similar to *Shiretoko* Class

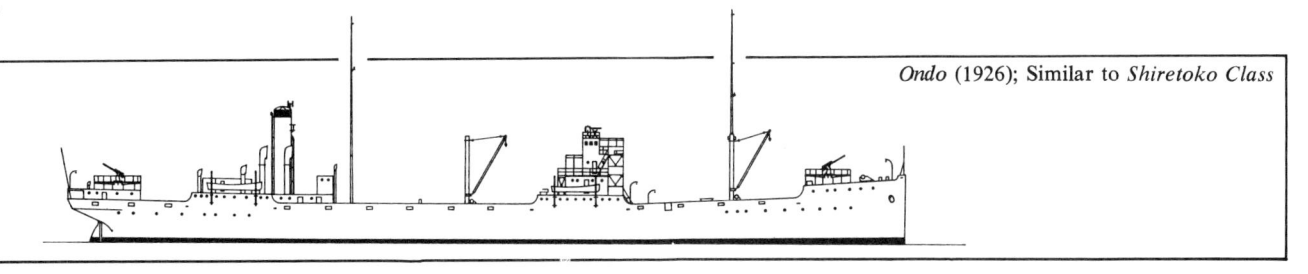

OILERS 249

GENERAL NOTES
Shiretoko class
1918–20 Building Programme: equipped for replenishment at sea. 1924: *Notoro* modified as Seaplane Carrier; *Tsurumi* as Aircraft Transport. (see pp. 61 - 66) 1928–32: all reboilered: *Naruto*, *Notoro*, *Shiretoko* and *Erimo* with 6 Hiyabara boilers; *Sata* with 4 Kampon Type '1' boilers; *Shiriya* and *Iro* with 4 Kampon Type 'Ro' boilers; *Tsurumi* with 4 Yarrow boilers. 1940: 140mm/120mm LA guns replaced by 2 × 80mm 40-cal HA, 4 × 13.2mm AA added.

CAREERS
Shiretoko
Launched 17 July, 1920; completed 20 September, 1920; 13 November, 1943: suffered severe damage as the result of a submarine torpedo attack NW of the Mariana Islands (18° 22′ N, 142° 50′ E) and taken to Singapore; sunk 1 February, 1945 in floating dock at Singapore by USAAF aircraft; raised and scrapped 29 November, 1946.
Notoro
Launched 3 May, 1920; completed 10 August, 1920; 1924: modified as Seaplane Carrier; 1942: reconverted to Fleet Tanker; suffered severe damage 20 September, 1943 as the result of submarine torpedo attack E of Palau (07° 23′ N, 150° 11′ E); heavily damaged 5 November, 1944 by air attack while under repair at Singapore; reduced to floating fuel oil tank; taken out of service and scrapped at Singapore 3 May, 1947.
Erimo
Launched 28 October, 1920; completed 16 December, 1920; beached 4 March, 1942 on Bali after torpedo attack by Dutch submarine *0.15*.
Shiriya
Launched 12, November 1921; completed 8 February, 1922; sunk 21 September, 1943 95 nm SE of Keelung, Formosa (26° 27′ N, 122° 40′ E) by US submarine *Trigger*.

Sata
Launched 28 October, 1920; completed 24 February, 1921; sunk 30 March, 1944 at Palau by aircraft from US TF 58.
Tsurumi
Launched 29 September, 1921; completed 14 March, 1922; 1924: modified as Aircraft Transport; 1931: reconverted to Fleet Tanker; sunk 5 August, 1942 S of Davao Gulf (05° 50′ N, 125° 42′ E) by US submarine *Cero*.
Iro
Launched 5 August 1922; completed 30 October, 1922; sunk 30 March, 1944 at Palau by aircraft from US TF 58.

GENERAL NOTES
Ondo group
1921 Programme: an unmodified continuation of the *Shiretoko* design, sometimes referred to as the '*Ondo* Class'.

CAREERS
Ondo
Launched 21 October, 1922; completed 12 March, 1923; beached 18 November, 1943 off Cavite, Luzon, after torpedo attack by US submarine *Bluegill*.
Hayamoto
Launched 4 December 1922; completed 18 May, 1924; 9 October, 1943: suffered severe damage as the result of a submarine torpedo attack in Sibutu Channel (05° 09′ N, 119° 18′ E); towed to Singapore with main propulsion machinery destroyed and subsequently used as bunker hulk; broken up at Singapore in 1945.
Naruto
Launched 30 January, 1923; completed 30 October, 1924; burned out 2 March 1944 at Rabaul following air attack.

The *Shiretoko* class oiler *Shiriya* was fitted with abeam-fuelling gear on the kingposts as early as April 1938, when this photograph was taken. Note that, although Japan was engaged in hostilities with China, no guns are mounted on the "bandstands". (Shizuo Fukui.)

Name	Builder	Date	Displ	Length ft in	Beam ft in	Draught ft in	Machinery	SHP	Speed	Fuel	Radius	Armament	Comp
OSE ex-*Genota*	Deutsche Werft, Hamburg	1935	7984 GRT	515 wl 502 pp / 11 0	65 11	29 0	1 8-cyl 2-st M.A.N. Diesel 1 shaft	6000	12	?	?	unknown	?

GENERAL NOTES
Dutch motor tanker. 12303 dwt.

CAREER
Launched April 1935 as Dutch *Genota* for La Corona, The Hague; captured 9 May, 1942 by Armed Merchant Cruisers *Aikoku Maru* and *Hokoku Maru*; 20 July, 1942; commissioned as Fleet Tanker *Ose*; sunk 30 March, 1944 at Palau by aircraft from US TF 58.

Name	Builder	Date	Displ	Length ft in	Beam ft in	Draught ft in	Machinery	SHP	Speed	Fuel	Radius	Armament	Comp
KAZAHAYA Class	Harima SB Co., Aioi	1941–?	20000 N 18300 S	460 0 pp	59 6	27 11	1 set GT 2 Kampon boilers	9500	16.5	?	?	3 × 120mm (4.7in) 45-cal HA and smaller	

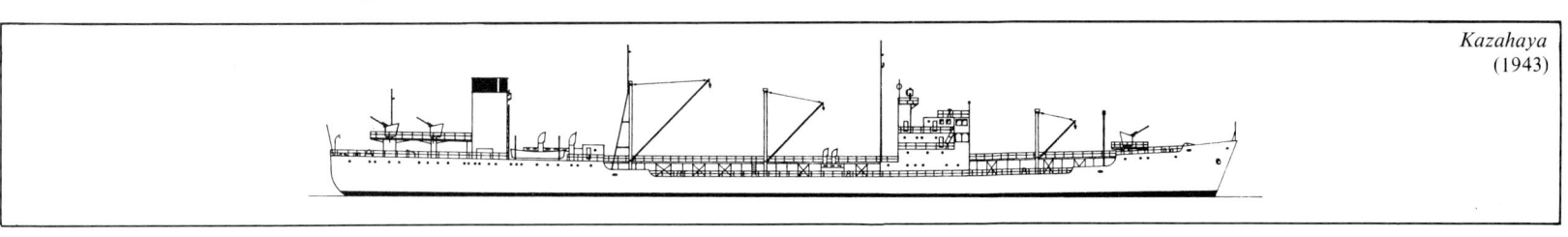

Kazahaya (1943)

GENERAL NOTES
1941 War Programme: Fast Fleet Tankers.

CAREERS
Kazahaya
Launched 1942; completed March 1943; sunk 6 October, 1943 240 nm NW of Truk (10° 01′ N, 148° 31′ E) by US submarines *Tinosa* and *Steelhead*.
Job No. 305. Cancelled.

Kariko class
Modified 1942 Fleet Programme. Fast Fleet Tankers, similar to *Kazahaya* class, but with 4 × 127mm guns.
Job Nos. 5381–5395. Cancelled.
Job Nos. 842–844
1942 Fleet Programme. Fast Fleet Tankers, improved *Kazahaya* class; 20000 standard ts. Not ordered.

Name	Builder	Date	Displ	Length ft in	Beam ft in	Draught ft in	Machinery	SHP	Speed	Fuel	Radius	Armament	Comp
HAYASUI Class	Harima SB Co., Aioi	1943–?	20000 N 18300 S	515 wl 502 pp / 11 0	65 11	29 0	1 set GT 2 Kampon boilers	9500	16.5	?	?	4 × 127mm (5in) 40-cal DP 6 aircraft 1 catapult	?

GENERAL NOTES
1941 War Programme. Fast Fleet Tankers and Seaplane Carrier.

CAREERS
Hayasui
Launched 1943; completed April 1944; sunk 19 August, 1944 80 nm NW of Cape Bolinao, Luzon (17° 34′ N, 119° 24′ E) by US submarine *Bluefish*.
Job No. 307: Cancelled.

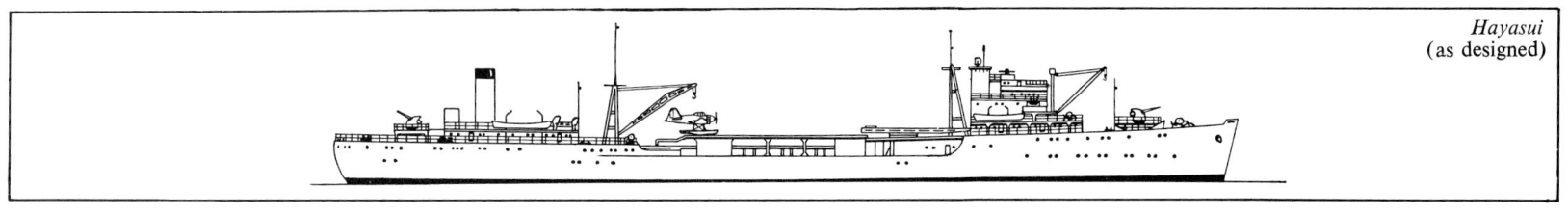

Hayasui (as designed)

Name	Builder	Date	Displ	Length ft in	Beam ft in	Draught ft in	Machinery	SHP	Speed	Fuel	Radius	Armament	Comp
TAMANO-Class	various		17500 N 15600 S	unknown			Geared turbines		17	?	?	4 × 127mm (5in) 40-cal DP 14 aircraft 1 catapult	?

Modified 1942 Fleet Programme. Fast Fleet Tankers and Aircraft Transports. To have been named *Tamano, Shiomi, Takahama, Oshu, Uma, Ryumai, Shiose*. Cancelled.

OILERS 251

Tamano class (as designed)

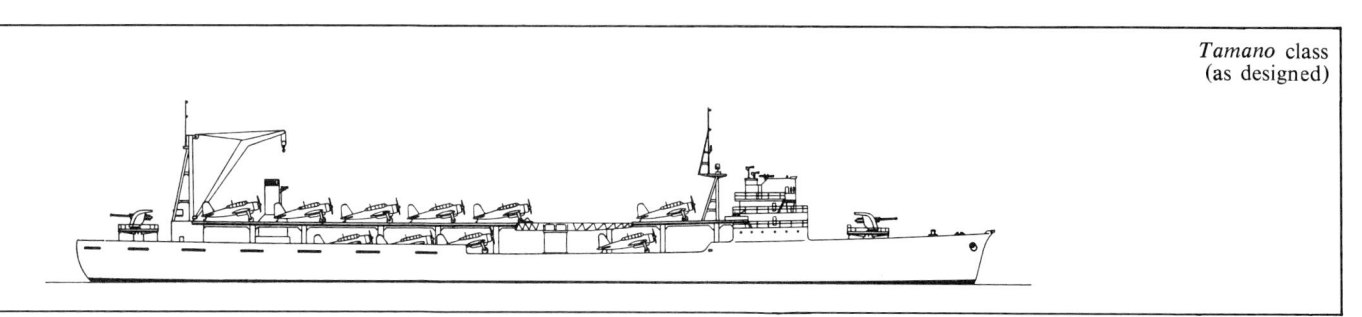

Name	Builder	Date	Displ	Length ft in	Beam ft in	Draught ft in	Machinery	SHP	Speed	Fuel	Radius	Armament	Comp
HARIO-Class	Harima SB Co.	1944–?	20000 N 18500 S	515 11 wl 506 4 pp	65 7	28 10	1 set GT 2 Kampon boilers 1 shaft	8600	16.5			2 × 120mm (4.7in) 45-cal HA	

GENERAL NOTES
1943–44 War Programme. Fast Fleet Tankers.

Hario
CAREERS
Launched 1944; completed December, 1944; sunk 3 March, 1945 off Cape Bastian, Hainan, by mine.
Job No. 4902. Cancelled.

Inatori class
1943–4 War Programme. New design Fast Fleet Tankers of 16350 standard ts, to be built by Harima SB Co.
Inatori (Job No. 4903) and *Job No. 4909*: cancelled.

Merchant Ships used as Fleet Tankers

The following merchant vessels were employed as Fleet Tankers or were converted when requisitioned. The latter comprise the first group:

Arima Maru
(7389 GRT) built 1936; sunk 3 April, 1943 N of Palau by US submarine *Haddock*.
Azuma Maru
(6646 GRT) converted to tanker 1942; sunk 3 December, 1943 NW of Sonserol by US submarine *Tinosa*.
Choko Maru
(1794 GRT) converted from Stores Ship 1943; sunk 24/5 February, 1944 off Saipan by US submarine *Tang*.
Goyo Maru
(8469 GRT) converted to tanker 1941–2; severely damaged and beached at Truk 16 May, 1942 after attack by US submarine *Tautog*; salvaged; sunk 3 February, 1944 NE of Formosa by US submarine *Tambor*.
Koryu Maru
(6680 GRT) converted to tanker 1943; sunk 22 April 1944 off Cape St Jacques by aircraft.
Kozui Maru
(7072 GRT) converted to tanker 1941; sunk 14 October, 1943 off Okiname by US submarine *Grayback*.
Matsumoto Maru
(7024 GRT) converted to tanker 1941–2; sunk 25 October, 1944 in Formosa Straits by US submarine *Tang*.

Merchant Tankers:
Akatsuki Maru
(10216 GRT) built 1938; sunk 28 May, 1943 in East China Sea by US submarine *Saury*.
Akebono Maru
(10182 GRT) built 1939; sunk 30 March, 1944 at Palau by TF 58 aircraft.
Amatsu Maru
(10567 GRT) built 1943 – Standard 1TL tanker; sunk 30 March, 1944 at Palau by TF 58 aircraft.
Choran Maru
(6000 GRT) built 1943; captured and used by Repatriation Service from August 1945.
Eiho Maru
(5068 GRT) built 1944 – Standard 1TM tanker; sunk 21 January, 1945 at Takao by TF 38 aircraft.

Enoshima Maru
(1942 GRT) built 1917 as British Admiralty Royal Fleet Auxiliary oiler *Ebonol*; captured at Hong Kong and renamed *Enoshima Maru*; returned in 1945.
Fujisan Maru
(9524 GRT) built 1931; sunk 17 February 1944 at Truk by TF 58 aircraft.
Gen'yo Maru
(10018 GRT) built 1937; scuttled by destroyer *Uzuki* W of Saipan after damage sustained in TF 58 air attack on 20 June, 1944.
Hishi Maru No. 2
(856 GRT) built 1936; sunk 9 November, 1944 in Mindoro Straits by US submarine *Haddo*.
Hoyo Maru
(8691 GRT) built 1936; severely damaged 6 November, 1943 by US submarine *Scorpion*; towed to Truk and sunk there 17 February, 1944 by TF 58 aircraft.
Itsukushima Maru
(10007 GRT) built 1937; sunk 27 October, 1944 in Balabac Straits by US submarine *Bergall*.
Juko Maru
(478 GRT) built 1938 as *Kamikaze Maru*; sunk 9 August, 1945 at Onagawa by TF 38 aircraft.
Kaijo Maru
(3270 GRT) built 1939; beached 10 March, 1943 at Butung, Celebes, after air attack; captured in 1945.
Kaijo Maru No. 2
(8632 GRT) built 1937 as *Kaijo Maru*; sunk 5 March, 1942 off Truk by US submarine *Grampus*.
Ken'yo Maru
(10024 GRT) built 1939; sunk 14 January, 1944 SE of Paulau by US submarine *Guardfish*.
Kinrei Maru
(867 GRT) built 1941; sunk 6 May, 1945 in Gulf of Thailand by US submarine *Hammerhead*.
Kiyo Maru
(7251 GRT) built 1930 as *Vigriol*; sunk 4 January, 1944 in South China Sea by US submarine *Rasher*.
Kokuyo Maru
(10026 GRT) built 1939; sunk 30 July 1944 in Sulu Sea by US submarine *Bonefish*.

252 OILERS

Koryu Maru
(820 GRT) built 1944; sunk by mine off Hasaki Light.
Kuroshio Maru
(10518 GRT) built 1938; sunk 9 January, 1945 S of Formosa by aircraft.
Kyoei Maru
(602 GRT) built 1937; sunk 16 November, 1944 off Tarakan, Borneo by aircraft.
Kyoei Maru No. 2
(1192 GRT) built 1940; sunk 27 July, 1944 in Sulu Sea by US submarine *Dace*.
Kyoei Maru No. 3
(1189 GRT) built 1941; sunk 19 July, 1945 in Gulf of Thailand by US submarine *Bumper*.
Kyoko Maru
(5800 GRT) built 1921 as Dutch *Semiramis*; sunk 15 February, 1942 at Pladjoe, Sumatra; raised, repaired and renamed *Kyoko Maru*; sunk 27 December, 1943 W of Celebes by US submarine *Ray*.
Kyokuto Maru
(10051 GRT) built 1934; sunk 21 September, 1944 at Manila by TF 38 aircraft; raised and repaired post-war; 1952: renamed *California Maru*; scrapped 1963.
Kyokuyo Maru
(17549 GRT) built 1938; sank 17 September, 1943 off Amami-O-shima in typhoon.
Manju Maru
(6515 GRT) built 1921; sunk 21 January, 1945 at Takao by TF 38 aircraft.
Mirii Maru
(10564 GRT) damaged 29 June, 1944 W of Luzon by US submarine *Bang* and laid up at Takao, where sunk 15 January, 1945 by TF 38 aircraft.
Nichei Maru
(10020 GRT) built 1938; sunk 6 January, 1945 in Gulf of Thailand by US submarine *Besugo*.
Nippon Maru
(9974 GRT) built 1936; sunk 14 January, 1944 S of Sorol Island by US submarine *Scamp*.
Nissan Maru
(6800 GRT) built 1938; sunk 19 June, 1942 in Kiska Harbour by aircraft.
Nisshin Maru
(16764 GRT) built 1938; sunk 6 May, 1944 off Borneo by US submarine *Crevalle*.
Nisshin Maru No. 2
(17579 GRT) built 1937; sunk 17 April, 1943 E of Formosa by US submarine (possibly *Seawolf*).
Nissho Maru
(10526 GRT) built 1938; sunk 25 February, 1944 in Davao Gulf by US submarine *Hoe*.
Ogura Maru No. 2
(7311 GRT) built 1930; sunk 16 September, 1944 S of Formosa by US submarine.
Ogura Maru No. 3
(7358 GRT) built 1916 as British Admiralty *Limeleaf*, mercantile *California* (1919), *Athelrill*, *Koyo Maru* then *Ogura Maru No. 3*; sunk 23 February, 1944 off Halmahera by US submarine *Cod*.
Omurosan Maru
(9204 GRT) built 1937; sunk 22 December, 1944 off Cape Batangan by US submarine *Flasher*.
Ryuei Maru
(5144 GRT) built 1943; sunk 2 January, 1944 in S China Sea by US submarine *Kingfish*.
San Clemente (Kuremente) Maru
(7335 GRT) built 1937; sunk 4 May, 1943 off Palau by US submarine *Seal*.
San Diego (Jiego) Maru
(7269 GRT) built 1928; returned to civilian owner 1944; scrapped Kobe 1961.
San Luis (Ruisu) Maru
(7269 GRT) built 1928; sunk 12 January, 1945 in Gulf of Qui Nhon by aircraft.
San Pedro (Pedoro) Maru
(7268 GRT) built 1927; returned to civilian owner 1944; sunk 25 June, 1944 off Cape Bolinao by US submarine *Jack*.
San Ramon Maru
(7309 GRT) built 1935; sunk 27 November, 1943 in East China Sea by US submarine *Sanraku Maru*
(3000 GRT) built 194?; sunk 15 June, 1943 off Sibutu by US submarine *Trout*.
Shinkoku Maru
(10020 GRT) built 1940; sunk 17 February, 1944 off Truk by TF 58 aircraft.
Shoyo Maru
(7498 GRT) built 1928; sunk 21 September, 1943 NE of Formosa by US submarine *Trigger*.
Takatori Maru No. 1
(878 GRT) built 1928; sunk 1 July, 1944 off Mokpo, Korea, by US submarine *Tang*.
Tarakan Maru
(5135 GRT) built 1943; sunk 6 January, 1945 E of Hainan Island by US submarine *Sea Robin*.
Tatekawa Maru
(10009 GRT) built 1935; sunk 24 May, 1944 S of the Saranagani Islands, Mindanao by US submarine *Gurnard*.
Teiyo Maru
(9849 GRT) built 1931; sunk 19 August, 1944 off Cape Bojeador, Luzon, by US submarine *Rasher*.
Tennan Maru
(5407 GRT) built 19??; sunk 23 October, 1943 N of the Admiralty Islands by US submarine *Silversides*.
Terukawa Maru
(6433 GRT) built 1934 as *Nora Maersk*; sunk 21 December, 1943 NW of Truk by US submarine *Skate*.
Toa Maru
(10050 GRT) built 1934; sunk 25 November, 1943 N of Ponape by US submarine *Searaven*.
Toei Maru
(10022 GRT) built 1938; sunk 18 January, 1943 100 nm SW of Truk by US submarine *Silversides*.
Toen Maru
(5332 GRT) built 1917 as *Aungban*; sunk 2 March, 1943 S of the Makassar Strait by US submarine *Thresher*.
Toho Maru
(9987 GRT) built 1936; sunk 29 March, 1943 in the Makassar Strait by US submarine *Gudgeon*.
Tonan Maru No. 2
(19262 GRT) built 1937; sunk 22 August, 1944 200 nm SE of Shanghai by US submarine *Bonefish*.
Tonan Maru No. 3
(19209 GRT) built 1938; sunk 17 February, 1944 at Truk by TF 58 aircraft.
Yamazuru Maru
(3651 GRT) built 1938; sunk 14 January 1944 300 nm S of the Kii Channel by US submarine *Seawolf*.

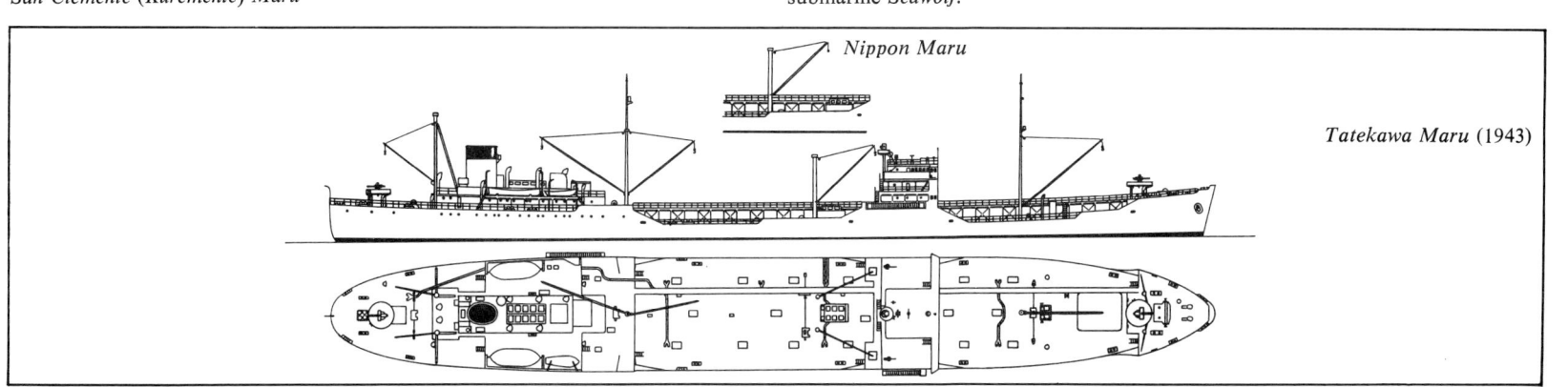

Nippon Maru

Tatekawa Maru (1943)

OILERS 253

Yuho Maru
(5266 GRT) built 1943 – Type 1 TM Standard; sunk 26 November, 1944 off Miri, Sarawak, by US submarine *Pargo*.

Honan Maru
(5542 GRT) built 1920 – requisitioned by Imperial Japanese Army; sunk 28 March, 1945 60 nm E of Nha Trang, Vietnam, by US submarine.

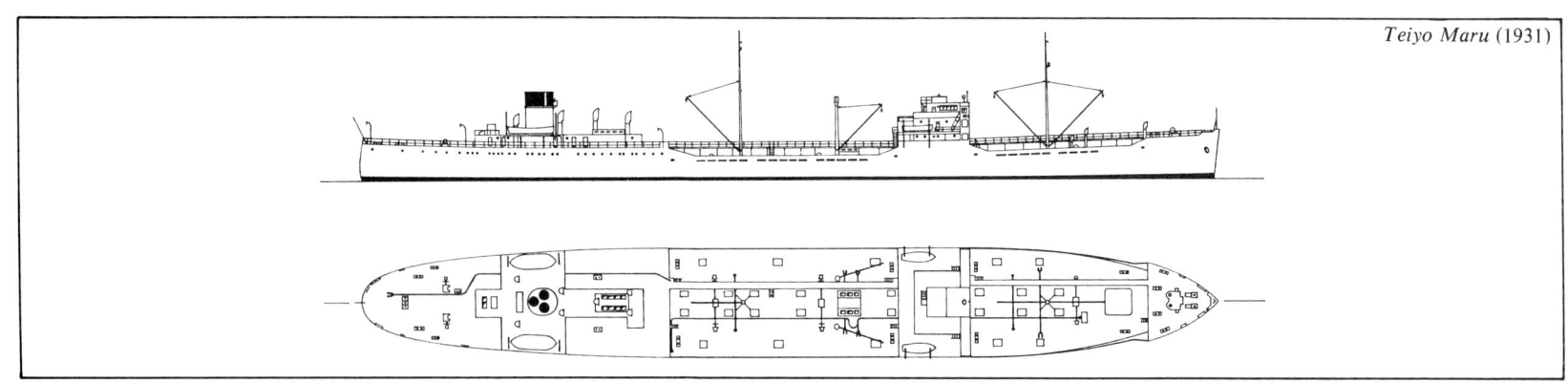

Teiyo Maru (1931)

Name	Builder	Date	Displ	Length ft in	Beam ft in	Draught ft in	Machinery	SHP	Speed	Fuel	Radius	Armament	Comp
ASHIZURI Class	Mitsubishi, Nagasaki	1941–1943	8400 N 7951 S	426 6 wl 413 5 pp	55 1	19 8	2 Diesel engines 2 shafts	6000	16			4 × 127mm (5in) 40-cal DP 4 × 25mm AA	

GENERAL NOTES
1940 Programme (*Job Nos. 219 & 220*); specialised underway replenishment vessels for supporting aircraft carrier task forces. In addition to supplying aviation gasoline and lubricant and aircraft spares, they were also fitted with aircraft repair workshops. Official designation – 'Kihatsuyu Umpankan'.

CAREERS
Ashizuri
Launched 16 May, 1942; completed 30 January, 1943; sunk 5 June, 1944 W of Basilan Island (06° 44′ N, 120° 55′ E) by US submarine *Puffer*.
Shioya
Launched 8 March, 1943; completed 9 November, 1943; sunk 8 June, 1944 120 nm NW of Manado, Celebes (03° 04′ N, 124° 03′ E) by US submarine *Rasher*.

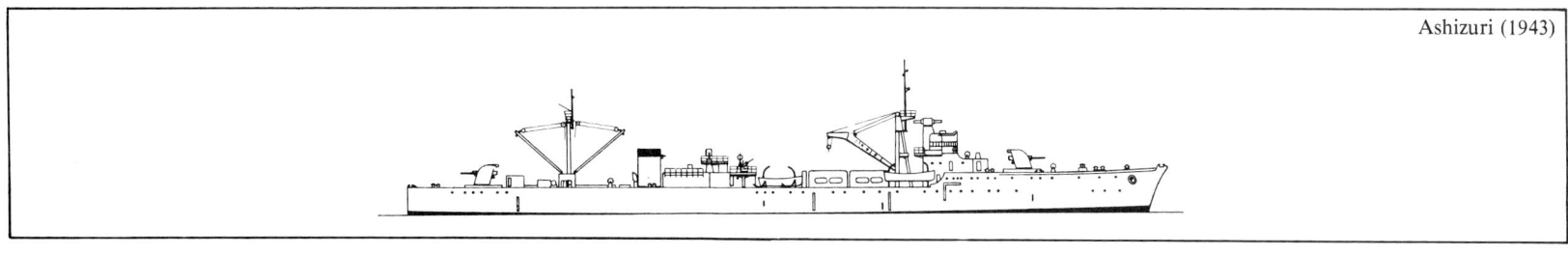

Ashizuri (1943)

Name	Builder	Date	Displ	Length ft in	Beam ft in	Draught ft in	Machinery	SHP	Speed	Fuel	Radius	Armament	Comp
SUNOSAKI Class	Mitsubishi, Yokohama	1942–1944	4700 N 4465 S	352 8 oa 347 9 wl 334 8 pp	49 3	16 5	2 Diesel engines 2 shafts	4500	16			2 × 120mm (4.7in) 45-cal HA	

GENERAL NOTES
1939 Programme (*Job No. 103 – Sunosaki*) and 1940 Programme (*Job Nos. 233–236*): aviation gasoline and lubricant tankers for carrier task force support.

CAREERS
Launched 28 December, 1942; completed 10 December, 1943; severely damaged 1 August, 1944 NE of Borneo by US submarine attack; sunk 21 September, 1944 at Manila by US TF 38 air attack.
Takasaki
Launched 3 May, 1943; completed 2 September, 1943; sunk 5 June, 1944 in company with *Ashizuri* by US submarine *Puffer*.
Job Nos. 234–236
Intended names – *Tsurugisaki*, *Shinasaki* and *Hijirisaki*; order cancelled before ships laid down (1942).

Stores and spare aero-engines could be carried by *Sunosaki,* necessitating the heavy-lift jib and large tripod foremast. (Shizuo Fukui.)

OILERS

Name	Builder	Date	Displ	Length ft in	Beam ft in	Draught ft in	Machinery	SHP	Speed	Fuel	Radius	Armament	Comp
500-ton COASTAL TANKERS	Ujina SB, Hiroshima Fujinagata, Osaka	1934–?	906 N	149 wl / 147 pp 11 / 8	31 2	11 2	1 Diesel engine 1 shaft	850	11			500 tonnes fuel oil	
150-ton WATER TANKERS	various	1940–?	233	89 oa / 85 pp 11 / 4	31 2	11 2	1 Diesel engine 1 shaft	100	7.5			150 tonnes water	

GENERAL NOTES

Coastal tankers carrying fuel from fleet bases to fitting-out yards. Official designation 'Juyusen'.

CAREERS

Juyusen No. 3128
Built 1934; immobilised hulk captured at Shingu.
No. 3829
At Kure in 1945, put into merchant service.
No. 3999
Under repair at Osaka in February 1947.
No. 3998
Nothing known of career or fate.
No. 4000
Possibly at Yokosuka in 1947.

GENERAL NOTES

Harbour service water tankers for service at Naval Dockyards and Fleet bases. Built by Yokosuka Naval Dockyard, Ominato Naval Repair Yard, Saizaki Dock Co., Kochi Shipbuilding Co. and Ishiwara Shipbuilding Co. among others. Official designation 'Suisen'. The number built and their fates are unknown, the only identified unit being *Suisen No. 3773*.

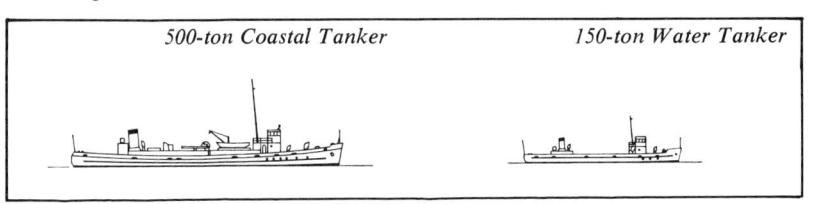

500-ton Coastal Tanker *150-ton Water Tanker*

24. Standard Merchant Ships

Japanese War Standard Construction

The Japanese Government followed a similar procedure to that of the United States in ordering a series of classes of merchant vessels to be built during the War to standard designs. Private shipyards provided the basic designs which were highly suitable for wartime construction and were further modified in order to hasten mass production.

1st War Standard Programme

Effective from 25 March, 1942 and included the different types of specialised vessels as well as cargo vessels and tankers. The various classes did not differ fundamentally from their peace-time counterparts and were intended to be economical vessels for post-war use. Approximately 12 units of the B, C, D and K-Classes were completed as auxiliary tankers during the first quarter of 1943.

2nd War Standard Programme

Initiated by the Naval Technical Office at the end of 1942, superseding the Transport Ministry's 1st Programme. The 2nd Programme was characterised by the abandonment of any considerations of commercial economy, so that mass production might be hastened and the maximum economy in building material might be achieved. The majority of ships built during the War were ordered under this Programme, and their noteworthy features included: total lack of camber on decks, reduced number of transverse frames, absence of double-bottom compartments, uncased funnels and counter stern. A specialised shipyard was completed at the time of this Programme, and construction of new yards for building the individual classes was commenced (see below).

3rd War Standard Programme

Initiated in September 1943, including seven classes with improved compartmentation and higher-powered machinery and greater speed to improve their defence against submarine attack. Only six of these large ships were completed, besides 36 coasters, before the end of the War.

4th War Standard Programme

Projected in 1945. These were to have been very fast ships, designed without regard for economical operation, to be used as independently-routed ships which could evade submarines. Work began on only three ships (coastal tankers) and they were not launched until after the end of the War.

Translator's note: The Japanese Naval Staff drew erroneous conclusions from the experience of the preceding three years of anti-submarine warfare in the formulation of this last Programme. The institution of the General Escort Command and the adoption of a widespread convoy system in November 1943 was a step in the right direction, but the lack of suitable long-range escorts and the haphazard application of the convoy system did not result in reduced sinkings, unlike the results obtained by the more efficient British and American organisations in the Atlantic theatre. The decision to revert to independent sailings was an unwise one, for even if the ships were faster than the submarines and presented difficult torpedo targets, they were still more vulnerable to air and surface gunfire attack than slower escorted ships. British experience showed that losses among 'independents' were double those among convoyed ships.)

In addition to the major classes described below, there were also a dozen classes of small vessels, such as tugs, fishery craft, etc., for which no data exist. The following shipyards, among others, were involved in the War Standard Programme:

Mitsubishi, Nagasaki: *1 TL, 1 TM, 2 TL, 3 TL, 3 D*
Mitsubishi, Yokohama: *1 TL, 2 TL, 3 TL*
Mitsubishi, Kobe: *1A, 2A, 3A*
Mitsui, Tamano: *1A, 2A, 3A*
Kawaminami, Koyakijima: *1A, 2A, 3A*
New shipyards for A-type construction:
Mitsubishi, Hiroshima/Hitachi, Kanagawa.
New shipyards for E-type construction:
Harima Shipbuilding Co., Matsunoura
Kawaminami Industrial Co., Fukahori
Mitsubishi, Wakamatsu
Tokyo Shipbuilding Co., Tokyo

1st Standard Programme
Deliveries

Year	A	B	C	D	E	F	K	TM	TL	TS
1942	7	5	10	7	6	8	12	6	—	3
1943	13	16	34	27	13	23	20	26	14	3
1944	—	—	10	6	4	4	—	—	6	2
August 1945: launched				—	1	—	—	—	3	—
building				—	—	—	—	—	—	—
total built	20	21	54	40	23	35	32	32	20	8

2nd Standard Programme
Deliveries

Year	A	D	E	TA	TE	TM	TL
1943	1	—	58	—	9	—	—
1944	49	52	296	34	112	29	21
1945	36	29	64	1	17	5	7
total built	86	81	418	35	138	34	28

Deliveries August 1945:	A	D	E	TA	TE	TM	TL
launched	4	3	3	—	—	4	2
building	1	15	—	—	—	5	3

3rd Standard Programme
Deliveries

Year	A	B	D	E	TA	TE	TL
1944	—	—	—	—	—	11	—
1945	1	—	1	25	1	—	3
August 1945: launched	1	1	2	13	1	—	1
building	3	2	11	20	—	—	1

The following Standard Ships were employed by the Navy. Certain units, marked '?', had similar characteristics but are not known to have belonged to the particular class in which they are included.

Name	Date	DWT	Length ft in	Beam ft in	Draught ft in	Machinery	SHP	Speed max/min	Radius

1 A
6400 GRT cargo steamer   1942–1943   9200   445 10 oa / 419 11 pp   58 5   32 2   VTE   3500 ihp   15 / 13.5   13000

CAREERS
Jokuja Maru
(6440 GRT) built 1943; sunk by submarine 1944.
?Nichizui Maru
(6584 GRT) built 1941; sunk by aircraft 1944.
Nisshun Maru
(6380 GRT) built 1941; sunk by submarine 1943.
?Shinnan Maru
(6417 GRT) built 1941; sunk by mine 1943.
Tatsuura Maru
(6420 GRT) built 1942; sunk by aircraft 1944.
Uyo Maru
(6376 GRT) built 1941; sunk by submarine 1943.

Name	Date	DWT	Length ft in	Beam ft in	Draught ft in	Machinery	SHP	Speed max/min	Radius

1 B
4500 GRT cargo steamer   1942–1943   6800   387 2 oa / 367 5 pp   51 10   24 2   GT   2400   14 / 11.5   7500

CAREERS
Awa Maru
(4532 GRT) built 1943; sunk by submarine 1944.
Bingo Maru
(4642 GRT) built 1943; survived (damaged).
Bisan Maru
(4667 GRT) built 1943; sunk by submarine 1944.
Bizen Maru
(4667 GRT) built 1943; sunk by submarine 1944.
?Daiten Maru
(4642 GRT) built 194?; sunk by submarine 1944.
Kokuyo Maru
(4667 GRT) built 1943; sunk by submarine 1944.
Meiryu Maru
(4793 GRT) built 1943; sunk by aircraft 1945.
Miho Maru
(4667 GRT) built 1944; sunk by submarine 1945.
?Misaku Maru
(4500 GRT) built 1942; sunk by submarine 1944.
Natsukawa Maru
(4739 GRT) built 1942; sunk by aircraft 1944.
?Toyu Maru
(4532 GRT) built 194?; sunk by aircraft 1945.
?Uragami Maru
(4317 GRT) built 1941; fate unknown.

Name	Date	DWT	Length ft in	Beam ft in	Draught ft in	Machinery	SHP	Speed max/min	Radius

1 C
2700 GRT cargo steamer   1942–1944   4300   321 5 oa / 305 1 pp   44 11   20 10   VTE   1800 ihp   14 / 11   5800

CAREERS
Anko Maru
(2907 GRT) built 1942; sunk by mine 1945.
?Bokuyo
(2726 GRT) built 1941; sunk by aircraft 1944.

STANDARD MERCHANT SHIPS

Daiji Maru
(2813 GRT) built 1943; sunk by submarine 1944.
Heijo Maru
(2627 GRT) built 1941; sunk by submarine 1943.
?Inari Maru
(2759 GRT) built 1944; sunk by mine 1945.
?Kashimasan Maru
(2825 GRT) built 1942; sunk by submarine 1944.
Komei Maru
(2857 GRT) built 1944; sunk by submarine 1944.
Kuniyama Maru
(2871 GRT) built 1943; sunk by aircraft 1944.
Masashima Maru
(2742 GRT) built 194?; sunk by aircraft 1945.
Meisho Maru
(2737 GRT) built 1943; sunk by aircraft 1944.
?Nittei Maru
(2728 GRT) built 194?; stranded 1945.
?Oakita Maru
(2704 GRT) built 194?; sunk by aircraft 1944.
Raizan Maru
(2828 GRT) built 1943; sunk by aircraft 1944.
?Reikai Maru
(2812 GRT) built 1943; sunk by aircraft 1944.

?Ryuko Maru
(2764 GRT) built 194?; sunk by aircraft 1944.
?Shinsei Maru No. 18
(2711 GRT) built 1941; sunk by aircraft 1944.
Shintai Maru
(2857 GRT) built 1944; sunk by mine 1945.
?Shin'yo Maru
(2634 GRT) built 194?; sunk by submarine 1944.
Shiramine Maru
(2857 GRT) built 1943; sunk by aircraft 1944.
Shirane Maru
(2825 GRT) built 1943; sunk by submarine 1944.
?Taiho Maru
(2720 GRT) built 194?; sunk by aircraft 1944.
?Taikoku Maru
(2633 GRT) built 194?; sunk by submarine 1944.
Unkai Maru No. 12
(2745 GRT) built 194?; sunk by submarine 1944.
Wayo Maru
(2726 GRT) built 1941; sunk by aircraft 1945.
Zukai Maru
(2700 GRT) built 194?; sunk by aircraft 1944.

Name	Date	DWT	Length ft in	Beam ft in	Draught ft in	Machinery	SHP	Speed max/min	Radius
1 D 1900 GRT cargo steamer	1942–1944	2800	285 oa 8 / 270 pp 0	40 0	20 4	VTE	1100 ihp	12.5 / 10	3800

CAREERS
Akishima Maru
(1933 GRT) built 1943; sunk by mine 1945.
?Hachijin Maru
(1918 GRT) built 1943; sunk by submarine 1944.
Hachirogata Maru
(1999 GRT) built 1943; sunk by submarine 1944.
Hakko Maru
(1948 GRT) built 1943; sunk by submarine 1944.
Matsutani Maru
(1999 GRT) built 1942; sunk by aircraft 1944.
?Nippo Maru
(1942 GRT) built 1943; sunk by submarine 1944.
?Nissho Maru No. 18
(1990 GRT) built 1942; survived.

?Nitcho Maru
(1942 GRT) built 1943; sunk by aircraft 1944.
?Shin'yo Maru No. 8
(1959 GRT) built 1941; sunk by submarine 1944.
?Shoken Maru
(1942 GRT) built 1943; sunk by submarine 1944.
Tatsuei Maru
(1942 GRT) built 1943; sunk by aircraft 1944.
?Tatsutagawa Maru
(1923 GRT) built 1942; sunk by destroyers 1944.
?Temposan Maru
(1970 GRT) built 1942; sunk by submarine 1943.
Un'yo Maru No. 8
(1941 GRT) built 1943; sunk by aircraft 1944.

Name	Date	DWT	Length ft in	Beam ft in	Draught ft in	Machinery	SHP	Speed max/min	Radius
1 E 830 GRT motor coaster	1942–1945	1265	213 3 oa / 196 10 pp	31 2	16 5	Diesel	750	12 / 10	6000

CAREERS
?Nagatsu Maru
(840 GRT) built 1942; survived.

Ujigawa Maru
(786 GRT) built 194?; sunk by aircraft 1943.

Name	Date	DWT	Length ft in	Beam ft in	Draught ft in	Machinery	SHP	Speed max/min	Radius
1 F 490 GRT motor coaster	1942–1945	700	175 0 oa / 164 0 pp	27 7	12 9	Diesel	550	12 / 10	3600

CAREERS
Fuchu Maru
(542 GRT) built 1943; fate unknown.
Heinan Maru
(661 GRT) built 1941; sunk by submarine 1942.
?Ryujin Maru
(495 GRT) built 194?; sunk by submarine 1945.
?Shinko Maru
(545 GRT) built 194?; sunk by aircraft 1943.

Name	Date	DWT	Length ft in	Beam ft in	Draught ft in	Machinery	SHP	Speed max/min	Radius
1 K 5300 GRT steam ore-carrier	1942–1943	7900	416 1 oa / 393 8 pp	54 2	24 7	VTE	2100	12/10	8700

CAREERS
Akikawa Maru
(5244 GRT) built 1943; sunk by submarine 1944.

Name	Date	DWT	Length ft in	Beam ft in	Draught ft in	Machinery	SHP	Speed max/min	Radius
1 M 9500 GRT Army attack transport	1941–1945	4000	501 0 oa / 465 10 pp	64 3	23 0	GT	10000	19/16	

1M (see p. 230).

Name	Date	DWT	Length ft in	Beam ft in	Draught ft in	Machinery	SHP	Speed max/min	Radius
1 W 2800 GRT steam ferry	1941–		436 11 pp	52 0		GT		12/10	

CAREERS
Taiho Maru
(2827 GRT) built 194?; sunk by aircraft 1944.
?Yanagawa Maru
(2813 GRT) built 194?; sunk by submarine 1944.

Name	Date	DWT	Length ft in	Beam ft in	Draught ft in	Machinery	SHP	Speed max/min	Radius
1 TL 10000 GRT steam tanker	1942–1945	15200	526 7 oa / 502 0 pp	65 7	29 10	GT	9500	18.5/15	10000

CAREERS
Amatsu Maru
(10567 GRT) built 1943; sunk by aircraft 1944.
Azusa Maru
(10022 GRT) built 1944; sunk by submarine 1944.
Hakko Maru
(10022 GRT) built 1944; sunk by submarine 1944.
Kyokuho Maru
(10059 GRT) built 1944; sunk by submarine 1944.
Kyuei Maru
(10171 GRT) built 1943; sunk by submarine 1943.
Mirii Maru
(10564 GRT) built 1943; sunk by aircraft 1945.
Nampo Maru
(10033 GRT) built 1943; sunk by submarine 1944.
Nichicho Maru
(10000 GRT) built 1944; fate unknown.
Nippo Maru
(10528 GRT) built 1944; sunk by submarine 1944.
Ominesan Maru
(10568 GRT) built 1943; fate unknown.
Otakisan Maru
conversion as escort carrier (see p. 62).
Ryoei Maru
(10016 GRT) built 1944; sunk by submarine 1945.
Seiyo Maru
(10536 GRT) built 1943; sunk by aircraft 1944.
Shimane Maru
conversion as escort carrier (see p. 62).
Taihosan Maru
(10536 GRT) built 1943; sunk by submarine 1944.

Type 1 TL

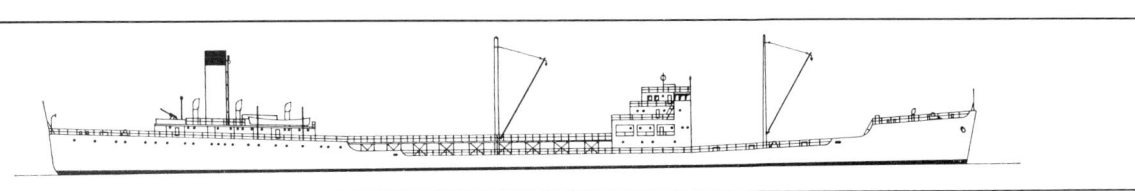

Name	Date	DWT	Length ft in	Beam ft in	Draught ft in	Machinery	SHP	Speed max/min	Radius
1 TM 5200 GRT steam tanker	1942–1943	7000	416 0 oa 393 8 pp	53 6	24 1	GT	3600	15 / 12.5	7000

Type 1 TM

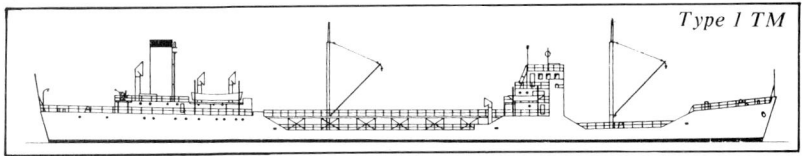

CAREERS

Asanagi Maru
(5141 GRT) built 1943; sunk by submarine 1944.
Asashio Maru
(5141 GRT) built 1943; sunk by aircraft 1944.
Ban'ei Maru
(5266 GRT) built 1944; sunk by submarine 1944.
Bokuei Maru
(5200 GRT) built 1943; sunk in collision 1944.
Eiho Maru
(5068 GRT) built 1944; sunk by aircraft 1945.
Eiyo Maru No. 2
(5061 GRT) built 1944; sunk by aircraft 1944.
Men'ei Maru
(5226 GRT) built 1943; fate unknown.
Mutsuei Maru
(5000 GRT) built 1943; survived.
Nichinau Maru
(5227 GRT) built 1943; fate unknown.
Ryuei Maru
(5144 GRT) built 1943; sunk by submarine 1944.
Shimpo Maru
(5135 GRT) built 1944; fate unknown.
Tarakan Maru
(5135 GRT) built 1943; sunk by submarine 1945.
?Tennan Maru
(5407 GRT) built 194?; sunk by submarine 1943.
Yuho Maru
(5266 GRT) built 1943; sunk by submarine 1944.

Name	Date	DWT	Length ft in	Beam ft in	Draught ft in	Machinery	SHP	Speed max/min	Radius
1 TS 1020 GRT steam coastal tanker	1942–1944	1250	213 6 oa 196 10 pp	32 2	15 5	VTE	950 ihp	12 / 10	3700

CAREERS

?Kyoei Maru No. 3
(1189 GRT) built 1941; sunk by submarine 1944.

Type	Date	DWT	Length ft in	Beam ft in	Draught ft in	Machinery	SHP	Speed max/min	Radius
2A 6600 GRT cargo steamer	1943–1945	10200	448 8 oa 419 10 pp	59 8	25 7	GT	2000	13 / 9.5	4000

2A
CAREERS

Azuchisan Maru
(6886 GRT) built 1944; sunk by submarine 1944.
Kisan Maru
(6859 GRT) built 1944; survived.

2 TA (tanker variant)
CAREERS

Einiu Maru
(6800 GRT) built 194?; fate unknown.
Hakushun Maru
(7112 GRT) built 194?; sunk by aircraft 1944.
?Tomei Maru
(4930 GRT) built 194?; fate unknown
Daiun Maru No. 2
(3000 GRT) completed post-war.

STANDARD MERCHANT SHIPS

Keisho Maru
(2840 GRT) built 1944; sunk by aircraft 1945.
?Shinroku Maru
(2857 GRT) built 1944; sunk by submarine 1945.
?Shinsei Maru
(2880 GRT) built 194?; sunk by aircraft 1945.
Sansui Maru
(10000 GRT) completed post-war.

Name	Builder	Date	Displ	Length ft in	Beam ft in	Draught ft in	Machinery	SHP	Speed	Fuel	Radius	Armament	Comp
2D 2300 GRT cargo steamer		1943–1945	3850	300 10 oa 278 10 pp	44 0	19 2	VTE	1000 ihp	11/9		4000		

CAREERS
Bujo Maru
(2270 GRT) built 1944; sunk by aircraft 1944.
Daiki Maru
(2217 GRT) built 1944; sunk by submarine 1945.
Doryo Maru
(2274 GRT) built 1944; sunk by submarine 1945.
Doshi Maru
(2274 GRT) built 1944; sunk by aircraft 1945.
Eijo
(Maru) conversion as minelayer (see p. 202).
Hakusan Maru No. 5
(2211 GRT) built 1944; sunk by submarine 1945.

Hino Maru No. 10
(2200 GRT) built 1945; fate unknown.
Kasei Maru
(2220 GRT) built 1944; sunk by mine 1945.
Ken'yo Maru
(2217 GRT) built 1944; sunk by aircraft 1945.
Mino
conversion as minelayer (see p. 202).
?Toan Maru
(2110 GRT) built 194?; sunk by submarine 1944.
Wakamiyasan Maru
(2211 GRT) built 1944; sunk by submarine 1945.

Name	Date	DWT	Length ft in	Beam ft in	Draught ft in	Machinery	SHP	Speed max/min	Radius
2 Ed 870 GRT motor coaster	1943–1945	1567	210 11 oa 196 10 pp	31 2	14 9	Diesel	430	9/7	2000

Type 2 Ed

Name	Date	DWT	Length ft in	Beam ft in	Draught ft in	Machinery	SHP	Speed max/min	Radius
2 Eh 870 GRT motor coaster			——as above——			Internal combustion	380	7	2000

Name	Date	DWT	Length ft in	Beam ft in	Draught ft in	Machinery	SHP	Speed max/min	Radius
2 Er 870 GRT steam coaster			——as above——			VTE	400 ihp	7	2000

2E
CAREERS
Hayabusa Maru
(873 GRT) built 1944; sunk by aircraft 1945.
?Ina Maru
(853 GRT) built 194?; sunk by aircraft 1944.

Kisaragi Maru
(873 GRT) built 1944; sunk by submarine 1944.
Koryu Maru
(873 GRT) built 1944; sunk by aircraft 1945.
Tobi Maru
(887 GRT) built 1944; sunk by mine 1945.

Name	Date	DWT	Length ft in	Beam ft in	Draught ft in	Machinery	SHP	Speed max/min	Radius
2 TL 10000 GRT steam tanker	1943–1945	16000	516 6 oa 485 7 pp	66 11	29 6	GT	4500	15/13	8000

Type 2 TL

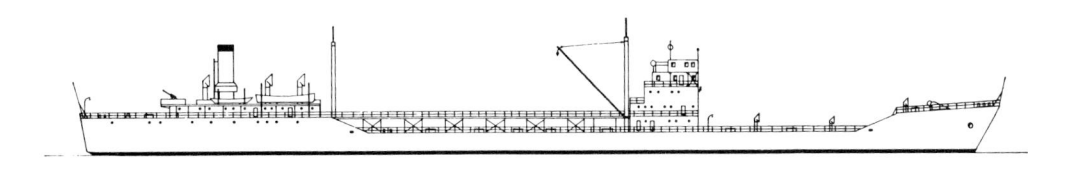

2 TL
CAREERS
Chigusa Maru
conversion to escort carrier (see p. 62).
Okikawa Maru
(10043 GRT) built 1944; sunk by aircraft 1944.
Seria Maru
(10000 GRT) built 1944; fate unknown.
Yamashiro Maru
conversion to escort carrier (see p. 62).

Name	Date	DWT	Length ft in	Beam ft in	Draught ft in	Machinery	SHP	Speed max/min	Radius
2 TM 2850 GRT steam tanker	1943–1945	4300	324 10 oa 305 1 pp	45 3	19 10	GT	1100	11.5 / 9.5	5000

2 TM
CAREERS
Aiten Maru
(2888 GRT) built 1943; survived.
Ayanami Maru
(2800 GRT) built 194?; fate unknown.
Kumanosan Maru
(2857 GRT) built 1943; sunk by submarine 1944.
Wakakusa Maru
(2850 GRT) built 1945; fate unknown.

Name	Builder	Date	Displ	Length ft in	Beam ft in	Draught ft in	Machinery	SHP	Speed	Fuel	Radius	Armament	Comp
2 TEd 870 GRT coastal motor tanker		1943–1945	1680	210 11 oa 196 10 pp	31 2	14 9	Diesel	430	9 / 7		4000		

CAREERS
Koryu Maru
(820 GRT) built 1944; sunk by mine 1945.
Murotsu Maru
(870 GRT) built 1943; survived.

Name	Date	DWT	Length ft in	Beam ft in	Draught ft in	Machinery	SHP	Speed max/min	Radius
3 A 7200 GRT cargo steamer	1945	11230	449 0 oa 419 11 pp	59 8	27 1	GT	4500	15.5 / 12	4000
3 B 5000 GRT cargo steamer	1945	6970	403 1 oa 377 4 pp	54 2	23 11	GT	4500	17.5 / 14	4000
3 D 3000 GRT cargo steamer	1944–1946	4700	342 0 oa 321 6 pp	46 11	20 0	GT	2000	14.5 / 12	4000
3 E 870 GRT steam coaster	1944–1946	1540	210 11 oa 196 10 pp	31 2	15 2	VTE	500 ihp	10 / 7.5	2000
3 TL 10000 GRT steam tanker	1944–1946	15467	516 1 oa 492 2 pp	65 7	29 6 ca	GT	9000	19 / 16	8000

STANDARD MERCHANT SHIPS 261

Name	Date	DWT	Length ft in	Beam ft in	Draught ft in	Machinery	SHP	Speed max/min	Radius
3 TA 7200 GRT steam tanker	1945–1946	11000	423 3 pp	59 9	28 0	GT	4500	13	4000
3 TE 870 GRT coastal motor tanker	1944	1608	210 11 ou 196 10 pp	31 2	15 2	Diesel	500	11 / 9.5	2000

Name	Date	DWT	Length ft in	Beam ft in	Draught ft in	Machinery	SHP	Speed max/min	Radius
4 B 3400 GRT cargo steamer		9500	367 6 pp	49 3		GT	8000	18	8500
4 TM 3400 GRT steam tanker		4400	367 6 pp	49 3		GT	8000	18	8500
4 TL 9600 GRT steam tanker		13800	492 2 pp	68 3	29 6	GT	18000	19	8000
4 TE 1150 GRT steam coastal tanker	1945	unknown	213 3 pp	35 5	15 9	GT?	750	13	2000
UTL 10200 GRT steam tanker		15467	492 0 pp	68 0		GT	9000	16	20000

25. Hospital Ships

No ships were built specifically as Hospital Ships for the Imperial Japanese Navy, but the following merchant vessels were requisitioned for the purpose:

CAREERS

Asahi Maru
(9326 GRT) built 1914 as Italian *Dante Alighieri*: 1937; commissioned into IJN as Hospital Ship *Asahi Maru*; damaged 5 February, 1944 in collision off Bizo Seto, Inland Sea; scrapped December, 1949.

Hakuai Maru
(2636 GRT) built 1898; 1904: requisitioned as Hospital Ship; 1905: returned to original owner; 1945: again requisitioned, as Transport; sunk 18 June 1945 E of Sakhalin (50° 23′ N, 155° 06′ E) by US submarine *Apogon*.

Hikawa Maru
(11621 GRT) built 1930; 1941: requisitioned as Hospital Ship; captured August 1945 and employed as Repatriation Transport until returned to original owners in 1947; for disposal 1961.

Hikawa Maru No. 2
(6067 GRT) built 1927 as Dutch liner *Op Ten Noort*; requisitioned as Hospital Ship 14 February, 1942; captured 1 March, 1942 40 nm SW of Bawean Island by *Amatsukaze*; late 1942: Japanese *Ten-No Maru*; 1 April, 1943: Hospital ship *Hikawa Maru No. 2*; lost c October 1944 to unknown cause.

Kosai Maru
(2635 GRT) built 1899; 1904: requisitioned as Hospital Ship; 1905: returned to owners; 1927: *Bifuku Maru*, later a floating crab-canning factory; sunk 8 August,

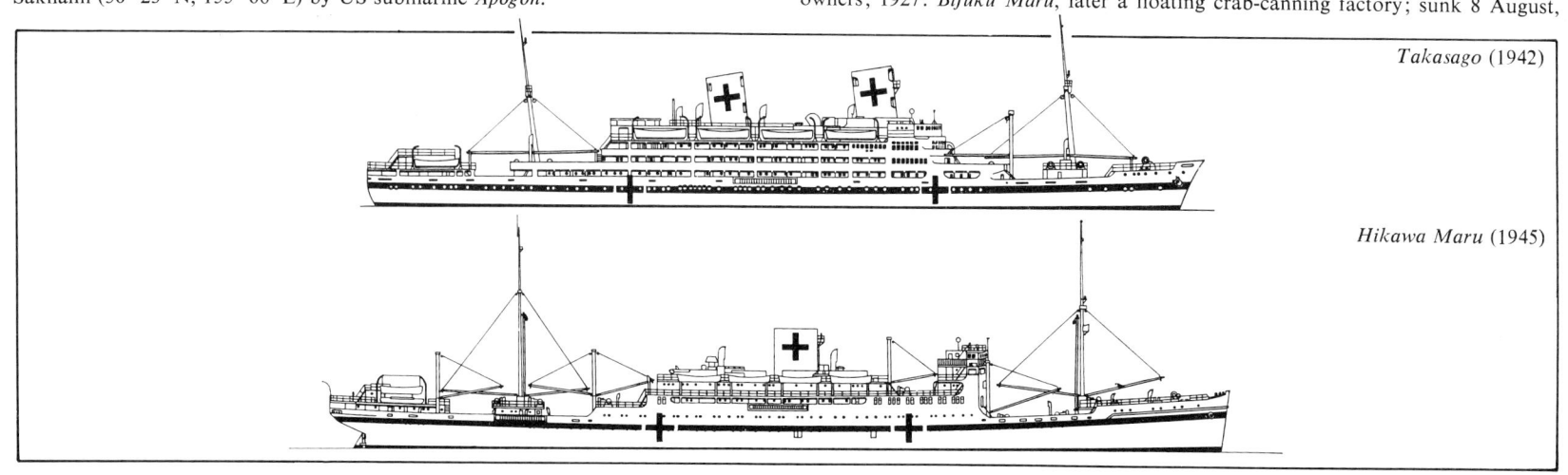

Takasago (1942)

Hikawa Maru (1945)

1942 in Tsugaru Straits by US submarine *Narwhal*.
Muro Maru
(1607 GRT) built 1926 as passenger vessel; 1938: requisitioned as Hospital Ship; sunk 13 November, 1944 in Manila Bay by TF 38 aircraft.
Rohira Maru
(3869 GRT) built 1880 as British *Rohilla*; 1904: Japanese Navy Hospital Ship; lost 7 July, 1905 by grounding on Manaita Rock, Ujina.

Tachibana Maru
(1772 GRT) built 1935; 1838: requisitioned as Hospital Ship; August 1945: Repatriation Service until returned to owners.
Takasago Maru
(9347 GRT) built 1936 as liner; 1941: requisitioned as Hospital Ship; August 1945: Repatriation Service until returned to owners, 1947.

26. Survey Vessels

Name	Builder	Date	Displ	Length ft in	Beam ft in	Draught ft in	Machinery	SHP	Speed	Fuel	Radius	Armament	Comp
HAYO ex-*Poyang*	Scott's SB & Eng., Greenock	1891	4600 N	287 7 pp	43 0	– –	2 sets VTE 2 shafts	6500 ihp	15	?	?	1 × 80mm (3in) 40-cal LA	
HAKUSA ex-*Fu Hsing*	W. Gray, West Hartlepool	1914	6799 N 6000 S	369 9 pp	51 2	12 2	1 set VTE 1 shaft	1830 ihp	11.4	?	?	2 × 80mm etc. HA	
CHOYO ex-*Tydeman*	Soerabaya DY	1916	1320 N 1160 S	226 4 oa 226 0 pp	32 0	11 0	2 Werkspoor Diesel engines 2 shafts	700	10	194	?	1 AA gun DCs	104
HEIYO ex-*Merry Hampton* ex-*Herald*	Blyth SB Co. Devonport DY	1918 1922– 1923	1320 S	276 7 wl 267 5 pp	35 0	12 0	1 set VTE 4 boilers 1 shaft	2500 ihp	17	260 coal	2600 @ 12	1 × 80mm etc. HA 2 × 7.7mm MGs DCs	133

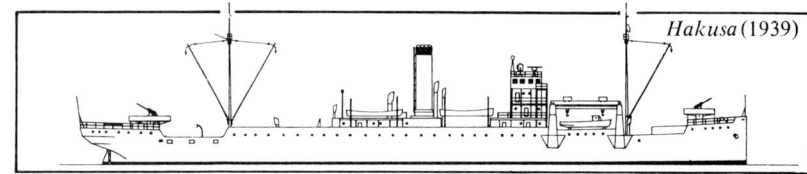

Hakusa (1939)

The heavy-lift hoist used to raise and lower fast patrol boats on the *Hakusa*. (Tappman Collection.)

CAREER
Hayo
(2551 GRT) built 1891 as British SS *Poyang* for the China Navigation Company Ltd., London; captured 1937 by the Japanese; 15 March 1940: Survey Ship *Hayo*; fate after 1942 unknown.

GENERAL NOTES
Hakusa
Former Chinese Customs Vessel equipped to carry boats on overhanging gantries on either side of the fore-deck, for ease of slipping and recovery while the parent vessel was under way.

RECONSTRUCTION AND ARMAMENT
September 1944: reconstruction as Repair Ship: boat gantry removed, 3 × 1-tonne, 1 × 5-tonne, 1 × 20-tonne derricks installed; armament: 1 × 120mm 45-cal HA, 20 × 25mm AA, 8 DCs; March 1945: reconstruction as Transport: workshops deleted, 2 kingposts and 2 × 2-tonne booms added.

CAREER
Built 1914 as Chinese Customs Vessel *Fu Hsing*; captured 1937 by Japanese; 20 February, 1938: commissioned as Survey Ship *Hakusa*; 25 September 1944: Repair Ship; 10 March, 1945: Transport; sunk 8 June, 1945 off Cape Camau (08° 56′ N, 105° 37′ E) by US submarine *Cobia*.

GENERAL NOTES
Choyo
Former Dutch survey ship, built for service in the Netherlands East Indies. The power provided by the Werkspoor Diesels was unreliable but although preparations were made for their replacement by two Enterprise Diesels, whose 800 hp was expected to give 14 knots, this work was not completed before the Japanese invasion of Java. 1944: amidships superstructure deck removed, tripod mast installed at rear of bridge.

CAREER
Launched 24 June, 1916 as Dutch Survey Ship *Tydeman*; sunk 4 March, 1942 at Tjilitjap by Japanese aircraft; raised and reconstruction begun on 25 March, 1944; recaptured August 1945 incomplete at Tandjong Priok; sunk 24 April, 1946 as target hulk by Dutch cruiser *Jacob van Heemskerck*.

GENERAL NOTES
Heiyo
Former British minesweeping sloop of the '24-class' or 'Racehorse-class'; converted to survey vessel 1922–3, renamed *Herald*.

CAREER
Launched 19 December, 1918 as Royal Navy sloop *Merry Hampton*; 1923: Survey Ship *Herald*; scuttled February 1942 by RN at Singapore; raised January 1943 and commissioned after repair as *Hieryu Maru* on 10 October, 1943 (maximum speed reduced to only 11 knots); 20 June, 1944: renamed *Heiyo*; sunk 14 November, 1944 by mine in the Java Sea.

SURVEY VESSELS 263

Name	Builder	Date	Displ	Length ft in	Beam ft in	Draught ft in	Machinery	SHP	Speed	Fuel	Radius	Armament	Comp
HOYO ex-*Pollux*	Verschure & Co., Amsterdam	1922	1012 N 946 S	195 6 oa 182 6 pp	31 2	10 0	1 set VTE 2 boilers 1 shaft	550 ihp	12	?	?	several AA MGs	50 approx

Hoyo
Former Dutch Lighthouse Tender.

CAREER
Launched 15 August, 1922 as Dutch *Pollux*; sunk 2 March, 1942 at Soerabaya; raised, repaired and commissioned as *Horai Maru* on 13 February, 1943; 20 June 1944: renamed *Hoyo*; recaptured August 1945 at Soerabaya, laid up after mine damage; scrapped.

Name	Builder	Date	Displ	Length ft in	Beam ft in	Draught ft in	Machinery	SHP	Speed	Fuel	Radius	Armament	Comp
TSUKUSHI Class	Mitsubishi, Yokohama	1940–1941	1600 N 1400 S	272 4 wl 260 2 pp	34 9	11 10	3 Diesel engines 3 shafts	5700	19.8	?	?	4 × 120mm (4.7in) 45-cal LA 1 floatplane	?

GENERAL NOTES
Tsukushi class
Tsukushi:
3rd Supplementary Fleet Programme 1937 and 1942 Supplementary Fleet Programme.
Official designation 'Sokuryo Kan'.

CAREER
Tsukushi
Launched 1941, completed December 1941; sunk 4 November, 1943 off New Ireland (02° 40′ S, 150° 40′ E) by mine.
Job No. 847
Not built.
Job No. 5418
(to be named *Miho*). Not built.

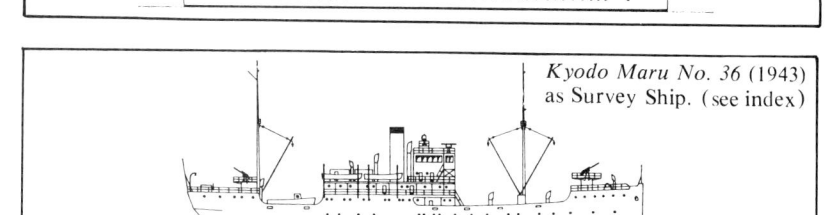

Tsukushi (1942)

Kyodo Maru No. 36 (1943) as Survey Ship. (see index)

27. Research Ships and Icebreakers

Name	Builder	Date	Displ	Length ft in	Beam ft in	Draught ft in	Machinery	SHP	Speed	Fuel	Radius	Armament	Comp
KAIYO Class	Mitsubishi, Shimonoseki	1939–1943	277 N 270 S	121 5 oa 111 7 pp	22 6	7 8	1 Diesel engine 1 shaft	400	11	?	7000 @ 10	3 × 13.2mm AA 2 × 7.7mm MGs DCs	?

GENERAL NOTES
'Kaiyo' means 'Ocean'. Oceanographic Research Vessels of trawler-type design. Speed on trials between 11.3 and 11.9 knots.

CAREERS
Kaiyo No. 1
Launched 1 July, 1939; completed 9 October, 1939; sunk 15 October 1944 off Soerabaya (06° 30′ S, 111° 35′ E) by US submarine *Dace*.
Kaiyo No. 2
Launched 4 October, 1939; completed 23 December, 1939; sunk 21 November, 1944 in the Celebes Sea by US aircraft.
Kaiyo No. 3
Launched 22 October, 1941; completed 17 June, 1942; August 1944: presumed lost after sailing from Shimoda.
Kaiyo No. 4
Launched 20 January, 1942; completed 17 July, 1942; captured August 1945; became MSDF Survey Vessel *HM 01*.

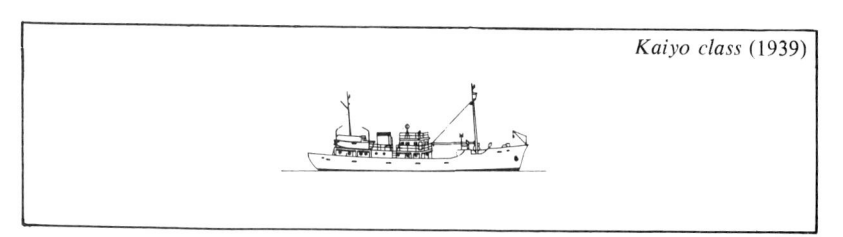

Kaiyo class (1939)

Kaiyo No. 5
Launched 12 November, 1942; completed 28 February, 1943; captured August 1945; became MSDF Survey Vessel; Autumn 1952: missing S of Sagami Bay, possibly due to underwater explosion of submarine volcano Myojin-Sho.
Kaiyo No. 6
Launched 12 December, 1942; completed 31 March, 1943; sunk 31 October 1944 off Murotsuki (32° 50′ N, 134° 21′ E) by US submarine *Gabilan*.

Name	Builder	Date	Displ	Length ft in	Beam ft in	Draught ft in	Machinery	SHP	Speed	Fuel	Radius	Armament	Comp
TENKAI No. 1 ex-*Nishizu Maru*	Mitsubishi, Shimonoseki	1936	150 N 145 S	88 7 pp	19 0	– –	1 Diesel engine 1 shaft	225	8	?	?	nil	?
TENKAI No. 2 ex-Dutch order	Miho SB, Shimzu	1942–1943	1200 N	149 3 pp	27 11	12 11	1 Diesel engine 1 shaft	550	11			several MGs DCs	
TENKAI No. 3 ex-*Fei Hsing*			625 N 600 S	139 9 pp	25 3	10 3	2 sets VTE 2 boilers 2 shafts	unknown	12 approx	?	?	1 × 47 mm (3pdr) several MGs	?
TENKAI No. 4 ex-*Majang*	NV 'de Maas', Slikkerveer	1928	1200 N 1000 S	167 6 pp	26 9	9 5	1 5-cyl 2-stroke Sulzer Diesel 1 shaft	122 nominal	10		3000 @ 10	2 × 7.7mm MGs DCs	?
TENKAI No. 5 ex-*Pulau Kidjang*	Taikoo Dock Co., Hong Kong	1936	400 N approx	114 10 pp	25 7	– –	1 6-cyl 4-stroke Deutz Diesel 1 shaft	70 nominal	10		?	2 × 7.7mm MGs 4 DCs	?

Tenkai No. 1
Hydrographic and Meterological Research Vessel. Requisitioned trawler.

CAREER
Launched 9 January, 1936 as 101 GRT trawler *Nishizu Maru*; September 1939: to Navy as *Tenkai No. 1*; captured August 1945 and handed over to the Hydrographic Department.

Tenkai Nos. 2 and 4
Hydrographic and Meteorological Research Vessels. Former Dutch motor coasters.

CAREERS
Tenkai No. 2
Under construction for Dutch (490 GRT); requisitioned by IJN and completed as *Tenkai No. 2* on 26 January, 1943; presumed lost June 1943 between Truk and Rabaul.
Tenkai No. 4
Launched 1928 as Dutch *Majang* (536 GRT); captured 15 February 1942 by Japanese and renamed *Nikko Maru*; 1944: converted to Research Vessel (also used temporarily as a Cable Layer); sunk 24 November, 1944 off Balabac, Philippines, by US aircraft.

Tenkai No. 3
Hydrographic and Meteorological Research Vessel. Former British Police Vessel.

CAREER
Built as Hong Kong Marine Police vessel *Fei Hsing* (450 GRT); captured December 1941 at Hong Kong; 10 October, 1942: commissioned as *Tenkai No. 3*; November 1943: converted as Training Ship for the Yokohama Harbour Defence Force; captured August 1945 and handed over to the Merchant Navy.

Tenkai No. 5
Hydrographic and Meteorological Research Vessel. Former British passenger vessel.

CAREER
Launched 1936 as British *Pulau Kidjang* (229 GRT); sunk December 1941 at Hong Kong; raised and repaired, renamed *Kissho Maru*; 1943: Research Vessel *Tenkai No. 5*; captured August 1945 at Singapore and returned to original owners; December 1946: *Pulau Kidjang* (Soon Bee SS Co., Singapore.)

Name	Builder	Date	Displ	Length ft in	Beam ft in	Draught ft in	Machinery	SHP	Speed	Fuel	Radius	Armament	Comp
ODOMARI	Kawasaki, Kobe	1921	2700 N 2330 S	211 0 oa 200 0 pp	50 0	18 4	2 sets VTE 5 boilers 2 shafts	4000 ihp	13			1 × 80mm (3in) 40-cal LA 2 × 25mm AA 2 × 13.2mm AA DCs	

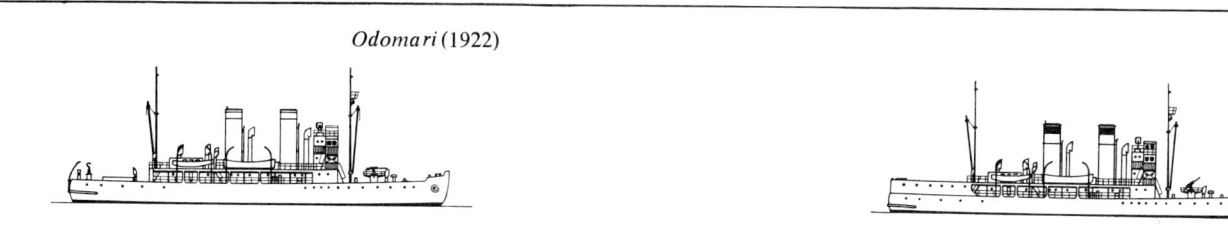

Odomari (1922)

Odomari (1945)

GENERAL NOTES
1920 Programme: first Japanese naval ice-breaker. Built without bilge-keel, later modified with strengthened bow and poop raised. 1937–8: 2 × 25mm AA, 24 × 13.2mm added.

CAREERS
Odomari
Launched 3 October, 1921; completed 7 November, 1921; captured August 1945 and intended for use as Repatriation Transport but not so employed; laid up at Yokosuka until 1947 and thereafter at Tsurumi; scrapped 1949.
Job No. 846
1942 War Programme. 6800ts standard. Not ordered.
Job No. 5419
1942M War Programme, to have been named *Esan*. 7400ts standard. Order cancelled before keel-laying.

RESEARCH SHIPS AND ICEBREAKERS

28. Tugs

Name	Builder	Date	Displ	Length ft in	Beam ft in	Draught ft in	Machinery	SHP	Speed	Fuel	Radius	Armament	Comp
600-TONNE Type	unknown	1914	597 N 600 S	145 0 oa 140 0 pp	27 0	10 2	2 sets VTE 2 boilers 2 shafts	1520 ihp	13.6	?	?	Nil	?

GENERAL NOTES
First Japanese naval salvage tugs – two funnels.

CAREERS
Sasebo No. 4
Built 1914; served with Sasebo Port Captain; captured August 1945 at Sasebo.

Kure No. 5
Built 1914; served with Kure Port Captain; 1938: transferred to the Yangtse (armed with 1 × 13.2mm AA MG); fate unknown.

Name	Builder	Date	Displ	Length ft in	Beam ft in	Draught ft in	Machinery	SHP	Speed	Fuel	Radius	Armament	Comp
HASHIMA-Class	Harima SB Co., Aioi	1937–1940	625 N 600 S	143 8 oa 131 3 pp	28 10	10 2	2 sets VTE 2 boilers 2 shafts	2200 ihp	14.5	?	?	2 × 25mm AA DCs	?

GENERAL NOTES
600-tonne salvage tugs with 2 × 2-tonne and 1 × 5-tonne derricks and salvage pumps. Designation 'Kyunan-sen ken Eisen'.

CAREERS
Hashima
Launched 1938; completed 26 May, 1938; to Yoko-suka Port Captain; sunk 25 January, 1945 (possibly) by US aircraft in the Formosa Straits.

Futagami
Launched 1939; completed 30 April, 1939; to Kure Port Captain; captured August 1945 at Truk.

Kasashima
Launched 1937; sunk 25 January, 1945 by US aircraft in the Formosa Straits.

Name	Builder	Date	Displ	Length ft in	Beam ft in	Draught ft in	Machinery	SHP	Speed	Fuel	Radius	Armament	Comp
OJIMA-Class *TATEGAMI* *NAGAURA*	Maizuru DY Harima SB Aioi	1936–1940	812 N 800 S	175 6 oa 160 9 pp	31 2	11 4	2 sets VTE 2 boilers 2 shafts	2200 ihp	15.3	?	?	2 × 13.2mm AA 6 DCs	?

GENERAL NOTES
800-tonne salvage tugs with 3 × 5-tonne, 1 × 10-tonne derricks, salvage pumps, compressors and workshops. 1941: 13.2mm AA replaced by 25mm AA.

CAREERS
Ojima
Launched 1940; completed 1941; lost 7 October, 1943 while assisting the burning *Kikukawa Maru* off Truk.

Tategami
Launched 1936; completed 25 January, 1937 as *Tategami Maru* for the Nippon Salvage Co.; requisitioned as naval salvage tug *Tategami*; captured August 1945 and returned to previous owners, renamed *Tategami Maru*.

Nagaura
Launched 1940; completed 31 October, 1940; sunk 22 February, 1944 W of New Ireland (00° 54′ S, 148° 38′ E) by US destroyers *Ausburne*, *Conway*, *Spence*, *Stanley* and *Dyson*.

Name	Builder	Date	Displ	Length ft in	Beam ft in	Draught ft in	Machinery	SHP	Speed	Fuel	Radius	Armament	Comp
MIURA Class	Mitsubishi, Shimonoseki	1944–1945	883 N 800 S	170 2 oa 160 9 pp	31 2	11 4	2 sets VTE 2 boilers 2 shafts	2200 ihp	12	?	?	2 × 25mm AA 6 DCs	?

GENERAL NOTES
Simplified Ojima-type: uncambered decks, no bilge-keel, upright funnel; 2 × 1000-tonne, 3 × 3/700-tonne, 3 × 2/500-tonne salvage pumps, 3 × 5-tonne, 1 × 10-tonne derricks, workshops, 2 diving tenders.

CAREER
Miura
Launched 7 September, 1944; completed 25 December, 1944; captured August 1945 at Kure and returned to Japanese Government as *Miura Maru*; 1949: MSDF *PL 01*, named *Miura*.

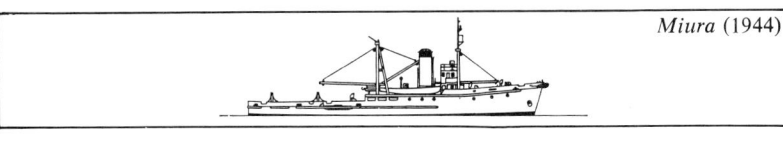

Miura (1944)

Yumihari
Launched 16 December, 1944; completed 12 March, 1945; captured August 1945 at Hakata, returned to Japanese Government as *Yumihari Maru*.

Hanashima
Under construction in August 1945; launched 5 December, 1945 as *Akama Maru* (593 GRT) for Mitsubishi Jukogyo KK, Tokyo.

Name	Builder	Date	Displ	Length ft in	Beam ft in	Draught ft in	Machinery	SHP	Speed	Fuel	Radius	Armament	Comp
20-TONNE Type	various	to 1940	20 N	55 9 oa / 55 9 pp	11 4	3 9	1 set VTE / 1 boiler / 1 shaft	200 ihp	11	?	?	nil	?

GENERAL NOTES
Harbour tugs and lighters. Designation 'Eisen ken Kotsu-sen'. Built in large numbers, hardly any numbers or fates are known apart from: Eisen Nos. 928, 1132, 1133, 1224–1229, all built by Mitsubishi between 1935 and 1940.

Name	Builder	Date	Displ	Length ft in	Beam ft in	Draught ft in	Machinery	SHP	Speed	Fuel	Radius	Armament	Comp
100-TONNE Type	various	1930–1945	106 N / 100 S	76 3 oa / 70 6 pp	17 9	6 9	1 set VTE / 1 boiler / 1 shaft	240 ihp	10.1	?	?	nil	?

GENERAL NOTES
Harbour tugs – 'Eisen'. Minor builders' differences between units: Harima SB Co., Aioi; Chosen Heavy Industry Co., Pusan; Hitachi SB Co., Kanagawa; Sakurajima, Osaka; Maeda SB Co., Osaka; Ujina SB Co., Hiroshima, among others. More than 100 units built, records of which are fragmentary. The following are known to have survived until 1945:

Eisen No. 770	No. 832	No. 1036	No. 1274
801	871	1112	1351
816	888	1113	1547
818	943	1273	1548

100-tonne Type

Name	Builder	Date	Displ	Length ft in	Beam ft in	Draught ft in	Machinery	SHP	Speed	Fuel	Radius	Armament	Comp
130-TONNE Type	Yokosuka DY	1939–1940	126 N	84 8 oa	18 0	6 3	1 Diesel engine / 1 shaft	400	11	?	1000 @ 10	1 × 13.2mm AA / 18 DCs	20 approx

GENERAL NOTES
Harbour tugs and basis for *Cha 1* auxiliary submarine chaser class (see p. 217). Slight differences in appearance between tugs and SCs. Copper-plated bottom.

CAREERS
Eisen No. 1182
Launched 1939; January 1940: to Yokosuka Naval District; May 1946: derelict at Uraga.

Eisen No. 1183
Launched 1939 by Ichikawa SB Co., Ujiyamada, fitted out at Yokosuka NDY; February 1940: to Yokosuka Naval District; 1947: laid up at Yokosuka.

Eisen No. 1648
Launched 1943; completed 24 August, 1943 as *Cha 43*; (see p. 218).

Eisen No. 1649
Launched 1943; completed 15 September, 1943 as *Cha 44* (see p. 218).

Name	Builder	Date	Displ	Length ft in	Beam ft in	Draught ft in	Machinery	SHP	Speed	Fuel	Radius	Armament	Comp
150-TONNE Type	various	1932–1945	150 N	87 0 oa / 82 0 pp	19 4	7 1	1 set VTE / 2 boilers / 1 shaft	400 ihp	10	?	?	nil	?

GENERAL NOTES
Harbour tugs; minor builders' differences between units. Built by Harima, Aioi; Chosen Heavy Industry, Pusan; Ujina, Hiroshima; Hakodate Dock Co.; Tohoku Dock Co., Shioggama; Kanazashi SB Co., Shimizu; Niigata Iron Works.

CAREERS
Eisen No. 789
Kure NDY; 1947: at Kure.
829
Maizuru Port Captain; 1947: at Maizuru.
880
fate unknown.
926
Ominato Naval Repair Yard; 1947: at Ominato.
942
Kure Port Captain; 1947: at Kure.
960
Yokosuka NDY; 1947: at Yokosuka.
983
Kure Port Captain; 9 December, 1946: to the Department of the Interior.
996
Sasebo Port Captain; 1947: at Kure.
1002
Yokosuka Port Captain; fate unknown.
1003
Sasebo Port Captain; fate unknown.
1029
1945: to Toyo Salvage Co., Osaka.
1030
Tokuyama Port Captain; 1947: at Tokuyama.
1031
Maizuru Port Captain; 1947 at Maizuru.
1033
Sasebo Naval Base; 9 December, 1946 to: the Department of the Interior.
1103
Sasebo Port Captain; 1947 at Sasebo.
1152
Kure Port Captain; 1947 at Kure.
1153
Sasebo Naval Base; 1947 in the Sasebo area.
1156
Sasebo Port Captain; 1947 at Nagasaki.
1181
sunk 1945 at Kagoshima by aircraft.
1343
Sasebo NDY; 1947 at Sasebo.
1344
Yokosuka Naval Air Technical Arsenal to 1947.

1455
1947 at Yokosuka.
1546
Kure Naval Base; 1947 at Kure.

1607
Sasebo Port Captain; 9 December, 1946: to the Department of the Interior.
3324
Kure NDY; 1947 at Kure.

Name	Builder	Date	Displ	Length ft in	Beam ft in	Draught ft in	Machinery	SHP	Speed	Fuel	Radius	Armament	Comp
150-TONNE Type (Wooden)	various	1944–1945	151 N	78 9 wl 73 8 pp	20 5	7 4	1 set VTE 1 boiler 1 shaft	400 ihp	10	?	?	nil	?

GENERAL NOTES
Simplified 150-tonne type for construction in small yards; no sheer or bilge-keel. Number and fate of completed units unknown.

150-tonne Type (Wooden)

Name	Builder	Date	Displ	Length ft in	Beam ft in	Draught ft in	Machinery	SHP	Speed	Fuel	Radius	Armament	Comp
250-TONNE Type	Mitsubishi, Shimonoseki	1941–1942	244 F 238 N	108 3 wl 108 3 pp	22 6	6 7	1 Diesel engine 1 shaft	400	10.9	?	1490 @ 10	nil	?

GENERAL NOTES
Officially designated 'Tug and Utility Craft' (Eisen ken Kotsu-sen, actually used as a sonar trials ship. Fresh water in double-bottom tanks for experimental purposes. Fitted for minelaying, but without separate mine-deck.

CAREER
Eisen No. 1434
Launched 12 August, 1941; completed 15 March, 1942; employed by the Numazu Research Establishment as *Fuji Maru*; captured August 1945 and employed at Uraga for Repatriation Service duties until 1947.

Name	Builder	Date	Displ	Length ft in	Beam ft in	Draught ft in	Machinery	SHP	Speed	Fuel	Radius	Armament	Comp
300-TONNE Type (Generating)	Kawasaki, Kobe	1936–1944	292 N	94 4 oa 86 11 pp	23 0	8 10	2 Diesel engines electric drive 1 shaft	700	12	?	?	nil	?

GENERAL NOTES
Designation 'Zatsueki-sen'. Tugs and floating electricity generators built to individual order by Kawasaki, Kobe, and requisitioned by the Navy. One 400 kw AC and 130 Kw DC Diesel-generators; compressors producing 28251 cu ft of air per hour.

CAREERS
Sumiyoshi Maru
Built 1936 for Kawasaki; 1937: requisitioned by the Navy and employed on the Yangtse.
Eisen No. 3496
Built 1939; Kure NDY; 1947 at Kure.
3498
Commissioned 1 April, 1940; fate unknown.

300-tonne Type (Generator)

6388
Completed 24 July, 1942; fate unknown.
6389
Completed 11 November, 1943; fate unknown.
6390
Completed 2 April, 1944; Yokosuka NDY; 1947: derelict at Yokosuka.
6391
Completed 8 July, 1944; fate unknown.
6741
Completed 14 December, 1943; fate unknown.

Name	Builder	Date	Displ	Length ft in	Beam ft in	Draught ft in	Machinery	SHP	Speed	Fuel	Radius	Armament	Comp
300-TONNE Type	various	1939–1944	300 N	121 5 oa 111 7 pp	23 0	8 1	2 sets VTE 2 boilers 2 shafts	800 ihp	12	?	?	nil	?

GENERAL NOTES
Tugs fitted with salvage pumps. Minor builders' variations between units. built by Fujinagata SB Co., Osaka; Hitachi, Kanagawa; Mitsubishi, Shimonoseki; Ujina, Hiroshima. Fifteen units built, details incomplete.

CAREERS
Eisen No. 841
Fate unknown.
1026
Kure NDY; 1947 at Kure.
1027
Maizuru NDY; 1947 at Maizuru.
1129
Kure NDY; 1946 at Kure, machinery unserviceable.

300-tonne Type

1130
as *No. 1129*.
1150
Sasebo NDY; 1947 at Sasebo.
1310–1312
(Ujina) fate unknown.
1543
(Ujina) at Shibayama in 1946.
1647
(Mitsubishi) launched 18 September, 1943; completed 30 April, 1944; in service as *Sasebo No. 9*; 9 December, 1946: to the Department of the Interior.

Name	Builder	Date	Displ	Length ft in	Beam ft in	Draught ft in	Machinery	SHP	Speed	Fuel	Radius	Armament	Comp
300-TONNE Type (Diesel)	Mitsubishi, Shimonoseki	1943	290 N	150 11 oa 141 1 pp	21 4	8 10	2 Diesel engines 2 shafts	800	13	?	?	nil	?

GENERAL NOTES
Tugs and utility craft of similar design to the Aircraft Salvage Craft (see p. 69), with two boats in place of the crane.

CAREERS
Eisen No. 1544
Launched 27 February, 1943; completed 5 June, 1943; employed by Tateyama Gunnery School as *Tateho Maru*; captured August 1945; 1945: bridge burned out, total wreck.

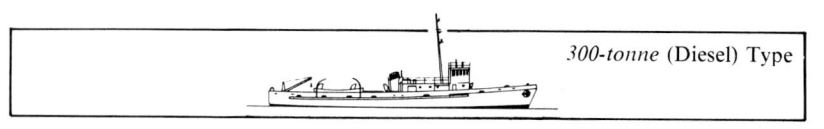

300-tonne (Diesel) Type

1545
Launched 27 March, 1943; completed 30 June, 1943; employed by Otake Submarine School; captured August 1945 and employed on Repatriation Service duties until 1947; 1948: rebuilt as ferry *Atada Maru*.

Name	Builder	Date	Displ	Length ft in	Beam ft in	Draught ft in	Machinery	SHP	Speed	Fuel	Radius	Armament	Comp
400-TONNE Type	Harima SB Co., Aioi	1942–1943	413 N 400 S	121 5 oa 111 7 pp	26 3	9 1	2 sets VTE 2 boilers 2 shafts	2200 ihp	14.3	?	?	nil	?

CAREERS
Eisen No. 1481
Launched 1942; completed 11 November, 1942; Kure Port Captain; employed by Allies from August 1945.

1482
Launched 1943; completed 27 April, 1943; Kure Port Captain; employed by Allies from August 1945.

1488
Fate unknown.

In addition to these major classes of tugs, there was a large number of older craft, mostly single units or small-scale classes for which neither the technical details nor service records exist. These include:

150–200 tons
Kure Nos. 1, 2, 6;   Maizuru Nos. 1 & 2;   Ominato No. 1;

Ryojun Nos. 1 & 2;   Sasebo Nos. 2–5;   Yokosuka Nos. 1–3, 5;
Eisen No. 453   No. 519   No. 667
        483   564   676
        509   598   705

250–300 tons
Kure Nos. 3 & 4; *Maizuru No. 3*; *Ominato No. 2*; *Sasebo No. 1* (*Eisen No. 617*, launched 22 November, 1890); *Sasebo No. 2* (launched 7 October, 1895); *Yokosuka Nos. 4 & 6*; *Eisen No. 488*, *No. 841*.

See also pp. 203 and 217 for details of tugs employed as Auxiliary Minelayers and Submarine Chasers.

29. Utility Vessels

Name	Builder	Date	Displ	Length ft in	Beam ft in	Draught ft in	Machinery	SHP	Speed	Fuel	Radius	Armament	Comp
MAIZURU	unknown	190?	300 N	117 11 pp	20 6		1 set VTE 2 boilers 1 shaft	400 ihp	8	?	?	nil	?
KOSAI	Kawasaki, Kobe	1904	1118 N 1000 S	219 10 oa	29 6		2 sets VTE 2 boilers 2 shafts	2480 ihp	8 approx	?	?	nil	?
ASUKA ex-*Yung Chien*	Kiangnang Dock Co., Shanghai	1914	1039 N 860 S	215 6 oa 205 1 pp	29 6	11 6	2 sets VTE 2 shafts	1400 ihp	13	?	?	1 × 80mm (3in) 60-cal AA 16 × 25mm AA 1 × 13.2mm AA 2 × 7.7mm MGs	145 approx
YUMIHARI ex-*Mata Hari*	C. Rennoldson & Co., South Shields	1915	1000 S	220 0 pp	35 3		1 set VTE 2 boilers 1 shaft	165 nominal	11	?	?	nil	?

Maizuru
CAREER
Built as steam passenger vessel; 1905: requisitioned by Navy as Utility vessel and tug and renamed *Maizuru*; transferred to the Naval Academy Etajima as a training ship; captured August 1945 at Kure; 1947 under repair at Osaka.

Kosai
CAREER
Built 1904 as Korean passenger steamer and lighthouse tender *Kosai*; purchased 1910 by Imperial Japanese Navy and employed as Utility vessel by the Port Captain,

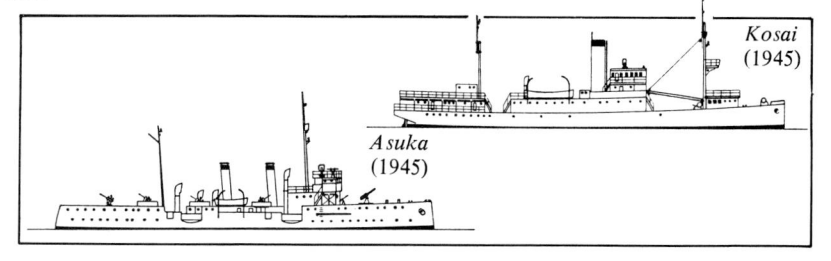

Kosai (1945)

Asuka (1945)

UTILITY VESSELS   269

Sasebo; captured August 1945 and employed by Repatriation Service until 14 May, 1947, when abandoned after running aground.

Asuka
CAREER
Built 1914 as Chinese gunboat *Yung Chien* (1 × 100mm, 1 × 80mm, 4 × 50mm guns); sunk 25 August, 1937 at Shanghai by Japanese aircraft; raised, repaired and commissioned as Torpedo Depot Ship *Asuka*; 1940: to Port Captain, Shanghai, as Utility vessel; 1945: converted to AA Ship (armed as in Table); sunk 7 May, 1946 in the Huangpo Estuary by aircraft.

Yumihar
CAREER
Built 1914 as British cargo steamer *Mata Hari* (P & O, London – 1020 GRT); sunk 28 February, 1942 in Sunda Strait by Japanese aircraft; salvaged and renamed *Yumihari*, employed running between Sasebo and Tsingtao; 1944: renamed *Nichirin Maru*; sunk 2 March, 1945 in East China Sea (27° 12′ N, 124° 22′ E) by US aircraft.

Name	Builder	Date	Displ	Length ft in	Beam ft in	Draught ft in	Machinery	SHP	Speed	Fuel	Radius	Armament	Comp
BUNSEI Class	Shanghai	1934	approx 450 N 400 S	142 9 pp	22 11	6 7	1 Diesel engine 1 shaft	800	12			2 × 13.2mm AA DCs	

Bunsei (1939)

Former Chinese Customs patrol vessels, built 1934.

CAREERS
Bunsei, Wen Hsing
Captured 1937 and used as Minesweeper Support Vessel and Utility vessel on the Yangtse; recaptured 1945 by Chinese Nationalists; sunk 1945 and salvaged by Communists.
Unsei, Yun Hsing
Captured 1937 and employed as survey vessel on the Yangtse and subsequently for miscellaneous tasks; 1944: redesignated as a transport, to serve with the Osaka Sea Transport Division; captured August 1945 and employed as a ferry between Kobe and Sunomoto.
Kotaka
see River Gunboats (p. 121).
Kuroshio Nos 1 & 2
see Landing Ships (p. 197–234).

30. Training Ships

GENERAL NOTES
Except for several sail training ships, the Imperial Japanese Navy had no ships designed as training ships until after 1945, the task being undertaken by active combatant units, as well as by several types of obsolete ships which saw out their useful life as training vessels.
Old battleships: *Fuji, Shikishima*.
Armoured cruisers: *Asama, Azuma, Yagumo, Izumo, Iwade, Kasuga, Nisshin*.
Armoured corvette: *Kongo*.
Protected cruiser: *Tsushima*, renamed *Haikan No. 10*.
Light cruisers: *Hirado*, renamed *Haikan No. 11. Yahagi*, renamed *Haikan No. 12*.
2nd class destroyers: *Kaki*, renamed *Osu. Nire*, renamed *Tomariura No. 1*.
Ashi, renamed *Tomariura No. 2. Sumire*, renamed *Mitaka*.
Patrol vessel: *P No. 101* (ex-*Thracian*), renamed *Toku I-go Renshutei*.

Name	Builder	Date	Displ	Length ft in	Beam ft in	Draught ft in	Machinery	SHP	Speed	Fuel	Radius	Armament	Comp
DAI-ICHI KAISO	not known		539 N	130 7 pp	26 3	10 6	sail					2 guns	

Dai-ichi Kaiso: Name means 'minesweeper No. 1'.
Built in 19th Century. Reputedly a Sail Training Ship until about 1910. Reliable details of the ship's origins or career are not available as the alternative transcriptions and translations of the original Japanese name are confusing.

Name	Builder	Date	Displ	Length ft in	Beam ft in	Draught ft in	Machinery	SHP	Speed	Fuel	Radius	Armament	Comp
ISHIKAWA	Ishikawajima, Tokyo	1874–1876	248 S	107 11 pp	21 4	10 2	sail					nil	
TATEYAMA	Kobe DY	1879–1880	543 N	113 10 pp	26 7		sail					2 × 57mm 40-cal	51
KANJU Class	Onohama, Kobe	1886–1888	877 N	134 5 pp	34 5	14 0	sail					2 × 20pdr 2 × 17pdr	102

Ishikawa
CAREER
Launched 1876; completed 1877; taken out of service about 1893.
GENERAL NOTES
Wooden, Sail Training Ship; Designation 'Renshu Hansen'.
Tateyama
GENERAL NOTES
Wooden, Sail Training Ship, schooner rig.
CAREER
Launched February 1880; completed April 1880; taken out of service 1897.
Kanju Class
GENERAL NOTES
Sail Training Ships, rig unknown.
CAREER
Kanju and *Manju*:
Launched August 1887; completed June 1888; withdrawn from service about 1898.

Name	Builder	Date	Displ	Length ft in	Beam ft in	Draught ft in	Machinery	SHP	Speed	Fuel	Radius	Armament	Comp
YURAGAWA Class	Boyd & Co., Shanghai	1900–1901	919 N 900 S	211 3 oa	29 4	14 1	1 set VTE 2 boilers 1 shaft	625 ihp	11			nil	

GENERAL NOTES
Former Russian passenger steamers.

CAREERS
Yuragawa
Launched 1901 as Russian SS *Bureia* (Chinese Eastern Railway Co., Vladivostok); sunk 1 November, 1904 at Port Arthur; captured and salvaged; commissioned 29 August, 1905 as Training Ship *Yuragawa*, attached to the Naval Engineering Academy Maizuru; 1964: converted to Transport and renamed *Yuragawa Maru*; sunk early 1945 in Maizuru Roads.

Nikogawa
Launched 1900 as Russian *Zeia* (Chinese Eastern Railway Co.); sunk 26 May, 1904 at Dalny; captured and salvaged; commissioned 29 August, 1905 as Training Ship *Nikogawa*, attached to the Naval Academy, Etajima; deleted from Active List about 1930.

Name	Builder	Date	Displ	Length ft in	Beam ft in	Draught ft in	Machinery	SHP	Speed	Fuel	Radius	Armament	Comp
ATADA ex-*Yat Sen*	Kiangnan Dock Co., Shanghai	1930	1520 N	275 0 oa 256 7 pp	34 5	11 2	2 sets VTE 3 boilers 2 shafts	2800 ihp	16	280 coal		3 × 80mm (3in) 40-cal HA 4 × 13.2mm AA	170 approx

GENERAL NOTES
Former Chinese gunboat. Original details: 1650ts standard, 1 × 152mm (6in) (Dutch). 1 × 140mm (5.51in) (Japanese), 4 × 76mm (3in) AA guns, 4000 SHP = 20 knots.

Atada (1940)

CAREER
Launched 12 November, 1930 as Chinese gunboat *Yat Sen*; capsized 25 September, 1937 and beached at Nanking after Japanese air attack; salvaged and reconstructed as Training Ship with tripod mast, new bridge, and cadet accommodation under raised quarterdeck; commissioned 12 May, 1938 as *Atada*, attached to the Naval Academy, Etajima; captured August 1945; refitted and handed over to the Chinese Nationalist Government at Shanghai on 25 August, 1946; renamed *I Hsien*.

Name	Builder	Date	Displ	Length ft in	Beam ft in	Draught ft in	Machinery	SHP	Speed	Fuel	Radius	Armament	Comp
TSUKUMO ex-*Nenette Moller* ex-*Iloilo* ex-*Sugbo*	J & K Smit's Scheepwerken, Kinderdijk	1898	1000 S	165 0 pp	29 0		1 set VTE 2 boilers 1 shaft	127 nominal	11 approx			unknown	

GENERAL NOTES
Former Philippines and British ferry steamer; low speed; poor stability required permanent ballast in hold.

CAREER
Tsukumo
Built 1898 as ferry *Sugbo*; later American *Iloilo* (de la Rama SS Co.); 1933: British *Nenette Moller* (Moller Towages Ltd., Shanghai); captured 10 December, 1941 in South China Sea; commissioned 28 September, 1942 as Training Ship *Tsukumo*, attached to the Naval Academy, Etajima; captured August 1945 and employed by Civil Transport Service as a collier; 1948: returned to former owners as *Edith Moller*.

31. Target Ships

Name	Builder	Date	Displ	Length ft in	Beam ft in	Draught ft in	Machinery	SHP	Speed	Fuel	Radius	Armament	Comp
HAKACHI	Harima SB Co., Aioi	1943	1900 N 1641 S	301 10 wl 286 11 pp	37 1	12 6	2 sets GT 2 boilers 2 shafts	4400	19.3		4000 @ 14	4 × 13.2mm AA	

CAREER
Launched 1943; completed 18 November, 1943; modified 1944 as an Escort vessel with 2 × 120mm 45-cal, 28 × 25mm AA guns and 36 DCs; captured August 1945 and employed by Repatriation Service until 1947, when scrapped at Fujinagata.

GENERAL NOTES
1941 War Programme (*Job No 660*). First ship to be designed specifically as an air bombing target. Designation 'Hyotekikan'.

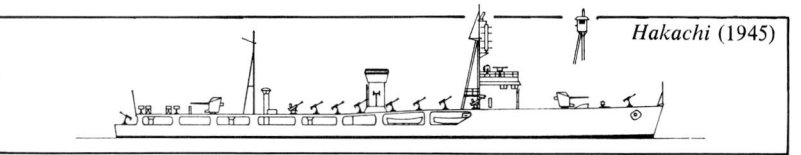

Hakachi (1945)

Name	Builder	Date	Displ	Length ft in	Beam ft in	Draught ft in	Machinery	SHP	Speed	Fuel	Radius	Armament	Comp
OHAMA	Mitsubishi, Yokohama	1943–1945	3070 N 2670 S	387 2 wl 367 5 pp	37 11	13 10	2 sets GT 3 boilers 2 shafts	52000	32.5		4000 @ 18	2 × 120mm (4.7in) 45-cal HA 32 × 25mm AA 36 DCs	
OSASHI		1944–	2950 N 2560 S	387 2 wl 367 5 pp	37 11	13 5			33			2 × 13.2mm AA 18 DCs	

GENERAL NOTES
1942M War Programme (*Job Nos. 5411–15*). Improved *Hakachi* type. 16-22mm armour on deck and superstructure.

CAREERS
Ohama
Launched 1944, converted while building to Escort vessel, completed 10 January, 1945; sunk 10 August, 1945 in the Onagawa area by American or British carrier aircraft.
Osashi
Launched 10 February, 1945; work suspended 29 June 1945 when 95% complete; sank 6 March, 1946 as a result of leaks, in Yokohama Harbour.
Job Nos. 5413–15: Orders cancelled before keels laid.
Converted battleship: *Settsu* (see p. 25).
Converted destroyer: *Yakaze* (*Minekaze* class, see p. 141).

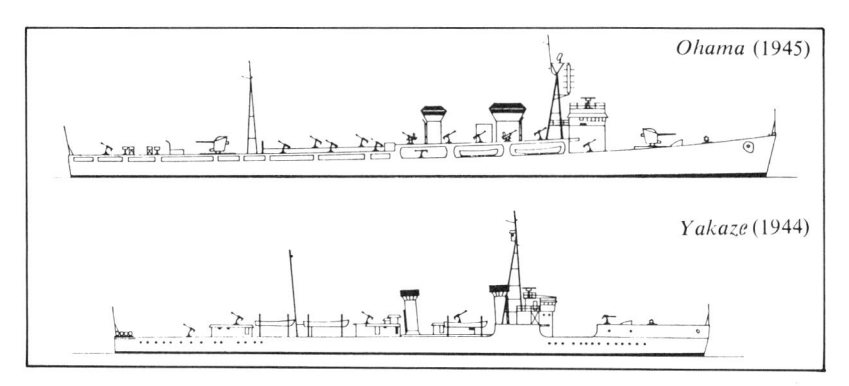

Ohama (1945)

Yakaze (1944)

32. Miscellaneous Assault Craft

Name	Builder	Date	Displ	Length ft in	Beam ft in	Draught ft in	Machinery	SHP	Speed	Fuel	Radius	Armament	Comp
TOKU 4-SHIKI NAIKATEI	Mitsubishi	1944 1945	19.2	36 1 oa	10 10	7 6	1 12-cyl Diesel motor	240 bhp	5	?	?	2 × 18in torpedo-launchers 2 × 13mm AA	3

GENERAL NOTES
Known as Naval Amphibious Tanks Type 4, these craft were designed to act as amphibious torpedo-boats, much like the German *Seeteufel*. They were for coastal defence and could be transported as deck cargo by submarines. Poor construction combined with lack of speed made them useless as a weapon, and none put to sea.

FATES
Parts for 18 units were assembled and trials took place off Kure in March 1944.

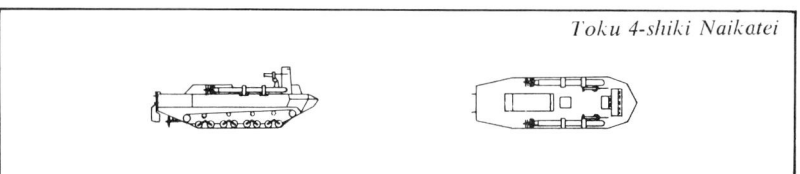

Toku 4-shiki Naikatei

Name	Builder	Date	Displ	Length ft in	Beam ft in	Draught ft in	Machinery	SHP	Speed	Fuel	Radius	Armament	Comp
SHINYO Type 1	Naval and private yards	1944–?	1.35	19 8 oa	5 6	1 1	1 gasoline engine	67 bhp	26	?	105 @ 26 125 @ 18	1 × 250kg explosive charge 2 × wooden RAK-12 rocket-launchers	1
SHINYO Improved Type 1		1944–?	1.35	16 9 oa	5 6	1 1			26	?			
SHINYO Type 1 No. 4		1944–1945	1.40	17 9 oa	5 6	1 1	1 gasoline engine	62 bhp	20	?	125 @ 20	1 × 13mm gun 1 × 250kg explosive charge	2
SHINYO Type 5		1944–1945	2.15	21 4 oa	6 1	1 2	2 gasoline engines	134 bhp	28	?	130 @ 12 115 @ 28 125 @ 18	2 × wooden RAK-12 rocket-launchers	

GENERAL NOTES
Explosive motor boats designed in 1944 to function in much the same manner as the German *fernlenk* (FL) boats of the First World War. Intended for suicide attacks, but there was provision for the helmsman to escape over the stern after locking the steering.
Known as Type 5 Division Boats, they were assembled by the Nippon SB Co., Tsurumi and Yokohama; Kimura Works; Kanagawa SB Co.; Nippon Sharyo Co.; Mitsubishi, Nagasaki; Yokohama Yacht Co.; Kariya Works, Toyoda; Nipponkai Dock; Naval Dock No. 1, Shanghai; Naval Yard No. 101, Singapore; Naval Yard No. 102, Soerabaya, etc.

MACHINERY
The shortage of engines made it necessary to engine the *Shinyo* types with ex-truck engines.

ARMAMENT
Some boats were experimentally armed with rocket-launchers in place of the explosive charge, and when these proved successful all boats were armed with the RAK type. From the Spring of 1945 they were fitted with 'jumping wires' to clear net obstructions.

FATES
About 400–600 boats per month were being built by the end of hostilities. War missions were carried out in the Philippines, and at the Iwo Jima and Okinawa landings.

Captured *Shinyo* suicide motor boats, in American hands after the fall of the Philippines. Hundreds were built, but they achieved little. (US Navy.)

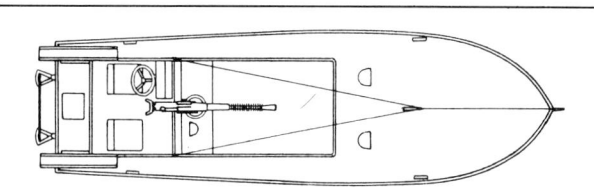

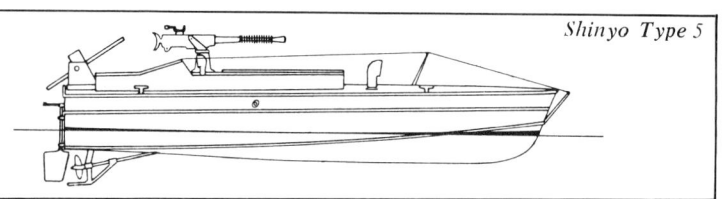

Shinyo Type 5

Name	Builder	Date	Displ	Length ft in	Beam ft in	Draught ft in	Machinery	SHP	Speed	Fuel	Radius	Armament	Comp
MARU-NI Type	various firms	1944–1945	1.6	18 4 oa	5 7 approx	1 2 approx	1 gasoline engine	80 bhp	25	?	?	1 200kg DC	1
K-GATA-TEI Type	various firms	1944–1945	1.2	18 0 oa	5 3 approx	1 2 approx	1 gasoline engine	80 bhp	30	?	?	1 200kg DC	1

GENERAL NOTES
These explosive motor boats were similar to the *Shinyo* but were built for the Army. They were intended to damage surface warships by dropping depth-charges close alongside as they lay at anchor. They were built in various yards in Osaka, Kobe, Tokyo and Yokohama.

MACHINERY
Some boats were fitted with an auxiliary rocket propulsion unit which produced speeds of 50 to 60 knots for about 30 minutes.

FATES
About 3,000 boats were built and they saw action at Lingayen, Okinawa and the invasion of the Philippines.

33. Royal Yacht

Name	Builder	Date	Displ	Length ft in	Beam ft in	Draught ft in	Machinery	SHP	Speed	Fuel	Radius	Armament	Comp
HATSUKAZE	Mitsubishi, Nagasaki	1901–1903	123 N	100 0 oa 90 0 pp	18 0	6 6	1 4-cyl quadruple-expansion engine 1 Miyabara water-tube boiler 1 shaft	230 ihp	11.3	?	?	nil	?

GENERAL NOTES
Shipyard gift to the Crown Prince. Composite construction, with certain of the frames being wooden. Trials speed 12.43 knots.

CAREER
Launched 4 October, 1903; completed 26 November, 1903; 193?: Training Ship; subsequent fate unknown.

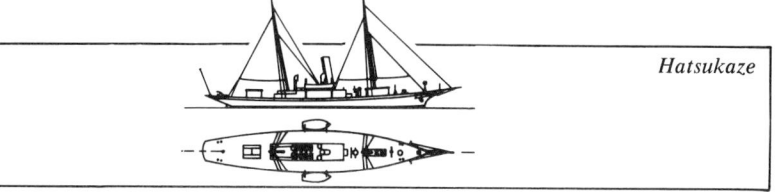

Hatsukaze

34. Miscellaneous Mercantile Auxiliary Vessels

Akashisan Maru (Transport): 4541 grt motor ship, built 1935; sunk 2/3 March 1944 west of Uruppu by US submarine *Sandlance*.

Aki Maru (Transport): 11,409 grt motor liner, built 1942; sunk 26 July 1944 320nm east of Hainan by US submarine *Crevalle*.

Aki Maru (Transport and Auxiliary): 6444 grt steamer, built 1902; requisitioned 1904, returned 1905; broken up 1934.

Akibasan Maru (Transport): 4603 grt steamer, built 1924; sunk 30 January 1944 south-west of Ujae Atoll, Marshall Islands, by US destroyer *Burns*.

Aiko Maru No. 20 (Guardboat): 51 grt steamer, built ?; sunk 11 August 1944 in Kaoe Bay, Halmahera Island by US aircraft.

Aikoku Maru (Blockship): 1773 grt steamer, built 1879; sunk in the entrance to Port Arthur 3 May 1904.

Aikoku Maru (Guardboat): 38 grt steamer, built ?; sunk about 30 June 1944 at Kwajalein by coastal artillery.

Akitsu Maru (Transport): 1038 grt motor ship, built 1936; sunk 28 May 1945 south of Kure by mine; salvaged 1945 and to mercantile service.

Akonoura Maru (Auxiliary): 1717 grt steamer, built 1900; requisitioned 1904; wrecked off Asesaki, Goto, 20 August 1904.

Amagisan Maru (Transport): 7620 grt motor ship, built 1933; sunk 17 February 1944 at Truk by US TF58 aircraft.

Amakusa Maru No. 1 (Water tanker): 1913 grt, built 1939; sunk 24 December 1942 5nm south of Wake Island by US submarine *Triton*.

America Maru (Armed Merchant Cruiser and Transport): 6069 grt steamer, built 1898; requisitioned as AMC 1904, returned 1905; requisitioned as Transport 194?; sunk 6 March 1944 south of Iwo Jima by US submarine *Nautilus*.

Amiji Maru (Guardboat): 107 grt steamer, built ?; torpedoed 22 April 1945 West of Torishima, 30° 50 N/138° 30 E by US submarine.

Amoi Maru No. 1, ex-*Carmen Moller* (Tug): 600 grt steam tug (British), built 1911; captured at Amoi 10 December 1941 and entered service 23 June 1942 as *Amoi Maru No. 1/Eisen No. 1447*; returned 1945.

Amoi Maru No. 2, ex-*Ready Moller* (Tug): 268 grt steam tug (British), built 1896; captured at Amoi 19(?) December 1941 and entered service June 1942 as *Amoi Maru No. 2/Eisen No. 1448*; returned 1945.

Amoi Maru No. 3, ex-*Visayas*, ex-*Illaroo* (Utility Craft): 1000 grt steam ferry (Filipino), built 1885; captured December 1941 and entered service 23 June 1942 as *Amoi Maru No 3/Eisen No 1449*; returned 1945.

Anshu Maru (Gunboat): 2601 grt steamer, built 1937; requisitioned 1941 as a gunboat; transport 1943; torpedoed 30 May 1944 in Davao Gulf, Mindanao (06° 42 N/125° 40 E) by US submarine *Gurnard*.

Arabato Maru (Salvage Vessel): 507 grt; requisitioned 1943; Repatriation Service 1945.

Aratama Maru (Ammunition Ship): 6783 grt turbine freighter, built 1938; requisitioned; sunk 8 April 1944 south of Guam by US submarine *Seahorse*.

Ariake Maru, ex-*Charters Towers* (Depot Ship): 2988 grt steamer, built 1890; requisitioned 1904, returned 1905; broken up 1934.

Ariake Maru, ex-*Kyosai Maru* (Guardboat): 167 grt passenger steamer, built 1913; sunk 22 April 1945 S of Honshu by US aircraft.

Arimasan Maru (Transport): 8696 grt motor ship, built 1937; captured 1945 and employed as Repatriation Transport until returned to original owners in 1947; 1966 *Katsuragawa Maru*; 1968 *Chokyu Maru*; 1970 Liberian *Locolina*.

Arizona Maru (Transport): 9683 grt passenger steamer, built 1920; sunk 14 November 1942 north of Guadalcanal by USMC and USN aircraft.

Asagao Maru, ex-*Asagawo* (Blockship): 2464 grt steamer, built 1888; sunk at Port Arthur 3 May 1904 (subsequently salvaged).

Asahi Maru (Auxiliary Scout): 4917 grt steamer, built 1884; requisitioned for scouting duties off Port Arthur February 1904, returned 1905; wrecked at Shana, Etorofu, 18 July 1928 (name changed to *Kinsei Maru* 1928).

Asahi Maru (Guardboat): 197 grt steamer, built 1917; wrecked 29 July 1945 E of Pusan.

Asahisan Maru (Transport): 4551 grt motor ship, built 1935; sunk 27 July 1944 off Halmahera by USAAF aircraft.

Asama Maru (Transport): 16975 grt motor liner, built 1929; sunk 1 January 1944 200 miles south-east of Hong Kong by US submarine *Atule*.

Aso Maru (Gunboat): 703 grt motor ship, built 1932; requisitioned 1938; torpedoed 9 May 1943 SE of Cayagan, Sulu Sea (09° 09 N/121° 50 E) by US submarine *Gar*.

Asuka Maru (Guardboat): 37 grt steamer, built ?; sunk 25 May 1943 in Macassar Strait by US submarine.

Atagosan Maru (Transport): 2043 grt steamer, built 1897; requisitioned 1904

Atlantic Maru (transcription — *Atoranchikku Maru*) (Transport): 5872 grt steamer, built 1920; requisitioned late 1943; sunk 30 March 1944 off Guam by US submarine *Picuda*.

Atlas Maru (Japanese transcription — *Atorasu Maru*); Army Transport: 7347 grt steamer, built 1920; requisitioned by Army 194?, transferred to Navy 1944; sunk 3 November 1944 in the Luzon Straits by US submarine *Pomfret*.

Atsu Maru (Transport): 499 grt, built 1911; requisitioned 194?; sunk 21 March 1944 north of New Guinea by US aircraft.

Augusta (Chartered Ship): Steamer (American), built 1867; chartered 1868 for operation against Enomoto; sold to Tosa-Han and renamed *Momijiga* (*Maru*) 1870; sunk about 1873.

Awa Maru (Transport): 11249 grt motor liner, built 1943; sunk 1 April 1945 in Formosa Straits by US submarine *Queenfish*.

Awaji Maru (Transport): 1948 grt, built 1944; sunk 21 September 1944 off Cape Bojeador, Luzon, by US submarine *Picuda*.

Ayanami Maru (Guardboat): 200 grt steamer, built ?; sunk 13 August 1943 in Korean Strait (approx. 34° 50 N/131° 10 E) by US aircraft.

Azumasan Maru (Transport): 7614 grt, built 1942; lost off Tassafaronga, Guadalcanal — beached and burned out after USMC and USN air attacks 14 October 1942.

Azusa Maru (Transport): 548 grt; sunk 29 December 1942 off New Georgia by US aircraft.

Bangame Maru No 3 (Guardboat): 99 grt steamer, built ?; sunk 18 March 1944 E of Japan (38° N/151° E) by US submarine.

Banri, ex-*Cosmopolite*: 699-ton steamer (British), built 1859; 1864 *Banri* — Higo-han; June 1868 *Banri Maru* — Ministry of the Interior; subsequently served with the Yubin Fleet and then sold to Mitsubishi as *Kagoshima Maru*; hulked between 1878 and 1882.

Banri Maru, ex-*Chogei Maru*, ex-*Dumbarton*: 1462-ton paddle steamer (British), built 1864; September 1864 *Chogei Maru* Shogunate Fleet; ran aground September 1866 and captured by Imperial Fleet, renamed *Banri Maru*; 1875 — Mitsubishi Fleet; hulked 1880.

Banshu Maru (Depot Ship): 983 grt motor trawler, built 1939; requisitioned 194?, returned 1945; 1954 reconstructed as 1066 grt refrigerated fish carrier.

Banshu Maru No 5, ex-*Banshu Maru No 15* (Depot Ship): 389 grt motor trawler, built 1933; requisitioned 194?; missing between Truk and Yokohama, presumed lost on 15 April 1943.

Banshu Maru No 13, ex-*Banshu Maru No 87* (Depot Ship): 363 grt motor trawler, built 1934; requisitioned 194?, returned 1945.

Banshu Maru No 15, ex-*Banshu Maru No 89* (Depot Ship): (details as *Banshu Maru No 13*).

Banshu Maru No 17 (Depot Ship): 459 grt steam trawler, built 1923; requisitioned 194?; sunk 19 November 1944 east of Hainan by US submarine *Gunnel*.

Banshu Maru No 31 (Transport): 748 grt motor trawler, built 1942; sunk 7 December 1944 north of Luzon by US submarine *Trepang*.

Banshu Maru No 92 (Guardboat): 95 grt fishing vessel, built ?; mined 17 April 1945 off Goto Rette.

Banshu Maru No 97 (Guardboat): 97 grt fishing vessel, built ?; requisitioned as subchaser (?); sunk 12 September 1944 off Cebu by US aircraft.

Banshu Maru No 98 (Guardboat): 97 grt fishing vessel, built ?; possibly requisitioned as subchaser; sunk 20 October 1944 W of Billiton (Belitung) 03° S/107° 30 E), cause unknown.

Batavia Maru (Japanese transcription — *Batabia M*) (Transport): 4642 grt passenger steamer, built 1919; requisitioned 194?; sunk 12 June 1944 160nm NNW Saipan by TF58 aircraft.

Benten Maru (Guardboat): 94 grt steamer, built ?; sunk 18 November 1944 off Tarakan, Borneo by US aircraft.

Benten Maru, ex-*Venus* (Transport): 3668 grt steamer (British), built 1896; seized as prize by AMC *Nippon Maru* in Etorofu Straits between 20 February and 4 March 1905; entered service 1 September 1905 as *Benten Maru*; subsequently to merchant service as *Daito Maru No 2*, *Ekisan Maru* (1939), *Mesuyama Maru* (1949).

Bingo Maru (Armed Merchant Cruiser): 6242 grt steamer, built 1897; requisitioned 1904, returned 1905; broken up 1934.

Bogota Maru, ex-*Bogota* (Transport): 1230 grt motor vessel (Dutch), built 1937; requisitioned May 1945; Repatriation Service September 1945; returned to Netherlands May 1950; subsequently Swedish *Astrid Sven* (1955), Greek Phrygia (1959), *Alkioni* (1964); sank after explosion 11 May 1964 north of St Louis, Senegal.

Bordeaux Maru (Japanese transcription — *Borudo Maru*) (Transport): 6567 grt turbine freighter, built 1923: requisitioned 194?; sunk 1 February 1942 at Kwajalein by USS *Enterprise* aircraft.

Boshin Maru, ex-*Filipino*: 316 (?) grt steamer (British); 1868 operated by Awa-Han in the service of the Imperial Fleet against Enomoto; lost off Sumoto, Awaji, 1874.

Bugen Maru (Transport): 691 grt; requisitioned 194?; sunk 12 September 1944 in Bohol Passage by US TF38 aircraft.

Buriat (River Gunboat): 193 tons (Russian), built 1907; seized 1918 and employed by the Amur River Flotilla; returned 1923.

Bushu Maru, ex-*Invertay* (Blockship): 1240 grt steamer, built 1883; sunk 24/25 February 1904 at Port Arthur as *Blockship 5*.

Busho Maru (Gunboat): 2569 grt passenger steamer, built 1921; requisitioned 1940; sunk 26 January 1944 in China Sea (08° 30 N/109° 10 E) by US submarine *Grevalle*.

Buyo Maru, ex-*Rosary* (Blockship): 1162 grt steamer, built 1889; sunk 24/25 February 1904 at Port Arthur as *Blockship 4*.

Canberra Maru (Japanese transcription — *Kambera Maru*) (Transport): 6457 grt motor vessel, built 1936; sunk 14 December 1942 west of Guadalcanal by USMC and USN aircraft.

Caroline Maru (Japanese transcription — *Karorainu Maru*) (Auxiliary): 320 grt motor coaster, built 1936; sunk 1 November 1944 west of Mindoro (with *Unkai M. No 12*) by US submarine *Blackfin*.

Ceylon Maru (transcription — *Seron Maru*) (Auxiliary; Transport): 4905 grt steamer, built 1904; requisitioned as Auxiliary 1904, returned 1905; requisitioned as Transport 194?; sunk 27 February 1944 in East China Sea by US submarine *Pogy*.

Chichibu Maru (Victualling Stores Ship): 1520 grt refrigerator ship, built 1923; requisitioned 194?; sunk 13 March 1942 120 miles south of Tokyo by US submarine *Gar*.

Chihaya Maru, ex-*Tjisaroea* (Transport): 7089 grt turbine freighter (Dutch), built 1926; captured 4 March 1942 south of Java and renamed; sunk 2 November 1943 north-west of the Bonin Is by US submarine *Seahorse*.

Chitose Maru, ex-*Coquette*: 620-ton steamer (British), built 1867; December 1867 Kurume-Han, 1868 Imperial Fleet; 1873 to Mitsubishi Fleet as *Seiro Maru*; lost 1913.

Chitose Maru (Guardboat): 177 grt steamer, built ?; requisitioned probably as subchaser; sunk 14 July 1945 4 miles off Kayabe, Hokkaido by aircraft of US TF 38.

Chitose Maru (Gunboat): 2668 grt steamer, built 1921; requisitioned 1941; returned 1945.

Chitose Maru No 6 (Guardboat): 165 grt steamer, built ?; probably requisitioned as a subchaser; sunk 22 January 1945 at Nansei Shoto, probably by air attack.

Chiyo Maru, ex-*Electra* (Blockship): 2708 grt steamer, built 1885; sunk 27 March 1904 at Port Arthur as *Blockship No 1*.

Chiyo Maru (Stores Ship ?): 657 grt motor trawler, built 1935; sunk 26 May 1944 west of Marianas by US submarine *Tambor*.

Chiyo Maru (Transport): 4700 grt; requisitioned 194?; sunk 2 June 1944 170 miles east of Parece Vela by US submarine *Shark*.

Chiyoda Maru, ex-*Parthian* (Transport): 1937 grt steamer, built 1883; requisitioned 1904, returned 1905.

Choan Maru No 2, ex-*Choan Maru* (Gunboat): 2632 grt motor passenger vessel, built 1927; requisitioned 1941; sunk 10 May 1944 N of Carolines (11° 31 N/143° 41 E) by US submarine *Silversides*.

Choei Maru (Guardboat): 39 grt vessel, built ?; sunk 3 March 1943 off Vella Lavella, Solomons by US aircraft.

Choei Maru: 86 grt vessel, built ?; mined 10 June 1945 off Shimineto.

Chohakusan Maru (Gunboat): 2120 grt passenger steamer, built 1928; requisitioned 1937; sunk 1 March 1945 NW of Naha, Okinawa (26° 30 N/127° 30 E) by US TF 58.

Chohei Maru (Minesweeper Depot Ship): 1718 grt motor passenger ferry, built 1920; requisitioned 1938; damaged 1 July 1945 at Wusung by US aircraft; returned 1945; MSA patrol vessel *Tsushima* 1950 (removed by 1957).

Chojusan Maru (Gunboat): 2131 grt passenger steamer, built 1928; requisitioned 1937; sunk 9 November 1944 in East China Sea (31° 15 N/129° 10 E) by US submarine *Queenfish*.

Chokai Maru (Guardboat): 135 grt fishing vessel, built 1936; sunk 2 March 1945 NE of Miyakejima, Izu-Shichito by gunfire from US submarine *Bowfin*.

Chokai Maru (Gunboat): 2658 grt motor passenger ship, built 1932; requisitioned 1940; sunk 1941.

Choko Maru, ex-*Seine Maru* (Transport): 6783 grt steamer, built 1920; requisitioned 194?; sunk 21 October 1942 off Kavieng, New Ireland, by US submarine *Gudgeon*.

Choko Maru (Transport): 3535 grt, built 1939; sunk 5 December 1943 off Kwajalein by aircraft from US TF50.

Choko Maru (Transport): 842 grt, built 1941; sunk 28 March 1942 off Macassar by US submarine *Sturgeon*.

Choko Maru No 2, ex-*Choko Maru* (Gunboat): 2629 grt steamer, built 1927; requisitioned 1941; sunk 12 January 1944 SW of Truk, Carolines (03° 37 N/147° 27 E) by US submarine *Albacore*.

Chokyu Maru (Guardboat): 116 grt vessel, built ?; sunk 18 April 1942 650 miles E of Japan by aircraft of USS *Enterprise*.

Chosa Maru (Gunboat): 2538 grt passenger steamer, built 1921; requisitioned 1940; sunk 20 August 1943 8 m SW of Penang (05° 09 N/100° 10 E) by Dutch submarine.

Choun Maru (Gunboat): 1914 grt Motor ship, built 1940; requisitioned 1941; fell into US hands 1945 and used on repatriation duties; returned 1947.

Choun Maru No 13 (Guardboat): 96 grt vessel, built ?; sunk 27 March 1945 in Kuchinoerabu Bay, Osumi-Gunto (30° 30 N/130° 05 E) by US TF 58.

Chowa Maru (Gunboat): 2719 grt vessel, built 1940; sunk 1 May 1945 SE of Erimosaki, Hokkaido (41° 02 N/144° 36 E) by US submarine *Bowfin*.

Choyo Maru No 3 (Guardboat): 94 grt vessel, built ?; sunk 15 February 1945 off Southern Japan (30° N/141° E) by US TF 58.

Choyo Maru No 8 (Guardboat): 103 grt vessel, built ?; sunk 13 May 1945 S of Korea (34° 28 N/127° 45 E) by US aircraft.

Chozan Maru, ex-*Fu Ping* (Auxiliary): 1393 grt steamer (British), built 1891; seized 12 October 1904 by torpedo boat Shiretoko; renamed and commissioned 14 February 1905.

Chozan Maru (Water Tanker): 1917 grt, built 1941; sunk 6 November 1943 west of Buka by USAAF bombers.

Chozan Maru No 6 (Guardboat): 91 grt vessel, built ?; sunk 26 April 1945 E of Kammon Strait, Shimonoseki by aircraft.

Chuetsu Maru, ex-*Trym* (Transport): 1196 grt steamer, built 1895; requisitioned 1904, returned 1905.

Chusa Maru, ex-*Tencer* (Transport): 2846 grt steamer (British), built 1890; Japanese merchant. *Chusa Maru* 1903; requisitioned 1904; lost August 1904.

Chutanzan Maru (Guardboat): 103 grt vessel, built ?; sunk 27 December 1944 off Mindanao.

Chuwa Maru (Gunboat): 2719 grt steamer, built 1940; requisitioned 1940; sunk 10 February 1942 off Keelung, Formosa (25° 23 N/122° 44 E) by US submarine *Trout*.

Conte Verde: 18765 grt turbine liner (Italian), built 1923; scuttled 9 September 1943 at Shanghai, salvaged and taken to Japan; sunk December 1944 while fitting out as troopship at Maizuru by US aircraft; salvaged June 1949 and sold to Mitsubishi Line.

Cuba Maru (transcription *Kyuba Maru*) (Transport): 5950 grt motor vessel, built 1926; requisitioned 194?; stranded 24 August 1942 south of Sakhalin.

Dai Nippon Maru No 15 (Guardboat): 36 grt vessel, built ?; sunk 13 August 1943 in Bismarck Archipelago by US aircraft.

Daido Maru (Guardboat): 69 grt vessel, built ?; sunk 12 June 1945 W of Wakkanai, Hokkaido by gunfire from US submarine *Spadefish*.

Daido Maru (Gunboat): 2962 grt passenger steamer, built 1935; requisitioned 1940; sunk 4 December 1943 NE of Ponape (9° 06 N/159° 02 E) by US submarine *Apogon*.

Daigen Maru No 7 (Gunboat): 1289 grt steamer, built 1937; requisitioned 1938; sunk 14 August 1944 SW of Inchon, Korea (37° 30 N/125° 50 E) by US submarine *Croaker*.

Daijin Maru No 1 (Guardboat): 143 grt vessel, built ?;

sunk 3 April 1945 SE of Japan (30° N/137° 30 E) by US aircraft.

Daikoku Maru No 3 (Guardboat): 74 grt fishing vessel, built ?; sunk 8 March 1945 E of Ogarijima by US aircraft.

Dairen Maru, ex-*Tenasserim* (Army Transport): 2926 grt steamer, built 1875; requisitioned 1904, returned 1905 broken up March 1908.

Dairi Maru No 10 (Guardboat): 74 grt vessel, built ?; sunk 25 July 1945 off Moji, Shimonoseki Strait, by US TF 58.

Daito Maru (Guardboat): 86 grt vessel, built ?; sunk 13 November 1944 at Cavite Pier, Manila Bay by aircraft of US TF 38.

Delhi Maru (Japanese transcription *Deri Maru*) (Gunboat): 2205 grt passenger steamer, built 1922; requisitioned 1937; sunk 16 January off Miyakejima (34° 12/V/139° 54 E) by US submarine *Swordfish*.

Denryu, ex-*Nagasaki*: 300-ton steamer (Dutch), built 1858; 1858 Sago-Han; 1868 flagship for the Imperial Fleet Review; 1871 Imperial Fleet.

Ebisu Maru No 3 (Guardboat): 46 grt vessel, built ?; sunk December 1944 off Manila.

Ebisu Maru No 5 (Guardboat): 46 grt vessel, built ?; sunk December 1944 off Manila.

Ebisu Maru No 5 (Guardboat): 131 grt vessel, built ?; sunk 30 April 1943 E of Japan (37° 34 N/155° E) by gunfire of US submarine *Scorpion*.

Ebisu Maru No 11 (Guardboat): Sunk 8 July 1944 off Saipan by US aircraft.

Ebisu Maru No 32 (Guardboat): 56 grt, built ?; sunk 11 August 1944 in Kaoe Bay, Halmahera by US aircraft.

Ebon Maru (Guardboat): 198 grt; sunk 2 January 1943 in Bismarck Sea (4° 30 S/151° 30 E) by US submarine, possibly *Gato*.

Eboshi Maru, ex-*Oakley* (Transport): 4098 grt steamer (British), built 1901; seized in Straits of Tsushima 18 January 1905 by cruiser *Tokiwa*, renamed and commissioned 12 April 1905; to merchant service 1 September 1905.

Edo Maru (Blockship): 1734 grt steamer, built 1884; sunk at Port Arthur 2 May 1904 as *Blockship No 7*.

Edo Maru (Gunboat): 1299 grt, steamer, built 1937; requisitioned 1940; sunk 13 August 1943 SE of Iojima (24° 04 N/142° 21 E) by US submarine *Sunfish*.

Eifuku Maru (Gunboat): 3520 grt vessel, built 1939; requisitioned 1941; sunk 8 February 1945 S of Cape Ca Mau, Indochina (7° 05 N/104° 50 E) by US submarine *Pampanito*.

Eifuku Maru No 8 (Guardboat): 94 grt; sunk 17 September 1944 in Western Pacific.

Ehimo Maru (Gunboat): 623 grt, built 1903; no details.

Eijo Maru, ex-*Altonower* (Army Transport): 2506 grt steamer, built 1880; requisitioned 1904, subsequently returned.

Eikichi Maru (Guardboat): 19 grt; sunk 30 March 1945 off Kagoshima, Kyushu by aircraft of US TF 58.

Eiko Maru (Gunboat): 3011 grt turbine passenger vessel, built 1937; requisitioned 1941; sunk 8 June 1944 NW of Penang (05° 59 N/99° 10 E) by British submarine *Stoic*.

Eiko Maru (Transport): 1843 grt passenger steamer, built 1903; requisitioned 1904, returned 1905; requisitioned 1944; damaged 23 February 1944 in Marianas by TF58 aircraft; sunk 24 October 1944 north-west of Luzon by US submarine *Seadragon*.

Eiko Maru, ex-*Kwongsang*, ex-*Valencia* (Transport): 1491 grt steamer, built 1880; requisitioned 1904, returned 1905.

Eiko Maru No 2 (Transport): 3535 grt, built 1940; requisitioned 194?; severely damaged 5 December 1943 at Kwajalein by TF50 aircraft and subsequently sunk by gunfire during assault on Kwajalein 30 January 1944.

Eikoku Maru (Guardboat): 99 grt; sunk 18 November 1944 off Tarekan by US aircraft.

Eitoku Maru No 18 (Guardboat): 171 grt; sunk 14 July 1945 off Cape Shiobuki, Hokkaido by US TF38.

Enju Maru (1941), ex-*Miraflores*, ex-*Onassi Socratis*, ex-*Canadian Miller* (Transport): 5374 grt steamer (Panamanian), built 1919; requisitioned 194?; sunk 4 August 1944 north of Chichi Jima by TF58 aircraft.

Esan Maru, ex-*Burma* (Auxiliary): 3071 grt steamer; requisitioned 1904, returned 1905.

Etorofu Maru, ex-*Aphrodite* (Transport): 3948 grt steamer (British), built 1898; seized between 22 February and 6 March 1905 in Etorofu Straits by AMC *Nippon Maru* renamed and commissioned 1 September 1905.

Florida Maru (transcription — *Furorida M*) (Transport): 5854 grt motor vessel, built 1925; requisitioned 194?; sunk 2 April 1943 in Kavieng harbour by USAAF aircraft.

Fuji Maru No 1 (Guardboat): 74 grt motor fishing vessel, built 1929; sunk 25 February 1945 off Torishima (31° 06 N/141° E) by gunfire of US destroyers *Hazelwood* and *Murray*.

Fujikawa Maru (Aircraft Transport): 6938 grt motor vessel, built 1938; requisitioned 1940; sunk 17 February 1944 at Truk by TF58 aircraft.

Fujisan: 600-ton steamer, built 186? in USA for Shogunate Fleet, commissioned 1864; 1872 Imperial Fleet Transport; 1876 machinery removed, employed as a sail training ship; hulked 187?.

Fuku Maru No 2 (Guardboat): 39 grt; sunk 22 February 1944 off Rabaul by US aircraft.

Fukui Maru, ex-*Abergeldie* (Blockship): 2944 steamer, built 1882; *Blockship No 2*, sunk off Port Arthur by Russian destroyer *Silnyii* before reaching scuttling position.

Fukuei Maru No 3 (Guardboat): 35 grt; sunk 8 July off Saipan by US aircraft.

Fukuei Maru No 10 (Gunboat): 847 grt motor ship, built 1936; requisitioned 1942; sunk 25 July 1945 in Bungo-Suido (approx. 33° N/132° 10 E) by US TF38.

Fukuichi Maru No 5 (Guardboat): 150 grt motor ship, built 1933; sunk off Torishima (30° N/141° E) by US destroyers *Barton*, *Ingraham* and *Moale*.

Fukuju Maru No 4 (Guardboat): 198 grt; sunk 12 September 1944 off Cebu by US TF38.

Fukuju Maru No 5 (Guardboat): 84 grt; wrecked 28 July, 1945 at Kujukurihama, Chiba Ken following attack by aircraft of TF38.

Fukuoka Maru, ex-*Denbighshire* (Transport): 2744 grt steamer, built 1885; requisitioned 1904, returned 1905; wrecked 23 January 1923.

Fukusei Maru No 2 (Guardboat): 47 grt; sunk 28 July 1945 at Kobe by aircraft of TF38.

Fukuyama Maru (Gunboat): 3581 grt screw steamer, built 1936; requisitioned 1940; sunk 22 February 1944 40m W of Saipan (14° 47 N/144° 50 E) by US submarine *Tang*.

Fukuyoshi Maru No 3 (Guardboat): 100 grt; no details.

Fukuyoshi Maru No 5 (Guardboat): 119 grt; wrecked 5 January 1944 at Wotje Atoll, Marshalls following US air attack.

Fusa Maru (Auxiliary): 177 grt motor coaster, built 1929; requisitioned 194?; written off following severe damage sustained 17 November 1944 south of Hachijojima when shelled by US submarines *Burrfish* and *Ronquil*.

Fusan Maru, ex-*Pemptos* (Blockship): 2502 grt steamer, built 1883; intended as *Blockship No 6* but not used in March 1904 operation due to boiler unserviceability.

Fushimi Maru No 2 (Guardboat): 46 grt; badly damaged 12 January 1945 in SE entrance to Vung Tan by aircraft of TF38.

Fushimi Maru No 2 (Transport): 779 grt; requisitioned 194?; sunk 21 March 1945 in Cam Ranh Bay by US aircraft.

Fuso Maru (Gunboat): 319 grt screw steamer, built 1895; requisitioned 1905 and later returned; BU at Osaka 21 September 1934.

Genkai Maru (Auxiliary): 1447 grt steamer, built 1891; requisitioned 1904, returned 190?; 1929 Chinese *I Chang*; 1934 *Nissho*.

Gion Maru (Guardboat): 40 grt; sunk 15 June 1945 in Cam Ranh Bay by US aircraft.

Gokoku Maru No 19 (Guardboat): 153 grt; sunk 16 March 1945 at Kikaigashima (approx. 28° 20 N/130° E) by US aircraft.

Goryu Maru (Water Tanker): 1912 grt, built 1940; sunk 4 February 1944 at Jaluit, Marshalls, by TF58 aircraft.

Gosei Maru (Transport): 1931 grt steamer, built 1937; requisitioned 194?; sunk 17 February 1944 at Truk by TF58 aircraft.

Goshu Maru (Aircraft Transport): 8592 grt, built 1940; requisitioned 1940; sunk 30 March 1944 at Palau by TF58 aircraft.

Goyo Maru, ex-*Hever* (Transport): 601 grt steamer, built 1884; requisitioned 1904; sunk 25 April 1904 in Wonsan harbour, Korea, by Russian torpedo boats *Nos 205* and *206*.

Gozan Maru (Transport): 3212 grt steamer, built 1919; requisitioned 194?; sunk 30 March 1944 at Palau by TF58 aircraft.

Haguro Maru (Transport): 3352 grt steamer, built 1928; requisitioned 194?; sunk 13 January 1944 north of New Ireland by US aircraft.

Hakkai Maru (Gunboat): 2921 grt steamer, built 1939; requisitioned 1941; sunk 5 May 1943 off Ise-Wan (34° 05 N/137° 35 E) by US submarine *Sawfish*.

Hakkai Maru (Repair Ship): 5114 grt motor vessel, built 1938; requisitioned 1942; sunk 17 January 1944 at Rabaul by US aircraft.

Hakkaisan Maru (Gunboat): 3311 grt, built 1937; sunk 22 October 1942 80 m SW of Tamana, Gilbert Islands (03° 30 S/175° 15 E) by gunfire of US destroyers.

Hakko Maru (Guardboat): 150 grt; sunk 31 March 1944 at Palau by aircraft of TF 58.

Hakonesan Maru (Transport): 6673 grt motor vessel, built 1929; requisitioned 194?; sunk 18 October 1942 south east of Sendai by US submarine *Greenling*.

Hakozaki Maru (Troopship):10413 grt turbine liner, built 1922; requisitioned 1940; sunk 19 March 1945 off the Yangtse estuary by US submarine *Balao*.

Hakurei Maru (Stores Ship): 407 grt motor trawler, built 1934; requisitioned 194?; no details of fate known.

Hakusan Maru (Troopship): 10380 grt turbine liner, built 1923; requisitioned 1940; sunk 4 June 1944 south-west of Iwo Jima by US submarine *Flier*.

Hakutetsu Maru No 7 (Auxiliary): 1018 grt steamer, built 1936; requisitioned 194?; sunk 12 September 1944 off Shiono Misaki by US submarine *Pipefish*.

Hakutetsu Maru No 15 (Auxiliary): 1339 grt, built 1941; requisitioned 194?; returned 1945 — minor damage when mined 3 June 1945 in Inland Sea.

Hakuun Maru, ex-*Sanogawa Maru No 2*, ex-*Sanogawa Maru*, ex-*Lauting*: 594 grt steam ferry (German), built 1906; German auxiliary minelayer *Lauting* sunk 29 September 1914 at Tsingtao, salvaged by Japanese; requisitioned as Transport 194?; mined and sunk 30 May 1945 off Hakata.

Hakuyo Maru, ex-*Atlantico*, ex-*San Bernardino*, ex-*Oriole*, ex-*West Jappa* (Transport): 5752 grt steamer, built 1920; requisitioned 194?; sunk 25 October 1944 north of Urup, Kurile Is, by US submarine *Seal*.

Hakuyo Maru (Transport): 2220 grt; built 1945; lost by stranding 12 June 1945 off Esansaki.

Hanakawa Maru (Transport): 4739 grt, built 1942; requisitioned 1942; sunk 17 February 1944 at Truk by TF58 aircraft.

Han'ei Maru No 2 (Guardboat): 19 grt; sunk 28 July 1945 at Aomori by TF38.

Hanshin Maru (Guardboat): 92 grt; sunk 7 June 1945 in Sea of Japan (43° 35 N/134° 59 E) by gunfire of US submarine.

Hao Maru: Barque; 1869 Imperial Fleet Transport.

Haruna Maru (Victualling Stores Ship): 1549 grt refrigerator ship, built 1923; requisitioned 194?; sunk 16 January 1944 south-west of Palau in collision with *Kyoei Maru*.

Haruta Maru (Guardboat): 18 grt; sunk 23 June 1944 off Pagan, Marianas by US aircraft.

Haruta Maru (Salvage Vessel): 1514 grt, built 1925; requisitioned 194?; sunk 21 January 1945 at Hong Kong by US aircraft.

Heiin Maru, ex-*Otentosama*: 94-ton steamer (British), built 1865?; 1866 Choshu-Han; 1869-(?)72 Imperial Fleet.

Heijo Maru (Gunboat): 1201 grt, steamer, built 1903; requisitioned 1905 and later returned; renamed *Shohei Maru* 1936 and sunk 6 February 1945 S of Lushun (38° 47 N/121° 28 E) by US submarine *Spadefish*.

Heijo Maru (Gunboat): 2627 grt steamer, built 1941; requisitioned 1941; sunk 4 September 1943 SW of Ponape, Carolines (05° 25 N/156° 37 E) by US submarine *Albacore*.

Heito Maru (Transport): 4468 grt turbine cargo-liner, built 1935; requisitioned 194?; sunk 23 August 1943 east of Car Nicobar by Allied aircraft.

Heiwa Maru (Guardboat): 88 grt motor fishing vessel, built 1933; sunk 18 June 1945 in East China Sea (30° 45 N/126° E) by gunfire of US submarine *Dentuda*.

Heiwa Maru (Transport): 313 grt motor coaster, built 1936; requisitioned 194?; sunk 24 January 1944 at Lorengau, Admiralty Is, by US aircraft.

Heiwa Maru (Transport): 5578 grt; requisitioned 194?; sunk 24 December 1943 in Kaoe Bay, Halmahera, by US submarine *Raton*.

Heiyo Maru (Troopship): 9816 grt motor liner, built 1930; requisitioned 194?; sank 21 January 1943 north-east of Truk following attack on 17th by US submarine *Whale*.

Hibari Maru (Ammunition Ship): 6550 grt, built 1940; requisitioned 194?; sunk 17 April 1943 off Shortland Is, Solomons, by US aircraft.

Higashinoyama Maru (Guardboat): 216 grt; sunk September 1944 in Leyte area.

Hijikawa Maru No 5 (Gunboat): 564 grt steamer, built 1897; requisitioned 1904; sank 11 August 1905 at Ulsan, and wreck later BU.

Hikade Maru (Transport): 5686 grt; requisitioned 194?; sunk 24 January 1944 south of Shiono Misaki by US submarine *Batfish*.

Himekawa Maru, ex-*Miyagawa Maru* (Auxiliary): 420 grt steamer, built 1894; requisitioned 1904, returned 1905; 1935 Chinese *Ying Chun*.

Hinko Maru (Transport): 5418 grt steamer, built 1936; requisitioned 194?; sunk 12 June 1944 off Chichi Jima by TF38 aircraft.

Hino Maru No 2 (Gunboat): 998 grt motor vessel, built 1935; requisitioned 1942; badly damaged 30 April 1944 at Truk (07° 20 N/151° 45 E) by US aircraft of TF58, and sank 4 May.

Hino Maru No 3 (Transport): 4389 grt turbine freighter, built 1937; requisitioned 194?; sunk 7 December 1942 west of Iwo Jima by US submarine *Kingfish*.

Hino Maru No 5 (Gunboat): 2935 grt, built 1940; sunk 10 October 1943 SW of Kazan-Retto (23° 59/N/138° 42 E) by US submarine *Kingfish*.

Hinode Maru No 1 (Guardboat): 55 grt; sunk 12 March 1945 E of Ryukyu Islands (20° 54 N/131° 38 E) by US aircraft.

Hinode Maru, ex-*Bellona* (Auxiliary): 1115 grt steamer, built 1872; requisitioned 1904; sunk 30 June 1906 in collision off Sasebo.

Hinode Maru (Transport): 5256 grt steamer, built 1930; requisitioned 194?; sunk 10 June 1943 north of New Ireland by US submarine *Silversides*.

Hinode Maru No 2 (Guardboat): 80 grt; sunk 15 April 1945 of Chezhudo (33° 19 N/127° 21 E) by US aircraft.

Hinode Maru No 6 (Guardboat): 245 grt; sunk 4 September 1944 E of Nampo Shoto (31° 55 N/152° E) by US submarine *Bowfin*.

Hiroshi Maru No 3 (Guardboat): 149 grt; sunk 10 July 1944 at Saipan.

Hirota Maru (Gunboat): 2922 grt, built 1940; requisitioned 1941; mined 14 August 1945 off Muture Lighthouse (33° 59 N/130° 52 E).

Hirotama Maru (Gunboat): 1911 grt, built 1933; requisitioned 1940; sunk 14 February 1943 in southern Makasar Strait (03° 59 N/117° 30 E) by US submarine *Trout*.

Hiryu Maru, ex-*Promise*: 590-ton steamer, built 1863; 1866 Shogunate Fleet; 1868-71 Imperial Fleet.

Hitachi Maru (Ammunition Ship): 6540 grt turbine freighter, built 1939; requisitioned 1941; beached as a total loss 14 February 1943 on Shortland Island after US air attack.

Hitachi Maru (Transport): 6175 grt steamer, built 1898; requisitioned 1904; sunk 15 June 1904 west of Pusan by Russian armoured cruiser *Gromowoj*.

Hiyo Maru: steamer, built 186?; 1869 Imperial Fleet Transport.

Hiyoshi Maru (Transport): 4046 grt turbine freighter, built 1937; requisitioned 194?; sunk 4 December 1943 north-east of Haha Jima by US submarine *Gunnel*.

Hiyoshi Maru No 2 (Gunboat): 1287 grt screw steamer, built 1936; sunk 18 February 1945 at Futami, Chichijima (27° 05 N/142° 11 E) by aircraft of TF58.

Hokkai Maru (Victualling Stores Ship): 407 grt motor trawler, built 1934; requisitioned 194?: sunk 200nm south-east of Tokyo by US submarine *Scabbardfish*.

Hokkai Maru (Transport): 8416 grt motor vessel, built 1933; requisitioned 194?; sunk 16 January 1945 at Hong Kong by US TF38 aircraft.

Hokko Maru (Victualling Stores Ship): 1521 grt refrigerator ship, built 1923; requisitioned 194?; sunk 20 March 1944 off Yap, Carolines, by US submarine *Picuda*.

Hokko Maru (Transport): 5385 grt, built 1940; sunk 19 November 1943 south-east of Iwo Jima by US submarine *Harder*.

Hokoku Maru, ex-*Straits of Belle Isle*, ex-*Lord of the Isles* (Blockship): 2698 grt steamer, built 1870; beached at Port Arthur 24/25 February 1904 as *Blockship No 2*.

Hokoku Maru (Gunboat): 1274 grt steamer, built 1936; requisitioned 1939 and re-rated as a transport 20 February 1944; sunk 14 July 1945 off Oma-saki, Tsugaru-kaikyo (41° 33 N/141° 08 E) by TF38.

Hokoku Maru No 2 (Guardboat): 36 grt; sunk 30 January 1945 off Ujae (08° 42 N/167° 44 E) by gunfire of US destroyer *Burns*.

Hokuan, ex-*Rokan* (Salvage Vessel): 558 grt motor coaster (Dutch), built 1929; sunk 5 March 1942 in East Indies by Japanese aircraft; salvaged 29 April 1943 and commissioned as Japanese *Hokuan*; sunk 22 April 1944 off Tebibong, Malacca, by HM submarine *Taurus*.

Hokuhi Maru (Transport): 1500 grt; requisitioned 194?; sunk 1 March 1945 at Makung, Pescadores, by US aircraft.

Hokuriki Maru (Transport): 8359 grt motor vessel, built 1930; requisitioned 194?; sunk 18 March 1944 230nm north-west of Lingayen by US submarine *Lapon*.

Hokuryu Maru No 1 (Guardboat): 148 grt; sunk 20 July 1944 off Torishima (28° 10 N/141° 36 E) by gunfire of US submarine *Cobia*.

Hokusho Maru (Transport): 4211 grt steamer, built 1937; requisitioned 194?; sunk 12 September 1943 off Nauru Is by US submarine *Narwhal*.

Hokuto Maru, ex-*Claverhill* (Transport): 2822 grt steamer, built 1896; requisitioned 1904; ran aground 10 May 1905 on Tsushima, subsequently salvaged.

Hokuyo (*Maru*), ex-*Kotic* (Salvage Tug): 400 grt steamer (Russian), built 1891; seized at Yokohama 10 February 1904; commissioned 14 July 1905 as *Hokuyo*; sold after 1919.

Hokuyo Maru (Transport): 4216 grt steamer, built 1936; requisitioned 194?; sunk 17 February 1944 at Truk by TF58 aircraft.

Hong Kong Maru (Armed Merchant Cruiser): 6169 grt, built 1896; requisitioned 1904, returned 1905.

Hong Kong Maru (Gunboat): 2797 grt turbine passenger steamer, built 1935; requisitioned 1941; sunk 21 June 1943 off Shirase Lighthouse by US submarine *Gunnel*.

Horaisan Maru, ex-*Daiho Maru No 1* (Transport): 1990 grt steamer, built 1920; requisitioned 194?; sunk 20 May 1944 north-west of Saipan by US submarine *Silversides*.

Horei Maru, ex-*Poolster* (Salvage Vessel): 1262-ton buoy layer (Dutch), built 1939; sunk 1 March 1942 while serving as MTB depot ship at Tandjong Priok; salvaged and commissioned 1 September 1943; sunk 15 January 1945 at San Fernando, Luzon, by TF38 aircraft.

Hosei Maru No 1 (Guardboat): 44 grt; sunk 8 July 1944 at Saipan by US aircraft.

Hosei Maru No 2 (Guardboat): 80 grt; sunk 3 April 1945 SE of Japan (30° N/137° 30 E).

Hoshin Maru (Salvage Vessel): 1000 grt; believed to be a captured vessel, commissioned 1943; sunk 25 July 1944 70nm east of Hong Kong by USAAF aircraft.

Hosho Maru: Barque, built 186?; Shogunate Fleet; 1869 Imperial Fleet.

Hosho Maru No 3 (Guardboat): 111 grt; sunk 25 February 1945 W of Miyakejima (34° 06 N/138° 28 E) by gunfire of US submarine *Piper*.

Hoten Maru, ex-*Mukden* (Transport): 1565 grt steamer, built 1891; captured 1904 and taken into Japanese service.

Hyakafuku Maru (Gunboat): 986 grt passenger steamer, built 1928; requisitioned 1938 but re-rated as a transport 1 January 1943; sunk 30 June 1944 NW of Chichijima (28° 20 N/141° 23 E) by US submarine *Plaice*.

Hyuga Maru (Victualling Stores Ship): 994 grt, built 1942; requisitioned 1942; sunk 16 March 1943 west of the Marianas by US submarine *Flying Fish*.

Ibaraki Maru (Guardboat): 150 grt; sunk 30 March 1944 at Palau by US TF58.

Ikushima Maru (Gunboat): 3943 grt turbine steamer, built 1936; requisitioned 1940, but re-rated as a transport 25 May 1942; sunk 30 April 1944 NW of Marianas (20° 41 N/143° 04 E) by US submarine *Stingray*.

Ikuta Maru (Gunboat): 2968 grt steamer, built 1936; requisitioned 1940; sunk 12 January 1944 at Kwajalein (08° 42 N/167° 44 E) by US aircraft.

Ikutagawa Maru (Victualling Stores Ship): 4013 grt; requisitioned 194?; sunk 12 January 1945 at Saigon by TF38 aircraft.

Imizu Maru (Gunboat): 2924 grt, built 1940; requisitioned 1940 and re-rated as a transport 25 May 1942; sunk

MISCELLANEOUS MERCANTILE AUXILIARY VESSELS 275

12 June 1944 at Saipan (17° 32 N/144° 10 E) by aircraft of TG58.4.

Inari Maru No 2 (Guardboat): 81 grt; sunk 28 July 1945 at Kobe by air attack.

Inari Maru No 20 (Guardboat): 81 grt; caught fire 7 October 1943 off Wake Island.

Ise Maru (Auxiliary): 1250 grt steamer, built 1883; requisitioned 1904, returned 1905; lost by stranding 28 May 1921.

Ishikari Maru (Collier): 3291 grt steamer, built 1938; requisitioned 194?; sunk 17 March 1942 off Chichi Jima US submarine *Grayback*.

Isobe Maru, ex-*Easby Abbey* (Transport): 2999 grt steamer, built 1892; seized 27 February 1905 off Etoroft by AMC *Nippon Maru*; commissioned as *Isobe Maru* 1 September 1905.

Isusan Maru (Submarine Depot Ship): purchased 1912; 1924 employed as Transport, deleted before 1930.

Isuzu Maru No 3 (Guardboat): 74 grt steamer; sunk 19 April 1945 S of Japan (30° 42 N/136° 42 E) by US submarine.

Isuzugawa Maru No 5 (Guardboat): 226 grt; sunk 1 July 1944 NW of Marianas (31° 26 N/141° 11 E) by US submarine *Batfish*.

Itahashi (*Maru*), ex-*Industrie*, ex-*Englishman* (Salvage Tug): 333-ton tug (Swedish), built 1889; seized 28 March 1905 and commissioned as *Itahashi*; deleted from Active List 1934.

Itsukushima Maru, ex-*Duke of Fife*, ex-*Fifeshire* (Transport): 3883 grt steamer, built 1887; requisitioned 1904, returned 1905.

Iwaki Maru (Guardboat): 122 grt; sunk 25 September 1944 in East China Sea (25° 10 N/125° 51 E) by US submarine.

Iwaki Maru (Guardboat): 3124 grt; later re-rated as transport; sunk 1 June 1944 off Matsuwa, Kurile Islands (48° N/153° E) by US submarine *Herring*.

Iwaki Maru (Transport): 3142 grt; requisitioned 194?; sunk 1 June 1944 off Matsuwa, Kuriles, by US submarine *Herring*.

Iwate Maru (Guardboat): 95 grt; sunk 18 April 1942 650m E of Japan by aircraft of USS *Enterprise*.

Izumi: Sailing vessel; 1869 Imperial Fleet.

Izumi Maru (Transport): 3229 grt, built 1893; requisitioned 1904; sunk 15 June 1904 west of Okinoshima by Russian armoured cruiser *Gromowoj*.

Izusan Maru (Submarine Depot Ship): WWII — no further details known.

Jimbo Maru No 12 (Guardboat): 192 grt; sunk 2 May 1943 in Makassar Strait (00° 35 S/117° 50 E) by US submarine (probably *Gar*).

Jinko Maru (Guardboat): 66 grt; sunk 15 June 1945 in Cam Ranh Bay by US aircraft.

Jinsen Maru, ex-*Moray* (Blockship): 2312 grt steamer, built 1877; *Blockship No 3* mined off Port Arthur 24/25 February 1904.

Jinsen Maru, ex-*Mogul* (Transport): 3654 grt steamer, built 1895; requisitioned 1904, returned 1905; 1907 Army Transport.

Josho Maru, ex-*Havenstein* (Transport): 7974 grt steamer (German), built 1921; purchased 1942; sunk 10 October 1944 at Takao by TF38 aircraft.

Jozan Maru (Transport): 1086 grt; requisitioned 194?; sunk 17 February 1944 between Truk and New Ireland by US submarine, possibly *Cero*.

Junkitsu Maru (Guardboat): 19 grt; sunk January 1945 in Corregidor area.

Jusan Maru (Guardboat): 3943 grt steamer; requisitioned 1941 but re-rated as transport in 1943; sunk 14 April 1945 W of Chezhudo (33° 25 N/126° 15 E) by US submarine *Tirante*.

Jusan Maru (Transport): 2111 grt steamer, built 1918; requisitioned 194?; sunk 16 December west of Chichi Jima Retto by US submarine *Finback*.

Kagawa Maru (Gunboat): 613 grt steamer, built 1903; requisitioned 1904 and returned 1905.

Kaga Maru (Transport): 6301 grt steamer, built 1901; requisitioned 22 April 1904; stranded 5 May 1904 Yontan Bay.

Kahoku Maru (Gunboat): 3311 grt motor passenger vessel, built 1921; requisitioned 1941 but re-rated as minelayer the same year; sunk 8 June 1943 N of Palau (08° 58 N/134° 14 E) by US submarine *Finback*.

Kaigyo Maru No 3 (Guardboat): 77 grt; damaged by mines, once on 19 June 1945 off Hezaki Lighthouse and a second time in July in Kammon Strait.

Kaihei Maru (Transport): 4575 grt motor cargo-liner, built 1934; requisitioned 194?; sunk 15 April 1943 north-east of the Marianas by US submarine *Seawolf*.

Kaiho Maru, ex-*Tsurugisaki* (Gunboat): 1093 grt, built 1917; requisitioned 1941; sunk 19 April 1945 off Shizunai, Hokkaido (42° 12 N/142° 21 E) by US submarine *Sunfish*.

Kaijo Maru (Gunboat): 284 grt, built 1902; no details.

Kaika Maru (Transport): 2087 grt; requisitioned 194?; sunk 16 April 1944 between the Carolines and New Ireland by US submarine *Blackfish*.

Kaiko Maru (Guardboat): 121 grt motor vessel, built 1933; sunk 15 September 1944 in Marshalls by US aircraft.

Kaiko Maru (Guardboat): 139 grt; sunk 14 March 1945 off Inubsoaki (35° 40 N/141° E) by gunfire of US submarine *Trepang*.

Kaiko Maru (Transport): 3548 grt, built 1941; sunk 23 February 1944 off Paramushiro by US submarine *Sandlance*.

Kaiko Maru (Transport): 851 grt; requisitioned 194?; sunk 25 April 1945 at Saigon by US aircraft.

Kaiko Maru (Victualling Stores Ship): 1514 grt refrigerator ship, built 1922; requisitioned 194?; returned 1946.

Kainan Maru, ex-*Makambo* (Transport): 1130 grt steamer, built 1907; requisitioned 194?; sunk off Phuket, Thailand, by HM submarine *Stoic*.

Kaianan Maru No 2 (Guardboat): 87 grt; badly damaged 28 July 1945 at Kobe by US aircraft.

Kainan Maru No 7 (Guardboat): 84 grt; sunk 23 January 1945 in Formosa Strait (27° N/120° 16 E) by gunfire of US submarine *Barb*.

Kairyu Maru (Guardboat): 180 grt; sunk 19 April 1945 off Namposhoto (30° N/145° E) by gunfire of US submarine.

Kaishin Maru (Guardboat): 106 grt; wrecked 26 May 1945 off Paramushir, Kuriles.

Kaisho Maru (Transport): 4164 grt turbine freighter, built 1938; requisitioned 194?; sunk 22 August 1943 between Truk and Guam by US submarine *Tullibee*.

Kaito Maru (Transport): 2745 grt; requisitioned 194?; sunk 20 December 1943 north of New Ireland by US aircraft.

Kaiun Maru (Guardboat): 129 grt motor vessel, built 1936; sunk 20 March 1945 at Rabaul by US aircraft.

Kaiwa Maru (Guardboat): 99 grt; sunk 24 July 1945 N of Himehima by TF38.

Kaiyo Maru (Guardboat): sunk 16 January 1944 at Maloelap Atoll, Marshalls by US aircraft.

Kaiyo Maru No 1 (Guardboat): 32 grt; wrecked 2 July 1942 at Guadalcanal.

Kaiyo Maru No 2 (Guardboat): 33 grt; wrecked 2 July 1942 at Guadalcanal.

Kaiyo Maru No 5 (Guardboat): 93 grt; sunk 2 September 1944 off Sumatra (03° 55 N/96° 20 E) by British submarine.

Kaiyo Maru No 6 (Guardboat): 93 grt; wrecked 29 July 1945 off Cape Wakamiya, Korean Strait.

Kamikaze Maru (Torpedo Transport and Repair Ship): 4918 grt turbine freighter, built 1937; requisitioned 1941; sunk 30 March 1944 at Palau by TF58 aircraft.

Kamishima Maru, ex-*Shinto Maru* (Transport): 2245 grt, built 1919; requisitioned 194?; sunk 12 June 1944 north-west of Saipan by TF58 aircraft.

Kamishima Maru (Transport): 527 grt; requisitioned 194?; stranded 25 May 1945 north coast of Java (slight damage — USSBS; total loss — Jentschura & Jung).

Kamitsu Maru (Gunboat): 2721 grt turbine steamer, built 1937; requisitioned 1941; sunk 26 June 1945 off Todo-saki (39° 35 N/142° 04 E) by US submarine *Parche*.

Kamo Maru (Guardboat): 131 grt motor vessel, built 1926; sunk 1 July 1944 NW of Marianas (21° 26 N/141° 11 E) by gunfire of US submarine *Batfish*.

Kamoi Maru (Transport): 2811 grt; requisitioned 194?; sunk 26 November 1943 north-west of New Ireland by US submarine *Raton*.

Kanayamasan Maru (Transport): 2869 grt, built 1942; sunk 12 November 1943 north of the Admiralty Is by Allied aircraft.

Kanko Maru (Gunboat): 909 grt, built 1938; requisitioned 1940; sunk 10 January 1942 off Cape San Augustin (06° 12 N/125° 55 E) by US submarine *Pickerel*.

Kanno Maru No 3 (Guardboat): 98 grt; badly damaged 14 February 1945 E of Nanseishoto (29° 50 N/135° 31 E) by gunfire of US submarine *Haddock*.

Kannon Maru (Guardboat): 115 grt; sunk 31 July 1944 in SW Pacific.

Kanto Maru (Aircraft Transport): 8606 grt motor vessel, built 1930; requisitioned 1942; sunk north-west of Cape Kendari, Makasar Straits by US submarine *Saury*.

Karimo Maru (Victualling Stores Ship): 233 grt steam trawler, built 1923; requisitioned 194?; sunk 9 May 1945 off Miyako Jima, Sakishima, by RN TF57 aircraft.

Kasado Maru, ex-*Kazan* (Transport): 6029 grt steamer (Russian), built 1900; sunk at Port Arthur by Japanese artillery December 1904; salvaged and commissioned as Transport 12 May 1905. USSBS lists 6003 grt *Kasado Maru*, sunk 9 August 1945 off Kamchatka by aircraft.

Kasagi Maru (Gunboat): 3140 grt passenger steamer, built 1928; requisitioned 1941; sunk 28 January 1944 off Mikurajima (33° 30 N/139° 35 E) by US submarine *Swordfish*.

Kashima Maru, ex-*Kano Maru* (Transport): 8572 grt motor vessel, built 1934; requisitioned 194?; severely damaged and beached 21 July 1942 on Kiska after attack by US submarine *Grunion*: 7 August 1942 shelled and set on fire by US cruiser gunfire; finished off by air attack on following day.

Kashima Maru No 3 (Guardboat): 34 grt; sunk 10 July 1945 40m N of mouth of Yangtse by US aircraft.

Kasuga Maru (Armed Merchant Cruiser, Torpedo boat Depot Ship): 3819 grt steamer, built 1898; requisitioned 1904 as AMC; 1905? torpedo boat depot ship; 190? returned.

Kasuga Maru No 2 (Transport): 3967 grt steamer, built 1936; requisitioned 194?; sunk 13 March 1943 off the Andaman Is by Royal Netherlands Navy submarine *O.21*.

Kasumi Maru (Transport): 1400 grt; requisitioned 194?; sunk 12 May 1944 east of Belawan, Sumatra, by mine laid by HM submarine *Taurus*.

Katori Maru (Gunboat). 1920 grt steamer, built 1938; requisitioned 1941 but re-rated as transport 1 January 1943; sunk 29 June 1944 NW of Cape Bolinao, Luzon (10° N/121° 42 E) by US submarine *Growler*.

Katsura Maru No 2 (Gunboat): 1368 grt steamer, built 1937; requisitioned 1941; sunk 12 September 1943 N of Urup, Kuriles (40° N/149° 20 E) by US submarine *S.28*.

Katsuragawa Maru (Salvage Vessel): 1428 grt; requisitioned 1943; lost 1945.

Katsuragi Maru (Aircraft Transport): 8033 grt motor vessel, built 1931; requisitioned 1940; sunk 1 October 1942 off Cape St George, New Ireland, by US submarine *Sturgeon*.

Katsuragisan Maru (Transport): 2427 grt steamer, built 1925; requisitioned 194?; sunk 4 January 1944 north-east of Truk by Japanese mine.

Kawachi, ex-*Kanakee*: 314-ton sailing ship (US revenue cutter), built 1863; February 1869 Imperial Fleet *Kawachi*; August 1869 to Okayama-Han; 1890 returned and broken up.

Kayo, ex-*Kofuyo*, ex-*Chusan*: 699 grt steamer, built 1852; 1866 Matsuyama-Han *Kofuyo Maru*; 1868 Choshu-Han *Kayo Maru*; 1871 Imperial Fleet; sold as hulk in Shanghai 1872.

Kazan Maru (also known as *Huashan Maru*) (Gunboat): 2103 grt steamer, built 1936; requisitioned 1937; badly damaged 31 May 1945 off Genkajima Lighthouse (33° 40 N/129° 57 E) and stricken.

Kazu Maru No 1 (Guardboat): 39 grt; sunk 15 September 1944 in Marshalls by US aircraft.

Keijo Maru (Gunboat): 2626 grt, built 1940; requisitioned 1941; sunk 21 June 1942 N of Guadalcanal (09° S/160° 80 E) by US submarine *S.44*.

Keiko Maru (Gunboat): 2929 grt steamer, built 1938; requisitioned 1941; sunk 8 November 1942 off Cape San Augustin (06° 24 N/125° E) by US submarine *Seawolf*.

Keishin Maru (Gunboat): 1434 grt, built 1940; requisitioned 1942; sunk 1 May 1943 off Iwaki (37° 04 N/141° 05 E) by US submarine *Pogy*.

Keisho Maru, ex-*Kowa Maru* (Transport): 5879 grt motor vessel, built 1929; requisitioned 194?; sunk 12 October 1943 at Rabaul by US aircraft.

Keiyo Maru (Aircraft Transport): 6442 grt motor vessel, built 1937; requisitioned 1941; beached 12 June 1944 on Saipan following damage by TF58 aircraft.

Keizan Maru, ex-*Crawl Keys* (Transport): 2116 steamer, built 1918; requisitioned 194?; sunk 10 March 1945 130nm north of Okinawa by US submarine *Kete*.

Keizan Maru (Transport): 2864 grt, built 1940; requisitioned 194?; sunk 26 October 1942 off Paramushiro by US submarine *S.31*.

Kembu Maru, ex-*Van Cloon* (Transport): 4519 grt steamer (Dutch), built 1911; beached in Java Sea after shelling by Japanese submarine 7 February 1942; salvaged and commissioned as *Kembu Maru*; sunk 12 January 1945 north of Quinhon, Vietnam, by TF38 aircraft.

Kembu Maru (Transport): 6816 grt; captured vessel, previous identity uncertain; sunk 5 December 1943 at Kwajalein by TF50 aircraft.

Kenan Maru (Transport): 3129 grt, built 1941; requisitioned 194?; sunk 3 May 1944 north-west of Tinian by US submarine *Sandlance*.

Kenko Maru, ex-*Kenko*, ex-*Stork*, ex-HMS *Beagle*: 523-ton steamer (British), built 1855; 1870 Imperial Fleet training ship; 1881 hulk, scrapped at Shinagawa 1889.

Kenryu Maru (Transport): 4575 grt motor vessel, built 1935; requisitioned 194?; sunk off Hachijojima by US submarine *Snapper*.

Kenshin Maru (Transport): 3126 grt, built 1940; requisitioned 194?; sunk 17 January 1944 at Rabaul by US aircraft.

Kensho Maru (Transport): 4861 grt motor vessel, built 1938; requisitioned 194?; sunk 17 February 1944 at Truk by TF58 aircraft.

Ken'yo Maru (Transport): 6486 grt turbine freighter, built 1938; requisitioned 194?; sunk 23 March 1943 130nm NNW of Saipan by US submarine *Whale*; see p. 260.

Kenzan Maru (Gunboat): 951 grt steamer, built 1938; requisitioned 1944; sunk 7 May 1945 off Manimbaja, Celebes (00° 08 S/119° E) by US aircraft.

Kiho Maru No 1 (Guardboat): 74 grt; burnt 6 May 1945.

Kiikawa Maru (Gunboat): 209 grt steamer, built 1892; requisitioned February 1905 and later returned.

Kikaku Maru No 6 (Guardboat): 137 grt; sunk 27 February 1945 NE of Keelung, Formosa by gunfire of US submarine *Scabbardfish*.

Kiku Maru No 16 (Guardboat): 118 grt; sunk 29 October 1944 at Rabaul by US aircraft.

Kikukawa Maru (Transport): 3833 grt turbine freighter, built 1937; requisitioned 194?; lost by fire 7 October 1943 at Truk.

Kikyo Maru (Guardboat): 274 grt; sunk 6 February 1944 at Kwajalein by TF58.

Kimishima Maru (Transport): 5193 grt turbine freighter, built 1938; requisitioned 194?; sunk 23 December 1944 off Torishima by US submarine *Plunger*.

Kimposan Maru (Transport): 3261 grt steamer, built 1936; requisitioned 194?; sunk 16 January 1943 west of Kavieng by US submarine *Greenling*.

Kinai Maru (Transport): 8360 grt motor vessel, built 1930; requisitioned 193?; sunk 10 May 1943 east of Saipan by US submarine *Plunger*.

Kinjo Maru, ex-*North Angela* (Transport): 2081 grt steamer, built 1883; requisitioned 1904; lost 23 August 1905 in collision with SS *Baralong* off Moji.

Kinjosan Maru (Gunboat): 3262 grt, built 1936; no details.

Kinsei, ex-*Kokuryu Maru*, ex-*Kumsing*: 467-ton steamer, built 1862; 1864 Shogunate Fleet *Kokuryu Maru*; 1868 Imperial Fleet training ship, at Kobe.

Kinsen Maru (Transport): 3081 grt steamer, built 1937; requisitioned 194?; slightly damaged by fire 6 November 1944; captured August 1945, returned to merchant service and sold to Korea 1946, as *Kumchhon*.

Kinshiu Maru, ex-*Kintuck* (Transport): 3854 grt steamer, built 1891; requisitioned 1904; sunk 26 April 1904 west of Wonsan by Russian armoured cruiser *Rossiya* *Kinshu Maru*, ex-*Mount Pentelikon*, ex-*Atlanticos*, ex-*Sylvia Victoria*, ex-*War Cavalry* (Transport): 5606 grt steamer, built 1919; requisitioned to 194?; sunk 17 June 1944 at entrance to Davao Gulf by US submarine *Hake*.

Kintoku Maru No 13 (Guardboat): 45 grt; sunk 5 June 1945 off Fujinaminohama by US aircraft.

Kiri Maru No 2 (Guardboat): 334 grt motor vessel, built 1935; sunk 23 July 1945 between Unoosaki and Shoyaskai by US submarine *Sea Pacher*.

Kiri Maru No 8 (Transport): 945 grt motor vessel, built 1937; requisitioned 194?; sunk 7 November 1944 off Irosaki by USS *Greenling*.

Kirikawa Maru (Transport): 3836 grt turbine freighter, built 1937; requisitioned 194?; sunk 27 February 1943 off Vella Lavella, Solomons, by US aircraft.

Kirishima Maru (Tanker): 5840 grt motor freighter, built 1931; requisitioned 1942 and converted to oil tanker (8267 dwt); sunk 25 September 1943 220nm south-east of Nha Trang by US submarine *Bowfin*.

Kisei Maru (Guardboat): 91 grt; sunk 8 January 1945 in Sunda Strait by US submarine, possibly *Cavalla*.

Kiso Maru (Gunboat): 703 grt motor vessel, built 1932; sunk 12 September 1944 off Cebu (10° 20 N/123° 58 E) by US aircraft.

Kisogawa Maru (Water Tanker): 1914 grt, built 1940; requisitioned 194?; sunk 10 November 1943 in Malakar Straits by HM submarine *Tally-ho*.

Kitami Maru (Stores Ship): 394 grt motor trawler, built 1930; requisitioned 194?; sunk 17 April 1942 south-east of Kavieng by US submarine.

Kizugawa Maru (Water Tanker): 1915 grt, built 1941; requisitioned 194?; severely damaged off Guam 8 April 1944 by US submarine *Seahorse*; sunk 27 June 1944 at Guam by TF58 aircraft.

Koan Maru (Water Tanker): 3217 grt steamer, built 1936; requisitioned 194?; sunk 24 January 1944 at Rabaul by US aircraft.

Kobe Maru (Transport, Hospital Ship): 2877 grt steamer, built 1888; requisitioned 1904 as Transport; 1905 Hospital Ship; returned to merchant service and lost by stranding 1 September 1923.

Kobe Maru (Transport): 7938 grt, built 1940; requisitioned 194?; lost 11 November 1942 off Yangtse estuary by collision with *Tenzan Maru*.

Kochi Maru, ex-*Takachi Maru* (Auxiliary): 329 grt steamer, built 1890; requisitioned 1904, returned 1905.

Kochi Maru No 1 (Guardboat): 70 grt; sunk 20 March 1945 E of Honshu by TF38.

Koei Maru (Guardboat): 19 grt; sunk 10 October 1944 10m SW of Bawean, Java Sea by gunfire from a submarine.

Kofuku Maru (Guardboat): 35 grt; sunk 8 July 1944 at Saipan by US aircraft.

Kofuku Maru No 1 (Guarboat): 35 grt; sunk 8 July 1944 at Saipan by US aircraft.

Kofuku Maru No 3 (Guardboat): 35 grt; sunk 8 July 1944 at Saipan by US aircraft.

Kofuku Maru (Transport): 3209 grt steamer, built 1934; requisitioned 194?; lost 6 September off Sado by collision.

Kogan Maru (Transport): 2965 grt steamer, built 1919; requisitioned 194?; lost 19 April 1944 off Hino Misaki, Honshu, by collision.

Kogyo Maru (Ammunition Ship): 6343 grt turbine freighter, built 1938; requisitioned 194?; sunk 24 September 1944 off Coron Bay by TF38 aircraft.

Kogyo Maru No 12 (Guardboat): 53 grt; sunk 30 July 1945 at Imaura by TF38.

Kojo Maru (Guardboat): 91 grt; sunk 16 November 1944 NW of Bonin Island (29° 59 N/139° 39 E) by gunfire from US submarine.

Kojun Maru (Transport): 1931 grt, built 1924; requisitioned 194?; sunk 13 August 1944 near entrance to Davao Gulf by US submarine *Bluegill*.

Kokai Maru (Transport): 3871 grt steam cargo-liner, built 1939; requisitioned 194?; sunk 21 February 1944 at Kavieng by US aircraft.

Koki Maru (Guardboat): 74 grt motor fishing vessel, built 1929; sunk 25 February 1945 off Torishima (approx. 31° N/141° E) by gunfire of US destroyers *Hazelwood* and *Murray*.

Koko Maru (Stores Ship): 1520 grt refrigerator ship, built 1922; requisitioned 194?; returned early 1945; mined 11 March 1945 off Shanghai.

Kokura Maru, ex-*Tartar* (Transport): 2590 grt steamer, built 1887; requisitioned 1904; proposed for May 1904 Port Arthur operation as *Blockship No 2*; returned 190?.

Komaki Maru (Aircraft Transport): 8524 grt motor liner, built 1933; requisitioned 1940; severely damaged 18 April 1942 at Rabaul by air attack; deleted from Active List 1 May 1942.

Kompira Maru (Guardboat): 35 grt; sunk 21 June 1944 off Tinian, Marianas by gunfire.

Kompira Maru No 1 (Guardboat): 94 grt; sunk July 1944 by aircraft of US escort carrier *Tinian*.

Kompira Maru No 2 (Guardboat): 89 grt; badly damaged 25 July 1945 off Moji by TF38.

Kompira Maru No 6 (Guardboat): 98 grt; sunk 18 November 1944 off Tarakan, Borneo by US aircraft.

Konei Maru (Transport): 2345 grt steamer, built 1930; requisitioned 194?; sunk 1 December 1942 north of the Bismarck Archipelago by US submarine *Peto*.

276 MISCELLANEOUS MERCANTILE AUXILIARY VESSELS

Kongosan Maru (Gunboat): 2119 grt passenger steamer, built 1927; requisitioned 1940; sunk 4 May 1942 24m SW of Daiozaki (33° 32 N/136° 05 E) by US submarine *Trout*.
Kosei Maru, ex-*Narenta*, ex-*Neganti* (Victualling Stores Ship): 8237 grt turbine refrigerator ship, built 1919; requisitioned 194?, returned early 1943; sunk 8 April 1943 north-west of Truk by US submarine *Tunny*.
Kosei Maru, ex-*Meiji Maru* (Transport): 2205 grt steamer, built 1924; requisitioned 194?; sunk 27 January 1944 south of Formosa by US submarine *Thresher*.
Kosei Maru (Transport): 3551 grt steamer, built 1937; requisitioned 194?; sunk 11 November 1943 east of the Nansei Shoto by US submarine *Sargo*.
Koshin Maru (Guardboat): 73 grt; sunk 21 December 1944, probably in the Gulf of Thailand.
Koshin Maru (Guardboat): 67 grt; badly damaged 11 July 1943 E of Kamchatka (approx. 55° N/164° E) by US aircraft.
Koshin Maru (Transport): 6530 grt turbine freighter, built 1938; requisitioned 194?; lost 9 August 1944 150nm north-east of Keelung, Formosa, by fire.
Kosho Maru (Gunboat): 564 grt steamer, built 1883; requisitioned from 6 to 19 June 1904 and then returned.
Kosho Maru (Gunboat): 1365 grt, built 1940; requisitioned 1941; sunk 22 May 1944 S of Penang (04° 52 N/100° E) by British submarine *Sea Rover*.
Kosho Maru (Victualling Stores Ship): 115 grt trawler; requisitioned 194?; sunk 28 July 1945 at Owase by TF38 aircraft.
Kosho Maru No 2 (Guardboat): 133 grt; sunk 15 April 1945 off Todo-saki (39° 35 N/142° 06 E) by gunfire of US submarine *Cero*.
Kosuku Maru, ex-*Fei Seen*, ex-*HMS Cowper*: 324-ton paddle steamer, built 1860; April 1864 Shogunate Fleet; 1869 Imperial Fleet; exchanged with J. Batchelor (American) for *Uncle Sam*.
Kotetsu Maru, ex-*Georges* (Auxiliary): 179-ton steamer (French); seized 19 August 1904 and commissioned as Japanese auxiliary.
Koto Maru, ex-*Glengarry* (Transport): 3182 grt steamer, built 1883; requisitioned 1904, returned 1905.
Koto Maru (Transport): 1053 grt steamer, built 1939; requisitioned 194?; sunk 31 May 1944 south-west of Paramushiro by US submarine *Barb*.
Koto Maru No 2 (Transport): 3557 grt steamer, built 1927; requisitioned 194?; sunk 7 July 1944 off Qui Nhon by US submarine *Flasher*.
Kotohira Maru (Guardboat): 39 grt; sunk 15 April 1944 at Truk, and wreck subsequently BU.
Kotoku Maru (Ammunition Supply Ship ?): 6701 grt motor refrigerator ship, built 1937; requisitioned 194?; sunk 29 July 1942 east of Buna by Allied aircraft.
Kotoshiro Maru (Guardboat): 90 grt; sunk 4 April 1945 in Marshalls by US aircraft.
Kotoshiro Maru No 8 (Guardboat): 109 grt fishing vessel; sunk 13 February 1945 S of Japan (30° N/136° 30 E) by gunfire from US submarine *Sennet*.
Kotoshiro Maru No 12 (Guardboat): 91 grt fishing vessel; sunk 4 April 1945 off Torishima (approx. 30° N/140° E) by US aircraft.
Kowa Maru (Gunboat): 1106 grt, built 1940; requisitioned 1941; sunk 21 February 1944 off Kavieng (02° 30 S/150° 15 E) by US aircraft.
Koyo Maru (Transport): 5471 grt steamer, built 1919; requisitioned 194?; sunk 23 February 1944 200nm NNW Haha Jima by US submarine *Snook*.
Kumagawa Maru, ex-*Nichiyo Maru* (Transport and Tanker): 7508 grt motor freighter, built 1934; requisitioned 1941; 1943 converted to oil tanker; sunk 12 January 1945 off Cap St Jacques by TF38 aircraft.
Kumano Maru (Armed Merchant Cruiser and Torpedo Boat Tender): 5076 grt steamer, built 1901; requisitioned 1904; lost 10 June 1927 off Takamatsu by collision.
Kunimiya Maru (Guardboat): 104 grt; sunk 18 March 1944 E of North Honshu (37° N/151° E) by US submarine.
Kunishima Maru (Transport): 4083 grt turbine freighter, built 1937; requisitioned 194?; lost 24 February 1944 off Katata by stranding.
Kunitsu Maru (Transport): 2722 grt turbine freighter, built 1937; requisitioned 194?; beached and written off 19 April at Sabang after attack by HMS *Illustrious*, USS *Saratoga* aircraft.
Kurihashi (*Maru*), ex-*Herakles* (Salvage Ship): 1040 grt steamer (Swedish), built 1897; purchased 21 May 1905 for Japanese Navy; captured August 1945 and employed by Repatriation Service until laid up in 1946; 1948 to Japanese Maritime Safety Agency (MSDF from 1953); deleted from List 1955.
Kuroshio Maru (Guardboat): sunk 12 June 1945 N of Sumatra (06° 20 N/95° 45 E) by British destroyers.
Kurushima, ex-*Christine Moller*, ex-*Titania*, ex-*Baikal* (Salvage Tug): 1000 grt steam tug (British), built 1917; captured 8 December 1941 at Shanghai; commissioned 6 May 1942 as *Kurishima*; August 1945 recaptured by British at Singapore and renamed *Christine Moller*; 1949(?) Chinese.
Kusunoki Maru No 2 (Guardboat): sunk 26 June 1945 S of Onekotan, Kurile Islands, (49° 40 N/155° 30 E) by US destroyers *Bearss*, *John Hood*, *Jarvis* and *Porter*.
Kusuho Maru, ex-*Orel* (Transport): 4880 grt liner (Russian) built 1889; captured 27 May 1905 by Japanese cruiser; commissioned 7 September 1905 as *Kusuho Maru*
Kyodo Maru No 36 (Survey Ship): 1499 grt passenger steamer, built 1929; requisitioned 1939; sunk 17 July 1944 north-west of Labuan by US submarine *Lapon*.
Kyoei Maru No 3 (Guardboat): 38 grt; sunk 29 October 1944 at Luzon.
Kyoraku Maru No 3 (Guardboat): 38 grt; sunk 20 July 1945 in Gulf of Siam (approx. 08° 08 N/103° 40 E) by US submarine *Bumper*.
Kyoshin Maru No 1 (Guardboat): 39 grt; sunk 3 February 1945 at Manila.
Kyoshin Maru No 2 (Guardboat): 39 grt; sunk 31 August 1944 off Halmahera by US aircraft.
Kyowa Maru, ex-*Helios* (Transport): 1917 grt passenger steamer (Norwegian); captured 8 December 1941 140nm south of Mekong estuary; commissioned 1942 as *Kyowa Maru*; sunk 23 October 1943 north-west of Buka by US aircraft.
Kyowa Maru No 2 (Guardboat): 108 grt; sunk 16 October 1944 5m NNW of Matsuwajima by gunfire from US submarine *Tilefish*.
Kyowa Maru No 3 (Guardboat): 154 grt; sunk 18 February 1945 S of Honshu (31° N/137° 30 E) by gunfire of US destroyers *Barton*, *Ingraham* and *Moale*.
Lüshan Maru (Gunboat): 2531 grt passenger steamer, built 1920; requisitioned 1937 and known also as *Rozan Maru*; sunk 5 February 1944 110m SE of Hong Kong by US aircraft.
Lyon(s) Maru (Aircraft transport). 7017 grt steamer, built 1920; requisitioned 1941; sunk 24 January 1944 at Rabaul (04° 13 S/152° 11 E) by US aircraft.
Magane Maru (Gunboat): 3120 grt steamer, built 1940; requisitioned 1941; sunk 24 January 1944 off Torishima (30° 06 N/141° 19 E) by US submarine *Snook*.
Maiko Maru, ex-*Kiel* (Transport): 1074 grt steamer, built 1891; requisitioned 1904; mined 11 May 1905 off Elliot Island (approx. 39° N/123° E).
Mamiya Maru (Stores Ship): 398 grt fishing vessel, built 1930; requisitioned during the war and later returned.
Manda Maru (Gunboat): 248 grt steamer, built 1900; requisitioned 1904 and returned 1905.
Mandasan Maru, ex-*Pembrokeshire* (Auxiliary): 4513 grt steamer, built 1901; requisitioned 1904 and returned 1905; BU 1933.
Man-Ei Maru (Oiler): 5226 grt turbine tanker Standard 1 TM type, built 1943; requisitioned 1944 and sunk 1945.
Manju Maru, ex-*Jufuku Maru* (Transport): 5874 grt steamer, built 1919; sunk 29 November 1943 W of Marianas (19° 38 N/139° 58 E) by US submarine *Pargo*.
Manko Maru (Stores Ship): 1502 grt steamer, built 1923; sunk 2 November 1943 off Rabaul (04° 15 S/152° 10 E) by US aircraft.
Manko Maru (Transport): 4471 grt turbine passenger vessel, built 1935; sunk 30 July 1944 NE of Cape Bojeador, Luzon (19° 08 N/120° 51 E) by US submarine *Parche*.
Manryu Maru (Transport): 1630 grt; sunk 16 April 1945 off Todosaki (39° 35 N/142° 06 E) by US submarine *Sunfish*.
Manshu Maru, ex-*Strathgyle* (Auxiliary): 5249 grt steamer, built 1894; requisitioned 1904 and returned 1905; wrecked 29 June 1913 on Okurishima.
Mantai Maru, ex-*Vancouver Maru* (Transport): 5863 grt steamer, built 1919; sunk 16 July 1944 off Cape Bojeador, Luzon (18° 20 N/119° 42 E) by US submarine *Guardfish*.
Man-Yo Maru (Gunboat): 2904 grt steamer, built 1937; requisitioned 1940; sunk 5 March 1945 in Java Sea (05° 50 S/113° 46 E) by US submarine *Sea Robin*.
Marudai Maru (Guardboat): 19 grt; sunk 17 June 1944 at Saipan by US aircraft.
Masajima Maru (Transport): 2742 grt steamer; sunk 13 March 1945 off Swatow (23° 30 N/117° 10 E) by US aircraft.
Matsuhouta Maru (Salvage ship): 383 grt, built 1941; requisitioned 1941; used for repatriation 1946-47 and transferred to Netherlands Navy on 3 May 1948 and renamed *Triton*; handed over to Indonesia in 1953.
Matsumoto Maru (Oiler): 7024 grt steamer, built 1921; requisitioned and rebuilt 1941-42 as an oiler; sunk 25 October 1944 in Formosa Strait (25° 07 N/119° 45 E) by US submarine *Tang*.
Matsutani Maru (Transport): 1999 grt steamer, built 1942; requisitioned 1942; sunk 17 February 1944 at Truk (07° 23 N/151° 05 E) by US TF58.
Meiho Maru (Guardboat): 108 grt; sunk 6 February 1944 at Kwajalein, Marshalls by US TF58.
Meiji Maru No 1 (Gunboat): 1934 grt steamer, built 1937; requisitioned 1941; sunk 20 April 1943 off Kinkazan (38° 10 N/141° 25 E) by US submarine *Scorpion*.
Meiji Maru No 2 (Guardboat): 80 grt; sunk 14 July 1945 off Hakodate by YF38.
Meiryu Maru (Transport): 4793 grt; Standard 1B type turbine steamer, built 1943; requisitioned 1943; sunk 2 January 1945 off San Fernando, Luzon (16° 37 N/120° 19 E) by US aircraft.
Meisho Maru (Transport): 2737 grt Standard 1C type steamer, built 1943; requisitioned 1943; sunk 16 January 1944 N of Bismarck Archipelago (02° 15 N/145° 35 E) by US aircraft.
Meisho Maru (Guardboat): 31 grt; sunk 19 May 1944 off Ogasawara-gunto by US submarine *Sturgeon*.
Meiten Maru (Transport): 4474 grt motor ship, built 1938; sunk 20 June 1943 W of Marianas (15° 57 N/140° 57 E) by US submarine *Tautog*.
Meiyo Maru (Transport): 5658 grt steamer, built 1940; sunk 8 August 1942 14m W of Cape St Georges (04° 52 S/152° 43 E) by US submarine *S.38*.
Menado Maru (Transport): 2165 grt passenger vessel, built 1922; sunk 20 January 1944 SE of Swatow (23° 10 N/118° 15 E) by US aircraft.
Mihairu Maru, ex-*Michael*, ex-*Clan Grant* (Stores Ship): 3643 grt steamer, built 1883; captured from Russians in 1905 and used as an auxiliary; BU in January 1929.
Mihara Maru (Transport): 697 grt motor passenger vessel, built 1925; sunk 9 September 1944 E of Mindanao (09° 45 N/125° 30 E) by US TF38.
Miho Maru (Transport): 515 grt passenger steamer, built 1913; sunk 15 July 1945 E of South Sakhalien (48° 29 N/147° 36 E) by US submarine *Skate*.
Miho Maru, ex-*Taganoura Maru* (Salvage Ship): 632 grt steam tug, built 1924; sunk 12 September 1944 off Cebu (10° 35 N/124° E) by US TF38.
Miho Maru (Transport): 4667 grt Standard 1B Type turbine steamer, built 1944; requisitioned 1944; sunk 30 April 1945 in Yellow Sea (34° 27 N/123° 48 E) by US submarine *Trepang*.
Miike Maru (Transport): 3364 grt steamer, built 1888; requisitioned 1904 and converted to a stores ship in 1905; later returned and lost 21 October 1929 near Tonnai, Sakhalien; later BU.
Miike Maru (Transport): 11738 grt passenger vessel, built 1941; sunk 27 April 1944 SW of Yap (08° 34 N/134° 48 E) by US submarine *Trigger*.
Mikage Maru No 3, ex-*Mifane Maru* (Transport): 3111 grt steamer, built 1928; sunk 13 July 1942 in collision 3m S of Tsurushima.
Mikage Maru No 18 (Collier): 4319 grt turbine steamer, built 1937; sunk 10 May 1944 N of Carolines (11° 26 N/143° 46 E) by US submarine *Silversides*.
Mikage Maru No 20 (Transport): 2718 grt steamer, built 1940; sunk 18 July 1943 50m S of Wake (18° 34 N/166° 20 E) by US submarine *Porpoise*.
Mikawa Maru (Blockship): 1968 grt steamer, built 1884; as *Blockship No 4* sunk 3 May 1904 at Port Arthur (38° 47 N/121° 14 E) by Russian shore batteries.
Mikuni Maru, ex-*Gerard* (Steamer): 663 grt screw steamer. built 1862; purchased by Satsuma Clan December 1865 and transferred to Imperial Fleet in 1868; in the same year she became the British *Alligator* and was later returned to the Prince of Satsuma.
Minato Maru (Stores Ship): 664 grt motor fishing vessel, built 1934; sunk 3 November 1943 at Ocean Island (00° 43 S/169° 10 E) by US aircraft.
Mino Maru (Stores Ship): 473 grt motor fishing vessel, built 1932; requisitioned during war but later returned.
Misaki Maru, ex-*Australcrag*, ex-*Strathleven* (Transport): 4422 grt steamer, built 1907; requisitioned in Second World War and sunk 14 November 1944 in South China Sea (15° 10 N/112° 40 E) by US submarine *Barbel*.
Misaki Maru No 2 (Transport): 769 grt passenger steamer, built 1917; wrecked 1 September 1944 at Shimushir, Kuriles (46° 55 N/152° E).
Misaku Maru (Transport): 4500 grt steamer, built 1942; requisitioned 1942; sunk 9 April 1944 W of Marianas (15° 32 N/145° E) by US submarine *Seahorse*.
Mishima Maru (Guardboat): 34 grt; sunk 12 October 1943 at Rabaul (04° 13 S/152° 12 E) by US aircraft.
Mitakesan Maru (Transport): 4441 grt turbine steamer, built 1937; sunk 11 May 1944 W of Marianas (14° 57 N/143° 30 E) by US submarine *Sandlance*.
Miya Maru (Guardboat): 81 grt; damaged 14 July 1945 in Eastern mouth of Tsugaru Kaikyo by aircraft of TF38.
Miyagi Maru (Guardboat): 248 grt; sunk 4 August 1944 off Sofu-Gan (29° 40 N/141°) by gunfire from US submarine *Sterlet*.
Miyasho Maru No 1 (Guardboat): 79 grt; sunk 19 June 1943 off Inubozaki (36° 40 N/142° 55 E) by gunfire of US submarine *Sculpin*.
Miyo Maru (Guardboat): 65 grt; damaged 11 February 1944 off Leyte by US aircraft.
Miyoshima Maru (Gunboat): 273 grt steamer, built 1902; requisitioned 1904 and returned 1905.
Moji Maru (Collier): 380 grt, built 1936; requisitioned 1941; mined 3 January 1942 SW of Hong Kong.
Moji Maru (Guardboat): 60 grt; sunk 8 July 1944 E of Borneo (02° 25 N/118° 14 E) by US submarine *Bonefish*.
Momokawa Maru (Transport): 3829 grt steamer, built 1941; sunk 17 February 1944 at Truk (07° 20 N/151° 53 E) by US TF58.
Mongol (Gunboat): 193-ton ex-Russian river gunboat, built 1907; captured 7 September 1918 at Habarovsk; not renamed, and returned 1922.
Montevideo Maru (Japanese = *Montebideo Maru*) (Transport): 7266 grt motor passenger vessel, built 1926; sunk 1 July 1942 NW of Luzon (18° 37 N/119° 29 E) by US submarine *Sturgeon*.
Muko Maru (Transport): 4862 grt steamer, built 1937; sunk 12 November 1943 N of Truk (09° 20 N/152° 46 E) by US submarine *Thresher*.
Mukogawa Maru (Gunboat): 418 grt steamer, built 1893; requisitioned 1904 and returned 1905.
Murotsu Maru (Oiler): 870 grt Standard 2 TE type motor tanker, built 1943; requisitioned 1943; used for repatriation in 1945 and later returned to commercial use.
Musashi Maru (Guardboat): 104 grt; wrecked 23 September 1944 at Bataan (20° 20 N/121° 58 E).
Mutsuei Maru (Oiler): circa 500 grt Standard 1 TM type turbine tanker, built circa 1943; requisitioned 1943, fate unknown.
Myojin Maru No 2 (Guardboat): 19 grt; sunk 6 November 1944 in Philippines.
Myojin Maru No 7 (Guardboat): 96 grt; sunk 13 July 1945 off Chichijima (27° 04 N/142° 11 E) by US aircraft.
Myojin Maru No 12 (Guardboat): 56 grt; sunk 27 March 1945 W of Torishima (30° N/139° 30 E) by US TF58.
Myoken Maru (Gunboat): 4124 grt turbine steamer, built 1938; requisitioned 1941; sunk 24 January 1942 N of Kema, Celebes (01° 22 N/125° 10 E) by US submarine *Swordfish*.
Myoko Maru (Transport): 5086 grt motor vessel, built 1937; sunk 17 June 1943 N of New Ireland (04° 04 N/154° 03 E) by US submarine *Drum*.
Myoro Maru, ex-*Harbarton* (Transport): 3265 grt ex-British steamer, built 1902; captured 18 March 1905 in Etorofu Strait by cruiser *Aktisushima*; requisitioned as naval transport 1 September 1905; fate unknown.
Nachi Maru (Gunboat): 1605 grt motor ship, built 1926; requisitioned 1943 but re-rated as submarine depot ship 20 January 1945; surrendered August 1945 and used on repatriation service before being returned to commercial service.
Nachiryu Maru No 12 (Guardboat): 97 grt; sunk 15 November 1944 NW of Ogasawara-gunto (30° 10 N/137° 23 E) by gunfire of US submarine *Sterlet*.
Nachizan Maru (Transport): 4433 grt motor passenger vessel; sunk 13 November 1943 in East China Sea (32° 55 N/125° 09 E) by US submarine *Trigger*.
Nagata Maru (Gunboat): 2969 grt steamer, built 1936; requisitioned 1940 but re-rated as a transport 1942; sunk 22 April 1944 off Cape St Jacques (10° 19 N/107° 05 E) by US aircraft.
Nagato Maru (Blockship): 1884 grt steamer, built 1884; requisitioned 1904 as *Blockship No 8* and earmarked for third attempt to block Port Arthur on night of 2/3 May 1904, but did not sail.
Nagato Maru (Guardboat): 90 grt; sunk 18 April 1942 650m E of Japan by aircraft of USS *Enterprise*.
Nagatsu Maru (Transport): 840 grt motor ship, built 1942; requisitioned during war and returned later.
Nagaura (*Maru*), ex-*Tatsura* (Submarine Depot Ship): built 1894.
Nagisan Maru (Transport): 4391 grt motor ship, built 1931; sunk 30 April 1944 at Palau (07° 30 N/134° 30 E) by US TF58.
Nagonoura Maru, ex-*China* (Transport): 1084 grt screw steamer, built 1865; requisitioned 1904; sunk 9 February 1904 10m off Henashizaki (approx. 40° 40 N/139° 40 E) by Russian Vladivostok Squadron.
Nakamura Maru (Transport): 102 grt steamer, built 1891; sunk 25 April 1904 off Shinpo by Russian torpedo boats *No. 205* and *No. 206*.
Namman Maru, ex-*Kuma Maru*, ex-*Fuji Maru* (Transport): 6550 grt steamer, built 1921; sunk 27 October 1943 in Philippine Sea (12° 02 N/134° 28 E) by US submarine *Flying Fish*.
Nampo Maru (Gunboat): 1206 grt steamer, built 1940; requisitioned 1941; sunk 15 June 1942 16m off Corregidor, Luzon (14° 20 N/120° 20 E) by US submarine *Seawolf*.
Nampo Maru (Oiler): 10,033 grt Standard 1 TL type turbine tanker, built 1943; requisitioned 1943; sunk 24 February 1944 E of Formosa (24° 20 N/122° 23 E) by US submarine *Grayback*.
Nana Maru (Transport): 6557 grt steamer, built 1940; sunk 23 January 1942 off Balikpapan (01° 20 S/117° 02 E) by Netherlands aircraft.
Naniwa Maru (Transport): 4853 grt steamer, built 1938; sunk 3 August 1942 W of Truk (07° 17 N/150° 46 E) by US submarine *Gudgeon*.
Nankei Maru (Transport): 8416 grt motor ship, built 1933; sunk 12 September 1944 in South China Sea (18° 42 N/114° 30 E) by US submarine *Sealion*.
Nankai Maru No 2 (Transport): 1960 grt steamer, built 1940; sunk 23 December 1943 at Mili Atoll, Marshalls (06° 05 N/171° 43 E) by US aircraft.
Nansatsu Maru No 3 (Guardboat): 149 grt; sunk 10 October 1944 in Naha harbour, Okinawa (26° 13 N/127° 41) by US TF38.
Nanshin Maru (Guardboat): 88 grt; sunk 18 April 1942 650m E of Japan by aircraft of USS *Enterprise*.
Nanshin Maru No 26 (Guardboat): 81 grt; sunk 1 February 1945 S of Japan (30° 05 N/135° 15 E) by US submarine, possibly *Threadfin*.
Nanshin Maru No 27 (Guardboat): 83 grt; sunk 15 September 1942 NE of Honshu (37° N/152° E) by gunfire of US submarine.
Nanshin Maru No 28 (Guardboat): 83 grt; sunk 3 October 1944, probably by a US submarine.
Nanshin Maru No 35 (Guardboat): 86 grt; sunk 18 February 1945 W of Torishima (30° N/137° 30 E) by gunfire of US destroyers *Barton*, *Ingraham* and *Moale*.
Nanshin Maru No 36 (Guardboat): 81 grt; sunk 16/17 February 1945 SW of Mikomoto Light by US destroyer *Haynsworth*.
Nanshu Maru No 2 (Guardboat): 43 grt; sunk 8 March 1944 off Duke of York Isle, St George Channel (04° 12 S/152° 30 E) by US aircraft.
Nan-Yo Maru, ex-*River Indus* (Transport): 3770 grt steamer, built 1884, requisitioned 1904; wrecked 28 March 1904 off Chezudo.
Naruto Maru (Ammunition Ship): 7148 grt motor passenger ship, built 1934; sunk 8 August 1943 NW of Marianas (23° 15 N/142° 45 E) by US submarine *Whale*.
Nasu Maru (Salvage Ship): 695 grt, built 1927; mined 12 July 1945 near Niigata.
Natsukawa Maru (Transport): 4739 grt steamer, built 1942; sunk 19 November 1944 off Brunei Bay (05° 20 N/115° 13 E) by US aircraft.
Neikai Maru (Transport): 2827 grt; sunk 27 January

MISCELLANEOUS MERCANTILE AUXILIARY VESSELS 277

1944 between Truk and New Ireland (03° 45 N/150° 38 E) by US aircraft.

Nichiei Maru (Transport): 2436 grt steamer, built 1938; sunk 12 September 1944 off Cebu (10° 20 N/124° E) by US aircraft of TF38.

Nichiei Maru (Guardboat): 78 grt; sunk 30 January 1944 off Ujae Atoll (08° 42 N/166° E) by US destroyer *Burns*.

Nichiei Maru No 2 (Guardboat): 78 grt; sunk 7 January 1945 in S Inland Sea by US submarine.

Nichiei Maru No 5 (Guardboat): 161 grt; sunk 11 June 1945 SW of Paramushir, Kuriles (approx. 50° N/155° E) by US aircraft.

Nichiho Maru (Oiler): circa 10,000 grt Standard 1 TL type turbine tanker, built circa 1944; requisitioned 1944, fate unknown.

Nichii Maru (Ammunition Ship): 6543 grt steamer, built 1939; sunk 21 November 1943 NE of Kavieng, New Ireland (02° S/149° 15 E) by US aircraft.

Nichiran Maru No 3 (Guardboat): 32 grt; sunk 12 July 1944 NE of Cape Engano, Luzon (18° 50 N/122° 40 E) by gunfire of US submarine *Apoggon*.

Nichiro Maru (Ammunition Ship): 6534 grt steamer, built 1939; sunk 17 February 1944 off Palau (08° 50 N/135° 40 E) by US submarine *Sargo*.

Nichiryo Maru (Transport): 2721 grt, built 1940; sunk 1 December 1943 in Celebes Sea (01° 30 N/120° 44 E) by US submarine *Bonefish*.

Nichizui Maru (Transport): 6584 grt steamer, built 1941; sunk 19 October 1944 S of Hong Kong (21° 11 N/114° 05 E) by US aircraft.

Nihonkai Maru (Torpedo Recovery Ship): 2684 grt motor passenger vessel, built 1932; sunk 17 June 1944 S of Mindanao (06° 36 N/127° 55 E) by US submarine *Flounder*.

Niigata Maru (Auxiliary): 2184 grt steamer, built 1903; requisitioned May 1905 and returned 1906.

Nikka Maru (Guardboat): 142 grt; sunk 23 June 1943 N of Bougainville (05° 34 S/155° 07 E) by US aircraft.

Nikkai Maru (Gunboat): 2562 grt steamer, built 1938; requisitioned 1940 and re-rated 1 October 1943 as transport; sunk 26 November 1943 SW of Truk (04° 12 N/148° 20 E) by US submarine *Ray*.

Nikko Maru (Escort/Armed Merchant Cruiser): 5823 grt steamer, built 1903; requisitioned as an armed escort in 1904 but re-rated as an AMC in 1905; wrecked 14 May 1905 off Pusan but salvaged and returned to commercial service; sunk 9 April 1945 in Manila Bay (14° 05 N/120° 37 E) by US aircraft.

Nikko Maru (Transport): 5949 grt steamer; sunk 20 November 1943 NE of Marianas (23° 10 N/147° 22 E) by US submarine *Harder*.

Nippo Maru (Water Carrier): 3763 grt turbine steamer, built 1936; requisitioned as water carrier and sunk 17 February 1944 at Truk (07° 20 N/151° 40 E) by US TF58.

Nippo Maru (Transport): 1942 grt steamer, built 1943; requisitioned 1943; sunk 16 July 1944 E of South Sakhalien (48° 29 N/147° 36 E) by US submarine *Skate*.

Nippo Maru (Oiler): 10,528 grt standard 1 TL type turbine tanker, built 1944; requisitioned 5 March 1944; sunk 27 October the same year in Balabac Strait (07° 17 N/116° 45 E) by US submarine *Bergall*.

Nippon Maru (Armed Merchant Cruiser): 6168 grt steamer, built 1898; requisitioned 1904 and returned 1905; later became the Chilean *Renaico*.

Nissei Maru (Transport): 333 grt, built 1935; requisitioned during war as a transport and also possibly as a minelayer; sunk 17 November 1942 off Christmas Island (10° 30 S/105° 40 E), possibly by US submarine.

Nisshin Maru (Guardboat): 111 grt; wrecked 15 May 1945 SW of Urup, Kuriles.

Nissho Maru No 2 (Gunboat): 1386 grt, built 1941; requisitioned 1941; sunk 3 March 1945 off Mijakejima (34° 05 N/139° 54 E) by US submarine *Trepang*.

Nissho Maru No 12 (Gunboat): 1199 grt steamer, built 1936; requisitioned 1938; re-rated as transport 1 April 1943 and returned later.

Nissho Maru No 16 (Gunboat): 1173 grt, built 1939; requisitioned 1941 but re-rated as a netlayer 1943; mined 1 February 1945 WNW of Mokpo, Korea (approx. 35° N/125° E).

Nissho Maru No 18 (Transport): 1990 grt steamer, built 1942; requisitioned 1942 and returned 1945.

Nisshun Maru (Ammunition Ship): 6380 grt steamer, built 1941; sunk 18 April 1943 W of Bismarck Archipelago (02° 02 N/148° 27 E) by US submarine *Drum*.

Nitcho Maru (Transport): 1942 grt steamer, built 1943; requisitioned 1943; sunk 12 June 1944 W of Marianas (17° 31 N/143° 10 E) by US TG58.4.

Nittei Maru (Collier): 2728 grt steamer, built 194?; ran aground on reef 6 January 1945 W of Noto-hanto (37° N/136° 40 E).

Nitto Maru (Guardboat): 69 grt; sunk 21 December 1944 in East Indies.

Nitto Maru No 23 (Guardboat): 90 grt; sunk 18 April 1942 650m E of Japan by aircraft of USS *Enterprise*.

Nojima Maru (Ammunition Ship): 7190 grt motor ship, built 1935; requisitioned 1941; damaged between 25 August and 15 September 1942 by various air attacks and ran aground in Trait Lagoon (51° 58 N/177° 33 E); subsequently stricken.

Noshiro Maru, ex-*Nordhav*, ex-*Bygdones*, ex-*General Morrison* (Transport): 2333 grt steamer, built 1919; requisitioned during war; sunk 26 April 1944 off Mikojima (28° 42 N/141° 26 E) by US submarine *Guavina*.

Oakita Maru (Transport): 2704 grt steamer, built 194?; sunk 12 September 1944 off Cebu (11° 21 N/124° 07 E) by US TF38.

Ogashima Maru (Transport): 1424 grt motor ship, built 1936; sunk 20 January 1944 off Namu Atoll, Marshalls (08° 07 N/168° E) by US aircraft.

Ojima Maru (Guardboat): 79 grt; sunk 14 July 1945 off Shiriyasaki (approx. 41° 30 N/141° 40 E) by US TF38.

Okikawa Maru (Oiler): 10,043 grt Standard 2 TL type turbine tanker, built 1943; requisitioned 1944; sunk 21 September 1944 at Manila (14° N/119° E) by US TF38.

Okitsu Maru (Transport): 6666 grt, built 1939; sunk 26 January 1944 N of Ponape (09° 30 N/157° 50 E) by US submarine *Skipjack*.

Okuyo Maru (Gunboat): 2904 grt steamer, built 1938; requisitioned 1941; sunk 31 December 1943 off Ambon Light (03° 51 S/128° 04 E).

Ominesan Maru (Oiler): 10,568 grt Standard 1 TL type turbine tanker, built 1943; requisitioned 1943, fate unknown.

Onoshi Maru (Guardboat): 148 grt; sunk 22 September 1944 off Cebu by US TF38.

Onoe Maru (Ammunition Ship): 6667 grt, built 1940; sunk 26 November 1944 N of Bismarck Archipelago (00° 40 N/148° 20 E) by US submarine *Raton*.

Onogawa Maru (Auxiliary): 319 grt steamer, built 1893; requisitioned 1904 and returned 1905; lost November 1926 off Nishitomari.

Oregon Maru (Repair Ship): 5873 grt steamer, built 1920; requisitioned 1941; sunk 17 November 1942 75m W of Manila (14° 16 N/119° 44 E) by US submarine *Salmon*.

Orotchanin (River Gunboat): 193 ton ex-Russian gunboat, built 1907; captured 7 September 1918 at Habarovsk but not renamed; wrecked in the Spring of 1918 in Upper Zeia; salvaged and repaired May 1920 in Nikolaievsk, but subsequent fate unknown.

Osaka Maru, ex-*Osaka* (Transport): 482 grt screw steamer, built 1866; requisitioned September 1869; sunk 25 December 1875 in the Inland Sea in collision with the *Nagoya Maru*.

Osei Maru, ex-*Castor* (Cable Layer): 641 grt ex-Netherlands buoy tender, built 1915; scuttled at Soerabaja 2 March 1942; raised 1943 and commissioned by Japanese as a cable layer; sunk 28 June 1945 3km SE of Jizosaki but raised, and later used for repatriation.

Otagawa Maru (Gunboat): 498 grt steamer, built 1893; requisitioned 1904; mined 8 August 1904 E of Port Arthur.

Otaru Maru, ex-*Dardanus* (Blockship): 2547 grt steamer, built 1886; requisitioned 24 January 1904 as an Army transport but returned; taken up again as *Blockship No 9* and sunk 3 May 1904 in third attempt to block Port Arthur (38° 47 N/121° 14 E).

Otome Maru (Guardboat): 199 grt motor vessel, built 1938; sunk 29 April 1945 SE of Borneo by submarine.

Otori Maru (Transport): 2105 grt; sunk 20 May 1944 SE of Cape San Augustin (05° 57 N/127° 11 E) by US submarine *Ray*.

Otori Maru No 2 (Guardboat): 302 grt; sunk 24 February 1943 in W Basilan Strait (06° 50 N/121° 25 E) by US submarine.

Oyo Maru (Transport): 5458 grt steamer, built 1921; sunk 20 October 1944 off Miri, Borneo (04° 11 N/113° 22 E) by US submarine *Hammerhead*.

Palau Maru, Japanese = *Parau Maru* (Guardboat): 35 grt; sunk 6 February 1944 at Kwajalein Atoll by US TF58.

Peking Maru (Gunboat): 2288 grt steamer, built 1937; requisitioned 1941; wrecked 21 July 1944 off Santa Cruz, Luzon (17° 31 N/120° 23 E).

Raizan Maru (Transport): 2838 grt Standard 1 C type steamer, built 1943; requisitioned 1943; sunk 30 March 1944 off Palau (07° 30 N/134° 30 E) by US TF58.

Rakuto Maru (Transport): 2962 grt passenger steamer, built 1935; sunk 12 September 1944 off Cebu (10° 35 N/124° 20 E) by US TF38.

Ramon Maru (Gunboat): 3514 grt, built circa 1942; requisitioned 1942 and sunk at unknown date.

Reikai Maru (Transport): 2812 grt Standard 1 C type steamer, built 1943; sunk 12 June 1944 NW of Saipan (17° 30 N/144° E) by US TG58.4.

Reiko Maru (Guardboat): 88 grt; sunk 18 June 1945 in East China Sea (30° 45 N/126° E) by gunfire of US submarine *Dentuda*.

Reiyo Maru (Transport): 5445 grt steamer, built 1920; sunk 17 February 1944 at Truk (07° 25 N/151° 45 E) by US TF58.

Rekisan Maru, ex-*Alexander*, ex-*Dunlossit* (Transport): 261 grt steamer, built 1900; captured from Russians 4 July 1905 and commissioned as a tender; rated as a transport in 1905 but became a submarine depot ship in 1909; stricken before 1930.

Risui Maru (Transport): 1500 grt; sunk 25/26 May 1945 E of Andaman Islands (10° 38 N/94° 42 E) by gunfire of British destroyers *Venus*, *Verulam* and *Virago*.

Ritsuzo Maru (Transport): Steamer; requisitioned in 1869, fate unknown.

Rokusan Maru (Minesweeper Depot Ship): 1059 grt, built 1917; requisitioned 1938; missing 27 July 1945 SE of Korea.

Roshu Maru (Guardboat): 99 grt; sunk 30 October 1942 S of Honshu by gunfire of US submarine *Drum*.

Ryoei Maru (Oiler): 10,016 grt Standard 1TL type turbine tanker; built 1944 requisitioned 1944; sunk 5 March 1945 off Da Nang (16° 47 N/108° 41 E) by US submarine *Bashaw*.

Ryofu Maru (Weather Reporting Ship): 1180 grt motor research ship, built 1937; requisitioned 1941 and later returned to commercial use.

Ryojun Maru (Gunboat): 499 grt steamer, built 1897; requisitioned 1904 and returned 1905.

Ryojun Maru (Gunboat): 123 grt; requisitioned 1941 but re-rated as a guardboat in 1942; sunk 26 July 1944 near Palau (07° 30 N/134° 30 E) by aircraft of US TGs 58.2 and 58.3.

Ryotaku Maru (Transport): 3843 grt steamer, built 1938; sunk 22 September 1943 NW of Marianas (20° 45 N/142° 10 E) by US submarine *Trout*.

Ryuei Maru (Guardboat): 207 grt; sunk 7 July 1944 off Tarakan, Borneo by gunfire from US submarine *Bonefish*.

Ryuhei Maru (Ferry): 727 grt motor passenger vessel, built 1910; requisitioned during war but later returned.

Ryujin Maru (Transport): 495 grt; sunk 4 June 1945 off Hachinohe (40° 54 N/141° 29 E) by US submarine *Tench*.

Ryuko Maru (Transport): 2764 grt steamer, built 194?; sunk 30 March 1944 at Palau (07° 30 N/134° 30 E) by US TF58.

Ryuosan Maru (Transport): 2455 grt, built 1940; mined 4 November 1943 off Edmago, New Ireland (02° 40 S/150° 40 E).

Ryusei Maru (Transport): 1230 grt screw steamer, built 1875; requisitioned 1904 and returned 1905.

Sabagawa Maru (Gunboat): 313 grt steamer, built 1890; requisitioned February 1905 and later returned.

Sachitaka Maru No 3 (Guardboat): 31 grt; sunk 8 July at Saipan by US aircraft.

Sado Maru (Transport): 6223 grt steamer, built 1898; requisitioned 1904 but re-rated as an armed merchant cruiser in July 1904; returned 1905 and BU 1934.

Sagami Maru (Blockship): 1927 grt steamer, built 1884; sunk 3 May 1904 as *Blockship No 11* in third attempt to block Port Arthur, with 13 dead (38° 47 N/121° 15 E).

Sagami Maru (Transport): 7189 grt steamer, built 1939; sunk 3 November 1942 by submarine.

Sagami Maru No 8 (Guardboat): 111 grt motor vessel, built 1938; sunk 11 May 1945 off Hong Kong (21° 52 N/113° 08 E) by US aircraft.

Saikyo Maru (Armed Merchant Cruiser/Transport). 2904 grt steamer, built 1888; requisitioned 1894 and returned 1895; requisitioned as a transport 1904 but re-rated as a hospital ship in February 1905; later returned to commercial service and BU in 1927.

Saikyo Maru (Gunboat): 1296 grt steamer, built 1936; requisitioned 1940; sunk 28 June 1942 in Philippine Sea (12° 34 N/136° 20 E) by US submarine *Stingray*.

Saisho Maru, ex-*Rossiya*, ex-*Wiltshire* (Transport): 2117 grt passenger steamer, built 1897; captured from Russia in 1905 and became a naval transport; sunk 3 January 1944 S of Honshu (33° 44 N/136° 23 E) by submarine.

Sakae Maru (Guardboat): 103 grt; sunk 10 August 1944 at Rabaul (04° 12 S/152° 15 E) by US aircraft.

Sakae Maru No 6 (Guardboat): 84 grt; sunk 13 July 1945 off Chichijima (27° 04 N/142° 11 E) by US aircraft.

Sakura Maru (Blockship): 2979 grt screw steamer, built 1887; sunk 3 May 1904 as *Blockship No 10* at Port Arthur with 20 dead in third blocking attempt.

Sakura Maru (Transport): 7170 grt motor ship, built 1939; sunk 3 March 1942 at Bantam Bay by shore batteries.

San Francisco Maru, Japanese = *S. Furanshisuko Maru* (Transport): 5831 grt steamer, built 1919; sunk 17 February 1944 at Truk (07° 22 N/151° 54 E) by US TF58.

Sanko Maru (Transport): 5461 grt turbinre steamer, built 1939; sunk 16 February 1944 off New Hanover (02° 24 S/150° 06 E) by US aircraft.

Sansei Maru (Transport): 3266 grt motor passenger vessel, built 1931; sunk 8 December 1943 SW of Chichijima (26° 32 N/141° 36 E) by US submarine *Sawfish*.

Santo Maru (Gunboat): 3266 grt motor passenger vessel, built 1931; requisitioned 1941; sunk 29 September 1943 off Saipan (15° 28 N/145° 58 E) by US submarine *Gudgeon*.

Santoku Maru No 2 (Guardboat): 146 grt motor vessel, built 1931; sunk 15 February 1945 S of Japan (30° N/143° E) by US TF58.

Sanuki Maru (Auxiliary): 6111 grt steamer, built 1897; requisitioned 1904 and returned 1905.

Sarushashi (Maru), ex-*Sars* (Salvage Tug): 610 grt tug, built 1904; requisitioned 8 May 1905; renamed *Sarushina* in 1946 and stricken 1947.

Satsuma Maru (Transport): 1946 grt steamer, built 1884; requisitioned 1904 and returned 1905.

Seia Maru (Ammunition Ship): 6659 grt steamer, built 1939; sunk 1 August 1944 in Moluccan Sea (01° 46 S/125° 32 E) by US aircraft.

Seian Maru, ex-*Chung Tai*, ex-*Kanna* (Transport): 1900 grt steamer, built 1911; sunk 1 October 1944 NW of Ogasawara-gunto (20° 20 N/139° 25 E) by US submarine *Snapper*.

Seian Maru (Gunboat/Oiler): 3712 grt motor ship, built 1938; requisitioned 1940; rebuilt as a naval oiler 1943 but returned to commercial service 1944; sunk off Subic Bay (14° 48 N/120° 17 E) by US TF38.

Seiei Maru No 2 (Guardboat): 113 grt; sunk 30 March 1944 at Palau (07° 30 N/134° 30 E) by US TF58.

Seikai Maru (Gunboat): 2693 grt steamer, built 1940; requisitioned 1941; mined 16 September 1943 off Kavieng (02° 30 N/150° 48 E).

Seiko Maru (Transport): 5385 grt steamer, built 1940; sunk 17 February 1944 at Truk (07° 22 N/151° 45 E) by US TF58.

Seikyo Maru (Gunboat): 2608 grt steamer, built 1934; requisitioned 1940; sunk 23 October 1942 at entrance to Kii-Suido (33° 12 N/135° 14 E) by US submarine *Kingfish*.

Seisho Maru (Guardboat): 128 grt motor vessel, built 1934; sunk 30 January 1944 off Celebes by US aircraft.

Seisho Maru No 3 (Guardboat): 76 grt; sunk 24 July 1945 at Kobe by US aircraft.

Seiun Maru (Guardboat): 39 grt; sunk 11 July 1943 E of Kamchatka (51° 20 N/164° 30 E) by US submarine *S.35*.

Seiun Maru No 5 (Guardboat): 146 grt; sunk 25 February 1945 off Torishima (approx. 31° N/141° E) by gunfire of US destroyers *Hazelwood* and *Murray*.

Seiyo Maru (Oiler): 10,536 grt Standard 1 TL type turbine tanker, built 1943; requisitioned January 1944; set on fire 20 June 1944 in Philippine Sea by US TF58; wreck sunk by destroyer *Yukikaze* (15° 35 N/133° 30 E).

Seizan Maru, ex-*Shinshu Maru No 2* (Transport): 955 grt steamer, built 1918; sunk 20 August 1943 in Makasar Strait (00° 58 N/119° 01 E) by US submarine *Gar*.

Seizan Maru, ex-*Shing Ho*, ex-*Barunga*, ex-*Cape Premier*, ex-*War Faith* (Transport): 4243 grt steamer, built 1918; sunk 23 February 1944 near Saipan (15° N/145° 30 E) by aircraft of US TGs 58.2 and 58.3.

Seizan Maru No 2 (Transport): 1898 grt steamer, built 1937; sunk 24 December 1943 27m E of Mikisaki (34° 02 N/136° 19 E) by US submarine *Gurnard*.

Sendai Maru (Stores Ship): 472 grt motor fishing vessel, built 1933; sunk 20 January 1942 in Davao Gulf, Mindanao in collision with destroyer *Inadzuma*.

Senkei Maru (Gunboat): 2101 grt passenger steamer, built 1926; requisitioned 1937 and re-rated as supply ship during war; sunk 7 October 1942 in S Carolines (01° 10 N/153° 31 E) by US submarine *Amberjack*.

Senko Maru (Transport): 4472 grt turbine passenger steamer, built 1935; requisitioned for war service but later returned.

Senshu Maru, ex-*Nan Yang*, ex-*Iphigenia* (Transport): 1570 grt steamer, built 1883; requisitioned 1904; sunk 22 September off Port Arthur.

Sen-Yo Maru (Gunboat): 2904 grt steamer, built 1937; requisitioned 1941; sunk 25 August 1942 off Takao, Formosa (22° 23 N/120° 10 E) by US submarine *Growler*.

Senzan Maru (Transport): 2775 grt motor ship, built 1929; sunk 18 January 1943 off Kavieng, New Ireland (03° 52 S/149° 20 E) by US aircraft.

Settsu (Steamer): 306 grt screw steamer, built 1854; purchased from USA July 1868 and renamed *Settsu*; presented to Okayama Clan in 1869 and armed in August 1870 for use by the Imperial Fleet; training ship in 1872.

Shibata Maru, ex-*Moyune* (Blockship): 2739 grt steamer, built 1886; requisitioned 3 May 1904 as *Blockship No. 1* for third attempt to block Port Arthur but not used.

Shiganoura Maru (Transport): 3512 grt steamer, built 1942; requisitioned 1942; sunk 30 November 1943 W of Marianas (18° 38 N/139° 35 E) by US submarine *Snook*.

Shigure Maru, ex-*Sigli* (Transport): 1579 grt steamer, built 1920; captured from Netherlands 2 March 1942 between Tjilatjap and Australia; sunk 10 October 1942 off Samarinda, Borneo (01° 07 S/117° 19 E) by US submarine *Seadragon*.

Shikoku Maru, ex-*Mongkut* (Transport): 1404 grt screw steamer, built 1883; requisitioned 1904 and returned 1905; burned out 28 January 1906 at Vladivostok.

Shikotan Maru, ex-*Tacoma*, ex-*Batavia* (Transport): 2812 grt screw steamer, built 1870; captured from Russia 14 March 1905 in Kunashiri Strait by cruiser *Takachiho*; requisitioned 1 September 1905; wrecked 3 October 1924 off Japan.

Shima Maru (Transport): 1987 grt steamer, built 1920; sunk 4 July 1944 at Takinoura-wan (27° 07 N/142° 12 E) by US TF38.

Shimane Maru (Guardboat): 93 grt fishery inspection boat, built 1934; sunk 4 June 1944 off Manokwari, New Guinea (01° S/134° 10 E) by US aircraft.

Shimpu Maru, ex-*Martin White* (Steamer): 189 grt screw steamer, built 1854; handed over to Imperial Fleet by Kurume Clan in October 1866 for use against the Enomoto rebels.

Shimpuku Maru (Transport): 2204 grt steamer, built 1908; sunk 19 December 1944 W of Luzon (13° 40 N/115° 50 E) by US aircraft.

Shinagawa Maru (Guardboat): 81 grt; wrecked 24 August 1943 E of Nemuro, Hokkaido (43° 22 N/145° 40 E).

Shinano Maru (Armed Merchant Cruiser): 6387 grt steamer, built 1900; requisitioned 1904 and returned 1905.

Shinei Maru (Guardboat): 69 grt; sunk 15 July 1945 off Shirojiri, Hokkaido by US TF38.

Shinko Maru (Oiler): 5135 grt Standard 1 TM type turbine tanker, built 1944; requisitioned 1944; torpedoed 12 August 1944 by US submarines *Puffer* and *Bluefin* and ran aground on Cape Calavite Mindoro (13° 18 N/120° 17 E).

Shinko Maru (Transport): 545 grt motor ship, built 194?; sunk 25 May 1943 at Rabaul (04° 13 S/152° 11 E) by US aircraft.

Shinko Maru (Transport): 3119 grt; sunk 2 November 1943 at Rabaul (04° 13 S/152° 10 E) by US aircraft.

Shinko Maru No 1, ex-*Shinko Maru* (Gunboat): 935 grt motor vessel, built 1938; requisitioned 1938 but re-rated as an auxiliary in 1944; sunk 9 January 1945 off Tandjung

Puting, Borneo (03° 41 S/111° 54 E) by Netherlands submarine *O.19*.

Shinko Maru No 2, ex-*Shinko Maru* (Gunboat): 2577 grt steamer, built 1939; requisitioned 1941; surrendered August 1945 and used for repatriation; returned to commercial service as *Shinko Maru*.

Shinko Maru No 6 (Guardboat): 55 grt motor fishing vessel, built 1933; sunk 17 January 1944 by US aircraft.

Shinko Maru No 10 (Guardboat): 72 grt; sunk 4 June 1944 E of Japan (35° 47 N/154° 54 E) by US submarine.

Shinko Maru No 15 (Guardboat): 55 grt motor fishing vessel, built 1933; missing 28 October 1944 on Yangtse.

Shinkoku Maru (Transport): 3991 grt, built 1941; sunk 18 February 1943 S of Saipan (15° 09 N/159° 30 E) by US submarine *Halibut*.

Shinkyo Maru (Gunboat): 2672 grt passenger steamer, built 1932; requisitioned 1940 but re-rated as a transport in 1943; sunk 25 March 1944 off Sarangani (05° 37 N/125° 58 E) by US submarine *Bowfin*.

Shinnan Maru (Transport): 6417 grt, built 1941; mined 17 April 1943 off Shortland (06° 50 N/155° 45 E).

Shinoshimasan Maru (Guardboat): 123 grt; ran aground 14 April 1945 on reef in Kagoshima Bay.

Shinrei Maru, ex-*Eisho Maru* (Transport): 993 grt steamer, built 1918; sunk 17 May 1944 off Soerabaja, Java by aircraft from British *Illustrious*.

Shinroku Maru (Transport): 2857 grt steamer, built 1944; requisitioned 1944; sunk 9 June 1945 off Esan-saki (41° 49 N/141° 11 E) by US submarine *Tench*.

Shinsei Maru (Guardboat):148 grt; sunk 20 March 1943 SE of Japan (32° 50 N/152° E) by US submarine.

Shinsei Maru (Stores Ship): 4746 grt steamer, built 1917; sunk 7 January 1945 in Formosa Strait (22° 40 N/118° 45 E) by US aircraft; in 1949 the hull was used for the conservation of crabs.

Shinsei Maru (Transport): 2880 grt turbine steamer; sunk 12 January 1945 off Cape St. Jacques (10° 20 N/107° 45 E) by US TF38.

Shinsei Maru No 18 (Transport): 2711 grt steamer, built 1941; sunk 30 March 1944 at Palau (07° 30 N/134° 30 E) by US TF58.

Shinsei Maru No 83 (Guardboat): 63 grt; sunk 24 July 1942 in Utasutu Bay, Hokkaido by gunfire of US submarine *Narwhal*.

Shinshu Maru, ex-*Gwalior* (Transport): 2839 grt screw steamer, built 1873; requisitioned 1904; wrecked 9 March 1904 at Inchon, Korea.

Shinshu Maru (Torpedo Recovery Vessel): 4836 grt steamer, built 1936; requisitioned 1941; sunk 9 July 1942 in entrance to Kwajalein Lagoon (08° 43 N/167° 33 E) by US submarine *Thresher*.

Shinshu Maru No 5 (Guardboat): 99 grt; sunk July 1945 off Japan by US aircraft.

Shinsoku Maru (Transport): 3202 grt steamer, built 1916; sunk 18 February 1944 NE of Wenshu-Wan (28° 22 N/121° 51 E) by US aircraft.

Shintai Maru (Transport): 2857 grt Standard 1 C type steamer, built 1944; requisitioned 1944; mined 18 June 1945 W of Noto-Hanto (36° 50 N/136° 43 E).

Shinwa Maru (Transport): 3328 grt; sunk 21 November 1943 off Manokwari, New Guinea (02° 24 S/134° 36 E) by US aircraft.

Shinyo Maru (Guardboat): 92 grt; sunk 30 May 1944 120m NE of Paramushir, Kuriles by US aircraft.

Shinyo Maru (Transport): 2634 grt steamer, built 194?; sunk 7 September 1944 off Lanboyan Point, Mindanao (08° 12 N/122° 40 E) by US submarine *Paddle*.

Shin'yo Maru No 5 (Gunboat): 1498 grt steamer, built 1937; requisitioned 1941; sunk 18 February 1942 W of Kyushu (32° 14 N/127° 14 E) by US submarine *Triton*.

Shin'yo Maru No 8 (Transport): 1959 grt steamer, built 1941; sunk 7 October 1944 off Vigan, Luzon (17° 50 N/119° 37 E) by US submarine *Cabrilla*.

Shinyu Maru (Gunboat): 414 grt steamer, built 1903; requisitioned February 1905 and later returned.

Shiramine Maru (Transport): 2857 grt Standard 1 C type steamer, built 1943; requisitioned 1943; sunk 12 September 1944 off Cebu (10° 34 N/134° 01 E) by US TF38.

Shirane Maru (Transport): 2825 grt Standard 1 C type steamer, built 1943; requisitioned 1943; sunk 5 May 1944 off Shionomisaki (33° 20 N/135° 32 E) by US submarine *Pogy*.

Shirogane (*Maru*) (Tug): circa 600 grt steam tug; requisitioned 191? and still in service after 1930.

Shirogane Maru (Transport): 3130 grt steamer, built 1938; sunk 19 September 1942 off Bougainville Strait (06° 30 S/156° 10 E) by US submarine *Amberjack*.

Shkval (River Gunboat): 946-ton ex-Russian river gunboat, built 1910; captured 7 September 1918 at Habarovsk but not renamed; returned 1922.

Shoan Maru (Transport): 5624 grt steamer, built 1937; sunk 23 February 1944 at Saipan (15° 15 N/145° 42 E) by US TF58.

Shobu Maru (Transport): 2002 grt; sunk 8 March 1944 in Malakar Strait (03° 38 N/99° 22 E) by British submarine *Sea Rover*.

Shoei Maru, ex-*General Lukin*, ex-*Oakwin*, ex-*War Oasis* (Transport): 3083 grt steamer, built 1919; sunk 19 December 1943 at Kwajalein (08° 42 N/167° 44 E) by US aircraft.

Shoei Maru (Gunboat): 1986 grt steamer, built 1936; requisitioned 1941; sunk 16 December 1944 in Sunda Strait by British submarine *Tally Ho*.

Shoei Maru (Gunboat): 3580 grt steamer, built 1936; requisitioned 1940; sunk 25 May 1943 off Rota, Marianas (14° 17 N/144° 50 E) by US submarine *Whale*.

Shoei Maru (Repair Ship): 5644 grt steamer, built 1937; requisitioned 1941; sunk 12 May 1942 9m off Cape St. Georges (04° 51 N/152° 54 E) by US submarine *S.44*.

Shoei Maru (Gunboat): 1877 grt steamer, built 1938; requisitioned 1941; sunk 30 March 1944 near Palau by aircraft.

Shoeki Maru (Netlayer): 897 grt motor vessel, built 1939; sunk 20 December 1944 in Banda Sea (06° 15 S/127° 30 E), probably by Netherlands aircraft.

Shohei Maru (Transport): Barque; captured 7 December 1868 and incorporated into the Imperial Fleet as a transport in 1869.

Shohei Maru (Transport): 7255 grt motor ship, built 1931; sunk 10 May 1944 off Luzon (15° 38 N/119° 32 E) by US submarine *Cod*.

Shoho Maru (Transport): 1358 grt; sunk 25 November 1944 in Balintang Channel (20° 18 N/121° 34 E) by US submarine *Pomfret*.

Shoho Maru (Transport): 1936 grt steamer; sunk 31 December 1943 in East Carolines (05° 40 N/160° 20 E) by US submarine *Greenling*.

Shoju Maru, ex-*Kyodo Maru No 26* (Transport): 1911 grt steamer, built 1920; sunk 5 August 1943 W of Marcus Island (24° 37 N/152° 45 E) by US submarine *Pike*.

Shoju Maru (Guardboat): 43 grt; sunk 21 December 1944.

Shoka Maru (Transport): 4467 grt turbine steamer, built 1935; sunk 25 May 1942 in Carolines (04° 05 N/144°) by US submarine *Tautog*.

Shokaku Maru, ex-*Yangtse* (Paddle Steamer): 359-ton paddle steamer, built 1857; acquired for the Shogunate Fleet December 1863 as *Shokaku Maru*; joined the Imperial Fleet 1868 but November 1868 was wrecked, off Ajiro.

Shokei Maru (Transport): 2557 grt, built 1938; sunk 8 September 1944 off Sakishima-gunto (24° 39 N/123° 31 E) by US submarine *Spadefish*.

Shoken Maru (Transport): 1942 grt, probably Standard 1 D type, built 1943; requisitioned 1943; sunk 29 May 1944 W of Marianas (16° 19 N/145° 25 E) by US submarine *Silversides*.

Shoko Maru (Gunboat): 1933 grt, built 1939; requisitioned 1941 but re-rated as a transport in November 1943; sunk 1 December 1943 N of Ulithi Atoll (14° 31 N/140° 18 E) by US submarine *Pargo*.

Shoriki Maru (Guardboat): 50 grt; sunk December 1944 at Manila.

Shosei Maru (Gunboat): 998 grt passenger vessel, built 1929; requisitioned 1938; sunk 20 May 1944 10m W of Guam (13° 32 N/144° 36 E) by US submarine *Silversides*.

Shosei Maru (Guardboat): 88 grt; sunk 12 March 1945 E of Ryukyus (26° 54 N/131° 38 E) by US aircraft.

Shosei Maru No 15 (Guardboat): 43 grt; sunk 13 May 1945 at Selat Bali (07° 05 S/114° 13 E) by US submarine *Baya*.

Shotoku Maru (Gunboat): 1964 grt steamer, built 1938; requisitioned 1941; sunk 28 June off Rota, Marianas (14° 07 N/145° 07 E) by US submarine *Tunny*.

Shoun Maru (Transport): 4396 grt; sunk 23/24 June 1944 at Rota, Marianas (14° 10 N/145° 10 E) by US TF58.

Shozan Maru (Transport): 5859 grt; sunk 26 June 1943 W of Hachijojima (33° 15 N/138° 56 E) by US submarine *Jack*.

Shozui Maru (Transport): 2719 grt; sunk 4 July 1944 in Takinoura Bay (27° 07 N/142° 12 E) by US TF58.

Shunzan Maru No 2 (Transport): 608 grt motor vessel, built 1934; sunk 24 February 1944 off Kusaie, Carolines (05° 20 N/162° 58 E) by US aircraft.

Shuri Maru (Gunboat): 1857 grt passenger vessel, built 1928; requisitioned 1937 but re-rated as a torpedo recovery vessel in 1939; sunk 21 January 1945 in Korea Strait (33° 45 N/128° 43 E) by US submarine *Tautog*.

Sonjo Maru, ex-? (Salvage Ship): 800 grt, probably Chinese; captured during 1930s and requisitioned and renamed in 1943; mined 17 April 1945 at Susung (31° 13 N/121° 52 E).

Soryu (Paddle Despatch Vessel): Built 1872; served as despatch vessel and yacht, but fate unknown.

Soshu Maru (Transport): 1283 grt steamer, built 1918; served during war and returned to commercial service in 1945.

Sugiyama Maru, ex-*Agios Vlasios*, ex-*Tysla* (Transport): 4379 grt steamer, built 1914; requisitioned 194?; sunk 15 November 1944 in South China Sea (15° 15 N/112° 10 E) by US submarine.

Suiten Maru, ex-*Schouten* (Transport): 1805 grt passenger steamer, built 1912; converted 7 December 1941 by Netherlands Navy to an anti-aircraft ship; sunk 28 February 1942 in Madura Strait but salvaged by Japanese on 26 February 1943; converted to a transport and renamed; sunk 22 April 1944 by US aircraft but raised again on 12 July that year; torpedoed 3 March 1945 off Bawean (06° 29 S/112° 48 E) by US submarine *Sea Robin* and ran aground.

Sumanoura Maru (Gunboat): 3519 grt, built 1940; requisitioned 1940 but re-rated as a transport later; sunk 24 January 1942 off Balikpapan, Borneo (00° 10 N/118° E) by US destroyer *Parrott*.

Sumatra Maru, ex-*Tomori* (Japanese = *Sumatora M.*) (Transport): 984 grt ex-Netherlands motor vessel, built 1929; sunk 2 March 1942 in Soerabaja Roads, but raised by Japanese in August 1944 and renamed; sunk 28 October 1944 at Phuket, Thailand (08° N/98° 15 E) by British submarine *Trenchant*.

Sumire Maru (Transport): 1729 grt motor passenger vessel, built 1928; surrendered in August 1945; used for repatriation and returned in 1947.

Sumiyoshi Maru (Guardboat): 94 grt; sunk 21 December 1944.

Sumiyoshi Maru No 10 (Guardboat): 49 grt; sunk 30 July 1945 8m N of Kohishima by US TF38.

Sumiyoshi Maru No 18 (Guardboat): 49 grt; damaged 30 July 1945 8m N of Kohishima by aircraft of TF38 and ran aground.

Suruga Maru (Stores Ship): 991 grt motor fishing vessel, built 1938; sunk 15 February 1943 in Bougainville Strait (06° 25 S/156° 05 E) by US submarine *Gato*.

Suwa Maru (Troopship): 10,672 grt passenger steamer, built 1914; requisitioned 194?; sunk 5 April 1943 at Wake Island (19° 18 N/166° 36 E) by US submarines *Finback* and *Seadragon*.

Taganoura Maru (Transport): 3521 grt; sunk 3 September 1943 off Mikura-jima (33° 43 N/140° E) by US submarine *Pollack*.

Taian Maru, ex-*Ta An*, ex-*Canadian Leader* (Transport): 5411 grt steamer, built 1921; surrendered in August 1945 and used for repatriation; returned 1947.

Taian Maru (Transport): 3670 grt steamer, built 1936; sunk 23 January 1944 S of Palau (05° 50 N/134° 14 E) by US submarine *Gar*.

Taichu Maru (Armed Merchant Cruiser): 3320 grt steamer, built 1897; requisitioned 1904 but re-rated as a minelayer in 1905; later returned and sunk 12 April 1944 in East China Sea (28° 08 N/128° 57 E) by US submarine *Halibut*.

Taiho Maru (Transport): 2720 grt steamer, built 194?; requisitioned 1941; sunk 17 October 1944 off Camiguin, North Luzon (18° 54 N/121° 51 E) by US TF38.

Taiho Maru (Transport): 2827 grt turbine ferry, built 194?; sunk 17 February 1944 at Truk (07° 22 N/151° 34 E) by US TF58.

Taiho Maru No 2 (Guardboat): 39 grt; sunk 20 March 1944 at Rabaul by US aircraft.

Taihosan Maru (Water Carrier): 1804 grt steamer, built 1937; sunk 12 March 1943 off Ponape, Carolines (07° 15 N/158° 45 E) by US submarine *Plunger*.

Taihosan Maru (Oiler): 10,536 dwt Standard 1 TL type turbine tanker, built 1943; requisitioned 1943; sunk 4 March 1944 in South China Sea (05° 29 N/108° 46 E) by US submarine *Bluefish*.

Taijun Maru (Transport): 1273 grt steamer, built 1918; burnt out at Truk 11 April 1942.

Taikai Maru No 3 (Guardboat): 95 grt; sunk 16 November 1944 SW of Torishima (30° N/139° 40 E) by gunfire of US submarines *Saury* and *Tambor*.

Taiko Maru (Gunboat): 498 grt steamer, built 1891; requisitioned February 1905.

Taiko Maru (Gunboat): 2984 grt steamer, built 1937; requisitioned 1937; sunk 14 July 1944 E of Salajar, Banda Sea (05° 56 S/121° 34 E) by US submarine *Sandlance*.

Taiko Maru (Guardboat): 66 grt; sunk 24 July 1945 at Kobe by US TF38.

Taikoku Maru (Transport): 2633 grt steamer, built 194?; sunk 17 May 1944 W of Marianas (14° 58 N/144° 49 E) by US submarine *Sandlance*.

Tainan Maru (Armed Merchant Cruiser): 3312 grt steamer, built 1897; requisitioned 1904 and returned 1905; sunk 25 June 1944 W of Kyushu (32° 42 N/129° 38 E) by US submarine *Tang*.

Tairyu Maru (Transport): 1913 grt, built 1940; mined 17 May 1945 off Wada-Misaki (34° 27 N/135° 11 E).

Taisai Maru No 5 (Guardboat): 95 grt; sunk 10 October 1944 off Naha, Okinawa (26° 13 N/127° 41 E) by US TF38.

Taishin (Guardboat): 89 grt; sunk 10 August 1944 E of Paramushir (50° 09 N/157° 03 E) by US aircraft.

Taisho Maru No 2 (Guardboat): 139 grt motor vessel; mined 23 July 1945 off Chinhä, Korea.

Taisho Maru No 5 (Guardboat): 47 grt; sunk 14 December 1944 in Pacific.

Taito Maru (Transport): 4466 grt turbine steamer, built 1935; requisitioned 1941; sunk 25 May 1944 N of Palau (11° 14 N/135° 12 E) by US submarine *Flying Fish*.

Taiwan Maru, ex-*Athole*, ex-*Inchrhona* (Transport): 2392 grt steamer, built 1881; requisitioned 1904; sunk 15 June 1904 off Korea.

Taiyo Maru (Supply Ship): 657 grt motor fishing vessel, built 1935; returned 1945.

Taiyo Maru No 1 (Guardboat): 47 grt; sunk 16 January 1945 E of Hainan by US TF38.

Taiyo Maru No 3 (Guardboat): 36 grt; sunk 16 January 1944 off Rabaul by submarine.

Tajima Maru (Guardboat): 89 grt; sunk 4 May 1944 N of Wake Island by gunfire of US submarine *Tuna*.

Takamiya Maru (Guardboat): 138 grt; sunk 6 July 1944 E of Ogasawara-gunto (28° 54 N/150° 50 E) by gunfire of US submarine, probably *Swordfish*.

Takasago Maru, ex-*Vostok*, ex-*Tai-Yick* (Auxiliary): 1789 grt, steamer, built 1897; requisitioned 1904 and returned 1905.

Takashima Maru (Transport): 319 grt steamer, built 1891; requisitioned 1904; sunk 20 July 1904 W of Japan by Russian cruisers *Rurik* and *Rossiya*.

Takatori Maru No 8 (Guardboat): 51 grt; sunk 11 July 1943 between Okinodaitoshima and Kazan-retto (24° N/135° 25 E) by gunfire of US submarine *Flying Fish*.

Takeura Maru (Guardboat): 26 grt; sunk 6 February 1944 at Kwajalein by US TF58.

Takunan (Supply Ship): 752 grt, built 1941; sunk 1 October 1944 N of Ogasawara-gunto (25° 30 N/142° 30 E) by US submarine *Trepang*.

Tama Maru (Transport): 3052 grt passenger steamer, built 1918; sunk 4 July 1944 off Palau (07° 44 N/133° 17 E) by US submarine *Guavina*.

Tama Maru (Guardboat): sunk 14 January 1944 at Wotje Atoll, Marshalls by US aircraft.

Tama Maru No 2 (Transport): 515 grt; sunk 24 December 1942 at Gasmata, New Britain (06° 18 S/150° 16 E) by US aircraft.

Tama Maru No 51 (Guardboat): 84 grt; sunk July 1945 in mouth of Yangtse by US aircraft.

Tamahime Maru, ex-*War Spray* (Transport): 3080 grt steamer, built 1918; sunk 5 June 1944 W of Marianas (18° 40 N/140° 35 E) by US submarine *Shark*.

Tamashima Maru (Transport): 3560 grt, built 1940; sunk 30 January 1944 NE of Marianas (21° 12 N/149° 18 E) by US submarine *Spearfish*.

Taro Maru, ex-*Redvers Hocken*, ex-*Armstor*, ex-*Lord Bangor* (Transport): 3117 grt steamer, built 1890; requisitioned 1904 and returned 1905; foundered November 1915 in Hainan Strait.

Tarushima Maru (Transport): 4865 grt steamer, built 1938; sunk 18 January 1944 in North Philippine Sea (22° 34 N/135° 46 E) by US submarine *Seawolf* and *Whale*.

Tatsuei Maru (Transport): 1942 grt Standard 1 D type steamer, built 1943; requisitioned 1943; sunk 4 July 1944 SW of Anijima (27° 07 N/142° 12 E) by US TF58.

Tatsugami Maru (Ammunition Ship): 7070 grt, built 1939; sunk 23/24 January 1942 in Balikpapan Bay (01° 18 S/117° 04 E) by US destroyers *Parrott*, *Paul Jones* and *Pope*.

Tatsuho Maru (Transport): 6334 grt turbine steamer, built 1938; sunk 22 August 1942 N of Formosa (25° 52 N/121° 29 E) by US submarine *Haddock*.

Tatsu Maru, ex-*Myrmidon* (Transport): 3,138 grt steamer, built 1900; requisitioned May 1905 and returned 1906; later became *Tenchu Maru*.

Tatsuta Maru (Transport): 16,975 grt motor tanker, built 1930; requisitioned 1941; sunk 8 February 1943 42m E of Mikurashima (33° 45 N/140° 25 E) by US submarine *Tarpon*.

Tatsutagawa Maru (Transport): 1923 grt, built 1942; requisitioned 1942; sunk 15 June 1944 E of Ogasawara-shoto (25° 02 N/144° 37 E) by gunfire of US destroyers *Boyd* and *Charette*, following air attacks from TGs 58.1 and 58.4.

Tatsutaka Maru (Guardboat): 246 grt; sunk 8 November 1944 S of Manila, possibly in typhoon.

Tatsuura Maru (Transport): 6420 grt steamer, built 1942; requisitioned 1942; sunk 13 November 1944 at Manila (14° 35 N/120° 55 E) by US TF38.

Tatsuwa Maru (Transport): 6345 grt turbine steamer, built 1938; damaged by mine 10 May 1945 (34° 05 N/132° 27 E) and sank in August 1945 off Kurahashijima.

Teia Maru, ex-*Aramis* (Transport): 17,537 grt French motor passenger ship, built 1932; captured in Indo-China in April 1942 and used as a transport; sunk 18 August 1944 N of Luzon (18° 12 N/120° 20 E) by US submarine *Rasher*.

Teiritu Maru, ex-*Lecomte de l'Isle* (Transport): 9877 grt French motor passenger ship, built 1922; captured June 1942; mined 27 June 1944 in Wakasa Bay; raised and surrendered in August 1945; returned to France and BU in Italy in 1956.

Teishu Maru, ex-*Quito* (Minesweeper Depot Ship): 1230 grt German motor vessel, built 1938; handed over by Germany in 1941; sunk 28 April 1945 off Tandjung Puting, Borneo (04° 11 S/111° 17 E) by US submarine *Bream*.

Teiyo Maru, ex-*Saarland* (Transport): 6801 grt German turbine steamer, built 1924; handed over by Germany in 1940; sunk 2 March 1943 W of New Guinea (06° 56 S/148° 08 E) by US aircraft.

Teiyo Maru (Oiler): 9849 dwt motor tanker, built 1931; requisitioned 1941; sunk 19 August 1944 SW of Cape Bojeador, Luzon (18° 09 N/119° 56 E) by US submarine *Rasher*.

Teizui Maru, ex-*Mosel* (Transport): 8426 grt German turbine steamer, built 1927; handed over by Germany in 1941; ran aground on reef 18 April 1945 in Kammon Strait (34° 04 N/130° 50 E).

Temposan Maru (Transport): 1970 grt steamer, built 1942; requisitioned 1942; sunk 29 December 1943 off Palau (08° 03 N/133° 51 E) by US submarine *Silversides*.

Tenjin Maru No 2 (Guardboat): 38 grt; sunk 22 February 1944 at Rabaul by US aircraft.

Tenjin Maru No 3 (Guardboat): 198 grt; sunk 26 March 1944 off Mapia (02° N/135° E) by US aircraft.

Tenryu Maru (Transport): 4861 grt turbine steamer, built 1936; sunk 25 December 1943 at Kavieng (02° 36 S/150° 49 E) by aircraft from US carriers *Bunker Hill* and *Monterey*.

Tenryugawa Maru (Transport): 3883 grt; sunk 12 June 1944 NW of Saipan (17° 32 N/144° 10 E) by US TG58.4.

Tenshin Maru, ex-*Worcester* (Blockship): 2942 grt steamer, built 1887; requisitioned as *Blockship No 1* and sunk 24/25 February 1904 3m SW of entrance to Port Arthur (38° 44 N/121° 12 E).

Ten-Yo Maru (Supply Ship): 657 grt motor fishing vessel, built 1935; wrecked 3 March 1944 S of Paramushir, Kuriles (50° 17 N/155° 55 E).

Tenzan Maru (Transport): 2775 grt motor ship, built 1929; sunk 8 July 1942 off Rabaul (04° S/151° 50 E) by US submarine *S.37*.

Teru Maru No 5 (Guardboat): 60 grt; mined at Wonsan

MISCELLANEOUS MERCANTILE AUXILIARY VESSELS 279

31 July 1945.

Terushima Maru (Gunboat): 3110 grt turbine steamer, built 1937; requisitioned 1941 but re-rated as an escort in 1943; sunk 18 May 1943 in Marshall Islands (08° 33 N/171° E) by US submarine *Pollack*.

Teshio Maru (Supply Ship): 398 grt motor fishing vessel, built 1930; sunk 26 March 1945 in East Andaman Islands (10° 38 N/94° 42 E) by British destroyers *Venus*, *Verulam* and *Virago*.

Toa Maru (Transport): 6732 grt motor ship, built 1939; sunk 31 January 1943 off Vella Lavella, Solomons (07° 50 S/156° 50 E) by US aircraft.

Toan Maru (Transport): 2110 grt; requisitioned 1944; sunk 24 August 1944 SE of Formosa (21° 29 N/121° 13 E) by US submarine *Sailfish*.

Tobi Maru (Transport): 887 grt Standard 2 E type, built 1944; requisitioned 1944; mined 25 May 1945 NW of Kyushu (33° 58 N/130° 52 E).

Toei Maru (Transport): 4004 grt turbine steamer, built 1937; sunk 1 February 1944 in Carolines (04° 24 N/143° 15 E) by US submarine *Seahorse*.

Toei Maru (Salvage Vessel): 433 grt Chinese vessel; captured in 1930s and converted to salvage vessel; sunk 6 March 1945 E of Sanmen Wan (approx. 29° N/122° E) by US aircraft.

Toho Maru, ex-*Ernemore*, ex-*Ardgay* (Transport): 4716 grt steamer, built 1918; sunk 1 June 1944 NW of Marianas (18° 08 N/141° 14 E) by US submarine *Pintano*.

Tokachi Maru (Collier): 1932 grt steamer, built 1939; mined 17 January 1943 40m W of Soerabaja (06° 50 S/112° 12 E) by Japanese mine.

Tokai Maru (Transport): 8359 grt motor passenger ship, built 1930; sunk 27 August 1943 at Apia by US submarine *Snapper*.

Tokio II (Guardboat): 221 grt British fishing vessel, built 1906; lent by RN from June 1917 to December 1918 and may have served as a guardboat.

Tokiwasan Maru (Transport): 1804 grt steamer, built 1937; sunk 9 September 1944 S of Japan (28° 58 N/137° 45 E) by US submarine *Bang*.

Toko Maru, ex-*Kia Kee*, ex-*Hwah Ting*, ex-*Deike Rickmers* (Transport): 4180 grt steamship, built 1908; requisitioned during Second World War; sunk 12 October 1944 near Cape Cavalite, Mindoro (13° 32 N/120° 21 E) by US submarine *Ray*.

Tokyo Maru (Transport): 1400 grt screw steamer, built circa 1872; requisitioned 1872.

Tokyo Maru (Transport): 6481 grt motor ship, built 1936; damaged by aircraft attack and sank in tow 10 November 1943 between Kavieng and Truk.

Tomitsu Maru (Gunboat): 2933 grt turbine steamer, built 1937; requisitioned 1937; sunk 22 October 1944 S of Akuseki-shima (29° 18 N/129° 44 E) by US submarine *Seadog*.

Tonei Maru (Transport): 4930 grt turbine steamer, built 194?; sunk 1 October 1943 in South Carolines (04° 01 N/143° 47 E) by US submarine *Peto*.

Tonegawa Maru No 1 (Paddle Despatch Vessel): 170 grt, built 1873; fate unknown.

Tonegawa Maru (Transport): 656 grt steamer, built 1897; requisitioned 1904; sunk 26 March 1904 in Yellow Sea (38° 25 N/120° 55 E) by Russian cruiser *Novik*.

Tosa Maru, ex-*Islam* (Auxiliary): 5823 grt steamer, built 1892; requisitioned May 1905 and returned 1906.

Tosei Maru (Transport): 5434 grt turbine steamer, built 1926; sunk 12 December 1943 N of Halmahera (02° 43 N/126° 56 E) by US submarine *Tuna*.

Toshi Maru (Guardboat): 19 grt; sunk January 1945 at Manila.

Toshu Maru (Gunboat): 1289 grt steamer, built 1937; requisitioned 1938 and re-rated as an auxiliary in 1943; sunk 23 September 1944 off Wowoni, Celebes (04° 23 S/122° 43 E) by US aircraft.

Totomi Maru (Blockship): 1953 grt steamer, built 1883; requisitioned 1904 as *Blockship No 5* and sunk 3 May 1904 at Port Arthur (38° 47 N/121° 15 E) with 3 dead.

Tottori Maru (Transport): 5978 steamer, built 1913; sunk 15 May 1945 in Gulf of Siam (09° 49 N/103° 31 E) by US submarine *Hammerhead*.

Toyo Maru (Transport): 4163 grt turbine passenger steamer, built 1937; sunk 26 June 1943 SW of Hachijo-jima (33° 10 N/138° 56 E) by US submarine *Jack*.

Toyo Maru (Transport): 2556 grt screw steamer, built 1873; requisitioned May 1905 and returned 1906.

Toyo Maru No 2 (Transport): 4162 grt turbine passenger steamer, built 1937; sunk 2 April 1943 W of Truk (07° 32 N/149° 18 E) by US submarine *Tunny*.

Toyo Maru No 3 (Transport): 985 grt passenger steamer, built 1925; sunk 24 August 1944 13m NW of Santiao (25° 13 N/121° 49 E) by US submarine *Ronquil*.

Toyohama Maru (Guardboat): 73 grt; wrecked 8 October 1942 at Wotje Atoll.

Toyohara Maru (Transport): 805 grt passenger steamer, built 1923; sunk 15 May 1942 65m off Sohuksando, Korea (33° 34 N/125° 09 E) by US submarine *Tuna*.

Toyokawa Maru, ex-*Seattle*, ex-*Bangor* (Transport): 5124 grt steamer, built 1911; mined 5 July 1945 near Mutsurejima (33° 56 N/130° 53 E).

Toyooka Maru (Transport): 7097 grt turbine steamer, built 1915; sunk 9 September 1944 NW of Babuyan, Luzon (19° 45 N/120° 53 E) by US submarine *Queenfish*.

Toyosaka Maru (Transport): 1956 grt, built 1940; sunk 1 March 1945 off Miyako-retto (24° 46 N/125° 30 E) by US TF58.

Toyotomi Maru, ex-*Graaf van Bylandt* (Transport): 1456 grt steamer, built 1876; requisitioned 1904; mined 15 June 1906 at Urago.

Toyotsu Maru (Gunboat): 2930 grt turbine steamer, built 1937; requisitioned 1941; sunk 1 February 1942 at Kwajalein Atoll (09° 12 N/167° 18 E) by aircraft from USS *Enterprise*.

Toyu Maru (Transport): 4532 grt turbine steamer, built 194?; sunk 12 January 1945 off Cape St. Jacques (11° 10 N/108° 55 E) by US TF38.

Tozan Maru, ex-*T'angshan Maru* (Gunboat): 2103 grt passenger steamer, built 1926; requisitioned 1941 but re-rated as a transport in 1942; wrecked in storm 8 August 1943 on S coast of Hokkaido (42° 25 N/143° 20 E).

Tsukiura Maru (Guardboat): 117 grt; sunk 17 March 1945 W of Torishima (30° N/137° 30 E) by gunfire of US submarine *Trepang*.

Tsunushima Maru (Transport): 2926 grt turbine steamer, built 194?; sunk 20 October 1943 between Truk and Kavieng (01° 26 N/148° 36 E) by US submarine *Gato*.

Udo Maru (Transport): 3936 grt; sunk 19 November 1943 N of Marianas (22° 28 N/147° 22 E) by US submarine *Harder*.

Ujigawa Maru (Transport): 786 grt motor vessel, built 194?; sunk 30 October 1943 near Kieta, Bougainville (06° 20 S/155° 45 E) by US aircraft.

Ujina Maru, ex-*Hackney*, ex-*Emir* (Transport): 4410 grt steamer, built 1889; requisitioned in May 1905 and returned 1906.

Ukui Maru (Guardboat): 39 grt; sunk 30 December 1943 off Rabaul by US aircraft.

Unkai Maru No 1 (Collier): 2250 grt steamer, built 1932; sunk 7 January 1942 off Mikomotojima (34° 27 N/138° 58 E) by US submarine *Pollack*.

Unkai Maru No 3, ex-*Kazan Maru* (Supply Ship): 3023 grt passenger steamer, built 1919; sunk 15 November 1942 at Rabaul (04° 12 S/152° E) by US aircraft.

Unkai Maru No 6, ex-*Venus* (Transport): 3220 grt steamer, built 1905; sunk 17 February 1944 at Truk (07° 25 N/151° 45 E) by aircraft of TF58.

Unkai Maru No 7, ex-*Yasokawa Maru*, ex-*Daishin Maru No 3* (Transport): 2182 grt steamer, built 1919; sunk 4 August 1944 at Chichijima (27° 40 N/141° 48 E) by US TG58.2.

Unkai Maru No 10 (Gunboat): 851 grt, built 1939; requisitioned 1939 as gunboat but re-rated as an auxiliary in 1943; sunk 17 July 1944 at Ogasawara-gunto (29° 15 N/139° 05 E) by US submarine *Cobia*.

Unkai Maru No 12 (Transport): 2745 grt steamer, built 194?; sunk 1 November 1944 W of Mindoro (12° 57 N/120° 12 E) by US submarine *Blackfin*.

Un'yo Maru No 1 (Gunboat): 2039 grt steamer, built 1936; requisitioned 1942 but re-rated as a transport in 1945; sunk 14 July 1945 off Muroran, Hokkaido (42° 21 N/140° 59 E) by US TF38; raised and returned to commercial service.

Un'yo Maru No 8 (Transport): 1941 grt Standard 1 D type steamer, built 1943; requisitioned 1943; sunk 4 July 1944 in Takinoura Bay (27° 05 N/142° 09 E) by US TF58.

Unzen (Ferry): 250 grt ferry, built 1943 by Mitsubishi; no other details.

Ukarami Maru (Salvage Vessel): 4317 grt turbine steamer, built 1941; requisitioned 1941; sunk 30 March 1944 at Palau (07° 30 N/134° 30 E) by US TF58.

Uwajima Maru No 5 (Auxiliary): 371 grt steamer, built 1895; requisitioned 1904 and returned 1905; wrecked 3 July 1910 off Shisojima.

Uyo Maru (Transport): 6376 grt steamer, built 1941; requisitioned 1943; sunk 21 December 1943 off Miyazaki (32° 29 N/132° 08 E) by US submarine *Sailfish*.

Votjak (River Gunboat): 244-ton Russian river gunboat, built 1907; captured 7 September 1918 at Habarovsk, but not renamed; returned 1922.

Vulcan (Paddle Steamer): 250-ton British paddle steamer, built 1863; bought in 1868 for the Shogunate Fleet but transferred to the Imperial Fleet for use against the Enomoto rebels; renamed *Naniwa Maru* in 1871 and *Riyo Maru* in 1888; BU in 1901.

Wakamiyasan Maru (Transport): 2211 grt Standard 2 D type steamer, built 1944; requisitioned 1944; sunk 14 June 1945 in Yellow Sea (37° 35 N/123° 30 E) by US submarine *Sea Devil*.

Wakayoshi Maru (Guardboat): 96 grt; mined 23 July 1944 at Hayatamono Seto, Inland Sea.

Wayo Maru (Water Carrier): 2726 grt steamer, built 1941; sunk 11 March 1945 in South China Sea (21° 31 N/112° 25 E) by US aircraft.

Yachiyo Maru No 3 (Guardboat): 151 grt motor fishing vessel, built 1934; sunk 29 September 1944 N of Torishima (31° 27 N/140° 07 E) by US aircraft.

Yahiko Maru, ex-*Glenelg* (Blockship): 2692 grt steamer, built 1888; requisitioned 1904 as *Blockship No 3*; sunk 7 March 1904 at Port Arthur (38° 47 N/121° 15 E) during second blocking attempt.

Yamabiko Maru (Repair Ship): 6799 grt turbine passenger steamer, built 1937; sunk 10 November 1944 SSW of Yokosuka (31° 42 N/137° 50 E) by US submarine *Steelhead*.

Yamafuku Maru (Transport): 4928 grt, built 1940; sunk 28 November 1943 NW of Marianas (18° 21 N/140° 08 E) by US submarine *Snook*.

Yamagiri Maru (Transport): 6438 grt motor ship, built 1938; sunk 17 February 1944 at Truk (07° 23 N/151° 51 E) by US TF58.

Yamaguchi Maru, ex-*Pak Ling* (Transport): 3321 grt steamer, built 1890; requisitioned 1904 and returned 1905.

Yamakisan Maru, ex-*Estero*, ex-*Point Estero*, ex-*Nelson Traveller*, ex-*Commercial Traveller*, ex-*Red Hook*: 4776 grt Panamanian steamer, built 1920; captured 1942 and renamed; sunk 17 February 1944 at Truk (07° 25 N/151° 45 E) by US TF58.

Yamakuni Maru (Transport): 6925 grt, built 1938; sunk 14 January 1944 off Hachijojima (33° 15 N/139° 38 E) by US submarine *Swordfish*.

Yamashimo Maru (Repair Ship): 6796 grt turbine steamer, built 1938; requisitioned 1943; sunk 22 February 1944 W of Saipan (14° 45 N/144° 32 E) by US submarine *Tang*.

Yamashiro Maru (Guardboat): 38 grt; sunk 6 February 1944 at Kwajalein Atoll by US TF58.

Yamatama Maru, ex-*Pleiades*, ex-*Munaires* (Transport): 46,426 grt steamship, built 1918; bought 1941 and converted; sunk 7 August 1944 SW of Mindanao (06° 04 N/124° 22 E) by US submarine *Bluegill*.

Yamato Maru No 2 (Transport): 439 grt, built 1941; missing 23 November 1943 between New Guinea and Palau.

Yamatogawa Maru (Transport): 776 grt; sunk 26 October 1943 at Hai'ou, Hainan (20° 05 N/110° 25 E) by US aircraft.

Yanagawa Maru (Transport): 2813 grt turbine ferry, built 194?; sunk 8 August 1944 W of Mindanao (08° 10 N/121° 50 E) by US submarine *Bashaw*.

Yawata Maru (Armed Merchant Cruiser): 3817 grt steamer, built 1898; requisitioned 1904; later re-rated as transport and returned.

Yawata Maru (Guardboat): 19 grt; sunk 20 May 1944 150m N of Marcus Island by US aircraft.

Yawata Maru No 2 (Guardboat): 39 grt; sunk 21 February 1944 at Rabaul by US aircraft.

Yawata Maru No 3 (Guardboat): 19 grt; sunk 27 May 1945 off Torishima (30° N/140° E) by gunfire of US submarine.

Yawata Maru No 5 (Guardboat): 61 grt; mined 6 June 1945 off Tsurumi.

Yayoi Maru (Transport): 495 grt motor vessel, built 1935; sunk 4 August 1944 at Chichijima (27° 05 N/142° 11 E) by US TG58.2.

Yeda Maru (Transport): 3221 grt steamer, built 1890; requisitioned in May 1905 and returned 1906.

Yehime Maru (Gunboat): 623 grt steamer, built 1903; requisitioned February 1905 and later returned.

Yobo, ex-*Yobo Maru* (Armed Merchant Cruiser): 3435 grt stream collier; requisitioned 1904 and converted; taken as Russian prize at Inchon 9 February 1904.

Yodobashi (*Maru*), ex-*Sylatch* (Tug): 870 grt Russian steam tug, built 1890; sunk 1 January 1905 at Port Arthur but raised by Japanese in October 1905; put into service as salvage tug *Shirachi* but renamed *Yodobashi* 25 March 1909; surrendered in August 1945 and returned to commercial service.

Yoko Maru (Transport): 1050 grt motor vessel, built 1936; sunk 12 September 1943 off Mikura-jima (33° 50 N/139° 33 E) by US submarine *Harder*.

Yoko Maru (Guardboat): 23 grt; damaged 24 February 1944 in Yangtse by US aircraft and probably stricken.

Yoneyama Maru, ex-*Accomac* (Blockship): 2693 grt steamer, built 1883; requisitioned 1904 as Blockship No 4; sunk 27 March 1904 at Port Arthur (38° 47 N/121° 14 E) by Russian destroyer *Blechitelny* during 2nd blocking attempt.

Yoneyama Maru (Transport): 584 grt steamer, built 1920; sunk 24 January 1945 NE of Iojima (24° 50 N/141° 22 E) by US destroyer *Dunlap* and *Fanning*.

Yoshida Maru (Gunboat): 2920 grt, built 1941; requisitioned 1941 but re-rated as an escort on 20 May 1942; reconstructed as an oiler in 1943; sunk 18 January 1944 W of Marcus Island (23° 44 N/151° 30 E) by US submarine *Flasher*.

Yoshidagawa Maru, ex-*Inegawa Maru* (Gunboat): 310 grt steamer, built 1890; requisitioned 1904 and returned 1905.

Yoshinogawa Maru (Transport): 1422 grt; sunk 9 January 1943 in Bougainville Strait (06° 10 S/156° E) by US submarine *Nautilus*.

Yuki Maru (Guardboat): 64 grt; sunk 10 January 1944 at Okinawa by US TF38.

Yülin Maru (Japanese = *Yurin M.*) (Guardboat): 97 grt; sunk 4 September 1943 in Northern Pacific (30° 40 N/159° 02 E) by gunfire of US submarine.

Yusho Maru (Salvage Vessel): 807 grt, built 1927; requisitioned May 1941 and converted; mined 5 September 1943 in Makasar Strait (05° S/119° E).

Zensho Maru (Guardboat): 99 grt; sunk 4 August 1944 off Sofu-gan (29° 40 N/141° E) by gunfire of US submarine *Sterlet*.

Zenyo Maru (Guardboat): 98 grt; sunk 21 April 1945 off Shiono-Misaki (31° 30 N/135° 40 E) by US aircraft.

Zuiho Maru (Guardboat): 35 grt; sunk 17 May 1944 off Duke of York Isle (04° 12 S/152° 20 E) by US aircraft.

Zukai Maru (Transport): 2700 grt steamer, built 194?; sunk 17 February 1944 NW of Truk (07° 46 N/150° 27 E) by US TF58.

Zuiko Maru (Gunboat): 2577 grt steamer, built 1939; requisitioned 1941; wrecked in storm 14 December 1941 at Matsuwashima, Kuriles (48° 05 N/153° 43 E).

Index

(Note: this Index does not include the ships listed in section 24, Miscellaneous Mercantile Auxiliary Vessels, since that section is already arranged in alphabetic order.)

A

A-Type (1945) escorts, see 186-187
A1, 2-Type (1938-44) submarines, 174-175
Abukuma (1923) cruiser, 107-108
Agano (1941) cruiser, 111-112
Agata Maru (1931) netlayer, 206
Aguni (1944) escort, 188-189
Aikoku Maru (1940) armed merchant cruiser, 235
Aiten Maru (1943) Standard Type 2TM tanker, 261
Ajiro (1943) minelayer, 201
Akagi (1888) gunboat, 115
Akagi (1925) aircraft carrier (ex-battlecruiser), 36, 44
Akagi Maru (1936) armed merchant cruiser, 234
Akashi (1897) cruiser, 99
Akashi (1938) repair ship, 240-241
Akatsuki (1901) destroyer, 132
Akatsuki, ex-*Riechitelny*, ex-*Kondor*, see *Yamabiko*
Akatsuki ex-*No 55* (1932) destroyer, 145
Akatsuki Maru (1938) tanker, 252
Akebono (1899) destroyer, 130
Akebono ex-*No 52* (1930) destroyer, 144-145
Akebono Maru (1939) tanker, 252
Akebono aircraft salvage craft, see *No 1332*, 70
Aki (1907) battleship, 23-24
Akigumo (1941) destroyer, 150
Akikawa Maru (1943) standard Type 1K transport, 258
Akikaze (1920) destroyer, 141-142
Akishima Maru (1943) standard Type 1D transport, 257
Akishimo (1943) destroyer, 150
Akitsu Maru (1941) Army landing ship and aircraft transport, 61
Akitsu Maru WWII submarine chaser, 224
Akitsushima (1892) cruiser, 97-98
Akitsushima (1941) flying-boat support ship, 67
Akizuki (1941) destroyer, 151
Amagi (1877) sloop, 90
Amagi ex-battlecruiser, aircraft carrier, 36
Amagi (1943) aircraft carrier, 56
Amagiri ex-*No 50* (1930) destroyer, 144-145
Amakusa (1943) escort, 187
Amami (1945) escort, 188-189
Amatsu Maru (1943) standard Type 1TL tanker, 252, 258
Amatsukaze (1916) destroyer, 140
Amatsukaze (1939) destroyer, 148-149
Anegawa, ex-*Angara*, (1898) transport, 244
Anko Maru (1942) standard Type 1C transport, 256
Anshu Maru (1937) gunboat, 123
Aoba (1926) cruiser, 80-81
Aoi (1920) destroyer, 137-138
Aoi Maru (1935) minesweeper, 211
Aotaka (1903) torpedo boat, 128
Aotaka (1940) minelayer, 201
Arare (1904) destroyer, 132-133
Arare (1937) destroyer, 147-148
Arisaki (1942) supply ship, 247
Arashi (1940) destroyer, 148-149
Arashio (1937) destroyer, 147-148
Ariake (1904) destroyer, 132-133
Ariake (1934) destroyer, 146
Arima Maru (1936) tanker, 252
Asadori unbuilt minelayer, 201
Asagao, ex-*No 10*, ex-*Kakitsubata*, (1922) destroyer, 138-139
Asagiri (1903) destroyer, 132-133
Asagiri, ex-*No 47*, (1929) destroyer, 144-145
Asagumo (1937) destroyer, 147-148
Asahi (1899) battleship, 18
Asahi Maru, ex-*Dante Alghierei*, (1914) hospital ship, 262
Asahi Maru No 2 (1934) minesweeper, 211
Asahi Maru No 9 (1939) submarine chaser, 224
Asaka Maru (1937) armed merchant cruiser, 234
Asakaze (1905) destroyer, 133
Asakaze, ex-*No 3*, (1922) destroyer, 142
Asakaze Maru (1938) collier, 248
Asama, ex-*Hokkai Maru*, (1868) screw corvette, 90
Asama (1898) armoured cruiser, 72-73; 270
Asanagi, ex-*No 15* (1924) destroyer, 142-143
Asanagi Maru (1943) standard Type 1TM tanker, 259
Asashimo (1943) destroyer, 150
Asashio (1902) destroyer, 131-132
Asashio (1936) destroyer, 147-148
Asashio Maru (1943) standard Type 1TM tanker, 259
Asatsuyu (1906) destroyer, 133
Ashi (1921) destroyer, 137-138; 270
Ashigara (1928) cruiser, 81-83
Ashizaki (1915) minelayer, 202-203
Ashizuri (1942) replenishment tanker, 254
Aso, ex-*Bayan*, (1900) armoured cruiser, 76
Aso (1944) aircraft carrier, 56-57
Aso Maru (1932) gunboat, 123
Asuka, ex-*Yung Chien*, (1914) torpedo depot ship, 269-270
Atada, ex-*Yat Sen*, (1930) training ship, 271
Atada Maru, see *Eisen No 1545*, 269
Atago (1887) gunboat, 115
Atago uncompleted battlecruiser, 36
Atago (1930) cruiser, 83-84
Ataka, ex-*Nakoso*, (1922) gunboat, 118
Ataka Maru (1921) minesweeper, 212
Atami (1929) river gunboat, 121
Atsu Maru (1934) minesweeper, 212
Awa Maru (1943) standard Type 1B transport, 256
Awaji (1943) escort, 187-188
Awashima (1945) minelayer, 202
Awata Maru (1937) armed merchant cruiser, 234
Ayanami (1909) destroyer, 133, 208
Ayanami, ex-*No 46*, (1929) destroyer, 144-145
Ayanami Maru (194?) standard Type 2TM tanker, 261
Ayase unbuilt cruiser, 110
Ayukawa Maru (1925) submarine chaser, 224
Azuchisan Maru (1944) standard Type 2D transport, 259
Azuma (1864) armoured ship, 12
Azuma (1899) armoured cruiser, 73; 270
Azuma Maru (1938) tanker, 252
Azusa (1945) escort destroyer, 153
Azusa Maru (1944) standard Type 1TL tanker, 258

B

B-Type (1945) escorts, 187-189
B1-4-Type (1938-) submarines, 175-177
Ban'ei Maru (1944) standard Type 1TM tanker, 259
Bangkok Maru (1937) armed merchant cruiser, 235
Banjo (1878) gunboat, 115
Banshu Maru No 18, ex-*Banshu Maru No 3*, (1922) minesweeper, 212
Banshu Maru No 51, ex-*Banshu Maru*, (1921) minesweeper, 212
Banshu Maru No 52, ex-*Banshu Maru No 2*, (1921) minesweeper, 212
Banshu Maru No 53, ex-*Meiji Maru No ?*, (1920) submarine chaser, 224
Banshu Maru No 56, ex-*Meiji Maru No 7*, (1920) minesweeper, 212
Basho unbuilt destroyer, 139
Bingo Maru (1944) standard Type 1B transport, 256
Bisan Maru (1922) minesweeper, 212
Bisan Maru (1943) standard Type 1B transport, 256
Bizen Maru (1943) standard Type 1B transport, 256
Bokuei Maru (1943) standard Type 1TM tanker, 259
Bokuyo Maru (1941) standard Type 1C transport, 256
Botan unbuilt destroyer, 139
Brazil Maru (1939) transport, 59
Bujo Maru (1944) standard Type 2D transport, 260
Bunsei, ex-*Wen Hsing*, (1934) utility craft, 270
Bunzan Maru WWII submarine chaser, 224
Busho Maru (1921) gunboat, 123
Byoritsu Maru WWII submarine chaser, 224

C

C-Type (1945) escorts, 189-191
C1-4-Type (1937) submarines, 177-178
CDa 1, 2 (1945) patrol craft, 194
CDa 101-157 (1945) patrol craft, 194
Ch 1-89 (1933-45) submarine chasers, 214-217
Cha 1-100 WWII auxiliary submarine chasers, 217-219
Cha 101-117 WWII captured submarine chasers, 222-223
Cha 151-253 WWII auxiliary submarine chasers, 219-221
Chiburi (1943) escort, 187-188
Chidori (1900) torpedo boat, 127-128
Chidori (1933) torpedo boat, 128-129
Chigusa Maru (1945) escort carrier, 62, 261
Chihiya (1900) sloop, 95
Chihaya uncompleted flying-boat support ship, 67
Chikubu (1944) escort, 188-189
Chikuma (1911) cruiser, 104-105
Chikuma (1938) cruiser, 87
Chikuto Maru WWII submarine chaser, 224
Chikuzen Maru WWII submarine chaser, 224
Chikuyu Maru (1934) submarine chaser, 224
Chinchu, ex-*Chen Chung*, (1880) gunboat, 116-117
Chimpen, ex-*Chen Pien*, (1880) gunboat, 116-117
Chin-Hoku, ex-*Chin Pei*, (1879) gunboat, 116-117
Chinnan, ex-*Chen Nan*, (1879) gunboat, 116-117
Chinsei, ex-*Chen Hsi*, (1879) gunboat, 116-117
Chinto, ex-*Chen Tung*, (1879) gunboat, 116-117
Chin'en, ex-*Chen-Yuan*, (1882) armoured ship, 14
Chishima (1891) cruiser, 93
Chitose (1898) cruiser, 100-101
Chitose (1936) seaplane carrier, 64; aircraft carrier, 57
Chitose Maru, ex-*Coquette*, (1867) screw steamer
Chitose Maru (1921) gunboat, 123
Chitose Maru (1937) minesweeper, 212
Chiyoda (1862) gunboat, 113
Chiyoda (1890) armoured cruiser, 71-72
Chiyoda (1937) seaplane carrier, 64; aircraft carrier, 57
Choan Maru 331 grt ferry, built 1935; requisitioned as minelayer 1941
Choan Maru No 2, ex-*Choan Maru*, (1927) gunboat, 123
Chogei (1924) submarine depot ship, 237
Chohakusan Maru (1928) gunboat, 123
Chojusan Maru (1928) gunboat, 123
Chokai (1887) gunboat, 115
Chokai (1931) cruiser, 83-84
Choko Maru (1923) stores ship converted to tanker, 252
Choko Maru (1940) netlayer, 206
Choko Maru No 2, ex-*Choko Maru*, (1927) gunboat, 123
Choran Maru (1943) tanker, 252
Chosa Maru (1921) gunboat, 123
Choun Maru (1935) minesweeper, 212
Choun Maru (1940) gunboat, 123
Choun Maru No 6 (1932) minesweeper, 212
Choun Maru No 7 (1934) minesweeper, 212
Choun Maru No 8 (1933) minesweeper, 212
Choun Maru No 18 (1935) minesweeper, 212
Choun Maru No 21 (1935) minesweeper, 212
Chowa Maru (1940) gunboat, 123
Choyo (*Maru*), ex-*Yedo*, (1856) corvette, 88
Choyo, ex-*Tydeman*, (1916) survey ship, 263
Choyo Maru WWII minesweeper, 212
Choyo Maru No 2 WWII minesweeper, 212
Chuhatsu -type naval landing craft, 233
Chuwa Maru (1940) gunboat, 123
Chuyo, ex-*Nitta Maru*, (1939) escort carrier, 58-59

D

D -Type (1943-45) escorts, 191-194
D1, 2 -Type (1943-) submarines, 180-181
Dai-ichi Kaiso (18??) sail training ship, 270
Daido Maru (1935) gunboat, 123
Daigen Maru No 7 (1937) gunboat, 123
Daihatsu landing craft, 233
Daiji Maru (1943) standard Type 1C transport, 256
Daiki Maru (1944) standard Type 2D transport, 260
Daiten Maru (194?) standard Type 1B transport, 256
Daito (1944) escort, 188
Delhi Maru (1922) gunboat, 123
Doryo Maru (1944) standard Type 2D transport, 260
Doshi Maru (1944) standard Type 2D transport, 260

E

Edo Maru (1937) gunboat, 123
Eguchi Maru No 3 (1935) minesweeper, 212
Eifuku Maru (1939) gunboat, 123
Eihimo Maru (1903) gunboat, 123
Eiho Maru (1944) standard Type 1TM tanker, 252, 259
Eijo (*Maru*) (1944) minelayer, 202
Eiko Maru (1937) gunboat, 123
Einiu Maru, standard Type 2TA tanker, 259
Eiryu Maru (1928) netlayer, 206
Eisen tugs, 203-204, 267-269
Eisen Nos 1650, 1651, 1658 (ex-*Ch 52, 53, 51*), 215
Eiyo Maru (1944) standard Type 1TM tanker, 259
Eiyo No 2 Maru (1944) standard Type 1TM tanker, 259
Enoki (1918) destroyer, 136, 208
Enoki (1945) escort destroyer, 153
Enoshima (1917) minelayer, 202-203
Enoshima Maru, ex-*Ebonol* (1917) tanker, 252
Ento (*Maroshima*) (1917) minelayer, 202-203
Erimo (1920) tanker, 249-250
Etorofu (1943) escort, 187

F

Fubuki (1905) destroyer, 132-133
Fubuki (1927) destroyer, 144, 231
Fuchu Maru (1943) standard Type 1F transport, 257-258
Fuji (1864) paddle frigate, 89
Fuji (1896) battleship, 16, 270
Fuji (1920) destroyer, 137-138
Fuji Maru (1929) minesweeper, 212
Fuji Maru (1932) netlayer, 206
Fuji Maru No 11 WWII submarine chaser, 225
Fujinami (1943) destroyer, 150
Fujisan Maru (1931) tanker, 252
Fukue (1943) escort, 187
Fukuei Maru No 7 (1934) minesweeper, 212
Fukuei Maru No 10 (1936) gunboat, 123
Fukuei Maru No 15 (1939) netlayer, 206
Fukuryu, ex-*Fu Lung*, (1885) torpedo boat, 127
Fukuyama Maru (1936) gunboat, 123
Fumi Maru (1938) submarine chaser, 225
Fumi Maru No 2 (1939) minesweeper, 212
Fumi Maru No 3 (1940) submarine chaser, 225
Fumi Maru No 5 (1942) submarine chaser, 225
Fumizuki, ex-*Silnyii*, ex-*Baklan* (1901) destroyer, 134
Fumizuki (1926) destroyer, 143
Furutaka (1925) cruiser, 79-80
Fushimi (1906) river gunboat, 120
Fushimi (1939) river gunboat, 122
Fuso (1877) armoured ship, 13
Fuso (1914) battleship, 25, 37
Fuso Maru (1895) gunboat, 123
Fuso Maru, see *Shinshu Maru*
Futagami (1938) salvage tug, 266
Futami (1929) river gunboat, 121
Futsutsu unbuilt minelayer, 201
Fuyo, ex-*No 16*, ex-*Ajisai*, (1922) destroyer, 138-139
Fuyutsuki (1944) destroyer, 151

G

G 6, 8, projected aircraft carriers, 47
Ganjitsu Maru (1926) submarine chaser, 225
Genchi Maru WWII minesweeper, 212
Gen'Yo Maru (1937) tanker, 252
Giso Maru No 40 (1945) standard trawler type submarine chaser, 225
Gokoku Maru (1941) armed merchant cruiser, 235
Goyo Maru (1939) tanker, 252
Gyoraitei -type motor torpedo boats, 154-158

H

H 1-61 (1940-45) motor gunboats, 158-159
Ha 1, 2 (1936) midget submarines, 183
Ha 3-76 (1938-44) midget submarines, 183-184
Ha 1-10 (1908-16) submarines, 160-162
Ha 101-279 (1944-45) submarines, 167-169
Habushi (1944) escort, 188-189
Habuto (1945) escort, 188-189
Hachijin Maru (1941) standard Type 1D transport, 257
Hachijo (1940) escort, 186-187
Hachirogata Maru (1943) standard Type 1D transport, 257
Hagi (1920) destroyer, 137-138
Hagi (1944) escort destroyer, 153
Hagikaze (1940) destroyer, 148-149
Hagoromo Maru (1920) minesweeper, 212
Haguro (1928) cruiser, 81-83
Haguro Maru (1928) transport,
Hakachi (1943) target ship, 271
Hakata Maru (194?) aircraft salvage craft, 70
Hakata Maru No 6 (1922) minesweeper, 212
Hakata Maru No 7 (1923) minesweeper, 212
Hakaze (1920) destroyer, 141
Hakkai Maru (1939) gunboat, 123
Hakkaisan Maru (1937) gunboat, 123
Hakko Maru (1943) standard Type 1D transport, 257
Hakko Maru (1944) standard Type 1TL tanker, 258
Hakko Maru WWII submarine chaser, 225
Hakuai Maru (1898) transport and hospital ship, 262
Hakusa, ex-*Fu Hsing*, (1913) survey ship, 263
Hakusan Maru No 2 WWII submarine chaser, 225
Hakusan Maru No 2, ex-*Hakusan Maru*, (1928) submarine chaser, 225
Hakusan Maru No 5 (1944) standard Type 2D transport, 260
Hakushan Maru, standard Type 2TA tanker, 259
Hakuyo Maru (1920) submarine chaser, 225
Hamakaze (1916) destroyer, 140
Hamakaze (1940) destroyer, 148-149
Hamanami (1943) destroyer, 150
Hanashima (1945) salvage tug, 266-267
Hanatsuki (1944) destroyer, 151
Hario (1944) tanker, 252
Harukaze (1905) destroyer, 133
Harukaze, ex-*No 5*, ex-*Tsumikaze*, (1922) destroyer, 142
Haruna (1913) battlecruiser, 31-35
Harusame (1902) destroyer, 132
Harusame (1935) destroyer, 146-147
Harushima, ex-*Harushima Maru*, ex-*Colonel GFE Harrison*, WWII cable ship, 205
Harutsuki (1944) destroyer, 151
Hashidate (1891) cruiser, 96-97
Hashidate (1939) gunboat, 118-119
Hashima (1937) salvage tug, 266
Hashitaka (1903) torpedo boat, 128
Hasu (1921) destroyer, 137-138
Hatakaze, ex-*No 9*, ex-*Soyokaze*, (1924) destroyer, 142
Hato (1903) torpedo boat, 128
Hato (1937) torpedo boat, 129
Hatsuharu (1906) destroyer, 133
Hatsuharu (1933) destroyer, 146
Hatsukari (1933) torpedo boat, 128-129
Hatsukaze (1903) yacht, 273
Hatsukaze (1939) destroyer, 148-149
Hatsuse (1899) battleship, 17-18
Hatsushima (1940) cable ship, 205
Hatsushimo (1905) destroyer, 133
Hatsushimo (1933) destroyer, 146
Hatsusuki (1942) destroyer, 151
Hatsutaka (1939) minelayer, 201
Hatsuume (1945) escort destroyer, 153
Hatsuyuki (1906) destroyer, 133
Hatsuyuki, ex-*No 41*, (1928) destroyer, 144
Hatsuzakura, ex-*Susuki*, (1945) escort

destroyer, 153
Hayabusa (1898) torpedo boat, 127-128
Hayabusa (1935) torpedo boat, 129
Hayabusa Maru (1944) standard Type 2E netlayer, 260
Hayabusa-Tei No 1 (1940) motor torpedo boat, 158
Hayabusa-Tei No 2-245 (1943-45) motor gunboats, 158-159
Hayanami (1942) destroyer, 150
Hayasaki (1942) stores ship, 247
Hayase, ex-*Chin Chiang*, WWII repair ship, 241
Hayashimo (1943) destroyer, 150
Hayashio (1939) destroyer, 148-149
Hayasui (1943) fleet tanker, 251
Hayate (1906) destroyer, 133
Hayate, ex-*No 13*, (1925) destroyer, 142-143
Hayatomo (1922) tanker, 249-250
Hayatori (1902) destroyer, 132-133
Hayo, ex-*Poyang*, (1891) survey ship, 263
Hazuki unbuilt destroyer, 151
Heian Maru (1930) submarine depot ship, 239
Heien, ex-*P'ing-Yuan*, (1890) armoured ship, 14
Heijo Maru (1903) gunboat, 123
Heijo Maru (1941) standard Type 2B transport (257) and gunboat, 123
Heinan Maru (1941) standard Type 1F transport, 257-258
Heiyo, ex-*Heiryu Maru*, ex-*Herald*, ex-*Merry Hampton*, (1918) survey ship, 263
Hibari (1903) torpedo boat, 128
Hibiki (1906) destroyer, 133
Hibiki, ex-*No 56*, (1932) destroyer, 145
Hiburi (1944) escort, 188
Hiei (1878) armoured ship, 13
Hiei (1912) battlecruiser, 31-35
Hie Maru (1930) submarine depot ship, 239
Hijikawa Maru No 5 (1897) gunboat, 123
Hikawa Maru (1930) hospital ship, 262
Hikawa Maru No 2, ex-*Ten-No Maru*, ex-*Op Ten Noort*, (1927) hospital ship, 262
Hikosan Maru, ex-*Carradale*, (1892) collier, 248
Hikoshima unbuilt minelayer, 201
Himeshima unbuilt minelayer, 201
Himeshima Maru (1927) minesweeper, 212
Himetaka Maru (1940) netlayer, 206
Hino Maru No 2 (1935) gunboat, 123
Hino Maru No 3 (1937) transport,
Hino Maru No 5 (1940) gunboat, 123
Hino Maru No 10 (1945) standard Type 2D transport, 260
Hino Maru No 25 (1945) submarine chaser, 225
Hino Maru No 43 (1945) submarine chaser, 225
Hino Maru No 63 (1945) submarine chaser, 225
Hinode Maru No 15, ex-*Daifuku Maru*, ex-*Daifuku Maru No 3*, (1920) submarine chaser, 225
Hinode Maru No 17, ex-*Inaba Maru*, ex-*Kakuwa Maru No 17*, (1919) minesweeper, 212
Hinode Maru No 18, ex-*Izumo Maru*, ex-*Kakuwa Maru No 18*, (1919) minesweeper, 212
Hinode Maru No 20, ex-*Kokusai Maru No 100*, (1930) minesweeper, 212
Hinoki (1916) destroyer, 135-136
Hinoki (1944) escort destroyer, 151-152
Hinoki Maru (1939) netlayer, 206
Hira (1923) river gunboat, 120
Hirashima (1940) minelayer, 200-201
Hirado (1911) cruiser, 104-105; 270
Hirado (1943) escort, 187
Hiro Maru (1927) netlayer, 206
Hirota Maru (1940) gunboat, 123
Hirotama Maru (1933) gunboat, 123
Hiryu (1937) aircraft carrier, 47-49
Hishi (1921) destroyer, 137-138
Hishi unbuilt escort destroyer, 153
Hishi Maru WWII tanker, 252
Hishi Maru No 2 (1936) tanker, 252
Hitonose, ex-*Ming Sen*, (1931) repair ship, 241
Hiyo, ex-*Izumo Maru*, (1941) aircraft carrier, 52-53
Hiyodori (1935) torpedo boat, 129
Hiyoshi Maru No 2 (1936) gunboat, 123
Hizen, ex-*Retvizan*, (1899) battleship, 20
Hodaka (1945) escort, 188-189
Hoei Maru (1919) minesweeper, 212
Hokaze (1921) destroyer, 141-142
Hoko (1940) minelayer, 200-201
Hokoku Maru (1936) gunboat (subsequently transport), 123
Hokoku Maru (1940) armed merchant cruiser, 235
Honan Maru (1920) Army tanker, 254
Hong Kong Maru (1935) gunboat, 123
Hosho (1868) gunboat, 114
Hosho (1921) aircraft carrier, 40, 41
Hoyo, ex-*Horai Maru*, ex-*Pollux*, (1922) survey ship, 264
Hoyo Maru (1936) tanker, 252
Hozu (1923) river gunboat, 120
Hyuga (1917) battleship and hybrid carrier, 26-28
Hyuga Maru (1944) landing ship (dock), 232

I

I.1-417 1st class submarines, 169-181
I.501-506, ex-German and ex-Italian submarines, 182-183
Ibuki (1907) armoured cruiser, 78
Ibuki (1943) cruiser, 87; aircraft carrier, 58
Ikara (1945) escort, 188-189
Ikazuchi (1898) destroyer, 130
Ikazuchi, ex-*No 57*, (1931) destroyer, 145
Iki, ex-*Imperator Nicolai I*, (1889) armoured ship, 15
Iki (1943) escort, 187
Ikino (1945) escort, 188-189
Ikoma (1906) armoured cruiser, 77
Ikoma (1944) aircraft carrier, 56-57
Ikuna (1944) escort, 188-189
Ikushima Maru (1936) gunboat, 123
Ikuta Maru (1936) gunboat, 123
Ina Maru standard Type 2E transport, 260
Inagi (1944) escort, 188-189
Inari Maru (1944) standard Type 1C transport, 257
Inatori unbuilt tanker, 252
Inazuma (1899) destroyer, 130
Inazuma ex-*No 58*, (1932) destroyer, 145
Io (1945) escort, 188-189
Ioshima, ex-*Ning Hai*, (1931) cruiser, 113
Irako (1941) supply ship, 247, 248
Iro (1922) tanker, 249-250
Ise (1916) battleship and hybrid carrier, 26-28
Ishigaki (1940) escort, 186-187
Ishikawa (1876) sail training ship, 270
Ishizake (1941) minelayer, 200-201
Isokaze (1916) destroyer, 140
Isokaze (1939) destroyer, 148-149
Isonami (1908) destroyer, 133, 208
Isonami, ex-*No 39*, (1927) destroyer, 144
Isuzu (1921) cruiser, 107-108
Itsukushima (1889) cruiser, 96
Itsukushima (1929) minelayer, 189
Itsukushima Maru (1937) tanker, 252
Iwade (1900) cruiser, 74, 270
Iwami, ex-*Orel*, (1902) battleship, 21
Iwashiro Maru (1939) collier, 248
Iwate, see *Iwade* (74)
Iwato Maru (1939) netlayer, 206
Izumi, ex-*Esmeralda*, (1883) cruiser, 98-99
Izumo (1899) armoured cruiser, 74, 270

J

Jingei (1875) corvette and yacht, 88
Jingei (1923) submarine support ship, 237
Jintsu (1923) cruiser, 108-109
Jokuja Maru (1943) standard Type 1A transport, 256
Juko Maru, ex-*Kamikaze Maru*, (1938) tanker, 252
Junsen-type (1923-38) submarines, 173-174
Junyo, ex-*Kashiwara Maru*, (1941) aircraft carrier, 52-53

K

Kaba (1915) destroyer, 135
Kaba (1945) escort destroyer, 153
Kaede (1915) destroyer, 135
Kaede (1945) escort destroyer, 151-152
Kaga (1921) battleship, 35; aircraft carrier, 42-43
Kagawa Maru (1903) gunboat, 123
Kagero (1899) destroyer, 131
Kagero (1938) destroyer, 148
Kagu Maru (1936) seaplane carrier, 67-68
Kahoku Maru (1931) gunboat, 123; minelayer, 204
Kaichu-type (1917-41) submarines, 164-166
Kaidai-type (21-43) submarines, 169-173
Kaido, see *Sawarabi*
Kaiho Maru (1941) gunboat, 123, 249
Kaii, ex-*Kashi*, (1916) submarine chaser, 225
Kaijo Maru (1902) gunboat, 123
Kaijo Maru (1939) tanker, 252
Kaijo Maru No 2, ex-*Kaijo Maru*, (1937) tanker, 252
Kaiko Maru (1921) submarine chaser, 225
Kaimon (1882) sloop, 91
Kainan Maru (194?) netlayer, 206
Kaio Maru No 2 WWII submarine chaser, 225
Kairyu-type (1945) midget submarines, 185
Kaishin Maru No 11 (1944) standard Type 2E transport, 260
Kaisho-type (1941-44) submarines, 167
Kaiten-type midget submarines, 185
Kaiyo, ex-*Argentina Maru*, (1928) escort carrier, 59
Kaiyo No 1-6 (1939-42) oceanographic research and weather ships, 264
Kaiyo Maru (1911) minesweeper, 212
Kaiyo Maru No 1 (1939) minesweeper, 212
Kaiyo Maru No 2 WWII submarine chaser, 225
Kaiyo Maru No 3 (1938) minesweeper, 212
Kaki (1919) destroyer, 137-138, 270
Kaki (1945) escort destroyer, 153
Kako (1925) cruiser, 79-80
Kali, ex-*Kashi*, 136
Kamakura Maru, ex-*Chichibu Maru*, (1930) transport and hospital ship; escort carrier (project), 60
Kamikawa Maru (1937) seaplane carrier, 67-68
Kamikaze (1905) destroyer, 133
Kamikaze, ex-*No 1*, ex-*Okaze*, (1922) destroyer, 142
Kamishika Maru, see *Shinroku Maru*
Kamishima (1945) minelayer, 202
Kamishima-class minelayers, 202
Kamitsu Maru (1937) gunboat, 123
Kamo Maru (1920) submarine chaser, 225
Kamoi (1922) seaplane carrier, 64
Kamoi Maru (1937) collier, 248
Kamoi Maru No 9 (1945) standard construction submarine chaser, 225
Kamome (1904) torpedo boat, 128
Kamome (1929) minelayer, 199
Kanawa (1944) escort, 188-189
Kanju (1887) sail training ship, 270
Kanju (1943) escort, 187
Kanko, ex-*Soembing*, (1852) corvette, 88
Kanko Maru (1938) gunboat, 123
Kanko Maru (1941) netlayer, 206
Kanran, ex-*Nemesis* (1910) destroyer, 137
Kanrin Maru, ex-*Kanrin*, ex-*Japan*, (1856) corvette, 88
Kanto Maru, ex-*Manchuria*, (1898) armed merchant cruiser, repair ship, 240-241
Karasaki, ex-*Ekaterinoslav*, (1896) submarine depot ship, 236
Karatsu, ex-*Luzon*, (1927) river gunboat, 122-123
Kari (1903) torpedo-boat, 128
Kari (1937) torpedo-boat, 129-130
Kariko-class tankers, 251
Karukaya, ex-*No 18*, ex-*Shion*, (1923) destroyer, 138-139
Kasado (1943) escort, 187
Kasagi (1898) cruiser, 100-101
Kasagi (1944) aircraft carrier, 56-57
Kasagi Maru (1928) gunboat, 123
Kasasagi (1899) torpedo boat, 127-128
Kasasagi (1935) torpedo boat, 129
Kasashima (1937) salvage tug, 266
Kasei Maru (1944) standard Type 2D transport, 260
Kashi (1916) destroyer, 135-136
Kashi (1944) escort destroyer, 151-152
Kashi Maru (1940) netlayer, 206
Kashii (1941) training cruiser, 111
Kashima (1905) battleship, 22
Kashima (1939) training cruiser, 111
Kashima Maru (1938) netlayer, 206
Kashimasan Maru (1942) standard Type 1C transport, 257
Kashino (1940) ammunition ship, 243
Kashiwa (1915) destroyer, 135
Kashiwa Maru, ex-*Mitsu Maru No 1*, (1918) netlayer and army transport, 206
Kashiwa Maru (1938) netlayer, 206
Kashiwara (1940) training cruiser, 111
Kasuga (*Kan*), ex-*Kiangtse*, (1863) paddle sloop, 89
Kasuga, ex-*Bernardino Rivedavia*, ex-*Mitra*, (1902) armoured cruiser, 75, 270
Kasumi (1902) destroyer, 132
Kasumi (1937) destroyer, 147-148
Katashima (1917) minelayer, 202-203
Katata (1922) river gunboat, 120
Katoku (1915) minelayer, 202-203
Katori (1905) battleship, 22
Katori (1939) training cruiser, 111
Katori Maru (1938) gunboat, 123
Katsura (1915) destroyer, 135
Katsura (1945) escort destroyer, 153
Katsura Maru (1934) patrol boat,
Katsura Maru (1938) netlayer, 206
Katsura Maru No 2 (1937) gunboat, 123
Katsuragi (1885) sloop, 91-92
Katsuragi (1944) aircraft carrier, 56
Katsuriki (1916) minelayer, 197
Kawachi (1911) battleship, 24-25
Kawakaze (1915) destroyer, 140
Kawakaze (1917) destroyer, 140
Kawakaze (1937) destroyer, 146-147
Kawasemi, ex-*Fungo*, (1906) torpedo boat, 126
Kaya (1919) destroyer, 137
Kaya (1944) escort destroyer, 151-152
Kazahaya (1942) tanker, 251
Kazan Maru (1936) gunboat, 123
Kazegumo (1941) destroyer, 150
Keihin Maru WWII submarine chaser, 225
Keijin Maru No 1-5 (1937) minesweepers, 212
Keijo Maru (1940) gunboat, 123
Keiko Maru (1938) gunboat, 123
Keinan Maru (1928) minesweeper, 212
Keishin Maru (1940) gunboat, 123
Keisho Maru (1929) submarine chaser, 225
Keisho Maru (1944) standard Type 3D transport, 260-261
Kenkai Maru (1902) transport and submarine depot ship, 239
Kenkai Maru WWII submarine chaser, 225
Ken'Yo Maru (1938) transport, 260
Ken'Yo Maru (1939) tanker, 252
Kenzan Maru (1938) gunboat, 123
Keyaki (1918) destroyer, 136
Keyaki (1944) escort destroyer, 153
Kibitsu Maru (1943) army landing ship, 232
Kii unbuilt battleship, 36
Kiikawa Maru (1892) gunboat, 123
Kiji (1903) torpedo boat, 128
Kiji (1937) torpedo boat, 129-130
Kiku (1920) destroyer, 137-138
Kiku Maru (1920) submarine chaser, 225
Kiku Maru (1929) netlayer and hospital ship, 206
Kikuzuki (1907) destroyer, 133, 208
Kikuzuki, ex-*No 31*, (1926) destroyer, 143
Kimikawa Maru (1937) seaplane carrier, 67-68
Kinezake, ex-*Nanshin*, (1940) supply ship, 247
Kinjo Maru (1935) minelayer, 204
Kinjosan (*Kinzyosan*) *Maru* (1936) auxiliary cruiser and gunboat, 123
Kinrei Maru (1941) tanker, 252
Kinryu Maru (1938) armed merchant cruiser, 235
Kinsui Maru WWII submarine chaser, 225
Kinu (1922) cruiser, 107-108
Kinugasa (1926) cruiser, 80-81
Kinugasa Maru (1936) seaplane carrier, 67-68
Kiri (1915) destroyer, 135
Kiri (1944) escort destroyer, 152
Kiri Maru (1941), ex-*Suikei No 22*, ex-*Kelena*, patrol craft, 224
Kiri Maru No 5 (1937) minesweeper, 212
Kirishima (1911) battlecruiser, 31-35
Kisan Maru (1944) standard Type 2A transport, 259
Kisaragi (1905) destroyer, 133
Kisaragi, ex-*No 21*, (1925) destroyer, 143
Kisaragi Maru (1944) standard Type 2E transport, 260
Kishin Maru (1941) netlayer, 206
Kishinami (1943) destroyer, 150
Kiso (1920) cruiser, 106-107
Kiso Maru (1932) gunboat, 123
Kitakami (1920) cruiser, 106-107
Kiyo Maru, ex-*Vigriol*, (1930) tanker, 252
Kiyokawa Maru (1937) seaplane carrier, 67-68
Kiyonami (1942) destroyer, 150
Kiyoshimo (1944) destroyer, 150
Kiyozumi Maru (1934) armed merchant cruiser, 234
Kiyotsuki unbuilt destroyer, 151
Koa Maru (1939) netlayer, 206
Koei Maru (1934) minelayer, 204
Koei Maru (1941) netlayer, 206
Kogi Maru (1940) netlayer, 206
Kohei-Go, ex-*Kuang P'ing*, (1891) torpedo-gunboat, 94
Kokko Maru (1938) netlayer, 206
Kokuyo Maru (1939) tanker, 252
Kokuyo Maru (1943) standard Type 1B transport, 256
Komahashi, ex-*Komahashi Maru*, (1913) submarine depot ship, 237
Komei Maru (1944) standard Type 1C transport, 257
Kongo (1878) armoured ship, 13, 270
Kongo (1912) battlecruiser, 31-35, 37
Kongo Maru (1934) submarine chaser, 225
Kongo Maru (1935) armed merchant cruiser, 235
Kongo Maru No 2 (1922) minesweeper, 212
Kongosan Maru (1927) gunboat, 123
Korei Maru (1939) netlayer, 206
Koryo Maru (1903) minelayer and gunboat, 204
Koryo Maru (1936) tanker, 252
Koryo Maru (1931) tanker, 252
Koryu-type midget submarines, 184
Koryu Maru (1944) standard Type 2E transport, 260
Koryu Maru (1944) standard Type 2TE tanker, 253, 261
Kosai (1904) lighthouse tender and utility vessel, 269-270
Kosai Maru (1899) hospital ship, 262-263
Kosan Maru (1934) minesweeper, 212
Kosei unbuilt minelayer, 201
Kosei Maru (1915) netlayer, 206
Kosei Maru (1933) collier, 248
Kosho Maru, ex-*Johann*, (1883) gunboat, 123
Kosho Maru (1940) gunboat, 123
Koshu, ex-*Michael Jebsen*, (1904) transport, 244
Koshun Maru (1928) submarine chaser, 225
Kotaka (1886) torpedo boat, 126
Kotaka (1930) river gunboat, 121
Kotobuki Maru No 3 (1936) netlayer, 206
Kotobuki Maru No 5 (1939) netlayer, 206
Kowa Maru (1940) gunboat, 123
Kozu (1945) escort, 188-189
Kozui Maru (1937) tanker, 252
Kuga (1944) escort, 188-189
Kuma (1919) cruiser, 106-107
Kumano (1936) cruiser, 85-86
Kumano Maru (1941) netlayer, 206
Kumano Maru (1944) army aircraft transport, 61
Kumanosan Maru (1943) standard Type 2TM tanker, 261
Kume (1944) escort, 188-189
Kumi Maru (1929) submarine chaser, 225
Kunashiri (1940) escort, 186-187
Kunikawa Maru (1937) seaplane carrier, 67-68; transport
Kuniyama Maru (1943) standard Type 1C transport, 257
Kurahashi (1943) escort, 187-188
Kurama (1907) armoured cruiser, 78
Kurama Maru (1921) submarine chaser, 212
Kurasaki, ex-*Oha Maru* (1928) supply ship, 247
Kure Nos 1-4, 6, tugs, 269
Kure No 5 (1914) salvage tug, 266
Kuretake, ex-*No 4*, ex-*Karukaya*, (1922) destroyer, 138-139
Kuri (1920) destroyer, 137-138
Kurihashi (*Maru*), ex-*Herakles*, (1897) salvage vessel,
Kurokami (1917) minelayer, 202-203
Kurosaki (1918) minelayer, 202-203
Kuroshima (1914) minelayer, 202
Kuroshio (1938) destroyer, 148
Kuroshio Maru (1938) tanker, 253
Kuroshio No 1, ex-*T.131*, (1944) landing ship, 228
Kuroshio No 2, ex-*T.149*, (1944) landing ship, 229
Kusagaki (1944) escort, 187-188
Kusentai No 101, ex-*I/DML 1062*, (1941) harbour patrol craft, 223
Kusentai No 111, ex-*ML 3??*, (1943) harbour patrol craft, 224
Kusentai No 102, ex-*ML 310*, (1941) harbour patrol craft, 224
Kusumi unbuilt supply ship, 247, 248
Kusunoki (1915) destroyer, 135
Kusunoki (1945) escort destroyer, 153
Kuwa (1918) destroyer, 136
Kuwa (1944) escort destroyer, 152
Kuzu (1945) escort destroyer, 153
Kyo Maru No 1 (1937) minesweeper, 212
Kyo Maru Nos 2, 6-8, 10, 11 (1938) submarine chasers, 225
Kyo Maru No 3 (1938) minesweeper, 212
Kyo Maru Nos 12, 13 (1941) submarine chasers, 225
Kyobun unbuilt minelayer, 201
Kyoei Maru (1937) tanker, 253
Kyoei Maru No 2 (1940) tanker, 253
Kyoei Maru No 3 (1941) tanker, 253, 258
Kyoko Maru, ex-*Semiramis*, (1921) tanker, 253
Kyokuho Maru (1944) standard Type 1TL tanker, 258
Kyokuto Maru (1934) tanker, 253
Kyukuyo Maru (1938) tanker, 253
Kyosai (1939) minelayer, 200-201
Kyosei Maru (1938) netlayer, 206
Kyuei Maru (1943) standard Type 1TL tanker, 258
Kyushu Maru (1936) netlayer, 206

M

Ma 1-4 (1940) minelayers, 203
Ma 101, ex-*Barlight*, (1941) minelayer, 203
Maeshima (1937) minelayer, 200, 201
Maikaze (1937) destroyer, 148, 149
Maiko, (ec-*Macao*), (1943) gunboat, 122, 123
Maizuru (1905) auxiliary, 269
Maizuru Nos 1-3 tugs, 269
Maki (1917) destroyer, 136
Maki (1942) destroyer, 151, 152
Makikumo (1904) torpedo gunboat, 117
Makikumo (1939) destroyer, 150
Makinami (1939) destroyer, 150
Mamiya (1920) supply ship, 247
Manazuru (1899) torpedo boat, 127, 128
Manazuru (1931) torpedo boat, 128, 129
Manju (1886) sail training ship, 270
Manju (1942) escort/sweeper, 187
Manju Maru (1941) oiler, 253
Manju Maru (1941) s/m depot ship, 239
Manshû (1901) transport, 244
'Maru-Ni' (1944) explosive motor boats, 273
'Maru-Se' (1945) rocket boats, 184
Matsu (1914) destroyer, 135
Matsu (1942) destroyer, 151, 152, 153
Matsue (1898) transport, 244
Matsukaze (1905) destroyer, 133
Matsukaze (1921) destroyer, 142
Matsu Maru (1941) netlayer, 206
Matsushima (1888) cruiser, 96, 97
Matsuwa (1942) escort sweeper, 187
Maya (1885) gunboat, 115
Maya (1928) heavy cruiser, 83, 84
Mayasan Maru (1941) landing ship, 231
Mejima Maru (1941) minesweeper, 212
Michishio (1935) destroyer, 147, 148
Mihara Maru (194?) transport,

282 INDEX

Mikasa (1899) battleship, 18, 19
Mikazuki (1905) destroyer, 133
Mikazuki (1924) destroyer, 143, 144
Mikuma (1931) heavy cruiser, 84, 85, 86
Mikura (1942) escort, 187, 188
Minakami Maru (194?) subchaser, 225
Minazuki (1905) destroyer, 133
Minazuki (1924) destroyer, 143
Minegumo (1935) destroyer, 147, 148
Minekaze (1918) destroyer, 141
Mino (1944) minelayer, 202
Mirii Maru (1943) oiler, 253
Misago Maru (194?) subchaser, 225
Misago Maru No 1 (1941) minesweeper, 212
Misago Maru No 2 (194?) subchaser, 225
Misago Maru No 3 (1941) minesweeper, 212
Misago Maru No 8 (1941) minesweeper, 212
Misago Maru No 11 (1941) minesweeper, 212
Mishima (1904) battleship, 15
Miura (1944) tug, 266, 267
Miyake (1942) escort, 187, 188
Miyako (1896) sloop/cruiser, 94
Miyo Maru (1941) minesweeper, 212
Miyuki (1926) destroyer, 144
Mizuho (1937) seaplane carrier, 65, 66
'M-Kanamono' (1944) midget submarines, 184
Mochizuki (1924) destroyer, 143, 144
Mochizuki (1939) destroyer, 150, 151
Mogami (1907) cruiser, 104
Mogami (1931) heavy cruiser, 84, 85, 86
Mogami Maru (194?) subchaser, 225
Mogamigawa Maru (1941) minelayer, 204
Moku Daihatsu Type (1944) landing craft, 233
Mokutu (1944) escort, 188, 189
Momi (1919) destroyer, 137
Momi (1942) destroyer, 151, 152
Momo (1916) destroyer, 135, 136
Momo (1942) destroyer, 151, 152
Moroshima (1937) minelayer, 200, 201
Moshun (1865) gunboat, 114
Murakumo (1897) destroyer, 131
Murakumo (1926) destroyer, 144
Murasame (1902) destroyer, 132, 133
Murasame (1933) destroyer, 146, 147
Muro Maru (1938) hospital ship, 262, 263
Muroto (1918) collier, 248
Murotsu (1944) escort, 188, 189
Musashi (1884) sloop, 91, 92
Musashi (1938) battleship, 38, 39
Musashi Maru (1941) minesweeper, 213
Mutsu (1918) battleship, 28, 29, 30
Mutsuki (1924) destroyer, 143
Mutsure (1942) escort, 187
Myoken Maru (194?) subchaser, 225
Myoko (1924) heavy cruiser, 81, 82, 83

N
Nachi (1924) heavy cruiser, 81, 82, 83
Nadakaze (1918) destroyer, 141, 142
Naganami (1939) destroyer, 150
Nagara (1920) cruiser, 107, 108
Nagara Maru (1941) netlayer, 206
Nagato (1917) battleship, 28, 29
Nagato Maru (1914) minelayer, 204
Nagato Maru (1914) minesweeper, 213
Nagato Maru No 3 (1914) minesweeper, 213
Nagatsuki (1905) destroyer, 133
Nagatsuki (1924) destroyer, 143
Nagaura (1936) tug, 266
Nagoya Maru (1932) submarine depot ship, 239
Naikatei No 1 Type (1938) motor gunboats, 159
Naikatei No 3 Type (1938) motor gunboats, 159
Naikatei No 615 (1920) motor torpedo boat, 154
Naikatei No 1149 (1920) motor torpedo boat, 154
Naka (1922) cruiser, 108, 109
Namikaze (1918) destroyer, 141, 142
Nan-Ho Maru (194?) subchaser, 225
Naniwa (1884) cruiser, 95, 96
Nankai (1942) gunboat, 119
Nanshin (1942) gunboat, 119
Nanshin Maru (194?) subchaser, 225
Nan-Yo (1941) gunboat, 119
Nara (1917) destroyer, 136
Nara (1942) destroyer, 151, 152, 153
Narumi, (ex-*Ermanno Carlotto*) (1943) river gunboat, 122, 123
Naruto Maru (1941) minesweeper, 213
Naruto (1922) oiler, 249, 250
Naryu (1937) minelayer, 200, 201
Nasami (1931) minelayer, 199, 200
Nashi (1919) destroyer, 137, 138
Nashi (1942) destroyer, 153
Natori (1920) cruiser, 107, 108
Natsugumo (1935) destroyer, 147, 148
Natsushima (1911) minelayer, 202, 203
Natsushima (1931) minelayer, 199, 200
Natsushio (1937) destroyer, 148, 149
Natsuzuki (1939) destroyer, 150, 151
Ne-no-hi (1905) destroyer, 133
Ne-no-hi (1931) destroyer, 146
Nichiei Maru (1938) oiler, 253
Nichirin Maru (1915) ferry/transport, 270
Nichiyo Maru (1940) minelayer, 204
Nigitsu Maru (1942) aviation transport, 61
Niitaka (1902) cruiser, 101
Niizaki (1937) minelayer, 200, 201
Niizuki (1939) destroyer, 150, 151
Niji (1897) destroyer, 130
Nikogawa (1905) training ship, 271
Ninoshima (1918) minelayer, 202, 203
Nippon Maru (1941) oiler, 253
Nippon Maru No 2 (194?) subchaser, 225
Nire (1919) destroyer, 137
Nire (1942) destroyer, 153
Nissan Maru (1938) oiler, 253
Nisshin (1869) screw corvette, 90
Nisshin (1902) armoured cruiser, 75, 76
Nisshin (1938) seaplane carrier, 66, 67
Nisshin Maru (1938) oiler, 253
Nisshin Maru No 2 (1937) oiler, 253
Nissho Maru (1938) oiler, 253
Nissho Maru No 3 (1941) netlayer, 206
Nissho Maru No 5 (1941) netlayer, 206
Nissho Maru No 16 (1941) gunboat, netlayer, 206
Nisui Maru (194?) subchaser, 225
Nitto Maru No 19 (194?) subchaser, 225
Nitto Maru No 20 (194?) subchaser, 225
Nitto Maru No 22 (194?) subchaser, 225
Niyodo (1942) cruiser (cancelled), 112
Nokaze (1918) destroyer, 141, 142
Noma (1919) oiler, 249
Nomi (1942) escort, 187, 188
Noshima (1918) collier, 248
Noshiro (1941) cruiser, 111, 112
Noshiro Maru (1933) armed merchant cruiser, 234, 235
Noshiro Maru No 2 (1941) minesweeper, 213
Notoro (1919) seaplane carrier, 63
Notoro (1920) oiler, 249, 250
Nowaki (1905) destroyer, 133
Nowaki (1937) destroyer, 148, 149
Nozaki (1939) supply ship, 247
Numakaze (1918) destroyer, 141, 142
Nuwashima (1937) minelayer, 200, 201

Numbered ships:
No 1, 2 (1934) midget submarines, 183, 184
Nos 1-44 (1914) minelayers, 204
Nos 1-263 (1943) escorts, 189, 190, 191, 192, 193, 194
Nos 1-9 (1904-07) submarines, 160
Nos 10-15 (1910-13) submarines, 161
Nos 11-16 (1918) battleships (cancelled), 36, 37
Nos 14, 16 (1945) aviation transports (cancelled), 62
No 14 (1918) submarine, 162
Nos 16-33 (1916-19) submarines, 161, 162, 163
Nos 34-43 (1920) submarines, 164, 165
No 44 (1921) submarine, 169
No 45 (1921) submarine, 165
Nos 46 & 47 (1920) submarines, 163
Nos 52-56 (1922) submarines, 169
No 57 (1920) submarine, 163
No 58 (1921) submarine, 165
No 59 (1921) submarine, 163
No 62 (1921) submarine, 165
Nos 68-71 (1921) submarines, 165
Nos 72, 73 (1921) submarines, 163
No 71 (1937) submarine, 168
No 84 (1921) submarine, 163
No 111 (1940) battleship (cancelled), 38, 39
No 114 (1939) motor torpedo boat, 156
Nos 300, 301 (1942) heavy cruisers (cancelled), 87
Nos 795, 796 (1940) battlecruisers (cancelled), 40
No 797-799 (1940) battleships (cancelled), 40
Nos 801-802 (1942) aircraft carriers (cancelled), 54, 55, 56, 57
Nos 810-814 (1942) cruisers (cancelled), 112
Nos 863, 864 (1942) seaplane carriers (cancelled), 66, 67
Nos 868, 869 (1942) gunboats (cancelled), 122
Nos 870, 872-873 (1933) aircraft recovery vessels, 69
No 887 (1934) aircraft recovery vessel, 69
Nos 901-903 (1935) aircraft recovery vessel, 69
Nos 929-932 (1936) aircraft recovery vessels, 69
Nos 1089-1091 (1939) aircraft recovery vessels, 69, 70
No 1264 (1939) aircraft recovery vessel, 69, 70
Nos 1332-1341 (1940) aircraft recovery vessel, 70
No 1440 (1940) aircraft recovery vessel, 70
No 1535-1541 (1940) aircraft recovery vessels, 70
No 1579 etc. (1940) aircraft recovery vessels, 70
No 1620 etc. (1940) aircraft recovery vessels, 70
Nos 3127-3136 (1944) aircraft recovery vessels, 71
Nos 3932-3934 (1941) aircraft recovery vessels, 71
No 4943 (1944?) aircraft recovery vessel, 71
Nos 5002, 5005, 5008-15 (1942) aircraft carriers (cancelled), 56, 57
Nos 5021, 5025 (1942) aircraft carriers (cancelled), 54, 555
Nos 5037, 5038 (1942) cruisers (cancelled), 112

O
O.1-3 (ex-U-Boats), (1919) submarines, 181, 182
O.4-7 (ex-U-Boats), (1919) submarines, 182
Oboro (1897) destroyer, 130
Oboro (1926) destroyer, 144, 145
Odake (1942) destroyer, 153
Odate (1940) cable layer/minelayer, 205
Odomari (1921) icebreaker, 265
Oga (1944) escort, 188, 189
Ogasawa Maru (1941) cable layer, 205
Ogura Maru No 2 (1943) oiler, 253
Ogura Maru No 3 (1942) oiler, 253
Ohama (1943) target ship, 272
Oi (1919) cruiser, 106, 107
Oi Maru (1941) minesweeper, 213
Oite (1905) destroyer, 133
Oite (1921) destroyer, 142
Ojima (1936) tug, 266
Oki (1942) escort, 187
Okikaze (1918) destroyer, 141
Okinami (1939) destroyer, 150
Okinawa (1944) escort, 188, 189
Okinawa Maru (1904) cable layer, 205
Okinoshima (ex-*Generaladmiral Apraxin*), (1904) battleship, 16
Okinoshima (1934) minelayer, 200
Okitsu (ex-*Lepanto*), (1943) gunboat, 119
Ominato No 1, 2 (?) tugs, 269
Omurosan Maru (1943) oiler, 253
Onami (1939) destroyer, 150
Ondo (1920) oiler, 249, 250
Osashi (1944) target ship, 272
Ose (1935) oiler, 251
Oshima (1889) gunboat, 116
Oshima Maru (194?) subchaser, 225
Oshio (1935) destroyer, 147, 148
Osu (ex-*Kaki*), (1919) training ship, 138, 270
Otaka Maru (194?) aviation transport, 70
Otakisan Maru (1945) aviation transport, 62
Otori (1902) torpedo boat, 128
Otori (1934) torpedo boat, 129
Otowa (1903) cruiser, 102
Otowa Maru (1941) minesweeper, 213
Otsu (1944) escort, 188, 189
Owari (1920) battleship (cancelled), 36
Oyashio (1937) destroyer, 148, 149
Oyodo (1941) cruiser, 112
Ozuki (1939) destroyer, 150, 151

P
P Nos 1, 2 (1939) patrol boats (ex-destroyers), 141, 142
P Nos 31-39 (1939) patrol boats (ex-destroyers), 137, 138
P No 46 (1942) patrol boat (ex-destroyer), 138, 139
P Nos 101-109 (1942) patrol boats, 195
P Nos 1-193 (1944) patrol boats, 196, 197

R
Raiden (1856) gunboat/yacht, 115
Ranzan Maru (1920) minesweeper, 213
Reisui Maru (1941) minesweeper, 213
Rikuzen Maru (1941) minesweeper, 213
Rio de Janeiro Maru (1930) s/m depot ship, 239
RO.1-5 (1917) submarines, 162
RO.11, 12 (1917) submarines, 164
RO.13-15 (1920) submarines, 164
RO.17-32 (1920) submarines, 164, 165
RO.33, 34 (1933) submarines, 165
RO.35-36 (1941) submarines, 166
RO.51, 52 (1918) submarines, 162
RO.53-56 (1919) submarines, 163
RO.57-59 (1920) submarines, 163
RO.60-68 (1921) submarines, 163
RO.75 (1941) submarine, 166
RO.100-117 (1941) submarines, 167
RO.500, 501 (1943) submarines, 182, 183
Rohira Maru (1904) hospital ship, 262, 263
Rokko Maru (1941) minesweeper, 213
Rozan (1904) transport, 244
Rumoe Maru (1920) subchaser, 225
Ryojun No 1, 2 (?) tugs, 269
Ryuei Maru (1943) oiler, 253
Ryuho (1941) aircraft carrier, 50, 51
Ryujo (1864) armoured corvette, 12
Ryujo (1929) aircraft carrier, 46, 47
Ryuko Maru (194?) collier, 248
Ryusei Maru (194?) subchaser, 225

S
Sado (1942) escort, 187
Saga (1912) gunboat, 117, 118
Sagami (1904) battleship, 19, 20
Sagara Maru (1940) seaplane tender, 67, 68
Sagi (1902) torpedo boat, 128
Sagi (1934) torpedo boat, 129
Sagiri (1926) destroyer, 144, 145
Sagyotei Type (1944) torpedo recovery vessels, 240
Sai-en (1894) cruiser, 99
Saigon Maru (1937) armed merchant cruiser, 235, 236
Saishu (1937) minelayer, 200, 201
Saishu Maru No 1 (194?) minesweeper, 213
Saishu Maru No 2 (194?) minesweeper, 213
Saishu Maru No 6 (194?) minesweeper, 213
Saishu Maru No 7 (194?) minesweeper, 213
Sakae Maru (1941) netlayer, 206
Sakaki (1914) destroyer, 135
Sakaki (1942) destroyer, 153
Sakaki Maru (1942) minesweeper, 213
Sakawa (1941) cruiser, 111, 112
Sakito (1944) escort, 188, 189
Sakura (1911) destroyer, 134, 135
Sakura (1942) destroyer, 151, 152
Samidare (1933) destroyer, 146, 147
Sanae (1922) destroyer, 138, 139
San Clemente (*Kuremente*) *Maru* (1937) oiler, 253
San Diego (*Jiego*) *Maru* (1928) oiler, 253
Sankyo Maru (194?) subchaser, 225
San Luis (*Ruiso*) *Maru* (1928) oiler, 253
San Pedro (*Pedoro*) *Maru* (1928) oiler, 253
Sanraku Maru (1943) oiler, 253
San Ramon Maru (1935) oiler, 253
Sansei Maru (194?) collier, 248
Sansei Maru (1942) collier, 248
Sanuki Maru (1939) seaplane carrier, 67, 68
San'yo Maru (1933) seaplane carrier, 67, 68
Sapporo Maru (1930) subchaser, 225
Sarushima (1933) minelayer, 199, 200
Sasebo Nos 1-5 (?) tugs, 269
Sasebo No 4 (1914) tug, 266
Sasebo No 9 (1943) tug, 268
Sata (1920) oiler, 249, 250
Satsuki (1904) destroyer, 134
Satsuki (1924) destroyer, 143
Satsuma (1905) battleship, 23
Sawakaze (1918) destroyer, 141
Sawarabi (1922) destroyer, 138, 139
Sazanami (1897) destroyer, 130
Sazanami (1926) destroyer, 144, 145
SB.101-128 (1943) landing ships, 229, 230
Seiki (1875) screw corvette, 90
Seiko Maru (1941) netlayer, 206
Seishu (1927) repair ship, 242
Seito (1915) transport, 244, 245
Seki Maru (1942) minesweeper, 213
Seki Maru No 2 (1938) subchaser, 225
Seki Maru No 3 (1941) minesweeper, 213
Sendai (1922) cruiser, 108, 109
Sendan (1917) destroyer, 137
Sensui Sagyo-Sen (1939) salvage submersible, 185, 186
Sen'yu Maru Nos 2, 3 (1941) minesweepers, 213
Seta (1920) gunboat, 120
Settsu (1909) battleship/target ship, 24, 25, 272
Settsu Maru (1942) dock landing ship, 232
Shiga (1944) escort, 188, 189
Shigure (1905) destroyer, 133
Shigure (1933) destroyer, 146, 147
Shii (1942) destroyer, 153
Shijiki (1916) oiler, 249
Shikinami (1893) torpedo gunboat, 117
Shikinami (1926) destroyer, 144, 145
Shikishima (1898) battleship, 17, 18
Shimakaze (1918) destroyer, 141, 142
Shimakaze (1941) destroyer, 149
Shimane Maru (1944) aviation transport, 62
Shimotsuki (1939) destroyer, 150, 151
Shimpo Maru (1941) minesweeper, 213
Shimushu (1937) escort, 186, 187
Shinan Maru (194?) subchaser, 225
Shinano (1940) battleship/carrier, 38, 39, 55
Shinkai (1944) midget submarine, 184
Shinko Maru (1940) minelayer, 204
Shinkoku Maru (1940) oiler, 253
Shinnan (1944) escort, 188, 189
Shinonome (1897) destroyer, 131
Shinonome (1926) destroyer, 144
Shinsei Maru No 6 (1938) collier, 248
Shinshu Maru (1935) landing ship, 231
Shinto Maru No 2 (1941) netlayer, 206
Shintohoku Maru (1941) minesweeper, 213
Shinyo (1942) aircraft carrier, 60
Shinyo (1944) explosive motor boat, 272, 273
Shinyubari Maru (1936) collier, 248
Shiokaze (1918) destroyer, 141, 142
Shioya (1941) aviation supply ship, 254
Shirakami (1937) minelayer, 200, 201
Shirakumo (1901) destroyer, 132
Shirakumo (1926) destroyer, 144
Shiranui (1897) destroyer, 131
Shiranui (1937) destroyer, 148, 149
Shirasaki (1942) supply ship, 247
Shirataka (1897) torpedo boat, 127
Shirataka (1927) torpedo boat, 197, 198
Shirataka Maru (1941) netlayer, 206
Shiratori Maru (1936) subchaser, 225
Shiratsuyu (1905) destroyer, 133
Shiratsuyu (1933) destroyer, 146, 147
Shirayuki (1905) destroyer, 133
Shirayuki (1926) destroyer, 144
Shiretoko (1920) oiler, 249, 250
Shiriya (1920) oiler, 249, 250
Shirotae (1905) destroyer, 133
Shisaka (1944) escort, 188, 189
Shofuku Maru (1941) netlayer, 206
Shohatsu Type (194?) landing craft, 232, 233
Shoho (1941) aircraft carrier, 49, 50
Shokaku (1937) aircraft carrier, 52
Shokaku (1922) carrier (cancelled), 40, 41
Shonan (1944) escort, 188, 189
Shonan Maru Nos 1-3 (1941) subchasers, 225
Shonan Maru Nos 2-3 (1914) minelayers, 204
Shonan Maru Nos 5-8 (1941) subchasers, 225
Shonan Maru Nos 10-12 (1941) subchasers, 225
Shonan Maru No 15 (1941) subchaser, 226
Shonan Maru No 16 (1941) minesweeper, 213
Shonan Maru (1941) subchaser, 226
Shosei Maru (1941) netlayer, 206
Showa Maru (194?) subchaser, 226
Showa Maru Nos 2-3 (194?) subchasers, 226
Showa Maru Nos 5-6 (194?) subchasers, 226
Showa Maru Nos 7-8 (1941) minesweeper, 213
Showa Maru No 10 (1941) minesweeper, 213
Shoyo Maru (1928) oiler, 253
Shuko Maru (1941) netlayer, 206
Shunsei Maru No 5 (194?) subchaser, 226
Shunsen Maru (1941) netlayer, 206
Shun'yo Maru (194?) subchaser, 226
S-Kanamono type (1943) midget submarines, 185
Sobun Maru (194?) subchaser, 226
Sokaitei Nos 7-12 (1926) minesweepers, 133, 208
Sokaitei Nos 7-8 (1930) minesweepers, 139, 208
Soko (1894) gunboat, 116
Sokuten (1913) minelayer, 202, 203
Sokuten (1937) minelayer, 200, 201
Sonobe Maru (1941) minesweeper, 213
Soryu (1934) aircraft carrier, 47, 48, 49
Soya (1904) cruiser, 102
Soya (1936) ammunition ship, 243
Soyo Maru (1931) collier, 248
SS.1-22 (1942) landing craft, 230, 231
Sugi (1914) destroyer, 135
Sugi (1942) destroyer, 151, 152
Suikei Nos 11-12 (1942) subchasers, 223, 224
Suikei Nos 21-22 (1942) subchasers, 224
Suikei No ?, (ex-*Rhu*), (1942) subchaser, 224
Suma (1892) cruiser, 99
Suma (1941) gunboat, 122
Sumida (1903) gunboat, 119, 120
Sumida (1939) gunboat, 122
Sumire (1919) destroyer, 137, 138
Sumire (1942) destroyer, 153
Sumire Maru (1917) oiler, 249
Sumiyoshi Maru (1936) tug, 268
Sunosaki (1917) oiler, 249
Sunosaki (1942) aviation supply ship, 254
Suo (1898) battleship, 19, 20
Susuki (1919) destroyer, 137, 138
Suzukaze (1933) destroyer, 146, 147
Suzunami (1939) destroyer, 150
Suzutsuki (1939) destroyer, 150, 151
Suzuya (1904) cruiser, 102, 103
Suzuya (1933) heavy cruiser, 85, 86
Suzuya Maru Nos 1-2 (194?) subchasers, 226

T
T.1-22 (1943) fast transports, 226, 227
T.101-176 (1943) landing ships, 227, 229
Tachibana (1911) destroyer, 134, 135
Tachibana (1942) destroyer, 153
Tachibana Maru (1941) hospital ship, 262, 263
Tachikaze (1918) destroyer, 141, 142
Tade (1919) destroyer, 137, 138
Taian Maru (1941) minesweeper, 213
Taigei (1933) s/m depot ship, 238
Taihei Maru No 3 (194?) minesweeper, 213
Taiho (1941) aircraft carrier, 54
Taihoku Maru (1904) minelayer, 204
Taiko Maru (1941) netlayer, 206
Taisei Maru (1941) minesweeper, 213
Taito Maru (1941) minesweeper, 213
Taiyo (1940) aircraft carrier, 58, 59
Takachiho (1884) cruiser, 95, 96
Takachiho Maru (1941) minelayer, 204
Takanami (1939) destroyer, 150
Takane (1944) escort, 188, 189
Takao (1886) sloop/cruiser, 92
Takao (1921) battleship, 36
Takao (1927) heavy cruiser, 83, 84
Takao Maru (1941) minesweeper, 213
Takasago (1896) cruiser, 100
Takasago Maru (1941) hospital ship, 262, 263
Takasago Maru (1941) minesweeper, 213
Takasaki (1902) transport, 244
Takasaki (1935) s/m depot ship, 238
Takasaki (1942) aviation supply ship, 254
Takashima (1937) minelayer, 200, 201
Takashima Maru Nos 2, 3 (1941) minesweepers, 213
Takatori Maru No 1 (1928) oiler, 253

INDEX 283

Takatsu Maru (1942) landing ship, 232
Take (1919) destroyer, 137, 138
Take (1942) destroyer, 151, 152
Takechi Nos 1-6 (1944) transports, 244, 245
Takunan Maru No 1 (1941) minesweeper, 213
Takunan Maru No 2 (1937) subchaser, 226
Takunan Maru No 3 (1941) minesweeper, 213
Takunan Maru Nos 5-8 (1937) subchasers, 226
Takunan Maru No 10 (1937) subchasers, 226
Tama (1920) cruiser, 106, 107
Tama Maru (1941) minesweeper, 213
Tama Maru (1941) minesweeper, 213
Tama Maru Nos 2-3 (1941) minesweepers, 213
Tama Maru Nos 6-7 (1941) minesweepers, 213
Tama Maru No 3 (1936) subchaser, 226
Tama Maru No 5 (1936) subchaser, 226
Tama Maru Nos 6-7 (1936) subchasers, 226
Tama Maru No 8 (1936) subchaser, 226
Tamanami (1939) destroyer, 150
Tamano (1942) oiler, 251
Tamatsu Maru (1941) landing ship, 231
Tamazono Maru Nos 1-3 (1941) minesweepers, 213
Tamura (1941) minesweeper, 213
Tango (1904) battleship, 19
Tanikaze (1916) destroyer, 140
Tanikaze (1937) destroyer, 148, 149
Tarakan Maru (1943) oiler, 253
Tatara (1941) gunboat, 122
Tategami (1936) tug, 266
Tateishi (1940) cable layer, 205
Tatekawa Maru (1935) oiler, 253
Tateyama (1879) training ship, 270
Tateyama Maru (1940) aviation transport, 70
Tatsu Maru (1941) netlayer, 206
Tatsuharu Maru (1941) minelayer, 205
Tatsui Maru (194?) subchaser, 226
Tatsumiya Maru (1941) minelayer, 205
Tatsuta (1893) torpedo gunboat, 93, 94
Tatsuta (1917) cruiser, 105
Teibo Nos 1-2 (1866) gunboats, 113
Teiyo Maru (1931) oiler, 253
Tenkai Nos 1-5 (1928-42) weather ships, 265
Tennan Maru (19??) oiler, 253
Tenryu (1878) despatch vessel, 91
Tenryu (1917) cruiser, 105
Ten-Yo Maru (1941) minelayer, 205
Terukawa Maru (1934) oiler, 253
Teruzuki (1939) destroyer, 150, 151
Toa Maru (1934) oiler, 253
Toba (1911) gunboat, 120
Tochi (1942) destroyer, 153
Toei Maru (1938) oiler, 253
Toen Maru (1917) oiler, 253
Togo Maru (1941) minesweeper, 213
Toho Maru (1936) oiler, 253
Tokachi Maru (1941) netlayer, 206
Tokitsukaze (1913) destroyer, 140
Tokitsukaze (1937) destroyer, 148, 149
Tokitsu Maru (1942) landing ship, 232
Tokiwa (1898) armoured cruiser, 72, 73
Toko Maru No 1 (1941) netlayer, 207
Toku Daihatsu type (194?) landing craft, 233
Toku 4-Shiki Naikatei (1944) amphibious tanks/torpedo boats, 272
Tokugata Unkato (1942) submarine stores vessels, 186
Tokuho Maru No 5 (1941) minesweeper, 213
Tokuho Maru No 10 (1941) minesweeper, 213
Tomariura Nos 1-2 (1919) training ships, 270
Tomoshiri (1944) escort, 188, 189
Tomozuru (1931) torpedo boat, 128, 129
Tonan Maru Nos 2-3 (1937) oilers, 253
Tone (1905) cruiser, 103
Tone (1934) heavy cruiser, 87
Torishima (1941) minesweeper, 214
Torpedo Boat Nos 1-28 (1878-1885), 124, 125
Torpedo Boats Nos 29-75 (1898-1902), 125, 126
Torpedo Recovery Vessels, 18-metre type, (1944), 240
Torpedo Transports, 150-ton type, (1936), 243
Tosa (1920) battleship, 35
Toseki Maru (194?) subchaser, 226
Toshima (1914) minelayer, 202, 203
Toshi Maru Nos 1-2 (1941) minesweepers, 214
Toshi Maru No 3 (1937) subchaser, 226
Toshi Maru No 5 (1941) minesweeper, 214
Toshi Maru Nos 7-8 (1941) minesweepers, 214
Toyohashi (1894) submarine depot ship, 236
Tsubaki (1917) destroyer, 136
Tsubaki (1942) destroyer, 151, 152, 153
Tsubame (1902) torpedo boat, 128
Tsubame (1928) minelayer, 199, 200
Tsuga (1919) destroyer, 137, 138
Tsugaru (1904) cruiser, 102
Tsugaru (1939) minelayer, 200
Tsukuba (1870) screw corvette, 89, 90
Tsukuba (1905) armoured cruiser/battlecruiser, 77
Tsukumo (1941) training ship, 271
Tsuskushi (1882) gunboat/cruiser, 92
Tsukushi (1940) survey ship, 264
Tsukushi Maru (1940) minesweeper, 214
Tsukushi Maru (1941) s/m depot ship, 239
Tsuruga Maru (1942) transport, 246

Tsurugisaki (1917) oiler, 249
Tsurugisaki (1935) s/m depot ship, 238
Tsurumi (1921) oiler, 249, 250
Tsurumi (1921) seaplane carrier, 63
Tsurushima (1940) cable layer, 205
Tsushima (1901) cruiser, 101
Tsushima (1942) escort, 187
Tsuta (1919) destroyer, 137, 138
Tsuta (1942) destroyer, 153
Tugs, 600-tonne type (1914), 266
Type 2 (194?) landing craft, 234
Type 3 (194?) landing craft, 234
Type 4 (194?) landing craft, 234

U

Uji (1902) gunboat, 117
Uji (1939) gunboat, 118, 119
Uji Maru (1941) netlayer, 207
Ujina Maru (1920) transport, 226
U-Kanamono (1944) midget submarines, 184
Ukishima (1937) minelayer, 200, 201
Ukishima Maru (1936) armed merchant cruiser, 235, 236
Uku (1944) escort, 188, 189
Ukuru (1944) escort, 188, 189
Ume (1914) destroyer, 135
Ume (1942) destroyer, 151, 152
Umikaze (1909) destroyer, 139
Umikaze (1933) destroyer, 146, 147
Umpoto type (1941) landing craft, 233
Unebi (1884) cruiser, 96
Unkato, L, M, S Types (1943) submersible stores carriers, 186
Unryu (1943) aircraft carrier, 56, 57
Unsei (1937) survey ship, 270
Un'yo (1868) gunboat, 114
Un'yo (1938) aircraft carrier, 58, 59
Un'yo Maru No 2 (1937) collier, 248
Urakaze (1913) destroyer, 140
Urakaze (1937) destroyer, 148, 149
Uranami (1905) destroyer, 133
Uranami (1926) destroyer, 144, 145
Urumi (1944) escort, 188, 189
Uruppu Maru (1926) subchaser, 226
Ushio (1915) destroyer, 133
Ushio (1926) destroyer, 144, 145
Usugumo (1897) destroyer, 131
Usugumo (1926) destroyer, 144
Uwajima No 6 (1904) minelayer, 205
Uzuki (1905) destroyer, 133
Uzuki (1924) destroyer, 143
Uzura (1902) torpedo boat, 128

W

W.1-6 (1922) minesweepers, 207
W.7-12 (1937) minesweepers, 209
W.13-18 (1931) minesweepers, 208, 209
W.19-41 (1939) minesweepers, 209, 210
W.101-102 (1941) minesweepers, 210
Wa.1-22 (1941) minesweepers, 210, 211
Wa.101-107 (1942) minesweepers, 211
Wafu Maru (1934) subchaser, 226
Wakaba (1905) destroyer, 133
Wakaba (1931) destroyer, 146
Wakamiya (1914) seaplane carrier, 62, 63
Wakamiya (1943) escort, 187
Wakamiya Maru (194?) netlayer, 207
Wakatake (1922) destroyer, 138, 139
Wakatake (1937) minelayer, 201
Wakatake Maru (194?) subchaser, 226
Wakatsuki (1939) destroyer, 150, 151
Wakazakura (1942) destroyer, 153
Warabi (1919) destroyer, 137, 138
War Standard Ships, 255-262
Washizaki (1920) minelayer, 202, 203
Water carriers, 150-ton type (1940) 255
Wen Hsing (1934) minesweeper support ship, 270

Y

Yachiyo Maru (1941) minesweeper, 214
Yachiyo Maru No 3 (194?) guardboat,
Yadake (1942) destroyer, 153
Yaeyama (1887) cruiser, 93
Yaeyama (1930) minelayer, 199
Yaezakura (1942) destroyer, 153
Yahagi (1910) cruiser, 104, 105
Yahagi (1941) cruiser, 111, 112
Yakaze (1918) destroyer/target ship, 141, 272
Yaku (1944) escort, 188, 189
Yakumo (1898) armoured cruiser, 73, 74
Yamabata Maru (1941) cable layer, 205
Yamabiko (1904) destroyer, 134
Yamagumo (1935) destroyer, 147, 148
Yamakaze (1909) destroyer, 139
Yamakaze (1933) destroyer, 146, 147
Yamasemi (1937) destroyer, 134
Yamashiro (1913) battleship, 25, 26
Yamashiro Maru (1944) aviation transport, 62
Yamato (1883) Sloop, 91, 92
Yamato (1937) battleship, 38, 39
Yamazuru Maru (1938) oiler, 253
Yanagi (1916) destroyer, 135, 136
Yanagi (1942) destroyer, 151, 152, 153
Yaryu Maru (194?) subchaser, 226
Yashima (1894) battleship, 16, 17

Yashiro (1942) escort, 187, 188
Yasoshima (1931) cruiser, 113
Yasukuni Maru (1930) s/m depot ship, 239
Yatsushiro Maru (1930) subchaser, 226
Yayoi (1905) destroyer, 133
Yayoi (1924) destroyer, 143
Yobai Maru (194?) subchaser, 226
Yodo (1908) cruiser, 103, 104
Yodogawa Maru (1939) collier, 248
Yoizuki (1939) destroyer, 150, 151
Yokosuka Nos 1-6 (?) tugs, 269
Yomogi (1919) destroyer, 137, 138
Yoshino (1892) cruiser, 98
Yoshino Maru (1941) minesweeper, 214
Yoshitomo Maru (1941) minesweeper, 214
Yoshun (1861) screw corvette, 89
Yu.1-12 (1943) submarines, 181
Yu.1001-1014 (1943) submarines, 181
Yu.2001 etc (1943) submarines, 181
Yubari (1922) cruiser, 110
Yubari Maru (1930) collier, 248
Yudachi (1905) destroyer, 133
Yudachi (1933) destroyer, 146, 147
Yugao (1922) destroyer, 138, 139
Yugiri (1926) destroyer, 144, 145
Yugumo (1939) destroyer, 150
Yugure (1897) destroyer, 131
Yugure (1905) destroyer, 133
Yugure (1931) destroyer, 146
Yuho Maru (1943) oiler, 254
Yukaze (1918) destroyer, 141, 142
Yukikaze (1937) destroyer, 148, 149
Yuki Maru (194?) minesweeper, 214
Yumihari (1915) despatch vessel, 269, 270
Yumihari (1944) tug, 266, 267
Yunagi (1905) destroyer, 133
Yunagi (1921) destroyer, 142, 143
Yun Hsing (1937) survey ship, 270
Yura (1921) cruiser, 107, 108
Yuragawa (Maru) (1905) training ship, 271
Yurijima (1937) minelayer, 200, 201
Yusen Maru No 3 (1944) subchaser, 226
Yusen Maru Nos 9-11 (1944) subchasers, 226
Yusen Maru No 16 (1944) subchaser, 226
Yusen Maru No 27 (1944) subchaser, 226
Yusen Maru No 31 (1944) subchaser, 226
Yusen Maru No 43 (1944) subchaser, 226
Yuzuki (1924) destroyer, 143, 144

Z

Zuiho (1935) aircraft carrier, 49, 50
Zuikaku (1938) aircraft carrier, 52